WITHDRAWN
NDSU

A TAXONOMY OF VISUAL PROCESSES

BOOKS BY WILLIAM UTTAL

Real Time Computers: *Techniques and Applications in the Psychological Sciences*

Generative Computer Assisted Instruction (with Miriam Rogers, Ramelle Hieronymus, and Timothy Pasich)

Sensory Coding: *Selected Readings* (Editor)

The Psychobiology of Sensory Coding

Cellular Neurophysiology and Integration: *An Interpretive Introduction*

An Autocorrelation Theory of Form Detection

The Psychobiology of Mind

A Taxonomy of Visual Processes

A TAXONOMY OF VISUAL PROCESSES

WILLIAM R. UTTAL

Institute for Social Research
University of Michigan

LEA LAWRENCE ERLBAUM ASSOCIATES, PUBLISHERS
1981 Hillsdale, New Jersey

Copyright © 1981 by Lawrence Erlbaum Associates, Inc.
All rights reserved. No part of this book may be reproduced in any form, by photostat, microform, retrieval system, or any other means, without the prior written permission of the publisher.

Lawrence Erlbaum Associates, Inc., Publishers
365 Broadway
Hillsdale, New Jersey 07642

Library of Congress Cataloging in Publication Data

Uttal, William R
A taxonomy of visual processes.

Bibliography: p.
Includes index.
1. Visual perception. 2. Visual perception—Physiological aspects. I. Title. [DNLM: 1. Visual perception. 2. Classification. WW15 U93t]
BF241.U86 152.1′4 80-18262
ISBN 0-89859-075-2

BF
241
U86

Printed in the United States of America

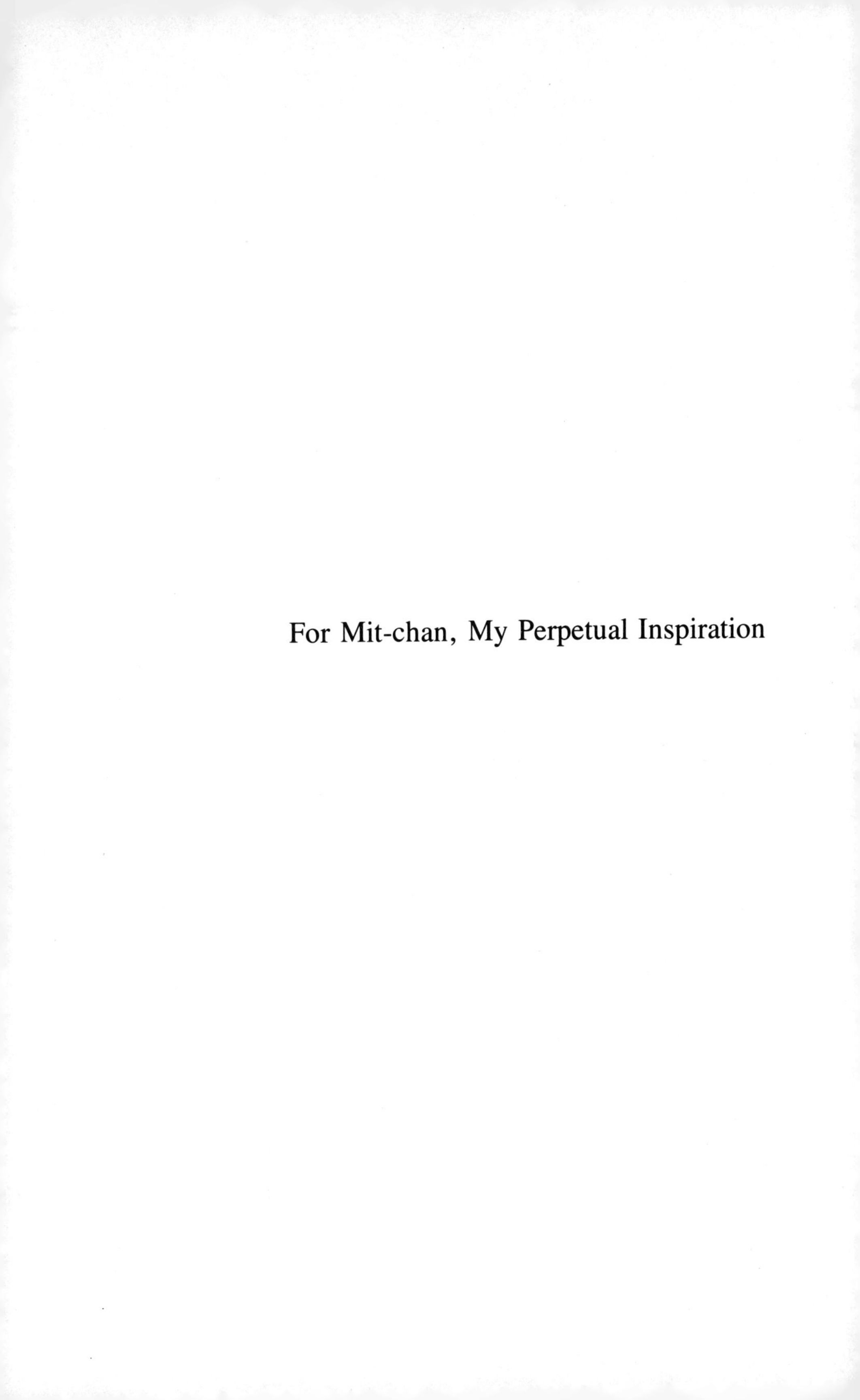

For Mit-chan, My Perpetual Inspiration

Contents

PART II: A TAXONOMIC LEVEL THEORY OF VISUAL PERCEPTION

Preface

At the beginning

This book is the third in a planned tetralogy on which I have been working through the decade of the 1970s. This third volume deals with the empirical data base and the theories concerning visual perception—the set of mental responses to photic stimulation of the eyes. As the book develops, I plan to present a general taxonomy of visual processes and phenomena. It is my hope that such a general perspective will help to bring some order to the extensive, but largely unorganized, research literature dealing with our immediate perceptual responses to visual stimuli. The specific goal of this work is to provide a classification system that integrates and systematizes the data base of perceptual psychology into a comprehensive intellectual scheme by means of an eclectic, multi-level *metatheory* invoking several different kinds of explanation.

Despite the ambitious nature of this goal, it should be made clear at the outset that the scope of this book is intended to be quite limited in several regards. I have constrained the topics discussed almost exclusively to those involving visual perception rather than dealing with perception in general. Even then, I consider only a limited portion of the full range of visual topics and concentrate on its more automatic and immediate aspects. I have chosen to so limit my discussion for several reasons. Not only are the eyes the most effective receptors of information (as well as being dominant in most multisensory stimulus conflict situations), but, more fundamentally, there is an enormous amount of generality among the senses and what is said, in principle, for vision is usually adequate to emphasize the essential concepts describing all of the other modalities as well. I believe that when proper and complete comparisons are made among the sensory modalities, only the mechanics and details turn out to be different.

Another compelling, though more pragmatic, reason to limit my discussion to a circumscribed range of topics is the totally unmanageable bulk of the published literature on visual perception. It is no longer possible within any individual's intellectual lifetime, to deal with all facets of this well-studied area of modern science. I shall, therefore, not attempt an exhaustive explanation or review of all of the data, phenomena, findings, and theory of even as limited a domain as visual psychology and psychobiology. Many other books do a fine job of summarizing the data base. The late Clarence H. Graham (1965a) left us with a legacy that still serves adequately as a detailed review of the perceptual literature that existed prior to 1964. A number of other excellent textbooks cover the various phenomena of visual perception. These include works by Kaufman (1974), Rock (1975), Forgus and Melamed (1976), and Dember and Warm (1979), to name only a few of those that I have personally found most thoughtful and useful. Detailed descriptions of the various phenomena going beyond what I have chosen to cover in this book can usually be found in any one of these books. There are also other more specific volumes available such as J. O. Robinson's (1972) extraordinarily good discussion of visual illusions and Julesz' (1971) or Ogle's (1950) books on stereopsis. Many articles in Carterette and Friedman's first (1974) and fifth (1975) volumes of their *Handbook of Perception* are also very useful, as are articles in Jameson and Hurvich's (1972) and Held, Leibowitz, and Teuber's (1978) volumes in the monumental *Handbook of Sensory Physiology*.

However, beyond the practical considerations of mass, there is an even more important reason for limiting the content of this work. I believe there is one contribution that I can make within these pages that will transcend all others—to present at least the beginnings of a systematic and ordered taxonomic metatheory of perceptual processes analogous to the classification of the basic particles of nuclear physics or atoms into periodic tables.

I acknowledge the ambitiousness of this task and perhaps even the uncritical grandiosity of it. But I am convinced that some step, however stumbling, in the direction of classification is demanded by the near chaos that exists in the literature of visual perception. This literature grows at an astonishing rate; the phenomena multiply like intellectual rabbits; and yet there is virtually no order, no system, and no organization to this huge body of knowledge, in spite of two and one half millenia of philosophical concern with the problems of vision and several centuries of formal empirical observation of these processes and phenomena. It remains, in most current texts, a science characterized by disorderly and encyclopedic enumeration rather than by orderly arrangement and abstraction of general principles.

If progress is to be made toward the goal of a satisfactory classification scheme, and thus toward a comprehensive metatheory of perceptual phenomena (since classification, itself, is a theoretical statement), it is necessary to constrain further the topics to be discussed here. Since classification schemes in visual perception are so undeveloped, I believe the chances of progress are enhanced if consideration is limited to the relatively immediate and automatic responses to photic stimuli rather than to the full range of topics that might otherwise be incorporated. Consequently, many topics that are intimately related to visual perception, especially those now in vogue in learning or cognitive psychology, will not be discussed until the next volume in this series.

I am thus intentionally excluding from this volume many of the topics that involve manipulation or storage of the visually acquired information subsequent to the immediate perceptual response. These excluded topics include such closely related but, from the point of view emphasized here, extraneous topics as memory, affective or motivational state, imagery, attention, search, complex visual problem solving, and image manipulation. While some examples of these important influences on perceptual response may be briefly mentioned, it should by no means be misunderstood that my goal was to consider them as deeply as some of the other visual areas. All of these topics fall into what I shall subsequently refer to as Level 5 processes. Although Level 5 is a part of the taxonomy I present here, it will not be discussed in detail.

The range of visual perception topics presented in this book, therefore, is little more inclusive than that usually included in any of a large number of other books that concern themselves with the same subject matter. What I hope to offer as my special contribution is a novel organizational synthesis that clarifies this body of scientific data and theory somewhat better than has been achieved by my predecessors.

The theme of this synthesis represents something of a novelty for me personally; it reflects a significant shift in the paradigm that has dominated much of my thinking in the past ten years. That shift is clearly evidenced by comparing this book with the first two volumes of the planned tetralogy of which this present book is the third part. The main theme in the two preceding books (*The Psychobiology of Sensory Coding,* Uttal, 1973, and *The Psychobiology of Mind,* Uttal, 1978) was neurophysiological reductionism—the philosophy that asserts that the phenomena of perception, in particular, and mind, in general, can best be explained in terms of the underlying neural processes and mechanisms. In the "Sensory Coding" book, I dealt mainly with the role of the peripheral nervous system in representing sensory and perceptual phenomena, and in the "Mind" book I dealt in a more general way with the central nervous system's role in our mental life.

In this third volume the reader will see repeated evidence of my gradual movement away from the hypothesis that perceptual processes can be "explained" in terms of or "reduced" to neural equivalences and toward the idea that given the state of our current technology and theory, most interesting perceptual phenomena are not at all amenable to this kind of reductionism. While this should not be construed as an outright rejection of the monistic principle that all mental phenomena must in some ultimate analysis be representable by neural mechanisms, it is an acknowledgment of the practical fact that we simply do not yet have any plausible psychobiological explanations of most perceptual phenomena.

In addition to thus revealing my own shift in personal perspective concerning the general concept of neuroreductionism (the idea that mental processes can be fully explained in terms of neurophysiology), I am also accepting a special responsibility as a critic concerning current psychobiological theories of perception. It is my belief that many members of the psychobiological community have too often assumed that numerous deceptively "simple" perceptual phenomena can be explained as the direct results of relatively peripheral transformations or coding processes. I shall attempt to convince my readers that most visual responses are, on the contrary, neither simple nor peripheral, even though they are certainly influenced by processes occurring in peripheral portions of the afferent communication system. While there are some processes (and some of my readers may be very much in disagreement with my view of how few there actually are) that do seem to depend largely upon identifiable peripheral physiological processes, I argue that, more often than not, and in spite of some superficial analogies between neurophysiological and psychological findings, visual perceptions are the result of central interpretive, inferential, or symbolic interactions that are so labyrinthine and involve so many neurons that no current (or even conceivable) neurophysiological analysis could begin to cope with their true complexity.

In this context, much of what has been presented as neurophysiological theory of perception, I believe, must be considered to be metaphor rather than valid reductive explanation. Other examples of the use of such metaphors are to be found in the psychological literature. For example, the computer is used as a metaphor to describe many of the findings of today's cognitive psychology. But it has become clear over the years to a few cognitive psychologists that the computer, though a useful heuristic, cannot provide an adequate reductive theory or model of human thought. There are substantial organizational differences between the von Neumann machine—the modern program-computer system—and the mind-brain system suggesting qualitative as well as quantitative discrepancies between the computer model and the actual brain-mind relationship.

I believe there is already a similar realization emerging concerning many of the less robust neuroreductionistic models of perception. Nevertheless, it must be acknowledged that there is an intrinsic seductiveness about these neural models of perception. If anything is axiomatic in modern psychobiology, it is that the nervous system is, in some way, the basis of all mental processes. However, I do not believe that we have yet linked the perceptual and neural domains to the degree necessary to assert that current electrophysiological wisdom actually explains as much about perception as has been suggested.

This is not to say that such metaphors are not useful and valuable heuristics that can guide and organize our thinking. But we must not overlook the fact that the useful heuristic is not the same as the valid reductive model. I have previously argued (Uttal, 1978), that the organizational level at which the essential elements or units of neurophysiological organization are identifiable with mental processes is the pattern of interaction of the great networks of neurons in the brain. And yet it is at exactly this level that our theory and technology fail us most completely. Our theoretical and mathematical tools are inadequate for studying the action of large networks of neurons in the brain. In sum, we do not well understand networks nor the links between these networks and the mental processes they represent, although these networks probably are the essential level of representation of perceptual processes.

I conclude from this state of affairs that a universal theory of visual perception must be an eclectic one incorporating both neurophysiological ideas on the one hand and psychological concepts and descriptive phenomenology on the other; each is used where it best serves theoretical needs. In this book, therefore, I propose a global taxonomy of perceptual processes that is, in fact, such a mixed model. The key to this multipronged approach is the definition of a series of levels or stages at which the critical events for the individual perceptual processes occur.

Should this approach prove to be successful; if my enthusiasm is sustained; if research support continues to be available; and if I am satisfied that I have been able to contribute something to our understanding of the more or less preattentive, immediate, and automatic perceptual responses to which I have restricted the scope of this book, the fourth volume of the tetralogy, dealing with subsequent cognitive processing or visual thinking, may be forthcoming. All four of these books, then, would collectively comprise my personal model or metatheory of the visual brain–mind complex as summed up in Fig. P-1.

In this diagram I have distinguished several stages of communication and integration between the respective physical, physiological, and psychological universes of discourse. The physical world, most easily understood because of its concreteness and face validity (but still fraught with complex interpretive and philosophical questions), is assumed to be the initial source of stimulus energy and information patterns. The main task of this series of books is: (1) to present a view of what happens after those patterned energies impinge upon the receptors; and (2) to describe the physiological and psychological transformations through which physical stimuli are converted to visual precepts.

Though there are identifiable preneural (geometrical and optical) transforms, the first physiological, as opposed to physical, stage of information processing occurs in the receptor where information is converted from the external physical energies to signals encoded in the electrochemical energies of the nervous system. These signals are then reencoded and communicated along the peripheral afferent nerves toward the brain. (These processes were emphasized in the first

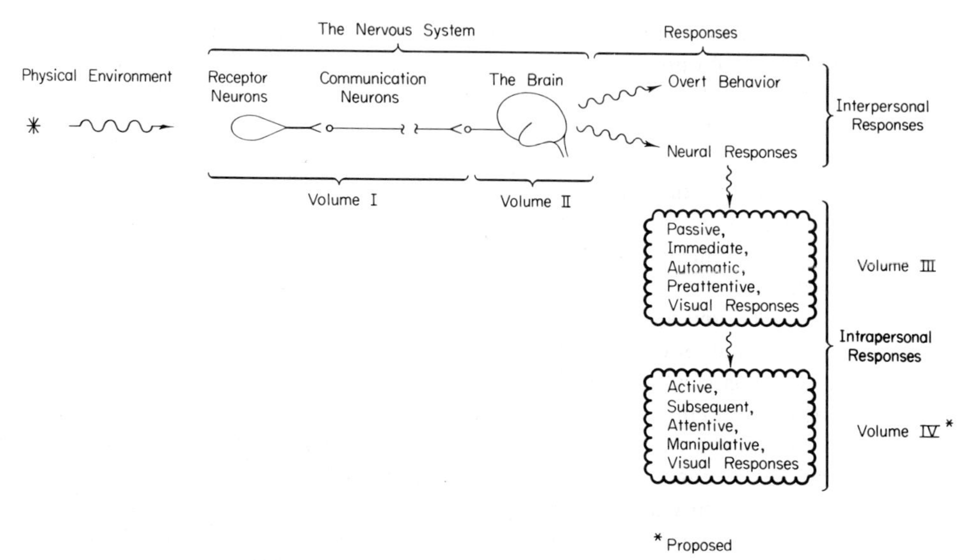

FIG. P.1. A model of the visual brain-mind system.

book in this series—*The Psychobiology of Sensory Coding,* Uttal, 1973). Subsequent stages of information processing are to be found in the central nervous system where this incoming information, already processed by peripheral mechanisms and transformed by the sensory communication system to at least a modest degree, is further modified and then integrated with past experiences into a neural state that becomes identifiable with the mental states we call mind. This second topic was emphasized in the *Psychobiology of Mind* (Uttal, 1978), the second book in this series.

In this third volume, the discussion becomes much more mentalistic and phenomenological. Although I do deal with many peripheral physiological processes, I pass on to consider a subsequent class of automatic perceptual responses that is only barely understood in neural terms. The fourth book, should it ever be written, will deal with the active manipulations of these incoming patterns of information—those subsequent processes psychologists call problem-solving, thinking, cognition, or, to be very modern, "attentive" manipulations.

The story I will tell in this third volume, obviously, cannot be totally nonphysiological. Indeed the main goal of this book is to attribute to the appropriate level of the nervous system the various influences on visual perception that are of importance. Nevertheless, the neural theory of perception, as an explanatory model, eventually passes from the scene in the development of this analysis and, as the reader shall see, I soon resort to the descriptive and mathematical language of the psychologist rather than the electrochemical language of the neurophysiologist. However, it is necessary to use some other languages as I progress toward this promised phenomenology. The vocabulary of optics and physics are very relevant to the story of how we see, as are the terminologies of biochemistry and cellular neurophysiology.

Most important of all, however, is the language of the philosopher. This is the vocabulary of words and ideas that provides the intellectual key that makes meaningful the babel of all of the other languages. Why are we interested in certain visual phenomena that seem to play such an inconsequential or trivial role in our daily lives or, even worse, can be demonstrated only in artificial laboratory situations? Some of the targets of investigation in the laboratory are so abstract as to have seemingly no relevance to any aspect of human existence. Only the terms, constructs, and analyses of philosophy can provide meaning to the otherwise bizarre behavior of laboratory scientists. Therefore, it is to the history of science and philosophy that I will frequently have to turn to understand why some psychologists are so vitally interested in some very peculiar experiments indeed. To preview briefly the answer to the perfectly valid question, ''Why do we study such seemingly unimportant aspects of behavior?'' is to note that the study of perception provides the empirical data necessary to unravel the profound perplexity—how it is that we acquire knowledge about the external world. Experimental perceptual psychology is truly nothing other than empirical epistemology.

This book, of necessity, thus transcends a number of different physical, biological, psychological and philosophical disciplines. Indeed, this variety of content continues to be one of the greatest pleasures in dealing with perception. But, beyond personal pleasure, this variety of approaches and issues reflects the unarguable fact that this topic is of substantial importance in our continuing quest for understanding some of the most important aspects of human nature. Visual perception is a field that certainly cannot yet be considered to be closed; few of the major visual problems that I pose in Chapter 1 have yet been solved. Rather, the study of seeing is as dynamic and active a field of scientific inquiry as visual perception is itself a dynamic and active processing of photic information. The often expressed (e.g., Gregory, 1970, and Gregory & Gombritch, 1973, pp. 63–68) analogy between perception by an individual man and science by the community of men is not, in my opinion, a farfetched one.

In this book, I attempt to isolate the intellectual issues and the significant conceptual (as well as technical) obstacles to full understanding, and to consider the relevant historical backgrounds and philosophical foundations more than is usual in a survey of a field so dominated by empirical research, methodology, and data. Needless to say, however, I believe that the scientific approach that has proven most effective in the past millenium has been the powerful multipronged strategy utilizing both an empirical examination of processes, events, objects, and phenomena, and an inductive-hypothetic-deductive theoretical analysis. Thus one of my major responsibilities as I wrote this book was to review selectively the currently available research literature even though the elucidation of broad concepts and general principles was my primary goal.

To any one familiar with the field, it should be obvious that I cannot deal with all of the experimental literature in visual perception; no single author could conceivably catalogue all of it even if he injudiciously set out to do so, nor would such an endeavor be intellectually satisfying. Rather, I hope to derive general concepts and identify the emerging principles by referring to rather arbitrarily chosen exemplars. Inevitably I will have to omit many important workers and contributions that others feel are equally compelling or even more significant. But, as many others have repeatedly noted, the only plausible strategy to achieve understanding in a field of inquiry such as this is to allow the *general principle* and the *illustrative example* to take the place of the *exhaustive list*.

As I embark on this next volume in the series, I have some hesitation, mostly attributable to the fact that in spite of the extended historical period of interest in the kinds of perceptual phenomena, there is still a remarkable absence of solid understanding in the field. Most perceptual phenomena have not proven susceptible to any satisfactory theoretical explanation, neurophysiological or otherwise, and most of the theories deal with only a very narrowly defined universe of discourse. I am not sure, as I set out on the continuing studies that must go on simultaneously with the writing of this book, that I will arrive at a synthesis that adds much to the wisdom already to be found in other studies of the subject. I will be better able to evaluate what I have achieved when I return to complete the next part of this preface sometime in the future.

At the end

And so two and a half years after writing the preceding pages, I now return to finish this preface. In the last few moments I have completed the last manuscript pages of the book I set out to write what seems to be so long ago. I have thus brought myself to the three-quarter mark in the proposed tetralogy. In this third volume I have proposed a taxonomic system, based on underlying processes rather than on phenomena. While not completely satisfactory, even to me, hopefully this system will at least partially fill the need that I detected at the outset of this project. It would have been especially satisfying if this taxonomy was internally consistent, exclusive, and inclusive, but I have no pretensions that I have met these high standards. There are many difficulties, not the least of which has been that the underlying processes are simply not known in many cases. It may be that any such effort is destined to fail to at least some degree. In particular, I am uncomfortable with the locations in this taxonomy at which I have placed such topics as stereopsis and hyperacuity. However, since there is still residual uncertainty, I have not moved these topics from my original placement; to do so would only raise other doubts.

In spite of such residual uncertainty, I am even more convinced that a taxonomy is essential in perceptual science, and that the only plausible solution to the problem posed by the need for a perceptual taxonomy is an eclectic one. Surely, our neurophysiological data base has explained much. But a rationalistic, inferential, and constructionistic approach is also absolutely necessary to pursue the study of perception. The probabilities of neural complexity compel that we deal with perception at the molar level at least in part, in spite of the progress that has been made in understanding the simpler and more deterministic transformations that occur in the peripheral nervous system. Whatever these peripheral transformations do, I am still convinced the interpretations and transformations that occur centrally are for the most part beyond neoreductionalistic analysis now and probably will be in the future as well. Psychologists need have no concern, therefore; our profession is not in danger of being supplanted by ever more efficient neurophysiological techniques.

I would also like to make a personal comment about the nature of the work that I have been involved in for the past several years. Frankly, I have been repeatedly astonished (perhaps naively so) at some of the opposition that I encountered when I chose to become an explicit generalist rather than a totally dedicated empirically oriented laboratory scientist. Some of the experiences encountered were nonsupportive to say the least. For these reasons, I have felt compelled to define my activities in a self-conscious way that is not usually required of scientists involved in more conventional empirical paradigms. It turns out, although I did not appreciate it at the outset, that what I have been doing is not without a name; the process of analysis, criticism, integration, and synthesis that I have attempted here is, in fact, a research speciality in its own right. I am now pursuing the profession of a *speculative psychologist*.

Although the adjective *speculative* has recently had a derogatory flavor among psychologists, I think the true essence of the process—my new professional specialty (after 20 years of laboratory research in experimental psychology)—has been captured by the philosopher Jerry A. Fodor (1975, p. vii) when he said: "What speculative psychologists do is this: They think about such data as are available about mental processes, and they think about such first-order psychological theories as have been proposed to account for the data. They then try to elucidate the general conception of the mind that is implicit in the data and the theories." However well or poorly I have done what I have done, at least I now know what I am doing: This book is an act of speculative psychology that was, in part, a response to the challenge of such scholars as Fodor and Alan Newell (1973) for someone to "put it all together."

The debts that I owe to many people for their support of one kind or another during the last two and one half years are numerous. It is not well appreciated by those who have not done it just how great are the costs in money and time to write a book like this nor how many people stand behind the single author who has the privilege of and responsibility for signing his name to the finished product. Writing this book was not a matter of evenings and weekends or a few bootlegged hours at the office; this book has been my full-time occupation and it could not have been completed without a great deal of financial, social, moral, and intellectual support. Financial support for this research project came from several sources. The Engineering Psychology Branch Office of Naval Research was the main source through the instrument known as Contract #N00014-77-C-0471. However, I am even more grateful for the confidence they expressed in me at a time that other agencies were unwilling to support any integrating and systematizing work in spite of the fact that all agree that there is a great need for it. I am particularly grateful to Dr. Martin Tolcott and Dr. John O'Hare for their help. John O'Hare, officially the Scientific Officer, became much more of a colleague as the months went by as he read manuscript pages and offered constructive advice and wisdom about the general direction that the work was taking. Other portions of the financial support for this project came from the Air Force Office of Scientific Research and the Aerospace Medical Research Laboratory at Wright–Patterson Air Force Base. The support of Dr. Alfred Fregley and Colonel Joseph Birt, respectively, in each of those organizations is also greatly appreciated.

I am also deeply indebted to the James McKeen Cattell Fund for its help in

To any one familiar with the field, it should be obvious that I cannot deal with all of the experimental literature in visual perception; no single author could conceivably catalogue all of it even if he injudiciously set out to do so, nor would such an endeavor be intellectually satisfying. Rather, I hope to derive general concepts and identify the emerging principles by referring to rather arbitrarily chosen exemplars. Inevitably I will have to omit many important workers and contributions that others feel are equally compelling or even more significant. But, as many others have repeatedly noted, the only plausible strategy to achieve understanding in a field of inquiry such as this is to allow the *general principle* and the *illustrative example* to take the place of the *exhaustive list*.

As I embark on this next volume in the series, I have some hesitation, mostly attributable to the fact that in spite of the extended historical period of interest in the kinds of perceptual phenomena, there is still a remarkable absence of solid understanding in the field. Most perceptual phenomena have not proven susceptible to any satisfactory theoretical explanation, neurophysiological or otherwise, and most of the theories deal with only a very narrowly defined universe of discourse. I am not sure, as I set out on the continuing studies that must go on simultaneously with the writing of this book, that I will arrive at a synthesis that adds much to the wisdom already to be found in other studies of the subject. I expanding my sabbatical leave (1978–1979) into a period of sufficient duration to allow me to finish the manuscript before I had to return to the hurly-burly of my usual ecological niche. The continued courtesy and help of Dr. Robert L. Thorndike, secretary-treasurer of the fund, throughout the course of that sabbatical were of an exceptional nature. My sabbatical was spent, both delightfully and productively, at the Department of Psychology of the University of Hawaii. I am also happy to acknowledge the support of Professor Robert Cole, the chairman of the department, who made this visit possible. While at The University of Hawaii I taught a seminar based on the manuscript. Through this seminar, and other less formal interactions, I was also able to come to know some of the exceptionally fine graduate students there. The lively discussion of professional matters, the intellectual and social support, and the personal friendship that wonderful people like Rosalie Tatsuguchi, Alan Yang, George Danko, Sally McIntosh, Mark Troy, Eugene Lee, Brenda Wong, Caleb (K. P.) Burns, Joyce Feld, Fran Lyons, LoRaine Dufy, Len Burns, Shinken Naitoh, Jean Nyland, Lanette Shizuru, Diane Nahl, Marlene Lindberg, Rod and Janice Calkins, Hugh Spain, Sharon Murakami, Mike Cap, Mary Soares, Maria Moctezuma, and many others offered to my wife and myself that year are now among our most treasured memories. They and our new faculty friends at the University of Hawaii made this an exceptional year, both personally and professionally.

The third source of support for this book came from my home base—The Institute for Social Research at the University of Michigan. As the years go by, I become ever more amazed that such an institution can possibly exist. ISR maintains the highest standards of academic excellence, of intellectual stimulation and freedom, of positive social support, and of cordial collegial relations. It is a model community of scholars, which many other departments and institutes might well emulate. I am ever grateful to Professors Angus Campbell and Robert Kahn for allowing me to join this community of social scientists and to Professors Thomas Juster and Steven Withey for maintaining this most unusual academic atmosphere.

A number of my colleagues have also helped me to complete this book in a more satisfactory fashion than would otherwise have been achieved. Daniel Weintraub, Yukio Tomozawa, Garth Thomas, Daniel Green, Ted Adelson, Angela Brown, Fred Kitterle, Maureen Powers, and John Jonides have read chapters and helped me smooth up roughness in both style and content. The book was also read in its entirety by Joseph Lappin, whose contribution to clarity and accuracy would be instantly appreciated by anyone who might have seen earlier drafts.

A number of secretaries and professional editors have worked with me over the years on this manuscript. I hereby acknowledge their entirely justified complaints about the roughness of some of my drafts, and also their important contribution to the completion of this project. Lucinda Quackenbush, Katherine Noto, Suzanne Gurney, and Christine Zupanovich have all performed prodigious feats with the manuscript. Judy Smith helped enormously with the reference list, and Toni Kennedy's editorial skills were critically important in smoothing my vagaries of style. Judy Emory did the subject index.

My publisher Larry Erlbaum continues to set high standards for the publishing industry and for cordial interactions with his authors. His willingness to trust in esoteric and advanced books of this sort is an especially important contribution to modern psychological communication.

Finally I must end this preface as I have ended all of my others. The one person who makes possible everything that I have done is my dear wife. To Mit-chan, as ever, this book is lovingly dedicated.

William R. Uttal

BASIC CONCEPTS

1 Introduction and Perspective

A. THE PROBLEM

1. An Orientation

How do human beings, endowed as they are with the mixed blessing of an intrapersonal conscious awareness, acquire information, knowledge, or understanding about the external world? This is the fundamental philosophical question underlying the study of perception and a nutshell expression of the challenge faced by technical epistemology. This issue has been a matter of explicit concern to philosophers and scientists since the pre-Socratic time of classical Greece. The question is framed in the vocabulary of philosophy, but it also underlies the entire current experimental thrust to understand how information is acquired, communicated, processed, and interpreted by the nervous system and thus responded to by the human mind.

The classic alternative answers to the question of how we acquire knowledge about the external world have long been concretized in the debate between rationalistic and empiricistic[1] philosophers. The details of this great controversy are dealt with later in this chapter and in Chapter 2, but, for the moment, I wish only to point out the following bias that will permeate much of this book, a bias that is also its major thesis.

Any modern metatheory of perception must be an eclectic one, invoking both neorationalistic and neoempiricistic concepts and premises in order to satisfy both the basic monistic psychobiological premise that all mental processes must be underlain by neural mechanism and the fact that most perceptual processes are so complex that they are beyond understanding in terms of the physiology of the involved networks.

It has been a great historic fallacy for philosophers to have considered the contributions of each of these two points of view as intrinsically antagonistic to each other. Man's psychological world is *both* empiricistic and rationalistic, depending only upon the measuring instruments that are used to observe it and the situations in which it is examined. Thus, any valid modern theory of perception must eclectically incorporate both the findings of neurophysiologists, who currently carry the banner of empiricism, and of cognitive psychologists, the contemporary champions of rationalism. To ignore either (and each is so often ignored by practitioners of the other field) is to develop a sterile metatheory of perception and a false epistemology.

It is very important that the reader keep in mind as he reads the following paragraphs that "rationalistic" and "empiricistic" are words that describe *theories*. In some ultimate metaphysical sense, both rationalistic and empiricistic processes must be embodied in the function of neural nets. The eclectic approach is required because neuroreductionism fails or, rather, our techniques fail, to provide the power necessary to understand networks involving tens, thousands, or billions of neurons. Theoretical rationalism is a practical outcome of complexity, not a denial of the basic tenet of monistic psychobiology. Later in this chapter, I suggest the broad outlines of such an eclectic approach that I develop more fully in Chapter 4. For the moment, however, let us only consider the

---

[1]I am going to take a little poetic license with this word. Although the adjectival form *empiricist* may be more correct, a poetic balance with *rationalistic* is achieved better by *empiricistic* than by *empiricist* and will keep clear certain distinctions I make later.

general nature of its neorationalistic and neoempiricistic components and the interrelation between them.

The central idea in the neorationalistic component of any viable metatheory of how we see is that perception must be considered to be a process in which a mental representation of the external world is constructed, not solely as a direct and deterministic result of a single aspect of an incoming stimulus, but rather as a result of complex symbolic interpretations, inferences, and integrations of a wide variety of currently arriving and previously stored patterns of information. This premise states that the perceiver is more than a passive responder to the physical characteristics of the stimulus but is also an interpretive agent who *uses* the meaning or implications of stimulus information to construct a percept. The dimensions of the mental responses are not, this point of view asserts, deterministically defined by the dimensions of the stimuli except in the simplest cases. It must be appreciated from the outset that this neorationalism expresses an idea that runs counter, in large part, to the prevailing deterministic paradigm of much current perceptual research and to the premises implicit in the very popular contemporary neurophysiological reductionism.

An epistemological neorationalism of this kind does not deny the primary importance of empirical research (that is clearly another use of the word empirical), the importance of the afferent flow of information, or the physicalist school of thought concerning external reality, but it does impel thinking in perceptual psychology toward a molar language and theory base that is increasingly non-neuroreductionistic, constructionistic, and inferential. Such a neorationalism asserts that most mental responses to stimuli may be better described as hypothetical and deductive rather than as automatic, inductive, and determined.

The central idea in the neoempiricistic component of perceptual theory, on the other hand, is that stimuli induce neural patterns of activity that have direct effects on the perceptual experiences of the observer. It is possible, according to this view, to explain on a strictly neuroreductionistic basis and to appreciate how stimuli may interact directly with the structure of the nervous system to produce specific experiences. This kind of explanation does not require any interpretation or inference on the part of the perceiver—the outcome is a direct function of the physical properties of the stimulus and the nervous system.

This other necessary component of an eclectic modern metatheory of perception is implicit in neural representation or coding theory[2]—the body of neurophysiological knowledge that describes how both external stimulus patterns and intrapersonal perceptual states are represented by patterns of nerve impulses within the nervous system. Sensory coding theory is one expression of the

[2]A full discussion of what I mean by *sensory coding theory* can be found in my earlier work, *The Psychobiology of Sensory Coding* (Uttal, 1973), that deals mainly with peripheral processes. The idea is extended to a more general central representation theory in Chapters 6 and 7 of *The Psychobiology of Mind* (Uttal, 1978).

monistic idea of psychoneural identity—the proposition that the state of the neural network is a sufficient substrate to explain all aspects of mental action. A very important corollary that feeds forward onto and links this essentially empiricistic idea with the constructionistic ideas of neorationalism is that these neural codes need bear little, if any, dimensional similarity to the original stimulus pattern. Thus, sensory coding theory, although an empiricistic idea, actually provides an important conceptual foundation for the neorationalism I invoke in this book. Indeed, it is the essential key to breaking the lock that the concept of isomorphic representation (the idea that there must be a dimensionally and geometrically similar—isomorphic in the sense I use the word—neural "toy in the head" corresponding to every "picture in the mind") has on so much psychobiological and psychological theorizing about perception. Coding theory makes many of the old questions meaningless (e.g., What is the significance of the inverted image? Is binocular depth a result of fusion or suppression of monocular images?) and stimulates new questions that were not previously possible to conceptualize (e.g., What neural dimensions correspond to perceived magnitude?). Coding theory and the neorationalism, or constructionism that some psychologists now find a more satisfactory synthesis of the great body of perceptual data, are intimately intertwined. Together they form the essential constructs of the global metatheory of perception that will be developed here.

Perhaps the significance of some of these ideas can be made more concrete by reference to a little allegory. Figure 1-1 depicts a model universe consisting of a murky lake, a rough bottom, and a man in a boat with a plumb bob on the end of a string. The man's task is to map the bottom of the lake by sounding it with the plumb bob. He is free to use any order of sounding he pleases as his strategy. From our omniscient viewpoint it is clear that the information that the man obtains about the bottom is going to be woefully incomplete without an exhaustive and impractical sounding of all points on the bottom. If his sample sounds are placed at regular intervals, he is very likely to miss irregularities in the bottom that are smaller than his sampling grid. If he samples irregularly (at random) he is very likely to miss the regular patterns that may exist on the bottom. Thus, at best, our allegorical *plumb-bobber* is going to have less than complete information about the bottom, and any map he makes will, of necessity, have to be an interpretive synthesis from the incomplete cues and clues that he was able to obtain.

The man in this little allegory is representative of some central perceiving process, and the plumb bob and line model the all-too-low-fidelity sensory communication channels through which we communicate with the external world (the lake bottom). The information about the bottom can be affected by the nature of the plumb bob, the string, or the dynamics of the boat. However, the main stress point of the allegorical relationship lies between the act of interpreting the incomplete plumbed data and the resultant percept. To the perceptual theorist, perhaps the most important part of the allegory is the murky water of the lake—

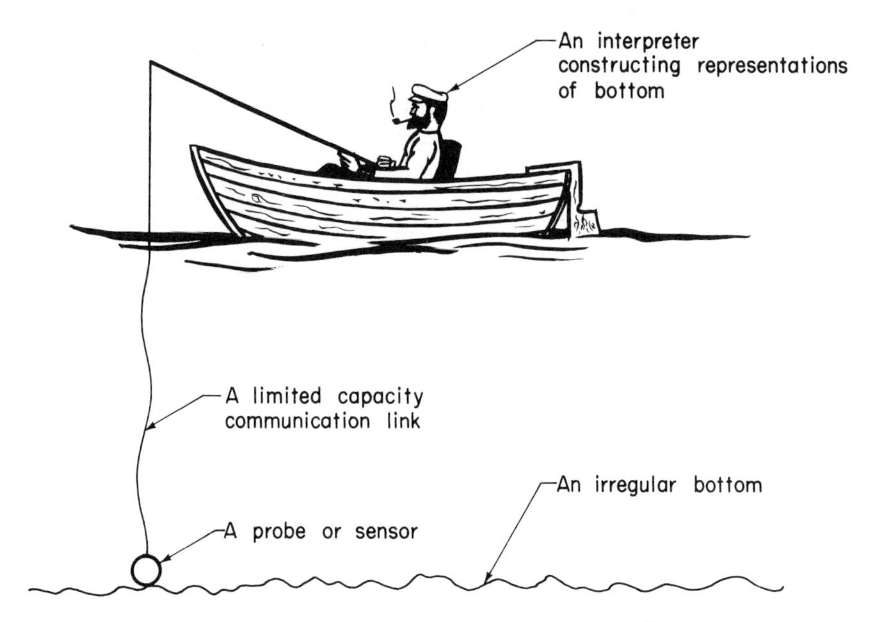

FIG. 1.1. A metaphorical representation of the processes of perception.

the barrier preventing our direct and complete apprehension of the external world. That part of the allegory, of course, represents the very limited capacity of our sensory communication channels.

Though it is a little frightening to contemplate, we are all cut off from the external world in a profound way. Whatever the "perceiving mind" is that makes up the essence of each of us, (and if there is anything certain in psychology it is that this fundamental concept of self-awareness or personal consciousness is far from being understood) each of us exists in an isolation that is penetrated and relieved only by communication along these very imperfect, and relatively low fidelity sensory communication channels. The old canard that we do not perceive the outside world at all but only the activity of our receptors has a very great degree of truth to it. The water is murky indeed.

As much as we have learned about these sensory pathways, this allegory also makes another important point concerning their relevance to the problem. The neural communication aspects of the nervous system, essential as they are for "plumbing the bottom," are not, in fact, identical with the integrative psychological act of perceiving. The essential part of this system, from the point of view of psychology, I believe, is the nature of the interpretive and inferential mechanisms modeled by the allegorical man in the allegorical boat. For these mechanisms we have not the slightest hint of a physiological model, and it is here that the neorationalistic and descriptive components of modern metatheory become essential if we are to achieve any understanding.

At this point the astute reader may feel that I am coming perilously close to the notion of the homunculus (the little man in the head so loved by medieval philosophers and despised by modern psychologists), but this is not what I mean, as shall be established later in this chapter. Rather, I am making a distinction between those parts of the peripheral nervous system that are mainly specialized for *communication* (with relatively modest integrative capacity) and those portions of the central nervous system that are specialized for *integrative* interactions and the synthesis of multiple inputs, as well as for the representation of mental processes in the sense modern theorists mean when they use the term *psychoneural equivalence*. For the communication processes, the neurophysiological or neoempiricistic component of a modern metatheory is the language of choice; the integration processes are better discussed in neorationalistic terms.

But what is perception? How are we to measure the intrapersonal responses that constitute these private experiences? What is the nature of a satisfactory "explanation" or "theory" of perception? What are the intellectual and conceptual problems and obstacles that stand in the way of our understanding this important aspect of the human mind? Each of these questions is both complex and continuously changing as new data are obtained or insights synthesized. This book, therefore, is capable only of presenting a snapshot of what the scientific community has to say about these issues in the late 1970s. Even then, it must be frankly admitted at the outset that most of the real fundamental issues remain both ill-formulated and unanswered at the present stage of development of perceptual science. Perception is but one part of the much more general mind-brain problem, which is itself both inadequately formulated and, as yet, unsolved.

Nevertheless, we do know some things about perception and we are accumulating a substantial (in fact, enormous) body of empirical knowledge (which I hope the reader appreciates is not the same thing as deep understanding) about both the phenomena of perception and the physiological mechanisms and processes that seem clearly to be related to the perceptual responses. And perhaps, at this time, it may be especially useful to step back from the details of laboratory investigation and attempt to achieve a broader perspective.

We are now very close to the sesqui-centennial of the origins of serious empirical research in perception (as distinguished from philosophical speculation and anecdotal reports). E. H. Weber's work dates from 1834 and G. T. Fechner's from 1860. It was only in 1879 that Wilhelm Wundt set up what is usually acknowledged as the first laboratory explicitly dedicated to experimental psychology. In the century that has passed, the data base has accumulated to such an abundance that its very mass is beginning to obscure the origins of this important scientific problem area.

There is, therefore, a serious need for a renewed consideration of the current conceptual, theoretical, and philosophical situation in perceptual sciences. Many of my colleagues are faced with such a variety of technical problems in their day-to-day activities in the laboratory that they often seem to forget *why* they are doing *what* they are doing. Theories seem to be increasingly microscopic in focus and consequently limited in what they have to say about the problem of perception in general. Such narrowness of perspective inevitably leads to "closed" microtheoretical systems that "explain" only within a narrowly circumscribed universe of discourse, or to experiments that, though technical tours de force, explain nothing. Indeed, the microtheories may actually be inconsistent with other relevant bodies of data and theory in many instances. Global understanding of the full range of perceptual problems cannot come from such externally inconsistent microsystems, but can only arise from a synthesis of what each subfield and each experiment says to us collectively. An explicit goal of this book, therefore, is synthesis and integration. It is a quest for a global view of what the laboratory's empirical data base tells us about the fundamental epistemological question of how we learn about the external world.

2. Toward a Definition of Perception

Before I can even begin to develop that global view, however, it is clear that a number of preliminary tasks must be at least tentatively considered in order to provide an adequate intellectual basis for the axioms of any synthetic theory. Primary among these preliminary tasks is the need to define what it is that is meant by the word *perception*. The perceptual literature is so vast and the variety of approaches to the problems so diverse that it is possible that all who consider themselves perceptual scientists (or who might teach a course by that name) may not actually be dealing with the same subject matter. I shall begin this discussion, therefore, with at least a tentative effort at defining the term and then follow up by a more operational approach in which I spell out the problems perceptual scientists seek to solve.[3]

As an initial thrust toward a definition of this elusive term, consider the following dictionary definition of perception from Webster (1963).

> *per-cep-tion*\pə(r) ′ sepshən\ *n*-s [L *perception-*, *perceptio* act of taking possession, obtaining, receiving, perceiving, fr. *perceptus* (past part. of *percipere* to take possession of, obtain, receive, perceive) + *-ion-*, *-io -ion*—more at PERCEIVE] 1: the receipt or collection of profits, rents, or crops—used chiefly in civil law ⟨the

[3]Over the years that I have been trying to define complex psychological terms, of which *perception* is but one example, I have finally come to the realization that the task is almost hopeless. At best, such definitions either reflect operational statements of the constraints put on the various topics by researchers in the relevant fields or simply call for some kind of commonsense agreement and, as a result, always leave much to be desired. Often they only provide some hints as to the connotation of the word rather than explicit statements of its denotation. My hope. therefore, here is only to emphasize certain salient aspects rather than to provide an exhaustive or exclusive definition of the term *perception*.

> lessee had the benefit of . . . the ~ of the profits for the whole term—C. G. Addison⟩ 2 *obs:* power of apprehension ⟨matter hath no life nor~, and is not conscious of its own existence—Richard Bentley †1742⟨ 3 a: a result of perceiving: OBSERVATION, DISCERNMENT ⟨it is a film bristling with sharp ~s but lacking in coherence—Arthur Knight⟩ b: a mental image: CONCEPT lyric ~s of friendship of love and lust—Edward Hubler⟩ ⟨endeavor to correct their~of what is beautiful by the opinions of other people—A. C. Benson⟩ 4 a: awareness of the elements of environment through physical sensation: reaction to sensory stimulus ⟨color~⟩⟨depth~⟩ ⟨since smell is a chemical sense, a contact is necessary for ~ — R. N. Shreve⟩ ⟨some sensation of ~ of the extremity after amputation is felt by 98% of patients—*Orthopedics & Traumatic Surgery*⟩ b: physical sensation is interpreted in the light of experience: the integration of sensory impressions of events in the external world by a conscious organism esp. as a function of nonconscious expectations derived from past experience and serving as a basis for or as verified by further meaningful motivated action 5 a: direct or intuitive recognition : intelligent discernment : APPRECIATION, INSIGHT ⟨a clear~of the uncertain boundary and the area in which there are bound to be limitations—F. L. Mott⟩ renewed ~ into the heart of human activity—H. V. Gregory⟩ b: a capacity for comprehension: intellectual grasp persecutors were ordinary reasonably well-intentioned people lacking in keen ~—C. H. Sykes⟩ [p. 1675].

My usage of the word *perception* in this volume is closest to the one given in 4a; namely, ''awareness of the elements of the environment through physical sensation'' or ''reaction to sensory stimulus.'' The subdefinition concisely incorporates many of the scientific meanings and uses of the word.

There is, however, one major regard in which I feel this part of the definition is quite inadequate. Implicit in this definition is what I believe to be the erroneous idea that sensory experiences and perception are separate and distinct processes, that is, that perception is a ''reaction to sensory stimulus,'' that perception is ''physical sensation as interpreted in the light of experience,'' or that it is the ''integration of sensory impressions.'' This dichotomization of input communication processes into simple sensations, or *sensa,* and complex perceptions, or *percepts,* is one that has had and continues to have quite a bit of currency in the psychological literature. Some psychological theories still implicitly assume that percepts arise from an associative synthesis of more primitive ''sensa.''[4]

Fortunately, the distinction between the two types of immediate responses, sensa and percepts, is finally passing out of favor. It is becoming increasingly difficult to maintain such a dichotomy as we begin to realize the unbelievable complexity of even the simplest *sensum.* About the only useful distinction that can currently be made between sensations and perceptions is that what is typi-

[4]The word *sensa* has been defined very loosely, but the general idea is that these are the most primitive and simple components of the perceptual response. This is an associationistic concept, however, that, as we shall see, has lost much of its credibility. For example, a particular color is a sensum. Feigl's (1958) term ''raw feels'' also connotes the same concept of a primitive, immediate element of sensory experience.

cally called sensory research is usually aimed more at determining the relationships between the mental response and a single dimension of the stimulus, whereas the perceptual scientist is usually more interested in the multidimensional aspects of both the stimulus and the response. Nevertheless, this is just another way of saying sensations are simple and perceptions are complex; it is not a meaningful way to dichotomize these very similar classes of phenomena.

Clearly any such distinction of these immediate mental responses into sensations and perceptions is especially inadequate because of the fluctuating state of knowledge in perceptual science. Such a dichotomy inevitably falls victim to the continuously changing boundaries of explanation. What had been considered simple often turns out to be more complex than once thought, and what had been considered complex often turns out to be simple as new insights are achieved in the laboratory or in the study. The actual processes underlying sensa and percepts, or sensations and perceptions, therefore, actually differ only in terms of trivial details of experimental design and not in any fundamental psychobiological manner.

Furthermore, I personally find it extremely difficult to make any satisfactory distinction between sensations, as mental responses that seem somewhat more amenable to neuroreductionistic analysis, and perceptual processes that are somewhat less analyzable. This, too, is a very labile criterion, and the change can go either way; we are only somewhat more likely to explain newly some percept in neurophysiological terms than we are to lose what had been a plausible neural model of some sensation.

Other themes struck in this dictionary definition, however, are insightful and useful. One of the most significant is that perception is a mental *response*. Perceptions, of course, are most often stimulated or triggered by some external event. Though the response may be modulated and modified by factors intrinsic to the organism, the essence of perceptual research is the study of the appropriate, congruent, and partially veridical mental responses to the pattern of stimulus information coming from the external world. Mental responses, such as percepts, from this point of view, take on most, if not all, of the attributes of any behavioral response with but one significant exception: They are not *inter*personally observable. Rather, perceptions are ultimately *intra*personal and can only be indirectly examined by an external observer through the medium of overt behavior or introspection.

Psychologists are gradually emerging from a rigid shell of radical metaphysical behaviorism that denies the measurability, if not the very existence, of those intrapersonal mental processes that we are coming to appreciate as the essential topics of perceptual inquiry. Though this may be called progress by some, by no means does it necessarily imply that we are close to solving one of the most fundamental problems of intellectual history—how we gain direct knowledge of other minds. This is the problem that Natsoulas (1978a) has referred to as that of "residual subjectivity" in his eloquent championing of the continued need for introspective techniques in modern psychology and his critique of any philosophy that suggested that it might be possible to develop a purely objective psychology.

Perceptual psychology, the science of some mental responses, is forced into a situation in which it is epistemologically, if not metaphysically, behavioristic; i.e., although it is strategically behavioristic, our science need not deny the ultimate reality of percepts or other mental processes. The allegorical murky waters that obscure an individual's view of the external world are equally effective in concealing the properties of an individual's mind from the probes of the psychological researcher. It is through a series of incomplete clues signaled over the low fidelity *efferent* communication channels and overt behaviors that we must plumb the mind of man, just as each mind can only partially discern the external world through equally poor *afferent* communication channels. Just as the perceiver has no direct contact with the environment, only with the responses of his nervous system, so, too, is there no direct evidence of the mental state or percept in the behavioral response. Behavior, like perception, is a heavily mediated interpretation of the intrapersonal mental awareness. "I see a blue circle," tells us nothing about the actual nature of the perceptual experience, only about the perceiver's encoded behavioral response to them. Joseph Lappin (in press b) has also eloquently considered this profound problem of direct reporting of perceptual experience. I refer the reader to this paper for a much more extensive discussion of this fundamental conundrum.

Another closely related aspect of this dictionary definition with which most contemporary psychologists would find general agreement is that perception is an active interpretive, inferential, and integrative process in which the properties of the organism strongly modulate whatever influences are exerted by the stimuli. The concept of a dynamic, rather than passive perceiver—one who actively processes incoming information—is another way of stating a key emerging principle of current perceptual research. Man does not perceive solely by passive, automatic, and empiricistic processes, but also by active manipulation of the meaning of the pattern of signals that pass along his afferent nerves. This is another phrasing of the neorationalistic theme that I have suggested must be a major component of any viable metatheory of perception.

There is, therefore, still another parallel between the role of the perceiver and the psychologist. Both the psychologist and the perceiver are capable only of inferring from partial information what the nature of the target doman is. While the psychologist concocts theories and hypotheses to describe and explain the nature of a mind that is not directly observable, the mind also concocts theories and hypotheses (i.e., percepts) to describe and explain the nature of the external world of which it has only partial information. Thus, the only partially permeable communication barrier between the inner and the outer worlds is at least symmetrical.

A further important point, also emphasized in this surprisingly coherent and effective part of the dictionary definition, is that perception is rarely a function of any single stimulus dimension or of even the simple aggregation of immediately available stimuli. Rather, we see, as the tale told in this book unfolds, that the percept, in many situations, is the result of an interactive combination and integration of multiple stimulus dimensions and of information that had been stored in the nervous system as a result of previous experience. This multidimensional and immediate-mixed-with-past determination of percepts is ubiquitously evidenced in the empirical data base; virtually no percept is independent of its present context nor of its relevant past. Whether it be motion, color, lightness, shape, or any one of the host of other dimensions of perception, our experimental findings repeatedly tell us that the currently apparent or perceived is always the result of the *interaction* of a number of different aspects of the immediate physical scene and the observer's previous experiences.

Though it is easy to accept this notion of multidimensional influences when presented in this context, it is somewhat disconcerting to see how many psychophysical experiments are carried out from what seems to be a unidimensional point of view. The words *psychophysical law* nowadays denote an observed functional relationship between one dimension of the stimulus and one dimension of the perceptual response. The lack of precise empirical validation of any psychophysical law in other than pooled data suggests that such an approach may, however, be largely fallacious. (See my discussion of this topic on pp. 260–273 in Uttal, 1973.)

This dictionary definition also suggests another subtle and complex general property of perception. It implies that the processes that led to the perception are themselves undetectable even by the perceiving organism. In other words, we perceive as a result of the function of information processing mechanisms of which we are not aware. Only the final result of the process is subject to perception, not the underlying neural, computational, cognitive, or inferential processes that led to that construct.

The final significant aspect of this dictionary definition is that perception is psychologically immediate. Whatever the mechanisms are that compute the final characteristics of the percept, they occur relatively rapidly following the presentation of the stimulus. This is particularly so for the class of experimental paradigms that constitute the subject matter of this book. If there is any single criterion that allows us to distinguish between perception (the topic of this volume) and cognition or thinking (the topic of the next book in this series), it is the degree of immediacy and automaticity of each. As is now also becoming well appreciated, the more immediate processes are also those that seem to be present at the earliest stages of perceptual development. Thus, another distinguishing criterion between perception and cognition may simply be the relative degree of growth or pasticity of each process over the individual's life course.

In sum, then, the word perception, as I shall use it within the context of this book is defined by the following paraphrase:

> *Perception is the relatively immediate, intrapersonal, mental response evoked as a partial, but not exclusive, result of impinging multidimensional stimuli, as modulated by the transforms imposed by the neural communica-*

tion system, previous experience, and contextual reasonableness. Each percept is the conscious end product of both simple computational transformations and more complex constructionistic "interpretations." However, the underlying neural and symbolic processes are not part of the observer's awareness.

The nutshell abstract of the dictionary definition concentrates on those aspects of the word that I shall emphasize in the rest of this book. I should acknowledge that this definition's restriction of perception to "relatively immediate" responses differs from the view of some of my colleagues who now would more closely unify these immediate aspects of perception with other subsequent cognitive processing tasks.

Obviously this brief definition has been tailored to fit my interests and the goals of this book. Equally obvious is the fact that a word like perception, which carries such heavy denotative and connotative baggage, is not easily defined within the confines of a nutshell. Many authors have filled entire books trying more or less successfully to clarify what this term means. For the reader interested in definitions of greater depth, I recommend a reading of the much more intense philosophical and historical literature (Armstrong, 1960; Boring, 1942; Hamlyn, 1961; Pastore, 1971; Russell, 1927; Smythies, 1956; Swartz, 1977; Warnock, 1967.)

I also appreciate the need to define further some of the vocabulary used in this definition of perception. Most of these *words* are translated into *operational concepts* by subsequent discussions in this book, but perhaps a word or two about the word *immediate* is in order at this point in our discussion. I have intentionally qualified the word by adding the adverb *relatively* and, by so doing, have left the classification of any response as a percept open to judgment. My own judgment, nevertheless, is that there are some mental responses that occur very automatically, are only weakly subject to experience, have very short reaction times, and involve little attentive manipulation. This is the context in which immediate is used and the criterion that I shall use to distinguish between a perceptual and cognitive process. In the following section I try to particularize the specific issues that confront modern research in perceptual psychology.

B. THE ISSUES

Now that I have briefly introduced the subject matter of this book and have made at least a step toward defining what is meant by perception, my next task is to sharpen our perspective of what the issues are in this scientific endeavor. Any science, no matter how empirical, does what it does in the laboratory each day in order to answer certain fundamental questions. Because these fundamental questions are rarely made explicit in the laboratory, there is often some doubt about the more serious reasons for pursuing a particular line of research: Defining the most immediate technical issues does not provide this answer. In its search for understanding of the full complexity of the world in which we live, science often uses abstractions of total reality, and because these abstractions themselves possess little of the relevance our times seem to demand, many researchers (as well as most students) lose track, at least part of the time, of what motivates the particular experiments that make up the "meat and potatoes" of their daily research activities. In this section I try to provide a sketch of the fundamental problems, questions, and issues motivating perceptual research. These issues will vary from the heights of the most profound and all-encompassing questions about the nature of man and/or reality down to a level just above the actual laboratory queries themselves.

None of these fundamental questions is, as yet, completely answered. This is why the field of perceptual research is still active. Many of the questions may never be answered—their breadth and profundity may prohibit any possibility of ever attaining a complete resolution of the intellectual challenge they represent. As we see many times in this book, it is far easier to pose a global question than it is to answer it. And although in some cases we do see the faint beginning glimmer of an illuminating answer, in the main, speculation and intuition are still the only answers to many of the issues that I list in this section.

As a result, a host of competing theories, schools, and points of view concerning perceptual theory have emerged over the years. It is clear that, as in so many other instances in science, no particular point of view is likely to triumph conclusively over all of the others. Rather, each perspective, each system, each theory will, far more likely, contribute to and be synthesized into a single, unified, global solution in which the differing explanations will be found to complement rather than exclude each other.

In this section, as I ask the questions, in some cases I allude to some answers about which my contemporaries seem to have reached some consensual perspective. Much of the later part of this book is intended to provide more complete empirical evidence for these possible answers and for the general principles that I believe best serve as a fair modern statement of what we know about visual perception today. At this point, the prospective answer presented also may serve to clarify my prejudices concerning the scientific study of perception. The questions proposed here are not mutually exclusive; they feed back and forth, mutually influencing each other and often including each other. I have tried to arrange them from the more general and philosophical to the more specific and technical, to provide, at least, some semblance of order.

1. How Do We Acquire Knowledge About the External World?

This question, as stated previously, is the most global expression of the fundamental epistemological issue of perceptual science and the query from which all of the others derive. However, this broad and all-inclusive statement of the problem of knowledge acquisition in general, and of perception in particular, is almost impossible to cope with experimentally as well as conceptually. As phrased, this question clearly does not represent a single question but rather an aggregate of subissues that interact strongly to affect the evolution of any particular global philosophical or scientific theory of perception. If there is any answer to this grand question, it would have to be formulated as a system of answers to each member of an intricate set of subquestions. Such a system of answers collectively would represent a comprehensive theory of perception, but clearly no such universal theory yet exists. To proceed further, it is necessary both to consider what might constitute a satisfactory explanatory theory and to partition the overall problem of perception into more manageable subproblems.

2. What Is the Nature of External Reality?

The classic philosophies of *rationalism* and *empiricism* have been in conflict for centuries over the means by which we perceive external reality. This is the foundation problem of epistemology. The corresponding foundation problem in metaphysics concerns the actual nature of that external reality. The major controversy, in this case, is between *physicalism* and *idealism*. Physicalism asserts that the fundamental level of reality is physical or mechanical; matter exists independently of its being perceived by any sentient being. Idealism, on the other hand, says that physical reality is secondary and that it exists only to the extent mental processes give it substance. This dichotomy is closely related to the disagreement between monistic theories that assert that all reality is of a single type and the dualisms (or pluralisms) that assert that mind and matter are separate forms of reality. But these two issues—(1) What is the nature of reality? and (2) What is the nature of mind?—are not the same. Monisms may be either physicalistic or idealistic. Bishop George Berkeley's (1685–1753) idealistic and monistic immaterialism, for example, asserted that external reality exists only to the extent it is perceived by some observer (Berkeley, 1709/1954) Gottfied Wilhelm Leibniz (1646–1716) idealism was also of this same genre. There was only one level of reality (a monism) but it was a mental one (an idealism). In the main, however, modern scientific monisms are physicalistic, rather than idealistic, and assert both explicitly and implicitly that, however difficult it is to understand, the physical world is real, continuous, and, in fact, essential to the existence of mental processes. To the radical physicalist, therefore, mental processes exist only as the functions of material (physical) entities.

Idealistic and physicalistic monisms thus differ completely in their respective emphases on the nature of the relationship between perception and the external universe. The idealistic view imputes primacy to the mental processes, the percepts, whereas the physicalistic view attributes primacy to the physical entities. In spite of the antiquity and familiarity of the debate, in this world of physical measurements of objects with demonstrable histories throughout which they must have existed, even though unobserved, it is difficult to think in terms other than those of physical realism without jeopardizing the entire scientific adventure. In the study of perception in particular, the physical stimulus must be taken as given, as a reference and as an anchor, possessing an independently measurable set of properties against which the responses of the human mind can be tested. The differences that obtain between perception and physical reality in this sense become the essential clues to understanding how the critical transformations are carried out on the incident information on its way to becoming perceptual experiences.

But how can we know the nature of the physical universe against which we can test the percepts for verdicality? The only answer to this question is that physical reality must be considered to be the most likely value emerging from a wide variety of measurements made with many different instruments. However, whatever instrument produced them, all measures must, of course, be introduced into the observer's nervous system through one or another of the sensory channels. Some measures, however, are more direct and easier for the organism to process than others. Thus, our senses can be supplemented and aided by rulers, spectroscopes, clocks, and scales. A consensus of all of these outputs from a wide range of measuring devices defines, at least for the moment, the physical reality against which perception must be tested in a world in which no direct verification is ever really possible. Mechanical measuring instruments help to define reality not because they bypass the sensory processes completely but because they simplify the information processing task required of the perceptual mechanisms. Instruments convert complex physical reality into a simpler and less ambiguous set of abstractions that do not strain the capacity of the sensory channel as much as would the full scope of the external stimulus world.

Another means of establishing a reference against which to test the verdicality of perceptions is provided by mathematics. Some physical entities are not directly observable because they are either too big or too small to fall within the range of the best microscope or balance. Mathematical models or descriptions can provide a model of these entities or situations in which the only observations that are possible may be ambiguous or misleading. For example, the counterintuitive physical nature of particulate matter is now best described in terms of mathematical statements, statistical probabilities, and consistency with a more general theory of physical reality. However, our perception of the effects of such matter is clearly deviant from the fundamental reality. Nevertheless, it is possible to understand the discrepancy in terms of the transformation between the characteristics of the mathematical model and those of the percept.

It is against the external reality defined by these simplified alternative measurements and mathematical models, therefore, that we must test the veridicality of our perceptions, not against any unambiguous, and totally independent measure of reality. Perceptual truth is nothing more than the maximum congruence between the perceptual models and the predictions that guide our subsequent interactions with the external world. Veridicality, therefore, is the confirmation of alternative models or predictions; it becomes nothing less than the most probable agreement among or between different modalities at a given time or within the same modality at different times. Whatever it is, veridicality is not agreement between percepts and some absolute references; it is, at best, agreement among different percepts.

In this regard, it is interesting to note that the prevailing concept of physical reality itself at any point in history is frustratingly impermanent. The idealists were not entirely wrong. What constitutes man's concept of physical reality, if not physical reality itself, is a product of the prevailing state of science. Physical models were once framed in terms of the four ''elements''—fire, earth, water, and air—but this was supplanted by the medieval awareness of the alchemists that different chemicals existed. Newton changed physical reality when he introduced a new view of physics, as did Einstein. Modern particle physics—dynamic, possibly probabilistic, and striving for a yet unseen order—is also very likely to revolutionize our perception of reality. In just the past few generations we have seen models of physical reality pass from those based on atomic units, to those founded on electrons and three or four intranuclear particles, and on to ideas based on a large number of different hadrons and leptons (subnuclear particles). Nevertheless, even this contemporary model of physical reality may already be obsolescent. Indirect evidence now suggests that some of the ''basic'' nuclear particles are themselves composed of a much smaller number of even more fundamental particles called quarks (see Chapter 3).

The question—What is the nature of physical reality that can be used as an anchor against which to reference perceptual responses?—must, therefore, be answered by another question—When? This is not to say that the ultimate nature of matter has changed. That would imply a radical idealism that, as I previously noted, is unpalatable to modern science; but rather that the current reference is not stable and that our percepts are not quite as solidly anchored to a concrete and permanent world of well-defined stimuli as some of us would like to believe.

A somewhat surprising outcome of this line of thought is the argument that it is only by accident and chance that any of our perceptions are ''veridical.'' Modern evidence concerning the manner in which sensory information is encoded and interpreted suggests that there is not necessarily a direct correspondence between the dimensions of the external world and the dimensions of our perception of it. Illusions, selective perception, and a host of other distortions of external reality all attest to the fact that the stimulus and the percept can be, and very often are, dimensionally quite different from each other just as nonisomorphic encoding is often the case for the mediating neural communication systems. Once it is shown that external physics and internal percepts can be dissociated in some cases, there is no further need to postulate that a direct linkage must exist in any other case. The percept is thus freed of the a priori necessity of any direct, deterministic, or causal relationship to the stimulus—it becomes, at least, a partial resultant, and, at most, only a symbolic, constructed inference or interpretation of the external world.

Many perceptual phenomena (particularly in the spatial and temporal dimensions) display a considerable amount of veridicality. However, for some phenomena, the dimensions of the percepts (colors, tones, and affects, for example) actually have no direct physical counterpart against which to test veridicality—the dimensions of the percept are only indirectly related to the pattern or "meaning" of the physical stimulus. The word *veridicality,* in these cases, loses much of its meaning and becomes more akin to some degraded form of response compatibility or consensual agreement. Our percepts are veridical to the extent that they produce responses that agree with the results of other means of measurement, or, in Hake, Rodwan, and Weintraub's (1966) terms, to the extent that they are coherent or internally consistent with the observer's previous experiences, set, and expectations or to the extent people agree about them. Beyond that, physical reality remains as elusive as the mind and "veridicality" an equally elusive and at best probabilistic criterion.

3. What Kinds of Scientific Theories of Perception Are Plausible?

It is important to reiterate that it is highly unlikely that any single theory of perception will ever completely supplant all the others. Current perceptual theories, in large part, are either microtheories dealing with some limited aspect of the total range of perceptual problems or broad macrotheories making some general statement about perceptual epistemology. It is highly unlikely that any of the microtheories proposed so far will ever be generalized sufficiently to answer the general epistemological question or that any macrotheory will be shown by logic or empirical observations to be correct at all levels. Rather, complementarity of perceptual theories is likely to continue to exist for the foreseeable future.

We can, however, ask certain general questions about theories in order to better understand their role in perceptual science. For example, what are the general approaches to theories of perception? If we ignore, for the moment, the philosophical accounts of possible epistemologies, we can distinguish three different classes or categories of perceptual theories that have originated within the psychological sciences: Neuroreductionistic, mathematical-descriptive, and cross psychological or semantic. Each class emphasizes a particular approach and point of view and is representative of the macrotheoretical theories that are detailed in Chapter 2.

a. Neuroreductionistic Theories

This category includes those models of perception that seek to explain perceptions by invoking the language and data of neurophysiology as theoretical constructs. Relationships are sought between the responses of neurons (and/or systems of neurons) and various perceptual phenomena. Such a theoretical approach is reductionistic in the sense that explanations of phenomena at one level of scientific analysis are sought in terms of the cumulative effects of components at a lower (i.e., more microscopic) level of analysis.

Three main varieties of neuroreductionistic theories can be discerned in the modern literature. The first, the single cell approach, emphasizes the responses of individual neurons as the unit of reductive analysis; the second, the neural network approach, emphasizes the action of networks of discrete neurons; and the third, the neuroelectric field approach, considers the actions of continuous fields of neuroelectric activity within the brain.

Single cell neuroreductionistic theories of perception, whatever the particular details of their formulation, share a number of common features. Generally they emphasize the selective response or filtering action of single cells or "channels" to particular spatiotemporal properties of the stimulus. Different neurons in different places become the essential equivalents of different percepts from the point of view of this type of theory. There is an implicit premise in such theories that the nervous system responds more or less automatically and passively to the properties of the stimulus. Activation of a particular set of neurons, it is almost always implied but rarely explicitly stated, is tantamount to the mental (perceptual) response. The individual features of the stimuli are usually the dominant factors in such theories of perception and though they may be modulated by the selective or filtering properties of the individual neurons, the stimuli are held to define totally the percept. The extrapolation of Hubel and Wiesel's (e.g., 1959, 1963, 1972) elegant physiological data to theories of perception by a very large number of psychobiologists is the most notable example of this class of explanation. Perhaps the most explicit statement of such a single cell neuroreductionistic theory is Barlow's (1972) paper. This particularly eloquent statement brings out into the open some of the dogma inherent in modern single cell neurophysiological models. I counter this approach with certain heresies in Chapter 9.

Neural network theories of perception, on the other hand, stress the more generalized ability of ensembles of neurons to process incoming information algorithmically, that is, by use of unspecialized neural mechanisms that do not respond specifically to specific features but that do execute general computational functions (algorithms) on whatever input patterns they encounter. Network theories may thus, in principle, respond either to the particular features of incoming stimulus patterns or to the overall arrangement of the features into a global form. But the essential aspect of this kind of theory is that the individual cell is not the important analytic agent; rather the collective action of an ensemble of neurons is fundamental. Once processed by the networks, the transformed pattern produces a neural network state which (according to some) must be decoded or (according to others) may itself represent the end product—the percept. The prototypical neural network theory is presented in Pitts and McCulloch's (1947) now classic paper, "How We Know Universals."

Those models that deal with the neuroelectric activity of the brain as a continuous field seek to emulate the successes of field theory in physics. An advantage of this approach is that the brain's aggregate electrical activity is dimensionally closer to the molar attributes of mental processes. A disadvantage is that such theories usually result in some sort of an expressed isomorphism. However, this "picture in the head" approach seems archaic given the concepts of symbolic encoding and representation that have gained credibility in recent years. The classic field theories were embodied in the now unacceptable models proposed by the gestalt psychologists. More modern field theories, such as that of Pribram, Nuwer, and Baron (1974) have rejuvenated some of these ideas.

A major problem with some field theories is that they are often not explanatory theories at all. Some workers have proposed "theories" that are no more than physical analogs of mental processes. Gross similarities in the form of the processes and formal mathematical tools are sometimes presented as explanations when in fact they explain nothing about the underlying mechanisms or transformations. A further problem is that such physical analogies very often carry with them a tremendous load of superfluous meaning that can seriously mislead the student of perception if they are taken without a full appreciation of the differences between the two analogous mechanisms.

Both neural network and neuroelectric field theories are also usually held to be implicitly passive in the sense that the response is thought to emerge almost automatically, following certain prescribed manipulations of the incoming stimulus information. Isomorphism of perceptual response states with the stimulus is often also an integral part of such theories, that is, the patterned neural response is usually thought to be of the same spatial or temporal "shape" as the percept.

b. Mathematical-Descriptive Theories of Perception

A second major category of perceptual theory includes mathematical or verbal descriptions of perceptual phenomena. Theories of this class are typically not neuroreductionistic; they themselves make no attempt to reduce the perceptual phenomena to their neural correlates or equivalents except as an incidental by-product or by using neural ideas as heuristic metaphors or as quite separable assumptions. Rather, their goal is the best possible formal description of the phenomena that occur so that predictions can be made from one type of stimulus situation to another. Theories of this kind also often seek to suggest sequences and pathways of interaction among processes that are only described functionally.[5] In this kind of theory the perceiving mind is often dealt with in much the same terms as a computer program and is assumed to grind out certain transformations in a lawful and regular manner. Many of the current

---

[5]This is sometimes not appreciated and some theoreticians have mistakenly assumed that the blocks or channels of information flow in some diagrams are real anatomical entities.

information-processing (computerized or not) models of perception fall into this class, as do some of the classic theories of color perception. Indeed all models that deal only with stimulus–response (psychophysical) data must necessarily be members of this class of descriptive theory.

I must emphasize that mathematical and neural assumptions in many theories are totally separable even when they are presented jointly. It is entirely possible to reject the mathematical assumptions and accept the neural ones and vice versa. Mathematics is the method of analogy taken to the extreme. Although it can help one to reject an implausible model, it can never specify a unique neural solution to the problem of underlying mechanism. Although a mathematical model may fit a phenomenon superbly, any attendent neural hypotheses are not necessarily supported by that good fit.

c. Cross-Psychological Models or Semantic Models

A third class of theory purporting to explain perceptual phenomena includes what may simply be referred to as cross-psychological models. In this case, there is no attempt either to reduce the phenomena to neural terms or to model formally or describe fully the processes. The effort to explain is limited to descriptions of perceptions as manifestations of other related psychological processes. The concept of perceptual defense (the perceptual suppression of words or pictures with negative affect or "immoral" overtone) in Directive State Theory (see Chapter 2) is an example of a cross-psychological model of perception.

Typically, theories of this sort deal with the more global and molar psychological aspects of perception of a level of complexity so great as to preclude any physiological reductionism, or of such great variability as to severely limit any mathematical description. Cross-psychological theories usually reference perceptual phenomena to such other aspects of the mind as intelligence, personality, emotion, and motivation and assume a much more active participation on the part of the observer in the perceptual process than do the previous two categories. The emphasis is on defining the cognitive significance and explaining the construction of percepts, partially on the basis of incoming stimulation, but with a heavy emphasis on past experience, meaning, and personal significance. What seems to the perceiver to be reasonable or logical is typically a major part of these cross-psychological or semantic models. The concept of symbolic representation (as opposed to isomorphic coding) is also usually more easily accepted within the context of these theories. The stimulus in such theories of perception also assumes less importance than the context in which it is embedded, the effect of past experiences, and the logical (or prejudicial) consistency with the organism's present "set." Obviously all cross-psychological level theories of perception operate at a nonreductionistic level in which it is easy to incorporate the ideas of the classic rationalistic philosophies.

What then are the criteria for a satisfactory theory of perception? In Chapter 4, I detail more completely my argument for an eclectic theory of perception that includes components from all three of the categories I have just described. I make the argument that each has a contribution to offer and that neurophysiological, mathematical, and psychological tools must all be brought to bear on the problem of perception for any real progress to be made toward achieving understanding in this complex field of science.

The definition of a satisfactory theory of perception, therefore, depends on many criteria: One's point in history, the subproblem being studied, and the available tools, as well as the practicalities of scientific explanation. There can be, therefore, no best theory of perception, but only a cluster of theories and certain broad points of view. Ultimately, any comprehensive perspective will be forced to invoke concepts and models from each of the three levels of theory that I have described here.

To speak more specifically to the matter of what constitutes a satisfactory theory of perception is to ask what the actual criteria are for judging between existing alternatives. Floyd Allport (1955), in one of the most remarkable and thoughtful analyses of the full range of perceptual theory, has suggested a set of six criteria for testing the relative validity of perceptual theories. Slightly paraphrased, his criteria are as follows:

1. Agreement with Facts:
   Does the theory agree with the data? Is it at least consistent, if not in obvious conflict, with the observed data?
2. Generality:
   Does the theory have explanatory value beyond the immediate data?
3. Parsimony:
   The fewer the postulates, the better the theory.
4. Immediate experimental availability:
   Can the theory be tested?
5. Logical consistency.
6. Explanatory value:
   Is the theory useful in explaining data by relating it to another level of discourse or does it simply "explain" by analogy or restatement of the data? [Paraphrased from pp. 8–9]

To Allport's six criteria, I would like to add a seventh:

7. Predictability and extrapolatability:
   Can the theory be used to extend our view of the world to data that may not yet have become available?

This criterion is not totally different from Allport's second and fourth ones but does add a somewhat different emphasis.

The three general approaches to theories of perception that I have discussed here, of course, encompass a very broad spectrum of radically different perspectives. Allport, for example, devotes over five hundred pages of his densely written text to a critical analysis of the most important historical theories of perception. In Chapter 2, I briefly consider the most notable global theories of perception, as well as some of the views of modern workers, and expand upon the tripartite scheme I presented here.

The basic question of what constitutes a satisfactory theory of perception, nevertheless, remains intractable. Perception is a word too poorly defined and with so many different ramifications that it is possible we would not be able to appreciate an optimum solution to the problem should we by some miracle fall upon it.

4. Is Any Theory of Perception Possible?

We are thus faced with an even more challenging question than that of the criteria of acceptability, namely, "Is any theory of perception possible?" Examples of the second (mathematical-descriptive) and third (cross-psychological) type of models described in the preceding comment can be certainly invented ad infinitum, and quasi-neural hypotheses concerning perception also abound. It is easy to draw analogies between different psychological processes, and there is literally no limit to the number of different mathematical models that can be used to describe individual perceptual phenomena. However, there is a real question whether it is possible to develop any theory of perception that would be: (1) broad enough to span several different, though indirectly related, phenomena; and (2) validly reductionistic in a neurophysiological or other structural sense.

Knuth (1976) and Stockmeyer and Chandra (1979), in considering the computability of complex processes, point out that there are many problems, some obviously and some subtly complicated, that exceed all conceivable computational power man could bring to bear on their potential solutions. Even problems concerning processes that are finite (in the formal mathematical sense) can require so many steps to be evaluated as to negate any hope that they will ever be practically solved. Interestingly enough, the type of problems that these computation theorists feel are potentially members of this unsolvable class often involve just the sort of logical networks that many others feel are most closely comparable to those neural networks that must underlie perception. Furthermore, Gödel's (1930) famous theorem that internal consistency within a system cannot be proven within the axioms of the system, has been interpreted by some mathematician philosophers to mean that the human mind can never understand itself or its foundation mechanisms. Whether or not these gloomy philosophies are valid, we must certainly not take for granted that the search for explanations of mental processes is a priori an achievable one. It simply *may not be possible* to do what we psychologists are trying to do—develop a comprehensive reductive theory of perception. This is not to say that *it is not possible* but only to keep the issue of the plausibility of theoretical explanation open. Of course, this does not deny that incomplete theories may be useful or interesting; it asserts only that in a theoretically ideal sense we may be facing some fundamental limits in explaining ourselves and the world we live in.

With this somewhat pessimistic view of the solvability of the perceptual theory problem let us now consider two corollaries of this general question that inquire into the specific difficulties encountered when attempts are made to develop either neuroreductionistic theories or psychological theories of perception.

a. Is a Purely Physiological Theory of Perception Possible?

As I have already noted, one dominant approach in current perceptual theory is to reduce the language of molar responses to the constructs of neurophysiological observations. However, the tests of necessity and sufficiency required to validate such neurophysiological models of perceptual responses have been made in only a few specialized instances.

A number of psychologists suspect that for many phenomena there has been a massive misinterpretation of the psychological significance of what may even be highly correlated neural responses. Although a few solidly established connections have been made between perceptual phenomena and a relevant body of neural data (the most obvious examples are between contour intensification phenomena and lateral inhibitory interactions in the retinal network or between receptor photochemistry and trichromatic color addition), many workers now believe that such phenomena as simultaneous contrast and geometric illusions, often attributed to peripheral mechanisms, are, in fact, not well modeled by any such simple peripheral neural processes. Nor for that matter is there universal agreement with the hypothesis that pattern recognition processes are adequately described by the dynamics of single neurons in the visual regions of the cerebral cortex.

The thesis that will be presented in this book is that, at best, the response of a single neuron can no better tell us about the molar behavior of the organism than the action of a single molecule of gas can describe the overall characteristics of a container filled with innumerable molecules. I, therefore, argue against such simplistic theories in my critique of single cell models of perception in Chapter 9. I assert that, all too often, both practitioners and proponents of the microelectrode technology seem to overlook the fact that the representation of any psychological process must be the resultant of the ensemble action of such a massive number of neurons that rigorous neurophysiological explanations of perceptual phenomena are likely to be the rare exception, rather than the usual result of our theoretical endeavors.

In this opinion I am not alone. Many other perceptual psychologists seem to appreciate the inadequacy of overly simplified neural theories of perception and are moving toward this same conclusion. For example, Lloyd Kaufman (1974), author of a particularly insightful text on perception, says:

> Though brain events must underlie events that are reported, brain events relevant to behavior are far more numerous than those associated with what can be reported. There is a many-one relation that makes it extraordinarily difficult to see how a unique configuration of brain activity can be arrived at from a particular set of experiences. The experiences are themselves more complicated than any report of experiment can reveal. The brain activity underlying the totality of behavior, including that which is reportable, is even more complicated. It is therefore unwise to say that because a particular tissue preparation gives an electrophysiological result that formally resembles the properties of a perceptual response, this particular physiological mechanism must therefore underlie or explain the perception [pp. 8–9].

Irwin Rock (1975) makes a very similar point:

> My most clearly identifiable bias is one which runs counter to the prevailing Zeitgeist, my belief that it is premature to seek to explain perceptual phenomena in terms of neurophysiological mechanisms (despite my agreement that in the final analysis psychological facts are explicable in terms of brain events). Because we seem to be in the midst of a revolution within sensory physiology, based on the discoveries of so-called neural feature-detector units, many teachers may consider this bias very serious. Yet the fact is that those who are making these discoveries (let alone their disciples in psychology) are by no means certain of the precise role of these mechanisms in determining perception. It seems to me that a careful consideration of the perceptual phenomena these detector mechanisms are presumed to explain is necessary, timely, and valuable [p. vi].

George Miller and Phillip Johnson–Laird (1976) add: "Moreover, the relation of our psychological results to the electrical and biochemical events that we can observe in the brain is so obscure that many philosophers suspect a fundamental conceptual error in the way most psychologists and neurophysiologists think about the relation [p. 36]."

A similar chord is struck by Peter Dodwell (1975) when he asserts:

> the point is to caution against overenthusiastic invocation of hypothetical physiological processes to explain psychophysical phenomena. A great many facts about visual perception are compatible with the neurophysiological findings, but the instances where an interpretation of the former in terms of the latter is forced on us by the tightness of the relationship are quite rare, and, for the most part, are at the first level of visual *detection*. The phenomena of scotopic and photopic vision and their relationship to rod and cone function are the outstanding example of such a tight association (see, e.g., Cornsweet, 1970). In particular the physiological findings on contour coding should be viewed with caution, so far as pattern and object recognition are concerned [p. 63].

A few of the more thoughtful neuroscientists such as Ragnar Granit seem to be moving in the same direction. Granit (1977), for example, says in his most recent book: "It would be a cardinal mistake to assume that "feature detectors" or for that matter "featureless detectors," such as spatial sine wave frequencies within a complex figure, are building blocks of perception in any other sense than as neural organizations making available "cues" for a central "interpreter" capable of matching them against other frameworks of reference [pp. 122–123]."

In all fairness I must note that all of these statements by these distinguished scientists have a somewhat defensive note to them. "Most perceptual theorists" and the "prevailing Zeitgeist," these authors tell us, seem to think otherwise and accept simple neuroreductionistic models of perception. If this is true (and it may not be—my experiences in recent years suggest that the simplistic neural models are well past their peak of influence),[6] then this book too will have to join the good company of this respectfully concerned, but critical, minority.

It should not be misunderstood that this negative attitude towards biological models of perception is only some sort of latter-day antireductionistic cryptonihilism or pseudodualism. The philosophy I champion here is quite antique. The view that biological models of perception may be neither epistemologically useful nor practically possible was part and parcel of the psychology of Thomas Brown (1778–1820). This was so in spite of the fact that the first volume of his greatest work dealt with the "physiology" of the Mind, a term that to him meant something quite different from what it means to modern psychobiologists. In Daniel N. Robinson's (1977) much appreciated compilation of and eloquent commentary on the most significant contributions to psychology from 1750 to 1920, Thomas Brown is quoted as saying:

> How much have we heard of images, and impulses, and traces in the sensorium, of vibrations, and vibratinuncles, of animal spirits, electricity and galvinism! There is scarcely a single new generalization of those phenomena of matter which have been long familiar to us, or a single power in matter inferred from the observation of new phenomena, which has not been immediately seized by philosophers, and applied to mind; as if it were the great business of metaphysical science to systematize the slight analogies of metaphor, and as if those internal processes, of which we are conscious, could be simplified, by the interposition of additional processes, of which we are not conscious, and which are themselves equally inexplicable, as the phenomena, which they are adduced to explain [Vol. I, p. xxxci].

Nevertheless, the fact that there are difficulties with all current neurophysiological theories of perception does not mitigate the argument that in the final analysis the basic premise of psychobiology is that these must be a

---

[6]See Chapter 9 for a more complete discussion of this matter including an extraordinary quotation from an extraordinary neurophysiologist—David Hubel—that make a similar point.

fundamental psychoneural equivalence of identity (Feigl, 1958) between the neural substrate and the perceptual experience. The question that I raise here about the long-range possibility of a neuroreductionistic model can be rephrased in a more positive manner, "How are the neural and the mental domains linked?" Though the question may not be answerable yet, this does not deny that both of the two domains of measurement exist even though this may be only one kind of reality. The point psychobiology makes is that it is a valid goal to attempt to link them.

Perhaps the true state of affairs, one in which the psychological and neurophysiological models must be seen to be complementary, has been most eloquently summarized by Peter Dodwell (1975):

> There is a creative antithesis between physicalist or reductionist theorizers on the one hand, and those with a leaning toward cognitive explanations on the other. To the extent that enormous advances in understanding visual physiology have occurred in recent years, one might argue that the former's star is in the ascendant. Yet detailed knowledge of visual physiology is only one step in the understanding of seeing. As understanding of the coding of visual sensory qualities progresses, the need to integrate them into coherent models of visual processing becomes pressing, and this is, in my view, one of the major contemporary issues [p. 64].

The point is, even given the fact that *in principle* all mental processes must be explicable in the language of neurophysiology, *in practice* it is clear that we do not yet have the mathematical or conceptual bridges to allow us to cross over in toto from the molar psychology of perception to the microscopic action of networks of neurons.

The great unsolved theoretical problem of perceptual psychology (along with all of the other psychobiological sciences), therefore, is to somehow find a basis for linking the network concepts of the neural microcosm to the molar concepts of the behaving oranism. How can a deterministic neuronal net rationalistically "construct" a percept? What does perception mean in the language of the neurons that we know must somehow underlie even the most complex "cognitive" process? Establishing the linkage between these two domains of discourse may, perhaps, be of the most important intellectual challenge facing mankind in the centuries to come.

Although sensory coding theory, the well-developed body of knowledge concerning afferent neural communication, is unlikely to speak to the general problem of the representation of complex perceptions, it can act as at least a first step toward linking the phenomenological and the neurophysiological domains. It can do so because of the way it highlights the fact that nonisomorphic (i.e., cross-dimensional and dimensionally dissimilar) representation is not only possible, but likely. In providing us with an escape hatch from many of the "bad questions" that have plagued psychology for centuries, sensory coding theory may also provide insights into more general psychological mechanisms that transcend the details of many of the individual microtheories. The ideas that symbolic representation is possible, that different signals must be integrated and related to each other to produce a meaningful message, and that relations, rather than absolutes, are the key criteria for encoding messages, are all concepts that transfer from the strictly neural domain of sensory coding theory to psychological models of perception. The concepts implicit in sensory coding theory, therefore, are powerful heuristics both in organizing data and in providing new insights into the processing of perceptual information in spite of the fact that in "explaining" the *phenomena* of perception they may be no more adequate than any other physiological model.

I hope that the reader appreciates how pervasive isomorphism is in current perceptual theory in spite of the fact that the traditional version in the gestalt tradition is so thoroughly discredited. We still spend a lot of time linking neural responses and percepts simply because of their dimensional similarity and more or less completely ignore the fact that dimensions such as color and tone can have no isomorphic relationship with the stimulus domain. Why then, one may ask, do we deify isomorphism in the spatial and quantitative dimensions?

The problem of internal representation is actually handled much better by cognitive psychologists who, while finessing the issue of neurophysiological reductionism, have explicitly concerned themselves with the alternative possible natures of the internal map. They have asked the question in a way that illuminates the issue in spite of the fact that there is a serious question whether or not the problem can even be resolved using behavioral measures alone (Anderson, J. R., 1978). Cognitive psychologists, at least, have dealt with the issue of isomorphic and symbolic representation explicitly, something that more reductively oriented perceptual psychobiologists have not yet done. Clearly, a corollary of the question asked in this section is one cognitive theorists ask: Is the nature of the internal representation of a percept pictorial (isomorphic) or is it propositional (nonisomorphic)?

The fundamental obstacle to a satisfactory neurophysiological theory of perception, however, is that any percept is most likely encoded or represented by the action of a network of neurons rather than an individual neuron. Indeed, it is not even the absolute magnitudes of the individual neural responses of the network, but rather the relation between the amounts and phases of activity in each neuron that is probably most significant. Thus, even a large number of snapshots of individual neural responses would not be very useful in "explaining" the action of the net. The overall state is still the essential aspect and to evaluate the overall state requires instruments and techniques that are not yet available. Since we have no adequate technology to study the simultaneous activities of networks sufficiently large to be relevant, it seems likely that a satisfactory neurophysiological explanation of most complex perceptual phenomena is no more imminent now than it was 2500 years ago.

b. Is a Psychological Theory of Perception Possible?

If a neurophysiological theory seems elusive for the more complex percepts, we have only the descriptive, mathematical, psychological, or phenomenological alternatives to which we can turn without removing ourselves entirely from the realm of scientific inquiry. To eliminate experiment and theory from the analytic armamentarium would be to cross over the fine line that separates the scientific analysis of natural phenomena from the superstitious and prescientific approaches that have proven to be so unfruitful in illuminating the nature of mind, matter, and man.

The question I must now ask is this—Does scientific psychology have more to offer than the neurophysiological panaceas that I have just rejected? To answer this question we have to know more about the psychological alternatives. One approach is that a scientific psychology of perception could be totally phenomenological and simply describe in precise and formal ways (through the medium of behavioral research techniques) the facts of perception without any explicit attempt at reductive explanation. Certainly many of the current texts in perception are nothing more than listings and descriptions of interesting and amusing visual phenomena. This may reflect limited perspective on the part of their authors, but it may also reflect an implicit accommodation to the fact that no perceptual theory is likely to be satisfactory and that a "barefoot" empiricism or phenomenism is all that is possible.

Another alternative base for perceptual theory is the enumeration of the psychophysical laws that formally describe the nature of the transforms achieved by the nervous system in converting physical stimulus patterns into experiences. Alternatively, a scientific perceptual psychology could be based on analogies to processes that exist in the other sciences. Distortions of visual space could be ascribed to the effects of "forces" that are "exerted" by the percepts on each other even though neither the percepts nor the forces may be definable in the more concrete terms sometimes achieved in the physical sciences.

Is any one of these alternatives sufficient? In my personal view, the answer to this question is no. Unless there is some success in reducing perceptual phenomena to simpler processes or in finding generalities among them (and these goals may be nearly synonymous), little progress toward understanding will have been accomplished. Integrative wisdom and deep understanding do not arise from the compilation of an encyclopedia or a dictionary. It is only when simplifying general principles emerge that progress toward understanding can be said to have been achieved.

So far, it seems clear that no all-encompassing psychological theoretical outlook in perception has been forthcoming. Many proposed psychological solutions to the problem of perception (or to any other part of the task of understanding the mind) turn out to be loose analogies to one or another aspect of the prevailing technology. The problem in these cases is to avoid mistaking the descriptive analogy for the solution. Other proposed solutions appear to be transformations of vocabularies that rename without achieving understanding. The problem in this case is not to mistake the nominal description for the analytic explanation.

One more promising set of alternatives, of course, is the ensemble of formalisms of mathematical theories and models. Although not reductive, mathematics provides a system of organization that clarifies and concretizes, and whether implemented in a notebook or in the form of a computer program, it requires a precision of language, premise, and concept that no verbal model can approximate. But mathematics is incomplete and, as I shall discuss in greater detail later, it cannot distinguish between equally plausible analogs. Nor, does a mathematic model by itself tell us anything about underlying mechanism. What mathematics does is to describe process; thus in an intrinsically nonreductionistic situation it may be the sine qua non of acceptable theory.

5. Is Perception Empiricistic or Rationalistic?—Direct or Mediated?

A persistent and fundamental controversy concerning the nature of perception has existed between classical empiricists[7] who assert that we perceive only by means of passive and direct manipulations of environmental stimuli and rationalists who champion the view that we perceive by active logical interpretations of these stimuli. Empiricism, usually but not universally, is associated with a metaphysical realism that assumes that perception is a more or less automatic response to the real stimuli provided by a real world. From a realistic and empiricistic point of view, the world as we perceive it is a direct functional result of the world as it is. Only through the direct effect on the mind of physical stimuli, can individuals come to know about the external environment by processes that are analogous to logical induction. Empiricism thus extols the sensory processes as the primary path to knowledge and usually asserts that there are no innate or a priori ideas or percepts; everything must be learned from experience.

Classic rationalism on the other hand assumes that our communication with the outside world is only partial and that we can never completely learn about reality from the sense datum alone. Rather it is necessary for the perceiver to act as a theoretical (hypothesis-forming) or deductive agent to synthesize knowledge from the partial clues coming from the external world in a way that is consistent with his previous experiences and logical reasonableness. A key aspect of

[7]The word *empiricism* is used in two somewhat different contexts. In the present instance it is used as an antonym to the philosophic school of *rationalism*. Empiricism in this sense connotes a direct, immediate, and unmediated kind of perception. In the nature–nurture controversy, however, the term *empiricism* is used as an antonym to *innateness*. The second connotation of the word is that experience is required to learn how to perceive. I develop more completely the differences between these two uses of the term in Chapter 2.

rationalism is that at least some part of this "rationally directing principle" must be innate.

Rationalism, the epistemology, is often, mistakenly linked to idealism, the metaphysic. Idealism asserts that the primary reality of the external world is the result of the perceiver's impression of it. This classic distinction between idealism and realism, however, like so many other scientific–philosophical schisms, may be a false one and simply reflect the "murkiness of the lake" and the low fidelity of the communication link between the physical world and the world of the mind. This distinction may only be another way of saying that various mental maps (idealistic models) of the external world are not always consistent with each other.

If one were to be so brash as to specify the contemporary resolution of the idealism—realism and rationalism—empiricism controversy, it would certainly have to be stated that most modern scientists tend to be empiricistic and realistic. However, as I have already suggested, a modified neorationalism now appears (to at least some of us) to be a necessary part of any perceptual theory describing the existing data base at the molar level for the most primitive of practical reasons—the complexity of the brain. The explicit statement of this practical fact reminds us that the fundamental epistemological paradox (How can a molar rationalistic system be composed of microscopic empirical units?) has not yet begun to be resolved.

6. To What Brain Mechanism May Rationalistic Construction Be Attributed?

If one embraces the position that an active rationalistic construction of some kind does occur in which a mental map (percept) is created from the barrage of partial clues and incomplete cues coming along the sensory channels, one is immediately led to the next logical question—what effects the actual mental construction? The classic answer to this question has been that a homunculus or "computational demon" (beset, unfortunately, with its own psychology) must serve this role. In recent years the notion of the "little man" in the head has, for good enough reason, come into disrepute. The issue has been replaced in the neurosciences by a modernized version phrased in the terms of sensory codes. Perkel and Bullock (1968), for example, asked "Who reads ensemble codes?" and then proposed a number of specific neural decoding mechanisms that might serve this function. In my opinion, this form of the question is as invalid as the concept of the homunculus. It is likely that nothing "reads" the code or does the construction. Rather there is a sequence of neural transformation processes that ultimately results in a particular neural network state. The pattern of neural activity to which I refer is a very complicated state indeed and need not be isomorphic with the stimulus or the percept, but it is that state, and that state alone, that constitutes the final neural equivalent of the mental responses we call perceptions. It is the state that *is* the final construction; it does not require any final processing by a homunculus or some super neural network to be decoded or interpreted. The concept of the homunculus (or the decoder) was (and is) an artifact invented only because the idea of symbolic or encoded representation was (and is) not accepted or appreciated by students of the mind–body problem.

From a molar point of view, the process of neorationalistic construction must be defined in other terms. It could be asserted that any particular perceptual construction is simply the most internally consistent solution to the problem posed by the sensory stimuli and current status of the organism. This, of course, is an incomplete description of what construction is; it simply restates the most profound perplexity of all—What is the mind? Furthermore, this description of constructionism as a hypothesis- or theory-generating mechanism finesses the all-important and completely unresolved question of how it is that the processes of the neural network state become the equivalent of the molar psychological state. Yet for practical reasons, some form of a molar inferential constructionism seems essential to the understanding of how we perceive; there seems to be no way yet developed to pass to this descriptive or psychological level from the neurophysiological level in spite of the fact that the mind-brain system must do exactly that.

Perhaps the difficulty is that we do not know what it really means to deal with ignorance. The information from which a percept must be constructed is woefully incomplete. Unfortunately, it is exceedingly difficult, if not impossible, to describe the explicit awareness of a lacuna or nonpercept. Thus, we tend to fill in or ignore these informational gaps in our perceptual response and thus "construct" a closed perceptual hypothesis of the world around us. The problem is that "filling in" and "ignoring" may not be empirically distinguishable mental strategies and thus both the homunculus and constructionism may be metaphors for our inability to perceive emptiness in our visual world.

7. Is Perception Innate or Learned?

Perceptual development, the changes in perceptual information processing that occur as infants become children, adolescents, adults, and the aged respectively, is a fruitful set of clues to the underlying nature of perceptual processes. The study of perception in infants, in spite of the very great difficulty in acquiring data and the low yield of usable responses (in this regard infants are very much like horseshoe crabs, which are also useful, but troublesome-to-work-with model preparations) is an especially popular area of perceptual psychology these days. One practical reason is that wisdom concerning the development of human perceptual skills would be extremely useful in helping us to improve the adequacy of our educational systems and possibly to solve many of the lingering social problems that confront modern urbanized society.

More important, however, to the conceptual understanding of perception is the fact that research in perceptual development speaks directly to one of the most perplexing and refractory problems in the history of human thought—the nature–nurture issue. Whatever the mechanisms of perception that are available to the adult to learn of the outside world, the thoughtful observer must also inquire whether they were innate and genetically programmed or learned as a result of the experiences the infant had in the early postnatal years. The ramifications of this question are profound, for the very nature of the mind is implicit in this particular form of the nature–nurture issue. As we shall see later, the degree of innateness is also a fundamental issue in the rationalism–empiricism controversy.

Must we learn to perceive or are the responses to visual stimuli innate, arising almost automatically from the organization of the neural circuitry? Does the neural circuitry itself respond to the experiences by reorganizing itself into new structural patterns? Are the particular portions of the retina, or the visual cerebral cortex for that matter, innately wired to respond with a fixed perceived localization? All of these are the perceptual corollaries of the more general nature–nurture issue.

Another problem, closely related to the problem of innateness, concerns the high degree of automaticity of the act of constructing percepts. It is remarkable that, even though percepts are very likely deductively constructed from incomplete afferent information, there is very little effect of contradictory knowledge on the nature of the percept. Geometrical illusions, for example, are remarkably stable even when contradicted by repeated straightedge comparisons or quantitative measurements. No matter how many times the two lines in the Müller-Lyer illusion may be shown to be identical, the illusion remains only modestly attenuated. Similarly, there is very little effect of volition on the magnitude of an illusion; we cannot will the disappearance of the Poggendorff illusion.

I think the answer to the conundrum posed by such implastic automaticity lies in the fact that most of the perceptual processes that I shall consider in this book reflect the function of more or less innate mechanisms. There is a rapidly increasing body of knowledge that supports the idea that many of the immediate perceptual phenomena are present even in newborn infants. It is possible that this is one criterion that can be used to distinguish between perception and cognition; cognitive processes may be more susceptible than perceptual ones to experiential variation.

There is a considerable amount of neurophysiological research that speaks to a corollary of this question: Is the neural substrate of perception fixed or plastic? Some very promising earlier work on cats (Hirsch & Spinelli, 1970; Blakemore & Cooper, 1971) that had suggested neural plasticity has recently been called into question (Stryker & Sherk, 1975) a point also made by some work on rabbits (Mize & Murphy, 1973). Although these studies were carried out on infrahuman preparations, some of the most interesting work in this field, however, has actually been done on humans. Dobelle, Mladejovsky, and Girvin. (1974), for example, have directly stimulated the cerebral cortex of congenitally blind subjects and found an excellent perceptual organization of the induced phosphenes suggesting a highly stable visual form perception even in cases of extreme sensory deprivation.

Obviously these are highly complex issues, and yet they are issues that are surprisingly amenable to empirical analysis. In spite of the great difficulty that one encounters when trying to disentangle the effects of experience from the mere passage of time, an extraordinary amount of progress has been made in the study of perceptual development. The question has not yet been fully resolved, of course, but considerable insight into the various stages of development has been achieved. The developmental work of such distinguished scholars as E. J. Gibson (1969) and J. Piaget (1969) make up some of the most universally admired contributions of modern psychology. Unfortunately, the range of topics in perceptual development is so great that I will not be able to give it any detailed attention in this book.

8. Is Perception Local or Global?

Another general conceptual issue facing the science of perception is whether the processes of perception are more influenced by the details of the local features of the stimulus or by its overall or global organization. Modern neurophysiological-reductionistic theories of perception, heavily influenced as they are by the feature selectivity of individual neurons that are observed at all levels of the visual nervous system with microelectrode technology, are heavily weighted in favor of local approaches. The impact of this particular conceptual model has stimulated many modern theories of pattern perception to emphasize the local or feature aspects of the stimulus. Computational models of perception, likewise (by virtue of the intrinsic nature of the modern digital computer—a serially organized machine) emphasize processes that concentrate on the local spatial properties of the stimulus rather than on its overall configuration.

A vigorous argument can be made that both of these technologies—the microelectrode and the serial digital computer—are actually ill-suited for the study of parallel processing in distributed sheets of interacting elements. However inappropriate, the findings from these technologies, stressing as they do local properties, have created a Zeitgeist that dominates theoretical thinking in this field. It seems increasingly likely to me, however, that distributed, parallel-processing mechanisms emphasizing global and configurational properties are actually more valid and fruitful models of perception. Indeed, it is mainly in the laboratories of psychologists, who are more intimately guided by their behavioral findings, that the press of the data compels the formulation of theories based upon more global, configurational, and parallel-processing orientations.

The rise of Gestalt psychology in the early years of the twentieth century was the most explicitly global theoretical interpretation of perceptual data and thus of the biology of the visual mind. Unfortunately, classical Gestalt psychology did not have the analytic tools to explore the empirical ramifications of their conclusions, no matter how astute their descriptions of perception or their insights into its global nature. Thus, this theoretical orientation did not prove to be a fertile source of new ideas and atomistic, local, feature-oriented theories came to dominate psychology for several more decades.

Even though the Gestalt theoretical approach generally failed, it is obvious that they were right in asserting that many findings in psychology speak to the fact that perceiving man is more heavily influenced by the arrangement of the parts of a stimulus than by the nature of the parts themselves. Perhaps nowhere is this made more clear than in the striking set of drawings shown in Fig. 1-2. Each of these forms (which have been designated ''random forms'' by their originator, Paul Kolers, 1970) is composed of totally different components, yet the classification of any of these forms into a collective conceptual framework (encoded by the concept ''chair'') is direct and easy.

FIG. 1.2. A collection of random shapes. (From Kolers, © 1970, with the permission of Academic Press.)

Many other perceptual demonstrations also emphasize the primacy of global pattern over local features. It seems highly unlikely, therefore, that component feature detection plays other than a secondary role in pattern perception. Thus, it is somewhat disconcerting to see how widely the neurophysiological and computer-based feature-type theories, emphasizing local rather than global properties of the stimulus scene, have been accepted. The only explanation for this anomaly is that our technologies have both misled us and proven to be inadequate to the task. Unfortunately, it is likely that techniques for studying parallel network, global processes are far off in the future in spite of the great need for them and what may be construed as their great suitability for modeling the processes of form perception.

9. How Do We Organize Visual Forms?

Closely related to the issue of the relative global or local nature of perceptual processes is a set of questions concerning the organization of visual forms by the observer. If perception is indeed based upon processing of local features, then the organization of molar percepts depends upon our ability to carry out higher levels of synthesis to convert this particulate information into the gestalts that we report we perceive. On the other hand, if the global form is perceived directly as a result of the overall configurational relationships of the stimulus, a different kind of higher-order processing must be hypothesized.

The problems of the organization of visual form were also brought into prominence by the Gestalt theoretical position and represent an active and important area of perceptual research. We are able to distinguish figures from background, to detect targets in noise, and to associate and group certain elements of a stimulus pattern with each other while excluding other elements from the perceived configuration. Organizational processes of this sort, as we shall see, represent one of the most important levels of classes of immediate visual processing. However, to this day, they also represent what many consider to be among the most refractory and least understood of all of the processes involved in visual perception. Although we have a considerable amount of descriptive information about target detection and grouping, we have virtually no idea how such extraordinary perceptual processes might be carried out. My discussion of these phenomena in Chapter 10 is, therefore, of necessity almost totally phenomenological and descriptive.

10. The Problem of Stimulus Equivalence

It has been repeatedly demonstrated that we do not have to have exactly the same stimulus presented after some initial familiarization to recognize any object. Rather, humans and other animals seem to have powerful ability to recognize complex patterns such as faces or solid objects regardless of the orientation, size, or position in which they may be presented. This also suggests that there is an equivalence among different ways in which a stimulus may be presented that depends upon some aspect of the configuration of its parts rather than local stimulus features per se. Such a result is strong evidence against any simplistic template matching or feature analysis explanation of pattern recognition. Nevertheless, whatever difficulties such phenomena may pose for such simple theories, they still do not help us to understand the nature of the mechanism that allows a variety of stimuli to be equivalent over what would be, for any conceivable mechanical system, a totally devastating transformation.

The problem of stimulus equivalence was first formalized by Karl S. Lashley (1942), a leading figure of both modern perceptual and psychobiological theory; he considered it to be the major bottleneck to our understanding perception in general. In recent years, the problem has been only rarely resurrected for study and few, if any, investigators have challenged this monumental perplexity. It is only recently that some of the Fourier (Pollen, Lee, & Taylor, 1971) and autocorrelation (Uttal, 1975a) theories have been developed that the beginning glimmering of an understanding of this major issue has been forthcoming. This should not be taken to mean, however, that great progress has been made. In fact, we are still pretty much in the same state as was Lashley when he acknowledged the central importance of the problem of stimulus equivalence to perceptual theory and its utter refractoriness.

11. Is Psychological Time Congruent with Physical Time?

It is obvious that psychological time plays some strange tricks on us. When we are busy, time "flies by," whereas a person in a boring situation can find brief periods of physical time extended into very long periods of perceptual time. Our perception of time, therefore, is, at least, elastic in a "temporal toplogical" sense; that is, it can be stretched and compressed without disrupting the order of events.

There is, however, a more fundamental noncongruity observed when one compares psychological and physical time. That difficulty lies in the fact that the perceptual distortion of time can sometimes violate not only the linearity of temporal intervals, but also the order or topology of events. If this interpretation is correct, the question arises of whether or not psychological time is even less congruent with physical time than a simple topological model would allow.

Lloyd Kaufman (1974), in his thoughtful textbook points out that there is an inherent paradox in some very simple apparent movement phenomena that suggest that psychological time may not be topologically isomorphic to physical time. He notes that in the apparent motion illusion (the phenomenal movement induced between two adjacent lights when they are sequentially turned on and off at an interval of about 80 msec) it is not at all clear what is the order in which they are perceived. To be aware of the direction and amplitude of the induced apparent movement, we must become aware of (perceive?) the position of the second of the two lights before we see (perceive?) it at that position! This is a highly paradoxical phenomenon, to say the least, and along with other similar paradoxical perceptual phenomena, it raises a serious question about the relationship of psychological time to physical time. As Kaufman suggests, the paradox posed by apparent motion seems best resolved by a constructionist model of the phenomenon, in which the entire perceptual response is but a meaiingful ex post facto interpretation or construction based on, but not determined by, the available stimulus clues.

The important point here is that the sequence of different parts of the percept is out of order with both the sequence of presentation of the parts of the stimulus and with what might be the neural order of events. The implications of this point are severe. If the order of psychological events can be demonstrated to be incongruent with the order of the physical events in at least some cases, then a number of serious problems are raised for any psychobiological theory of perception.

One of the problems is especially significant because it presumably also involves what must be an internal shift in temporal order of the representative neural events at different levels of the nervous system. There is little doubt that in the periphery the neural events are in the same order as the physical stimulus. On the other hand, to assume that the central neural events were out of order with the percept would be to reject the very basis of the monistic identity theory that lies at the foundation of modern psychobiology. Therefore, there must have been a transformation of order in the neural events between the peripheral and central mechanisms. What this means is that the perception of certain information must be temporarily suppressed without any loss of its perceptual significance. In other words, the apparent motion paradox suggests that the perceptual awareness can be semantically suppressed without its representation being extinguished to the point of irretrievability. This dissociation of the order of the central and perceptual events from both that of the physical world and of the peripheral neural events is an enormously complex problem, and I make no claim to possessing even the beginning of a solution to it. The question of the relationship between psychological and physical time posed by this paradox is a fundamental one, however, that cannot be overlooked in our tabulation of the major issues in perceptual science.

12. Is Perception Separable from the Other Aspects of Mentation?

There are two strong and somewhat contradictory traditions abroad in psychology today with regard to the unification of the various subareas of experimental research. One tradition vigorously champions the idea that to make any progress in the laboratory toward the understanding of mental processes, we psychologists must dissect out, or abstract, a single aspect from the totality of the mental influences and processes for isolated study. It is only in this way that the multidimensional causal relations can be disentangled, it is said. In the laboratory, therefore, psychologists are required, this point of view asserts, to study the most elemental examples of stimulus input, processing, and storage as well as response output. The magnitude of an illusion, the persistence of a memory, the mental rotation of an image, and the trade-off between reaction time and response accuracy are the kinds of tasks that characterize most current psychological experiments on mental processes.

This approach to the problem by fractionation or partition is by no means unique to psychology. Arnold Pacey in his interesting book on the intellectual history of technology reminds us that the "method of detail" (another name for the isolation technique I have just described) has been a fundamental strategy used by all areas of science since medieval times and was one of the foundation axioms of John Stuart Mill's empiricism. Specifically, according to Mill, as quoted in Pacey (1975), the key to progress in science: "may be shortly described as the method of detail; of treating wholes by separating them into parts . . . and breaking every question into pieces before attempting to solve it [p. 138]." In Chapter 2, where I discuss René Descartes' philosophy and his discussion of the methods of science, we see (on p. 79) that the classic rationalistic orientation also invokes partition and analysis as a necessary method of science in much the same way.

In spite of the purported desirability of isolating individual psychological processes, there are both practical and theoretical considerations that argue that the method of detail should not be applied carelessly to the solution of the problems of mind. One practical difficulty is that the same experimental test can often be used to probe perception, learning, or problem solving. What is being studied is often more a function of the emphasis the experimenter places on a specific part of the response than of actual differences in the task being performed. Furthermore, a fundamental logical difficulty has been raised by modern cybernetics and the other system sciences. They question the validity of dissecting into its component parts any complex system in which there is a significant degree of feedback, feedforward, or lateral interaction. To do so, it is asserted, is to lose exactly that which is being studied—the result of the complexity.

The antithesis of the method of detail (and one rapidly increasing in popularity particularly in the 1970s) is oriented toward a unification of psychological processes. For example, Forgus and Melamed (1976), who have written an eminently readable text in this field, feel that a more wholistic model of human information processing better describes human mentation. Mind is a unitary process, from their point of view, from which we separate out a particular subelement only at the potential cost of losing the essence of what the global mind is all about.

Clearly, the possibility of losing the "baby with the bath water" is the major difficulty created by the injudicious application of the method of detail. It is entirely possible that the essence of the process under examination is to be found in the concatenation, the integration, and the interaction of and among the parts of the whole, rather than in the nature of the parts. By reducing the problem to one in which the parts are emphasized, we may have oversimplified the problem to the extent of having, in fact, tossed it out. This persistent problem of the unity of mental processes—what some authors like Michael Posner (1978) have called the problem of "isolability of codes"—will probably continue to perplex researchers and to complicate studies of psychology for years to come.

It will soon become clear to the reader, however, that I, like all other students of perception, have, for more or less practical reasons, also had to accept the analytic method of detail as a strategy in the development of this book. The taxonomy of process levels that I propose depends on the premise that these levels are separable. I have also assumed that perceptual processes can be experimentally isolated from cognitive ones. Not to have made these assumptions would have made any review and discussion of the empirical literature virtually impossible. Nevertheless, the problem remains, and I am able to offer no guarantee that the separations I have made have not also thrown out some critical essence of the problem.

13. Are Perception and Consciousness Identical or, at Least, Inseparable?

The existence of intrapersonal consciousness poses an enormous difficulty for any psychological theory. Not only is a matter as important as monistic physicalism itself brought into question by our individual awareness of our own being (see Uttal, 1978, and for a contrary view, Popper and Eccles, 1977), but the very methodology of psychology is challenged when confronted with the problem. All too often in the past this science has been driven to the nihilism of behaviorism or positivism and away from the acknowledgment that the proper topic of psychology is, in fact, the study of exactly this intractable problem, consciousness.

It is extremely difficult to define exactly what we mean by the terms *consciousness* and *perception*. In different contexts the formal denotations of the two words overlap and the meaning of each becomes confused. The critical question considered here is whether this confusion is irreconcilable in principle (are the concepts denoted by each, in fact, identical?) or whether the two terms denote demonstrably different concepts.

I believe the answer to this question is primarily a matter of lexigraphic and classification inadequacies rather than one reflecting any fundamental biological or psychological distinction between *perception* and *consciousness*. The two terms are simply not precisely enough defined to allow a complete separation of the domains they denote. Indeed, one possible (though incomplete) definition of perception is that it is *self-awareness* (or consciousness) of experience (see the definition on page 9 from Webster [1963]). Consciousness is defined in nearly the same terms in that dictionary. For example:

> *con-scious-ness* \-nəs *n*-es 1a: awareness or perception of an inward psychological or spiritual fact: intuitively perceived knowledge of something in one's inner self b: inward awareness of an external object, state, or fact ⟨a~ . . . of what really is at stake in modern philosophy—Hannah Arendt⟩ c: concerned awarness: INTEREST, CONCERN—often used with an attributive noun ⟨tax~⟩ ⟨class~⟩ ⟨rank~⟩ 2: the state or activity that is characterized by sensation, emotion, volition, or thought: mind in the broadest possible sense: something in nature that is distinguished from the physical 3: the totality in psychology of sensations, perceptions, ideas, attitudes, and feelings of which an individual or a group is aware at any given time or within a particular time span—compare STREAM OF CONSCIOUSNESS 4: waking life (as that to which one returns after sleep, trance, fever) wherein all one's mental powers have returned ⟨the ether wore off and the patient regained~⟩ 5: the part of mental life or psychic content in psychoanalysis that is immediately available to the ego—compare PRECONSCIOUS, UNCONSCIOUS 2 [p. 482].

Obviously, many of the terms used in this definition are identical to those used in defining perception. The question of the distinction between perception and consciousness, therefore, is probably a bad question. It is operationally resolved in this book simply by the circumscription of the area of inquiry germane to those more immediate conscious responses to visual stimulation. In sum, if there is any difference between the denotation of the two words, it is that perception is a subset of the full range of processes and phenomena encompassed by the word consciousness.[8]

14. Can Valid Psychophysical Laws Be Formulated?

One of the main arenas of activity in the study of perceptual processes is the determination of the functional relationship between changes in an observer's responses and variations in the stimulus dimensions. The formal mathematical functions that model the transform between the dimensions of the stimulus and the dimensions of perceptual responses are referred to as psychophysical laws. The two most famous of these, of course, are the Weber–Fechner logarithmic law (Fechner, 1860) and the Stevens power law (Stevens, 1957) relating subjec-

---

[8]Natsoulas (1978b) has delved more deeply than I have here into the meaning of the word *consciousness* using a similar lexigraphic approach. Referring to the 1933 edition of the Oxford English Dictionary, he discerns six different meanings, some of which also seem to be well within the meaning of perception as I have used it here.

tive magnitude to the intensity of the physical stimulus. Other "laws," less formally named and often only developed as graphs or charts, relate other physical dimensions such as photic wavelength to such continua of psychological response as hue.

In spite of the near universal acceptance of the concept of simple psychophysical laws and the successful paradigm exhibited by the law approach in physics, formulations of this sort may be misleading for psychological science on a number of counts. Most serious is the fact that most "laws" usually purport to relate the psychological response to a single dimension of the stimulus. It is clear that this is not the case for most perceptual phenomena, but rather that virtually all perceptual dimensions are determined by the interaction of multiple stimulus dimensions. For example, auditory subjective magnitude, or loudness, is a function of the wavelength of the acoustic stimulus as well as of its intensity, and apparent size is related to both retinal size and the stimulus factors that also determine apparent distance at least. Multidimensional determination of responses seems to be the rule throughout the perceptual domain, yet this fundamental fact is erroneously de-emphasized by the very act of formulating any unidimensional psychophysical law.

Another difficulty with the formulation of simplistic psychophysical laws is that they are usually empirically incorrect. Deviation from each proposed psychophysical law is the rule rather than the exception. The law for pooled data often does not fit the responses of individuals (Luce & Mo, 1965). Similarly some psychophysical laws can be approximated only under very highly circumscribed rules of data acquisition. When detailed attention is given to their microstructure, the response curves almost always are found to involve points of inflection that are not reflected in the first-order logarithmic or power expressions that were postulated during the past century of perceptual research.

Michel Treisman (1970) has also reminded us that the existence of such phenomena as constancy and contrast (see Chapter 11) makes a shambles of any attempt to specify a simple and valid deterministic relationship between the physical attributes of the stimulus and the dimensions of a percept.

We must accept the fact that either we do not yet understand the full impact of multidimensional stimuli on the percept, or to put the same idea in other words, the proposed laws are not yet good predictors of the biological facts. Typical psychophysical laws, especially those dealing with the relationships between stimulus intensity and subjective magnitude, seem to work best when they are interpreted only as general descriptors of the central tendencies of pooled data without giving too much concern to the individual's responses or to the detailed microstructure of the functional relationship. The simple unidimensional laws, therefore, are only gross approximations of individual performance that approach validity only when all other parameters of the experiment are held constant.

It should not be overlooked, in this regard, that any ability on the part of either a power or logarithmic law to represent a given perceptual domain may in large part be attributed to the essential generality of the mathematical function invoked rather than to the validity of the theoretical assumptions. The power law, in fact, is not derived from any particular theoretical premise, but rather, is an empirical construct that depends entirely on the fact that this particular mathematical expression is able to represent a family of monotonic functions over wide ranges of positive and negative accelerations. To a first approximation, many psychophysical functions also display nearly constant second derivatives. Power laws thus can roughly model (describe) the family of subjective magnitude functions but in a way that is only loosely linked to any explanatory insight or reductive explanation.

The intrinsic weakness in the "general law" approach is made clear when it is realized that even finer fits can be obtained with more generalized polynomial functions, because *any* function can be perfectly fit by a polynomial of sufficiently high order. The absurdity of pursuing this kind of a theoretical mathematical modeling was made abundantly clear in a satirical article recently published by "Sue Doe Nihm" (1976) of the "Chang Ri Law" University, to wit:

> A new theory proposed that sensation grows as a polynomial function of physical intensity. The theory reproduced all of the published data perfect without error. The degree of the polynomial is independent of whether category ratings or magnitude estimations are used as the dependent variable; it is independent of stimulus range, number of categories, value of the standard, first stimulus, modulus, stimulus spacing, and all other contextual features of the experiment except the number of stimuli. Because the polynomial law always provides a superior fit to the data, it should supersede the logarithmic and power laws of sensation [p. 808].

The cutting edge of this satirical *reductio ad absurdum* is so keen that it lays the concept of the psychophysical law open to the bone and points up the difficulties embedded in the assertion that any such simplistic law of perception can be valid. The idea that a unidimensional psychophysical law may be formulated to precisely represent multidimensional psychophysical functions is probably itself an illusion.

In general, therefore, it seems certain that psychophysical laws of the unidimensional type proposed by Fechner or Stevens can be, at best, only gross approximations to the true dynamics of the perceptual response. Furthermore, any two-dimensional graph plotting the relationship between a single stimulus dimension and a single dimension of a behavioral response is, by the same criteria, only an approximation and works only to the degree that experimental controls can hold constant all other contributing variables. Although they can be useful in some restricted ways, a more multidimensional analysis is certainly required to fully elucidate the determinants of even the simplest perceptual phenomena. We must begin to think in terms of functions of the form:

$$\begin{aligned}\text{Subjective magnitude} = f(&k_1 \times \text{stimulus intensity} + \\ &k_2 \times \text{stimulus quality} + \\ &k_3 \times \text{temporal sequence} + \\ &k_4 \times \text{location in space} + \\ &k_5 \times \text{organism's experience} + \\ &k_6 \times \text{organism's set} + \ldots)\end{aligned} \quad (1\text{-}1)$$

as more adequate descriptors of perceptual reality than such simple monodimensional relationships as

$$\text{Subjective magnitude} = f\ (\text{stimulus intensity}) \quad (1\text{-}2)$$

The point in this case is that as equations of the form of Eq. 1-1 become more and more widely accepted, the plausibility of monodimensional empiricistic models of perceptual performance become less and less credible.

15. How Are Multiple Stimulus Dimensions Integrated to Produce a Unified Percept?

In discussing the previous question (Are valid psychophysical laws possible?) I argued on both logical and empirical grounds that most percepts are based on multiple dimensions of the stimulus scene. A wide variety of empirical evidence strongly supports this same argument. Color contrast, shape constancy, apparent size, stereopsis, and a host of other perceptual phenomena (many of which are extensively discussed in Chapter 11) are well known to be influenced by multiple aspects of the stimulus. Striking changes, for example, can occur in the apparent lightness of an object by simply placing a reference object in the same scene without any change in the luminance of the original object. The emergence of depth when the views from the two eyes are integrated is another example. The perceptual response, in all such phenomena, is a result of an integrative concatenation of multiple dimensions of incoming information.

Having established the empirical fact and the logical reasonableness of multidimensional influences on perception, we are now faced with the more difficult problem of determining how such computations can be carried out by the nervous system. What sort of interactions occur between the dimensions of the stimuli to allow them cooperatively to determine the percept? Do the percepts vary continuously, gradually changing as the magnitudes of the two or more interacting stimuli are modulated, or are there sharp discontinuities between distinguishable perceptual states? How are the invariances and statistical properties of aggregated stimuli extracted?

An important aspect of this cluster of problems is that it is typically the relationship between the dimensions of the stimulus information, rather than the absolute magnitude of each of the contributing stimulus attributes, that seems to determine the distinctive properties of the percept. In this case there is a suggestive analogy between the idea of stimulus dimensional relationships and what is known of the relational nature of neural codes that further supports the idea that there is little absolute in the stimulus–percept relationship. This analysis further adds to the arguments that precise psychophysical (functional) laws may be in some ways logically inappropriate and that the general idea of a neorationalistic or inferential constructionism in perception may have much to say for it.

16. How Are We Able to Suppress Afferent Information So That Spurious or Inconsistent Signals Do Not Lead to Erroneous Percepts?

When complex real stimuli are integrated in order to avoid internally inconsistent percepts, certain aspects of the pattern must be suppressed. Suppression, in the sense that I use it here, does not necessarily mean that the neural signals themselves must be completely turned off or extinguished. Rather, it is possible that the afferent information's significance, meaning, or contribution to the final constructed percept, may be altered without the signal being physically extinguished.

To concretize this difficulty, consider the case of the apparent position in visual space of an object as the eyes move across a scene. There is a continuous change in the retinal position of the image of any fixed part of the scene. Yet the rationally constructed percept is not of a moving object but of a stationary one. Somehow information about the movement of the eyes (perhaps proprioceptive feedback from the ocular muscles) has been combined with the moving image on the retina to produce a percept of an object fixed in space. It has thus been possible to dissociate *retinal position* from *apparent position* in space (i.e., to suppress the retinal position cue to perceptual localization), yet the external object may still be perceived. This process exemplifies a type of complex computational process in which specific aspects of the afferent stimulus information are altered in their significance without all of its information content being totally lost.

Expressed in this way, the question I pose in this section clearly can be seen to encompass the controversy that has raged for nearly a century over Lotze's (1841/84) theory of the local sign. In professing this theory Lotze proposed that the apparent direction of an object in space was uniquely tied to a particular retinal locus. He argued that each retinal locus generated specific patterns of activity encoding the actual physical direction of the object. It is clear that demonstrations like the one just mentioned make a simple retinal position theory of local signs totally untenable. Nevertheless, retinal position is an important factor in specifying apparent direction in many instances. The only theory that makes sense of this phenomenon is that the retinal position is an influential contributing clue to perceptual localization but is not rigidly locked to that phenomenon in any fixed way comparable to the classic idea of the local sign.

The fact that there is a possible dissociation of retinal locus and percept in at least some cases makes any theory incorporating a fixed empiricistic and automatic relationship between stimulus and response very difficult to support. A corollary of this question then immediately arises. If there is no fixed relationship between stimulus and response in this case and so much evidence of cognitive, constructionistic interpretations of stimulus patterns of all sorts, why then is it so difficult to overcome the distortions introduced by one or another kind of illusion-generating stimulus by an act of volition? Why, after a ruler has been placed along the lines in the Poggendorff or Hering illusory stimuli, are we unable to overcome the compelling distorting force of these displays? I have no answer to these perplexities and indeed they may be beyond experimental resolution. The problem posed by the failure of volition in this specific case may well remain unanswerable, as will the question of how the automatic suppression of the awareness of a stimulus can occur without the destruction of its information content.

17. How Do We Construct Percepts When the Stimuli Are Not Physically Present?

A question closely related to the issues of integration or suppression of actual stimuli concerns the nature of the compelling and powerful percepts that occur in situations in which a physical stimulus is not actually present. The phenomena of subjective surfaces and apparent motion are among the most intriguing examples of the class of percepts to which I refer (see Figs. 10-34 and 11-33. In these cases a powerful percept of a contour of or motion can occur even though there is no equivalent physical contour or moving object present. To complicate the matter further, there is some psychophysical and neurophysiological evidence suggesting that no isomorphic neurophysiological correlate of such "subjective events" is present, either. For example, Paul Kolers (1964) has shown that apparently moving objects do not inhibit the detection of dim targets inserted in the illusory trajectory, even though a real moving object of similar phenomenal properties passing along the same trajectory will "mask" a target under comparable conditions. We must therefore ask: Can two quite different neural processes produce the same perceptual experience?

A related perplexity concerns the compelling perception of the parts of a background figure hidden behind a foreground object. Verbally, such a perceptual process has been described by Gestalt psychologists as the tendency toward "good continuation," but this is hardly a satisfactory explanation of this intriguing phenomena. What conceivable kinds of mental computation or symbolic encoding could account for the observer's perception of implied, rather than actually present, stimuli remains another major perceptual question.

18. What Are the Phenomena and Processes of Perception?

Next in this list of important questions in perception, I turn to much less philosophical and more mundane matters—to the more immediate targets of empirical research. However mundane, these are the matters that actually occupy the preponderance of energy and time of most perceptual researchers. These are the "meat and potatoes" of the current effort to understand perception. Although the need and importance of an explicit effort to organize perceptual science are clear, very little research effort or thought is explicitly directed at the questions I have listed so far. Rather, more researchers concentrate on discovering and describing new phenomena, developing microtheories to explain them, and inventing new methods to observe the extraordinary processes that make up the substantive content of perceptual psychology.

The discovery of a new illusion, or the plotting of the functional relationship between some stimulus and some perceptual dimension, occupies the attention of most perceptual scientists. Others are interested in building what might be called microscopic theories of the various perceptual processes that have been discovered and described previously. Still others are searching for the answers to somewhat more general questions such as:

How do we see form, color, brightness, or flicker?
How does form emerge from background?
How do we locate objects in space?
How is movement detected?
How do we see depth, direction, location, size, or shape?
How do we recognize forms?
What are the influences on perception of emotion, prejudice, or learning?
How do we adapt to changes in luminance?

Beyond these substantive questions there is also an enormous interest in the development of methodology, statistical procedures, instruments, and psychophysical techniques that may help to minimize the inevitable bias interjected into the study of any problem by its methodology. Ideally, our knowledge and understanding should reflect psychobiological reality not the method used to probe that reality.

Others have also asked: What are the salient phenomena of perception? Two of the most notable answers to this question are to be found in the work of Allport (1955) and Gregory (1974). Their approaches differ from each other, as well as from the one that I develop in this book, to a degree sufficient to warrant attention to their views at this point.

Allport (1955) suggests that the phenomena of perception can be classified into six broad classes (paraphrased from pp. 59–66):

1. Perceptual Qualities. The dimensions of the stimulus such as color, smell, subjective magnitude, duration, and extensity. In this category Allport refers to aspects of perception that are, in large part, defined by the particular physical parameters of the stimulus. I believe, after reading his analysis, that he is speaking to many of the same issues that I dealt with in my earlier work (Uttal, 1973), namely, the problems involved in a dimensional analysis of sensory processes into spatial, temporal, quantitative, and qualitative parameters, even though Allport has incorporated all of these terms into the single rubric of quality.

2. *Figural or Configurational Aspects.* The parameters of form or organization, as emphasized by the Gestalt tradition.

3. *Constancy Phenomena.* The tendency for objects to appear with constant properties even though the percept may be evoked by varying physical stimuli.

4. *Relational or Frame-of-Reference Phenomena.* The tendency for elements to be judged in relation to other examples sampled from the same dimensional continuum.

5. *Concrete Object Character.* The meaning of significance of the perceived object.

6. *The Effect of Prevailing Set or State.* Those effects on perception that are due to the momentary state of the observer. According to Allport, these influences may vary from something as simple as frequency to more profound variations in vigilance, familiarity, or attentiveness of a kind familiar to current students of attention and cognition.

Frankly, I find Allport's categorization of the basic phenomena of psychology not too useful and both nonexclusive and very incomplete. Too many well-known phenomena do not fit into his schema. Furthermore, a curious mixture of organismic and stimulus processes confuses his list. In fact, his list seems to be a combination of perceptual processes (1, 2, 3, and 5) of the type I seek to enumerate in this book and a pair of items that deal more with the subjective conditions that affect perception (4 and 6) than with the percepts themselves. His list is also redundant; from at least one point of view, items 4 and 6 mean exactly the same thing.

A more complete, but also somewhat restricted list of perceptual phenomena has been proposed in Gregory's thoughtful defense of a constructionistic theory of perception. He sought to challenge alternative theories of perception by testing them against what he referred to as the "facts of perception." I believe his phrase denotes concepts that are very similar to the perceptual phenomena I seek to enumerate in this section. Gregory (1974) cites the following "facts" (paraphrased from pp. 260–267) as being most central in contemporary perceptual research:

1. Perception of objects goes beyond available sensory inputs.
2. Appropriate behavior can continue through gaps in sensory inputs.

3. In skills there may be no delay between sensory input and output behavior.[9]
4. Probable objects are perceptually favored over improbable objects.
5. Intense pattern stimulation of the retina may produce corresponding aftereffects (afterimages) added to any immediately subsequent perceptions.
6. Spatial distortions occur with some figures.
7. Spontaneous changes of perception (perceptual ambiguity) occur with unchanged sensory input, with many figures and objects.
8. There can be impossible (paradoxical) perceptions.
9. There can be illusory contours.
10. Visual distortions occur across illustory contours.

Obviously, this list of visual phenomena is not complete either, but it is more extensive than the one provided by Allport and does have the advantage that it is totally a list of relevant perceptual phenomena drawn from the same level of discourse.

A more complete listing of phenomena of perception can be culled from the many books written on the subject. The following totally unclassified and unordered list, based on a very random sampling, is presented to enumerate more fully the types of phenomena with which perceptual science is concerned:

1. Constancies.
2. Geometric illusions and illusory contours.
3. Figure–ground organization.
4. Figural aftereffects.
5. Color perception.
6. Brightness perception.
7. Lightness perception.
8. Simultaneous and metacontrast effects.
9. Flicker, afterimages, and other temporal interactions.
10. Depth, size, and distance perception.
11. Pattern and form detection and recognition.
12. Real and apparent movement.
13. Phenomenal localization of objects in extrapersonal space.
14. Contour enhancement.
15. Absolute thresholds.
16. Orientation perception.
17. Filling in, closure, grouping, and continuation.
18. Prediction and extrapolation.
19. Rivalry and suppression.
20. Mirages.
21. Dark adaptation.
22. Acuity.

---

[9] I do not agree that this is a well-established fact of perception.

23. Visual direction.
24. Entophthalmic phenomena.
25. Suprathreshold functions.
26. Perceptual duration.
27. Subjective contours and surfaces.
28. Masking.

This list is only partial, at best, and some of these phenomenal categories are overlapping and redundant. Some are well understood both as phenomena and in terms of the responsible underlying processes whereas others are poorly understood in both regards. All, however, demand much deeper analysis.

It is important to remember that it is the aggregate of the theories that have evolved to explain these phenomena that is intrinsically important rather than the description of the individual phenomena themselves. Collectively, the theories explaining these phenomena are our best current answer to the fundamental epistemological question of how we acquire knowledge about the world in which we live. Because of the anchor provided by the stimulus, the relative simplicity of afferent pathways, and the mainly monodirectional flow of information, the perceptual macrotheory or perspective that our explanatory theories collectively define represents the closest approach yet available to a comprehensive physiological and psychological understanding of the nature of the mind.

In this brief comment I can hardly do justice to the enormous data base of perceptual psychology nor was it my intent to do so. Clearly, the phenomena and processes to which I have only briefly alluded constitute the empirical foundations that add concreteness, meaningfulness, and ultimately, validity to any theoretical and philosophical effort. A considerable portion of the remainder of this book is devoted to the description, analysis, and classification of these phenomena and processes, as well as the methodology used to study them.

19. Is It Possible to Develop a Comprehensive Classification Scheme of Perceptual Phenomena?

Finally, in this survey of the fundamental issues of perceptual psychology I come to what may indeed be the crux of whatever novel contribution I am able to make in this book. As one scans the list of perceptual phenomena tabulated in question 18 or looks at any of the many textbooks of perceptual psychology, one notes the absence of any broad classification scheme. Any attempt to provide some order, to categorize, or to classify the range of perceptual phenomena that I have just tabulated is rare to the point of nonexistence.[10] Quite the contrary, the rambling and disordered way in which perceptual phenomena are usually presented makes

[10]Indeed, only a few other perceptual psychologists have even attempted such a task for more restricted areas of perception. One exception is found in Chapter 13 of Coren and Girgus' (1978) work on visual illusions, a book I encountered as I was finishing the manuscript of this volume.

any course of instruction in the subject an exercise in rote learning rather than an elucidation of broad general principles and comprehensive understanding. At the present time, virtually the only simplifying schema introduced into any discussion of perceptual phenomena is one that segregates the senses into the different modalities (e.g., vision, hearing, and touch), or one that separates the various classes of phenomena (e.g., space, flicker, and form perception) into their own chapters. Other than that, most textbooks in the field are disordered, though often encyclopedic compendia of perceptual phenomena.

Perhaps the most important question faced in this regard is whether there is, in fact, some intrinsic underlying disorder to perceptual phenomena that prohibits their being organized. There is a pressing urgency to determine whether or not it is possible to emulate other sciences and to develop a taxonomy of the percepts, or if the empirical chaos will have to be accepted as a permanent part of the perceptual literature.

Man's urge to organize is great. Very few of us are satisfied with the unsystematic "understanding" that comes in the form of an encyclopedia or dictionary. In physics, chemistry, and biology the value of classificatory taxonomies has been profound. The key to the understanding of chemical processes in terms of atomic models was the periodic table of the elements developed[11] by Dimitry Ivanovitch Mendeleyev (1834–1907). The realization that the root causes of the chemical regularities ordered by the periodic table could be explained in terms of atomic orbital structures has enriched and literally illuminated all of our lives. Similarly, the classification of fundamental physical "basic" particles into distinct categories (photons, gravitons, leptons, baryons, and mesons) on the basis of the forces to which they are sensitive has now led to the hypothesis that a set of a small number of even simpler particles could bring order to this level of analysis. When the number of hadrons increased unreasonably and early classification schema broke down, a further taxonomy of these even more microscopic constituent subparticles (humorously called quarks because of their elusiveness) clarified and disentangled the confused state of affairs. (See Chapter 3 for a more detailed discussion of the modern view of physical reality.)

In the history of the biological sciences, an equally profound influence of taxonomic systems can be discerned. The grand theories of evolution of the nineteenth century championed by such luminaries as Chevalier de Lamarck (1744–1829), Charles Darwin (1809–1882), and Alfred Russell Wallace (1823–1913), depended on and were stimulated by the classification of species suggested by Carolus Linnaeus (1707–1778) in the eighteenth century in spite of the fact that the latter's system (Linnaeus, 1735) for plants was based on the

[11]Mendeleyev's achievement is in no way mitigated by the fact that some of his contemporaries were also proposing similar classification schemes. But for a quirk of fate the periodic table might have been attributed to such now-forgotten names as Johann Döbereiner or William Olding. See Newman (1956) for a complete discussion of this matter.

"artificial criterion" of flower parts. Current understanding of the genetic puzzle is largely based upon the unraveling of the code for DNA and RNA. These codes, comprised of ordered arrays of basic units, may be thought of as direct biochemical analogs of the species classification systems in biology, physics, and chemistry.

I assert here the proposition that perceptual science is badly in need of a similar effort to classify its pertinent phenomena. The data base is enormous and rapidly proliferating, yet these empirical facts remain unrelated by a systematic ordering scheme. As a result, similarities between superficially different phenomena go unrecognized, and misleading qualitative analogies are invoked between processes that are not actually as intimately related as they may at first glimpse appear. I am convinced that this state of affairs is not a necessary condition for this science and that it is possible to develop a comprehensive classification scheme for perceptual phenomena. I hope that this book demonstrates that such schemes can be developed and that they can help to illuminate the generalities and define broad principles even if the one I propose here turns out to be less adequate than I hope it will be. I am equally convinced that systematic understanding of percepts is possible and that the schema that does ultimately evolve will be qualitatively different from the "British Museum" type of exhaustive enumeration of phenomena that seems to characterize so much of perceptual science today.

The intended goal of this book is premised on the assumption that such a classification scheme is feasible and that an effort to spell out at least one possibility is a worthy enterprise. The schema that I propose here is certainly going to be at least internally incomplete and, possibly, also internally inconsistent in some parts; it will certainly be subject to extensive criticism, correction, and modification. Nevertheless, I believe that the very presence of an overt attempt at a systematic taxonomy of perceptual phenomena will help to crystallize some of the difficulties inherent in such an enterprise and may serve as the stimulus for the development of a better overall theory of perception than is available today.

The taxonomic theory that I propose here is rooted in several different traditions. It is an outgrowth of the known anatomy of the nervous system, the theory of sensory coding in peripheral nerves, and the general information-processing Zeitgeist that has such wide currency in modern psychology. It is, however, also influenced by the wholistic approaches of the Gestalt psychologists as well as the neorationalistic and constructionist influences of current cognitive approach. In particular, it is a stage or level model that assumes that there are separable stages of perceptual processing that can be assayed and examined independently with appropriate techniques and tasks.

Level models of perception are not universally accepted these days. Posner (1978), for example, raises several cogent criticisms of level theories, but in a way that I do not believe is actually in conflict with the general approach that I follow here. Posner's critical concern is with the processes that I classify here as the third, fourth, and fifth levels of the model. The hierarchy of levels I suggest is also based upon a concept of a sequence of levels of information saturation that I feel Posner might not find incompatible with his criticism. On the other hand, many others (Attneave, 1962; Craik & Lockhart, 1972; Dodwell, 1975; Forgus & Melamed, 1976; Hebb, 1949; Neisser, 1967; Powers, 1973; Treisman, 1970; and Turvey, 1973) have found one kind or another of a hierarchical level model acceptable. Such an approach is also implicit in the thinking of many contemporary researchers even when it is not so explicitly formalized.

The level scheme proposed here is based on the concept that there is a hierarchy of sequential neural and psychological information-processing levels (which are not necessarily correlated with specific neuroanatomical levels) involved in visual perception. Each stage is assumed to set boundary conditions for the succeeding stages; but once the properties of the stimulus pattern exceed a threshold of information saturation for any of the preceding stages, it is assumed that the contribution of the earlier stage to the processing of visual information becomes of secondary consequence.

Specifically, this model assumes that there are six separable, sequential stages in the visual processing of patterned information. Level 0 is designed to incorporate all of the preneural and prepsychological processes that occur prior to sensory transduction within a single major category. Level 1 incorporates those processes that occur in the visual receptors, the rods or the cones of the eye. Level 2 is defined in terms of interactive processes that occur mainly within the neural network of the retina. Level 3 consists of processes that are related to the separation of signals from noise, of figures from ground, or in general with the organization of the different functional regions and objects of the stimulus scene. Level 4 incorporates perceptual information processes that depend on the integration of multiple aspects of the stimulus scene for the establishment of the percept and that result in quantifiable dimensions of experience. (A definition of exactly what is meant by "perceptual quantification" is deferred until Chapter 11.) Finally in this scheme, Level 5, which is not discussed in this book, consists of attentive and effortful manipulative processes that occur subsequent to the immediate, more passive preattentive and automatic processes of the first four levels.

Levels 1 and 2, both in practice and principle, can be linked to neuroanatomical concepts and vocabulary. I believe, however, that the complexity of the third, fourth, and fifth levels is such that no neurophysiological model is, in fact, appropriate. A different theoretical paradigm involving constructionistic, inferential, rationalistic, and symbolic (as opposed to isomorphic) encoding and the interrelation of perception to other behavioral mechanisms becomes the theoretical approach of choice at these levels.

The emphasis in this taxonomy is upon criteria of *underlying processes* rather than of the *phenomenology* of the responses themselves, that is, I have collected phenomena together into separate classifications, not on the basis of the similarity between the mental responses but rather on the basis of the processes that can best be invoked to explain them. In so doing, I have made a large number of judgments about what constitutes the best currently available theoretical explanation. There is ample opportunity for error, of course, but hopefully most of my judgments can and will be adequately buttressed by citation of appropriate empirical facts.

The reader will, therefore, find phenomena collected together (e.g., color blindness and acuity) that are phenomenologically dissimilar but share common underlying mechanisms. He or she will also find widely scattered references to some phenomena (e.g., hue will be discussed both in the context of peripheral color blindness, Level 1, and color contrast, Level 4) that may seem, from the perspective of a phenomenological analysis, to be more closely related than such a dispersed discussion implies. For better or for worse, this is a specific outcome of the emphasis on process rather than phenomenon.

The taxonomy that I propose is also based on some other important assumptions that should be made explicit at this point. I have assumed that the processes can, in general, be isolated from each other in the laboratory in a way that allows independent evaluation of their contribution to the various phenomenon. I have assumed that multilevel processing can and does occur and that the transformations that occur at different levels are often redundant. Finally, except for the fifth level, with which I do not deal in this volume, this entire scheme of taxonomic levels deals with the more immediate and automatic aspects of perceptual response.

This is but the bare skeleton of the taxonomic theory of visual perception, the assumptions of which are discussed more fully in Chapter 4. However, it should also be appreciated that the complete elaboration of this theory is actually the goal of this entire book, and Chapter 4 alone is not complete either. In order to flesh out these bare bones, it is necessary to examine many perceptual phenomena and their underlying processes to decide into which of these six levels each fits best.

It is clear to me at the outset that both the general approach and the specific attribution of the phenomena to particular processing levels will not achieve universal agreement. Not all of my colleagues will even accept the general idea of a hierarchical theory of processing levels such as the one described here. And, even among those who will accept the concept, there is likely to be an enormous amount of disagreement about the details of the system, concerning both the particular taxonomic levels I have chosen and the location of any particular phenomenon within the six-level schema. For example, my personal bias is that simultaneous contrast is probably a Level 4 phenomena. Many of my colleagues, however, are firmly committed to the idea that simultaneous contrast is but another expression of lateral inhibitory effects at Level 2. This is the sort of controversy that continues to keep perceptual science rich, challenging, and highly stimulating. It is also an example of the type of controversy I hope to resolve specifically in the critique presented in Chapter 9.

In spite of these potential problems, I believe that this schema does offer a concrete, useful, and, I hope, fruitful means of introducing some order into the science of perception—an order that is very much needed and that may ultimately lead to some deeper understanding of perceptual phenomena.

C. THE PLAN OF THE BOOK

So far in this introduction I have discussed, in broad philosophical terms, the problem, and issues faced in seeking to understand the visual means by which humans gather information from their external environments. I have tried to define what is meant by perception, to identify some of the more specific conceptual issues that motivate research in this field and to spell out some of the assumptions that guide (and bias) this book. Clearly, however, if a useful contribution is to be made by this work, this general introduction must be detailed with more specific materials. Now that I have expressed the nature of the problem faced and have briefly introduced the logical schema that will constitute the framework of this book, I hope some of the specific intellectual issues encountered in the study of perception are more obvious than they had been previously.

The main goals of this book are to search out the general principles of perceptual psychology and to develop a general, process-oriented taxonomy of perceptual phenomena. It is clear that I cannot discuss every topic and all known experiments; rather, selected experiments will be presented as exemplars of the general principles I seek to elucidate and as sample elements in the taxonomy.

This book will be guided by a number of themes and premises, most of which have already been alluded to in the previous discussion; these are now abstracted for emphasis:

1. The set of automatic aspects of visual perception is the vehicle I have chosen to convey general perceptual principles. However, it should be remembered, that most of what I have to say with regard to vision is generalizable, in principle, to the other perceptual modalities (with due consideration given to the differences in relevant physics, adequate stimuli, and anatomy).

2. All perceptual phenomena, as well as all other psychological processes, are, in principle, identifiable with the functions of specific, though highly complex, neural networks. This basic monistic and reductionistic premise is the keystone of all of psychobiology; it is not denied, by the assertion that a neural

explanation of some particular process is, in practice, unlikely, simply because of complexity.

3. Neurophysiological reductive explanations of perceptual processes are possible only in certain restricted cases. These restricted cases are mainly those that are strongly affected by peripheral neural mechanisms. No satisfactory neurophysiological models yet exist for any of the phenomena that are more sensitive to central processes.

4. Central aspects of visual perception are better examined by neorationalistic models that assume an active construction of percepts from partial and ambiguous information. This constructionistic or inferential approach, surprisingly, is a speculative outgrowth of sensory coding theory—a highly neuroreductionistic approach to peripheral neural communication processes. The concept of perceptual constructionism is also intimately related to the emerging principle that multiple aspects of the stimulus scene are almost always used in the construction of the best perceptual solution to the cognitive problem posed by even relatively simple stimulus scenes.

5. Order is both required and possible in perceptual psychology. One way to achieve this order is to concentrate on general principles and the conceptual basis of the experimental literature, rather than the details of individual experiments. Another way is to classify the phenomena in a manner that will best exhibit and emphasize these general principles. In this book, the organizing taxonomic scheme is the six-stage model of visual processing that is briefly introduced in the previous section.

These, then, are the overall themes, organizing principles, and goals of this work. The explication of these themes and principles is divided into two parts. The first part, consisting of Chapters 1, 2, and 3, provides an introduction to the field. In Chapter 1 I spell out the nature of the problem and identify psychological research in perception as the main empirical approach to the solution of the general epistemological perplexity. I also establish certain general premises and prejudices affecting the presentation of relevant material.

In Chapter 2, I review the history, philosophy, and global theoretical approaches that have been taken by others both in the distant past and in recent years to explain perceptual phenomena. This second chapter is not concerned with microtheories or data in any depth but rather with those broad psychological and philosophical perspectives (metatheories) that have been proposed to explain perception in general. I try to analyze the essential premises and concepts of each approach and to classify, to the limited extent possible, the various types of theories within a subsidiary taxonomy of its own.

Chapter 3, on the other hand, deals with technical material, at a much more microscopic (literally) level. Perceptual science is not all esoteric theory and philosophy. It also involves a highly sophisticated technological methodology and depends upon the detailed knowledge gained in some of the other sciences. It is impossible to discuss the process of visual perception without giving some attention to the anatomy of the eye or to the organization of the visual portions of the central nervous system. The physics of light, as well as a brief allusion to the nature of physical reality as it is currently understood by particle physicists, also seem to be essential parts of the general wisdom necessary to understand fully perceptual processes.

In short, Chapter 3, is intended to help make this book self-standing by providing the background, technical, and methodological materials that are essential to understand fully the experiments that are discussed in later chapters. But there is also another more fundamental reason for the inclusion of the materials of Chapter 3. It is almost a truism that the theories, as well as the data, that are generated in any program of research are heavily dependent on the measuring instruments (both mechanical and conceptual) used to examine the phenomena under consideration. Ideas, particularly conceptual and physical analogies, feed back and forth between the sciences and it is sometimes quite illuminating to note how theories develop because of some similarity between two quite distant domains of inquiry.

The second part of the book is both a survey of the phenomena and the data and the concrete expression of my particular theoretical perspective—the process taxonomy. It is designed to explicate general principles by attributing the variety of perceptual phenomena to the six levels of perception. Chapter 4 presents the detailed framework of the taxonomic level theory that I develop in the rest of this book and deals with the specific attributes of the theory, its advantages, and disadvantages and the difficulties faced by anyone seeking to develop a comprehensive and global metatheory of visual perception.

Chapter 5 presents a discussion of the Level 0 preneural and prepsychological transformations imposed between the distal stimulus generated in the external world and the proximal stimulus that actually exists on the retina just prior to photoreceptor transduction. Chapter 6 deals specifically with these processes that seem to be mainly influenced by Level 1 receptor processes. Chapter 7 is a multilevel digression. It is here, for unavoidable and practical empirical reasons, that the level theory fails completely and one is forced to deal with certain peripherally mediated temporal phenomena in terms of several inseparable levels of processing. As I studied the material, it became clear that it is very difficult to discriminate between Level 1 and Level 2 influences on such phenomena as temporal summation or visual persistence. The discussion, therefore, necessarily crosses both of these levels of analysis.

Chapter 8 concerns itself with those perceptual phenomena that I believe are clearly the result of relatively simple network (Level 2) interactions in portions of the nervous system only slightly more central than the receptor. Chapter 9, on the other hand, is a transition discussion, a mezzolog, bridging the conceptual gap between the materials of Chapters 6, 7, and 8, which were so dependent on neurophysiological models and concepts and Chapters 10, and 11 for which the appropriate vocabulary is much more molar and psychological. Chapter 9 is also intended to spell out some specific arguments against the application of a neuroreductive level of analysis to the majority of perceptual phenomena. In Chapter 9, I take a particularly critical stance towards some popular contemporary neuroredictionistic theories of perception and attempt to clarify what I believe is some terribly muddy or equivocal psychobiological thinking by alluding to some compelling counterindications to such theories.

Chapter 10, dealing with Level 3 processes, is the first to deal with phenomena that are not, in general, amenable to neurophysiological explanation. In particular, the emphasis in Chapter 10 is on such topics as the processes of signal extraction from background interference, the organization of form in two and three dimensions and figure–ground differentiation.

Chapter 11, on the other hand, deals with Level 4 processes that seem to be better described as the result of the interaction of multiple dimensions of the stimulus scene. These are the processes in which the first-order relationship between a single dimension of the stimulus and the perceptual process is patently inadequate to explain the phenomenon. The stimuli in these cases often seem only to be no more than vehicles for the dimensional information rather than direct deterministic antecedents of responses themselves. There is often no isomorphism of the stimulus scene and the percept. This chapter introduces a kind of perceptual relativism that I assert is essential for the generation of quantitative experience.

Finally, Chapter 12 provides the epilog in which the broad emerging principles of perceptual psychology, as I see them, are extracted and listed. This list of emerging principles and metaprinciples will itself constitute, from some points of view, a specific expression of one theory of perception. It is heavily *based on* the empirical data, as must any viable theoretical construction in science, but it is not *composed of* the empirical data. Each principle will, hopefully, transcend the individual experiments and abstract some more fundamental attribute of perception.

In this first chapter I have spelled out the fundamental issues of perceptual science and have outlined the intended scope of this book. Before a new synthesis can be meaningfully presented, however, it is necessary to consider the perspectives of those who have preceded this work to place it properly in its intellectual and historical context. That is the purpose of the next chapter.

2 Theories of Perception

- A. Introduction
  - 1. The Role of Theory
  - 2. Macrotheories and Microtheories
  - 3. On the Resolution of Apparently Incompatible Macrotheories
- B. Dimensions of Perceptual Theories
  - 1. Is Perception Innate or Learned? The Nativism-Empiricism$_1$ Dimension
  - 2. Is Perception Direct or Logically Mediated? The Rationalism-Empiricism$_2$ Dimension
  - 3. Is Perception a Function of the Global Configuration of the Pattern or of its Constituent Parts? The Wholism-Elementalism Dimension
- C. Macrotheories of Perception
  - 1. The Rationalistic Macrotheories of Perception
    - a. The Classic Rationalistic Tradition
    - b. Modern Rationalisms
      - —Bruner and Postman's Directive State Theory (The New Look in Perception)
      - —Helson's Adaptation Level Theory of Perception
      - —Constructionism
  - 2. The Empiricistic Macrotheories of Perception
    - a. The Classic Empiricistic Tradition
    - b. Modern Empiricisms
      - —Gibson's Ecological Optics
      - —Other Direct Realisms
  - 3. Wundt and Titchener's Structuralist Macrotheories of Perception
  - 4. The Functionalist Macrotheories of Perception
    - a. Brunswik's Probabilistic Functionalism
    - b. Dewey and Ames' Transactional Functionalism
  - 5. The Gestalt Macrotheory of Perception
  - 6. The Behavioristic Approach to Perception
  - 7. Cybernetic, Information-Processing, Computer and Automata Models of Perception
    - a. Cybernetic Theories of Perception
    - b. Information-Processing Theories of Perception
    - c. Computer Models and Artificial Intelligence
  - 8. Neurophysiological-Reductionistic Models of Perception
    - a. Single Neuron Theories of Perception
    - b. Spatial Frequency Filter Theories of Perception
    - c. Neural Network Theories of Perception
    - d. Neuroelectric Field Theories of Perception
  - 9. Mathematical-Descriptive Theories of Perception
- D. An Interim Summary

A. INTRODUCTION

1. The Role of Theory

In the previous chapter I consider some of the perplexing issues that constitute the substance of perceptual science and spelled out a few of the concrete questions through which science addresses the general and, indeed, much too broad, epistemological issue of how we acquire information from the external environment. It is only in the more narrowly defined context of such specific questions that perception becomes amenable to experimental research and specific theoretical modeling. The purpose of the present chapter is to present a historical survey of some of the many global theories that have been previously proposed as general answers to the problem of perception.

It is a truism that the individual experiments in any field of science, and particularly in psychology, are by themselves rarely of lasting importance. Their contribution is to signal answers to the broader questions and to generate global perspectives. That overall psychological perspective usually arises from a synthesis of the mass of detailed data obtained from extensive programs of empirical research rather than from particular findings. What inevitably happens, unfortunately, is that in reducing any complex, real-world situation to an abstraction that is manipulable in the laboratory, a great deal of generality is necessarily lost. Each experiment has only a blurred and partial view of the full scope of the problem. Fractionation of this sort is a serious limitation of the experimental method and most thoughtful scientists would agree that if science were only a matter of experimenting with such abstractions, it would be sterile indeed. A major and important role of an integrative theory encompassing a wide variety of data is, therefore, to reconstitute the broader meaning and significance of the results of individual experiments designed (for reasons of control and manipulability) to abstract narrowly defined aspects of reality. It is this global or reconstitutive role of theory to which this chapter is dedicated.

In spite of this very important integrative role, the word *theory* is often used as a pejorative—as a synonym for an untested and speculative idea that is not substantiated by empirical observations: Some would say, "I can't accept that idea; it is only a theory." My use of the word here, however, is the more positive one commonly used in the scientific community. Theory, as used in the present context, denotes a comprehensive, meaningful, and synthetic integration of a diverse set of empirical findings in a way that, hopefully, leads to a deep and broad understanding of the pertinent substance of the science. Simple aggregation of data is not theory building from my point of view; it is only when one goes beyond the immediate observation to general understanding that a theory, in the sense I use the word, has been built. Integrative theory thus refers to the outcome of the ultimate stage of the scientific process—the interpretation of aggregates of data to extract general meaning—rather than the popular concept of idle armchair speculation as a substitute for active exploration and data acquisition.

The variety of points of theoretical view and the unresolved controversies among different schools of thought in science reflect an important fact: Powerful, fertile, and elegant theories are *intended* to go beyond the available data. Theory breeds controversy because it is an extension beyond observation. It is a simple fact of scientific life that extrapolative interpretations can differ among reasonable men and women. Obviously, therefore, commitment to a particular point of view or perspective must be, at least to a certain extent, a matter of taste and value concerning the elegance, simplicity, or completeness of the theory rather than quantitative measures of its explanatory value. Theories (outside of highly mathematical ones) typically are not replaced because they have been shown to be incorrect in some formal way but rather, more often, fall into disfavor because some glaring empirical inconsistency has been introduced by some new observational tool[1] or because scholarly interest has gradually shifted away from the particular phenomena with which a given theory dealt. This is not to say that there are not some general criteria that can be used to evaluate theories, but most of the criteria suggested (e.g., F. Allport's list on page 23 of Chapter 1) are more suitable for the comparison of quantitative models of highly restricted intent than for the verbal explanations that usually characterize the perceptual theories discussed in this chapter.

Another aspect of this problem of achieving understanding of perceptual processes that should not be forgotten is that both experimental data and theory are labile and transient. Theories, it is well appreciated, come and go; and the attention of scholars is quite inconstant. Different theories emphasize different aspects of perception; different periods in history find different phenomena in vogue and emphasized by researchers; and ideas dismissed or ignored 25 or 50 years ago may be enthusiastically restored to favor by contemporary scholars. For example, the modern cognitively oriented explanations of perceptual phenomena can be considered as rejuvenations of the rationalistic and functionalist theories that were dormant during the heyday of twentieth-century positivistic behaviorism.

It is not so well appreciated, however, that the impact and influence of a considerable portion of the empirical data base itself also waxes and wanes in conjunction with the theory that it was originally designed to support. Since most experiments must be abstractions of full-blown behaviorally and ecologically relevant situations, many data are collected with the intent of being specifically relevant to a particular theoretical perspective. The data explained by one theory

---

[1]For an eloquent discussion of such revolutions in scientific paradigms, or as he now calls them—discrepancy matrices—see Thomas Kuhn's book *The Structure of Scientific Revolutions* (Kuhn, 1962) and Wade's (1977b) interpretation of its impact. For a semi-autobiographical account of his own development as a historian of science, see Kuhn (1978).

are very often not the same as those explained by another. Rather, each theory sets up a particular corpus of experimental evidence to support its particular point of view; very often the different copora for the different theories do not even overlap. Surprisingly often, superficially "competitive" points of view simply do not concern themselves with the same processes and phenomena.

It is, therefore, far more often the case that theories in perception are not competitive as much as they are complementary. Finding the conceptual basis for such complementarity is another important goal of perceptual science. It should not be forgotten that one of the most important contributions made by any perceptual theory is the attention it calls to a particular class of phenomena that may not previously have been a part of the collective consciousness of the psychological community.

Each perceptual theory, by defining a set of relevant experiments and by virtue of the built-in constraints on its intended scope, thus becomes, to a very great extent, a closed system dealing only with a limited universe of data. When, for one reason or another, the theory loses its attractiveness and is supplanted by some other theory, there is often a vacuum of relevance created with regard to the experiments that have been carried out in support of the now-defunct theory. They may become "classic" demonstrations in a textbook or introductory lecture; or, at some later time, arguments for a modified and resurrected form of the theory; but theory-free data, even if they are in sharp disagreement with the prevailing Zeitgeist, usually have little influence on the newly dominant perspective. The data are not incorrect, inconsistent, or contentious; they are simply no longer of interest and relevance to contemporary science.

Most theories in perceptual psychology deal with only a small portion of the full range of perceptual phenomena. This narrowness of perceptual theories is both a strength and a weakness. By limiting the theory to a restricted domain, localized explanation is made possible, whereas trying to encompass all perceptual phenomena into a master and universal theory almost always turns out to be an elusive and futile task. On the other hand, the closed and restricted systems of thinking that are articulated in most perceptual theories often constrain new insights and impede the realization of the conceptual linkages that do exist between related phenomena.

There is another compelling force toward theory building that is particularly important with regard to the study of perception. Perceptual phenomena, to a very substantial degree, are nonveridical; that is, the percept very often diverges from the straightforward response that would have been predicted on the basis of a direct or automatic processing of the stimulus. If percepts were totally determined transformations of the stimulus, there probably would be no need for any of the perceptual theories that I shall consider in this chapter. Indeed, there would be little for perceptual psychologists to explain other than the straightforward communication of information from one point to another in the communication channel. On the other hand, illusions, as one impressive set of otherwise trivial examples, are of interest just because they are nonveridical responses to the stimulus not because of any substantive importance of the perception of an obscure illusion.

That visual stimuli produce percepts deviating in major ways from the direct implications of the retinal image is the essential and interesting substance of perceptual science, not the nonneuronal and nonperceptual, but linear and easily understandable transformations that occur within the optics of the eye. The nervous system–mind complex is not a simple lens that straightforwardly transforms the stimulus into a mental image, but is rather a system that exerts its own sometimes very substantial influences on the incoming signals.

The role of perceptual science, in this context, is to define, describe, and, most important of all, explain the often exceedingly complex transformations carried out by this psychoneural system. It is not, as so many of today's perceptual psychologists seem to think, simply to collect data. When theory and explanation are absent, the laboratory is inevitably sterile.

My colleage, Joseph Lappin (in press a) reminds us of the words of Albert Einstein in 1950 concerning the role of theory in science in this citation:

> Why do we devise theories at all? The answer to the latter question is simply: Because we enjoy 'comprehending,' i.e., by reducing phenomena by the process of logic to something already known or (apparently) evident. . . . There exists a passion for comprehension, just as there exists a passion for music. . . . I believe that every true theorist is a kind of tamed metaphysicist, no matter how pure a 'positivist' he may fancy himself. The metaphysicist believes that the logically simple is also the real. The tamed metaphysicist believes that not all that is logically simple is embodied in experienced reality, but that the totality of all sensory experience can be "comprehended" on the basis of a conceptual system . . . built on premises of great simplicity.

These somewhat romantic views of the role of theory should, however, be tempered with some realistic caveats. Most perceptual theories are at once too broad and too narrow. With regard to their breadth, many of the most prominent global theories of perception deal with all perceptual phenomena as if they were uniformly explicable. The multilevel analysis followed in this book, as well as all other comparable stage and level theories, attempts to clarify the difficulties introduced by this uncritical fusing of what are fundamentally different kinds of processes into single categories.

With regard to their narrowness, on the other hand, many theories of perception deal with such highly restricted classes of phenomena that they lose the one asset any theory must possess: the foundation of a sufficiently broad class of related phenomena to allow generalization and synthesis. It is only in this way that progress can be made towards the ultimate goal of psychological science—man's understanding of the nature of man.

Another fundamental problem for perceptual theory builders is the simple fact that in many cases the conceptual, logical, and empirical foundations essential for the construction of a satisfactory theory are lacking. It is very easy to theorize about the nature of perception and to conjure up many different models to deal with various classes of phenomena. On the other hand, any current discussion of theory must acknowledge that there still remain imponderables and unanswerables. Lacunae in our knowledge and in our understanding prevent us from formulating a complete and satisfactory model of perception. As examples, we do not yet adequately understand the link between the neural mechanism and the phenomenological response; we do not yet understand the relationships among diverse perceptual phenomena; and we do not yet have any means other than overt behavior to examine the covert mental responses we call percepts.

2. Macrotheories and Microtheories

Theories of visual perception can be divided into two major categories—*macro*theories and *micro*theories—depending on their intended breadth. The category of macrotheories includes those explanatory models that spell out a global view of the general way in which perceptual mechanisms work. Macrotheories typically make an overt intellectual commitment to a particular philosophical point of view concerning the general nature of perception and propose an overall answer to the general epistemological question. The typical macrotheory, for example, would assert a position with regard to the very broad issues of the degree of innateness of perceptual processes and the mediation of the causal link between stimulus and percept by the perceiver but would typically ignore the details involved in explaining any specific illusion. It would attempt to provide an overall explanation of a very wide body of empirical knowledge. An example of a modern macrotheory is J. J. Gibson's system (described later in this chapter) of *ecological optics*. In developing his macrotheory, Gibson's attention was directed to the general relationship between environmental stimuli and the percepts they generate and not to a particular stimulus–process–phenomenon relationship.

Microtheories, on the other hand, are concerned with the detailed explanation of a single perceptual phenomenon or a small, closely related set of phenomena. Microtheories are typically concerned with the derivation and description of a functional relationship between a single dimension of a stimulus and a single dimension of some particular perceptual response. A microtheory, for example, might attempt to explain the nonveridical illusion called the Mach band (the psychoneural enhancement of physical contours; see Fig. 8-29) by invoking some known neural interactive process but would not necessarily make an explicit statement with regard to the major epistemological issues that are the core of macrotheory. It should not be forgotten, however, that all microtheories always exist within a context of some particular macrotheory whether or not the commitment is explicitly made.

Having made this distinction between macro- and microtheories, I now am in a position to define more specifically the purpose of this chapter. Its intended aim is to survey macrotheories of perception and to spell out the salient aspects of these global views. Microtheories, on the other hand, are so specialized that it is more appropriate to describe them, wherever they are relevant to the particular discussions of the various levels of perception, in the second part of this book. In developing that part, I am explicitly attempting to categorize and classify the levels at which each of the many perceptual phenomena have a critical influence exerted on them. By the simple act of so classifying the phenomena, I am implicitly asserting in each case a particular microtheory for each of the phenomena. It should be mentioned at this point that the entire classification system of levels itself constitutes a more or less novel macrotheory that guides the organization of this book.

3. On the Resolution of Apparently Incompatible Macrotheories

In the following review of the various macrotheories that have graced perceptual science, it may seem that many of these global models take diametrically opposed positions with regard to the answers they propose to certain key issues. Does this controversy mean that there is, in fact, a "correct" theory and that only that one point of view will ultimately survive in some wisely adjudicated final analysis? I believe that this is not the case. In perceptual science, as in most others, theories that seem at first to be totally incompatible often turn out to be complementary. This actual complementarity may result from the fact that the apparently antagonistic theories do not, in fact, deal with the same aspects of perception (i.e., they do not exist in the same universe of discourse), or it may result from the fact that there is a logical equivalence at some deeper level of the superficially inconsistent languages used by each theory. In either case, it is important not to read conflict into logical obscurity or antagonism into different realms of concern.

A classic example of the eventual resolution of such an apparent incompatibility, and a constant reminder that we should remain flexible, was the rationalization of the controversy over the quantum and wave theories of light in the physical sciences. As it turned out, there is now an eclectic acceptance of both models in a single comprehensive quantum-field theory. Wave and particle principles and concepts are respectively useful or complementary, each in its respective place, as advocated by Niels Bohr (1885–1962). Similarly, I believe that many superficially contradictory theories of visual perception will all ultimately be shown to be actually complementary, each in its own appropriate context, as long as the linguistic terms of each are not uncritically mixed in the same sentences.

This potential complementarity is most likely to emerge with regard to the antagonism some perceive to exist between neurophysiological reductionistic theories, on the one hand, and cognitive theories, on the other. One of the main factors that leads to an apparent, but false, antagonism between neural and cognitive perceptual theories is that only a few phenomena have yet been satisfactorily subjected to neurophysiological reductionism. Other phenomena seem to result from mechanisms that operate at levels of complexity that exceed any plausibly conceivable form of neurophysiological reductionism in the foreseeable future. Thus, there is a natural schism between those phenomena that can be adequately described in neurophysiological terms at present and those that must be described in the less reductive language of rationalism, phenomenology, and behavior. Unfortunately, there is also an associated ideological schism between the respective analytic theories—micro-neuroreductionistic and molar-psychological—that deal with each category of phenomena. Of course, the dividing line between these two types of phenomena and the two respective theoretical approaches is labile and subject to change as new concepts of neurophysiological organization emerge, but the existence of these two schisms does represent, at any given moment, a serious source of pseudocontroversy. In my opinion the neural and the molar approaches are not intrinsically antagonistic, but both are necessary to encompass the broad range of perceptual phenomena already identified.

B. DIMENSIONS OF PERCEPTUAL THEORIES

As noted, the main purpose of this chapter is to review the various macrotheories of perception and to organize them so that both their similarities and their distinctive differences can be discerned. The development of a classification scheme for theories requires identification of the relevant dimensions or axes to specify the criteria upon which the classification is to be based. A preliminary analysis of the various theories I will discuss encouraged me to assume that it is actually possible to identify a small number of cogent dimensions or criterion axes. Indeed, I now believe that the development of a satisfactory classification scheme capable of encompassing most perceptual macrotheories requires only three major dimensions. The theories to be described, of course, do not pay equally explicit attention to all three axes, and their positions with regard to those axes that are ignored must often be inferred indirectly. Furthermore, some secondary issues are important to some theories that do not fall within the range of the three main dimensions I later propose. Nevertheless, these three variables can account for most of the variance between perceptual macrotheories.

Ideally, the three classification axes should be orthogonal. That is, they should be independent and exclusive; each should measure a concept that is totally unrelated to each of the others. As we shall see, this is not entirely possible with the tridimensional classification of perceptual theories that I invoke in this chapter; correlations exist among the positions taken by the various theories with regard to each of the three axes.

Now, to make this schema more concrete, we need to define more specifically the three dimensions or axes that I believe collectively characterize theories of perception. These dimensions can be best characterized as representing the potential range of answers to the following three questions:

1. Is perception mainly innate or is it mainly learned?
2. Is perception mainly a direct and automatic outcome of the stimulus information acting on a passive perceptual system, or is it mainly mediated by deductive, epistemic, logical, symbolic, inferential or rational processes in a highly active system?
3. Is perception mainly influenced by the overall configuration of stimuli, or are percepts mainly the results of processes more sensitive to the individual features or parts of stimuli?

My task, after more precisely defining exactly what is meant by each of these three issues and briefly describing the prototypical positions that can be taken on each, will be to describe how each of the major historical theories of perception as well as a sample of modern views fits, into this three-dimensional schema.

Before I begin my discussion of the three dimensions of perceptual theories, it is important to point out that there is an important distinction that should be made between two uses of the word *empiricism*. The word will occur in two different contexts: the empiricism–rationalism and the empiricism–nativism controversies, respectively. However, the meaning of the term in each context is different and it is not logically necessary, nor has it been the case historically, that empiricists concerned with one issue be empiricists concerning the other. I will, therefore, distinguish in this chapter between the two meanings of the word by adding a subscript to indicate its intended usage. The term *empiricism*$_1$, therefore, will be used to denote the antonym of nativism, while the term *empiricism*$_2$ will be used to denote the antonym of rationalism. The following discussion more fully details the connotations of each of these two terms.

1. Is Perception Innate or Learned? The Nativism–Empiricism$_1$ Dimension

The developmental issue of interest here concerns the position taken by the various macrotheories of perception with regard to the degree to which an infant must learn to perceive. Traditionally, a radical nativistic philosophy asserts that the more immediate kind of mental responses to physical stimuli (the kind on which I concentrate in this book) are built into the organism as a result of its genetic heritage and evolutionary processes. According to this position, the infant observer is able to perceive visually as soon as the optics of the visual system are adequately developed, and the musculature of the eyes under sufficient mechanical control to allow good image formation on the retina.

The antagonistic empiricistic$_1$ philosophy stresses, to the contrary, that most aspects of perception must be learned. This empiricistic$_1$ tradition is usually closely related to an associationism that asserts that the primitive and simple sensory responses of innate mechanisms are combined or "associated" as a result of experience to produce complex perceptual phenomena.

However, it must also be appreciated that many empiricists did not assume that *all* perceptions are learned and formed from association of more primitive sensory elements. Even the most committed empiricists have generally accepted the fact that there must be some primitive experiences available to the perceiver before any learning or association can take place. Two-dimensional form perception, for example, was an innate and primitive sensory element even in the perceptual theory of such a confirmed empiricist$_1$ as John Locke (1632–1704). Thus it is important to reiterate that the empiricistic, and nativist positions are not always in total opposition and, like so many other theoretical stances, may differ more in emphasis than in substance.

Modern nativistic philosophies can be traced back to the concepts of "innate ideas," "eternal truths," and "a priori givens" proposed by a number of seventeenth and eighteenth century rationalistically oriented philosophers as well as to certain critical physiological developments. Benedict de Spinoza's (1632–1677) concept of "innate intuitions" and Immanuel Kant's (1724–1804) concept of "a priori ideas" are examples of the philosophical concepts underlying the nativistic point of view. Johannes Müller's (1801–1853) law of the "specific energy of nerves" and Ewald Hering's (1834–1918) opponent-color perception theories were both also attempts to demonstrate an anatomical-physiological, and thus innate, basis for the perception of sensory qualities and thus also fall within this rubric. The opposing empiricistic$_1$ view, emphasizing the role of experience and learning, is largely traceable to the British empiricist school pioneered by John Locke. Perhaps the arch-empiricist$_1$ of relatively modern times was William James (1842–1910), who coined the phrase "blooming, buzzing confusion" to describe the perceptual world of the newborn. Only through experience, James asserted, could such a confusion be made orderly and discriminative abilities sharpened.

Though its origins are antique, the nativist–empiricist$_1$ controversy is certainly not dead. The high contemporary degree of interest in developmental psychology and, in particular, perceptual development, is a modern expression of the persistent interest in establishing just what part of perception may be attributed to our genetic heritage and what part is acquired along with the rest of our cultural baggage as a result of experience.

2. Is Perception Direct or Logically Medicated? The Rationalism–Empiricism$_2$ Dimension

I have already dealt briefly with the controversy between rationalism and empiricism, in Chapter 1. To recapitulate, an empiricistic$_2$ theory asserts that perception is a more or less direct and automatic response to the stimuli provided by the world to a more or less passive organism. The aggregation of experiences is the main route to understanding, and thus the main logical model underlying empiricism$_2$ is an inductive one. Very often a direct spatiotemporal isomorphism is asserted to exist between the stimulus, the neural representation, and the percept in theories emerging from this tradition. Rationalistic philosophies, on the other hand, have traditionally asserted that, although the perceptual response is indirectly triggered by the stimulus, the resulting signals must be elaborately processed by cognitive or symbolic mechanisms that are neither direct nor isomorphic. The prevailing state of the organism, it is often asserted by the rationalists, is more important in dictating how an incoming set of stimuli will be perceived than is the stimulus itself. Without that rational and symbolic mediation, they suggest, our minds would forever be nothing but that confusion of meaningless, disorganized, and primitive sensory responses that William James proposed. Because of the need for some kind of indirect mediation, rationalists have a strong tendency to emphasize the fact that stimuli are ambiguous and incomplete and to base their logical models on deductive rather than inductive processes.

It is difficult to define simply and exactly what is meant by the two terms "direct" and "mediated" in the context of this controversy. Merely saying that a percept is direct or that it is mediated does not adequately characterize the process in terms of any sharply defined criteria. These are simply alternative words, which help to suggest the connotation, rather than clarify the denotation, of the two theoretical approaches. Perhaps a better way to define these antonyms is to note that the empiricism$_2$–rationalism dichotomy is closely linked to the different cognitive strategies suggested by another pair of terms—synthesis and analysis. Empiricists$_2$ typically describe perceptual processes as being analytic with regard to the way that the stimulus is treated. The single-cell neurophysiological reductionists (who, as we shall see, clearly are in the empiricist$_2$ camp) emphasize the feature analysis processes carried out by the individual elements of the nervous system. According to their theories, a straight moving line that is part of a more complex pattern is more or less passively extracted (i.e., analyzed) from the stimulus scene by tuned neural mechanisms, and this analysis of the whole into its features is thus the key to the perceptual response. Indeed, some highly empirical psychologists would define perception as nothing more than "the process of information extraction."

On the other hand, a long tradition among the rationalistic theorists asserts that the process of perception is not analytic but synthetic. This position asserts that, in order to be perceived, the elements or parts of the scene must be processed and given significance by active integrative mechanisms. Such a synthetic and rationalistic philosophy asserts that perception is an act of construction in which elements of the scene interact according to reasonable rules to provide a set of cues to some "cognitive theorizer" that, by acts of indirect construction, interpretation, or unconscious inference creates a coherent mental model of the outside world. It is the organization of the parts that is emphasized by the rationalistic theorists.

Closely related to this synthesis–analysis controversy is another facet of the issue that may be designated as the realism–idealism schism. The classic concern in this traditional debate has been the nature of external reality; that is, does it exist independently of being perceived or is it dependent upon observations? Clearly the modern direct realism to which most of us adhere asserts that objects exist independent of their being perceived, although controversy is brewing in this direction, too.

Another aspect of this main issue is: To what are we actually responding when we perceive—the external object or the coded representation of it in our nervous system? The causal chain from object to neural code to percept has no natural break points, but if we do adopt the stance of the school of thought known as representational realism (i.e., we respond to the neural representation) then, clearly, there is a much greater requirement for interpretive, rationally mediated processes than if we stress the direct effect of the external object. In sum, representational realists tend to be more rationalistic and direct realists tend to be more empiricistic$_2$.

3. Is Perception a Function of the Global Configuration of the Pattern or of its Constituent Parts?—The Wholism-Elementalism Dimension

The wholism–elementalism controversy is waged between associationists (otherwise known as connectionists, elementalists, or atomists) who assume that perception occurs as a result of the connection or association of the individual elements of a scene on the one hand. and the wholists (often referred to as configurationists or Gestaltists), who believe that the global pattern or organization of a scene is more important than the nature of the parts of which it is composed. Wholistic theorists of perception emphasize the overall configurational properties of a visual stimulus scene as elementalistic theorists concentrate their theoretical and experimental attention on such problems as the features, components, or local regions of the stimulus pattern.

Associationism, which asserts that simple sensory elements are concatenated into complex perceptions, has had a long history in perceptual theory, and was a keystone of the British empiricist philosophy epitomized by the works of John Locke and James Mill (1773–1836). The associationistic and elementalistic perspective has been extremely persistent and can be discerned in the neurophysiological theories that dominate much current thinking about perceptual theory. Donald Hebb's (1949) neurophysiological redictionistic theory of the organization of the mind is founded on the associationistic idea of the development of cell assemblies and, subsequently, of phase sequences from lower-level units of analysis. The principle of associationism is also implicit in most neurophysiological research on perceptual problems today, even when this tenet is not made explicit. Much of the classic emphasis on learning of conditioned responses or nonsense syllables is also an outgrowth of the associationistic and antinativistic philosophies espoused by the empiricistic$_2$ philosophies.

The roots of wholism, on the other hand, are to be found in the work of Immanuel Kant, whose philosophy dominated so much of nineteenth century thought. Kant was perhaps the first modern philosopher-psychologist to articulate the a priori importance of the whole form as opposed to the parts of which it seemed to be composed when examined in (too great) detail. The basic concept of wholism was further developed by Christian von Ehrenfels (1859–1932) who was the first to introduce the idea of pattern and melody into the discussion. Ernst Mach (1836–1916), the great physicist–physiologist–psychologist, though also a major contributor to neurophysiological reductionism at the cellular level, was also one of the main contributors to modern wholistic theory. His suggestion that multidimensional spatial and temporal patterns were "senations" as valid as the unidimensions of color and tone was especially important in this intellectual sequence. The epitome of wholistic thinking, however, was the very influential Gestalt psychology that took these early ideas of configuration and made them the keystone of a macrotheory of perception. The three most significant names in that tradition were Max Wertheimer (1880–1943), Wolfgang Kohler (1887–1967), and Kurt Koffka (1886–1941). In brief, the main premise of the wholistic approach is that the organization of the parts is more important than the nature of the parts.

The wholism–elementalism debate has recently been framed in another context by Kinchla and Wolfe (1979). Those psychologists noted that many theories exist that are oriented in terms of "top-down" processes while many others are framed in terms of "bottom-up" processes. The bottom-up approach stresses features and their extraction by simple neural mechanisms. Rumelhart (1970) proposes a modern example of this point of view. Selection rules based on primitive feature extraction processes can then be brought into play by the nervous system to categorize stimuli in a way that bottom-up theorists assert is comparable to pattern recognition. Kinchla and Wolfe go on to note that the top-down approach stresses the recognition of global forms prior to the identification of features. Modern theoreticians of this persuasion include Broadbent (1977) and Navon (1977).

I believe the difference between the bottom-up and top-down antagonists in this controversy are virtually identical to those I have just been discussing. Clearly, this modern dispute is but another aspect of the hoary old wholism–

elementalism issue. Interestingly, Kinchla and Wolfe found in their experiments that neither approach was really adequate, but rather that a "middle-out" strategy seemed to be followed by observers; the first parts of the stimulus to be processed were those aspects of an intermediate size.

Most of the macrotheories of perception that I discuss in subsequent portions of this chapter take up a particular position on each of these three axes. The classification criteria of the theories that I use here may thus conveniently be conceived of as a three-dimensional space, as shown in Fig. 2-1. As I have noted, the axes are not completely orthogonal and there are certain correlations that appear more frequently than not between pairs of the three axes in the various macrotheories. For example, empiricism$_2$—the antithesis of rationalism—is often associated with an elementalist point of view that assumes that local features are the major focus of the perceiving system. Rationalism, on the other hand, is quite more often than not associated with a wholistic point of view. It must be reiterated that these correlations are only general tendencies; as we see later, almost any combinations of positions on the three axes is in principle possible and in practice identifiable.

To demonstrate more clearly my estimate of the positions taken on these dimensions by the various theories, I shall use the type of diagram shown in Fig. 2-2. The three axes have been separated in this display for clarity (two-

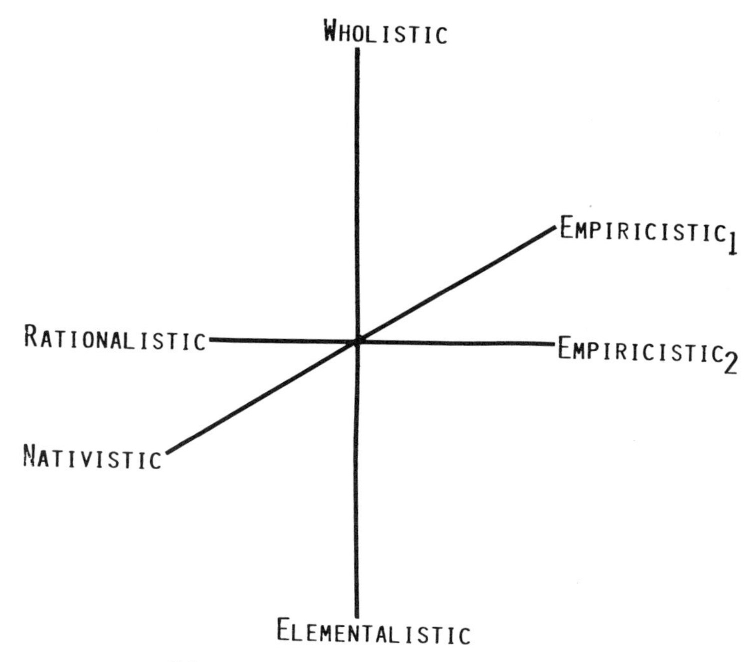

FIG. 2.1. The theory space of visual perception.

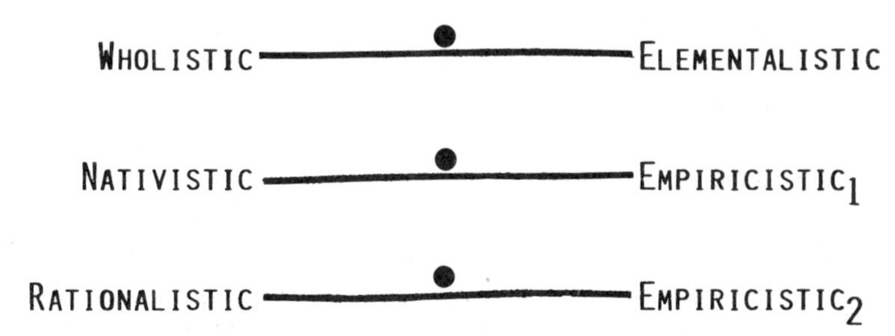

FIG. 2.2. The three dimensions of the theory space separated for clarity. The position of the dot indicates the conceptual position of the theory in later figures.

dimensional projections of three-dimensional diagrams are sometimes susceptible to perceptual ambiguities).

C. MACROTHEORIES OF PERCEPTION

To maintain conceptual order in this discussion of perceptual macrotheories, it must be emphasized that the arrangement of the various schools and theoretical positions can be represented in a logical and historical sequence. It is possible to trace a path through the maze of ideas that I present here. Many of the later theories actually originated in large part as either critical responses to the arguments and propositions, or as positive responses to the key premises, of the earlier ones. It is also clear that the timely introduction of novel and influential ideas, concepts and events also played an important role in guiding the development of the sequence of theories. The following list summarizes some of the most notable and important intellectual developments of perceptual theory in the last 300 years but makes no value judgments of their respective validity for the moment:

1. The expression of a mechanistic philosophy professing the idea that cause and effect relations occurred in all aspects of the natural universe, including the psychological ones, by Thomas Hobbes (1588–1679).
2. The separation of the study of mental processes from theology and the removal of the theological issues of soul and God from psychological protoscience by Thomas Hobbes and Rene Descartes (1596–1650), among others.
3. The development of experimental science as a means of examining natural phenomena under the influence of such intellects as Robert Grosseteste (1168–1253), Leonardo da Vinci (1452–1519), and Francis Bacon (1561–1626).
4. The emphasis on logical-rational-meaningful functions of mind by the early rationalists.
5. The emergence of the British empiricist tradition, emphasizing sensations and feelings as elements of mind, and the association of these elements into more complex mental processes by processes of experiential learning.

6. The linkage of physiology and psychology and the beginnings of the experimental basis of a theory of physiological psychology that could be invoked to provide possible answers to the mind–body problem.

7. The establishment of laboratories exclusively dedicated to the study of psychological phenomena by Wilhelm Wundt (1832–1920) in 1879 and others.

8. The emphasis on psychological processes, rather than contents, by the Act psychologists.

9. The emphasis of the early structuralist tradition on mental experiences as the subject matter of psychology and of introspection as the proper method to study mind.

10. The emphasis on the adaptive and functional role of mental processes as stressed by the American functionalists.

11. The emphasis on the nature of the configuration or pattern of the stimulus scene by the German Gestaltists and their predecessors.

12. The subsequent rejection of intrapersonal mental processes of mind as the proper topic of psychology (and introspection as the proper method) by the positivists, logical positivists, and American behaviorists, and their substitution of interpersonally observable behavior as both the subject matter and method of a proper psychology, also their reemphasis of learning and, in some extreme cases, their complete rejection of reductive explanation.

13. The reemphasis on intrapersonal mental process and the introspective methods by modern cognitive psychologists. The emergence of the constructionist school as a modern neorationalism.

14. The information-processing computer as a heuristic metaphor for understanding mental processes.

15. The flood of data from twentieth-century neurophysiology and the resulting impact on current neuroreductionistic views of sensory coding and perceptual representation.

Guided by the context established by these important developments it is possible to develop an intellectual genealogy for the various theories of perception that have been developed over the last few hundred years. Figure 2-3 represents one, but by no means the only, possible way, of concretizing this heritage of ideas.

In so diagraming this genealogy of perceptual metatheories (and in the discussion that follows) I have specifically excluded any consideration of those prototheories that deal with perceptual problems prior to the times of Bacon, da Vinci, Hobbes, and Descartes. Much of that classic thinking was not formalized sufficiently to be considered as scientific theory or was so interspersed with theological issues that it can be omitted for our purposes here. The reader interested in the classic pre-Hobbesian and pre-Cartesian views may wish to look at the work of D. N. Robinson (1976a) or Hamlyn (1961) for comprehensive historical discussions. The present discussion is limited to what many feel is the beginning of the modern scientific era.

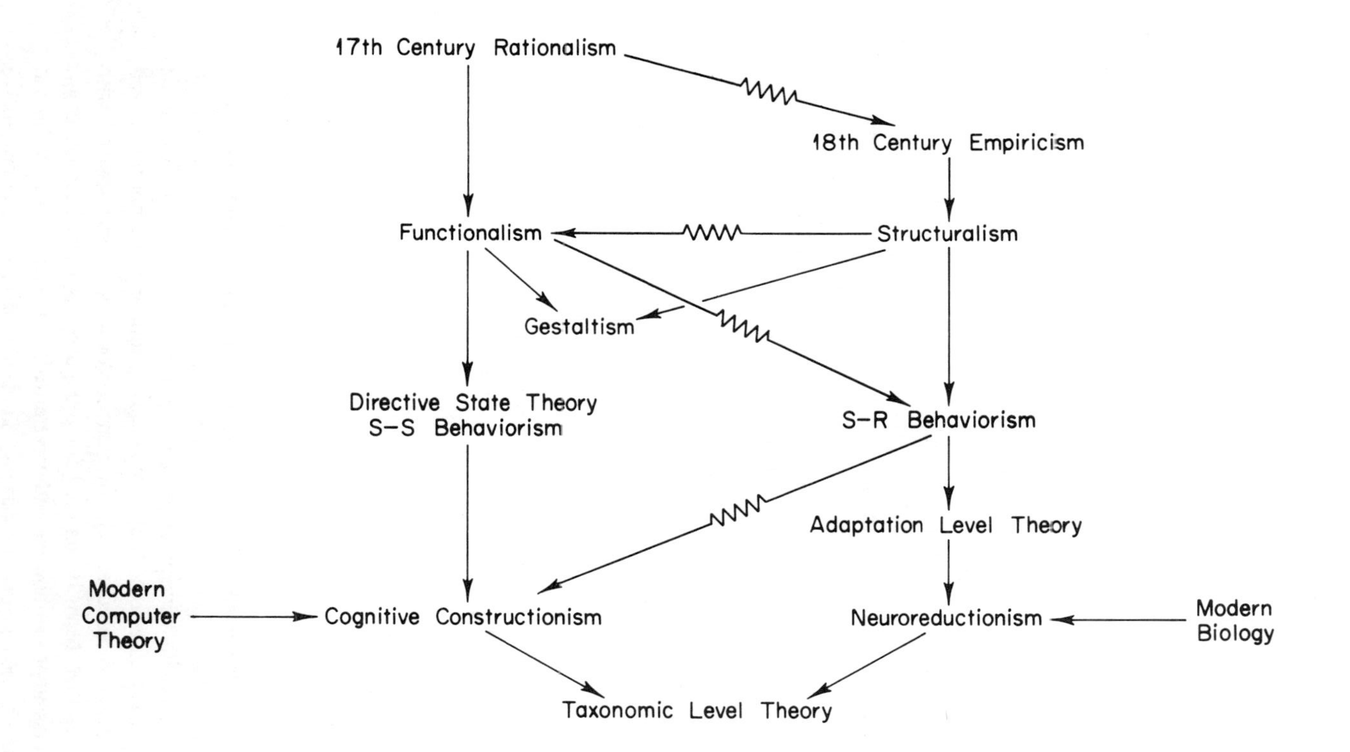

FIG. 2.3. One possible genealogy of perceptual theories.

Another extensive tradition of perceptual theorizing that I have omitted is the work of many distinguished modern philosophers. Much of this work is insufficiently based on empirical evidence or is so distant from current scientific psychology that I have intentionally reneged on what some may perceive to be a responsibility of this chapter. The reader who is interested in the important interpretations of philosophers per se, as opposed to those psychologists who are less expertly considering the philosophical issues, might find more of interest to them in the works of Smythies (1956), Hirst (1959, 1965), Warnock (1967), Armstrong (1970), and Swartz (1977). The reader is also particularly advised to refer to the sections on perception, realism, and idealism in the *Encyclopedia of Philosophy* (1967).

Also excluded from this discussion, as I have indicated earlier, are the patently psychological theories of cognitive processing that do not adequately emphasize immediate perceptual phenomena. Although this exclusion may be somewhat artificial, my aim in this book is to deal with the preattentive responses to stimuli. This is in some ways unfortunate; some important modern views of cognitive psychology that clearly involve perception as a central theoretical component—for example, Michael Posner's (1978) exciting new book—go beyond the range of the more conventionally defined perceptual problems with which I deal in this book. However, limits on space suggest that such topics may be better dealt with in another volume in this series.

In preparing these descriptions of perceptual theory, in addition to the cited primary sources, I have depended upon a number of secondary sources to which the reader who wishes more detailed discussions of the various theories is referred. These include the works of F. H. Allport (1955), Avant and Helson (1973), Boring (1950), Carterette and Friedman (1974), E. J. Gibson (1969), Hamlyn (1961), Lana (1976), Marx and Hillix (1973), Murphy and Kovach (1972), Pastore (1971), D. N. Robinson (1976a), Schultz (1975), and the *Encyclopedia of Philosophy* (1967).

1. The Rationalistic Macrotheories of Perception

a. *The Classic Rationalistic Tradition*

Modern philosophical and psychological theories of perception are both usually dated from the time of René Descartes, clearly one of the most extraordinary intellects of human history. In addition to his many contributions to philosophy and psychology, Descartes also contributed important ideas to mathematics and psychology and would have won immortality for either his invention of analytic geometry or his modern conceptualization of the mind–body problem in a way that made it susceptible to naturalistic observation and empirical investigation. Descartes' dualistic concept of separate but interacting body and mind has few adherents today among psychologists, but it did represent a sharp line of demarcation between the theologically dominated scholasticism of the medieval years and the monistic philosophy of mind that evolved subsequently in psycholobiological thinking. Descartes, perhaps better than anyone else, should be identified as the first modern psychologist.

Descartes' major contribution to the problem of perception was his advocacy of the rationalistic point of view. The major premise of a rationalistic philosophy is that man gains information and knowledge about the world around him not by a passive and inductive aggregation of his sensory experiences but by an active, deductive, and logical interpretation of the incoming sensory information. To the rationalist, this epistemology implied that the incoming information had to be evaluated by mental processes that were in some way already built into the system. Thus, there is often a close association between the classic rationalisms and the idea that many ideas are innate.

The rationalistic philosophies of perception are often misunderstood in the psychological literature. Daniel N. Robinson (1976a), among others, has noted that the rationalists did not totally reject the premises of empiricism and associationism that I will discuss shortly. The main argument between the rationalists and the empiricists, quite the contrary, concerned their respective attitudes toward the innateness of ideas. The great rationalists, including Descartes, Benedict de Spinoza (1632–1677), Gottfried von Leibniz (1646–1716), and Immanuel Kant (1724–1804), all believed that there were certain innate "eternal truths" or "a priori concepts" that make possible the interpretation and understanding of the rich variety of sensory experiences enjoyed by the individual during his development. Thus, whereas there was a strong emphasis on the innate ideas that contributed to the establishment of the meaning of the sensory data (as an alternative mechanism for experiential associations), an important role of sensation and perception was not denied by the classic rationalists. The mind was prepared by certain basic intellectual properties, according to the rationalist emphasis, to make sense out of sensations. They did not deny, however, that sensations were necessary and important to the acquisition of knowledge about the outside world.

As one explores the writing of these great rationalistic philosophers it is clear that they did actually agree in most regards concerning their acceptance of this fundamentally empiricistic epistemology. Descartes, the dean of rationalists, was thoroughly empiricistic in some of his writing. He believed that the sensory mechanisms (about which he wrote in remarkable anatomical detail, considering the state of scientific knowledge at the time) were the primary source of all complex perceptions. He also accepted the idea that sensations were stimulated by a realistic (in the formal, philosophical sense of the word) external environment. Indeed, it is possible to see the intellectual antecedents of the subsequent elementalist and associationistic tradition that were to follow in his writing as well as in that of Locke. In describing his method of scientific inquiry, for example, Descartes repeatedly referred to the necessity to reduce complex problems to their components. Knowledge, to Descartes, as to the British empiricists, came from an accumulation of information about small elements into larger intellectual structures. Such an epistemology differs in only minor respects from the associationistic tradition toward which he is so often considered to be the antagonist. This emphasis on reductionism to simpler entities was coupled with a very strong call to orderly, "nonprejudicial" (could he have meant nonrationalistic?) thinking. Consider Descartes' own words (quoted in the *Encyclopedia of Philosophy,* 1967) on the rules of scientific method:

> The first of these was to accept nothing as true which I did not clearly recognize to be so: that is to say, carefully to avoid precipitation and prejudice in judgments, and to accept in them nothing more than was presented to my mind so clearly and distinctly that I could have no occasion to doubt it.
>
> The second was to divide up each of the difficulties which I examined into as many parts as possible, and as seemed requisite for it to be resolved in the best manner possible.
>
> The third was to carry on my reflections in due order, beginning with objects that were the most simple and easy to understand, in order to rise little by little, or by degrees, to knowledge of the most complex, assuming an order, even if a fictitious one, among those which do not follow a natural sequence relative to one another.
>
> The last was in all cases to make enumerations so complete and reviews so general that I should be certain of having omitted nothing [Vol. 2, p. 345].

The special essence of Descartes' rationalism can thus be found in the first of his methods, which gave priority to his own logical, rational, and reasonable mental processes, rather than in a radical rejection of empiricism. He does imply that there are innate ideas and that these ideas, by the methods he has described, could be illuminated and developed but only by the application of the latter three rules that sound so profoundly empiricistic.

Descartes' description of his personal scientific method also illustrates another important characteristic that distinguishes the rationalistic school of thought from the classic empiricistic one; that is, the emphasis on deduction rather than on induction, which would later be so strongly stressed by the empiricists. This emphasis on deductive methods, and perhaps his entire rationalistic philosophy, some historians believe, may have been an outgrowth of what is likely to be the longest-lasting and most important practical contribution of his illustrious career—the invention of analytic geometry.

The other classical rationalistic philosophers, Spinoza, Leibniz, and Kant, all express similar attitudes toward the senses and the role of empiricism and elementalism. None of them rejected the idea that most knowledge had to be acquired by the senses in some way before it could be assimilated into human thought. They did, however, all agree on the existence of innate ideas and principles and that it was necessary for there to be some sort of built-in mind present before the sensory experiences could become meaningful. There is a fundamental need, they collectively asserted, for some eternal intuitive truths to exist before the experiences. Our concepts give us our perception, not vice versa!—was the essential assertion of the classic rationalists as it is of today's constructionalists.

Beyond this essential agreement on the nativism–empiricism axis, there was little in common among the rationalists with regard to the other two axes I have proposed for classification of these macrotheories of perception. One can find wholistic approaches (e.g., Leibniz' idea of the mind as an irreducible monad) or elementalistic notions (e.g., Descartes' surprisingly modern perceptual neurophysiology). There were further differences among the great rationalists with regard to the degree to which they would accept any mechanism as a model of mind. Descartes was supremely mechanistic (once past the theological commitment that appears to have been pro forma, for his time), whereas Spinoza's concern with innate "intentions" and "passions" represents a much weaker commitment to a mechanistic philosophy of the human spirit.

The rationalistic and empiricistic traditions have usually been placed in opposition to each other. It is clear from this brief analysis, however, that the differences are matters of degree, and that the essence of any residual distinction revolves around the innateness of perception. Figure 2-4 sums up how the classic rationalisms can be characterized in the tridimensional space of perceptual macrotheories.

b. Modern Rationalisms

Until recent years, the empiricist tradition has clearly been dominant and the rationalistic position I have just described has been dormant. This is so, not only in terms of the enormous emphasis placed on empirical laboratory experimentation and a strong inductive approach to perceptual theorizing, but also in terms of the selection of particular research topics and the emphasis on the role played by

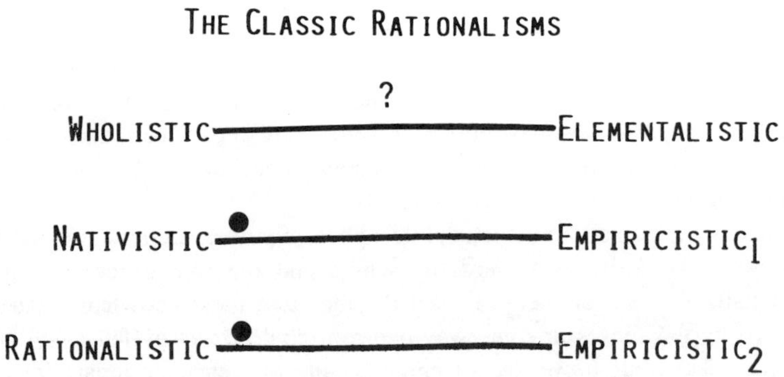

THE CLASSIC RATIONALISMS

?

WHOLISTIC —— ELEMENTALISTIC

NATIVISTIC —— EMPIRICISTIC$_1$

RATIONALISTIC —— EMPIRICISTIC$_2$

FIG. 2.4. A characterization of classic rationalism in the theory space.

the stimulus environment in defining perceptual phenomena. However, the recent trend toward cognitive psychology, with its heavy emphasis on the mental processing of stimulus information, suggests a resurgence of the classic rationalistic tradition. The continuing influence of seventeenth- and eighteenth-century rationalism is seen, I believe, in the shift of interest among psychologists from problems that seem amenable to physiological reductionism (e.g., sensory processes and motivational states) to those that seem better described in terms of attention, problem solving, imagery, and other cognitive processes.

This reemergence of a rationalistic perspective can also be seen in another aspect of modern theory. In addition to the generally agreed-upon premise of innate or a priori ideas, rationalists as a group have always tended to describe mental activity in active rather than passive terms. They believed, to a much lesser degree than did the empiricists, in a passive automaton model of the mind and played down the stimulus as the unique determinant of the perception. As I have noted, the rationalists assert that internal mental processes actively manipulate the incoming sensory experiences and what is perceived depends upon the observer to a greater extent than upon what is observed. Such a philosophy is also implicit in the theories and experimental paradigm of modern cognitive psychology. Attribution of an active information-processing role for the mind can be discerned in any modern cognitive theory that proposes some sort of a preexisting (either innate or learned) schema (Arbib, 1975; Bartlett, 1932), plan (Miller, Galanter & Pribram, 1960), frame (Minsky, 1975), or script (Abelson, 1973). The roots of constructionism or "hypothesis" theory (Gregory, 1970, 1974; Neisser, 1967) are also to be found in the tenets of classic rationalism.

Furthermore, several explicit modern theories of perception emphasize the role played by the observer and his momentary internal mental state in determining the nature of the percept, and I believe these also approach a modern expression of the classic rationalist philosophy. Although as a group these theories emphasize the active cognitive role played by the observer in interpreting the incoming stimuli, there are some important individual differences in perspective among them. Bruner and Postman's directive state theory emphasizes the role of affect and experience in perception; Helson's adaptation level theory emphasizes the role of the temporal and spatial surround in defining perception; and current constructionistic theories stress the role of the perceiver in interpreting ambiguous clues. In the following sections I elaborate on these capsule summaries of each of these important perceptual macrotheories.

Bruner and Postman's Directive State Theory (The New Look in Perception). Directive state theory, or as it was popularly known a few years ago, "The New Look in Perception," is a contemporary rationalistic approach, formally structured in terms of the central cognitive, motivational, and experiential influences on perception. Though no longer of major interest to perceptual theorists, the major thesis of directive state theory as proposed by Jerome Bruner and Leo Postman (Bruner & Postman, 1947, 1948, 1949; Postman, 1951) is that of classic rationalism; namely, that our perceptions of the external environment are more dependent on the high-level state or set of the perceiving organism and the transformations it applies to the afferent information than they are on the stimulus itself or on the automatic mechanisms of the peripheral nervous systems. Directive state theory thus emphasizes the ambiguity of the stimulus, the lack of veridicality between stimulus and percept, and the differences between the cognitive responses of different perceivers to identical stimuli because of individually determined differences in meaning, significance, or emotional overtone of the stimulus.

The essential elements of directive state theory are needs, values, set, previous experience, and the dynamics of learning. On the other hand, the actual physical dimensions of the stimulus are almost inconsequential from this point of view. Stimuli simply provide a vehicle to convey information cues. From the point of view of the directive state theoriest, the physical stimulus information is almost always ambiguous and is significant only to the degree it is interpreted by a cognitively active observer.

According to the directive state theorists' point of view, perceptions are internally generated hypotheses concerning the nature of the outside world. Perceptual hypotheses are confirmed by such processes as consensual validation (agreement among different observers), frequency of past confirmation by the individual, and rational evaluations of the number of plausible alternative hypotheses (Postman, 1951).

Directive state theory is easily classifiable within the three-dimensional macrotheoretical space as shown in Fig. 2-5. With regard to the wholism–elementalism axis, there is a heavy emphasis on the meaning and significance of the entire stimulus scene as defined by the internal cognitive state of the observer. From this point of view, it is almost inconsequential to the observer what

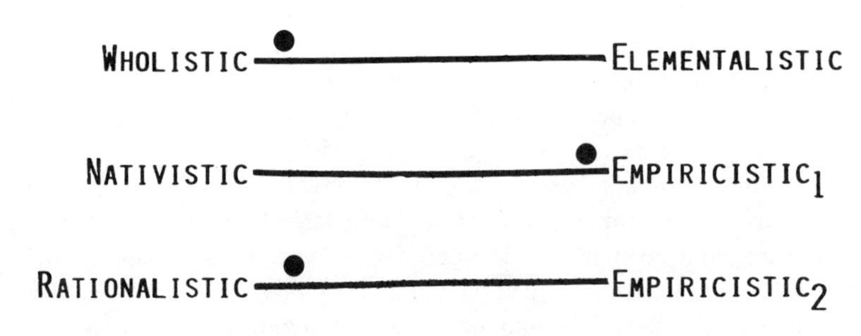

FIG. 2.5. A characterization of directive state theory in the theory space.

the stimulus elements are, or even what the nature of the configurational geometry of the stimulus is. For the directive state theorist the important aspect of perception is the semantic content of the stimulus, rather than its geometrical–physical properties. In this regard, the approach is seen to be wholistic in a manner that transcends any previous use of the term.

Furthermore, the theory is clearly empiricistic$_1$ in its heavy emphasis on learning and experience as the main source of the internal mental states of the organism. Finally, directive state theory is a radical rationalism in its definition of the causal processes in perception. It asserts a cognitive, and thus indirect or mediated, processing of stimulus information and relegates such factors as retinal size and luminosity to a very inconsequential role. What is seen is what is consistent with the organism's central state not with what is forced on it by the stimulus. Processes such as *perceptual defense* (the ability to block or suppress "offensive" significance) and *resonance* (the ability to select from among a number of alternative hypotheses the one most consistent with the organism's needs) are the key intervening variables. Perception, according to the directive state theorist, is not passive and automatic but active and rationally mediated.

It is clear from these comments that directive state theory seeks to deal only with a somewhat limited portion of the total problem of perception. It is, by intent, applicable to the more molar aspects of perception that involve semantic and affective content. The theory concentrates research attention on those instances in which the response can be modulated as a result of the inner states of the perceiver and ignores those areas when the stimulus physics and geometry are sufficiently powerful and unambiguous to be adequate to define the percept. The concept of a psychophysical law (in the sense proposed by Fechner, 1860; or Stevens, 1957) is relatively unimportant to directive state theorists. Such simple perceptual phenomena as absolute thresholds and spatial inhibitory interactions do not typically come under their scrutiny.

Bruner and Postman's original formulation of directive state theory subsequently ran into a hornets' nest of opposition and criticism on empirical, methodological, and theoretical grounds. The major issues revolve around the question of whether or not it is a perceptual theory at all or, quite the contrary, merely a description of perceptual response processes. Other technical issues of word familiarity and frequency were also raised (Solomon & Howes, 1951), and of response suppression (M. J. Goldstein, 1962) as well as a wide variety of issues that dealt with the various controls and balancing of experimental design in the critical experiments supporting this approach.

Indeed, the controversy was so great that the directive state idea has gradually lost attractiveness, and little research is done on the many remaining questions revolving around it, in spite of its great influence in the 1940s and 1950s. For the reader who would like to learn more about directive state theory, an exceedingly insightful analysis of the fundamental assumptions of directive state theory can be found in F. Allport (1955).

Helson's Adaptation Level Theory of Perception. Bruner and Postman's directive state theory is similar in certain key regards to an important theory of perception proposed by Harry Helson. Helson's adaptation level theory (Helson, 1948, 1964) was also built upon the premise that the immediate stimulus conditions alone cannot and do not define a percept. But Helson suggested a somewhat different solution to the problem. He proposed the idea that all percepts were affected by the immediate temporal and spatial surround of the stimulus as well as by the sequence of experiences that had been previously encountered by the observer. Helson's approach is thus a kind of psychological relativism based upon the idea of the establishment of an internal reference norm that operates on many different aspects of the stimulus scene to produce the final phenomenal state.

Helson's aim was to develop a quantitative theory of perception that could deal with such phenomena as visual illusions, brightness constancies, sequential order effects, and other related phenomena. These were among the most perplexing of the perplexing phenomena that had repeatedly demonstrated that there generally was no simple unidimensional relationship between a stimulus and a response. Helson suggested that any perceptual response to a stimulus scene was heavily influenced by a prevailing adaptation level or reference norm maintained within the observer. The adaptation level, in turn, was the result of pooling many different aspects of the stimulus, including current physical variables such as background luminance, but also including preceding events that specified the value of such factors as the relevance of the object being examined to preceding events in time. All dimensions were pooled, according to Helson, in a simple additive manner that differentially weighted the various dimensions. Therefore, depending upon the momentary adaptation level determined by these preceding semantic, temporal, and spatial factors, a given physical stimulus might have quite different effects from one presentation to another.

The emphasis in Helson's theory, as in the directive state model and all other rationalisms, is that the state of the organism is critical. The stimulus dimensions alone are not able to specify uniquely the perceptual response. Another important aspect of this adaptation level theory was the computational and statistical notion that is implicit in the pooling functions proposed to account for perceptual phenomena. Both of these aspects, the organismic determination of the percept and the multidimensional origins of the percept, provide the basis for characterizing this theory on the rationalism–empiricism$_2$ axis as a new expression of rationalism. With regard to the nativism–empiricism$_1$ axis. adaptation level theory is, on the other hand, thoroughly empiricistic$_1$ in its assertion that perception is strongly dependent upon the sequence of experiences encountered by the observer.

With regard to the third dimension of our classificatory trichotomy, it is not obvious whether adaptation level theory should be considered to be wholistic or elementalistic. The general idea of a perceptual relativism, as suggested by

Helson (among many others, as we see later in Chapter 10) is, in principle, analogous to the configurational aspects of the prototypically wholistic Gestalt theory. However, Helson's idea of an arithmetic pooling of the effects of various stimulus dimensions is similar in concept to the associationism of the classic elementalistic theories. I have summed up my characterization of adaptation level theory in Fig. 2-6.

Constructionism. Throughout the history of rationalistic macrotheories, the main theme has been that mental responses or percepts are not direct and deterministic results of stimuli, but rather are created by an act of mental construction from or interpretation of very incomplete and noisy sets of signals or cues from the external environment. According to this philosophy, the fact that the percept is more than is directly allowed by the stimulus is reflected in the considerably less than absolute veridicality of the percept for the individual, as well as by the lack of agreement among different individuals about their perceptions of exactly the same stimulus environment. Modern constructionism, which responds to these observations in much the same way as do the other neorationalisms I have just discussed, is a molar theoretical model of perception founded on the language, data, and perspectives of the psychologist. There is usually no attempt made to link the inductive process it emphasizes to the reductionistic terms used by neurophysiologists to describe the underlying mechanisms. Constructionist theories, furthermore, like most other molar approaches, are usually incomplete. Whereas they reject a direct and automatic response to stimuli as the causal process in perception, they usually do not describe any alternative mechanisms for the logical and inductive constructive processes they invoke.

Perhaps the earliest modern formulation of a constructionist theory is to be found in Hermann von Helmholtz (1821–1894) concept of "unconscious inference." He states (as cited in Warren & Warren, 1968):

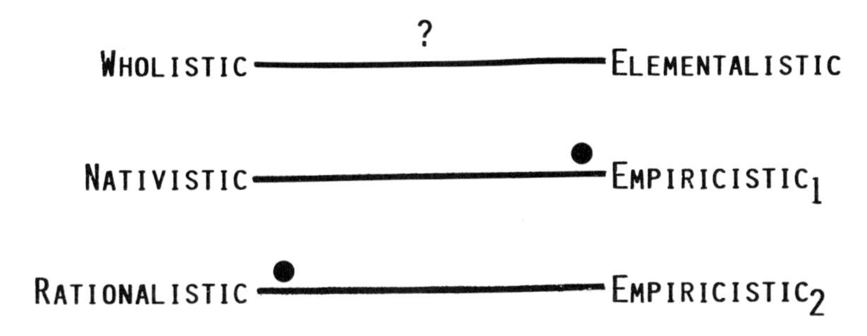

FIG. 2.6. A characterization of adaptation level theory in the theory space.

> Now we have exactly the same case in our sense-perceptions. When those nervous mechanisms whose terminals lie on the righthand portions of the retinas of the two eyes have been stimulated, our usual experience, repeated a million times all through life, has been that a luminous object was over there in front of us on our left. We had to lift the hand toward the left to hide the light or to grasp the luminous object; or we had to move toward the left to get closer to it. Thus, while in these cases no particular conscious conclusion may be present, yet the essential and original office of such a conclusion has been performed, and the result of it has been attained; simply, of course, by the unconscious processes of association of ideas going on in the dark background of our memory. Thus, too, its results are urged on our consciousness, so to speak, as if an external power had constrained us over which our will has no control.
>
> These inductive conclusions leading to the formation of our sense-perceptions certainly do lack the purifying and scrutinizing work of conscious thinking. Nevertheless, in my opinion, by their peculiar nature they may be classed as *conclusions,* inductive conclusions unconsciously formed [p. 195].

Thus, Helmholtz succinctly characterizes many of the major attributes of contemporary constructionistic theory and helps to classify it in the tridimensional theory space. His version of constructionism is clearly a rationalistic theory in diametric opposition to a mechanistic and empiricistic$_2$ philosophy. His reference to "association of ideas," however, indicates, somewhat unexpectedly, a compatibility with an empiricistic$_1$ approach as well as an intrinsic elementalism. With this emphasis on experience, Helmholtz, like many of the later constructionists, differs from the classic rationalistic positions.

A strong constructionistic tone is also discernible in the several psychological philosophies that emphasize perceptual *processes* rather than the perceptual *phenomena* themselves. Franz Brentano's (1838–1917) Act psychology (Brentano, 1874/1973), with its stress on the "act" or process of perceiving, and Fredric Bartlett's (1866–1969) theory of remembering (Bartlett, 1932, 1958) as an active process, are both examples of this same point of view although neither explicitly uses the word *construction*. Overtones of the same point of view can also be discerned in the writing of Henri Bergson (1911) and William James (1890).

Currently, there has been a resurgence in constructionistic thinking and a number of modern psychologists have been vigorous champions of this kind of neoratinalistic ideology. Among the most notable modern theorists whose ideas are compatible with the constructionist school of thought are M. D. Vernon (1955), George Miller, Eugene Galanter, and Karl Pribram (1960), K. J. W. Craik (1967), Ulric Neisser (1967), Jean Piaget (1969), Richard Gregory (1974), and Irvin Rock (1975). The reader is directed, as one exemplar of the latter's constructionistic approach in the laboratory, to the report by Rock, Shallo, and Schwartz (1978).

Difficulties with the constructionistic approach can, however, also be detected in the Helmholtz quote. Helmholtz reference to the "dark background of memory" reneges on the theorist's responsibility to specify, as exactly as possible, what is happening in the system under investigation. But even today, the details of where or what a constructing mechanism might be remain elusive; no theory included within this rubric adequately comes to grips with it. The reader interested in a more critical analysis of modern constructionist (or as this particular direct realist calls them, "epistemically mediated" models) theories would be well advised to read Michael Turvey's (1977) analysis of the problem.

In conclusion, I must note that many contemporary perceptual psychologists present their work in a way that is implicitly, if not explicitly, constructionistic. Often this becomes a mere waving of the hands, for the analysis is sometimes purely descriptive, atheoretical, and nonreductionalistic. By acknowleding the great complexity of the underlying process, we limit ourselves to verbal and mathematical "theories" that really do not help us to understand how it is that we perceive. This is one of the serious pitfalls confronted in the later chapters of this book.

Figure 2-7 sums up the stance of constructionists on the three dimensions of our macrotheoretical space. Constructionism is elementalistic, in a certain sense, when it asserts that the elements of sensory experience must act as clues for the construction of a mental map. However, this macrotheory is also wholistic in assuming both that the resulting map must fit into a coherent pattern and that the impact of the input stimuli depends on their coherence. I have, therefore, placed constructionism in a middle position on this axis. The other two axes are much less equivocal. Modern constructionism is highly empiricistic$_1$ in assuming that the experiences encountered by the observer are predominant in dictating the nature of the construction and, of course, it represents the prototype of the rationalistic approach.

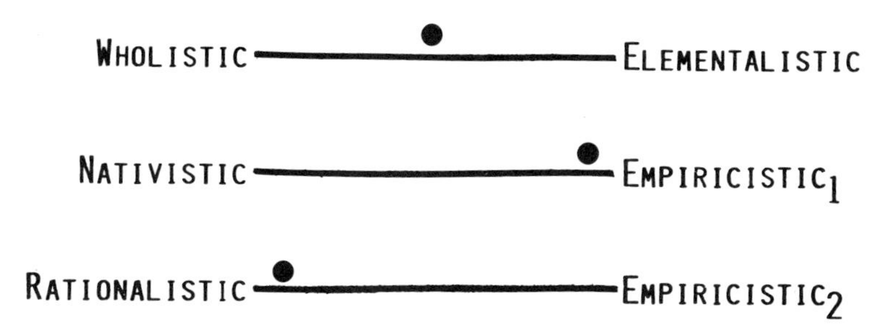

FIG. 2.7. A characterization of constructionalism in the theory space.

2. The Empiricistic Macrotheories of Perception

a. The Classic Empiricist Tradition

The rationalist epistemology was, to a major degree, an outgrowth of the medieval scholastic tradition that was dominated by problems of theology and that considered the human soul (mind) as a separate and virtually supernatural entity operating outside of the scope of natural laws. However, during the Renaissance another strong intellectual current—observational science—stimulated the evolution of quite a different epistemology, now known as empiricism. In its most extreme form, empiricism was characterized by three basic premises: (1) no knowledge is innate; (2) all knowledge is gained by sensory experience; and (3) percepts are the more or less automatic responses to the environment by a deterministic mind. A closely related corrolary that complex ideas arise from association of simpler ones is also usually a part of any empiricistic doctrine. The historical antecedents of empiricism are obvious in the scientific and philosophical developments of the sixteenth and seventeenth century. The realization by Francis Bacon (1561–1626) of the importance of scientific experimentation (empiricism of another kind) and the need for the pragmatic relevance of knowledge was one important influence. But this intellectual development was strongly stimulated by and coupled with the emergence of commerce and contemporary advances in the conception, design, and construction of useful mechanisms of one kind or another (e.g., clocks, printing presses, and navigational instruments). Theories of both the external physical world and the internal anatomical and mental worlds changed rapidly in concert with the emergence of means for controlling the environment.

The intellectual analogy between epistemological empiricism and scientific method has been noted many times, and the historical roots of these two traditions are strongly intertwined. Perhaps even more important, however, was the de-theologization of inquiry and knowledge in general. The sixteenth and seventeenth centuries saw the full flowering of the trend towards dealing with biological and psychological issues as parts of the natural scene (rather than as metaphysical or supernatural events not subject to the usual rules governing material entities) that had been seeded in earlier centuries. The artists, craftsmen, naturalists, and social critics of the Renaissance contributed subtly to this revolutionary idea. Thomas Hobbes laid other important foundation stones of empiricism in *Leviathan* (Hobbes, 1651/1962), articulating a mechanistic philosophy in which mental acts were depicted as direct physical reactions (even as motions) to the "pressures" exerted by physical stimuli. Henceforth, man was to be dealt with as another object of nature and not a divine creation.

René Descartes (1596–1650), the father of rationalism, also contributed to this emerging awareness that the methods of science could be expanded to examine the relationships between the mind and the body. Though the Cartesian dualistic interactionism was significantly different in fundamental philosophy from Hobbes' monistic mechanism, it is clear that Descartes too conceived of mental processes as part of the natural world, though he clothed much of what he had to say in theological garments.

The emergence of these materialistic, mechanistic, and, some would say, positivistic points of view concerning mind in general led to the development of British empiricism—a school of thought that has had much to say about epistemology and perception in particular. The evolution of the several sequential intellectual stages of this school are well known. British empiricism is usually dated specifically from the work of John Locke (1632–1704) who set the stage for the later development of empiricistic epistemology by spelling out a number of fundamental principles which have had an enduring effect in the intellectual life of our civilization.

Locke's (1690/1975) theory of perception (best summed up in 1690 in his work *An Essay Concerning Human Understanding*) was highly mechanistic, elementalistic, and empiricistic. In strong reaction to Descartes' rationalism and belief in innate ideas, Locke asserted that *all* human knowledge was acquired solely as the result of experience. Most students of his work believe that by experience he specifically meant the individual's history of sensory inputs and impressions. The mind, Locke proposed, was a *tabula rasa*—a clean slate—prior to experience; there were no innate ideas. Locke was perhaps the first to advocate explicitly the concept that ideas more complex than simple sensations were created by aggregating or associating the basic sensory experiences through a process of "reflection." Locke's reflection, reminiscent of Helmholtz's unconscious inference, was itself, however, a quasi-rationalistic concept that contrasts somewhat with the more automatic associationistic premises of the later empiricists. Nevertheless, according to Locke, these "reflections" must necessarily operate on the material provided by sensory experience. Thus, Locke was in fact proposing a prototype of a hierarchical or level theory of knowledge, but one in which the intelligent mind built increasingly complex ideas from the most primitive sensory elements. It should be obvious to any student of modern psychology that the concept of association of simple experiential elements into complex mental events has probably been the most influential single theme of psychological research in the last century. The importance of this particular idea—associationism—in directing the intellectual evolution of psychological science is all-pervasive, and should never be underestimated.

The next major figure in the development of British empiricism, Bishop George Berkeley (1685–1753), was in general agreement with Locke's idea of associationism. Berkeley's major point of contention with Locke dealt with the latter's concept of primary and secondary qualities. Locke had asserted that each physical object had two different sets of properties. One set, consisting of the primary qualities (e.g., length), was a basic characteristic of the object itself, whereas the other set, made up of the secondary qualities (for example, color), was meaningful only when expressed in terms of and referenced to the observer's mental processes. In other words, Locke had said that secondary qualities were inferred by the observer. Berkeley, however, believed that there were only secondary qualities and that all properties of a perceived object were meaningful only when defined in terms of the observer. Berkeley thus holds a particularly interesting position in the empiricist school because he was not a materialistic monist but an immaterialist monist, for the assertion that all qualities are secondary is equivalent to that kind of radical idealism.

Berkeley did not believe, as is popularly misconstrued, that matter dematerialized when not observed, but he did have to fall back onto theological arguments when faced with the question of the unobserved external environment. To *Bishop* Berkeley, the persistence of objects possessing only secondary qualities when not viewed by men was easily explained because of the presence of an omnipresent observer—God. Except for this aberration and his immaterialism, Berkeley's philosophy was generally consistent with the other British empiricists. He was an associationist who believed that knowledge was gained solely by experience, and complex ideas, by the subsequent concatenation of the immediate sensory impressions. Berkeley's (1709/1954) most important work on perceptual theory was his book, *An Essay Towards a New Theory of Vision,* first published in 1709. A modern discussion of this work can be found in Armstrong (1960).

David Hume (1711–1776) attempted to remove Berkeley's theological and idealistic metaphysics from the otherwise mechanistic philosophy of empiricism. Hume made an especially important contribution in his suggestion that the mind was better considered as the *process* by which the various sensations, ideas, and memories circulated from one point to another than as a *thing*. His most important books, *A Treatise of Human Nature* (1739/1941) and *Enquiry Concerning Human Understanding* (1748/1966), are critically analyzed with regard to his perceptual theory in Price (1940). Hume was particularly concerned with the causal connections between the stimuli and mental percepts. He carried Locke's associationistic philosophy forward to a new high of mechanism by proposing that the laws of association were of exactly the same nature as the laws of interaction between physical objects.

Both Hume and David Hartley (1705–1757), the next important figure in the development of British empiricism, concerned themselves with the problem of how the associations between the elemental sensory impressions developed. Each at one time or another in their writings expressed the idea that simple contiguity in time and similarity in meaning or significance were sufficient to establish associative bonds between these elements of the mind. This same kind of simple associationism was championed by James Mill (1773–1836), who added the idea that the association of sequential sensations established a temporal order that was preserved when more complex ideas were regenerated. In this regard he was partially anticipating Hebb's theory of phase sequences (discussed later in this chapter). Unfortunately, one implication of Mill's notion of temporal order and of a synchrony between stimulus and percept was to emerge again in later psychologies as a rather uncritical acceptance of the idea that psychological time was isomorphic with physical time.

James Mill's simplistic and direct associationism may be thought of as the epitome of the mechanistic point of view among the British empiricists. Simple contiguity was all that was required for a "mental chemistry" to convert simple sensations into complex ideas. Meaning and similarity were concepts that were ejected from his philosophy.

Next in this chronology, James Mill's son. John Stuart Mill (1806–1873), proposed an elaborate taxonomy of associationistic mechanisms: contiguity, frequency, similarity, intensity, and inseparability. In expanding the conditions for association of sensory elements, he went far beyond the simple contiguity-based associationism of his father and set the stage for the modern approach to learning by expressing the need to determine the varied set of conditions under which learning occurs.

Curiously, John Stuart Mill was not a radical realist in his metaphysics. His philosophy differed little from Berkeley's; Mill expressed the idea that matter was nothing more than the "permanent possibility of sensation." This form of immaterialism led him to postulate that the mind was capable of expectations concerning sensations and to propose that these expectations were equivalent to what we today would call perception. This deviates somewhat from the radical tradition of the other British empiricists, who proposed that perceptions were simply direct aggregates of sensation. John Stuart Mill, like Descartes before him, thus plays a bridging role between the empiricist and the rationalist view of epistemology.

British empiricism, however, mainly evolved into a strict sensory associationism. Interestingly, at about the same time in France, Etienne de Condillac (1715–1780) proposed a much more extreme empiricism that did not involve the concept of associationism. Condillac asserted that sensations alone were all that were required for mental processing and awareness. Condillac's philosophy was thus an extreme empiricistic elementalism that did not involve the concatenation or association of primitive sensory experiences into more complex perceptions or ideas.

It is clear that although there was considerable difference of opinion concerning specific issues, there was also a strong thread of agreement among all of the empiricistic philosophers. Their virtually unanimous rejection of the innateness of ideas and (although the recurrent allusion to "reflection" or "expectation" by some of the British empiricists makes this comment somewhat equivocal) their usual rejection of rationalistic deduction as a means of acquiring knowledge make this important group of philosophers both empiricistic$_1$ and empiricistic$_2$ in terms of our tridimensional macrotheoretical space. The most persistent contribution of the empiricists, particularly in terms of their impact on modern learning theory, has been the emphasis on connectionism or associationism of primitive elements into complex ideas. These characteristics of the British school are summed up in Fig. 2-8.

Another important lasting contribution of empiricism was its role in perpetuating those mechanistic foundations of modern psychobiology that were originally suggested by Hobbes and Descartes. According to the empiricist tradition and its intellectual descendants (structuralism, behaviorism, and neurophysiological reductionism) mental responses to the stimuli are more or less direct and automatic. The perceiver is, to a very great extent, a passive transducer operating by means of simple mechanical and deterministic processes. In this context can be seen another important distinction between the basic positions of the empiricists and the rationalists.

As I have noted, empiricism and associationism have had an enormous impact on modern Western psychology. The influence of these theories of mind and perception can be traced through William Hamilton (1778–1856),[2] Alexander Bain (1818–1903), Herbert Spencer (1820–1903), Hermann Ebbinghaus (1850–1909), Wilhelm Wundt (1832–1920), William James (1842–1910), and the behaviorism of John B. Watson (1878–1958) to the current analytic and biological views of mind. It is only in recent years that the cognitive approach has begun to diverge from the associationistic empiricism initiated in the philosophical treatises of Locke, Berkeley. and the two Mills so many years ago. Whatever the future holds, the empiricistic tradition must always be appreciated to have been an exceedingly important stepping-stone to most current theories of mind.

b. Modern Empiricisms

As noted, the classic empiricistic tradition has had a powerful influence on modern theories of perception. Its influence is now so ubiquitous that one has only to look about at the procedures, methods, and approaches of modern perceptual research to see its persistent traces. The selection of the research problems, many of the implicit assumptions, and some of the most fundamental concepts (e.g., the notion that a functional relationship can be established between a stimulus scale and a mental response scale) are only a few of the profound residual effects of the empiricist influence on contemporary psychology. Furthermore, several specific theoretical positions are modern versions of this point of view. Typically these neoempiricistic theories stress the role of the stimulus in determining the percept and pay less attention to the state of the observer than do the neorationalistic theories. However, in choosing to incorporate these particular theories into this section, I should not be understood to be asserting that I believe that these are the only areas in which the empiricistic influence is exerted.

---

[2]Hamilton, although a confirmed direct empiricist, and not a rationalist, did not accept associationism. Quite to the contrary, as we later see, he was clearly in the line of thought that led to Gestalt psychology.

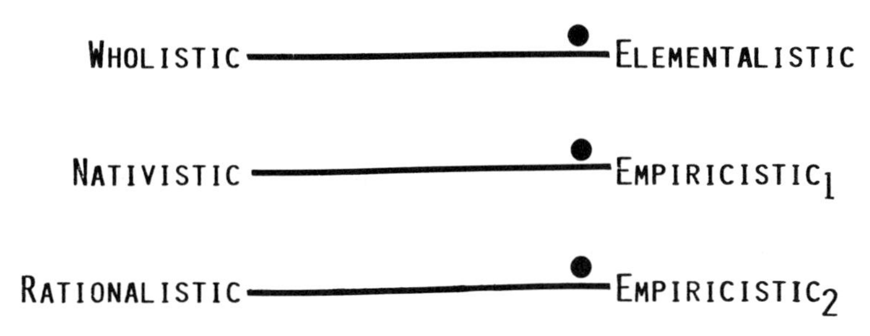

FIG. 2.8. A characterization of classic empiricism in the theory space.

Subsequent discussions in this chapter on neuroreductionistic and behavioristic approaches are also clearly latter-day versions of the empiricistic philosophies.

Gibson's Ecological Optics. The most explicitly empiricistic modern macrotheory of visual perception is that suggested by J. J. Gibson (1950, 1966, 1979), and known as ecological optics. Ecological optics is a radical direct realism, by which I mean that it emphasizes the direct causal effect of the stimulus in generating the percept almost to the exclusion of the properties of the observer. The observer, in Gibson's terms, attends to the information in the "optic array." but does not create the meaning or significance that is attendant to the percepts; that is largely predetermined by the environmental stimulus scene itself. Meaning is thus inherent in the role played by the stimulus in the external environment (i.e., its ecological function).

Gibson's theory is sufficiently well-structured to allow its major premises to be abstracted and tabulated. The following summary of the major points of his theoretical position is abstracted from a particularly fine discussion by Gibson (1950) of his own theory:

1. The world is real and is a source of information-filled stimuli, which are the direct antecedents of perception.

2. The purpose of perception is to communicate ecologically valid information about the external environment.

3. Sensation and perception are separate and distinguishable processes of systems. An example of a sensation is "blueness" and an example of a percept is "texture."

4. Perceptions are not based on the concatenations of simpler sensations nor on any organizing on the part of the perceiver but rather on the direct extraction of information from the optic array—the pattern of light at the retina, which is a linear transform of the external environment.

5. There can be "sensationless perception."

6. When perception occurs, there is a more or less direct detection on the part of the perceptual system of invariants of the stimuli, but no construction from sensory elements occurs. Perception, furthermore, is not a triggering of recall of previously learned patterns of knowledge but a new and direct response to the attributes of the stimulus scene.

7. Perception is improved by experience; there is such a thing as perceptual learning even though learning is not essential for the perceptual experience itself. In other words, we learn to perceive, but we do not need prior experience to perceive some new stimulus.

Gibson's theory can be seen in terms of these basic premises to be a reaction against both an $empiricistic_1$ associationism that suggested that perceptions were created by the aggregation and concatention of simpler sensations and a rationalism that suggested that some organizational, rational, or logical processes within the observer were required to construct perceptions from incomplete or ambiguous stimulus information.

A particularly important aspect of Gibson's theory is in the calling of attention to the invariants in the stimulus scene, and for this reason, Gibson expends much of his attention on such stimulus factors as texture, perspective, and outline. These and other aspects of the stimulus form are especially important to him because they collectively convey information about the whole stimulus scene. In other words, stimuli signal the *invariant* aspects of the stimulus even though texture, for example, may be continuously varying in terms of its projected retinal image.

Another especially significant aspect of Gibson's theory is his rejection of a role for stimuli as triggers to elicit previously stored memories or internal mental processes. For Gibson, the stimuli, which are themselves produced by the environment, are the direct antecedents of the percept, and thus merely reflect the primary role of the external environment in the causal chain from stimulus to perception. Ecological optics is thus also nonrationalistic.

Gibson's antiassociationism has been extended to what I believe is an erroneous dichotomy between sensation and perception. Gibson considers the two terms to be unrelated in a way that leads to such difficult-to-interpret concepts as "sensationless perception" (Gibson, 1966, p. 2), made even more obscure by the fact that Gibson does not, to my knowledge, define either sensation or perception in a sufficiently precise way to clarify the denotation of the words as he uses them.

How can ecological optics be characterized in our tridimensional space? First, Gibson clearly is not an $empiricist_1$. He does not believe in either the fundamental premise of associationism of sensory elements into perceptions nor does he believe that past learning uniquely determines knowledge and present perceptual impressions. But he is also not quite a nativist in a simplistic sense of the term. In his acceptance of the principles of perceptual learning (i.e., we must learn to perceive—the process is not innate) he diverges significantly from classic nativism. Gibson, rather, is closely associated with the position that perceptual learning is an act of differentiation (Gibson & Gibson, 1955), possibly of a system of innate alternatives, but in a way that is distinguishably different from both the associationism of the $empiricists_1$ and the constructionism of the rationalist. We must place him at the midpoint of this axis.

In his extreme rejection of the constructionist ideology, Gibson's ecological optics is, however, very much in the $empiricist_2$ tradition. The external world provides complex and, to Gibson, informationally complete stimuli to which there is a more or less direct psychobiological response we call perception. There is no interpretation, rationalizing, constructing, or hypothesizing. The perceptions are the direct resultants of the stimuli and arenot mediated either by sensory primitives or by any form of epistemic inferences. Characteristics of the stimuli such as texture and contour themselves become the direct antecedent conditions of perception in Gibson's (1951) highly $empiricistic_2$ system.

Where does ecological optics stand on the elementalistic-wholistic axis? Helson (1967) abstracts ten kinds of configurational or global variables that Gibson had emphasized:

> 1. Solid form: The margin or contour formed by two solid objects.
> 2. Surface form: Flat physical surfaces and their edges at various degrees of slant.
> 3. Outline form: The tracings of objects by means of pencil or pen on a surface.
> 4. Pictorial form: Photographs, paintings, and drawings.
> 5. Plan form: A plan view of the edges of a surface as in engineering drawings.
> 6. Perspective form: Outlines indicating a perspective projection or view of an object.
> 7. Plane geometrical form: An imaginary closed line on an imaginary plane, although in actual representations composed of finite lines in given planes.
> 8. Solid geometrical form: Geometrical forms in three dimensions.
> 9. Projected form: A form in one to one correspondence with another form, e.g., an object and its shadow.
> 10. Nonsense form: Tracings on a surface which do not represent recognizable objects [p. 318].

By calling our attention to these and other stimulus parameters, such as texture and pattern, and the direct perception of these complex aspects of the environment, Gibson has joined with the Gestalt psychologists as a champion of a wholistic point of view and reawakened modern interest in these important global aspects of stimuli. Figure 2-9 summarizes his position on the axes of our tridimensional model of perceptual macrotheories.

A keen critique of this Gibsonian direct realism has been presented by John Gyr (1972). Arguing that perception and voluntary motor responses are very

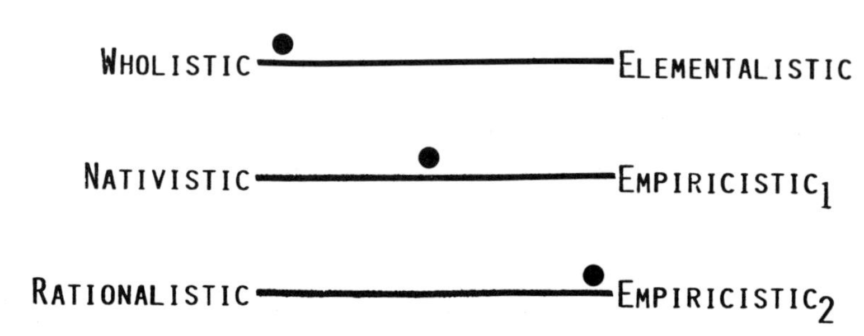

FIG. 2.9. A characterization of ecological optics in the theory space.

similar, Gyr suggests that the organism does not passively respond to the stimuli in the way that Gibson proposes but that the essential aspects of perception are more akin to self-organizing processes carried out by the central nervous system of the perceiver on the afferent stimuli. Gyr notes the enormous amount of attentive selection on the part of the perceiver depending on his current state. He believes that such stimulus selection is tantamount to a prima facie rejection of Gibson's strong premise of an external-stimulus-dominated perceptual response and his radical $empiricism_2$. This specific response to Gibson should be read to sharpen the distinction between Gibson's highly $empiricistic_2$ ecological optics and Gyr's more conventional neorationalism.

Gibson has recently become more interested in the perception of two-dimensional pictures (Gibson, 1971) such as outline drawings and photographs. His ideas have been championed in an interesting paper (Hagen, 1974) that attempts to develop a programmatic test of these new ideas. The main thrusts of this new work are: (1) to identify the similarities between the picture and the real three-dimensional scene that are used in developing the percept; and (2) to understand how the observer disregards those aspects of the scene (e.g., stillness and point of view) that are different in a picture from those in the real world.

Other Direct Realisms. Gibson's theory—ecological optic—of perception has had a significant impact on current theoretical thinking. Neisser's (1976) most recent book attempts to incorporate many of Gibson's ideas into the framework of contemporary cognitive psychology. But the work of Shaw and Turvey seems to me to be the most important step forward from Gibson's original position. Shaw and Turvey have begun to develop a radical direct realism in a series of articles (Shaw & Bransford, 1977; Shaw & Turvey, in press; Turvey, 1977; Turvey & Shaw, 1979; Turvey, Shaw & Mace, 1978). They have presented a deeply thoughtful argument that perception is not the result of a distant relationship between the external physical environment and the perceiving observer as mediated by nonisomorphically encoded signals, but rather that it is a much more intimate transactional relationship between the perceiver and the environment. In Shaw and Turvey's (in press) words "the objects of perceptual knowing are functionally ascribed directly to objects in the knower's environment." Direct realism of this sort asserts that the experience is not of the brain state triggered by the stimulus, but of the "functionally specified environment" itself. Shaw and Turvey's theory postulates that this interaction is in the form of a "coalition" between the observer and the environment. Their approach, therefore, ties together the observer and the observed into a unified entity; perception is not understandable, according to them, without consideration of both observer and observed and the interactions between them.

Although there are many novel and interesting ideas raised in Shaw and Turvey's discussions, it should not go without specific mention that I personally am not comfortable with their idea of a "direct" perception of the world without the mediation of the coded neural signal. And because sensory coding exists, one can argue that perception must necessarily be indirect in a way that their theory does not allow. The kind of interaction that Shaw and Turvey invoke, seems, therefore, to be virtually in violation of the most intuitive of physical laws. By de-emphasizing everything between the perceived and the perceiver, Shaw and Turvey have cast out the important physical role of sensory communication as a necessary part of perception. On the other hand, one cannot read their eloquent articles without some appreciation of the quality of their argument. Agree with them or not, I earnestly suggest that any one interested in this problem carefully study these papers. The reaction they stimulate transcends the specifics of their argument. But, the reader should also consider a sharp criticism (Hayes-Roth, 1977) of this kind of direct realism for balance.

3. Wundt and Titchener's Structuralist Macrotheories of Perception

The controversy between the classic rationalists and the classic empiricists went on for almost 200 years in a totally nonexperimental context: The arguments used to buttress each side of the controversy were, for the most part, philosophical and speculative. In the middle of the nineteenth century, however, some important intellectual events occurred that led to a change in the way in which the debate was carried out. Franz Brentano (1838–1917), in his book *Psychology from an Empirical Standpoint* (1874/1973), proposed an *Act* psychology championing the idea that the processes or acts of perceiving were more important than the percepts or phenomena themselves. One important aspect heavily emphasized by Brentano's Act psychology was that psychological processes were amenable to laboratory experimentation and could be manipulated equally as well as physical events. Gustav Fechner (1801–1887) had already contributed to this idea when he formalized Ernst Weber's (1795–1878) qualitative psychophysical observations into a system of quantitative relations between physical stimuli and mental processes. All of these precursors of a fully experimental psychological science came to fruition when the first laboratory exclusively dedicated to the experimental study of psychological processes was set up by Wilhelm Wundt (1832–1920) in 1879 at the University of Leipzig. Wundt's contributions to the experimentalization of psychology were enormous, however, and went far beyond the surface aspects of this administrative and organizational contribution. In setting up his laboratory, Wundt not only explicitly gave concrete form to the rapidly emerging idea that psychology is a natural science and that its subject matter is as analyzable as any other area of biology or physics but also spelled out the general scope of the research problems to be dealt with by experimental psychologists. It is remarkable to note that in 1979, the centenary of Wundt's laboratory, most of our colleagues were still studying many of the same problems as Wundt a century earlier.

Wundt was a prolific scholar. His most important works, however, were *Principles of Psychological Psychology* (1874/1910) and *Lectures on Human and Animal Psychology* (1894/1907). In spite of these titles, Wundt's work was predominantly in the field we now would call human experimental psychology, and his research included such topics as sensation, learning, reading, and response-processing time.

Wundt's longest-lasting contribution, however, was that he spelled out the premises of the first truly modern scientific and fully psychological theory of mind, the theory that was later to be called *structuralism* by his most famous student, E. B. Titchener (1867–1927). Structuralism owed an enormous intellectual debt to the empiricistic and associationistic traditions of the previous century, but it was Wundt who established and interpreted this intellectual movement in terms of a scientific psychology rather than a speculative philosophy. Wundt emphatically stated that the proper subject matters of this new laboratory-based psychology were the mental processes and phenomena themselves, and that the method to study such mental processes was specifically *subjective introspection*. Though this is not too unsettling today, at his time such a perspective was truly revolutionary.

The new science of experimental psychology, of course, did not spring full-blown from nothing; it was traditionally empiricistic in asserting that complex thoughts were created from simple sensations and feelings by associationistic processes. Although this elementalistic approach to the problems of psychology was later to be challenged by succeeding schools of functionalist, Gestalt, and constructionalist psychologists, many of the introspectionistic and mentalistic aspects that dominated the Wundt school have persisted. Furthermore, with the emergence of the modern cognitive tradition they have recently been regaining importance.

Heavily influenced by his training in Wundt's laboratory, Titchener spent his career at Cornell University championing the structuralist approach to psychology. Titchener's psychology was also based first, foremost, and irrefutably upon the Wundtian ideas that the proper subject matters of psychology were mental responses and conscious experiences, and that the only method that could profitably be used to study these intrapersonal responses was laboratory experimentation, using carefully controlled and analyzed introspection. Titchener was also, like Wundt, a thorough going elementalist in the associationist tradition, believing that all percepts, images, and affective states were composed of elementary psychological units. For percepts, the topic of the present discussion, the elements were the primitive sensations produced as a direct result of the stimulating environment. Titchener's structuralistic elementalism went to extremes in championing this notion of sensory elements. In one of his books, *An Outline of Psychology* (Titchener, 1896), it is reported that he calculated that there were 44,000 sensory elements from which percepts were formed! The physiological elements of Titchener's theory were also influenced by Johannes Müller's (1801–1858) doctrine of the specific energies of nerves. Whatever the elements, psychological or physiological, the concept of the analyzability of complex events into elements was the keystone of both Wundt's and Titchener's structuralism.

Structuralism is easily categorized in our three-dimensional space of macrotheories as shown in Fig. 2-10. It is obviously a deeply committed elementalism in its most rigorously held form. Elements are combined or associated by experience to form more complex perceptions, according to both Titchener and Wundt; the school is thus clearly empiricistic$_1$. It is also empiricistic$_2$ in its general adherence to a view emphasizing the role of direct experience in defining percepts. In other words, structuralism can be seen as a psychologizing of the traditional empiricistic view and to be its lineal intellectual descendant.

The reactions against structuralism described in the following sections arose primarily because of its heavy emphasis on inner mental processes and lingering doubts about how valid introspection was as a measure of inner psychological

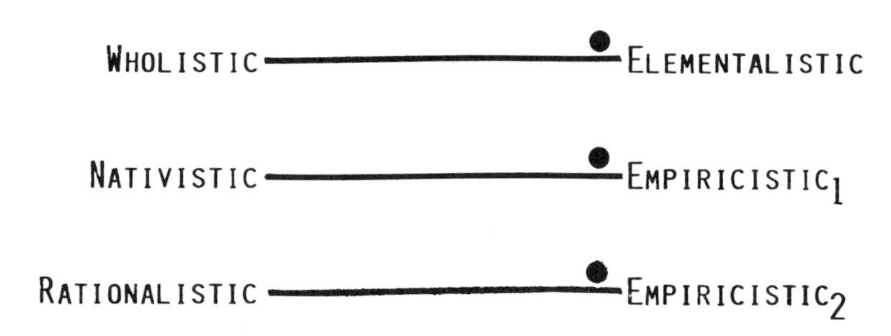

FIG. 2.10. A characterization of structuralism in the theory space.

processes. These weaknesses laid structuralism open to an attack by the strong evolutionary and positivistic movements in the twentieth century and led inevitably to behaviorism, radical positivism, and functionalism, the latter being a kind of psychological evolutionism.

Nevertheless, structuralism had lasting influences on theoretical and experimental psychology that should not be underestimated in spite of its lack of formal adherents today. Many of the ideas championed by Wundt and Titchener have been appropriated into modern theories. Whether these ideas are considered to be novel contributions made by the structuralists or were merely ideas handed on by them from their empiricistic past, this movement played a key role in the history of psychology. The emphasis on psychological experimentation, the formalization of the first organized theory of psychology, and the introspective method (surprisingly resurgent in today's cognitive psychology) were all major contributions. However, the reader interested in a very recent attack on the validity of the introspective process would profit from a careful reading of Nisbett and Wilson's (1977) interesting paper in which they argue that people can only poorly evaluate their own cognitive processes.

4. The Functionalist Macrotheories of Perception

Powerful intellectual forces at work in the scientific community during the early twentieth century were also to make changes in ideas in perceptual theory inevitable. Charles Darwin's (1809–1882) theory of organic evolution, as put forth in his monumental work *Origin of Species* (1859/1975), suggested to many psychologists that the adaptation of perceptual and thought processes to the exigencies of the immediate environment might be the most important role of the mind. A considerable number of theoreticians began to think of psychological processes, therefore, in terms of the general *adaptive functions* they performed in developing environmentally or ecologically appropriate mental states, rather than as *passive responses* to the stimulating environment.

The resulting "functionalist" school of psychology, a school which included such notable psychologists as William James (1842–1910), James McKeen Cattell (1860–1944), and John Dewey (1869–1952). American functionalism was a pragmatic response to the myriad problems posed by the interplay between the human mind and its environment. However, none of the psychologists I have just mentioned emphasized the problem of perception in their writings. Much more typical of their functional approach was a strong emphasis on learning and on establishing relevant and situationally adaptive responses to the environment as a result of experience in common with the yet-to-be-developed spirit of American behaviorism. One perceptual concept emphasized by the functionalist tradition, however, which was to have a lasting impact on perceptual theory, was that sensory stimuli were more than simple physical energies. The functionalists made the important contribution that stimuli are symbols and cues of a meaningful and relevant environment or ecology. In this regard they shared a common emphasis with Gibson's subsequent ecological optics.

The portions of functionalist theory that dealt specifically with perception can be considered to be specializations of the more general stress on adaptive responses championed by this school of thought. Two perceptual theories closely linked to American functionalism are Egon Brunswik's (1903–1955) probabilistic functionalism and John Dewey and Adelbert Ames, Jr.'s (1880–1955) transactional functionalism. Let us first consider Brunswik's ideas.

a. *Brunswik's Probabilistic Functionalism*

Egon Brunswick (1955) stressed the importance of the external world in determining percepts to a degree that seems almost to violate the laws of physics. It was his assertion that the main emphasis in studying perception should be on the objects of the environment—the distal stimuli—in much the same way as stressed by Turvey and Shaw's direct realism and J. J. Gibson's ecological optics, which are of this same genre. In this regard Brunswik minimized the role of the patterns of physical energy impinging upon the receptors—the proximal stimuli. For Brunswik, all that was important about the proximal stimulus was that it provided information about the physical object in the environment. Brunswik thus relegates to a secondary level of importance and interest all that is known of sensory and neural communication processes. To him, as to Gibson, it was the virtually unmediated interaction between the mind and the environment that mattered.

Brunswik made this emphasis diagrammatically clear by suggesting as an analogy for his theory, the lens model shown in Fig. 2-11. This figure shows an

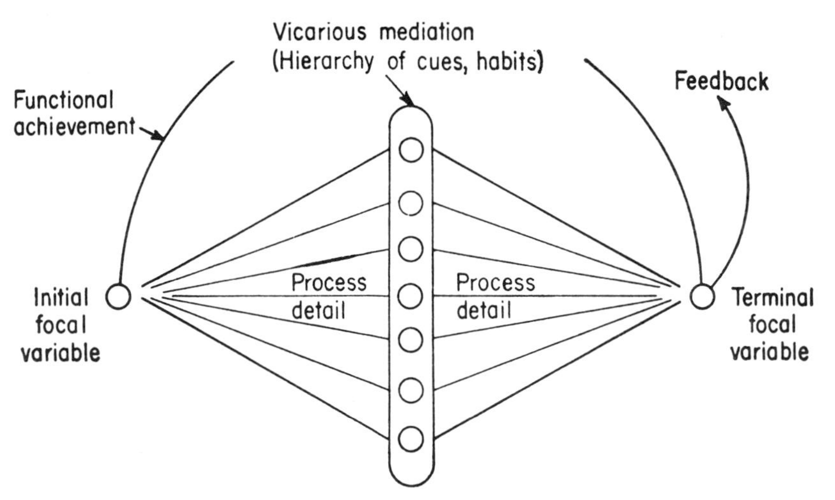

FIG. 2.11. The lens model of probablistic functionalism. (From Postman and Tolman, 1959, with the permission of McGraw-Hill, Inc.)

external object in the physical environment as the source of a system of stimulus rays analogous to, but not necessarily identical with, the light rays emanating from an object in optical space. The system of rays is "defocused" (in a metaphorical sense) by the act of being encoded as physical energies. The hypothetical rays pass through various sensory pathways in this defocused and imperceivable form. It is only when the relevant mental process "refocuses" the system of stimuli into a meaningfully reconstructed pattern that the psychological process of perception occurs. Thus, Brunswik does not deny the presence of the coded sensory signals but deals with them as secondary processes, as merely a medium that simply conveys suggestive information rather than as the primary deterministic substance of perception. In other words, whereas neural signals convey information just as do the electromagnetic waves that carry television pictures, they are not the essential determinant of the percept, which to Brunswik was the external object of referent itself. The critical relationship was between the mind and the external object, not between the mind and the available sensory cues. It is the latter relationship that is stressed by the more modern psychophysical or psychobiological traditions in perceptual theory.

Thus, according to Brunswik, the sensory (proximal) stimuli actually constitute only a disjoint set of cues or clues, each of which conveys some partial information about the distal object, but none of which are the primary causal precursors of the act of perception. The observer's task is to process cognitively (i.e., interpret rationally) the array of cues and to form a conclusion about the nature of the external object. Because the array of proximal stimuli produced by the distal object is, in principle, very large, each component representing only one of its many aspects, the act of perception becomes a statistical process more than an arithmetic one in Brunswik's theory. The perceiver is required to make a probabilistic estimate of the nature of the perceived structure from among the many alternatives opened to him by the system of "rays." Clearly there is a strong rationalistic theme permeating Brunswik's theory.

b. Dewey and Ames' Transactional Functionalism

Transactional functionalism, the other predominantly perceptual theory in the functional school, has been described either as a theory of perception or merely as a set of perceptual demonstrations. The demonstrations that traditionally have been invoked to exemplify the transactional approach are the very familiar ones (e.g., the distorted room) invented by Adelbert Ames Jr. to show how easily the eye can be fooled into misperceiving the environment when stimuli are made ambiguous or internally inconsistent. These amusing and interesting demonstrations are of lasting importance because they highlight an important class of perceptual phenomena that have not yet been well treated by contemporary theory. They have also often been denoted as concrete and prototypical expressions of ideas inherent in the theory of transactional functionalism most clearly and formally spelled out by John Dewey and A. F. Bentley (1949).

This interpretation is not universally accepted, however. Robert Shaw and Michael Turvey have suggested (in a personal communication conveyed to me by Joseph Lappin) that whereas Dewey was initially very interested in Ames' demonstrations, he subsequently came to realize that Ames' conception of the meaning of these experiments was fundamentally different from his own. One story is that Dewey actually wrote to Ames requesting that he refrain from using the words *transactional functionalism* because he felt it misrepresented his (Dewey's) position. Thus, there are substantial doubts now being raised as to whether Ames and Dewey should be linked in the way usually suggested and whether Ames actually thought about his demonstrations in this same theoretical sense.

In common with probabilistic functionalism, the primary premise of transactional functionalism was the idea that the stimulus was not the direct causal determinant of perception, as it is considered to be in the psychobiological and stimulus–response traditions. The transactionalists did not place the causal responsibility solely on the distal stimulus, however, as did Brunswik or Gibson. Rather, in their more radical rationalism, the transactionalists suggested that the perceiver cognitively created a percept by establishing an interactive, or transactional, relationship between his mind and the environment. What is seen by a perceiver, from the point of view of this theory, is the immediate response of the mind to its past experiences, assumptions, and expectations much more than it is a response to the immediate stimulus scene. Though the word *transactional* appears both here and in Shaw and Turvey's discussion (see page 96), it seems to me that this is not a direct realism in the sense that they use the word.

The essential aspect of this kind of transactional functionalism, therefore, is that perception is strongly dependent upon the cognitive state of the observer. Perception is interpreted by this theory to be an active process in the tradition of classic rationalism and Helmholtz' unconscious inference. Where the stimulus–response oriented psychologist attributes the highest importance to the flow of information from the stimulus to the perceiver and the pure idealistic rationalist sees the mind's action on the environment as the most important aspect, the transactionalist sees the process as one with strong feedback properties in which information flows in both directions between mind and environment. What stimuli are accepted and that which is perceived depend as much on the motor responses and the set of cognitive assumptions of the observer as it does on the nature of the stimuli themselves. Thus, in the distorted room, the perceiver creates the illusion of the size-distorted occupants because of his mistaken assumption that the room is a normal one—an assumption based on his previous experience and resulting expectations.

Both probabilistic and transactional functionalism can thus be seen to be cognitive, rationalistic theories having little or no use for neurophysiological or stimulus–response reductionism. Classifying these two theories within the tridimensional macrotheory space is, therefore, relatively easy. They are both, in the context of their strongly cognitive orientation, rationalistic rather than empiricistic$_2$. The repeated references to the importance of learning in establishing probabilities or assumptions about the stimulus scene, or the role of the observer's set, makes it clear that they are also empiricistic$_1$ rather than nativistic. With regard to the elementalistic–wholistic axis, however, the situation is somewhat cloudy. The functionalistic emphasis on cognitive assumptions, meaning, and ecological relevance is suggestive of a concern with pattern and functional organization, but Brunswik's notion of the probabilistic evaluation of an aggregate of relatively independent cues each independently bearing information about the different aspects of a stimulus is, I believe, fundamentally elementalistic and associationistic in overview. Figures 2-12A and 2-12B depict my view of an appropriate description of probabilistic and transactional functionalism respectively.

5. The Gestalt Macrotheory of Perception

The method of detail, the concept that understanding of a complex event could come about only by analysis of the event into ever simpler components, was the key premise of the associationistic, empiricistic, structuralistic, and (as we see later) behavioristic theories of perception. In each of these theoretical positions, the problem of perception was reduced to the problem of the analysis of percepts into more "primitive" sensations, which were thought to be the elements making up the more complex, but semantically and cognitively more significant, percepts. Developing parallel to the elementalistic theme in this set of theories, however, was a diametrically opposed viewpoint that stressed the overall configuration of the stimulus pattern rather than the elements of which it was composed.

This parallel wholistic development point of view was, in the main, dormant for many years, hidden behind the dominant elementalistic and associationistic traditions. At first, indications of this configurationistic philosophy were not even identifiable as a specific and separate point of view. Kant, for example, stressed the idea that the act of perception was not a passive concatenation of individual ideas to produce perceptions but rather an active processing of the information communicated by the overall stimulus pattern. In other words, he stressed the "melody" rather than the "notes" of the symphony of perceptual experience. In doing so he implicitly suggested the vital importance of the pattern itself without rejecting the fundamental elementalism implicit in the associationistic philosophy. Similarly, Ernst Mach (1838–1916) and Christian von Ehrenfels (1859–1932) both made singularly important contributions by suggesting, more or less independently, that, in addition to the elemental sensory qualities and properties already considered by the associationistic tradition, there were *other* properties that could be defined in terms of the overall spatial and temporal form of stimulus patterns and sequences. Both Mach and von Ehrenfels

PROBABILISTIC FUNCTIONALISM

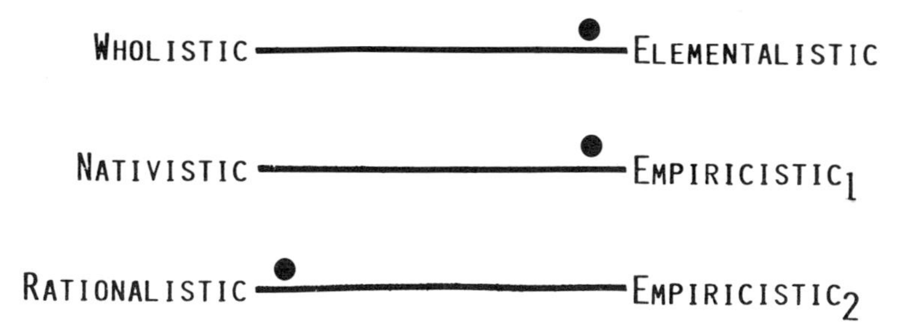

FIG. 2.12. (A) A characterization of probabilistic functionalism in the theory space.

alluded to the emergenistic idea that these global properties contained more information than did the sum of their parts. Thus they asserted that the properties of patterns transcended any simple arithmetic summation of the properties of the separate components. Another important, though earlier, antecedent of modern Gestalt psychology can be discerned in the writing of Thomas Reid (1710–1796). According to D. N. Robinson (1976b), Reid was one of the earliest to develop the idea of the relations among the parts as a central theme in perception. Another who argued that we perceive by a process of analysis "from the whole to its parts" was William Hamilton (1788–1856) thus also contributing to the wholistic tradition of Gestalt psychology.

The essence of this emerging new configurationalistic school of thought revolved around the radically different approach (compared to the associa-

TRANSACTIONAL FUNCTIONALISM

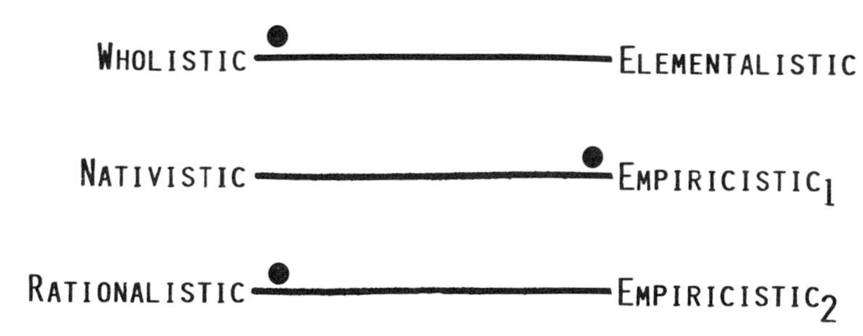

FIG. 2.12. (B) A characterization of transactional functionalism in the theory space.

tionistic–structuralist tradition) it took with regard to the problem of the nature of the relationships between the whole and the part in determining perceptual experience. The wholistic school of thought ultimately crystallized in the Gestalt (best translated as "pattern" or "structure") theories under the leadership of Max Wertheimer (1880–1943), Kurt Koffka (1886–1941), and Wolfgang Kohler (1887–1967) in the first half of the twentieth century, first in Germany and then after the dismal days of 1933 in the United States.

The essential premise of this new Gestalt school of thought, which most sharply distinguished it from the structuralism of Wundt or Titchener, was its vigorous adherence to the notion that the global configuration of the stimulus was neither just another property of the stimulus nor the sum of the parts of which it was composed. Rather the central dogma of Gestalt psychology was that the overall form of a pattern was the essential causal influence on perception. In this regard the Gestalt theory was obviously a strong reaction to the associationist and structuralist idea that combination of the sensory elements (or the details of the retinal mosaic) was the determinant of perception.

The Gestalt psychologists carried out a large number of experiments demonstrating the important role of the global pattern and what they believed to be the lesser role played by the individual components. Many of their experiments were nonquantitative, however, in that they were often unique demonstrations that made some point concerning the global pattern but were not suitable for parametric experimental manipulation or a high degree of control over the full range of the salient stimulus dimension. "Form," unfortunately, was as poorly quantified then as it is now, and thus this centerpiece of Gestalt theory was never adequately defined in most of their experiments. As a result, this configurationalistic approach was at odds in many ways with the quantitative and reductionistic tradition of modern science.[3]

What the Gestalt psychologists did contribute, and what remains their major gift to modern perceptual theory, is their emphasis on a wholistic approach in a science that had previously been totally dominated by an elementalistic tradition. Whether or not the particular Gestalt data base or theory is totally incorrect or not is almost beside the point; the Gestaltists called attention to an important set of perceptual phenomena that deserve explanation and consideration by any and every theory of perception, and to a wholistic viewpoint that has much to say about the ways in which humans perceive. In eschewing most forms of structural analysis in perception, however, the Gestalt tradition denied itself one of the most powerful methods of scientific explanation. As a result the laws of perception suggested by the Gestaltists are shallowly descriptive and do not explain perceptual phenomena in any theoretical sense. These laws or principles were

[3]Efforts (Attneave & Arnoult, 1956; Brown & Owen, 1967; Leeuwenberg, 1969, 1971, 1978; Buffart, 1974) to quantify, and thus to rigorously define form, remain unsatisfying. These methods typically do not uniquely define a form; they usually only classify categories of forms.

formally expressed by Max Wertheimer (1923) and I discuss them in detail in Chapter 10.

Beyond their descriptive set of principles, Gestalt perceptual theory did associate itself with a specific and equally molar physiological model invoking neural representations of perceptual processes by isomorphic electrotonic brain fields. There are two main premises of this wholistic neural theory of perception that should be kept separate—wholistic neuroelectric fields, and isomorphism. First, in accord with the general adherence to wholistic processes, the Gestalt brain theory strongly supported the idea that it was the overall field of brain action, rather than the action of individual neurons, that was critically important in the representation of psychological function. However, it was later definitively shown (Lashley, Chow, & Semmes, 1951; Sperry, Miner, & Myers, 1955) that these fields of electrical activity in the brain could not possibly account for perceptual phenomena. Metal foils and pins inserted into the brain in a way that would certainly have short-circuited any neuroelectric field seemed to have little effect on any behavioral measures of perceptual responses in experimental animals.

However, the second premise of the Gestalt brain field theory, which asserts that the relevant brain responses must be isomorphic to the associated psychological processes, still exerts a powerful, though usually unacknowledged, influence on thinking with regard to models of perceptual process. The Gestalt theoreticians did accept a "rubber sheet" kind of topological distortion but were not willing to accept any coded or symbolic representation of perceptual responses in the brain. This belief in spatial and temporal isomorphism is also often a component of many current neuroreductionistic theories of perception, especially ones emphasizing single neurons, but is honored implicitly rather than overtly. Surprisingly, on close examination, the idea of isomorphism is actually contrary to the ideas of neural coding and symbolic representation that have become popular in interpreting modern neurophysiological data. This conflict between the concepts of isomorphic and symbolic coding remains one of the most perplexing issues of contemporary theory, and, as we see later in this book, one of the main difficulties in developing adequate perceptual theories.

How, then, does the Gestalt theory fit into the tripartite classification system of macrotheories that I have proposed to organize the perceptual theories described in this chapter? The most obvious characteristic of the Gestalt theory is its essential and irrevocable commitment to the wholistic approach, so its position on that axis is self-evident. With regard to the nativism–empiricism$_1$ dimension, my analysis suggests that this problem was not directly faced in the Gestalt tradition. In large part, most Gestalt theorists have emphasized the fact that the organization of the percept was driven by the configuration or "pragnanz" of the stimulus but was only modestly dependent upon the current state of the perceiving organism. All of Wertheimer's laws, for example, are really descriptions of the stimulus. Innate mechanisms and learning, though not explicitly rejected by the Gestaltists, were just not considered by them to be a major part of the perceptual problem. In my opinion, however, the Gestalt psychologists were more concerned with genetic factors than with experiential ones and, in the main, therefore, should probably be classified closer to the nativist end of that axis than to the $empiricist_1$ end.

The most difficult aspect of the problem in classifying Gestalt theory is in regard to the $rationalism–empiricism_2$ area. It is here that I believe that the Gestalt tradition is ambiguous. The Gestalt psychological theory, particularly as developed by Köhler (1929/1947), though a field theory, is very much an automatic and direct process that is best described as $empiricistic_2$. The laws of Gestalt psychology (described in detail in Chapter 11) are, as I noted, mainly described percepts that are best considered as resultants of the intrinsic properties of the stimulus rather than as derivatives of the psychology of the observer. Thus, from this point of view, Gestalt theory is thus more $empiricistic_2$ than it is rationalistic. On the other hand, when Koffka spoke of the importance of the meaning of the stimulus or when Köhler spoke of the importance of the past experiences of the observer directing and organizing the perceptual experience, I believe both psychologists came very much closer to the rationalistic tradition than is often appreciated in recent analyses of these theories.

In sum, the Gestalt tradition, the archetypical wholism, is equivocal on the other two axes of the tridimension categorization scheme of perceptual macrotheories as shown in Fig. 2-13.

6. The Behavioristic Approach to Perception

Structuralism can be considered to have been highly fertile if measured in terms of how many counterreactions it generated. We have just seen one example of this reaction, the Gestalt theory, that was aimed at counteracting the extreme elementalism of structuralism. There was, however, another much more power-

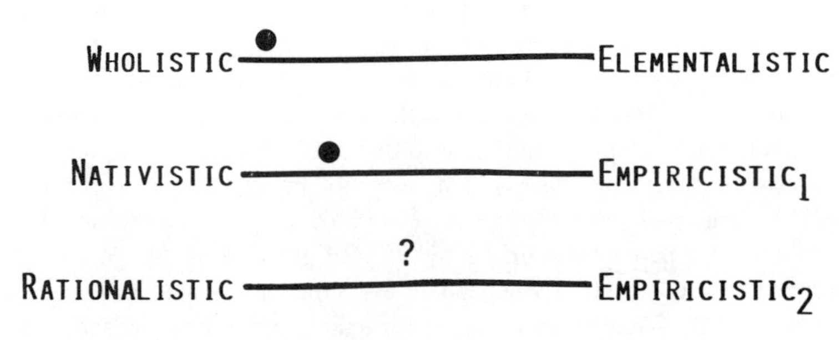

FIG. 2.13. A characterization of Gestalt theory in the theory space.

ful reaction against the structuralist ideas that concentrated its attack on its other main premise—the radical commitment to introspection that characterized both Wundt's and Titchener's views as well, incidentally, as those of the Gestalt school. This reaction against introspective research techniques and its implied mentalism reached a pinnacle in modern American behaviorism under the leadership of John B. Watson (1878–1958).

The behavioristic tradition in psychology, however, has never been deeply concerned with perception. It was primarily a learning psychology, but even then the roots of this learning were usually not analyzed deeply. Behaviorism ignored the physiology of learning for the most part (as it did most of the rest of physiological reductionism) and emphasized the current stimulus and past experiential determinants of changes in behavior rather than the internal processes by which learning occurred. Since the key premise of the behavioristic theoretical position was that the inner experiences, the mental responses, were intrapersonal and thus intractable in terms of scientific observation, patently private responses like percepts played only a minor role in Watson's psychology.

The most important theoretical behaviorist was Clark L. Hull (1884–1952) who proposed a formal mathematical theory of human behavior (Hull, 1943; 1951; 1952). Although primarily concerned with human learning, Hull did pay some small amount of attention to perception. Hull considered percepts to be very much like conditioned responses of the more overt kind. However, perception is not a topic of interest in either of two of his earlier books (Hull, 1943, 1951). In a subsequent volume Hull dealt with the problem posed by perception by merely acknowledging it as a major issue and adding it to his list of work yet to be completed. Specifically, Hull (1952) states:

> Passing to the more qualitative aspects of systematic behavior development, toward which we may look forward with considerable confidence, we turn first to that traditionally known as *perception*. Now, perception appears to be based on sensory stimulation (S), together with stimulus generalization, and the results of previous learning (${}_SH_R$), ... The best makeshift we have been able to achieve so far has been to treat S and ${}_SH_R$ separately. Perhaps one of the reasons why the failure to distinguish sharply between stimulation and perception does not interfere any more markedly with the validity of the present deductions is that the elements of both stimulation and generalization are explicitly included in the system.
>
> Perception has ordinarily been reported by means of speech symbolism. Perhaps because of this connection between speech and introspective reports, the *Gestalt* psychologists have specialized in this field, and have made notable contributions to it. In the present work it is conceived that the whole subject should be reworked from a behavioral point of view, and that the various laws peculiar to perception should be deduced in terms of ${}_SH_R$, ${}_S\bar{H}_R$, D, S, R, and so on. Thus a real scientific unity would be attained [p. 354–355].

It is clear that Hull, the radical behaviorist, did not deal with perception, the prototypical mental response, in the same way as did some of the other theoreticians I have already discussed. He redefined it rather in terms of stimuli, learned discriminative response, and stimulus generalization; that is, in the linguistic and theoretical constructs of a learning theorist. Hull, like most of the other behaviorists, did not totally reject the reality of these mental phenomena, but in choosing to define them in terms of "response strengths" and "reaction potentials" he recoded these concepts in a way that makes it very difficult to translate them into the phenomenological language more common among perceptual psychologists. Whereas analogies can be drawn between some perceptual phenomena and some of the terms of Hull's model, there is little evidence that anyone has yet been able to achieve the "scientific unity" that Hull called for. Quite to the contrary, his formal model began to decline in influence in the 1950s when it became clear that it was a relatively closed system, overemphasizing learning and underemphasizing many other important mental processes of which perception is only one.

The Hullian and other behavioristic philosophies can be characterized in terms of the three dimensions that I have used to organize perceptual macrotheories in this chapter. There is no question that, with their heavy emphasis on learning, they would be empiricistic$_1$ in the extreme and eschew nativism. Stimulus–response behaviorism is also, without any question, extremely elementalistic in its outlook. In this regard it accepted the classic associationistic and structuralist ideas and, some would say, even adopted a more radical position than those predecessors with regard to this axis. There is a very substantial commitment in behaviorism to the philosophy that stimuli, habit strengths, and the other units of the internal and external environment must be connected or associated to form more complex forms of behavior. The Hullian model, in particular, considering the specific formulation of its quantitative laws, suggests a literally arithmetic associationism quite unlike the probabilistic mental processing suggested by Brunswik. From this same point of view behaviorism can also be seen to be, in the main, an empiricistic$_2$ philosophy with the various elements of the stimulus, the internal milieu, and the experiences of the organism leading directly, without any rationalistic mediation, to the response. This characterization of Hullian behaviorism is summed up in Fig. 2-14.

Hull's heavy stress on the direct determination of the perceptual response by the stimulus, however, was not universally accepted even by other behaviorists. For example, the behaviorism of Edward C. Tolman (1886–1961), as expressed in Tolman (1932), was considerably more cognitive and mentalistic than that of Hull. Rather than a direct stimulus–response causal relationship. Tolman proposed that intervening psychological processes, which he referred to as behavior determinants were the actual causal agents in defining behavior. Terms like *cognition* and *purpose* were both a part of his theoretical system, although they would have been anathema to the radical stimulus–response behaviorists like Hull and Watson. By incorporating into his theory such concepts as purpose and cognition, Tolman clearly placed himself among the rationalists rather than the

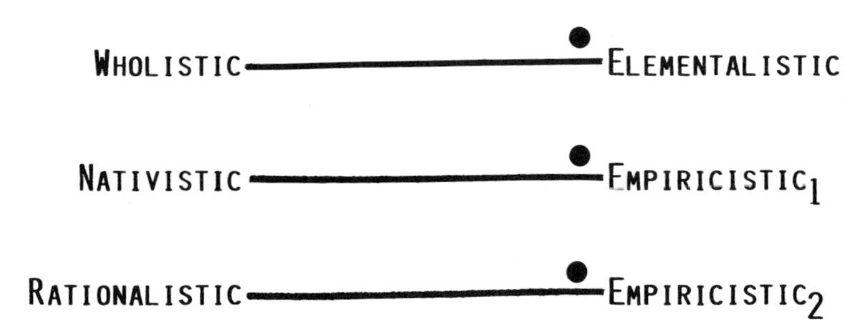

FIG. 2.14. A characterization of S–R behaviorism in the theory space.

empiricists$_2$. Tolman was also influenced by Gestalt psychology to the extent that a field or wholistic approach would more accurately describe his position on the wholistic–elementalistic axis. With regard to the third dimension, however, Tolman still must be considered to be a learning theorist and thus implicitly antinativistic. The characteristics of his version of behaviorism are summed up in Fig. 2-15.

Behaviorism, by de-emphasizing intrapersonal mental responses, placed itself in a position in which it could not (or would not) play a significant role in exploring or understanding the phenomena of perception. It also negatively influenced the study of perception by its rejection of both the experimental accessibility of mental responses and the value of verbally reported introspective response. There was, in general, a powerful constraining impact on the type of experimental research that could be carried out as a result of this limitation of the object of inquiry to externally observable behavior. Linguistic, physiological, and cognitive studies were all squelched during this time. Most germane to this discussion was the fact that from the decline of the Gestalt tradition in the late 1930s until the rise of modern cognitive psychology in the late 1960s, relatively little attention was paid to the more complex perceptual processes. Rather, a highly behavioristic and psychophysical tradition was substituted, in which unidimensional analyses of relatively simple sensory mechanisms dominated the attention of most workers in the field. Psychology, the study of the mind, has yet to recover fully from this behavioristic parody of experimental physics.

7. Cybernetic, Information-Processing, Computer, and Automata Models of Perception

Throughout history one of the richest sources of new theories of perception has been the contemporaneously available technology. As each new engineering advance was made or mechanism invented, someone was quick to note that it

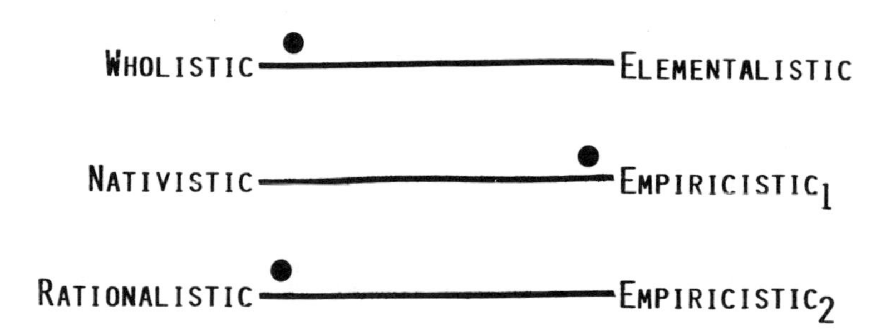

FIG. 2.15. A characterization of S–S behaviorism in the theory space.

exhibited properties that in some way were analogous to human behavior or thought. It is not surprising, therefore, that in the present highly technological age of analog and digital computers and automatic control systems there has been an especially intense interest among perceptual theoreticians to use servomechanisms or computer technologies as the basis of their models of perception.

This enthusiasm has been manifested in a number of different manners. The cyberneticists proposed the use of control theory; computer advocates suggested that the computer could serve both as a model of perceptual processes and as a "theory machine" on which various ideas could be tested for plausibility; and other theoreticians have simply drawn upon the vocabulary and concepts of information theory or information-processing machinery as sources of ideas with which to flesh out their hypotheses. All of these approaches, however, share certain common features. In the following sections I mention briefly some of the more significant of this mixed bag of approaches to theories of perception and point out their similarities.

a. Cybernetic Theories of Perception

Since the publication of Norbert Wiener's (1894–1964) classic book, *Cybernetics* (Wiener, 1948), itself based upon the engineering developments that occurred during the Second World War, there has been a continuing interest in applying the mathematics of control systems to the problem of behavior in general and perception in particular. The concepts of information feedback and feedforward, regulation, and the control of complex systems by patterns of communication among functional units all have an a priori face validity when compared to the arrangement of the brain nuclei and the communication pathways between them. There is no avoiding the simple fact that common features such as inhibitory feedback and latticelike plans of organization are to be found in both electronic and neural cybernetic systems. Similarly, the adaptive behavior of men and servo control systems compellingly suggest process analogies between the electronic and organic domains.

There is, however, a substantial difficulty in conceptually linking cybernetic theories and the mental responses we call percepts. The facts of the matter are that the mathematics of cybernetics is designed to describe the function of relatively simple mechanical systems. The differential equations used for this type of analysis are, in general, inadequate for the analysis of the much more complex networks underlying perceptual processes. Although cybernetics and closely related information theories may serve as useful heuristics in describing some aspects of perception, in my opinion, they have not yet successfully been applied to the solution of any problem other than motor responses.

There is another fundamental mathematical reason that any approach that reasons by analogy will always be unsatisfactory: The solutions to particular differential equations may often be unique, but the converse is not true. A given form of solution does not reflect back on a unique differential equation. In other words, a particular response dynamic[4] can be the output of a literally infinite number of different, though feasible, mechanisms.

However, cybernetic and control system analogies do provide the basis for two different and extremely helpful kinds of contribution to the problem of perception. First, they provide a most welcome and desirable highlighting of the effects of the complexly interconnected network of neural units that is most certainly involved in even the simplest perception. Second, this approach has laid the groundwork for information flow models of mental processing such as that shown in Fig. 2-16, in which the individual processing units are not in any way linked with anatomical structures but rather are descriptors of cognitive processes of unknown neuroanatomic origins.

Cybernetic theories, however, do find themselves in difficulty when the two kinds of organization, neuroanatomy and psychology, are not kept distinct. A clear example of how this confusion can lead to logical difficulties is found in the work of William T. Powers (1973). His model of perception and behavior is founded explicitly on cybernetic control theory with extensive consideration given to the use of feedback and control system dynamics as analogs of behavioral functions. However, like many other contemporary cybernetic theorists, Powers is forced by the nature of the model and the lack of an adequate conceptual linkage between the anatomy and the mental states to fall back on premises that, from my point of view, will satisfy neither cognitive psychologists nor neuroanatomists. For example, Powers (1973) defines perception in the following way:

---

[4]The word *dynamic* here is borrowed from physics and refers to the function describing some process over the full range of variation of some independent variable (such as time).

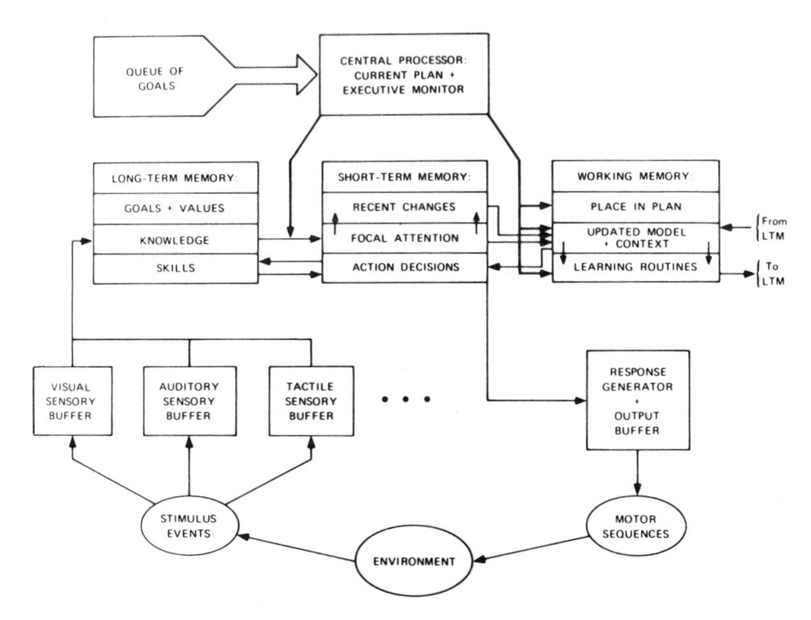

FIG. 2.16. An information processing model of perception. (From Bower, © 1975, with the permission of Lawrence Erlbaum Associates, Inc.)

When I refer to perception, I mean in general the entire set of events, following stimulation, that occurs in the *input* part of the brain, all the way from sensory receptors to the highest centers in the cerebral cortex.

More specifically, *perception* is to be distinguished from *conscious perception*. A perception is occurring if the neural current corresponding to that perception has a magnitude greater than zero. The perception is *conscious* if there is reason to believe that awareness is involved also. Thus we can speak of perception as a brain phenomenon, and leave the subject of consciousness for later discussion. Clearly there are often sensory responses going on in nerves with no consciousness of the presence of these signals; for example, consider the pressure sensation from the seat you are in. Presence of perceptual neural currents is a necessary prerequisite of conscious perception, but is not sufficient to assure consciousness of that perception. Thus many perceptions may be involved in behavior even though the subject is not always paying attention to them.

A "perception" means a neural current in a single fiber or bundle of redundant fibers which has a magnitude that is related to the magnitudes of some set of primary sensory-nerve stimulations [p. 35].

It appears to me that in this passage Powers is confusing the neurophysiological language with the psychological one and, in fact, rejecting the challenge of the more recalcitrant combined psychoneural problem. He is not even attempting to deal with the physiological substrates of perception, but rather has redefined the highly mentalistic word *perception* in quasi-neural terms in a way that finesses any possibility of a step toward a reductionistic explanation of perception.

The distinction he makes between conscious perception and other perceptual phenomena simply avoids, rather than solves, the fundamental issue of neuroreductionistic theories of perception. I believe Powers is thus violating a fundamental distinction between two kinds of neural signals—signs and codes[5] (see pp. 223–226, Uttal, 1973)—by assuming that any neural response in the nervous tissue is tantamount to a perception. I have argued that this is not an acceptable strategy, though it is a very common one, and that each candidate neural code (or perception in Powers' terminology) must be tested to determine if it has any mental or behavioral significance.

Based upon this highly questionable definition of perception. Powers then proposes a hierarchical multistage theory of mental processes in which each of the early stages are controlled by feedback signals from subsequent stages. The early stages are specifically linked to anatomical stages. For example, "second-order control systems" controlling sensation are mainly linked to the brain stem nuclei while "third-order systems" controlling what Powers calls "configuration" (i.e., processes like walking), are localized in the cerebellum and the higher sensory nuclei of the thalamus. Higher levels of processing are disassociated in his model from specific anatomical structures, as they are in the conceptual model I present in this book, but he retains the specific metaphorical connection with electronic control system theory at all of his levels.

The main contribution of Powers' version of a cybernetic theory of mind is his emphasis on the fact that the observer adapts to the stimulus environment, and is an active participant in the perceptual process, and on the role of feedback in governing mental and behavioral responses. In this regard Powers' ideas are clearly related to the rationalistic, functionalist (particularly the transactional approach), and ecological viewpoints, although with a cybernetic and information-oriented perspective that is unusual in the rationalist tradition. Powers' model, however, is far too specific, and thus vulnerable, in its neuroanatomic premises to be simply lumped with these other mentalistic theories. It serves as an extreme example of what I believe is erroneous thinking by analogy in psychology.

b. Information-Processing Theories of Perception

Cybernetic theories are closely related to the information-processing models proposed by psychologists such as Atkinson and Shiffrin (1968) and Bower (1975), as well as a host of others in recent years. Both the cybernetic and the information-processing approaches involve the specification of functional units

[5]Briefly, a sign is a stimulus-driven dimension of the neural response at one level of the nervous system that is not actually interpreted at a higher level. It is merely a concomitant change that is not significant in all subsequent information processing. A code, on the other hand, is functionally significant at higher levels, and is not just a low-level concomitant. Specific tests must be made to distinguish whether a candidate code (any observed neurophysiological transient) is a sign or a code. To be a true code, a candidate code must be shown to be necessary and sufficient to produce some effect at the behavioral level.

(some defined only as psychological processes and some associated with specific neuroanatomic structures) interconnected by specific patterns of intercommunicating lines of information flow, and both use flowcharts or block diagrams to represent the critical aspects of what would have been verbal models in an earlier time. These pictorial means of representing the organization of psychological processes and mechanisms, introduced into our thinking by computer and cybernetic technology, now play a major role in this type of theoretical systemization. It is important to remember. however, that flowcharts are not merely intended to be *aide-mémoires* by their originators, but are explicit expressions of the premises of the various theorists concerning the specific lines of flow and processes involved in information manipulation within the perceptual system.

The information-processing approach to perceptual theory now is one of the mainstreams of research activity in modern experimental psychology. Programs of the meetings of the Psychonomic Society, a major scientific association of experimental, mathematical, and physiological psychologists, are dominated by multiple and often simultaneous sessions on "information-processing" psychology. In spite of this nearly universal enthusiasm, it is still not easy to specify what is meant by an information-processing approach to perceptual theory. All psychological and neural processes are, from one point of view, information-processing activities. Indeed, psychology can be considered to be nothing more (nor less) than the science of organic information processing.

Although a precise definition of what is meant by an information-processing view is elusive, the perspective denoted by these words is sufficiently coherent that a history of its major intellectual milestones can bc traccd. Thc origins and critical experimental and cognitive ideas that stimulated this current burst of interest in information-processing theories among psychologists have been extensively discussed by Haber (1974); his discussion of the main antecedents and important conceptual milestones can be summarized (from pp. 314–319) as follows:

1. Shannon's (1948) and Wiener's (1948) work on communication theory establishing a quantitative measure of information.
2. Hebb's (1949) book on the organization of behavior with its plausible, but now known to be inaccurate, physiological theory of perception.
3. Miller's (1951) book on language.
4. The development of computers and the associated mathematical and engineering technologies during the 1950s and 1960s.
5. Tanner and Swets' (1954) theory of signal detection.
6. Stroud's (1949) paper on the quantitization of psychological time (the psychological moment), also no longer believed to be tenable.
7. Broadbent's (1958) book introducing the notion of selective attention.
8. Sperling's (1960) work on poststimulus cuing and masking.
9. The neurophysiological work of Hartline and his co-workers (Hartline &

Ratliff, 1957; and Hartline, Wagner, & Ratliff, 1956), that of Hubel and Wiesel (1959, 1963), and of Lettvin, Maturana, McCulloch, and Pitts (1974).

To this list, I would add some of the germinal research papers that decorated the early days of information-processing psychology. Most notably these included Miller and Frick's (1949) paper on the application of information theoretical measures to patterns, Aborn and Rubenstein's (1952) application of these ideas to human learning, and Garner's (1953) information–theoretic approach to hearing problems.

Not all of the ideas behind each of these contributions have remained viable over the years. For example, the hopeful promise expressed in Attneave's (1954, 1959) work that the quantitative measures of information quantity that had proven so successful in the engineering sciences could be simply and directly applied to psychological processes has been largely unfulfilled. It has been replaced by a more enlightened acceptance of the idea that the vocabulary and concepts of information theory provide a useful metaphorical language to describe perception but not a formal system of measurement. Similarly, Stroud's concept of a discrete and discontinuous psychological moment have been in large part replaced by ideas of a continuous or traveling moment within which signals can be integrated each and every moment in time (D. Allport, 1968; Turvey, 1977; and Uttal, 1970b). Nevertheless, the information-processing paradigm still permeates much of modern psychology and is a major feature of some of the more important current theories of perception.

It is, perhaps, an unfortunate semantic error that the information theoretical approach to psychological problems has come to be referred to as a "theory" of psychology. In fact, in its current form, it is far from a theory at all, but instead should be considered to be a particular language and orientation towards psychological processes.

The outstanding review of the basic ideas of psychological information theory is still Wendell Garner's (1962) important volume *Uncertainty and Structure as Psychological Concepts*. It is interesting to note that Garner himself never actually refers to the information approach as a theory of any facet of psychology. Rather he defines the relevant mathematical concepts (e.g., uncertainty and redundancy), and then shows how these concepts can be applied in a qualitative way to the description and measurement of a number of important psychological problems. Garner discusses a variety of experiments in which redundancy is varied and the resulting effect on some discriminative response evaluated. But this is not a psychological theory in the usual sense, and information theory is not a theory of perception in the same sense as are most of the other theories I have described so far. It is rather an approach, a set of organizing concepts and, perhaps most influentially, a metaphor for the kind of information processing that goes on inside the perceiver. As used currently, it is more akin to a physical analogy than an interpretive and explanatory explanation.

Reed (1973) provides an excellent and still up-to-date review of the information–theoretic approach to perception. Estes' (1978) fifth volume in the important *Handbook of Learning and Cognitive Processes* is also a useful discussion of both the general area and of a number of special subtopics in this central field of contemporary psychological research. A host of other more microscopic theories of "form perception" based on information–theoretic ideas abound at present. But they are not germane, other than as exemplars of the general approach, to the present discussion of macrotheories.

I believe that in the long run the most important contribution of information theory will be its re-emphasis of the exceedingly important idea that the semantic content (information in a general sense) of a message is not the same as the physical code (information in a particular sense) conveying that message. This emphasis can also be seen as another expression of the equally important idea that the representation of concepts can be carried out by dimensionally nonisomorphic codes. That is, it is possible to map variations in one dimension in a code conveyed by variations in a totally different dimension (e.g., magnitude may be encoded by place).

c. Computer Models and Artificial Intelligence

Another closely related set of perceptual theories that heavily emphasizes computer programs as models of perception is often intermixed and confused with the information-processing or cybernetic models I have just described. However, I believe that the fundamental premises of these quite distinct computer programming, artificial intelligence, and automata approaches are considerably different from the two classes of theories I have just discussed. These computer-based theories have crystallized around more formal methods of analog or digital computer programs, logical analyses, or conventional mathematics, rather than simply paying lip service to the metaphor of control or information processes.

Two distinct goals can be discerned in this computer-oriented theoretical work. The first is indistinguishable from those of theoretical psychologists. Here are stressed understanding and explanation, in the usual scientific tradition, without any particular regard for possible engineering applications of the phenomena, mechanisms, and processes under investigation. The second, and quite distinct, goal of this type of research is to use human perceptual process as a suggestive source of ideas for the development of artificial systems that can achieve the same functions as the human (detection, classification, recognition, etc.), but not necessarily by a direct imitation of the processes carried out by the human. This approach is a practical and applied one; it is concerned less with understanding than it is with the development of useful tools and procedures. It uses what it can but does not demand that the models it builds be valid descriptors of psychological processes.

Sometimes, unfortunately, the goals of these two approaches are confused, and what is only useful engineering is sometimes misrepresented as valid explanatory psychobiological theory. The problem inherent in this confusion is that computer programs that imitate some sort of cognitive process may do so by the use of mechanisms that are analogous in process to mechanisms used by the human brain but that are totally different in fundamental operating principle. For example, computer programming systems using list-processing languages can simulate semantic similarity by substituting propinquity in long lists stored in a computer memory. However, it is a farfetched and unjustifiable logical leap to assume that this particular mechanism—ordered lists of items—must necessarily be the same mechanism for encoding similarity of meaning that is likely to be found in the brain.

The recent interest in computer or automata models of perception was in large part stimulated by the pioneering work of Oliver Selfridge (1958) and the late Frank Rosenblatt (1928–1971). Rosenblatt's (1962) classic work, *The Principles of Neurodynamics* in particular, spelled out a theory of random networks that were capable of simple forms of learning and that, as a result of this learning, were able to discriminate between patterns. Though Rosenblatt's premise—the idea that random networks were advantageous in adaptive processes of this sort—is no longer considered to be either necessary or even desirable, the general idea of networklike, problem-solving perceptrons is now a major line of inquiry in the artificial intelligence field. Minsky and Papert's (1969) book brings the field nearly up-to-date and provides a formal mathematical structure for many of the basic ideas that were not fully developed in Rosenblatt's earlier work. They also formally prove that the specific type of random net proposed by Rosenblatt was very limited, even under ideal conditions.

A wide variety of other computer models of perceptual and other cognitive processes now exists. A number of recent examples can be found in Schank and Colby (1973) or Sutherland (1976), both of which are useful summaries of the current state of automata theory. The former book also includes an extraordinarily good review (Newell, 1973) of the general philosophy behind the use of computer programs as theories of cognitive processes.

One particularly interesting example of a computer model of perception has been presented by Leonard Uhr (1974). Uhr's model is diagrammed in Fig. 2-17. In this figure the cone represents the successive levels of the computer program that simulate sequential processing stages in which information is extracted or abstracted from the two-dimensional pattern that originally activated the receptor mosaic of the model. As proposed by Uhr, this model is a flexible one in that the number of information-processing layers and the degree to which the information is coalesced (thus defining the pitch of the cone) can be varied from one version of the model to another.

Uhr's computer operates on the basis of several relatively simple transforms, such as averaging and feature extraction, to arrive at a final classification of the object, a point which he considers to be the equivalent of recognition. The final "cell" at the tip of the cone, therefore, contains a highly compressed description of the stimulus input based on information that has been "extracted, abstracted

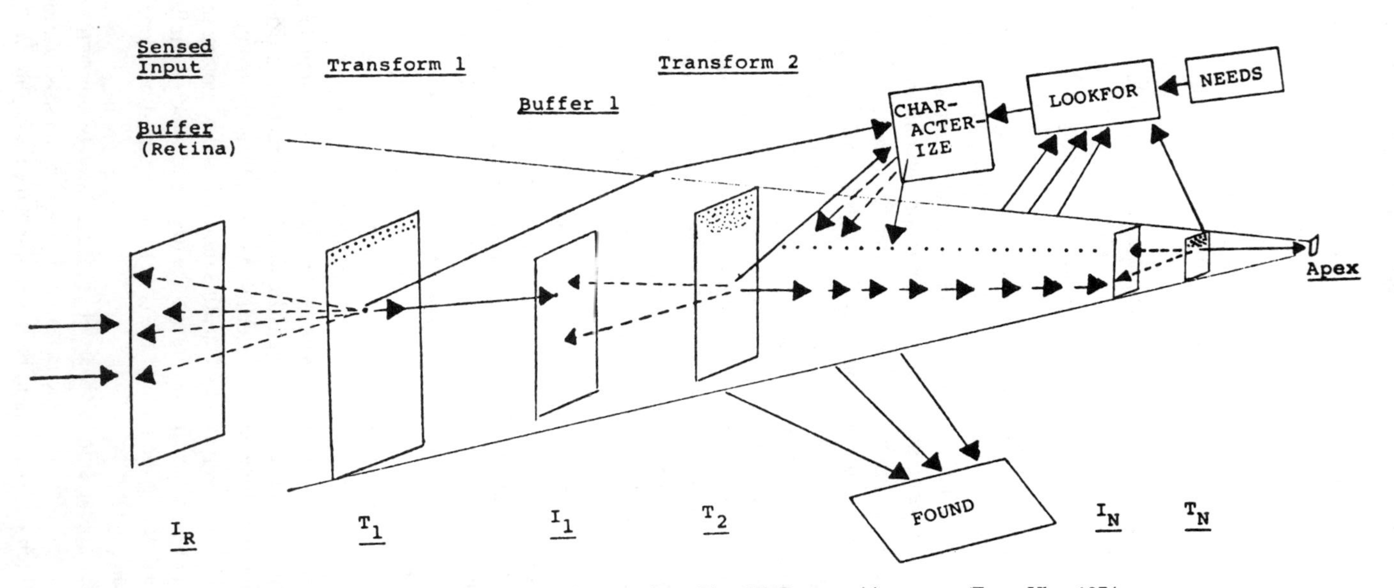

FIG. 2.17. Uhr's model of visual perception—The SEER recognition cone. (From Uhr, 1974, courtesy of Dr. Leonard Uhr of the University of Wisconsin.)

and coalesced'' from the original stimulus pattern by the earlier stages of the model.

Uhr's model is, in principle, heavily dependent upon the parallel processing that goes on within each of the sequential abstracting levels. He reminds us of an all-too-often forgotten fact, however; the modern digital computer, on which such theoretical models have to be developed and tested, is intrinsically a serial machine. It is always inefficient, therefore, according to Uhr, to execute a parallel model such as the one he proposes on a currently available computer. His own program runs, therefore, are artificially elongated by this procedure. This basic incompatibility in the organization of computers and brains remains a serious impediment in both the design and the conceptualization of computer models of perception.

Other examples of computational models of one or another aspect of visual perception can be found in the work of Arbib and Riseman (1976), who sought to simulate visual scanning behavior and Hanson and Riseman (1976), whose more general computer model of visual perception is designed to develop a symbolic representation of any scene presented to it. The work of David Marr and Gian Poggio, which I discuss later, is more specifically a model of what they presume are the early, peripheral stages of human visual perception, but is of this same genre.

The application of computers to simulate perceptual-like information processing has become a major tool in the development of psychological theory as well as a major activity of computer science. The reader interested in further information on the role of such programs in computer science will find an abundance of material on computer pattern recognition and picture processing. Specifically, reference shall be made to Uhr (1966), Kolers and Eden (1968), Reichardt (1969), Rosenfeld (1969), Watanabe (1969), Andrews (1970), Lipkin and Rosenfeld (1970), Meisel (1972), and Uhr (1973). Anyone who pursues this line is cautioned, however, to be sure to keep clear which of the many procedures and techniques are presented as practical tools, and which are specifically intended to be theoretical models of human perception. The reader is especially cautioned against accepting the all-too-glib assertion sometimes made by the authors of these programs that, because their model simulates some human perceptual behavior, it is, therefore, a satisfactory explanation of the associated perceptual response. A solid argument can easily be made that no such extrapolation from *useful simulation* to *valid explanation* is necessarily justified.

How, then, can we classify all of these cybernetic, computer, or information-processing theories of perception in terms of the three dimensions I have utilized in this chapter to categorize the various macrotheories of perception? The basic idea of an interacting network of functional units can be considered either as an expression of a wholistic philosophy (the arrangement is the essence) or as an elementalistic one (the nodes or functional units are the essential aspects), depending upon one's emphasis. I do believe, however, that there is a mechanistic and associationistic overtone to all of the cybernetic, information-processing, and automata theories that suggest that they are, in the main, elementalistic.

The position of these theories on the empiricism$_1$–nativism axis is somewhat less easy to define. The emphasis on learning (adaptation to previous experience) in many of these theories not only reflects the behavioristic tradition that was dominant in psychology during the time the computer and cybernetic models germinated but also an inherent tendency for any such theory to ignore the initial state of the system. In this regard, all of these theories are classically empiricistic$_1$ rather than nativistic, if it is at all appropriate to apply such organismic terms to computer programs and automata. However, since these programs all embody an original organization or algorithm at the outset of processing, to a certain extent, they also implicitly assume a nativistic philosophy on the part of their originators.

With regard to the third dimension, the rationalism–empiricism$_2$ axis, the categorization is more direct. All of these theories, in attempting to produce explanatory models of the perceptual processes, frame their explanations of the molar psychological processes in terms of automatic, deterministic processing elements analogous to computer instructions, discrete feedback processes, or units of information. Thus they all provide a deterministic, mechanistic, and, I believe, empiricistic$_2$ explanation of perceptual processes. Because each global process is explicable in terms of well-defined algorithms, there is no place for any analog of rationalism or any of its semantic overtones among this class of theories in spite of the claims of their originators in my opinion. Figure 2-18 sums up this tridimensional classification of these approaches.

It is not inappropriate to comment at this point that should this approach succeed in providing processing algorithms that do satisfactorily explain (and not just simulate) complex cognitive processes in human beings, the rationalist ap-

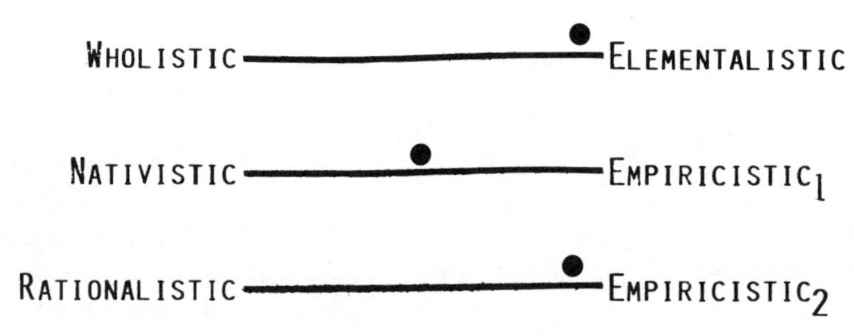

FIG. 2.18. A characterization of cybernetic, information-processing, and process models in the theory space.

proach would in fact, cease to be meaningful. A valid linking of simple logical processes on the one hand, and molar "thought" processes on the other, is exactly the long-term goal of any psychobiology. Whether it can be achieved in the foreseeable future is another question, and some form of rationalism, therefore, probably will continue to play the same role in perception that statistical measures (e.g., pressure) play in molecular mechanics.

8. Neurophysiological-Reductionistic Models of Perception

An explosion in knowledge of the biology of the nervous system in the nineteenth and twentieth centuries led directly to some significant developments in the theory of perception. It is possible at this point in our discussion to look back at the various theories of brain localization or the developments in neuronal physiology that led to such important concepts as Müller's Law of Specific Energy of Nerves, but to do so would be to recapitulate unnecessarily the entire history of the neurosciences. The reader interested in that line of discussion might want to look at my earlier work (Uttal, 1978). A more appropriate starting point for the present discussion with regard to modern neural theories of perception, however, can be found in the work of Ernst Mach (1828–1917) and his efforts to explain the peculiar perceptual contour intensifications (shown in Fig. 8-29) now known as the Mach bands.

The relevant aspect of Mach's theory of contour enhancement (beyond the highly unusual fact that recent research has tended to continue to support its main premises) is that this hypothesis was probably the first example of a totally neuronal explanation of a perceptual phenomenon. Mach explained the sharpening of the contours by attributing them to specific interactions among the neural elements of the retina, and specifically, lateral interactions occurring at what he believed was a peripheral anatomical level. Mach must have been influenced by the same earlier work on reciprocal interaction that led Karl Ewald Hering (1834–1918) to enunciate his opponent theory of color vision, another contribution to perceptual theory that has been both significant and lasting.

Mach not only localized the critical anatomic locus of the phenomena, and defined a specific neurointegrative mechanism that accounted for these illusory bands, but also laid out the framework of what has become one of the main conceptual foundations of modern psychobiology—reciprocal inhibitory interactions (the best modern discussions of which can be found in Ratliff, 1965, and von Békésy, 1967). The impact of Mach's ideas is still clearly evident in the most current theories of the integrative action of the retina. The reader is referred to Graham and Ratliff's (1974) lucid review for a comprehensive discussion of current derivatives of Mach's ideas. Trained as a mathematician and physicist, Mach was able to discern the mathematical regularity of the process and to provide a formal quantitative model that still stands as one of the outstanding examples of neurophysiological reductionalistic theory in perceptual science. Mach thus set the stage for what has clearly become one of the main modern themes of perceptual theory—quantitative neural net theories of perception.

Let us turn for a moment to a broader overview of the neurophysiological models of the class of which Mach's theory was but the original exemplar. There is, with all neuroreductionist theories, one common premise about which there is no debate. All theories of this class are monistic and assert that in some final level of analysis, practically obtainable or not, there is a neural equivalent of every perceptual process. Whether the process under examination is actually analyzable in neural terms or not (and, indeed, most real neural networks are beyond computability and analysis, according to some scholars such as Pippenger, 1978), this premise of an ultimate neural reductionism is not only a part of these theories, but also the keystone of contemporary psychobiology.

In spite of the incontrovertibility of this premise, I, too, feel that most perceptual phenomena, in present fact, remain refractory to such neural explanations. Nevertheless, this premise of ultimate reducibility itself attaches a compelling seductiveness to any putative neural model of sensory or perceptual phenomena, regardless of how well it actually fits the behavioral data.

A highly monistic philosophy of perception championing this idea of psychoneural identity is called representational realism (Brain, 1959; Smythies, 1956). It is based on the chain of causal relations (reflected light, receptor processes, neural transmission codes, brain response, percept) that most certainly exist in the afferent pathways. Representational realism may be thought of as a kind of radical neuroreductionism since its premises are consistent and overlapping with those of the more explicit neural theories described later in this book, but it is couched in the vocabulary of a philosophical language. It is also quite close in concept to Feigl's (1958) identity theory, which is also highly neuroreductionistic and representational in the same way. Another important facet of representational realism, or any comparable sensory coding theory, is its implication that we can only perceive patterns of nervous activity and not external objects directly. The same point is made by my metaphor of the man in the boat described on page 7. The sinker and line in that case is directly analogous to the retina and optic nerve in the real visual situation.

Another pragmatic argument supporting such neuroreductionistic models of perception results from the nearly overwhelming abundance of data that have been forthcoming from neuroscientific laboratories concerning sensory-driven responses in the central nervous system. Findings describing the characteristics of the component building blocks of the brain are exceedingly influential when so many agree that these building blocks, in some way, must be the elements of perception even when we do not yet have direct knowledge of how they interact to produce the molar process.

The result of all these forces has been the postulation of a substantial number of neural theories of perceptual phenomena, many of which, however, are loosely drawn and uncritically accepted. Furthermore, most neural theories of perception, like the Mach theory of lateral interaction among retinal neurons, are microtheories that deal with but a single perceptual phenomenon or, at best, a very few closely related ones. Within this environment of neural micromodels of perception four distinguishable major classes of theory can be discerned. They are based, respectively, on feature-sensitive single neurons, spatial–frequency-sensitive channels, neural networks, and neuroelectric fields. I mention them briefly here but return in Chapter 9 to analyze their essential premises more critically.

a. Single-Neuron Theories of Perception

The first class of neurophysiological theory includes those models based upon the performance and transformational properties of single neurons. This class of theory was strongly stimulated by the seminal work of Hubel and Wiesel (1959 and 1963, in particular) and Lettvin, Maturana, McCulloch, and Pitts (1959) in the late 1950s and early 1960s. The essential premise of this first class of theory is that single neurons of the nervous system exhibit highly selective trigger-feature sensitivities to particular aspects of the spatiotemporal pattern of stimuli that limit the range of stimuli to which they will respond. When an appropriate trigger stimulus is present, however, the individual neuron responds with a high level of activity.

An important corollary of this premise is that it is not the absolute amount of energy that determines the response but rather that the neuron is more sensitive to the way that the physical energy of the stimulus is arranged in time and space. The neuron, then, is selective with regard to the pattern of the stimuli that will best trigger it to respond. Thus, stimuli must have some ecological significance to the neuron before they will activate it. For example, a stationary dot of light might be totally ineffective in eliciting a response from a neuron in the tectum of a frog's brain, but should that dot begin to move (simulating a fly), the cell will actively respond.

Implicit in this type of theory is a concept of microlocalization. Though usually unexpressed, most neuroreductionist theories of this class do assume that the actuation of a particular "pontifical" neuron, or an aggregate of neurons with common trigger features and located in particular places, is equivalent to the perception. Though the implications of such a single-cellular theory of perception are almost never made explicit, theories of this class often strongly, but I believe incorrectly, imply that the demonstration of a neuron's sensitivity to some spatial or temporal attribute of the stimulus pattern is tantamount to a demonstration of the psychoneural equivalent of the perception, regardless of the level of the nervous system at which the electrophysiological responses may have been collected. As noted earlier, I believe there is a considerable amount of confusion regarding the interpretation of these data, and a good bit of misunderstanding of their actual role in mediating visual perception. At the very least the confusion of the communicative and representational role played by these highly pattern-selective neurons must be resolved. At the worst, a massive misunderstanding of the significance of these data may have occurred.

Another premise of these single-neuron theories, and one that bridges them to the network theories of the next class, is the emerging awareness that the activation of a single neuron by a particular spatiotemporal stimulus pattern is mediated by the integrative action of the network of cells feeding into that neuron. Furthermore, it is now specifically thought (Pettigrew and Daniels, 1973) that it is mainly the pattern of inhibitory connections that accounts for the selective sensitivity of the four basic kinds of visual cortical neurons. Such neurons have been classified as simple, complex, lower-order hypercomplex, or higher-order hypercomplex by Hubel and Wiesel (1965).

The single-cell theories of this first neuroreductionistic class are all, of course, highly elementalistic from the cellular point of view. But they are also elementalistic in the other sense that I have used the term in this chapter; the selective neurons are generally described as responding to specific features or parts of the stimulus scene rather than to its overall configurations. Thus, feature-sensitive, single-cell theories are prototypically associationistic: The perception of more complex scenes arise from a hierarchical concatenation of the responses of simpler neurons to the elements of the scene according to this theoretical perspective.

Perhaps the most extreme theoretical extension of the associationistic and elementalistic ideas implicit in a single-neuron theory of perception has been postulated by Jerzy Konorski. Pursuing the conclusion that the four types of visual cortical neurons I mentioned earlier were formed by a hierarchical convergence of the "simpler-level" neurons onto more "complex" ones, Konorski (1967) attempted to extend the neurophysiological observations of Hubel and Wiesel to explain much more complex psychological processes. He assumed that the four classes of visual cells are only the first of a more extended hierarchy in which increasingly complex integrations of the incoming information ultimately led to cells of cognitive "complexity." Ultimately these integrative processes culminate in a neuron (or set of similar neurons) that is actually capable of what Konorski called "gnostic" functions. Such gnostic neurons, he further assumed, are actively formed by plastic neural mechanisms that are reflected in the molar behavior of the organism as learning. The essential part of Konorski's theory is that all psychological processes, no matter how complex, can be understood in terms of the activity of single neurons that are conceptually identical in function and organization to the single neurons hypothesized to underlie feature sensitivity in the more peripheral portions of the visual system.

Konorski's foundation premise that the visual nervous system is organized hierarchically, however, has recently been challenged. A considerable amount of evidence (e.g., Kelly & Van Essen, 1974) has accumulated that suggests that even the purported hierarchical arrangement of the four Hubel and Wiesel types of visual neuron is, perhaps, an illusion. Kelly and Van Essen have shown that the higher-order units are not formed by a convergence of sensitivities of lower-order ones. Rather, they simply represent parallel, but different, kinds of neural organization. Indeed, they may represent the terminal units in totally separate chains or channels from different classes of ganglion cells (*W*, *X*, and *Y*) in the retina.

Single-cell theories are also easily classifiable along the other two dimensions that I have been using to characterize perceptual theories. It is obvious that there is not the slightest hint of any rationalistic overtone in any single-neuron theory of perception; these theories are all strongly empiricistic$_2$. With regard to the nativism–empiricism$_1$ axis, most neurophysiological theories emphasizing the function of single neurons are inherently nativistic. Although some empirical evidence in recent years supports Konorski's hypothesis that learning may play a role (Blakemore & Cooper, 1970; Hirsch & Spinelli, 1970, 1971) in defining the feature sensitivity of those single neurons that comprise the sensitive elements in such a neuronal theory, other recent research (Stryker & Sherk, 1975; see also Chapter 9) has raised questions concerning the validity of these experiential effects on receptive field organizations. Although there appears to be continuing controversy, the consensus may be swinging away from receptive field plasticity to a view asserting that the trigger features of the individual visual neurons are largely genetically determined. Therefore, at present, single-cell theories are probably best classified as being nativistic.

b. Spatial Frequency Filter Theories of Perception

The idea that distinct neuroanatomic channels exist in the nervous system to convey information about specific spatial features of the stimulus is closely related to the single-cell hypothesis just described. It differs, however, in that the elements of this theoretical structure are often anatomically less well-defined entities than are the easily observable neurons. Spatial filter channel theories, however, are similar in attributing an analytic function to highly localized parts of the nervous system and, thus, are also place theories of the same persuasion as many of the single-cell theories. Currently the most influential and highly developed version of a channel model is based upon the idea that spatial patterns can be analyzed into their spatial frequency components in accord with the Fourier theorem. The classic one-dimensional Fourier theorem asserted that any function that met certain conditions of continuity could be analyzed into a set of sinusoidal functions of varying frequency and amplitude. Conversely, the theorem asserts that one could always find a subset of sinusoidal functions that could be added together to reproduce any other wave form. Specifically, the Fourier theorem can be stated as follows:

$$f(x) = \sum_{n=0}^{\infty} (a_n \cos nx + b_n \sin nx) \tag{2-1}$$

where

$$a_n = \frac{1}{n} \int_{-\pi}^{\pi} f(x) \cos nx \, dx \quad \text{and} \quad b_n = \frac{1}{n} \int_{-\pi}^{\pi} f(x) \sin nx \, dx \qquad (2\text{-}1)$$

About 10 years ago, on the basis of some psychophysical studies, Campbell and Robson (1968) suggested that the nervous system might be organized as a multichannel Fourier analytical system for two-dimensional pattern perception. They assumed that the afferent nervous system was organized into a large number of quasi-anatomical channels, each of which was selectively sensitive to a particular spatial frequency rather than one channel differentially sensitive to the various spatial frequencies. Form, according to this model, would be encoded by the relative amount of activity in the various channels just as color was supposed to be encoded by the relative amount of activity among the three photochemically defined chromatic channels.

The Fourier theory proposed by Campbell and Robson and subsequently elaborated by Blakemore and Campbell (1969) and Blakemore, Nachmias, and Sutton (1970), among many others, has attracted a considerable amount of attention in recent years and many attempts have been made to find neural correlates of the channels. Although there is still a great deal of controversy concerning this theory, its popularity makes it a serious contender as a major new innovation in neuroreductionistic theory building.

It is very important to note that the perceptual Fourier theory goes far beyond the idea that the mathematical nomenclature embodied in the Fourier analysis can be used to represent functions in some descriptive sense. Quite to the contrary, Campbell and Robson's original hypothesis is an anatomical and physiological one asserting the existence of a Fourier analysing mechanism within the nervous system. One obvious difficulty with the Fourier model is that the very generality of the mathematics (anything can, in theory, be represented by orthogonal functions) may eventually become a handicap in its evaluation. It is at once necessary and difficult to distinguish between the mathematical analyzability of a function and the anatomical presence of a neural mechanism within the nervous system that actually performs that analysis.

There are, however, many other logical and empirical difficulties with the Fourier model of perception. These difficulties are discussed in great detail in Chapter 9, wherein I critique the neuroreductionistic theories, in general, and the single-cell and spatial frequency theories, in particular.

c. *Neural Network Theories of Perception*

Neural network theories of perception are characterized by an emphasis on the collective information processing performed by an aggregate or network of neurons. The fact that the spatiotemporal feature selectivity of individual neurons is now considered to be determined by the organization of their interconnections with other neurons is an important conceptual link between single-cell theories and network theories. The foundation premise of neural network theories of perception, however, is that, even though the individual neurons may be unspecialized, in the aggregate they assume the ability to respond selectively to various stimulus situations. The specialized sensitivity or information-processing ability is assumed to arise from the pattern of interconnections among the individual neurons in the same way that a collection of simple logical units within a computer system can be interconnected to execute much more complicated algorithms than can be executed by the units individually. Prototypical of this neural network approach are the now classic models suggested by Mach, which I have already mentioned, and by Donald O. Hebb (1949).

Hebb, for example, proposed that neurons in a network functioned collectively in a two-stage manner to synthesize perceptual processes. He proposed that the first stage was the formation of a network of individual neurons, which he called cell assemblies, that began to function as an integrated unit as a direct result of their experience with the local features of the stimulus. Thus, each corner, line, or curve in a geometrical figure sensitized a network of neurons in the brain of the observer to that particular feature. According to Hebb, these cell assemblies are made semipermanent by the action of plastic synaptic mechanisms on the basis of simple use. Hebb (1949) formally stated this premise: "When an axon of cell *A* is near enough to excite a cell *B* and repeatedly or persistently takes part in firing it, some growth process of metabolic change takes place in one or both cells such that *A*'s efficiency, as one of the cells firing *B*, is increased [p. 62]."

The second phase of Hebb's model hypothesizes the combination of these cell assemblies into a temporarily ordered string of neural and motor responses, which Hebb referred to as a "phase sequence." The phase sequence is a succession of cell assemblies in which each cell assembly leads progressively to the next in an overall manner directly representative of the more molar time–order of perception and thought. Hebb also suggested that the phase sequences were formed as a direct result of the eye movements involved in scanning a figure. Thus a phase sequence representing a triangle would be made up of three cell assemblies associated with each of the three critical features—the corners—as well as an overall cell assembly whose "activity in the schema, is perception of the triangle as a distinctive whole (Hebb, 1949, p. 97)." In general, however, tachistoscopic studies of pattern perception make a shambles of any theory involving eye movements; therefore, this aspect of Hebb's theory is not taken seriously today.

A recent network theory that draws heavily upon both Hebb's idea of cell assemblies and Konorski's (1967) idea of a hierarchy of neurons is Bindra's (1976) concept of gnostic assemblies. Bindra has developed an elaborate theory based upon the premise that higher levels of mental complexity are encoded by successively more complex networks of neurons, rather than by a progressive convergence on a more specialized single neuron. In this way, many of the criticisms that can be lodged against Konorski's theory are mitigated. Figure

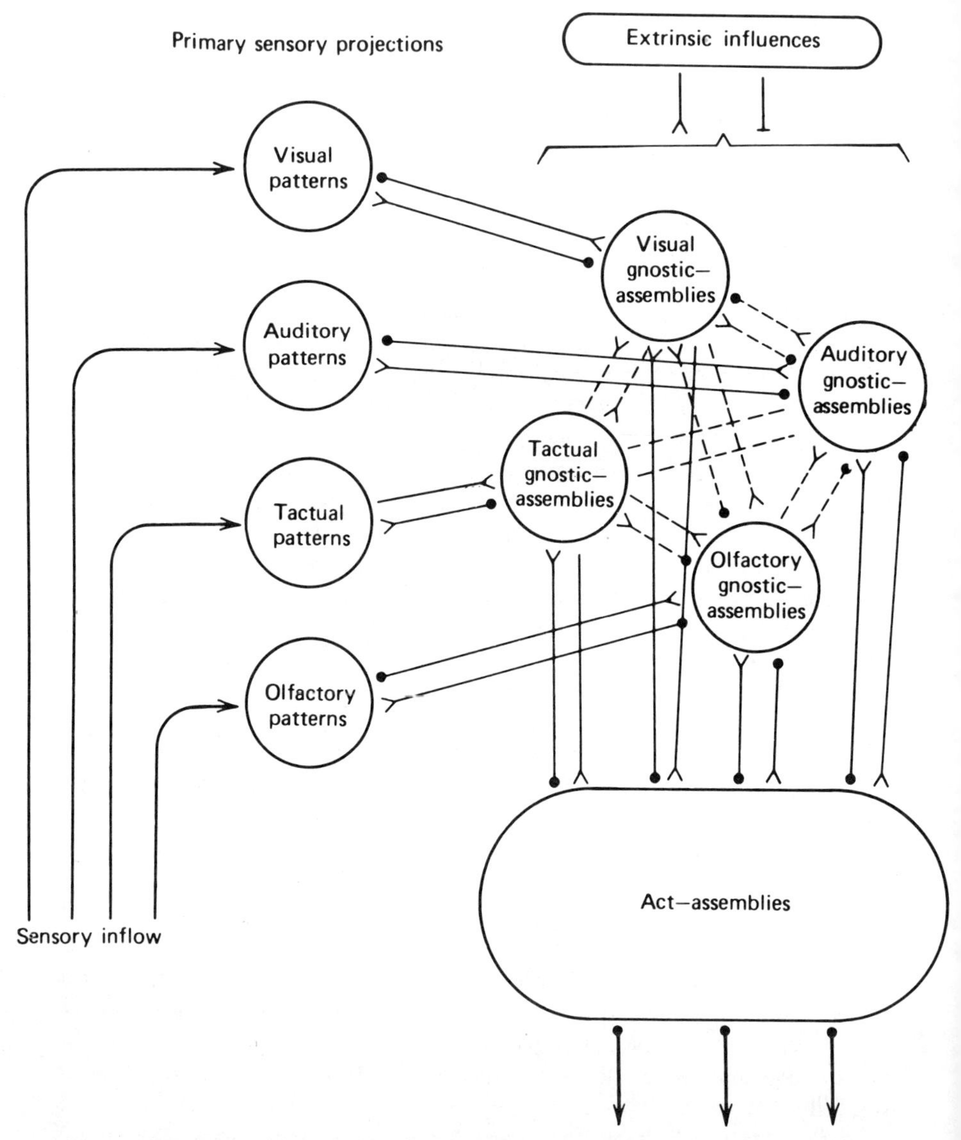

FIG. 2.19. A model of perception and response interaction. (From Bindra, © 1976, with the permission of John Wiley & Sons, Inc.)

2-19, for example, indicates how signals from many different sensory modalities may be integrated with previous experience within Bindra's hypothetical nervous system. Not only do networks of neurons make up the gnostic assemblies, but networks of gnostic assemblies are also interacting with each other.

Most network models, of which Hebb's is the prototypical and classic example and of which Pitts and McCulloch (1947) and John (1967, 1972) are other prominent examples, are distinctively different from the single-cell theories with regard to their characterization in the tridimensional space of perceptual macrotheory. Network models are typically more concerned with the overall configuration of both the stimulus pattern and the neural network rather than with the elements of either. Many network theories, therefore, are more patently configurational than was Hebb's, which did assume that stimulus elements were associated into cell assemblies and phase sequences. In a recent work (Uttal, 1975a; also the more extensive discussion in Chapter 10 of this book), I proposed an autocorrelation theory of form detection incorporating a neural network approach that heavily emphasizes the overall configuration of the stimulus scene rather than its features. Indeed, the properties of the neurons of the hypothetical network implementing that autocorrelation function were totally undifferentiated. The obtained differences among the alternative responses of the network to different stimuli were dictated solely by the pattern of interconnections among the neurons and not by any feature selectivity on the part of the individual cells. Even more fundamentally wholistic, however, was the nature of the network's response to patterns. The individual features of the stimulus pattern were quite unimportant in affecting the algorithmic process by which the network evaluated stimuli. The global arrangement of the parts was instead the critical factor to which the autocorrelation process was shown to be most sensitive. This sensitivity to overall configuration on the part of the algorithm embodied by this particular neural network was paralleled by similar patterns of sensitivity in the psychophysical responses. A good recent compendium of modern network theoretical studies can be found in Metzler (1977).

d. Neuroelectric Field Theories of Perception

A fourth class of neurophysiological theories of perception includes those that deal with the mass action of a very large number of neurons, rather than with individual neurons or even aggregated networks of cellular units. Such mass action theories are generically referred to as field theories. To field theorists, neither the function of the individual neurons nor the connections between them is important; their attention is directed solely toward the global and integrated measures of the electrical activity measured on the surface or within major chunks of the brain.

The theoretical roots of such a field approach are to be found in the work of the nineteenth-century physicists who originally developed the mathematics of fields of physical forces. More recently, the experiments of the distinguished physiological psychologist Karl Lashley (1890–1958) showed that no particular regions of the brain were specially involved in learning or memory. Rather, Lashley often observed equipotentiality among the different regions—the magnitude of a deficit depending upon the amount of tissue removed. To a very great extent, however, this equipotentiality varied with the specific behavioral task used to assay the effect of a brain lesion. These findings led him to speculate that mental processes were encoded by interference patterns among waves of electrical activity within the brain (Lashley, 1942)—an idea that has recurred many times in the subsequent literature.

At present the most active proponent of a modified neuroelectric field or interference theory as an explanation of perception is Karl Pribram. He has hypothesized (e.g., Pribram, Nuwer, & Baron, 1974) that the electrical fields of the brain operate in a manner analogous to processes underlying the optical hologram. Pribram does not propose that optical mechanisms are actually found in the head, but rather that neuroelectric interference patterns, which can be described by the same mathematics as those optical ones, are present there. When analyzed closely, however, Pribram's concept of brain fields is seen not to be inconsistent with single-cell physiology, as I have already shown (Uttal, 1978); his fields are related to neurons in the same way a field of wheat is related to the individual stalks.

Field neurophysiological theories of this sort are easily classified as wholistic and empiricistic$_2$. They are by definition anti-elementalistic and, by the overwhelming intention of their originators, antirationalistic. Most theories of this genre, furthermore, are indicative of considerable interest in the problems of learning both to the extent of the experiences set up the various fields of neural activity and in terms of the interference patterns as a storage media for memories. Thus they may also be classified as empiricistic$_1$.

In sum, it is clear that there is a strong thread of empiricism$_2$ in all four classes of neuroreductionistic theories of perception. They are, almost without exception, mechanistic in their description of the processes by which afferent information is transformed into sensory and perceptual experiences, at least to the extent they deal with this issue. All neurophysiological theories, in their extreme and radical reductionism, implicitly or explicitly champion a direct relationship between the observed function of the nervous substrate and the mental act and between the stimulus input and the subsequent perceptual response. Such a philosophy is not so much antirationalistic as it is simply totally unrelated to the concepts, tradition, and significance of the terms of that molar language.

With regard to the nativism–empiricism$_1$ axis, neural theories of the first class (i.e., those oriented toward single-cell approaches) are generally nativistic in asserting that the nervous substrate underlying the field is the result of normal growth and development processes. However, neural network theories and field theories often introduce concepts of learning and adaptation into their models of perceptual processes that make an exact placement on this axis equivocal.

Finally, neural theories diverge considerably among themselves concerning the elementalistic–wholistic controversy. Single-cell theories, heavily influenced by the microelectrode technology and the data that have flowed from its extensive application, are strongly elementalistic and stress local features of stimuli. On the other hand, theories invoking neuroelectric nets or fields are characteristically wholistic and stress the overall configuration of stimuli. Figure 2-20 sums up these characteristics in terms of the tridimensional scheme.

What all four classes of theory do agree upon is that mechanistic neuroreductionism is a fruitful model and approach and that some portion of human perception can be explained by its application. To a very large extent, however, much of this enthusiasm is still an expression of faith. There is still a great deal to be learned before the radical neuroreductionism expressed by these theories can be accepted for the many phenomena to which they have been applied in recent years.

9. Mathematical-Descriptive Theories of Perception

In Chapter 1, I briefly introduced the concept of a mathematical–descriptive theory as one of the main ways scientists have of representing any body of phenomena. The study of perception is as amenable to the highly precise language of mathematical analysis as any other science. Indeed, it takes only a brief survey of the literature to ascertain that an enormous amount of mathematical modeling goes on in perceptual research. I make no attempt here to survey these theories in particular but concentrate my attention on what these theories do and do not do as a generic class.

Mathematical theories typically describe processes. That is, they allow us to represent the behavior of some phenomena or body of data in terms of an analytic

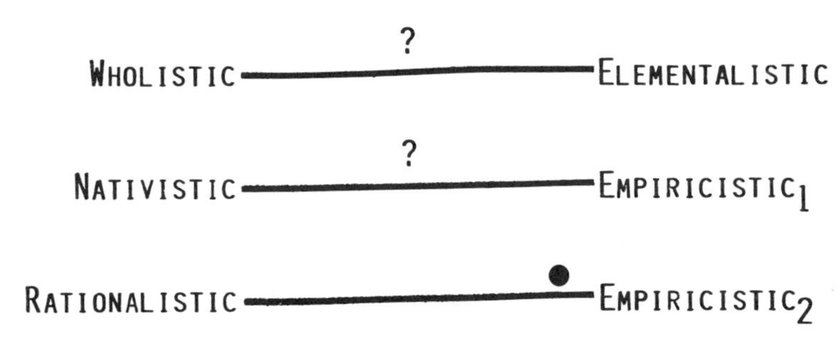

FIG. 2.20. A characterization of neurophysiological reductionism in the theory space.

function. But mathematical models also provide a highly specific matrix within which to trace the effects of particular assumptions. The most sophisticated kind of mathematical modeling, therefore, is a theory that starts from certain premises and predicts the shape or form of some response function by deriving the descriptive expression best fitting the data from those premises. Such "models" play a very important role in perceptual theory because of the precision of the language in which they are couched.

Mathematical models are not all-powerful, however. The analytic tools needed to carry out the derivations from assumptions to response functions often do not exist, and approximation methods (statistical or otherwise) must be used. These approximation methods do not *necessarily* imply that the mental process is also statistical but may only indicate the limits of our analytic capabilities. Some mathematical functions involve so many interactions that they are not practically computable. This may be so even though the problem is finite and can easily be expressed in either formal equations or as verbal statements.

Another major limitation of mathematical models is that they are, in fact, not able to give any direct support to any one of the many possible mechanisms that could implement the processes described by a single set of formal equations. It must not be forgotten that any mathematical model can, in principle, represent an infinite number of different mechanisms that exhibit a common response form. The set of mechanisms described by the model is referred to as the set of *analogs*. Analogs need not be the same mechanism; i.e., they need not be homologs, no matter how strong the analogy.

Some mathematical models have led their authors to infer specific neural structures. Luce and Green (1972), for example, suggest that their model of loudness supports a timing explanation of neural coding as opposed to a counting hypothesis. They are thus using the mathematical model to support a particular neural coding hypothesis. In principle, I do not believe that this inference is justified. The lessons of both sensory coding and computer theory (any mechanism or code can in principle represent any process) or of analog computers (different physical devices can produce the same response form), suggest that their extrapolation from their powerful mathematical model to a specific neural mechanism is too great a leap of logic.

A very important limitation of mathematical theory that is all too often overlooked must therefore be emphasized: There is no valid way to go from behavior to a unique statement of internal codes or structure, just as there is no way to tell what verbal language was used to represent internally an idea in a train of translators knowing only the input and output. Luce and Green's work, although highly distinguished in other regards, provides only the weakest intuitive support for any statement of internal mechanism. All that can be shown with certainty is that the implications of a particular mechanism are not incompatible with the processes represented by the mathematical relationships. Mathematical models therefore, although they may test plausibility, do not provide justification for any statements of unique internal structure. When phrased in these terms, I doubt if Luce and Green would disagree with this point. The structure of their paper, however, does suggest the implicit assumption that their experiments do distinguish between timing and counting mechanisms within the nervous system.

The work of the mathematician, William Hoffman, is a particularly important mathematical model of perceptual phenomena. Hoffman (1966) originally proposed the use of an existing mathematical system (the Lie algebra of transformational groups) on which work independent of vision had been done for many years (Mostow, 1950; Cohn, 1957; Auslander & Mackenzie, 1963) as a model of visual perception. Hoffman noted the many similarities between the transformations that were describable by the abstract mathematics of the Lie algebra and those that occurred in visual perception. These are summarized in Fig. 2-21. In light of these analogies, he suggested, therefore, that the Lie algebra would prove to be a powerful means of describing and analyzing visual processes. Hoffman (1970, 1971, 1978) has pursued this line of inquiry extensively in recent years applying the model to movement perception, constancies, and perceptual development. In the most recent of these reports, he has extended his model by

Transformation groups on $\mathbf{R}^2 \times \mathbf{T}$

Perceptual invariance	Lie transformation group	Orbits
Shape Constancy	*Unimodular Group* SL($\mathbf{R}$, 3)	
Location in the field of view	Horizontal translations	
	Vertical translations	
(Form memory)	Time translations	
Orientation	Rotations, SO_2	
Afferent binocular vision	Pseudo-Euclidean Rotations	
(Efferent binocular function)	Pseudo-Euclidean Rotations in plane-time: $\mathbf{R}^2 \times \mathbf{T}$ (Invariant: xyt)	
Size constancy	*Dilation group (Homotheties)*	
Motion-invariant perception	*Lorentz group of order 2*	
Cyclopean, egocentered perception	Group of rotations, SO_3, in Plane-time: $\mathbf{R}^2 \times \mathbf{T}$	

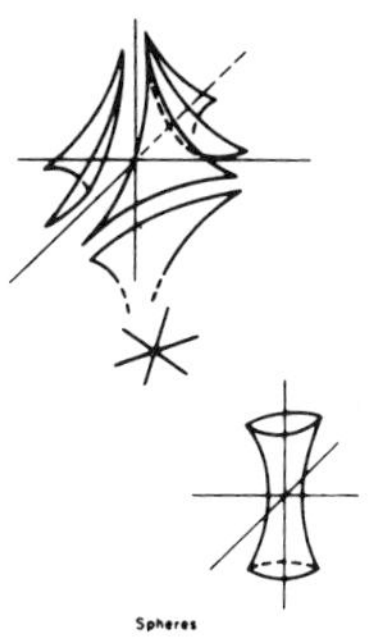

FIG. 2.21. Relationships between certain visual illusions and the Lie transformation algebra. (From Hoffman, © 1978, with the permission of John Wiley & Sons, Inc.)

invoking possible nerual explanations of perceptual transformations (largely dependent on the discovery by Hubel and Wiesel of the orientation-sensitive detectors. Although the use of the Lie Algebra as a descriptive model of vision seems appropriate, I believe there is less support for the neural hypotheses Hoffman proposes. And though it is possible that the neural–network-mediated transformations invoked by Hoffman are the basis of the perceptual transformations he describes, it is also possible that such percepts are the result of higher-level processing. The point is that the mathematical model and approach used by Hoffman cannot resolve this issue; it can only test the plausibility of his premise that the cumulative effects of a manifold of orientation detectors are responsible for such processes as constancy. It is neither a test of necessity nor sufficiency, however, and other quite distinct, though analogous, assumptions (e.g., that the transformations occur as the result of constructionistic interpretations mediated by exceedingly complicated and very high-level neural nets) also remain viable.

Other similar mathematical models of visual perception are described in a new book edited by Leeuwenberg and Buffart (1978). Although most of the theories presented there are mathematical, few have anything to say about the underlying neural mechanisms. The previously cited work of Joseph Lappin (1979), calling attention to some analogies between some visual phenomena and the mathematics of Einstein's special theory of relativity, is also of interest in this same context.

D. AN INTERIM SUMMARY

In this chapter I have reviewed some of the major positions in perceptual macrotheory. A wide variety of different points of view and emphases have been presented. Obviously I have not exhausted all possible macrotheories of which I might have written. Some were excluded because I feel they do not offer much to our understanding. For example, in my opinion, motor theories of perception only transfer the basic problems from the visual to the somesthetic and proprioceptive modalities without coming to grips with the fundamental problem. Some other theories, characteristically the philosophical ones, are too vague for inclusion and are not founded on an adequate empirical base. Still others are simply not macrotheories in the sense I use the term here.

Of those I have discussed, I must reiterate my view that it is not necessary for the reader to consider any to be antagonists of any other. The actual situation is that each macrotheory presents a global view that stresses a particular set of phenomena or facets of the overall process of perception and, to a fairly great degree, they do not interact. Although I am sure some readers may wish to quibble over details, I believe perceptual theorists on the whole will finally agree that all of these theories are valid interpretations of some part of the problem and that none of the perspectives I have discussed here is subject to total rejection or invalidation by any conceivable body of empirical evidence. This may distress some rigorous students of the philosophy of science who feel that the lack of complete rejectability is tantamount to bad theory, but it should be remembered that these macrotheories are all intended to be expressions of very broad perspectives and do not, in general, involve detailed explanations of the kind I have called microtheories. The main contribution of macrotheories, therefore, is not so much to explain the mechanisms of a particular illusion, for example, as it is to provide the premises of a general perspective concerning the total perceptual process. Often they can make this contribution by doing no more than calling attention to and describing a class of perceptual phenomena that may not previously have been of interest to the perceptual research community.

There are major differences in overall perspective among the macrotheories of course, but they are not so much contradictory as they are complementary. The following summary is an attempt to identify some of the major differences of approach or perspective.

One of the most radical schisms we have seen is between those who are psychologically oriented and those who are oriented toward the tools and concepts of the cellular neurophysiologist.[6] The former approach the problem from a molar behavioral point of view, emphasizing the cognitive and rationalistic processes that are so compellingly evident in so many psychological findings, whereas the latter approach the problem from the point of view of the tip of a microelectrode, emphasizing the neurophysiological details of the mechanism that all (even the most molar) agree must be responsible for the perceptual process in some ideal reductionism. This dichotomy of views has been referred to as the schism between the top-down (i.e., psychological) approach and the bottom-up (i.e., neurophysiological) approach.[7]

The essence of the problem faced by perceptual theory is, therefore, not so much to resolve controversy between the top-down and bottom-up approaches but rather to find a means of bridging the two main approaches by invoking explanatory theories that, to the greatest extent possible, actually link the language of the psychologist with the language of the neurophysiologist. In principle, it has been well established by formal mathematical theorems (Turing, 1936) that it is possible to do so to the extent that it is possible to describe psychological propositions in a formal language. In practice, however, the problem of linking the neurophysiological and psychological approaches remains what is perhaps the most intractable problem in science. Though many would disagree with this latter generalization and assert that great progress has been made in developing

---

[6]The reader should not confuse this orientation with the professional training of the practitioner. Some of the most cellular-oriented theoreticians today are psychologists and some of the most molar were originally neurophysiologists.

[7]The same words—bottom-up and top-down—are used in a slightly different context later. The reader is cautioned to keep the two meanings separate.

neural theories of perceptual phenomena, I believe many such theories will ultimately prove to be spurious and founded more on wishful thinking than on rigorous experiment and theory. Only in the rarest instance is a well-substantiated neurophysiological theory available for a perceptual phenomenon. Both top-down and bottom-up approaches must therefore remain a part of the perceptual scientist's strategies.

Another major conceptual difference among the many theories I have discussed concerns the nature of the causal chain that is assumed to result in the perceptual phenomena. There is a discernible schism between those theories that lay great stress on the stimulus determinants of behavior and those that stress the role of cognitive or central processes in defining what is perceived. This, of course, is another way of expressing the continuing debate between rationalistic and empiricistic$_2$ theories of perception. However, as we have seen, the rationalistic theories are not entirely rationalistic, and the empiricistic theories are not entirely empiricistic. Upon close analysis, however, the major distinction between the two seems to lie in the degree to which each accepts the innateness of certain a priori ideas.

A concern with the primary causes of perceptual phenomena does, however, permeate all of the macrotheories discussed in this chapter. For those theories stressing stimulus determination, the nervous system is conceived of as operating mainly in an automatic and mechanistic manner. It responds to afferent information patterns by transforming and modulating the incoming information in accord with its neuronal organization, but, according to this view, within the limits determined by its ability to adapt to experience, the same response will be produced at one time as the next. The classic empiricistic, computer, ecological-optical, and neurophysiological theories all express such a direct stimulus determination of perception either implicitly, or (less often) explicitly.

On the other hand, classical rationalisms, cognitively oriented theories, constructionistic, cybernetic, functional, and directive state approaches stress the active determination of the response by the needs and state of the central portions of the organism. The essential message of proponents of this view is that we see what we need to see, what we want to see, or what is consistent with our current state. They do not reject the role of the stimulus, but they do assert that the stimulus is only a partial contributor to the finally constructed percept.

Closely related to this distinction between external stimulus and central organismic determinants are the different ways in which the stimuli themselves are treated by various theories. From one point of view, that of ecological optics or probabilistic functionalism, the proximal stimulus is almost irrelevant. The interaction between the mind and the external environment is such, these theories propound, that the physical action at the receptor itself is reduced to a trivial aspect of the problem. The emphasis is on the meaning and significance of the external object—the distal stimulus. From a neuroreductionistic point of view, the role of the proximal stimulus is, to the contrary, essential. It is the only physical means of conveying environmental information and it, rather than the distal stimulus, is thus all-important. If the environment is not able to convert stimulus attributes into the physical energies that constitute the proximal stimulus, it does not exert any psychologically significant effects.

Another closely related facet of the controversy surrounding macrotheories concerns the different approaches of the various theories regarding the assumed degree of completeness of the stimulus in determining a perceptual response. From some points of view, mainly the empiricistic$_2$ or behavioristic ones, the stimulus is assumed to be more complete than incomplete and to provide most of the essential information leading to the elicitation of the perceptual response. The causal chain from stimulus to perceptual response is direct. A contrary view, typically found in those theories stressing the cognitive or rationalistic construction of perceptual responses, asserts that the stimulus is always incomplete and *suggests* a percept to an actively deductive mind rather than directly *causing* it in a passive neural network. From this point of view, available stimuli are but partial cues to the nature of the outside world; we live in awful and drastic isolation from our fellows and from the external world in which we are embedded. Accordingly, we construct hypotheses concerning what we are to see from what are at best partial cues and are not driven to a unique perceptual experience by a nearly complete set of stimuli.

In reality, all of these views are probably equally correct or incorrect, in spite of a strong tendency to view these "opposite" positions as antagonists. Each point of view, each theory, or each expression of the nature of perceptual processes deals with its own universe of discourse, its own experiments, and its own limited range of insight and wisdom gleaned from its own perspective. This is so in spite of the fact that perception is actually a complex and multifaceted response that is at once rationalistic, empiricistic$_2$, nativistic, empiricistic$_1$, wholistic, and elementalistic. Due to narrowness of scope, the various theories do not really communicate with each other, nor do they relate to more than a part of the total process of perception. It is not difficult to see some reasons for this lack of communication. One of the most critical points at which communication has broken down is at the intersection of the neuroreductionistic and cognitive schools of thought. These two approaches literally have nothing to say to each other because the conceptual or intellectual linkages that are necessary to establish a common arena in which to interact do not yet exist.[8]

Just as there is no neurophysiological model of cognition yet at hand, the psychophysical data can say nothing direct about the nature of the neural coding mechanisms that represent perception within the nervous system. All psychophysics can do is suggest certain constraints and identify certain process-

[8]Once again I have to acknowledge that many perceptual scientists will disagree with the thrust of this paragraph. I hope it will be accepted as a responsible point of view after the reader has read the whole book.

ing requirements. Yet the idea that there is such a neural process underlying each and every mental process is as unassailable a premise of modern psychobiology as is the fact that, viewed at the macroscopic level, the human mind acts as a rational modeler of the external world.

Further evidence for the eclectic argument that virtually all macrotheories of perception have some understanding to contribute, and that each speaks to different classes of phenomena, can be seen in the course of their historical development. There has obviously been an ebb and flow of the intellectual tide from one extreme to the other and then back again. Rationalism gave way to empiricism, which subsequently gave way to mentalistic theories, followed by a swing to behaviorism, and then back once again to a current constructionalism that is hardly distinguishable (except in the technical sophistication of its experimental paradigms) from classic rationalism. I believe that this ebb and flow of the attention of perceptual scientists reflects the fact that the problems with which epistemology, perceptual theory in general, and this book in particular, are concerned are, for the most part, yet unresolved. We change our attention to a new set of data; we drain the last bit of fruitfulness from a given theory or point of view; and then we return to a theoretical position that the scientific community had all but rejected years ago. The cycle then recycles! The return to the older paradigms of thought and theories concerning perception occurs because the older views were fruitful and useful, because each had an intrinsic validity, and because their decline was not the result of a progressive empirical rejection but of a change in interest patterns.

Now to conclude this chapter, I would like to alert the reader to my biases by stipulating what I believe to be the consensus emerging from modern research concerning the three dimensions of classification of perception theory. These stipulations do not follow directly from the material presented in this chapter. Much of the remainder of this book is dedicated to a presentation of the data that support my particular perceptual macrotheory. In my view, the sum of modern psychological research supports the following assertions:

1. With regard to the nativism–empiricism$_1$ dimension: There is increasing evidence that the more immediate aspects of perception are probably more innate than had previously been thought, and also that the more cognitive, manipulative, and interpretative aspects are very strongly heavily influenced by learning and experience.

2. With regard to the rationalism–empiricism$_2$ dimension: In spite of the enormous amount of interest in the intrinsically empiricistic$_2$ processing of afferent information by the nervous system, an increasing body of psychophysical evidence suggests that human beings create a model of the external world by constructionistic and interpretive processes that are comparable to rationalistic processes. The specific problem this book must deal with is where to place the dividing line between relatively peripheral, empirical$_2$ mechanisms and more

central, constructionistic ones, both of which must be invoked to explain the full range of perceptual phenomena.

3. With regard to the wholism–elementalism dimension: Even though the Zeitgeist (mainly due to progress in computer modeling and neurophysiological research) is heavily elementalistic, the weight of the evidence suggests that what people see is defined more by the overall stimulus configuration than by the features of which it is composed.

Now that a historical foundation of theory has been provided, I can comfortably turn to some much more concrete matters. The esoteric, theoretical, and philosophical aspects of perception become meaningful only when matters of speculation are attached to mundane empirical data. Current research in perceptual science utilizes a highly sophisticated technology and has resulted in a body of important background knowledge. The next chapter briefly summarizes the physics of stimuli, the anatomy of the visual system, and some relevant neurophysiological findings in order to lay a solid technical foundation for the chapters to follow.

3 Foundations of Perceptual Science[1]

A. An Introductory Comment
B. The Nature of Physical Reality—A Descent into the Microcosm
   1. The Classic Particles
   2. The Forces of Nature
   3. The Observed New Particles
   4. The Unobserved (?) New Particles
   5. The Identity of Matter and Energy
C. Photic Energy as a Stimulus
   1. The Concept of the Stimulus
   2. Measurement of the Stimulus
      a. Measures of the Quality of Photic Stimuli
      b. Measures of the Quantity of Photic Stimuli
         —Radiometric Measures
         —Photometric Measures
   3. Sources of Photic Stimuli
D. The Anatomy of the Visual System
   1. Macroanatomy of the Visual System
   2. The Microanatomy of the Retina
      a. General
      b. The Photoreceptors
      c. The Outer Plexiform Layer
      d. The Inner Plexiform Layer
   3. The Macroanatomy of the Higher Levels of the Visual System
      a. The Lateral Geniculate Body of the Thalamus
      b. The Cerebral Cortex
E. Visual Optics
   1. Image Formation by the Eye
      a. Some Simple Optics
      b. The Optics of the Eye
   2. The Visual Angle and Retinal Size
   3. Visual Stimulus Intensity Control
F. Transducer Action in the Photoreceptor
   1. The Primary Sensory Action in Vision
   2. The Production of the Photoreceptor Potential
G. A Summary

A. AN INTRODUCTORY COMMENT

Perceptual psychology is a multifaceted problem area that requires contributions from many different fields of science to achieve insight and understanding. The perceptual scientist thus has compelling reasons for simultaneously approaching the problem from the point of view of a widely diverse set of other sciences: Other methodologies and sources of knowledge play an important, and in some cases essential, part in understanding visual processes. The substantial amount now known about the physics of the photic stimulus, the optics of the eye, and about the anatomy, photochemistry, and neurophysiology of the visual system has already been the key to understanding certain perceptual phenomena. In other instances, information from some other science seems to have brought us to the verge of explaining some otherwise intractable visual problem. Perceptual science, in principle, could be carried on without reference to these other areas of science, but, in fact, most modern theoretical developments in visual theory are closely interdigitated with progress in related fields of inquiry. It is the purpose of this chapter to provide a brief review of this supportive background.

In the following sections of this chapter I am concerned with the methods and knowledge relevant to the search for answers to the following questions:

1. What is the nature of physical reality?
2. What is the nature of the photic stimulus?
3. What is the anatomy of the visual system at both macroscopic and microscopic levels?
4. What are the nonneural optical phenomena occurring in the eye?
5. How is transduction mediated in the eye to convert photic energy to the electrochemical energy of the nervous system?

B. THE NATURE OF PHYSICAL REALITY—A DESCENT INTO THE MICROCOSM

The basic epistemological question asked in this book is: How does man come to know about the external world? Without some appreciation of the nature of the external world, of course, this question is meaningless. It is important, therefore,

---

[1]A few portions of this chapter have been extracted, adapted, and updated from earlier works of mine. Frankly, I must admit that it proved psychically impossible for me to rewrite completely material on which I had previously achieved closure and for which there has been little conceptual change in the recent literature. Yet, I believe this material is necessary for full understanding of the material to follow and thus I have included it to make this book relatively self-contained. Some updating, considerable editing, and the insertion of major new sections has made the task bearable for me.

that the reader be aware of recent concepts and current ideas among physicists concerning the actual nature of matter and energy, the elements that constitute the physical world with which the mind interacts by means of the visual system. Considerable change is currently occurring in physicists' interpretation of the nature of matter and energy as well as in the meaning of the "interaction" between the physical world and the nervous system. This section is intended to provide a brief, qualitative discussion of the current status of physical reality as it is perceived today. I must warn the reader that because of the rapid rate of conceptual change in particle physics, much of it will probably be obsolescent before publication of this book.

To understand current views of physical nature and the photic stimulus, it is necessary to know a little about the history of particle physics. The relevant part of the story begins in the latter years of the nineteenth century. The classic view of matter and energy, prior to that time, can be summed up fairly quickly. Matter was defined simply as anything that had the ability to occupy space. In turn, matter was thought, in those days of classical Newtonian physics and pre-Mendelevian chemistry, to be composed of various compounds of a relatively large family of indivisible and indestructible particles called atoms. About 80 elemental atoms were thought to exist in 1900, but about all that was known was that they were of variable weight and divergent chemical properties. Although Dmitri Ivanovich Mendeleev (1834–1907) had proposed his periodic table of the chemical elements in 1868,[2] and the regular arrangement of the properties of the known atoms in his system was already apparent, it was not clear what the underlying reasons for this order could be. The fact that fractional atomic weights existed (as measured with chemical procedures and expressed in terms of the number of equivalent hydrogen atomic weights) presented a profound obstacle to any simple explanation of subatomic structure. Chemical reactions were explained in terms of the reactions of the different elements with each other, but the detailed nature of the interaction was at best an object of speculation.

Energy, on the other hand, was thought to be a separate property that could be acquired by matter as a result of its movement (kinetic energy) or its position (potential energy) in some electrical or gravitational field of interaction between different pieces of matter. Matter and energy were considered to be two quite different attributes of reality, and the total amount of each had to be conserved in any reaction between pieces of matter. Most germane to the present discussion, the system of atomic elements was thought to be the set of indivisible and fundamental building blocks of physical matter.

Within a very few years, these two basic premises, the separate conservation of matter and energy and the elemental status of chemically active elements, were to be replaced by concepts with startlingly different implications. What are

---

[2]Interestingly, it was first presented in the pages of his chemistry *textbook*.

now thought to be the truly fundamental particles are actually several structural steps below the atomic elements, and all physicists accept the fact that there is a fundamental identity between matter and energy. In modern theory, the two forms of reality are intraconvertible and equivalent.

In the following pages I briefly review the history that led to the presently accepted model of physical reality and then spell out a few qualitative details of that model.

1. The Classic Particles

In the last years of the nineteenth century some critically important experiments began to suggest that atoms may indeed be divisible. Physicists had detected the presence of ionized gases and metals and had, on the basis of very limited evidence, correctly interpreted this fact to mean that ''parts'' of some sort could be broken off from the ''indivisible'' atoms. A particularly curious phenomenon was ''Crooke's Ray''—a negatively charged stream of particles produced by applying a high voltage between metallic electrodes embedded in an evacuated glass tube. The fact that these invisible rays could be bent by magnetic or electrostatic fields indicated that they were charged. The way in which they were produced suggested that these ''rays'' might actually consist of discontinuous streams of some kind of subatomic particles.

In 1895 and 1896, two accidental discoveries further contributed to the rejection of the concept that the atomic elements themselves were the fundamental building blocks of matter. In 1895, while studying the effects of applying very high electrical voltages to evacuated tubes, Wilhelm Roentgen (1845–1923) discovered the existence of an extremely penetrating and mysterious ''X ray'' that was emitted from a Crooke's-type tube when the voltage was raised to a sufficiently high level. In the next year, a French physicist, Henri Becquerel (1852–1908), inadvertently laid some uranium salts on a photographic plate in a drawer in his laboratory. Tradition has it that a key lay between the salts and the plate and that a natural photograph of the key was visible when the plate was developed. Subsequent research showed that three different kinds of emission were present in such ''radioactive emissions.'' The first, called alpha rays, turned out to have an atomic weight of 4, to be positively charged, and probably, therefore, to be an ionized (i.e., electron depleted) form of helium. The second emission, called beta rays, was negatively charged but was very light and seemed to be the same as Crooke's rays. The third emission was uncharged and appeared in many ways to be similar to Roentgen's X rays. The important thing about these two discoveries was that they provided highly suggestive evidence that the stimulus for the exposure of the photographic plate was the emission of particles from within the atomic elements of the uranium salts because there was no evidence of a chemical reaction. The atomic ''elements,'' therefore, were not in fact elemental, but themselves must be composed of even smaller particles.

Within a few years, such evidence led to the hypothesis that atoms were made up of different numbers of two kinds of smaller units—the negatively charged particles that were subsequently named electrons and another more massive particle with a positive charge that was equal, but opposite, to that possessed by the electron, which came to be called a proton. A great deal of experimental attention was directed toward the determination of the exact properties of these newly discovered "fundamental" electrons and protons. Late in the nineteenth century J. J. Thomson (1856–1940) was able to measure the ratio of the charge to the mass of the electron (Thomson, 1897), and a few years later in 1907 he was able to determine the same ratio for the proton. The next important step came in 1916 when Robert A. Millikan (1868–1953) was able to measure directly the charge of electrons by an ingenious technique in which charged oil drops were suspended in an electrical field. The strength of the field required to support a charged oil drop indicated that the charge on the drop was always a multiple of a precisely defined unitary value, which was assumed to be the charge on the individual electron. Once the charge on the electron was known, it was easy to determine its mass from the charge–mass ratio figure determined earlier by Thomson. The mass of an electron was thus shown to be approximately 1/1800 of the mass of a hydrogen atom. Because the charge on the electron was equal to the charge on the proton, and the charge–mass ratio was also known for the proton, the mass of the proton could also be specified as being approximately the same as the mass of the hydrogen atom.

After the discovery and measurement of the electron and proton, the theory quickly evolved that the naturally atomic elements were actually made up of aggregations of these particles. Neutral (in charge) atoms were produced by the combination of an equal number of positive and negative charges—the characteristic properties of protons and electrons respectively. Though there were some minor discrepancies (the weights of atoms also did not exactly equal the weights of integral combinations of electrons and protons), the approximate values were close enough that most physicists were willing to accept the idea that electrons and protons were the major constituents of atomic structures. As we later see, it was not discovered until 20 years later that another particle, the neutron, equal in mass to the proton but with a zero charge, was also a constituent part of atomic structures, and another 30 years had passed before it was appreciated that the minor discrepancies in the masses of the atomic elements indicated that many, many particles other than the electron, proton, and neutron were involved in constructing atomic structures. Even more fundamental was the discovery that mass was interconvertible with energy during interactions among these particles.

At the time, however, a vigorous debate arose concerning the way in which electrons and protons were arranged within the atom. Some proposed a plum-pudding sort of model in which pointlike electrons were embedded in a distributed mass of positively charged protons. In 1912 Lord Ernest Rutherford (1871–1937) and Fredrick Soddy (1877–1956) carried out what many consider to be one of the most influential experiments of the twentieth century. They bombarded metal foils with alpha particles and, from the distribution of the particles after they passed through the foil, determined that positive charges had to be concentrated in a central nucleus within the atomic structure. The negative charges, on the other hand, appeared to be orbiting around this central, positively charged nucleus. It is now known that only certain orbits are possible (due to the particulate or quantal nature of energy), and that each orbit can contain only a certain characteristic number of electrons. This planetary model of the atom was formalized by Niles Bohr (1885–1962) in 1913.

The Bohr planetary model of the atom remains today the theoretical keystone explaining a host of different chemical and physical phenomena. It explained the lines in the emission spectra from radiant matter, the nature of the groups in Mendeleev's periodic table (and thus chemical reactions), and perhaps most important, provided empirical support for the very important idea that energy is not available at continuous values but can only take on discrete "quantal" values. The idea of a quantum had been suggested earlier by Max Planck (1858–1947) in 1900 and Albert Einstein (1870–1955) in 1905, but Bohr's application of this idea in modeling the planetary atom was probably one of the most spectacular intellectual achievements of the twentieth century. Quantum mechanics, as it came to be called, developed into an elegant model of reality under the direction of such eminent physicists as Werner Heisenberg (1901–1976), Paul Dirac, and Erwin Schroedinger (1887–1961).

In 1930 another fundamental particle was discovered when Walter Bothe (1891–1957) and his colleague Becker bombarded beryllium with alpha particles and observed a new emission with enormous penetrating power. Two years later in 1932 this new emission was shown by Sir James Chadwick (1891–1974) to be made up of streams of an uncharged particle—the neutron—much like the proton in mass. In 1933 Carl Anderson discovered a fourth particle, identical to the electron in mass but with a positive charge—the positron. Then in 1935, Hideki Yukawa predicted, on theoretical grounds, the existence of a fifth fundamental particle—the π meson. Indeed, such a particle was actually observed in cloud chamber tracks in 1948 in the nuclear debris created by a cyclotron-accelerated particle colliding with other particles. By then, however, another kind of meson, the μ meson, had already been observed.

Thus, by the middle 1930s there was a relatively small number of fundamental or basic particles—electrons, protons, neutrons, positrons, and several kinds of mesons—that were collectively assumed to be the indivisible constituents of all of the rest of the material universe. These tiny indivisible "billiard balls" were, according to this theory, combined in various ways to account for the diverse kinds of atomic structures and chemical and molecular reactions. This theory, particularly in terms of the role of the meson, provided a fairly good explanation of the structure of the atomic nucleus and thus seemed to explain satisfactorily Becquerel's fortuitous observations of natural radioactivity.

Following the Second World War and its stimulation of practical, though particularly horrible, applications of these ideas of atomic structure, however, some surprising developments occurred that were to alter radically this simple model of physical reality. Very-high-energy accelerators were developed that could produce streams of one or another of the small number of "fundamental" particles with extremely high energies. One kind of particle could thus be smashed against another at enormous speeds. Rather than simple rebounds, as would have been expected if the fundamental particles had been indivisible "billiard balls," such collisions often resulted in the emission of an embarassingly large number of other previously undetected and apparently equally indivisible particles of varying mass and charge. These new particles also varied enormously in their longevity. Some were relatively stable but others decayed rapidly and spontaneously into other more stable particles in very small fractions of a second following their creation.

By the mid-1970s several hundred different "fundamental" particles had been discovered by means of such collision experiments. The simple model of the atom composed of a few basic particles could no longer explain all observed phenomena and had to be modified. To attempt to do so, in the context of the disordered chaos of several hundred particles, would be tantamount to leaving us with a model of fundamental particles reminiscent of the state of atomic theory prior to the time Mendeleev proposed his periodic table to order the 80 or so different "fundamental" elements then known.

The solution to this problem has proven to be exactly the same in concept as the strategy that ultimately explained Mendeleev's table. It was to invoke a universe of a smaller number of even more fundamental particles that are combined to produce the much larger families of particles at the next higher level of reality. In order to understand these new sub-subatomic particles and how they combine, it is necessary to introduce a new set of concepts, dealing not with these particles per se but with the forces by which they interact.

2. The Forces of Nature

In recent years, physicists have taught that there are four different forces mediating interactions between material objects.[3] A key premise of the modern theory is that the exertion of these forces involves other particles of matter. Each of the four forces is thought to be mediated or exerted by an action that can best be described as the exchange of a particular kind of particle. It should not pass without explicit comment that this concept is intimately related to an exceedingly important idea; matter and energy are but different aspects of a single level of physical reality. I have more to say shortly concerning this very important point.

[3]But see how even this four-force theory is in the process of being modified as described later in this section.

The four different types of forces invoked in this modern physical theory are designated as electromagnetic, gravitational, strong, and weak. Each of these four forces is characterized by a particular range, the particles of matter on which it effectively operates, a characteristic relative strength, and the particle or particles exchanged. Electromagnetic energy, for example, is exerted over great distances but acts only on charged particles. The particle that is exchanged in an electromagnetic interaction is, however, an uncharged particle called a photon. Gravitational energy is also exerted over very great distances. Gravitational force operates on all the many different particles of matter not on charged particles alone. It is mediated by the transfer of a particle called a graviton. The effects of both gravitational and electromagnetic energies decrease with distance as a function of the reciprocal of the square of the distance between the interacting bodies.

Unlike the gravitational and electromagnetic force, which can influence objects at great as well as at short distances (and thus can affect events in the macroscopic world as well as at the level of electron orbits in atoms), the strong and weak forces exert their influence only over very short distances typical of those within the nuclei of atoms. Thus they are believed to account for the highly localized, but powerful, events occurring either within the nucleus of an atom or within comparably short distances when free particles interact. The strong forces in particular are invoked to explain the binding together of the subnuclear particles into more or less stable nuclear structures. The strong forces do not seem to affect all matter, however, but only a class of particles (to be defined more completely later) called *hadrons* and their component parts called *quarks*. Hadrons include the now-familiar proton and neutron, various kinds of newly discovered mesons, as well as a host of exotic newly discovered particles with such unfamiliar names as sigma hyperon or the upsilon particle. When a strong force is exerted between hadrons, mesons are thought to be exchanged. When a strong force is exerted between quarks, a particle called a *gluon* is thought to be exchanged. The strong force, which operates over only intra-atomic distances, does not display a simple inverse square law analogous to that describing the action of electromagnetism and gravity. Rather, within the narrow range in which they work, contemporary physicists believe that gluon-mediated strong force (between quarks) may remain relatively constant for substantial distances greater than 10^{-13} cm, whereas the meson-mediated strong force (between hadrons) may decline abruptly to trivial values at this same distance.

In this new world of forcelike matter and matterlike forces, it is hypothesized that the fourth type of force, the weak force, is conveyed by a hypothetical particle called the intermediate-vector or *W* boson. The weak force is the explanatory mechanism for the spontaneous transformation, breakup, or decay of a particle into others in the absence of any interaction with some other particle. The weak force is exerted on hadrons as well as on another class of particles called *leptons;* it is attractive, but it is exerted only over the very short range of 10^{-15} cm.

The various particles exchanged when a force is exerted vary in their mass, and the distance over which the exchanged particle can act is inversely proportional to the mass of that exchanged particle. Thus gravitational and electromagnetic energy, which are exerted over infinite distances, are conveyed by particles of zero mass—the graviton and photon, respectively. Gluons are also believed to be massless. On the other hand, the mesons exchanged in a strong force reaction range in weight from approximately 270 electron masses up to very heavy particles that may weigh 4000 electron masses or more. The intermediate vector boson, which has not yet been directly observed, is probably even heavier, perhaps 100 times the mass of the proton.

Another important difference between the forces is their respective strength. True to its name, the strong force is considerably stronger than any of the others. Electromagnetic forces are only 1/137 and the weak force is but 1/10,000 of the strength of the strong force. Weakest of all is the gravitational attraction. It is thought to be only 10^{-40} as powerful as the strong force. Table 3-1 sums up all of these characteristics of the four forces.

A continuing goal of physics has been to provide a single unified theoretical explanation of all four of these forces. Freedman and van Nieuwenhuizen (1978) have presented a highly intelligible discussion in which they describe the progress that has been made over the years in unifying force theory. Newton, they note, had unified celestial and terrestrial gravity; Maxwell had linked electricity and magnetism; Einstein had spent the latter years of his life trying to link gravitation and electromagnetism; and the quantum electrodynamic theory proposed by Glashow, Weinberg, and Salam had linked the weak force with electromagnetism. Now, they suggest, physics is on the verge of a single all-inclusive theoretical explanation—a universal and global unified field theory[4]—of the four forces I have described here. This new unified theory would be framed in terms of a single "super gravity" force that represents both a conceptual and mathematical breakthrough in physical thought. But the problem is not yet solved and the taxonomy of the four forces still provides a useful way of organizing four quite distinct bodies of physical measurement. The best that we have accomplished so far is to model all four forces with the same kind of mathematics—the so-called *local gauge theory*.

3. The Observed New Particles

During the past 20 years, as I noted earlier, the family of fundamental particles has continued to grow as more powerful accelerators have been developed. There are now known to be several hundred different particles that can be generated in

[4]It is important to understand what physicists mean by a unified theory is a mathematical model that describes the behavior of two or more of the four kinds of forces. Many more physical assumptions and processes are involved in a unified model than in any single model, but the unified model is more parsimonious in explaining more with less than are the aggregated independent theories.

TABLE 3.1
The Four Physical Forces and Their Properties

Force	*Relative Strength*	*Range*	*Particle Exchanged*	*Mass of Exchanged Particle*	*Particles Influenced*
Gravitational	10^{-40}	∞	Gravitons	-0-	All
Weak	10^{-5}	10^{-15} cm	Intermediate Vector Bosons	Very Heavy	Hadrons and Leptons
Electromagnetic	10^{-2}	∞	Photons	-0-	Charged Particles
Strong	1	10^{-13} cm	Gluons, Mesons,	Variable	Hadrons and Quarks

Adapted from Freedman and Nieuwenhuizen, 1978.

high energy accelerators that survive for at least a brief lifetime before spontaneously decaying, in addition to the few stable ones that were known in 1940.

The discovery of new particles continues on with each improvement in accelerator energy and each new improvement in collision procedure. In 1974 came the discovery of the Ψ, of J particle, a very heavy object with a mass equivalent to about 3500 electron masses. This particle was discovered nearly simultaneously by two groups and a highly exciting account of each of their experiences has been written by Richter (1977) and by Ting (1977), the respective leaders of the two research projects. Still another new particle (the tau), has recently been reported (Perl & Kirk, 1978). Even more recently (1978) has described the discovery of an enormously heavy particle—the upsilon—which in some of its several forms seems to weigh as much as 19,000 electron masses. This is by far the heaviest particle discovered so far. It is highly likely, however, that these new discoveries do not exhaust the possibilities.

This plethora of newly discovered "fundamental" particles has created chaos in physical theory. Where once three, four, or five fundamental particles could be invoked to explain the nature of all matter, there now are so many "building blocks" that the older, simplistic theory has all but totally collapsed. Furthermore, the very large number of particles so far observed itself cries out for some sort of classification and ordering. Is it possible that the many fundamental and indivisible particles so far observed are not quite so fundamental and indivisible, but are, in fact, themselves composed of even more fundamental particles? This is the challenge faced by modern physical theory; the chaotic array of particles is not aesthetically pleasing!

The best way to begin to search for some more fundamental set of smaller building blocks is to see if there is some order within the larger family of observed particles. The initial problem is then to develop a classification schema of the large number of observed particles just as Mendeleev did for the atomic elements. A first step in this direction can be made by classifying the various particles in terms of the four physical forces to which each is sensitive. Using this criterion, four major categories of particles can be defined. The first includes only the graviton, sensitive only to gravitational forces. The second category includes only the photon; it alone is sensitive to both electromagnetic and gravitational forces but not to weak or strong forces. (The predicted influence of gravitation on photons was one of the great successes of Albert Einstein's general theory of relativity published in 1916.) Leptons, the taxonomic name for the particles of the third category, do not respond to strong forces but do take part in weak reactions, gravitational reactions, and, if they are charged, electromagnetic interactions. The fourth category of particles includes only hadrons, which are influenced by gravitational, strong, weak, and, for those hadrons that are charged, electromagnetic forces. Together, most of the hadrons (excluding mesons) and leptons are referred to as fermions, honoring one of the pioneers of nuclear physics, Enrico Fermi (1901–1954). The mesons and photons are called bosons. Table 3-2 summarizes the energetic potential interactions for the four classes of particles.

Leptons and hadrons differ in another way. The very small number of leptons—the electron, the muon, the tau particle, the three kinds of neutrino, and six respective antiparticles—all appear to be pointlike entities: They appear to have no physical extent (as indicated by particle-scattering experiments) and, therefore, no possibility of any internal structure. Hadrons, on the other hand, have a measurable physical extent, which though small is not pointlike. For this reason, among others, hadrons are thought to be made up of other, smaller, and more fundamental particles.

One difficulty with this schema is that there are still unpleasingly large numbers of particles included within the single category of hadron. As I mentioned, several hundred different kinds of high-energy reactions have been observed that are believed to involve one or another hadron. This dichotomy between the particles called mesons and those called baryons in the hadron classification was

TABLE 3.2
The Particles Exchanged During the Exertion of a Physical Force and the Particles Each Force Acts Upon

Force / *Particle*	*Gravitational*	*Electromagnetic*	*Strong*	*Weak*
Graviton	X			
Photon	X	X		X
Hadron	X	⊗		X
Lepton	X	⊗	X	X

⊗If charged
Adapted from Weinberg, 1974.

also originally made on the basis of a certain physical property that differed between the two groups. The property that distinguishes between fermions and bosons is their spin. Fermions have a half-integer spin (½) whereas bosons have integer or zero spin (0 or 1).

This then brings us to the important point in this discussion. On what basis do we distinguish between the various particles? The answer to this question is complex because it involves not a single dimension or parameter of their physical attributes but, instead, a system of physical properties—the quantum numbers.

The set of quantum numbers describing any one of the particles that I have so far enumerated is a list of a set of physical properties of those objects. Some of these physical properties are relatively familiar. Most of us have some sort of an intuitive idea of what may be meant by mass or spin. However, at the subatomic level at which these particles exist, there are other properties with which we are far less familiar, that are virtually only mathematical abstractions (as are, in the final analysis, even those we think we can intuitively understand). As the explorations into the nature of matter have progressed, more and more of these physical properties or quantum numbers have been discovered, so that we are now faced with such distant abstractions that some of the newly identified quantum numbers have been given such strange names as *flavor* or *charm* simply to have a word to describe them. Regardless of what these properties actually represent, it is a basic law of physics that any two particles having exactly the same set of quantum numbers are indistinguishable from each other. There are now enough known quantum numbers to allow the classification of a very large number of particles. Table 3-3, the partial summary of the current classification system of known particles, indicates some of the entities that have been observed so far.

4. The Unobserved(?) New Particles[5]

Although it is now believed that the gravitons, photons, and leptons are actually indivisible and truly fundamental particles, the disarray introduced into theory by the discovery of such a large number of hadrons and the increasing appreciation of their physical diversity led physicists to hypothesize that hadrons were, in fact, not indivisible but were made up of combinations of even more fundamental units. In 1964 two theoretical physicists, Murray Gell-Mann (1964) and George

---

[5]Although I have framed my discussion in this section in terms of quark theory, it is interesting to note that not all physicists accept the premise implicit in the search for ever more fundamental particles. Some, like Chew and Rosenzweig (1978) and Capra (1979), have suggested that there are no such particles but that the role served by quarks in most modern theories can be alternatively served by ''patterns of interactions'' among existing particles, particularly as mediated by the strong forces. A formal mathematics known as S-matrix theory has been developed to support this point of view. In so doing, Chew, Rosenzweig, and Copra are eschewing physical reductionism in much the same way that I criticize neuroreductionism in Chapter 9. There may be some conceptual linkage here that transcends the specific technical details involved in each science.

TABLE 3.3
The System of Basic Particles as Known About 1980

	Class	*Particle Class*	*Sub Class*	*Examples*
Indivisible Particles	I	Particles sensitive only to gravitational force		Graviton
	II	Particles sensitive to electromagnetic and gravitational forces		Photon
	III	Leptons—particles sensitive to weak, gravitational, and, if charged, to electromagnetic forces		Electron Muon Tau Neutrino (3 kinds) and 6 respective antiparticles
Divisible Particles	IV	Hadrons—particles sensitive to gravitational, weak, strong, and, if charged, to electromagnetic forces, and made up of quarks	Mesons	Pions Kaons ETA Rho Omega
			Baryons	Proton Neutron Deltas Sigmas Lambda Cascade

Zweig, independently suggested the existence of an even more fundamental building blocks that Gell-Mann called *quarks* in honor of their elusiveness. According to this theory, all the large number of observed hadrons and their quantum number properties could be explained by various combinations of a small number of a few different kinds of quarks. Quarks, Gell-Mann and Zweig suggested, would have their own characteristic quantum numbers, and some of these physical properties might be very different from the ones used to describe the hadrons of which they were the constituent parts. Among the most deviant properties of quarks was the suggestion that their charge could take on fractional parts, either ⅔ or −⅓, of what had been considered to be the indivisible unit charge found on the electron or proton.

Recent experiments, in which highly energetic electrons were directed at and scattered by protons, provide direct evidence for the existence of quarks. The way in which the electrons was scattered indicated that there are smaller pointlike objects within the proton; these presumably are the quarks.

At present, the theory of quarks, or as it is known among physicists, quantum chromodynamics, is in a state of extreme flux. Each new experiment or discovery of a new particle leads to a slightly different interpretation of how many quarks there may be. In 1977 the accepted theory was that there were four different kinds of quarks and four different kinds of antiquarks. The eight different quarks were denoted by arbitrary names simply to designate that they are thought to be different in some of their quantum properties. The eight classes of quark were referred to as the up quark, the down quark, the strange quark, and the charmed quark, to which must be added the four corresponding antiquarks. The quantum properties—upness, downness, strangeness, and charm—were referred to as quark "flavors." These quarks also have other quantum properties, some of which are intuitively familiar and others which represent esoteric mathematico-physical characteristics for which our conventional vocabulary has yet derived no name. We therefore refer to these quantum numbers by such poetic terms as *strangeness, charm, flavor,* or *color* to have some way of discussing them simply when we do not care to use their more complicated mathematical formulations. Table 3-4 describes one possible set of quarks, the respective quantum numbers, and the alternative values they are believed to possess.

Recent experiments (as summarized by A. Robinson, 1977, 1978; and Lederman, 1978) involving the discovery of new hadrons with unexpected properties, particularly the very heavy upsilon particle, have suggested to some physicists the existence of a fifth and perhaps even a sixth kind of quark flavor that may make even the very recent 1977 model already obsolete. The flavor names suggested for these two new quarks are bottomness and topness, or according to some more romantic types, truth and beauty. Thus, with the respective antiquarks, there may be 12 rather than 8 quarks. Furthermore, quarks can also vary in their electrical charge, or *color,* as that particular quantum property is known. Three different colors corresponding to three possible states are thought to exist. If so, there would have to be room in the quantum chromodynamic theory for as many as 36 different kinds of quarks and antiquarks (6 flavors × 3 colors × 2). It may be that we are approaching the same kind of accumulation as occurred with the hadrons. Are there even more fundamental particles than quarks? Certainly by the time this book is published, this rapidly changing theory may be very different indeed; but, for the moment, the story of quarks can be summarized by the brief qualitative comments in the previous paragraphs.

As I noted, the basic motivation behind this quark model was to simplify the model of physical reality. The hope was that combinations of a small number of truly elemental particles with a modest number of quantum properties might be able to account for the very large and disordered variety of hadrons. One version of the present theory is that the two different kinds of hadron are produced by two different combinatorial rules from constituent quarks. Baryons, according to this

TABLE 3.4
A Taxonomy of Quarks

		Quark "Colors"		
	Quark "Flavors"	*Red*	*Green*	*Blue*
Quarks	Up			
	Down		J, B, S, Q*, C, T, P	
	Strange			
	Charm			
	Top			
	Bottom			
Anti-Quarks	$\overline{\text{Up}}$			
	$\overline{\text{Down}}$			
	$\overline{\text{Strange}}$			
	$\overline{\text{Charm}}$			
	$\overline{\text{Top}}$			
	$\overline{\text{Botton}}$			

*Each of the thirty-six Quarks is defined by a particular pattern of Quantum Numbers (e.g., J = Spin, B = Baryon Number, S = Strangeness, Q = charge, C = Charm, T = Topness, and P = Bottomness).

theory, are produced by a combination of either three quarks or three antiquarks. The mesons, on the other hand, are produced by the combination of one quark and one antiquark.

The hypothetical quarks have some very peculiar physical characteristics. One of the most surprising is that quarks have proven to be extremely elusive and difficult to observe in isolation. Quarks are not detectable in the debris left when a hadron, of which they are supposed to be the constituent parts, breaks up. The current theory is that quarks are "confined to the structures of which they are a part and that they cannot exist independently outside of a hadron. Recently, however, a group of researchers at Stanford University (Metz, 1977), using a modification of the Millikan oil drop experiment (in which small niobium balls were substituted for the oil droplets), claimed to have found that two of their sample balls displayed an electrical charge that was not a multiple of the unit electrical charge but was a close approximation to the ⅓ unit charge predicted for the quark by Gell-Mann. There is considerable question about these experiments—only a pair of the balls was found to be so charged—and most physicists do not accept these data. However, if they can be replicated, these studies will represent the first direct experimental evidence of the existence of a free and unconfined quark, a development that for the moment runs counter to conventional theory.

One new explanation of the confinement of quarks is that, because of the increase of the gluon-mediated strong force with distance, the quarks are actually enclosed within an impenetrable bag or bubble of this force (K. Johnson, 1979). But, to say the obvious, this is the frontier of physical knowledge and many more surprises are in store for us in the years to come. Whatever happens, this new science of quark interactions and properties—quantum chromodynamics—is one of the most exciting fields of modern science.

In this section I have very briefly reviewed the current state of basic particle physics and thus the nature of external physical reality as it is perceived by physical scientists at the beginning of the 1980s. This is, of course, a view of reality that differs greatly from the one that was in vogue 50 or 200 years ago. The material that I have discussed is in a rapid state of flux and to my knowledge much of it is not yet in conventional textbooks. The reader who would like a more complete discussion of these interesting topics will find no better reference than the following collection of papers from the journals of *Scientific American* and *Science:* Weinberg (1974), Schwarz (1975), Drell (1975), Nambu (1976), Cline, Mann, & Rubbia (1976), Metz (1977), Schwitters (1977), and K. Johnson (1979). These articles have provided the basis for most of the preceding discussions.

Even for those of us trained in more classical physics, many of the concepts I have mentioned here are extremely nonintuitive. It is not easy to conceptualize exactly what is meant by the "exchange of a particle" when force is exerted, a particle that exerts a forceful influence over intergalactic distances, or the "flavor" of a quark. Ideas such as the ones described here, it should be appreciated, are the outgrowth of mathematical models of a microcosm that we humans cannot experience directly and thus cannot easily translate into commonsense verbal descriptions. Even at what may seem to be the simplest level, the intuitively acceptable notion of the most basic particle, whatever it is, as a coherent and indivisible "marble" or "billiard ball" may be an inaccurate metaphor. The particle of matter being discussed here may be better described as regions in space that possess a high probability of interaction with some other equally vaguely defined region in space. It is likely to be many years before our society has built such a new set of intuitions into our educational system, however. For the moment all of us will have to suffer from the difficulty in conceptualization that this new physical theory imposes upon us.

There are many illuminating analogies between the development of this modern physics and the problems of perceptual psychology. The handicap of invisibility of the objects of concern is common both to particle physics and psychology. The resolution by compromise and unification of the debate between the wave and particle theories of matter and the realization that there is no fundamental difference between matter and energy may have something quite profound to say to those of us interested in the relations between neural codes and percepts, or between rationalistic and empiricistic theories. Similarly, the successes and difficulties enjoyed by psychologists over the past century in their attempts to conceptualize the nature of an intrapersonal mind may be instructive to physicists searching for some way to make an equally intangible physical universe intuitively understandable.

5. The Identity of Matter and Energy

The fact that forces are exerted by the exchange of a particle between interacting bodies is but another way of expressing the fundamental equivalence of matter and energy that is now a foundation of modern physical theory. Another way to express this same idea is the well-known equation proposed by Albert Einstein in his special theory of relativity published in 1905:

$$E = \frac{m_0 c^2}{\sqrt{1-(v/c)^2}} \tag{3-1}$$

where E is the energy associated with a mass m, m_0 is its mass at rest, v is its velocity, and c is the velocity of light.

A second important relationship defines the momentum (p) of a particle in the same terms.

$$p = \frac{m_0 v}{\sqrt{1-(v/c)^2}} = mv \tag{3-2}$$

Third, the wavelength (γ) associated with a particle with momentum (p) is defined by the deBroglie equation:

$$p = \frac{h}{\lambda} \tag{3-3}$$

where h is Planck's constant (with a value of 6.624×10^{-27} erg). Therefore, setting the two values of p equal to each other, we see that

$$mv = \frac{h}{\lambda} \tag{3-4}$$

$$m = \frac{h}{v\lambda} \quad \text{(3-5}$$

thus linking the wavelength and the mass (m) of a particle at velocity v.

Because the mass of a particle varies as a function of its velocity in accord with the relation,

$$m = \frac{m_0}{\sqrt{1-(v/c)^2}} \quad (3\text{-}6)$$

Equations 3–5 and 3–6 can also now be substituted into Eq. 3–1 to give

$$E = \frac{hc^2}{V\lambda} \quad (3\text{-}7)$$

This final expression relates wavelength and energy just as Eq. 3–5 related wavelength and mass. Mass, wavelength, and energy, therefore, are all interchangeable and intertransformable. It should be noted that these expressions also hold when the medium through which the light is being transmitted is not a vacuum. Both the velocity and the wavelength of the light change concurrently in such situations, keeping the equation balanced.

Thus modern physics makes it clear that there is no real reason for any controversy between particle and wave theories of light or any physical difference between matter and energy. Matter, both in mathematical theory and practical fact (as witnessed by the existence of nuclear bombs and power sources), is interchangeable with energy. Measures of matter, energy, and wavelength are simply different ways of describing a single physical reality. Using these equations, we may calculate either an energy equivalent or a corresponding electromagnetic wavelength for any object for which the mass can be determined, and vice versa. Indeed, the wave and particle models of matter–energy together may be a complete description of physical reality, or in Niels Bohr's words, may "exhaust all definable knowledge about the objects concerned" [quoted in Sambursky, 1975, p. 538].

This new perspective, acknowledging both the wave and particle aspects of matter–energy, has been formalized in what is now called quantum field theory. This is the mathematics of quantal fields or, equivalently, of the spatial distribution of quanta. The history of this important reconceptualization of the nature of matter and energy has been well described by Steven Weinberg (1977).

This excursion into modern views of the nature of physical reality has been carried out for two reasons. First, the basic epistemological question that has been posed over the centuries asks how the human mind gains knowledge about the external world. This discussion is an attempt to define that external world. Understanding external reality as it exists in terms of the latest theory of the external world requires that we understand something about quarks, photons, gravitons, leptons, and the other players on the stage of contemporary physics.

The second reason for this discussion has been that it is also the basis for understanding the nature of the interactions between our sensory receptors and the external world. It is clear that any receptor system must be able to respond to at least one of the four forces to "learn about," "interact with," or "sense" the external world. Clearly our vestibular and joint receptors are at least indirectly activated by gravitons, even though the interaction must be most directly mediated by electromagnetic interactions. Touch, too, is an electromagnetic interaction based upon repulsion and attraction of electric charges within solid objects. Vision, though, is the epitome of electromagnetic sensitivity with its exquisite sensitivity to photons. In the next section of this chapter I link these preceding physical concepts with the process of photostimulation that occurs in the rods or cones of the retina.

C. PHOTIC ENERGY AS A STIMULUS

1. The Concept of the Stimulus[6]

So far I have considered the nature of matter and energy solely from the point of view of the physicist. To biologists, among whom I would place psychologists, however, the significance of this physical matter–energy lies in the extent to which it exerts an influence on living organisms. The direct interaction of photic energy with living matter occurs in a number of essential ways. Light can communicate sensory information, control periodic behavior, stimulate plant growth, and regulate hormone levels in animals. Two mechanisms in particular, however, can be singled out as virtually essential to the continuation of life, as we know it, on the face of the earth. The first is photosynthesis, the solar light-driven production of carbohydrates from carbon dioxide and water that ultimately underlies all food cycles on the face of the earth. Photosynthesis not only provides the plant food that animals need to eat, but it also regenerates the oxygen they need to breathe. Indirectly, photoreactions also account for all fuel sources whether they be water, wind, combustion, or photoelectrically driven.

Our attention here, however, is mainly directed at the other important interaction between light and organisms, the one that occurs between photons and sensory receptors. It is not too farfetched to say that it is this ability of light to communicate information to responsive organisms that ultimately leads to the cognitive processes of perception and thought. Although conceivable, it is hardly likely that we would be the intellectualizing creatures that we are today in the absence of vision.

A precise specification of the stimulus for sensory photoreception plays an important conceptual role in any discussion of perception. Any model or theory that is posed to answer the epistemological question must be, to some degree, closed. That is, it cannot incorporate all of the topics, ideas, and materials that constitute the total universe of physical reality without becoming unusably cumbersome. Each theoretical perspective in perception, as in any other scientific or mathematical system, therefore, must have some kind of a starting point, which may consist of some a priori axioms and premises from which theory may be developed or some physical reference measure against which to anchor empirical

[6]Some of the material in this section is adapted from Uttal (1973).

data. Thus, even though any system of measurement or explanation may involve an arbitrarily large number of derived measures, at some primitive level, it must refer back to some simpler set of fundamental measures or axioms that must be accepted a priori.

Systems of measurement of energy, length, mass, and time in physics thus have been developed with many levels of derived units. However, some place in some obscure Parisian vault, or in the setting of some standard spectroscope, there must be a primary reference on which all the rest of the system is based. Either the frequency associated with a particular spectroscopic line or the length of the king's foot must be present at some point in any system of measurement or any theory of nature.

In the study of perception exactly the same situation obtains. There must be established, at some point, a primary reference with which all other attributes of the perceptual process are compared. Without this reference, concepts like veridicality become meaningless. From time to time throughout the history of psychology, the particular reference used by perceptual scientists has varied. Most perceptual theorists now agree that the physical configuration of the stimulus is the most appropriate candidate to serve as this primary reference for perceptual processes.

The word *stimulus,* therefore, must have a very specific meaning in perceptual psychobiology. It is best defined as a pattern of physical energy that produces activity in the sensory pathways. There are a number of restrictions implicit in this definition, which I should explicitly mention. First, note that I have not said that a stimulus is a pattern of physical energy that is *capable* of producing activity. To be a stimulus rather than just free-floating energy, the physical energy must actually *produce* activity. Therefore, I distinguish between those patterns of physical energy that are *potential* stimuli and those that are *actual* stimuli. Potential stimuli are physical energies that lie within the range of sensitivity of some receptor organ but that have not yet produced activity in the neural portions of the sensor. Actual stimuli are those stimuli that are transduced into forms of neural energy and thus have initiated some chain of events in the nervous system.

An important point implicit in this definition is that it implies that, to be an actual stimulus, a physical energy must have some measurable effect on an organism. The organism is constantly receiving a wide variety of physical energies, not all of which produce electrical activity in the receptors and transmission pathways; therefore, simple impingement is insufficient to define any energy as an actual stimulus. Furthermore, not all of these neural responses that are physiologically effective are perceptually meaningful. Thus it is desirable to discriminate further between physiologically significant and behaviorally significant actual stimuli. Some actual stimulu may be effective only in a limited physiological way and not psychologically. Electrophysiologists might be unhappy with this definition, but it is necessary for psychobiologists to further restrict the meaning of a psychologically significant actual stimulus in order to avoid the kind of logical difficulty to which Powers' cybernetic theory (described in Chapter 2) fell victim.

Another important point to note concerning the definition of a behaviorally significant stimulus is that I have made no specific limitation on the temporal dimension of the term *subsequent*. The response, which is engendered by a stimulus, may be relatively immediate—occurring within a few milliseconds of the time the signal arrives at an appropriate anatomical level—or it may be greatly delayed, even for as long as a lifetime.

A further consideration, when one considers the meaning of an actual stimulus, is that the mere presence of physical energy does not always constitute an effective stimulus even if the physical energy is well within the limits of sensitivity of, and does properly impinge on, the appropriate sense organ. The physical energy, in many cases, must be patterned or modulated both temporally and spatially to be effective. The importance of spatiotemporal pattern is emphasized for very specific empirical reasons. Continuous or unchanging modes of physical stimulation typically lose their efficacy as stimuli very quickly, even if they did elicit some response, unless there is some fluctuation along one or another of their dimensions. This fluctuation may be introduced by the perceptual system itself; small movements of the eyes tend to introduce some spatiotemporal fluctuation. Thus for example, Riggs, Ratliff, J. Cornsweet, and T. Cornsweet (1953) have shown that when visual patterns are projected into the eye in such a way that they do not move with respect to the retina, they tend to disappear very quickly. The stimulus itself may also generate the necessary fluctuation. Hubel and Wiesel (1959) and Lettvin, Maturana, McCulloch and Pitts (1959), and literally thousands of other more recent studies have also shown that physical energy patterns, differing only in their shape, speed, or direction of movement and absolutely constant in total light flux, may be either vigorously effective or totally ineffective in activating certain specialized neural elements depending on the way the light is distributed in time and space.

Another important aspect of the definition of the word *stimulus* is the concept of the adequate stimulus. Each receptor is very sharply tuned to respond to only a narrow range of all possible physical energies—a range that is defined by the properties of the receptor rather than by the physics of the stimulus. The kind of physical energy that produces a receptor response with the minimum amount of equivalent energy is known as the adequate stimulus of the receptor.

The adequate stimulus for the eye, for example, is obviously but a tiny portion of the total range of matter–energy. It is instructive to pare down successively the full range of matter–energy to the much narrower effective range. To start, of the four forces and the many kinds of fundamental particles, only the electromagnetic energy conveyed by photons can be considered to be the adequate stimulus for vision. We cannot directly respond to either leptons or hadrons. Even then it is only an extremely narrow region (the visible spectrum) of the full range of possible electromagnetic wavelengths and photon energies that is capable of stimulating the eye.

The relevant stimuli for visual perception can be pared down even further by invoking the concept of potential and actual stimuli at this point. The visible spectrum constitutes the range of potential stimuli, but most photons in this range, of course, are nothing more than potential ones. The physiological process of transduction (the conversion of external electromagnetic energy into the internal electromagnetic energy of ionic concentrations) occurs only when there is a conjunction of a potential stimulus and a sensitive receptor. Even this is not the final step in the paring-down process. I have already alluded to the distinction between those stimuli producing neurophysiological responses that are behaviorally significant and those stimuli that produce neurophysiological responses that are concomitant, yet, in fact, irrelevant to the perceptual experiences. Physical stimuli, therefore, must be further distinguished in terms of their ultimate psychological contributions. In the final analysis each *psychologically significant stimulus* is a highly selected sample of the full range of possible physical matter–energies.

It is clear, in the light of this discussion, that the word *stimulus* is a highly complex one used in many different ways. So far I have distinguished between potential, actual, adequate, psychologically significant, and psychological insignificant "stimuli." Figure 3-1 illustrates the progressive reduction from the full range of matter–energy to the electromagnetic spectrum, to the visible spectrum (the potential stimuli), to the actual stimuli, to those that are physiologically effective, and finally to that small portion of the original range that is psychologically effective and thus germane to perceptual theory.

2. Measurement of the Stimulus

Now that I have considered the various meanings of *stimulus,* I can turn to more mundane matters concerning the measurement of the potential visual stimulus. Any visual stimulus must be defined in terms of the four basic stimulus attributes—quality, quantity, space, and time. In the following sections I describe how these dimensions are actually measured in order to provide the proximal stimulus referent in any particular perceptual research project.

a. Measures of the Quality of Photic Stimuli

Light is one of the easiest of the potential stimuli for which to specify quality. The importance of light to our physical sciences over the decades and the almost unique singularity of the wavelength dimension as a correlate of psychophysical qualities have led to a very high degree of sophistication for specifying visual potential stimulus quality. Figure 3-2 shows the color names associated most commonly with various wavelength bands of the visual spectrum. Although the most commonly used single physical measure of photon quality is wavelength, as

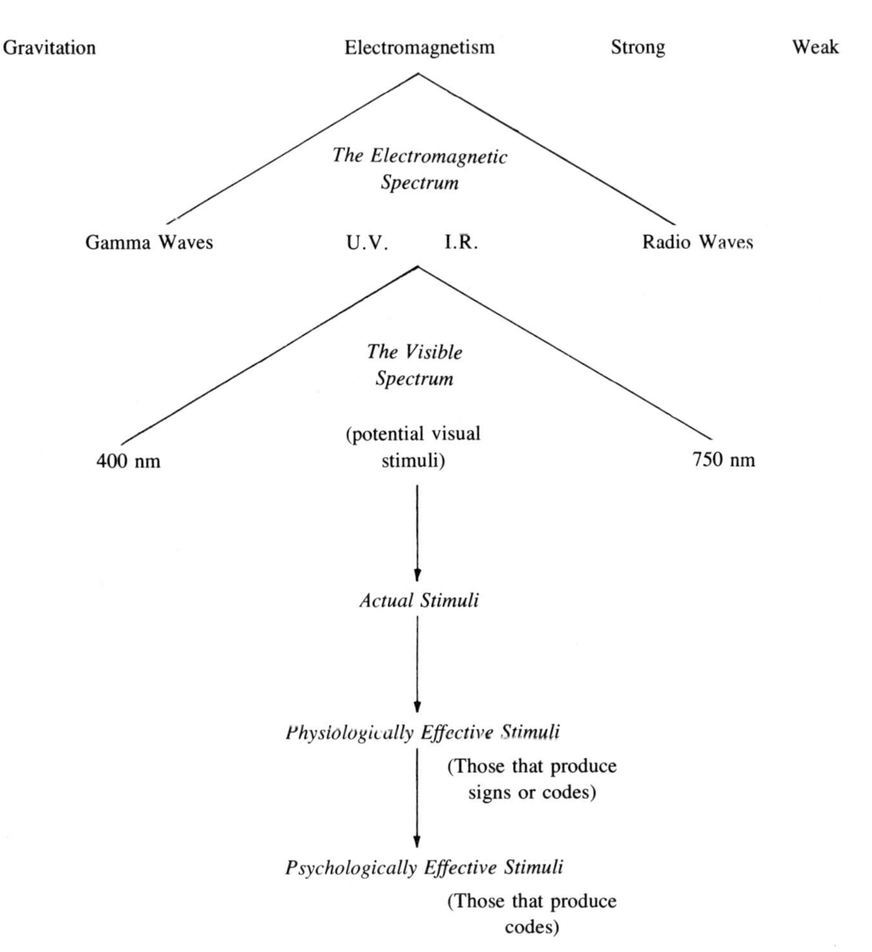

FIG. 3.1. A hierarchy of spectra showing the narrow range of matter-energy to which the visual system responds.

I have noted earlier, wavelength measures may easily be converted to equivalent frequencies or even to the energy content of single quanta.

The wavelengths of light to be used as a stimulus are measured by spectroscopes, devices that segregate light of different wavelengths, either by selective refraction (as in a prism spectroscope) or by selective interference of wave fronts (as in a grating spectroscope). A spectroscope that has its own internal source of light, any narrow-wavelength band of which can be chosen by a dial setting, is called a monochrometer. Narrow spectral bands of relatively pure light can also be produced by use of special filters transmitting only certain portions of the

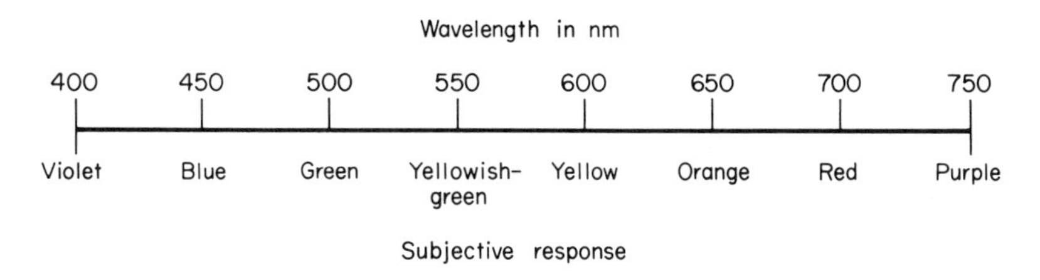

FIG. 3.2. A 3.2. Associations between wavelength and perceived color names.

visible spectrum. Such filters may be based on either selective absorption or interference principles.

Other secondary characteristics might also be considered as additional ways of specifying the quality of a given visible light. For example, the degree of polarization (i.e., the direction of oscillation of the wavelike properties of light), specifies a certain characteristic of light, which has a large number of physical implications.

To make the concept of polarization clearer, remember that all electromagnetic radiation can be considered in terms of its wavelike properties. The waves of this energy can be thought of as an electric oscillation occurring at right angles to a magnetic wave. Figure 3-3A displays such a perfectly polarized electromagnetic wave with only a single electric component at right angles to a single magnetic component. If, as shown in Fig. 3-3B, the light is randomly and equally oscillating in all directions normal to its direction of travel (i.e., both the electric and magnetic vectors are equally present in all directions), then it is said to be unpolarized. If, on the other hand, as shown in Fig. 3-3C, it has a preferential, but not exclusive, axis of oscillation, then it is said to be partially polarized.

From the point of view of the perceptual scientist, there are only a few phenomena in which polarization is important. Some insects seem to be able to utilize the angle of polarization of sunlight as navigational aids. The so-called Haidinger's Brushes—radical bluish and yellowish lines observed when viewing the sky through a polarizing filter—have been cited as effects of polarization sensitivities in human vision; but only a few other similar oddities exist; and none seem to be of any special significance in man's adaptation to his environment.

b. Measures of the Quantity of Photic Stimuli[7]

Whereas a single dimension—wavelength (and its derivitive—polarization)—completely specifies the quality of light for all cases, specification of the amount or quantity of light is not so simple. Not only are there several different units used to specify the amount of light, depending upon special viewing conditions, but there are also two completely different systems for measuring light intensity—radiometry and photometry. The radiometric system

---

[7]Some of the material in this section is adapted from Uttal (1973).

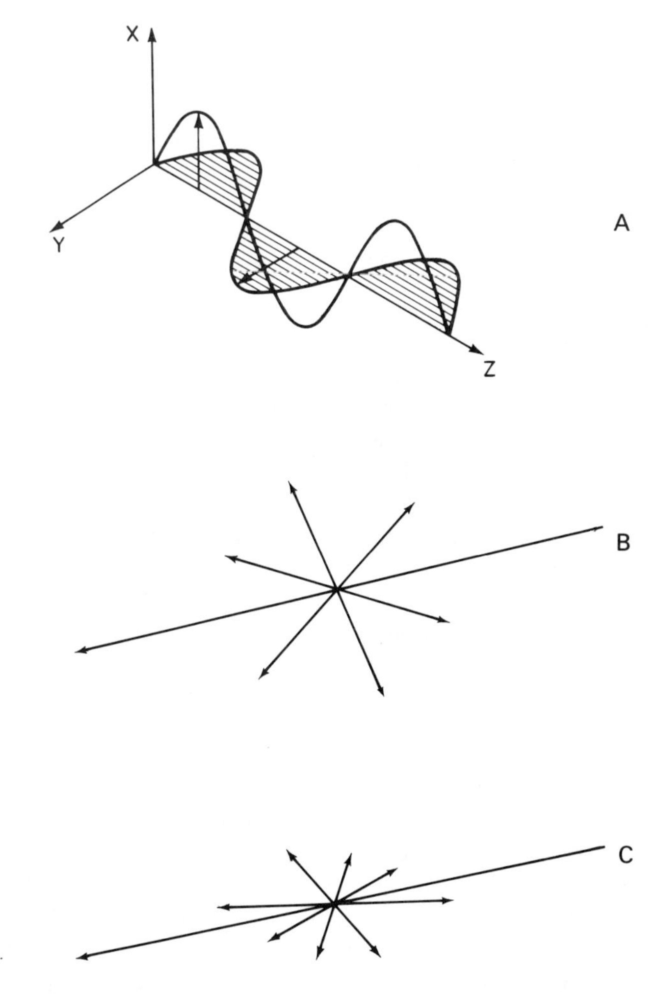

FIG. 3.3. (A) A perfectly plane polarized light wave. (B) A system of perfectly unpolarized light waves. (C) A system of partially polarized light waves.

is an uncorrected physical energy measurement system, which is used primarily by physical scientists to specify the actual amount of physical energy present, irrespective of its ultimate use. Radiometric measurements are made with instruments that have been corrected for their own differential sensitivities as a function of wavelength so that an absolute energy reading can often be directly obtained.

In the photometric system, measurements of light quantity are obtained using a built-in correction factor that makes stimulus measurements dependent on the potential visual effectiveness of the light. The standard correction factor for visual effectiveness is the photopic (light-adapted) luminosity curve of the human eye; however, alternative systems using the scotopic curve as a correction factor have also been suggested.

Measurements in photometric units are, therefore, limited to wavelength values between 390 and 760 nm, in agreement with the limits of sensitivity of the human photoreceptor. Thus, light with a wavelength of, say, 1300 nm, even though of very high radiometric intensity, will necessarily have zero photometric intensity. It would simply cook the eye before it could be detected by the human visual system. To repeat this very important point: *Any light, no matter how intense radiometrically, that has a wavelength outside of the range of visible light has a photometric intensity of zero and is not a potential visual stimulus.*

Figure 3-4 is a cut-away diagram of a fine modern visual photometer, which produces a compound field of view as shown in the inset. A central reference spot is produced by the optical system constructed into the handle of the instrument. The spot is surrounded by a view of the external scene that is to be photometrically evaluated. The observer's task is to adjust the reference spot so that it is the same subjective brightness as the surrounding scene. The value of brightness can then be read off the scale inscribed on the handle of the photometer that is coupled to the optical system.

Figure 3-5 is a photograph of a radiometer that converts photic energy to electrical signals. This device acts by the absorption of photic energy by a medium that does not usually have the same spectral characteristics as the human eye but rather, in the ideal instrument, has a flat response curve (absorbing all wavelengths equally well). Unlike the photometer, which incorporates the human observer into its measuring system, the radiometer is not corrected for the spectral absorption characteristics of the human eye in any way and thus gives only absolute values of the incident energy when connected to an appropriate indicator such as a galvanometer.

Table 3-5 summarizes and previews the entire system of photometric and radiometric units, which are discussed in detail in the following sections of this chapter. This table and the following discussion are based on Riggs' (1965) article.

Now that I have briefly defined the difference between these two systems of quantity measurements, I would like to continue by considering in detail the various units that are used to measure light quantity for the various viewing conditions. There are four basic viewing conditions for measuring the amount of light. For each of these "points of view," a separate standard unit has been developed for use in either the radiometric or the photometric system. The four viewing conditions specify units that measure:

1. The total amount of light being emitted from a point source.
2. The amount of light passing through 1 steradian (defined as the unit solid angle) from a point source. (Because there are 4Π steradians making up the sphere around a point source, viewing condition 1 measures 4Π times the amount of light

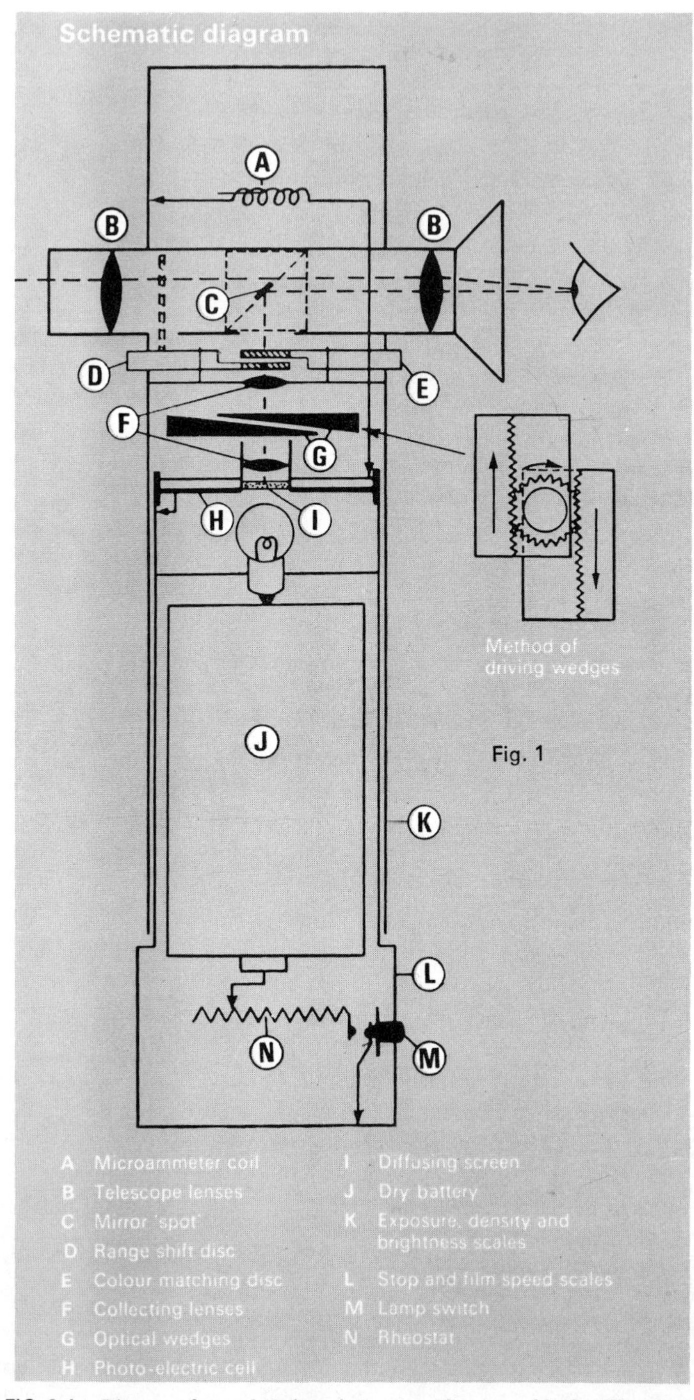

FIG. 3.4. Diagram of a good modern photometer. (Courtesy of Salford Electrical Instruments, Ltd., Lancashire, England.)

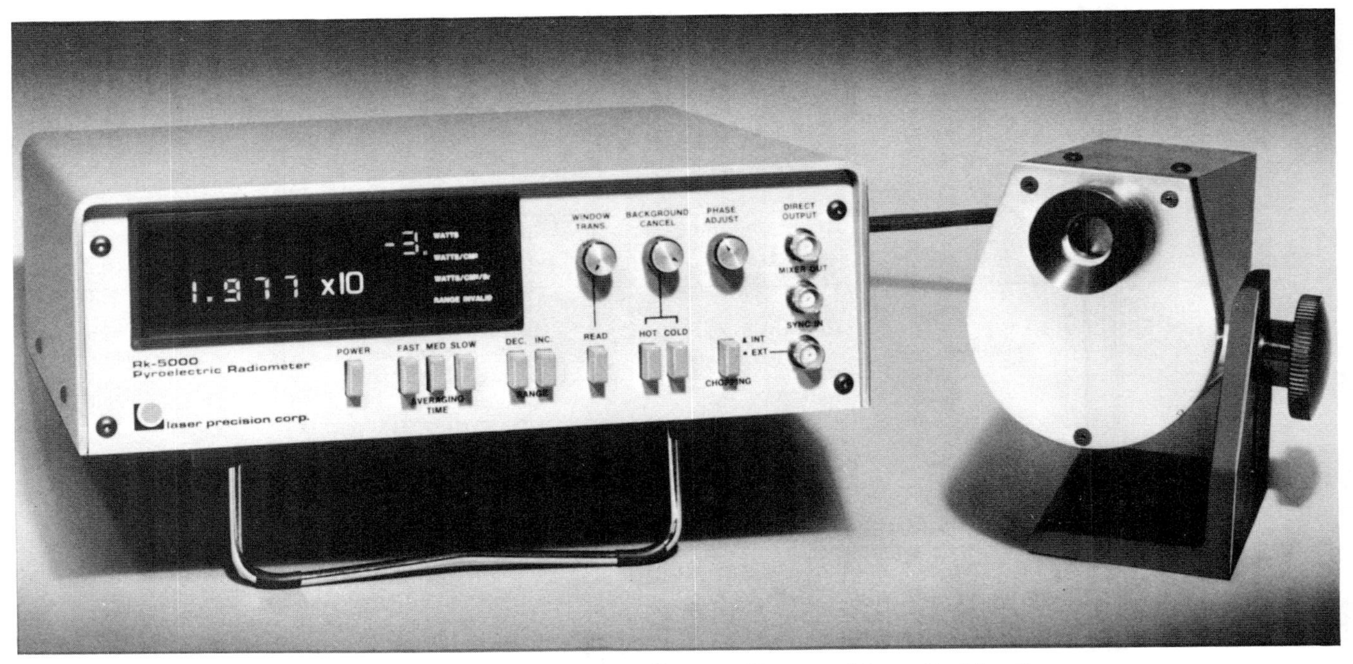

FIG. 3.5. A good modern radiometer. (Courtesy of Laser Precision Corp., Utica, New York.)

TABLE 3.5
The Radiometric and Photometric Units Used to Measure Visual Stimulus Quantity

(1 lumen = $685 \sum_{0}^{\infty} P_\lambda V_\lambda \Delta_\lambda$)

	Radiometric				Photometric			
	Symbol	Name	Unit	Relating Equation	Symbol	Name	Unit	Relating Equation
Total Light	P	Radiant flux	Watt (erg/sec)		F	Luminous flux	lumen	
Light Through 1 steradian	J	Radiant intensity	W/steradian	$P = 4\pi J$	I	Luminous intensity	lumen/ steradian (1 candle)	$F = 4\pi I$
Light Falling on Extended Surface	H	Irradiance	W/m^2	$H = \frac{J \cos\theta}{r_2}$	E	Illuminance	lumen/m^2 (1 lux)	$E = \frac{I \cos\theta}{r^2}$
Light Being Emitted from Extended Surface	N	Radiance	W/steradian/ m^2	$N_{actual} = N_{max} \cos\theta$	L	Luminance	lumen/ steradian/ m^2	$L_{actual} = L_{max} \cos\theta$

From Uttal, 1973, as adapted from Riggs, 1965.

being emitted through a single steradian as is measured in viewing condition 2. This holds only if the light is coming from an isotropic source (i.e., one radiating equally in all directions).

3. The amount of light falling on a unit surface at a given distance from a source.

4. The amount of light being emitted per unit area from an extended source.

Radiometric Measures. First consider the radiometric or energy-based units that have been developed for these four viewing conditions:

1. Radiant flux (P): If an observer is able to measure the total amount of light being emitted from a point source with some spherical radiometric measuring instrument that completely surrounds that source, he would then be able to specify the total *radiant flux* from the source. It would not matter if the source were isotropic or very irregular in its emission depending on the direction. The measurement of total energy emitted by the source would still be accurate, since all emitted energy would intercept the measuring surface surrounding the source. Radiant flux is usually measured in watts (W) or ergs per second (1 W is equal to 10^7 ergs/sec).

2. Radiant intensity (J): However, there are few such spherical flux measuring instruments. The receptive area of most real measuring instruments intercepts only the amount of light passing through a much smaller section of the space around the light source. A practical measure of this sort, one that measures the flux through a solid angle of a given size, is called *radiant intensity*. Radiant intensity is measured in units of watts per steradian where the steradian (ster) is the unit solid angle.

It should be noted that J is independent of both how far the measuring instrument is from the source and the size of the measuring instrument only if one corrects for the area of the measuring surface and the distance between the source and the instrument. Furthermore, most practical light sources do not emit light equally in all directions and are thus said to be anisotropic. For this reason, radiant intensity measurements cannot usually be extrapolated to radiant flux directly by simple multiplication by 4π. It is true only for perfectly isotropic sources that the theoretical relation $P = 4\pi J$ holds true.

3. Irradiance (H): The unit of irradiance has been developed in a further effort to find a practical unit of light intensity. *Irradiance* is defined as the radiometric measurement of the amount of light energy falling on a surface. This measurement is, of course, dependent on the distance between surface and source, as well as on the magnitude of the source itself. But because it is measured at the destination rather than at the source, it is usually a better measure than radiant intensity for evaluating the amount of energy really involved in some stimulus situation. Irradiance has basic units of watts per square meter. Because the solid angle projection of a given surface is dependent on its deviation from

perpendicularity to the line from the source to the surface, and the proportion of a steradian which is cut is also inversely dependent on the square of the distance of the surface from the source, it is possible to calculate the radiant intensity from an irradiance value by use of the following equation:

$$H = \frac{J \cos \theta}{r^2} \tag{3-8}$$

where r is the distance of the surface from the source, and θ is the angle of deviation from the perpendicular in this case. It must be emphasized that, in this case, this equation is precisely accurate, given a good value for H. However, it cannot, in general, be extrapolated to a total estimate of the flux for the same reasons that radiant intensity cannot—the possibility of anisotropy in the emmission.

4. Radiance (N): All three preceding measurements have been specified in terms of an idealized point source of light. However, many light-emitting sources are extended surfaces rather than points. Such distributed light sources also require a unit that takes into account the fact that the light is coming from a broad region. Radiance is such a unit, having the physical dimensions of watts per steradian per square meter. The amount of light being emitted by such a surface also must be corrected for the angle of view. When the plane of a surface is parallel to the line connecting the observer and the surface, any surface subtends a vanishingly narrow horizontal line of no measurable surface area, and, therefore, no light emitted from it should be seen directly. As the plane subtends a greater and greater angle, then more of the luminous surface is exposed to the observer. This process is represented by the following equation:

$$N_{\text{actual}} = N_{\text{max}} \cos \theta \tag{3-9}$$

where N_{actual} is the amount of light measured; N_{max} is the amount that would have been measured by an instrument situated perpendicularly to the radiant plane; and θ in this case is the angle between the surface and the line of sight.

Photometric Measures. An equivalent set of photometric measures exists. The only difference between these photometric measurements and the radiometric measurements just described is that all photometric measures are corrected by the average *visual* effectiveness of each wavelength of light. The visual effectiveness of light is defined by the scotopic or photopic luminosity curves of human rod and cone vision; data discussed in detail later in this book. For the present, let us simply consider the photopic luminosity curve shown in Fig. 3-6 as a set of measures indicating the effectiveness of light of different wavelengths for a light-adapted eye. This curve tells us, for example, that it takes a much more physically energetic source of red light to produce a given subjective brightness (complicated, of course, by a difference in hue) than to produce a

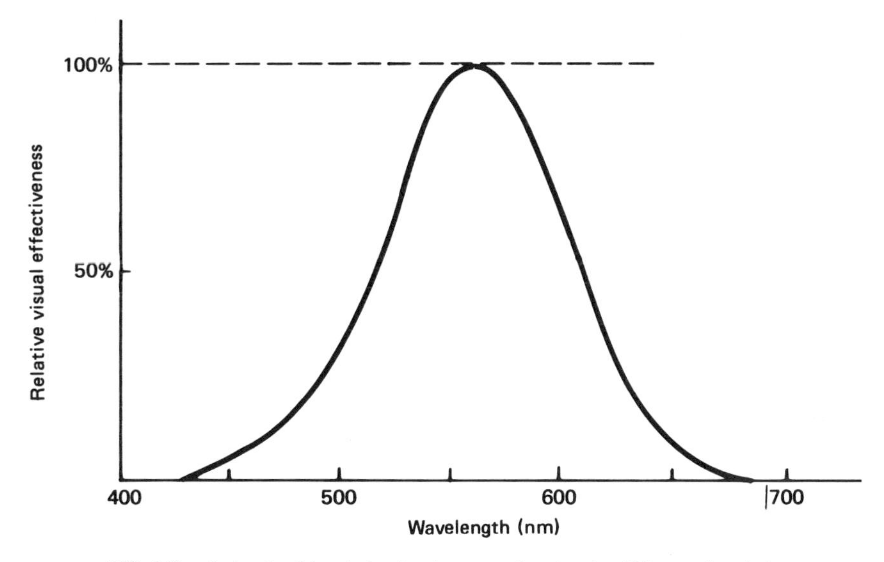

FIG. 3.6. A simple photopic luminosity curve showing the difference in relative visual effectiveness of light of varying wavelengths. It is this curve that is used to convert radiometric energies to the photometric units. (From Uttal, 1973.)

yellowish sensation of the same brightness. Thus, the luminosity (i.e., the visual effectiveness of equal energy stimuli) need not be the same.

The process of tying the radiometric and photometric systems together is a transformation from the units of radiant to luminous flux. With this transformation we are able to calculate the luminous flux produced by a given amount of radiant flux. Because the transformation is based on the photopic luminosity curve, which is equivalent to a set of constants (one for each wavelength or wavelength band used), rather than a single constant, and because light brightnesses sum (approximately, but see Chapter 6) as the colors are mixed, the total luminous flux can be calculated as a sum of all the corrected wavelength effects. The formal relation transforming watts to lumens (the lumen being the basic unit of luminous flux) is:

$$\text{Number of lumens} = 685 \sum_{0}^{N} P_\lambda V_\lambda \Delta_\lambda \qquad (3\text{-}10)$$

where 685 is the number of lumens per watt of the most effective stimulus for the light adapted eye (i.e., light with a wavelength of about 555 nm); $P\lambda$ is the radiant flux at each wavelength component λ; V_λ is the photopic luminosity coefficient (the proportional height of the luminosity curve at λ) for each component; and Δ is the width of each of N wavelength bands. Such a transformation has the mathematical effect of superimposing the visual sensitivity of the eye onto the measurements of radiometric intensity. Other instruments, which actually involve the visual process or which correct radiometric measures by appropriate filters, can also be used. In either case, the units of the photometric system that describe the same four basic viewing conditions used in radiometry are as follows:

1. Luminous flux (F): Luminous flux is defined as the total amount of visually effective light being emitted in all directions by a point source. The standard candle is the basic unit of the photometric system and it, by definition, emits 4π lumens. Originally, a candle was literally that, but nowadays standardized electrical sources are used to calibrate photometric devices.

2. Luminous intensity (I): Luminous intensity is defined as the amount of visually effective light being emitted through 1 steradian. It is measured in lumens per steradian. One standard candle emits 1 lumen through each steradian.

3. Illuminance (E): Illuminance is defined as the amount of visually effective light falling on a surface. The unit of illuminance is the *lux,* which is defined to be equal to 1 lumen per square meter. As in the definition of irradiance, the angle of deviation from the perpendicular (θ) and the distance (r) from the light source determine the illuminance according to the following rule:

$$E = I \frac{\cos \theta}{r^2} \tag{3-11}$$

4. Luminance (L): Luminance is defined as the amount of visually effective light emitted by an extended source. The units are, therefore, measures of luminous flux per square meter, or lumens per steradian per square meter. Other units of luminance are commonly used; for example, 1 lumen per steradian per square meter is equilavent to 3.14 millilamberts (mL). As in the definition of radiance, the angle of view of the source is critical in defining the amount of light that can be seen according to the following rule:

$$L_{\text{actual}} = L_{\text{max}} \cos \theta \tag{3-12}$$

where L_{actual} is the amount of visually effective light which can be seen at an angle θ from a source whose emission is equal to L_{max} when viewed perpendicular to its surface.

Both photometric and radiometric units are measures of the amount of light being emitted by light sources, either in terms of physical energy or visual effect, and do not include in their formulation any information about the optical characteristics of the eye. From time to time various investigators have attempted to define units that include the necessary ocular optical corrections and, thus, to specify more precisely the light that actually falls on the retina. The absorption characteristics of the ocular media and the size of the pupil are two additional factors that one would ideally like to have included in the definition of the visual stimulus amplitude. Photometric measures do, implicitly, include estimates of the passive absorption of the visual system because of their correction by the luminosity curve, but fluctuations in the size of the pupil add a parameter of uncertainty about luminosity measurements in those instances in which total stimulus energy is important.

As an approach to such a measure of retinal, rather than corneal, illuminance, Troland (1930, p. 110) proposed a unit, defined as the luminance of a one candle per square meter light source viewed through a one square millimeter pupil. This unit, now known in his honor as the *troland,* has a number of limitations in its application but is frequently used by investigators as a more convenient way of specifying the actual and significant amplitude of the stimulus rather than the purely physical properties of the light source.

Another means of controlling retinal illuminance is to insert an artificial pupil, a small aperture, in the optic pathway close to the natural pupil. The size of the artificial pupil is usually chosen to be slightly less than the minimum size attainable by the most constricted pupil—about 2 mm for humans. When the artificial pupil is used, the magnitude of a stimulus is unaffected by the continuous fluctuations in the natural pupil and thus retinal stimulation can be held more constant than otherwise. This is particularly important in situations in which adaptive or situational variations in pupil diameter might be present.

An alternative way to guarantee that the pupil fluctuations do not inadvertently affect the light intensity is to bring all of the light to a focus exactly at the center of the pupil. Thus in an ideal situation all of the light would then pass through this focal point, and pupil contractions would have no effect on the available amount of light. Such an optical arrangement, designated a Maxwellian view, is diagramed in Fig. 3-7.

Regulation of the intensity or luminosity of the light source is usually achieved by inserting neutral density filters formed from thin sheets of plastic or wedges of varying optical density in the pathway of a constant light. The control of the light source itself is almost always ineffective because color changes usually occur with changes in driving voltage and temperature.

3. Sources of Photic Stimuli

There are several physical means of producing the particular range of photons that make up what we call ;"light." All, however, are alike in that they involve the acceleration of some kind of charged object. Indeed, all electromagnetic energy, not just the narrow range we call the visible spectrum, is created in exactly the same way—changing the velocity or direction of some moving charged particle. This act of acceleration creates photons where energy did not previously exist in this form or alters the constituent wavelengths of those that may have previously existed. All of this must be done at the expense of other energy or mass to maintain the physical balance.

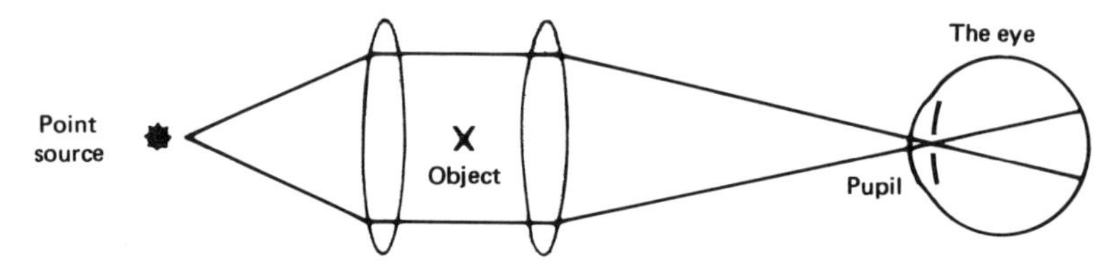

FIG. 3.7. A Maxwellian view optical system. The incident light is focused at the entrance pupil so that fluctuations in the pupil size have no effect on stimulus intensity. Objects to be imaged on the retina must be placed between the two converging lenses to be seen in sharp focus. (From Uttal, 1973.)

Five main types of photon generation processes are known.

1. Incadescence
2. Luminescence
3. Synchrotron radiation
4. Bremsstrahlung radiation
5. Inverse Compton scattering

Of these five types, only incandescence and luminescence are practical sources of controlled stimuli for perceptual experimentation.

Incandescence involves the thermal agitation of molecules. This process can be accomplished by any device capable of heating a material to the point at which it can give off light. Because the thermal agitation of molecules is a random process, all frequencies (photons of all energies) are emitted by the acceleration of the particles in an incandescent source. The spectrum (a plot of the component wavelengths of the light) is, therefore, said to be continuous. Although the spectrum may shift its peak and increase its amplitude as the temperature rises, it does remain continuous over the entire wavelength range in which the source is emitting light. The shift in the peak of the distribution is the reason that most materials, as they are heated to higher and higher temperatures, tend to shift through a precisely defined series of colors from red to yellow to bluish white. These shifts in peak emission and the increasing total amount of energy emitted are in accord with Wien's displacement law and the Stefan–Boltzmann law, respectively.

Wien's displacement law specifies the peak of the continuous emission spectrum of any incandescent source in the following manner:

$$\lambda_{peak} \cdot T = \text{Wien constant} \tag{3-13}$$

where λ_{peak} is the peak of the emission spectrum, T is the temperature in degrees Kelvin, and the Wien constant is equal to .2897 cm per degree.

The Stefan–Boltzmann law specifies that the total amount of energy (E_{Tot}) being emitted by an incandescent source varies in the following manner:

$$E_{\text{Tor}} = CT^4 \tag{3–14}$$

where C is a constant equal to 5.672×10^{-7}. Note that the energy emitted is a function of the fourth power of the temperature and thus rises very rapidly with modest increases in the temperatures of the source.

The second means of producing light is by a process called *luminescence*. Luminescent sources emit light as electrons in the atomic orbits drop from a higher orbit to a lower one. Higher orbits require more energy than lower ones, so that when such a shift occurs, surplus energy is given off, partly in the form of visible light. It should be remembered that the initial energy required to move an electron to a higher orbital level has to come from some external energy source. It may come from a chemical reaction, such as that used by luminescent insects and fungi, or from photon or electron bombardment.

The nature of luminescence is best illustrated by some brief comments on the operation of the cathode-ray tube (CRT) such as that shown in Fig. 3-8. Within a CRT, a stream of electrons is produced by applying a voltage across a resistive filament. The negatively charged electrons, "boiled" off by the thermal heating of the filament, are accelerated by a positive voltage and directed in the general direction of a luminescent material on the face of the CRT. After the electrons are properly focused and positioned by other electrostatic or electromagnetic electrodes, they impinge upon a particular point on the luminescent screen. There, the accelerated electrons, arriving at relatively high velocities, are able to "kick" other electrons out of the atomic orbits of the salts composing the screen. The vacancies so created are filled by free electrons dropping into the empty orbital

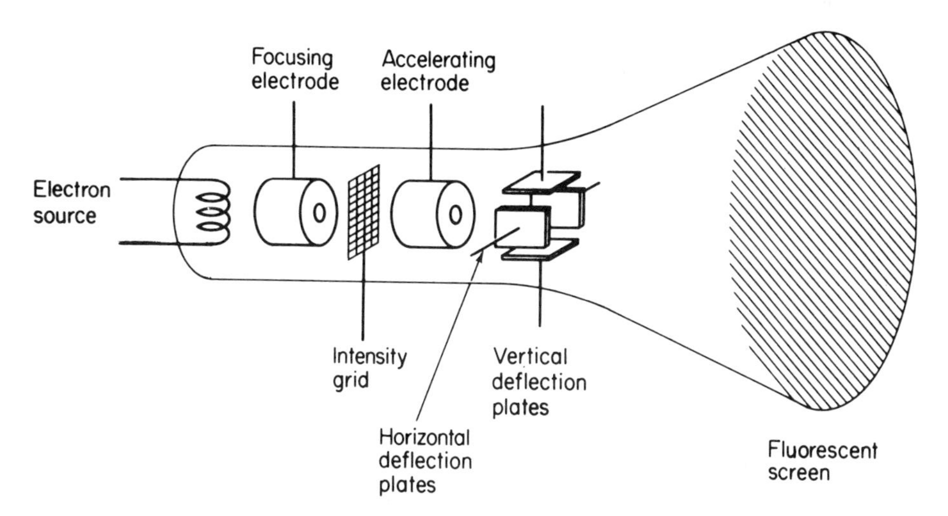

FIG. 3.8. Drawing of a cathode ray tube used in an oscilloscope. (From Uttal, 1975b.)

positions under the attractive force of the newly positively ionized atoms. In so doing, these replacement electrons must give up the excess energy that allowed them, at least temporarily, to remain outside of the atomic orbits. If the salts constituting the phosphor are correctly chosen, a substantial part of this excess is in the form of those quantum values that constitute visible light, and it is this visible light that emerges as the trace on the CRT display.

Because, in accord with quantum principles, only certain energy values are possible as the electrons fill the empty orbital positions, the light from a luminescent source, if analyzed with a spectroscope, will be found to be a series of lines rather than the continuous spectrum produced by an incandescent source. The particular lines that are present will be a function of the materials that make up the luminescent material. The deposition of different materials on the surface of a CRT can result in different wavelengths of emitted light and, therefore, such delights as color television. An excellent source of practical and useful information concerning the uses of *CRT*s in perceptual research can be found in a series of papers by George Sperling (1971a, 1971b, 1971c).

In addition to oscilloscope phosphors, light-emitting diodes (*LEDs*), lasers, and electroluminescent panels also operate on the basis of luminescent processes with the particular electron transitions in solids, gases, and fluids determining what particular wavelength lights will be emitted.

The third physical means of producing light—synchrotron generation—is hardly a practical means for carrying out psychophysical experimentation. It requires that electrons be injected into a very powerful particle accelerator and rotated in a circle at velocities very close to the speed of light. The angular acceleration involved in changing the otherwise linear path of the electron by a strong magnetic field is also able to produce visible electromagnetic radiation. Electromagnetic radiation produced by the synchrotron method is indistinguishable from radiation produced by luminescence, incandescence, or any other method, as are the outputs of any of the other methods from it. Although it has some useful properties (continuous spectra like those produced by incandescent sources can be generated from the relatively low frequencies of the far infrared to the very high frequencies associated with gamma radiation), the expense of the equipment involved makes the synchrotron method an unlikely light source for inclusion in the run-of-the-mill visual experiment. A good introduction to the characteristics and possible uses of synchrotron radiation can be found in Watson and Perlman (1978).

Synchrotron radiation can also occur naturally in cosmological situations as can the other two photon-generating processes previously mentioned—bremsstrahlung radiation and the inverse Compton effect. Bremsstrahlung radiation occurs when an electron passes close enough to an atomic nucleus so that its trajectory is changed by electromagnetic attraction or repulsion. The change in the direction of the moving particle, even if the magnitude of its velocity is not changed, is an acceleration and thus some photons must be given off. The inverse

Compton scattering process, on the other hand, occurs when a photon and an electron collide such that the electron gives up some of its energy to the photon with a resulting change in its wavelength. Though in this latter case a new photon is not created, an old one has changed its characteristic wavelength.

For obvious practical reasons, none of these latter three kinds of photon-generating processes are likely to be used in the perceptual laboratory, and the decision left to the experimenter is simply one of choosing between an incandescent and a luminescent source. Because of the low-level light intensities generally available from luminescent sources, incandescent sources have, in the past, been more often used in psychophysical experiments. But the use of incandescent sources has a number of inherent disadvantages primarily associated with their temporal and thermal characteristics. Incandescent sources must be heated to emit light, and due to the thermal inertia of the constituent parts, this often requires turn-on and turn-off periods which are quite long in comparison with the visual processes under investigation. The timing of incandescent light patterns is, therefore, generally done with shutters of one sort or another (tachistoscopes), which mechanically obscure the light. On the other hand, some fluorescent sources, which have rapid ignition times of the order of a few microseconds, have now been developed and such sources are regularly used in tachistoscopes to expose an image for a brief period of time. Even this sort of device, however, suffers from certain problems. Often these sources have an initial ultrabright transient, which, although lasting for only a millisecond or so, may interfere with the stimulus requirements of many visual threshold experiments. Oscilloscope screens themselves are often used as tachistoscopes. Phosphors, which have ignition times as short as fractions of microseconds and extinction times of a few tens of microseconds, can be chosen, but luminous intensity is usually low, and only discrete points can be plotted at high speeds. Newly available high-speed electrooptical shutters capable of manosecond flashes have just begun to be used in perceptual laboratories.

D. THE ANATOMY OF THE VISUAL SYSTEM

1. Macroanatomy of the Visual System[8]

The visual system, as I define it in this book, consists of the eyes, the ascending visual pathways, and substantial portions of the brain and brain stem. However, neural responses to photic stimuli can be detected in almost all parts of the brain. Therefore it is somewhat difficult to demarcate an exclusively visual brain from the other portions of the central nervous system. Nevertheless, the determination of the general arrangement of the major visual pathways and brain regions has

[8]Some of the material in this section is adapted from Uttal (1973) and Uttal (1978).

been a major goal of neuroanatomy and electrophysiology for hundreds of years (Lindberg, 1976), and a considerable amount of progress has been made in this regard. In this section I consider the macroanatomy of the visual system, and in the next a more microscopic analysis of the various nuclei and centers.

Figure 3-9 is a diagramatic presentation of the macroanatomy of the primary visual pathway. Beyond the retina there are at least four different pathways through which signals can pass from the retinal photoreceptors to the cerebral cortex. The "classical" geniculo-striate pathway passes through the optic nerves and tracts to the lateral geniculate bodies of the thalamus. From there, visual signals project to the occipital or striate cortex—the primary visual projection region. To add to the complexity, this major geniculo-striate pathway is probably made up of several functionally separate subpathways. These subpathways are characterized by the presence of three types of neurons that have been referred to as the *W*, *X*, and *Y* type units, respectively. The *X* and *Y* neurons were first identified on the basis of their distinctive receptive field properties by Enroth-Cugell and Robson (1966). The ganglion cells of each of these three subpathways, in addition to the differing properties of their selective sensitivity, also seem to be characterized by differences in their respective conduction velocities; *W* cells conduct slower than *X* units that themselves are slower than the *Y* units.

Another variation among the three different classes of ganglion cells, however, was in terms of the characteristic of the receptive fields. Enroth-Cugell and Robson originally reported that certain *X*-type ganglion cells had receptive fields

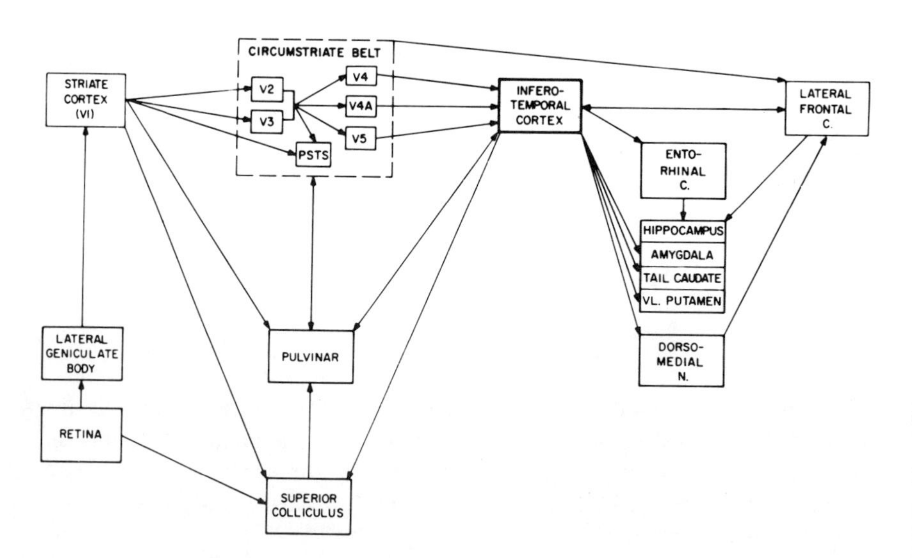

FIG. 3.9. An anatomical theory of the organization of the primate visual system. (From Gross, Bender, & Rocha-Miranda, © 1974, with the permission of the MIT Press.)

that were organized such that there was a null position somewhere in the receptive field at which a stimulus grating pattern could be presented without producing a neural response. All other portions of the receptive field did lead to a response when such a grating stimulus was presented. For *Y*-type ganglion cells, which conducted faster, there was no such null position in the receptive field, and the presentation of a grating stimulus always led to the elicitation of a response.

The third (*W*-type) class of cells was originally discovered by Hoffman, Stone, & Sherman (1972) and further described by Wilson and Stone (1975). These cells exhibit very slow conduction velocities and receptive fields that are continuously excited or inhibited by a stable contrast between different portions of the field rather than onset or offset of the stimuli.

An important fact about the *W, X,* and *Y* classification of ganglion cells is that comparable neurons have now been found in the lateral geniculate body (Sherman, Wilson, Kaas, & Webb, 1976) and thus, as noted, this trichotomous classification of neurons may actually represent three distinct communication subpathways to the visual cerebral cortex, even within the conventional geniculate–striate pathway. The *X* subpathway, it is proposed, runs from *X*-type ganglion cells in the retina to *X*-type cells in the lateral geniculative body, and thence to what are known as Hubel and Wiesel (1965) simple cells in the cerebral cortex. *Y*-type ganglion cells in the retina, on the other hand, it has been suggested, project through similar *Y* cells in the lateral geniculate body to Hubel and Wiesel complex cells in the visual cortex. The final destination of the *W* channel has not yet been established.

The velocity criterion for the *W, X, Y* trichotomy has recently been supplemented by the realization that another characteristic of ganglion cells—their response to stimulus contrast—may also represent another criterion distinguishing between the systems. Cleland, Dubin, and Levick (1971), Cleland and Levick (1972, 1974), and Ikeda and Wright (1972) have all suggested that a more fundamental distinguishing criterion for the *X–Y* dichotomy is that these cells characteristically respond with a sustained tonic or transient (phasic) response respectively. The sustained and transient characteristics of the *X* and *Y* cells have been the conceptual basis of a number of theories of visual phenomena (Breitmeyer & Ganz, 1976; Enoch, 1978).

Another important distinction between the transient responding *Y* units and the sustained responding *X* units has recently been uncovered by Cleland, Levick, and Sanderson (1973) and Ikeda and Wright (1974). These investigators have shown that the *Y* units respond best to temporal discontinuities in low spatial frequency stimuli, whereas the *X* units respond best to high spatial frequency stimuli that are continuously presented.

It is even possible that the three types of cells that were originally classified in terms of their physiological properties may also be structurally different. Boycott and Wässle (1974) have suggested an anatomical trichotomy that seems to overlap with the three functional categories. They believe *W,X,* and *Y* cells can be distinguished on structural grounds as γ (gamma), β (beta), and α (alpha) types, respectively. The problem that arises then is upon which of these several characteristics of the three categories should the classification be primarily based. Perhaps the best discussion of the problem of how to classify the W, X, and Y neurons of the visual system has been given by Rowe and Stone (1977). They point out that, in fact, all the distinguishing dimensions that I have mentioned here should contribute to the definition of the three categories rather than any single one.

A second major visual pathway passes through the ascending reticular system of the brain stem. This "reticular activating system" collects signals from several sensory modalities and is thought to be associated with nonspecific activation of most portions of the cortex. It is probably mainly associated with arousal and, therefore, is not considered in detail at this point. Its perceptual significance appears to be that it is necessary for a reticular response to occur, along with the primary projection region response, for us to be "aware" of a stimulus (Uttal & Cook, 1964).

A third visual pathway, although less well known, has received increasing attention in the past decade. G. Schneider (1969) and Trevarthen (1968) have outlined an important pathway from the retina that passes through the superior colliculus and thence to the pulvinar nucleus on its way to the cerebral cortex. The properties of this collicular pathway are somewhat different from those of the geniculo-striate pathway. The collicular pathway is characterized by neurons with very large receptive fields, and seems to be more involved in gross spatial localization than in fine form perception. Kaplan (1970) has suggested that it serves a number of functions, which are quite important and which he believes are observable in human psychophysical processes, such as walking or texture sensitivity. Schiller and Koerner (1971) have also shown this pathway to be important in the positioning of the eyes and the foveation of images rather than precise form perception. In general, the collicular pathway is thought to be involved in spatial orientation and image centering in the fovea. In addition to the retinal afferents, many other brain regions are heavily interconnected with the superior colliculus. Kurtz (1977) has summarized the anatomy of this important visual center.

Graybiel (1972, 1974) has also described a fourth visual pathway to the brain that passes through the pretectal region on its way to the pulvinar and thence to the cortex. Its function is still obscure.

Within the cortex there are many regions to which visual signals are conducted, as shown in Fig. 3-9. This figure also indicates that some of the signals initiated in the retina project directly to the striate cortex and then pass to various other visual regions of the peristriate or circumstriate cortex (V_1, V_2, V_3, etc. as described by Zeki, 1971), and from there to the inferotemporal cortex. The work of Allman and Kaas on the visual area of the owl monkey brain also points in the same direction. They (Allman and Kaas, 1974a, 1974b; 1976) have identified ten separate visual regions in this animal, all of which appear to be topographically organized.

It is important to emphasize at this point that even the fourfold set of pathways from the retina to the cortex I described here is probably incomplete. Although such demonstrations have not yet been made for primates, in frogs it is now known (personal communication from Glenn Northcutt of The University of Michigan) that there are more than 15 different pathways from the peripheral retina to the central nervous system. The specific function of each of these pathways has not yet been established (nor for that matter is it certain that they are all functional), but obviously the vertebrate visual system is a good bit more complicated than was thought even a few years ago.

According to Charles Gross and his colleagues (Gross, Bender, & Rocha-Miranda, 1974), visual pathways from the inferotemporal cortex then pass to both the frontal lobes of the brain and to subcortical areas of the brain stem, including those especially interesting ones of the limbic system. Obviously, according to current anatomical evidence, in most mammals a very large portion of the brain is potentially involved in visual function.

There are a number of other extremely important points of macroanatomy that contribute to our understanding of visual perception. For example, though the ganglion cell axons pass without synapse to the lateral geniculate body, there is a most important and significant sorting out of these fibers at the optic chiasma, the transition point that separates the part of the visual pathway known as the optic nerve from that known as the optic tract. Each retina, therefore, is functionally divided into two regions, which gather visual information from the left and right visual field, respectively. In the right eye, the right field of view is mediated by the nasal hemiretina. In the left eye, the same right view is mediated by the temporal hemiretina. On the other hand, the left-hand view for the right eye is mediated by the temporal hemiretina and in the left eye by the nasal hemiretina, as shown in Fig. 3-10.

So many different perceptual phenomena are mediated by fusion of the corresponding images from the two left- or the two right-viewing hemiretina that it is not surprising to discover that the evolutionary forces operating have produced a system in which the necessary crossovers provide exactly the anatomy needed for this image conjunction. Ganglion cell axons from the left temporal and the right nasal hemiretina project to the left cerebral hemispheres, and ganglion cell axons from the right temporal and left nasal hemiretina project to the right cerebral hemisphere. Interhemispheric connections almost certainly exist through the corpus callosum, but such processes as stereoscopic depth perception in at least half of the field could presumably be handled from each field of view within a single hemisphere without such interhemispheric communication. There is no known synaptic interaction between neurons from the two eyes at any level more peripheral than the geniculates of the thalamus.

Now consider the macroscopic structure of the eye itself. Figure 3-11 is a

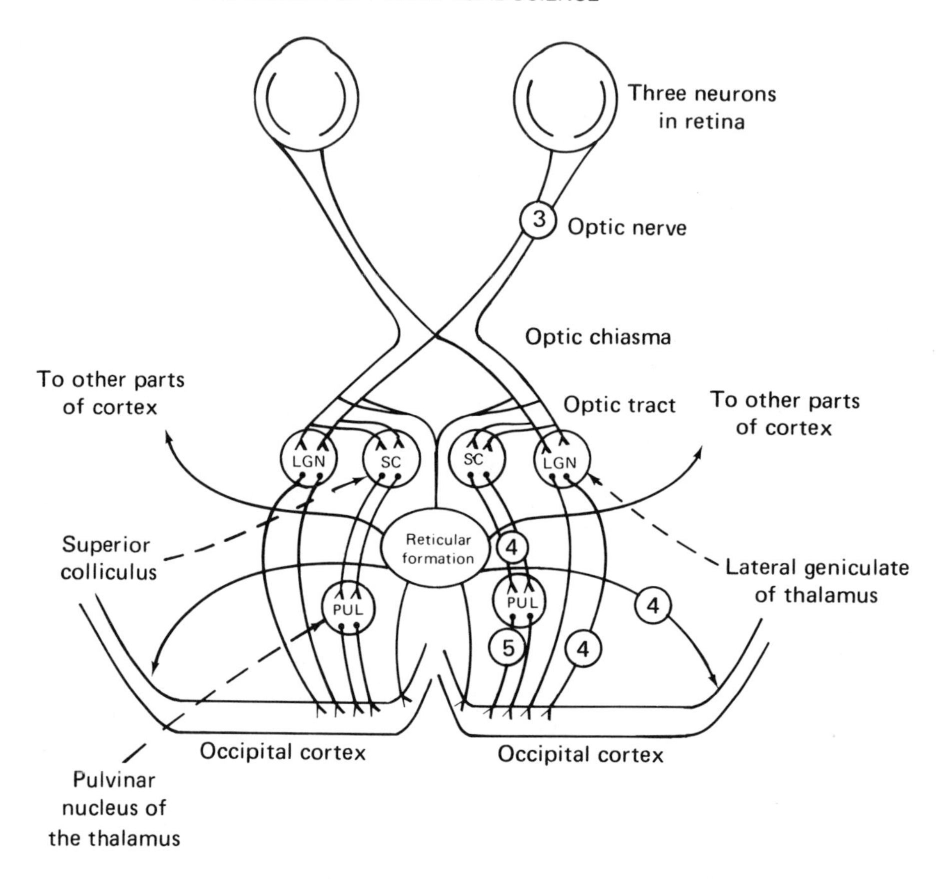

FIG. 3.10. A schematic drawing of the entire ascending visual pathway. Small circled numbers indicate the order of the neuron in the chain from the receptor to the cortex. (From Uttal, 1973.)

cross section of the human eye observed from the top. The most anterior portion of the eye is the transparent cornea, the interface between the external and internal worlds. The cornea performs passive optical functions—refraction and selective transmission—in addition to the protective and supportive functions it shares with the two other layers of the eye, the sclera and the choroid. Behind the cornea lies the anterior chamber of the eye, filled with a clear watery fluid known as the aqueous humor. Behind this anterior fluid-filled chamber lie two mechanically active units of extraordinary capability—the iris and the crystalline lens.

The iris, colored by the deposition of varous pigments, is a diaphragm composed of two counteracting muscular bands, the sphincter and the dilator. The sphincter is the anterior layer composed of muscle fibers running parallel to the perimeter of the circular iris. It is capable, upon contraction, of reducing the diameter of the pupil—the aperture in the iris—to less than 25% of its relaxed dimensions—from a maximum of about 8 mm to a minimum of about 2 mm. The dilator, on the other hand, is composed of radial muscle fibers which, when contracted, tend to pull the pupil to its maximum opening.

Pupil diameter is a function of many different variables. The amount of incident light can directly affect pupillary diameter, but the internal emotional state of the animal can also have dramatic effects. Kahneman and Beatty (1966),

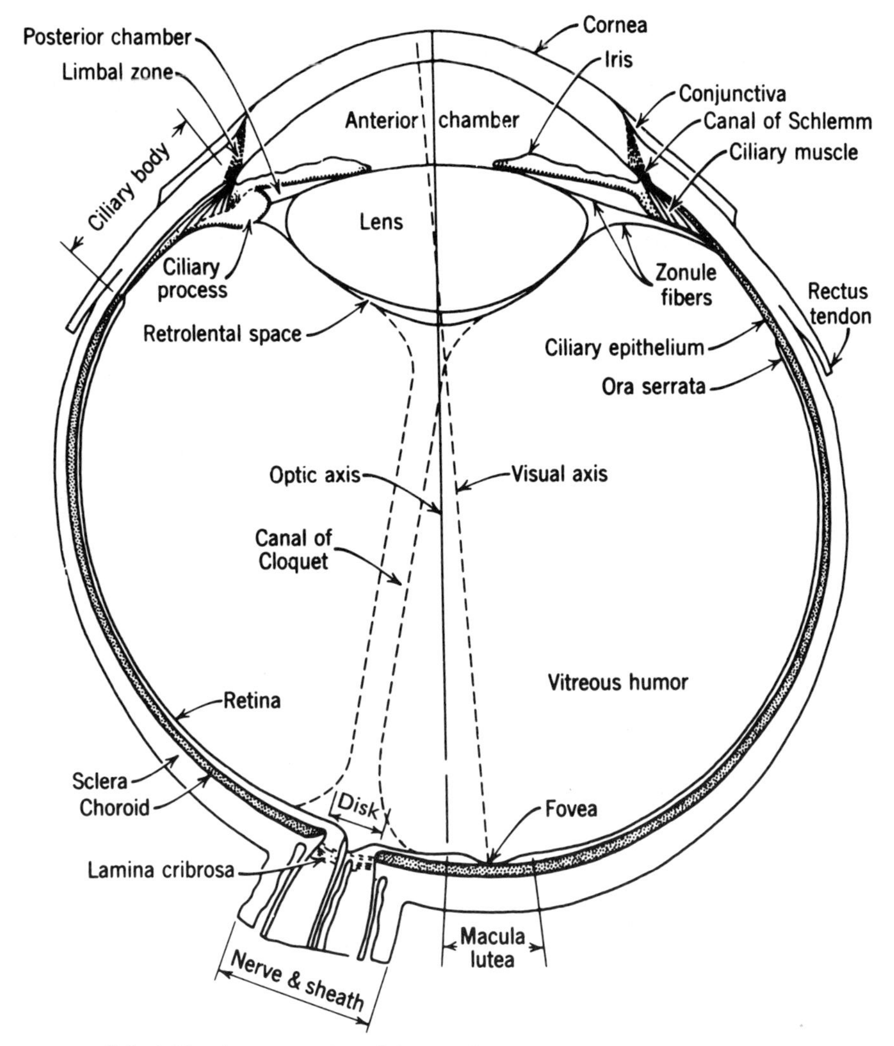

FIG. 3.11. A cross section of the eye from the top, showing many of the important structures involved in the visual process. See text for full details. (From Uttal, 1973, after Brown, 1965, after Walls, 1942, as modified from Salzmann, 1912.)

for example, have shown that such intellectual activities as mental arithmetic affect the pupil diameter. It is not too surprising then to realize that the muscles of the iris are smooth muscles controlled involuntarily by the autonomic nervous system. Dilation is stimulated by sympathetic signals, and the constrictor action of the sphincter muscle, by parasympathetic nerve action.

The action of the iris, like any other mechanical diaphragm in an optical system, can control the amount of light entering the eye. However, pupil area can vary only over a range of about 16 times the minimum size. Other neural and photochemical factors must be invoked to explain the enormously wide range of light adaptation observed in perceptual experiments. Reducing the size of the pupil, furthermore, can also increase the depth of field of clear vision and the overall sharpness of the retinal image by cutting off the rays coming from the periphery (see Chapter 6). These peripheral, oblique rays contribute more to the spherical, cylindrical, and astigmatic aberrations of the visual image than the central direct rays. Their absence, therefore, greatly decreases the amount of blur, and in a situation in which precision perception may be required this may be a truly useful advantage for an animal.

Another mechanically active tissue behind the anterior chamber is the crystalline lens. Its actions are equally as remarkable as those of the pupil but are mainly associated with image-focusing on the retina rather than with the control of stimulus intensity. The lens, as it necessarily must be, is a transparent object in the normal eye and is made up of a series of laminae very much like those of an onion. The lens is suspended by a series of ''zonule'' fibers from another muscular ring, the ciliary muscle, which lies just under the sclera below and to the outside of the iris. Details of the anatomy of the lens and its muscles are also shown in Fig. 3-11. The action of the ciliary muscle is to adjust automatically the shape of the lens to provide the appropriate focusing action for objects at differing objective distances. The lens must be flattened to provide increased focal length for objects that are far away. This is achieved by a relaxation of the ciliary muscle, producing an increased tautness of the zonule fibers in turn, overcoming the natural elasticity of the lens and thus flattening its shape. For near objects, the focal length of the lens must be shortened by making the lens less flat. This is achieved when the ciliary muscle contracts with a resulting decrease in the strain on the zonule fibers. Then the lens' natural elasticity tends to make it more spherical.

The ciliary muscle is, like the iris, also a smooth muscle controlled by the autonomic nervous system. Information about the degree of retinal blur is conducted from the central nervous systems to the autonomic nervous efferents and then to the muscles that control the lens' shape. The exact nature of this impressively effective communication link is not known.

Behind the lens lies the great posterior cavity of the eye, which is filled with the gelatinous vitreous humor. The canal of Cloquet, the dim structures shown running through the posterior chamber from the lens to the retina in Fig. 3-11, is a vestige of the pathway of the hyaloid artery, which actually connected the lens to the blood supply during the embryonic development of the eye. It degenerates during childhood.

Other gross features are also visible without magnification to an observer when he views the retina through an opthalmoscope. One of these features, which can also be seen in Fig. 3-11, is the optic disk or as it is better known, the "blind spot." It is in this region that the retinal blood vessels and the optic nerve both enter or leave the eye through a region in which there are no photoreceptors present. The eye is literally blind in this region. Another easily seen feature is the tiny bright spot, which indicates the position of the fovea. The fovea is a highly specialized region of the retina, mediating the most spatially and chromatically acute visual processes, due mainly to the fact that it is here that the maximal density of cones occur. A reddish-yellow region surrounding the fovea is also apparent. This is the macula, of which I have considerably more to say in Chapter 5.

2. The Microanatomy of the Retina

Now that the general arrangement of the visual system has been described, we can descend to a considerably more microscopic universe in which the individual neurons become the target of the discussion rather than nuclei or entire nerves.

a. General

Most important of all ocular structures, and the *raison d'être* for the presence of all the other accessory structures, is the retina. This tissue, visible only as a slight discoloration at the gross level at which I have been discussing ocular anatomy up to now, contains the critically important receptor cells and the neural plexus, mediating transduction and initial neural information processing, respectively. To appreciate the structure and the significance of this highly important receptor tissue, we must take our first step down into the microscopic world. Our guide in this exploration initially will be the two volumes that sum up the monumental work of Steven Polyak (1941, 1957). Polyak dedicated his entire life to the study of the optical micrography of the primate retina. Recently an equally formidable modern coverage of the same subject has been written by R. W. Rodieck (1973). This new volume is also an important modern source of information on retinal anatomy and physiology.

Figure 3-12 is a pair of microphotographic cross sections of the human retina taken from a region near the fovea. First, note the optic nerve and the foveal "pit." Then the reader should note the thinness of this tissue. The retina is exceedingly delicate, varying in thickness from 125 μ at the fovea to about 300 μ at the periphery, and even then, this frail tissue contains 10 distinguishable structural layers. Even more surprising than the delicacy of the tissue, however, is the fact that the retina seems to be inverted. Light comes in from the outer

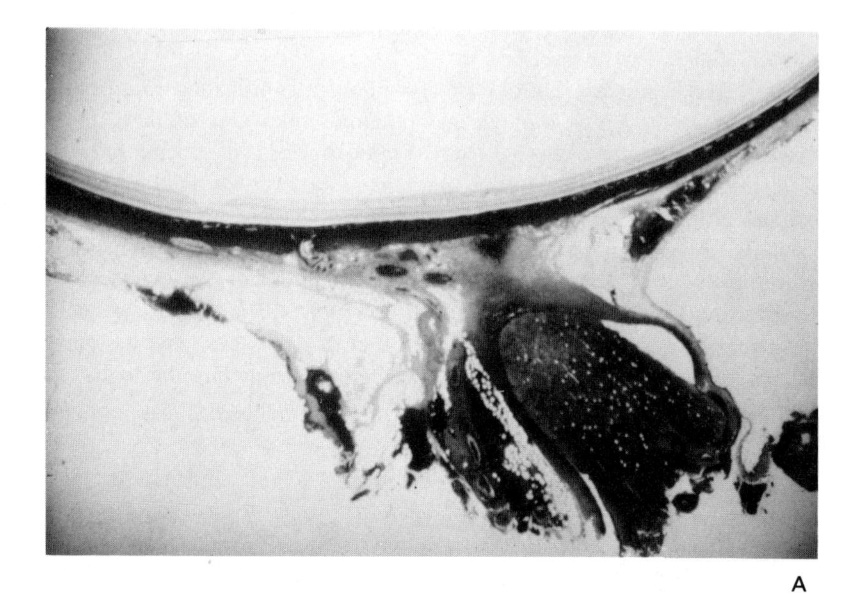

A

B

FIG. 3.12. A photographic cross section of the foveal region of a monkey retina. (A) Low magnification—note, the stump of the optic nerve and the foveal cup. (B) High magnification in the region of the foveal cup. Courtesy of Professor Mitchell Glickstein of Brown University.

world after having passed through the ocular media. Before the light arrives at the photoreceptors themselves (the delicate vertical lines at the bottom of Fig. 3-12B), it must traverse the entire thickness of the other neural and supporting cell layers of the retina. The absorption of visible light by these initial layers is relatively slight, fortunately, for they are nearly transparent in the normal living eye. Nevertheless, it is measurable and, therefore, it is especially important that the absorption spectrum of this tissue, as well as that of the lens and vitreous, be understood and corrected for in any calculations that attempt to distinguish absorption spectra of the retinal receptors from that of the whole eye.

Looking at Fig. 3-12B once again, we see that there are three main cellular layers in the vertebrate retina. The initial cellular layer (the term *initial* is defined here in functional terms) consists of the photoreceptors. The second cellular layer is composed of short bipolar cells, which convey information from the receptors to the third layer, the ganglion cells, whose axons make up the optic nerve and pass without a synapse to the thalamus.

Interspersed among the bipolar cells are certain newly discovered neurons, structurally quite similar to the bipolar cells, but conducting in the opposite direction. These "interplexiform" cells (Boycott, Dowling, Fisher, Kolb, & Laties, 1975; Dowling, Ehinger, & Hedden, 1976) convey information from the inner to the outer plexiform layers, i.e., in a centrifugal rather than afferent direction.

Figure 3-13 is a much more diagramatic sketch, from Ruch's (1965) modification of a Polyak drawing, which defines the 10 different regions of the retina to which I have referred. This division is based upon the cellular anatomy and also indicates some other structures I have not described in detail. Figure 3-13 shows the presence of various kinds of laterally connecting horizontal cells at the intersection of the receptors and bipolars (the outer plexiform layer) and amacrine cells at the intersection of the bipolars and the ganglion cells (the inner plexiform layer). But this drawing is highly diagramatic and induces a gross underestimation of the real microscopic complexity of the retina.

b. The Photoreceptors

The photoreceptor layer in all vertebrate eyes is made up of one or both of two highly specialized types of neurons. These cells have been distinguished on the basis of their shape, and named rods and cones. However, it is clear from surveying the anatomical literature that this dichotomy refers to what is actually a continuously graded series of cells of varying shape. There are both rodlike cones and conelike rods to be found in the primate retina. The two types of cells do differ in their function, and retinal electrophysiology and psychophysiological findings are frequently explained in terms of the presence of two kinds of photoreceptors (the theory of the duplex retina). They also differ in the respective densities with which they are distributed across the retina. The rods and cones themselves have only minimum axons, if their terminal axonal brushes can be

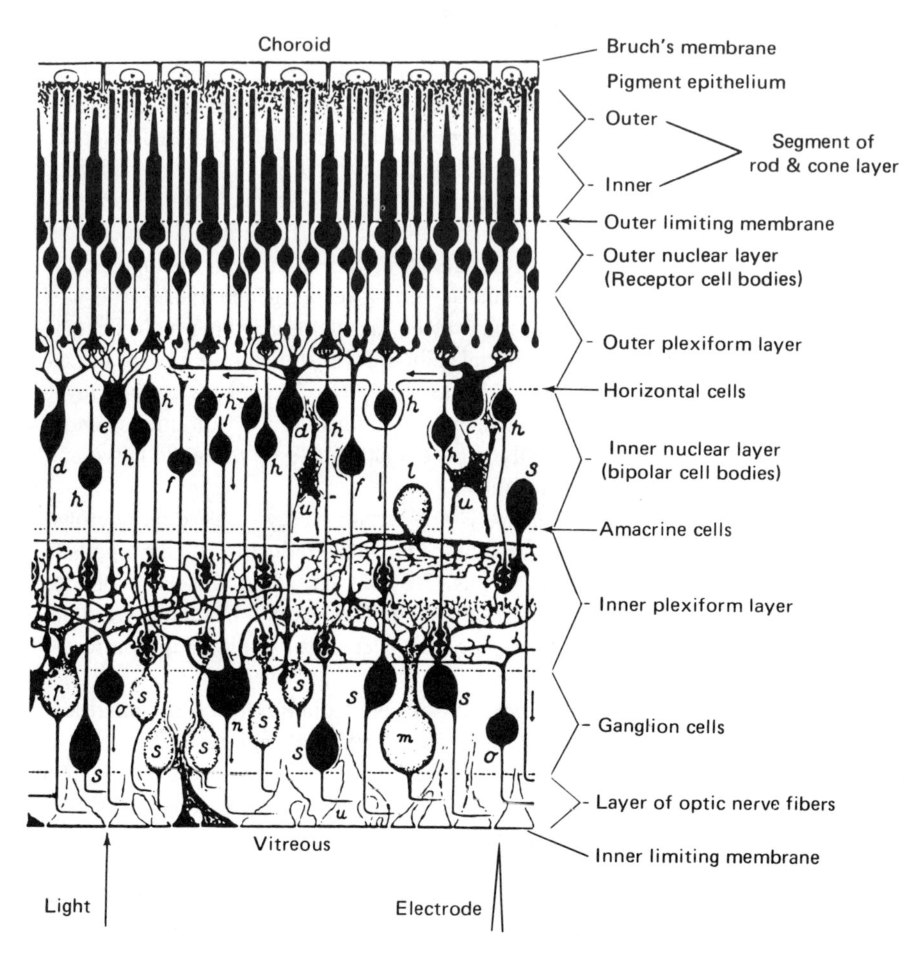

FIG. 3.13. Diagrammatic rendition of a cross section of the retina at a region that has both rods and cones present. The normal direction of incident light and of an electrode penetration are shown. (This diagram, from Ruch and Patton [1965] has been modified from an earlier drawing by Polyak [1941] and is used through the courtesy of Mrs. Stephen Polyak.)

dignified at all with that nomenclature. They synapse almost immediately with the layer of bipolar cells and other horizontally interconnecting cells.

It is now well established that there are three different kinds of cones (most directly characterized by the differences in the peak absorption wavelength of the absorption spectra of the photochemicals they respectively contain) in the primate and teleost retinae, as determined by microspectrophotometric measurements of individual cones (Marks, W., Dobelle, & MacNichol, 1964; Brown, P., and Wald, 1964; Marks, W., 1965). The differences in the absorption spectra of the three different cones are attributable to the different photochemicals contained within the outer segment of each receptor, but these receptor cells do not appear to differ at all with regard to their shape. They do, however, differ with regard to their distribution across the retinal mosaic as has been shown by Marc and Sperling (1977). These researchers perfused the retina of ennucleated baboon eyes with nitroblue tetrazolium chloride (NTC), a chemical possessing the highly useful property of being converted into another substance, nitroblue tetrazolium chloride diformazon (NTCD), in those cones that have been activated by light. Thus, by stimulating the eye with long-, medium-, and short-wavelength light, respectively, Marc and Sperling were able to map out the loci of those cones that were sensitive to the three wavelength bands by staining the retina with dyes specific to NTCD. Sample results of their studies are shown in Fig. 3-14. The overall conclusions drawn by Marc and Sperling from their analysis of these maps were that there were many more "green" cones than "red" ones, more "red" ones than "blue" ones, and that the "red" and "green" cones were distributed randomly across the entire retina. The "blue" cones, on the other hand, appeared to be present predominantly in the annular region surrounding the fovea. The estimated density distributions are shown in Fig. 3-15.

Another important development in recent years has been a substantial increase in knowledge concerning the microstructure of the rods and cones themselves. The typical microanatomy of a rod and of a cone are illustrated in Fig. 3-16 and, somewhat magnified, in Fig. 3-17. These figures illustrate a number of important points. Both the rod and cone are seen to be composed of two main parts: (1) an inner segment containing the cell nucleus; and (2) the foot (on which lie the synaptic contacts) separated by a thin stalk from an outer segment containing disks in which the light-sensitive photochemicals are enclosed. The structure of the rod, however, can be seen to be not only architecturally different from the cone, but a close examination also suggests a developmental difference of considerable importance. Figure 3-17 shows that the outer segments of rods, like those of cones, are composed of a series of disks or plates. These intracellular disks are, according to current theory, produced by invaginations of the cell membrane at the base of the outer segment in both rods and cones. In the rod the disks are totally disconnected from the outer membrane of the cell; in the cone, one edge remains connected to the plasma membrane of the outer segment.

Careful microscopic examination of the region beyond rod outer segments has shown debris apparently made up of fragments of cast-off, free-floating rod disks, as diagrammatically exemplified in Fig. 3-16. Radiographic tracer techniques that track the development of rod disks, show that new protein is first incorporated into newly forming disks near the bottom of the outer segment, and then these new disks gradually migrate to the end of the outer segment, there to disappear. The ultimate disappearance of the labeled disk at the terminus of the outer segment is apparently associated with its "casting off" at the end of its useful lifetime. In sum, it seems that the disks in the outer segments of rods are in

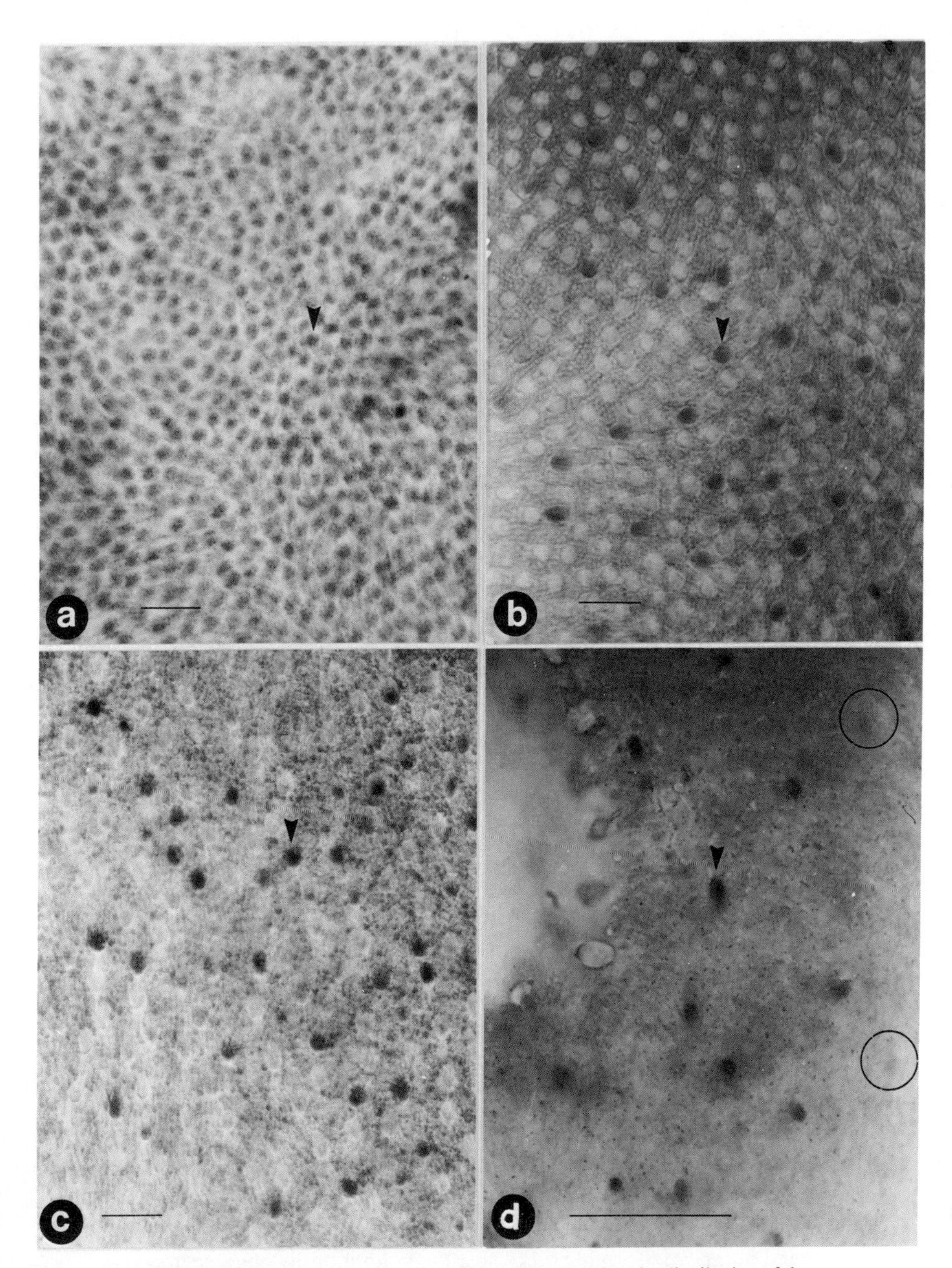

FIG. 3.14. Photomicrographs of a baboon retina showing the distribution of the three different kinds of cones. (A) White light exposure at 10 deg eccentricity; (B) blue light exposure at 25 deg eccentricity; (C) red light at 40 deg eccentricity; and (D) blue light at the center of the fovea. Arrows indicate stained cones (sample). Circles indicated out of focus stained cones (sample). (From Marc and Sperling, © 1977, with the permission of the American Association for the Advancement of Science.)

a constant state of disintegration at their apical end and reconstitution from their basal end. Disks in the rods, unconnected to either the rod outer segment plasma membrane or to each other are therefore transient structures in a constant state of replacement.

Disks in the outer segment of the cone, on the other hand, are always partially attached to the cell membrane and to each other and are probably open to the external environment, as shown in Fig. 3-17. These disks do not migrate but are

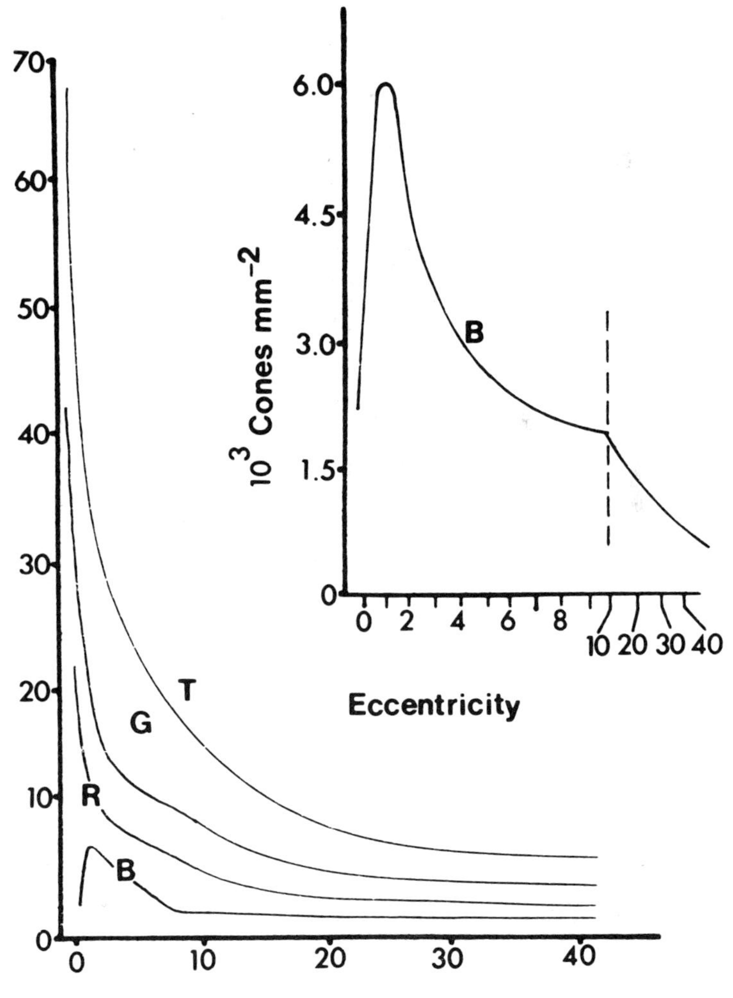

FIG. 3.15. Cone density as a function of eccentricity (T = total; R = long wavelength sensitive cones; G = medium wavelength sensitive cones; and B = short wavelength sensitive cones). Insert is an enlargement of B curve. (From Marc and Sperling, © 1977, with the permission of the American Association for the Advancement of Science.)

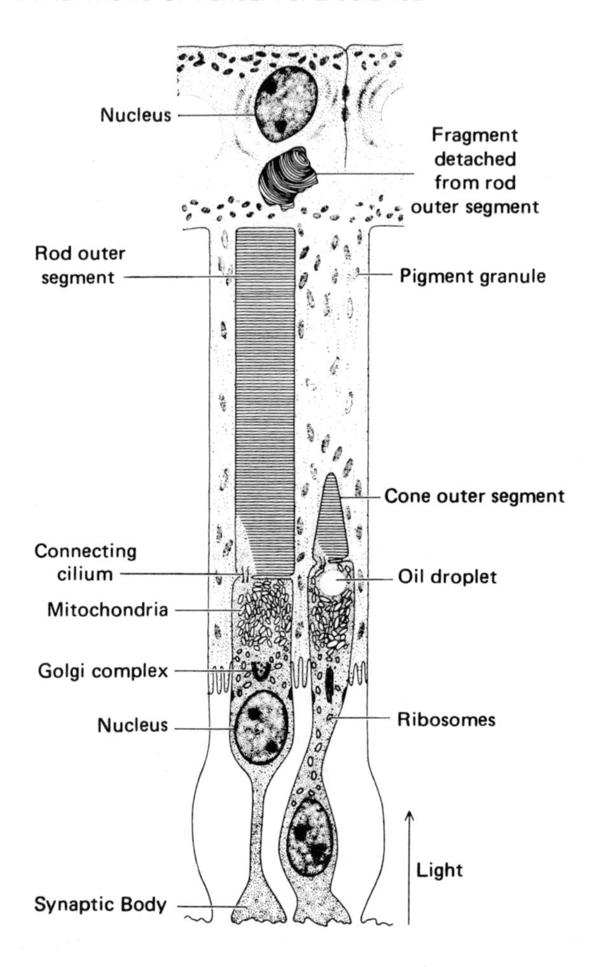

FIG. 3.16. Drawing of a single rod and a single cone from a frog, showing the characteristic difference in shape. This figure also shows the connecting cilium, a feature not visible until electronmicrographs were taken of this cell. (Courtesy of Dr. R. W. Young of the University of California at Los Angeles.)

fixed in their initial position. The intradisk photochemicals are replenished by a circulation of nutrient materials through the cone's outer segment. In fact, it is believed that the cones are predominantly cone-shaped primarily because the outermost segments were created early in the life of the animal and the more proximal larger ones later in its development. No further development of new disks occurs in cones after the animal has matured. Support for the idea that only cone disks are, in fact, open to the extracellular fluids comes from a study by Laties and Liebman (1970), using a dye that has the property of not being able to cross the plasma membrane of a cell. The dye was taken up by cone outer segments but not by those of rods.

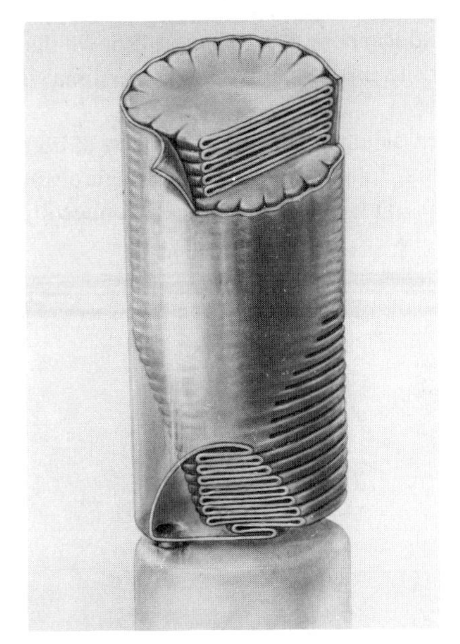
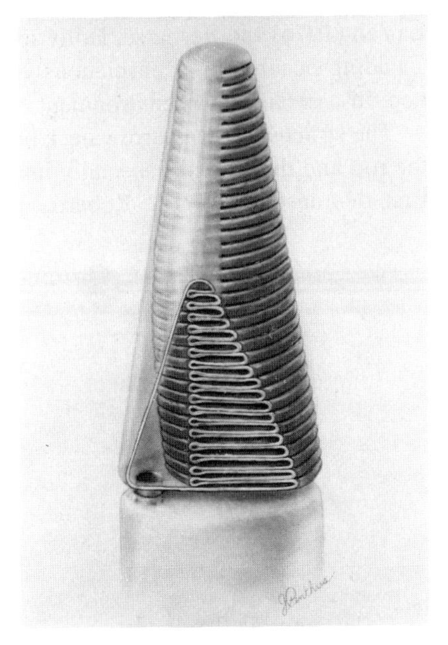

FIG. 3.17. Drawing at an even further magnification of the outer segments of a rod and of a cone. There is a characteristic difference between the two in the manner the disks are formed. In a rod the disks are formed from invaginations of the cell membrane, but gradually become detached from it as they migrate toward the terminal end. In the cone there is no such disk migration, and the disks remain fused to the outer cell membrane throughout the life of the cell. (Courtesy of Dr. R. W. Young of the University of California at Los Angeles.)

Major differences in the embryological development of the rods and cones of the tadpole have been brilliantly demonstrated by Nilsson (1964, 1969), whose work on photoreceptor ontogeny is considered to be definitive. Figure 3-18 shows the development of a cone, and Fig. 3-19 shows the development of a typical rod and the different stages in the growth of the disks.

The generally accepted dogma that cone and rod disks have substantially different structural properties has, however, been recently challenged. Anderson and Fisher (1975) have suggested that both rods and cones shed the outer discs and, in at least some vertebrates, that both can regenerate new disks by invagination near their base. In the tree squirrel, the animal they studied, however, the cones and rods are very similar. Figure 3-20 shows the similarity between these two and also the manner in which the shedding is believed by Anderson and Fisher to occur. It is possible that in this animal the two types of receptor are more alike than usual, not only in their anatomy, but also in their development, and that this animal represents an anomaly rather than a good general model of disk structure.

Other recent evidence has begun to point to the photostimulation process itself as the initiating factor for the shedding of rod (and perhaps cone) outer disks.

LaVail (1976) and Besharse, Hollyfield, and Rayborn (1977) have all shown that shedding occurs most conspicuously after the onset of light when an animal is kept in a cyclically lit environment.

The structure of the narrow neck between the inner and outer segments of both the rod and the cone is especially interesting. Its ultramicroscopic structure was first demonstrated by de Robertis (1956). This narrow neck, or connecting

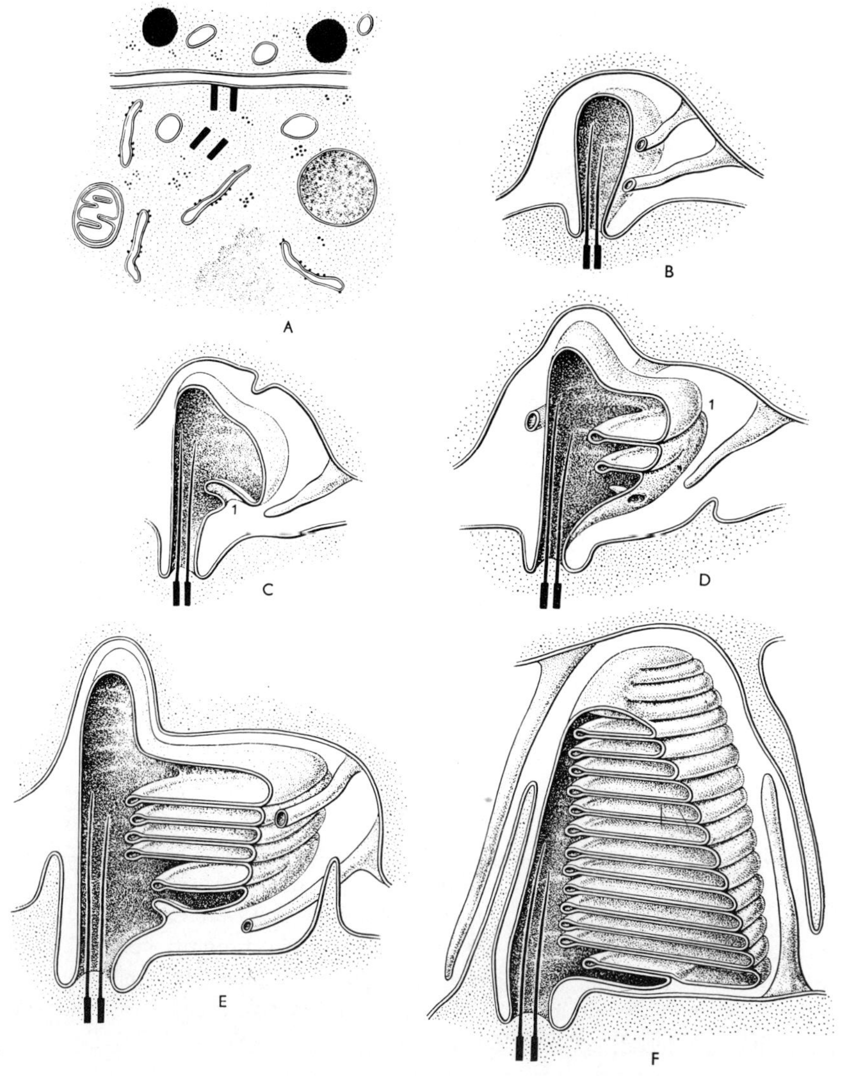

FIG. 3.18. A series of figures showing the embryological development of cone outer segments in the tadpole retina. (From Nilsson, © 1964, with the permission of Academic Press.)

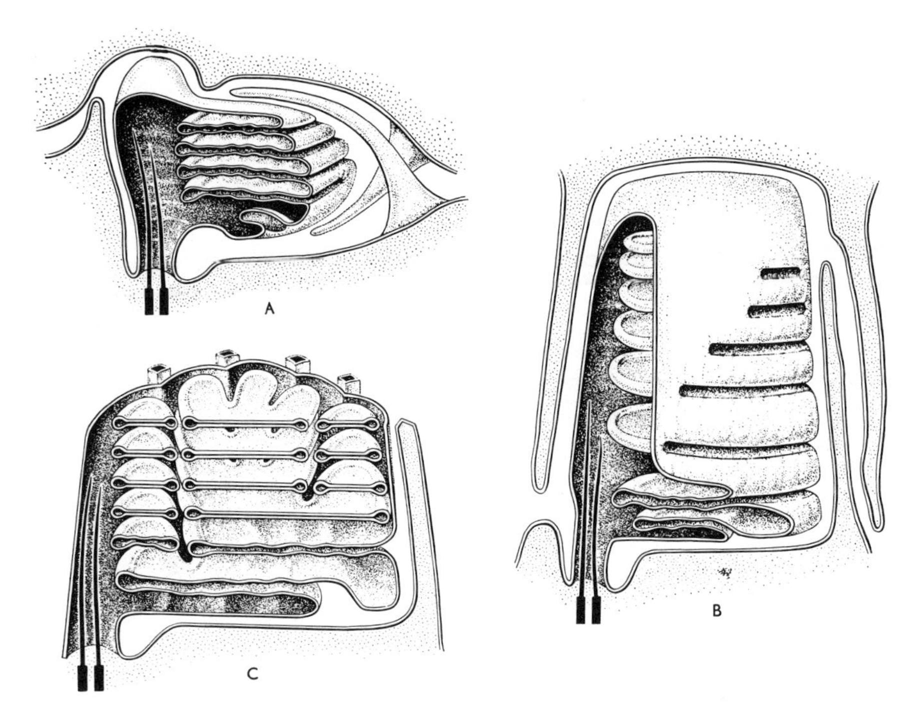

FIG. 3.19. A series of figures showing the embryological development of rod outer segments in the tadpole retina. (From Nilsson, © 1964, with the permission of Academic Press.)

cilium, shown greatly enlarged in Fig. 3-21, has a rather complex structure of its own; it is threaded with fine filaments. In spite of its small cross section, all the nutrient materials necessary for normal cell metabolism and for the regeneration of photochemicals following visual stimulation must flow through this narrow cilium because the metabolic factory and controller, the cell nucleus, is located in the inner segment, and it is there that the nutrients are produced.

Figure 3-22 illustrates the fineness of the microscopic scale at this level of cellular ultramicroscopy. The smallest discriminable structures are the membranes of the disks within the outer segment. These are only about 40 angstrom units in thickness.

c. *The Outer Plexiform Layer*

The outer plexiform layer is the tangle of receptor cell feet and dendritic arborizations at the junction between the photoreceptors, the horizontal cells, and the bipolars. What so far may have seemed to be a relatively straightforward and simple organization is belied by the actual complexity of this thicket as it has been unravelled by Sjöstrand (1969, 1974, 1976). Sjöstrand's work is clearly a

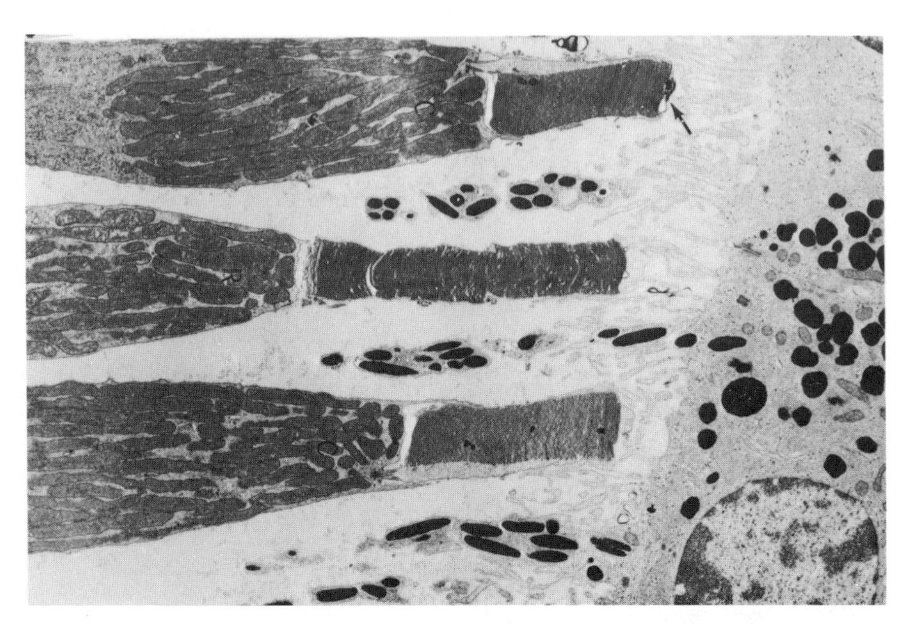

FIG. 3.20. Rods and cones from the ground squirrel showing possible shedding of cone discs. × 7200. (From Anderson and Fisher, © 1976, with the permission of Academic Press.)

tour de force of modern neuroanatomy, involving as it did a nearly complete synaptic analysis of what proved to be the extremely complex network of interaction of a single photoreceptor cell from the retina of an individual rabbit.

Sjöstrand's technique was so unusual that it is worthy of some special comment. His approach to this ultramicroscopic neuroanatomic problem, as I have said, was to concentrate all of his attention on the synaptic connections at the foot of a single photoreceptor. To achieve this, he prepared and examined a sequential series of sections of the neuropil (the tangle of neural structures) at the foot of a single receptor with conventional transmission electronmicroscopy. From the electronmicrographs, prints of successive sections were made on sheets of transparent plastic. These enlarged prints were then actually physically assembled into a three-dimensional model of the region, representing a magnification 24,000 times the size of the original portion of the outer plexiform layer. Though I have not been able to reproduce the color photographs of this model in this book, the interested reader is strongly advised to look at Fig. 16, 17, and 18 in Sjöstrand (1974) for a view of his extraordinary achievement.

Based upon the map that this model represented, Sjöstrand then made drawings of the arrangement of the network as he interpreted them from the micrographically constructed model. Finally a schematic circuit diagram was prepared indicating the specific details of the large number of synaptic connections at the base of the photoreceptor neuron.

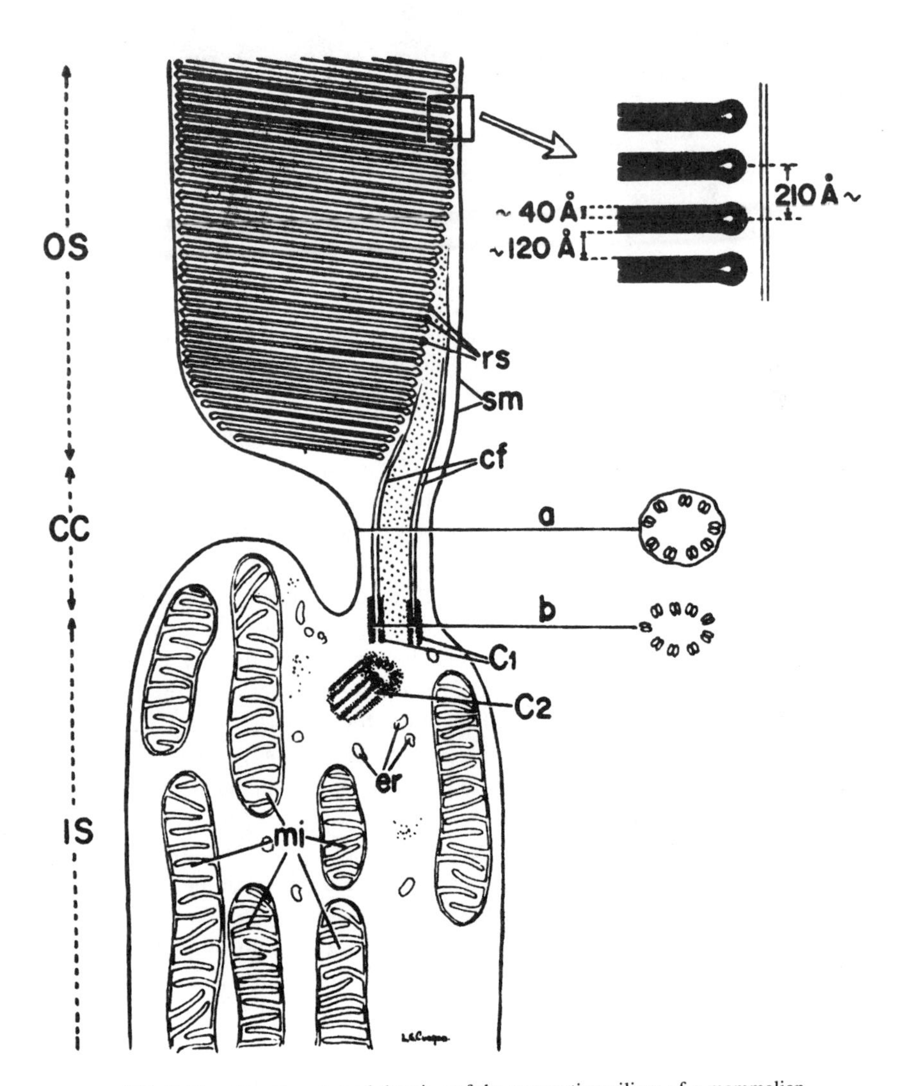

FIG. 3.21. Greatly enlarged drawing of the connecting cilium of a mammalian rod: OS = outer segment; CC = connecting cilium; IS = inner segment; cf = ciliary filaments; sm = plasm membrane; rs = rod discs; mi = mitochondria; er = endoplasmic reticulum; C_1 and C_2 are side and cross-sectional views of the basal bodies. Note the ultramiscroscopic dimensions of the discs shown in the inset. (From De Robertis, © 1956, with the permission of the Rockefeller University Press.)

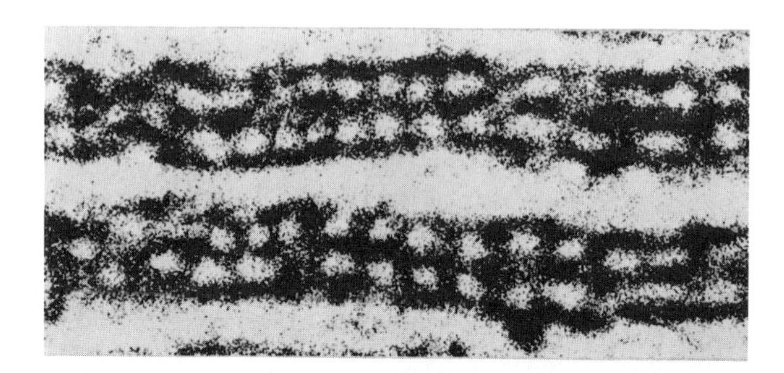

FIG. 3.22. Ultramicrographs of the fine structure of rod disc membranes showing the triple layer characteristic of all plasma membranes. × 800,000. (From Nilsson, © 1965, with the permission of Academic Press.)

Now that I have briefly described Sjöstrand's general method, let's look in more detail at the specific arrangement of this single portion of the outer plexiform layer that was produced by his Herculean effort. Sjöstrand denoted the particular receptor cell with which he worked by the code *β-RC1*, where β (beta) referred to a cell type, *RC* indicated that it was a receptor cell, and 1 was its serial code number. It is possible but could not be confirmed by Sjöstrand that all β-type photoreceptors were cones. A second class of receptors, denoted as α- (alpha) type cells, were possibly rods, but the microscopy did not allow simultaneous examination of the outer segment and the subreceptor neuropil to make this tentative identification positive. Below the foot of β-*RC*1, lay the complicated neuropil of processes from this receptor and from horizontal and bipolar cells. Sjöstrand also tagged each of these processes that could be identified with a particular serial number.

Many of the subprocesses made synaptic contact with the photoreceptor cell itself, but in contrast to the apparent randomly tangled thicket of the neuropil, the actual junctions were structures of a highly regular form called *synaptic ribbon complexes*. In the retina of the rabbit, at least, synaptic ribbon complexes seemed to be the standard junction for β-type receptor cells. Figure 3-23 is a sample drawing of one such ribbon complex and, it can be seen that the synaptic junctions are actually made within an invagination of the receptor membrane itself. In the particular case pictured, the complex consists of junctions from two horizontal cells and a single bipolar cell, but other more or less standard synaptic types involving larger or smaller numbers of neurons were also observed by Sjöstrand. A particularly interesting point is that the three nonreceptor cells involved in this region of neuropil were actually synaptically interconnected with each other, in addition to their synapse with β-*RC*1, thus providing a locus for a high order of integrative information processing even at this most peripheral synaptic level. Some other types of synapses were also present on β-*RC*1; single processes made both invaginated and superficial contact with the photoreceptor foot.

The most important general point, so eloquently emphasized by Sjöstrand's work, is that, at least in the region of the rabbit's retina he studied, each photoreceptor is interconnected with many bipolars and horizontal cells. Sjöstrand measured 10 bipolar processes and 9 horizontal processes making contact with *βRC*1, by means of 16 distinguishable synaptic ribbon complexes. Considering all the combinations of these neurons and their constituent processes, the potential for information processing is obviously very great.

These words, however, do not convey the full impact of Sjöstrand's discoveries; the magnitude of his contribution can be supported most effectively by Fig. 3-24 and 3-25. Figure 3-24 is a transmission electron micrograph showing a sample of his original electron micrographs. In this figure each number represents a particular connecting process, and each letter indicates a single synaptic ribbon complex. A large number of microphotographs of this sort were made at different depths and at different lateral positions to construct the three-dimensional model.

From that model, interpretive drawings like that shown in Fig. 3-25 were prepared. This particular drawing is a reconstruction of the neuropil below *β-RC* 1. The complexity of this neuropil is obvious, but even this picture underestimates the situation. The portion of the neuropil shown is only a part of the full picture. Not only are other processes involved that are not shown, but the synaptic junctions with the photoreceptor are not indicated in this drawing. By drawing a large number of such pictures, however, Sjöstrand (1974) was able to track down each process and to develop for each the following kind of verbal description:

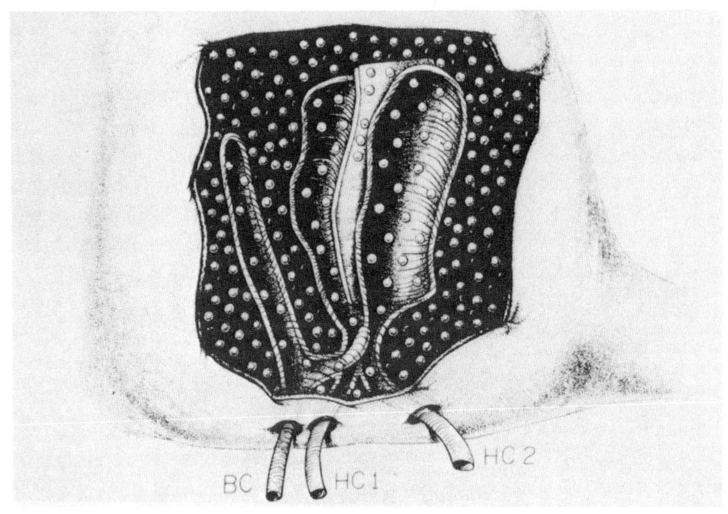

FIG. 3.23. A diagram of a typical synaptic ribbon complex. HC1 and HC2 are horizontal cell endings, and BC is a bipolar cell ending. (From Sjöstrand, © 1976, with the permission of Pergamon Press.)

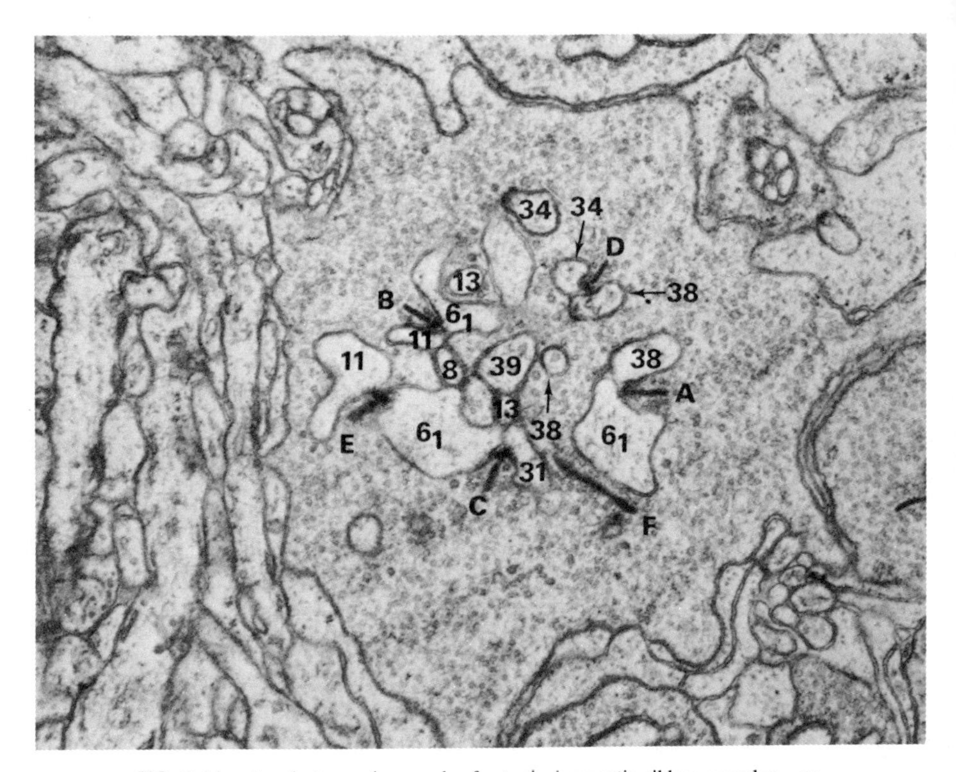

FIG. 3.24. An electron micrograph of a typical synaptic ribbon complex—an example of the raw data in Sjöstrand's heroic study. (From Sjöstrand, © 1976, with the permission of Pergamon Press.)

Process 11 (Fig. 1–14, 16–21) was a large (diameter 2 μm) horizontal cell process extending in a west-to-east direction which sent off a large branch south of the terminal. This branch extended in a south-to-north direction and passed directly vitread to the subsynaptic neuropil of the terminal. Here it sent off a thin branch in a sclerad direction into the subsynaptic neuropil. This branch split up into a number of end branches contributing endings to the following synaptic ribbon complexes: *B, E, F, G, H, L, N, O,* and *P;* that is, to nine such complexes.

The terminal of *β-RC*1 was the first terminal contacted by this branch after branching off from the main trunk. [p. 149]

Figure 3-26 presents a more schematic circuit diagram summarizing the arrangement of all 19 processes and all 16 synaptic complexes as traced out by this method. It should not be forgotten that this complex circuit diagram is only of the synaptic connections of a single photoreceptor! This typical network is repeated for hundreds of thousands of other receptors in each eye. Sjöstrand, understandably, notes that it is unlikely that this approach will become a common procedure for the analysis of photoreceptor structure. He also wisely emphasizes the enormous variety of integrative mechanisms that is possible in a network such as this. The outer plexiform layer, he therefore suggests, probably has been underestimated in terms of its possible neural information-processing power. In fact, Sjöstrand concludes that it is actually more complex than the microscopically more conspicuous and thicker inner plexiform layer, which, because it is composed of relatively larger cellular processes, may actually be simpler in its network organization.

d. The Inner Plexiform Layer

No comparable study of the inner plexiform layer comparable to Sjöstrand's heroic effort has yet been carried out. A less richly detailed study of inner plexiform organization, however, has been reported by M. W. Dubin (1970) on that retinal layer where the bipolars, the amacrine, and the ganglion cells of the retina interact. Although Dubin notes that there is considerable difference among

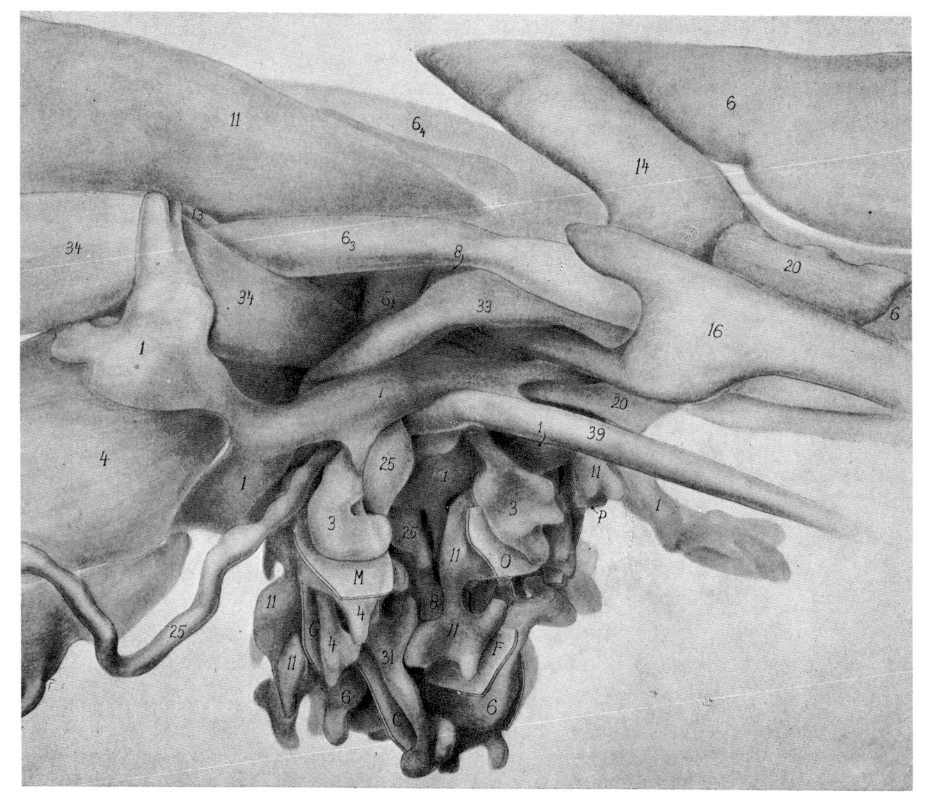

FIG. 3.25. A three-dimensional reconstruction of the neuropil at the base of a single rabbit receptor cell. (From Sjöstrand, © 1976, with the permission of Pergamon Press.)

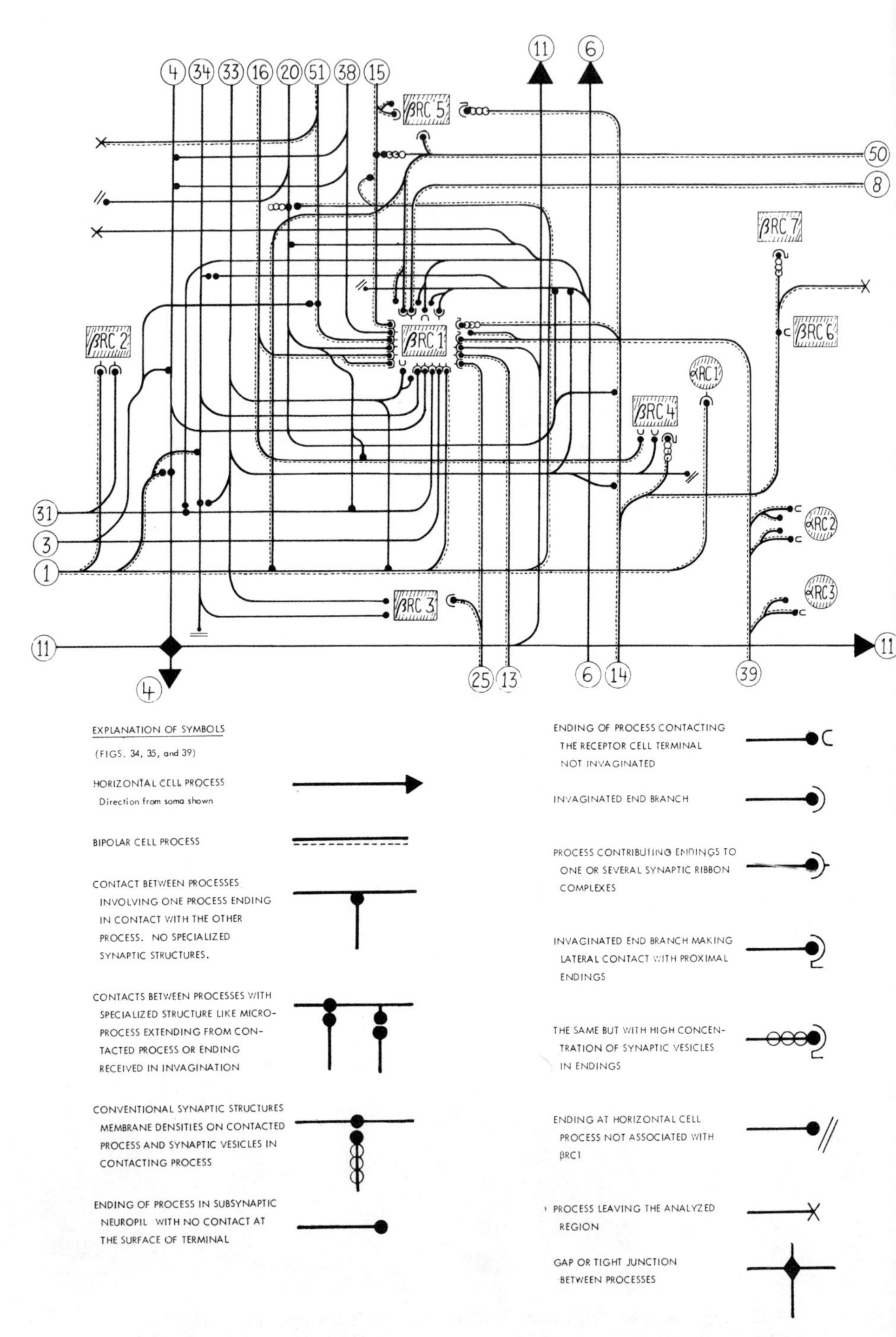

FIG. 3.26. A circuit diagram of the neuropil shown in Fig. 3.24 and 3.25. Numbers here decode the number used in Fig. 3.24 and 3.25. (From Sjöstrand, © 1976, with the permission of Pergamon Press.)

species with regard to the structure here, he believes that a general pattern of organization is found in all vertebrate retinal inner plexiform layers. Typically, several distinct types of synaptic junctions are to be found in this region. These have been classified by Kidd (1962) as conventional, spine, ribbon, and serial types: The relative proportion of each of the different types is known to vary between species. Dubin, on the basis of quantitative measures of the proportion of these different types of synapses proposes that the inner plexiform layer is organized as shown in Fig. 3-27. Some of the interesting facets of this detailed characterization are that there can be both direct and indirect communication between the bipolars and the ganglion cells. In the indirect route, one or more amacrine cells may serve as the intermediary links in the communication chain. We also now know of the centrifugally conducting interplexiform cells. If we extrapolate the work on the outer plexiform layer to this inner one, it is likely that a much more complex network is likely to be present than is actually indicated by the relatively modest magnification used in this drawing.

In concluding this section, I should note that I have concentrated on the anatomy of the neurons of the retina and did not intend so spend very much time reinstructing my readers in general neurophysiology. There is one special

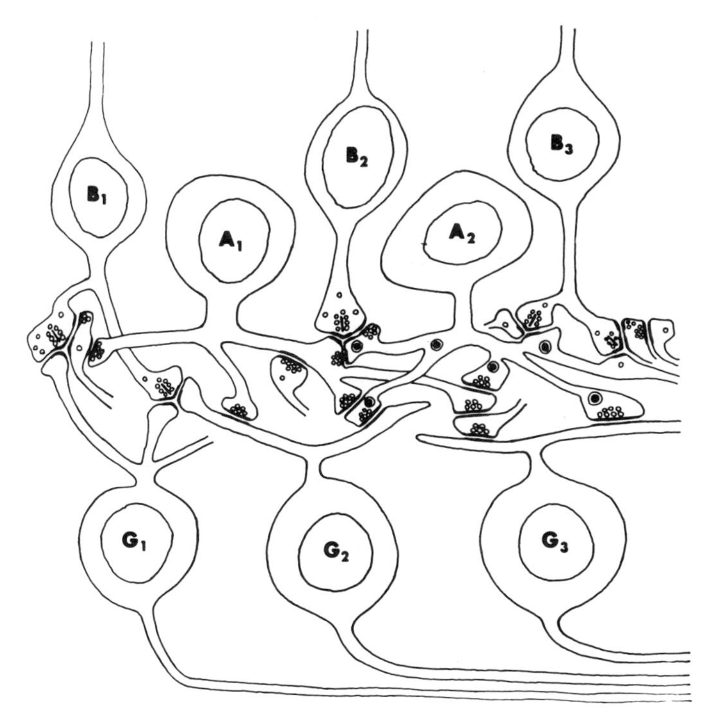

FIG. 3.27. The organization of the inner plexiform layer. (From Dubin, © 1970, with the permission of The Wistar Institute Press.)

neurophysiological detail particular to the retina that must be mentioned, however. The neurons of the retina are not all capable of producing the same kind of neural responses. Receptors, horizontal cells, and bipolars respond only with a graded, non-propagating electrophysiological response. It is only when one records from the amacrine cells and the ganglion cells that the classic, propagating, nondecremental spike action potential is first obtained. The characteristic response of each of the main retinal neurons is shown in Fig. 3-28.

Finally, the serial reconstruction method used by Sjöstrand has recently been applied by Stevens, McGuire, and Sterling (1980) to study the anatomy of ganglion cells in a cat's retina. Following Boycott and Wässle's (1974) nomenclature, ganglion cells were classified into three different categories (α, β, γ) on the basis of their size and dendritic branching patterns. The α ganglion cells were the largest with the β and γ progressively smaller. Some sample shapes falling into each of these categories are shown in Fig. 3-29. Each of the black dots in this figure indicates a synaptic contact, once again illustrating the ample and elaborate opportunity for neural integration in the retina.

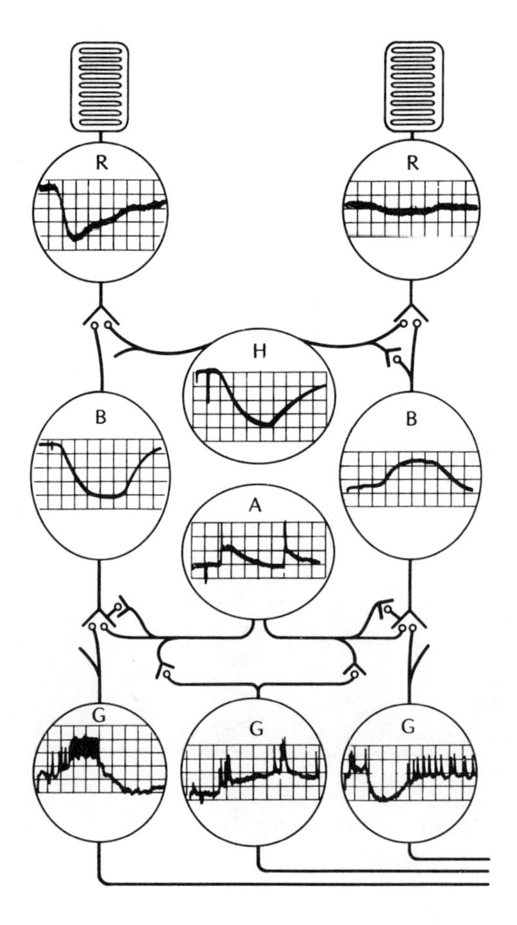

FIG. 3.28. A graphic representation of the types of responses of which each of the retinal neurons is capable. Only amacrine and ganglion cells produce spike action potentials. (From Dowling, © 1970, with the permission of C. V. Mosby Company.)

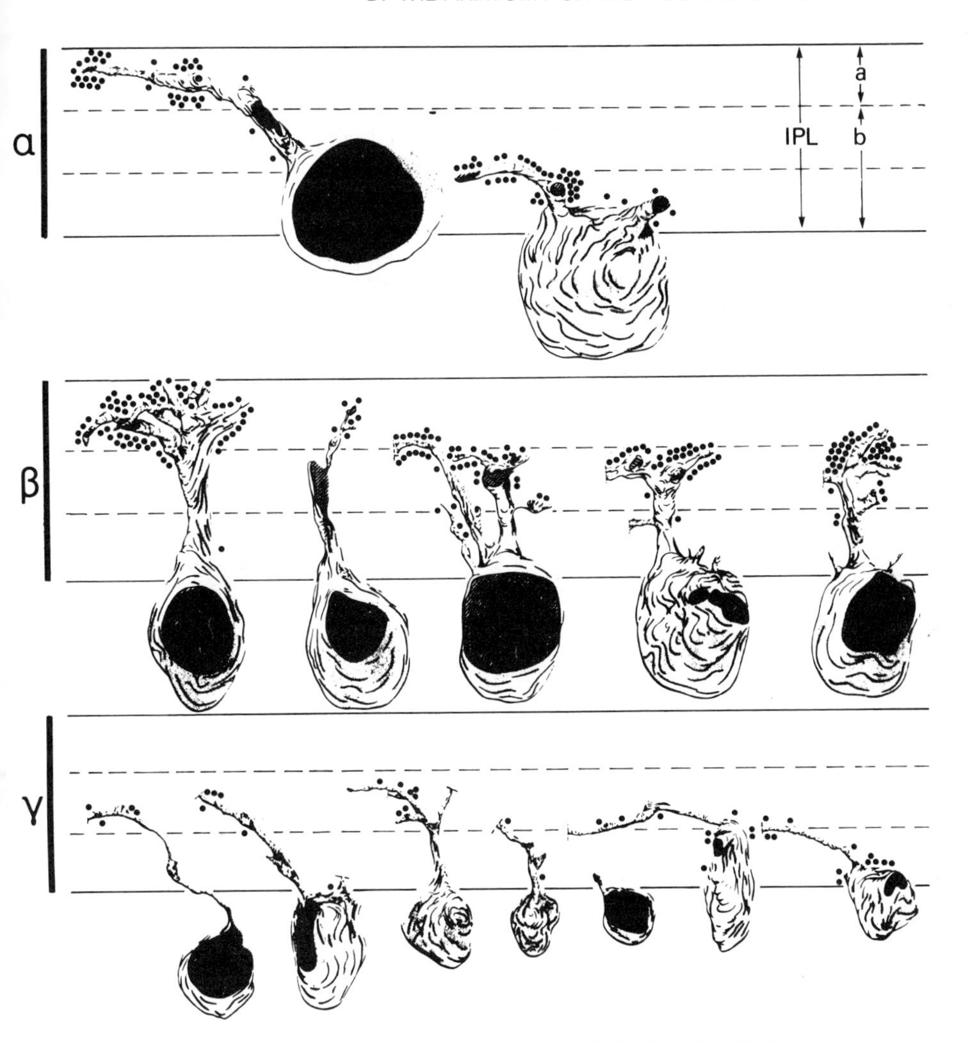

FIG. 3.29. Three different types of ganglion cell bodies in the retina. Black dots represent synaptic contacts. (From Stevens, McGuire, and Sterling, © 1980, with the permission of The American Association for the Advancement of Science.)

3. The Microanatomy of the Higher Levels of the Visual System[9]

We now also know a considerable amount more than we did only a few years ago about the microscopic organization of higher levels of the visual nervous system, primarily as a result of the combination of artistic and neuroanatomic talents of an extraordinarily gifted man, Janos Szentágothai. Szentágothai's genius, both as

[9]Some of the material in this section is adapted from Uttal (1978).

an anatomist and as an artist, has been almost unique in modifying our concept of microanatomy of the higher levels of the nervous system. Primarily because of his work we now appreciate that, although the nervous system is very complex, it is not randomly structured but is highly ordered and in some cases structured with almost crystalline regularity. In the following sections I discuss the cellular organization in the lateral geniculate body of the thalamus and the striate cortex. Similar analyses, to the best of my knowledge, are not yet available for the other visual areas of the brain.

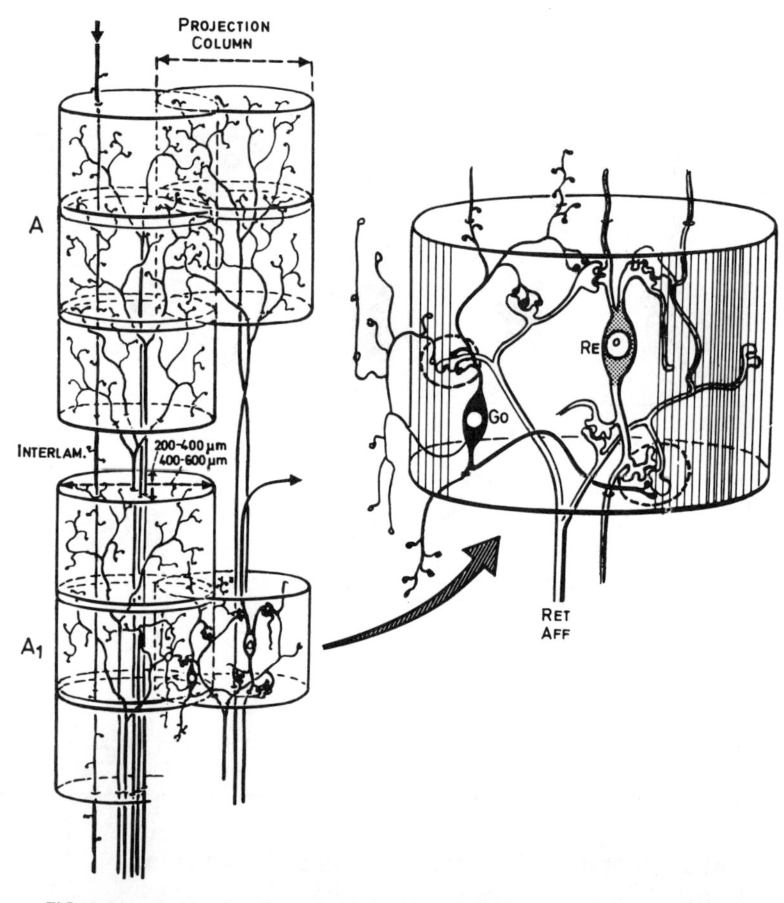

FIG. 3.30. A schematic drawing of the regular organization of the neurons in the lateral geniculate body. Abbreviations indicated are: Ret Aff = retinal afferents; Re = relay cells; and Go = Golgi type II cells. Note that in spite of the apparent disarray there is a great deal of order in this structure if one properly considers the volumes defined by the dendritic arborizations of the various neurons in general rather than the idiosyncracies of each cell. (From Szentágothai, © 1973a, with the permission of Springer-Verlag, Inc.)

a. The Lateral Geniculate Body of the Thalamus

The lateral geniculate nucleus is the first synaptic relay point in the pathway from the retina to the visual neocortex. It is here that the long axons of the retinal ganglion cells synapse with the neurons that project to the visual cortex. Figure 3-30 depicts Szentágothai's (1973a) conceptualization of the way in which the neurons are organized in the cat's three-layered lateral geniculate. Axons of the ganglion cells emerge from the optic nerve and rise in almost perfect vertical lines through the various layers of the geniculate. At various levels in this ascent, a certain proportion of the incident axons terminates in an arborization roughly filling in a cylindrical space. These conceptual cylinders demarcate functional and structural regions in which elaborate synaptic interactions occur and thus define the limits of the communication effects of each ganglion cell.

The general arrangement of the cylinders is that of a group of parallel columns, each column consisting of a stack of these cylinders. The cylindrical regions are variable in height, and Szentágothai (1973a) believes synaptic contacts are to be made at all levels within each column. Consequently there is considerable overlap of the synaptic inputs to each cylinder both vertically and horizontally (i.e., ascending neurons terminate in several layers of cylinders).

Within each cylinder, each ascending ganglion cell axon makes synaptic contact with two types of cells. One of these is the next transmission neuron—an afferent relay cell—in the chain to the cortex. The other is a characteristically shaped neuron, which Szentágothai refers to as a Golgi-type cell, specialized for lateral (horizontal) transmission among the cylinders. These Golgi-type cells, therefore, provide a potential means for lateral interaction and neuronal integration between cylinders at all of the layers of the lateral geniculate nucleus.

One other very important type of neuron is found in these synaptic cylinders. Descending from the cortex are long axons with multiple synaptic contacts within all laminae of the lateral geniculate nucleus. These neurons provide an anatomic means through which centrifugal (efferent) signals could be integrated with the centripetal (afferent) signals from the retina, although such a physiological process has not yet, to my knowledge, been demonstrated. The details of the neuronal interconnections are shown in Fig. 3-31 (Szentágothai, 1970).

b. The Cerebral Cortex

The striate cerebral cortex in the occipital region (Brodmann area 17) is the primary projection destination of the thalamic relay neurons—the terminal of the geniculo-striate pathway. Here the interconnections are both far more intricate and numerous than at any lower level of the nervous system. Furthermore, there are many more different types of cells in the cerebral cortex than in any of the lower portions of the visual pathway. Over 50 cell types have already been identified in the primary visual cortex. The problems in comprehending its functional organization are considerably more complex, therefore, than elsewhere in the nervous system.

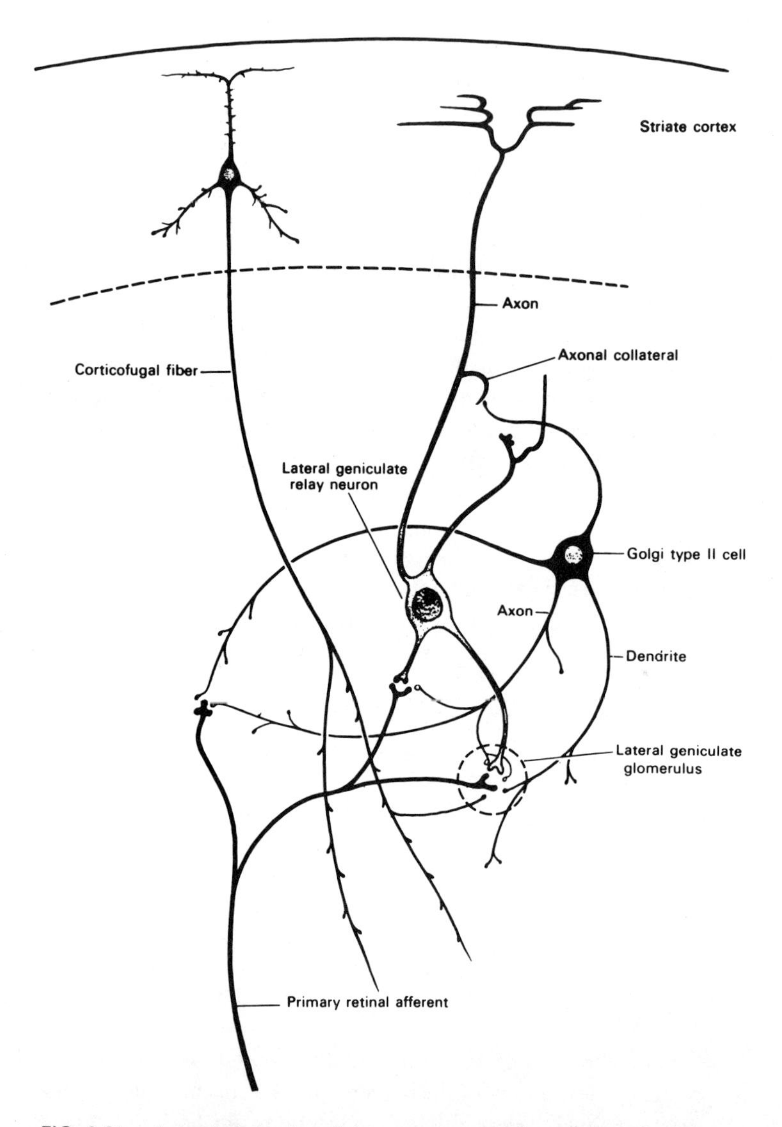

FIG. 3.31. A detailed drawing of the arrangement of the cells in a single volumetric cylinder (see Fig. 3.30) in the lateral geniculate body. (From Carpenter, © 1976, after Szentágothai, 1970, with the permission of Williams & Wilkins Company.)

To understand the structure of the cerebral cortex in this part of the visual system, it is first necessary to appreciate that it, along with many other cortical regions, is a laminated structure. Fig. 3-32 (Szentágothai, 1973b), for example, shows the arrangement of the laminae at Brodmann's region 17. An important anatomical fact is that the afferent fibers that convey information into this visual cortex do not enter and synapse at either the highest or lowest of the six layers. Instead, most of the axonal fibers that come from the thalamus pass without

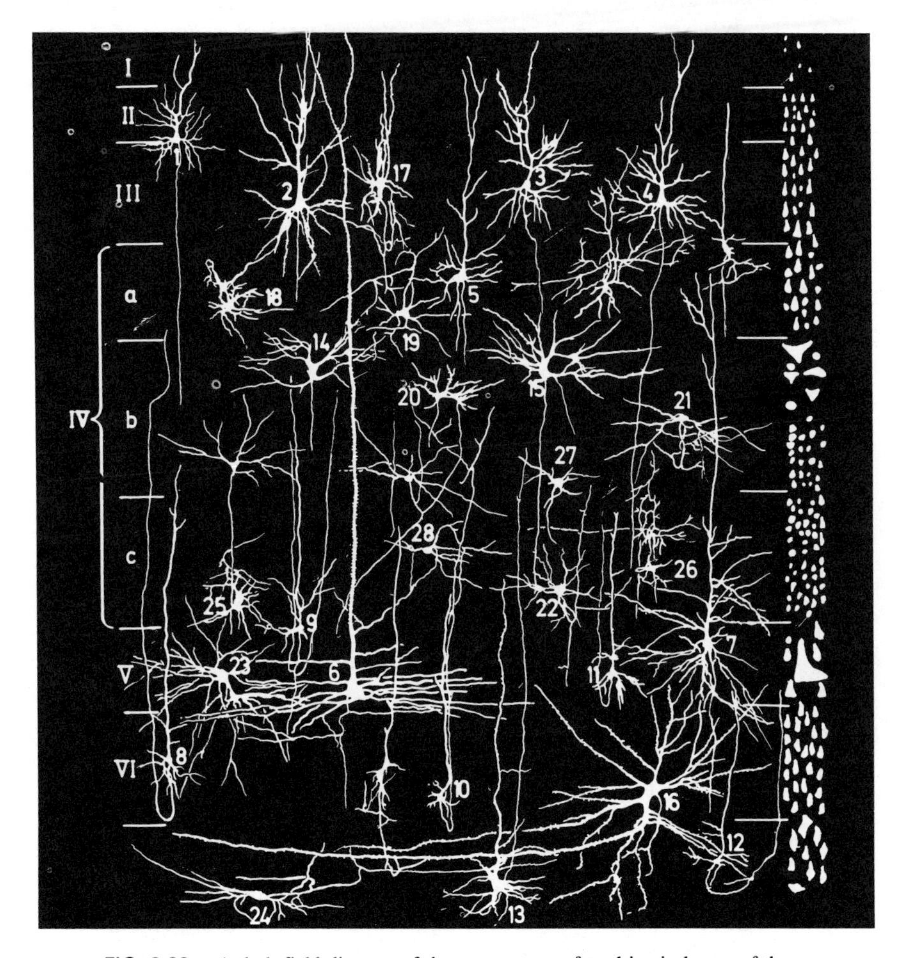

FIG. 3.32. A dark field diagram of the neuron types found in six layers of the human visual cortex. On the right-hand side, only the cell bodies have been drawn to illustrate the different distribution of cell sizes found in the different layers: typical pyramids (1-7), short pyramid—mainly with ascending axons (8-13), large Category I stellates of Cajal (14, 15), giant fusiform lamina VI (16), Category II stellates (17-24), and midget stellates (25-28). (From Szentágothai, © 1973b, after Skolnik-Yarros, with the permission of Springer-Verlag, Inc.)

synapsing through the bottom two layers (layers V and VI) of the cortex. It is only in the central layer IV that these fibers terminate by synapsing with cortical integration neurons. Only a small proportion of the afferent fibers passes through all the cortical laminae and synapses within the outermost Lamina I.

In spite of the complexity of the cerebral cortex, Szentágothai has proposed some general organizational principles that greatly simplify the superficial complexity of cellular arrangement within it. Figure 3-33 is an up-to-date schematic of cerebral cortical cytoarchitectonics (Szentágothai, 1975) typical of that found in the primary visual region. The most notable feature of this figure is its emphasis on the specification of the three-dimensional spaces that are defined by the regions of influence of particular cell types and clusters.

The reader should note that in this figure a number of horizontal planes have been added for clarity. These planes, however, are simply aides to three-dimensional visualization and, as Szentágothai emphasizes, they do not represent the boundaries between the different cortical laminae. Only the visual afferents are shown in this figure, but even in the visual cortex there are usually other afferent and collateral fibers terminating in this region. The sensory afferents terminate on four different types of cells. The critical point, in the context of the present discussion, is that the information that terminates on one of these cell types is more or less restricted to a sharply defined vertical column in the cortex as indicated by the large column in Fig. 3-33.

Physiological evidence for cortical columnar organization of this kind was observed first by Mountcastle (1957) in somatosensory cortex and then later by Hubel and Wiesel (1962) in visual cortex. In both cases, these workers observed that electrode penetrations along these perpendicular (to the surface of the cortex) columns recorded neuronal responses activated by a single highly limited class of peripheral stimuli (i.e., lines oriented in only one direction). These electrophysiologically defined columns, it has now been suggested, may be the functional expression of the columnar organization of the cortical neurons now demonstrated anatomically by Szentágothai.

In addition to this vertical columnar form of organization, there are also two other vertical organization patterns of the neurons found throughout a typical portion of the visual cortex. Two vertical planes identified by Szentágothai (1975) are also shown in Fig. 3-33. These two planes are oriented perpendicularly to each other, and their particular shapes are defined by the orientation and projection of the axons and dendrites of the neurons contained within them.

The first of the two planes, shown on the left side of Fig. 3-33, is defined by the arborization of basket neurons, one of the many types found in the cerebral cortex. The dendrites and axons of basket neurons of this class are flattened and, although they run both up, down and across the plane, they do not pass out of the indicated plane. On the right side of Fig. 3-33, the second plane is defined by a peculiar *H*-shaped stellate neuron. Although the orientation of the plane is different, the arborization of this neuron is also limited to the indicated space.

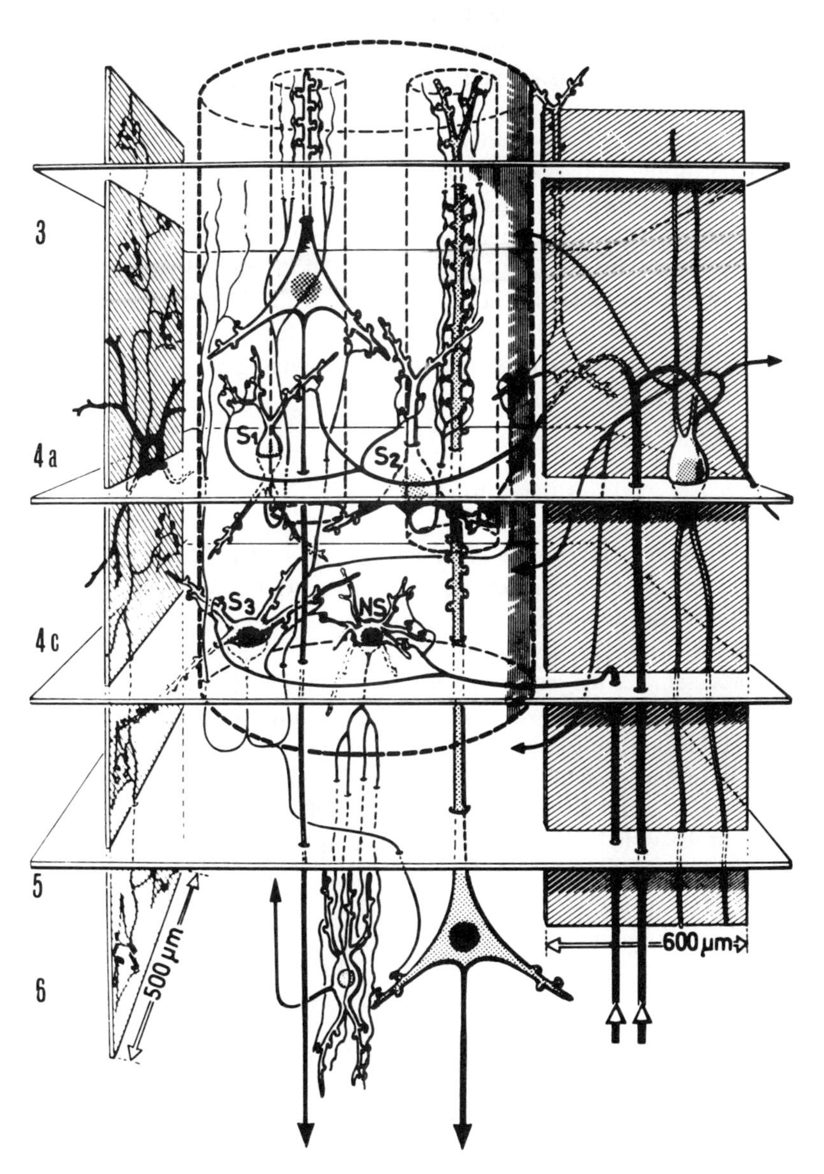

FIG. 3.33. A simplified block diagram of the organization of the cerebral cortex as defined by the volumes of interaction of the individual neurons. The Roman numerals on the left indicate the cortical lamina. S_1 and S_3 are two kinds of spiny stellate neurons; S_2 is a "star pyramid." NS is another kind of stellate cell characterized as being nonspiny and neurogliform. Note the entry of the afferents into the system at level 4. The other major cell types are defined in the text. (From Szentágothai, © 1975, with the permission of Elsevier Scientific Publishing Co.)

Szentágothai believes that the first of these two planes, the one on the left, specifically represents the region of inhibitory influence exerted by the basket neurons, that he thinks selectively inhibit pyramidal neurons—the large cells with the long descending axons. The *H*-shaped stellate neurons, on the other hand, are more probably excitatory units and may act to integrate the responses of a number of pyramidal neurons as well as other cell types.

In conclusion, I must emphasize that these conceptual planes, cubes, and columns are not visible anatomical entities; they are merely regions of influence, and they certainly are not as sharply demarcated in the real tissue as in these idealized drawings. They do, however, attest to the fact, as Szentágothai so elegantly emphasizes, that the visual cortex, like other portions of the brain, is a highly organized structure and is not arranged in anything remotely like a random order.

E. VISUAL OPTICS

The eye, composed as it is of several refracting surfaces, a gain-controlling diaphragm, and absorbing media, is an optical, as well as a neuronal, organ. Its main biological functions are the transduction of photic energy from the external world into the electrochemical energy of the nervous system by the receptor cells and the processing of the resulting patterns of transmitted neural information by the rest of the retina. However, the eye also performs a number of other non-neural modifications of the incident photic stimulus prior to receptor transduction. The most important of these preliminary transformations, and the ones that I consider briefly in this section, are associated with refractive image formation, geometry of the visual angle, and stimulus intensity control.

1. Image Formation by the Eye

a. Some Simple Optics

It is necessary, before I begin this discussion of the optical properties of the eye to review briefly some basic geometrical optics—the physical science of lenses and light rays. The main process that must be understood in this science is refraction—the bending of light rays by optical elements. The basic fact is that light rays or wave fronts tend to be altered in the direction they are moving when they pass at oblique angles across an interface between two materials with different indices of refraction. The resulting change in the direction of a light ray is called refraction, and the degree of refraction depends upon the indices of refraction of the two materials and the wavelength of the lights, as well as the angle of incidence of the light ray on the interface, as shown in Fig. 3-34. The index of a

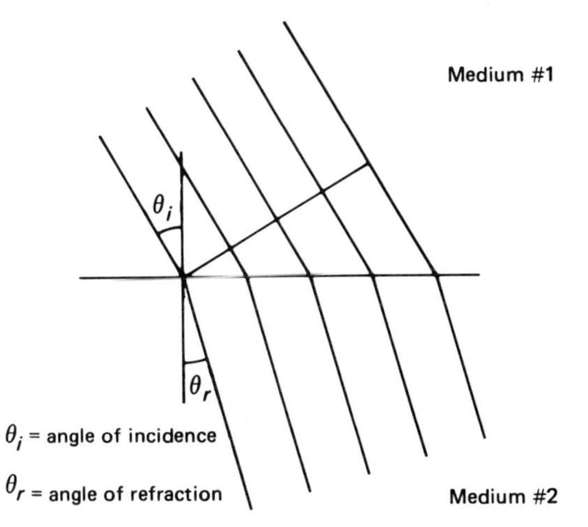

FIG. 3.34. Diagram showing the change in the direction (refraction) of a beam of light as it enters a medium possessing a different index of refraction than that of the one in which it had been traveling. Refraction is the basis of all optical lens effects including magnification. (From Uttal, 1973.)

refraction of any material can be shown to be equal to the ratio of the speed at which light moves through the material and the speed of light in a vacuum.

The analogy has often been made between a platoon of marching men and the light wave front. If one corner of the metaphorical platoon hits a muddy field (corresponding to a medium with a relatively low index of refraction) before the other corner (corresponding to an oblique angle of incidence), which is still on a hard surface (corresponding to a medium with a relatively high index of refraction), then the entire front will be changed in direction as the earlier-arriving troops are slowed before the other portions of the march. When the army (or the light) approaches the new medium absolutely perpendicular to the interface, then all portions are slowed at the same time and equally, and there is no change in direction (i.e., no refraction).

The angle of refraction produced at any interface between two media can be calculated from Snell's law. This classic relationship states that the ratio of the sine of the angle of incidence (Θ_i) to the sine of the angle of refraction (Θ_r) is the inverse of the ratio of the velocities of light in the two media (V_1, V_2), or

$$\frac{\sin \theta_i}{\sin \theta_r} = \frac{V_2}{V_1} \tag{3-15}$$

which is also, of course, equal to the ratios of their respective indices of refraction. As the velocity of a light also depends on wavelength as well as on the index of refraction of the material, these two variables are also implicit in the Values V_1 and V_2.

Lenses are optical surfaces that are curved in order to provide a continuously varying oblique angle and thus to refract differentially an incident front of light rays. Ideal lenses can thus be considered to be a single surface with a varying angle of incidence that acts selectively to refract a parallel bundle of light rays in a way that brings all the light rays to a common focal point as shown in Fig. 3-35A. The distance from the lens to the common focus point is called the focal length of a lens (F).

The parallel incident light rays shown in Fig. 3-35A may be thought of as coming from a light source that is an infinite distance away from the lens. Equivalent optical infinity, however, is easy to achieve; one simply has to place a point light source at the focal point of any lens and use the lens "backwards" to produce a parallel bundle of light rays as shown in Fig. 3-35B. When the object is at some distance less than infinity, then the waves are not parallel and the image will come to a focus at a distance that is not solely a function of the strength of the lens but also of the distance of the object from the lens. Figure 3-35C depicts this more general optical situation. In this figure an actual physical object located at a distance D_o from a lens produces an image at a distance of D_i from that lens. The general lens quation, allowing the exact determination of either D_o, D_i, or F when the other two terms are known, is

$$\frac{1}{F} = \frac{1}{D_o} + \frac{1}{D_i} \tag{3-16}$$

Clearly, a lens with a short focal length is going to refract the rays of light more substantially than one with a long focal length; that is, the greater the power, the shorter the focal length. The true power of a lens, therefore, is usually defined as a reciprocal of its focal length. If the focal length of a lens is measured in meters, the units of power so defined are called diopters. More formally,

$$\text{Power (in diopters)} = \frac{1}{F \text{ (in meters)}} \tag{3-17}$$

Another important aspect of the geometrical optics of such simple lenses is that the image is always inverted as also shown in Fig. 3-35C. More complex systems of lenses, mirrors, or prisms, rather than a single lens, are required to produce an erect image of an object. Though the inverted image is important in the optics of a system, contrary to popular mythology, it could not matter less to the nervous system. The question—Why do we see the world right side up when the retinal image is inverted?—given the otherwise highly encoded nature of the afferent signal is nonsensical.

These few general comments concerning geometrical optics set the stage for the following particular discussion of the optics of the eye.

b. The Optics of the Eye

The eye can also be considered in terms of the same geometrical optical concepts and principles introduced in the previous section. The optical eye is composed of two refracting lenses, the cornea and the crystalline lens, and three

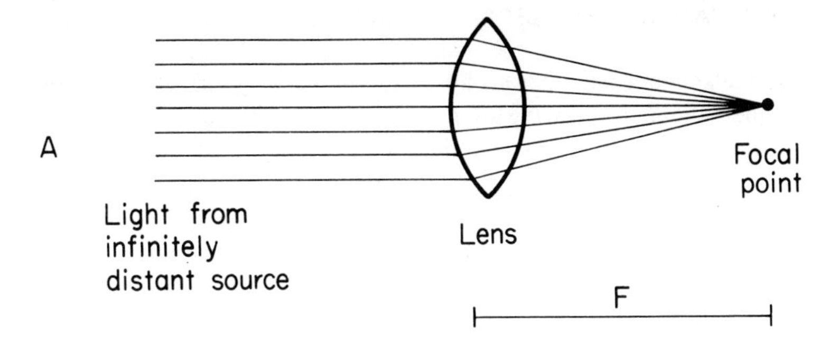

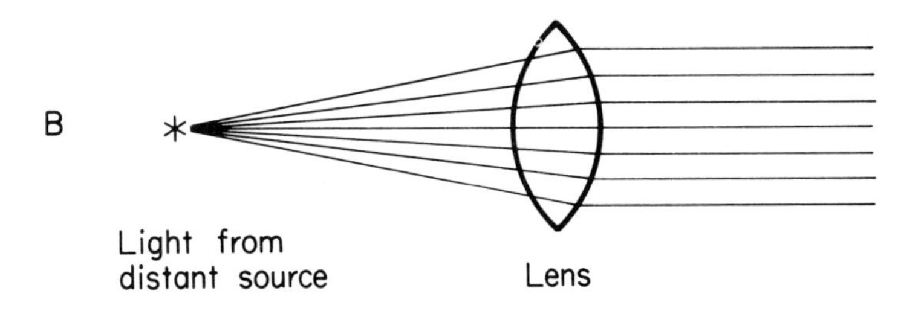

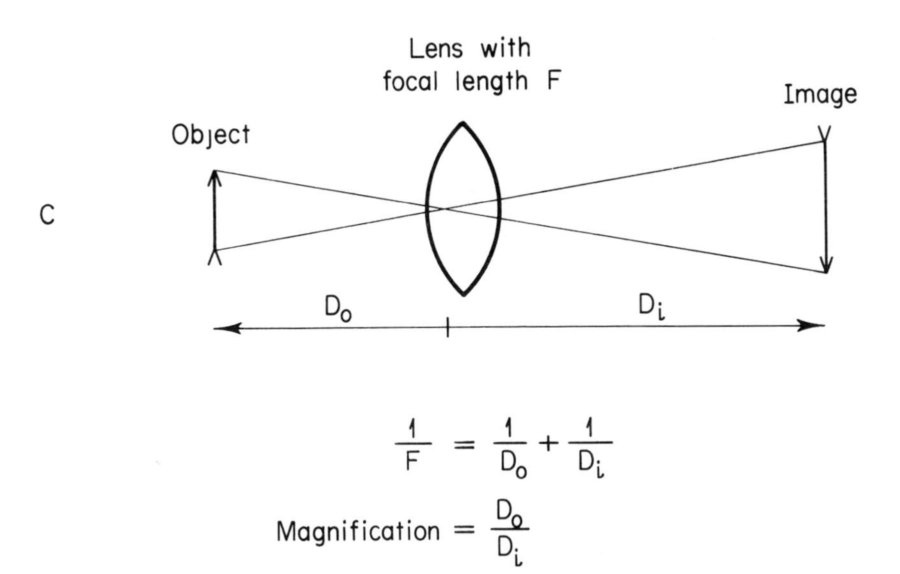

FIG. 3.35. The action of an optical lens. (A) Convergence of parallel rays of light to the focal point of the lens. (B) Divergence of rays from a point source at the focal point of the lens to a parallel system of rays. (C) The lens equation.

fluids, air and the aqueous and vitreous humors, with varying refractive indices, as shown in the schematic drawing of Fig. 3-36. In combination with these fluids, the two refracting structures give the eye the ability to produce a crisply focused, reduced, and inverted image of an object on the retina, which is normally 17 mm from the posterior surface of the lens. (The whole eye of a normal human is typically 24 mm from retina to corneal surface.) Applying the lens formula we can thus estimate the overall optical power required for a well-focused eye in the following way by assuming an object at optical infinity (∞):

$$\frac{1}{F} = \frac{1}{D_o} + \frac{1}{D_i} = \frac{1}{\infty} + \frac{1}{.017} = 58.82 \qquad (3\text{-}18)$$

Thus the power of the normal eye must be about 59 diopters when the cornea–lens system has a focal length of about 17 mm. The cornea and crystalline lens are not ideal thin lenses, however. There are four active refracting surfaces (the front of the cornea, the back of the cornea, the front of the lens, and the back of the lens) that must be considered. The ratios of the refractive indices on either side of these four surfaces also differ (according to Westheimer, 1972, the refractive index of air is 1; of the aqueous humor 1.336; of the vitreous humor, 1.336; of the cornea, 1.376, and of the lens, 1.554). Because the curvature of the

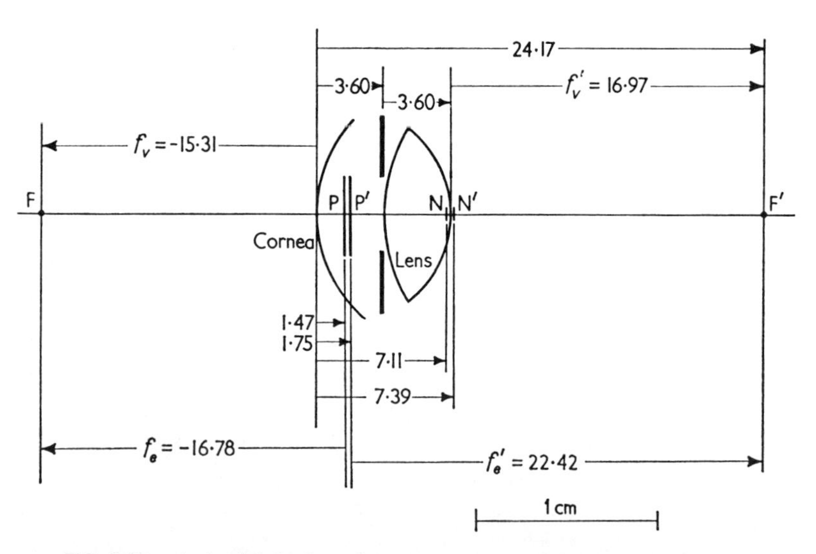

FIG. 3.36. A simplified schematic eye in the unaccommodated state. F = anterior principle focus. F′ = posterior principal focus. f_e = anterior equivalent focal length. f'_e = posterior equivalent focal length. f_v = anterior vertex focal length. f'_v = posterior vertex focal length. P and P′ = first and second principal points. N and N′ = first and second nodal points. (All distances in mm.) (Figure and caption labels from Bennett and Francis, © 1962, with the permission of Academic Press, Inc.)

four surfaces also differs, they have widely varying refractive effects. The anterior convex portion of the cornea accounts for most of the power of the eye (about 49 diopters) whereas the posterior portion actually reduces the overall power by about 6 diopters because of its concavity. The anterior surface of the lens adds about 6 diopters of power and the posterior about 9 diopters to the entire refractive system, giving a total of approximately 59 diopters. This information is summed up in Table 3-6. Thus it is the refractive power exerted by the anterior portion of the cornea that accounts for most of the optical power of the eye. This power is in turn accounted for, not by any unusually great curvature, but by the relatively large difference in the refractive indices of air and the corneal tissue.

So far I have been considering the eye as a relatively perfect instrument. I have asserted that if the distance from the retina to the posterior surface of the crystalline lens is 17 mm and the refractive power of the cornea lens system is 59 diopters, then a sharp image with negligible blur will be projected on the retina. In that case, the eye is said to be emmetropic. However, if the cornea–lens system does not have 59 diopters of power or if the eye is too long or too short, the physical image of the external object or scene will be blurred at the plane of the retina and defective vision will occur. If the focus occurs beyond the retina (i.e., if the eye is physically too short or its dioptric power is low), vision is said to be hypermetropic (farsighted) and near objects cannot be seen clearly. Adding additional positive diopters of optical power by spectacles or contact lens can cure this aberration. If, on the other hand, the focal plane occurs in front of the retina (i.e., the eye is too long or its dioptric power too high), the image is also blurred and the vision is said to be myopic (nearsighted) and distant objects are blurred. In this case the reduction in blurring must be accompanied by reducing the total dioptic power of the eye by adding lenses with negative dioptric power.

TABLE 3.6
The Optical Characteristics of the Human Eye

1. Refractive Index	
Air	1.000
Cornea	1.376
Aqueous humor	1.336
Lens	1.386
Vitreous humor	1.336
2. Dioptric Power of Surfaces	
Anterior Surface of Cornea	+49D
Posterior Surface of Cornea	−6D
Anterior Surface of Lens	+6D
Posterior Surface of Lens	+9D

After Westheimer, 1972.

Most such corrections are small compared to the total power of the eye, however; only two or three diopters either way are needed to cure all but the most extreme aberrations.

Even normal eyes are not always correctly focused for all viewing conditions. The focal power of the system, however, can be adjusted by the visual system itself. The lens can be mechanically distorted in shape by the ciliary muscles thus changing its dioptric power. This process—accommodation—plays an important role in providing sharp and well-focused images in the various viewing conditions encountered by the normal eye. However, as a person ages there is a progressive decline in accommodative power. Whereas a teenager's lens may be able to vary its power by as much as 15 diopters, a 50-year-old person must find other optical means of supplementing his limited 2 diopter accommodative range. Although the exact neural processes controlling accommodation are not known, it now appears that there is a voluntary (Provine & Enoch, 1975) as well as a reflexive component to this control system.

2. The Visual Angle and Retinal Size

Another important geometrical aspect of the eye is the visual angle subtended by the stimulus object. The visual angle is defined as shown in Fig. 3-37. The visual angle (α) of an object of size h at a distance (d) is derived from the expression:

$$\text{arc tan } \frac{\alpha}{2} = \frac{h}{2} \cdot \frac{1}{d} \tag{3-19}$$

Because the eye uses a relatively high-power positive diopter lens system to form the retinal image, it acts as a demagnifier producing a very much reduced image of the external object. The retinal size of this image is given by the following expression:

$$\text{Size of image on retina (in mm)} = \tan \alpha \text{ (visual angle of object)} \times \text{focal length of eye, (17 mm)} \tag{3-20}$$

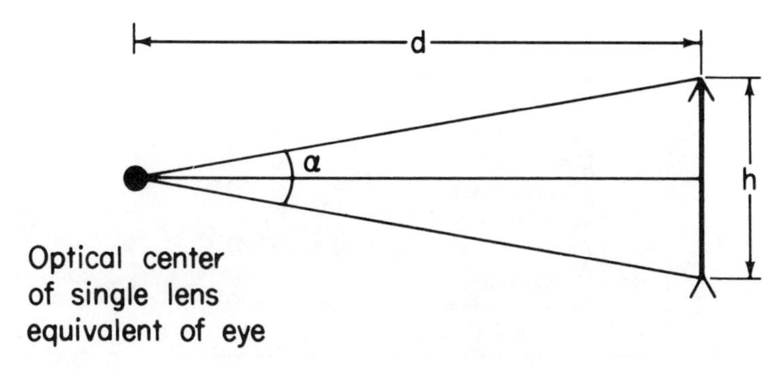

FIG. 3.37. Definition of the visual angle.

However good the visual image, acuity is not totally dependent on the stimulus visual angle but also depends on a number of other factors, for example, the size of the entrance pupil and aberrations of one sort or another in the transparent media. How good the resolution of two lines can be also depends in large part on the density of the photoreceptor elements in the retinal mosaic. Specifically, the theoretical maximum resolving power of the eye is proportional to the square root of receptor density. These topics are discussed in much greater detail in Chapter 5.

3. Visual Stimulus Intensity Control

In addition to neural and photochemical effects that can control the sensitivity of the visual system (to be considered in later chapters), the eye is also able to modulate directly the amount of light falling on the retina by varying the size of its entrance pupil. The defocused rays from each point of light pass through all portions of the pupil; thus the total amount of light brought to a focus at each point after passage through the eye will vary depending upon the size of the pupil. Variations in pupil size, therefore, do not cut off or add to any particular portion of the image but dim or brighten the entire image uniformly and thus act as a mechanical stimulus-intensity control.

The fluctuation in pupillary diameter is controlled by a reflex from the central nervous system that is stimulated by the stimulus luminance itself. The reflex, therefore, acts as an automatic gain control partially regulating the amount of light falling on the retina. However, only a small portion of the range of perceivable brightness can be regulated by the pupil. Most of the gain control of the eye, as we see in later chapters, must be attributed to neural and biochemical effects.

F. TRANSDUCER ACTION IN THE PHOTORECEPTOR[10]

The photochemical transductive process in vision may be thought of, in general, as consisting of two different, though sequential, stages. The first stage is a nonneural process—the primary sensory action—the last physical act performed by the stimulus. It is the direct antecedent of the processes by which photon energy is converted into neurochemical signals but is not directly a part of that conversion. In hearing, the primary sensory action is the mechanical deformation of a portion of the receptor cell membrane at the foot of a cilium or hair. In touch, it is probably also the direct mechanical deformation of a specialized terminal

---

[10]This section is an adaptation and modification of material from my earlier books (Uttal, 1973 and 1975b).

portion of a cutaneous axon. In vision, however, the primary sensory action is a most unusual process. It is the chemical stereoisomerization (change in spatial geometry) of a large molecule that is triggered, but not energized by the incident light.

The second stage of the transductive process is the actual production of the initial neurochemical electropotential. Following the successful consummation of the primary sensory action, some change must occur in the membrane of the receptor cell which allows ions of sodium and potassium to redistribute themselves across the membrane. This membrane permeability change and the resulting ionic flow lead to the creation of an electrochemical potential (in the case of the photoreceptor in the eye, a receptor potential) that is the first truly neural event. How these processes occur in the various senses is discussed in general in one of the earlier books (Uttal, 1973) in this series. How the two stages of the transductive process are thought to occur in the photoreceptors of the eye is the topic of this section.

1. The Primary Sensory Action in Vision

On the basis of the work of a number of distinguished biochemists but most notably that of the Nobel laureate George Wald and his colleagues, the story that can be told about the primary sensory action in vision is virtually complete at the level we need for the purposes of this book. To preview the tale very briefly, the picture of the transductive process in vision, which Wald and others have developed over the years, asserts that the outer segments of the rods and cones contain large photosensitive molecules that break into two parts under the influence of incident light. The breakdown products resulting from the photodecomposition of these molecules in some unknown way induces a change in the membrane permeability. It is this permeability change that is the direct antecedent of the receptor potential. Wald's most important contributions to our understanding of the process lie in his elucidation of the mechanisms initiating the breakdown of the photochemical and the subsequent steps in its decomposition. In short, he has shown that a series of intermediary substances are produced by a string of spontaneous decompositions following the initial configurational change in the photosensitive macromolecule.

Now let us consider the story in a little greater detail. For a number of years, it had been known that a curious violet chemical is involved in the visual process. Boll, in 1877, had discovered this substance and had named it rhodopsin. The general idea that there was a cycle, which involved rhodopsin and its breakdown products, had been suggested by Selig Hecht in the 1930s. Wald (1968) states (in his Nobel acceptance speech) that it was under the influence of Hecht that he began a search for the chemical constituents, which had appeared as only hypothetical structures in Hecht's theories. In 1933 Wald made the initial, though not unexpected, discovery that vitamin A was present in large amounts in the retina and shortly thereafter followed this up with another important discovery: Wald (1933) reported the presence of another organic substance, closely related to Vitamin A, that he at that time was to call retinene. Retinene ultimately turned out to be an aldehyde of vitamin A. These substances are treated in more detail later, but first let us skip ahead a few years and alter the terminology to the more modern one. Wald and others have now agreed that vitamin A should be called *retinol,* and retinene, its aldehyde, should be called *retinal,* to emphasize their very important roles in the visual process. (An aldehyde is a chemical product produced by the oxidation of a precursor such as retinol.)

Wald next defined the chemical steps in what is now known as the "Rhodopsin Cycle." He and his students and colleagues identified the specific molecules and the nature of the reactions that occur under the influence of incident light. In doing so, they provided moern visual science with a very specific statement of the primary visual action.

The still generally accepted Wald model is that the visual pigment found in each of the receptor cells of the eyes of a wide variety of animals consists of a typical kind of photosensitive molecule composed of two essential parts or moieties. One part—a carotenoid (so named because pure suspensions often have a typical orange-red color)—is a relatively simple structure. In fact, the carotenoid in man is one isomeric form of retinal. The other part of the visual pigment is a much larger organic structure—a protein with a molecular weight of 30,000 to 40,000. Though we now appreciate that there are many different kinds of this large proteinaceous moiety Wald has coined the generic name *opsin* for all of these complex structures regardless of the animal or photoreceptor in which they might be found.

Opsins differ in two ways. Details of the organic structure vary from species to species and are, therefore, said to be species specific. There are corresponding differences in the absorptive properties of the photosensitive pigments in these animals. A relatively complete list of the peaks of the absorption spectra of the visual pigments of many vertebrates can be found well summarized in a review by Lythgoe (1972). But even within the nervous system of a single animal, there are frequently several different kinds of opsins. In man, one opsin is responsible for the compound visual pigment found in the rods, and the trio of photochemicals observed in the three types of cones suggests that there are three different cone opsins. All four pigments in man, however, are combined with the same kind of retinal (retinal$_1$) to complete the photosensitive molecule.

The model of a composite molecule composed of a large proteinaceous moiety (an opsin) bonded to a smaller structure (a retinal) is now believed to be the standard configuration of all vertebrate visual photopigments and the key to understanding the primary sensory action in vision as it is modeled by the presently accepted Wald theory. Let us next consider some of the chemistry of the smaller part—the carotenoid—as an initial step in elucidating the full details of this most important theory of the primary sensory action in vision.

Retinol exists within the body in a balanced equilibrium between itself and its aldehyde, retinal. The structure formula of one kind of retinol–retinol$_1$—and one kind of retinal–retinal$_1$—are shown in Fig. 3-38A and 3-38B. It can be seen that the two differ very little. Only the bonding of the terminal *OH* or *O* group differs. Retinol$_1$, however, is not an active participant in the visual process. Its main importance is in the role it plays as a precursor of retinal$_1$. The quantities of retinol$_1$, only weakly determine the availability of retinal$_1$, and thus retinol$_1$ (Vitamin A) deficiencies in the diet lead only indirectly, if at all, to visual inadequacies.[11] The equilibrium between retinol$_1$ and retinal$_1$ is balanced such that the oxidation process producing retinal$_1$ has the lesser chemical rate constant of the two reactions; thus retinal$_1$ is produced and maintained only as it is used in the visual cycle and only, it is thought, in the highly specialized chemical engines of the retina.

A structure analysis of retinal$_1$ is further complicated by the fact that it can exist in several different stereoisomeric forms. All of the isomers of retinal$_1$ have the same chemical formula $C_{19}H_{27}CHO$, but they differ in the three-dimensional pattern into which the molecules are arranged. The physical shape of the whole molecule is a function of the angles assumed at bonding points between adjacent carbon atoms. The various stereoisomers of retinal$_1$, therefore differ principally because of differences in bonding angles at carbon-to-carbon junctions. An important fact, upon which visual photochemistry is based, is that the chemistry of stereoisomers can differ even though their formulas are identical.

The two most important of the several stereoisomeric forms in which retinal$_1$ can exist are the *all-trans* and the *11-cis* shapes. The all-*trans* form was illustrated by the drawing in Fig. 3-38B. The shape of its tail is essentially straight because all the carbon-to-carbon bonds in that tail are in the same direction.

The 11-*cis* stereoisomer of retinal$_1$ is illustrated in Fig. 3-38C. In this form there is a bend at the eleventh carbon atom, which puts a kink in the tail. As Wald points out in a now classic discussion of his model (Wald, 1968), the 11-*cis* configuration should not be expected to exist at all because molecular dynamics suggest that it is intrinsically unstable. The extraordinary fact, however, is that 11-*cis*-retinal$_1$ does exist and does maintain this stable stereoisomeric form, *but only as long as it is kept in the dark.* This deceptively simple statement is, in fact, the key to all vision.

There are two very important reasons for the key role of 11-*cis*-retinal$_1$. First, this is the only stereoisomer of retinal$_1$ that is capable of forming a stable bond with the organic macromolecule, opsin. Second, the action of light on the rhodopsin molecule serves to stereoisomerize 11-*cis*-retinal$_1$ into its all-*trans*

---

[11]Because there must be a massive deficiency of Vitamin A (retinol) to affect vision, and the body contains appreciable stores, eating carrots to improve night vision would be in vain.

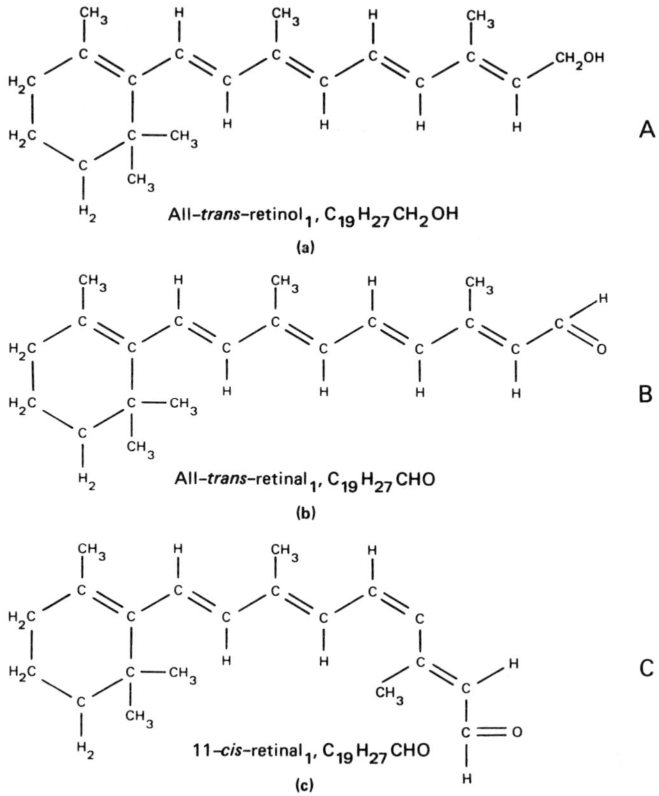

A

All-*trans*-retinol$_1$, $C_{19}H_{27}CH_2OH$

(a)

B

All-*trans*-retinal$_1$, $C_{19}H_{27}CHO$

(b)

C

11-*cis*-retinal$_1$, $C_{19}H_{27}CHO$

(c)

FIG. 3.38. The structural formulas of three of the important molecules involved in the photochemical cycle. See text for details (adapted from Wald, 1968).

form, thus forming an unstable substance that spontaneously goes through the various stages of the visual cycle without the necessity for any other external energy source.

The net effect of these very special characteristics of retinal$_1$ is that the primary sensory action in vision can be specifically identified as the straightening or stereoisomerizing of the 11-*cis* to the all-*trans* form of retinal$_1$. No other action of light is necessary once this triggering process has occurred.

When 11-*cis*-retinal$_1$ is stereoisomerized by light and the combined photo-molecule breaks down, a complex series of spontaneous further decompositions occur. The rhodopsin molecule, for example, does not immediately degenerate into all-*trans*-retinal$_1$ and rhodopsin but rather goes through a number of intermediate states, each of which has its own specific properties. These intermediate states occur very rapidly, and it had been extremely difficult to determine their characteristics by the ordinary spectral absorption techniques used for the stable final breakdown products. A remarkable innovation, also introduced by Wald's group, however, has made it possible to take "temporal snapshots" of the intermediaries. The technique, which is called *freeze chemistry*, took advantage of the fact that the sequence of intermediary photochemicals are produced by reactions with different temperature thresholds. That is, each of the processes can occur only at a successively higher temperature. Thus, the initial breakdown of rhodopsin into an intermediary called prelumirhodopsin will lead to a stable mixture of rhodopsin and prelumirhodopsin if the experiments are carried out at −195°C. If the temperature is allowed to rise to −140°C, then prelumirhodopsin will spontaneously decay further into another intermediary called lumirhodopsin.

At −40°C, lumirhodopsin further decays spontaneously into a substance called metarhodopsin I which, in the presence of H^+ ions, is converted into another substance known as metarhodopsin II. There is now thought to be another intermediary—metarhodopsin I′—formed between the I and II stages. Metarhodopsin II is subsequently decomposed into pararhodopsin, which then, under the proper *ph* conditions, becomes *N*-Retinylidene-opsin, which then decomposes into the final breakdown products, all-*trans*-retinal$_1$ and opsin, through two alternative routes.

The whole process is diagramed in Fig. 3-39, which is adapted from Rodieck's (1973) book. In addition to showing the sequence of breakdown products, this figure also shows the key temperature at which each sequential step is "unfrozen" as well as two other very interesting and important sets of data. First, the peak wavelength of the absorption curve of each of the intermediates is indicated. It should be noted that each of these chemicals absorbs maximally at a different part of the visual spectrum. This placement of the absorption peak is the most useful measure identifying each breakdown product and the main way of showing that they are really separate and distinct chemicals. A better characterization of the absorption spectra of the breakdown products is shown in Fig. 3-40.

Second, the figure also indicates which reactions are spontaneous and will occur in the dark (straight lines), and which reactions must be driven by light (wavy lines). It is important to note that there is only one light-driven breakdown reaction, and this means that the visual response only requires light initially to trigger the string of dark reactions that ultimately lead to the free final breakdown products—retinal$_1$ and opsin. The other light reactions, interestingly enough, are all in the opposite direction and contribute to the regeneration of rhodopsin from the various intermediaries and thus to the final equilibrium mixture of the various substances.

The main advantage of the technique of freezing the chemical reactions is that processes that normally last for only a few microseconds and that are, therefore, too brief to be examined at body temperature can be stopped for a sufficiently long period so that measurements of their optical and chemical properties can be made. Of course, it is not at all certain that each of the processes isolated in this manner is not really itself a combination of several subprocesses with the same or similar threshold temperature. Indeed, some investigations have suggested that, in fact, lumirhodopsin may also actually be two substances (now known tentatively as lumirhodopsin *A* and *B*), but the details are not yet completely established.

The story of the biochemistry of the visual photopigments is complicated further by the fact that just as there are many different types of opsins found in different species and four different kinds of opsins (i.e., one rod and three cone types) found in humans, there are also known to be two different types of retinol and thus two different retinals. The two different kinds of retinal are usually found in different species of animals, but some animals seem to be able to change from a retinal_1 system to a retinal_2 system (or vice versa) as they mature. The structural formulas of retinol_2 and retinal_2 are shown in Fig. 3-41 A and B, respectively.

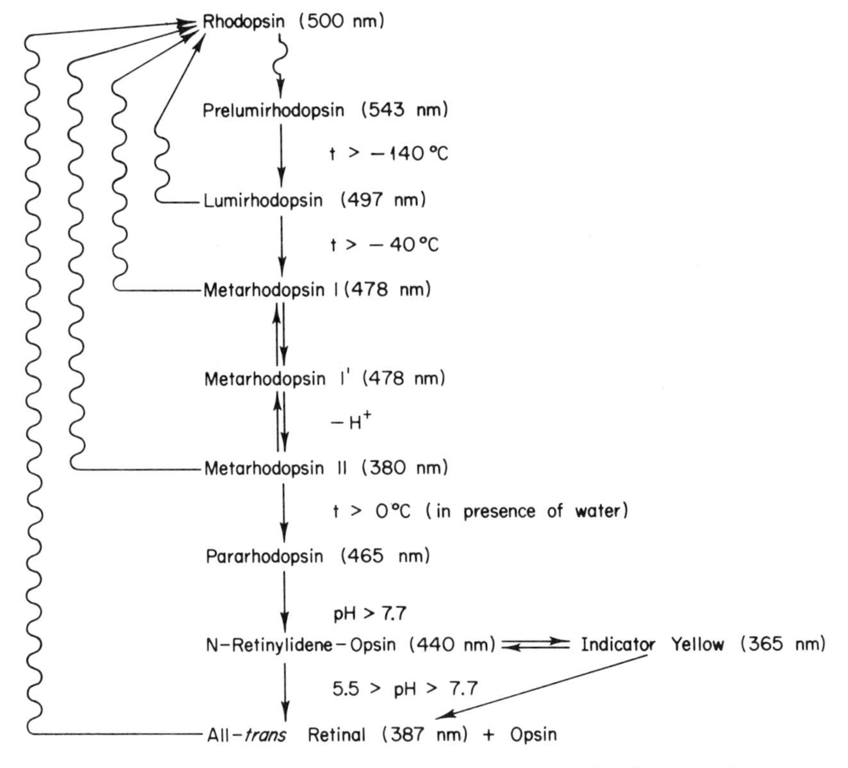

FIG. 3.39. The sequence of breakdown products as revealed by freeze chemistry following isomerization of rhodopsin. A wavy line indicates a light driven reaction and a straight line indicates a reaction that can be driven by thermal energy in the dark. (Adapted from Rodieck, © 1973, with the permission of W. H. Freeman & Co.)

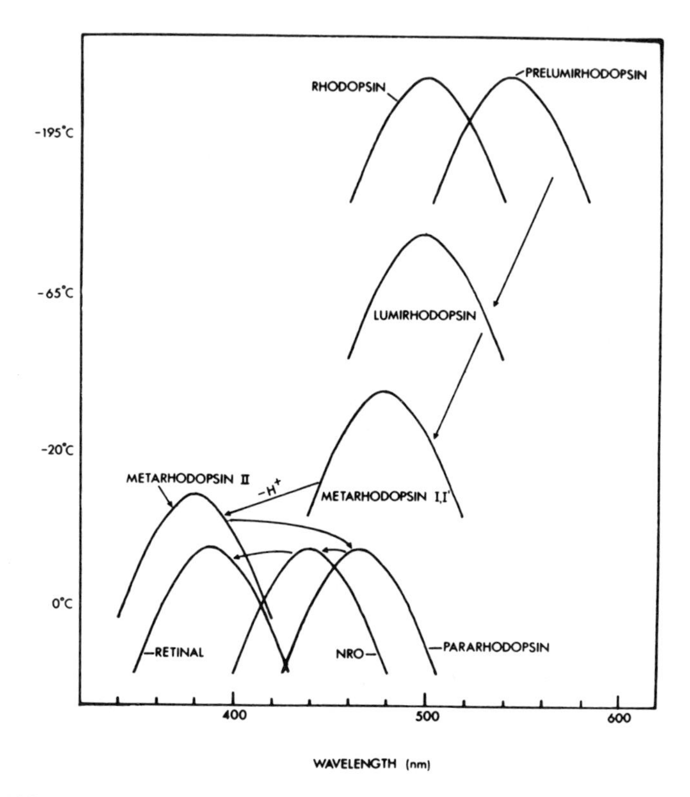

FIG. 3.40. The absorbtion curves of the breakdown products of rhodopsin. (From Rodieck, © 1973, with the permission of W. H. Freeman & Co.)

Retinal$_1$ and retinal$_2$ and their respective retinols are not simple stereoisomers of each other, but are distinct chemical structures with differing formulas. Retinal$_1$ has a formula of $C_{19}H_{27}CHO$ as we have seen, whereas retinal$_2$ has a formula of $C_{19}H_{25}CHO$. The critical structural differences can be observed in the benzene ringlike body of the molecule, where a double bond between two carbons in retinal$_2$ replaces a pair of auxiliary hydrogen atoms in retinal$_1$.

I have suggested earlier a further and very important complication concerning color vision in some animals. Because the retinal in each of the cone pigments would presumably be the same, the observed differences in absorption spectra must be due to the fact that there are three different kinds of cone opsin. According to a modern theoretical consensus, each single cone has one, and only one, of each of these photopigments, which Rushton (1962) has named chlorolabe, erythrolabe, and cyanolabe, respectively.

The exact nature of the three cone pigments has been one of the most perplexing and persistent problems in visual science. It had long been appreciated that in practice only three colors are necessary to reproduce any other perceivable color.

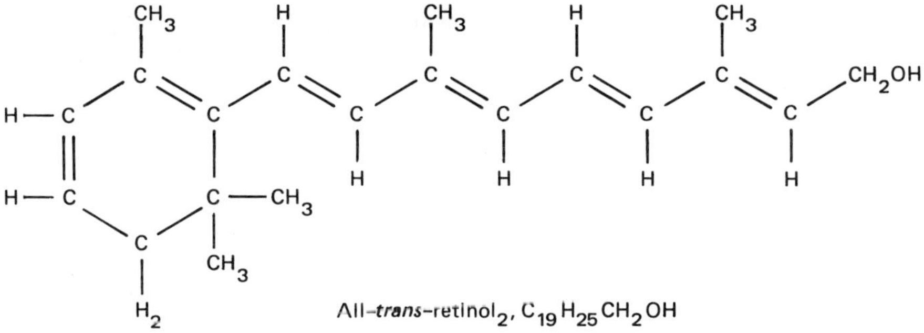

All-*trans*-retinol$_2$, $C_{19}H_{25}CH_2OH$

A

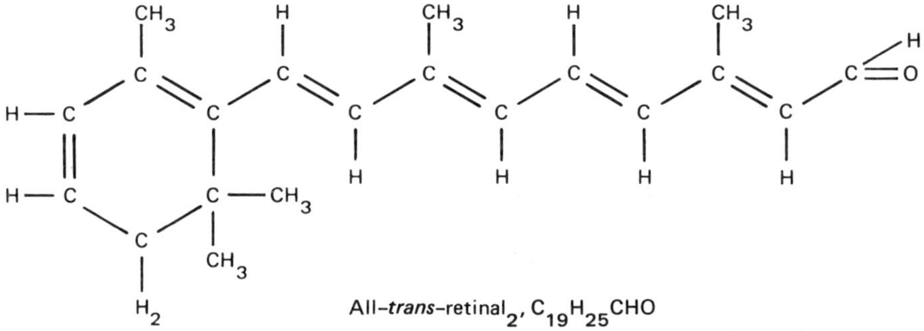

All-*trans*-retinal$_2$, $C_{19}H_{25}CHO$

B

FIG. 3.41. The structurals of retinol$_2$ and retinal$_2$. (From Uttal, 1973, after Wald, 1968.)

Artists and printers had made use of these rules for centuries. Since the time of Thomas Young's (1773–1829) postulation of a trichromatic theory of color vision and Hermann von Helmholtz' (1821–1894) modernization of the concept, in which he specifically asserted that the receptors differed because of their varied spectral absorption (Helmholtz referred to this property as the cone's "resonance"), a wide variety of mathematical models of the three fundamental receptor absorption curves has been proposed. Each of these models suggests a different set of fundamental spectral characteristics for these receptors. Even within the exclusively trichromatic receptor theories (and ignoring for the moment the opponent-color theories), almost every possible type of spectral curve seems to have been proposed at one time or another for the three receptors. Some theorists suggested very narrowly tuned spectra with closely spaced peaks, and others proposed broadly responsive receptor sensitivities with widely spaced peaks.[12] Such theoretical attacks on the problem were collectively beset by a common empirical problem—the cones were so small that it did not seem possible to measure their spectral absorption directly.

In 1964, however, this task was accomplished and an exceedingly tedious and difficult experiment was performed that resolved this century-old debate. This experiment was actually carried out on man and other primates nearly simultaneously by two groups (Brown & Wald, 1964; Marks, Dobelle, & MacNichol, 1964) using newly developed and nearly identical techniques of microspectrophotometric measurement.

Marks, Dobelle, and MacNichol's data indicated peaks at 445, 535, and 570 nm, respectively. Brown and Wald's data were quite similar for a smaller sample of cones. The major significance of this latter work lies in the fact that it directly and definitely specifies the width and peak sensitivity of the absorption spectra of the photochemicals underlying trichromatic vision in primates. There is no further basis for the controversy among the alternative tuning curves that could underly color vision.

The general model I have presented of the primary sensory action in human vision can be summarized as follows. It is, simply, a light-driven stereoisomerization of a very particular bond in one common part of four kinds of photosensitive molecules—the eleventh carbon-to-carbon bond in the retinal moiety. This particular kink (and only this one) is straightened by light, changing 11-*cis*-retinal$_1$ from a stereoisomer that bonds stably to opsin, to an isomeric form—all-*trans*-retinal$_1$—that spontaneously disassociates itself from the protein. This is all that the light does in the visual process. Although the carotenoid may be either one of two kinds, and the protein may be any of several different kinds found either in different receptor cells or in different species of animals, the story seems to be essentially the same in all instances. Differences in absorption spectra between receptor cells or between species are primarily explicable in terms of the chemical differences between opsins. (Shifts in the absorption spectrum of retinal as a result of chemical combination are called bathochromic shifts.) Once the stereoisomerization has occurred, the rest of the sequence of breakdown stages is a dark reaction; that is, it occurs spontaneously without further photic stimulation.

Now that I have considered this remarkable story, we can move on to the next stage: How is it that this chemical reaction can produce a receptor potential?

---

[12]Although the idea of some kind of selective photoabsorbtive tuning of receptors is the basis of most current theory, the concept is not universally accepted for all species. In a thought provoking paper, Gerald Wasserman (1973) has suggested that very broad-band sensitivity in invertebrates may invalidate this explanatory hypothesis for color vision in some of these animals. Wasserman's point of view on this particular issue is not generally accepted, but it is worthy of consideration. His new book (Wasserman, 1978) is also an excellent source of the history and current status of color theory.

2. The Production of the Photoreceptor Potential

So far I have been mainly concerned with the characteristics of the retinal part of the large photosensitive molecule. The structure of this relatively small portion of a molecule of rhodopsin, or of any of the other photopigments, determines the characteristics of the primary sensory action—the decomposition of the pigment due to the photoisomerization of the retinal to its all-*trans* form. To explain the next step in the chain, the production of the receptor potential, however, I must shift the focus of the discussion to the opsin moiety. It is this much larger part of the photosensitive molecule that is now thought to be critical in the actual production of the receptor potential.

George Wald originally expressed the chemical bonding between the retinal and opsin moieties by the following chemical equation:

$$C_{19}H_{27}HC = O + H_2N\text{-opsin} \rightleftharpoons C_{19}H_{27}HC = N\text{-opsin} + H_2O$$
$$11\text{-}cis\text{-retinal} + \text{rhodopsin} \rightleftharpoons \text{rhodopsin} + \text{water} \qquad (3\text{-}21)$$

The key portion of this reaction is the substitution of all of the retinal molecule (with the exception of the oxygen atom) for the two hydrogen atoms that had been attached to the nitrogen atom on the opsin. Whereas the oxygen and hydrogen form a free molecule of water, the opsin and the retinal are attached by a carbon to nitrogen double bond—a condition that can remain stable only if the retinal remains in the 11-*cis* stage. However, in addition to the availability of the double-bonded oxygen on the retinal molecule and the H_2N group on the opsin as indicated in this equation, another atomic sidechain known as a sulfhydryl group —SH— is also required for the combination to occur and is likewise exposed when decomposition occurs. Under the action of the stimulating light, the rhodopsin molecule fractures and "exposes" two of these highly reactive sulfhydryl groups. At a later stage, in the sequence of the intermediate breakdown products, a hydrogen bond is also exposed, but, according to Wald, apparently this occurs too long after the time the actual excitatory process occurs to play a very significant role in the actions yet to follow. Specifically, the opsin fragment with its exposed sulfhydryl groups is supposed to affect membrane permeability directly, even though it must penetrate the disk membrane to get to the cell membrane.

"Exposure" of the sulfhydryl groups is a somewhat ambiguous notion, for they apparently are not part of the actual bonding reactions holding retinal to the opsin. Wald suggests that the exposure is a function of the stereogeometry of the opsin moiety. Where previously the sulfhydryl groups had been buried deep within the molecular structure of the rhodopsin molecule, the structural changes occurring in the structure of the opsins during the photodecomposition actually bring them to the surface where they are available for chemical interaction. Whether this sort of stereogeometrical change is a metaphor for a much more complicated catalytic or direct chemical reaction is hard to say. The important fact is that, shortly after the initiation of the bleaching process, the opsin is no longer an inert and unreactive part of the rhodopsin complex but is altered to a reactive structure capable of participation in other processes by mechanisms other than those produced by the rupture of C═N bond.

However, this model does not yet explain the production of the graded electrical receptor potential. Wald suggests another plausible mechanism that might be involved in the production of the receptor potential, which some investigators have suggested is observed as the *A* wave of the electroretinogram. If they are correct, the *A* wave may be properly referred to as the *late receptor potential* (LRP).

Wald's suggestion is that the exposed sulfhydryl groups on the opsin immediately begin to react chemically with either the outer cell membrane of the receptor itself or with the more immediately available interior membranes of the lamella of the receptor outer segment, as shown in Fig. 3-22. If the opsin in some way did change the permeability of either membrane, there would be a resulting depolarization or hyperpolarization as passive forces redistributed, at least in this local region, the ions whose concentration differences produced the resting potential. A local current sink or source would thus be produced that could lead to action at a distance—presumably at the synapse at the base of the receptor cell. Such a hypothetical system would explain one adaptive reason for the presence of the platelike lamellae in the outer segments of photoreceptors. The lamella might act as amplifiers of a sort. A local depolarization in one region might summate with those in others to produce a receptor potential magnitude far greater than that which could be produced by the single cell membrane.

Hagins, Penn, and Yoshikami (1970) have discovered that in the vertebrate eye the action of the photobreakdown products is to reduce, rather than to increase, the permeability of the rod or cone membrane and thus to reduce a continuous ionic current observed when receptors are in the dark. The decrease in permeability leads to a hyperpolarization of the membrane potential of vertebrate photoreceptors when they are exposed to light. (Invertebrate photoreceptor potentials are more usually found to be depolarizations.)

There is a second process that may be involved in transduction. K. T. Brown and Murakami (1964) have shown that if the photically driven voltage (the electroretinogram) between the front and the back of a dark-adapted vertebrate eye is recorded with the use of very high stimulus energies, a rapid voltage shift, which seems to be associated with the initial stages of the photochemical breakdown, occurs with a latency of only a few microseconds.

This fast visual response, the *early receptor potential* (ERP), appears to be dependent upon parallel alignment of the rhodopsin molecules in the outer segments of the intact eye. It will not occur in solutions of the photochemical in a test tube (Cone & Brown, 1967). Almost no other change in the physics of the situation seems to affect the amplitude or latency of the response. Because the signal is measurable only at very high stimulus intensity, it is not clear what role it might play in normal vision. Nevertheless, the ERP is of great interest in suggesting that there may be a direct electrical action produced by some of the steps in the breakdown of the photochemical, one not mediated by an intermediate membrane permeability change due to the presence of the breakdown products.

Cone (1967) feels that the ERP is a direct result of the redistribution of charges as the rhodopsin molecule goes through the intermediary stages of decomposition following the initial photoisomerization. Cone and Cobbs (1969) were able to evoke a distinctive pattern of the *ERP* at different times, following a strong preliminary conditioning flash. They believe that the shape of the *ERP* in these cases is characteristic of the presence of one or another of the breakdown products. Because the threshold for the ERP is at least a million times greater than that of the LRP, the ERP does not appear to be the direct antecedent of the receptor potential per se. It probably will continue to be an important measure of the photochemistry of retinal pigments.

Obviously, the problem of transduction in the vertebrate visual receptor is still not fully understood. Nevertheless, we are beginning to learn some things about the involved subcellular mechanisms in the vertebrate eye. In summary:

1. The process is initiated entirely by the action of the light that alters the stereoisomeric state of the retinal portion of the photochemical.
2. The ultimate intracellular result of the breakdown in the photochemical is to produce a reduction in the permeability to sodium ions of the plasma membrane of the outer segment of the receptor cell, thus hyperpolarizing the cell.
3. This membrane permeability change can be recorded as the *LRP,* which is probably the same as the *A* wave in the electroretinogram.
4. The *ERP,* on the other hand, is an indication of the processes that are occurring within the pigment molecule rather than at the membrane and is probably not related to the rod or cone receptor potential per se.

G. A SUMMARY

In this chapter I have tried to provide the technical foundations necessary for understanding the taxonomic theory of visual perception presented in the remainder of this book. As I noted at the outset, it is both one of the delights and one of the complications of this subfield of psychology that so many other fields of science contribute to it. In this chapter, we see how anatomical, physiological, physical, and chemical knowledge all must be invoked in understanding the psychological problems intrinsic to the study of visual perception. Yet it must never be forgotten that, from the point of view of the perceptual scientist, these are but the technical tools and media one must use to develop theoretical models. The true object of study of perceptual *psychology* is the perceptual experience itself—the mental response to the incident stimuli—and not the physics of light or the anatomy or physiology of the eye. All the rest of this material is cognate, supportive, and indirect, however useful and valuable it may be as we attack the psychological problem of how we perceive. Thus the material presented in this chapter should be appreciated for what it is, prerequisite and preparatory, but not mistaken for the main issue at hand. No matter how elegant the neurophysiology or intriguing the biochemistry, it is the psychological problems inherent in the study of perceptual phenomena that are most germane to the theme of this book.

Certain summary generalizations concerning this supportive material can profitably be made explicit at this point. The brief review of background material has clarified and emphasized certain points that are particularly relevant to an understanding of the general state of perceptual science in the second half of the twentieth century.

My review of the current view of the physics of external reality should have been particularly important in reminding us that there is still much to be learned about the nature of the external world. Many of the models that were discussed are in a rapid state of flux and seem to change literally by the week. It is certain that by the time this book is published much of what I have said concerning quark theory, for example, will be obsolete, or at least amended.

But there is something more profound, transcending individual theories and models of physical reality to which perceptual scientists should be especially sensitive. The mathematical models and the bizarre quantum numbers or physical properties ascribed to the constituent particles of matter and energy are all but meaningless abstractions to most of us. Our Newtonian intuitions are simply not adequate to comprehend what a "confined quark" actually is, or indeed if the commonsense notions that we have of the existence of "particles and forces" are actually valid. Many of these entities are so thoroughly cut off from our sensory experience by the gross difference in magnitude between the scales of man and the basic particle microcosm that certain of their properties such as "strange flavors" and "charmed colors" may always remain elusive concepts and never take on any more substantial intuitive meaning. Our fragile link to the external world is once again placed in sharp focus.

Another important general point that I hope this chapter has made is that the physical energies that constitute actual stimuli for our sensory apparatus represent but very small portions of the total range of energies that exist. Some forces simply do not interact with our receptors. Even electromagnetic energy, the one force that is responsible for almost all of our sensory processes is, in the main, insensible. Only a very small window of the electromagnetic spectrum—visible light—affects our visual apparatus.

My discussion of the anatomy of the visual system was also intended to lay the foundation for another general point, which is probably not going to be very popular among visual psychobiologists but which I still believe to be true. The current state of neuroanatomy and neurophysiology is much farther away from explaining most perceptual phenomena than many of my colleagues seem willing to admit. It is terribly difficult to appreciate the existence of lacunae in our knowledge, and most of us tend to fill in our ignorance with fancy and all-too-glib analogies. Yet one cannot look at the incredible complexity of the inner plexiform layer of the retina as elucidated by Sjöstrand, or the cerebral cortex as analyzed by Szentágothai, without appreciating how very far our neuroanatomic wisdom is from explaining the complexities of psychological processes such as those measured by Tanner and Swet's signal detection theory. The simplistic neurophysiological theories of perception that had grown out of some extraordinarily distinguished neurophysiological research are now appreciated to be quite limited in explanatory power. Neurophysiological research is no longer championed as the panacea it once seemed to psychologists hungry for any reductive explanation. Receptive fields and hypercomplex cells are no longer unquestionably accepted as the neural correlates of some very complex perceptual phenomena. I expand greatly upon this general point in Chapter 9.

We have also seen how the visual process is triggered by a structural change in a particular bond in a very specialized molecule. This process, in addition to providing the key to the transductive process, also gives evidence of the extraordinary success of the selective mechanisms that have guided the evolution of organic processes for billions of years. What sort of creatures we would have been without the specific photosensitivity of 11-*cis* retinal is not determinable, but the degree to which we can attribute our species' success to this peculiar chemistry is awesome. It is probably not too much of an exaggeration to say that without this chemical quirk the human race as we know it would not exist!

With this background now in hand, the scope of this project can now properly be shifted. I leave this technical material, the survey of perceptual problems, and the historical review of perceptual theories that have been proposed as answers to the great epistemological perplexity and begin a presentation of the taxonomic, multilevel theory that is intended to be the main contribution of this book.

II A TAXONOMIC LEVEL THEORY OF VISUAL PERCEPTION

4 Prolog

A. AN INTRODUCTORY COMMENT

The remainder of this book reviews perceptual microtheories and presents an eclectic, multilevel, and taxonomic theory of visual perception. Underlying this attempt to bring some initial order to the widely diverse phenomena and data making up the empirical substance of this field is a basic premise that assert that there are identifiable levels (the six briefly introduced in Chapter 1) at which afferent signals undergo some critical information processing or transformation in a way that affects some subsequent perceptual response. I believe that, to the extent it is possible, specification of these critical informational processes or transforms is the best way to explain the various aspects of each perceptual phenomenon. Because I anticipate that this emphasis on process and processing levels may be the subject of a considerable amount of criticism, it is necessary to make explicit certain caveats and to clarify certain premises that have guided my thinking about this matter. It is also necessary to consider certain logical, empirical, and conceptual obstacles to theory development in perceptual psychology in order to appreciate some of the difficulties faced by anyone undertaking a macrotheoretical attack on perception. The purpose of this chapter, therefore, is to introduce some of the basic thinking that underlies the rest of the book and to detail more specifically the nature of the taxonomic level theory of visual processes that is its essential internal structure.

It is critically important to the following argument that I present for the reader to understand that my specification of a critical level of processing for any phenomenon is not meant to imply that I am asserting that any perceptual response, so assigned, is exclusively encoded, represented, and processed *only* at that critical level. I appreciate that all of the other levels of communication and integration, both external to and within the perceptual nervous system (as defined by the five psychoneural—omitting Level 0—levels of the model), must be involved to some degree in the establishment of the final percept.

As we shall see, virtually every perceptual dimension is affected by multiple factors often representing processes and transformations occurring at many different levels. The different processes interact and concatenate to define the final percept. Therefore, no process at any level is sufficient to define totally a perceptual experience. The premise that a critical level exists asserts only that there are loci of incident information transformation that are the principal determinants of subsequent perceptions but not the sole determinants. Some of these critical processes that I describe occur very peripherally, whereas others are the result of the integration of information that could occur only in the deepest and most complex portions of the brain. Simple anatomic reasons make the argument for the central localization of some processes very straightforward indeed; others place critical processes in the periphery equally solidly. Some critical processes, such as lateral inhibitory interaction, affect the actual isomorphic spatiotemporal geometry of the afferent signal. Others, such as the processes underlying geometric illusions, are probably more properly understood in terms of symbolic alterations of the "significance" or "meaning" of the stimulus. I demonstrate later in the book that any critical level can lead to immediate powerful, compelling, and virtually automatic perceptual responses, not just those most closely associated with periperhal mechanisms.

I must stress again the idea that the critical level accounting for any given phenomenon does not preclude the involvement of other levels of this hypothetical perceptual system, nor does it deny that several levels may redundantly exert the same critical effect on a given afferent signal. Thus, although trichromatic analysis in the retina, for example, does lead to a set of chromatically encoded information-bearing signals communicated upward through all anatomic levels of the nervous system, these signals may be subject to subsequent processing at other levels that may further modulate them. Color contrast, for example, which can also affect perceived hue, appears to be explained by processes occurring at a much higher level than that underlying color addition phenomena; yet the contrast effect also strongly modulates our perception of color and may, in fact, totally override the effects of the peripheral processes that seem more directly responsive to the physics of the stimulus. Furthermore even this dual-level description is insufficient to explain all hue phenomena; knowledge of what a color "should be" can also affect perceived hue. It is very important to note, therefore, that the trichromatic color addition and contrast phenomena that I discuss do not tell the entire story of color vision. Rather, each represents only a highly circumscribed subportion of the global process called color vision. Many vigorously articulated controversies have been ridden into the ridiculous because the simple fact was overlooked that processes at different levels (like the wave and particle theory in physics) may be complementary rather than mutually exclusive and antagonistic.

The unavoidable fact is that all processing levels are involved in almost every phenomenon and most phenomena are influenced by more than a single factor or aspect of the stimulus configuration. Stereoscopic vision, for example, which is later identified (admittedly with some residual doubt) as a Level 4 process, could not occur unless the initial transductive processes of Level 1 occurred earlier, and the monocular information so generated was communicated and processed by

Level 2 processes so that it could be organized as a form by Level 3 mechanisms. But the *critical* processing stage for stereopsis, the level at which the essential pattern of neural information is first available as a necessary and sufficient equivalent of the perceptual response of apparent depth, is probably that cortical level at which a merger of previously independent monocular information occurs. Below that, the necessary neural conditions for stereoscopic depth simply do not exist; there has been no joining in the same locus of monocular information to allow an integrative response.

In this context, it is equally essential to remember that the determination that some property of the stimulus is *implicitly encoded* at any level of the nervous system is not equivalent to an identification of the critical level. The critical level is defined as the level at which the essential information underlying a related phenomenon *first* became *explicitly available* in a perceptually usable form. Thus, for example, the transformed signals that are the coded representation of the Mach band first emerge as an explicit pattern of coded signals in the retina. Though the precursor information (i.e., the geometrical properties of the proximal stimulus) was present prior to that level as a pattern within the receptor mosaic, the bands themselves do not become manifest until the retinal network interactions (which in this case are the critical processes) operate on the flow of afferent information. For this phenomenon the critical level is defined by the act of combining the stimulus geometry and the processing algorithm that is built in the retinal plexus level. Prior to that level, the critical processes had not occurred and the responses were not manifest in any coded form and subsequent to that level, the neural information representing enhanced contours is explicitly present in all further coded representations unless subsequently reprocessed back to its original form. Though the codes may change from one neural language to another, or even from an isomorphic to a symbolic representations, the explicit information pattern indicative of enhanced contours remains available and could, in principle, be detected by an ideal external measuring device up to the highest level of neural and perceptual equivalence. In sum, the critical level may also be defined as the level at which the encoded representation of a phenomenon became explicit in the neural dimensions of the communicated message.

The next issue to be dealt with is—identification of the criteria for distinguishing between the levels of the taxonomic theory proposed here. As a preliminary answer to this question, it should be noted that the criteria I have used are predominantly theoretical and explanatory and, in a very direct sense, psychological. I have approached the problem from a perspective that asks, "Given a phenomenon, what is the most plausible and effective level of analysis that can account for it?" rather than, "What phenomena are explained by this or that neuroanatomic level?" Thus what may appear to be closely related phenomena (e.g., trichromatic addition and color contrast) are often attributed to widely divergent levels within this taxonomy. There is, it must be appreciated, no direct correspondence between the critical processing levels I invoke here and anatomic stages beyond the obvious one of Level 1.

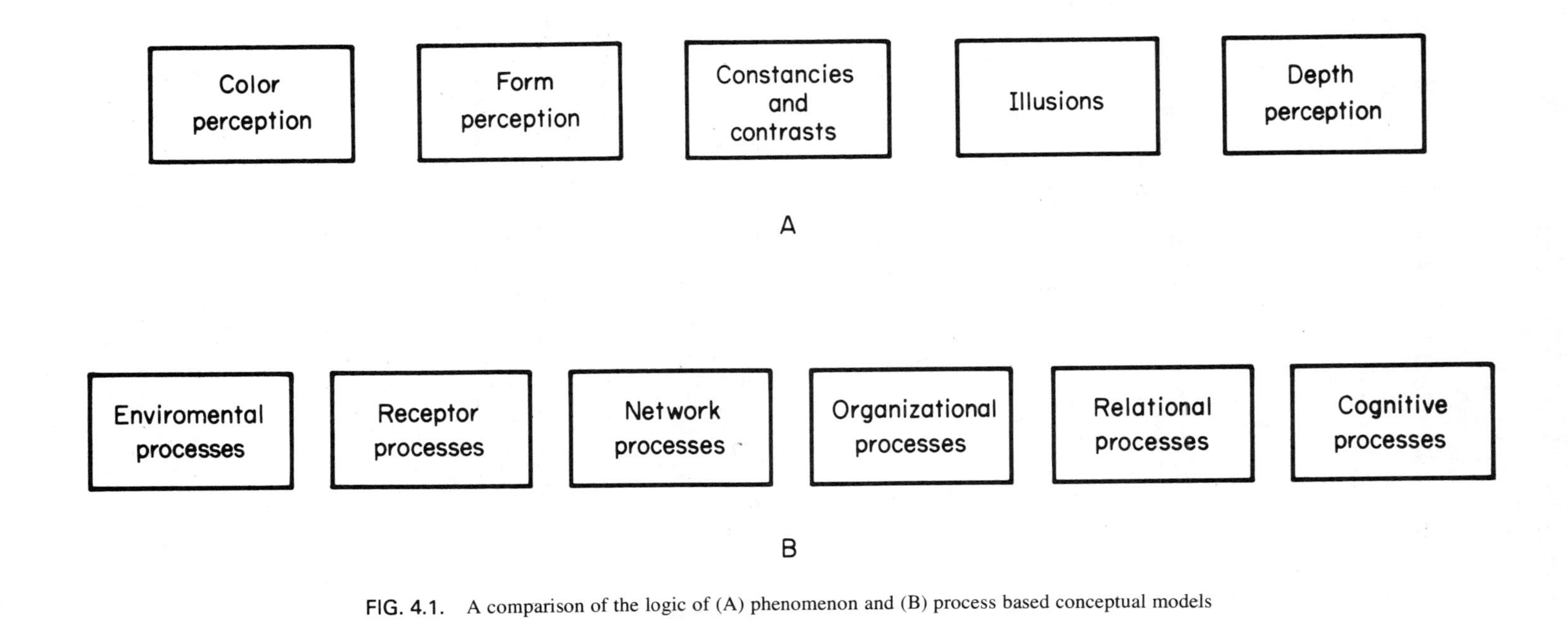

FIG. 4.1. A comparison of the logic of (A) phenomenon and (B) process based conceptual models of perceptual science.

The fundamental philosophy behind the dissection of what some may consider to be global processes into more sharply defined subprocesses can be made clearer by considering a few simple block diagrams of the logical organization of some alternative approaches. The complex of processes collectively referred to as color perception must, as I have noted, be accounted for by actions that probably occur over several levels of the multilevel perceptual system. If one clusters all similar phenomena together, the conceptual model underlying a typical text would look like Fig. 4-1A. However, if the complex of processes is broken down to the individual influences on color perception, as I do in this book, then the conceptual model would look more like that shown in Fig. 4-1B. Here, a block indicates one of the conceptual and processing levels at which a critical transformation may take place and the entire process of color perception becomes an aggregated manifestation of the influence of many factors and levels.

In this section, I have briefly introduced some of the general premises and assumptions of the multilevel taxonomic theory of visual percepts that I develop in this book. There are, however, many logical, conceptual, and empirical obstacles and difficulties that make this task challenging and difficult, and in the next section I discuss some of these obstacles to progress toward a general macrotheory of perception.

B. EMPIRICAL, LOGICAL, AND CONCEPTUAL OBSTACLES TO MACROTHEORY DEVELOPMENT IN PERCEPTUAL SCIENCE

Most previous attempts to develop a global theory of visual perception are disappointing in one common way: Few, if any, seek to provide the taxonomic order so greatly needed by perceptual psychology. There are multiple reasons for this enormous error of omission in perceptual theory, and many of these reasons are still relevant and impede new effort towards a perceptual taxonomy. As I spell out the details of my level theory in the subsequent pages of this book, I am fully aware that my effort, too, will be subject to hindrances, restrictions, obstacles, and difficulties of the sort that have plagued previous attempts. This section identifies those difficulties that have impeded progress in theory building in the past and that are likely to limit the effectiveness of the new model I propose here.

Three different general classes of obstacles to perceptual macrotheory development can be discerned. The first includes empirical and factual difficulties based simply upon the presence or absence of data or with the practical problems of data collection. The second includes logical limitations, those more fundamental difficulties based upon the organizational and relational aspects of the various components of the puzzle. The third consists of some conceptual or cognitive limitations on the part of theorists themselves.

1. Empirical Obstacles

Empirical obstacles include those difficulties in macrotheory development in perceptual psychology that pertain to the current availability of data and measurements that are necessary for the construction of any theoretical structure in perceptual psychology or to the practical difficulties of obtaining that data. This category of obstacles can be a function either of an inadequate or, somewhat surprisingly, of a superadequate store of observations, either a plethora or a dearth of data can inhibit theory development.

a. A Plethora of Data. The amount of relevant data now available to the perceptual theorist is indisputably enormous! In the English language alone, a dozen or so journals speak monthly to the problems of perceptual psychology. If each issue of these journals published only a dozen papers (and most publish more), every month would produce over 100 new articles, all relevant to the problems of the field encompassed by this book, for a total approaching 2000 articles each year. Clearly no one, *absolutely no one,* can read even a modest proportion of these papers. Equally likely, most individual papers are ignored by most beyond a brief glance at their titles. There is, therefore, an enormous glut of data, much of it representing a huge waste of human effort precisely because most of it is presented in a disorganized and disjointed form without relevance to a guiding intellectual superstructure.

Because of its essentially empirical and atheoretical orientation, I believe this problem of data proliferation is particularly crucial to perceptual psychology. It is as if an army of mad botanists had gone out to collect plants and continued to do so without any effort to find out what the family interrelationships were among the various collected items. The botanists at least seem to have been limited by a relatively modest number of species. Perceptual phenomena are virtually innumerable and ubiquitous.

The situation in current perceptual psychology is as it must have been in botany prior to the revolution embodied in the Linnaean taxonomic system. This flood of often meaningless data and the lack of a clear statement of what constitutes a critical experiment establish both the need for and the obstacle to the development of a general taxonomy of the perceptual data base. The obstacles to theory building, so generated, then arise for the simplest of practical reasons; there are so many phenomena and so many unrelated, redundant, and pointless observations that it is simply logistically difficult to begin to encompass all of them within the confines of a single global theory.

The number of perceptual phenomena that can be observed in the laboratory is equally enormous. There are so many possible targets of interest that, of the substantial number of working experimental psychologists, few ever seem to be attacking a common problem. Physics, on the other hand, if current statements may be believed, seems to be organized according to a completely different paradigm. Relatively few active problems are currently circulating within the physical community, and large numbers of physicists are simultaneously and highly competitively working on the few that are momentarily popular. The babble of the perceptual literature displayed in the pages of the journals of the Psychonomic Society or the American Psychological Association is quite different from the concentrated attention displayed in the publications of the American Physical Society. In sum, although this lack of concentrated attention and the resulting plethora of unrelated data constitute a major obstacle to the development of a systematic view of perceptual phenomena, they simultaneously present one of the best arguments for establishing such a taxonomy.

b. Redundant and Multiple Discoveries of Phenomena. Greatly accentuating what I believe to be a genuine glut of findings and data in perceptual psychology is the redundant discovery of the same phenomena under slightly different conditions. Many phenomena reported as novel results are actually identical (in terms of the underlying mechanisms, processes, and responses) to others repeatedly described in the earlier literature. Some classic observations have been discovered or described anew in slightly different experimental contexts time after time. They are represented as novel discoveries by very well-meaning researchers unaware of their redundancy because of the absence of an organizing taxonomy of percepts.

Redundant discoveries often arise as a result of the application of a multiple or more complex version of the stimulus conditions that led to an earlier reported phenomena. Nevertheless the complex process so invoked is, in principle, the same as the simpler one. It is particularly distressing when, as so often happens, the earlier report of the prototypical phenomenon is not even cited by the psychologist who stumbles upon the more complex version. A critical conceptual commonality between the prototype and the more complex version is thus obscured, and the Parthenon of perceptual events becomes unnecessarily crowded with repeated discovery of the same basic phenomenon. Thus, absence of clear criteria and a conceptual superstructure leads to a host of redundant "discoveries." The process then feeds back on itself and these redundancies impede the development of the conceptual system.

Methodological differences alone, regardless of how elaborate, should not justify describing what properly should be considered to be identical perceptual phenomena under two or more quite different names. To divide so falsely exemplars of the same class of process multiplies the already superabundant perceptual data base without clarifying the fundamental relationships among the various phenomena.

c. An Absence of Critical Experiments. However abundant the perceptual data base is, in general, there is also, paradoxically, a shortage of those particularly critical experiments that are essential in discriminating between different classes of phenomena or in choosing among alternative theoretical explanations. This difficulty, the shortage of critical experiments, also is related to the absence of a schematic or taxonomic model of perceptual phenomena: The absence of even a tentative classification scheme (which does help to clarify meaningful questions) makes it difficult for the theoretician to propose significant experiments just as the shortage of particularly critical experiments impedes the development of the classification scheme. To break such a refractory cycle, one must enter the system at some point. An argument can be made that the most effective point of entry would be to develop an organizing taxonomic theory or schema. Critical experiments would then emerge almost automatically even if the schema were not perfect. Only within the framework of such an organized theoretical or classificatory structure can perceptual psychology approach the ideal target of applying "strong inference" to this science as so eloquently championed by John R. Platt (1964) and thus fill in the critical gaps in our knowledge created by the shortage of the very special, very seminal, and very decisive studies that are the essence of scientific theory building.

d. The Difficulty of Obtaining Direct Electrophysiological Evidence from Human Subjects. The dearth of experimental data obtained from humans concerning the neurophysiological foundations of perception presents a further empirical difficulty in developing global macrotheories. Because at least two of the six levels I propose here are couched in patently neurophysiological terms, it would be especially useful to be able to carry out comparative studies of the same phenomena in the same animal using both psychophysical and neural indicators. Indeed, it would be particularly valuable to use the animal from which most of the psychophysical data has been collected—the human being. This is not generally possible, however, for a host of worthy ethical and practical reasons. Thus psychobiologists frequently resort to model preparations in lower vertebrates and invertebrates.

Many psychobiologists are now becoming aware, however, that model preparations in infrahuman preparations, although displaying analogous overt behavior, may do so on the basis of mechanisms that are quite different from those underlying the human phenomena. For example, lateral inhibitory interaction between neural responses may be analogous to the inhibitory interactions observed between *concepts or ideas* in perceptual defense experiments, but it is hardly likely that identical or even similar neural mechanisms account for the two behaviors.

Human single-cell electrophysiological studies are rare: A few examples of such studies do, however, exist: those of Marg (1973), within the brain; Hensel and Boman (1960), in peripheral somatosensory nerves; and Weinstein, Hobson, and Baker (1971), in retinal ganglion cells. Other than those electroencephalographic studies that measure compound, cumulative action potentials, there are few other reports that speak directly to the electrophysical basis of perception in man himself. The absence of this particularly critical data base is especially frustrating, and a major empirical obstacle in distinguishing among some equally plausible alternative explanations of certain perceptual phenomena. The only mitigation of this frustration is that, so far, nothing has appeared in the few human studies to suggest that man is very different from his mammalian cousins with regard to his neurophysiology.

e. The Difficulty in Discriminating Between Closely Related Psychological Processes. The fact that any psychological function—be it a perceptual phenomenon, a motivational state, or a progressive improvement of behavior as a result of experience—must necessarily incorporate all of the other functions, to at least some degree, means that there will always be a certain amount of empirical difficulty in distinguishing between the contribution of each of the different components of our mental life to any particular phenomenon. There are many instances in the perceptual literature in which two contributory factors were not appreciated as being essentially separate influences until very late in the historical development of the topic. As one very salient example, the fact that both peripheral neural and central criterion factors are involved in absolute threshold measurements was not fully appreciated until the development of signal-detection theory in the 1950s, even though thresholds had been an explicit topic of interest since the 1850s. Of course, psychologists were aware of judgmental factors, but the change in perspective introduced by signal detection theory was profound.

A closely related empirical difficulty is that current laboratory methodology still does not provide us with an unequivocal way of determining at what time a percept occurs. I have already alluded to the continuing problem faced by psychologists in deciding whether psychological and real time are congruent. Those few measures of timing psychological processes (e.g., Efron, 1970b, Wasserman & Kong, 1979) that have been suggested are not without their limitations; all such attacks on the problem are more or less indirect.

Finally, the human mind is so constructive and creative in its responses to partial and poorly structured stimuli that the perceptual scientist faces a fundamental empirical difficulty in distinguishing between a percept that is a more or less direct response to some stimulus dimension and one that is rationally "constructed" as a solution to the "problem" posed by a less-than-complete stimulus configuration. All of the matters mentioned here pertain to the difficulty of isolating and then precisely defining the psychological state under examination.

2. Logical Obstacles

Theory development in perceptual psychology is not only impeded by the empirical difficulties described in the previous section but is also strongly hindered by certain logical obstacles intrinsic to the nature of the problem. Many of these logical obstacles are common to other sciences as well (e.g., an indeterminacy principle operates in psychology as well as in physics; the measurement process often alters the state of the measured experience), but some are especially aggravating in psychology, characterized as it is by multivariate causes and the interpersonal privacy of mental responses. Some of the difficulties I describe in this section are so refractory that it is possible that, unlike the empirical difficulties, they may never be satisfactorily overcome. For others, resolution may possibly only await new analytic techniques and conceptual approaches.

a. The Intrapersonal Nature of Perception. Perhaps the most difficult problem faced by psychologists, along with other scientists who do not have immediate access to the objects of their science (e.g., astronomers), arises from the fact that perceptions, as *intrapersonal* subjective or mental responses, are themselves inherently invisible to the external observer and can be only indirectly evaluated through the medium of *interpersonally* reported communications or observed behavior. It is, however, unfortunately true that explicit behavior does not always directly and accurately reflect implicit mental response. People act, lie, deceive themselves, or even grossly misunderstand their own mental processes (Nisbett & Wilson, 1977). The positivistic and behavioristic concept that a description of behavior was essentially all the knowledge that could be obtained about mind is clearly incomplete but, equally clearly, it is also true that our knowledge of the relation between internal mental states and behavior still remains incomplete. There is, therefore, a continuing difficulty in analyzing and fully understanding what can only be seen through the murky medium of language or other behavior. The characteristics of the efferent medium must be filtered out before we can define the residual characteristics of the obscured underlying mental processes. In short, the fundamental intrapersonal privacy of the perceptual response remains a major logical obstacle to achieving understanding in this important field of experimental psychology.

b. The Absence of Well-Defined Dimensions of Categorization and Measurement in Perceptual Psychology. Another major logical obstacle hindering the development of any macrotheory of perception arises from the fact that many perceptual phenomena do not have well-defined dimensions or units of measurement, and may not be well anchored to other dimensions that do enjoy better-defined metrics. Although most perceptual phenomena are studied in relation to the stimulus conditions which elicit them, it is clear from the literature that there is, in general, no direct correspondence between the dimensions of the external world and those of the mental response. Rather, in most perceptual experiments a lack of "veridicality" is very often found between the stimulus dimensions and the perceptual dimensions. For example, variations in photic wavelength are perceived as variations in hue. Thus the anchoring provided by the physical stimulus domain is very often looser than it may at first seem.

Traditional efforts to provide some sort of metric or unit for the perceptual dimensions (e.g., sones, dols) have rarely been satisfactory and usually have been quickly forgotten. It is now far more common to deal in a kind of dimensionless space–time in which proportions, ratios, or other forms of quasi-numerical relationships are used instead to describe the variation of some perceptual response produced by a variation along some physical stimulus dimension.

In the absence of any simple, direct, or rigorously defined units or dimensions (comparable to the wavelength of light in the stimulus domain), many perceptual phenomena have come to be classified on the basis of distinctions that are less easily formularized and defined. After all, the name categories of red, blue, yellow, and green are not quantitative values along a single continuously varying perceptual dimension that is directly equivalent to the continuously varying wavelength of the light that evoked the experiences we tag with these names. Even when the analogy between the perceptual dimension and the stimulus dimension is more direct (e.g., when one is comparing perceptual magnitude estimates to stimulus intensities), there is always a sufficient degree of nonlinearity present in the relationship to make a precise definition of the psychological units of experience an elusive, if not impossible, task.

c. Constraints on Analysis of Internal Structural Imposed by Input–Output Methods. Another major logical obstacle to understanding perceptual processes and phenomena is that an analysis of the internal mechanics of any multistage, multiprocess, and multicomponent closed system (closed in the sense that internal structure is not directly observable) cannot, in principle, be carried out solely by observing the external performance of the whole system. Yet, the only approach available to students of perception is the paradigm of comparing stimulus–input and behavioral response–output in a correlative manner. As I noted earlier, no conceivable direct neurophysiological approach can unequivocally demonstrate the existence of mental responses.[1] I now call the reader's attention to the fact that behavioral observations are equally inadequate to solve the problem of internal structure.

What we have here is an intrinsic logical limit on how effective input–output methodology can be in unraveling the inner workings of complex interactive

---

[1]The absoluteness of this remark may upset some of my readers. However, I maintain that most of the perceptual responses described in the latter chapters of this book are not amenable to electrophysiological examination in the direct way often proposed without an enormous leap of faith and logic as yet unjustified by rigorous scientific observation. No matter how complex the machine nor how detailed our knowledge of its structure (and the operations of that structure), it is impossible to establish definitively that sentience is present. Mental activity can only be inferred from behavior and cannot be deduced from the correlated workings of the mechanism. Determining which of the brain activities (observed with electrophysiological techniques) are equivalent to perceptual processes that have been independently demonstrated (with behavioral techniques) thus remains a refractory problem in psychobiology.

systems If nothing else is known except the nature of the transform between the input and the output, it is axiomatic that nothing can be said with certainty about internal structure, no matter how simple and how direct the relation between the stimulus and the response may appear to be. This is so simply because there is an infinite number of possible mechanical arrangements that could produce the same transform within an intact "black box."[2] However, we usually do know something else beyond the bare bones of the input–output relation and can make some plausible inferences that can help point the way towards at least a glimmering of understanding about the internal organization of the perceptual system. The progress that can be made, however, should not be overestimated. It is terribly easy to deceive one's self into believing that one of many *plausible* and *possible* internal models is, in fact, a *unique* and *definitive* explanation of some perceptual process.

d. No Phenomenon Is Truly Isolatable to a Single Level. A further logical obstacle to model building in perceptual science emerges from the fact that no matter how hard we may strain to develop a hierarchical theory of perception, no individual phenomenon is, in actuality, totally isolatable to any one stage of psychoneural processing. Every perceptual phenomenon (with the possible exception of totally endogenous images and hallucinations) is linked at some point in its history to a stimulus transduction. Every percept, thus, must bear some relationship to the receptor, neural network, and communication processes of the peripheral stages of psychoneural processing that must be a part of any kind of a hierarchical model of perception. The fact that a percept comes to conscious awareness is a further indication that it is also being processed at higher levels and must, therefore, also be represented there. It is, furthermore, hardly possible to conceive of a perceptual response that has not been affected to some degree by the prior experience of the subject and which, therefore, involves some psychological processes that are not an explicit portion of the multilevel model I propose here.

The escape hatch from this considerable difficulty lies, I believe, in the joint impact of the definition of a *critical level* of processing and the fact that the taxonomy I present here is based on processes, not phenomena. As I noted in the introduction to this chapter, the critical level is the stage at which the information processing of the perceptual nervous system first performs the essential action that gives rise to an explicit manifestation of the patterned neural signals that are the necessary and sufficient equivalents of any given perceptual process. The key point here is that it is this process that is isolated to a single level, not the phenomena; and processes can in principle be sharply isolated even if phenomena cannot.

---

[2]For a discussion of what is meant by a "black box," see Chapter 9.

3. Conceptual Obstacles

Now I come to the third and final category of obstacles to the development of comprehensive macrotheories of perception. This third set of difficulties, which I classify as conceptual, is not data-oriented, nor does it entail the logical difficulties inherent in the subject matter itself. Conceptual obstacles arise instead out of the cognitive characteristics of the practitioners of this ambitious art of perceptual theory building. These conceptual impediments are the blocks to the free flow of inventive, consistent, and creative thinking to which we are all subject and for which the major cure is simply to make them as explicit and obvious as possible. However explicit they may be made, there is an amazing adherence exhibited by each of us to our own conventional modes of thought. Thomas Kuhn (1962), in his now-classic work on scientific "paradigms," has eloquently discussed the powerful, persistent, and compelling forces exerted on scientific thinking by the contemporary millieu at any instant in scientific history.

This intellectual conservatism, however, is not entirely a negative force. It is relatively easy to make the case that conservatism in science is also a very positive attribute of this particular aspect of human endeavor. Without some reasonable degree of conservatism (which might otherwise be defined as an extreme unwillingness to change one's beliefs in the absence of an inordinately powerful argument) the entire scientific system, as we know it, would be unstable, continuously falling victim to every half-baked idea that emerged in print or on the podium. Thus there is a necessary and, from some points of view, a constructive tension between the desire for novelty and progress on the one hand and the absolute necessity for stabilization in science on the other hand. This is so in spite of the fact that conservatism sometimes engenders in scientists a disconcerting unwillingness to diverge from the conventional views held by the majority of their contemporary colleagues. It is a value judgment, of course, as to what is to be considered a destructive conceptual block and what is to be considered to be a healthy conservatism. In the following subsections, a through f, I discuss what I believe are the major conceptual constraints to progress in theory building in the perceptual sciences. The reader must evaluate for himself whether they are unnecessarily debilitating to the growth of science or examples of valid reasons for cautious hesitation.

a. A Conceptual Predilection for Isomorphic Models. Until the fifteenth or sixteenth centuries the major conceptual blocks to theory building in what has since come to be called psychology arose out of the antagonism on the part of the then dominant theological philosophies towards studies of the mind. Indeed, even today, most of the world's people still approach the concept of mind with a religious or, at least, dualistic bias that impedes acceptance of theories and data directed towards solution of the problem of the biological origins of mental processes. Today, however, most conceptual difficulties arise, not directly from this religious bias but rather as a response to the *reaction* to that bias. The intellectual reaction, which counterbalanced and overcame the constraints imposed by the dualistic theological philosophies of medieval and earlier times, was a mechanistic metaphysics in which physical and biological processes were suggested to underlie mental processes. This revolutionary mechanistic theory, championed originally by Thomas Hobbes, was exceedingly straightforward, allowing explanations only to the extent that the mechanical models directly, isomorphically, and deterministically recreated the form of the mental process.

According to this point of view, to represent a mental process a mechanism had to exist that actually reproduced the geometric and temporal form of the process. The concept of symbolic or coded representation was neither appreciated in the abstract nor incorporated into any of the many theories of perceptual reductionism that had been forthcoming in the last few hundred years. This led to a search for "pictures in the head" to match "pictures in the mind," a search that has gone on continuously since the rejection of the medieval theological theories. The pre-eminent criterion for acceptibility of a theoretical model, which even now can be discerned in much current theory, was spatial–temporal congruency of the mental process and the neural mechanism. This criterion has biased psychobiological theoreticians either to accept or to reject theories of perception purely on the basis of the degree to which the isomorphic form of the percept is reproduced in the form of the neural response. It has also led to some spurious attempts to explain processes, such as depth perception, in terms of the actual creation of *solid* images in three-dimentional chunks of the visual cortex sensitive to inputs from both eyes. In my opinion, such an approach is based upon an inadequate appreciation of the concepts of coding and analogy.

Despite this conceptual propensity among psychobiologists for isomorphic models, there is ample evidence (as much of the rest of this book attempts to show) that the coding processes underlying percepts must, in very substantial portion, be of a symbolic rather than isomorphic nature. Not only do the psychophysical data speak to this point but increasingly so also do the neurophysiological data supporting the multidimensional sensory coding theory that is rapidly gaining currency today. To the extent that the predilection for isomorphic models prevails, there will be a conceptual block to the development of macrotheories of how percepts are represented in the nervous system. Others who have argued against the idea of a strict spatial and temporal isomorphism in perception include Skinner (1945) and Shepard and Chipman (1970).

b. The Impact of the Prevailing Scientific–Technological Zeitgeist. Theory building in psychology has historically been strongly influenced by the scientific and technological Zeitgeist. At various points in history, technology offered up concepts originating in pneumatics, hydraulics, mechanics, electricity, and telephonics as models of mind. Continuing this tradition of influence, the relevant intellectual environment today consists of concepts and ideas from computer theory and practice on the one hand, and single-cell neurophysiology on the other. There is, as a result, a powerful and compelling tendency to build models of mind, in general, and perception, in particular, based on the tenets, concepts, premises, and axioms of these sciences. Yet these technological and scientific sources can be very limited indeed and possibly grossly misleading when applied to perception. For example, concepts emerging from studies of single-cell neurophysiology are being imposed upon perception, but these concepts reflect the limits of the specific technology regulating the kind of data that is collected in, typically, a microelectrode experiment. With rare exception the neurophysiologist is limited to examining the behavior of a single point (the single neuron at the tip of his microelectrode) in space as a function of time (as defined by the trace of the typical oscilloscope display). These technological limits, which at first glance may seem almost incidental, have led almost directly to the emergence of what I believe are overly simplistic single-cell theories of perception. Recent thinking[3] makes it seem far more likely that a technology emphasizing the simultaneous activity of many interacting neurons would be a far more appropriate technological basis on which to develop neural models of perception. However, such a network-oriented paradigm is probably not within the grasp of current laboratory or theoretical practice. We thus remained locked into what may be a very inappropriate paradigm of perceptual theory defined by the highly circumscribed technology of the neurophysiological laboratory rather than by the actual biology of neural mechanisms.

The power of the present neurophysiological Zeitgeist to mislead can perhaps best be epitomized by noting the broad currency of a kind of pseudoneurophysiology and pseudoneuroanatomy that permeates so much of current theory. Hypothetical neuroanatomical structures such as "channels" and "feature detectors" are very often invented nowadays as possible mechanisms by which various perceptual phenomena may be implemented. Elementalistic feature-detecting psychological processes are invoked as hypothetical constructs by extrapolating the properties of the actual single cells that have been observed in the visual cortex by a large number of neurophysiologists, even when the psychophysical data suggest that molar, wholistic, and Gestalt-type mental processing is the more likely mode of action.

A similar argument can be made that concepts emerging from the development of the modern digital computer are also often misapplied to perceptual theory. The modern digital computer, or "von Neumann Machine," implements a very particular kind of logic organization. It is largely a serial device with well-defined lines of sequential communication between its different components. The various stages of a program are processed in strict order; indeed, the

---

[3]A number of psychologists and philosophers have questioned current thinking about such radical single-cell theories of perception. See Chapters 1 and 9, and Uttal (1978) for a more complete discussion of this central problem of perceptual theory.

typical computer program itself is also another example of a serial logical organization. The problem is that it is not at all certain that the serial logical organization of the contemporary digital computer can be universally applied to all forms of information-processing systems. In particular, it is not at all certain that the logical structure and conceptual organization implicit in the computer, as we know it, is appropriate for theory building in perceptual psychology. Yet the influence of digital computer concepts on perceptual theory is ubiquitous. The most widely accepted models of many perceptual processes are patently derived from the logic and theory that has been presented to us by the digital computer engineer.

The effects of such an influence can be subtle and pervasive. One seductive aspect of this analogy is that it has established among psychologists a predilection for models based on manipulation, storage, and representation of *discrete* symbols. This is in sharp contrast to the influence of the analog computer technology that led to ideas of continuous processes and symbols.

Whether or not the single-neuron and computer models of visual perception are ultimately going to be acceptable as satisfactory explanations of perceptual processes is not the point to which I am speaking here. (History will have to make that determination, and I elaborate my personal view in Chapter 9.) Rather, the germane point here is that these two technologies are examples of how very strongly we are influenced by the scientific and technological environment in which we are embedded. To be forewarned that sometimes we may uncritically accept these ideas without considering some of the fundamental discrepancies between those technologies and the findings of perceptual psychology is the first step in avoiding some rather serious conceptual pitfalls in macrotheory development.

c. Propensity for Peripheral Models. Another powerful conceptual constraint on perceptual theorizing can best be summed up as propensity towards unwarranted (by the data) peripheral (as opposed to central) neuroreductionistic models. A substantial portion of the tendency to peripheralize our theories is based upon the simple fact that we know quite a bit more about the peripheral nervous system than we do about the deeper portions within the central nervous system. With the exception of the occipital cortex (area 17, without stretching the term too much, may actually be considered a part of the peripheral visual system) we know very little about the details of the function of the extremely complex visual central nervous system. We simply have not made enough empirical progress in understanding the highly complicated neural coding processes underlying symbolic representation in the deep central nervous system to allow incorporating those principles into our models of perceptual phenomena. Yet psychological experiments provide strong arguments that this more central tissue is in fact the locus of most perceptual processes of interest to contemporary researchers. Unfortunately we have no assurance that the organization of the actual structures is based on the same principles as the peripheral ones.

The peripheral nervous system is, without question, simpler in organization than the central nervous system. The structure is better ordered and does embody a more direct isomorphic and mechanistic set of operating principles that are particularly appealing as first approximations to an explanatory model. The alternative approach, the use of very much more complex central network models, leads us into a truly stupefying labyrinth. Thus even though complexity may be the true state of affairs, there is a powerful and compelling tendency on the part of all of us to seek simple (and perhaps simplistic) explanatory models.

Controversy between peripheralist and centralist models of perception has a long history. Elements of the peripheralist tradition can be traced back to the associationalist tradition of the British empiricist school of Hobbes, Locke, and the Mills. Ignoring even older, more naive ideas of the role of the eye in vision, the concept that minute sensory elements can be concatenated into complex percepts can be thought of as being antecedent to the concept that simple additive or inhibitory processes, typical of those occurring in the peripheral nervous system, regulate the formation of complex percepts.

The centralist position, on the other hand, reflects a rationalistic approach in the great tradition of Descartes, Leibnitz, and Spinoza. The centralist theories emphasized a more mediated and less automatic kind of mental processing—an intellectual paradigm that found expression both in Helmholtz' concept of unconscious inference and in modern cognitive psychology's rediscovery of the constructivistic ideas of mind that are clearly only a new form of classic rationalism.

Other historical traditions within psychology also contribute to the conceptual block leading to this overemphasis on peripheral explanations. On one hand, we see the psychophysical tradition in which the proximal stimulus is considered to be the main determinant of the percept. On the other, we see the remnants of an antithetical tradition in which the object and its appearance (the distal stimulus) are given priority. It does not take too great a logical step to appreciate that the psychophysical-proximal stimulus tradition would be highly conducive to the evolution of peripheral theories, and that the object-appearance-distal-stimulus tradition more immediately suggests concepts that are more central.

d. Semantic Confusion in the Use of Keywords. Another block to progress in the development of perceptual theory is a semantic one. Certain keywords in perceptual psychology are used in different contexts to describe some very different concepts. The word *threshold* for example, links together several quite different phenomena including the absolute and the differential threshold. Yet there is a reasonable argument for assuming that the absolute threshold and differential threshold represent processes at the opposite and extreme ends of the taxonomic schema I develop in this book. The absolute threshold is primarily defined by the peripheral and microscopic details of the quantum catch by the receptor; the differential threshold seems to be better characterized as a phenomenon of Level 5, where subsequent manipulative, attentive, and active processing (in this case, discriminative judgments) of the perceptual experiences take place.

I suggest that the use of the same word to describe such disparate phenomena is a result of a common psychophysical methodology rather than a common biological or psychological basis of the two situations. Both kinds of thresholds are measured by psychophysical procedures that are often nearly identical. But the processes themselves, at least within the context of the hierarchical model I have invoked here, are not nearly as similar as they appear to be initially. The absolute threshold is psychologically defined in terms of the establishment of a minimum level of experience. The differential threshold is an active comparison of two suprathreshold levels. Such a comparison is more akin to a cognitive process in which criteria of similarity and dissimilarity are applied[4] that go beyond the simple concept of the absolute threshold.

Often an extra effort as simple as asking the question ''What is the subject actually doing?'' helps to distinguish two quite different uses of a word with multiple meanings. However in other instances the semantic confusion may be very great indeed and not so easily unraveled. The word *masking*, for example, actually is a ''super'' category that incorporates many different levels of perceptual processing. The only thing that the many different kinds of masking experiment have in common is that each represents an example of a type of interaction between sequential visual stimuli. In terms of the actual underlying psychoneural processes they may be very different indeed. Lumping all masking phenomena into a single category based on similarity in experimental design rather than underlying biological or psychological processes is hardly a satisfying solution to the taxonomic problem.

Different types of stimuli and interstimulus intervals may activate a number of mechanisms that can be classified at virtually all of the different levels of the taxonomic system proposed here. Specifically, I distinguish at least seven distinct kinds of masking among the cluster of experiments that have been lumped within this single term:

1. The effect of a bright flash on a dim preceding stimulus due to variations in receptor potency as a function of stimulus intensity.
2. Figural summation as a result of response persistence.
3. Lateral inhibitory effects of one stimulus on a nearby one.
4. The camouflaging of an ordered dot pattern by patterns of random dots or other contextural confusions.

---

[4]I am aware at this point of the difficulties implicit in this separation of absolute and differential thresholds into two such divergent levels. Both types of thresholds can, from another point of view, be considered to be discriminations of a similar kind. In one case the observer is asked to discriminate between two suprathreshold levels; and in the other, he is asked to discriminate between spontaneous background activity and the response to the stimulus.

5. Masking because of functional fixedness in Gestalt groups.
6. Metacontrast—the "suppression" of the perception of a stimulus by central processes in a way that may not involve any diminution in actual neural signal strength. In this case it is often possible to retrieve the suppressed information, even though it is not reported.
7. The misidentificatian of letters because of their contextual position in a printed word. (How many readers, to make this point graphically clear, saw the misspelling of the second word in the previous sentence?)

The aggregation of these very different processes into a single rubric—masking—is, therefore, a conceptual error in the context of an analytic or taxonomic theory of visual perception. It is more likely that each of these forms of masking is explicable in terms of mechanisms and processes that are quite dissimilar from those underlying the others. The result is that many pseudocontroveries have developed over the years because one or another of these masking phenomena has been compared to another with which it, in fact, shares no common mechanism.

e. Obstacles of Aesthetics and Parsimony. Next I come to a set of conceptual difficulties that perhaps should not be represented as obstacles as much as criteria of excellence. I refer at this point to those intangible aspects of pleasingness and simplicity that make a theory acceptable to the scientific community. A world of uncertainty, such as that of perceptual theory building where absolute proofs of each theory are not available, requires criteria other than simple statistical tests (e.g., of the proportion of variance that is explained) or the degree to which empirical data can be predicted, as the scientific community picks and chooses from among the alternative explanations. Thus some arbitrary criteria must necessarily be utilized that involve social and personal values, subjective estimates of the elegance or beauty of a theory, judgments of its consistency with the rest of the contemporary scientific enterprise, and appraisals of the "simplicity" or "parsimony" of any proposed theoretical explanation.

Considerations of this kind may lead to a particular theory bcing rejected at the outset. For example, some of the modern psychobiological theories of mind at still not acceptable to some laymen (and even some psychologists) because they conflict with strongly held personal theological values. Other theorists are rejected because they are judged to be unnecessarily complex or to involve too many assumptions to allow them to pass some personal test of plausibility or parsimony. These evaluative processes represent a class of conceptual obstacles whose influence should not be underestimated. They are, perhaps, the most difficult and refractory hindrances to progress in perceptual macrotheory at any point in history.

f. The Absence of a Good Taxonomy of Percepts. My final example of a persistent conceptual block to successful theorizing in perceptual psychology is exactly the one that this book seeks to overcome: the absence of a satisfactory classification scheme for perceptual phenomena. A good taxonomy of percepts could serve perceptual psychology in the same way that Mendeleev's periodic table served chemistry or Linnaeus' schema served biology. Such taxonomies of scientific subject matter are absolutely vital preliminary steps towards any generalized theory building. Hopefully this deficiency will be at least partially alleviated by the remaining portions of this book.

C. ATTRIBUTES OF THE TAXONOMIC LEVEL THEORY

1. General Premises of the Taxonomic Level Theory

So far in this chapter I have spoken in general of the difficulties and problems faced by the perceptual scientist attempting to develop a macrotheory of visual experience. In the following sections I discuss the particular attributes of the specific multilevel model of visual perception within which the material in the remainder of this book will be organized. An understanding of these attributes or premises is fundamental to an appreciation of the advantages and disadvantages of this taxonomic model. The following comments make explicit some of the concepts and premises that are implicit in the model.

a. The Range of Topics Covered. The subject matter of this taxonomy is limited to the more immediate perceptual responses or phenomena. It is likely that a unified theory of visual processing processes stressing the indivisible interrelationships among both attentive and preattentive mental phenomena would have much to say for it. Nevertheless, tradition and practicality demand that certain classes of psychological processes be abstracted from the entire mental aggregate for separate study if progress is to be made in understanding how the perceiving mind works. The range of psychological topics that I have decided to consider in this volume spans only the more immediate perceptual responses to stimuli. The range of these topics is close to what Herbert Feigl (1958) has referred to as the class of "raw feels"—the primitive, initial, and immediate sensory-perceptual responses that constitute the first stage of mental activity following stimulus presentation. My sixth level, which transcends this class of immediate responses, is only briefly mentioned in this volume.

Obviously there is a wide range of other mental processes that overlap with and border on the topics that I have chosen to emphasize in this book. It is clear that few perceptual experiences ever develop unaffected by the social, motivational, cognitive, or experiential contexts of which they certainly are a part. The assumption behind the limits that I have arbitrarily placed on the topics that I discuss here is that these other variables can be held more or less constant within the type of experiments that provide the data base analyzed in this book. I do not believe this limitation does too great violence to the psychobiological reality of the situation.

b. Phenomenon Defined. The term *phenomenon,* as I use it in this book, referes to any percept, finding, observation, functional relationship, law, or other experiential descriptor of the intrapersonal mental responses produced by stimulus scenes. The awareness of red is a phenomenon, as is either the algebraic or graphic function corresponding to the dark-adaptation curve. The perception of depth, size, and the functional effects on the threshold of the manipulation of such dimensions as the wavelength of a light stimulus are all included within the rubric I have chosen to call "phenomena." Measurements of phenomena constitute the empirical data base of perceptual psychology. They are the analogs of the molecules, cells, organs, animals, and plants that make up the observational data base of the other biological sciences.

c. Process Defined. The term *process* refers to any transformation or integration at any of the six levels of the proposed taxonomy that acts to alter the nature of afferently flowing information in a perceptually significant way; that is, to alter the meaning or significance of the signal. In the present context, the mere representation (or re-representation) of some sensory message by different patterns of candidate neural codes is not the kind of perceptually significant "process" I intend to include within this rubric.

d. The Premise of Isolability. Any classification schema or level theory of the sort proposed here is based upon the assumption that it is possible to isolate the critical levels of perceptual processing by appropriate experimental procedures. The idea that process isolability is achievable is an essential premise of the global theory of vision presented here. Without such empirical separability the levels are a priori meaningless and the categorized processes mythical.

The practical degree to which different level processes can be isolated from each other depends upon experimental task and design. Many psychological experiments are intrinsically incapable of selectively measuring the effects of a single processing level. Rather, they record responses that reflect the influence of multiple levels of perceptual processing. For example, in a highly ingenious study of the span of perception, Oyama (1978) designed a paradigm that simultaneously assayed the combined effects of several different levels of processing. The observer was required in his experiments to report how many dots were flashed in a tachistiscopic display as a function both of the number of dots and the interval between the test stimulus and a visual mask composed of a rectangular array of similar dots. For very short stimulus–mask intervals, reports by the observers indicated that they simply did not see all of the dots. At somewhat longer intervals, but for smaller numbers of dots, there appeared to be a kind of contrast between the numerosity of the dots of the test stimulus and those of the mask. At higher numbers of dots and longer intervals the subjects seemed to be having difficulty counting the number of dots. The important point here is that this single experimental design spanned at least three different levels of processing (as I define them in this book) as the interval between the test stimulus and the mask was varied. Whether or not this design should properly be considered to be three different experiments (incorporating short, medium, and long intervals, respectively) is another question.

This example stresses the fact that exactly the same experimental paradigm can either be inadvertantly or intentionally used to study several different levels of processing. Furthermore, it is often possible to pass from one level of processing to another, without changing the way the stimuli are presented or the responses collected, simply by instructing the observer to attend to a different aspect of the stimulus scene. Great care must be taken to achieve a true isolation of level of processing, and there is the ever-present danger that the levels that emerge from a body of research may reflect the methods used, rather than psychobiological reality.

In sum, isolation seems to be possible and necessary for any taxonomic effort but is by no means achieved in all experiments. Experimental designs that do mix levels of processing can sometimes help to illuminate the rich multiple influences on any perceptual phenomenon, but can also obscure the existence of fundamental levels of processing in other instances.

e. The Premise of Redundancy. As I noted earlier in this prolog, the fact that a particular phenomenon is affected by a process at a given level does not mean that the percept or phenomenon may not be represented or affected in other manners at either prior or subsequent levels. The underlying assumption of levels of this taxonomy, therefore, means only that each phenomenon may be influenced by a critical process in the multilevel hierarchy, but it does not mean that the phenomenon loses its sensitivity to influence at any other level. Neural signs of all visual perceptual phenomena are present at all levels; however, not all levels contribute to the essential transformations that are responsible for one or another aspect of visual perception. Some nonessential levels simply pass on the incident information passively or recode it in a trivial way that maintains the pattern of communicated information as it was at earlier stages even though the language is different.

A further corollary of this premise is that processes at multiple levels may affect a given phenomenon either redundantly or summatively. Thus it is further possible, within the framework of this schema, that identical (or indistinguishable) perceptual effects may be produced by processes occurring at several different levels. There are many instances of the considerable redundancy built into the perceptual system. For example, as I previously mentioned, limited visual acuity may be introduced by nonneural effects of image degradation due to the optics of the eye, the size of the retinal mosaic defined by the cross section of the individual rods and cones, as well as by the convergent neural interactions in the retina. By far the most difficult area of redundant processes is that including temporal interactions among stimuli. The difficulties in isolating processes are so great in this case that I found it impossible to segregate them and had to pool my discussion of these topics in a multilevel digression in chapter 7.

f. The Premise of Sequential Thresholds—Information Saturation. The level hypothesis embodied in this proposed taxonomic theory is based upon a system of sequential thresholds. Below the threshold[5] for a given level the relevant critical processes cannot begin to operate, and the response of the system is totally defined by the lower level. After the threshold for a given level has been exceeded, however, the processes at the lower level are presumed to be functionally constant. This does not mean that activity at that lower level is totally inconsequential. Quite the contrary, the prior level's function must always be continued for the phenomenon to be maintained. The point is that, once having crossed a threshold for a higher level, the significance of the activity of the lower levels should only be considered as constant, not null. It is as if the processing at the lower levels had achieved a kind of saturation of significance or meaning, and although further modulation of the codes or representations of the signal flow could occur, they would be without functional (i.e., perceptual) impact. This saturation of information is analogous to the saturation occurring in receptors in which increasing stimulus intensity finally arrives at a level at which the receptor is no longer able to respond more robustly. In the case of information saturation no further alteration in the meaning of the encoded message occurs, even though the dimensions of the coded signals may still be changing. Over a certain range of the signal all variations mean exactly the same thing. Indeed, there may be kinds of information saturation situations in which the coded signals are quite different and yet functionally identical. These ideas are summed up in Fig. 4-2.

To make this point clear, consider the following situation. Garner (1974) has described experiments in which multidimensional information is carried by such complex stimulus patterns as those shown in Fig. 4-3. The observer's task in these experiments may be to classify the various patterns according to some common features (e.g., position of the black dot or the side containing the opening). The point is that neither the particular pattern nor the size of the pattern

[5]The word *threshold* as I use it here refers not only to the absolute energy threshold but also to all of the minimum geometric configurations of any signal that must be achieved before the higher levels can be activated.

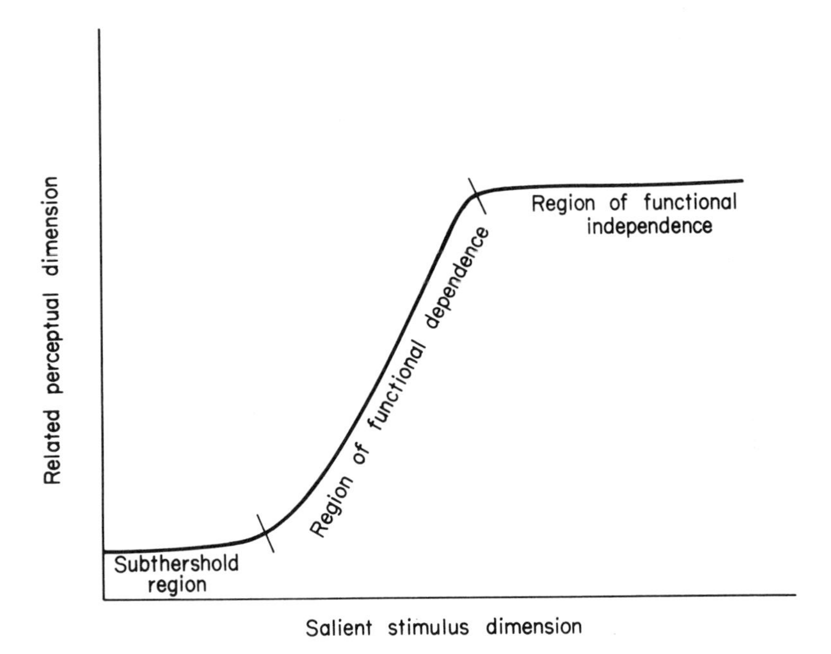

FIG. 4.2. Hypothetical graph relating the informational significance of some salient stimulus dimensions to some related perceptual dimensions.

is an essential part of this experiment. All such cues convey the same information and collectively exist above some information-saturation threshold. Information processing at all lower levels is, of course, required to convey the stimulus information in this case. There is some luminance level below which the pattern will not be discernible; the figure must be organized; and it must not be inhibited by a Level 4 type of metacontrast, for example. However, once these threshold levels have been exceeded, any further increase in illumination or any further reorganization of shape and pattern is of no consequence to the perceptual processing of the relevant dimensions that observers utilize for their judgments in this type of experiment. If the flow of visual information is cut off, of course, the observer will not be able to perform in Garner's experiment, but above those lower-level thresholds wide variations in the stimulus conditions are without influence on his performance. In fact, there is really no need to use these particular patterns in this experiment. The salient features of these stimuli are only symbolic relationships, and any other equivalent set of symbols (e.g., an acoustic sequence) could be used to convey exactly the same information. The particular patterns used in this case are only the media—not the messages—and the details of their physical attributes that do affect processing at lower levels are, for most of Garner's purposes, irrelevant.

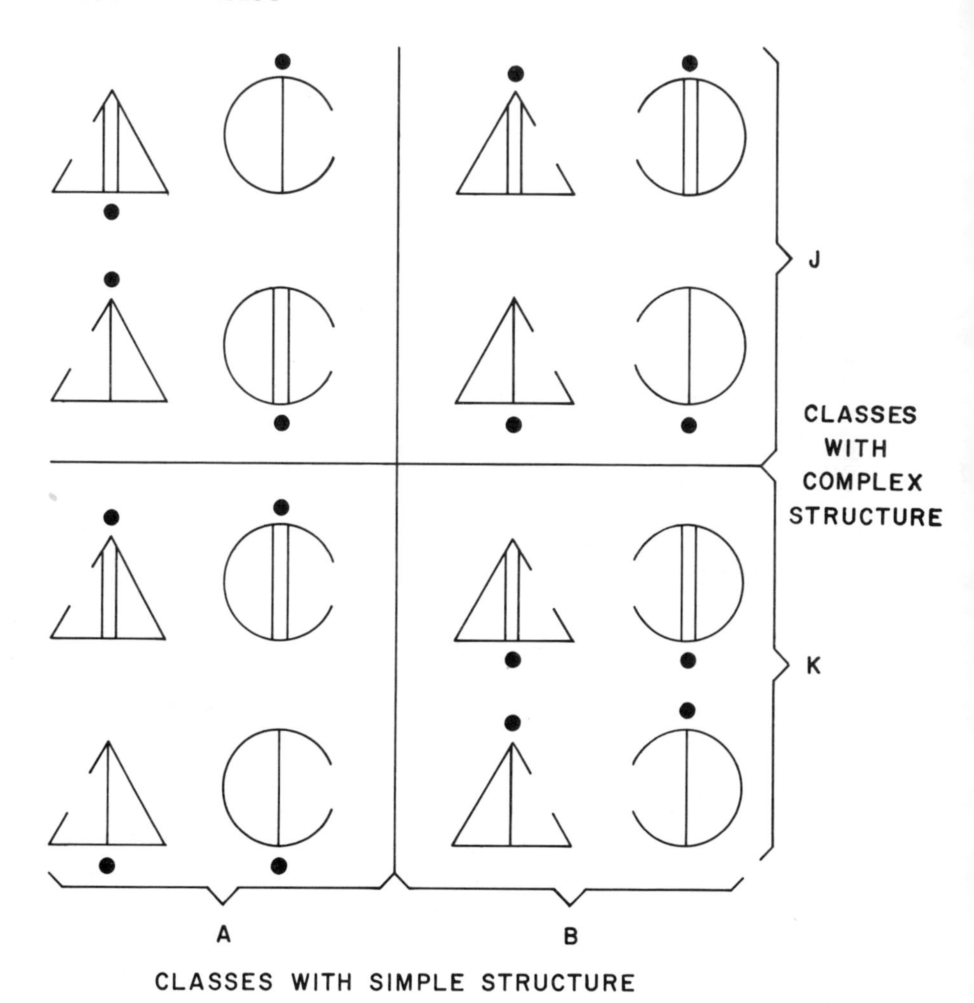

FIG. 4.3. An illustration of some stimuli that may informationally saturate. (From Garner, © 1974, with the permission of Lawrence Erlbaum Associates, Inc.)

g. The Limited Range of Neuroanatomical Reductionism. The proposed hierarchy of levels is uniquely linked to anatomic levels only at Levels 1 and 2. Levels 3, 4, and 5 are patently psychological, involving models of explanation which I believe are beyond any hope of promise of neurophysiological reductionism. Thus the schema of a hierarchical series of processing levels proposed here is a mixed and eclectic psychological and neurophysiological metatheory of perception, but with somewhat lower expectations for the latter than is usually assumed.

h. Rejection of Isomorphism. It is likely that only the processes incorporated into Levels 0, 1, 2, and 3 of this schema need maintain any semblance of isomorphic representation. Beyond Level 3, a host of experiments tells us that symbolic and nonisomorphic representation is probably more likely.

i. A Taxonomy of Processes, not Phenomena. A vitally important premise of this multilevel theory is that the hierarchical scheme of levels proposed here is a taxonomy of processes and not directly of phenomena. Although many phenomena will be closely, and in some cases uniquely, linked to particular levels, the taxonomy is of processes operating at each level, and not of the phenomena themselves.

j. The Practical Need for Molar Terms. The terms *symbolic, interpretive, inferential, constructionistic,* and *rationalistic* are all used as interchangeable synonyms in developing this taxonomy. Although the denotation of these terms is difficult to express precisely, they all refer to highly complex and nonlinear neural network computations by means of which responses can be generated that are not predictable in terms of the passive, linear, deterministic transformations typical of simpler nets. Because we cannot presently understand how these processes work at the microstructural level, we are obligated to study and describe them at the overall molar level. Psychology's future seems assured.

k. Attribution to Levels Is the Goal of This Endeavor. Finally, the main goal of this entire enterprise is to classify the processes that act on the various psychological phenomena and to assign them to the most appropriate levels. I believe it is with regard to these specific assignments that most further controversy is likely to ensue.

2. Specification of the Processing Levels of the Taxonomic Theory

Now that some of the attributes and premises of this taxonomic theory of visual perception have been made explicit, it is necessary to make equally manifest exactly what is meant by the single level of preneural, and each of the five levels of neuropsychological, processing that are used as the framework for discussion in the remainder of this book.

a. Level 0 Processes. From the point that photons are reflected or emitted by an object and begin their course towards the point in the receptor where the primary sensory action occurs, there are innumerable opportunities, both external and internal to the eye, for the stimulus to be modulated in ways that have perceptual consequences. Though these modulations or transformations of the stimulus by the optical and spatial properties of the external environment and the eye are not, strictly speaking, perceptual processes, they are often confused with transformations occurring within the nervous system and do exert equally powerful influences on our response to the distal stimuli. It is necessary, therefore, to include a separate category for these physical processes in the proposed taxonomy. In Chapter 5, in which these Level 0 processes are presented, I distinguish between *mirages* (failures in perceptual veridicality that are produced by physical transformations) and *illusions* (failures in perceptual veridicality produced by transformations within the perceptual nervous system).

b. Level 1 Processes. Level 1 is concerned with the transductive processes of the photoreceptor and is, therefore, almost exclusively influenced by the actual physical energetics of the interactions between the photons of the stimulus and the photoreceptor chemicals or by the distribution and neurophysiology of the receptor cells themselves. Luminous, chromatic, and acuity thresholds are, at least in part, controlled by processes categorized within this first level. Level 1 includes processes that are largely determined by the photoabsorptive properties of the chemicals located in the most peripheral portion (the outer segments) of the receptor units. A light must be of a certain intensity and of a certain wavelength and the receptor must be in a certain state before a visual experience can be elicited. However, except for some modest temporal and spatial summation (within the confines of a single receptor), nothing about the geometric form of the stimulus is essential to processes at this level; most of the characteristics of this stage of processing are defined by simple energy and chemical considerations. Absolute threshold measurements using appropriate psychophysical procedure have been the usual experimental paradigm of choice in studies of Level 1 phenomena. However, there is increasing recent interest in suprathreshold phenomena, which, it is now appreciated, are also substantially defined by mechanisms within the receptor cell. Some temporal properties of the perceptual response (e.g., visual persistence) may also be attributable to this stage of information processing.

c. Level 2 Processes. Level 2 processes include those specifically affected by neural network interactions in the retina and perhaps also in the more peripheral portions of the central nervous system. Both the thresholds and the magnitude of the resulting perceptual response may be either suppressed or enhanced as a result of interaction effects between neighboring portions of neural networks more central than the receptor itself. Contour enhancement effects, such as the Mach band or the gray spots in the Hermann grid, are the most clear-cut examples of perceptual phenomena thought to result from Level 2 spatial interaction processes, but spatial summation effects on the threshold and some aspects of visual acuity and the dark-adaptation curve also are categorizable at this level. Many temporal properties of vision are also now thought to result from Level 2 processes.

Specifically, many of the processes I classify as Level 2 processes are probably mediated by feedback and lateral interactions in the inner and outer plexiform layers of the retina. To observe the effects of such interactions, however, the boundary conditions determined by the energy thresholds of Level 1 must have been sufficiently exceeded so that they are no longer of consequence. In some of the phenomena resulting from processes at this level, the geometrical relationships among the components of the stimulus may be very important. A general outcome of Level 2 interactions is the alteration of the brightness of restricted local portions of the visual field in strict dependence on the distance between the interacting segments. Global brightness changes (e.g., simultaneous contrast) without functional dependence on distance between the various portions of the figure seem more likely to be mediated by more centrally located mechanisms classifiable within Level 4.

d. Level 3 Processes. Level 3 processes, like those of Level 2, also include critical operations that are exquisitely sensitive to the detailed geometry and microstructure of the stimulus. However, Level 3 processes do not necessarily result in any change in the apparent magnitude of a stimulus-induced perceptual response. Instead the effects on form at this level are more often exhibited as variations in the organization or detectability of an entire form rather than in terms of the absolute detectability of its elements.

Level 3 processes are often assayed by experimental techniques that involve the separation of a target from its background, as exemplified by several of the currently popular noise-masking paradigms, as well as by the classic observations of figure–ground abstraction. At this level of processing, all the component parts of the stimulus and the interfering visual noise are considerably above the absolute luminosity thresholds, as well as beyond (or excluded from) the constraining influences of the lateral interaction processes characteristic of Level 2 processes. The essential criterion identifying a Level 3 process is the detection or establishment of a percept due to the organization of a form rather than to some response to its energy distribution. Therefore, at this stage, some process that is sensitive to geometry, configuration, organization, form, or order is critical to the discrimination of the signal from the background.

The level processing of global properties in a way that involves the separate components of a form is sometimes well modeled by quasi-statistical mechanisms. Although we know virtually nothing about the neurophysiology of the mechanisms that may be related to this level of processing, the central tendency of all of the elements of a complex field seemed to be evaluated in establishing the percept of the whole form. In other instances we have to depend upon the descriptive rules of classic Gestalt theories to organize the phenomenon of Level 3. In most cases, Level 3 processes seem to result in prequantitative organization rather than in quantitative dimensions for the respective responses. Figures may be distinguished from grounds, but the values of brightness, color, etc. are still relatively undetermined. Demonstrations, as opposed to formal experiments, often typify the study of Level 3 processes.

At both Levels 2 and 3, as noted, visual processes are characterized by a strong dependence on the specific geometry of the stimulus. As such they are likely to be represented by neurological codes and maps that are still *isomorphic* to the original stimulus patterns. Stimulus dimensions, originally specified in terms of distances or other spatial relationships, presumably must still be represented in a similar manner at the neurological levels at which these stages of processing occur, in order for the geometrical organization to continue to be an effective determinant of the response. It seems certain that at least topological organization must be preserved at this level even though the stimulus may be highly distorted in the coded representation. Level 2 processes are definitely mediated by neural mechanisms that are still geometrically consistent with the original stimulus. Level 3 processes probably are but the latter are so complex as to be beyond plausible neuroreductionism.

e. Level 4 Processes. Level 4 processes, however, are the first in which nonisomorphisms and nonveridicalities are almost always observed between the dimensions of the stimulus and the dimensions of the evoked perceptual experience. At this level, geometry must be subservient to other aspects of the stimulus. Processing of signals at Level 4, I believe, exemplifies the first level of predominantly symbolic (i.e., nonisomorphic) processing and, therefore, is undoubtedly accomplished by highly complex neural mechanisms that no longer represent the stimulus in a maplike fashion.

The main property of responses affected by processes of Level 4 is that they are characteristically multidimensionally determined: Aspects of the percept change as a function of the joint influence of multiple aspects or dimensions of the stimulus. Relationships among the different dimensions of the stimulus are very important at this level, and there may be gross discrepancies between what might have been the single physical dimension initially thought to be most closely associated with the phenomena and the perceptual response itself. For example, as I noted at the outset, it would not have been unreasonable to associate apparent size with retinal image size. However a long history of research has shown that apparent size is, in fact, jointly affected by the same stimuli that determine apparent distance. This is but one example of the many "constancy" effects that will be classified as Level 4 processes. These processes define phenomena in which deviation from some aspect of veridicality occurs in a way that suggests that the physical stimulus is more important as a symbol or clue to the solution of a perceptual "problem" than as a direct transformational determinant of the response in the sense stressed by a naive stimulus—response psychology.

As with Level 3, neural models for this stage are weak and implausible and descriptive, phenomenological, and mathematical theories seem much more appropriate here. For example, all models of illusions that invoke Level 2 types of network interactions as the explanatory process appear to have little validity. In many examples of Level 4 phenomena the stimulus configuration seems merely to be used as a vehicle to convey a system of cues regarding certain multidimensional information; and any one of several informationally equivalent, but not necessarily isomorphic stimuli, can achieve the same end. The methodological emphasis employed to explore Level 4 is also characteristically different. Detection tasks are no longer used as the prototypical research tool; the emphasis shifts to the quantitative description of the responses (e.g., shape, size, brightness) created by the multiple interacting dimensions of the stimulus pattern. Indeed the relational, comparative process of Level 4 seem to be necessary for the establishment of the quantified magnitudes or specific quality of a percept.

Level 4 processes are, therefore, frequently nonveridical with the physical characteristics and spatial geometry of the stimulus and depend upon them only to the extent that these dimensions limit the ability of the stimulus pattern to symbolically convey dimensional information. The stimulus pattern must be detectable with regard to energy, must be unaffected (or at least constantly affected) by its immediate neighbors, and must clearly be detectable or emerge as a figure or a ground before Level 4 processing can be studied in isolation from the effects of the earlier stages. Only when all three of these thresholds have been exceeded and the relevant information saturation levels achieved can the unencumbered influence of Level 4 relational processes on perception be measured. Even when the response is as complex as depth perception a little thought suggests that the integration of the stereoscopic response is not a direct manifestation of the information conveyed from the individual eyes. The monoptic ''images'' are only clues to be interpreted in the establishment of the perceptual response.

f. Level 5 Processes. Levels 0 to 4 of psychoneural processing in this taxonomic scheme are collectively characterized by a single criterion—they all represent relatively immediate, even though multidimensional, preattentive responses to the stimulus scene. These five lower level sets of processes set up the raw sensory-perceptual experiences that can be processed by subsequent attentive mental information manipulations. Decisions must be made, criteria evaluated, comparisons carried out, classifications and categorizations established, and discriminations between the raw experiences made; these are the manipulative processes that are characteristic of what I claim is the sixth level of perceptual processing.

Level 5 processes may be distinguished from the preceding ones, therefore, on the basis of the criterion of active or attentive mental manipulation. This stage of visual processing consists of active cognitive manipulations that are carried out subsequent to the more immediate response mediated by the earlier processing levels. Level 5 visual processes may be divided into the following sub-categories: (1.) acquisition and attention; (2.) classification; (3.) decision-making; (4.) spatial thinking; and (5.) storage and retrieval.

The category of acquisition and attention incorporates those cognitive processes that deal with the pickup of visual information. These processes, all subsequent to the more immediate responses I have previously categorized as perceptual processes, include among other topics, attention, search, vigilance, and encoding. This subcategory includes those processes that regulate or lead to the acceptance of the raw perceptual information into the framework of the subject's cognitive system.

Once information is acquired, other Level 5 processes become more germane. The classification, recognition, and conceptualization of the acquired information collectively represent what I believe is another separate subcategory of cognitive processes. Next is the subcategory of decision processes and the nature of the mental manipulations that deal with subjective probabilities, problem-solving behavior, and choosing among alternative responses: in short, the topics associated with cognitive decision making. A distinct and separate cluster deals with spatial cognition—the active manipulation of images and the interpolation and extrapolation of partial spatial information into "closed" cognitive maps. Finally, there is, of course, a great interest in memory and retrieval in the cognitive literature.

All Level 5 processes differ from the earlier levels in requiring more effort on the part of the perceiver. They are not automatic and immediate but instead require appreciable amounts of time to run their course and a deliberate and active mental attention on the part of the observer. The criterion aspects of perception identified in a signal-detection theory type of experiment are also Level 5 processes, and thus there are Level 5 effects that can influence even as primitive a phenomenon as the absolute threshold. Some processes that may be assayable by relatively simple psychophysical procedures and that may seem at first glance to be the results of processes occurring at earlier levels on closer analysis often turn out to be better categorized at this sixth level. For example, the differential threshold phenomenon can be characterized as a comparison of two samples of visual experiences, subsequent to the immediate processes that define the individual magnitudes of those quantitative experiences. Thus, according to this point of view, differential threshold measurements would better fit into Level 5 than an earlier one.

Clearly, the kind of subsequent manipulation of perceptual responses characteristic of Level 5 involves psychological processes that are much further removed from the stimulus anchor than are those underlying the geometrically isomorphic visual representation of Levels 1 and 2. These processes, like those of Levels 3 and 4, are also probably forever beyond any possible application of neurophysiological reductionism. Imagining, pattern recognition, and other semantic and symbolic information-processing tasks are among the most typical of Level 5 processes categorized in this scheme. Social and affective factors that alter percepts probably also operate at this level. Level 5 perceptual processes overlap and may be identical with what otherwise are called cognitive processes. This level includes as broad a range of topics as those of all of the lower levels combined. It is not covered in this book, therefore, but will be considered in the next volume in this series.

In brief, then, this is the skeleton of the comprehensive metatheory or macrotheory of visual perception that is used to organize this volume. In this book I am specifically trying to classify and categorize the various processes contributing to the large family of reported and observed phenomena. Table 4-1 summarizes many of the essential and salient aspects of the taxonomic level theory proposed here. One major dichotomy in this classification system is between the more or less immediate responses of Levels 0, 1, 2, 3, and 4 and the subsequent responses of Level 5 that require some sort of active mental manipulation by the perceiver. In addition, a second major dichotomy can be discerned between Levels 0, 1, 2, and 3 where it seems likely that a high degree of isomorphism is maintained between the stimulus and its internal representation, and Levels 4 and 5 that are more likely to be encoded by symbolic mechanisms. The characteristics of each level in this taxonomy are also indicated and some sample processes and their related phenomena listed.

The matrix in Tab. 4-2 provides another way to look at the problem inherent in this attempt to build a perceptual process taxonomy. Filling in this matrix is a general goal of the level theory that I developed here. The main idea embodied in this matrix is that particular processes are selectively invoked by distinguishable aspects or dimensions of the stimulus. The measure of the impact of the selected processes on the particular dimensions is the degree of immediate influence exerted on the establishment of the perceptual phenomena. In an earlier work, I proposed a similar chart to represent the analogous problem faced by the sensory-coding theorist interested in relating sensory dimensions and neural codes. Although there are some similarities between this diagram and that one (Tab. 5-1 in Uttal 1973), the two are substantially different in concept. The sensory-coding matrix sought correlations between stimulus patterns or percepts and the neural codes that were used to represent them at the various anatomical levels of the afferent communication pathways. In this case, relationships are sought between the *percepts* and the processes at the six levels where the relevant information processing act occurs.

3. Advantages of the Taxonomic Level Theory

Now that I have made the premises and the general outline of the taxonomic level theory more explicit, it is appropriate to consider how this model might be able to relieve or resolve some of the difficulties and obstacles confronting the perceptual theorist. Of course, not all of the difficulties that were noted in the earlier pages of this chapter can be overcome either in part or entirely. Many of them

TABLE 4.1

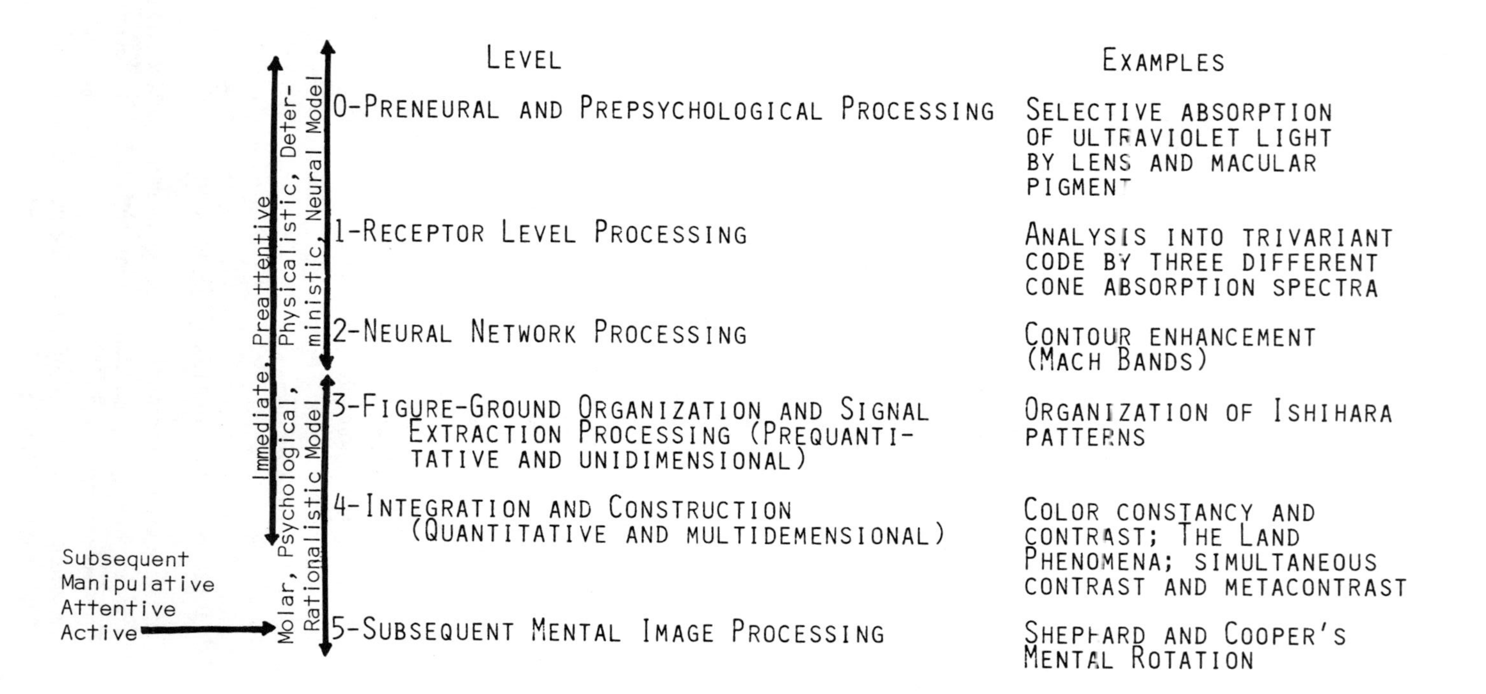

Level	Examples
0-Preneural and Prepsychological Processing	Selective absorption of ultraviolet light by lens and macular pigment
1-Receptor Level Processing	Analysis into trivariant code by three different cone absorption spectra
2-Neural Network Processing	Contour enhancement (Mach Bands)
3-Figure-Ground Organization and Signal Extraction Processing (Prequantitative and unidimensional)	Organization of Ishihara patterns
4-Integration and Construction (Quantitative and multidemensional)	Color constancy and contrast; The Land Phenomena; simultaneous contrast and metacontrast
5-Subsequent Mental Image Processing	Shepfard and Cooper's Mental Rotation

TABLE 4.2

Processing level

Perceptual phenomena	0	I	II	III	IV	V
1						
2						
3						
4						
5						
6						
7						
8						
9						
10						
11						
12						
13						
14						
15						
• • •						
N						

remain unmitigated and unalleviated problems for the theorist. The eclectic level theory that is the framework of this present work, however, does have certain advantages that at least partially overcome these obstacles and sustain the theoretician in his quest for order and explanation.

The most important of these advantages are:

1. A taxonomic level theory provides a conceptual framework for a classification of the perceptual processes. It does so by seeking to identify the critical level at which a particular phenomenon is affected by an influential process. Thus it also potentially provides a framework within which the microtheories relevant to the individual phenomena may be ordered and equivalences and relationships among the individual phenomena can be identified. The current segmentation of perceptual science into unintegrated and isolated phenomena and processes is virtually lethal to the development of a broad universal understanding of the problems of this science, just as it would be for any other. An eclectic taxonomic level theory of the kind proposed here may not itself be the ultimate and universal explanatory theory some would desire. However, some such taxonomy is clearly a necessary first step towards introducing classificatory order into the chaotic description of perceptual phenomena that now fills the literature and represents the only present hope of making progress towards a solution to the problem by the sheer mass of data.

A systematic taxonomic schema, which points up the similarities between various phenomena, is necessary for identifying redundant discoveries and reducing the plethora of data to a more manageable body of knowledge composed of general principles rather than merely an encyclopedic listing of experimental findings. But most important is the fact that a classification system elucidating the relationships among the various processes and phenomena is an absolutely necessary prerequisite for the development of those comprehensive macrotheories of perception that must surely follow.

2. The taxonomic level theory presented here is a mixed neurophysiological and phenomenological model that acknowledges the contributions of both methodologies to the existing body of empirical knowledge and theoretical understanding in perceptual science. It incorporates both the top-down and the bottom-up perspective. Therefore, it intrinsically provides a means of rationalizing various points of view that are often in superficial conflict. Although the level theory in itself is not capable of solving the problem of the dearth of direct electrophysiological evidence, at least it postulates in an explicit, rather than an implicit manner, the line of demarcation between those phenomena that are potentially explicable in neurophysiological terms and those that are not. In doing so it can help enormously to filter out the pseudoneurophysiological and pseudoneuroanatomical ideas that have gained such wide currency in modern perceptual theory.

3. A taxonomic level theory does not deny the fact that each phenomenon of perception is represented and processed at all levels of the system. It does assert, however, that each phenomenon may be critically influenced at only one or a few of these levels.

It must be explicitly restated here that this concept of a critical level of processing is the key, essential, primary, and definitive premise upon which almost everything subsequently to be said in this book is based. It is the keystone of the classification schema of perceptual processing that I have proposed here.

It is especially important, therefore, that the concept of a critical process be clearly understood. *A critical process,* in the context of this book, *transforms the ongoing signal in such a way that after that process it has a different meaning, information content, or significance than it had prior to that process.* A critical process is not simply a translation of a message to a different code in some other neural language; it is a process that transforms the information *content* of that neural message so that some ideal decoder capable of reading all neural languages would interpret the posttransformation message differently from the pretransformation message. It is, in short, a change in the value of the message, not just in its communication language.

To make this concept more concrete, consider these examples. The integration of the monoptic visual signals into a perceived stereoscopic space is a critical process. On the other hand, the conversion from a graded neural action potential to a regenerative spike action potential at the interface of the bipolar cell and the ganglion cell is not, in the sense it is used in this book, a critical process. The first involves a perceptually significant transformation of the information contained in the message; the latter only converts the same message from one communication language to another.

4. A taxonomic level theory broadens the universe of discourse to incorporate all perceptual processes. Better than any other approach, it avoids defining an artificially closed and narrowly constrained theoretical system; its eclecticism is useful both theoretically and empirically.

5. A taxonomic level theory incorporates many of the fundamental premises originally invoked by predecessors but in a way that does not necessarily lead to any inernal inconsistencies. The neuroreductive, information–theoretical, cognitive, or motivational approaches are all reasonably well contained within its overall scope, without requiring any new premises. Each classic theory contributes to the global perspective by emphasizing its own kind of data, its own methodology, and its own insights; yet the relationships between the different theories are crystallized and clarified. Level theory accepts all of these bodies of knowledge and helps to identify the inconsistencies whenever they occur.

6. A taxonomic level theory provides a concrete and tangible issue for constructive debate (in terms of the level of each critical process) as a substitute for vacuous arguments between what are actually nonexclusive points of view. The key problem becomes an empirically testable one of determining which critical levels influence each phenomenon rather than one of resolving false conflicts between what have classically been misperceived as antagonistic positions. A specific set of issues and tests concerning particular phenomena, processes, and levels is profitably substituted for the arrogant ''pseudocontroversies'' that have been so typical among radical adherents to each narrowly defined extremist position. For example, perceptual psychobiologists oriented toward peripheral (retinal) explanations have often rejected, out of hand, the arguments for central or cognitive explanations of various phenomena. On the other hand, cognitive psychologists have often invoked complex interpretive and symbolic mechanisms to explain processes that could be more simply explained by peripheral neural processes if they were familiar with them. By calling attention to the multiple possible stages of processing, a taxonomic level theory establishes an arena of eclectic consideration in which disagreements concerning the origins of various phenomena can be more reasonably adjudicated. It thus provides a compelling intellectual pressure toward synthesis, integration, and thus, global understanding—a pressure that is notably missing from much of perceptual science today. In sum, perceiving man is both rationalistic and empiricistic in a complementary sense and this taxonomic level theory explicitly acknowledges that complementarity.

7. Because the taxonomic level theory proposed here concentrates on the processes rather than the phenomena of perception, it permits us to conceptualize the fact that the effects of several different processing levels may be exerted

to define a single phenomenon. This is an important advantage of this type of theory for two reasons. First, it calls to mind the fact that such phenomena as the absolute threshold and the perceived color of an object are actually determined by processes at multiple levels, and thus compels the theoretician to think of such complex responses as color perception as being influenced by multiple determinants. By doing so, a level theory removes, almost a priori, the basis for many other pseudocontroversies that have plagued perceptual psychology for years. The controversy between trichromatic and opponent-color theories is a hollow one from this perspective; both mechanisms are important contributors to color vision and both processes leave their trace in measurable phenomena.

Second, a level type of theory helps to demonstrate dissimilarities between phenomena that may at first glance seem to be closely related on the basis of analogous response patterns. A dimensional and process-oriented analysis such as the one proposed in this taxonomic level theory, for example, quickly makes it quite clear that simultaneous contrast and the Mach band phenomena are quite different entities that depend upon different processes occurring at substantially different levels of the perceptual system.

8. Another specific advantage of the taxonomic level theory is that it does not demand the same kind of sequentiality of the constituent processes in the way that some other superficially similar level theories do. In Chapter 2, I discussed some of the antecedent level theories that have influenced the development of the present one. Many of these earlier versions of level theory are derivatives of ideas inherent in computer or information-processing technology. In those technologies, as I noted earlier, there is a ubiquitous overtone of serial order because of the nature of the von Neumann-type computer architecture. Rather uncritically, some psychologists have transformed the serial electronic architecture into a theory of the human mind. It seems clear, however, that many of these theories have a great deal of difficulty with the problem of how the information is sequenced between the various levels of their respective models.

The taxonomic level theory that I propose here is, however, free of many of the difficulties associated with serial sequencing. It does not require that each stage of processing exert its influence on perception before the next one can be invoked. All that is required is that the process modulate the information pattern in a way that inserts the *necessary conditions* (i.e., produces the appropriate transformations) for the phenomenon to be evoked *at some later level*. The fact that lateral interactions occur in the retina does not mean that the Mach band is *perceived* in the retina. Instead the various processes produce latent transformations that may not become phenomenal realities until some much higher level of interpretation. Thus, for example, within the context of this taxonomic level theory of perceptually significant processes, it is entirely possible for contours to be critically processed at Level 2 prior to Level 3 at which a figure is actually extracted from the ground.

9. A related advantage of a taxonomic level theory is that it also allows for feedback effects from higher levels to lower ones. Experience, attitudes, and knowledge of what *should be seen* can be contributory factors that determine the nature of what is seen within Level 4 in particular. Centrifugal neurophysiological processes are also containable within the macrotheory that this taxonomy represents. In general, feedback processes can be simply thought of as alterations by higher levels of the transformational properties of lower levels.

10. Another advantage of the taxonomic level theory that I propose here is that it is consistent with modern theories of classification. Both Tyner (1975) and Rowe and Stone (1977) have pointed out that there has been a major shift in recent decades among taxonomists with regard to the criteria used in classifying any system of entities. Traditionally the emphasis had been on the identification of the essential characteristic or ''essence'' of each class. Modern taxonomists, however, search for multidimensional schema to categorize the species and genera of any taxonomy. Rowe and Stone note that this multidimensionality allows for a flexible system that can incorporate new observations as they accumulate. I believe that the perceptual process taxonomy that I present here is in step with this modern approach. The categories that I have suggested are, for the most part, defined in a relatively open fashion and without invoking such specific criteria that a few new observations could require its complete reorganization. The emphasis on process, whether it be well accepted or simply a best guess emerging from whatever data is available rather than phenomena, is perhaps the most important step in achieving this multidimensional and adaptive taxonomic scheme.

11. Finally, whereas it must be acknowledged that this taxonomic level theory does not contribute anything beyond that offered by any other theoretical perspective to overcoming the logical obstacles I mentioned, it does go well beyond many of the others in highlighting some of the conceptual problems that have blocked theory building in this area. It does this to the extent that it emphasizes some of the preconceptions, propensities, and conceptual tendencies that have plagued theory building in this field in the past, and to the extent that it contributes to the continuing evolution of a new Zeitgeist.

In conclusion, I should also balance this discussion by acknowledging that the proposed taxonomy suffers from several unavoidable disadvantages. It is ''inelegant'' in that it incorporates within the same structure two quite distinct areas of psychoneural discourse—the neurophysiological (which characterizes Levels 1 and 2) and the molar psychological (which characterizes Levels 3, 4, and 5). The mixed model I propose will simply not please those whose thinking is dominated by the criteria of a purer philosophy of science. The very act of incorporating concepts from these two levels of explanatory discourse admittedly violates principles of parsimony. As much as I found this distasteful, I am firmly convinced, however, that there is no way to resolve this difficulty short of either manufacturing patently false neurophysiological theories or giving up all hope of reductive explanation of those perceptual processes that do seem amenable to a reasonable kind of neural modeling. The multilevel theory I propose is, in my judgment, a realistic expression of the current state of affairs in perceptual science. Simply put, we have no satisfactory neurophysiological models of most of the important aspects of perception and *must* fall back on the artifact of creating a system that incorporates multiple levels intentionally defined to include both neural and phenomenological explanations.

The special practical difficulties involved in developing a global theory of perception, therefore, make violation of the canons of parsimony unavoidable in this particular case and require that neural and phenomenological concepts be mixed into a single macrotheory. Failure to do so is tantamount to simply denying any possibility of a comprehensive schema of perception and would relegate us to an endless and exhaustive search for a virtually infinite number of unrelated and unclassified perceptual phenomena. That is a kind of science that would obviously be sterile and unsatisfying.

There is one factor that, at least to some degree, mitigates this inelegance and minimizes some of this lack of parsimony in proposed taxonomic level theory. That is the conceptual relief offered by the key idea of the critical level of perceptual processing. This intellectual device, which plays such a central role in this model, is neither a purely physiological nor a purely psychological construct. It is, in itself, an eclectic and mixed theoretical entity that can be used equally well in the neural as well as the mental universes of discourse.

D. A COMMENT

Whether or not the particular taxonomic scheme and the concept of the critical level I present here are ultimately accepted as useful contributions is almost immaterial. What is material is that some self-conscious effort to develop a classification scheme for these processes and phenomena is absolutely necessary now to prevent perceptual psychology from falling into a total theoretical disarray that would be more characteristic of philately than the search for orderly understanding that is the ultimate goal of a true science. Furthermore, in a certain sense, I do not feel it is critically important whether the assignment of any process to a particular critical level is correct in detail or not; science is an adaptive process, and whatever assignment errors are made now will quickly be corrected.

Indeed, I am sure that many of my colleagues will find plenty of room for disagreement concerning my level assignments. Not only is there a substantial probability that, either because of ignorance or an incorrect evaluation of the relevant data, I will differ from the consensus concerning the processes underlying a given phenomenon, but also in many cases there simply is no consensus—only a vigorous, stimulating, and seminal disagreement that dignifies the profession. This controversy often results from the fact that the data have not yet been adequately accumulted to resolve some of the more subtle issues and sometimes from the fact that reasonable men can differ in their interpretations even when sufficient data are available.

It is not inappropriate that I end this chapter by once again stressing the need for classificatory order. Whatever the obstacles and no matter how obstructive are the theological, empirical, logical, and conceptual difficulties that lie in the way of the theorist, there is little argument among perceptual scientists that understanding should be our main goal. Progress may be slow and in some instances criteria of elegance and simplicity may be violated; but in the long run each step, no matter how small, toward a comprehensive macrotheory is a step towards a purer, more elegant, and more satisfying understanding of this exceedingly important aspect of the human mind.

The remaining chapters of this book speak to the five preattentive processing levels in turn. In Chapter 5, I begin a detailed discussion of perceptually influential processes with a consideration of those Level 0 processes that can be accounted for in terms of the physical modulations of the stimulus stream prior to the initial transductive encoding.

5 Level 0: Preneural and Prepsychological Processes Affecting Perception

A. INTRODUCTION

The multilevel taxonomic classification scheme of perceptually significant processes that I propose in this book is aimed at describing and classifying the significant neural and psychological[1] transforms imposed upon the stream of

[1]It is essential for the reader to appreciate that when I use the word *psychological* in this context, I am not presupposing any fundamental metaphysical difference between the processes at these levels

information defined by the proximal stimulus scene. However the first, and not necessarily the least powerful, influence on visual perception occurs prior to the sensory transduction that converts the physical energies of the external environment to the electrochemical energies of the nervous system. This chapter considers those preneural stimulus transformations that occur either in the external environment or within the optical components of the eye that have been shown to be of measurable perceptual significance. I refer to these transformations as Level 0 processes to emphasize that although these transformations are perceptually influential, and in many cases may even be the result of biological mechanisms within the eye, they are mediated by predominantly linear physical processes, not by the more complex psychoneural ones.

There is a very important reason for discussing these essentially physical processes in this treatise on visual perception. The topics themselves are of considerable intrinsic interest, but all too often many phenomena, which I believe are best explained in terms of preneural and prepsychological Level 0 processes, are mistakenly attributed to neural and psychological processes occurring at higher levels of the taxonomic scheme. Such kinds of fallacious arguments are often made despite the fact that there may actually be a high degree of veridicality between the percept and the proximal stimulus—a degree of veridicality that indicates that, in fact, there have been no informationally significant transformations of the afferent information stream between the *relevant* proximal stimulus and the perceptual experience.

The fact that the psychological processes may be in substantial agreement (i.e., veridical) with the pattern of physical energies that impinges upon the receptors (even though there may be considerable differences between the percept and the external scene on the one hand, and the external scene and the proximal stimulus on the other) is a compelling argument for the use of the proximal (the receptor image), rather than the distal stimulus (the object in external space), as the anchor against which perception should be referenced. Indeed, the transformations that occur at Level 0 can best be characterized as the result of those geometrical and optical factors that account for the differences between the proximal and distal stimuli. Level 0 processes, therefore, are not biological in the same sense as the processes associated with the other levels even when they occur within the eye. They do not occur as the result of transformations imposed by the information-processing algorithms of the perceptual system on the flow of afferent information, but rather are more direct physical transfor-

---

and those simpler peripheral processes that can be more explicitly analyzed in neurophysiological terms. The use of this word *psychological* is only meant to imply that these phenomena are of such extreme neurophysiological complexity that there is no present hope of applying the same reductive philosophy to their analyses and description as can be used for some other simpler phenomena. The eclectic nature of the taxonomic theory I present here is an expression of this practical fact and is not intended to be some kind of a cryptodualism furtively implying a nonmonistic metaphysical position.

mations of the energetics of the stimulus by the geometrical, refractive, reflective, or absorptive properties of the environment or the eye.

From the point of view of this distinction, there are two kinds of nonveridical visual perceptions. The first kind includes those percepts that are produced by neural and psychological transformations imposed by the perceptual system. I shall refer to this kind of nonveridicality by the generic term *illusion*. Transformations of afferent information at Levels 1–5 produce illusions. The second kind of nonveridicality is a disagreement between our perceptual experiences and the distal stimulus due to modifications that occur between the external world and the proximal stimulus. This kind of nonveridical response includes such phenomena as classic desert or sea mirages, rainbows, and the floating patterns we sometimes see in our visual field. There is probably no generally accepted generic term to encompass these phenomena, so I shall use the word *mirage* as shorthand for this kind of Level 0 mediated perceptual response.

Both illusions and mirages are driven by certain stimulus conditions; they can be, therefore, said to be exogenous. There is another related class of phenomena called *hallucinations* that can be described as endogenous (i.e., they occur in the absence of an external driving stimulus). Hallucinations are thought to result from aberrant activity in the perceptual nervous system, such as may be induced by drugs, tumors, injuries, or even from prolonged isolation (stimulus deprivation). A fourth class of perceptual response—*images*—may also be considered to be endogenous. It includes the normal perceptual constructions that arise as a result of long-delayed stimuli or as a response to a highly symbolic stimulus. The spoken word "square" for example, may lead to the perception of a □ equally as easily as seeing the geometrical form itself.

For the present, however, let us consider an important issue concerning the first two kinds of nonveridicalities. What is the exact dividing line between a physical mirage and a psychoneural illusion? There is a very specific answer to this question. The sharp line of demarcation between the two kinds of nonveridicalities lies at the interface defined by the point of transformation from the photic energy of the stimulus to the electrochemical energy of the nervous system. It is the point at which the primary sensory action occurs. For vision, this is the point at which the isomerization of the retinal moiety of the receptor photochemical occurs in the outer segment of the rod or cone. Prior to this primary sensory action, all transformations of the stimulus stream are strictly environmental, physical, and optical; and any nonveridical perceptual phenomena attributed to these processes must be considered to be mirages rather than illusions in the broader sense of the words as defined here. Processes associated with optics of the eye or even of the optics of the outer segments of the photoreceptors themselves fall within the Level 0 rubric as would any effects produced by selective absorption or optical obstructions in the ocular media. Similarly, the classic desert mirage, an optical aberration produced by thermal gradients in the external atmosphere would also be considered to be the result of a Level 0 process as would any perceptual response resulting from the natural geometry of the visual scene. On the other hand, processes modulating encoded information subsequent to this primary sensory action would be considered, according to this criterion, to be illusions and explicable within the limits of the five psychoneural levels of processing.

Level 0 may be considered to consist of three major divisions. The first includes those stimulus aberrations that are produced in the external environment (i.e., outside of the eye). Within this major subcategory there are three further subdivisions. The first subdivision includes those processes that arise from the intrinsic spatial nature of the environmental scene. For example, the extraordinary visual effect—linear perspective—can be best understood in terms of this natural geometry of the environment. Such processes often can powerfully distort the perception of a given scene and make parallel lines appear to converge, but a close examination usually shows that "illusions" of perspective actually are not illusions (in the sense I use the word here) at all but are veridical responses to a retinal image that is, in fact, nearly congruent with the perceptual experience. The second subdivision of perceptually significant processes of the external environment includes those that affect the stimulus as a result of some optical aberration. Whereas in the first subdivision the distortions were intrinsic to the geometry of the visual space, in this case some property of the optical pathway of the environment acts to distort the path of the light rays. Such optical aberrations by the external environment can alter what would be an otherwise straightforward stimulus scene into a wildly bizarre one. A thermal inversion layer spuriously reflecting or refracting light waves or a polluting haze scattering the light passing through would be examples of processes incorporated within this subdivision. The third subdivision includes those probabilistic quantal effects that arise from the statistics of photon generation and availability. These effects are particularly pronounced at low light levels where the law of large numbers cannot operate to smooth out the random fluctuations in the number of quanta that may be present in any locus at any given time.

The second major Level 0 division includes those optical processes that modulate the path of incident light rays as they pass through the eye. This division includes, for example, such processes as the spherical and chromatic aberrations of the eye. In terms of the classification scheme presented here, it also seems appropriate to include with this division such intrareceptor optical processes as the Stiles–Crawford effect—an alteration of the effective absorption of light as a function of the angle of incidence of the stimulating light upon the external segment of the receptor.

The third major division of Level 0 is also ocular but is not so much concerned with processes that alter the paths taken by light rays (geometrical optics) as it is with selective absorptions by the ocular media or physical obstruction of light from the receptors. Thus, for example, this division would include the process reflected in the fact that under some conditions it is possible to see the shadows of the blood vessels of the retina. Another example of this third division is the finding that presence in the ocular media of selectively absorbing pigments may produce aberrant results in color mixture experiments.

It is important to remember, however, that although these physical Level 0 processes themselves can lead to modifications of the proximal stimulus such that a nonveridical perceptual response (nonveridical in terms of the distal stimulus) will be produced, it is also possible that the resulting distortion of the stimulus can lead to a response that itself can be a cue for a higher level of perceptual processing. For example, areal haze can lead to a blurred retinal image and thus directly to the phenomenon of blurred vision. This is clearly a Level 0 process. However, differences in the degree of that blurred vision can themselves also be cues for depth perception. The relative amount of blur of objects at different distances is well known to be a monocular cue for depth. In this latter case, however, the stimulus condition (image blur on the retina) was not the direct antecedent of the visual response (the perception of depth) as it was in the former case (where the perceptual response was a blurred mental image). The subsequent interpretation of such a pattern of relative blur clues leading to the experience of depth, therefore, is better classified as a Level 4 transformation.

To emphasize a concept central to this book, I must note again that it is not the particular dimension of the stimulus nor the resulting phenomenon per se that defines the level of analysis. It is the kind of *process* or *transformation* of the stimulus information that is the critical criterion in defining each level in the taxonomic scheme I present here. In the case I am considering here, the transformational process that is the *physical blurring* of the stimulus image on the retina defines a Level 0 process, and the conversion of the *configurational information implicit in the relative amount of blur* into an experience of depth denotes a Level 4 process. Now that I have generally introduced the range of processes that are classified as Level 0 processes, let us consider the various categories in separate detail.

B. PERCEPTUALLY SIGNIFICANT ENVIRONMENTAL DISTORTIONS OF THE STIMULUS

1. Geometrical Processes

a. Transformations Due to the Natural Geometry of the Environment. In Chapter 3, I defined the visual angle α by the following relation:

$$\text{arc tan}\ \frac{\alpha}{2} = \frac{h}{2}\cdot\frac{1}{d} \qquad (5\text{-}1)$$

where h is the height of the object and d is the distance of the object from the eye. This simple algebraic relation provides a means of measuring the projected retinal size of a stimulus object. For obvious reasons, this is vastly superior to a definition phrased solely in terms of the physical size of the object. The fact that the visual angle (and thus the retinal size in millimeters, since retinal size = visual angle × 17 mm) subtended by any physical object varies inversely with the distance of the stimulus from the eye is, itself, one of the most powerful factors in our perception of the external world. The perceived spatial shrinkage of distant objects is a direct result of the natural geometry of space and has nothing to do with any psychoneural processing. Although, as I describe in Chapter 11 when I discuss size constancy, the size of the retinal image is not the sole determinant of the perceived size of an object, it is a major one. Therefore, at least to a first approximation, any physical object (particularly one that is ambiguous with regard to its distance from the observer) will appear to be smaller the farther it is from the observer. Pirenne (1970) refers to this basic law of visual perception as "apparent diminution with increasing distance."

This diminution in apparent size is, however, only one of innumerable perceptual effects resulting from the natural geometrical properties of the environment that can be summed up by the expression for visual angle. Consider for a moment a somewhat more complicated stimulus-perceptual response situation. Two railroad tracks that are physically parallel (in an euclidean geometric sense) over the full extent of their construction[2] appear to merge at the limits of vision. Because the tracks are physically equally spaced at all points on their course, the visual angle subtended by the intertrack distance must decline continuously the greater the actual distance from the eye. Thus the width of the retinal image representing the intertrack spacing must linearly contract the further away the track is from the observer. This contraction in the retinal image size and visual angle with distance is referred to as *linear perspective*. Linear perspective, in the extreme limit, leads to the phenomenon of the vanishing point. At some distance the visual angle subtended must become so small that it passes beyond the limits of visual acuity and becomes interpretable only as a point in space.

Vertical and horizontal perspective operate in exactly the same way, and simultaneously. The explicit introduction (discovery would be too strong a word) of perspective into Western art in the fourteenth and fifteenth centuries added enormously to the perceptual realism of two-dimensional depiction of three-dimensional objects. Figure 5-1, for example, shows an early etching by Leonbattista Alberti (1404–1472), dated 1436, in which perspective has been powerfully used to convey depth cues. Figure 5-2 is a more recent painting, on the wall of the Star of the Sea Church on the Puna coast of the island of Hawaii. This painting also produces a powerful illusion of depth on what is actually a flat wall. One of the most interesting of baroque perspective works is the drawing by

[2]In Australia this hypothetical situation takes on an awesome reality. The Indian–Pacific Railroad line runs across the Nularbor Plain for 300 miles without a turn and with but the barest change in elevation.

FIG. 5.1. An early example of linear perspective from a fifteenth century book on architecture by Leonbattista Alberti (1404–1472).

Giovanni Battista Gaulli (Baciccio) (1639–1709) on the ceiling of Il Gesu Church in Rome. Here, as shown in Fig. 5-3, the artist has used linear perspective to produce a remarkable effect—an ascending column of angels rising completely out of the confines of the church's dome. Figure 5-4 illustrates how this column of angels would appear if one were standing in the nave of Il Gesu Church.

This kind of perspective painting, so capable of producing a strong impression of apparent depth on a virtually flat surface, is referred to as *trompe l'oeil* art. Other artists have striven for the same effect and have accomplished a level of three-dimensional realism that is often quite compelling and always quite interesting. But the main point that I wish to make in my discussion of this art is that these paintings lead the visual system to a perceptual response by incorporating into the proximal stimulus a synthetic perspective identical with the perspective that would have been produced by a real three-dimensional scene. Thus, the *trompe l'oeil* paintings mimic the transformation between the real physical situation and the projected retinal image created by the natural geometry of the environment.

In the case of such deceptive art, it is important to remember that the perspective is simulated; it is an artificial perspective, which the artist has introduced to provoke a depth response, and is not the natural linear perspective produced by a real three-dimensional scene. After all, a canvas is but a two-dimensional world and the artist's use of this false perspective to create the impression of depth is part of his bag of artistic skills used to suggest rather than totally re-create natural scenes. It is an intentional substitute for the natural contraction with distance that would have occurred as a result of the geometry of the environment if that

FIG. 5.2. The wall of the Star of the Sea Church on the island of Hawaii showing an extremely effective use of linear perspective to achieve a strong impression of depth in a very small space. The wall behind the altar is actually flat.

FIG. 5.3. The ceiling of the Il Gesù church.

environment had been there. These paintings are attempts, in other words, to simulate the two-dimensional retinal image of a three-dimensional space on a two-dimensional canvas. (The reconstruction of the three-dimensional percept, of course, cued by this perspective is a Level 4 process.)

M. H. Pirenne (1970) has reminded us of another dramatic example demonstrating how linear perspective can evoke some extraordinary perceptual effects. He notes the perspective effect in the ''sunburst'' phenomenon that has played such an important role in art and religion for millenia. As they approach the earth, the rays of the sun are almost exactly parallel because of the great distance between the sun and the earth. Because of their parallelism, the individual beams pouring through breaks in a cloud *must* exhibit the same sort of perspective effect seen in the converging railroad track. Those portions of the sunbeam that are closer to the observer will subtend a larger visual angle than those further away. The beams will appear to be convergent, therefore, just like the railroad tracks, but in all directions, not just in one plane. Thus the sunburst phenomena results from exactly the same natural geometry as does the convergence of parallel railroad tracks and can be accounted for in exactly the same terms of varying visual angle. The process occurs as a necessary result of the natural geometry of the environment; it cannot be avoided; and this phenomenon has been obvious to humans at all stages of their evolutionary development.

Finch (1977) has noted that if the perspective is based on an euclidean space, some unavoidable distortions are introduced into drawings. On the other hand, if

FIG. 5.4. A diagrammatic side view of the Il Gesù church showing the impression of an ascending column of angels obtained when one is stationed properly to take advantage of the perspective painting shown in Fig. 5.3.

a hyperbolic perspective is utilized, the spatial distortion does not occur and a drawing is more veridical with our percepts. A comparison of these two kinds of perspectives is shown in Figs. 5-5A and 5-5B. The implication of this finding is that our visual space is hyperbolic (non-euclidean) according to Finch.

Another related effect of the natural stimulus geometry concerns the perceptual placement of more distant objects in higher regions of the visual field. We can state a corollary to Pirenne's law of diminishing size with distance that states that distant objects, under ordinary circumstances, tend to be localized higher in the visual field than those nearby. There is nothing mysteriously neural or psychological about this elevated localization to be explained. It is entirely a result of the natural geometry of the environment in exactly the same way as is linear perspective. Objects at a distance appear high because our eyes are on our heads; our heads are on the uppermost portion of our bodies; and we usually stand on the top of a surface rather than hang from the bottom due to the geocentric directionality introduced into our life by the earth's gravity. This set of standard conditions defines a characteristic retinal projection geometry such that there is a greater declination from the horizontal for objects that are closer to us than those that are further away. The elevation of distant objects is, therefore, an entirely veridical perceptual response in which nearby objects are perceived as below distant objects. This is the reason why railroad tracks converge to a vanishing point at the top of the scene rather than at its bottom. If we stood under a bridge bearing a similar railroad track (an extraordinary situation), or beneath a ceiling in a long corridor (an ordinary situation), then the reverse arrangement would be true and the vanishing point would be situated below the nearer positions of the visual scene. The natural geometry of these two viewing situations is shown in Fig. 5-6.

A similar situation obtains concerning visual movement parallax—the change in relative position as the observer moves past multiple objects located at different distances from his viewpoint. Figure 11-36 shows the resulting change in relative position perceived by the observer in a multi-object scene. In this situation, as in the preceding one, the change in relative position is totally explained as a result of the external geometry defining visual angles.

The artistic trick of foreshortening—the intentional reduction in the size of objects in the foreground—is required to compensate for distortions produced by variations in the visual angle. Without a foreshortened image, objects in the near field will be unrealistically enlarged simply because they are subtending a spuriously large visual angle. This distortion would result in a picture in which close objects appeared out of proportion to the ones farther away. The implications of foreshortening have been eloquently analyzed by Rudolf Arnheim (1971). His book *Art and Visual Perception* is considered a modern classic of intercommunication between the two important fields of visual perception and artistic expression.

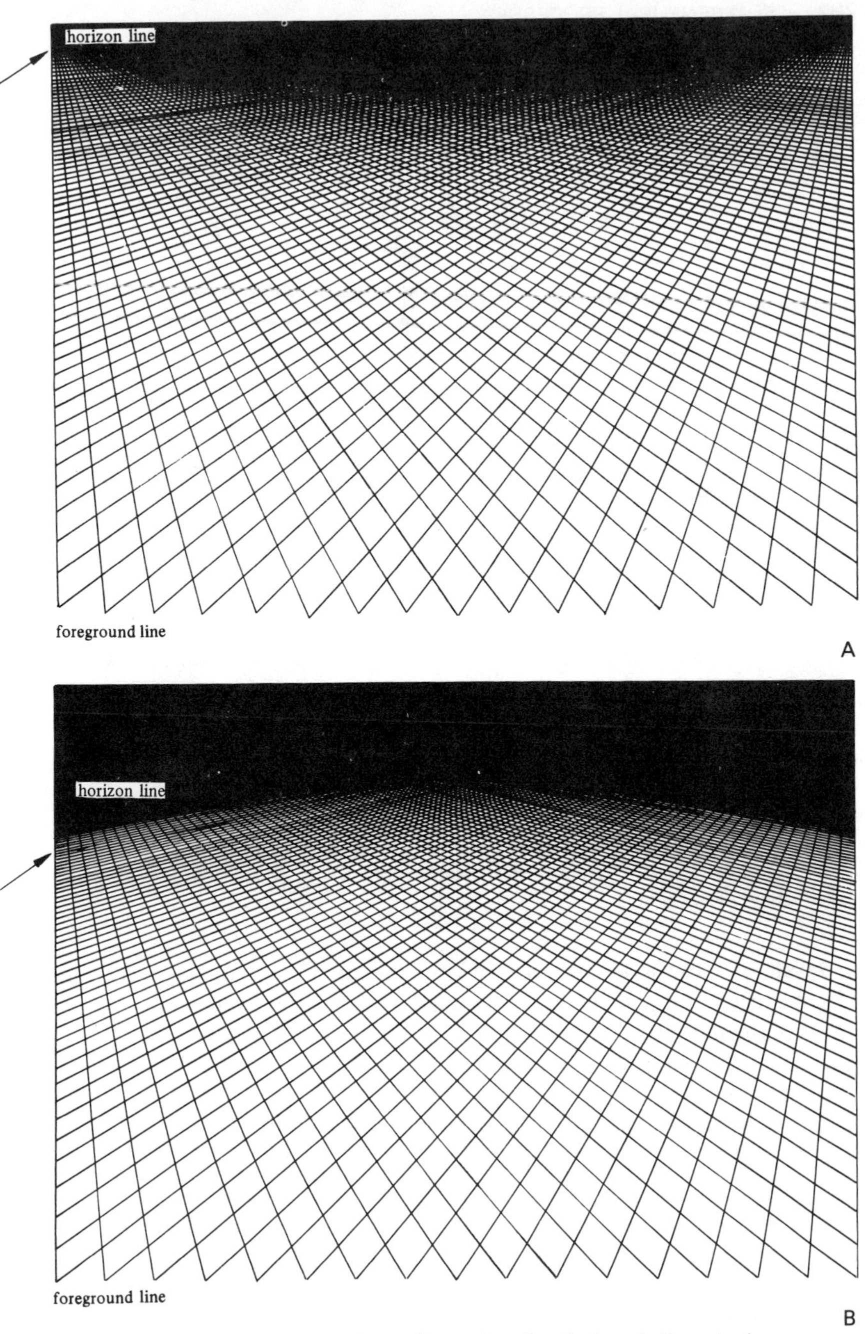

FIG. 5.5. (A) A plane plotted according to the rules of a hyperbolic projection. (B) A plane plotted according to the rules of a linear perspective. The arrows in each figure show the point of maximum distortion in the linear projection. (From Finch, © 1977, with the permission of Pion, Ltd.)

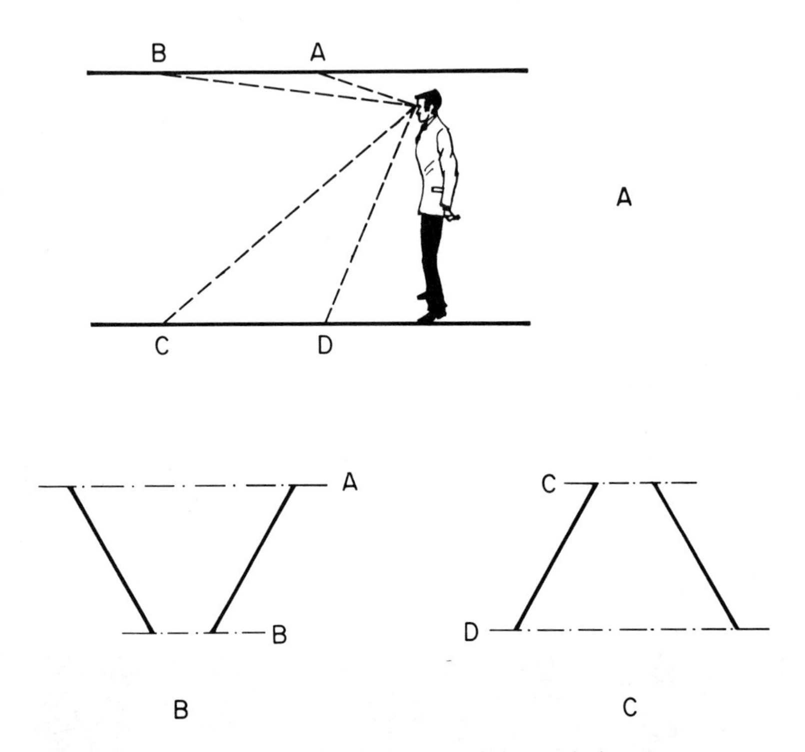

FIG. 5.6. Figures showing the effect of point of view on the important cue to depth known as relative height. (A) The observer standing above and below the viewing plane. (B) More distant points on the upper plane appear to converge below closer ones. (C) More distant points on the lower plane appear to converge above closer ones.

In all of these examples of the influence of the natural geometry of the stimulus scene on perception, the possibility for further processing by higher levels of the perceptual system also remains. For example, the linear perspective illustrated by the example of the converging railroad tracks or, alternatively, the phenomenon of motion parallax are both powerful cues that can be used by higher levels of the perceptual system to elicit the experience of depth. The transformation of these inherently two-dimensional cues into a three-dimensional experience is not a direct result of natural geometry, as is the linear contraction of perspective itself, but requires a further integrative processing of the afferent information by higher levels of perceptual processing.

In sum, it should be understood that the experience of depth is, in a fundamental sense, not veridical with the proximal stimulus even though it may be with the distal stimulus. The critical process that transmutes two-dimensional coded information projected on the retina into a three-dimensional experience requires further processing by higher levels of the visual system.

b. Anamorphoses. The perception of an anamorphosis provides another example from the world of fine arts of a visual phenomenon that is entirely determined by the geometry of the external environment. The word *anamorphosis* is a generic term for a variety of perceptual effects that have been developed over the centuries as artistic curiosities. The word itself is a composite form of the Greek stems *ana* (again) and *morphe* (shape), the implication being that the observer's perceptual system must process a distorted version of a scene to reconstitute the original and more natural form of some wildly distorted stimulus scene. In recent years an interesting art show entitled "Anamorphoses: Games of Perception and Illusion in Art" has been touring the world. The items in this collection have been described in an elegant book (Schuyt & Elffers, 1975). In fact, the games played by anamorphotic artists are not illusory in the sense I defined the word earlier. They too are mirages resulting from the natural geometry of space and the visual angle. All of the anamorphoses depicted in Schuyt and Elffers' book can be understood entirely either in the geometrical terms invoked to explain the perspective effects or in the equivalently simple and straightforward terms of distortions produced by regular optical reflections in unusual mirrors. In either case, an anamorphotic illusion is never a result of any perceptual processing on the part of the observer (other than that accounted for by his assuming the proper viewing position). Anamorphoses are, in their entirety, the results of geometrical and optical transformations occurring in the external environment, and the percept is veridical (i.e., nonillusory) with the proximal stimulus even though it may be a distortion of the distal stimulus. Perhaps this point can be made most clearly by referring to specific examples of anamorphic art.

There are actually only two classes of anamorphic art. The first class includes distorted pictures that are reconfigured into a nondistorted percept as a result of visual perspective transformations. The distorted geometry of the anamorphotic painting is corrected in this case by establishing an appropriate viewing condition that imposes a perspective capable of compensating for the real distortions in the picture. For example, Fig. 5-7A is a hardly recognizable figure of a horse (to give away its anamorphotically hidden secret). When viewed from the bottom of the figure, the perspective transformation compensates for the artist's distortion and the figure is seen (within the limits of the clear depth of field) as shown in Fig. 5-7B. The correction of the distortion, however, is hardly the result of a perceptual process; it can be totally accounted for in terms of the perspective contractions that arise as a result of the natural geometry of the viewing situation—in other words, linear perspective. The perception of the horse is, in fact, veridical with the proximal stimulus when viewed at an oblique angle, but not with the original (distal) scene so nonlinearly represented by the highly distorted anamorphosis.

Another type of anamorphosis is illustrated in Fig. 5-8. Here the painting has been distorted in accordance with the rules of a conical reflection. If, as has been

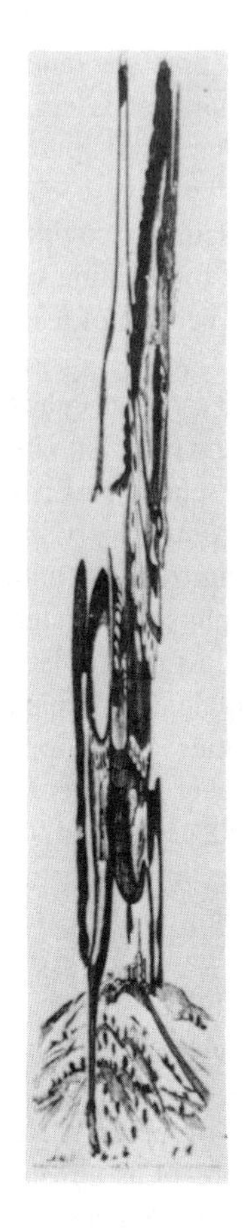

A

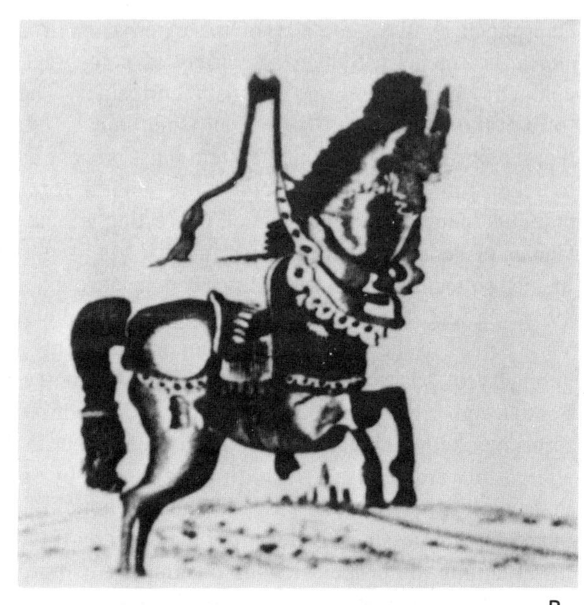

B

FIG. 5.7. (A) An anamorphosis containing a hidden figure. When this figure is viewed from the bottom at a steep angle the natural geometry of the viewing situation converts it into the figure shown in (B).

done in this composite figure, a conical mirror is placed at the center of the figure, the pattern of reflections produced by the cone will compensate exactly for the distortions introduced when the artist painted the picture.[3] When viewed directly from the top through this type of mirror, the properly proportioned figure is seen. Other anamorphoses have been drawn distorted in a way that allows a cylindrical mirror to reconstitute the proper proportions.

Not all anamorphoses require a mirror or perspective transformation in order to be seen as reconstructed forms. Wildly distorted objects such as the "broken"

---

[3]It is highly likely that the artist actually painted the anamorphosis by using a similar distorting cone-shaped mirror to guide his brush.

ladder shown in Fig. 5-9A can appear from one (and only one) viewpoint to be whole and intact structures as a result of the clever use of interposition. Fig. 5-9B shows the perceptual mirage of a wholly intact ladder as it would appear to an observer stationed at the single proper point of view.

The important point about these anamorphotic demonstrations is the same one made previously; they are not illusory transformations mediated by critical processes within the perceptual system. In each of the three types of anamorphoses that I have described, the process that transforms some wildly distorted painting or object into a coherent perceptual experience occurs as a result of the clever use of the natural geometry of the external environment. It is the geometry of perspective, interposition, or optical reflections that produces what is essentially an appropriate and properly structured proximal stimulus, leading directly to a highly veridical perceptual response.

c. Natural Geometry of the Eyes. Just as the natural environment of the external environment sets certain limits on what we see and modulates the nature of the proximal stimulus in a way that has direct perceptual consequences, there are also some geometric features of the anatomy of the visual apparatus itself that

FIG. 5.8. An anamorphosis that must be corrected for proper viewing by use of a conical mirror placed in its center. This figure shows both the anular anamorphosis and the corrected image in the centered conical mirror.

FIG. 5.9. An anamorphosis of a ladder. The actual physical "mess" is seen in (A). (B) shows the perceptual experience as it can be both seen and photographed if one is stationed at the proper viewing point.

directly contribute to certain perceptual responses. Consider the following: It is a truism that normal human beings have two eyes arranged in a bilaterally symmetrical arrangement on either side of the nose. The two eyes in this binocular system are horizontally rather than vertically displaced. This particular expression of the general bilateral symmetry of the human body is the immediate antecedent structural condition underlying and making possible stereoscopic vision. Stereoscopic phenomena is the topic of an extended discussion in Chapter 11. For the moment, however, I consider only the Level 0 implications of the simple geometrical fact that the two eyes are arranged on a horizontal axis rather than a vertical one.

The horizontal displacement of the two eyes constrains all binocular processes to be sensitive only to the vector component of the differences between the two monocular images that is oriented along the horizontal axis. To make this somewhat cryptic concept clearer, I must briefly consider certain aspects of stereoscopic vision—a Level 4 process.

Consider the following gedanken experiment: Suppose that a flagpole is dichoptically[4] viewed through two tubes so that its bottom and top cannot be seen. The dichoptic observer's view of this stimulus situation is shown in Fig. 5-10A. Such an observer would be able to obtain information about the distance to the flagpole from this display because of the slight horizontal difference in viewpoint of each eye. This difference in viewpoint produces a difference between the optical images on the two retinae that is called relative retinal disparity.

If the flagpole is progressively rotated so that the view is as shown in Fig. 5-10B and then to the extreme horizontal position shown in Fig. 5-10C, there will be a gradual reduction in the ability of the subject to discriminate the distance to the pole if he is limited only to the single depth cue of binocular retinal disparity. The reason for this reduction in stereoscopic competence is that the two images are decreasingly disparate in the horizontal direction as the flagpole is rotated from the vertical to the horizontal orientation. Because of the horizontal displacement of the eyes on the face, it is *only* the horizontal disparity of the two images produced by the vertical stimuli that can possibly provide the cues necessary for stereoscopic depth perception. Vertical disparity does not exist as a usable cue because the eyes are at the same vertical level; any information that might have been obtained from the increasingly horizontal flagpole by a vertical-disparity-sensitive system are simply not available to the normal horizontal-disparity-sensitive human observer as a cue for depth.

---

[4]By dichoptic I refer to a viewing condition in which each eye sees a different scene as is the case in normal three-dimensional viewing. The word binocular is reserved for the condition in which both eyes are seeing the same thing—a condition that would obtain, for example, when the same two-dimensional scene is viewed with both eyes. Monocular viewing refers to the situation in which only one eye is viewing a scene. Cyclopean perception, a term coined by Herman V. Helmholtz and rejuvenated by Bela Julesz (1971), refers to the usual perception that we are looking at the world through a single "eye" located in the middle of the forehead.

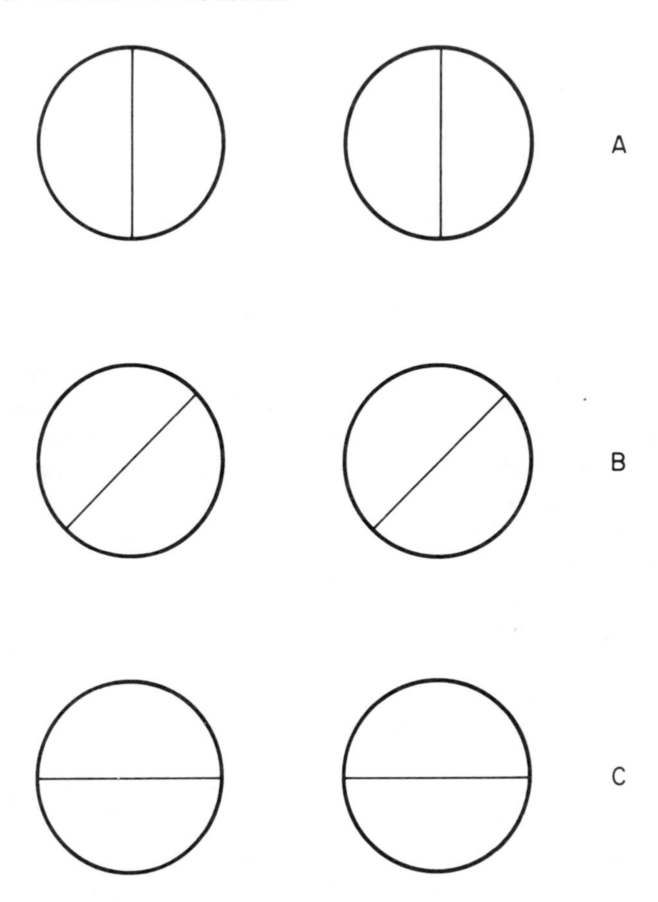

FIG. 5.10. The paradigm of the tilting flag pole experiment demonstrating the decline in available horizontal disparity as the flag pole is tilted. The reduction in depth judging competence is due to the reduction in the stimulus cue; it is not a characteristic of the visual system.

It would be entirely possible to carry out this experiment[5] and actually plot the decrease in the ability of the subject to make the desired horizontal disparity-dependent distance discrimination. Furthermore, the results would be valid and reliable. We might predict[6] that there would be a decreasing ability to discriminate depth with the increasingly horizontal position of the flagpole in accord with a cosine law. However reliable the data, it must be understood that the resulting data do not reflect any perceptual processing of the visual cues. Quite to the

[5]Some years ago I was called upon to referee a manuscript just like this gedankenexperiment. That manuscript had been submitted to a journal for possible publication. This experience was the stimulus for my special appreciation of the conceptual misunderstanding described here.

[6]But see later statements.

contrary, the measured decline in depth discrimination would be a direct result of the natural geometry of the viewing situation as defined by the laterally displaced positions of the two eyes on the head. The key variable in this gedankenexperiment would simply be a gradual reduction in the magnitude of the critical stimulus dimension—horizontal disparity—and would not reflect any property of the perceptual system. The experimenter in this case would be measuring nothing more than the proportion of the vector defined by the flagpole that is vertical—a change in a totally physical stimulus variable—using the subject's more or less constant stereoscopic sensitivity as an indicator of the horizontal component. It is for this reason that any idea obtained from this kind of experiment would necessarily follow the cosine law.

Perhaps this point can be made more concrete if one thinks how obviously fallacious such a result might be if placed in a slightly different context. Suppose that one presented a stimulus spectrum that was composed of very irregular energies at each wavelength. Obviously the perceived brightness at each wavelength of this unusual spectrum would, in part, be a function of the variable stimulus energies themselves. The shape of the response curve would, therefore, be a composite of the spectral sensitivity *of the eye* and the energy distribution *of the stimulus spectrum*. To infer that such a brightness function represented the relative sensitivity of the human eye would obviously be absurd and would clearly represent a serious confounding of the true relationship between brightness and stimulus wavelength that would have been measured with an equal energy spectrum.

As usual, however, nothing is as simple as it may at first seem in the field of visual perception. A newer study of the interaction between vertical and horizontal disparity has been carried out in a much more thoughtful manner by Friedman, Kaye, and Richards (1978). They showed that the decline in stereoscopic depth did not simply follow a cosine law, but that, in fact, observers were progressively less sensitive than they should have been as horizontal disparity decreased and vertical disparity increased. They suggested that this progressive decrement, beyond that predicted by natural geometry, was due to an attenuation of the effectiveness of horizontal disparity by vertical disparity. This interaction, it must be appreciated, may be the result of a real psychophysical process, and not a Level 0 process, even though the major effect of declining horizontal disparity is solely attributable to the stimulus environment.

I now turn to yet another aspect of binocular vision that, I believe, is more appropriately classified as a Level 0 process resulting from the stimulus geometry defined by the horizontal displacement of the eyes. Consider the horopter, a sample of which is shown in Fig. 5-11. Shipley and Rawlings (1970), in what is an outstanding historic and conceptual analysis of this important visual concept, have critically considered the various meanings of the term *horopter*. They note that different visual scientists have used the term with what are substantially different meanings. Some look upon the horopter as the apparent fronto-parallel

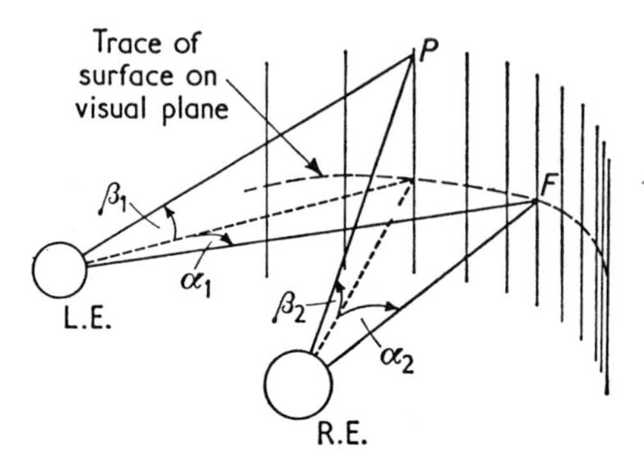

FIG. 5.11. The horopter depicted as a cylindrical field. (From Ogle, © 1962, with the permission of Academic Press, Inc.)

plane; some define it in terms of corresponding points; and others consider it to be the surface on which single vision is obtained. These various criteria are not simply irrelevant abstractions; they lead to practical differences in the measurement of the horopter in various viewing conditions.

Shipley and Rawlings, however, believe that none of these criteria is fully adequate to specify what it is that should actually be measured in a valid horopter experiment. Their analysis, quite to the contrary, leads them to the conclusion that the horopter is really nothing more (nor less) than another manifestation of the geometry of the lateral spatial arrangement of the eyes in the binocular observer. Shipley and Rawlings note that Linksz (1954) had previously shown that the apparent fronto-parallel surface measured psychophysically is only indirectly related to the horopter as defined geometrically. They also quite properly note that singleness of vision is not a critical criterion for depth perception; stereoscopic depth can be generated by the observer from two images so disparate that the images are not single but diplopic. Thus Shipley and Rawlings (1970) believe the horopter is actually better defined as "the locus, in physical space, of intersections of the two sets of monocular lines of common visual direction [p. 1241]." In other words, they assert that the idea of a horopter is strictly a geometrical concept (Level 0) that does not depend on higher-level processes involving corresponding points, single vision, etc. The horopter, they go on, is thus only indirectly a measure of the locus of corresponding points or of single vision. They suggest that once the eyes are fixed at a particular distance, it is exclusively the geometry of the lines of sight that properly defines the surface that is called the *horopter*.

Shipley and Rawlings distinguish further between the "frontal geodesic" (the surface that appears to the subject to be equidistant from his egocentric localization in space—a point closely corresponding to the position of a perceptually fused "cyclopean eye" located in the middle of the two eyes) and the horopter, which is more closely related to the map of the corresponding points that has evolved to best match the common lines of sight defined by this geometry.

Though the corresponding points in both eyes are those retinal loci that produce the best single vision, from Shipley and Rawling's point of view these are secondary relations due to the correlation among these factors. According to their model, even if the visual system could not stereoscopically fuse the two images, the horopter would still exist as a geometrical construct showing where the corresponding points should be located when they finally do evolve.

Recent evidence has suggested that the concept of the horopter as a frontal parallel plane or surface must be modified. Geometrical relationships suggest that the actual fronto-parallel surface should look more like that shown in Fig. 5-12, according to W. Hoffman (1978). Furthermore, other investigators have even suggested that the actual horopter is not a surface, but rather a circle (corresponding to the classic Vieth–Müller circle) oriented horizontally with a single inclined vertical line that passes through the center of the circle. It is only on this line and circle that the criteria for the horopter are actually met, according to this point of view.

The important general point for the purposes of the present discussion of the horopter is that the geometrical arrangement of the eyes on the head is the critical factor in defining the meaning of this important perceptual construct. Like the natural geometry of the external space, the geometry of the eyes determines some of the phenomena of visual perception. These eye–arrangement-determined

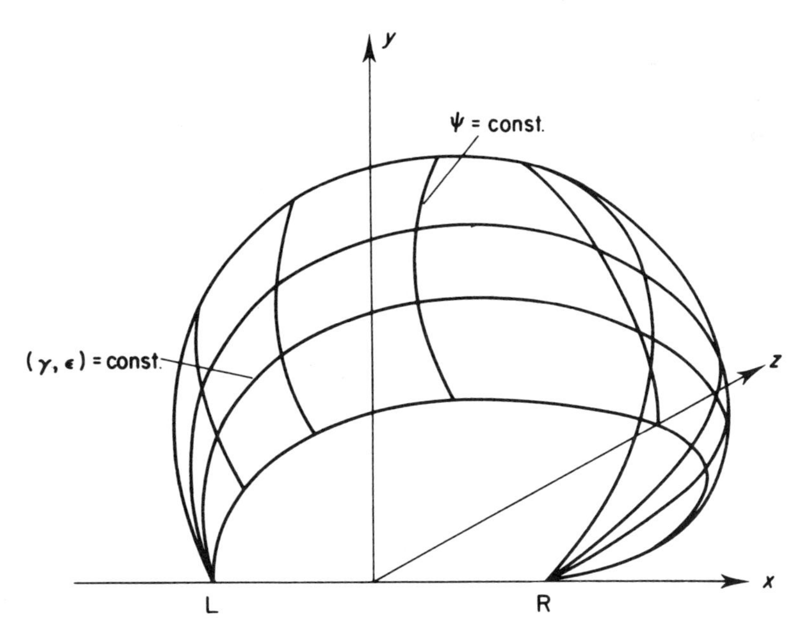

FIG. 5.12. The horopter depicted as a torus. (From Hoffman, © 1978, with the permission of John Wiley & Sons, Inc.)

phenomena are not the results of transforms carried out in the perceptual system but, like the other Level 0 processes described in this chapter, the results of natural geometry—in this case, the geometry of the visual apparatus itself.

To say that these perceptual effects arise directly from the natural geometry of the eyes (which must be also considered as a part of the external environment), however, is not to say that the perceptual space so defined is identical to the external physical space. Indeed, one of the classic theories of binocularly perceived space (A. Blank, 1958, 1978; Luneberg, 1947, 1948, 1950) suggests that all of the geometrical, anatomical, neurophysiological, and psychological factors interact to produce a perceived space that is substantially different from the external physical space. The human-sized external space is euclidean, i.e., it is a space in which parallel lines never meet; in which the sum of the angles of a triangle equal 180 deg; and in which the curvature is zero. However, Luneberg asserts that in the same scale universe in which the phenomena of binocular perception are measured, perceptual space exhibits quite a different metric. The space of the binocularly perceiving human is a non-euclidean one, better modeled in terms of convex hyperbolic or Lobachevskian mathematics than in terms of a strictly linear Cartesian coordinate system. In being non-euclidean, visual space is similar to the macrocosm of cosmological interactions. In the macrocosm, space is made non-euclidean by the gravitational forces operating within it; in perceptual space, analogous transformations result from the aggregate effect of all higher levels of processing and therefore are not, strictly speaking, Level 0 effects.

The Luneberg theory states that visual space is only locally (i.e., over very short distances) euclidean and that for long distances it is hyperbolic. (A hyperbolic space is one in which the component angles of a triangle add to less than 180 deg, the component angles of a square add to less than 360 deg.) The coordinate system so defined is curved like a saddle and, thus, parallel lines do meet at distances that depend upon the degree of curvature of the space. A coherent discussion of the specific postulates of Luneberg's theory of visual space can be found in Blank (1959). Many of these same properties are to be found in Hoffman's Lie algebra description of visual space that I have already described in Chapter 2. This is probably also the explanation for the non-euclidean nature of linear perspective as discussed on page 290.

Luneberg's hypothesis that perceptual space is non-euclidean is now generally accepted by most perceptual scientists. However, debate continues over the exact nature of the deviation from a euclidean space. Battro, Netto, and Rozestraten (1976), for example, have suggested the basis of large field experiments that the perceived curvature of visual space can vary from less than 1 (a saddle—the Lobachevskian or hyperbolic space suggested by Luneberg) for small fields to greater than 1 (a bowl) in large fields. Such a space would have to be represented by a much more general Riemannian geometry that allowed such a range of curvatures.

It must be kept clear, of course, that both Luneberg's and Hoffman's theories are not, in fact, solely the result of Level 0 processes. They are descriptions of the overall outcome of the full range of transforms applied to external space by all levels of the psychoneural system.

2. Optical Aberrations by the Environment

In the previous sections I have considered a number of perceptual effects that depend upon the natural geometry of the physical environment or of the eyes. These effects are the end products of processes that depend on the spatial relations of the viewing situation and would occur even in an optically perfect environmental medium. There are, however, other perceptually significant alterations of the stimulus information that result from optical aberrations created by the medium through which the light rays travel before impinging upon the eyes. These other processes are not naturally geometrical in the same sense as those previously discussed, though they may simulate some altered and bizarre spatial geometry as the light pathways are optically distorted. Optical aberrations of this sort may be thought of as distortions of the visual space by the geometrical optical properties of the media that make up that environment.

This class of Level 0 transformations due to optical aberrations by the external environment includes a wide variety of processes affecting the optical signals that constitute the communication links between the stimulus object and the retinal image. Light may be selectively absorbed, scattered, reflected, or refracted in a way that leads to a perceptual experience that is not consistent with the independently measured physical nature of the original environmental object that was the origin of the stimulating light rays. The spectrum of light incident on the eye may be broken up by internal reflections in water droplets; light may be scattered in a way that gives rise to unusual colors or blurred images; or objects that are, in physical reality, linear (or nonlinear) may appear nonlinear (or linear) because of distorting refractions and reflections. Colors may appear where only white light had been present and so on. All these processes are examples of optical aberrations by the environment and all of them can have perceptual significance and often do result in some extraordinary visual phenomena.

All the phenomena that fit into this division of the Level 0 category can be considered to be the direct results of the optical processes of selective reflection, refraction, and absorption by the environment. Reflection, to review briefly some elementary physics, refers to the bending of the path of a light ray so that it passes back within the same medium from whence it came. Refraction, on the other hand, refers to a bending of the path of a light ray at an interface between two media (due to differences in the indices of refraction of the two materials) in a way such that as the path passes from one medium to the other, it changes direction. Refracted light thus leaves the interface through the second medium, not the first medium through which it approached the interface. Selective absorption, on the other hand, refers to the capacity of a medium to absorb spectral wavelengths unequally from the incident light. Figure 5-13 depicts these three different processes.

These three optical processes, reflection, refraction, and absorption account for most of the optical aberrations that I describe in this section. I now consider some of the simpler visual phenomena produced by reflective and refractive aberrations, then phenomena resulting from selective absorption, and in turn, the special problem of blur.

a. Perceptual Effects of Refraction and Reflection in the External Environment. A large group of perceptual phenomena arise directly from the refractive

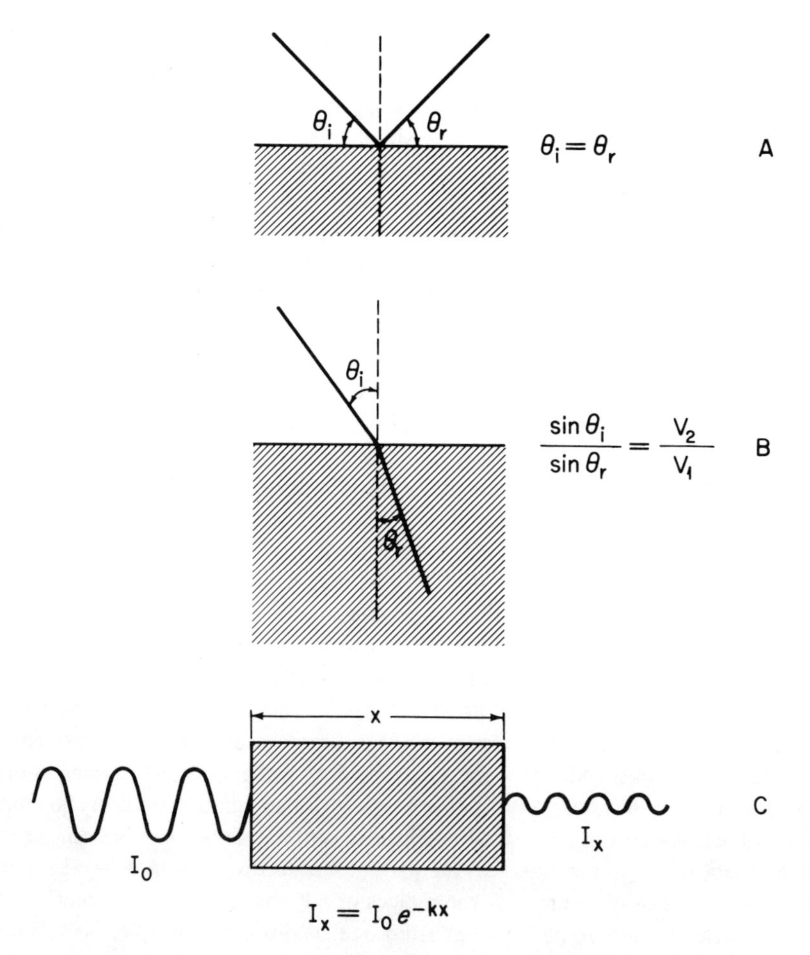

FIG. 5.13. (A) The light pathway in reflection. (B) The light pathway in refraction. (C) The effect on light of absorption.

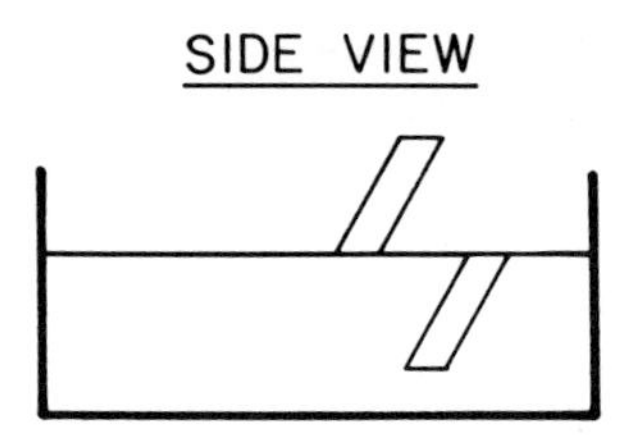

A

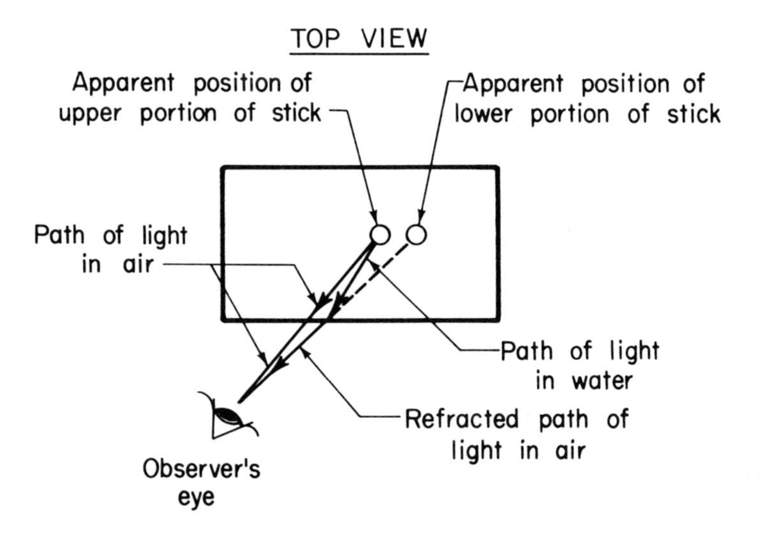

B

FIG. 5.14. The effect of refraction on the continuity of physical objects. (A) Side view; (B) top view showing the pathway of the light rays through air and through water.

aberrations imposed on light waves traversing interfaces between different media in the external environment. This section considers these processes and attempts to show how these phenomena are interrelated or even equivalent in terms of the optical process that account for them.

One of the simplest phenomena of visual perception is the apparent distortion, due to refraction, of an object partly immersed in a pool of water. Figure 5-14A illustrates this optical distortion of a perfectly linear (in terms of independent physical measures) object; it ''appears'' to be broken into two parts. The percept, in this case, is nonveridical with the physical reality of the object. When withdrawn from the water, the stick is straight, and no one would accept the contention that it may have actually been deformed in the water. Indeed, when probed with a nonoptical measuring device (such as another rod or a hand), the stick can easily be demonstrated to be mechanically straight.

The explanation of this visual phenomenon is relatively straightforward. The respective refractive indices of air and water have selectively influenced the pathways taken by the light. As shown in Fig. 5-14B, the light rays from the lower portion of the stick have been refracted at the water–air interface so that they appear to come from a position to the left of the unrefracted light rays from the upper portion of the stick.

This is only a simple example of the perceptual effects of refraction and is generally appreciated by all concerned. More impressive or complicated visual phenomena may also depend, however, upon exactly the same refractive properties of the environment medium and not be so clearly self-evident. For example, there is an apparent displacement[7] of the positions of celestial objects due to the refraction that occurs as light waves pass from the near-vacuum of interplanetary space, with its characteristic index of refraction, into the earth's atmosphere with its own often irregular refractive properties. Figure 5-15 shows the nature of this celestial distortion for an object near the horizon. An identical refractive process also explains how the sun can be visible near the horizon well after the officially announced time of sunset when it should be out of the direct line of sight. Postsunset redness can also be understood in similar terms, but, in this case, the explanation is complicated by a wavelength-dependent factor. Long-wavelength light is refracted more strongly than short-wavelength lights. Thus the reds can be seen after the blues have disappeared in a typical sunset.[8]

A number of the optical applicances intentionally designed to alter the external optical pathway taken by the visual stimulus do so as a result of their refractive properties. Spectacles have been used for hundreds of years to improve the optical properties of the retinal image, and more recently, scleral and corneal contact lenses have been introduced. It is now even possible to insert corrective applicances into the gap left after the removal of a cataract-plaqued lens of the human eye. The correction of the refractive errors of the ocular optics, therefore, has become almost a routine practice. Optical errors, both in the locus of the focal point (myopia and hypertropia) and in the differential focus of stimuli at different orientations (astigmatism), can be corrected by appropriate lenses.

Lenses and prisms have also been used for many years by perceptual scientists to distort visual stimulus scenes experimentally. These studies have generally

---

[7]There is also a similar displacement due to gravitational attraction between light and a massive object like the sun. But this general relativistic effect is not germane to our present discussion.

[8]The blueness of the sky, however, is not a result of simple refraction but, results instead from another wavelength-dependent optical effect—scattering by particulate matter in the atmosphere. A perfectly dust-free sky would look black except in the immediate region of some celestial light source. The dust that exists in considerable amounts in our atmosphere, however, scatters (irregularly reflects) light in a way that functionally depends upon its wavelength. Short wavelengths are scattered considerably more by the small dust particles than are the longer wavelengths. Thus there is a more homogenous and even distribution of the short-wavelength than of the long-wavelength light, and for this reason the color of the clear sky is predominantly blue.

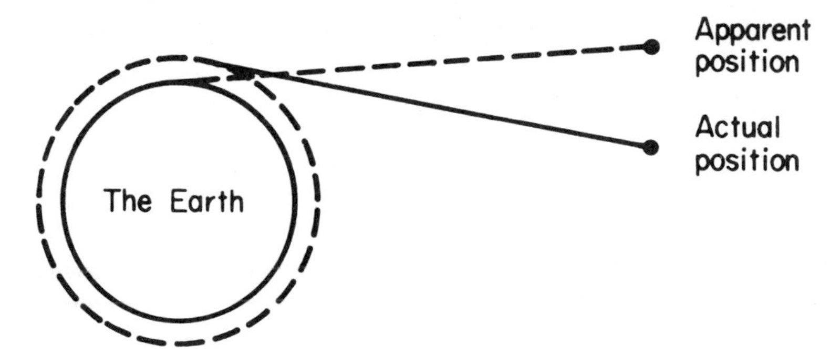

FIG. 5.15. The effect of refraction on the apparent position of the sun. The sun may appear to be above the horizon after it has actually "set" in a geometrical sense, because of this refractive effect.

been aimed at determining whether or not the relationship between perceived space and the neural representation (i.e., the retinal projection) is innately structured or whether, to the contrary, it adapts as a result of experience.

A novel, interesting, and very powerful all-electronic means of producing the same kind of image distortions produced by prisms has recently been developed by Gourlay, Gyr, Walters, and Willey (1975). This group programmed a computer to simulate the effects of prism distortion and then to plot, on an oscilloscope screen, visual patterns as they would have appeared to an observer who was wearing equivalently distorting prisms. In an actual experiment, the subject may, for example, be told to follow a straight line on the face of the oscilloscope. However, the computer processes the straight line image in such a way that the path on which it is plotted is actually curved (simulating the effect of some distorting prism). Thus the subject must move his point of fixation in a curve to follow the straight line. To achieve this simulation requires that the subject's eye position be constantly monitored and this ability was also a part of the computer system hardware and software.

Reflective processes can combine with refractive ones to produce some extraordinary perceptual phenomena. The most notable of these, of course, is the rainbow produced by the water that is particularly abundant in the atmosphere following a rainstorm. It has long been appreciated (perhaps since medieval times) that the rainbow phenomenon can be explained in terms of the internal reflections and refractions of light rays within the confines of a single droplet of water. The amazing story that is now understood of the passage of light within these tiny droplets is even more incredible when one appreciates that not one, but perhaps a dozen or more different "orders" of rainbows can actually be generated by droplets of water. Though few of us have even seen an atmospheric rainbow with more than twin bows because of the required viewing angles, laboratory simulations can develop these higher-order dispersion phenomena so that they can be photographed.

According to a theory worked out by Nussenzveig (1977), the many orders of rainbows arise as a result of multiple reflections within each droplet of water. Figure 5-16 shows his analysis of the pathways of rays of light within a single droplet. Nussenzveig asserts that some of the light is reflected at the first encounter with the atmospheric water droplet interface. These initially reflected portions of the incident beam are defined as Class 1 rays. Other portions of the incident light are refracted slightly as they enter the water droplet. Some of this light emerges immediately from the droplet, once again being refracted at the interface by the different indices of refraction of water and air. These light beams are categorized as Class 2 rays.

A third portion of the incident light, however, is internally reflected at the point the Class 2 rays emerge. A portion of these internally reflected rays also subsequently emerges, once again being refracted by the water–air interface to make up the set of Class 3 rays. Other portions of the original incident light are subject to even further internal reflections and emergent refractions to make up higher-order packets of rays. The Class 3 rays are particularly important; they constitute the light that is seen as the main rainbow that dominates this colorful effect in intensity and saturation.

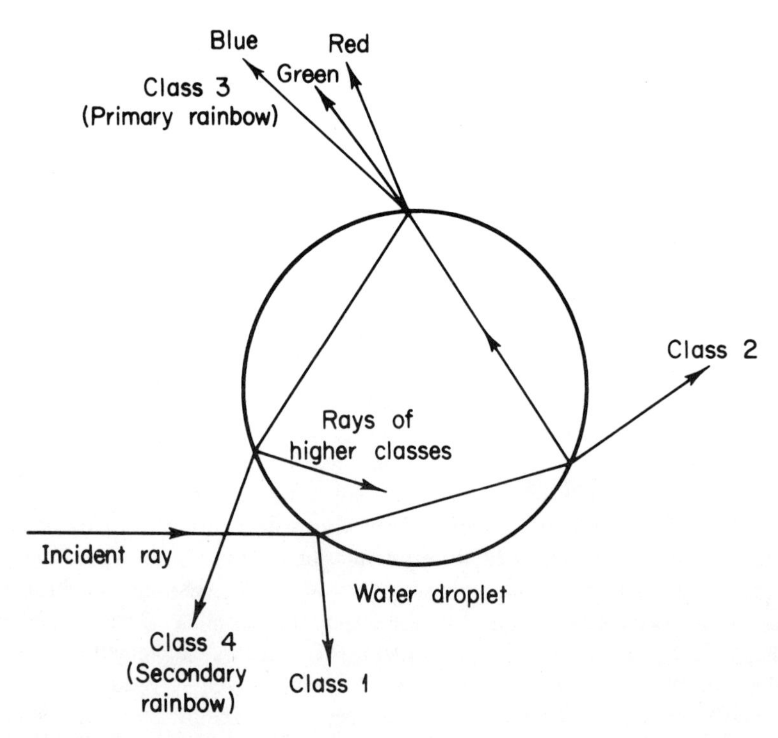

FIG. 5.16. The production of rainbows by individual droplets of water. (Redrawn from Nussenzveig, © 1977.)

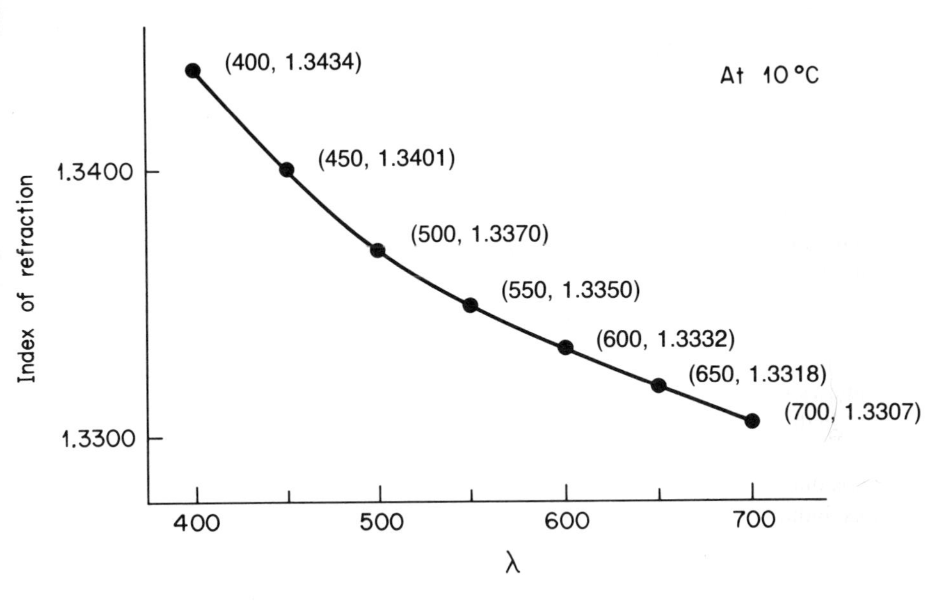

FIG. 5.17. The change in the index of refraction of water as a function of the wavelength of the incident light.

So far I have not said anything about the most conspicuous feature of the rainbow—its apparent color. Why is it that the light rays are segregated as a function of their wavelength? The answer to this question is exactly the same as the answer that would be necessary to explain the spectral dispersion of light by any prism spectroscope. The dispersion of the incident light into a colorful rainbow results from the fact that different wavelengths of light are refracted differentially at any interface between water and air.[9] In this case, the angle at which the different wavelengths of the Class 3 rays of light emerge from each droplet is dependent upon the different degrees of refraction imposed on the various wavelengths of light at the entry and exit points. The water droplet is, in fact, acting very much like a miniature prism spectroscope.

This brief discussion of rainbows is not intended to completely explain all of the phenomena of these beautiful effects. The reader who would like more detail is referred to Tricker (1970), Boyer (1959), or Nussenzveig's (1977) paper itself for an especially clear and well-illustrated explanation.

If rainbows are examples of natural optical aberrations produced by water droplets acting like prism spectroscopes, it is also possible to find similar color

[9]See Figure 5-17 for a plot of the effective indices of refraction of water for light of different wavelengths.

effects due to natural processes imitating interference or diffraction spectroscopes. Colored bands comparable to rainbows are seen when thin films of oil float on water or when optical distortions occur in glasses. The colors in this case are not due to selective refractions but to interference patterns that occur when thin films approximate the wavelength of light in thickness. A more complete description of the interference effects underlying this kind of spectral dispersion can be found in any text of physical optics. Perhaps the most interesting of these natural interference spectroscopes can be found in the iridescent colors from the cuticles of insects. Either multiple layers of regularly spaced cells or a pattern of closely spaced fine lines in the chitonous epidermis of many species of beetles can produce the optical interference patterns that underly the iridescent mini-rainbows (Hinton & Gibbs, 1969, 1971).

Whether the colorful phenomena are water–droplet-produced rainbows or flights of shimmering colors from a beetle's carapace, however, the important fact is that they are optical tricks of the external environment and not transformations induced within the perceptual system of the perceiver. These Level 0 processes, like the geometrical ones described in earlier sections of this chapter, produce essentially veridical responses to the proximal stimulus even though there is a considerable discrepancy to the distal stimulus.

Another closely related and enormously interesting class of phenomena includes those phenomena traditionally referred to as mirages. The classic mirages are also totally explicable in terms of the refractive effects of the environment on transmitted light rays without recourse to any psychoneural transformations. In the case of mirages, because of their scale, the chromatic effects are usually negligible or secondary, and the main aspect of the phenomenon is some distortion of spatial geometry. Distances may contract; objects may apparently be inverted; and other aberrations of shape or topology occur. The classic mirages, like rainbows, can be photographed, and this simple fact is clear proof that they are environmentally determined and, like other Level 0 based phenomena, the result of processes that occur external to the nervous system.

I had a memorable personal experience with a well-known type of mirage known as the *Fata Morgana*. The Fata Morgana is the spurious perception of a nonexistent wall with many vertical discontinuities. It usually occurs when the observer is looking out over a large body of water at a distant coastline. My family and I had been sailing north on the Red Sea on the MS *Victoria* out of Hong Kong prior to a transit of the Suez Canal. On a very hot morning of the day we were to arrive in Port Suez, the southern terminus of the canal, I suddenly became aware of a very large "city" to the starboard of the ship. The city consisted of many typical desert "houses"—the square, white, small-windowed, flat-roofed homes that are ubiquitous in that Mediterranean area. I could even see "laundry" hanging in the streets and courtyards and had a very strong impression of human and cart traffic in the alleys between the houses. My first reaction was enormous awe; the city I was looking at was huge and extended for miles. I had not been aware that any city existed on the east coast of the Red Sea; I had previously thought that that was the forlorn and uninhabited west coast of the Sinai Peninsula. How wonderful, indeed, had been the Egyptian government's urban development!!

My second reaction, however, was a vague feeling that the "laundry" and "houses" and "traffic" were "not quite right." My third reaction was the dawning realization that this whole perceptual experience was absurd. The Sinai coast of the Red Sea IS uninhabited desert, and the city that I saw extending for miles along the coast could not have been other than a classic case of the Fairy Morgan's "castle." Until I came to my rational, logical, and knowledgable psychological senses, I had been badly misinterpreting these visual stimuli. When the relatively small city of Port Suez finally did truly appear on the horizon, it was clear just how absurd my perceptual response had been. Yet, my sense organs had been doing just what they were supposed to be doing, providing me with information about the external world that was painted, however, distorted, on my retinae. Had my camera been with me, it too would have been able to record the fairy city without any difficulty. With the exception of some of the more intricate details, such as the laundry, which had to be attributed to my very overheated imagination that day, the distortions in the scene were entirely accounted for by aberrations in the hot air over the sea and desert.

If the fairy city I saw was not actually there, then to what kind of optical aberration can I attribute this bizarre perceptual experience? The answer to this question arises from exactly the same explanation as that encompassing spectacles, the rainbow, and the apparently bent stick in the glass of water. The Fata Morgana is a result of thermal gradients and discontinuities that make the atmosphere act as a huge, although poor quality, lens. This lens refracts, in sometimes complicated and anisotropic ways, the rays of light that pass through it. The full story of the thermal atmospheric lens has been told most eloquently by Fraser (1975) and Fraser and Mach (1976). These authors point out that the index of refraction of the air is almost totally determined by its density, which in turn is almost entirely a function of the temperature of the air at any point. Therefore, in any atmosphere in which a thermal gradient exists there will be a tendency to refract transient rays of light to different degrees depending upon their physical location. In almost all practical situations there is, in fact, a gradient of temperature distribution and, in some situations, sharp discontinuities such as are found in inversion situations where cold air may sit on top of hot air. The net effect of these thermal gradients, and the resulting variations in refraction indices, is that the atmosphere can act as an optical lens to bend the pathways of rays of light passing through it. Indeed, the atmospheric lens need not be exceptionally powerful in terms of its local refractive power. Because of the great distances usually involved, only a slight refractive effect per unit distance is required to produce enormous aberrations of a scene.

This, in essence, is all there is to atmospheric mirages. They are the result of the refraction of light by a giant thermally created lens with a nonhomogenous index of refraction that can differentially bend the rays of light coming from distant objects. The effect of this kind of optical aberration may be that of spuriously raising or lowering an object in relation to other objects, magnifying or diminishing (towering or stooping in the vocabulary of the mirage buffs) an object in size. Objects may even be differentially magnified so that distant portions of a scene may appear to be closer than nearby objects. Spurious reflections may produce stimuli suggesting the presence of extensive sheets of water where it is actually very dry, or distorting regularly shaped physical objects into bizarre shapes.

A more detailed and formal explanation of mirages is given in Figs. 5-18A and 5-18B. The following discussion is based on the particularly lucid paper by Fraser and Mach (1976). The diagrams on the left of each of the two figures show the relationship between air temperature and altitude. If the temperature is higher closer to the ground than at greater elevations (as shown in Fig. 5-18A), then the image of the surface[10] of the earth will appear to be bent increasingly downward by the refractive effects, with increasing distance from the portion of the surface being considered. Fraser and Mach have placed three objects in this diagram to illustrate the varying effects of this refractive situation on images of objects at different distances. The object closest to the observer is simply displaced downward, and because the optical rays are divergent at the point at which it is located, it is slightly magnified. On the other hand, an object at an intermediate distance produces a double image because of the great curvature of the optical pathways produced by the refractive effects of the atmospheric lens. Two images—one upright and one inverted—are often seen. In both cases the images are also substantially magnified because of the divergent ray paths from that point. The inversion of one image is a strong factor in producing the impression of water since the inverted image looks very much like a reflection image. The respective magnifications of the two images of these objects at intermediate distances also contribute to the impression that the objects are much closer to the observer than, in fact, they actually are, an effect that can have disastrous consequences for a traveller in a desert environment. Finally, the even more distant third object is totally invisible because the rays forming its image have been bent totally out of the line of sight of the observer.

If the temperature–elevation relationship is reversed, however, with the temperature increasing with elevation rather than decreasing, and if there is a point of inflection in the temperature curve then the bending of the light rays will be in the direction opposite to that shown in Fig. 5-18A. This new thermal configuration is shown in Fig. 5-18B. In this instance a triple image is often formed by an object at intermediate distance as a result of the refraction effects. The magnification, however, for such an object may be very irregular and the three images may all be of different sizes. Objects closer to the observer in this second thermal situa-

[10]This ignores the natural curvature of the earth. In the model cases described here, the surface of the earth is considered to be flat.

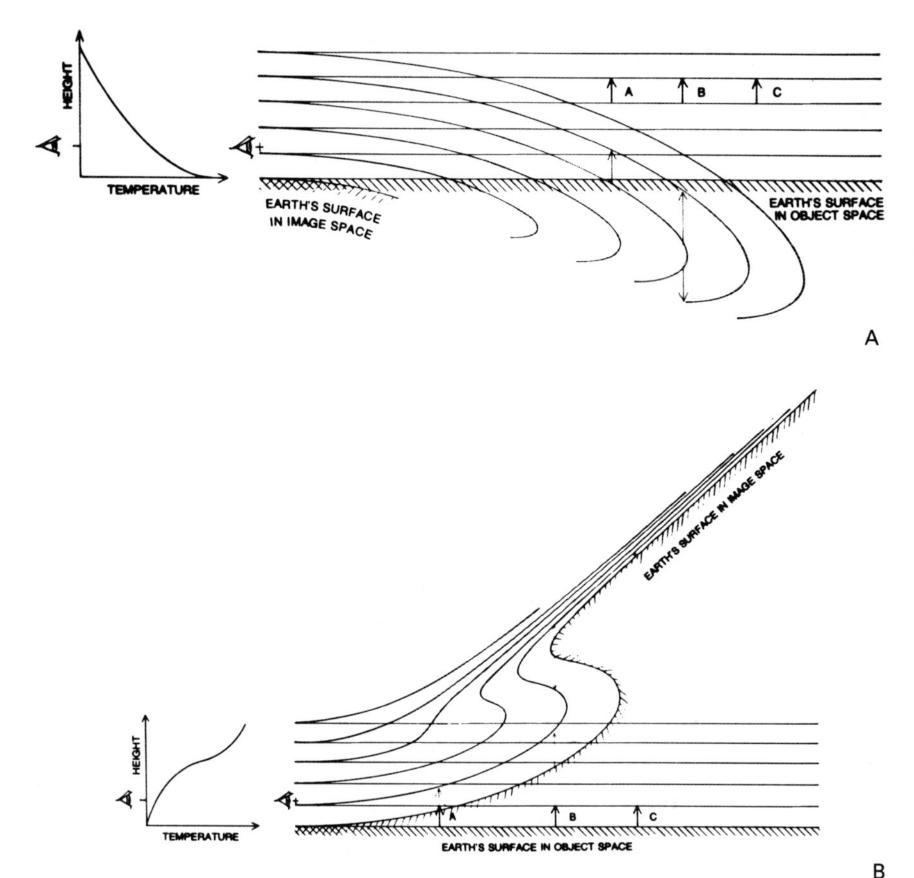

FIG. 5.18. (A) The optical effect of a temperature inversion system with colder air at higher levels. The object space depicts the physical situation; the image space depicts the apparent percept or, as it is otherwise known, the mirage. (B) In this case the atmospheric optics are also aberrant, but the critical feature is the inflection point in the function relating height and temperature. Both the object and image space are also shown here for this alternative atmospheric lens. (From Fraser and Mach, © 1976, with the permission of Scientific American, Inc.)

tion may be elevated but not substantially distorted. However, an object at a very great distance may be very much smaller than would be predicted by a simple application of the law of visual angle (Eq. 5-1).

These, then, are only the rudiments of the theory of mirages as developed by Fraser and Mach. It is not necessary that the reader of this book fully understand all of the detailed mathematics and optics of these aberrations of the stimulus situation. The point that I wish to make in this perceptual context of mirages, once again, is that they are not illusions produced by transformations within the psychoneural perceptual system but are phenomena entirely explicable in terms of environmentally produced aberrations. Mirages, like rainbows, are the veridical responses of the perceptual system to the proximal stimuli that impinge upon it.

b. Perceptual Effects of Selective Spectral Absorption by the External Environment. There are other perceptual phenomena produced not by the refraction or reflection of light rays by the environmental optical medium but by the selective absorption of portions of the spectrum of the incident light by the medium. Environmental absorption of light is explained in terms of quantal, atomic, and molecular energy interactions in the absorbing medium that are tuned to particular wavelengths of the incident light. When the appropriate wavelength light falls on a molecule or atom, the energy of the light photon is converted into a shift of the orbital energy of some electron or into heat. In either case, the energy of the quanta of that particular wavelength is absorbed and is no longer available to play any role in the proximal stimulus.

The gaseous components of the atmosphere are selective absorbers of the electromagnetic energy coming from the sun over wide ranges of photic wavelength, much to our comfort and longevity. Recent interest (e.g., Hammond & Maugh, 1974; Tukey, 1976) in the absorption of ultraviolet wavelengths by the ozone layer of the stratosphere has highlighted the fact that selective absorption by this portion of the atmosphere protects us from dangerously high levels of this radiation. Figure 5-19 shows the absorption spectrum of ozone and illustrates how it can act as a protective blind to ultraviolet radiation because of its absorption of these potentially dangerous wavelengths. (Note also, however, its sharp cut-off and excellent ability to pass visible light.) Water vapor, on the other hand, selectively absorbs the longer (red and infrared) wavelengths. Water thus protects us and our environment from the damage that could be produced by too high levels of these longer electromagnetic waves. Other natural and contaminant gases in the atmosphere can also selectively absorb other portions of the solar spectrum, either to our detriment or to our benefit. It is interesting to note how dependent we are on the narrow transparent window between the ozone and water absorption spectra. Except for that window, animals with our characteristic photosensitivity would live in a world of darkness. Of course, if the window were elsewhere, we probably would have evolved some other suitable absorption spectrum.

Another striking practical example of the perceptual effects of selective absorption can be found in the effects on vision when the viewer is underwater. In recent years commercial and recreational use of the underwater part of our environment has grown enormously. The SCUBA system (self-contained underwater breathing apparatus) has allowed man to spend hours rather than just a few seconds underwater. But this is a new visual environment as well, and some attention is warranted to possible perceptual effects when one is submerged.

The optical properties of water are relatively straightforward and well understood, but their effect on vision has not been an object of study until recently.

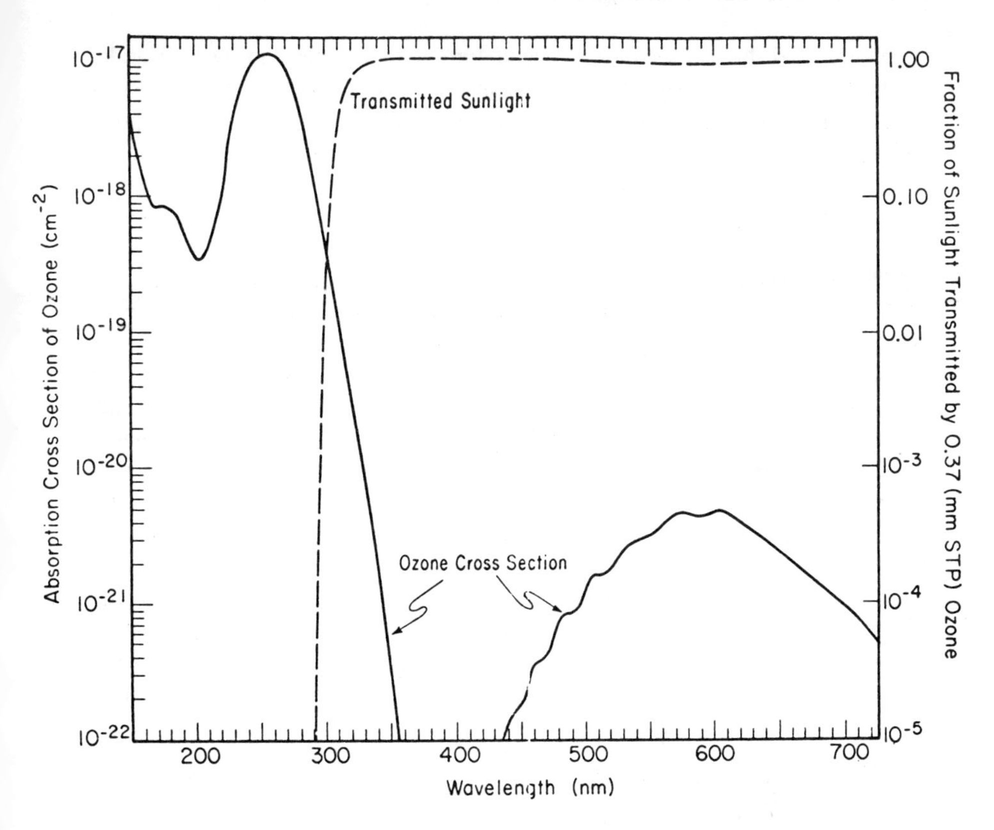

FIG. 5.19. The absorption properties of ozone as a function of wavelength. Note that the ozone blocks out substantial amounts of ultraviolet light between 350 and 430 nanometers. Depletion of ozone would allow larger amounts of this dangerous radiation to pass through to the surface of the earth. (Courtesy of Dr. Harold S. Johnston of the Lawrence Berkeley Laboratory of the University of California.)

Luria and Kinney (1970) have recently made an important contribution to the problem of underwater color vision and have shown how selective absorption can profoundly affect our perceptual experience. As in any other experiment, they wished to have an independent variable that could take on a number of different values so that functional relationships between the absorptive properties of several different underwater environments and perception could be determined. To meet this need, Luria and Kinney ingeniously measured the absorption spectra of several quite different bodies of water to provide them with an independent variable. They found that the absorption spectra of various bodies of water differed greatly from that of very pure water vapor (as shown previously in Fig. 5-17). Depending upon the body of water studied, the transparency to various wavelengths of visible light could vary from almost a perfect fit to a pure water-absorption curve to almost total opacity.

Figure 5-20 shows their measurements for a naturally clear spring in Florida, the Gulf of Mexico, Long Island Sound, and the terribly polluted Thames River in Connecticut. It is obvious that the differences in relative spectral absorption indicated in this figure are not just quantitatively different; they vary in the overall shape of the respective curves as well. In some cases, the qualitative difference could be extreme. The transmission spectrum in the Thames River is actually reversed from that of ordinary water; it absorbs most strongly in the short wavelengths and passes proportionately more of the longer wavelength light.

Luria and Kinney used a color identification task to determine the effects of these varying spectral absorptions on vision. Figure 5-21 shows the results of one of their experiments. The subjects were asked to identify either a nonfluorescent or a fluorescent version of eight different colored paints. The luminous intensity of each paint sample was made roughly equal by placing the samples at different distances corresponding "to the limits of visibility" in each of the four underwater conditions. Some painted panels (gray and black) were never correctly identified; obviously their lack of chromatic properties made them so much like the prevalent color of the background that they remained essentially invisible even at the short distances at which all other colors were always correctly recognized.

Figure 5-21 indicates that nothing can be said in general about a single "best" color for underwater vision. In some environments the yellows and oranges were

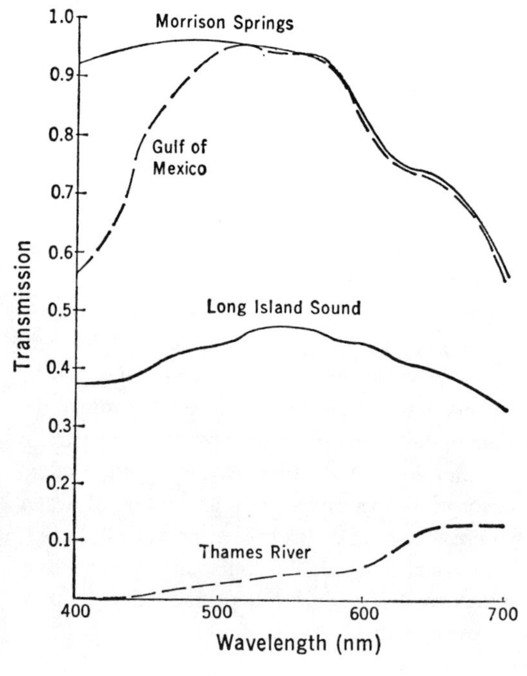

FIG. 5.20. Transmission of light as a function of wavelength through four different bodies of water. (From Luria and Kinney, © 1970, with the permission of the American Association for the Advancement of Science.)

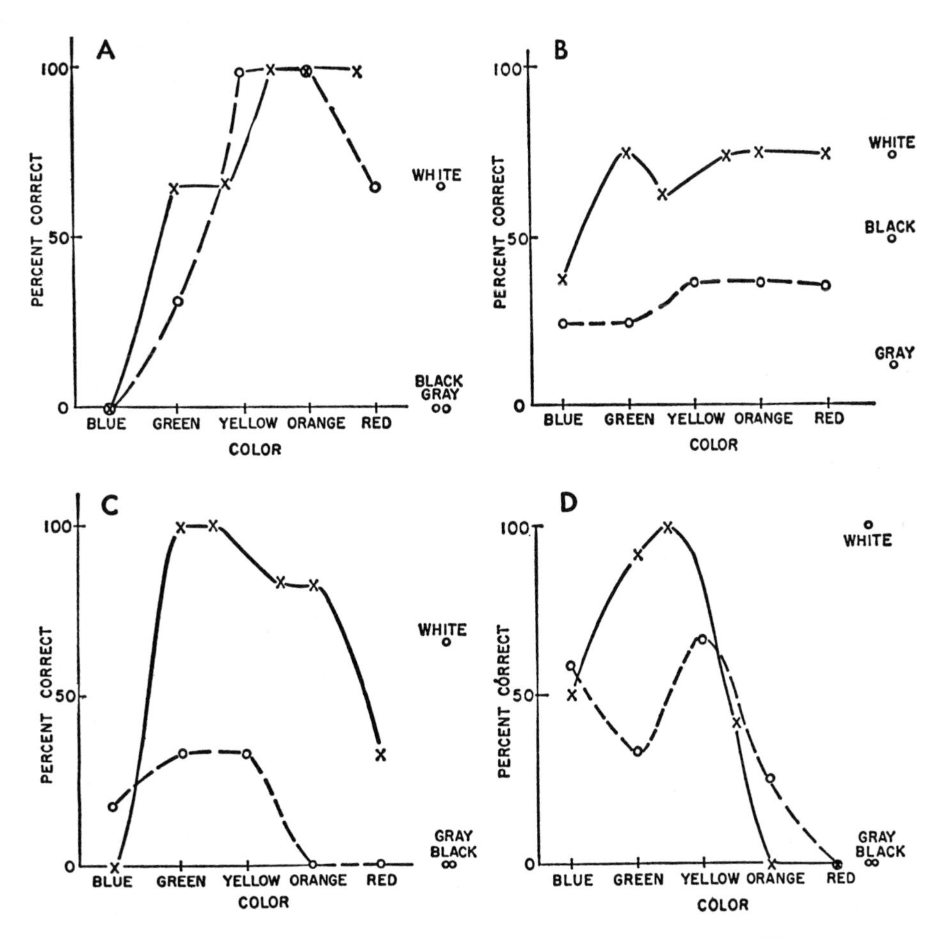

FIG. 5.21. The relative identifiability of various colors in the four different bodies of water whose absorption spectra are shown in Fig. 5.20. (From Luria and Kinney, © 1970, with the permission of the American Association for the Advancement of Science.)

most often correctly named; in other environments green was more often correctly identified. Underwater color vision is thus affected in a qualitative manner by the spectral absorbance of the medium. However complex the perceptual results of Luria and Kinney's experiment, the important fact is that the critical process underlying this anomalous color perception is absorption by this particular watery environment—another Level 0 transformation.

c. Perceptual Effects of Environmentally Produced Blur. Optical blurring produced by scattered light in the external environment can also modulate visual perception. In the most extreme conditions, the overlap of the blurred images of two or more stimuli may be so great that an observer will not be able to discriminate the presence of multiple objects. This breakdown in object detectability due to retinal image blur is superimposed upon the limits on visual acuity defined by anatomy and physiology of the observer's eye. Though the effects are, in principle, indistinguishable, environmentally induced blur actually says nothing about the capabilities of the observer. Externally induced blur simply sets limits on what even an ideal observer with a perfect eye and a perfect nervous system would be able to discriminate in the stimulus scene. Obviously, environmentally induced blur is another example of a Level 0 process rather than a psychological or neural process of a higher level.

Nevertheless, the effect of externally induced stimulus blur, though totally nonneuropsychological, can be considerable. It is not only possible to lose the crisp outlines of an object but it is also possible to lose the ability to discriminate critical features as well. Figure 5-22, for example, shows the visual effects of blurring concentric ring patterns as demonstrated by Fry (1957). As the blur increases, double rings become spots, and in at least the case of the pattern in the lower right hand corner of this figure, the central spot can disappear into the blur entirely.

Whereas it is relatively easy to simulate this kind of blur by simply defocusing a projector, a more efficient means of introducing controlled blur gradients in projected images was developed by Fry. His system is shown in Fig. 5-23A. The subject views an image rear projected on a frosted glass screen located at A. This screen is also diffusely front-illuminated by light sources located at C and D. The subject sees what is essentially a bipartite screen with the right half illuminated from the rear by the projector shown at the left of the figure. The left half of the screen is blocked from the projected light, however, by a shield placed at H. The vertical line between the left and right half of the screen is a blurred intermediate region whose gradient is defined by the shape of the aperture placed at G. A blur gradient that approximates a probability curve is defined by an aperture like the one shown in Fig. 5-23B; near-linear blur gradients such as those required for the classic Mach band phenomenon (see Chapter 8) can be produced by the aperture shown in Fig. 5-23C. This device is a highly useful means of producing a controlled blur pattern of any desired gradient. Fry suggested that other apertures could be used to simulate astigmatism or even the kind of blur produced by an out-of-focus camera.

Whatever experimental use to which it is put, however, the blur produced by this device remains an environmental modulation of light stimuli. Although the effects of this environmental blur may be profound, this transformation is not the result of any psychoneural processing but is simply another Level 0 process. The blurred percept may be used by some higher level of processing and serve as an important trigger for some other critical process, but the perception of the blur itself is clearly the result of an environmental and not a psychoneural transformation.

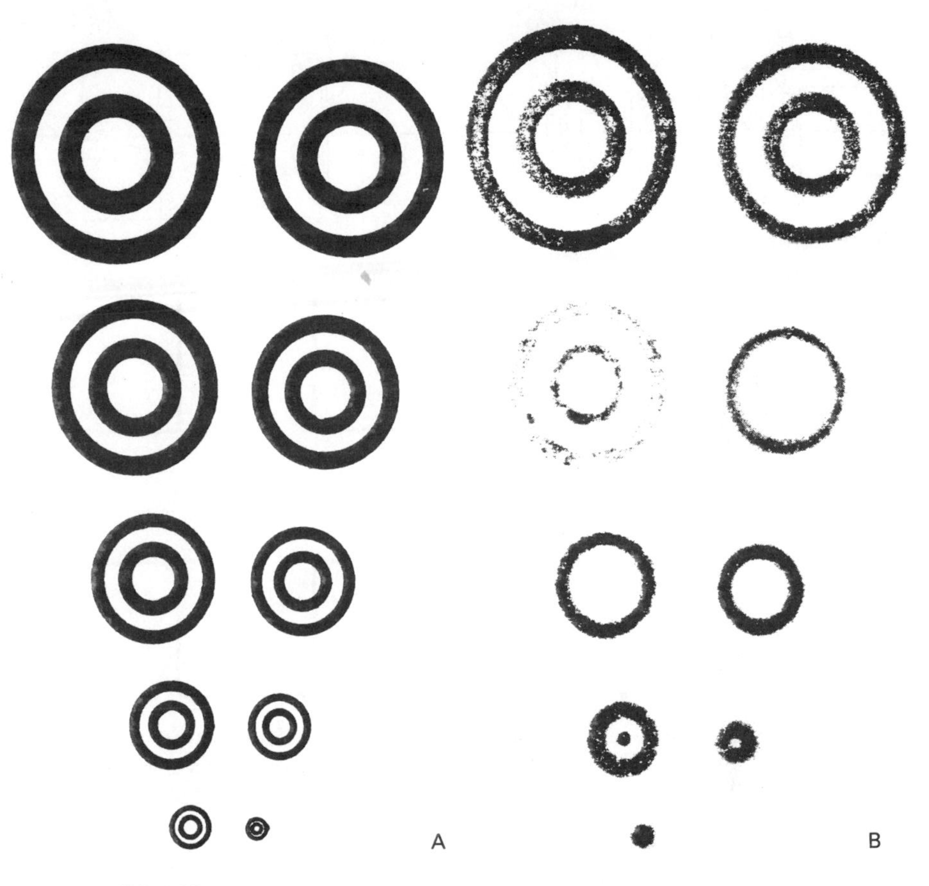

FIG. 5.22. The degradation in image quality resulting from an increase in blur. A. Unblurred stimuli. B. Blurred stimuli. (From Fry, 1957.)

Some psychologists, such as Coren (1969b; Coren & Girgus, 1978) have proposed that blur is an important factor in some of the geometrical illusions. However this seems to be something of a second order effect, if that, and perhaps only a Level 0 simulation of these illusions. In general, though the Müller-Lyer, or Poggendorff, illusion may be enhanced by increasing blur, the major component of the phenomenon seems to be a relational judgment that is better classified within Level 4.

3. Quantum Statistics

Finally, in this discussion of the environmental distortions of the stimulus that can influence the perception of a visual scene, it is important to note that at low

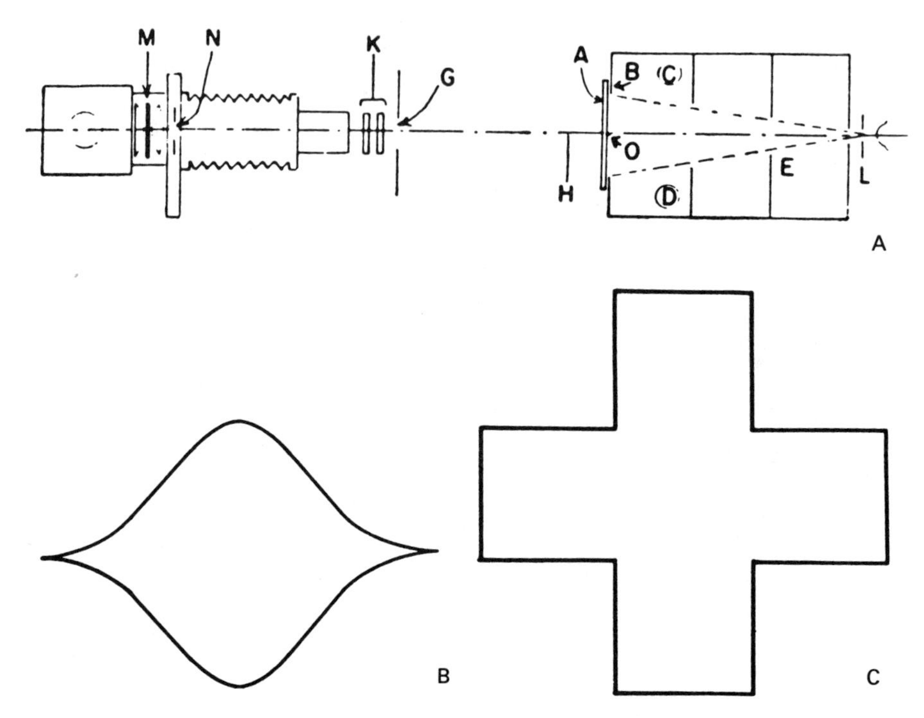

FIG. 5.23. (A) The optical equipment used by Fry to produce controlled amount of blur. (B and C). The apertures used by Fry to regulate the blur edge characteristics. (From Fry, 1957.)

stimulus intensities the quantum nature of light itself becomes an important variable. Because this topic is so closely related to the absorption processes of the receptor, I choose to discuss these quantum statistical effects in the next chapter. However it is not inappropriate at this point to at least note that statistical fluctuations in the number of quanta in a dim and brief flash of light may properly be considered to be one of the prime determinants of the absolute threshold.

The fact that statistics of the number of quanta available were influential in determining the lower limits has been emphasized by Hecht, Shlaer, and Pirenne (1942), and by Barlow (1964). The important fact for the reader to keep in mind when reading my discussion of their work later in Chapter 6 is that the statistical fluctuation in the number of available quanta is itself a physical process that does not result from any property of the visual system but arises directly out of the elemental nature of light itself. That such quantum statistical effects are now understood to play an important role in the determination of the threshold is one of the great intellectual breakthroughs in unifying the physical and biological theories of light and vision.

C. PERCEPTUALLY SIGNIFICANT OPTICAL PROPERTIES OF THE EYE

In the previous sections of this chapter, I discussed a number of stimulus transformations that result either from the natural geometry of the environment or from optical aberrations occurring within that external environment. These effects modulated and distorted the distal physical stimulus into what was often a substantially different proximal stimulus. The external environment, however, is not the only preneural medium capable of altering stimulus information as it passes between the distal object and the site at which the transductive process in the receptor is activated. Between the external environment and the mapping on the receptor mosaic there lies another set of optically active elements, those of the eye itself.

These optical elements introduce changes or transformations that are neither properly considered as psychoneural nor externally environmental. Instead they should be considered as internally environmental. Clearly, however, the processes I consider in the following section are indistinguishable, in physical principle, from the ones previously discussed in this chapter. Both are transformations that occur without any change in the nature of the stimulus energy. Their segregation into separate sections is intended only to emphasize the fact that the processes now under discussion are mediated by the anatomic structure of the organism itself, rather than external physical processes.

The purpose of this section, therefore, is to consider these intra-ocular optical processes and their influencese on visual perception. In doing so, I will be considering the refractive, reflective, and absorptive effects of the cornea, aqueous humor, lens, and vitreous humor as well as those of the entire retina and the individual photoreceptors themselves. In addition, the spherical geometry of the eye, also a source of image distortion, is relevant to this discussion.

In an ideal optical world, all lenses would possess perfect refractive properties; image space would be isomorphic to object space; and no media would selectively absorb any portion of the incident light. However, in the biological reality of the eye (as well as in the external environment) optical properties are never perfect. Lenses are not perfect refractors; the retina is not actually a flat surface; and all colors are not refracted or absorbed equally.

Furthermore, even in perfect lenses there are optical distortions introduced due to the wave aspect of the fundamental dual nature of light. Interferences between light waves are referred to as optical diffractions. The net result of diffraction is to produce wavelike fringes that represent the additive and subtractive interaction of wavefronts. Small apertures or objects, slits and lines, and double slits and double opaque lines are the prototypical cases of diffraction usually considered in physical optics texts, but in fact, all objects and apertures of any shape produce diffraction patterns at their edges at the very least. The diffraction patterns are usually quite small, but given the magnification inherent in the optics of the eyes and the close spacing of the receptors, these tiny effects can produce a fundamental limit on the perception of very small objects. Diffraction patterns produced by the interference of wave fronts, therefore, are most likely to be a source of aberration in visual acuity tests. Diffraction effects produced by objects and apertures within the eye can degrade contours, spread the image, and lead to what is essentially a microscopic blurring of the tiny images on the retinal mosaic. Figure 5-24 displays some sample diffraction patterns.

Diffraction effects become visually significant when the pupil is nearly as small as it can be. Indeed, when the pupil is near its minimum size (about 2 mm), the diffraction effects, which are inversely related to pupil size (i.e., the smaller the pupil, the more blur due to diffraction), become more significant than the blur due to the other optical aberrations, which are directly related to pupil size (i.e., the smaller the pupil, the less blur due to optical effects). It is for this reason—the crossing over of the two curves—that the best visual acuity and smallest blur circles occur for pupil sizes of about 2.4 mm, rather than for smaller apertures (Campbell & Gubisch, 1966).

Diffraction effects have been very well known for years and were originally described formally by Airy in 1834. These interference patterns are now called Airy patterns in his honor and are represented by the following equation:

$$L = kr^4 \left[1 - \frac{1}{2} m^2 + \frac{1}{3} \left(\frac{m^2}{2!} \right) + \frac{1}{4} \left(\frac{m^3}{3!} \right) + \ldots \right] \quad (5\text{-}2)$$

where L is the light intensity at any point, k is a constant, r is the radius of the aperture, and m is equal to $\pi r/\lambda \sin \alpha$, in which λ is the wavelength of the light used and α is the angle defined by the center of the aperture, the center of the diffraction pattern and the point. This represents a typical diffraction pattern—in this case a system of concentric light and dark rings (see Fig. 5-24), each of which can be attributed to either a constructive or destructive interference of the light waves. The diameter of the central spot ($2r_D$) which contributes most to the blur circle and sets the minimum size of the point spread function, can be calculated from the following expression:

$$r_D = \frac{.61\ \lambda}{n \tan \theta} \quad (5\text{-}3)$$

where r_D is the radius of the central spot, n is the index of refraction of the medium, and θ is the angle subtended by the aperture. It is this latter factor (θ) in the denominator of the equation that describes the inverse relation between the blur circle radius (r_D) due to diffraction and the size of the aperture.

Any lack of homogeneity in the optical pathway (including the edge of the iris) can lead to diffraction effects, and these effects cannot, in principle, be overcome by any corrective action. They represent a fundamental limit of the

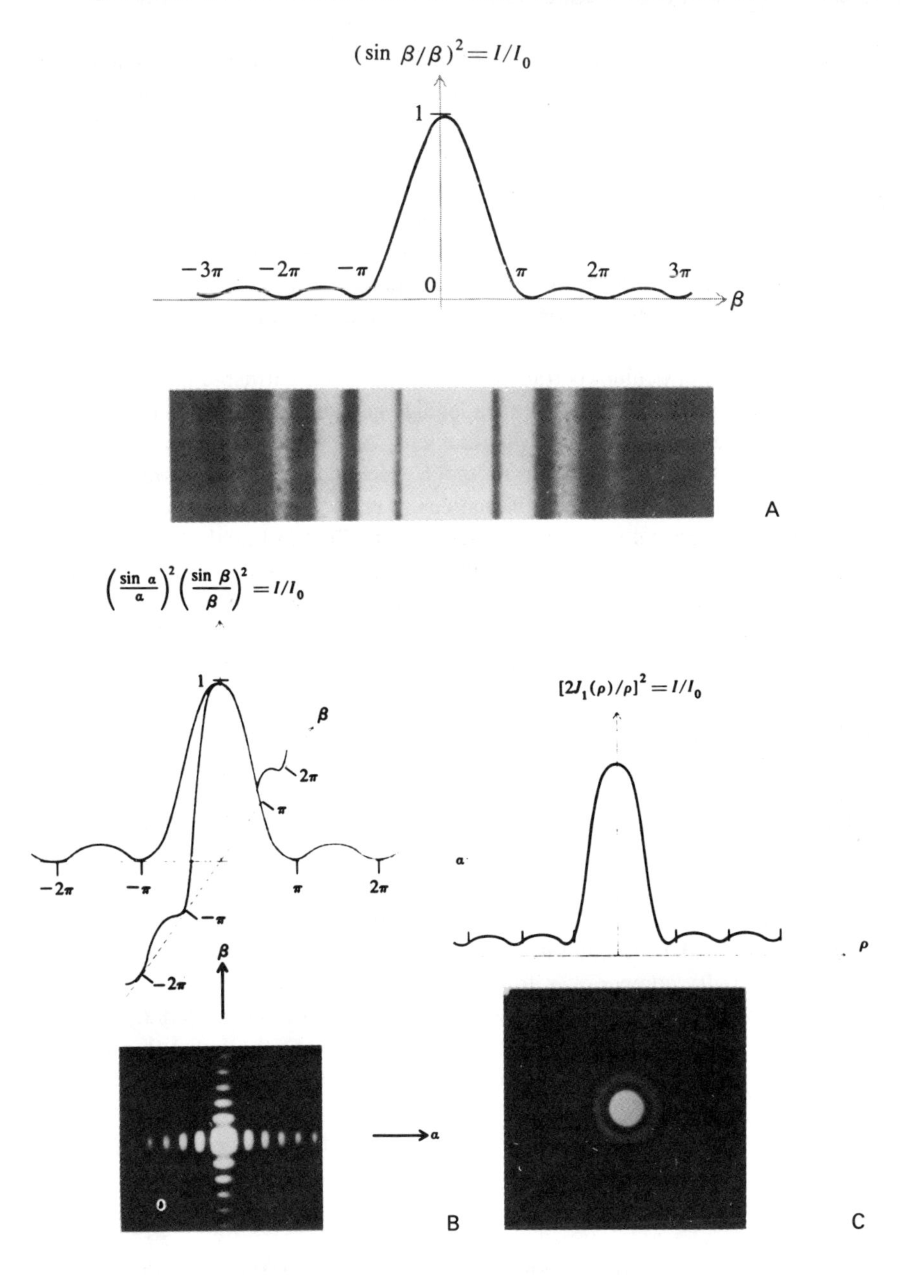

FIG. 5.24. Diffraction patterns produced by various kinds of apertures. In each case a photograph and a plot of the intensity of the light are shown. (A) The pattern produced by a slit. (B) The pattern produced by a rectangular aperture. (C) The pattern produced by a circular aperture. (From Fowles, © 1975, with the permission of Holt, Rinehart, and Winston, Inc.)

information-bearing properties of light itself, and no lens design, no matter how subtle, can correct for such diffraction effects. It is fascinating to note that the minimum pupil size that has evolved over the millenia is just about the size at which this unavoidable limit becomes manifest.

The net result of all of these failures to achieve optical perfection is a degradation of the image that falls on the photoreceptor mosaic and ultimately a reduction in the ability of the visual system to process information. This section of the chapter considers the various ways in which the eye fails *as an optical instrument* to achieve perfect information transmission and thus introduces blur into the retinal image.

The sources of ocular aberrations are of five distinguishable kinds. The first, geometric aberration, is due to the inadequate geometry of the eye's two focusing elements—the cornea and the crystalline lens. As we see later, there are also five different kinds of geometric aberration. The second, chromatic aberration, is due to a wavelength-dependence of the indices of refraction of the material of which the cornea and crystalline lens are constructed. The third kind of ocular aberration is due to the overall geometry of the eye and, in particular, to the fact that the imaging surface—the retina—is not a flat surface. The fourth arises as a result of the obstruction or absorption of some portion of the incident light. The optics of the outer segments of the receptors themselves also lead to certain selective sensitivities and thus to certain perceptual phenomena, as can their movement, and this process can be defined as a fifth kind of optical distortion within the eye. All of these processes are, however, similar in that they are preneural and explicable in terms of specific physical mechanisms within the eye. They are, in short, all intraocular Level 0 processes and are among the topics to be discussed in the remainder of this section.

It should be noted in preview, however, that the visual system has other processing mechanisms at higher levels of processing that can compensate for some portion of the aberrant intraocular optical effects. Contour intensification at Level 2 partially compensates for blur, and color-constancy effects at Level 4 partially compensate for the absorptive properties of the ocular media. Be that as it may be, it is necessary to understand this nature of the Level 0 intraocular aberrations to comprehend fully the range of transformations of which the eye is capable.

1. Ocular Geometrical Aberrations

Image distortions due to the shape and nonisotropic refractive indices of real lenses are referred to as optical or refractive aberrations. Optical aberrations are present in all less than ideal optical devices (which for all practical purposes means all lenses) including the optically imperfect human eye. Indeed, after one learns just how poor the eye actually is as an optical instrument compared to the fine grain of the retinal receptors, it is something of a surprise that we see as well as we do. One has only to compare the multiple-lens system found in a good 35 mm camera with the much simpler duplex lens system of the human eye to appreciate how amazing it is that we "see" with any degree of clarity at all. As many as a dozen separate pieces of glass are often used to correct for the slight optical irregularities in a complex camera lens in order to reproduce a sharp image on a flat film surface in the camera. In our eye there are only two focusing lenses—the cornea and the crystalline lens. Though the two simple optical lenses must account for all of the dioptic power of the eye, they are fraught, as we later see with substantial optical aberrations.

To appreciate fully an aberrant optical system, however, we must first understand what is meant by an optically perfect system. The classic definition of a perfect optical lens that exhibits no aberrations was suggested by the great nineteenth-century physicist, James Clerk Maxwell. He asserted that:

1. A perfect lens is so designed that every ray of light emerging from a point on an object converges at a point on the image.
2. A perfect lens produces a plane image of a plane object.
3. A perfect lens produces an image that is geometrically similar to the object even when there is magnification or demagnification.

Obviously, the lens system of the eye does not, in general, meet these three criteria and, therefore, is, to a greater or less extent, aberrant.

More specifically, it is now believed that there are just five kinds of geometrical optical aberrations exhibited by less-than-perfect lenses. These five geometrical aberrations collectively or individually lead to violations of the three criteria of a perfect lens suggested by Clerk Maxwell (in addition to chromatic aberration, a topic that is discussed separately in the next section). The currently accepted mathematical theory of geometrical aberrations of lenses is attributed to Phillip Ludwig von Seidel (1821–1896). His mathematical theory of geometrical aberrations consisted of a set of five equations, each of which had to be balanced for perfect optical quality. Each of von Seidel's five equations was equivalent to a particular kind of geometrical aberration. In establishing his equations as mathematically independent of each other, von Seidel was also essentially hypothesizing that the various kinds of aberrations were also independent of each other.

The von Seidel theory has important practical applications because it is still used as a means for calculating how an optimum (maximally aberration-free) lens can be constructed in advance of its actually being ground. All one has to do is to compute the appropriate parameters of the formula for each of the five lens aberrations and to shape a lens in accord with these parameters.

Specifically, von Seidel considered the five basic kinds of aberrations to be:

1. Spherical aberration.
2. Coma.
3. Astigmatism.
4. Field curvature.
5. Distortion

Spherical aberration is illustrated in Fig. 5-25. The key evidence for the presence of spherical aberrations is that the light rays passing through the lens along different axial pathways converge at different points as shown. Spherical aberrations may result in an almost random image blur for different portions of the stimulus object or for objects at different distances from the lens, or they may be systematic if it is bad enough (like the proverbial bottom of a soft drink bottle). Another way of interpreting spherical aberration is to note that a point source located at the focal point of a spherically aberrant lens will produce a system of nonparallel light rays after they emerge from the lens as shown in Fig. 5-26. Spherical aberrations can only be corrected by grinding the lens to a proper shape. Because there will always be some limits on the mechanical ability to grind lenses, no lens can ever be perfectly free of spherical aberration.

Coma is a similar geometric aberration of lenses. In the case of coma, however, the blurred images are produced by objects that lie off the central axis of the lens. Coma typically produces a pear-shaped image as shown in Fig. 5-27.

Astigmatism has already been briefly introduced in Chapter 3. To reiterate briefly, it is a lens aberration such that the focal distance depends upon the orientation of the image. When a lens brings an image to a focus at different focal distances depending upon its orientation, the lens is said to be astigmatic. Figure 5-28 shows the effect of this kind of aberration.

Any lens that is corrected so that these three aberrations (spherical, comatic, and astigmatic) have been overcome will satisfy the first of the three Clerk Maxwell criteria; the image of any point in the object space will be another point

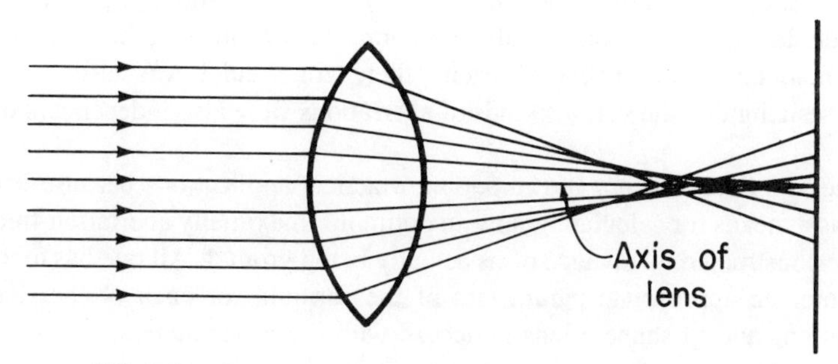

FIG. 5.25. Ray paths of a lens displaying spherical aberration.

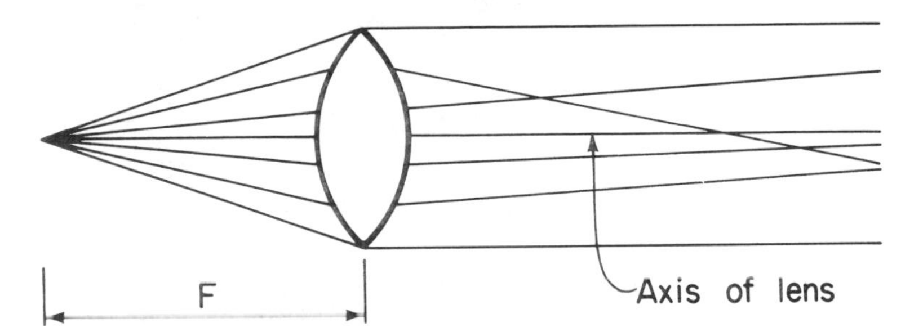

FIG. 5.26. An alternative means of displaying the ray paths of a lens displaying spherical aberration.

in the image space. The correction of these three aberrations by proper lens grinding, however, can often result in the introduction of other kinds of geometric aberrations. Specifically, the correction of astigmatic aberration often results in the introduction of the fourth aberration—curvature of the field as shown in Fig. 5-29. *Field curvature* constitutes a violation of Clerk Maxwell's second criteria (i.e., a curved image field will transform a plane in the object space to a curved surface in the image space). Such an aberration can be a severe nuisance in a camera using flat film. However in the eye it is not so serious. Because the retina itself is curved, optimum imaging must depend upon some degree of field curvature so that the image surface matches the retinal surface. Obviously, the match is never perfect. Although field curvature may contribute, in part, to the reduced acuity and increased blur of the peripheral visual field, much of this kind of aberration in the eye is ignored or compensated for by higher-level processes or is lost in the confusion caused by the increasing neural convergence as one moves away from the fovea.

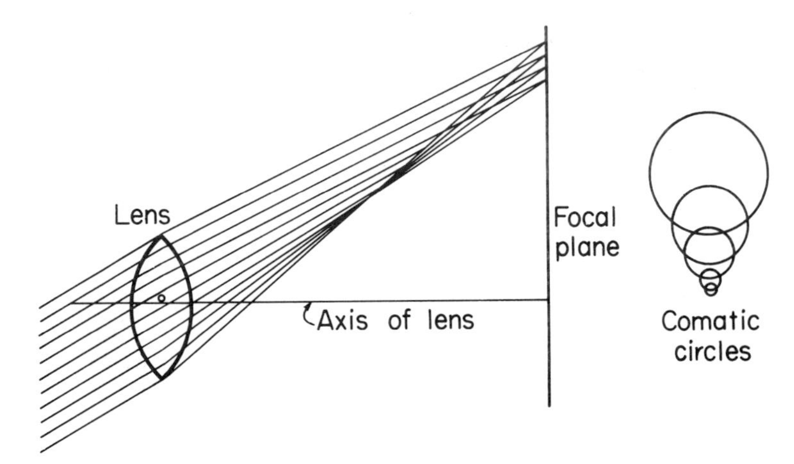

FIG. 5.27. Ray paths of a lens displaying comatic aberration.

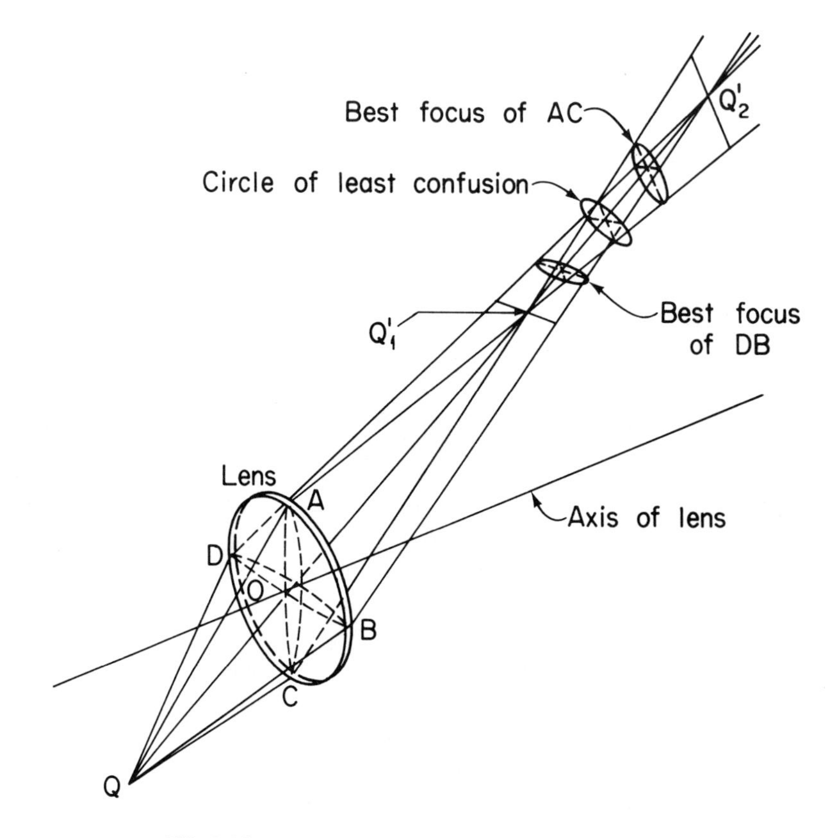

FIG. 5.28. Ray paths of a lens displaying astigmatism.

The fifth form of geometric aberration in lenses is called *distortion*. Distortion does not involve the sharpness of focus of the image, as do the first four kinds of aberration, but rather measures the degree to which the overall image is deformed. For example, Fig. 5-30 shows both pincushion and pillow distortion of a square produced by two lenses that had been inadequately designed in opposite directions. These topologically deformed images may, in fact, be composed of very sharply focused straight lines.

The perceptual system, however, is remarkably capable of compensating for image distortions—which must inevitably occur in the human eye because of its simple lenses and curved retinae. Because the response to artificial distortions by prisms seem to be highly plastic (a few days of adjustment to the distorted scene is all that is needed for the observer to become almost totally unaware of any such distortion), it is highly unlikely that we are affected to any significant degree by the ubiquitous, but slight, distortion introduced by the optics of our eyes. Our continued need, however, for lenses and spectacles to overcome blur-causing aberrations is quite evident. We do not adapt adequately to these kinds of aberra-

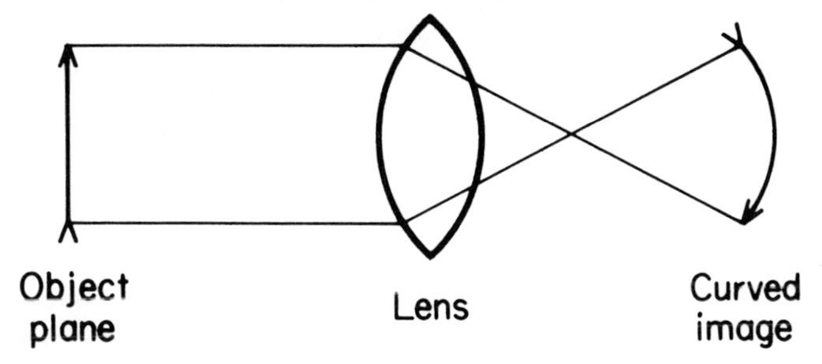

FIG. 5.29. The optical properties of a lens displaying field curvature.

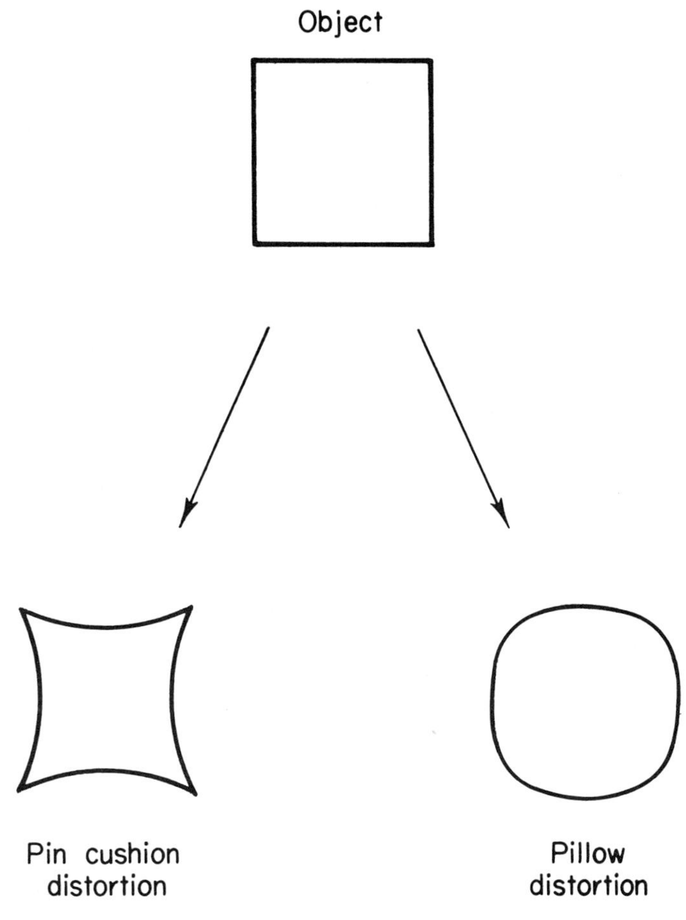

FIG. 5.30. The result of a lens displaying pillow or pincushion distortion.

tions in which high-frequency information is lost, not just transformed into another image from which it can be recovered. Thus though great efforts are made to correct blur due to spherical, comatic, astigmatic, and field curvature aberrations, little attention is given in human visual therapy to correcting distortion.

2. Ocular Chromatic Aberration

A lens may be as perfect as mechanically possible, have all five geometrical optical aberrations discussed in the previous section totally compensated, and yet still display another kind of optical anomaly—chromatic aberration. I have already introduced the concept of chromatic dispersion in my discussion of the rainbow. The reason for this dependence of the focal length of a lens on the wavelength of the incident light can be understood best by considering the index of refraction as a function of wavelength for several different kinds of glass, as shown in Fig. 5-31. The fact that none of these curves is flat over the visual spectrum means that the different wavelengths will be refracted to a greater or lesser extent even by the same portion of an otherwise geometrically perfect lens. Chromatic aberration, therefore, differs from the five types of geometrical aberration in terms of its fundamental source. It is dependent on the materials from which the ocular media are made rather than on their geometry. The very same

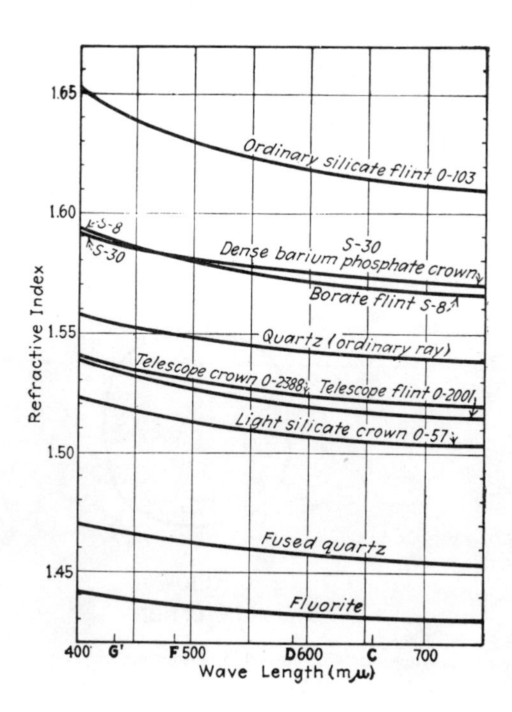

FIG. 5.31. The refractive index of various glasses as a function of the wavelength of the incident light. (From Hardy and Perrin, © 1932, with the permission of McGraw-Hill, Inc.)

color effects observed in a water droplet or a prism due to the different indices of refraction that are exhibited when various wavelengths of light pass through those materials are also observed when light passes through the media of the human eye. Chromatic aberrations are thus anomalous optical processes in which different wavelengths of light are brought to focus at different distances from the lens. This process is illustrated in Fig. 5-32.

The eye's chromatic aberration can lead to some peculiar but little known perceptual phenomena. Colored objects may be differentially magnified by the differing indices of refraction exhibited by the lens, and colored fringes may be created around a point source of light. Perhaps most amusing and dramatic, however, is the fact that chromatic aberrations can lead to differential depth effects as the images of different colored objects are diverted to fall on different corresponding points in the two eyes. The most amusing of these *chromatostereoscopic* effects is the oft-told and probably apocryphal story of the little old lady who thought that a miracle had occurred—all the red letters were standing out above the pages of her Bible! The miracle was, of course, the result of chromatic aberration, a phenomenon that most scientists would consider to be more of a nuisance than a miracle.

Chromatostereoscopic phenomena go under other names. Helmholtz (1856) referred to this same effect as the "fluttering hearts phenomenon." Red stimuli on a blue background appear to float in front of the background. However romantic, the effect is due to exactly the same transformation—chromatic aberration—as the somewhat more theological version just described. Research on chromatostereopsis has been reviewed by Oyama and Yamamura (1960), who have also shown that the effect is independent of stimulus luminance but quite dependent on the purity of the chromatic stimuli. They also showed a decline in the separation (in depth) of different colors when color-blind observers were used.[11]

Chromatic aberrations in the eye may be measured in several ways. Psychophysical tests have traditionally been used (Bedford & Wyszecki, 1957). In recent years, however, increasing use has been made of objective measurement procedures using opthalmoscope-like devices (Bobier & Sivak, 1978; Charman & Jennings, 1976). In these objective procedures, direct measurements are made of the light reflected back from the retina as a function of the stimulus wavelength. Bobier and Sivak, for example, found that there could be as large as 0.8 diopter difference in refractive power of the eye for red and green lights, and my colleague, Daniel Green of the University of Michigan, suggests that the difference may be as great as 2.8 diopters for red and blue lights under certain

[11]I should also note that Oyama and Yamamura (1960), at least at the time their paper was published, were among the few who did not believe that the sterochromatic phenomenon was due to chromatic aberration. They attributed it to a putative variation in "color sensation," basing this conclusion on the decline of the effect in color-blind observers.

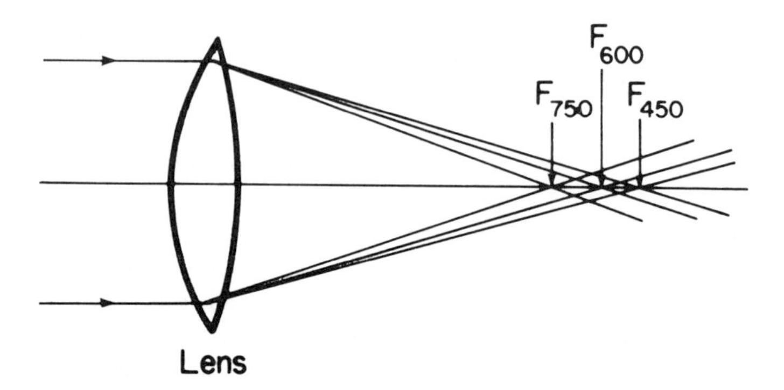

FIG. 5.32. Ray paths of a lens displaying chromatic aberration.

conditions. Obviously, chromatic aberration is not a negligible process even if it is evidenced only in obscure instances such as those just described.

3. The Effects of Pupil Size

The diameter of the pupil of the human eye is controlled by a pupillomotor reflex that depends in part on the level of the incident light, the level of mental activity of the subject, and other psychological factors. Some factors influencing pupil size are stimulus-related, and some are controlled by higher-order cognitive interpretive processes. Alpern and Campbell (1962), for example, have studied the influence of stimulus luminance on pupil size; they observed that both the rods and the cones contribute signals that lead to the control of pupil diameter by demonstrating that the peak of the spectral sensitivity of the pupillary reflex occurs at about 535 mm—a value that is intermediate between the scotopic and photopic sensitivity curves. The relation between stimulus intensity and pupillary diameters is shown in Fig. 5-33.

On the other hand, it has been shown that the pupillary diameter is also affected by mental arithmetic tasks (Kahnemann & Beatty, 1966) and general intelligence (Ahern & Beatty, 1979). Hess (1965) has demonstrated that the diameter of an observer's pupils is also affected by such intangible factors as the attractiveness of a member of the opposite sex or, even more surprisingly, simply by the diameter of the pupils of the person who is being viewed. Hakerem and Sutton (1966) have shown that the level of vigilance demanded of a subject also affects the pupillary diameter in a way that is totally independent of whether or not a visual stimulus is present. Painful stimuli will also evoke pupillary responses (Bender, 1933). Thus it is clear that the diameter of the pupil actually is an indicator of a complex response to many exogenous and endogenous factors at the several different processing levels of the taxonomic theory that I present in this book.

Over the last 20 years, Lawrence Stark of the University of California and his colleagues have presented a compelling case that the pupil can be modeled as a

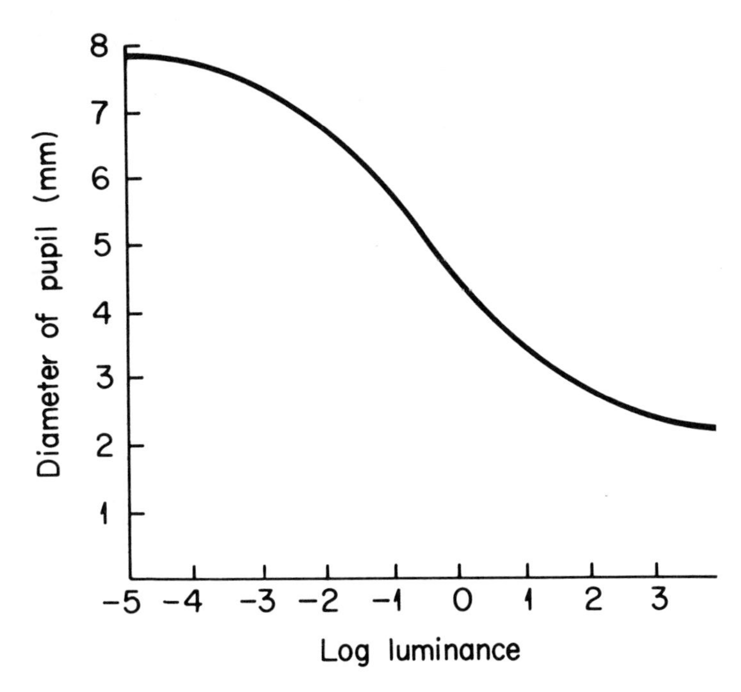

FIG. 5.33. Variation of the pupil diameter with light intensity. (This figure is a rough approximation, as great individual differences are always present.)

nonlinear dynamic servomechanism. (Stark, 1964, 1968; Stark, Campbell, & Atwood, 1958; Terdimen, Smith, & Stark, 1969; Usui & Stark, 1978). Thus, though the influences on pupil size are manifold, the sum total is a smoothly operating system. We now appreciate some of the complexity of this system even if we do not fully understand all of the involved neural pathways.

Regardless of the origin of the forces and the neuromotor mechanisms that regulate the diameter of the pupil, it is obvious that the pupil is an important link in the optical chain within the eye and that its diameter can significantly contribute to changes in the quality of the retinal image. The size of the pupil is particularly important in accentuating any intrinsic refractive errors of the various components of the eye. It is for this reason that an artificial pupil the size of the most tightly constricted natural pupil or a maxwellian optical system in which all light rays pass through the center of the pupil are desirable adjuncts in any experiment in which measurements are made of visual acuity as well as in those in which it is necessary to control retinal illuminance.

For any eye that is not perfectly refracted, the size of the blur circle due to optical aberrations[12] produced by a theoretically perfect point source of light will

---

[12]Of course, there will also be diffraction-induced blur, growing as the aberration-induced blur diminishes with reduced pupil size.

depend on the pupil size. Optical scientists have derived the following relation for the effect of the pupil size on the blur circle size:

$$\text{Blur circle diameter} = \frac{\text{pupil diameter} \times \text{diopters of refractive error}}{\text{total dioptric power of eye}} \quad (5\text{-}4)$$

Thus if the eye is perfectly corrected (i.e., the refractive error = 0 diopters), there will be no blur, other than that due to diffraction, no matter what size the pupil is. On the other hand, if there is any refractive error, then the size of the pupil will be a major factor in determining the size of the blur circle.

The nature of this equation also suggests that even a badly refracted eye can produce relatively sharp vision if the pupil is small. It is for this reason that highly myopic or hypermetropic viewers can obtain much clearer vision by looking through a pinhole. It is for this reason also that as the light dims at the end of the day and pupillary reflex expands the pupil diameter, visual acuity typically diminishes. This effect is known as night myopia. However, low luminance as such is not a necessary cause in this situation. If, for example, the pupil is dilated with drugs or if the contrast of a sinusoidal stimulus is reduced (as done by Green & Campbell, 1965), the same sort of reduction in visual capability occurs. Low luminance is not, in other words, the immediate antecedent of night myopia. Factors that increase blur or contrast are the immediate causes, and "night" myopia can occur even in relatively bright lights.

Pupil size also affects the range of depths over which clear vision can be obtained. Images are not in focus at all distances from the eye when it is accommodated for clear focus at any one depth. In general, the wider the pupil, the smaller the depth of focus. Specifically, this relationship is described by the following equation:

$$\text{Depth of focus} = \frac{\text{acceptable blur circle diameter} \times \text{focal distance}}{\text{pupil diameter}} \quad (5\text{-}5)$$

4. The Point Spread Function and the Modulation Transfer Function

All the geometrical optical aberrations discussed so far in section C result in the degradation of an image (of point, line, or object) projected on the retina, by spreading the region onto which the incident light falls. The particular form of this degradation may be measured in several ways. The two most often used metrics of less than perfect retinal imaging are the *point spread function*[13] and the

[13]In the discussion that follows I use both the terms *point spread function* and *line spread function*. For our purposes these two terms may be considered to be identical. The cross section of the line spread is a good approximation to a point spread. Formally, the line spread function is simply the integral of the point spread function in the direction of the line. Practically, one obtains a point spread function if one's stimulus is a point, and a line spread function if one's stimulus is a line.

modulation transfer function. The point spread function is a measure of the spread of the image of a point source of light. The modulation transfer function is the measured reduction in *contrast* of a spatial sine-wave stimulus pattern; that is, the decrease in the relative intensity of illumination of the peak and trough of waves of the projected spatial sinusoid on the retina due to the aberrant spread in the light.

Before I discuss the details of these two means of measuring the effect of optical aberration on image quality, it is important to make two preliminary points. The first is that the point spread function and the modulation transfer function can both be objectively measured in a way that does not require any psychophysical judgment on the part of the subject. The devices used to measure the objective optical properties of the images on the retina can be an opthalmoscope and a photometer and do not necessarily involve any psychophysical procedure. Indeed, it is not even necessary that the subject in such an experiment be alive! One early study (DeMott, 1959) of the point spread function was actually carried out on the ennucleated eye of deceased cattle.

A different kind of point spread function and modulation transfer function can, however be measured psychophysically. It is possible to ask subjects to rate or discriminate the degree of blur of the image by specifying tasks for them to perform that require acuity judgments of patterns of small dots. It is also possible to present subjects with sinusoidal light patterns and to determine the degree of contrast that must be present for the grating to be perceived as a grating for different spatial frequencies. In either case the entire perceptual system is being used as a measuring instrument. This procedure, however, does not determine the degree of retinal image degradation as does the ophthalmic photometer used in the objective procedure. The psychophysical procedures measure the overall effect of the entire visual system. And indeed the two curves are very different; the objective test produces a monotonic function while the subjective one peaks at a central value (see Fig. 5-37).

The important principle here is that the objective and psychophysical procedures do not measure the same thing! The objectively measured point spread function and modulation transfer function are exclusively measures of the Level 0 transformations that have been imposed upon the image by the optics of the eye. They say nothing about the neural or psychological processes that may be involved in establishing the related perceptual phenomenon; they are simply excellent descriptions of the properties of the proximal stimulus. The psychophysical measurements, on the other hand, measure these optical effects in combination with the effects of other levels of processing. These higher levels of processing can further degrade the ability of the eye in tasks that involve visual acuity and the detection of spatial sinusoidal patterns. Surprisingly, however, they can also reduce the impact of quality reduction by compensating contour intensification processes. In a later chapter I discuss the modulation transfer function and related spatial interaction effects as measured psychophysically.

Any differences between those data and the findings described here must be interpreted as the additional effects of other higher levels of psychoneural processing.

The second preliminary point to be kept in mind is that the point spread function and the modulation transfer function are totally equivalent in terms of the information that they represent. The modulation transfer function can be directly obtained from the point or line spread function by performing a Fourier transform upon it. Thus, neither method will produce any ''better'' description of image degradation than the other. One of the methods of measuring image degradation may be more convenient than the other in a particular instance, but neither is inherently superior to the other.

Because the point spread function is somewhat more intuitively direct, let us consider it first. The image of a point source, as noted previously, will not be perfectly imaged on the retina as a point if the eye exhibits any optical aberrations; that is, the image will be blurred (spread out) on the retina if any of the von Seidel lens equations do not balance or if the retina is not exactly at the focal distance of the ocular duplex focusing system. The task faced, when one attempts to measure the point spread function, is then how to evaluate the image produced on the retina by a theoretically perfect point light source. Note that I have used the word *theoretically* here. In fact, one need not have a perfect point source to carry out this experiment. An equivalent to a *mathematically* or theoretically perfect point source can be approximated by a less than real physical point source placed at a distance such that it subtends a visual angle of less than the one-half minute of visual angle, which is the average cross-sectional diameter of a foveal cone. For all practical purposes, even if the optics of the eye were perfect, no smaller point source could produce an image that would have any greater physiological significance. It now seems certain that a given number of quanta crammed into even as small an area as .0001 of a minute of visual angle would produce exactly the same neural effect as the same number of quanta distributed over a full half-minute of visual angle. A theoretical or mathematical point, therefore, is established by any stimulus that subtends a visual angle less than the width of a photoreceptor.

The first objective measurements of the spread function in human eyes were made only recently by Flamant (1954). She used a graphical means of reconstructing the reflected image on the retina obtained with an opthalmoscope. Her measurements led to the discovery that the spread function, although not negligible in the human eye, was not as bad as might have been expected, given the previously assumed sloppy optics of the cornea and lens. This good report card for the optics of the eye has since been replicated a number of times (Campbell & Gubisch, 1966; Krauskopf, 1962; Westheimer, 1963; Westheimer & Campbell, 1962, among others). In each case the eye was shown to have impressive optical properties and to display a spread function that was quite modest considering the assumed lack of homogeneity of the optical media of the eye.

The actual shape of the blurred image produced by a real eye will depend on the dioptic details and the angular subtence of any object greater than one-half minute of visual angle. For a optimumly refracted (emmetropic) eye and a close approximation to a theoretical point source, the retinal image will be distributed over approximately 2–3 min of visual angle by residual optical aberrations. For a somewhat larger stimulus (for example, a 1.6-min-wide line), the optical image will be spread over approximately 6 min of visual angle. In both cases, the width of the point spread function will depend on the size of the pupil in the manner described in the previous section.

To measure the spread function, Krauskopf (1962), for example, set up an elaborate opthalmoscope that projected a stimulus line (1.6 min of visual angle in width) onto the retina. He then photometrically measured the reflected image. Because the reflected image consisted of light rays that had passed through the optical system of the eyes twice, the actual retinal light distribution had to be reconstructed by taking the inverse Fourier transform of the product of the individual Fourier-analyzed components of the original stimulus and the square root of the calculated sine-wave responses for each frequency.[14] This technique is based on several assumptions. For example, the success of such a calculation depends upon the validity of the assumption that the optical pathway is symmetrical and reversible (i.e., that the effects of the aberrations will be much the same for the light entering the eye as for the light leaving the eye). Using this assumption, Krauskopf computed what the distribution of the light must have been on the retina from the measurements that were made of the light emerging from the eye. These reconstructed spread functions (which are cross sections of the light distribution from a line rather than exactly of a point in this particular study) are shown in Fig. 5-34. The several curves in this figure are parametric with the diameter of the pupil. The 1.6-min-wide physical stimulus has been spread by the optical properties of the eye into a wider blur region that varies from about six min of visual angle for a 3 mm pupil to about 12 min for an 8-mm pupil.

Of course, the decrease in the point spread function with decreasing pupil size shown in Fig. 5-34 is only part of the story. At the same time that the optical aberration effects are decreasing the effects of diffraction are increasing and the minimum size of the point or line spread function actually is at a minimum at about 2.4 mm where the two curves cross over. Not surprisingly, it is at about this diameter also that visual acuity is greatest (S. Shlaer, 1937).

A powerful property of the calculated spread function, as Krauskopf points out, is that it makes it possible to compute the retinal image produced by any stimulus. To do so, one must carry out the mathematical transform known as *convolution,* which is represented by the following equation:

---

[14]The reader should consult Krauskopf (1962) for details of how this procedure was actually carried out.

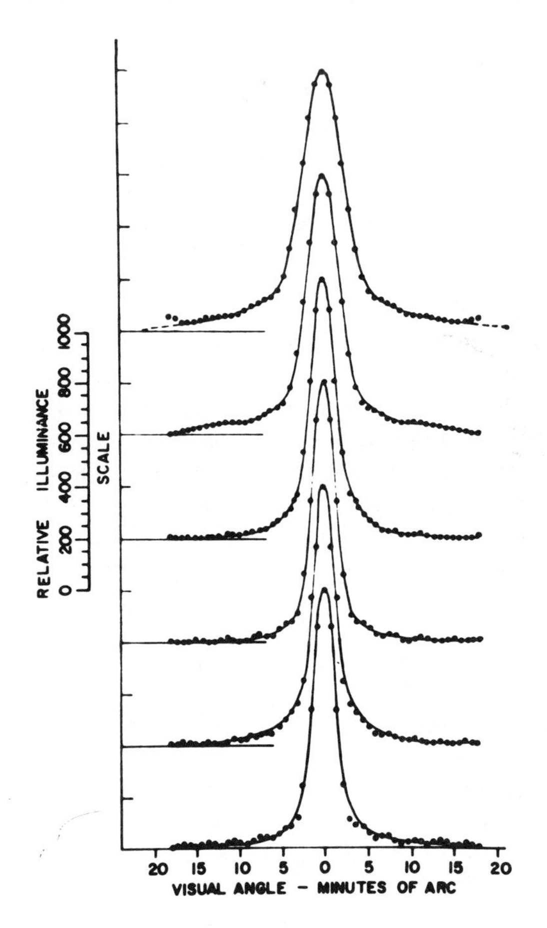

FIG. 5.34. Effect of pupil size on the retinal line spread function. The set of parametric figures presented here depicts the results for (from bottom to top) pupil sizes of 3, 4, 5, 6, 7, and 8 mm. (From Krauskopf, © 1962, with the permission of the American Institute of Physics.

$$I(x,y) = \int_{-\infty}^{+x} \int_{-\infty}^{+y} PSF(x - x', y - y') \times O(x',y')\, dx'\, dy' \qquad (5\text{-}6)$$

where $I(x, y)$ is the luminance distribution on the retina produced by $O(x, y)$, the luminance distribution of the stimulus object, $PSF(x, y)$ is an analytic expression for the point spread function[15] and x' and y' are shifted coordinates. Though this sounds complicated, the convolution can be thought of as nothing more difficult than a point-by-point multiplication of the point spread function and an inverted version of the stimulus. Having carried out such a calculation, one

[15]For those interested, $PSF(x, y)$ for the normal human eye has been approximated by Flamant (1954) and by Westheimer and Campbell (1962) as being represented by the expression e^{-kd}. For the cat the point spread function was found by Bonds (1974) to be of the form $1/(d/k)^{5/2}$, and by Robson and Enroth-Cugell (1978) as $1/1 + (d/k)^{3/2}$, where d is the distance from the center of the image and k is a constant in all cases (and e is the base of the natural logarithm).

approaches much closer to an exact specification of the proximal retinal stimulus against which to anchor the perceptual process than is possible knowing only the physical properties of the stimulus.

As Flamant had originally discovered, it also turned out in Krauskopf's experiment that the optics of the eye were rather good. The latter's measurements suggested that the spread of the image due to optical aberrations was probably less than the spread due to neural convergence in many portions of the retina. Furthermore Bonds, Enroth-Cugell, and Pinto (1972), have neurophysiologically confirmed that the convergence of receptors onto the ganglion cells as measured by the size of their respective fields in most parts of the eye is much larger than the point spread function in the cat's eye.

A similar outcome has been obtained in a psychophysical experiment reported by Campbell and Green (1965b). Using an image projected on the retina with a laser, they determined that the optical properties of the eye were far better than suggested by the conventional ophthalmoscopic methods using noncoherent light. Obviously there are also retinal effects contributing to the reduction in image quality. These two contributions to the spread function—the optics of the eye and those of the retina—have also been teased apart by Gorrand (1979). He used a new method of measuring the modulation transfer function (to be discussed later) to separately measure the scattering in the retina and the aberration due to the optics of the eye. In this way he was able to attribute to each its proper role in image degradation.

The improved estimates of the quality of the optics of the eye does not mean that we now think they approach perfection. In recent years more direct means of measuring the point spread function have been developed that do not require the assumptions of the indirect mathematical transformation methods based on data obtained during a double transverse of the light nor the additional complexities of a psychophysical judgment. For example, Robson and Enroth-Cugell (1978) developed a technique for inserting a tiny optical fiber into the eye so that the light distributions could be measured directly at the retina. Although they did confirm that the light intensity produced by the aberrations of the ocular optics did diminish quite rapidly (most of the light was contained within a few minutes of arc as previous workers had found), they were also able to establish that some lesser amount of light could be measured as far out as 20 deg from the center of the image.

The alternative means of specifying the optical properties of the eye is to plot its Spatial Modulation Transfer Function (*SMTF*). The *SMTF* is a graph that relates the spatial frequencies (into which any spatial pattern can be analyzed by a two-dimensional Fourier analysis—see Weisstein, 1980 for a good introductory tutorial on this topic) to the relative ability of the optics of the eye to maintain the contrast between the peaks and the troughs of the consistuent spatial sine waves of differing frequency. The contrast or contrast ratio (CR) is conventionally defined as

$$CR = \frac{\text{peak height} - \text{trough height}}{\text{peak height} + \text{trough height}} \tag{5-7}$$

To make this concept clear, consider three different spatial sine waves that, for example, have spatial frequencies of 1, 10, and 20 cycles/degree of visual angle, respectively. The lowest frequency spatial sinusoid (1 cycle/degree) will pass through the optics of the eye with relatively little degradation. The peaks and troughs are so far apart that they are affected very little by the optical aberrations of the eye. However, the high-frequency (20 cycles/degree) spatial sine waves tend to lose their contrast as they pass through the eye. The dark troughs tend to have some light refracted, diffracted, and scattered into them (and thus to be less dark), and the light peaks tend to have some light refracted, diffracted, and scattered out of them (and thus to be less light) by the optical aberrations of the eye. Intermediate values will be affected to some intermediate degree. Thus, to a first approximation, the reduction in contrast depends directly on the spatial frequency of the stimulus; the higher the frequency, the greater the reduction in contrast. The *SMTF* is the function representing the specific relationship between the contrast ratio and the frequency of these spatial sine waves.

Ideally the *SMTF* would be measured by applying a family of spatial sine waves to the eye and measuring the contrast for each presented spatial frequency at the retina itself. In actuality one usually has to reason backwards in exactly the same way as Flamant and Krauskopf did in their pioneering studies of the point spread function because it is difficult to place measuring instruments on the retina itself (despite the highly unusual accomplishment of Robson and Enroth-Cugell, 1978). Thus the usual way to determine the objective *SMTF* from the details of the known stimulus pattern and the measurements of the doubly transited reflected image requires virtually the same kind of mathematical manipulations just described for the point spread function. Figure 5-35, based upon research by

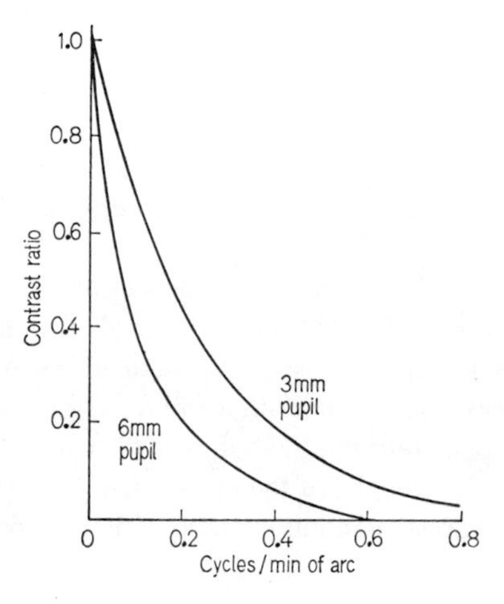

FIG. 5.35. The effect on contrast of the spatial frequency of the stimulus pattern. This is the objective spatial modulation transfer function. (From Westheimer, © 1972, with the permission of Springer-Verlag, Inc.)

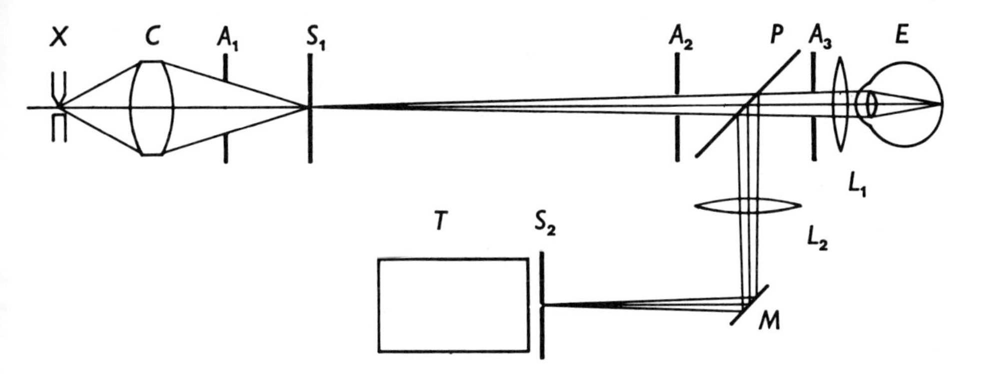

FIG. 5.36. The optical equipment used to measure the objective spatial modulation transfer function. X, Xenon arc lamp; C, collecting lens; A_1, aperture; S_1, source slit; A_2, aperture; P, beam-splitting pellicle; L_1, lens in outgoing beam; M, front-surface mirror on rotating mount; S_1, analyzing slit; T, photomultiplier. (Figure and caption codes from Campbell and Gubisch, © 1966, with the permission of *The Journal of Physiology*.)

Campbell and Gubisch (1966) and Westheimer (1963), shows the objective *SMTF* produced with both a 3-mm and a 6-mm pupil. The kind of research opthalmoscope used in this kind of experiment is shown in Fig. 5-36.

The degree to which the optics of the eye blurs the optical image of an external object will be reflected in the retinal image degradation measured with these objective techniques. Retinal blur will also be reflected in the limits on visual acuity and contrast sensitivity obtained in purely psychophysical experiments. But it should not be forgotten that there are other factors—the size of the receptor; the density of the receptor matrix; the neural interactions in the various networks, including such high level processes described by the words *criterion* and *subjective*—that also will limit the observer's ability to utilize the pattern of the retinal information. Indeed, as we later see and as shown in Fig. 5-37, these higher-level processes not only change the magnitude but also the shape of the function. The retinally measured *SMTF* is a monotonically declining function, whereas the psychophysically measured *SMTF* has a peak at an intermediate spatial frequency. Nevertheless, the optical aberrations do establish a maximum limit that even an ideal nervous system cannot exceed. No information-processing system will be able to perform better than the input signal allows, and one that does as well as that maximum must be considered as an ideal observer.

The *SMTF* of the various components of the eye can be determined independently. We should like to know what portion of the blur can be attributed to the optical properties of the lens, cornea, and ocular media. We should also like to know what part of the blur can be attributed to scattering in the retina, and finally, what part can be attributed to the neural processing that occurs subsequent to transduction. The procedure for determining each of these contribu-

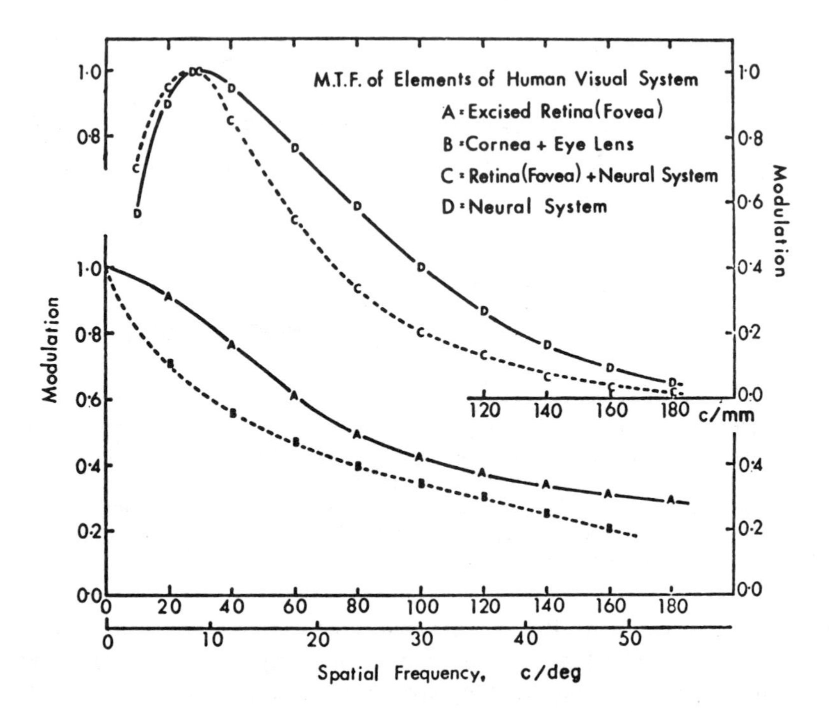

FIG. 5.37. The objective and subjective modulation transfer functions (MTF) of the human visual system. (A) The MTF of a retina with the image projected directly upon it (i.e., all other components have been removed). (B) The MTF of a retina as modulated by the eye's optic. (C) The psychophysical (subjective) MTF. (D) C divided by B to give an estimate of the MTF produced by the neural portions of the visual system. (From Ohzu and Enoch, © 1972, with the permission of Pergamon Press, Inc.)

tions is different. For example, to determine the blur due to retinal scattering, Ohzu and Enoch (1972) took a freshly ennucleated human eye and removed the retina. They then measured the blur of the light image emerging from the back of the retina when a sharply focused image was projected on the front of the retina. This procedure gives the *SMTF* of an isolated retina. In other experiments, Campbell and Green (1965b) have determined both the objective *SMTF* (as measured with the double transit ophthalmoscopic procedure previously described), and thc psychophysical SMTF (as determined by a contrast threshold experimental procedure). Ohzu and Enoch have proposed that by normalizing the psychophysically obtained SMTF by dividing it by the objective whole eye *SMTF*, an estimate can be obtained of the contribution of the neural system alone. All four of these curves are shown in Fig. 5-37. Clearly, the nervous system and not the optics of the eye, is totally responsible for the nonmonotonic aspect of the psychophysically obtained function.

5. Binocular Optical Effects

In an earlier part of this chapter I discuss some of the perceptual consequences of the geometrical fact that the two eyes are located at different locations on a horizontal rather than a vertical line. In this section, I pursue this discussion of the binocular processes further by considering how differences in the optical properties of the two eyes may affect visual perception.

I have already alluded to two very obvious facts of vision. First, structurally the normal human observer has two eyes; and, second, his visual perception is functionally singular. These two facts compellingly state that our perception must result from the construction of a single perceptual interpretation out of the signals from the two eyes by some central integrative mechanism. However this intermixture of binocular signals occurs, it is a subtle and complex process that goes far beyond simplistic concepts of "suppression" of the information from one eye or a simple additive "fusion" of the information from both eyes. Rather, the two-dimensional information coming from each eye must be intermingled and interpreted such that a new, previously nonexistent three-dimensional percept can be created. Differences between the two monocular images, therefore, may be very important in defining the generated percept. In fact, as we see in Chapter 11, they are critical to stereopsis, and any distortion of the retinal image is likely to have a profound effect. It is the purpose of this section to consider specifically those optical conditions that can lead to image size differences between the two eyes—a condition originally referred to as *aniseikonia* by Lancaster (1938).

I have already noted the simple fact that the two eyes do not have the same viewpoint and that most real-life scenes are filled with three-dimensional objects. This means that the simple geometry of the binocular viewing mode will directly lead to slightly disparate (different) images on the two retinae. Such binocular disparities are the basis of stereoscopic depth perception, the mental reconstruction of the real three-dimensional scene. In the normal viewer, there are broad regions of single three-dimensional vision in those portions of visual space in which there is appropriate convergence of the lines of sight. This single vision appears to be that of a cyclopean eye (Julesz, 1971) as I have already noted.

There are, however, some abnormal situations in which the lines of sight of the eyes may not be adequately under control, and proper convergence and registration on corresponding points may not occur. In this situation, diplopia (double vision) is likely to occur. In some advanced cases, one of the diplopic images may be powerfully suppressed to overcome this distracting effect of double vision leading to a functional monocular blindness referred to as strabismic amblyopia.

The differing viewpoints of even the normal eyes can also lead to another optical condition that can also have significant perceptual consequences. The fact that the two eyes view the world from two different viewpoints means that, with the exception of those two-dimensional objects lying exactly equidistant from the two eyes, all objects will produce different-sized images on the two retina. Different-sized retinal images can also be produced by an entirely unrelated process—unequal magnifying powers in the two eyes—even when the object is equidistant from the two eyes. Optical magnification imbalances may be due to transient factors such as momentary accommodation differences or to semipermanent magnification differences existing between the two eyes. A further source of what may be functionally equivalent to different image retinal sizes could also arise from differences in the anatomical packing of the photoreceptors themselves. If the receptor density is greater in one eye than in the other, the effect of even perfectly equal-sized images might not be the same because the mapping onto the retinal mosaic could activate the equivalent of a larger projection area at higher levels of neural encoding.

Whatever the source of the asymmetrical magnification on the two retinae, whether it be the geometry of the viewing situation, unequal magnification by the optics of the two eyes, or receptor density differences, the result is aniseikonia. The outstanding student of such image size differences was Kenneth N. Ogle who presented what is still generally accepted to be the master discussion of the topic in his magnum opus, *Researches in Binocular Vision* (1950).

Aniseikonia can lead to major visual disturbances if not corrected. If the retinal images are very different in size, fusion is not possible; and one eye or the other may fall into disuse. Aniseikonia is especially severe when one of the lenses is removed to treat cataracts; in that case the difference in image size may be 10% or more. The main effect of more moderate aniseikonia, however, is on the perception of depth. Although stereoscopic depth is a topic dealt with more fully in Chapter 11, aniseikonic interference with stereopsis is properly considered as a Level 0 process and can, therefore, be considered at this point.

Understanding the perceptual effects of aniseikonia is made difficult by the fact that only the horizontal components of the magnification error should produce a stereoscopic distortion. Yet, surprisingly, it turns out that both the vertical and horizontal components of aniseikonia are perceptually effective. If the magnification differences of an aniseikonic eye are limited to the horizontal plane (as would occur if the retinal image were distorted by a cylindrical lens with the long axis oriented vertically), then substantial distortions of the stereoscopic space would be expected. Figure 5-38 illustrates a cylindrical lens and its effects. An example of a stereoscopic distortion induced by the predominantly horizontal aniseikonia produced by such a lens is shown in Fig. 5-39. This type of spatial distortion results directly from the horizontal disparities produced as a result of unequal image size and can be predicted on a purely geometrical basis from the magnitude of the aniseikonia.

On the other hand, if the magnification is equal in all orientations (as would be produced by a spherically magnifying lens), then a very surprising result occurs.

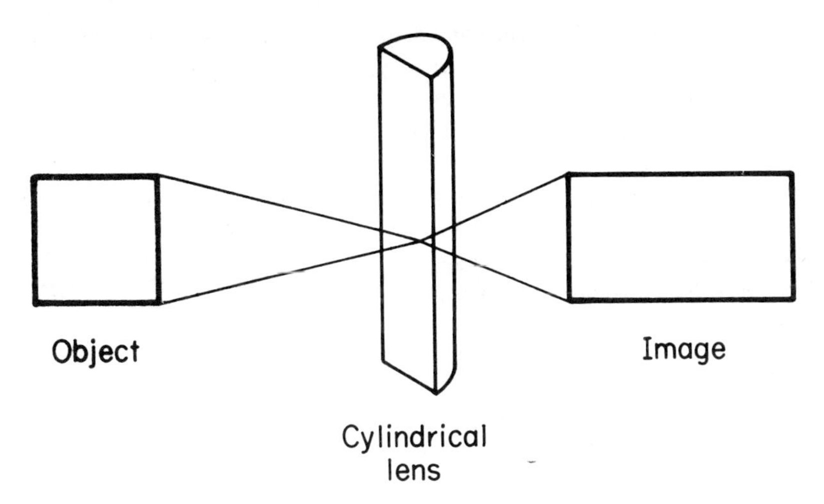

FIG. 5.38. The effect on an image of a square object when the light rays are passed through a cylindrical lens.

Very little distortion of the stereoscopic scene is produced. What seems to be happening is that the visual system has developed a powerful compensatory process that can adapt to wide ranges of intraocular differences in spherical magnification. This is a highly useful and adaptive process, because the differences in magnification between the two eyes would always be expected to be very much greater than the very small differences in retinal position associated with proper registration on corresponding points. This adaptive process, and the insensitivity to what may be substantial differences in spherical magnification, is

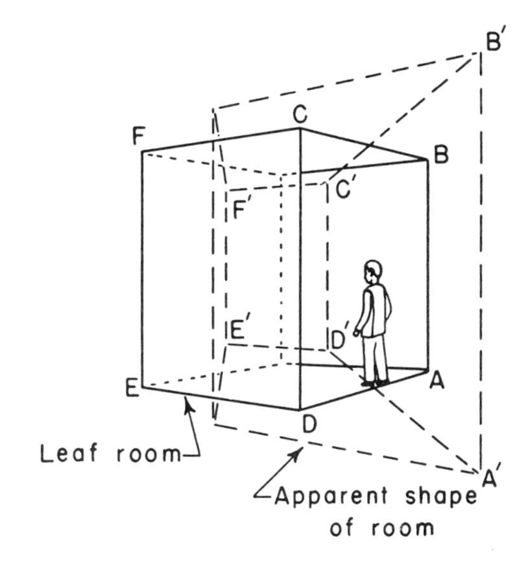

FIG. 5.39. The effect on the image of a room with ill defined contours (a "leaf room") when it is viewed with a cylindrical lens in front of the right eye, only magnifying the image in the horizontal direction. (From Ogle, © 1950, with the permission of W. B. Saunders Co.)

a strong argument that the corresponding points may not have any "hard-wired" or fixed relationship at all, but rather may represent only flexible, and perhaps even transient, functional relationships among the retinal loci.

Thus even though a purely vertical magnification difference between the two eyes should not produce any distortion in a stereoscopic space from a purely theoretical point of view (binocular stereopsis should be insensitive to vertical disparities), it does turn out that there is, in fact, a strong effect of vertical magnification asymmetries. Ogle described the strong distortion effects produced by vertical aniseikonia as the "induced effect." He characterized the induced effect of a vertical magnifying cylindrical lens placed before one eye as a "simulation" of the effect of an equivalent horizontal magnification placed *before the other eye*. Thus, spherically magnifying lenses produce surprisingly small effects even though separate horizontal and vertical magnifications produce substantial perceptual effects.

It is interesting to note that the processes underlying the counterbalanced effects of equal horizontal and vertical (i.e., spherical) magnifications before one eye must be assigned to different levels of the taxonomic schema that I have proposed as an organizing schema for this book. The distortion produced by horizontal aniseikonia is totally explicable in terms of the geometry and optics of the situation, and thus properly belongs in this chapter dealing with Level 0 processes. Ogle, however, could find no equivalent geometrical or optical explanation of the induced effect produced by unequal magnification along a vertical axis, and had, therefore, invoked a "psychic" or "psychological" explanation that I believe is quite comparable to the interpretive, symbolic processes I have incorporated under the Level 4 rubric. Specifically Ogle (1950) says:

> Since the evidence as presented in the previous chapter generally denies the existence of any physiologic compensatory change of vertical magnification, we are forced to fall back upon a hypothesis of a psychical change which results in a reorientation of the frame of reference for stereoscopic localization, partially in the sense of a rotation of the entire binocular perceptual space about the fixation point.
>
> This phenomenon, which basically must arise from the vertical disparities of images in the two eyes, which point of fixation from the two eyes or unequal magnification by the ocular optics, provides a basis for an explanation for the induced effect. When one increases the magnification of the image of the right eye in the vertical meridian by a suitable lens, an apparent distortion of space occurs in the sense that objects at the right of the fixation point appear nearer, those on the left farther—a clockwise rotation of the field. Thus the stereoscopic reference surface must have been rotated counterclockwise. This is the direction in which the reference surface must also be rotated when the eyes are asymmetrically converged to the right, if egocentric stereoscopic localization is to be maintained. This rotation of the subjective binocular visual field is not a pure rotation alone, but is the principal aspect consistent with an increase in the magnification of the image of the left eye in the horizontal meridian [p. 223].

Thus Ogle invokes what in the present context would be called an integrative, symbolic, interpretive Level 4 process. He believes that this process has evolved to overcome what necessarily must be a rather substantial difference in the magnification of the images on the two retinae by even normal eyes. The response to the naturally occurring aniseikonia thus is, in a very true sense, nonveridical with the actual image distortion on the retina. This compensatory process—the induced effect—helps us to overcome the disparities produced by spherical magnification differences between the two eyes. Yet without the horizontal component of magnification the induced effect of a purely vertical magnification is still so compelling that it can actually overcompensate and produce a perceptual distortion for which no compensation was actually required. Unfortunately, the nature of the induced effect remains obscure; and though the effect probably exists as described, it does little to help us understand what are the underlying mechanisms.

6. The Spherical Shape of the Eye

The retina is not a plane. The fact that it is distributed over the interior surface of the globe of the eye means that the retina must necessarily deviate from the idealized planar projection screen required by Clerk Maxwell's criterion of a perfect nonaberrant lens. No matter how good the optics of the eye, therefore, there is no image plane on which to project an ideal object plane. There are, however, both advantages and disadvantages to the nearly spherical retinal shape and, in general, the curved retina has rather inconspicuous influences on our perceptions of the external world.

One of the main advantages of a strongly curved retina on which to project the ocular image is that the field of view of the eye can be very much wider than it would be without such a construction. Figure 5-40, for example, shows a perimetric field measurement for a subject with normal vision. Such perimetric charts have become standardized tests of visual function. They are usually plotted in the following way: A small spot of light is used to explore the visual field, and the subject reports when it disappears from view. Obviously a flat retina would have to be unrealistically wide to have the same field of view.

Perimetric measurements of this kind often indicate that the field of view of the human eye is actually somewhat greater than it would be expected to be and in some instances the field of view can actually reach around more than 90 deg from the line of sight. This result is initially surprising but totally explicable in terms of the relevant optics. Pirenne reminds us of the reasons that such an apparent violation of line-of-sight optics is possible. In this elegant book, *Optics, Painting, and Photography* (1970), Pirenne reproduces a drawing (see Fig. 5-41) originally presented by Hartridge (1919) showing the refractive effects of the cornea and the lens when hit at a near-grazing angle by a ray of light from an object that is objectively behind the eye. Our ability to see an object so far "out

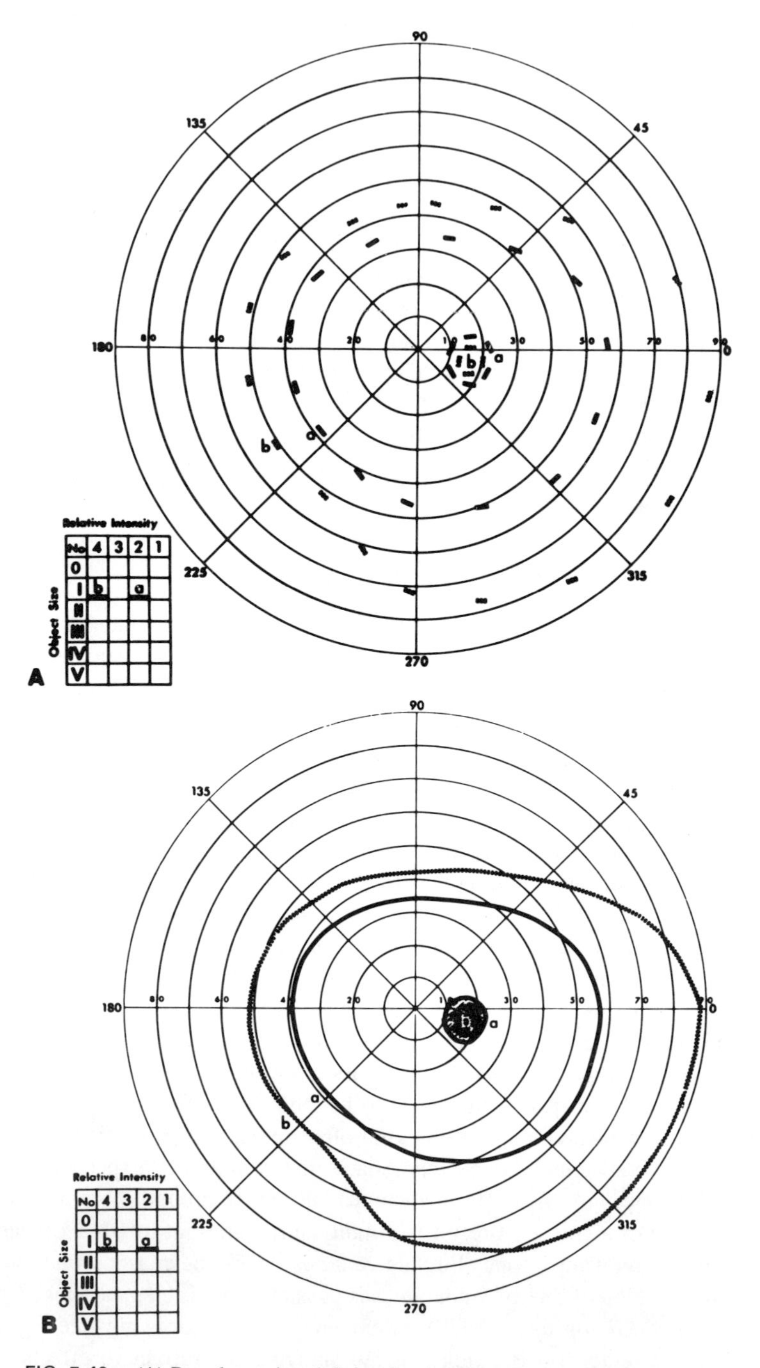

FIG. 5.40. (A) Raw data points defining the visual field for two different intensities of an exploring test spot. (B) Completed perimetric charts of the visual field for the two different intensities. (From Tate and Lynn, © 1977, with the permission of Grune and Stratton, Inc.)

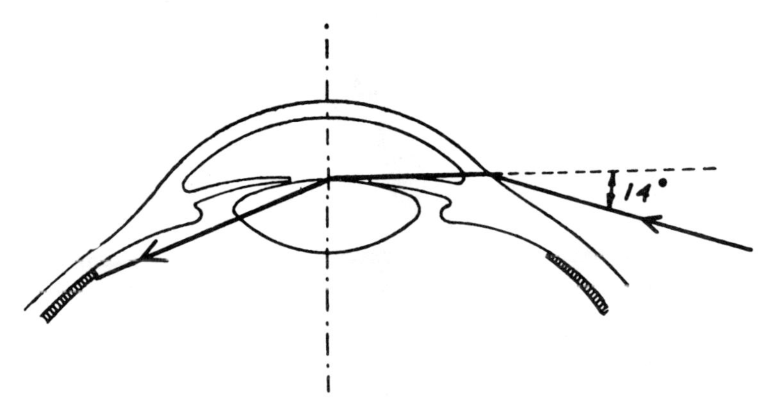

FIG. 5.41. Diagram showing how the visual field can in some extraordinary circumstances actually be larger than 180° as a result of the strong refractive effects on light hitting the cornea from a point greater than 90° from the line of sight. (From Pirenne, © 1970, after Hartridge, with the permission of Cambridge University Press.)

of the corner of the eye'' is totally explained in terms of the refractive bending of rays of light by the cornea. The dioptric power of the cornea is sufficiently great that light coming from an angle greater than 90 deg to the line of sight can be bent back to pass into the eye and impinge upon the edge of the retina.

Somewhat surprisingly, it turns out that it is relatively difficult to identify any perceptual penalty paid by the observer for the curvature of the retina. There is no question that there is considerable optical distortion of the *optical image* produced on peripheral portions of the retina, but like the optical inversion of the image by the optics of the eyes, this distortion, in general, is of little consequence with respect to how the world is perceived. Compensatory neural coding and cognitive interpretive processes apparently overcome these distortions in the reconstruction of the perceptual experience. It is only in the most unusual circumstances, as Pirenne points out, that the perceptual effects of the curved retina can be detected. The association between the cognitive ''image'' and the retinal ''image,'' therefore, is not likely to be a linear one but at best only a topological one.

One rather obscure demonstration of the effects of the spherical shape of the eye is shown in Fig. 5-42. This figure, also cited by Pirenne (1970) after an earlier demonstration by Helmholtz (1856), shows a distorted checkerboard. When the eye is placed at a position approximately 2 inches from the center of the figure, the checkerboard assumes a more linear and ordered appearance. The perceived correction of the pattern is largely due to the optical distortion of the portions of the retinal image that are farthest from the fovea.

In general, however, it is clear that the degree of perceptual distortion produced is nowhere near the degree of image distortion on the retina. The percep-

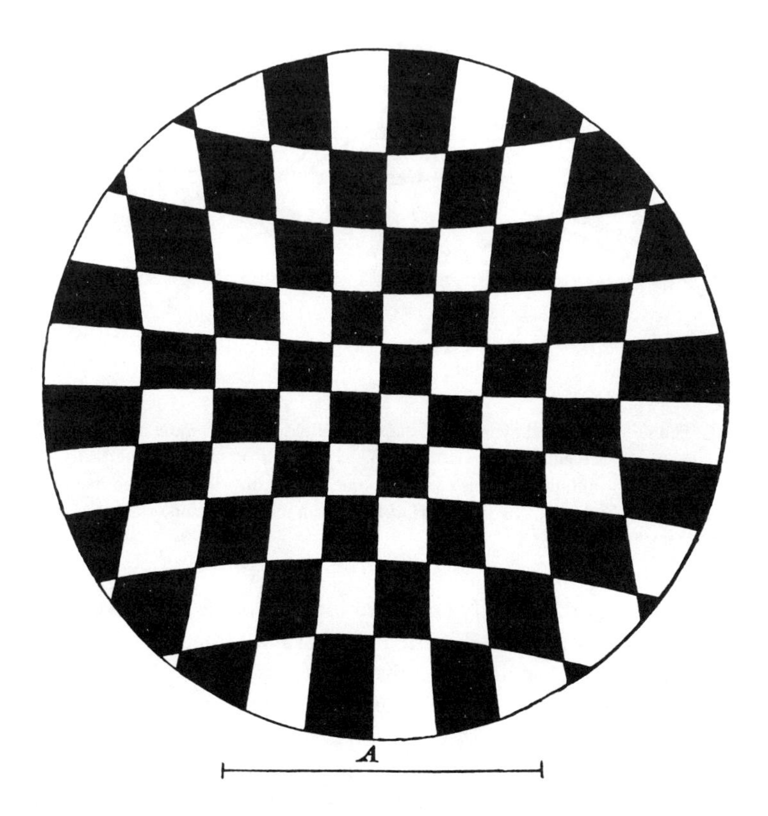

FIG. 5.42. A stimulus that appears to be a rectangular checkerboard as a result of the optical distortion in the eye. To observe this phenomenon this stimulus should be viewed at a distance equal to the length of line A with one eye. (From Pirenne, © 1970, with the permission of Cambridge University Press.)

tual nervous system is a highly encoded system and there are many other higher-level processes that can compensate for many kinds of peripheral distortions including those introduced by such factors as the spherical retina. A fundamental explanation of compensatory processes leading to the linear and upright perception of a topologically distorted and inverted image can be found in the language of sensory coding theory (the idea that a stimulus message may be represented by any dimension, no matter how distorted or scrambled, as long as decoding operations are available to unravel the representations), and in terms of a constructionistic perceptual psychology in principle, if not in detail. These compensatory processes are so effective that the perceptual effects of what can sometimes be very profound topological distortions in the retinal mapping of an object scene are often very difficult to detect.

7. The Stiles–Crawford Effect

Even though the perceptual system can compensate for many kinds of distortions, there are other optical effects within the eye—in fact within the receptor—that can lead to significant uncompensable perceptual phenomena. One example is the Stiles–Crawford effect (Stiles & Crawford, 1933), a substantial variation in absolute visual threshold as a function of the portion of the pupil through which the ray enters the eye. This effect is generally attributed to the angle of incidence of the light ray upon the outer segment of the photoreceptor rather than pupil entrance point per se, but the former follows directly from the latter.

The optical situation giving rise to this anomoly is shown in Fig. 5-43. The effect, to put it simply, is that the visual effectiveness of a stimulus is progressively less the greater the deviation from the axis of the photoreceptor outer segment with which that stimulus impinges. Typical results from one of Stiles and Crawford's early experiments are shown in Fig. 5-44. The effect was first reported as a unique characteristic of cones and was thought to be very weak in rods if it existed at all. However, there is now little question nowadays that it also does occur in rods: Daw and Enoch (1973), using a blue-cone monochromat, and Van Loo and Enoch (1975), as well as Webb (1972), and Flamant and Stiles (1948) have all irrefutably demonstrated its presence in rods. They also demonstrated that rods have a less constrained directional sensitivity than do cones. Figure 5-45 shows a comparison of the scotopic and photopic functions to illustrate this difference and to indicate why the lesser rod effect was missed in the early experiments.

The Stiles-Crawford effect is definitely not due to any additional absorption by the ocular media in the longer pathways traversed by these light rays entering the perimeter of the pupil compared to those entering through its center. Such additional absorption could, in any case, amount to only a few percentage points

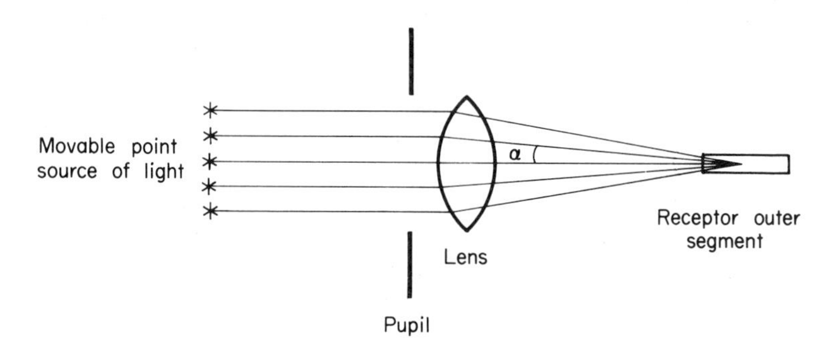

FIG. 5.43. Diagram depicting the variation in the angle of incidence of light on a receptor as a function of the point of entry into the pupil.

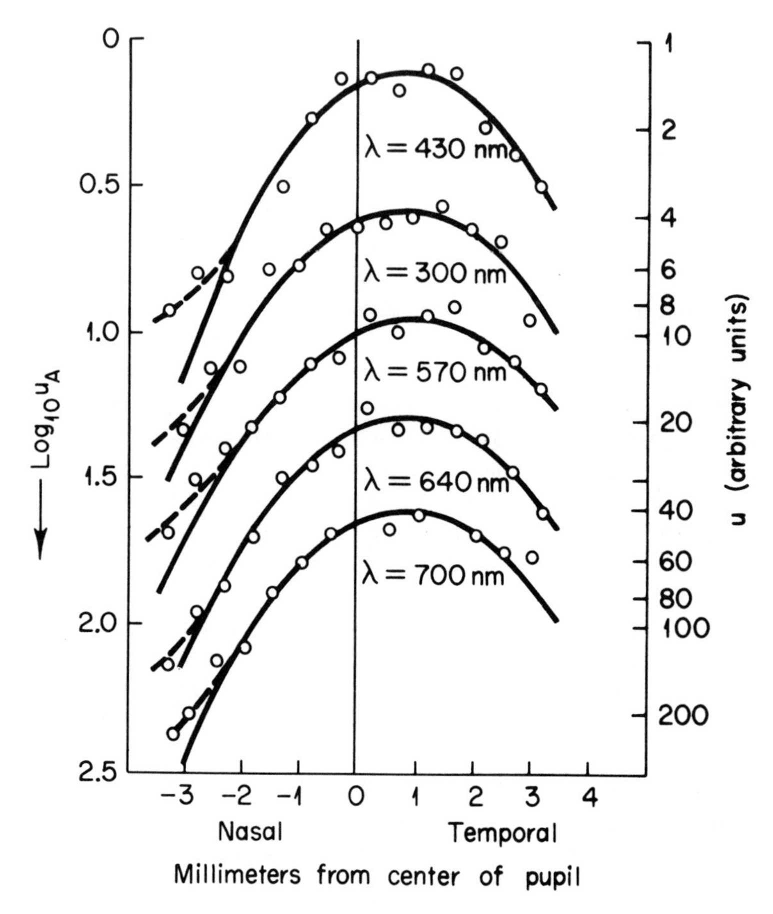

FIG. 5.44. The Stiles-Crawford effect shown as a function of wavelength in the dark adapted fovea. Nasal or temporal displacement of the stimulus from the center of the pupil degrades the detectability of the stimulus. (From Stiles, © 1939, with the permission of The Royal Society of London.)

in the available amount of incident light; the effect itself, on the other hand, may lead to a reduction in visual sensitivity of as great as 80% in some situations.

In fact the actual decrement in visual effectiveness that is measured in the classic Stiles–Crawford experiment may actually be much stronger than that indicated in Fig. 5-44. There is another intraocular counterbalancing process that at least partially compensates for the effect. The crystalline lens, belying its name, is not completely colorless even in a young normal eye. There is a considerable amount of pigment present in it; and that pigment has a decided yellow tint, indicating that it absorbs some portion of the shorter wavelength of light passing through it. Weale (1961), noting that the lens is an oblate object thicker at the center than at the edges, suggested that there should be a differential absorption by the pigmented materials of the lens such that more of a ray of light passing through the center of the pupil should be absorbed than of one passing through the periphery. This differential absorption should produce a decrement in visual performance at the center of the lens—an effect contrary to the Stiles–Crawford effect; and therefore, if this differential absorption existed, it would tend to diminish the measured strength of the associated phenomenon. Thus it is unlikely that the measured magnitude of the effect is, in fact, an underestimate of the actual influence of the angle of incidence on photoreceptor absorption in vision.

The Stiles–Crawford effect is also dependent on the wavelength of the incident light. The absorption of short-wavelength light is most greatly influenced by the angle of incidence and long and medium wavelengths are, respectively, less strongly affected. Van Loo and Enoch (1975) have also shown this to be the case for rods. Because such a differential effect of the wavelength of the incident light exists, it is not surprising that there are also chromatic phenomena associated with the effect. Indeed, in some of the early experiments on this phenomenon, Stiles (1937; 1939) reported that the color of a beam of light consisting of a

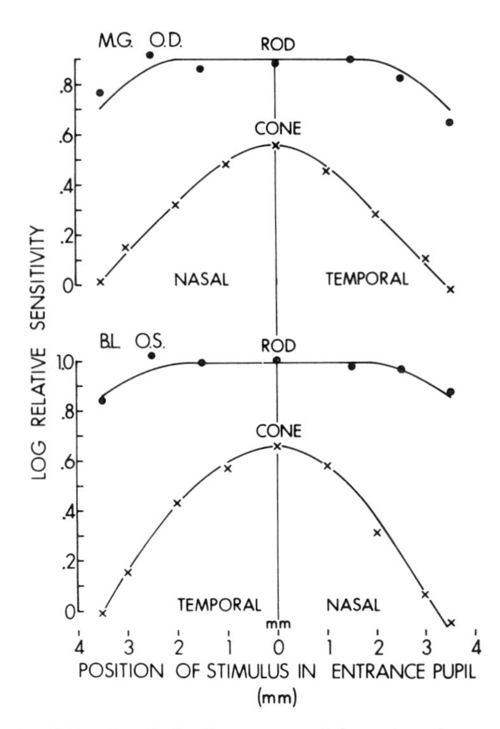

FIG. 5.45. The Stiles-Crawford effect measured for rods and cones for two different observers. (From Enoch, © 1976, with the permission of John Wiley & Sons, Inc.)

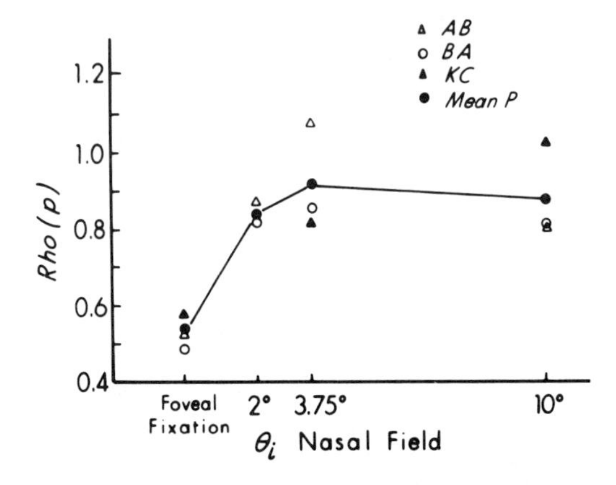

FIG. 5.46. An index (Rho) of the Stiles-Crawford effect plotted as a function of retinal location. (From Enoch and Hope, © 1973, with the permission of the Association for Research in Vision and Opthalmology.)

mixture of wavelengths varied as a function of the part of the pupil through which it entered. Vos (1960) has also summarized a large body of data that indicates that a monochromatic beam of light also changes hue depending upon the entrance point of the pupil. The explanation of Van Loo, Enoch, and Stiles' observations is obvious. If the proportions of the different wavelengths in the incident beam are altered by the wavelength-selective Stiles–Crawford effect, then the relative composition of the light absorbed by the retinal receptors will also vary. The explanation of the data summarized by Vos is less obvious but must have to do with a differential amount of Stiles–Crawford absorption shift by each of the three types of cones. As we see in Chapter 6, this is also a sufficient condition for a change in perceived chromaticity.

The Stiles–Crawford effect also varies in magnitude as a function of retinal position. Enoch and Hope (1973) have compared the effect at the fovea and at three locations, 2, 3.75, and 10 deg respectively, from the fovea. They found that the fovea was less directionally sensitive than these three extrafoveal regions but that there was little difference between directional sensitivity in the three extrafoveal regions. Figure 5-46 shows this result for the four retinal locations.

In other studies, Blank and Enoch, 1973; Blank, Provine & Enoch, 1975; Enoch, 1975) have shown that the peak of the Stiles–Crawford curve (i.e., the point on the pupil through which light must pass for maximal visual effectiveness) shifted substantially during accommodation. They attribute this to an actual stretch of the retina (up to 0.5 cm) when the ciliary muscle contracts, resulting in an actual physical reorientation at the receptors' optical axes.

The Stiles–Crawford effect is now thought to be best explained in terms of the optical properties of the outer segments of the photoreceptors. Enoch (Enoch, 1960; 1961; 1972; Enoch & Horowitz, 1974) has suggested that because the size of these microscopic receptor cells are so close to the dimensions of the wavelengths of the incident light, the outer segment may act very much like a waveguide, or an optical fiber to produce a directional sensitivity that depends on internal reflections. Properly shaped microwave antennas also display a comparable directional sensitivity to the angle of incidence of the appropriate (much longer), but analogous, wavelengths of electromagnetic energy to which they are sensitive.

Enoch and his co-workers have tested the plausibility of this model in two ways. In an earlier paper, Enoch (1960) reported how he built an enlarged model of a photoreceptor and bombarded it with appropriately elongated wavelengths of microwave radiation. A directional sensitivity comparable, although enormously scaled upward, to that observed in the psychophysical experiment was also observed in this model experiment. In another more recent study (Tobey & Enoch, 1973), light was passed backwards through an isolated rod from the retina of a rat. This experiment showed that the light emerged, presumably as a result of the internal reflection typical of waveguide action, in a narrow beam. Because the outer segment of a rat's rod could be expected to be optically identical in either direction, this supported the idea that the normal directionality was explained in terms of its waveguide properties.

Although from time to time other theories have been proposed to explain the Stiles–Crawford effect, most of the alternatives either fail to handle the data well or turn out to be equivalent to Enoch's model. The reader who is interested in a more complete and fairly up-to-date discussion of the alternative theories and a comprehensive set of references will find nothing better than Crawford's (1972) summary article in the multivolumed *Handbook of Sensory Physiology*.

Given the existence of the Stiles–Crawford effect, it is obvious that the orientation of the individual rods and cones is critical to maximization of the efficiency of the eye. For ideal visual performance, all of the photoreceptors, regard-

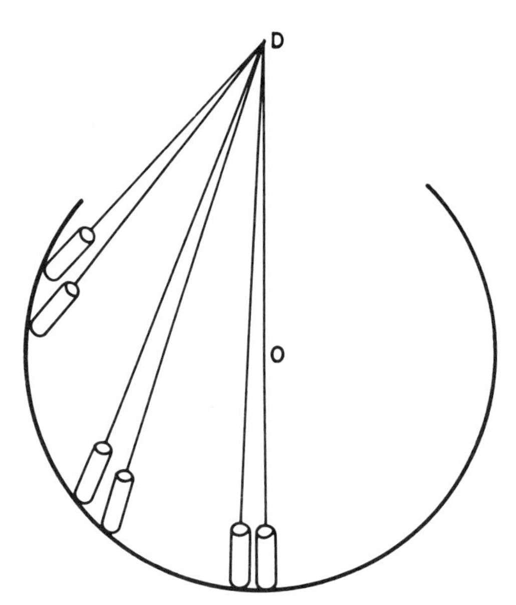

FIG. 5.47. Diagram showing the necessity for the photoreceptors to be oriented differentially on the retina for proper aiming at the center of the pupil (D) relative to the center of the eye (O) to produce maximum visual efficiency. (From Enoch and Hope, © 1972a, with the permission of C. V. Mosby Co.)

less of retinal locus, should be pointing at the center of the pupil. The receptors are not, in general, oriented perpendicularly to the retina. Figure 5-47 shows why they cannot be and all still point at the center of the pupil. Microscopic examination of the retina makes it clear that the retina has in fact advantageously evolved so that the receptors are all aligned with the pupillary center thus maximizing the eye's sensitivity to light. Figure 5-48 shows this for two portions of the retina.

The actual anatomic variation of receptor orientation in the eye was first demonstrated by Laties (1969). In recent years he has collaborated with Enoch and Hope in a series of important papers on the psychophysical and clinical implications of receptor orientation (Enoch & Hope, 1972a, 1972b; Enoch & Laties, 1971; Laties & Enoch, 1971). This work has been crisply summed up in an excellent review by Enoch (1976) that is probably the most appropriate resource for readers who are interested in pursuing the visual implications of receptor orientation further.

8. The Dynamics of Retinal Movement[16]

The eye, in general, is not stable in its orbit but is usually exhibiting some kind of movement. Therefore there is a constant movement of the position of an optical image on the retina. These eye movements, or *saccades,* may be either voluntary or involuntary. Large movements are usually elicited by elaborate central "voluntary" or reflexive orientation processes that seemingly have as their goal the centering of the retinal image on the fovea. Such foveation processes tend to bring the most relevant aspects of a visual scene into focus on the portion of the retina that is best suited for fine pattern discrimination and color perception. Small involuntary movements (physiological nystagmus) also occur. These microsaccades seem also to play an important functional role,[17] since totally stabilized images rapidly fade from view. However this phenomenon is best attributed to levels of processing higher than the optical Level 0 and I shall discuss it later.

Both the small and large movements of the eye do, however, also produce some optical effects that can properly be classified as Level 0 processes. The perceptual effect most often suggested to be closely related to eye movements is a process known as saccadic suppression. Briefly stated, the question posed by the term *saccadic suppression* is "does the visual system "see" as well when the eye is moving as when it is standing still?" The problem was first formulated at the turn of the century in terms of a controversy in which both sides accepted the

---

[16]Some of the material in this section is adapted from Uttal and Smith (1968).

[17]An interesting and novel contrary view can be found in Steinman, Haddad, Skavenski, and Wyman's (1973) discussion of the general role of such small saccades. They believe that these "miniature" eye movements are, in fact, artifacts, occurring only in the laboratory as a result of artificial conditions of attending.

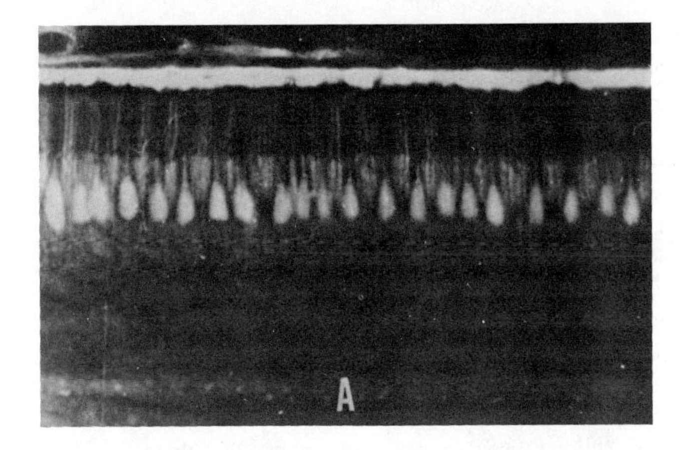

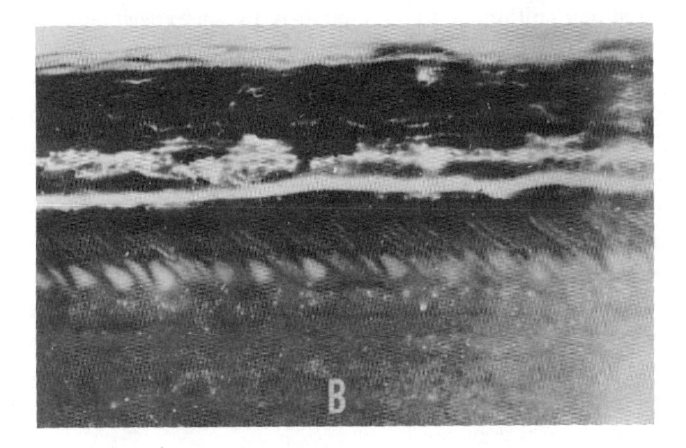

FIG. 5.48. Photomicrographs showing the actual difference in receptor-retina orientation in two different locations. (A) Receptors near the posterior pole of the eye. (B) Receptors near the periphery of the retina. (From Enoch, © 1976, with the permission of John Wiley & Sons, Inc.)

assumption that vision was indeed suppressed during eye movements. The controversy at that time concerned which of two possible mechanisms—retinal blurring or central inhibition—was responsible for the assumed phenomenon. Dodge (1900, 1905) championed the notion that the effects were in part caused by peripheral factors that blurred the image, but his antagonist Holt (1903) believed they were due to some more central inhibitory process.

An examination of more recent experiments carried out under a wide variety of experimental conditions by a number of investigators raises a number of issues that go beyond the initial assumptions and formulations of Dodge and Holt. Support for the phenomenon itself is not unequivocal. On one side, Latour

(1962) reported a complete suppression over a wide range of times both during and preceding the eye movement itself, and Ditchburn (1955) reported complete blanking of a cathode-ray trace during involuntary saccades. However, on the other side, Krauskopf, Graf, and Gaarder (1966) reported little suppression of visual perception during involuntary eye movements, as did Frances Volkmann (1962) who showed that the effect, though statistically significant, is very small and appears to be merely a slight increase (0.5 log units) in absolute thresholds. This value has been corroborated with a technique using electrically induced phosphenes by Riggs, Merton, and Morton (1974). A further complication is that Zuber and Stark (1966) and Zuber, Stark, and Lorber (1966) have reported that the suppression, which can be measured using either visual thresholds or the pupillary reflex as indicators, actually occurs mainly during the period preceding eye movement.

Uttal and Smith (1968) showed furthermore that there was a high level of visual pattern-recognition ability maintained in an experimental situation in which the eye movement itself was *required* to produce the horizontal scan of patterns plotted on the face of a cathode-ray tube. This experiment was particularly significant because it contains an absolute control that the correct identification could occur only during the eye movement. Figure 5-49 shows the stimulus display used in the Uttal and Smith experiment. The appropriately timed vertical line of dots was spread out into a two-dimensional alphabetic character by eye movements. The eye movements were electrooculographically detected to trigger the presentations of each vertical column in the same position, but at successive intervals. Without the eye movement nothing could be seen except a single vertical line of dots. This procedure thus guaranteed that any reported spatial pattern perception could occur only during the eye movement itself. Given the high level of character recognition that was observed, it is obvious that total suppression during eye movements does not occur.

This minireview of relevant experiments presents a picture of a great deal of empirical disagreement. However, upon careful inspection of the methodological details and experimental conditions, it becomes clear that a wide variety of different experiments have been subsumed under the general rubric of vision during eye movements. On the basis of such an inspection it seems safe to conclude that if the phenomenon occurs at all, it is very much a function of the intensity of the stimulus. A distinction, therefore, must be made between a movement-induced elevation of the absolute intensive threshold of the eye to a flash of light per se and a reduction in the ability of the observer to process patterned information that is above threshold.

Ethel Matin (1974), in a comprehensive review of the literature of saccadic eye suppression, suggests that actual causes of any suppression measured during eye movements are multiple. Specifically she refers either explicitly or implicitly in her review to the following factors that may be involved in saccadic suppression:

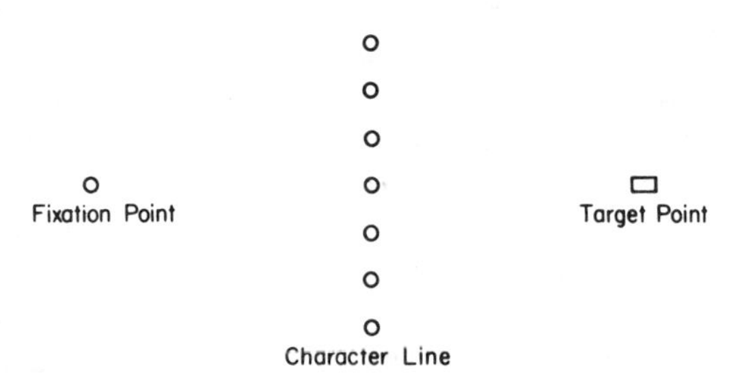

FIG. 5.49. The stimulus display used in the Uttal and Smith experiment. The observer voluntarily moves his view from the fixation point to the target point. The target letter was triggered at a variable delay following the initiation of the eye movement as determined electrooculographically. (From Uttal and Smith, 1968.)

1. Retinal smear of low-intensity lights.
2. Mechanical distortion of the retina during accelerations.
3. Metacontrast and other forms of backward masking.
4. Velocity sensitivities of X and Y cells in the visual pathways.
5. Contour intensification due to lateral inhibitory interactions.
6. Central inhibition resulting from information overload.
7. Central inhibition resulting from oculomotor feedback.
8. An increase in background noise.
9. Central inhibition due to discrepancies between perceived position and actual retinal position.

The first two of these possible causes of saccadic suppression are Level 0 processes, and it is the possible contributions of these two mechanisms, smear and retinal distortion, that I should like to consider in this section.

Retinal smearing (distribution of incident light over a number of photoreceptors) was first suggested as a possible source of saccadic suppression in one of the earliest papers describing the phenomenon (Dodge, 1900). Dodge's ideas with regard to this movement-induced spread of light lay essentially dormant for many years as other researchers concentrated on theories emphasizing more central aspects of saccadic suppression. In recent years, however, attention has been redirected towards the possible contribution of smear to the suppression of vision during eye movements. Mitrani and his colleagues (Mitrani, Mateef, & Yakimoff, 1970, 1971) and Uttal and Smith (1968) have also taken the theoretical position that champions the contention that a substantial portion of the suppression effect can be attributed to this Level 0 process—smear—even if some central suppression is also involved. Let us now consider one argument for smearing as a major contribution to the elevation of the threshold during eye movements.

First, let us make an estimate of the angular velocity of eye movement. The conditions of the Uttal and Smith experiment were such that the time of motion was about 125 msec to traverse a 25 deg path. At these values, the velocity of eye movement can be calculated to be 1 deg per 5 msec; or, because 1 mm of retinal length is approximately equal to 3 deg of visual angle; ⅓ mm of retinal length in 5 msec. This is equivalent to 6.6 micra in 100 μ sec. The typical diameter of the cross section of a rod or cone is about 1.5 micra, thus such a velocity suggests that exposure times as short as 10 or 20 μ sec could allow brief stimuli to be shifted across the boundaries of single rods and cones. Thus the amount of light falling on a given receptor at the edge of a visual pattern could be reduced on the average to about half the available light during this brief period of time, particularly in the fovea where spatial interactions are modest.

This simple physical analysis is admittedly incomplete. But it does suggest that for dim stimuli, the statistics of the available quanta may interact with the distribution of the minute receptors during an eye movement to lower the probability of a stimulus being detected. Because it seems unlikely that a total suppression ever occurs and that the effect on near-threshold stimuli actually represents only a fraction of a log unit of reduced visibility, this idea of image smearing, or better, quantal distribution, may account for a considerable portion of the observed phenomenon. This is not to deny that there may be some additional cognitive or central contributions, particularly at high luminance levels, but rather that in the case of discrete, pointlike, near-threshold stimuli, the effect is largely accounted for in terms of retinal dynamics and quantal distribution.

Richards (1969a) describes another possible Level 0 effect that could contribute to the suppression of vision during eye movements. In an especially interesting experiment, he demonstrated that the retina is actually physically sheared (bent) by the accelerative forces produced by an eye movement just as it was distorted by accommodation (Blank & Enoch, 1973; Blank, Provine and Enoch, 1975). Richards attributes the reduced sensitivity during eye movements to both the actual physical distortion of the retinal plexus and to the resulting induction of a higher than normal level of background activity induced by the mechanical shear. To prove that the physical distortion actually occurred, Richards, like Blank and Enoch, demonstrated that there was a shift in the peak of the Stiles–Crawford effect that corresponded to a shift in the actual physical position of the

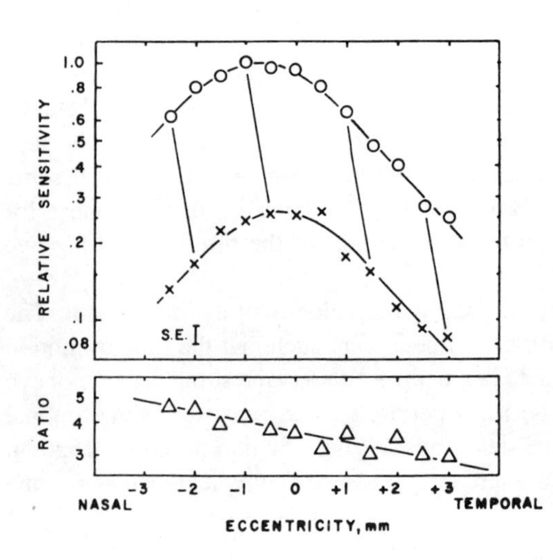

FIG. 5.50. The effect of eye movements on the Stiles-Crawford effect. The circles indicate the usual effect for a stable eye. The x's indicate the lessened magnitude of the effect measured 40 msec after the beginning of an eye movement. (From Richards, © 1969a, with the permission of the American Institute of Physics.)

photoreceptors. This effect is shown in Fig. 5-50. Though Richards does not explicitly make the point, it seems conceivable that some portion of the saccadic suppression effect could indeed also be in part attributed to the Level 0 Stiles–Crawford effect itself. As the retina is sheared and the receptors distorted, the optical axes of the photoreceptors might be misaligned with the optical axis of the eye. The net effect would be to tilt the outer segments of the rods or cones to an angle at which they would be less responsive to incoming light and thus to further reduce the ability of the eye to detect a dim stimulus when the eye is moving, just as when it is markedly accommodated.

These, then, are two Level 0 effects that may contribute to the phenomenon known as saccadic suppression. As indicated, however, these Level 0 effects are probably not capable of completely explaining the phenomenon, and other more central effects must also be invoked to explain it fully.

D. PERCEPTUALLY SIGNIFICANT PROPERTIES OF THE OCULAR MEDIA—ENTOPHTHALMIC PROCESSES[18]

In the previous section I consider some of the optical and mechanical properties of the eye that affect perception. My discussion so far has assumed that the eye is composed of more or less ideal optical media and that it displays only those refractive or geometrical aberrations that might be found in any more or less perfectly transparent glass lens. The media from which the optical elements of the eye are composed, however, are not ideal and perfectly transparent. They are, like all other biological tissues, imperfect to a substantial degree in youth and display an unfortunate tendency to become further degraded in their optical quality as the individual grows older (much to the dismay of those of us who are already beyond the prime years of our visual powers). In this section, therefore, I discuss those properties of the ocular media that tend to alter visual perception or to introduce perceptual phenomena that are not veridical with the stimulus scene as defined by independent estimates. The kinds of effects that I am considering in this section include: (1.) mechanical obstructions of the line of sight; (2.) scattering of light and media opacity; (3.) selective polarization; and (4.) selective spectral absorption by the media.

1. Mechanical Obstructions

The pathway traversed by light rays from the outer surface to the cornea to the receptor cells is not entirely clear and homogeneous. Several mechanical obstructions can partially block light and thus cast a perceivable shadow on the retina as

[18]Tyler (1978b) calls attention to the fact that the traditional use of the word *entopic* is incorrect in this context. That word correctly refers to the whole visual system and *entophthalmic* correctly refers to processes occurring only within the eye.

a result of their aberrant indices of refraction and abnormal transparency. The vitreous humor, for example, is not a perfectly uniform medium. It contains tiny threads and clumps of cellular debris that can be perceived under the appropriate conditions. These tiny shadows have traditionally been referred to as *muscae volitantes* (Southall, 1937). Most of these intravitreal objects are microscopic in actual size but the optics of the eye are such that it acts as a powerful magnifier for intraocular objects and thus can produce a relatively large image of even a very small object. For example, the magnification of intraocular objects can easily occur if an intravitreal object lies between the node of the lens and the retinal projection. Therefore, objects positioned at a point where the light rays are divergent will throw shadows that are much larger than the object itself as shown in Fig. 5-51A. It should not be forgotten in this context that the acuity of the eye is very fine, comparable to the width of a foveal cone (1.5 micra) and that an image of even this small size would theoretically be detectable. For similar reasons, debris on the surface of the cornea or imperfections in the cornea or lens can also be seen under certain conditions, as is shown in Fig. 5-51B.

Objects floating in the vitreous humor are usually perceived as dark and transient spots in the visual field because they act as impediments to the free passage of the light rays from an external illuminant. However under other conditions the debris in the media may appear as a bright object, particularly if the external light enters the eye at an oblique angle. This is the biological equivalent of a dark field microscope.

Moving bright spots can also occur. These phenomena usually result from an interruption in an otherwise continuous obstruction. One of the most interesting of these is seen when the eye is stimulated with a large diffuse stimulating field. Brindley (1960) suggests that, in this case, the perceived moving bright spots of light are actually the gaps between single files of red blood corpuscles in the very narrow capillaries of the retina.

It is also possible to see the shadows of the larger blood vessels in one's own eyes. If a small bright light (e.g., the beam from an opthalmoscope) is directed into the eye from its corner and the light moved about, a treelike shadow (of the retinal blood vessels) can be perceived. This is in fact not so surprising. These blood vessels are relatively large and are filled with densely pigmented red blood cells. Indeed, the most interesting question is why these blood vessels' shadows are not seen under ordinary conditions. The answer to this question lies at another level of processing and discussion, but briefly, it has been assumed that the retinal blood vessels are not perceived because they represent an ideal *stabilized retinal image*. (See p. 783 for a complete discussion of this topic.) Stabilized retinal images are well known to fade quickly from view. The reason that the blood vessels are seen in the highly unusual experimental situation I just described is that their shadows are no longer stabilized when a moving light is directed into the eye from a moving oblique light source. The shadows of the blood vessels under these unusual conditions move about on the retina, de-

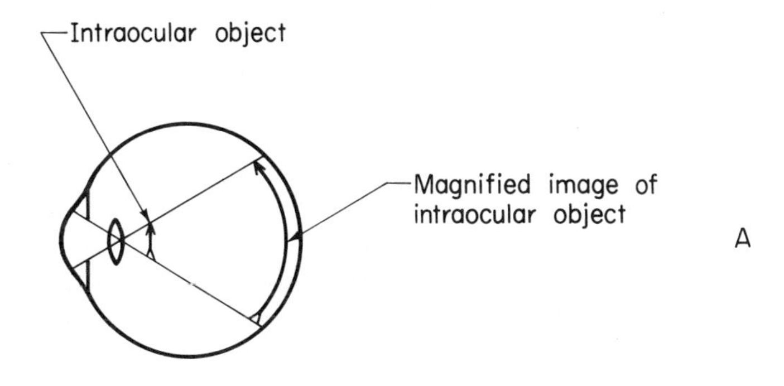

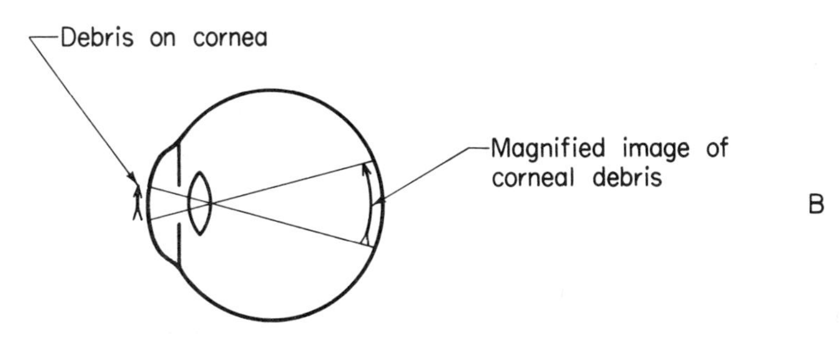

FIG. 5.51. Diagrams showing how small objects in the optical pathway of the eye can produce relatively large images on the retina. (A) The optics for an intraocular object. (B) The optics for debris on the cornea.

stabilizing the image, and thus continuously regenerate the appropriate perceptual experience.

2. Scattering of Light

Another source of visual artifacts occurs when the natural transparency of the various components of the optical pathway of the eye becomes degraded. Translucency can take the place of transparency as the lens thickens, becomes opaque, or accumulates pigment, or when minute particles capable of scattering light accumulate anywhere in the ocular media. The most obvious, as well as the most disastrous, defect of this kind occurs when the crystalline lens loses its transparency in whole or in parts. Such a region of opacity is referred to as a cataract and can totally blind an afflicted person to everything except overall changes in luminosity.

The exact cause of cataracts is not yet known. Even though it is generally accepted that cataracts result from some kind of metabolic disruption of the epithelial cells that make up the body of the lens and the subsequent production of an abnormal lamina, there is considerable controversy as to what leads to these errors of cellular reproduction. Treatment with X rays or cortisone can produce cataracts, and it has often been suggested that the reason that this disease is most common in older people is their lifelong exposure to ultraviolet radiation. However, some recent data contradicts this suggestion. (See my discussion of this topic later in this chapter.) What is definitely known is that when sufficiently large numbers of damaged epithelial cells are produced that are individually opaque to light, almost total blurring of the retinal image may result.

It is interesting to note, however, that cataracts, even when they involve the whole lens, need not prevent psychophysical testing of the acuity of what may be the perfectly normal retina underneath. An ordinary incandescent light source cannot be used to project an image on the retina for opthalmoscopic examination in the case of extensive cataract, but a laser opthalmoscope can do so. Daniel Green (1970) of the University of Michigan has developed just such a system. His device can be used to test the residual visual acuity of the retina even though the lens is totally opaque. The reason that a clear image can be projected on the retina by a laser is that the pattern of fringes produced by this highly coherent light source is dependent solely upon interference effects and not upon the actual optical clarity of the pathway. Thus even unfocused coherent light passing through an imperfectly refracting and transluscent optical pathway can produce sharp retinal images. It is for this same reason that those of us who suffer from myopia can also enjoy the pleasures of at least a sample of clear vision, a laser "speckle pattern," without our glasses or contact lenses. It is a surprisingly reinforcing and satisfying experience that is impossible to the uncorrected myope in ordinary noncoherent light.

This curiosity can be combined with the Badal optical principle[19] to produce an optometer (a device for measuring the accommodative state of the eye) with some highly useful properties (Hennessy & Leibowitz, 1972). This device is shown schematically in Fig. 5-52. The major advantage of such a system is that it allows the experimenter to measure the state of accommodation without interfering with that state.

Whereas a translucent lens produces the most dramatic disruption of visual clarity, almost all the other ocular media scatter some light due to anisotropies and irregularities in their optical properties. The cornea both reflects and scatters an appreciable amount of the light impinging upon it (Boynton & Clarke, 1964).

---

[19]The Badal principle can be defined as follows: If the eye is placed so that the focal point of a positive lens coincides with the anterior focal point of the eye, then the centers of the blur circles from two points in the image of an object located anywhere behind the positive lens will always subtend the same visual angle. It should also be noted that the Badal principle also can be used in conjunction with a polarizing system in much the same way as with the laser system to give direct measurements of the accommodative state of the eye (Simonelli, 1979).

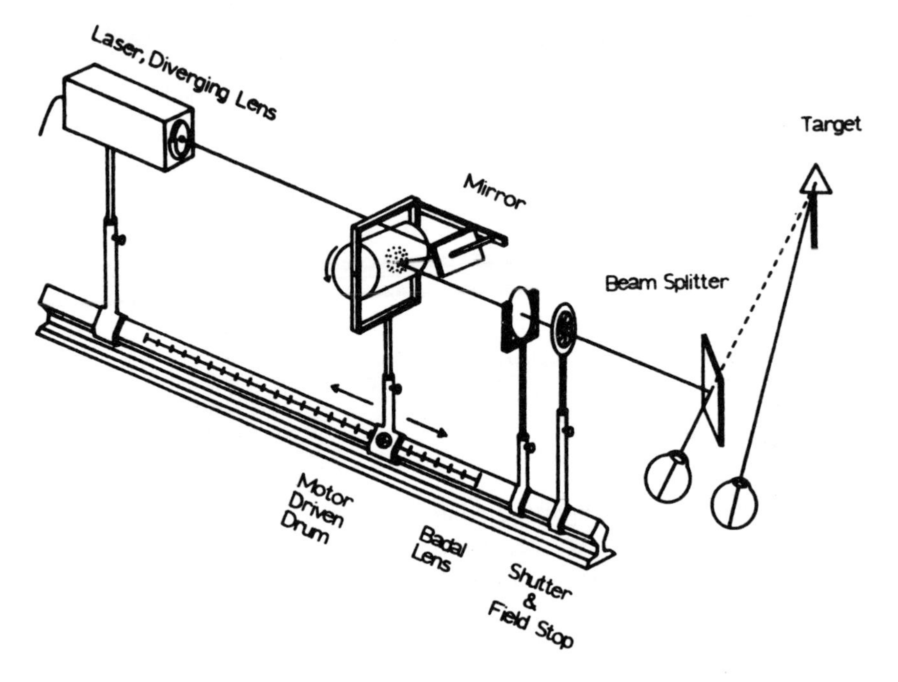

FIG. 5.52. The Badal optometer. (From Hennessy and Leibowitz, © 1972, with the permission of The Psychonomics Journals, Inc.)

The other ocular media also scatter substantial portions of incident light (Wolf & Gardiner, 1965). Because the retina is inverted and incident light must pass entirely through it before impinging upon the photosensitive outer segments of the rods and cones some additional scatter can also be expected even at this level.

The net result of all this intracoluar scatter is that there will be a substantial amount of stray light spuriously distributed around the retina even when a stimulus spot is very small. Scattered light of this sort is always a potential artifact in any visual experiment in which low-level stimuli are being used, and particularly in detection-type experiments. Studies that are designed to be tests of lateral neural interactions can also be easily confounded by the light scattered by the less-than-perfect optical properties of the ocular media.

An important aspect of scattering is that it need not be uniform for all wavelengths of light. Scattering can also add to the chromatic aberration of the optics of the eye because it too is slightly dependent upon the wavelength of the incident light. Thus there is an intraocular chromatic effect comparable to the wavelength-dependent scattering of light in the atmosphere. Figure 5-53 shows the wavelength dependence of scattering by the entire eye. Because short wavelengths are scattered more than long wavelengths, there is a tendency for the ocular media to look bluish, like the sky.

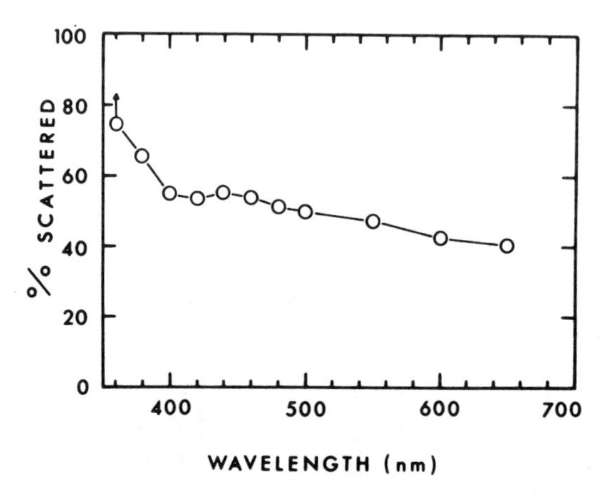

FIG. 5.53. The relationship between scattering and the wavelength of the incident light. (From Rodieck, © 1973, with the permission of W. H. Freeman & Company.)

The major result of a light scattering within the eye, however, is to further degrade optical images. The process is distinguishable in principle from the optical aberrations of lenses described earlier, but in practice some of the effects may be much the same. Scattered light probably acts to maintain a low level of illumination throughout the entire eye for all practical levels of illumination.

3. Polarization Effects

Scattered throughout all the layers of the retina in a nearly circular disk with a radius of about 4 deg of visual angle around the fovea[20] are optically significant amounts of a chemical called lutein. Because this pigment absorbs short-wavelength light, it produces a reddish and yellowish circular region around the fovea that is observable in opthalmological examinations. This region is called the *macula lutea* or, in brief, the macula.

In addition to its selective absorption of short wavelengths (which is discussed in the next part of this section), the molecules of lutein appear to be highly regularly arranged. The molecules of lutein are apparently oriented with their axes along the radii of the macula lutea. As a result of this orientation, lutein exerts a selective filtering action on any incident light that is to any degree polarized (i.e., that is not circularly or isotropically polarized). This selective absorbance as a function of the degree of polarization of the incident light is another Level 0 critical process that is the antecedent condition leading directly to certain perceptual phenomena.

---

[20]Though, in the past, there has been considerable dispute concerning this point (see Graham, 1965a, p. 366), it seems most likely that there is very little lutein present over the fovea itself. This accounts for the ringlike appearance of some of the phenonema attributed to the macular pigmentation.

The most famous perceptual effects produced by the regular molecular arrangement of lutein are referred to as *Haidinger's brushes,* after their discoverer, Wilhelm von Haidinger (1795–1871). Haidinger (1844), in the exciting days in which physical optics was staging its great period of discovery and development, observed that when the blue sky or some other evenly illuminated blue field was observed through a nicol crystal (a birefractive crystal producing two separate beams of polarized light because the index of refraction depends upon the angle of polarization of the incident light), a small hourglass-shaped figure, usually yellowish in color and perpendicular to blue wingshaped regions would be briefly perceived. The figure could be continuously regenerated in various positions by rotating the nicol crystal. This figure could be seen in polarized monochromatic illumination (except at longer wavelengths, where the brushes are not visible) but, in that case, the brushes vary only in terms of the relative brightness of various portions of a uniformly colored field.

The yellow hourglass is thought to be due to the absorption (and thus the selective removal) of the portion of the incident short-wavelength light that is polarized along axes perpendicular to the lutein molecules. Along this axis, therefore, the appropriately polarized shorter wavelengths of the blue stimulus will be blocked (in addition to the short wavelengths that are also absorbed by the macular pigment simply because of its wavelength sensitive absorption). The net result will be that the region surrounding this axis will be receiving less short-wavelength light than does the rest of the macular region in which the lutein molecules are oriented differently. The effect of the depletion of short-wavelength light is to make this region (the hourglass) appear yellowish, because it has a disproportionate amount of longer wavelengths. The visual system can adjust to these changes in stimulus color, but it takes some time. During that adjustment period Haidinger's brushes are seen. The bluish regions near the neck of the hourglass, according to the conventional theory, may be contrast effects occurring as a result of Level 4 processes.

Quantitative determinations of the spatial extent of the brushes indicate that they are very close to the same size as the macular pigmentation. It is mainly for this reason that this effect has been generally attributed to the selective polarization sensitivity of the partially oriented molecules of lutein. This orientation is not complete, however, and thus the partial natural polarization of skylight is insufficient to elicit the perception of Haidinger's brushes. It is only when the partial polarization of the sky is enhanced by a birefringent crystal or some other polarizing material that the modest polarization selectivity of the circumfoveal region of the human eye can lead to the production of this interesting perceptual experience.

A recent development in the study of the eyes' sensitivity to polarized light is the discovery that the cornea may also exhibit some polarization properties (Shute, 1974). The cornea contains large amounts of regularly organized collagen fibers that apparently act as a birefringent mechanism, just as does the nicol prism, to produce two images of a single object. These images are made up from light rays that are perpendicularly polarized to each other. In conjunction with other optical devices called "quarter-wave plates" that can shift the phase relations between the two images, this corneal birefringence can lead to the 90 deg rotation of the Haidinger's brushes.[21] A brief, very clear discussion of this phenomenon can be found in J. Walker (1977).

Though the most generally accepted explanation of Haidinger's brushes is that they are produced as a result of the selective absorption of light with various angles of polarization due to the regular orientation of lutein molecules, this theory has not been subscribed to universally. Cogan (1941) has attributed them to the orientation of fibers in the lens. Most recently, Hochheimer (1978) has argued that the source of the brushes cannot be the macular pigment because the macular pigment does not absorb light at the long wavelengths (525–685 nm) at which an objective polarization effect can actually be photographed in a monkey's eye. He also argues against the corneal or lens explanation on the basis of the optical placement of the brushlike images he was able to photograph. Hockheimer, therefore, attributed the effect to the selective absorption of short-wavelength lights by Henle's layer—the layer of the ganglion cell fibers—which is also radially organized. Regardless of the specific site of the selective absorption, most theorists (with a few exceptions noted by Hochheimer) do feel that the explanation of Haidinger's brushes must be framed in terms of a physical (Level 0) process rather than that of any higher levels.

In some animals there appears to be a much greater sensitivity to even smaller degrees of anisotropic polarization than that to which the human is sensitive. Many arthropods seem to be more highly sensitive to the slight amount of natural polarization and can use this weak cue as a means of orientation and navigation (von Frisch, 1967; Meyer-Rochow, 1975; Waterman, 1973; Wehner, 1976).

A related phenomenon has been observed that cannot be accounted for in terms of the selective sensitivity to polarized light of the macular pigment. Boehm (1940) has observed perpendicular bands, one light and one dark in peripheral vision where lutein is presumably absent, that are also produced when the observer views an evenly illuminated field through a rotating nicol prism or other polarizing device. This phenomenon suggests that there may be some other optically oriented material present in the peripheral portion as well as in the macular region of the human retina. What specifically this material is, if indeed it does exist, is not yet known.

4. Selective Spectral Absorption

Finally, in this discussion of entophthalmic processes, it is important to remember that the various portions of the ocular media have also been shown to

---

[21]This does not mean, however, that the corneal collagen can account for Haidinger's brushes themselves, as Shute (1974, 1978) so emphatically states.

display selective spectral absorbances that can lead to measurable psychophysical phenomena. In general, all the ocular media absorb especially strongly in the short-wavelength range of the visual spectrum and some even well into the ultraviolet. Because ultraviolet radiation may cause damage to various elements of the eyes, this is a highly adaptive and useful evolutionary outcome.

The perceptual effects of selective spectral absorption are, in general, elusive and difficult to observe in the human but have been measured in a number of psychophysical procedures. Stiles (1959) used the absorption curve of the entire eye to correct measured trichromatic addition data and was thus able to develop an improved estimate of the spectral absorption curves of the individual color receptors. The difference accounted for by this selective absorption is the type of perceptual effect to which I allude here. Incidentally, Wald (1949) earlier made the same correction to produce the almost perfect match between the absorption spectrum of rhodopsin and the average human scotopic sensitivity curve. The absorption properties of nonphotoreceptor pigments can also lead to drastic discrepancies between electrophysiologically determined spectral sensitivity from the whole eye and the action spectra of extracts of the photochemical. However in these cases it is also possible to rationalize the two sets of data by correcting the electrophysiological results for the absorption properties of the media as has been done by Goldsmith (1978).

The relationship can also be conceptualized is psychophysical terms; one of the most useful means of estimating the absorption of the optical elements of the entire eye is to determine their effect on metameric matches. Stiles and Burch (1959) originally developed this technique in a well-controlled laboratory environment and it was later developed into a mass screening procedure for large samples of subjects by Coren and Girgus (1972).

Most of the absorption of shorter wavelengths of light in the human eye is accounted for by the absorption spectra of the lens and the macular pigmentation. As I mentioned earlier, when removed from the eye, the lens typically displays a yellowish color indicating substantial absorption of the short-wavelength light transmitted through it. There is a gradual increase in the yellowishness, and thus the absorption, of the lens with advancing age. The classic data describing this change are to be found in a paper by Said and Weale (1959). Some controversy has recently developed concerning whether or not this phenomenon is due to ultraviolet-induced injury to the lens, or whether it was in fact an inevitable result of the normal growth of additional layers of the lens itself. Recently, in an interdisciplinary experiment combining sample survey techniques to obtain estimates of lifetime exposure to ultraviolet light and psychophysical tests of lens density, Girgus, Coren, and Porac (1977) collected data suggesting that there is almost no relation between lifetime exposure to ultraviolet light and yellowing of the lens. The yellowing, according to them, is a relatively normal process attributable to the more or less natural accumulation of pigments with age for other reasons. However, according to others (Zigman, 1978), their experiment is inconclusive, and the debate continues.

Support for the visual effectivensss of the macular pigment-mediated differential absorption comes from other psychophysical and neurophysiological studies. For example, Ruddock (1963) has shown that there is a measurable effect on color-matching phenomena that seems to be associated with the macular pigmentation. By far the strongest evidence, however, for a macular absorption effect comes from an electrophysiological study of the response of ganglion cells in the monkey eye by de Monasterio (1978). He showed that the spectrally opponent responses obtained from certain red–green ganglion cells located under the macular pigment were narrower than similar cells located sufficiently far extrafoveally to be free of the macular filtering effect. Blue–yellow sensitive ganglion cells displayed a similar flattening of their spectral sensitivity curves. Both effects were attributed by de Monasterio to the absorption of short-wavelength light by the macular pigment.

Another classic visual phenomenon—Maxwell's spot—is also traditionally attributed to the selective absorption of short-wavelength visual light, but in this case, from the wavelength-dependent filtering action of the macula lutea. Maxwell's spot was first described in the mid-nineteenth century by James Clerk Maxwell (Maxwell, 1856). The phenomenon appears to the observer as a colored spot when a diffuse white field is observed through a blue filter following an adaptation period with some other color filter. The particular color of the spot will depend upon the color of the second filter; but typically, if the adapting filter is yellow, Maxwell's spot will appear as a darker region on the blue background. After viewing the white field through a purple-adapting filter, on the other hand, it will appear pink, The spot (or, more correctly, the ring, for it does not appear over the fovea—probably because there is little, if any, lutein there) appears quite strongly for a brief period following the shift from the adapting filter to the blue one.

Maxwell's spot has been traditionally explained as the result of a selective adaptation of the long-wavelength–sensitive receptors of the retina by the predominantly long-wavelength light passing through the adapting filter. When shorter-wavelength light is then used as an illuminant (the stimulus light passing through the blue filter), the depressed responsiveness of the adapted long-wavelength receptors enhances the blue response according to the classic explanation. The darkness of Maxwell's spot is, therefore, due to the fact that the rest of the retina is producing neural responses to short-wavelength stimuli (which had been missing from the yellow filtered light) that are abnormally high while the region of the macular retina is still deficient in the short-wavelength light it receives due to the absorption by lutein.

Although I have some reservations about the particular aspects of this adaptation theory, it is clear that Maxwell's spot is most likely a direct result of the selective absorption regulated by the macular pigment and therefore is the result of a Level 0 process. The proposed neural mechanisms are, however, somewhat more equivocal than the contributions of the selective absorptions and may be much more complicated than the traditional theory suggests.

It is clear that with all the absorptive, reflective, scattering, and refractive attenuation of light produced by the ocular media, only a very small portion of the light that impinges upon the eye actually leads to a visual response. The selective absorption spectrum of the receptors themselves further limits the visually effective proportion of the stimulus to a relatively narrow region of the full spectrum of incident light.

E. AN INTERIM SUMMARY

In this chapter I have surveyed the Level 0 processes that are of perceptual significance. We have seen how the optical and geometrical properties of the external environment as well as those of the eye can influence our visual experience. In each case in which there was some kind of perceptual effect of a Level 0 process it could be accounted for in terms of a more or less passive or physical modulation of the electromagnetic energies being communicated from the stimulus object or scene to the receptor photochemical. The processes that I have discussed in this section, therefore, are best considered as transformations in the signal as it passes from what constitutes the distal stimulus to what constitutes the proximal stimulus—the latter being the pattern of photic energy that is actually transduced by the receptor photochemicals.

The processes I have discussed, therefore, whether they occur within or external to the organism itself, are not psychoneural in origin. They do not in any instance involve a transformation of the kind of energy in which the stimulus information is encoded. In all cases Level 0 processes represent quantitative modulations or spatial distortions of the electromagnetic energy of the stimulus. Light rays may be bent; spatial patterns may be deformed; or selected portions of the light stimulus may be removed from the incident beam. But the stimulus that falls on the photoreceptors is still the same kind of electromagnetic radiation as it was when it was first emitted or reflected from the stimulus object.

There is, therefore, a sharper point of demarcation between these Level 0 processes and those of higher levels than will be found between the other levels of processing; that point of demarcation is the primary sensory action. Prior to the primary sensory action—the photoisomerization of $retinal_1$—all changes in the visual stimulus are what I have called Level 0 processes involving only quantitative shifts in photon availability. Beyond that point the afferent information pattern is encoded in an entirely different medium—the electrochemical energies of neurons and synapses.

It was the purpose of this chapter to outline the preneural and prepsychological influences on visual perception and to make clear that even though an experience may differ greatly from the distal environmental object, there still may be a great deal of veridicality between the percept and the pattern of proximal stimulation. In such cases, the nervous system is operating in a more or less straightforward manner; the responses are not illusions—a term I reserve for psychoneural aberrations. No matter how bizarre the mirage—a term I reserve for the perceptual effects of Level 0 processes—the explanation of these phenomena is not to be found in the perceptual system but within the physics of stimulus modification prior to the neural transduction.

The major general point I hope the reader will take from this chapter is that Level 0 processes do not provide the perceptual scientist with any information concerning the nature of the transforms and operations that take place within the perceptual system. Ignorance of this fact can seriously confound our appreciation of the nature of mind.

It is also important to appreciate that there is a remarkable ability on the part of subsequent levels of psychoneural perceptual processing to compensate for many of the distortions or aberrations produced by Level 0 processes. This compensatory ability is evidence for the powerful coding and interpretive mechanisms that are characteristic of the perceptual system itself and constitute the subject of the remainder of this book.

Finally, it must be remembered that there is a host of distal stimulus variables that also affect perception in a way that has little or nothing to do with transformations occurring either in the external environment or the nervous system. Our totally verdical response to some property that is actually present in the distal stimulus should not be confused with a nonveridical response that is the result of some process classifiable within some higher level of the taxonomic scheme I have proposed here. Many visual responses are neither mirages nor illusions, but are instead appropriate responses to some aspect of the intrinsic organization of the stimulus. Moiré patterns, for example, produce visual experiences that are not the result of any *critical* processing (in the sense I have defined the term) by the environment or the visual system. These patterns are in fact the direct result of the actual physical summation of superimposed periodic stimuli. Although the visual system sometimes responds to these stimuli in peculiar ways (e.g., by evoking scintillations), the essential transformation has occurred in the external stimulus world and not within the perceptual processing system. Moiré patterns would be equally well detected by an ideal and perfectly linear system. In sum, in this example and in many other level 0 situations the percept is actually veridical with the distal stimulus and should not be misattributed to either environmental or psychoneural transformations.

6 Level 1: Receptor Processes Affecting Perception

A. INTRODUCTION

Chapter 5 reviews many of the ways in which the natural geometry and the optical properties of the environment and of the eye led to critical processing of the stimulus in ways that resulted in perceptually significant phenomena. In each case the phenomenal indication that some alteration of the distal stimulus has occurred is a lack of veridicality between the resulting percept and some independent measurement of the "objective" properties of the stimulus scene. The Level 0 critical processes discussed in Chapter 5 are all physical transformations occurring prior to the transduction of the photic energy into the neurochemical energy of the afferent nervous system.

We saw how a sharp line of demarcation can easily be drawn between those perceptually significant transformations in the external environment (Level 0) and those perceptually significant processes that result from transformations within the nervous system (Levels 1-5). This line must be placed at the point of the primary sensory action, the point at which the photons of light are actually absorbed by the photochemical materials in the outer segments of the rods and the cones of the eye. Beyond this line, there is a profound difference in the nature of the information transformations occuring at high levels of critical processing. No longer do the relatively simple linear physical laws of continuous external environment and the optical pathways determine the nature of the transformations. Rather the biochemical, organizational, and integrative properties of a discontinuous, interactive, and generally nonlinear nervous system now predominate. Thus the primary sensory action not only demarcates regions of different energy media but also distinguishes between two distinct kinds of critical processing that differ in their fundamental nature as well.

In this chapter, I concentrate on the first of the neural information-processing levels—the family of transformations that occurs as a result of the properties of the receptor cells. Level 1 critical processes, as I define them, are explicable in terms of neurochemical mechanisms that are confined within the spatial extent of single receptors or in terms of the locus and distribution of ensembles of these highly specialized neurons.

Many of the information transformations that occur in receptors can be attributed to two quite different aspects of the photoreceptor's function. The first aspect concerns the nature of the photochemical absorption process itself. It is profoundly humbling to realize how much of our nature is determined by the characteristic dynamic[1] of a particular chemical bond between two carbon atoms in retinal, one of the two components (opsin and retinal) of an only moderately complex organic molecule (rhodopsin) in the photoreceptors. Absolute thresholds, trichromatic color addition, and spectral luminosity phenomena are but a few of the phenomena that can best be understood in terms of the energetics of that particular carbon-to-carbon bond in rhodopsin's molecular structure.

The second aspect of photoreceptor processing that profoundly affects perceptual phenomena is the mechanism that leads to the generator potential following the photon absorption event by the photochemical. The receptor potential, as many experiments now show, usually does not grow linearly with stimulus

[1]The word *dynamic* is used in this chapter as a noun. It denotes the functional association between two variables, (one independent and one dependent) in the sense of an input-output relationship.

intensity. Its nonlinear and generally compressed response dynamic is now believed to be a major contributor to the establishment of the molar suprathreshold functions that describe the psychophysical relationship between the stimulus intensity and perceived magnitude.

The dynamic function relating stimulus intensity and receptor potential response is an example of a nonlinearity in the intensive dimension. But there are also temporal characteristics of the receptor potential that can also contribute to perceptually significant transformations at this level. A brief stimulus can elicit a receptor potential that starts later and lasts longer than the stimulus itself. This persistence of the receptor response seems to provide at least a partial explanation of a number of perceptual phenomena in the temporal domain. I expand upon this point extensively in Chapter 7.

In addition to these processes, it is also the case that the size, shape, and location of the photoreceptors themselves can be the direct causal antecedents of behaviorally measurable perceptual effects. These phenomena are sometimes more subtle than those arising from variations in photochemical sensitivity or from a nonlinear generator potential dynamic. At the limit, the size of the cross-sectional area of the receptor cell presented to light must determine the ultimate ability of a sense organ to distinguish between two nearly adjacent stimuli. Different parts of the retina may also exhibit different properties, depending upon the kind and number of receptors present. All of the resulting phenomena are attributable to the class of critical processes incorporated within the Level 1 rubric.[2]

Thus a number of perceptually influential critical transformations are exerted on the stream of afferent information by the neurochemical and distributional properties of the receptors. These transformations are the result of processes intrinsic to the nature and distribution of this particularly important class of neurons. It is important to note, however, that it is only fortuitous that this first level of processing directly corresponds to the first level of cellular neuroanatomy in the visual system; this association of neuroanatomic and processing levels will not continue at higher levels. Level 2, which deals with integrative interactions in the peripheral networks of neurons, is not directly comparable to any one of the next sequential levels of visual neuroanatomy. Quite to the contrary, Level 2 processes may be represented by simple network interactions that occur at several anatomic levels within the retina and perhaps at other more central levels of the visual nervous system as well. The lateral interaction process, for example, is probably not restricted to any single anatomical level of synaptic interconnection. Rather, the processes that I attribute to such interactions are probably common to the outer and inner plexiform layers of the retina, the lateral geniculate body of the thalamus, as well as the primary projec-

[2]From another point of view, the distribution and size of receptors can also be thought of as contributing to Level 0 processes, and they could have been so categorized.

tion regions of the cerebral cortex. In all these regions Level 2 type processes can and probably do occur. Subsequent levels of perceptual processing, as defined by the taxonomy used in organizing this book, are probably even more discordant with particular anatomical levels.

As we later see, Level 1 processes are primarily influenced by the energetics rather than the organization of the stimulus. The stimulus factors that are most influential in activating and altering Level 1 processes are the luminosity of the stimulus, its spectral properties, its duration, and the time and place at which it is presented. The dimension of quality of the visual stimulus, of course, is directly associated with the wavelength of the incident photons, and this independent variable will reappear again and again as an effective agent in much of the following discussion. Many Level 1 processes are straightforward reflections of the fact that different wavelengths are absorbed by different photochemicals with different degrees of efficiency. Out of this relationship arise most of the explanatory theories of trichomatic color addition, for example, as well as those of the absolute threshold.

Phenomena mainly attributable to Level 1 processes are, on the other hand, almost totally insensitive to the form, organization, or meaning of the stimulus. The receptor dynamic operates to modulate and transform the stimulus-borne information, but there is nothing in what is known about such receptor effects that indicates that the geometry or the semantic burden of the stimulus is a significant factor in determining the receptor response. There remains, of course, the possibility that higher-level processes may further modulate the afferent information stream in a way that is highly dependent on the shape of the stimulus (contrast effects mediated by adjacent regions of different wavelength can change the apparent chromatic properties of a perceptual response to a stimulus), but for all practical purposes there is virtually no evidence suggesting that receptor-mediated transformations depend on anything other than the physical properties of the stimulus that I have already mentioned.

An even more startling aspect of the Level 1 processes is that they often are as sensitive as they can theoretically be. An abundance of information gleaned from four decades of research on the absolute threshold indicates that visual sensitivity should be measured in terms of very small numbers of quanta—the indivisibly small units of photic energy—and perhaps even single ones. The human observer seems literally to "count every quantum," in Barbara Sakitt's (1972) colorful phraseology. Thus it is highly unlikely that there is any actual lower limit on visual sensitivity; the term *absolute threshold* is probably better considered as a metaphor for the results of a class of experiments studying the detection of very low-level stimuli than as a dividing line between ranges of subthreshold and suprathreshold stimuli. From one theoretical point of view, there is simply no such thing as a permanent "subthreshold stimulus." The facts of the matter are that the molecular aspects of quantal absorption by the receptor are discrete; they operate on the basis of single events corresponding to the rupture of single chemical bonds by single quanta. The extraordinary fact is that, even as molar psychological entities, it seems likely that we can respond to such individual and discrete ultramicroscopic events.

At this point, it would be well for the reader to review the section of Chapter 3 dealing with the primary sensory action process in vision. An appreciation of the perceptual material discussed in this chapter depends on an adequate understanding of many of those biochemical details.

The overall purpose of this chapter is to explore all the relevant perceptual phenomena attributable to these Level 1 (receptor) critical processes. In this chapter I consider the low-level, or quasi-threshold, processes that seem to be a function of the catch of individual quanta, the chromatic responses that depend upon the photochemical's selective absorption, and the secondary effects of the distribution of the receptors themselves. The dynamic relating stimulus intensity to the receptor response also has specific perceptual consequences and a discussion of that topic is included in this chapter as well.

B. PERCEPTUAL IMPACT OF THE QUANTUM CATCH

This section is concerned with several different perceptual phenomena that seem to be the direct result of the receptor photochemical's ability to absorb quanta of different wavelengths selectively. First, I discuss what is known concerning the absolute threshold of vision and then the phenomena of trichromatic color addition. Both of these categories of molar perceptual phenomena are currently considered to be the outcome of the specific ways in which incident light is absorbed by the four retinal photopigments. My discussion of the absolute threshold will be primarily limited to a discussion of the absorption of the rod photochemical, rhodopsin, because this material is by far the most sensitive of the four retinal photopigments and it is for rhodopsin that the analysis has been most complete. Trichromatic color phenomena, on the other hand, are primarily discussed in terms of the absorption of relatively large numbers of quanta by the much less sensitive triad of cone photochemicals. Figure 6-1 shows the spectral sensitivities of these four photoreceptors plotted in a particularly clear manner to emphasize both the differences in their absorption spectra and their relative sensitivities.

1. Some Physical Background

There are several basic and fundamental ideas that are of critical importance in understanding the subsequent discussion of the perceptual impact of the quantum catch. Most important is that the reader's understanding of the nature of the quantum be adequate to follow this material, and for this reason I now digress to a brief review of the principles of the absorption of quanta of light by chemicals.

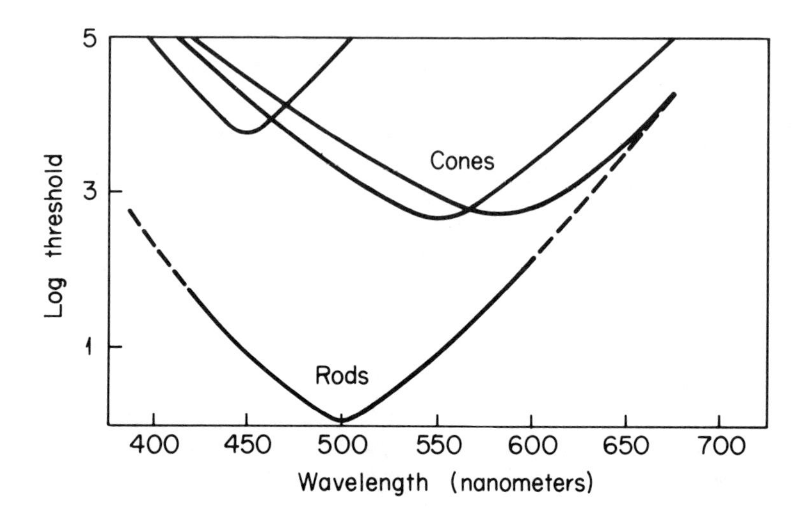

FIG. 6.1. The spectral sensitivities of the four different kinds of retinal photoreceptors showing the effect of the wavelength of the incident light on the thresholds of the four different photochemicals.

The basic idea of the quantum or photon of light energy, as noted in Chapter 3, is that light can exist only as an indivisible unit whose energy was given exactly by Eq. 3-7. There are several facts that derive directly from this fundamental unity of the quantum:

1. Quanta are either absorbed in their entirety or not at all; they are not subdivisible.
2. The total energy of absorbed light is always an integral multiple of the energies of the individual quanta involved.
3. The basic photochemical reaction is between a single molecular bond and a single quantum of incident light.
4. Because the eye is so sensitive, statistical fluctuations in the number of available quanta provided by the light source at very low stimulus intensities are behaviorally significant.

However there are also other considerations that can lead to what appears to be a nonquantal continuum of photic effects when one is studying vision. When stimulus intensity levels are greater than a few dozen quanta, as they are in most practical cases, it becomes virtually impossible to discriminate the essentially quantal nature of the energy source because the energy of the individual quantum is so small. Statistical fluctuations are smoothed over by the law of large numbers and the quantal energy unit value drops below the precision of measurement. In most practical suprathreshold experiments, therefore, light intensity can be treated as a continuously varying dimension that may assume all practically measurable values and that is free from the statistical anomalies just mentioned. As we later see, however, this approximation to continuity does not hold when one is dealing with those experiments using exceedingly low levels of light intensity in studies of the visual system's extraordinarily low absolute sensitivity.

It is at the higher levels where statistical smoothing and apparent continuity are the rule that we may comfortably use the molar law of photoabsorption postulated by J. H. Lambert (1728–1777):

$$I_x = I_0 e^{-kx} \tag{6–1}$$

where I_x is the intensity of a light at a distance x into an absorbing medium, I_0 is its initial intensity when it first impinges upon the medium, k is the coefficient of absorption of the medium (the percentage of the light absorbed per unit thickness), and e is the base of the natural logarithm.

This classic version of Lambert's law, on the other hand, is inapplicable at very low stimulus levels in which only a few quanta are involved. In that case, statistical effects on the absorption of individual quanta predominate, and one cannot be sure that any particular proportion of an equally variable number of incident quanta will actually be absorbed. It is more likely that the number of absorbed quanta will vary from trial to trial in some stochastic fashion.

Another major point concerning quantal absorption of light is a modern expression of the classic law of specific nerve energies first postulated by Johannes Peter Müller (1801–1858). Müller's law originally stated that the neural response of a sensory fiber was the same regardless of the nature of the stimulus. In other words, once generated, the response was specific to the neuron and not to the stimulus. Though the intensity of the energy required to activate that neuron might differ from one kind of stimulus to another, once the neuron had fired there was no residual information concerning the kind of stimulus that had evoked the response.

In the context of quantal catches that is the present topic of discussion, a corollary of the Müllerian law of specific energies has also been enunciated. This is the law of *univariance* first postulated by Naka and Rushton (1966). The law of univariance, like Müller's law, states that the visual nervous system's response, once evoked, does not contain any information concerning the quality (wavelength and/or energy) of the quanta that excited a photoreceptor. The neural code, according to this law of univariance, only conveys information about the number of quanta that were absorbed by a receptor and nothing else about their properties. Thus, long-, medium-, or short-wavelength quanta may be absorbed with different proclivites depending upon the spectral absorption curve of the pigment, but once absorbed each of these events will be dealt with identically, and a given number of long-wavelength quanta will convey exactly the same information as the same number of short-wavelength quanta. There will, of course, be differences in the number of quanta absorbed as a function of their respective wavelengths, but this does not violate the principle of univariance. Quite to the contrary and most importantly, it does provide the basis for the differential coding of stimulus quality. Should one somehow be able to force equal numbers of quantal absorptions by each of the three cone pigments for two different wavelengths, there would be no way to distinguish between the two events within the confines of the visual system as we know it.

Difference in neural coding thus depends only on the number of quanta caught, and all information about quality must, therefore, be represented in terms of the *relative* amount of activity in the different channels activated by receptors with varying probabilities of absorption for different-wavelength quanta. The fundamental basis of color coding is that information is differentially borne in these three channels rather than through the absolute sensitivity of any one channel. With this background information concerning quantal absorption in hand, it is now possible to move on to the perceptual implications of Level 1 processes.

2. The Absolute Threshold

Perhaps the first question (in some logical rather than historical sense) that should be asked about vision is What is the smallest amount of light that can be seen? This apparently simple and relatively direct question has motivated a considerable amount of research in the last hundred years—indicating that it is not as easy to answer this question as it is to pose it. To a very great extent, the difficulties encountered in the search for an answer to this question arise out of the quantum effects that I have just discussed, but the problem is also compounded by issues of the variable decision criteria employed by observers, the latter being an issue that was not even appreciated until the advent of modern signal-detection theories. The empirical facts of the matter are that the eye is so sensitive to electromagnetic energy that the experimenter is dealing with amounts approaching the minimum physically conceivable energies. The problem encountered is that absolute threshold energy levels are close to or at that carried by a single quantum.

Furthermore, as I also noted earlier, light stimuli at these low levels do not come from neatly controllable sources of illumination that may be continuously cranked up and down in intensity at will and with great precision by the experimenter. But because of the quantal nature of light, experimentally manipulated stimuli become stochastic rather than determinate events, and the experimenter cannot say with certainty just how many quanta were actually presented in any single trial. Furthermore, the photoreceptive process might not be constant but may also vary with similar probabilistic characteristics. Thus there is a fundamental indeterminacy both in the generation of a stimulus and in the absorption by the rod or cone that will probably forever complicate the search for the answer to the deceptively simple question posed at the outset of this section.

Because of the extreme sensitivity of the human visual system, it turns out that we are not dealing with a small statistical fluctuation superimposed on a relatively high value when the absolute sensitivity of vision is determined. Quite to the contrary, the signal and noise levels are very close to each other. The uncontrolled variation in the amount of light presented in a near-threshold stimulus (under optimum viewing conditions) may be as great as the mean threshold value. The reason for this very poor signal-to-noise ratio is the astonishing one to which I have already alluded—it turns out that we are sensitive to luminance levels that approach the energy of an individual quantum.

The extreme sensitivity of the human eye has been appreciated for almost one hundred years. The earliest studies of the absolute threshold were made in the late nineteenth and early twentieth centuries (Langley, 1889; von Kries & Eyster, 1907) even before the quantal nature of light was appreciated. Even these early studies, however, were approximately correct in specifying the minute amounts of light involved in just-detectable visual stimuli. Langley overestimated the amount of light needed to produce a threshold visual experience by an order of magnitude, but von Kries, Eyster, and a number of others (see Hecht, Shlaer, and Pirenne, 1942, for a complete historical review) properly estimated the very small magnitude of an optimal threshold stimulus.

It was, however, the classic and still definitive study of Hecht, Shlaer, and Pirenne only four decades ago that finally and convincingly demonstrated just how extraordinary visual sensitivity is, and it is this study that forms the backbone of the following discussion. Hecht and his colleagues specifically set out to measure the smallest amount of light that could be detected by the human eye under optimum conditions. They appreciated that there were a number of different factors affecting the absolute threshold, and their experiment was designed to optimize each of these several factors. They chose, for example, a stimulus wavelength of 510 nm—the wavelength of the peak of the scotopic or rod sensitivity curve, the most sensitive of the four retinal photoreceptors. They allowed their observers to dark-adapt for 30 minutes before testing their sensitivity to maximize the possibilities that all influences of previous stimuli had been minimized. They chose a location on the observer's retina 20 deg in a temporal direction from the fovea. This is near the point at which the well-known peripheral sensitivity advantage was thought to be at a maximum. They chose to use a test spot that subtended 10 min of visual angle—a value maximizing the spatial-intensity reciprocity relationship known as Ricco's law—to take full advantage of spatial summation. They also chose a stimulus duration of 1 msec to be sure that they were well within the time region in which stimulus intensities would be minimal in accord with Bloch's law of intensity-duration reciprocity.[3]

---

[3]I have prematurely introduced a number of new ideas into the present discussion without adequate background information at this point. The reader may wish to skip ahead to other sections of this chapter or the next to preview the significance of each of these ideas.

By optimizing all these variables, Hecht and his co-workers hoped to produce an experimental situation that reflected the receptor's maximum capacity. Of course, other levels of processing might also affect the threshold values, but this paradigm accentuated the measurement of the Level 1 quantum catch factors that are of concern to us here.

After all these stimulus and organismic factors had been controlled, Hecht and his colleagues carried out a series of measurements using a straightforward psychophysical procedure. A series of different stimulus intensities (emitted from a light source calibrated by a thermopile and regulated in intensity by placing neutral-density filters in the optical pathway) was presented to a group of observers by means of an appropriate optical system. The intensity of the stimulating light had been measured in a preliminary calibration run at the position in the optical system at which the observer's pupil would be located in the actual experiment. They then measured the proportion of times that the subject reported that he saw the dim light as a function of a variety of settings of stimulus intensity and arbitrarily assumed that the threshold was the intensity that was seen 60% of the time. Table 6-1 shows their results for seven subjects. The initial calibrations of the optical system indicated that between 54 and 148 quanta of the 510-nm light used as a stimulus must fall on the cornea of an observer to produce a perceptual response.

So far, this seems a fairly straightforward procedure. However, as I have already suggested, there are a number of complications in interpreting their results. Hecht, Shlaer, and Pirenne were aware of the fact that there were also what I have called Level 0 processes influencing the proportion of the incident

TABLE 6.1
The Original Threshold Data from the Hecht, Shlaer, and Pirenne (1942) Experiment

Observer	*Energy*	*No. of quanta*	*Observer*	*Energy*	*No. of quanta*
	ergs × 10^{10}			*ergs* × 10^{10}	
S.H.	4.83	126	C.D.H.	2.50	65
	5.18	135		2.92	76
	4.11	107		2.23	58
	3.34	87		2.23	58
	3.03	79			
	4.72	123	M.S.	3.31	81
	5.68	148		4.30	112
S.S.	3.03	79	S.R.F.	4.61	120
	2.07	54			
	2.15	56	A.F.B.	3.19	83
	2.38	62			
	3.69	96	M.H.P.	3.03	79
	3.80	99		3.19	83
	3.99	104		5.30	138

light that was actually effective in producing a visual response. Because their measurements of stimulus intensity were made prior to the point at which light entered the eye, the number of *visually effective* quanta was probably being substantially overestimated. The cornea reflects some light; there are various selective absorptions of light by the intraocular media; and a substantial amount of light that actually makes its way to the retina simply passes through it without being absorbed. The number of quanta actually absorbed by the rhodopsin of the rods being stimulated in this experiment, therefore, was without question considerably less than the 54–148 range indicated by the measurement made at the equivalent of the corneal surface. In fact, their calculations of the combined reflectances, absorbances and losses in the eye led Hecht and his colleagues to believe that only 10% of the light incident on the cornea was actually absorbed by the rods in a visually effective way. A more modern re-estimate of this value was made by Rushton, 1956; however, according to some informal communication, there recently has been considerable controversy as to whether this might not have been an underestimate of the receptor's ability to catch quanta. It was on this basis, nevertheless, that Hecht and his colleagues concluded that, in actual fact, only 5 to 14 quanta of light were required to produce a threshold response under optimum visual conditions.

This is an extraordinarily small number, and yet there is one other factor that suggested that even this low value may have been, from one point of view, too high. Recall that the width of the test spot was about 10 min of visual angle. Assuming that the stimulus spot was roughly circular, this visual angle defines a retinal area that encompasses approximately 500 rods at the portion of the retina 20 deg in the periphery used by Hecht and his colleagues in their study. From simple statistical considerations, therefore, it is hardly likely ($< 5\%$) that more than a single quantum of the 5 to 14 effective quanta was absorbed by a single rod. Thus the visually effective stimulus to a single rod is unlikely to be more than one quantum even though 5 to 14 rods must be nearly simultaneously activated to produce a threshold visual response under these optimized conditions. This fact emphasizes that, although the absolute threshold is properly defined as a Level 1 process in terms of the individual rod, a Level 2 process—the spatial summation that pools the responses of 5 to 14 rods—is also involved.

Thus it is quite likely that it is the collective impact of the generator potentials of the approximately 5 to 14 rods that have absorbed single quanta at threshold that leads to the conduction of a coded neural signal capable of being detected and reported as a molar psychophysical response. It also seems unlikely that within the pool of 500 rods the spatial distribution of the quanta is at all important. It is more probable that exactly the same sort of threshold response would have been produced even if all 5 to 14 quanta had been concentrated on a single rod. All that is really required is that a sufficient accumulated level of activity be transmitted to a region in which there is the possibility of lateral summative interaction.

So far in this discussion, I have used the magic value 5 to 14 quanta (a direct quote from the earlier portions of Hecht, Shlaer, and Pirenne's 1942 paper) as the range required for a threshold experience. These numbers, though, are only approximate in two further regards. First, the very vagueness of the numbers "5 to 14" suggests that the threshold varies over a relatively wide range between trials and between observers, second, these values are the average values for experiments in which a number of repetitions of the same stimulus intensity value were presented to several different observers. These estimates of the threshold are, therefore, very much averages of averages, and a further analysis is required to estimate more rigorously the number of quanta actually required to produce a threshold experience. Hecht, Shlaer, and Pirenne pursued such an analysis in their seminal paper. They noted that the statistics of quantal availability provided by the light source was also an important consideration in defining the actual stimulus. They also acknowledged the possible impact of momentary variations in the sensitivity of the subjects on the measurements they obtained. They astutely noted that both of these probabilistic factors had to be considered to deepen the understanding of just what was actually happening in the photochemical microcosm underlying the threshold situation.

To pursue this line of analysis, Hecht and his co-workers organized their data in a slightly different manner. Instead of taking the single value of the threshold as the energy level (i.e., number of quanta) that was affirmatively reported 60% of the time they replotted the entire data set obtained in their experiments in the form of a frequency-of-seeing curve. This type of display plots all the stimulus intensities presented in the experiment against the proportion of times that each intensity was seen. Samples of their frequency-of-seeing curves for three subjects are shown in Fig. 6-2. These curves plot the proportion of yes-I-see-it responses

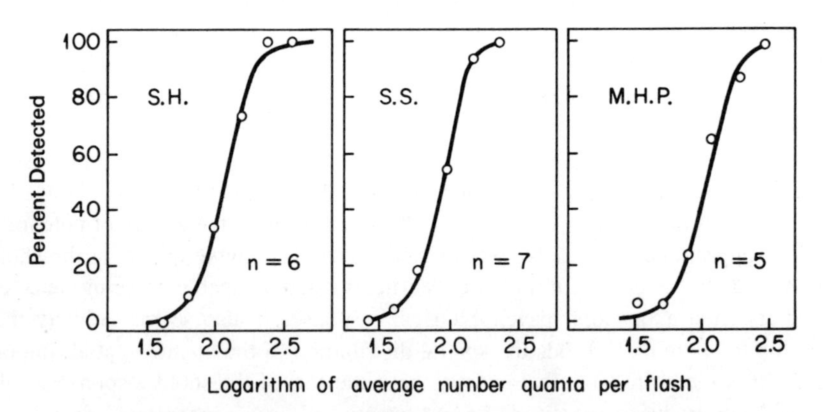

FIG. 6.2. The data from the Hecht, Shlaer, and Pirenne experiment for three different observers showing the proportion of stimulus flashes detected as a function of the average number of quanta per flash. (Redrawn from Hecht, Shlaer, and Pirenne, 1942.)

as a function of the average number of quanta per flash—a value that is a direct derivative of the thermopile energy measurements and the densities of the neutral filters used to attenuate the light intensity.

These frequency-of-seeing curves were then compared with a nomograph that was constructed[4] based on totally independent probability estimates of the number of quanta that should be present in a flash of light under the condition that the number of quanta emitted by a very dim light source in any particular flash was purely random. Such a nomograph is shown in Fig. 6-3. The shape of the family of curves represents the cumulative probability that a certain number of quanta will be delivered to the retina by light sources that emit randomly varying numbers of quanta. Each curve represents a particular average number of quanta and reflects a Poisson distribution of the number of quanta that may be emitted in each trial. The Poisson distribution is the appropriate one in this case because it is especially suited for representing distributions of a very small number of events.

The creative logical leap made by Hecht, Shlaer, and Pirenne was in realizing that these probability nomographs might also be interpreted as being equivalent to the frequency-of-seeing curves; that is, if one assumed a perfect observer (who always responded yes when the number of captured quanta was equal to or above the threshold number and no when it was below), then these curves would be identical to idealized frequency-of-seeing curves. Thus one only had to take the empirical frequency-of-seeing curves, slide them along the nomograph until a perfect fit was obtained between one of the curves of the nomograph and the obtained psychophysical data, and the best fitting curve would then represent the number of quanta being used by the observer to demarcate his yes-I-see-it responses from his no-I-don't-see-it responses. If one seeks to achieve a fit of the experimental data with the frequency-of-seeing curves for the three subjects shown in Fig. 6-2, the threshold values of the curves turn out to be 5, 6, and 7, respectively.

There is a further complication, however, that was further developed by Cornsweet (1970). If one does not assume that the observer is a perfect detector, always reporting an experience of light when the number of quanta is greater than 5, 6, or 7 and never when it is less, but rather that his threshold also randomly varies, then the picture is somewhat more complicated. In that case, one would expect that a random variation of the observer's threshold would be confounded with the random distribution of the number of quanta in a dim flash of light. The assumption that both processes are, in fact, random leads to another nomograph,

---

[4]The clearest written development of the way in which this nomograph was constructed is to be found in Cornsweet's (1970, pp. 68–75) lucid discussion of the matter. I shall not try to replicate it here, only guide the reader through the high points and direct the reader to Cornsweet's excellent clarification of the rather opaque and incomplete presentation made by Hecht, Shlaer, and Pirenne (1942) in their original paper.

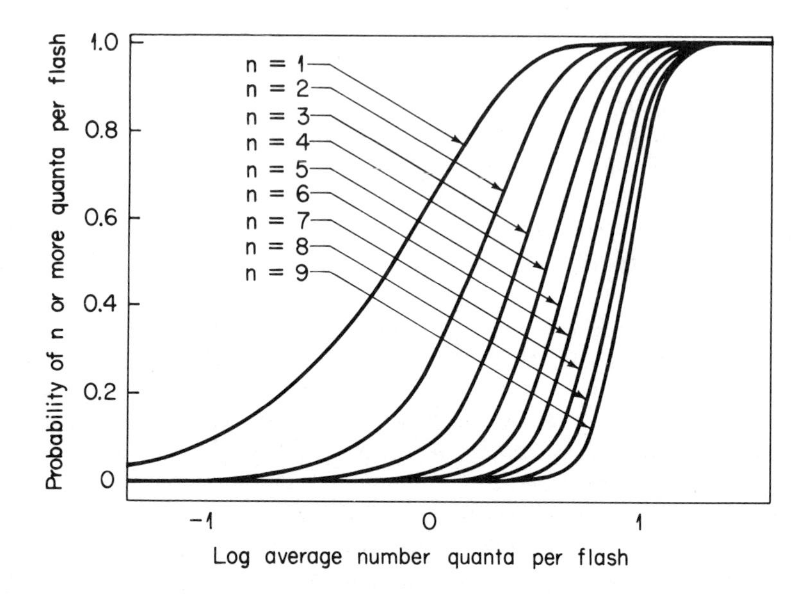

FIG. 6.3. A nomogram showing the expected shapes of the frequency of seeing curves for observers with fixed threshold indicated as number of quanta. In this case, the variability in response is due to stimulus variability. (Redrawn from Hecht, Shlaer, and Pirenne, 1942.)

such as that shown in Fig. 6-4. In this case, the fit between the psychophysical data and the nomograph is quite different and the number of quanta required for threshold is now best fit by curves corresponding to 12, 13, or 14 quanta.

How, then, do we distinguish between these two models—one that assumes a perfect observer and one that does not? A plausible answer to this question can be arrived at on the basis of the direct energy measurements shown in Table 6-1. These data do not involve any of the statistical assumptions of the two models just described. One has only to compare the actual physical energy measured for the threshold experience (5, 6, and 7 quanta) to the two sets of nomographs. Obviously the former one showing best-fits at 7, rather than the second nomograph indicating 14 quanta, is a better approximation. It turns out, therefore, that the best-fit with the nomograph is based upon the dual assumptions that the number of quanta is randomly varying and that the observer is an ideal one.

The extraordinary conclusion that we must come to on the basis of this analysis is that the observer in these visual detection tasks is performing very close to the ideal and that the variability reflected in the obtained frequency-of-seeing curves is largely due to the statistics of the emission of quanta from the light source. This is a highly surprising result from two points of view. First, we know that there is a substantial variability on the part of the human observer in most situations; second, modern signal-detection theory tells us that subjective variability (criteria fluctuations) should play a significant role in any signal-in-noise detection task. Nevertheless, in Hecht, Shlaer, and Pirenne's experiment, in which they made no attempt to control criterion levels, this ex post facto analysis makes it appear that the observers were actually performing more like ideal observers than the light source was performing like an ideal quantum emitter. The variability in the thresholds measured in this important study seems, therefore, to be more a function of the stimulus than the observer.

3. "Counting Every Quantum"

Considerable progress has been made in both empirical data collection and theoretical understanding of the problem of absolute thresholds since Hecht, Shlaer, and Pirenne's (1942) seminal study. One of the most important breakthroughs has been the rationalization of their data and theory with the modern signal-detection theory approach. Though there still seems to be little question that their findings and analyses are robust and that observers performing under their experimental conditions did perform as they described, we now appreciate that the yes–no paradigm they used may, in some cases, be misleading. Even considering the small number of quanta they measured, their methods would be

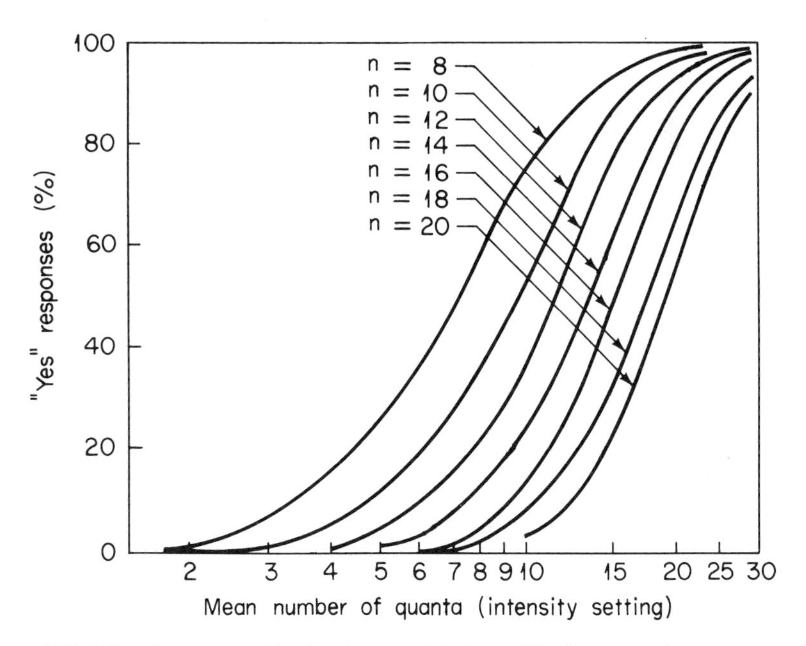

FIG. 6.4. A nomogram showing the expected shape of the frequency of seeing curves for observers exhibiting randomly fluctuating thresholds. In this case response variability depends upon the observer as well as the randomly distributed stimulus intensities. (Redrawn from Cornsweet, 1970.)

expected to reflect a somewhat higher threshold value than would be obtained in a forced-choice procedure according to standard dogma. The yes–no psychophysical procedure is also limited by the fact that it does not provide the kind of data (separate recording of the false alarm and either hit rates or rank order) that allows modern theoreticians to compute the discriminative and criteria factors separately using a signal-detection theoretical approach.

In a report that has attracted a great deal of attention, Barbara Sakitt (1972) has carried forward the signal-detection line of analysis of the quantal effects in a way that has added greatly to our understanding of the problem of the absolute threshold. Sakitt performed an experiment in much the same tradition as Hecht and his coworkers; however, instead of asking for yes–no responses as they had done 30 years before, Sakitt required her observers to rank the magnitude of the perceptual experience according to a 7-point scale varying from ''nothing seen'' (0) to a ''bright'' experience (6). The stimulus itself, however, did not vary continuously over the intensity range but was controlled to assume only one of two values corresponding to either 55 quanta (a ''weak'' stimulus) or 66 quanta (a ''strong'' stimulus) at the cornea. A large number of blank trials were also inserted in the protocol to gauge the false alarm rate.

By allowing her observers to use this rating form rather than merely providing a yes or no answer, Sakitt ingeniously allowed them to shift their criteria downward so that any residual sensitivity to even smaller numbers of quanta than that value determined by Hecht, Shlaer, and Pirenne could be detected. In doing so, Sakitt reminds us that the method used by Hecht and his colleagues should have led to an overestimation of the actual value of the threshold. She suggests that the instructions given to the observers in the older experiment actually biased them to make very few false alarms and thus to overestimate the number of quanta that were actually required for a just-detectable response—a surprising statement in light of the very few quanta determined to be required for a visual experience by Hecht, Shlaer, and Pirenne.

The possible implications of Sakitt's experiment are, therefore, enormous. Because her use of a rating scale distinguished various magnitudes of psychophysical response that were actually even finer than that magnitude defining the yes-I-saw-it response, she pushed the measured sensitivity of the whole visual system, not just the individual rod, very close to the ultimate level at which individual quanta are significant determinants of the global response.

There are two exceedingly important implications to such a finding, one general and one particular. The particular implication is that the human observer, as a molar entity, is, in fact, sensitive not to 5 or 6 quanta integrated over time and space but actually to the impact of an individual quantum! The general implication is that the absolute threshold does not, in fact, exist for these optimum visual conditions, even for an individual receptor, and thus may not be a meaningful concept in this context. The sensitivity of the overall visual process, not just that of a rod, is as fine as the smallest amount of light that can exist. This finding would mean that the human observer is, in fact, able to respond differentially to each individual quantal absorption. Indeed, the results of Sakitt's experiment suggest that this is exactly what is happening in the human visual system. The rating scale did highlight differences between the response to a blank, the weak, and the bright stimuli, respectively, in accordance with the expected random distribution of quanta produced by optical equipment producing these stimuli.

Hecht, Shlaer, and Pirenne's estimate of the ultimate visual sensitivity thus has been pushed even lower by Sakitt's experiment. It is no longer even necessary to assume that the integrated response of 7 rods is required to produce a discriminable experience. Sakitt found that for at least one of her observers, a single rod response was apparently detectable, although with a lower level of certainty for the responses that resulted from larger numbers (2, 3, 4, etc.) of quanta. The new lower "threshold" value using the forced-choice procedure was, according to Sakitt's estimates, 0.4 log units below that obtained with the yes–no procedure. There was an even more surprising result however. Although the minimum number of quanta that could be detected by the three observers in her experiments were 1, 2, and 3, respectively, all three displayed a sensitivity to the increment of a single quantum once their respective minimum number was exceeded. Barbara Sakitt's subjects were literally "counting" every quantum.

Of course, the validity of all this elegant story depends on the correctness of the assumption of how few of the quanta falling on the cornea were actually being absorbed by the photochemicals. If, as has been suggested recently, more than the 10% of incident quanta assumed by Hecht, Shlaer, and Pirenne, and also by Sakitt are being absorbed, then the estimate of the effective number of quanta in both experiments would have to be raised. The Poisson distribution curves suggest that only a few "events" are involved, but perhaps the events are not absorptions of individual quanta but neural events of some other sort.

Regardless of what the events are, other implications of these important findings are also of interest. Such an extreme sensitivity requires that we postulate some sort of cascaded amplification system in the visual system that can magnify the energy of a single photon to a level capable of producing a receptor potential; then, subsequently, a propagated action potential in the ganglion cell fibers; and, ultimately, a much more highly amplified response in the form of the verbal articulation, "yes, I see it." Furthermore, these results support the contention that the limits on the low-level visual experiments are actually defined by the absorptive properties of the receptor and that they are, in fact, as I have indicated, properly classified as Level 1 processes.

4. The Problem of Background Noise

Sakitt's analysis of the twin problems of the lowest levels of light that can be seen and the smallest differences that can be detected both solves and raises some difficult problems. The fact that observers apparently can be as sensitive to as little as a single quantum and can reliably distinguish between stimuli that on a statistical basis seem likely to differ by only a single quantum conflicts with what we now know about spontaneous or intrinsic activity within the nervous system. It seems undeniable that there should be a measurable amount of spontaneous decomposition of rhodopsin molecules simply because of the thermal agitation. How then can an observer distinguish between a stimulus-driven decomposition and a spontaneous one? Is there some mechanism that provides for discriminably different neural responses in the two cases? If not, how is the observer able to distinguish between the two nearly identical events in the outer segment of the rods of his retina?

These questions are probably not answerable at present (unless it turns out that the events are not quantal absorptions but more energetic neural responses), but they do lead to another way of looking at the problem. The task of the absolute threshold can be thought of as a signal-in-noise detection task comparable to the signal-detection process. Indeed this has been the theme of a body of thought on thresholds that has persisted since the time of Fechner (1860). The outstanding modern proponent of the hypothesis that the absolute threshold is constrained by the signal-to-noise ratio of the neural responses is Horace Barlow of Cambridge University. For almost two decades he has been pursuing support for this theoretical position (e.g., Barlow, 1956, 1957; Barlow & Levick, 1969; Barlow, Levick, & Yoon, 1971). The full details of his experiments need not be presented in the present discussion, but in brief, Barlow has consistently argued[5] that spontaneous activity in the retina, generated by either thermal decomposition of the photochemical or other spontaneous neural events, poses a complex signal-in-noise discrimination problem for the nervous system in the context of the detection of low-level signals. As in any signal-detection task the visual system must in some way be able to adjust its criterion so that it is able to respond affirmatively to a signal even when the signal-to-noise ratios are poor; yet not do this so easily that its false alarm rate is maladaptively high. The analogous neurophysiological problem, of course, is one of discriminating additional spikes in a stream of ongoing neural activity.

It is a highly reinforcing fact that both Barlow's theoretical analysis and his data support the contention that the number of additional spike action potentials required for reliable detection is very small and may vary within "a range of 1 to 20" (Barlow & Levick, 1969, p. 21). Because a single quantum may, in many instances, produce a single graded action potential in a receptor, this sensitivity would, in agreement with Sakitt's psychophysical study, also support the plausibility of single-quantum sensitivity on the part of observers.

The anatomical–physiological situation is also supportive of the extraordinary finding of sensitivity to single quanta. The nervous system's coding scheme has been definitively shown not to operate on the basis of single fibers. Instead, activity in any individual ganglion cell is likely to be accompanied by simultane-

---

[5]Along with others such as Rose (1948) and Clark-Jones (1959).

ous activity in other parallel axons of the optic nerve. Even a single quantum could, in principle, produce such parallel activity as a result of neural divergence. Because there is a high degree of interconnectivity of receptors with second- and third-order cells in the peripheral portions of the retina in which these responses are measured, it is likely that a substantial number of fibers would be simultaneously activated.

This spatial amplification of neural signals suggests another mechanism that may help to distinguish signal from noise that is not easily measured with single-cell microelectrode type experiments—namely, the coincident activation of a family of parallel fibers. Some more central neural decoder would then not have to base its judgment on the reception of a single quantum of light or on the addition of a single response in a single neuron but would have the much richer information provided by the criterion of coincidence of responses in a parallel bundle of fibers. Although this mechanism would not fully overcome the difficulties injected by the spontaneous decomposition of a molecule of rhodopsin or some comparable early spontaneous action, the criterion of coincident responses would satisfactorily overcome any difficulties introduced by spontaneous activity in individual higher-level neurons.

In sum, an amplifying system that passed messages indicating the reception of a quantum of light down a bundle of parallel axons would be relatively insensitive to the spontaneous activity in those communication axons compared to a comparable single-channel system. The difficulty of appreciating how a single spike in a single cell could be detected (as suggested by Sakitt's data) by a detection system that had to operate on the basis of a single fiber would then be at least partially overcome.

The reader should not overlook the fact that this signal detection approach emphasizing the absolute detection of signals in spontaneous neural noise is not universally accepted. Baumgardt (1972), for one, remains unconvinced that the signal-to-noise ratio is the definitive factor in determining the subject's lower limit of visual sensitivity. His criticism of this theoretical perspective is well worth reading for a coherent expression of an alternative point of view. In an earlier paper (Baumgardt & Smith, 1965) he stated what is essentially the classic threshold view; namely, that there is a lower limit below which the signal will never be seen. The perspective of Barlow and his followers, on the other hand, is clearly within the school of thought that says that there is, in fact, no threshold. Instead they assert that the false alarm rate simply gets higher as the subject lowers his criterion.

In formalizing this position, Barlow and Levick (1969) state that three of the most important factors affecting the absolute threshold are:

1. The number of quanta required to produce a spike.
2. The duration of the neural response produced by a spike.
3. The intrinsic irregularity of the nerve impulse pattern and the degree to which it becomes more regular as a result of a stimulus.

All three of these factors are closely associated with the signal-to-noise ratio, the aspect of the problem that Barlow and Levick believe is the fundamental limit on the perception of dim stimuli. It should be noted in passing that while Barlow's emphasis is on a criterion spike action potential, given what we now know about the graded action potential and its unique role in the first two neuronal layers of the retina, it is not all certain the spike action potential criterion is essential. Nevertheless, the concept is valid even if the criterion is changed to a "significant graded potential."

This discussion may be summed up by expressing a very important point concerning receptor function. I have chosen to place this discussion of the absolute threshold in this section because I believe that, in the limit, the threshold is determined by the quantum catch. The emphasis on criteria, experimental task, and signal detection theory, which permeates this entire discussion, reminds us, however, of the fact that higher-level processes, including Level 5 decision criteria, are also very important in specifying when a subject will say—yes, I see it.

Finally, it should be briefly mentioned that the conditions under which Hecht and his colleagues and Sakitt measured the absolute threshold were selected to minimize the amount of energy that would be detected. There is, of course, a virtually infinite number of other combinations of conditions in which the visual system would not exhibit the same extreme sensitivity. The choice of a different wavelength stimulus, a change in the state of dark adaptation, a change in the stimulus duration of spatial extent, or a shift in the stimulus to another point on the eye would degrade this extreme sensitivity.

What I have emphasized here are the optimum conditions and that, a priori, means limiting my discussion to the extrafoveal regions where rods predominate. In the fovea the situation is quite different. There rhodopsin and rods are in short supply, and three different kinds of cones filled with photosubstances that have quite different quantal absorption properties predominate. In the fovea the number of quanta that are required to produce a threshold response is much higher than in the peripheral retina. Indeed, at the wavelength corresponding to the peak of the photopic sensitivity, the number of quanta required to exceed foveal threshold appears to be about 10 times higher for foveal cones than for peripheral rods (Marriott, 1963; Baumgardt & Smith, 1967). However, when stimuli are used that differ from the wavelengths of the peak sensitivity of both the cones and the rods, the threshold values would of course increase substantially.

The fact that the cone-rich fovea is so much less sensitive than the peripheral retina does not necessarily mean, however, that the individual cones themselves are very much less sensitive than individual rods. After all, the primary sensory action is the absorbence of a single quantum of light by a single molecule of the photochemical even though the probability of catching this single quantum may vary. The fact that as many as 50 or 60 quanta are required to produce a response when the stimulus is presented to foveal cones, as opposed to only a few quanta when it is presented to peripheral rods, may possibly be explicable in terms of the lesser amount of spatial summation at the feet of the foveal cones than at those of the peripheral rods as well as in terms of this lower probability of photoabsorption. For example, it is well-known that foveal cones are in virtually a one-to-one proportion to ganglion cell axons in that region but that the spatial convergence of the rods on ganglion cells is much greater. To produce the same level of energy amplification, even with photochemicals that are equally sensitive, therefore, would require that the individual cone be activated much more frequently within some temporal integrating period to allow temporal summation at a single point in space to take the place of the spatial summation at an instant in time that occurs in the periphery.

Thus, temporal summation at a particular point in space (the cone) may substitute for spatial summation among rods only when the individual cone receives a sufficiently large number of quanta. The statistics of the matter are simple. To get the necessary number of quantal effects in a single foveal ganglion cell, it is necessary to have a large number falling on a single cone to which it is uniquely connected, but a smaller number of quanta *per rod* are required in the periphery where convergent mechanisms allow the quantal effects from several rods to converge and summate. This hypothesis could be tested by stimulating individual cones with much smaller stimuli than have been previously used and determining whether or not the threshold dropped substantially when the stimulus approximated the size of a single cone.

C. PERCEPTUAL IMPACT OF WAVELENGTH-DEPENDENT ABSORPTION[6]

We have already seen in Chapter 3 that the absorption of the photochemicals that are found in the four kinds of receptors of the primate retina varies as a function of the wavelength of the stimulus. In this section I argue that the absorption spectra of these four photochemicals (rhodopsin in the rod, and erytholabe, chlolabe and cyanolabe in the three types of cones, respectively) are the basic factors in determining the nature of certain molar perceptual phenomena.

There is one chemical fact, however, that deserves a brief comment prior to this perceptual discussion. It is, when one thinks about it a bit, not immediately obvious why there should be a spectral sensitivity curve with varying absorption at different wavelengths for these photochemicals. Materials in the gaseous state do not absorb in this way, for example; they absorb only at sharply defined frequencies and thus produce dark lines of absorption when light is passed

---

[6]Some of the material in this section has been adapted and updated from similar sections in Uttal (1973).

through them. In the liquid state, however, most materials exhibit a wide absorption band with some central peak of maximum absorption and decreasing absorption on either side of that peak. Because the act of photon absorbence is, in fact, nothing more than the elevation of an electron to an excited (higher-energy) state, it is somewhat surprising why this intrinsically quantal process should be differentially sensitive in this way to different wavelengths.

The answer to this dilemma is probably related to the stereochemistry of the retinal portion of the rhodopsin molecule. In solution, the typical retinal moiety is much more frequently colliding with other molecules than it would if the compound of which it is a part was in a gaseous state. This high level of collision occurs as a result of the fact that the average intermolecular distance is much smaller in solutions than in gases. It is thought that these collisions structurally deform the involved molecules. These deformations represent changes in the stereogeometry of the photoabsorbent structure, and thus of the energy required to hold the constituent atoms in their respective locations. Such a hypothesis asserts that in different stereogeometric configurations different amounts of energy are necessary to maintain an interatomic bond and thus different quantal energies would optimally alter a photoreceptor molecule from the 11-*cis* state to the all-*trans* state. According to this line of analysis, this variation in the energy required for isomerization (reflecting the random collision-determined deformations) is what accounts for the fact that a wide spectrum of different energy photons (with appropriately varying wavelengths) can be absorbed by different rhodopsin molecules. Because this process is the result of random collisions (within the constraints of the allowable molecular structures—some configurations are said to be "hindered" by the structural interrelationships of the various bonds), it is not too surprising that the absorption curves are vaguely reminiscent of probability distributions like the normal or Poisson distribution curves.

An explanation of the particular shape of the absorption curves of the retinal photochemicals, therefore, should not be framed in terms that state that some wavelengths of light are better absorbed by one kind of molecule than are other wavelengths. Rather, the explanation should be phrased to reflect the fact that there is a random distribution of various kinds of molecular structures, each of which absorbs in a narrowly defined but different region of the spectrum. The range of the absorption spectrum of any photochemical is, according to this analysis, determined by the overall distribution of the allowable states into which it can be deformed by relatively random intermolecular collisions.

In these terms it can be seen that the particular spectral sensitivity of the visual system is determined by a more or less fortuitous set of circumstances. Even though all four photoreceptor substances are compounds of $retinal_1$, and the specific bond responsible for the quantal absorption is on that $retinal_1$ molecular moiety, four distinctly different absorption spectra are produced by the presence of the four different kinds of opsins and the random collisions.

It is also important to remember that even though the four retinal pigments specify a particular distribution of spectral absorptions, the same neural information (with the exception of the limits of the visual spectrum) could be encoded by almost any set of four differentially absorbent photochemicals. There is, therefore, nothing intrinsically special about the pigments found in the human photoreceptors except for the fact that they *are* the ones found there. In other animals the pigments vary in composition and spectral properties from human values, and yet many other species have equal or even more excellent visual capabilities. All that is really required for color vision is that there be some pigments with sufficiently different spectral properties to allow measurably different relative levels of activity to be established.[7] It is this fundamental fact that makes it so difficult to tell from psychophysical data alone what is the absorption spectrum of any of the retinal photochemicals. It required the direct measurements of individual cone absorption spectra by Brown and Wald (1964) and Marks, Dobelle, and MacNichol (1964) to finally resolve the issue of the actual absorption spectra of retinal receptors as I discussed more fully in Chapter 3.

Much is now known concerning the spectral sensitivities of vertebrate photoreceptors. Over 25 years ago H. J. A. Dartnall (1953) suggested that the spectral absorption *bandwidths* of all visual pigments that were composed of a combination of any opsin and $retinal_1$ (the form found in humans) were exactly the same. However, Dartnall's hypothesis is no longer thought to be correct and has been replaced by a somewhat more elaborate theory. Ebrey and Honig (1977), for example, have suggested that there are actually three subfamilies of pigments that must be considered separately. They suggested that the three subfamilies display maximum sensitivities occurring at about 617, 530, and 438 nm and that they are progressively narrower in their bandwidth with decreasing peak wavelength. To test their theory, Ebrey and Honig measured the bandwidth of absorption spectra from many different vertebrates by determining the width in nanometers of the absorption curve at a value that was one-half of that of the peak absorption.

After comparing the data from a large number of animals, Ebrey and Honig proposed a new nomograph (a graphical calculator) that could be used to compute the percentage absorption relative to the peak absorption for any wavelength in any pigment from the three $retinal_1$ groups. Figure 6-5 reproduces their nomograph and explains how this useful device can be used to calculate the absorption coefficient of any stimulus wavelength, given only the most sensitive wavelength of the relevant photochemical. (A separate nomograph is available in their article for those animals that use $retinal_2$ in their photopigments.)

[7]Indeed, in an extreme case it is not even necessary to have two photopigments for rudimentary color vision. Kong, Fung, and Wasserman (1980) report that in the eye of the grasshopper *Phlaeoba,* there exists only one photoreceptor pigment, yet this insect can discriminate colors. The trick is that there are bands of another pigment, not a photochemical, present in the chitenous ''cornea'' of the grasshopper's compound eye. These bands alternate with clear areas. Thus there are actually two absorption curves—one for the photopigment alone and one for the photopigment as screened by the ''corneal'' pigment. This is sufficient, as behavioral tests confirm, to allow a simple ''dichromatic'' color discrimination ability.

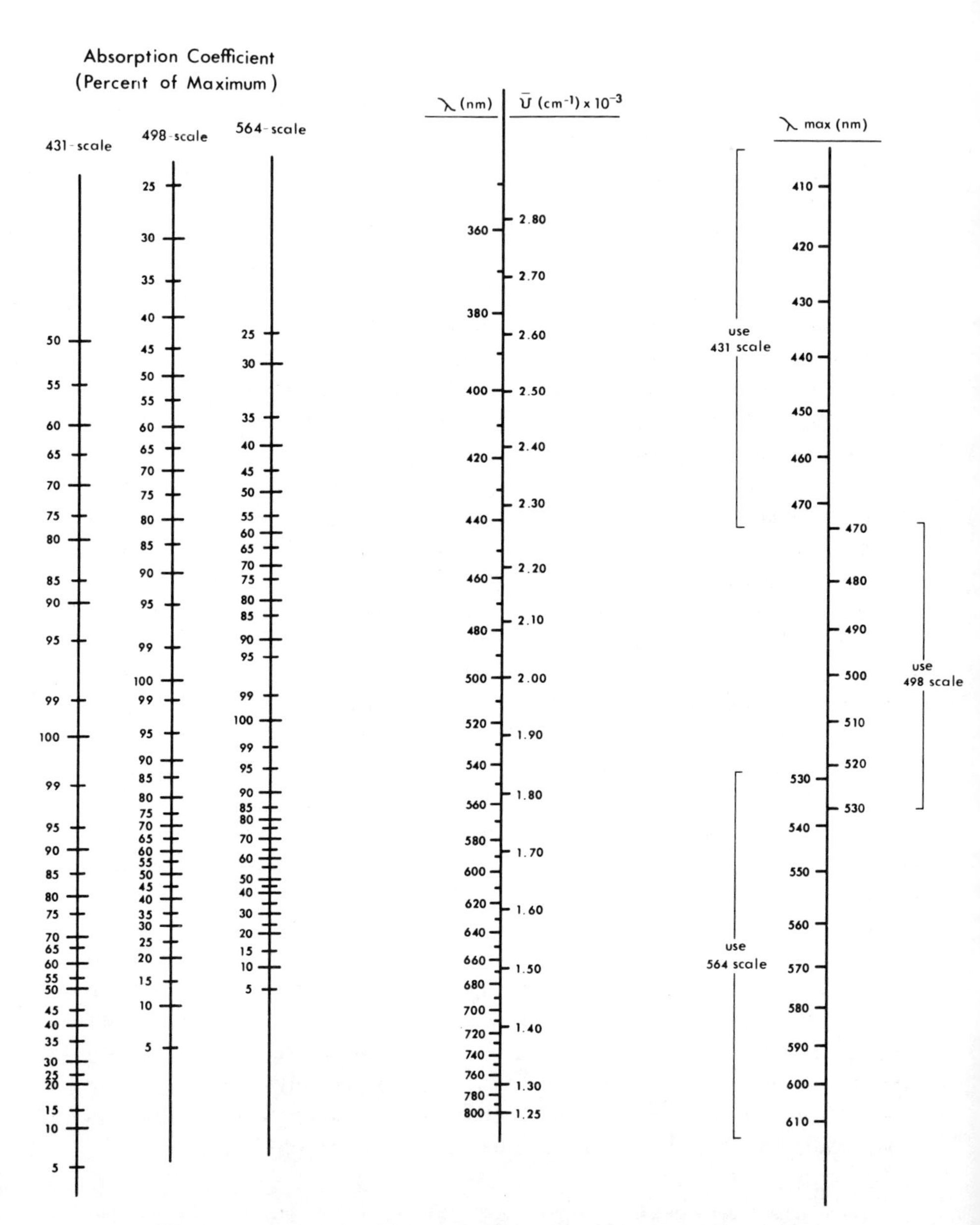

FIG. 6.5. A nomogram for determining the value of the absorption coefficient for Retinal$_1$ based pigments. To use this analog calculating device, one constructs a line from the point on the right hand line indicating the peak of the absorption spectrum through the point on the center line indicating the appropriate wavelength and then reads from the appropriate one of the three scales on the left. (From Ebrey and Honig, © 1977, with the permission of Pergamon Press, Inc.)

Once again, it should be remembered, only the relative amount of neural activity is important in encoding chromatic information. Therefore any animal that has more than one pigment, or one pigment and a selectively absorbing screen as we saw on p. 395, is *theoretically* capable of discriminating between at least some different stimulus wavelengths. Whether it actually perceives color or not is, of course, another question over which a considerable amount of controversy has raged in the past. To illustrate the differences of opinion concerning the color sensitivity of the cat, see for example Meyer, Miles, and Ratoosh (1954), and J. Brown, LaMotte, Shively, and Sechzer (1973) for two opposing views. It is possible, however, that both arguments—one for feline color vision and one against—are correct but in different contexts. Loop and Bruce (1978) and Loop, Bruce, and Petuchowski (1979), for example, suggest that color discrimination in the cat is observable only when the stimuli are relatively large and note that the studies showing no color vision in the cat typically use small stimuli. Furthermore, there is solid neurophysiological evidence that the afferent visual system of a cat does differentially encode wavelength. Ringo, Wolbarsht, Wagner, Crocker, and Amthor (1977) have shown that stimulus wavelength is differentially encoded in ganglion cell responses. However, neither an explanation of why the empirical color discrimination data were so contradictory nor a demonstration of the neural apparatus mitigates the impossibility of directly determining the nature of the cat's visual experience when it is presented with a stimulus that would produce a chromatic experience in man.

In spite of the generality of the basic fact of trichromaticity from a theoretical point of view (any set of three pigments could do essentially the same job), the practical facts of the matter are that there are three very particular cone pigments found in the human retina. This biological reality of three pigments constrains, at least to a certain extent, the nature of some of the psychophysical responses. In the following sections of this chapter I consider the perceptual consequences of the particular nature of the four (three cones plus one rod) pigments found in the human eye.

1. The Luminosity Curves

The human retina consists of two quite different receptor systems. The first receptor system is the one mediated by the single pigment found in the rods. This system is characterized by an extremely high sensitivity to low levels of illumination but, because it contains only one photopigment, an inability to differentially encode stimulus wavelength. The second system, the tripartite one mediated by the three cone pigments, can encode wavelength differences but displays a much lower sensitivity to dim stimuli.

Thus, this system, although conventionally referred to as a duplex retina, is actually a quadriplex one. The more restricted notion of a duplex retina has been forced upon us by the practical difficulty in most psychophysical experiments of distinguishing between the separate properties and responses of the three cone subsystems. Measurements made at moderate light intensities in the fovea, because of the considerable overlap of the spectral sensitivities of the three kinds of cones (see Fig. 6-1), represent composite functions that are almost always mixtures of the response functions of at least two of the three cones. Later in this chapter I speak of some attempts that have specifically been made to psychophysically study the responsiveness of the individual cone systems, but even then the separation is rarely ever complete and considerable doubt remains as to the relationship between the so-called π mechanisms and the four receptor systems.

For the moment, however, I will concentrate on the two easily and directly measurable response functions that reflect the rod and aggregate cone sensitivities, respectively. If one determines the relative spectral sensitivity of human vision at high illuminances, it is the spectral sensitivities of the cones that predominate. As I noted in Chapter 3, such a spectral sensitivity curve is referred to as the photopic luminosity curve. If, on the other hand, the spectral sensitivity is determined in a dark-adapted subject at low light intensities (less than 0.001 cd/m^2), then the data, referred to as the scotopic luminosity curve, exclusively reflect the spectral absorption characteristics of the rods.

There are two ways in which these two luminosity curves can be plotted. If both the photopic and scotopic data are normalized on a graph in such a way that the full scale represents the maximum response for the optimum stimulating wavelength of each, then the curves appear as shown in Fig. 6-6. This representation, however, is often quite misleading; for although it emphasizes the difference in peak spectral sensitivity, it ignores the fact that the absolute sensitivity of the scotopic curve is so much greater (i.e., so much less light is needed to elicit a response) than the photopic one. A somewhat better way of plotting these same data that avoids this difficulty is to utilize an absolute radiant energy vertical axis rather than a relative or normalized one. This was done by Wald (1945), for example, and his version has been replotted in Fig. 6-7. In this plot the difference in absolute levels of sensitivity is much more clearly shown, and thus the true relationship between the two curves is made clear. In these experiments the difference in the peak sensitivity of the two curves is about 2 log units or approximately 100 times greater for the rods than for the cones. This difference is an order of magnitude larger than the tenfold difference described earlier in our discussion of the absolute thresholds. This additional factor of 10, however, is due to different experimental conditions. The Wald study sought not to measure the greatest degree of sensitivity but rather to compare the two curves under standardized, but less than ideal, conditions.

The photopic luminosity curve can be seen to peak at about 560 nm and the scotopic curve, at about 507 nm. This difference in the peak absorption of the rhodopsin, on the one hand, and the mixture of the three cone pigments, on the other, leads to several other important effects. In addition to the break in the dark-adaptation curve shown in Fig. 6-22, there is also a shift in the peak

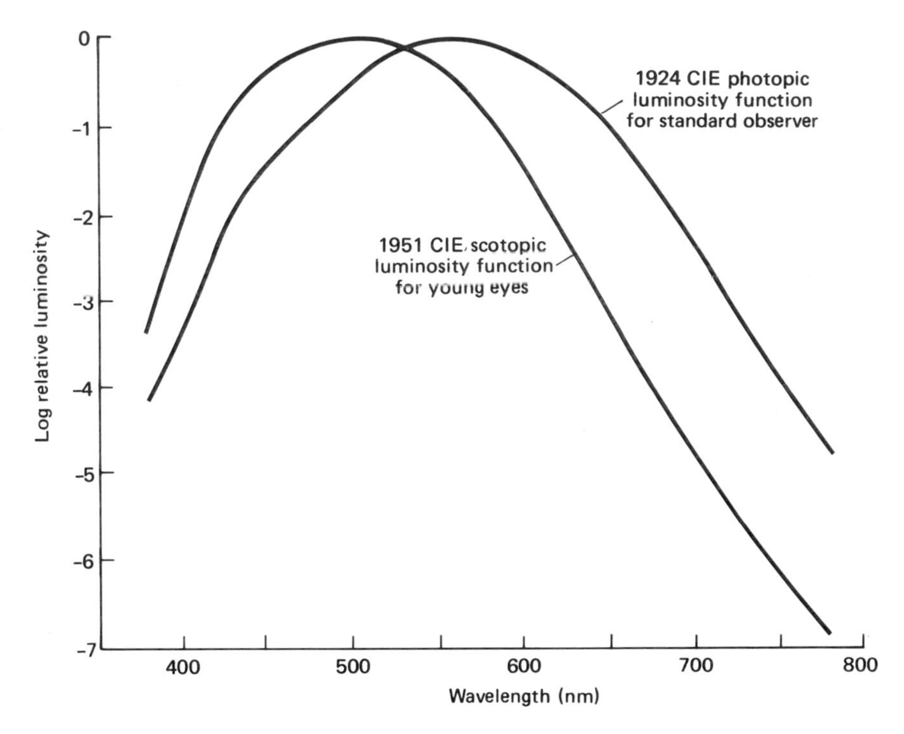

FIG. 6.6. The CIE relative luminosity curves for scotopic and photopic vision normalized by assuming equal maximum sensitivities for rods and cones and plotted as a logarithmic attenuation from that reference level. But see also Fig. 6.1 and 6.7. (From Uttal, 1973, redrawn from Graham, 1965b.)

wavelength—the Purkinje shift—to which the eye is relatively most sensitive as the eye dark-adapts and becomes more sensitive. A light-adapted eye is most sensitive to lights in the yellowish-green region of the visual spectrum, and a dark-adapted eye is most sensitive to green lights. The effects of this shift as one gradually dark-adapts can be remarkable. If red and blue stimuli are matched for equal photopic brightness in intense light, the blue will become subjectively much brighter than the red under scotopic condition.

Lights composed of mixed wavelengths tend to change chromatically as their intensity changes because of this shift in peak sensitivity. Combinations of wavelengths corresponding to yellow, orange, and red experiences tend to be yellowish at high intensities but to take on definite blue and green tones at low intensities. This phenomenon is known as the Bezold–Brücke phenomenon (or shift) and is probably related to the change in the relative contribution of the rod and cone retinal photopigments to the luminosity function at differing levels of light adaptation. I have more to say concerning this and related subjects later in this chapter.

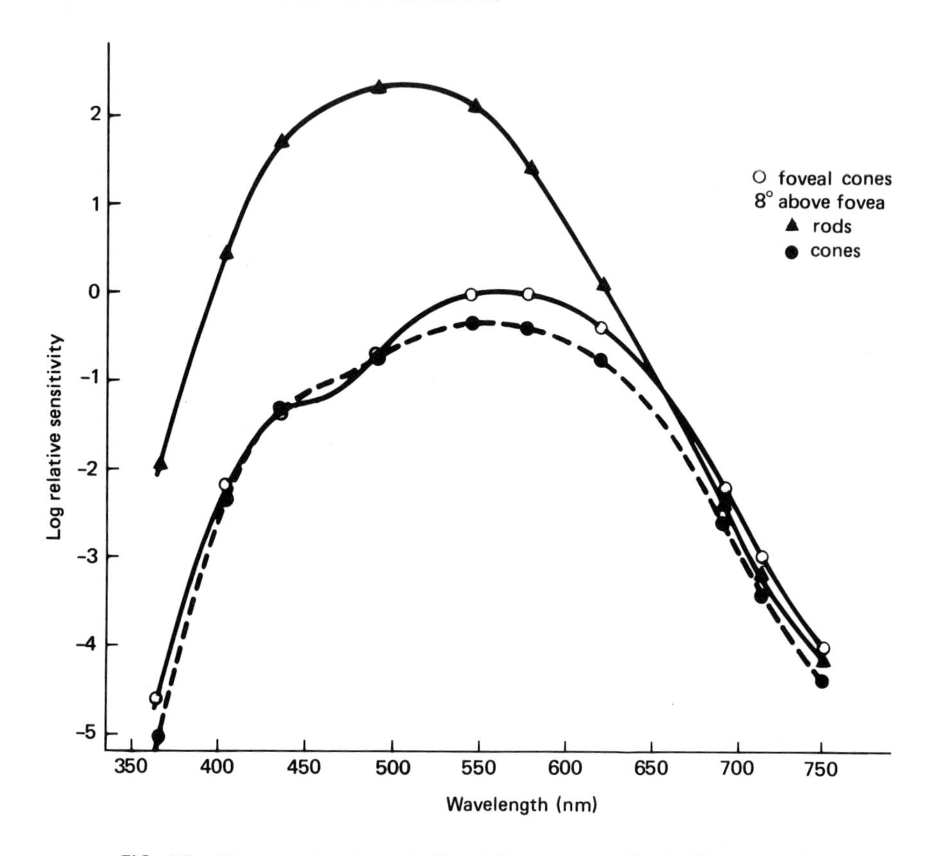

FIG. 6.7. The same data shown in Fig. 6.6 but not normalized. This means of graphing the scotopic and photopic curve emphasizes the fact that cone vision is three log units less sensitive than rod vision. Data for cones at the fovea and at 8° from the fovea are shown. Rod measurements are taken 8° from the fovea. (From Uttal, 1973, redrawn from Wald, 1945.)

Between the threshold luminance of cone vision and the luminance at which the rods are responding maximally lies a region in which both rods and cones contribute to a mixed or mesopic luminosity curve. Because there is, as we see later in Chapter 8, substantial interaction between rods and cones, there is no simple way to combine the four pigment absorption curves to predict the specific shape of any of the mesopic curves that may exist at the various luminances in this middle region.

Finally, I should also remind the reader that these characteristic photoreceptor absorption spectra are totally responsible for the fundamental perceptual fact that there is a limited visual spectrum and thus a relatively sharply circumscribed range of photic wavelengths over which vision is possible. We are able to see electromagnetic wavelengths that vary from about 400[8] to about 750 nm. Only in exceptional circumstances does the vision of the normal human eye extend further into the ultraviolet or infrared and then only at such high stimulus intensities that there is serious danger of actual tissue damage.

2. Trichromatic Color Addition

The perception of color results, as do all other phenomena, from a complex concatenation of the critical processes and transformations that occur at several levels of the taxonomic schema I have proposed in this book. Nevertheless the initial analysis of the wavelength of a photic stimulus is a direct result of the varying spectral sensitivities of the three different cone pigments. It is also true that there are measurable perceptual phenomena that are the direct results of this initial receptor analysis.

I have used the word *direct* several times in the preceding paragraph and it is not inappropriate for the more philosophically oriented reader to ask what is meant by that term. Though I am not sure that an exact answer can be given to this question, I should comment on what the connotation of the term is in the context in which I have used it.

The word *direct* is a derivative of the idea of the *critical process* that has guided the organization of this book. If a phenomenon can be entirely attributed to a particular transformational process, it is, in my lexicon, "directly" determined by that process and the process is critical to that phenomenon. The word *direct* connotes that the transformation that occurred at some level was essential and sufficient to alter the afferent flow of information so that sensory signals must be interpreted in a corresponding altered manner at some appropriate higher level (unless further transformed at some intermediate level back to the original information pattern). To say that the psychophysical data of trichromatic color addition are directly determined by the cone absorption spectra is to say that man is behaviorally trichromatic (and not dichromatic or tetrachromatic) specifically because there are three differentially sensitive dimensions of encoding in the receptors. Though different and more elaborate coding schemes may be present at other levels in the nervous system (e.g., the opponent mechanisms that appear even in the second-order bipolar neurons), these higher-level codes do not create additional information or dimensions of encoding. The fact that the mind of man is, in at least some aspects, trichromatic is a result of the maintenance of the initial informational tridimensionality by whatever code is used at higher

[8]The limit of 400 nm on the short-wavelength end of the visual spectrum is mainly due to the absorption of short wavelengths by the lens (remember, light passing through the lens looks yellowish). Observers with aphakic eyes (eyes in which the lens has been removed or eyes with artificial acrylic lens implants) can sometimes see well into the ultraviolet.

neuroanatomic levels. The critical transformation in this case is the receptor analysis by the three cones, and trichromatic vision is the direct result of this initial analysis. No other process must be invoked to explain why we are trichromatic.

In practical as well as theoretical fact, however, the psychophysical data of trichromatic color addition, even though they are a direct result of the receptor analysis, do not, as I have mentioned previously, allow us to calculate the spectral properties of the three cone pigments. Practically, there is too much overlap of the three spectral absorption spectra to allow them to be individually separated out of the complex response. Theoretically, the problem is an example of the classic asymmetry of mathematics; it is usually possible to go from a problem to a unique solution but almost always impossible to reverse the process and go from a solution to the particular problem that gave rise to that solution. I know what 2 + 2 equals, but there is no way to determine the mathematical origins of any particular number such as "4."

The nature of the three actual cone spectral absorption curves would, therefore, remain obscure if it were not for electrophysiological and spectrophotometric measurements of individual cones. As I indicated in Chapter 3, we have known the actual spectral sensitivities of individual cones since 1964, and now appreciate that, even though the psychophysical data do not uniquely specify three cone pigments, there are indeed three and only three types of cones in the eye displaying very particular absorption bandwidths and peak sensitivities. Table 6-2 shows the results of a series of experiments which have in one way or another attacked the problem of cone pigment spectral sensitivities in a variety of species. Many of these experiments provide support for an important conclusion: The three types of cones in the human are broadly tuned and peak at about 450, 530, and 560 nm, respectively.

What the psychophysical data of trichromatic color addition can and do tell us, is that there can be *no fewer than three mechanisms* of one kind or another operating to encode all chromatic experience and that, at some early stage of processing, all information was encoded in no more than three dimensions. They also say that only a trivariant theory is necessary to explain all color mixture data. However, a virtually infinite number of triads of spectral sensitivities could all model these same psychophysical data, and the wide differences of theoretical opinion with regard to the primary colors or fundamentals in the pre-1964 era reflects this innate uncertainty.[9]

---

[9]Although trichromaticity is the most general expression of color addition, it should also be appreciated that not all vision is necessarily trichromatic. We do very well looking at black and white (monochromatic) television and many useful color experiences can be produced from the mixture of only two of the fundamentals. In addition, useful tests of the quality of human color vision can be made with only two colors. For example, a classic means of testing human color vision has been to have an observer match a standard yellow with a mixture of red and green in an adjacent area. This is the famous Rayleigh (1881) match method named after John William Strutt, Lord Rayleigh (1842–

TABLE 6.2
The Peak Spectral Sensitivities of Trichromatic Retinas Derived from Several Sources.*

Study	Species	"B"	"G"	"R"
Brown and Wald, 1964	Man	450	525	555
Marks, Dobelle, and MacNichol, 1964	Man Monkey	445	535	570
Marks, 1965	Goldfish	455	530	625
Witkovsky, 1968	Carp	482	517	580, 660
Burkhardt, 1968	Goldfish	450		620
Tomita *et al.* (1967)	Carp	462	529	611
Stiles (Psychophysics) (1949, 1959)	Man	440	540	575
Wald (Psychophysics) (1964, 1966)	Man	430	540	575

*Note particularly that there are only two different groups of animals involved—primates and teleost fish—and that two of the studies are psychophysical ones. This table clearly shows that widely spaced visual primaries with peak sensitivities as indicated must now be accepted. Trichromatic retinas have not, however, yet been demonstrated in other animals. From Uttal, 1973.

The trivariant theory of receptor absorption, then, is the keystone underlying a large number of chromatic psychophysical phenomena. Most obvious and important among these phenomena is a result so ubiquitous and compelling that we may actually call it the trichromatic fact; namely, that a normal observer can match any chromatic stimulus with a mixture of *no more than three* other fundamental or primary chromatic stimuli. In the normal observer the corollary is also true; *no fewer than* three chromatic stimuli are required to match all other possible color experiences. These empirical "facts" can be expressed formally by the following expression:

$$C \equiv aC_1 + bC_2 + cC_3 \qquad (6\text{-}2)$$

where C is the chromatic stimulus to be matched and $\equiv$, in this case, represents the notion of "can be matched by" rather than any notion of numerical equality. In this equation, the coefficients a, b, and c represent (to a first approximation)

1919). Deviation from certain normal proportions of red and green in the matching mixture suggest particular color deficiencies of one kind or another in the observer's vision. Rayleigh matches must be used if one is using monochromatic lights as the fundamentals, as we soon see.

the proportions of the three stimuli C_1, C_2, and C_3—the set of three primaries—that have been chosen to achieve the match.

In both practice and theory, virtually an infinite number of sets of three chromatic stimuli can be used as the fundamentals, be they monochromatic lines, broad spectral distributions, or bizarre mixtures of various wavelengths. All that is necessary is that they are independent and sufficiently broad based. Thus, the basic premise of the trivariant theory has often been phrased in the following manner: Any chromatic stimulus can be matched by appropriate amounts of any fixed set of three other nonidentical chromatic stimuli. The only restriction is that the set be psychophysically orthogonal or linearly independent; that is, no one of the three matching stimuli may be matched by a mixture of the other two. The choice of what the triad of primary stimuli is to be used, therefore, is theoretically as well as practically arbitrary. Indeed they need not even be equal in brightness and all three could come from one portion of the visual spectrum.

However there are some practical restrictions in the way certain sets of fundamentals may be used to match another stimulus. For example, if three fundamentals are chosen, all of which are in the long-wavelength end of the visual spectrum, then one of the coefficients a, b, or c will have to be negative. A negative coefficient means that one of the triad of fundamentals has to be added to the color that is being matched rather than to the other two members of the triad. Negative coefficients[10] are absolutely necessary when monochromatic fundamentals are used or, in some instances, when one is trying to match a monochromatic light, but the need for a negative coefficient does not diminish the basic power of the fact of trichromaticity. To be very rigorous, this fact asserts only that three and only three variable light sources must be manipulated to match the chromatic properties of any other light source by the normal human observer. In other words, this empirical ''trichromatic fact'' obtained from psychophysical studies means that color vision is dimensionally trivariant in its internal codes.

The choice of the triad of primaries, as I have said, is completely arbitrary if one depends only on psychophysical data for their specification. The triad may consist of any three broad bandwidths of the visual spectrum. However, the choice of a particular triad will determine the magnitude of the associated coefficients a, b, and c of Eq. 6-2 that represent the proportion of each fundamental

[10]Since the $\equiv$ symbol in Eq. 6-2 is not an equal sign, it is not exactly correct to say that the mixture of one of the fundamentals with the color to be matched (rather than with the other two fundamentals) is equivalent to a minus sign. Some modern expressions of this process (Boynton, 1971) propose an alternative law which is not precisely a mathematical derivative of Eq. 6-2. The form of this alternative formulation is

$$C + aC_1 \equiv bC_2 + cC_3$$

If one is using monochromatic fundamentals, then this is the expression of choice.

that has to be used for the match. These coefficients may be interpreted from a number of different point of view. Given a particular triad of fundamentals, these coefficients may be considered to be nondimensional ratios defined by the following three equations:

$$a = \frac{C_1}{C_1 + C_2 + C_3} \tag{6-3}$$

$$b = \frac{C_2}{C_1 + C_2 + C_3} \tag{6-4}$$

$$c = \frac{C_3}{C_1 + C_2 + C_3} \tag{6-5}$$

C_1, C_2, and C_3 reflect, in this case, the absolute intensities of the three fundamentals in a given mixture. Because each of the coefficients is defined in terms of the proportion of one light to the sum of all three, it is immediately clear that the sum of the coefficients must be equal to 1. Thus:

$$a + b + c = 1 \tag{6-6}$$

Another way in which the same information may be represented has been most clearly presented by Cornsweet (1970). Rather than a formula specified in terms of the relative intensities of the three primaries, he describes a system of chromatic stimulus matching that is specified in terms of the quantal absorption of three retinal pigments. This model of color space is based upon the idea that a mixture of three fundamentals will match some other chromatic stimulus only if the number of quanta absorbed by each member of the set of three photosensitive pigments is the same for the matched and the matching stimuli. Or, expressed formally;

$$N_{a0} = N_{a1} + N_{a2} + N_{a3} \tag{6-7}$$

$$N_{b0} = N_{b1} + N_{b2} + N_{b3} \tag{6-8}$$

$$N_{c0} = N_{c1} + N_{c2} + N_{c3} \tag{6-9}$$

where N, in general, refers to the number of quanta of light absorbed by one of the three photopigments. Each of the three pigments (subscripted a, b, and c) will absorb a certain number of quanta from each of the four involved lights: the unknown (subscripted 0) and the three primary stimuli used in the color match (subscripted 1, 2, and 3). Thus, the number of quanta absorbed by the b photoreceptor when stimulated by the first of the fundamentals would be indicated N_{b1}. A light will be matched by adjusting the intensities of a set of primaries until the quantal absorption in each of the three photopigments is equal for the unknown and the combined effect of the three matching primaries.

Both of these formulations, one in terms of the ratio coefficients of luminances and one in terms of quantal absorption counts, are, of course, equivalent, and it is possible to go directly from one to the other. Each is an equivalent expression of the basic fact that I am emphasizing here, namely, that trichromacy is the basic characteristic of normal color vision.

The tridimensionality of color space allows us to represent it in a three-dimensional spatial plot in a compressed and simple manner. There are two ways in which this can be done, one based upon the ratio coefficients and one based upon the concept of quantum absorption.

The method based upon ratio coefficients allows us to display in a two-dimensional plot (the chromaticity diagram) many of the three-dimensional features of color mixing and trichromatic vision. One form of this plot, the CIE (Commission Internationale de L'Eclairage—International Lighting Commission) chromaticity diagram is illustrated in Fig. 6-8. This particular chromaticity diagram is based upon a set of what have been called *imaginary primaries*. In other words, they were chromatic stimuli that existed outside of the region enclosed by the locus of spectral points—the continuous curve plotted in this figure. These primaries, which of course are not physically obtainable, were used to keep a, b, and c all equal to positive numbers. A different set of physically realizable primaries would produce an equivalent chromaticity diagram, but one differing in shape to the degree that the primaries differ from the standard CIE set. One very important chromaticity diagram is the one shown in Fig. 6-9. It is based on monochromatic primaries of 435, 546, and 700 nm, respectively. In this diagram the points labelled X, Y, and Z represent the three imaginary primaries underlying the CIE diagram. Although this curve does have negative values of r, q, and b (the equivalent of a, b, and c in the CIE nomenclature), it does have the advantage of being based on real and monochromatic primaries.

An important practical criterion for the choice of a set of primaries is that when they are mixed in equal proportions, the mixture will produce a relatively good white. On any of the chromaticity diagrams, the horizontal coordinate represents one of the coefficients of the trichromatic equation (Eq. 6-2), which specifies how much of the long-wavelength fundamental is present. The vertical coordinate, in turn, represents the coefficient of the intermediate-wavelength fundamental. Given these two numbers, the coefficient of the third short-wavelength component is uniquely specified, because $a + b + c = 1$; thus, no third dimension need be graphically specified on the diagram.

The CIE chromaticity diagram, as well as any of the others, is packed with an astounding variety of information. One of the most important subsets of data contained within it is the definition of the coefficients (a, b, and c) that must be used to match pure spectral stimuli, that is, nearly monochromatic stimuli. The continuous curve shown in Fig. 6-8 is the locus of the coefficients required to reproduce the experience produced by narrow-band spectral stimuli ranging from the near-infrared to the near-ultraviolet. This locus of points also essentially represents the outer limits of the color world, for each related color experience theoretically represents the purest or most saturated color possible. Under some

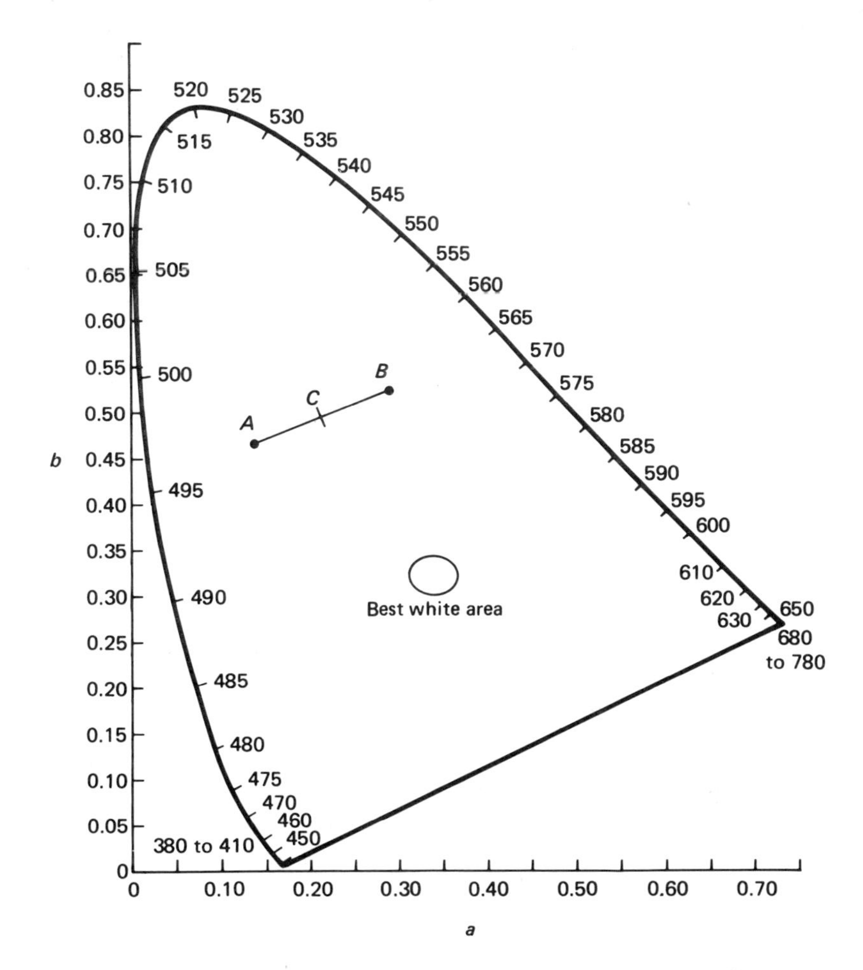

FIG. 6.8. The standard 1931 CIE chromaticity diagram plotting the a coefficient against the b coefficient. Since a + b + c = 1, c is also thus uniquely defined. The circled center region approximates the most white of the whites obtained in a three-color mixture experiment. The straight line shows a means of calculating the chromatic resultant C of the mixture of two colors, A and B. (From Uttal, 1973, after the Optical Society of America, 1953.)

conditions, such as those following chromatic adaptation, combinations of coefficients are required that represent points that lie outside of the spectral locus. Such combinations of color coefficients from one point of view represent "supersaturated" colors; but the interpretation of such phenomena is equivocal; and I do not feel that there is anything very meaningful to say further about them.

Points lying along this outer line represent narrow-band spectral stimuli and produce experiences that vary in hue. But chromatic experiences will also vary in

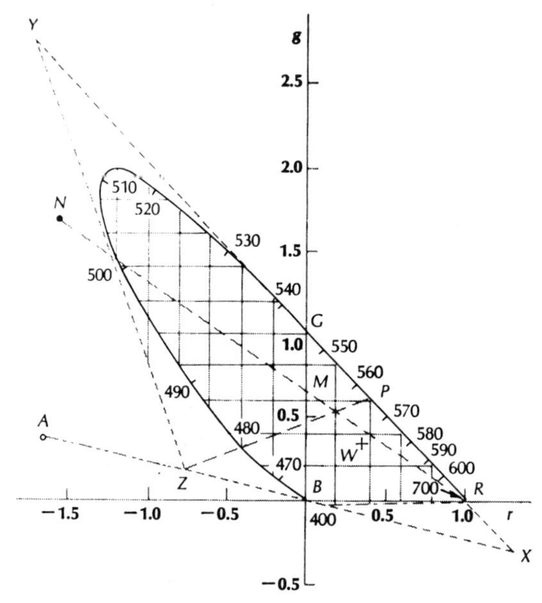

FIG. 6.9. An equivalent chromaticity diagram based on real primaries. (From Boynton, © 1971, with the permission of Holt, Rinehart and Winston, Inc.)

saturation[11] and this dimension is also represented on this chromaticity diagram. As one moves along any line connecting the locus of the coefficients representing narrow-band spectral stimuli and the center of the chromaticity diagram, one is moving along the saturation continuum from a highly saturated color experience to the whitest white in which no color tones are observable.

The perceptual effects of mixing two chromatic stimuli represented by points anywhere on the chromaticity diagram are also easily calculated, as shown in Fig. 6-8. The chromaticity coordinates of a mixture are represented by the center of gravity[12] of a straight line joining the points that represent each of the constituent components of the mixture. For these special cases, in which the two components lie at the ends of a straight line passing through and having its center of gravity in the white region, the two component chromatic stimuli are said to be complements of each other.

---

[11]I define *hue* and *saturation* more precisely a few pages later in this chapter.

[12]The center of gravity, or more correctly the center of chromatic gravity, in this case is defined as the point on a line connecting two colors such that

$$X \times C_1 = Y \times C_2$$

where C_1 and C_2 are the luminances of the two colors and X and Y are their chromatic distances to the center of gravity.

Another interesting and useful set of data, included on some versions of the chromaticity diagram, is the family of MacAdam ellipses. MacAdam (1942) had shown that there were areas on the chromaticity diagram within which the normal human observer could not distinguish any difference between any of the enclosed mixtures. MacAdam demonstrated that these areas were in the form of ellipses, but that the orientation of the major axis of each ellipse varied systematically depending upon where they were located on the chromaticity diagram. Figure 6-10 shows a system of MacAdam ellipses. The small size of the ellipse in the lower left-hand corner of the curve suggests a very great sensitivity to color differences when the slightest changes are made in the proportions of the fundamentals. But the very large ellipses at the top of the chromaticity diagram suggest

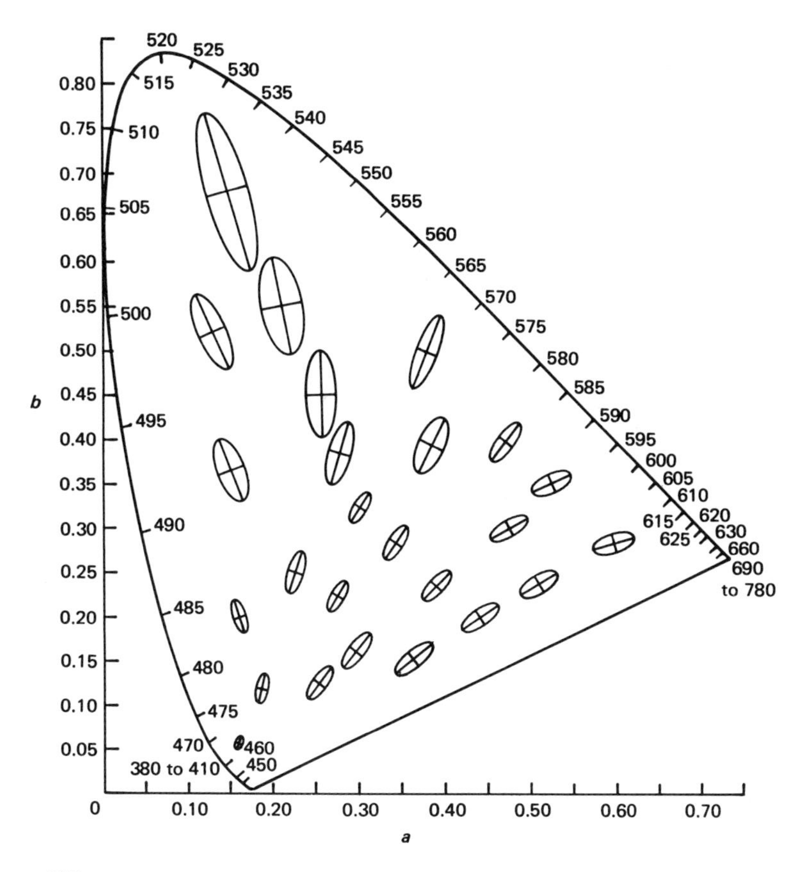

FIG. 6.10. The system of MacAdam ellipses, which show the regions in which colors are not differentiated from one another. The dimensions of the ellipses are defined by a measure of the standard deviation of the wavelength of indiscriminable colors in a two-color discrimination experiment. Note: All ellipses are magnified ten times for clarity. (From Uttal, 1973, redrawn from MacAdam, 1942.)

that in this region there is a reduced sensitivity to changes in the proportions of the fundamentals. The wide horizontal axis indicates an insensitivity to the long-wavelength fundamental. However the very elongated vertical axis of the ellipse indicates that even less effect on the perceived color would be induced when very substantial changes are made in the amount of medium—wavelength light in the mixture. The middle-size ellipses in the lower right-hand corner of the chromaticity diagram indicate that the observer's sensitivity to changes in any of the three fundamentals is intermediate in that region. (The reader should keep in mind, when estimating the size of any differential threshold from this figure, that the ellipses in this diagram are enlarged 10 times for clarity.)

The chromaticity diagram can also be used as a starting point for discussing many other more detailed rules of chromatic stimulus mixture. It is quite obvious that any given point on the diagram can be produced by a number of different combinations. For example, any point on the CIE chromaticity diagram can be produced by the combination of any of the pairs of stimuli at the ends of any of the family of straight lines that pass through and have their center of gravity at that point. Yet regardless of the nature of the pair of components used to produce that same set of chromatic coefficients represented by that point, all of the mixtures are indistinguishable. Combinations that produce equal color experiences, regardless of how widely the component stimuli may vary, are called *metameric matches*.

The experiments and data concerning chromatic stimulus mixture are varied and extensive. Much of the data have been summarized in a set of approximately accurate rules generally known as Grassman's laws, and over the years, the rules have been extended and rephrased to reflect current theory and experiment. Though as we shall see later the ''laws'' are not exact, they are useful first approximations in describing how chromatic stimuli add together. Perhaps the best modern statement of these rules has been summarized by Graham (1965b, p. 372) and are paraphrased thus:

1. Any chromatic mixture, no matter how it is composed, must have the same appearance as the mixture of some portion of the spectral locus, and a point corresponding to a white (Helmholtz, 1867).

2. When the appearance of one of the two kinds of light that are to be mixed together changes continuously, the appearance of the mixture also changes continuously (Helmholtz, 1867).

a. For every point on the CIE diagram, there can be found another complementary or antagonistic point representing a chromatic stimulus that, if mixed with it in the right proportion, gives white or gray; and if mixed in any other proportion, gives an unsaturated color having the hue of the more intense component (Titchener, 1915).

b. The mixture of any two chromatic stimuli that are not complementaries produces an intermediate chromatic experience varying in hue with the relative amounts of the two original stimuli and varying in saturation with their nearness or remoteness on the CIE diagram (Titchener, 1915).

3. The mixture of any two combinations that match will itself match either of the original combinations, provided that the illumination of the colors remains approximately the same (Titchener, 1915).

4. The total brightness of the mixture is the sum of the brightness of the light mixed (Grassman, 1854). (This law, as we later see, is perhaps the least accurate of the four presented here.)[13]

Although the CIE chromaticity diagram has been the standard spatial representation of the data of color mixture, the quantal trivariance representation described by Cornsweet (see Eq. 6-7, 6-8, and 6-9) presents an alternative that may prove to have considerable advantages in years to come. The basic assumption underlying Cornsweet's approach is that all quanta that are absorbed by any of the three cone pigments have an equal physiological effect, regardless of the wavelength of the illuminating light. This is another way of expressing the law of univariance for each of the cones. Because it uses absolute numbers of quantal absorptions, the Cornsweet plot must be a true three-dimensional one, for the quasi-two-dimensionalization inherent in the equation $a + b + c = 1$ is not present in this situation. The number of quanta absorbed by each of the three photopigments is not normalized, and each absorption count must, therefore, be represented as independent degrees of freedom. Figure 6-11 shows an example of Cornsweet's method of plotting the chromatic trispace. This figure also displays the locus in this quantal catch space of the spectral stimuli.

Although at first glance the curve representing the locus of the spectral stimuli looks as if it were simply a two-dimensional plot, this is merely a consequence of the fact that the absorption coefficient of the short-wavelength receptor substance is quite small compared to the others. It is a general result that the short-wavelength light contributes less per incident quanta to the overall luminous experience than does the medium-wavelength or the longer-wavelength sensitive lights.

Each point on the spectral locus on Cornsweet's chromaticity diagram (Fig. 6-11) is plotted by determining the relative absorption of each spectral wavelength by the three photopigments. Three coefficients of absorption are thus defined. It is then assumed that 1000 quanta/sec of any particular wavelength compose the incident signal. To specify the three coordinates, one need only multiply each of the three determined coefficients by 1000 to specify the number of quanta absorbed by each of the three chromatic color pigments for any spectral

[13]An exceedingly interesting reformulation of Grassman's laws of chromatic mixing has been proposed by Krantz (1972). Krantz takes these verbal statements and proposes logical equivalents in a way that allows him to specify a formal "Grassman structure" that more precisely describes this set of phenomena than do the verbal laws.

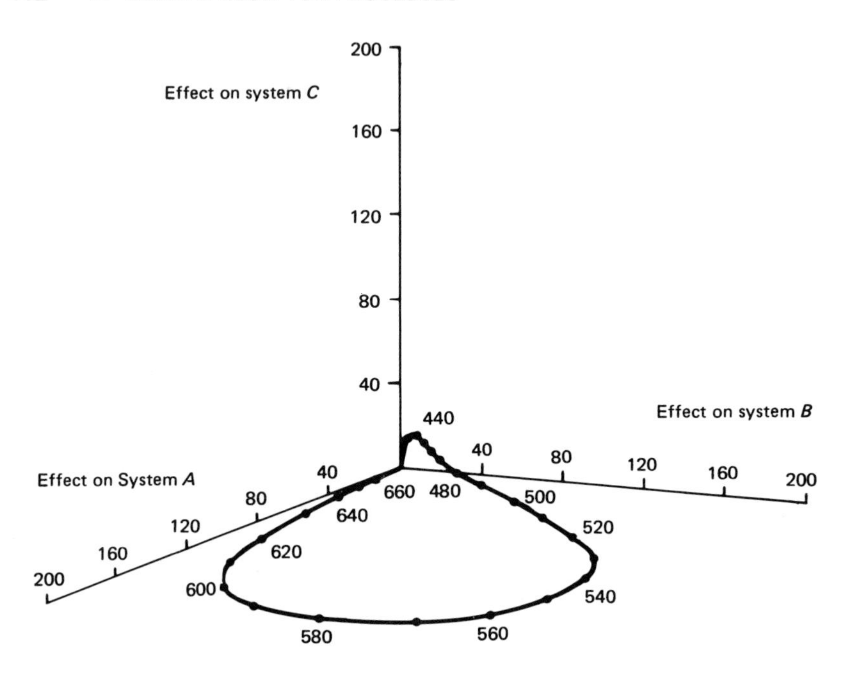

FIG. 6.11. An alternative means of plotting the chromaticity diagram in a three-dimensional space. The three coordinates indicate the proportion of 1000 quanta, which are absorbed by the three photochemicals, respectively. Though the curve appears to be primarily in the A-B (red-green) plane, it is truly three-dimensional. The distortion is due to the low level of absorbance of the blue (C) system. (From Uttal, 1973, redrawn from Cornsweet, 1970.)

stimulus wavelength. In Cornsweet's words, this is the "effect on system A, B, or C" of any given wavelength and the locus of all of these points constitutes the coordinates of the entire visual spectrum.

The locus of the spectral stimuli represents the same information as the locus of spectral colors on the CIE chromaticity diagram; each must be translatable into the others. Many of the other aspects of chromatic stimulus mixture can also be developed in Cornsweet's plot in a similar manner.

3. Increment Thresholds and the π Mechanisms

It would be nice if the data of trichromatic color addition allowed us to say something about the individual absorption spectra of cones, but as I have noted, the color-addition data obtained in psychophysical experiments are highly equivocal; the fact is that almost any wavelength simultaneously activates all three of the cone systems to at least a certain degree. The three types of cones have absorption spectra that extend across most of the entire visual spectrum and thus there is a virtually infinite number of ways in which $a + b + c$ can be made equal to 1. The problem is to separate each of the three individual cone responses from the aggregate response represented by the photopic luminosity curve. One way in which this might, in principle, be accomplished is to preadapt the eye with a stimulus that would selectively fatigue two of the cone mechanisms so that any residual response would reflect the remaining unadapted cone response in an enhanced manner relative to the adapted pair.

In practice, however, this selective preadaptation cannot be fully accomplished. The curves overlap so much that any wavelength effective on one or two of the cone systems would also necessarily activate the third, though to a lesser degree. It is only possible to bias or weight the responses of the triple system so that one cone system is somewhat more sensitive than the other two, such that the composite result is more a reflection of the activity of that one cone absorption system than it would be in the normal unadapted system.

If, however, threshold measures are taken following adaptation, and the thresholds of two of the cone systems have been elevated more than the third one, the residual response may mainly reflect the response of the third system if stimulus levels are kept low. The resulting function would be very much like the two-limbed dark-adaptation function shown in Fig. 6-22 but hopefully would exhibit several discontinuities comparable to the rod–cone break as the stimulus intensity was increased; the multiple limbs of the function so defined would be, in principle, equivalent to the envelope of the sensitivity curves of the several receptor systems in the retina.

Such a procedure has been developed by Stiles (1939, 1949, 1959) and has proved to be a powerful tool in analyzing human color vision over the years. Stiles' technique involved the presentation of a small test spot of one wavelength on an adapting background of another. The subject's task was to detect the slight additional light on the background. For this reason the phenomenon measured has been referred to as the increment threshold rather than the absolute threshold.

With this preadaptation technique, Stiles was actually able to demonstrate, as predicted, a multiple-segment curve. He interpreted the multiple segments in this function to be the result of differences in the absorption spectra of the three cone photochemicals. From these multisegment curves Stiles was able to calculate an additional set of curves that, he believed, are closely related to the actual spectral sensitivities of the three photoreceptors.

Let us consider Stiles' technique and findings in somewhat greater detail because of the very special role they played as putative psychophysical indicants of receptor photoabsorption characteristics and in the history of this problem. In his experiments, the background stimulus consisted of a continuous 10 deg wide background-adapting field of one wavelength, and the incremental test stimulus consisted of a briefly illuminated 1 deg wide test flash of another wavelength. The amount of energy of a just-perceptible test stimulus is then simply measured as a function of the intensity of the background. This is usually done for many combinations of the test and background wavelengths to evoke the response functions of the several different receptors.

As noted, the theory behind this procedure is that the background illumination acts selectively to adapt the three photoreceptors. Thus, a red adapting light will tend mainly to diminish the sensitivity (i.e., raise the threshold) of the long- and medium-wavelength receptors but should leave the short-wavelength-sensitive cone relatively unchanged because it is much less responsive to longer wavelengths than the other two. The overall threshold response of the whole system is obviously a function of the pooled influences of the three receptor types, and this selective adaptation will have the effect of enhancing the relative contribution of the short-wavelength receptors in comparison to the long and medium ones. The overall response will be biased more in the direction of the unadapted short-wavelength receptor than it was when none of the three was light-adapted. Thus, just as workers once obtained a break in the adaptation curve by using different levels of white light or different durations of dark-adaptation to bias the response of that function selectively, Stiles used chromatic adaptation to obtain the sort of functions shown in Fig. 6-12. In this particular case, a relatively short-wavelength test light (476 nm) was superimposed on a medium-wavelength adapting light (578 nm). The curve shows distinct response

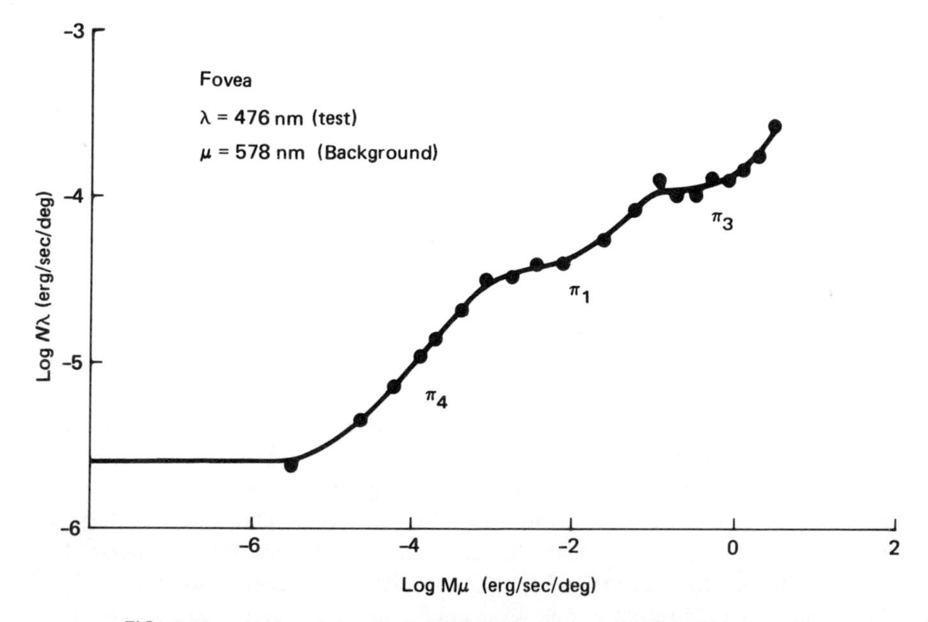

FIG. 6.12. A plot of the threshold of the test stimulus as a function of the background illumination level. The curve obtained in this experiment is a multi-faceted one, in which each segment reflects some aspect of multiple receptor mechanisms. See text for details. (From Uttal, 1973, redrawn from Stiles, 1959.)

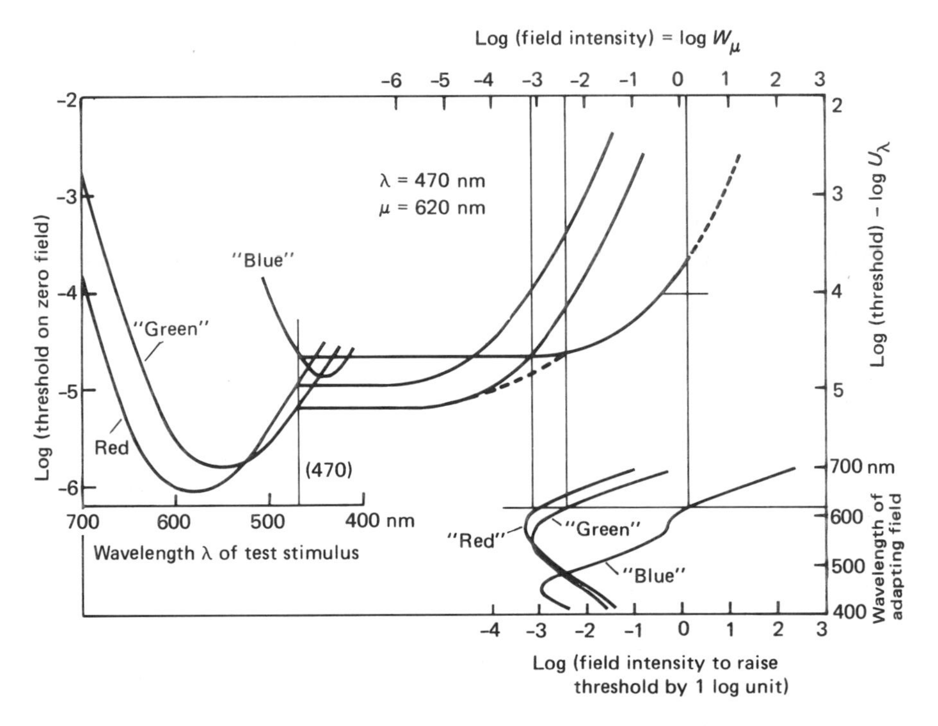

FIG. 6.13. A graphical means of showing how the individual photoreceptor spectral absorption curves are derived from the increment threshold data shown in Fig. 6.12 (From Uttal, 1973, redrawn from Stiles, 1959, after Stiles 1949.)

segments, which Stiles believed were reflections of the activity of several receptor mechanisms. He referred to these mechanisms by the codes π_1, π_2, π_3, π_4 and π_5. The π_1, π_2, and π_3 mechanisms reflected in the results of these and other related experiments were all thought by Stiles to be equivalent to the action of the short-wavelength-sensitive cone. Stiles originally attributed the π_4 mechanism mainly to the action of a medium-wavelength-sensitive cone and π_5 mainly to the action of a long-wavelength-sensitive cone.

The critical next step is to go from the ''adaptation'' curves, of which Fig. 6-12 is one example, to the individual spectral sensitivity curves of the photoreceptors. Unfortunately, this involves a number of mathematical considerations and some intervening assumptions. The full details of Stiles' derivation are beyond the scope of our present discussion,[14] but fortunately he has summed them up graphically in Fig. 6-13. Assume that the three curves on the left-hand side of this figure are the three spectral absorption curves for the three photo-

---

[14]The reader interested in a more detailed statement of the method Stiles used in going from the adaptation data to the implied photoreceptor spectral absorption curve is referred to in Enoch's (1972) article in Volume VII/4 of the *Handbook of Sensory Physiology*.

receptors. Assume also that there is another spectral function involved, which is displayed by the three curves in the lower right-hand corner. This second set of three curves represents the change in the background field intensity that has to be made to raise the threshold for a test flash by one log unit as a function of wavelength for each of these three receptor systems. These two spectral functions will then be related by the third set of "linking" functions in the right-hand quadrant of the figure. Due to the fact that this is a mixed system involving three different photoreceptor sensitivities, the threshold in the increment experiment will be determined by the lower value of any of these three linking functions. The bottommost envelope indicated by the combined dotted and solid line is the current example. This combined envelope is exactly the sort of curve that was obtained and displayed in Fig. 6-12.

By processing a large set of such adaptation threshold curves (typified by the dotted curve of the present case) and making certain assumptions to which I have already alluded, Stiles attempted to reason backward to the shape of the three photoreceptor curves. His conclusions are tabulated in Table 6-3, which shows his view of the general characteristics of the spectral response of the three cone types as well as the rod as computed from increment threshold data.

TABLE 6.3
The Relationship Between Stiles' "π" Components of the Adaptation Curve and the Four Photoreceptor Mechanisms.*

Mechanism	Symbol	Remarks	Wavelength of Maximal Sensitivity (nm)
Rod	π_0	Absent at the fovea	503
"Blue" cone . . .	π_1	at approx. 2.6 log units	440
	π_2	at approx. 1 log unit	? (Between 440 and 480 mμ)
	π_3	at approx. 4.0 log units	440
"Green" cone . .	π_4		540
"Red" cone . . .	π_5		575 (very flat max.)

*This table also indicates the peak sensitivities of the spectral absorptions of the four photoreceptors in the human eye.

From Uttal, 1973, as adapted from Stiles, 1959.

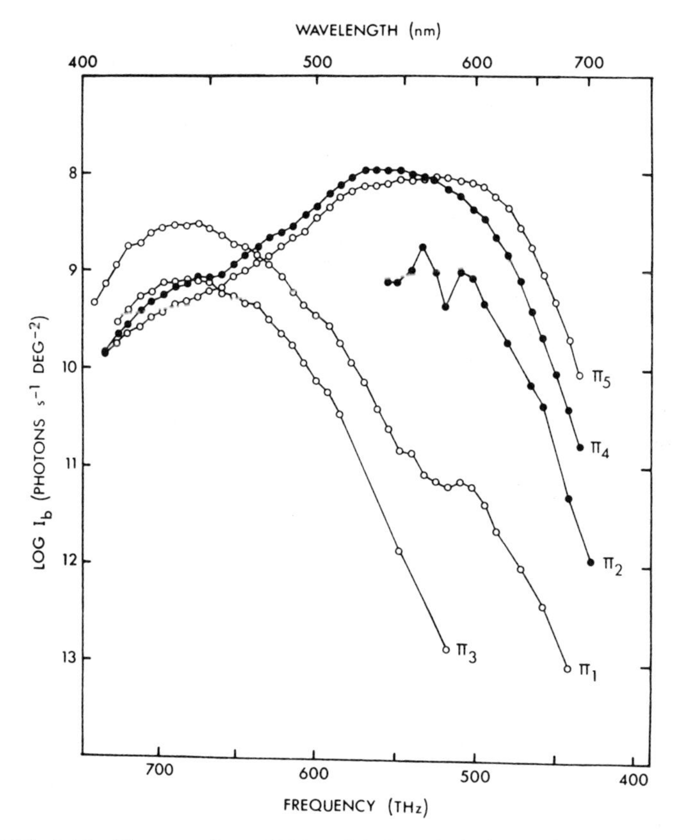

FIG. 6.14. The spectral sensitivities of the hypothetical π mechanisms. (From Rodieck, © 1973, with the permission of W. H. Freeman and Co.)

Whereas it is most important to note that Stiles' π functions are not currently considered to be completely identical to the individual cone absorption curves, it is on the basis of these π functions that he was able to derive one of the few plausible sets of cone spectral sensitivities that is based purely on psychophysical data. His three spectral sensitivity curves for the cones have peaks at 440, 540, and 575 nm. These values should be compared with the biological data presented earlier in this chapter in Table 6-2. Figure 6-14 is a composite of the spectral sensitivities curves of the π mechanisms produced by further analyses of the increment threshold data (Stiles, 1959; Wyszecki & Stiles, 1967).

A newer hypothesis (for example, Estevez and Cavonius, 1977) is that π_2 is actually a composite function resulting from interactions of the long- and short-wavelength-sensitive receptors; whereas π_1 and π_2 are both possible candidates to be expressions of the short wavelength sensitive receptor alone. It is therefore very important to reiterate that most recent investigators do not believe that any of the π mechanisms can be uniquely identified with the triplet of cone pigments. Rather, all of the π mechanisms are now thought probably to be composites of the three receptor absorption functions as mediated by interactive processes. In this regard, Pugh and Mollon (1979) have now suggested that the π functions do not reflect receptor photochemical properties alone but also adaptive processes occurring higher in the visual pathway and involving both feedforward and feedback interactions from all types of cones.

It is now agreed by most workers in this field that it takes an unacceptably large number of assumptions to go unequivocally backwards from the π functions to the pigment spectral absorption, as was done by Stiles in preparing Fig. 6-13. We must also not forget that the Stiles data are entirely psychophysical and that in principle no analysis, so based, can ever be uniquely descriptive of a triad of photochemical absorbances.

It should not be surprising that the psychophysically determined π mechanisms do not replicate the objectively obtained photoreceptor absorption spectra very well. Even at the level of the ganglion cell, the measured spectral sensitivities (Spekreijse, Wagner, & Wolbarsht, 1972) do not agree with those measured electrophysiologically (Tomita, Kaneko, Murakami, & Pautler, 1967) or with microspectrophotometry (W. Marks, 1965) at the receptor level, even in the same type of animal.

Both the ganglion cell records and the psychophysical responses, therefore, do not indicate the true spectral properties of the receptors. These false estimates have been called *pseudopigments* by Sirovich and Abramov (1977), who have provided what they propose to be a means of resolving the spatial properties of the pseudopigments into the properties of the true receptor photopigments. I shall not try to present their procedures here but note only in passing that to the degree they work, they would be a most important contribution indeed.

It would have been an absolute theoretical joy if we could also have gone directly from Stiles' π mechanisms to predict the data obtained in color-addition experiments. But this too is an extremely difficult thing to do. Some recent attempts to make this predictive transition, however, have shown considerable progress (Estevez & Cavonius, 1977), especially when the observer's own measured π mechanism curves are used to predict his own color-addition data rather than pooled data from a number of subjects.

In conclusion, I should note that if in fact it is correct that the π phenomena are the result of neural interactions among the outputs of the three-cone system, it would be appropriate to attribute these phenomena in part, at least, to Level 2 processes.

4. Shifts in the Chromatic Response as a Function of Variations in Dominant Wavelength, Purity, and Luminance

Because stimulus wavelength information is first encoded in terms of the relative response levels of the three cone systems, each with its own spectral properties, any shift in the stimulus that leads to a change in the relative amount of activity in each system would be expected to produce a corresponding change in the perceived color. Furthermore, the spectral sensitivities of the three systems are not identical, and it is likely that almost any kind of a shift in the nature of the stimulus will lead to a shift in the relative response as well as the absolute response. To understand the meaning of these statements fully it is necessary to remind ourselves of the definitions of the basic perceptual dimensions along which chromatic stimuli can vary. The family of discriminable colors can be well-mapped as a three-dimensional spindle-shaped solid such as that shown in Fig. 6-15. This spindle represents a phenomenal space. Its dimensions are the chromatic dimensions of the perceptual response. It is not a physical or stimulus space; for any point on it can be achieved by a wide variety of metameric

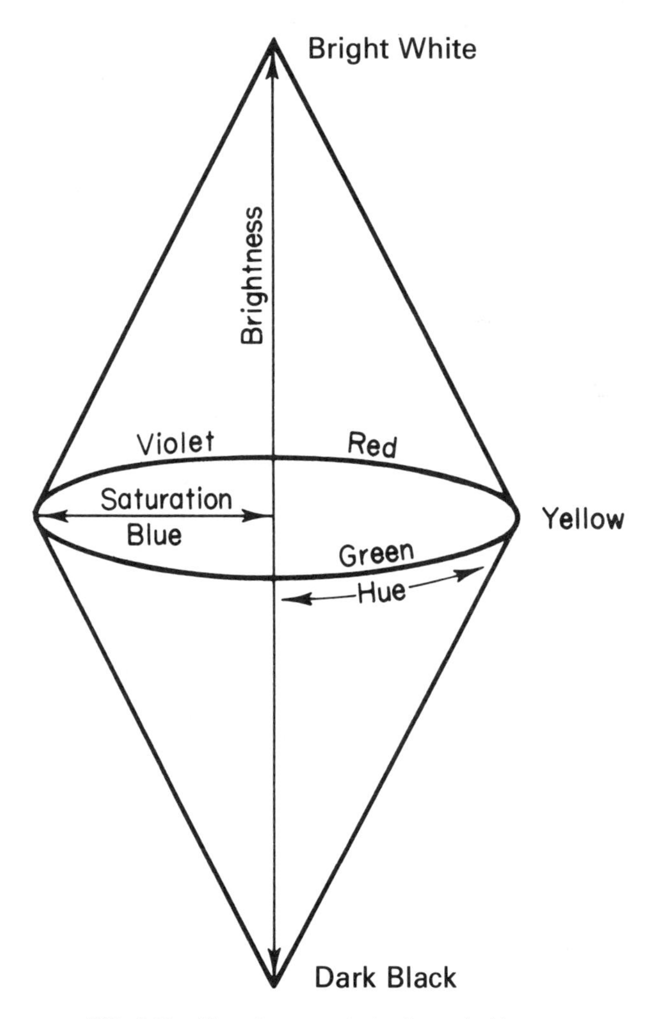

FIG. 6.15. The color space depicted as a double cone.

matches; and the color space is by no means as regular as is suggested in this drawing.

The first chromatic response dimension—hue—is depicted on this spindle as a set of concentric rings at various radia from the vertical axis. Each corresponding position on each ring represents the hue of a particular chromatic stimulus. Hue is best defined as the dimension of experience denoted by our use of color names. Like all other qualitative dimensions, it is extremely difficult to define precisely what is meant by hue, but we can say that as we vary the wavelength of a monochromatic light source, the correlated experiences pass through a continuum of different perceptual values that vary from one hue to another. The experiences associated with the words *red, green, blue,* and *yellow* are sample hues, and the stimulus dimension most closely related to those perceptual responses is the dominant wavelength of the stimulus light.

The second chromatic response dimension—saturation—is represented not by the positions in a circle at a constant radius, as is hue, but by position along a radius of the spindle. Different positions along a single radius represent different saturation values for a particular hue. Colors that are very close to the experiences produced by the spectral colors are said to be highly saturated and are found near the periphery of the spindle. A completely desaturated light, on the other hand, is one that appears white and is represented by a point near the central axis. For example, red is a highly saturated color; pink is less saturated; and white is a totally desaturated color. These colors are represented by points that are progressively closer to the axis, but all are aligned on a single radius. A useful nontechnical term connoting what is meant by desaturation is *paleness.* The major stimulus variable in determining the saturation of a chromatic stimulus is the degree to which the spectrum contains many wavelengths other than the dominant one. This stimulus dimension corresponding most closely to saturation is, therefore, referred to as purity.

I have previously discussed how both hue and saturation are represented on the CIE chromaticity diagram earlier in this chapter. Indeed, any of the chromaticity diagrams may be considered to be cross sections through the spindle at particular luminance levels. The shape of the CIE chromaticity diagram, for example, is a more precise statement of the actual shape in color space of a cross-section near the point at which the two cones making up the spindle join. The color spindle, however, is better able to illustrate the third dimension of the chromatic response in a way that cannot be made explicit in a chromaticity diagram. This third dimension, running vertically along the long axis of the spindle, represents the brightness produced by the stimulus. Brightness varies from a very dark region at the bottom point of the spindle where all stimuli of low luminance produce an equally dark blackness, to the top peak where all stimuli of high luminance are an equally bright white. It is for these two reasons—the contractions of all dim stimuli to black and the contractions of all bright stimuli to white, regardless of dominant wavelength or purity—that the color space represented by this three-dimensional artifice is approximately spindle-shaped. The stimulus dimension most closely corresponding to brightness is stimulus intensity or luminance.

Thus, to a first approximation, hue is a function of the dominant wavelength of the stimulating light; saturation is a function of the degree of mixture (impurity) of other wavelengths into the dominant wavelength; and brightness is a function of the luminance of the stimulus. However there are many other secondary factors that determine the hue, saturation, and brightness of a stimulus; it is these second-order effects that constitute the main topic of this section.

The secondary influences on color perception that I am about to consider are not those higher-level (Level 4) processes such as contrast, which will be taken up in Chapter 11, but those that reflect the effects of the three most elementary stimulus factors—wavelength, purity, and luminance themselves—on the two dimensions of chromatic experience other than the one upon which they exert their main influence. The general implication of the material I am about to discuss is that all three dimensions of chromatic experience are to some extent influenced by all three stimulus dimensions. In addition to the primary effects of dominant wavelength, purity, and luminance on hue, saturation, and brightness, respectively, each stimulus dimension also secondarily affects the other two response dimensions. Table 6-4 summarizes this statement. In this table I have indicated the major effect with an asterisk. The secondary effects are indicated by either the classical name of the effect (where it has been so dignified) or simply a description of the phenomenon.

a. The Effects of Dominant Wavelength. The main effect of the dominant stimulus wavelength, as I have indicated, is to vary the hue of the stimulus. Hue

TABLE 6.4
Primary and Secondary Interactions Between Stimulus Dimensions and Perceptual Dimensions in Vision

Stimulus Dimension / ψ *Response Dimension*	*Dominant Wavelength*	*Purity*	*Luminance*
Hue	* Hue Discrimination	Aubert Effect	Bezold-Brücke Phenomenon
Saturation	Priest-Brickwedde Effect	* Saturation Discrimination	Helmholtz Effect
Brightness	Luminosity Curves	Helmholtz-Kohlrausch Effect	* Brightness Discrimination

*Primary effect.

can be measured in two principal ways. One is to use a color-naming type of experiment, asking the subject to categorize the chromatic experiences on the basis of the names already familiar to him. This task, which involves considerably higher levels of processing, is hardly satisfactory to measure the fine color discrimination exhibited by the visual system. As was shown in Fig. 3-2, data consisting of simple probabilities of the use of the few available color names are usually obtained. Unfortunately our vocabulary of color names is nowhere near adequate to indicate the very large number of colors that we can actually discriminate. Therefore the alternative procedure, a color discrimination experiment in which the subject's task is to distinguish between two similar colors, is preferable to color-naming techniques in evaluating the discriminative limits of hue perception. Hue discrimination has been a classic experimental paradigm for decades, and, therefore, the well-agreed-upon data can be summed up in Fig. 6-16. It is interesting to note that the best sensitivities measured in these experiments are of the order of only 1 or 2 nm.

The dominant wavelength of the stimulus thus affects the perceived hue with a high degree of precision; very small changes produce perceptually distinguishable responses. But it is also true that the dominant wavelength affects other

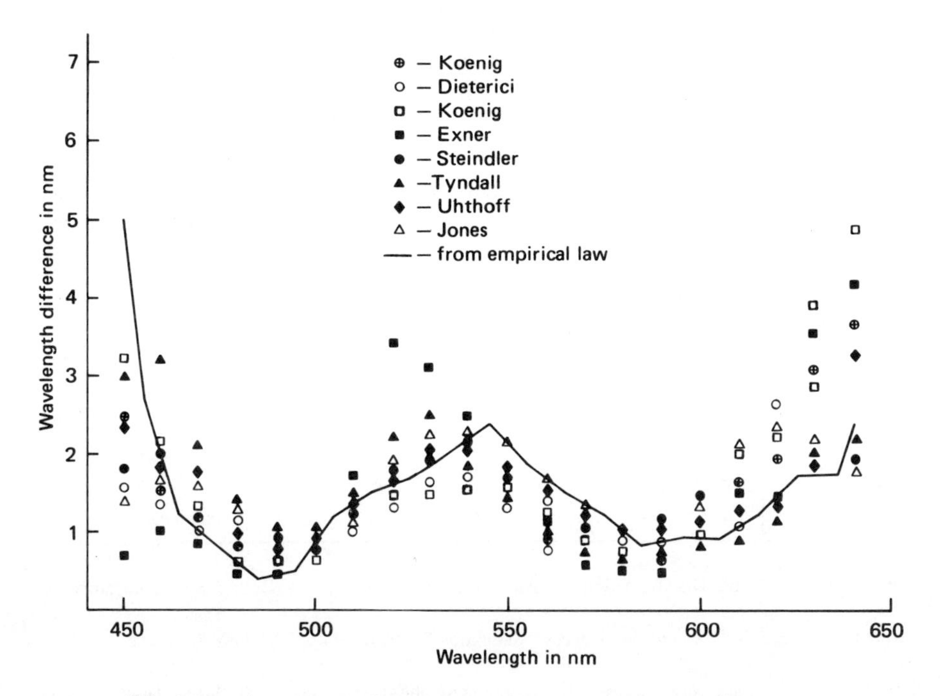

FIG. 6.16. A summary of several experiments measuring the differential threshold for changes in stimulus wavelength as a function of wavelength. (From Uttal, 1973, redrawn from Judd, 1932.)

chromatic properties as well; both the saturation and brightness of a test spot also vary as a function of the dominant wavelength. Furthermore, even pure spectral colors vary in their intrinsic saturation as a function of the stimulus wavelength. Very-long-wavelength reds and very-short-wavelength blues appear to be more highly saturated than do the middle-wavelength yellows. This is probably largely due to the fact that equivalently energetic medium wavelengths produce higher levels of activity in all three receptor systems than do the long and short wavelengths, thus simulating the effects of a broader (or more impure) spectral mixture. More quantitatively, it is possible to measure the minimum detectable chromatic impurity (i.e., the just-noticeable desaturation), and these measurements show the same thing—a greater propensity toward desaturation at the middle wavelengths, even when luminances are kept constant and the stimuli at all tested wavelengths are equally monochromatic.

The classic study of the intrinsic saturation of spectral colors is to be found in the work of Priest and Brickwedde (1938). Figure 6-17 shows their results. The chromatic purity (CP) of a mixture of white and spectral colors (with luminances equal to W and SC, respectively) was defined in their experiments as

$$CP = \frac{SC}{W + SC} \tag{6-10}$$

Thus, the criterion for plotting their findings was the amount of the spectral color that had to be added to white light to give a just-noticeable difference from the totally desaturated white light. Low numbers on the vertical axis of this curve therefore indicate high intrinsic saturation (i.e., a strong ability to produce saturated color experiences by adding only a modest amount of monochromatic light to a white light), and high values indicate relatively low intrinsic saturation. (A substantial amount of the monochromatic light must be added to white to produce a chromatic effect.) Overall, a surprisingly small amount of monochromatic light was required to produce a shift in saturation away from white in Priest and Brickwedde's experiment. The luminance of the monochromatic light had only to be about 0.1% of the luminance of a moderately bright white light to produce a detectable color in the very-long and very-short-wavelength ends of the spectrum.

The effects of dominant wavelength on brightness are largely hidden, but they also are profound. The reason that they are hidden is that most psychophysical experiments use photometric rather than radiometric measures of the stimulus intensity. Thus though an equal amount of energy of different-wavelength light will produce major differences in the apparent brightness, this factor has been already accounted for when the radiometric measures were transformed by cross-multiplication with the scotopic or photopic luminosity curves. Though the threshold responses represented by these luminosity functions are not directly extrapolatable to suprathreshold values, they do give an approximate picture of the differential effectiveness of various wavelength stimuli in producing bright-

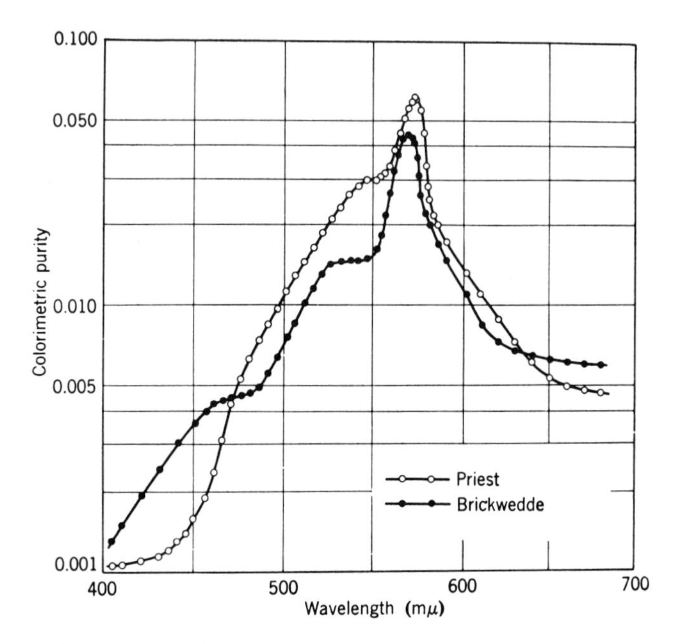

FIG. 6.17. The effect of wavelength on the intrinsic resistance to desaturation. (From Graham, © 1965b, with the permission of John Wiley & Sons, Inc.)

ness differences. Figure 6-18 shows the relation between brightness and wavelength for various levels of adaptation. The dependent variable in this case is radiometric energy, it should be noted. The shape of the uppermost curve closely approximates the photopic threshold curve, and the shape of the lower one closely approximates that of the scotopic function. The others are super-threshold mesopic luminosity curves as described earlier.

A considerable amount of research also indicates that when the various wavelengths are matched for threshold luminance, their suprathreshold brightness functions (i.e., the relations between brightness and stimulus intensities) are very much alike. Magnitude estimation experiments of the growth of brightness with proportional increases in luminance indicate that shape of the function seems not to be affected in any significant way by the wavelength of the stimulating light. A number of psychophysical studies of this problem, including that of Ekman, Eisler, and Kunnapas (1960), indicated that a common exponent for the best-fitting Steven's power law is obtained regardless of the wavelengths utilized. Figure 6-19, summarizing the data obtained by B. Wilson (1964), displays the same finding. The parallel curves indicating the brightness function for a set of five wavelengths all reflect an exponent of approximately 0.5.

b. The Effects of Purity. Now let us consider the effect of stimulus purity on the three chromatic response dimensions. The hue of a visual stimulus is well

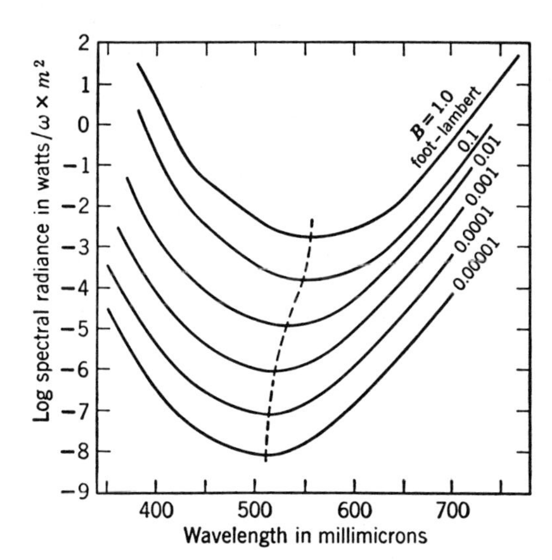

FIG. 6.18. The effect of wavelength on brightness. (From Judd, © 1951, with the permission of John Wiley & Sons, Inc.)

known to change with the purity of the stimulus. This phenomenon is known, in general, as the Aubert effect, but in special cases it may have other names. For example, the increase in redness when white is added to a blue light is sometimes referred to as the Abney Effect.

The main effect of spectral purity, however, as I have indicated previously is on the perceived saturation. Saturation discrimination experiments can be carried out in essentially the same way as are hue discrimination experiments. Subjects may be asked to discriminate between two stimuli having a slightly different proportion of the monochromatic spectral component at various wavelengths, or to discriminate between a white and a white mixed with a small amount of some

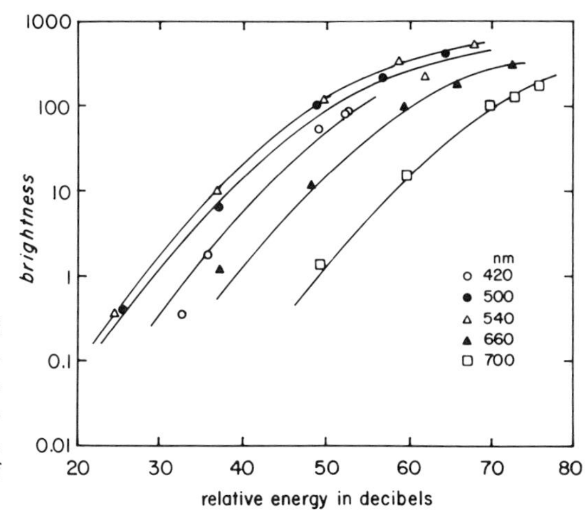

FIG. 6.19. The dynamic of monochromatic lights for the indicated wavelengths. This function relates stimulus intensity to suprathreshold brightness. (From Marks, © 1974, with the permission of Academic Press, Inc.)

monochromatic wavelength. The procedures used in such a study of the effects of purity are operationally very similar to those used in the Priest and Brickwedde study that measured the effect of wavelength on perceived saturation. Although it would be cumbersome to design an experiment that would scan all possible combinations of mixed wavelengths, data have been obtained in the case where a single wavelength was mixed with white. Martin, Warburton, and Morgan (1933), among others, carried out such an experiment and obtained some of the data summarized in Fig. 6-20.

The purity of a mixed-wavelength stimulus can also affect its apparent brightness. In general, the purer the spectrum of a stimulus the more likely it is to produce a brighter perceptual experience even when the luminance of the component wavelengths in a pure and impure stimulus have individually been

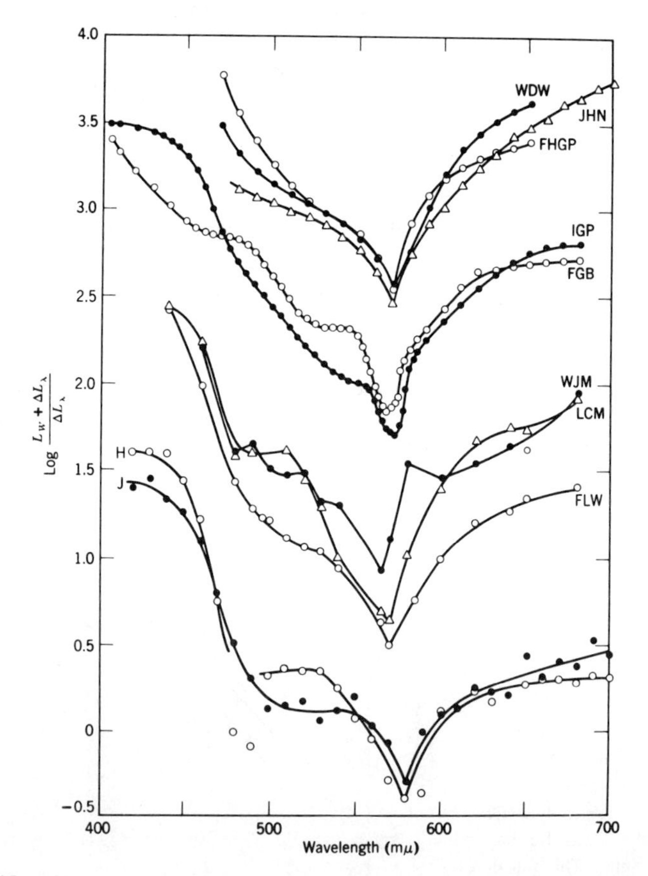

FIG. 6.20. The resistance to desaturation plotted as a function of wavelength. The results of several experiments are plotted together to show the general data. A theoretical curve is also plotted at the bottom. (From Graham, © 1965b, with the permission of John Wiley & Sons, Inc.)

equated. This deviation from a strict luminance addition is known as the Helmholtz–Kolrausch effect. Final interpretation of such data is, however, very much complicated by the measurement procedures that have to be used to carry out this comparison. It is not possible, of course, to measure directly the luminance of a pure spectral color and the equivalent mixture of wavelengths necessary to carry out this experiment. That would beg the question being experimentally asked. Instead one has to depend upon the laws of chromatic luminance addition (see Grassman's laws on pg. 410) to set up what *should* be two equivalent stimuli. Thus, on reflection, it becomes clear that an experiment seeking to relate stimulus purity and apparent brightness is, in fact, a further test of Grassman's fourth law.

Grassman's law of brightness additivity, or as it is known in its heterochromatic form, Abney's Law (1913), has been severely challenged in recent years, most notably by Sherman Guth and his co-workers (e.g., Guth, 1967; Guth, Donley, & Marrocco, 1969). To the extent that Abney's law does not hold when luminances are added, then there is an effect of stimulus purity on perceived brightness. Such a failure of Abney's law seems to be exactly the empirical fact. Guth, Donley and Marrocco (1969) have further shown that if one adds together two lights of the same luminance and the same wavelength, the sum generally appears to be brighter than the sum of two lights of the same luminance but different wavelengths. This finding is both a violation of Grassman's (or Abney's) law and a precise quantitative statement of the fact that the purity of a stimulus does influence perceived brightness.

c. The Effects of Luminance. The third stimulus dimension to be considered in terms of its effect on the subjective dimensions of hue, saturation, and brightness is luminance or stimulus intensity. The main effect of luminance is on brightness, of course. In general, however, we also observe that luminance has secondary effects on the hue and saturation of a chromatic experience. The major effect of luminance on hue is referred to as the Bezold–Brücke phenomenon—the change in the hue as a function of the luminance of the stimulus. As the light dims, mixed stimuli look greener and bluer and less yellow and red than they did in brighter light.

The major, and now classic, studies of the Bezold–Brücke effect were carried out by Purdy (1929, 1937). Purdy measured the phenomenon in the following way: He simply picked a given wavelength, varied its luminance, and measured the resulting hue by matching the manipulated stimulus on one side of a bipartite field with the other side on which was projected a monochromatic light of constant intensity. The results of his experiment are shown in Fig. 6-21. There is no single pattern in these findings. The response to some wavelengths shifted so that shorter wavelengths were required to match the resulting color at high luminances, but at lower luminances longer wavelengths were required for a match of the same wavelength. Some spectral colors, on the other hand, did not

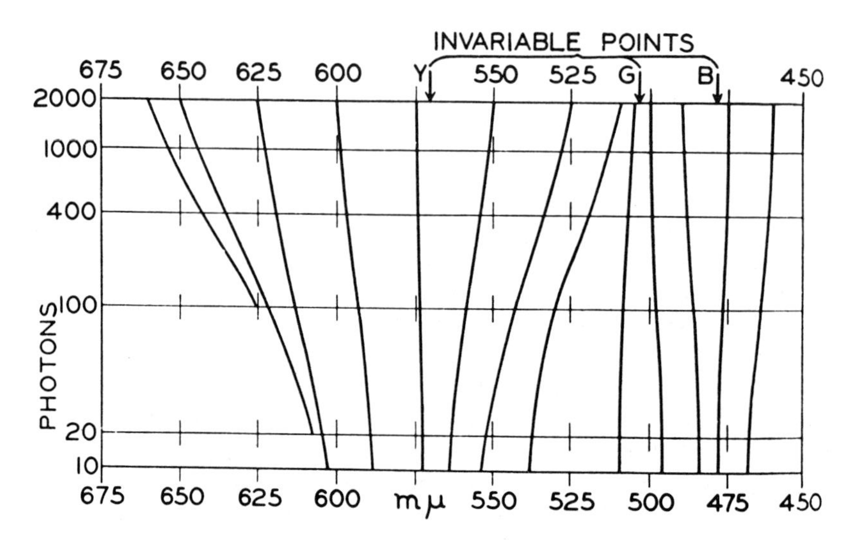

FIG. 6.21. These curves show the wavelength that is required to maintain a constant hue as the intensity of the stimulating light is increased. Note the three neutral points. (From Purdy, © 1937.)

change their hue to any measurable amount as a function of stimulus luminance. Such stimulus wavelengths have been referred to as the invariant points on the spectrum and have been used as arguments (for example, Hurvich & Jameson, 1955) that the Bezold–Brücke and Purdy phenomena may be due to opponent-coding mechanisms deeper in the retina rather than the receptor processes to which I have attributed them here. Cicerone, Krantz, and Larimer (1975) and Larimer, Krantz, and Cicerone (1975) have pursued this idea and have developed an opponent (and thus Level 2) mathematical model of these phenomena.

There is also, of course, a shift in the portion of the spectrum to which the eye is most sensitive as the intensity of the stimulus changes (as evidenced by the dashed line in Fig. 6-18). At low light intensities and good dark adaptation the rods determine the scotopic threshold, and peak sensitivity occurs at about 507 nm. In bright light the cones determine the threshold, and the photopic curve peaks at about 560 or 570 nm. This shift in sensitivity with luminance level is called the Purkinje phenomenon. Color mixture data also change substantially as a function of luminance of the stimulus, both in the fovea and in the extrafoveal regions (Gilbert, 1950; Stiles, 1955; Richards & Luria, 1964). Reds turn into yellows at high luminances, for example, and violets lose their red tinge.

The spindle shape of the color solid depicted in Fig. 6-15 also reflects another secondary influence of luminance—its powerful effect on saturation. As I noted earlier, all very dim stimuli fade into black achromatic responses at very low stimulus intensities, and all bright ones fade into a total whitish desaturation at very high luminances. It is only in the intermediate region that the saturation dimension has any appreciable extent.

Nevertheless, the strongest effect of stimulus luminance, of course, is exerted directly on brightness—the perceptual dimension with which it is most directly correlated. The more intense the illumination, the brighter will be the response and the larger the size of the just-detectable luminance difference. I discuss this general relationship later when I consider the receptor (Level 1) influences on suprathreshold functions. The shape of these suprathreshold functions appears to be controlled less by the spectral absorption of the receptors than by the postabsorptive processes within the receptors that lead to the development of the receptor potential.

In sum, in this section I have concentrated on the perceptual impact of the characteristics of the absorption curves of three cone photochemicals. The first analysis of the spectral properties of the stimulus is carried out as a direct result of the varying spectral absorption curves of these three substances. The coded neural information pattern generated by this process is thus represented in terms of the relative amount of activity in the signals within the three cone systems. This differential or relational (between channels) representation is essential; otherwise the nervous system would have no means to discriminate, for example, between a bright red light and a dim yellow light, both of which might produce the same response in an isolated receptor system. The various shifts (particularly the secondary influences) in hue, saturation, and brightness that occur as a result of changes in the wavelength, purity, or luminance, I believe, also reflect this shift in the balance of the transmitted neural signals elicited by the receptor absorption characteristics.

However, there is one somewhat disconcerting caveat that should be mentioned at this point. In the preceding discussion I have more or less concentrated on the classic theory that the cones, and the cones alone, are responsible for color vision. However in recent years a number of investigators have observed experimental situations in which it seems that the rods may also be contributing to color vision. That they should do so is not out of the question from a theoretical point of view. As we saw in Fig. 6-1, the absorption spectrum of rhodopsin is different from that of the three cone pigments. Therefore if the rods and any one or more of the cone systems were active, there would at least be a possibility that sufficient information was being conveyed to encode stimulus wavelength and to provide the differential interchannel information necessary for chromatic discriminations.

Some of the experiments invoked to demonstrate such rod involvement in color vision have evolved from the Land Retinex theory of color perception (see Chapter 11). Specifically, McCann and Benton (1969), McCann (1972), and McKee, McCann, and Benton (1977) have attempted to show that if a long-wavelength light activating one set of cones, and a short-wavelength light activating only rods, are presented to an observer, the observer ''sees'' colors and makes color discriminations. Because their experimental setup was designed to activate only one cone system and the rod system, the classic trichromatic theory would predict that only a monochromatic scene would be detected. The fact that varied color experiences were produced supports a possible involvement of rods in the color system and thus suggests that the visual system (if not the psychophysical data) may actually be tetrachromatic. Trezona (1974), in further support of this idea, has presented evidence that supports a ''tetrachromatic'' theory of color vision. U. Stabell and B. Stabell (1973) have reviewed the literature pertaining to the problem of alternative models of color perception for those who wish to delve deeper into the topic.

A possible role of the rod as the single short-wavelength receptor had for long been an object of extensive debate in visual science. However, the work of Brown and Wald (1964) and Marks, Dobelle, and McNichol (1964) has made it clear that there are distinct rod and short-wavelength receptor spectral absorption curves, so it is unlikely that the rod is the short-wavelength receptor and that rhodopsin is cyanolabe. The question of the possible contribution of the rod as a fourth channel to color vision, however, certainly remains open.

The discussion in this section has essentially been a classic one. I have concentrated, as intended, on the role played by the relative spectral absorbences of the three photochemicals on the determination of the color experience. However it must not be forgotten that this is only one level of processing that can affect color experiences. Indeed, some researchers (Land, 1977) feel that the trichromatic story is only a highly special subcase of the total color-vision problem and that in more realistic scenes many of the generalities that I have presented here, do not in fact hold. Indeed, Land has demonstrated that there are many instances in which vastly different color names can be applied to exactly the same spectrum of physical energies. Thus the trichromatic addition story (and the deviations from it that I have indicated here) may hold only for small isolated stimuli for which there is no opportunity for the observer to make estimates of the reflectances or lightnesses of the objects or in which the possibility for simultaneous contrast comparisons do not exist. In studying these ideas, therefore, the reader should be especially diligent not to overgeneralize these results for a highly abstract experimental situation (color addition) to more realistic scenes in which wide divergences from simple trichromatic laws may predominate. Chapter 11 considers this matter in greater detail.

D. PERCEPTUAL IMPACT OF PHOTOCHEMICAL AVAILABILITY

Considering the extreme importance I have placed on the absorptive properties of the photochemical in determining so many different aspects of visual perception, it is obvious that if one or more of the retinal photochemicals is absent or depleted for some reason, the availability of the photochemical itself may then very well become a determining factor in many visual phenomena. Nevertheless, many experiments have indicated that the effect of a diminished supply of photochemical becomes measurable only when the amount remaining is very small. Otherwise the general nature of the receptive process is such that the observer can compensate for and adapt to wide ranges of photochemical availability.

Further, there are several different sources of diminished availability of the photochemical that can and do influence visual perception. Deficiencies due to congenital, pathological, nutritional, or adaptational causes may all produce perceptual phenomena. In the following two sections I briefly consider the perceptual consequences of the two of these four sources of lower than normal photochemical supply that are most germane to the present context—congenital and adaptive deficiencies.

1. Congenital Deficiencies in Photochemical Availability

In many instances, due either to hereditary or prenatal environmental influences, individuals are born with abnormal photoreceptor chemistry in the retinae. A complete absence of the retinal photoreceptors and the inevitable blindness that would accompany such a deficit is only rarely reported. By far the most common congenital photochemical anomaly is an absence of or a reduction in the amount of one, two, or three of the normal complement of four photochemicals. The most striking perceptual defect associated with this kind of photochemical deficiency is color blindness, or as it should more properly be designated, an other than normal trichromatic color-addition response. Color blindness is most often a genetically transmitted defect that is more likely to be expressed in the male than in the female phenotype. Most kinds of defective color vision are transmitted by a recessive gene (with the possible exception of rod monochromatism according to Jaeger, 1972). Thus, males (X, Y genetically) more often exhibit the defect because only one of the pairs of genes determining sex need be affected. Females, on the other hand, (X, X genetically) will exhibit this defect only if both X chromosomes are affected, a much less likely occurrence. Only rod monochromatism is found equally often in males and females.

A precise operational definition of color blindness, necessitated by the many different ways in which this anomaly may become manifest, is based on the number of degrees of freedom required by a observer to match all the colors in the chromaticity space. Normal trichromatic vision, as I have indicated, requires the presence of three independently controllable chromatic stimuli in any mixture for the matching of all other stimuli. In short, normal color vision is trivariant.

However, the converse is not true; not all trichromatic vision is normal. Various forms of weak or anomalous trichromatic color vision have been observed that are still trivariant. Observers may be protanomalous (these so called *protans* have a lowered sensitivity to long wavelengths and the peak of their photopic luminosity curves are shifted downward by about 10 nm) or deuteranomalous (these so called *deutans* exhibit a lowered sensitivity to the middle range of wavelengths and the peak of their photopic luminosity curves are shifted upward by anywhere from 10 to 40 nm). In both forms of anomalous trichromatism, the observer still needs three different chromatic stimuli to match all samples of the chromatic visual space, but wide deviations are found from the normal amounts of the three primaries required to match a given chromatic stimulus by an anomalous trichromatic subject. A protanomalous trichromat will tend to use far more than normal amounts of long wavelengths for his matches, for example. A deuteranomalous trichromat will use more middle-wavelength light than normal for his color matches. *Tritans,* tritanomalous trichomats, exhibiting lowered sensitivity to short wavelengths, have been reported, but they are apparently very, very rare.

On the other hand, there also exists a group of observers with deficient color vision such that only two chromatic stimuli are required to match any other stimulus in the chromaticity space. People with such a deficiency are called *dichromats* and are functionally bivariant in their color vision. As was the case with anomalous trichromats, there are several distinguishable types of dichromatism. Observers may exhibit behavior that classifies them as suffering from dichromatic protanopia, deuteranopia, or tritanopia. As is the case with anomalous trichromats, the dichromats (*protonopes, deuteranopes,* and *tritanopes*) exhibit deficiencies in other psychophysical tests such as hue discrimination as well as in color mixing. Hue discrimination in dichromats may be 10 times as insensitive as in normal trichromats (i.e., 10 times the normal wavelength difference is required for a chromatic difference to be reported). This is an important factor in diagnosing the specific biological basis of each condition as well as the nature of the chromaticity confusion. On the other hand, the specific nature of the changes in the luminosity curves of dichromats has been a matter of considerable debate over the years. Protanopes, like protans, also seem generally to exhibit a diminished sensitivity at the red end of the spectrum; deuteranopes exhibit a weakness corresponding to the deutan deficiency in the green region; and tritanopes, like tritans, seem to have a diminution in the sensitivity of their luminosity curves at the blue end of the spectrum.

A somewhat different scheme of classifying dichromats based upon an opponent-color model (see Chapter 8) is often proposed in which both protanopes and deuteranopes are characterized by weak red–green discrimination, but with somewhat different characteristics. A second condition, weak yellow–blue discrimination, is also dichotomized into two classes—tritanopia and tetranopia—by such workers as Hurvich (1972).

Though these two classification systems differ, the greater familiarity of the trichromatic schema should not be misunderstood to mean that it is necessarily the correct one. Both models are generally viable. One, the trichromatic, attributes the deficiency mainly to photoreceptor function, as I have here, but the other, the opponent model, is much more likely to stress the abnormal functions of neural mechanisms located deeper in the retina.

Sufferers from the most extreme form of color blindness, monochromats, are for all practical purposes, incapable of discriminating among visual stimulus on any basis other than brightness differences—all wavelength stimuli produce the same phenomenal quality. Thus any stimulus can be used to match all other stimuli anywhere in the chromaticity space simply by varying its luminance. Two types of monochromat can be distinguished on the basis of their luminosity curves. One displays a light-adapted luminosity curve that is indistinguishable from the scotopic luminosity curve. The other type displays a light-adapted luminosity curve that is different from both the normal scotopic and the normal photopic luminosity curves. It has been suggested that the first type of luminosity curve is produced by a retina with no functional cones at all, whereas the second type is produced by a retina with only one of the three normal types of cones present. For this reason the term *rod-monochromat* has been used as a descriptor of the former type, and the term *cone-monochromat* as a descriptor of the second type. For purposes of color mixture, both types behave as if a single stimulus wavelength could match any other wavelength in color-mixing experiments, even though theoretically a person with only one cone might be able to discriminate colors if the rods were also present.

Both kinds of monochromats also typically show many other kinds of visual difficulties related to their abnormal receptor complement. Rod-monochromats are characterized by a syndrome known as congenital achromatopsia, which typically includes some degree of photophobia (i.e., bright light is very painful to them, even though their vision in dim light may be virtually normal). These monochromats may also suffer from poor visual acuity due to an absence of the usual density and configuration of foveal cones. Cone-monochromats, on the other hand, have relatively good acuity, can see well in bright lights but are very deficient in dim light, and typically exhibit high absolute thresholds in the few cases in which they have been observed.

It is not known whether there are three different kinds of cone-monochromats—a possibility suggested by the fact that any one of the normal three types of cones might be present alone in this system. There have been reports of "blue" cone-monochromats and "green" cone-monochromats. As expected, blue cone-monochromats have a luminosity curve that peaks at a much shorter wavelength than the scotopic curve. The relative rarity of this type of color blindness makes any such hypothesis extremely speculative, and a definite answer will have to wait until a sufficiently large sample of monochromats have been studied.

It should not be overlooked, however, that there is still a great deal of uncertainty as to whether or not the various forms of color blindness are *entirely* explained by the presence or absence of the three cone photochemicals. The simple trichromatic theory presented here holds that a monochromat should have only one cone pigment or none, a dichromat two, and an anomalous trichromat some peculiar proportion of cone pigments or abnormal cone pigments. However, Alpern (1974) reports that in some reliably diagnosed cases of what appear psychophysically to be rod-monochromatism, there appears to be a normal complement of at least two of the cone pigments, and possibly all three, when

Rushton-type densitometry measurements (Rushton, 1958) are made of the reflectance of these observers' retinae. He asserts, therefore, that in these cases, deficiency in color vision must be due to abnormalities in the neural interconnections at the level of the retinal network or even higher. Although these cases in which normal photopigments are apparently present are unusual, it is obvious that the same psychophysical discrepancies in color matching could occur either as a result of the deficiency of certain photochemicals or as a result of abnormal postreceptor network interaction processes even when the receptors and their photochemicals are totally normal. In both cases the critical coded information—differential levels of activity in parallel channels—is lost; in the former case, because of the lack of a distinction between the absorption spectra of the photopigments; and in the latter, because of the pooling of the information from two or more channels. It would not, of course, be possible to distinguish between the two explanations on the basis of any psychophysical evidence alone. As we see in Chapter 8, it does seem likely, however, that the normal color blindness of the peripheral retina, at least, is due to such neural convergence rather than to an absence of any of the three types of cones.

Various kinds of aftereffects can also produce color-blindlike phenomena apparently unrelated to receptor photochemistry. For example, Stiles (1949), Mollon and Polden (1976; 1977), and Valeton and Van Norren (1979) have all demonstrated a transient tritanopia that was induced following adaptation with yellow lights. This temporary color blindness, in the opinion of Valeton and Van Norren, resulted from some neural process "beyond the level of the bipolar cells."

Alpern (1974) also reports that in some exceptional cases of cone monochromacy (i.e., color-blind cases in which color-matching data, as well as direct measurements of the pigment in the retina using reflection densitometry procedures, suggest that the patients possess only the long-wavelength-sensitive cone pigment), alternative psychophysical techniques (such as the increment threshold procedure of Stiles, 1949, 1959) indicated that there may also be some residual response of what appears to be a short-wavelength-sensitive receptor. Thus the possibility that more than one type of cone is present even in well-diagnosed cone-monochromats cannot be unequivocally denied.

To sum up, although it appears that most color blindness is a Level 1 phenomenon clearly attributable to abnormalities in the nature and proportions of the cone photopigments, other *functionally* identical visual defects may also arise from coding and network errors better classified as Level 2 processes. Thus, as one very likely possibility, if the outputs of two or three normal cones were all pooled into a single information channel, the effect would be exactly the same as having one or two, rather than three, functioning pigments. It is further possible that some abnormal absorption in the ocular media could also distort normal color vision, but this type of Level 0 process is usually considered to be only a secondary perturbation.

In spite of the possible impact of other levels of processing on color vision, it is clear that the predominant critical process underlying normal trichromatic vision is the initial analysis of incident light into the relative amount of activity within three parallel channels of communication as a result of the particular spectral sensitivities of the three photochemicals. If the absorption spectrum of any individual cone-type is different from the normal one, this difference could be a necessary and sufficient cause of abnormal color vision. If there were more, fewer, or different types of cones, the data base of human color psychophysics could be profoundly different.

It is also appropriate to note that the dual possible origins of defective color vision—abnormal receptor absorption or abnormal neural interactions, pooling—should flag another important point about perceptual coding in general. That point is that although the trichromatic characteristic of normal human vision originates in the initial analysis of the stimulus spectrum by the absorption properties of the three photochemicals, it also depends upon the continued ability of the nervous system to maintain the tridimensional information up through all of the more central levels of the visual pathway. If information concerning the tridimensionality of the stimulus is lost at any point, so, necessarily, must also be lost the psychophysically demonstrated ability to match all colors with no more and no less than three fundamentals. However, normal chromatic vision would be maintained even if the information were re-encoded in some neural language other than a trichromatic one, as in fact it is, but only if that new scheme maintained the tridimensionality of the information in its own symbols. Once the tridimensionality is lost, for example, by convergence of the three channels to a one- or two-dimensional encoding scheme, it can never be regenerated at any higher level of the nervous system by any restorative process.

Thus in conclusion, congenital deficiencies in the availability of the normal tetrad of retinal receptor photochemicals governed by hereditary or, possibly, prenatal mechanisms can lead to deficiencies in color vision in particular but also to difficulties with encoding the full range of light intensities and even acuity. Though these perceptual abnormalities may also be mimicked by neural network encoding errors at higher levels, at least the initial analysis of the chromatic information depends upon the availability of these photochemicals.

2. Adaptation and Its Relation to Photochemical Availability

The ability of the human eye to detect small amounts of light varies as a function of the intensity of the background light and the immediate visual experiences that precede the threshold test. The momentary state of the visual system as a result of its immediate environment and history is referred to as its state of *adaptation*. Generally there is a gradual increase in the visual system's ability to detect small dim targets as the background luminance is reduced and the longer the observer has been in the dark. Repeated measurements over the years have shown that under certain conditions the increase in sensitivity during this dark-adaptation process is a two-limbed curve with a noticeable break occurring after about 7 minutes in the dark. The conditions necessary to produce this double function include:

1. Use of a sufficiently intense preliminary adapting light.
2. Illumination of an area of the retina that includes both rods and cones.
3. Use of a broad spectral band to light-adapt all of the photoreceptors of the eye prior to the dark-adaptation.
4. Use of an observer without any form of color deficiency that might obscure the break. At least one cone system and the rod system must be functioning.

Figure 6-22 shows a typical decrease in threshold as a function of time in the dark. This process is known as *dark adaptation*. The earlier part of the curve is assumed to be due in large part to a rather rapid decrease in the absolute threshold

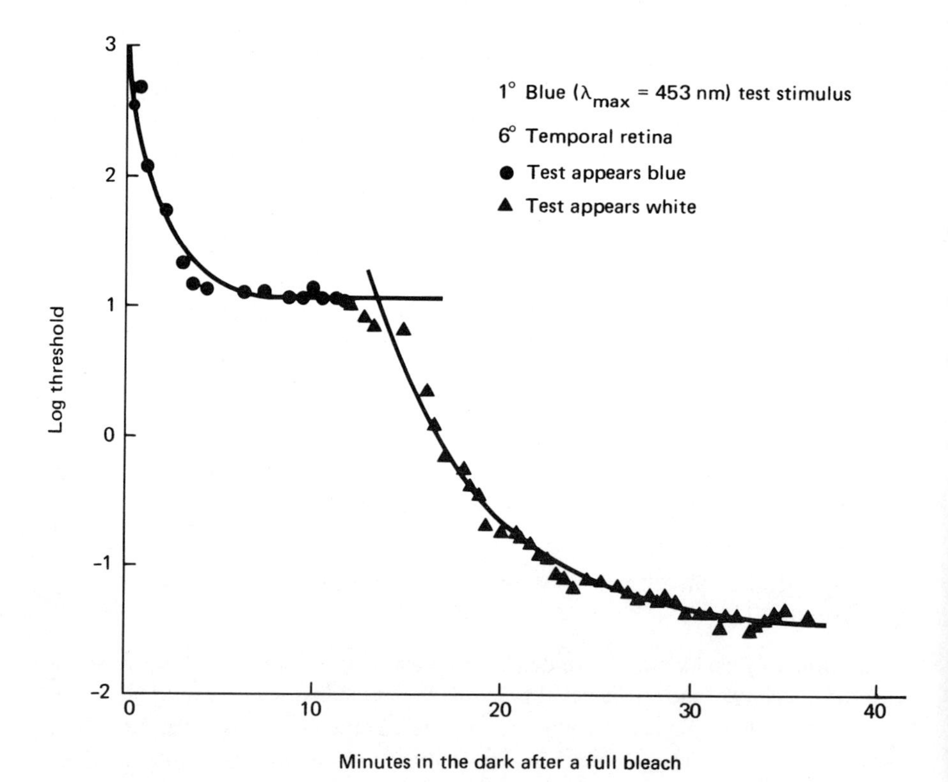

FIG. 6.22. A typical two segment dark adaptation curve clearly showing the rod-cone break. (Courtesy of Dr. Mathew Alpern, University of Michigan.)

of the low-sensitivity cone system, and the later part of the graph is in large part attributable to the decreasing threshold of the slower-adapting but far more sensitive rod system. The break in the cumulative dark-adaptation curve is assumed to be caused by the crossover of the adaptation curves of the rods and the cones, respectively. This classic theoretical explanation of the dark-adaptation curve is based, in part, on data obtained from subjects who presumably suffer from a congenital absence of all three kinds of cones (rod-monochromats) and who thus exhibit only the slow segment attributed to rod dark-adaptation, or obtained from peripheral regions of normal retinae where only rods are present. Foveal dark-adaptation curves also support this hypothesis because they are presumably almost pure cone responses and display only the earlier, more rapid, portion of the curve before becoming asymptotic at a relatively high level. Similarly, if long-wavelength light is used to light-adapt the eye prior to the dark adaptation, the resulting function is almost solely the product of the more rapid cone response.

A fundamental problem that has been present since the earliest observations of this duplex dark-adaptation phenomenon has been to identify the processes that account for it. Although there is still some controversy, in general, it is agreed by most authorities in the field that the shape of the dark-adaptation curve actually reflects several processes. Contributing to the variations in sensitivity are, among other factors, thought to be the amount of photochemical available, non-photochemical neural effects in the photoreceptor, and neural network effects in the more central portions of the retinal plexus. To be entirely consistent with the context of this section, I consider here only the first two of these three factors, which are demonstrably Level 1, and defer my discussion of the neural interaction (Level 2) aspects of the problem of adaptation until Chapter 8.

The discovery of visual pigments in the photoreceptors occurred during the second half of the nineteenth century. Franz Boll (1849–1879) was the first[15] to formally describe the visual role of photochemical of the rods, a substance that has come to be called rhodopsin. Boll and his contemporary, Friedrich Kühne, (1837–1900), both realized that vision depended on the chemistry, and thus the availability, of rhodopsin. Over the next half century, most theories of visual adaptation simply generalized this idea and ascribed the phenomenon to the

[15]A highly informative discussion of Boll's contribution, along with an excellent translation of his classic 1877 paper, has been published in *Vision Research* (Vol. 17, No. 11/12). This issue also describes another of these unfortunate controversies over scientific priority between Boll and Kühne. Kühne, a little too quickly and from some points of view unethically, pursued (see Kühne, 1977 for a reprint of the 1879 paper) the obvious research implications of Boll's original report. This issue of *Vision Research* is of particular interest to those among us who have an interest in the history of visual science. Kühne's contributions, it should not be misunderstood, were profound (he clarified the chemical basis of rhodopsin's color change), but the credit for the initial observation of rhodopsin as a visual photochemical clearly should go to Boll in spite of the fact that he did not follow up his original discovery.

momentary quantity of photochemical. This trend finally culminated in the form of a theory (Hecht, 1937) that quantified the relationship between the amount of photochemical and the threshold sensitivity of the eye. In the years following Hecht's model, however, it became increasingly clear that the hypothesis that photochemical availability completely explained dark adaptation could not possibly be true, and what should have been obvious became, in retrospect, the new dogma. That new dogma is that there are also neural factors not depending directly on photochemical availability, in both the receptor and the underlying neural network, that also contribute to the adaptation process. (For an excellent discussion and clear expression of the new dogma, see Green, Tong, & Cicerone, 1977.)

One of the most clean-cut analyses of the problem of the relative contribution of photochemical and neural factors to adaptation can be found in the report of a very important experiment carried out on the rat's visual system by John Dowling (1967). He showed that there was no measurable change in the photochemical concentration over a range of 5 log units of background intensity above the threshold level. This absence of a measurable photochemical concentration difference occurred in spite of the fact that there was a very great difference in the threshold as measured with an electroretinographic procedure. (Changes in the *b*-wave of the electroretinogram are known to parallel closely the adaptation process measured psychophysically in humans.) Measurable concentration differences in the photochemical did not occur until much higher luminance levels were used.

Dowling thus provided strong support for the hypothesis that there are, in fact, at least two mechanisms working simultaneously in the dark-adaptation process. One was a very rapid mechanism primarily accounted for by the recovery of responsivity of neural mechanisms. This high-speed process was apparently responsible for most of the change in sensitivity at those low light levels at which only a very small proportion of the photochemical was bleached. The second adaptive mechanism is one that does depend upon the availability of the receptor photochemical but is called into play only at the higher stimulus intensities at which bleaching is substantial enough to deplete photochemical concentrations measurably. This mechanism has a much slower time constant and thus accounts for the later phases of dark-adaptation of even a single chemical like rhodopsin.

Dowling's experiments were carried out on the rat, an animal that has a predominantly rod retina (although whether it is completely cone-free has been questioned by D. Green, 1971), so that there was no likelihood of a rod–cone break such as that shown in Fig. 6-22. In the human eye the situation is obviously more complicated, but it appears likely that the dual neural and photochemical processes observed in the rat also parallel the course of the adaptive processes in its fellow vertebrate—man. Indeed, early rapid fluctuations in dark adaptation in the human, comparable to the fast neural response observed by Dowling in the rat, had even earlier been psychophysically described and attributed to a similar neural mechanism by H. Baker (1963). Figure 6-23 presents Baker's summary drawing of the mechanisms that might possibly contribute to the human dark-adaptation cycle. The fast components of the adaptation process he describes are obviously ignored in the classical dark-adaptation curve shown in Fig. 6-22. Baker's paper also reviews a number of the other early psychophysical studies that indicated there were rapid, early processes that could not easily be associated with the amount of the photochemical available. The reader is directed there for details of some of these important early experiments. Dowling (1967) also lists some of the early psychophysical results supporting the general hypothesis that the availability of the photochemical alone was insufficient to explain the dark- and light-adaptation cycles.

Other types of data also support the contention that photochemical availability has little to do with determining the sensitivity of the eye at low and moderate light levels. For example, one implication of Rushton's (1961, 1964) retinal densitometry procedures is that the photochemical depletion can account for only a small portion of the shift in threshold.

Photochemical availability has a corresponding lack of influence on supra-threshold rod-mediated brightness as evidenced in studies of the apparent brightness of a stimulus as a function of the level of dark adaptation. This experiment was originally carried out by Craik (1940a), but more recently replicated by Geisler (1978) with the same results. When the brightness of a light presented to one eye (that is in various degrees of dark adaptation) is compared with the

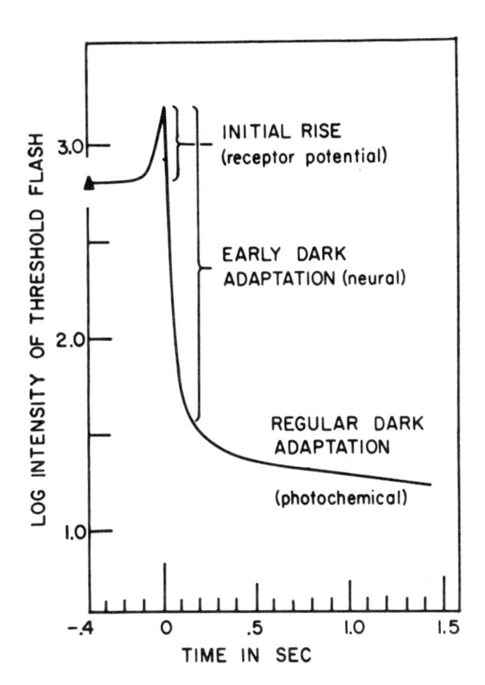

FIG. 6.23. A hypothetical model of three stages of the dark adaptation cycle. (From Baker, © 1963, with the permission of the American Institute of Physics.)

brightness to the other eye, the comparison light must be increased to obtain a match as the adaptation field increases, but only up to a limit. After that, the curve is relatively flat, as shown in Fig. 6-24. The explanation for this bipartite result, according to Geisler, is that it is only above an adaptation level of 4 log trolands that the photochemical is depleted sufficiently to affect the apparent brightness of a stimulus. Below 4 log units, the shift in brightness is largely determined by the neural (as opposed to photochemical) processes of the receptors.

I can summarize this discussion by noting that it is highly unlikely that the availability of the photochemical has anything to do with the sensitivity to dim

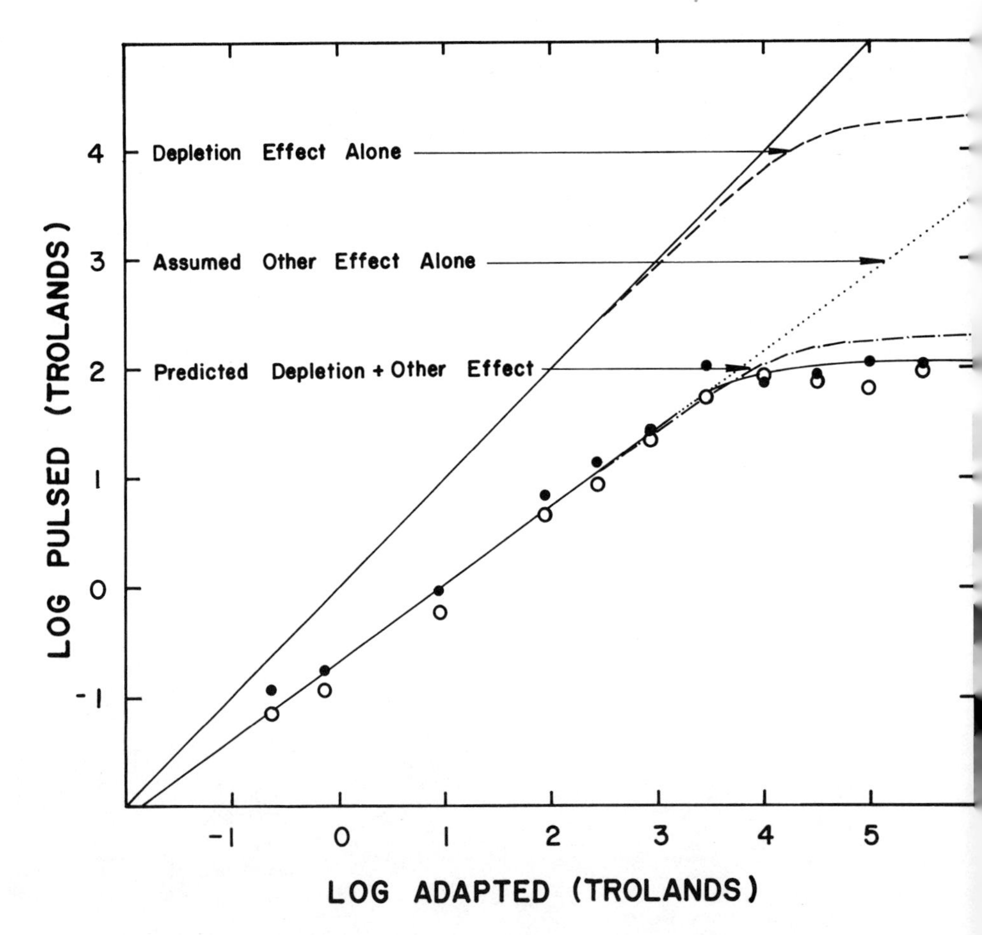

FIG. 6.24. Another model showing the multiple causes of dark adaptation. Note the relatively small contribution of the photochemical depletion effect; depletion is negligible until relatively high levels of light adaptation are reached. (From Geisler, © 1978, with the permission of Pergamon Press.)

stimuli within about 4 or 5 log units of the optimized absolute threshold. At these low levels the adaptive changes in threshold levels are almost totally accounted for in terms of neural (i.e., nonphotochemical) processes. It is only at high stimulus intensities that photochemical availability becomes influential and that appreciable amounts of the very large number of available molecules of the photochemical are bleached. (Dowling, 1967, estimates that there may be as many as 30,000,000 molecules of rhodopsin in each rod in the rat's eye).

At high stimulus intensities, however, where there is an appreciable amount of bleaching, both Rushton (1956) and Dowling (1960) have determined a fairly straightforward relationship between the amount of photochemical that is bleached and the stimulus energy required to produce a just-detectable difference from a background. They propose that under conditions of strong light adaptation, and thus substantial photopigment bleaching, the incremental threshold is simply a logarithmic function of the amount of photochemical present. This specific relationship between the threshold and the available photochemical can be represented as

$$\log \frac{\text{adapted threshold}}{\text{unadapted threshold}} = kR \tag{6-11}$$

where k is a constant and R is the proportion of the original amount of rhodopsin remaining after a bright bleach.

Geisler (1978) also concurs with this judgment. In the paper just discussed, he asserts that when light levels are high enough to activate the cone photochemicals and we are therefore dealing with photopic processes, the effect of photochemical depletion becomes substantial. He lists the following photopic phenomena that appear to have a functional dependence on photochemical depletion per se:

1. High level light-adaptation threshold.
2. Brightness of high-level stimuli.
3. Increment thresholds with high-level backgrounds.
4. Simultaneous brightness contrast at high levels (a conclusion with which I do not agree—see Chapter 9).

The time constants of various neural and photochemical adaptive processes may, as we have seen, be quite different. The neural components of both dark and light adaptation occur at a more rapid rate than does the photochemically based dark-adaptation process. However, even though the photochemical process of dark adaptation (the replenishment of the photochemical) takes a considerable period of time (see Fig. 6-25), the initial breakdown of the photochemical (light adaptation occurring when a stimulus impinges on the photochemical) probably occurs in submicrosecond fractions of a second and may actually be the fastest of the four processes (i.e., neural light and dark adaptation, and photochemical light and dark adaptation).

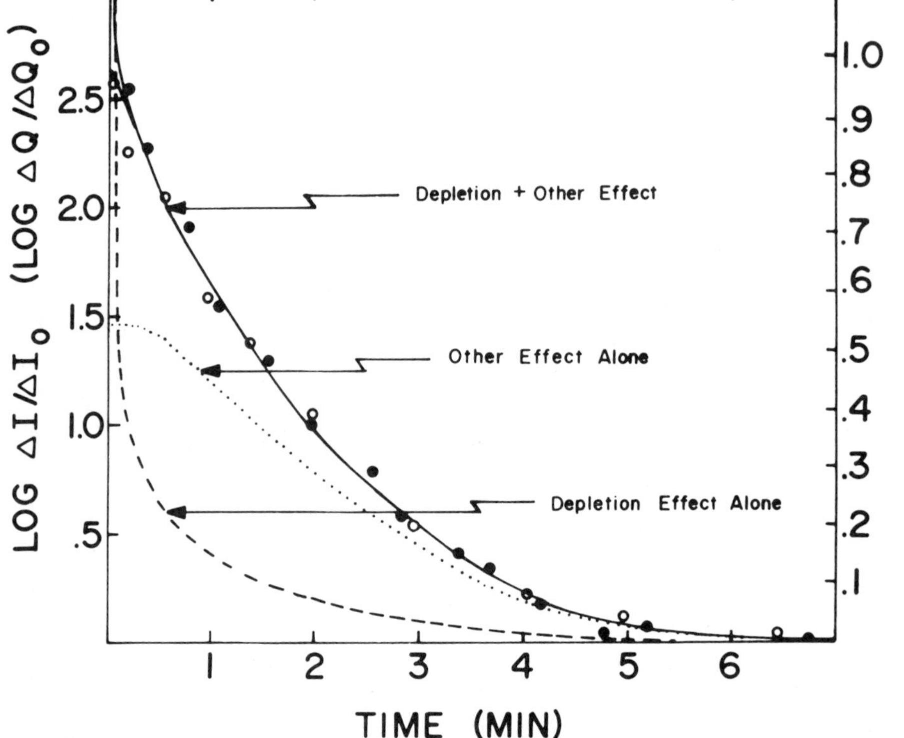

FIG. 6.25. The possible time courses of the photochemical (depletion) and neural contributions to dark adaptation. (From Geisler, © 1978, with the permission of Pergamon Press, Inc.)

It is also important to remember that there are two quite distinguishable neural mechanisms operating in adaptation, neural effects in the receptor itself (which should be classified as Level 1 processes), and neural effects in the retinal network beyond the receptors (which should be classified as Level 2 processes). Although the photochemical and the nonphotochemical neural effects that occur in the photoreceptor are extremely difficult to disentangle with intracellular recordings (even when the electrode is in the receptor itself), it can be done. One example of a study in which this was accomplished was that of Kleinschmidt and Dowling (1975). They discovered that the threshold of a rod in the gecko's eye (measured in terms of a criterion differential receptor potential response magnitude of 0.5 mv) and the absolute magnitude of the receptor potential following a bleach were approximately correlated only during the first 5 minutes of the dark adaptation cycle. This important result is shown in Fig. 6-26. After that initial period the absolute level of the membrane potential remained virtually constant (suggesting that the fast neural processes had fully recovered), but the threshold of the photoreceptor was still elevated and only gradually became asymptotic to its original dark-adapted state many minutes later. This is further evidence that there are at least two different adaptive mechanisms—one neural and one photochemical—even within the photoreceptor itself that can be at least partially disassociated.

Other fast neural adaptive processes more likely to be functions of interactive processes within the retinal plexus (or higher) are discussed when I consider Level 2 processes in Chapter 8. The reader interested in an up-to-date collection of current research on visual adaptation would do no better than to refer to the April issue of Volume 19 (1979) of the journal *Vision Research*.

E. PERCEPTUAL IMPACT OF RECEPTOR AND PHOTOCHEMICAL DISTRIBUTION

In my discussion of the impact of the availability of the photochemical on certain chromatic and adaptive phenomena, in the previous section, I necessarily ignored another important variable—the retinal location of the photoreceptor that was being stimulated. Instead I dealt with the problem of photochemical availability as an abstraction, assuming a more or less idealized locus somewhere on the

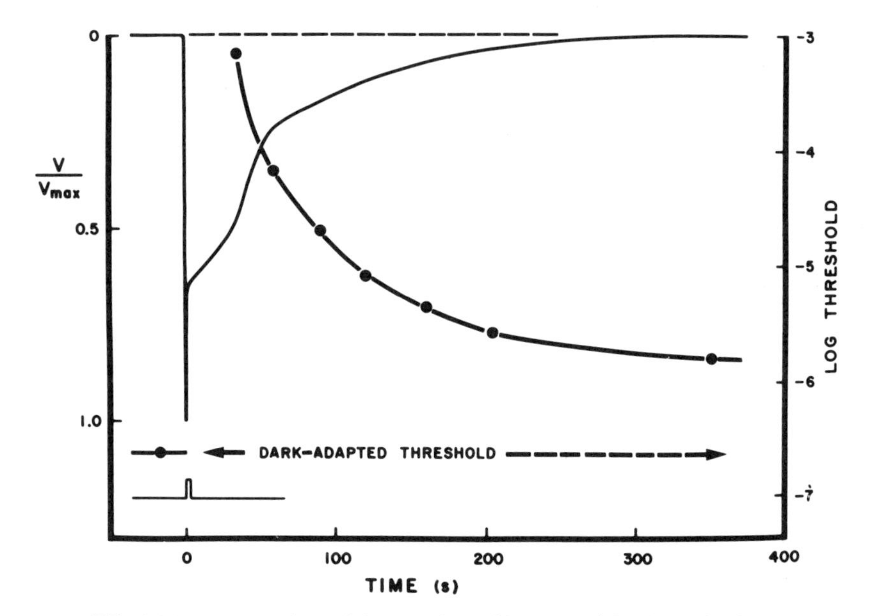

FIG. 6.26. A comparison of the neural membrane potential and the threshold stimulus intensity (for a criterion evoked potential) in the gecko photoreceptor. (From Kleinschmidt and Dowling, © 1975, with the permission of Rockefeller University Press.)

retina. In fact, however, the spatial distribution of the photoreceptor material, and indeed of the photoreceptors themselves, is also a highly influential determinant of a number of perceptual phenomena. Location and distribution, therefore, must be considered in greater detail in order to round out our understanding of the role of the receptor in perception.

Figure 6-27A shows the distribution of the rods and cones across the retina plotted in terms of the number of receptors per unit area. To appreciate this curve properly it is necessary to remember that the size of the receptors remains relatively constant over the entire surface of the retina, and therefore it is the packing density of the receptors that must be varying. The cross-sectional diameter of the outer segments of the receptors, the surface presented to the stimulus, is usually considered to remain more or less constant at about 1.5 micra. This figure clearly illustrates the predominance of cones in the central (foveal) portion of the

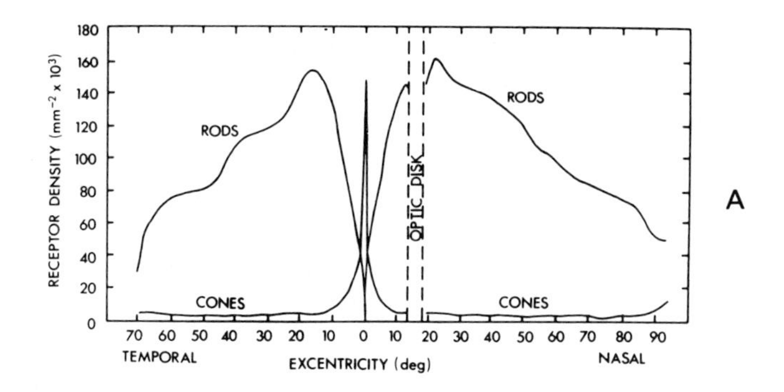

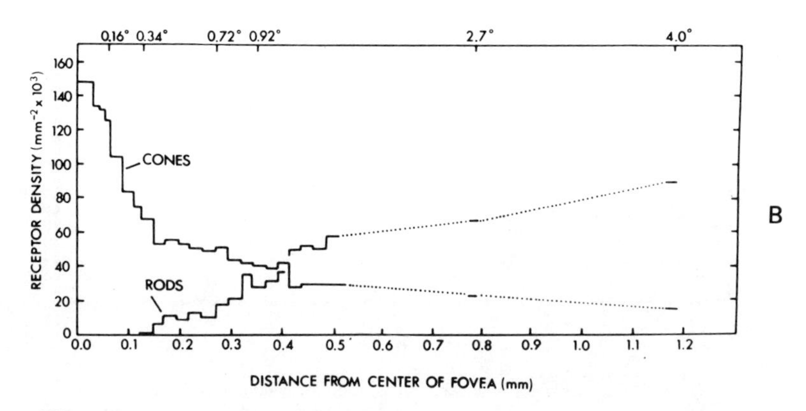

FIG. 6.27. The results of a study of the density of receptors in the eye of a single rabbit. (A) Across the entire retina. (B) In the foveal region. (From Rodieck, © 1973, after Osterberg, 1935, with the permission of W. H. Freeman & Company.)

retina and the ring of highest rod density at about 20–25 deg from the fovea. Also indicated is the optic disk—the region through which the blood vessels and the optic nerve fibers enter and leave the retina—that is totally devoid of receptors.

Figure 6.27B shows the density of the rods and cones on a more highly magnified scale. A particularly interesting breakpoint occurs at a radius of about 1 deg of visual angle (corresponding to about 0.4 mm on the retina), a value equivalent to what is usually considered to be the maximum extent of the fovea. It is here that the curves representing the density of the rods and cones cross; at 1 deg, therefore, the retina changes from cone to rod domination. However it should be noted that the totally rod-free portion of the fovea is a much smaller central disk (about 0.1 mm in radius) than the whole fovea. It is also equally important, in the context of our subsequent discussion, to note that cones are probably present out to the limits of the retina, although in very low densities. These two figures, Fig. 6-27A and 6-27B are, themselves, historically very interesting because they represent the outcome of a unique study of a single human retina carried out almost fifty years ago by Osterberg (1935) that apparently has never been replicated. In spite of the lack of confirmation, these graphs have been the anatomical foundations of a number of retinal theories of a wide variety of perceptual phenomena.[16]

It is clear that this distribution of photoreceptors is going to affect visual perception in some very direct ways. For example, perimetric vision is delimited largely by the physical extent of the carpet of photoreceptors. Interestingly, this distribution extends out to more than 135 deg measured from the fovea. I have already mentioned how this greater than hemispheral orb, coupled with the high refractive power of the air–cornea interface, allows peripheral vision greater than 90 deg from the optical axis of the eye (see p. 349).

Another major phenomenon directly attributable to the distribution of receptors is the blind spot—a region in the visual field in which the eye is blind. This blindness results from the complete absence of any photoreceptors in the region referred to as the optic disk—the region of the retina through which the blood vessels and optic nerve enter and leave the eye. It is one of the great paradoxes of perception that the blind spot is, in general, invisible in spite of the fact that it represents approximately a 5 deg wide lacuna in the visual field. It takes special conditions to demonstrate its phenomenal existence. A stimulus scene must be viewed through only one eye, and the object (or parts of it) introduced into the field must be discrete and small enough so that cognitive filling does not occur in the region of modest acuity in which the blind spot resides.

---

[16]Somewhat to my amazement, I discovered recently that this paucity of background data for solidly entrenched visual standards is not unusual. Both the standard 1931 CIE chromaticity diagram and the photopic and scotopic luminosity curves are based on only a few dozen observers. Although the difficulty of collecting such data makes this understandable, it seems that a concerted effort to provide a surer foundation for such basic standards would be well justified.

The shape of the dark-adaptation curve also depends upon the retinal locus and therefore is also functionally related to the distribution of receptors upon which the light falls. In the periphery, the dark-adaptation curve mainly reflects rod function, and in the fovea it is mainly influenced by cones. It is only in some intermediate region in which the rods and cones are both present that the "typical" adaptation curve showing the characteristic rod–cone break shown in Fig. 6-22 can be evoked.

Visual acuity may also be influenced to a degree by the distribution and nature of the photoreceptors. But it is also affected by Level 0 optical factors, Level 2 neural interaction processes, and probably even by higher-level criterion and judgmental processes. The discussion of acuity, therefore, is necessarily one that spans several levels of processing. Nevertheless, the role of receptor distribution is important in acuity. To a first approximation, the density of the retinal mosaic (or the interreceptor spacing or the receptor size) will determine the maximum high spatial frequency band-pass capability of the visual system.

But the reader should be forewarned; a functional dependence of some phenomenon on retinal locus, however, is not necessarily an indication that the receptor distribution itself is critical. As we later see, the variation in both color vision and absolute threshold with retinal locus are only indirectly associated with the differential availability of receptor types at different loci. Level 2 processes may in fact be the most important aspects of the locus effects on these phenomena. In other words, there may be systematic changes in the retinal network as a function of locus that can mimic changes in receptor type or distribution.

In the following discussion I concentrate on those phenomena that are locus-dependent and that do seem to depend on the properties or distribution of the receptors per se. In Chapter 8 I return to locus-dependent topics, but in that case I deal with those that seem to depend upon the organization of the retinal network.

1. Perimetry. Perimetry is the measurement of the extent of the visual field of view. Perimetric measurements can be made with a number of different methods, but somewhat surprisingly, various procedures may give somewhat different results. The classical method of bringing a spot of light in from the peripheral visual field until it can just be detected results in the definition of a field of view that is different from that obtained by tests using chromatic or flicker thresholds. Pupillary responses have also been used as an "objective" measure of the visual system's ability to respond to visual stimuli even though they may not come to conscious awareness.

Figure 5-40, presented earlier, displayed a normal perimetric chart. That diagram provided an approximate description of the limits of the human visual field. Perimetric measurements of this sort can also be used to demonstrate abnormalities in the visual field. The blind spot is a natural *scotoma,* but other abnormal scotomas or visual lacuna can precisely locate sites of neural degeneration or lesions at the retina or higher levels of the visual pathway. Perimetric measurements of the visual field will also depend on the current state of the receptors as well as the particular parameters of the stimulus. For example, a perimetric chart determined with a small bright spot in a dark-adapted eye is likely to be much larger in extent than one in which a light-adapted eye was confronted with the task of detecting a dim light or a dark spot on an illuminated background. The color of the stimulus will also be an important determinant of the perimetric measurements as will the practice that a subject has had in this sometimes difficult discriminative task. On the other hand, there is relatively little effect of the refractive state of the eye on the size of the visual field.

In sum, the shape and size of the visual field, although strictly limited by the distribution of the visual receptors, will also be very much affected by the means by which it is measured and the nature of the stimulus used to determine its limits. In the final analysis, however, the extent of the visual field is totally dependent upon the distribution and availability of receptors to receive the photic stimulus. A full and comprehensive discussion of the current state of perimetric research and theory can be found in Aulhorn and Harms (1972).

2. The Absolute Threshold. The minimum amount of light necessary to produce a just-detectable response also varies systematically as a function of the locus on the retina onto which the stimulus falls. Figure 6-28, for example, shows the change in the threshold luminance as a function of the position on the retina for the four quadrants of the visual field as measured by deGroot, Dodge, and Smith (1952). If the two curves corresponding to a horizontal axis across the eye are plotted end to end, they at first appear to be very similar to the curve of rod density shown in Fig. 6-27. A superficial comparison of the two figures shows many correspondences. There is a depression in the sensitivity of the eye at the fovea and a peak on either side of the blind spot and fovea, respectively; and the general course of the two functions is in agreement. However, a closer examination discloses that the loci of the two peaks are not the same and there are also differences in relative heights that suggest that the two curves do not fit together as perfectly as may have seemed at first glance. For this reason the simplest hypothesis explaining the absolute threshold, namely, that the threshold function is strictly dependent upon the density of the rods, has never been universally accepted. The general shape of the two curves is close enough, however, and because the rod-density measurements presented in Fig. 6-27 by Osterberg were for a unique preparation, it may be that the discrepancies are not as great as indicated.

Unfortunately, the alternatives to this simplistic association of threshold with rod density (e.g., the degree of neural convergence) are insufficiently developed to allow the issue to be definitively adjudicated. I think it is sufficient to note that

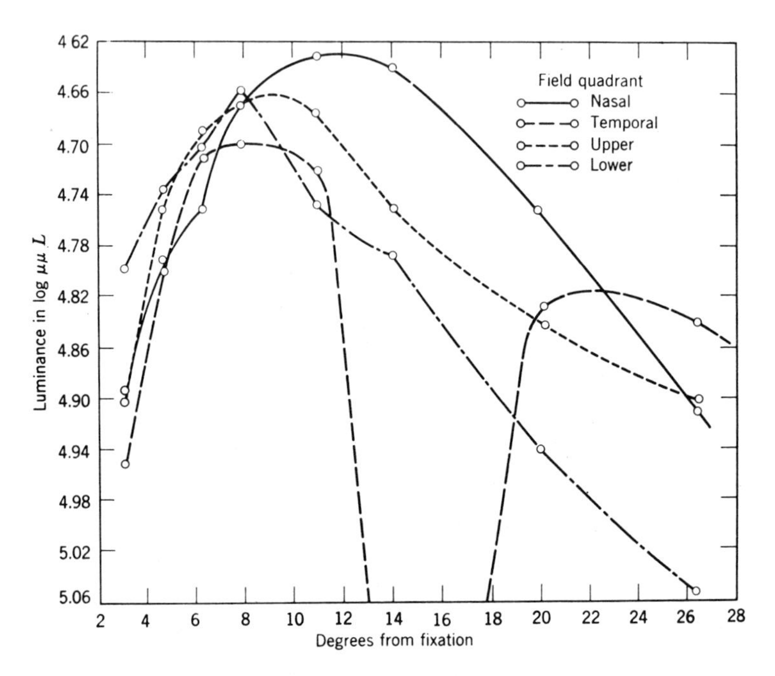

FIG. 6.28. Absolute thresholds as a function of retinal location. (From Bartlett, © 1965, with the permission of John Wiley & Sons, Inc.)

threshold data are very similar to rod density, and that until something better comes along, rod density is probably a first approximation to an answer to the question of why absolute thresholds vary as a function of the retinal locus.

It should also be noted in this context that the effect of retinal locus on the function describing the magnitude of the visual response (i.e., the apparent brightness) is relatively small even though the receptor dynamic, as we see later in this chapter, strongly affects the relationship between brightness and luminance. Figure 6-29 shows that this is the case except for the initial portion of the curves that are constrained by threshold effects. The implication of these data is that the absolute threshold and the suprathreshold functions are mediated by separate, though interacting, aspects of receptor function.

3. Adaptation. The particular shape of the dark-adaptation function is also closely related, as I have mentioned, to the fact that two basic kinds of receptors are present in the eye. Because the relative proportions of the receptor types varies as a function of locus, the shape of the dark-adaptation curve varies when measured at different points across the retina. This variation of the adaptation function with retinal locus is a classic observation that in fact has been considered to have been a closed issue for over forty years. I have not been able to find a reference to any study of the effects of retinal position on the dark-

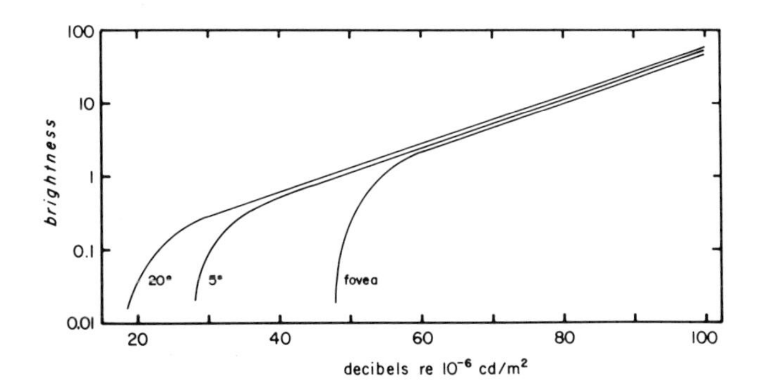

FIG. 6.29. The suprathreshold dynamic as a function of retinal position. (From Marks, © 1974, with the permission of Academic Press, Inc.)

adaptation curve more recent than the one reported by Hecht, Haig, and Wald (1935). Figure 6-30 shows their findings concerning the effect on the shape of the dark-adaptation curve of placing the test spot in four different loci on the retina. The adaptation function approximates the prototypical two-segment dark adaptation curve (shown in Fig. 6-22) only in the middle extrafoveal regions. Within the fovea, the region in which few if any rods are thought to be present, the adaptation curve quickly falls to the threshold level defined by the maximum sensitivities of the cones. It is only as the test spot is moved more toward the

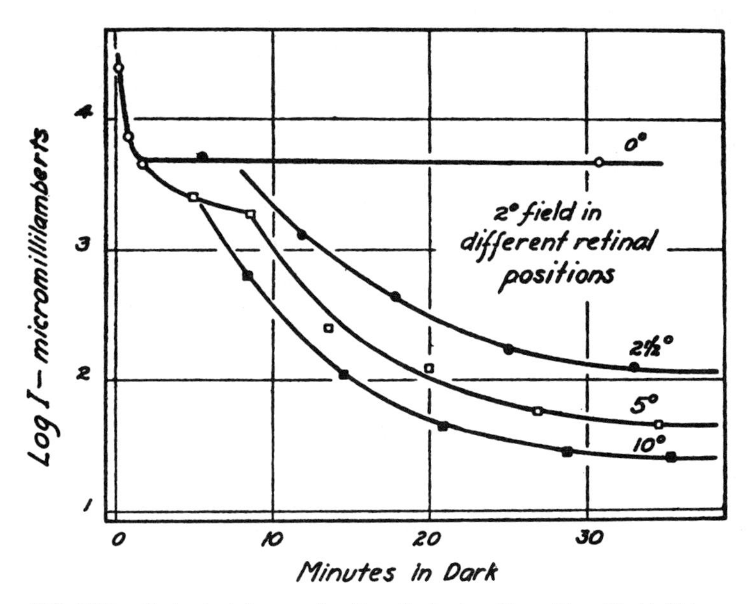

FIG. 6.30. Dark adaptation as a function of retinal position. (From Hecht, Haig, and Wald, © 1935.)

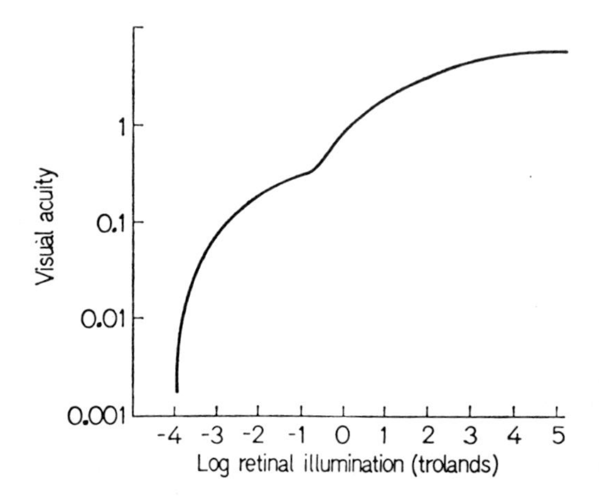

FIG. 6.31. Acuity as a function of retinal illuminance. (From Westheimer, © 1972, after Pirenne, © 1962, with the permission of Academic Press, Inc.)

periphery that the function begins to exhibit the classic rod–cone break indicative of a mixed population of rods and cones. The faster-adapting, but less sensitive, cone curve is more and more quickly bypassed by the slower-recovering, but more sensitive, rod response until in the extreme periphery a single-limbed function totally reflective of rod function is obtained.

In spite of the apparent lack of recent interest in this problem, however, it is clear that the family of functions obtained when one varies the retinal locus is not completely explained in the simple terms of the distribution of the photoreceptors. This is so for exactly the same reasons that the absolute threshold is not completely explained in terms of photochemical concentration; there remains a significant possibility that there is some other contribution to these phenomena by the processes embodied in neural network interconnections below the receptors.

4. Acuity and the Information Capacity of the Retinal Mosaic (A Multilevel Digression).[17]. Acuity, the ability to discriminate adjacent loci, is known to depend upon the intensity of the stimulating light, as well as on the wavelength of the stimulus and its background as shown in Fig. 6-31 and 6-32, respectively.

[17] I have had some difficulty deciding where to put this section. From one point of view, the size and spacing of the receptors are at the base of a Level 1 process in the same way that photoreceptor distribution is. On the other hand, the informational analysis that I pursue in this section actually reflects pretransductive processes in much the same way as does the Stiles–Crawford effect. Therefore it might have been equally easy to place this section in the discussion of Level 0 in Chapter 5. I suppose the best way to handle this dilemma is merely to point out the existence of the problem, to note that this probably reflects a weakness in the selection criteria of the taxonomic theory that I have presented, and to let the reader choose where to place this material in his own personal schema. Personally, I prefer to place it at this point, but I must acknowledge that the fact that Level 2 neural interactions get involved in the discussion in a few pages even further confounds the dilemma.

The effect of stimulus intensity on acuity is a function, in part at least, of the signal-to-noise ratio defined in terms of the proportion of receptors in the mosaic that are stimulated. Pirenne (1967) has graphically demonstrated this important concept in Fig. 6-33, showing how the detectability of a spot depends, in fundamental principle, upon the activity in the surrounding receptors and thus upon the overall level of activity.

Two important anatomical factors that theoretically should influence visual acuity are the size of the receptors and density of the retinal mosaic. Simple considerations from information theory say that there should be a theoretical limit on the ability of a multireceptor system such as the human retina to detect a difference between one and two stimuli. That limit is reached when the spacing between the centers of the receptors is less than half the spacing between the two targets. This is but another way to phrase the well-known sampling theorem of information theory that generally asserts that any wave form (in time or space) can be adequately represented if samples are taken at no less than twice the highest constituent frequency of that wave form. In fact, within 2 degs of the fovea, receptor spacing does seem to define precisely the limit of the precision of acuity for pointlike objects.

A formal theory of the limit on acuity imposed by receptor size and spacing has been developed by Snyder, Laughlin, and Stavenga (1977), who have ingeniously derived a quantitative statement of the information capacity of an idealized retinal mosaic from the basic sampling theorem. One of the most important ideas added to our understanding of acuity by Snyder and his col-

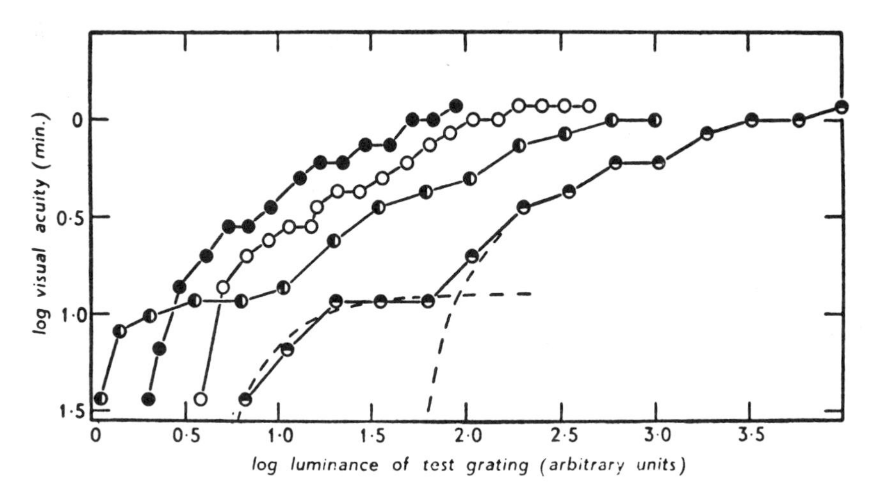

FIG. 6.32. Variation of visual acuity with luminance and with the spectral properties of the test and background stimuli. Solid circles = 548 nm grating on 680 nm background; vertical semicircles = 454 nm grating on 548 nm background; horizontal semicircles = 454 nm grating on 680 nm background. (From Brindley, © 1960, with the permission of Williams and Wilkins, Inc.)

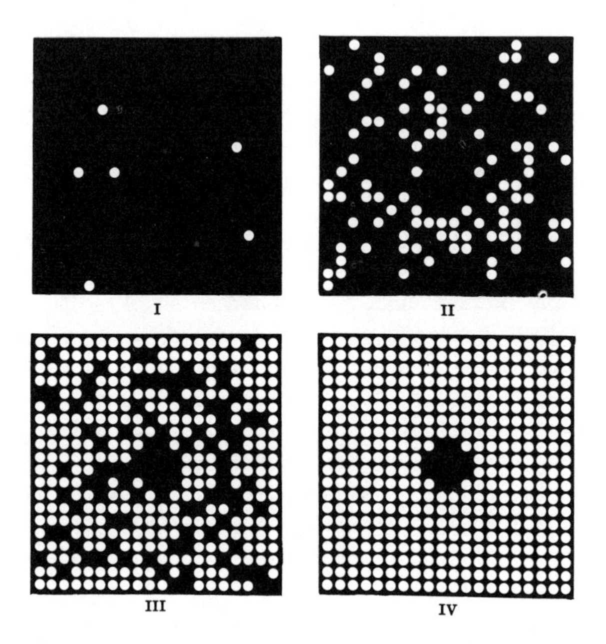

FIG. 6.33. Pirenne's demonstration of why the retina exhibits higher acuity as light intensity is increased. (From Pirenne, © 1967, with the permission of Chapman and Hall, Ltd.)

leagues is that the amount of information that can be carried by a given density of receptors of a given size is not only a function of the dimensions of the receptors but also of the intensity of the light. I have already considered the psychophysical implication of this statement in presenting Fig. 6-31, which displays the psychophysical relationship between acuity and luminance.

Snyder, Laughlin, and Stavenga begin their analysis of this problem by reminding us that the most important contribution of Hecht, Shlaer, and Pirenne's (1942) experiment was its recognition that the ability of the receptors to capture quanta is the critical factor in defining the limits of low-level visual processes. If a stimulus is very dim, then the same width receptors that were functional in a brighter light no longer will be able to convey the same amount of information due simply to the statistical distribution of the quanta of incident light. The advantage of the large receptors is that their increased cross-sectional area receives a larger number of quanta for any given intensity, and therefore a larger receptor will display a superior signal-to-noise ratio than will a smaller receptor. However, the price paid for this ability to discriminate low levels of stimulus intensities better is that the larger receptor is less sensitive to spatial patterns because the details of form information are essentially lost within the homogeneous receptive area of a single rod or cone. Acuity and absolute thresholds, therefore, are in a compensatory balance with each other. Figure 6-34 illustrates this relationship for idealized receptors of different sizes.

The compensatory interaction between the receptor size needed for optimum discrimination of lights of different intensities and the size needed for optimum fine spatial discrimination is the conceptual heart of Snyder, Laughlin, and Stavenga's analysis. They show how the smaller the receptor, the finer the spatial acuity; but the larger the receptor, the better the unit is able to deal with low light levels and thus to distinguish dim stimuli from the quantum and physiological noise of the visual system.

Snyder, Laughlin, and Stavenga define the spatial information capacity (H) of a receptor mosaic as a function of both the receptor size (or for a closely packed mosaic—its equivalent—the spacing between the centers of the receptors) and the ability of the receptor to encode different intensity levels as follows:

$$H = \frac{\ln n_i}{(\Delta\, \phi)^2} \qquad (6\text{-}12)$$

where $\Delta\phi$ is the spacing in degrees of arc between receptor centers, and n_i is the number of possible intensity levels that can be represented by the neutral code of the receptor. In this case, Snyder and his colleagues note that H is equivalent to the number of different "pictures" (i.e., the number of patterns in space and

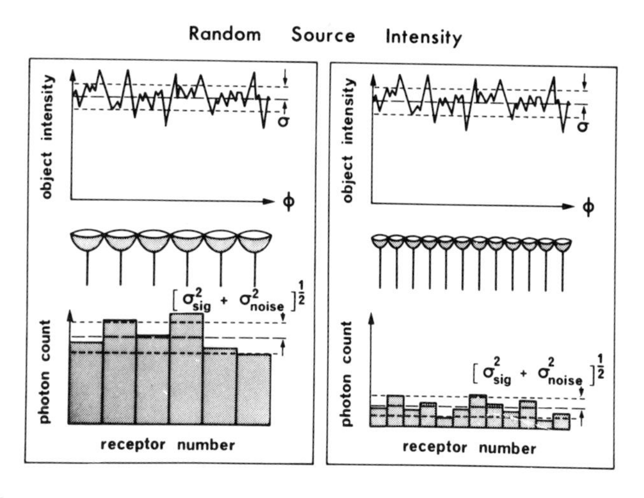

FIG. 6.34. Diagram indicating the compensating advantages and disadvantages of receptor size. Large receptors each capture larger number of quanta and, therefore, have a better signal to noise ratio. Small receptors have a finer grid and thus have better acuity, but poorer signal to noise ratios. The two properties thus act in opposition and improving one capability necessarily must degrade the other. (From Snyder, Laughlin, and Stavenga, © 1977, with the permission of Pergamon Press, Ltd.)

amplitude) that can be encoded by a field of receptors with this spacing and this number of levels of possible intensity discrimination.

The interaction between the two independent variables—spacing and possible intensity levels—is shown in Fig. 6-35. Here the information capacity (H) has been plotted for different receptor spacings as a family of curves that are parametric with the intensity of the stimulus. Obviously, a higher intensity stimulus would permit a smaller receptor spacing and thus a finer intrinsic acuity. But these small receptors will necessarily be poor encoders of low-intensity stimuli. Therefore, Snyder and his colleagues suggest that the ideal eye must have several different kinds of receptors. It should have large receptors for regions in which it is working at low light levels (where it would exhibit only modest acuity but be able to encode many different intensity levels), and it should have small receptors where the light levels are high (with a resulting increase in the visual acuity, but a tolerable degradation in the number of discrete intensity levels).

This is an idealized model of an optimum retina, however, that probably does not obtain in the human eye. With high sensitivity and poor acuity typical properties of the periphery, and poor sensitivity and good acuity characteristic of the foveal regions, this does not appear to be the result of different-size receptors. The foveal cones and the peripheral rods are very similar to each other in terms of the diameter of their outer segments.

There is, however, another factor that may actually simulate large receptors in the peripheral retina and thus approximate the ideal retina conceptualized by Snyder and his colleagues. That additional factor is the degree of neural con-

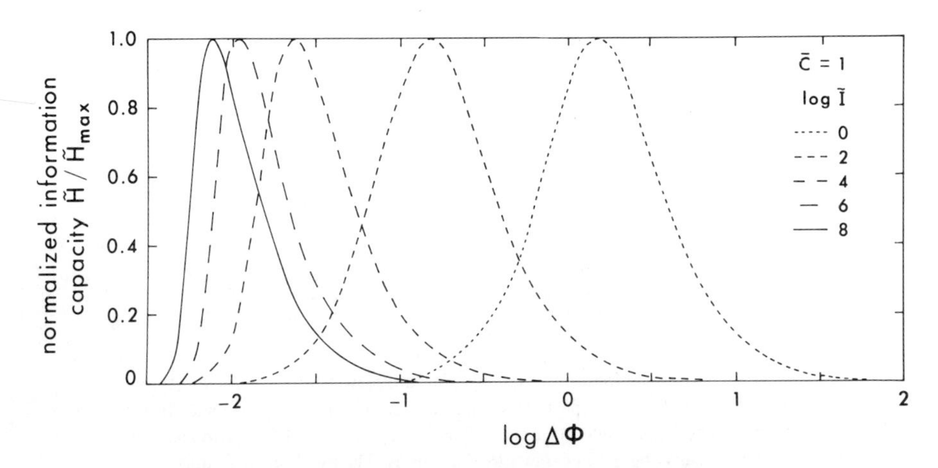

FIG. 6.35. A graphical construction making the same point as Fig. 6.34. The relationship between the receptor spacing (Δ Φ) and possible information capacity is plotted for different stimulus intensities. (From Snyder, Laughlin, and Stavenga, © 1977, with the permission of Pergamon Press, Ltd.)

vergence typical of the more peripheral regions. In the periphery the outputs of many of the receptors converge onto a single ganglion cell. The resulting situation is functionally equivalent to a single large receptor in much the same way that a large array of suitably interconnected small antennas can mimic a single large one in radio astronomy. This mechanism may have evolved to provide different regions of the retina with the ability to display optimum sensitivities to different visual conditions and thus to be maximally adaptive to the widest possible range of information processing. It is a highly adaptive solution to the need for different-sized receptors (either actual or functional) resulting from the compensatory requirement for high acuity and multiple levels of magnitude representation.

An interesting further insight into Snyder, Laughlin, and Stavenga's analysis of the effect of different-size receptors can be obtained from a comparison of acuity mediated by eyes that actually contained different-size receptors. Comparative anatomists and psychologists have now carried out such studies. Birds of prey, such as the falcon, have been shown by anatomists to have a density of receptors three times greater than do humans (Polyak, 1957); by physiologists, to have eyes in which the optical line-spread function is half that found in humans (Shlaer, 1972); and by psychologists, actually to display behavioral indications that their acuity is almost three times as good as that of humans (Fox, Lehmkuhle, & Westendorf, 1976). The psychologists have demonstrated that the falcon has good acuity for spatial frequencies up to about 0.2 min of visual angle as compared to about 0.6 min for the human. This comparison is shown in Fig. 6-36.

It is not possible to say that the packing density of the falcon's photoreceptors is the sole determinant of this animal's enhanced acuity because its optical properties are also so much better than a human's, but it is clear that the dimensions of the receptor do play an important contributory role. From an evolutionary and adaptive point of view the optics, receptor size, and neural interactions can all be thought of as having evolved an interacting composite of properties such that each is supportive of the others, but not wasteful, in making available competencies that could not possibly be utilized by the less capable elements in the system.

It is also interesting to note that the decline in the acuity of the falcon when the stimulus luminance decreases was much steeper than in the human according to Fox and his co-workers. This finding is entirely consistent with the Snyder, Laughlin, and Stavenga predictions discussed earlier in this section. The smaller receptors in the falcon would be expected to be especially sensitive to the interfering effects of the compensatory balance between the demands for good acuity and the demands for magnitude representation. Both this prediction and the psychophysical findings are, therefore, in complete agreement on this score.

Acuity, of course, must also be influenced by many other factors beyond those associated with receptor density and ocular optics that I have mentioned so

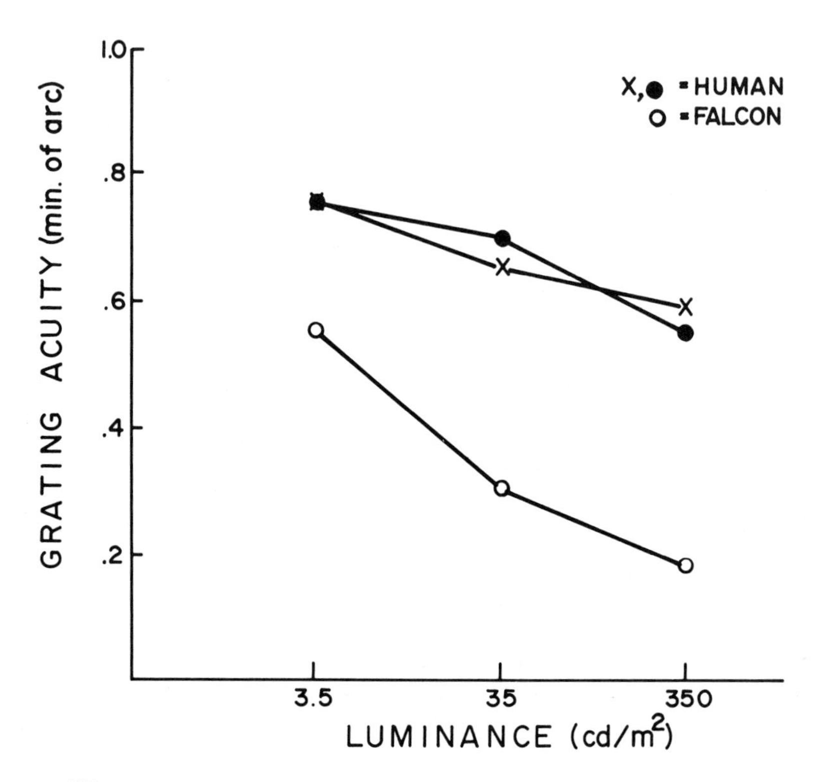

FIG. 6.36. The effect of luminance on acuity in the falcon and in the human. (From Fox, Lehmkuhle, and Westendorf, © 1976, with the permission of the American Association for the Advancement of Science.)

far. Burg (1966) reports that there is a progressive decline in visual acuity with age. Even more surprising, he notes that men have significantly better visual acuity than women—a result that remains unexplained and somewhat disconcerting in this day of equality between the sexes.

Remarkably, acuity is only minimally affected by target motion. A number of investigators have shown that there is little effect of stabilizing a retinal image on acuity (Keesey, 1960) and that the function relating target velocity to acuity is also quite flat when the velocity of a Landolt C target is varied over a range of 0–3.0 deg/sec (Westheimer & McKee, 1975), as shown in Fig. 6-37. This insensitivity to velocity also held for a vernier acuity target.

It should not go unremarked that while I have generally alluded only to the spatial resolvability of two or more objects as the main measure of acuity in this discussion, the Spatial Modulation Transfer Function (*SMTF*), measured psychophysically as opposed to optically (see p. 339), must also be informationally equivalent to the two-object acuity measure and provides an alternative means of quantifying the visual resolution capacity. Since the psychophysical

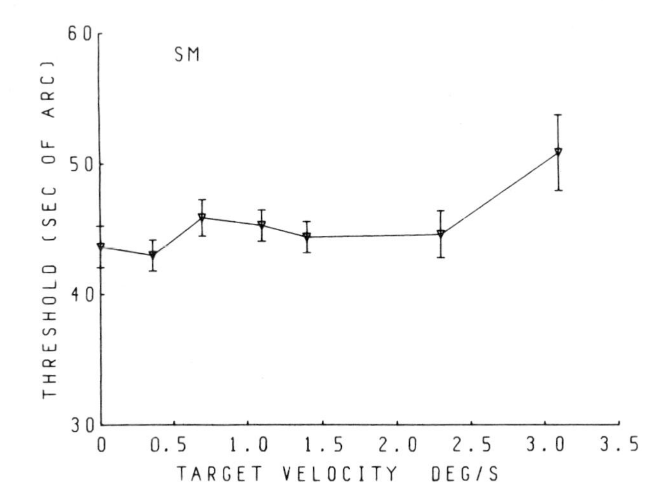

FIG. 6.37. Graph showing the surprisingly small effect of target motion on visual acuity. (From Westheimer and McKee, © 1975, with the permission of the American Institute of Physics.)

SMTF was first introduced the general finding has been replicated a number of times. The surprising thing about such psychophysically obtained SMTFs is that they do not even qualitatively match the optically measured ones. Figure 5-37 in Chapter 5, for example, displayed both "objective" and "subjective" *SMTF*. *One* major difference was immediately evident. The psychophysical *SMTF* is not monotonic like the optical one. Instead, there is clearly a peak present (comparable to the resonant peak of a tuned filter) that is not characteristic of the *SMTF* obtained by an objective measurement of image spread. This psychophysical result is so nonveridical with the proximal stimulus pattern, as defined by the objective *SMTF,* that it must be a result of higher levels of perceptual processing. There is no plausible optical or receptor property that could account for this phenomenon, and it therefore must be considered to be the result of processes at a higher level where neural interactions provide a more plausible explanation.

F. PERCEPTUAL IMPACT OF RECEPTOR DYNAMICS

Now that I have considered some of the ways in which the chemistry, availability, and distribution of the photochemical can influence perceptual functions, it is appropriate to look at other receptor (Level 1) processes that are not directly photochemical or associated with receptor size but which can also exert a profound influence on the molar perceptual experience. This class of processes includes actions that reflect the neurophysiological properties of the receptor rather than its anatomy or photochemistry. One process of particular importance is the transformation represented by the functional relationship between the stimulus intensity and the neural response—the graded receptor potential—produced by the rod or cone. This mathematical relationship is referred to as the receptor dynamic response or, in brief, the receptor dynamic. In the subsections that follow, I consider the neural basis of the receptor dynamic and its perceptual implications, particularly as they have been theoretically described by Ernst H. Weber (1795–1878) and Gustav T. Fechner (1801–1887) in the last century and S. S. Stevens (1906–1973) in this one.

In general, as I soon show, both the neural and psychophysical functions are nonlinear in the same way. Both lead to a "range compression" that allows a very wide range of signals to be represented and differences between both low and high levels of stimulation to be discriminated. How and where this highly adaptive transformation occurs are the questions I discuss next.

1. The Neural Basis

Although a great deal is known about the primary sensory action leading to the stereoisomerization and ultimately the disruption of the rhodopsin molecule that triggers the transduction process, relatively less is known about the mechanisms responsible for the production of the generator potential itself—the first specifically membrane-mediated representation of the stimulus within the nervous system. The consensus now is that the breakdown of the photochemical in the vertebrate photoreceptor leads to the release of some kind of an "internal transmitter substance" that blocks the sodium channels in the plasma membrane of the outer segment (Baylor, Hodgkin, & Lamb, 1974; Penn & Hagins, 1972). The effect of this transmitter substance is to reduce the permeability of the membrane and thus to hyperpolarize the receptor. It is this hyperpolarization that is the actual information carry signal, according to this hypothesis, in the vertebrate.

There has been considerable interest in this problem since Wald's (1968) suggestion that the exposed sulfhydryl bonds on the opsin moiety of the fractured rhodopsin molecule might directly alter the membrane in a way that produces a change in its ionic permeability. In fact, the sequence of thermal decompositions of the family of light-driven breakdown products of rhodopsin is so complicated that it is not even certain which step in this sequence is critical for triggering the membrane changes nor which component in the breakdown series (if any single one) is the essential chemical one. What is known is that at some point in the cycle, one of the breakdown products must do something to the intrareceptor disk, which contains the photochemical, in order to allow information concerning the chemical processes going on in that disk to be conveyed to the outer membrane of the receptor itself. The actual messenger may be either an electrical signal that directly activates the synapse at the foot of the receptor or a chemical process that leads to a change in the permeability of the receptor membrane via some specialized receptor site.

The possibility that some sort of an ionic messenger exists that must pass from the disk to the cell membrane has stimulated a number of workers (Heller, Ostwald, & Bok, 1970) to postulate one or another chemical model comparable in principle to the chemical transmitters of synaptic transmission (see also Adolph, 1964). The difference in the case of the receptor potential is that the transmitter chemical process is going on totally inside the confines of the single receptor cell rather than extracellularly as it does at a synapse. The idea is that the photochemical-containing disk is acting as if it were a separate "presynaptic" neuron even though it is enclosed within the confines of its "postsynaptic" partner—the outer membrane of the receptor cell itself.

Opposition to Wald's original hypothesis that the opsin moiety is the important factor in developing the membrane potential has also been forthcoming. Bonting and Bangham (1967), for example, in developing their chemical model of the origin of the graded receptor potential, attribute the key role to the all-*trans* retinal that is isomerized from the 11-*cis* form by light rather than to the opsin. An excellent review of this work can be found on pp. 328–337 of Rodieck's (1973) comprehensive book on the vertebrate retina.

The lack of definite knowledge concerning the relationship between the breakdown products of the photochemicals and the generation of the receptor potential is not the sole source of difficulty in understanding the function of these important cells. Far more obstructive to our understanding the perceptual impact of photoreceptor neurophysiological processes is the extreme difficulty in recording directly from these very fine and delicate cells. It was not until 1967 that the first reports of intracellular recording from cones began to emerge from the Japanese laboratory of Tsuneo Tomita (Tomita, Kaneko, Murakami, & Pautler, 1967) following their ingenious invention of the jolting device shown in Fig. 6-38. This jolter accelerated the receptor–electrode interface in a way that allowed very small microelectrodes to penetrate the surprisingly elastic and resistant plasma membrane of the vertebrate photoreceptor. Prior to that invention most recordings from the retina had either been poor extracellular recordings from receptors or had been obtained from the more easily penetrated bipolar or ganglion cells of the retina.

Unfortunately, recordings from secondary neural levels lead only to information about the pooled characteristics of two or three levels of neural information processing and not to definitive information about the functions of receptors in isolation. Only in the last few years have intracellular studies of receptors themselves begun to appear that speak directly to the problem of receptor neurophysiology (Baylor & Hodgkin, 1974; Fain & Dowling, 1973; Kleinschmidt & Dowling, 1975). Thus we are only now beginning to appreciate that the neural properties of the receptor, independent of its photochemical processes, may also represent critical processes that influence perception. I have already mentioned the possible role of receptor neural (as opposed to photochemical) processes in dark adaptation. In addition, the neural properties of the recep-

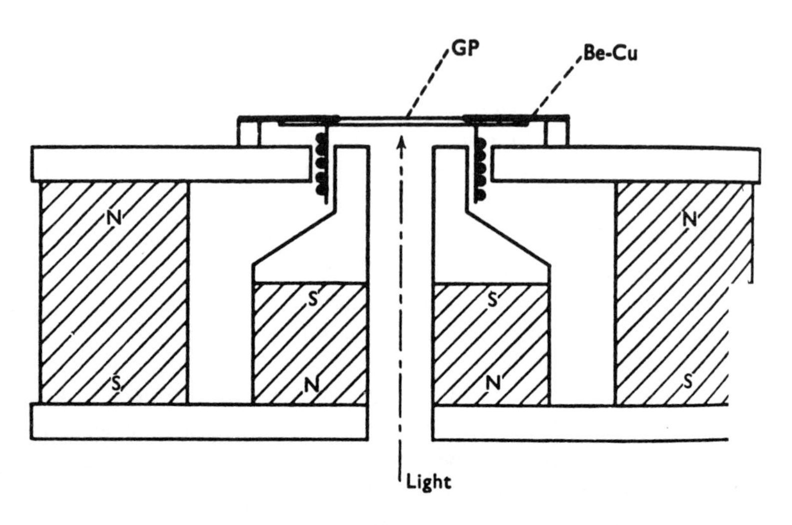

FIG. 6.38. Tomita's device for "jolting" the retina to allow microelectrodes to penetrate individual photoreceptors. GP is a glass plate on which the retina is mounted. Be-Cu is a beryllium-copper plate through which a 10kHz current is passed to produce the oscillations. (From Tomita, © 1970, with the permission of Cambridge University Press.)

tor have also been implicated in the definition of the shape of the suprathreshold function relating stimulus intensity and subjective brightness.

The possible neural mechanisms that may underlie these processes are still only partially understood, but a most unusual hypothesis has been presented by Thorson and Biederman-Thorson (1974). They suggest that both dark adaptation and the suprathreshold function may be accounted for in terms of the distributed properties of the neural membrane. In other words, they suggest that the local properties of the membrane may differ from point to point on the surface of a receptor. Yet when accumulated, these local properties may add together to produce, in the transforms imposed on signals passing through the receptor cell, composite nonlinearities that are critical to higher-level behavior. Though the mathematical complexities of the Thorson and Biederman-Thorson model are beyond the scope of the present discussion, the important concept in their hypothesis is that it provides a unified explanation for both the nonphotochemical component of dark adaptation and the nonlinear range-compression properties exhibited by the receptor.

Regardless of whether the details of this distributed receptor hypothesis are correct, it is now generally agreed[18] that the overall dynamics of the photoreceptor process do display a nonlinear relationship between the intensity of the

[18]With the exception of the Kleinschmidt and Dowling study that I describe shortly.

stimulus and the intensity of the membrane response. Baylor and Fuortes (1970) have been able to record the receptor potential from single cones in the retina of the turtle by the use of an especially small micropipette. As usual, they found that a sustained negative resting potential, which hyperpolarized when stimulated with light, was recorded upon penetration. It should not be forgotten that the hyperpolarizing receptor potential has been found to be characteristic of all vertebrate receptors, although most invertebrate receptor potentials seem to depolarize when stimulated.

Figure 6-39 is a log–linear plot of the height of the potential recorded by Baylor and Fuortes for stimuli of various luminances relative to the maximum potential evoked with a "very bright light." To compare this data with the other data discussed in this section of this chapter, I have converted Baylor and Fuortes' data (as represented by the dotted curve) to log–log coordinates and replotted this converted data in Fig. 6-40. These data are best fit by a two-segment power function with an exponent of 0.58 for lower intensities and one that approaches zero for higher ones.

Tomita and his colleagues also measured this relationship between stimulus intensity and receptor membrane potential in the carp. Figure 6-41 shows their data as they initially reported them; they are more useful when converted to a log–log plot. The slope of this function, according to this transformation, is

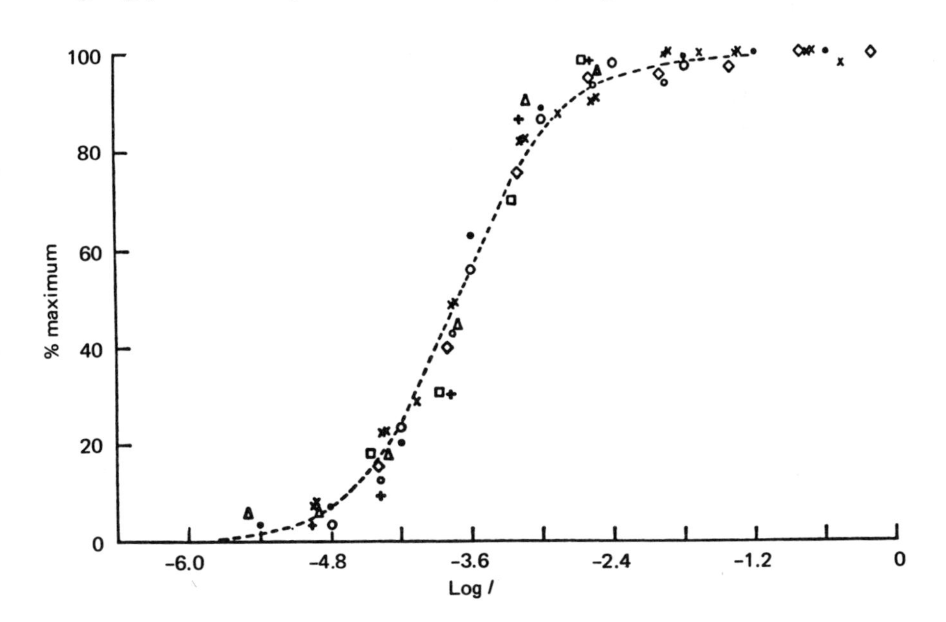

FIG. 6.39. The visual receptor potential amplitude from turtle cones as a function of the logarithm of stimulus intensities. (Redrawn from Baylor and Fuortes, 1970.)

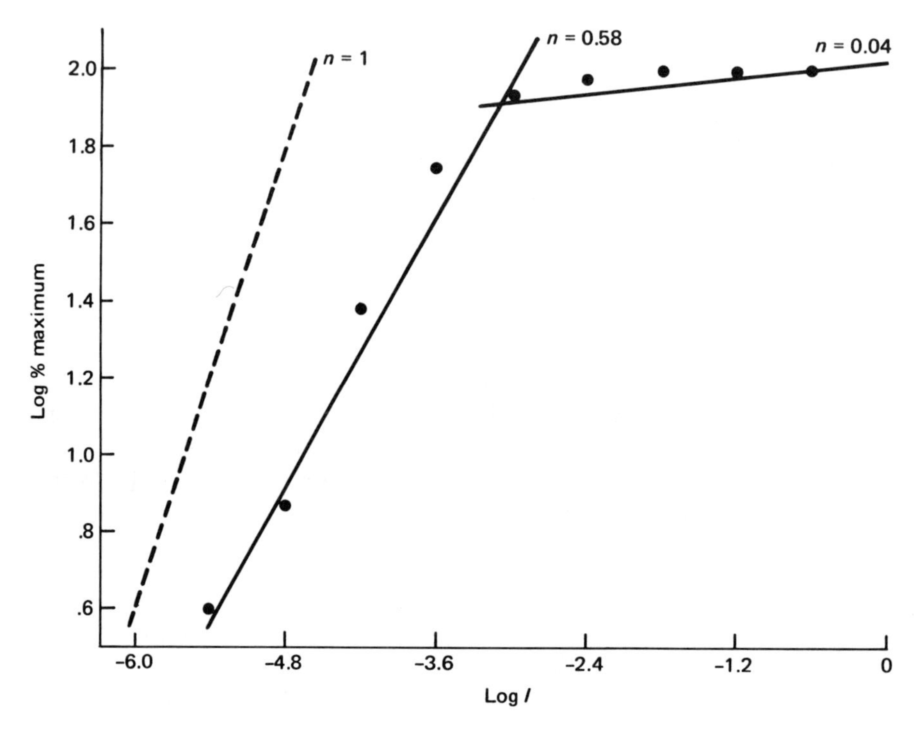

FIG. 6.40. A sample of the data of Fig. 6.39 converted to log-log coordinates displaying a two-segment range with power function exponents of 0.58 and 0.04, respectively. (From Uttal, © 1973.)

approximately 0.55. Thus, two independent measures of the nonlinear transformation between stimulus intensity and receptor potential suggest that the relationship is a nonlinear one with a compression factor equivalent to a power function with a slope of about 0.6. As we shall see, this is very close to the exponent obtained for the function relating the apparent brightness of a brief flash of light to the intensity of that flash (S. S. Stevens, 1971).

The compression of the receptor response in the photoreceptor is not, as I have mentioned, universally observed. Recently, the intracellular response of gecko rods and turtle cones have been studied by Kleinschmidt and Dowling (1975). They observed that in these animals, the relationship between the normalized (obtained by dividing the voltage in any trial with its maximum possible voltage) rod receptor potential and stimulus intensity was not compressed but was rather more closely approximated by a linear function (i.e., one that displayed a slope of 1.0 on a log-log plot) as shown in Fig. 6-42. At present it is not possible to say whether species or procedural differences account for the difference between this study and the others I have cited.

Recent evidence has indicated that the ascending portion of the receptor compression function can be generally represented by the function

$$V = V \max \frac{I^n}{(I^n + I_{0.5})} \tag{6-13}$$

where V is the value of the induced receptor potential by a stimulus of intensity I raised to an exponent n, V max is the maximum receptor potential, and $I_{0.5}$ is the stimulus intensity producing V max/2. This expression was first empirically developed for horizontal cells in the retina by Naka and Rushton (1966), but has now been shown to hold also for receptor potentials (Grabowski, Pinto, & Pak, 1972; Fain & Dowling, 1973). For brief flashes n approaches 1, but for longer flashes n can decrease to a value as low as 0.7. This difference in stimulus duration may be the difference accounting for the apparent discrepancy between Kleinschmidt and Dowling's data and those from other laboratories.

I shall not pursue the neurophysiology of the receptor dynamics further at this point. I have already discussed this topic extensively in an earlier work (Uttal, 1973) and other reviews such as those by Lipetz (1969) are also available. In general, most of the data seems to support the conclusion that the nonlinear response of the receptor introduces a range compression and nonlinear dynamic into the visual process that accounts in large part for related phenomena reported

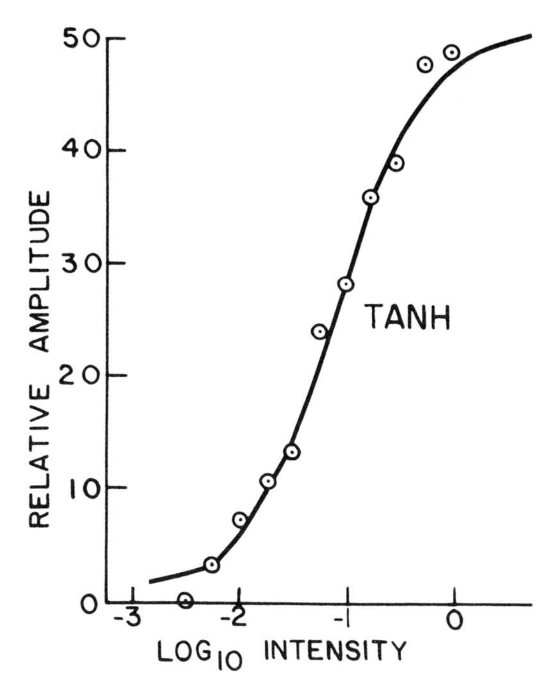

FIG. 6.41. The relationship between stimulus intensity and the response magnitude from a cone of a carp. This function exhibits a slope of approximately .55. (From Lipetz, © 1969, after Tomita, Kaneko, Murakami, and Pautler, 1967, with the permission of Pergamon Press, Ltd.)

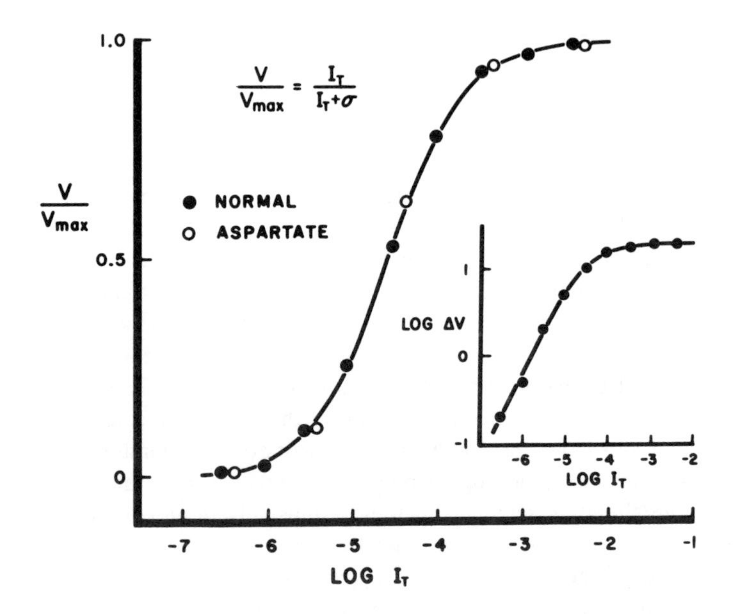

FIG. 6.42. The relationship between stimulus intensity and the Gecko photoreceptor's evoked potential. Open circles are for aspartate treated cells and the filled circles are for normal cells. The former condition produced 25% larger maximum voltages, but this absolute information is lost in computing the ratios shown on the vertical axis. The inset shows the data for the normal conditions plotted on log-log coordinates. This inset curve displays a slope of 1. Thus, in this case the relationship between the stimulus intensity and the response magnitude is linear. (From Kleinschmidt and Dowling, © 1975, with the permission of Rockefeller University Press.)

at the most molar level by psychophysical methods. Therefore it is probably appropriate in large part to attribute the compressed suprathreshold characteristic of molar human vision to the neurophysiology of the first-order neuron—the receptor—and this phenomenon is thus the result of a Level 1 process. This does not, however, preclude the contribution of higher levels to the final determination of the psychophysical function.

It is clear, however, that we do not yet understand the nature of the intracellular processes that more often than not produce a nonlinear, compressed relationship between the stimulus intensity and the receptor membrane potential. Rushton (1965) has suggested that response compression may be the result of an intrareceptor feedback mechanism that acts like a mechanical governor to regulate the amplitude of the potential that is produced. It may, on the other hand, represent an intrinsic nonlinearity in the photochemical breakdown process (small stimuli might produce relatively larger amounts of breakdown products than would larger ones) or reflect the nonlinear properties of the amplification mechanism that converts the energy of a single photon into as many as two million unit electrical charges (Hagins, Penn, & Yoshikami, 1970).

It is clear, however, that the range compression introduced into the visual signal, whatever it origin, does represent an enormously advantageous evolutionary development for human vision. It is the main factor accounting for our ability to deal with stimuli that range over very wide ranges of intensity. The brightest lights that humans can perceive without retinal damage may be as great as 10 billion times more intense than the lowest energy levels of a few quanta that can be detected at threshold. Furthermore, our visual system can both tell the difference between two stimuli that differ by only a few quanta and also discriminate between light levels, billions of times more intense, that differ by huge numbers of quanta. This highly useful ability to vary the size of the differential threshold as a function of the absolute stimulus intensity is a common attribute of most human sensory functions.

What I have just said, of course, is a verbal expression of what, perhaps was the first great mathematical generalization in psychophysics—Weber's law. Weber's law expressed this dependence of differential thresholds on stimulus intensity levels in the following way:

$$\frac{\Delta I}{I} = K \tag{6-14}$$

where ΔI is the just-detectable difference, I is the absolute stimulus intensity level, and K is a constant. Whereas this generalization is now known to be an inadequate description of the psychological function, it is the generalized idea of compression that it represents, rather than the specifics of the law, that has led to its persistence for almost a century of psychological theory and experimentation.

In sum, the neuroreductionistic point that I want to stress here is that both the enormous intensity range of human vision and its ability to discriminate differences at both low and high light levels seem most likely to arise directly out of the compressed transform of the mechanism responsible for the production of the initial receptor potential. Although it is not certain that all of the compression exhibited psychophysically can be accounted for by these receptor processes, so many sensory receptors exhibit comparable compressed functions that the generalization that stimulus intensity-response magnitude compression mainly reflects a receptor transformation seems secure.

It would, of course, be enormously surprising if all measures in all species reflected exactly the same degree of compression. It would also be too much to expect that the compression should be solely a function of the intensity of the stimulus. Indeed we know that other stimulus factors affect the degree of compression measured neurophysiologically. For example, the duration of the stimulus plays an important role in the degree to which the response dynamic is compressed in psychological experiments just as it does in neurophysiological experiments. With prolonged stimuli the compression seems to be greater than it is with brief flashes (S. S. Stevens, 1971; Mansfield, 1973). The particular response measure used also affects the degree of compression that is measured. Neurophysiological data obtained using evoked brain potentials as indicators (Stevens, 1971) suggest that the exponent for the composite response may differ from both the single-cellular and psychophysical ones. Boynton and Whitten (1970) have also studied the response dynamic of the composite receptor potential evoked from monkey cones and found that a power function with an exponent of 0.7 almost always describes the data obtained with an extracellular, but microscopic, electrode; and this value does not agree exactly with either the psychophysical or evoked brain potential exponents. Notwithstanding these disagreements, which speak more to the problems of interpreting neural codes than to the locus of compression, the response compression displayed in the psychophysical data now seems to be best explained as a direct result of the critical process represented by the receptor dynamic.

A remaining issue concerns whether the compression is instantaneous (and dependent upon the initial stages of transduction) or is delayed while some adaptation mechanism acting as an automatic gain control process is brought into action. The latter mechanism would imply that the compression function was mediated by some other mechanism that depended upon the level of the stimulating light. Although no complete resolution to this issue has yet been forthcoming, it seems likely that both sources of compression occur.

Having considered the likely receptor origins of response compression, I can turn now to a discussion of the perceptual consequences of these early receptor transformations. The following discussion concentrates on the suprathreshold dynamics as observed at the perceptual level.

2. Mathematical Descriptions of Suprathreshold Dynamics[19]

a. The Weber–Fechner Relation—A Logarithmic Law. It was not too many years ago that the Weber–Fechner description of the relationships between stimulus amplitudes, incremental thresholds, and subjective magnitudes described in this section was considered to be "The Psychophysical Law." Though it is no longer accepted as more than only an approximately valid model of psychophysical performance, the Weber–Fechner formulization is of particular interest for two reasons. First, it historically represents one of the first formal expressions of the emerging belief in the quantifiability of mental processes. Second, it is very often today the specific critical target of some of the newer approaches to psychophysical modeling. Although it is quite clear that the

[19]This section has been adapted and expanded from my earlier discussion (Uttal, 1973).

Weber–Fechner law can no longer adequately represent the abundance of data obtained in the last century, it is important to understand the assumptions that underlie its formulation. In the following section, I review the history of Fechner's mathematical development of some empirical observations made by Weber and the impact these ideas had on many decades of perceptual research.

In the middle of the nineteenth century, Ernst Weber reported the results of some experiments on differential thresholds, which asked the general question: What is the size of the increment that has to be added to a given stimulus intensity to produce a just-noticeable difference? Weber's experiments were initially carried out using weight estimations as a model experiment, even though there was no applied interest in this particular type of judgment at the time. His experiments involved the measurements of the differential weight that had to be removed from or added to a standard weight for the change to be detected by either active (with hand movements) or passive (without hand movements) examination. Weber's general conclusion was that the amount of weight that had to be removed was a constant proportion of the total weight originally in hand.

Weber himself probably never used the explicit mathematical equation that I presented in Eq. 6-14. It was Fechner who quantified the qualitative notion expressed in Weber's verbal statements. Even then, Weber was probably not even the first to mention the ratio relationship in sensory studies. Fechner (1860) mentions that the mathematician Euler, 100 years earlier, had noted the relationship for the musical scale. Fechner also noted that the astronomers Steinheil and Pogson had appreciated the same reciprocal relationship as characteristic of the scales of stellar magnitudes. Nevertheless, Weber was the first to proclaim its general applicability to sensory magnitudes in many different modalities. Fechner himself, however, was among the first to mention that the relation was not of universal validity, his comment being a portent of criticisms to be made 100 years later.

Fechner, a mathematical physicist by training, derived another distinctly different psychophysical law by mathematically manipulating the algebraic expression of Weber's Law expressed in Eq. 6-14. To do so, however, required several very important assumptions that have made his derivation controversial for many years. First of all, he assumed that because the just-noticeable *stimulus* difference ratio was constant; changes in the *subjective magnitude* should be also directly proportional to the Weber ratio. He expressed this idea in the following relation:

$$\Delta\Psi = k\,\frac{\Delta I}{I} \tag{6-15}$$

where $\Delta\Psi$ is the perceived change in subjective magnitude for a just-noticeable difference; K is a scaling constant; ΔI is the change in stimulus intensity for a just-noticeable difference; and I is the absolute magnitude of the stimulus. This equation is not (and this is most important) directly derivable from Weber's law, which involves only stimulus intensities. It is a separate idea and one of the two key assumptions in Fechner's development. It is most important to appreciate that Fechner only assumed that all just-noticeable differences ($\Delta\Psi$s) are equal in size.

The other key assumption in Fechner's development is that this statement (Eq. 6-15), formulated at the level of macroscopic finite differences, can be taken to the limit and reduced to the infinitesimal differential form

$$d\,\Psi = \frac{dI}{I} \tag{6-16}$$

From this point on, all of the mathematics is straightforward enough, even if the final equation is empirically invalid. Eq. 6-16 may be integrated on both sides to give

$$\int d\,\Psi = k \int \frac{dI}{I} \tag{6-17}$$

or

$$\Psi = k \ln I + Q \tag{6-18}$$

where Q is a constant of integration. Q may be removed by formulating the equation in terms of the absolute threshold. At threshold $\Psi = 0$ and $I = I_0$, therefore,

$$0 = K \ln \mathrm{I}_0 + Q \tag{6-19}$$

or

$$-Q = K \ln I_0 \tag{6-20}$$

which may be substituted into Eq. 6-18 to give

$$\Psi = K \ln I - K \ln I_0 \tag{6-21}$$

or

$$\Psi = K \ln \frac{I}{I_0} \tag{6-22}$$

which is the final form of what has now become well known as the Weber–Fechner "law." Specifically, this expression states that the subjective magnitude of a sensation is a function of the logarithm of the ratio of the stimulus intensity and the absolute threshold stimulus intensity. It is, therefore, a law of suprathreshold subjective magnitudes that asserts a logarithmic compression dynamic relating, for example, brightness and luminance. Weber's law, on the other hand, is a description of the size of the differential threshold.

Admittedly, the derivation is based on a pair of quite controversial assumptions, and some contemporary mathematical psychologists claim that both are, in fact, invalid. Furthermore, the Weber–Fechner law is not a good predictor of empirical data. Nevertheless, as I have said before, the generality of the compression function implicit in the logarithmic relation between stimulus intensity and perceptual magnitudes gave it wide currency for many years in psychological thinking.

b. The Stevens Power Law. In recent years, some of the discrepancies of the Weber–Fechner law as an experimental predictor have begun to become more disconcerting. Not all psychophysical intensity functions turned out to be even approximately logarithmically compressed, and therefore new formulations have been suggested. Perhaps the most vigorous champion of a systematic new point of view was S. S. Stevens (1906–1973), who proposed (Stevens, 1961) that intensive functions are better modeled by a power law than by a logarithmic function.[20] Stevens' formularization of his "psychophysical law" differs considerably from the Weber–Fechner relation in that it allows both expanded and compressed response dynamics.

Stevens' theory, if one can call his descriptive curve fitting a theory, is that all sensory magnitudes can be described by the following form of a generalized power function:

$$\Psi = K(I - I_0)^n \tag{6-23}$$

where the terms have the same meaning as in Eq. 6-22 above. The only new term—n—is simply the exponent or power to which the stimulus term is raised. A key concept of Stevens' law is that there is a particular power for each sensory modality and, for that matter, many different tasks in the same modality.

Before we consider the implications of this idea in detail, let us consider for a moment the effect of variations of the exponent. If the exponent is equal to 1, sensory magnitude is simply a linear function of the stimulus intensity scaled by the coefficient K. If the exponent is less than 1, however, the function is compressed or decelerated so that the same absolute increment at low levels of stimulation produces a greater differential response than when the intensity is high. If, however, the exponent is greater than 1, we have a situation in which expansion of the response occurs. That is, a given increment (ΔI) in stimulus intensity at high stimulus levels causes a larger change in sensory magnitude than when the stimulus intensity is low. Figure 6-43 illustrates on a linear–linear scale the effect of such variations in the exponent.

There is a convenient graphical test to distinguish among the three types of response curves that we have so far discussed: (1) the linear, (2) the logarithmic, and (3) the power function. A linear curve will appear as a straight line on graphs in which both coordinates are plotted on linear scales—a linear–linear plot. A

[20]A similar exponential relationship had been proposed much earlier (Plateau, 1872) and had been the object of considerable research in the latter part of the nineteenth century.

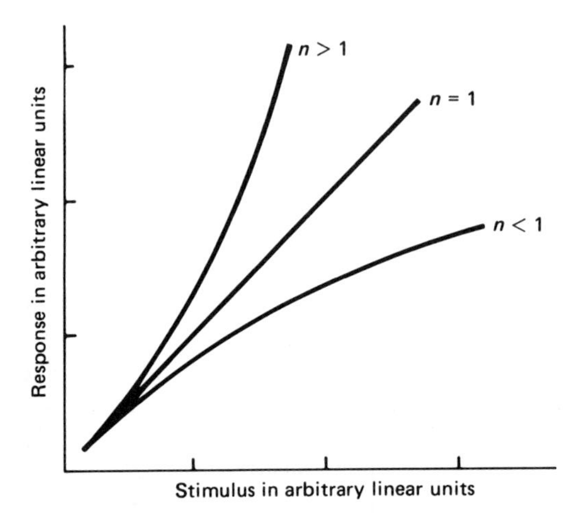

FIG. 6.43. A drawing of a linear (n = 1), compressed (n < 1), and an expanded (n > 1) power function plotted on linear-linear coordinates. (From Uttal, 1973.)

logarithmic function will appear as a straight line on a graph in which the vertical coordinate is plotted linearly and the horizontal axis is plotted on a logarithmic scale—a log–linear scale. A power function, on the other hand, will appear as a straight line on a graph in which both axes have been plotted along logarithmic scales—a log–log plot. The slope of the straight line representing a power function on a log–log plot is equal to the exponent of that power function. Thus, when the slope of a linear function is 1 on a log–log scale (and its exponent is also 1), a straight line will, in fact, represent a true linear function. The relationship among the expanded, linear, and compressed functions on the linear–linear and log–log plots can be seen if one compares Fig. 6-43 and 6-44. Expanded curves are accelerating, and compressed curves are decelerating on a linear–linear plot. All are straight lines on a log–log plot but with slopes that vary according to the degree of curvature. Accelerating (expanded) curves have slopes greater than 1; decelerating (compressed) functions have slopes less than 1.

It should also be appreciated that logarithmic functions also come very close to overlapping some of the power functions with exponents much less than 1, and in certain instances some investigators have had to apply statistical tests of the closeness of fit to determine which function is, in fact, able to account for more of the variance. That such tests are required to discriminate between two such very general models is, itself, an indication of the frailty of seeking simplistic laws of psychophysical correspondence. At the very best, psychophysical laws can be no more than gross approximations simply because many additional stimulus and situational factors (rather than, for example, stimulus intensity alone) determine the dimensions of any subjective experience. There is also the very serious conceptual problem inherent in the fact that these laws are all too general. Any monotonic function can be fit by a power function of some kind, and such extreme generality is itself a plausible argument against its utility as a

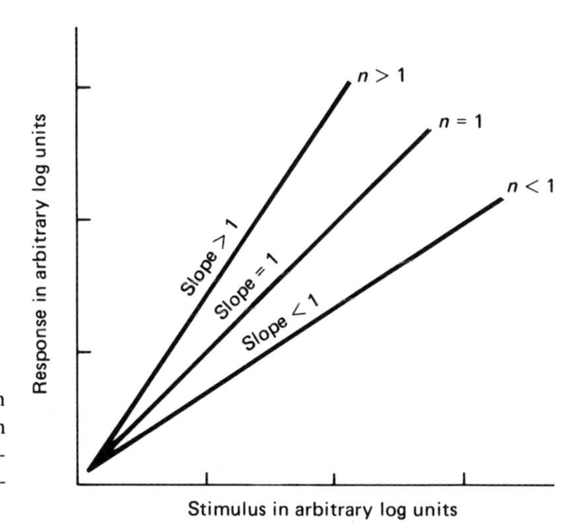

FIG. 6.44. A drawing of a linear (n = 1), a compressed (n < 1), and an expanded n > 1) power function plotted on log-log coordinates. (From Uttal, 1973.)

specific psychological theory. Another most severe criticism is that the data do not fit either the Weber–Fechner nor the Stevens formulation very well, particularly when obtained from individual subjects.[21]

Finally, this approach to the formulation of psychophysical laws also suffers from the fact that it overemphasizes the relationship between the stimulus intensity and the subjective magnitude. There are many other dimensions of both the stimulus and the response that have to be considered in perceptual research, and to assert that this particular relationship is "the psychophysical law" is to ignore all of those other dimensions and associations. I refer the reader to my earlier work (Uttal, 1973, pp. 266–273) for a more extensive critique of the power law idea. A more supportive view of the efficacy of a general power law can be found in Marks (1974).

Clearly, however, these brief comments only scratch the tip of a massive problem that is of great concern to a number of contemporary psychophysicists. The rationale underlying the representation of sensory information by real numbers is an exceedingly deep problem, but I will have to leave it to others with a far greater degree of expertise in this field than I possess to elucidate these subtleties.

The most important general point that I hope the reader will carry away from this discussion is that the compressed dynamic, which does seem to be a valid description of sensory magnitude functions and which is generally fit by either

---

[21]An interesting new point of view is that Fechner and Stevens may both be correct to the extent that either is; each procedure may measure a different aspect of the response. Wasserman, Felsten, and Easland (1979) raise this possibility and note that the peak amplitude and the area under a curve give slightly different functions that may be separately assayed by magnitude estimate and increment techniques, respectively. One may be best fit by a log function, the other by a power function.

the logarithmic or exponential laws, is most likely to be the outcome of a receptor (Level 1) process.

G. AN INTERIM SUMMARY

In this chapter I have surveyed the first level of psychoneural processing, the variety of Level 1 processes occurring within receptors, that alters the flow of afferent information in ways that lead to corresponding perceptual phenomena. It has not been possible to exclude all discussion of other level processes entirely from this chapter. I have alluded to the fact that some Level 1 processes might just as well be classified as Level 0 ones. There are also peripheral transformations that are not yet fully understood and cannot yet be exclusively attributed either to Level 1 or a higher-level transformation. There is a particular difficulty in disentangling the Level 1 processes from the Level 2 processes. Both share many common features, and the relevant processes may be either redundant or may mimic the transformation of the other level.

I believe, however, that in this chapter I have been able to support the hypothesis that there exist molar perceptual phenomena that are attributable to transformations that occur in the most peripheral neuron in the afferent chain—the receptor itself. To express the inverse corollary of this statement, the transformational properties of the receptor are discernible in the molar psychophysical response. This is a powerful statement; it is awesome to consider that we are able to discuss with such confidence the role of microscopic biophysical and biochemical events in the context of the molar behavior of the entire organism.

Nevertheless, a number of the topics I have discussed depend upon just this approach. We have seen, for example, that the absorptive properties of four very special photosensitive chemicals contained within the outer segment of the receptors define the nature of the interactions between photons and neurons. In doing so, these photochemical reactions establish certain neural codes within the peripheral nervous system that represent the dimensions of photic stimulus. The range of the visible spectrum, a phenomenon of great interest to psychologists, is uniquely determined by the range of quantum energies that can be absorbed by these photochemicals. Similarly, the absolute threshold, especially because of the extreme sensitivity of the human visual system, is largely determined by the way in which the molecules of these photochemicals absorb quanta on a one-for-one basis. In fact, as we have seen, the sensitivity of the human eye is so great that it appears that under optimum conditions, we may be differentially sensitive to each individual quantum of light. This hypersensitivity changes the problem of the variability of the threshold from one that emphasized the intrinsic variability of the visual system to one that emphasizes the statistical variability of the emission of quanta from a light source. The relationship between the background activity in an unstimulated retina and the amount of activity induced by a near-threshold stimulus thus becomes of extreme importance in the analysis of the threshold problem.

We have also seen in this chapter that the absorption spectra of the chemicals in the photoreceptor at this initial level of transduction impose constraints on the encoding of the wavelength spectrum of a stimulus that have persistent and residual effects up to the level of the molar perceptual response. The differences between the luminosity curves obtained in bright and dark lights are totally explained in terms of the shift from one type of receptor to another as are many of the features of the dark-adaptation curve. Equally profound is the persisting effect of the absorption spectra of the three cone photopigments (a Level 1 process) on psychophysically obtained color-mixing data. Whereas other levels of processing are involved in color perception (as we see in later chapters) and reflect higher levels of encoding and transformations, the important fact is that it is possible to design psychological experiments whose results are sensitive to the absorptive properties of the photochemicals themselves.

The discussion in this chapter also pointed out that the photochemical must be extremely depleted before there is any perceptual effect of its availability. This insensitivity to photochemical concentration in the face of wide variation in the intensity of stimuli probably also results from the fact that the absorptive process is mediated on a one-quantum-for-one-molecule basis. Because there is an enormous amplification of the absorption of even this slight amount of energy and because so little of the photochemical is utilized in a normal visual process, the bleaching or depletion of photochemical must be extensive before it can exert any measurable effect. This generalization leads directly to the corollary that because there are substantial psychophysical effects of dark adaptation even at low light levels at which only a small proportion of the photochemical is bleached, these effects must be mediated by neural processes, some of which occur in the receptor, that supplement the adaptive effects of photochemical depletion.

There are, however, other phenomena that do depend on the distribution of the receptor elements if not the local concentration of the photochemical. The absolute threshold obtained at any point on the retina seems to be closely related to the density of the rods, and the *shape* of the dark-adaptation curve depends in large part on the relative contribution of rods and cones in the fovea and the peripheral retina respectively.

On the other hand, the well-known "abnormalities" in color vision in even normal eyes in different regions of the retina (e.g., the peripheral retina is dichromatic) may not be what they might seem. The initial judgment was that such color blindnesses are easily explained in terms of differing distributions of the three receptors. Now, however, the consensus is that these anomalies are more dependent upon the convergent network interactions that pool, and thus lose, the differential information from the three types of cones. Strong evidence for this conclusion is provided by the observation that all three types of cones are present in equal proportions though in reduced numbers across the entire retina.

For this reason, I have classified these effects of retinal locus on color vision as a Level 2 phenomena and discuss them in Chapter 8. (I should note in passing, however, that the tritanopia of the central fovea is, in fact, usually associated with the observed absence of the short-wavelength-sensitive cones there.)

The general point made by this mimicking of Level 1 processes by Level 2 transformations is that it is often exceedingly difficult to determine the actual level of critical processing for phenomena that are patently peripheral. It takes the combined experimental resources of the psychologist and the neuroscientist to make that correct level attribution.

The next topic discussed was the theoretical impact of the receptors on the ability to encode various levels of intensity and of spatial patterns. Both abilities are strongly dependent on receptor size, but the effects are of opposite polarities. The larger the receptor, the better able it is to catch larger numbers of quanta and thus to discriminate between more levels of intensity. On the other hand, the larger the receptor the poorer it will be in representing spatial patterns in accord with the sampling theorem. Therefore, there is a compensatory interaction between the receptor size best suited for encoding intensity and that size best suited for encoding spatial patterns. What would be an optimum size for multilevel intensity representation would be inappropriate for spatial pattern representation and vice versa. It turns out that, in fact, there is little variation in receptor size across the retina, and thus evolutionary forces have not altered us to meet this need by stimulating the emergence of variable size receptors. We now appreciate, however, that the convergent mechanisms of the peripheral retina may simulate the function of large receptors by pooling the outputs of a number of individual small receptors into a single neural fiber. Thus, ideal conditions for pattern discrimination can be maintained in the fovea while at the same time peripheral loci may be organized by convergent mechanisms for optimum intensity discrimination even though receptor size actually remains constant.

Finally, we saw that the molar response dynamic—the compressed relationship between stimulus intensity and response magnitude—is probably also due to another neural process in the receptor. That process is the compression inherent in the electrochemical process that leads to the production of the receptor's graded potential. The actual source of the neural compression in the receptor is not certain, but it may be related to intrareceptor feedback gain control processes that we are just beginning to understand.

In sum, there are a number of well-known and identifiable processes in the receptor itself that have subsequent phenomenological outcomes. The purpose of this chapter has been to explore those perceptually influential receptor (Level 1) processes and to describe the associated molar phenomena.

In considering Level 1 processes, I have encountered a substantial difficulty with one special class of phenomena—those involving temporal interactions. For reasons that are highly specific to the dimension of time, it is much more difficult to disentangle the Level 1 and Level 2 processes contributing to temporal interactions than it is with the intensive, qualitative, and spatial ones that were emphasized in this chapter. I have necessarily bowed to this discrepancy in our understanding and in the next chapter have separated the temporal phenomena from those other topics. This constitutes a multilevel digression that violates the general theme of the taxonomic theory I present here. It is, however, unavoidable. To do otherwise would violate the limits of current scientific knowledge.

7 Temporal Interactions: A Multilevel Digression

A. A COMMENT

In the previous chapter I dealt with a number of phenomena that are directly associated with transformations occurring in the receptors. For that level of critical processing, it was comparatively easy to establish the links between perceptual responses and critical processes. In this chapter, I turn to another cluster of phenomena, all of which are involved in one way or another with the dimension of time. Unlike the relatively unequivocal associations between phenomena and receptor level processes, there is a substantial amount of uncertainty concerning the level of processing to which these temporally related phenomena should be attributed. As we later see, most perceptual theoreticians agree that the phenomena of interest in this chapter are the result of relatively peripheral processes; however, there are few satisfyingly rigorous means of disentangling the Level 1 and Level 2 contributions.

As a consequence, this chapter represents a substantial digression from the taxonomic schema that I have sought to maintain in this book. Given the present state of our knowledge and the logical complexity of the problem of disentangling receptor and neural network temporal responses, any alternative to the course I now pursue would become objectionably arbitrary and therefore aesthetically unacceptable. The taxonomic model would be strained too far for credibility should I try to force these phenomena uncritically into either Level 1 or Level 2 explanations exclusively. Therefore, this chapter is a multilevel discussion that cuts across both levels and leaves any more detailed analysis for future researchers. The insertion of this chapter simply and, I believe, fairly acknowledges the fact that modern psychological theory and experiment have not yet been able to provide a microtheory or technology of process localization that can handle these particular phenomena. In the following section, I consider the nature of the difficulty encountered in attempts to explain the temporal interaction phenomena in terms of any single level of processing.

B. BACKGROUND

The electrophysiological response of the nervous system to a brief flash of light is not necessarily equally as brief as the stimulus flash. Quite the contrary, a large number of experiments have demonstrated that a brief stimulus produces a prolonged response in a rod or a cone as well as at higher levels of the nervous system. Figure 7-1 displays in a diagramatic fashion the prototypical time course of a receptor response to a brief stimulus. I have drawn this figure with the response downward to emphasize that in the vertebrate the photoreceptor response is usually a hyperpolarization of the membrane potential rather than the depolarization characteristic of other higher-level vertebrate neurons and invertebrate photoreceptors. This prototypical receptor response can be seen to have several features that collectively characterize its temporal course. First, there is a definite latent period subsequent to the presentation of the stimulus and prior to the beginning of any observable neural activity. Second, the initial response has a measurable rise time. Third, there is an initial, but transient, level of activity during which the response magnitude may be substantially greater than the level arrived at following the initial transient. Fourth, there is a prolonged period of response that may show a progressive decline in amplitude. Finally, there is a decline in the response to the resting level following the offset of the stimulus. This off response is often associated with other transient shifts in the membrane potential. Most important of all, however, in the context of our present discussion is the fact that the overall duration of this phototypical neural response may

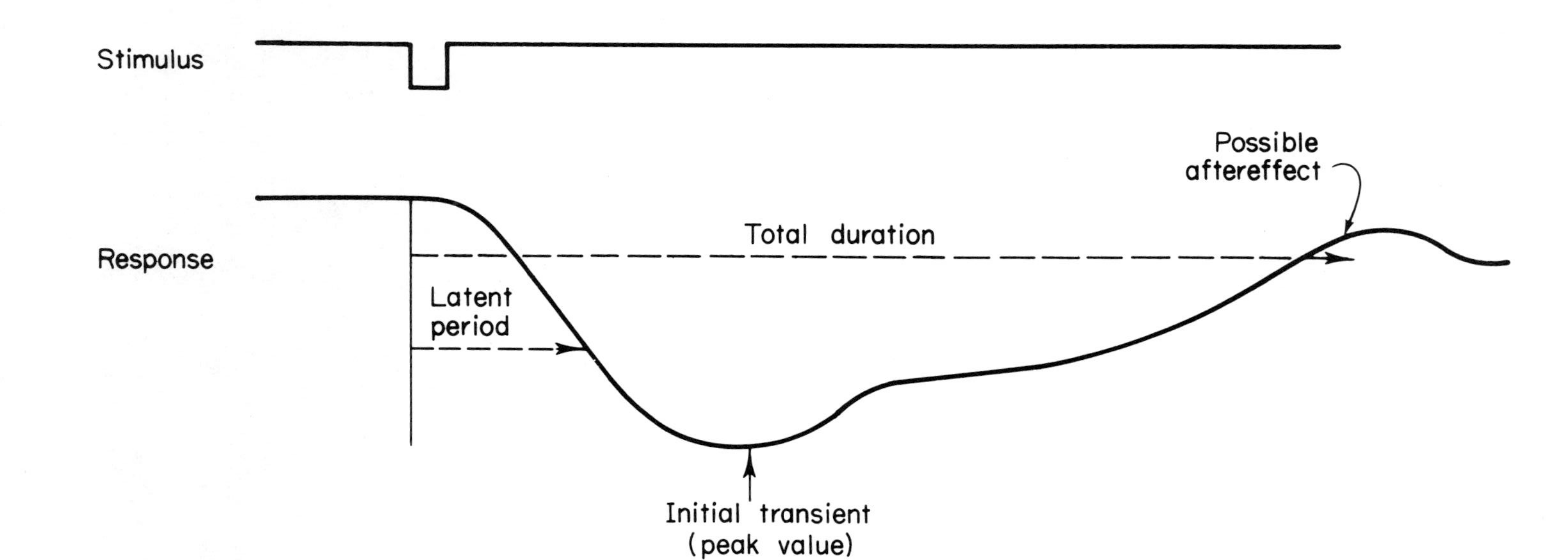

FIG. 7.1. A schematic representation of the prototypical prolongation of a neural response to a brief stimulus. Note particularly the latent period, the initial transient, and the prolonged persistence of the response beyond the duration of the stimulus. Each of these features is associated with certain properties of the perceptual response.

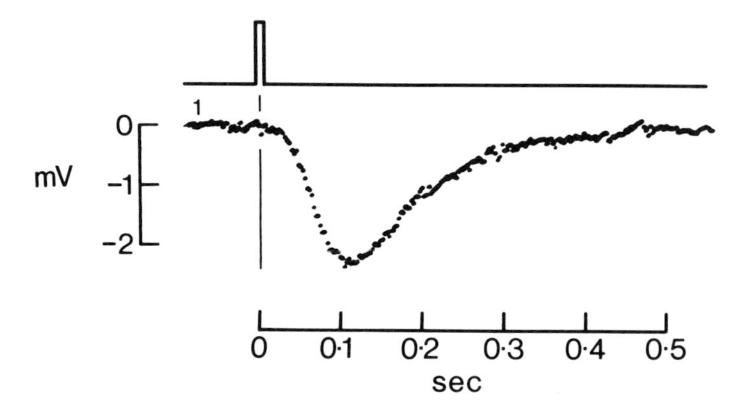

FIG. 7.2. The response of a long wavelength sensitive cone in the turtle retina to a brief (10 msec) visual stimulus. (From Baylor and Hodgkin, © 1974, with the permission of the Journal of Physiology.)

be very much longer than the stimulus that evoked it. As we later see, these features of the receptor response are both typical of other levels of neural encoding and are often accompanied by equivalent perceptual phenomena.

Another important general point is that there is a progressive increase in the duration of the response as one ascends the sensory pathway. In order to demonstrate this fact, let's consider a series of figures from successively more central loci in the visual pathway. Figure 7-2 shows the time course of an actual photoreceptor response to a brief stimulus. This is the first step in the chain. The prolonged response of the receptors to brief stimuli has been confirmed in a number of studies of the vertebrate retina (Baylor & Hodgkin, 1974; Fain & Dowling, 1973; Kleinschmidt & Dowling, 1975).

Figure 7-3 displays a typical electroretinogram also showing a similar prolongation of the response to a brief stimulus at the next anatomical stage—the entire retina. The electroretinogram is a complex response most certainly reflecting the activity of several different mechanisms in the retina. Rodieck (1973) has proposed that it is composed of the linear electrical sum of the following: (1) a *late receptor component* that appears to arise in the receptors themselves; (2) a *direct current component* that appears to result from bipolar cell activity; (3) a *b component* that appears to arise from certain interstitial (nonneuronal) cells in the retina known as Müller cells; and (4) an *r component* that is associated with electrical activity in the retinal epithelium. This particular component analysis of the electroretinogram is a modification of an earlier model suggested by Granit (1933). Regardless of which model is correct, and both are, in principle if not in detail, quite similar, the important point for the present discussion is that the potentials reflecting electrical activity of the whole retina, which would thus

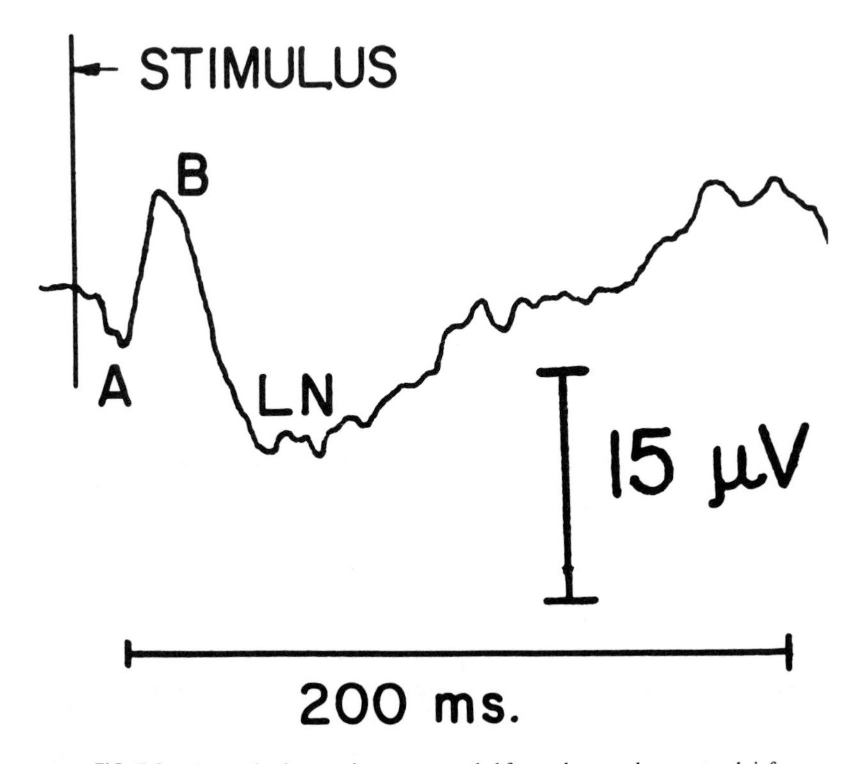

FIG. 7.3. A sample electroretinogram recorded from a human observer to a brief visual stimulus. A and B denote early components and LN denotes the late negative wave. (Courtesy of Dr. John C. Armington of Northeastern University.)

incorporate both Level 1 and 2 processes, are prolonged even beyond the observed duration of the receptor potentials themselves.[1]

Figure 7-4, a reproduction of the compound brain potential elicited by a visual stimulus, carries this sequence to the level of cerebral cortical macropotentials. The characteristics of this compound-evoked brain potential emphasize how a very brief, low luminance stimulus may be elongated by the properties of the perceptual system into a neural response that is enormously magnified, not only in the number of involved neurons, but also in duration.

---

[1]Although I do not consider the response patterns of individual mammalian ganglion cell fibers in this discussion, it is important to remember that the ganglion cells' responses are typically highly idiosyncratic. These neurons may exhibit some continuing spontaneous activity, but their functional response to a stimulus is usually a highly selective one triggered by some spatiotemporal feature of the stimulus that is congruent with some property of the receptive field of the neuron. In general, ganglion cells respond with brief bursts of spike action potentials that do not reflect the overall course of the stimulus but rather some transient or discontinuous feature such as its onset, offset, direction of movement, or contours.

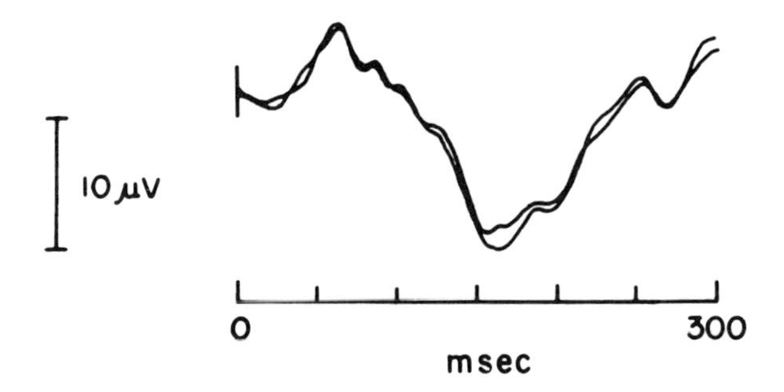

FIG. 7.4. A sample evoked brain potential from a human observer to a brief, diffuse flash of light. (Courtesy of Dr. Kenneth Kooi of the University of Michigan.)

Because the receptor produces a response that is longer than the stimulus and the response at higher levels of the nervous system is so much longer than any conceivable single neuronal response, it is clear that both Level 1 and Level 2 processes must be contributing to the observed prolongation at the very least.[2] The duration of the response of a single neuron reflects its own characteristic impulse response (of which I have more to say later). On the other hand, the duration of a compound action potential that incorporates the activity of a large number of neurons can result only from the temporal spread of response in a network. Feedforward, feedback, and reverberatory neuronal circuits are all network processes that can lead to the prolongation of activity in a network for a period that is vastly longer than the duration of even the longest lasting single-cell response. All of these mechanisms must be incorporated into any explanation of the temporal phenomenon that constitute the subject matter of this chapter.

In this chapter, I argue, that the progressive prolongation of the neural response at each subsequent level of the nervous system, whatever its cause, can and does contribute to a variety of visual phenomena that involve temporal interactions. Many of these phenomena can be thought of as arising directly from the fact that the response to any visual stimulus, no matter how brief, outlasts that stimulus by a considerable time, so that traces of two nonoverlapping physical events can exist simultaneously within the perceptual system. As we soon see, this simple concept ties together a substantial portion of the psychological literature on the temporal aspects of perception.

The effect of a persistent neural response, outlasting the stimulus, is ubiquitous and is exerted on many visual processes. Nevertheless the existence of this strong common thread of explanation, potentially capable of tying together many of the findings concerned with the temporal dimension, is often overlooked. This

[2]Higher level processes of course may also be involved in temporal psychophysical judgments.

is so in spite of the fact that such a unifying principle is extremely useful. Without it experimental paradigms that are only slightly different are often attributed to totally different mechanisms. For example, in developing a plan for the Volume VII/4 of the *Handbook of Sensory Physiology,* Dorothea Jameson and Leo Hurvich requested that two separate articles on temporal interactions by two different authors be prepared. One was entitled "Discrimination of Homogenous Double Pulses of Light" (Boynton, 1972) and the other, "Flicker" (Kelly, 1972). Though these articles covered topics that are distinguished by being procedurally different in the laboratory, I believe that this sort of methodology-based compartmentalization is conceptually incorrect. It ignores the fact that, when viewed as an intermittency detection task, a two-pulse experiment is but a reduced case of the more general flicker experiment and the findings of each must, in principle, be consistent. In the former case, the subject is asked to discriminate an intermittency between two pulses of light, and in the latter he is asked to discriminate intermittencies in a series of pulses. The former is a *reductio ad simplicitum* of the latter; it is but one point on a continuous function relating intermittency detection to the number of pulses in the stimulus. From this point of view, it would be extremely surprising if there were not a common explanation linking the two types of experiments. Nevertheless we are indeed faced with a theoretical surprise when reading these two articles. The artificial compartmentalization suggested by Jameson and Hurvich seems actually to have led to the worst possible theoretical result! Whereas Boynton attributed the two-pulse results to a photoreceptor process, Kelly attributed the closely related flicker phenomena to a retinal neural network transformation.[3] Regardless of the basis for either attribution, this discrepancy represents the kind of unfortunate conceptual dichotomization that leads progress directly away from any unified explanation of what should be considered to be very similar phenomena.

A possible solution to the problem engendered by such an arbitrary dichotomy of what may be essentially equivalent phenomena arises if one analyzes such phenomena in terms of the underlying processes rather than in terms of trivial procedural differences. If the common process underlying all of the sequential temporal interaction phenomenon is considered to be the prolongation of response, not only do both flicker and the two-pulse experiments fall into a common conceptual category, but so also do a number of other less obviously related phenomena such as short-term visual storage, critical duration, and temporal summation.

In the following pages of this section, I consider those perceptual phenomena that do appear to arise as a result of the persistence of the visual response. Although it would greatly simplify my discussion to be able to ascribe persistence phenomena directly and fully to a Level 1 process, as I noted at the outset of this chapter, the taxonomy, based as it is on the premise of isolable levels, has

[3]As we see in this chapter, however, Kelly's view is currently somewhat more eclectic.

a great deal of difficulty with any attempt at such an attribution. The factors underlying this difficulty are both empirical and logical. Not only is there a paucity of relevant neurophysiological analysis that can definitively tell us at what level the critical processes are occurring; but even if such data were available, it would be difficult to tell which of two comparable prolongations is the critical one or if they were, in fact, redundant.

When one considers the logic of the situation it becomes clear that it is virtually impossible to separate the various levels of temporal processing from each other and to assign perceptual phenomena uniquely to any particular level even if all of the conceivably useful data were available. All one can say is that some earlier prolonged response is not a candidate to explain some temporal interaction if the earlier response is of a lesser duration than the period over which that interaction occurs. In the case of cascaded neural network interactions, many of which exceed the period of psychophysical interaction, it is conceptually impossible to determine that any particular level is uniquely critical in the sense I have used the term here. It is for this reason that, in spite of Kelly's appropriately cautious speculations, for all practical purposes the data of flicker fusion have never been satisfactorily attributed to any particular level of processing. It is for this same reason that phenomena that are very likely identical in terms of underlying mechanisms can erroneously be attributed to different processing levels. It is also for this reason that, in the absence of a firm empirical and logical basis, any attempt on my part artificially to allocate the phenomena of sequential temporal interaction exclusively to either Level 1 or Level 2 would be inappropriate and would assume a state of knowledge that does not currently exist.

The organization of this chapter, therefore, explicitly acknowledges the empirical and logical difficulties that are so particularly obstructive when one is dealing with temporal phenomena. What we can say is that it is likely that the topics to be considered here are probably best explained on the basis of Level 1 or Level 2 processes and that it is, therefore, likely that the most relevant processes occur in the periphery. Thus this chapter represents a very appropriate transition zone as we pass from those processes that are clearly Level 1 to those that are clearly Level 2.

A brief list of the topics to be considered in this chapter includes:

—Latency effects
—Transient effects
—The duration of a percept
—Afterimages
—Iconic storage
—Sequential interactions
—Intermittency detection
—Subjective colors

C. LATENCY EFFECTS IN VISUAL PERCEPTION

Above and beyond simple persistence, however, there are other features of the prototypical neural response shown in Fig. 7-1 that are known to have specific perceptual consequences. One of these influential features, defined as the latent period, is the time that passes subsequent to the presentation of the stimulus but before the initiation of the neural response. This neural latent period seems to be a contributing antecedent to a comparable latency in psychophysical responses. The purpose of this section is to review the phenomenology of response latency and to consider possible explanatory mechanisms of it.

It is interesting to note in passing that it is highly unlikely that the very earliest steps in the visual process display any measurable latent period. The photochemical processes initiated by the breakdown of the receptor photochemical by light (as reflected in the early receptor potential described by Brown & Murakami, 1964) are virtually instantaneous following presentation of a stimulus. The molecular events—stereoisomerization of 11-*cis* retinal—that contributes to the early receptor potential probably occur in fractions of microseconds, and any measured latency at this level, more often than not, is more a reflection of the limited band-pass characteristics of the recording amplifier than of the photochemical process itself. However, the late receptor potential, which reflects permeability changes in the receptor membrane elicited by a less intense stimulus, has an appreciable latency that may be as long as a tenth of a second (Baylor & Hodgkin, 1974, Fig. 2).

1. Reaction Time

As a result of this neural latency, and barring the intervention of some totally unexpected means of extraneural, even extraphysical, communication, there can never be a psychological response that precedes or occurs simultaneously with the stimulus. The nontrivial latent period of the receptor combined with the nontrivial conduction time of the afferent pathway makes perceptual simultaneity with the stimulus a physical impossibility. Thus even at this early information processing level, the concept of the reaction time is introduced into psychological theory; that is, the overall (molar) latent period that occurs between the onset of the stimulus and the subsequent behavioral responses. The perceptual latent period, it must also be understood, is not mapped exactly by the behavioral reaction time. The reaction time is a composite delay that consists of a series of sequential steps. These steps include the latencies of the individual neural components, the conduction time of the afferent pathways, and any central processing or integration time. To these contributions to the molar latency must be added all of those further delays produced by the efferent neural conduction times, the latency of the neuromotor unit interface, and finally the inertial delays of the effector mechanism itself.

There should be no misunderstanding on this point: the behaviorally measured reaction time is far greater than the latent period of the afferent system. It is also essential to appreciate that the minimum effect of the latency of the receptor and the afferent neural conduction times is to disassociate mental time from physical time in a profound way. At the very best, the two will be separated by a constant amount of time; at the very worst (as appears to happen in such phenomena as apparent movement), psychological time is not even topologically consistent with physical time, and the perceived order of events may differ from the order defined by physical measurements of the stimulus.

Reaction time measurements, nevertheless, have played a persistent and significant role in psychological research for many decades since they were first introduced as an explicit experimental paradigm by F. C. Donders (1818–1889). Donders had been impressed by some observations made in astronomical observatories and popularized by the great mathematician F. W. Bessel (1784–1846) "as the personal equation." Bessel was, in turn, impressed by the fact that different observers gave substantially different readings in marking the transit of stars across reference lines in telescopes. Even in the 1880s when Donders did his pioneering work it was clear that the behavioral reaction time must be a composite of many different latent periods—some peripheral and some central. Not only did the brief latencies of the peripheral receptor apparatus play an obvious role, but Donders also appreciated that central decision-making factors must also contribute to the individual variations in the delay between a stimulus and a response. Measurement of human reaction times with the earliest nineteenth-century psychophysical methodologies clearly supported this composite nature of the behavioral reaction time. Even the best observers could not reduce the simple responses to less than a few hundreds of milliseconds—a period considerably longer than the most extravagant estimates of the latent periods of the receptors.

The basic stimulus determinants of visual reaction time have been well understood for many years. Perhaps the most regular stimulus parameter in determining the response latency when all other factors are held constant is the luminance of the stimulus. Figure 7-5, for example, shows the function obtained when reaction times are measured as a function of stimulus intensity. Though this functional relationship has been repeatedly studied by many psychologists, I present here the findings of a particularly well-done version of the prototypical experiment reported by Ueno (1977).

The tight relationship between stimulus luminance and reaction time can also be exhibited in other, less direct, ways. For example, Fig. 7-5 also demonstrates the relationship between the intensity of the stimulus and the behaviorally measured reaction time for a short and a long stimulus (as well as for a monocular and a binocular viewing condition). Even though one parameter in this experiment is the duration of the stimulus, in fact, the relationship between duration and reaction time is mediated by the same intensity-reaction time relation just de-

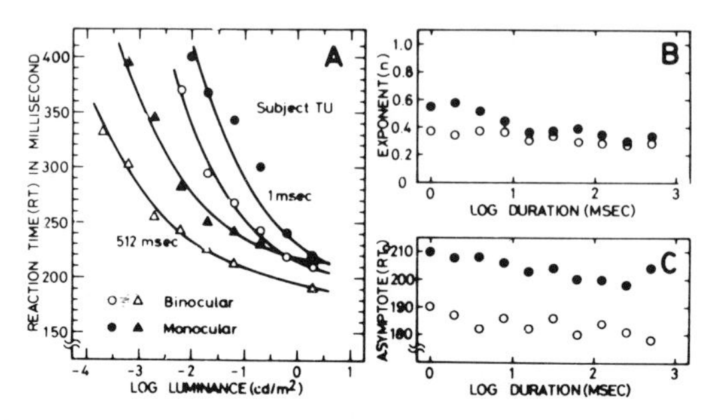

FIG. 7.5. The reaction time to a brief visual stimulus plotted as a function of the luminance for two stimulus durations (1 and 512 msec). The open symbols represent data obtained from a binocular viewing condition. Note that there appears to be some binocular advantage. (From Ueno, © 1977, with the permission of Pergamon Press.)

scribed. Duration simply serves as a surrogate for luminance by allowing a distributed (in time) amount of light to be temporally summated into a unitary but more effective stimulus. The visual effect of increasing the stimulus duration, in other words, is to increase the total amount of photic energy absorption in a way that directly simulates a more intense stimulus.

Stimulus factors other than luminance are known to be effective in altering the reaction time and thus also appear to be affecting peripheral latencies. Arden and Weale (1954), for example, examined the effects of retinal position. Their results comparing foveal and extrafoveal locations clearly demonstrate a major difference in the response time for stimuli placed in the foveal and extrafoveal regions, respectively. Within the fovea, luminance exerts a much weaker effect on the reaction time—the major changes occur at the low luminance end of the stimulus range. Even then, the magnitude of the change of reaction times in the fovea for the range of luminances used is less than a third of the maximum change in the extrafoveal regions.

Stimulus wavelength can also affect molar reaction times. A number of workers (Lit, Young, & Shaffer, 1971; Pollack, 1968) have studied the effect of the wavelength of a stimulus on the molar reaction time under conditions in which all of the stimulus wavelengths were presented at equivalent luminance values. A typical result is shown in Fig. 7-6. The displayed function shows a double-limbed structure that, like the dark adaptation curve, is thought to be a characteristic of the duplex (rod-cone) retina. As shown in Fig. 7-6, shorter reaction times are found, as expected, at the higher stimulus luminances, where cone vision presumably predominates. Responses at these luminance levels seem to exhibit little sensitivity to the wavelength of the stimulating light. On the other hand, there is a surprising and substantial effect of wavelength at the lower stimulus luminances where the latency is presumably mediated by the rods even though luminances were controlled.

Collectively, these data demonstrate that neural latencies exert a powerful influence on the molar reaction time. The variation with luminance wavelengths, retinal locus, and retinal luminance—the basic physical properties of the stimuli—suggests a relatively peripheral locus for the relevant critical processes.

The fact that the experimental design and other factors that affect criteria interact so weakly in studies of visual reaction times (Grice, Nullmeyer, & Schnizlein, 1979) is further evidence for the peripheral locus of this phenomenon.

To reiterate an essential point, however, the absolute values of the measured reaction times are so great that they obviously only partially reflect the contribution of peripheral latent periods. Proper estimates of the magnitude of the peripheral latencies can be obtained only by indirect methods or by using difference measures (i.e., reaction time at Condition 1 minus reaction time at Condition 2 equals peripheral latency) that implicitly assume that central latencies remain constant as these stimulus variables are manipulated. This last assumption is not without its own intrinsic difficulties, and objections to it can also be raised. For this reason, some of the indirect procedures, relying upon some dependent variable other than reaction time per se, are often particularly useful in estimating peripheral neural latencies. Apparent depth and motion are two latency-dependent phenomena that have been invoked to provide alternative estimates of the peripheral latencies.

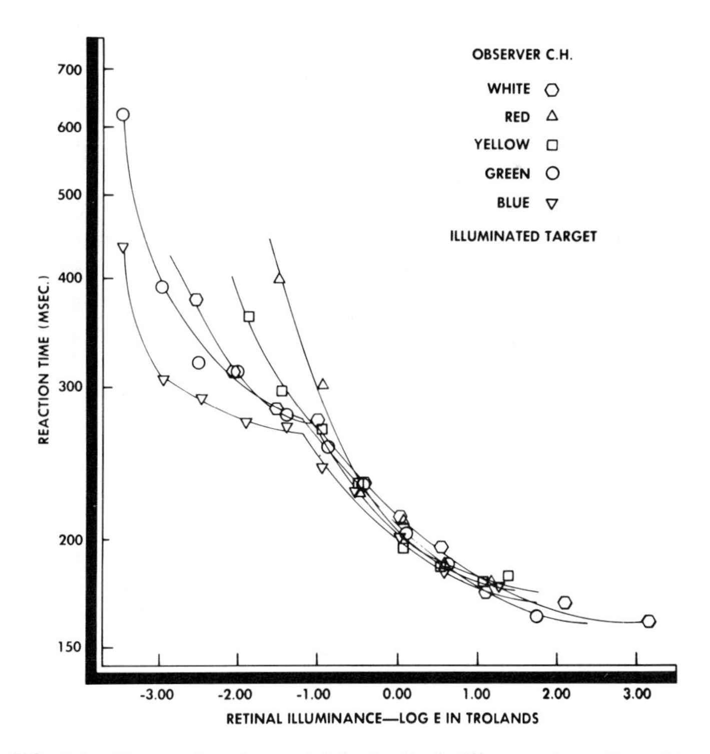

FIG. 7.6. The reaction time to brief stimuli of different colors. (From Lit, Young, and Schaffer, © 1971, with the permission of The Psychonomics Journals, Inc.)

2. Apparent Motion and Depth

Let us consider apparent motion first. More than a half century ago it had been observed by Korte (1915) that a "reversed" apparent movement (i.e., from the later to the earlier stimuli) would be perceived between two spatially separate light stimuli if the second of the two stimuli was much more luminous than the first. The mechanism he invoked to explain this reversal of the usual apparent motion phenomenon was the variation in latencies of the peripheral retinal mechanisms as a function of the stimulus intensity. He assumed that latency differences could be so great that the more intense stimulus could actually produce an earlier neural response than the dimmer one, even though, in physical fact, the dimmer stimulus occurred earlier. Reversed apparent movement of this kind is often referred to as *delta movement*. Calculation of the derived intensity differences at which apparent movement reverses can lead to an estimate of the relationship between intensity and latency.

The Pulfrich phenomenon (Pulfrich, 1922), a dramatic illusion of depth induced by stimulus motion, is also traditionally attributed to exactly the same sort of strong latency–luminance relationship. In this illusion, the path of a pendulum bob that is actually moving in a fronto-parallel plane appears to be traversing a path that moves in and out of the plane. This illusion occurs when a neutral density filter is placed over one eye but not the other. The physical and apparent paths characteristic of various kinds of oscillatory motion are shown in Fig. 7-7 following Efron (1963).

Traditional theories (Lit & Hyman, 1951; Pulfrich, 1922) have ascribed the Pulfrich effect to the increased latency of the neural response to the stimulus in the eye in which the image luminance has been diminished by the filter. Thus, the conventional explanation goes, at any point in time an equivalent spatial retinal disparity is produced that is functionally dependent upon the velocity of the bob. In other words, because of the difference in latency resulting from the difference in monocular stimulus luminances, at any moment in time there is a "simulated" spatial disparity present in the dichoptic images. At some central point the image from one eye is seen at the same time as the delayed image from the other eye. When the bob is moving, the simultaneous neural responses are not from corresponding points, but rather are from noncorresponding points due to the unequal latencies. The greater the speed, the greater the simulated disparity; and the greater the simulated disparity, the greater the apparent depth. Thus, the paths of the bob appear elliptical in depth as shown in Fig. 7-7A because the simple harmonic motion typical of an oscillating pendulum is greatest at the center and diminished at the ends of its travel. The other paths shown in Fig. 7-7 are explained in similar terms.

Alfred Lit, in a 30-year series of experiments that has established him as the modern master of the Pulfrich phenomenon, has extracted a great deal of information about visual latency effects from this perceptual illusion (Lit, 1949, 1960;

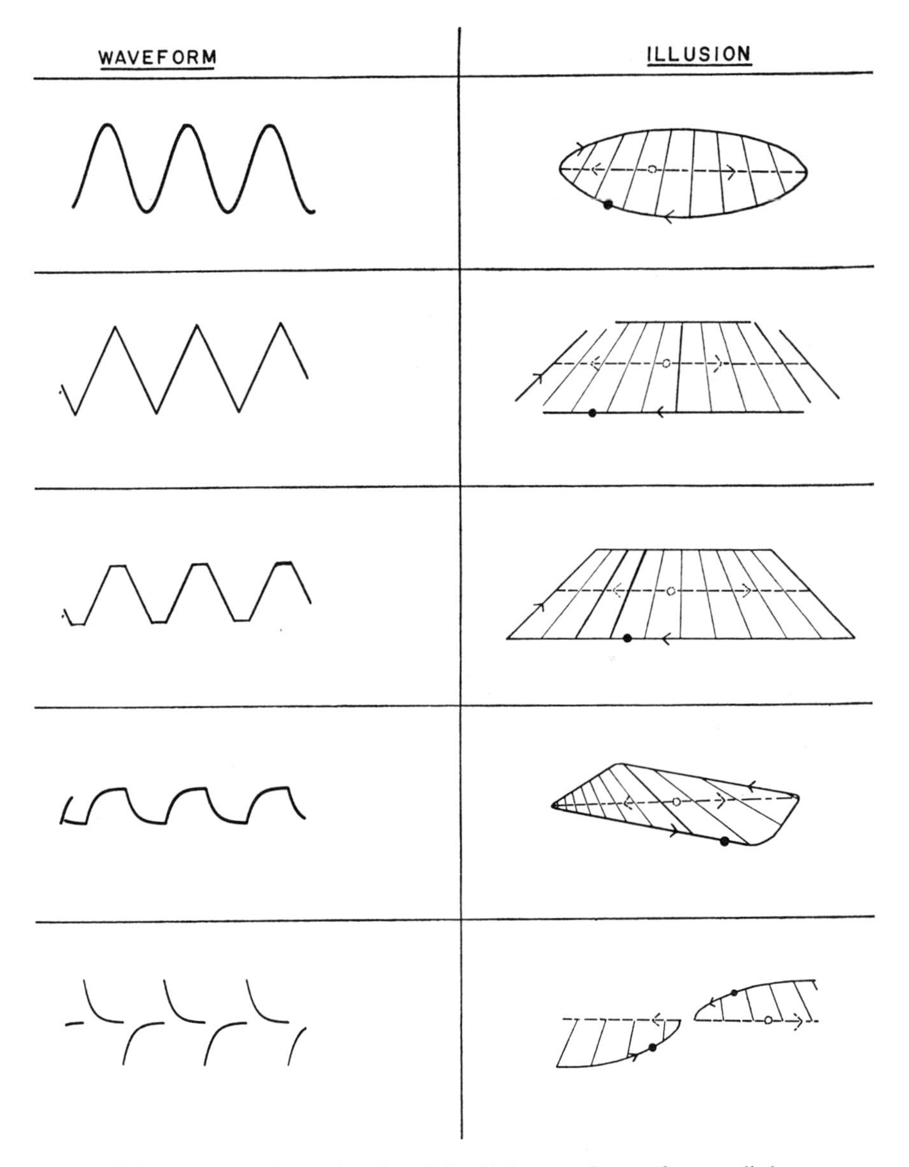

FIG. 7.7. These figures show the relationship between the waveforms applied to an oscilloscope to control the horizontal displacement of an oscillating dot and the shape of the evoked Pulfrich phenomenon. (From Efron, © 1963, with the permission of St. Martin's Press, Inc.)

Lit, Finn, & Vicars, 1972; Lit and Hamm, 1966). Figure 7-8 shows the results from a recent experiment (Brauner & Lit, 1976) in his laboratory. Brauner and Lit estimated the neutral density filter-induced latencies from judgments of the apparent depth of the illusion using the method described in Lit (1960b). They then compared these latency estimates with the reaction times to a simple visual stimulus. This graph clearly emphasizes the difference between the "simple reaction time" (actually a composite of the effects of various levels of processing) and the differences in perceived depth that seem more reasonably to be associated specifically with variations in the peripheral latencies. Latency changes varying up to 50 msec are suggested by this method.[4] The important point of this experiment is that the use of an indirect measure (the experimenter is measuring a spatial dimension—apparent depth—to estimate a difficult-to-measure temporal one—latency) may produce a highly precise estimate of the actual latency changes that are occurring in the afferent pathway.

Lit has also systematically explored the effect of other dimensions on the Pulfrich effect and has found, for example:

1. A monotonic increase in the magnitude of the effect as a function of increasing luminance difference between the two eyes (Lit, 1949);
2. A monotonic increase in the effect with increases in target velocity (Lit, 1960b);
3. A monotonic increase in the effect with viewing distance (Lit, 1968).
4. No effect of target thickness (Lit, 1960a).

The classic latency explanation of the Pulfrich phenomenon, however, has been criticized by a number of researchers in recent years (Harker, 1967). Perhaps the strongest attack, however, has been presented by Wist, Brandt, Diener, and Dichgans (1977). They demonstrated that the amplitude of the Pulfrich phenomenon (which could be evoked with an oscillating grating as well as a bob) was strikingly affected by the spatial frequency of the grating. The depth illusion increased monotonically as the spatial frequency of the grating

[4]There is another comparable illusion in which a bob that is actually moving in a fronto-parallel plane is perceived as moving along a similar elliptical (in-depth) path. This other phenomenon, the Mach–Dvorak illusion (see, for example, Michaels, Carello, Shapiro, & Steitz, 1977), however, results not from a difference in stimulus intensities to the two eyes but from differences in the time of arrival of the physical stimulus regulated by alternating the times at which each eye can see the bob. The alternation between the viewing times of the two eyes may be accomplished by an episcotister (as in the Michaels et al. study), or by means of electronic delays in the plotting cycle of the stimuli on the face of an oscilloscope (as in comparable studies by Burr & Ross, 1979; Ross, 1974). The Mach–Dvorak illusion is phenomenally similar to the Pulfrich effect but at first appears to be due to a quite different integrative process. However, this may not be the case; both may actually be due to the same "time of arrival" difference. In the latter case, retinal latency differences due to stimuli luminance differences probably explain the effect; in the former case, short-term visual storage effects may lead to spurious disparities for monocular stimuli that cannot be seen simultaneously.

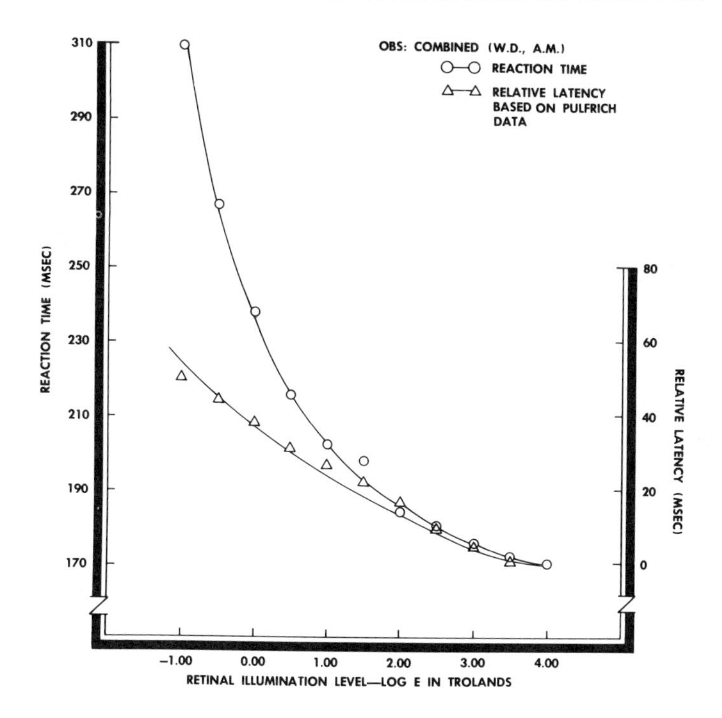

FIG. 7.8. A comparison of the simple reaction time and the latency computed from the Pulfrich phenomenon. Obviously the reaction time involves other factors than simple latency. (From Brauner and Lit, © 1976, with the permission of the University of Illinois Press.)

increased. Wist and his colleagues believe that this result is incompatible with a latency difference hypothesis. In a previous study (Diener, Wist, Dichgans, & Brandt, 1976), they had shown that the perceived velocity of a moving grating was a function of its spatial frequency. The inference they drew from these combined findings is especially significant because they actually suggested that this form of dynamic stereopsis is not mediated by the effective simultaneous stimulation of corresponding points, the idea that is the mainstay of the conventional theory, but rather by differences in the perceived velocity between the two eyes. Their suggestion would place the process underlying the Pulfrich phenomenon at a much higher level than that invoked by conventional theory.

3. Apparent Simultaneity

Another useful indirect means of examining the effects of peripheral latency differences as a function of various stimulus dimensions is to measure the stimulus conditions under which stimuli physically occurring at different times can be made to appear to be simultaneous. One such simultaneity method involves the movement of two stimulus traces of different luminances across an oscilloscope screen as shown in Fig. 7-9A. Because the stimulus luminances differ, a latency difference will occur, with the dimmer stimulus arriving in the central nervous system after a longer delay than the brighter one. If the two stimuli are actually physically moving together, the less intense one will appear to be trailing behind the more intense one because of the latency differences as shown in 7-9B. Within limits, an observer who has control over the physical displacement of the two stimuli should be able to adjust the spacing between the

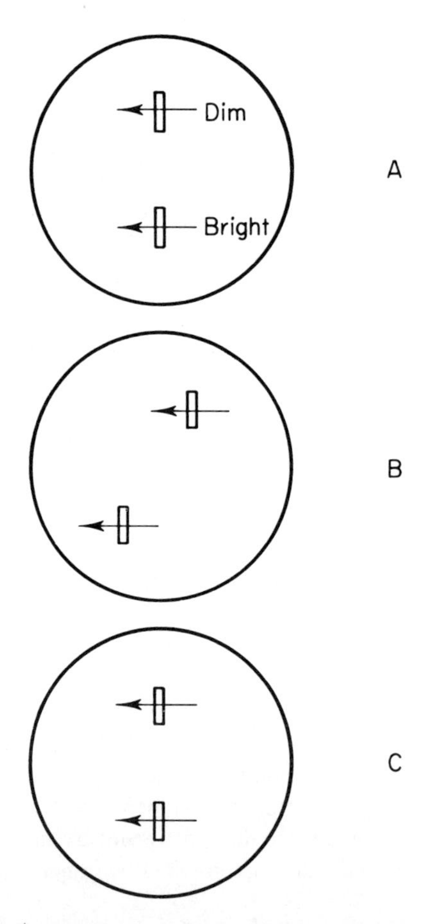

FIG. 7.9. The simultaneity experiment. (A) Two moving lines, one bright and one dim, on an oscilloscope screen shown in their actual physical relationship to each other. (B) Because of the latency-luminance relationship, the dim one appears to lag behind the bright one when both are moving at the same speed. (C) If a time delay is inserted so that the bright line physically lags behind the dim one, they are perceived as occurring at the same locations. The physical lag that is introduced can be used to compute visual latency.

two so that they appear to be occurring at the same place and at the same time, as shown in Fig. 7-9C. Knowledge of the velocity of the moving stimuli, the actual physical spacing between them, and their respective luminances allows the experimenter to calculate in a simple manner the relationship between luminosity and latency. With all other aspects of the experimental situation held constant, the differential spatial displacement set by the subject should be a fairly direct measure of the peripheral latency attributable to luminance differences. This technique has been used for almost a century. Charpentier had reported an early observation of the phenomenon as early as 1893. Recently Guth (1964) has used this same procedure to study the effects of wavelength on the latency of the visual response. Unlike some others (Liàng & Piéron, 1947), Guth did not find any effect of wavelength, but the data generated did reflect latency differences for different stimulus luminances.

Other studies using the apparent simultaneity of two nonmoving dots (Alpern, 1954) or the absence of apparent motion (Roufs, 1963) between lights of differing luminances at intervals that should produce the illusion also speak to the question of the dependence of latency on stimulus luminance and are explained in the same terms. The general result of Roufs' experiments, for example, suggest peripheral latencies as great as 25 msec, a value that is in good accord with the results of Lit's studies on the Pulfrich phenomenon. Figure 7-10 shows Roufs' data for one subject and also illustrates why he concluded that the relationship between stimulus luminance and latency was virtually a perfect logarithmic function.

A fascinating aspect of figure–ground relations that may be related to latency differences of this sort is that even though the relative position of the two parts of the stimulus (i.e., the figure and the ground) may be fixed in the stimulus space, it is possible to produce an apparent spatial separation between the two parts if there is a substantial luminance difference between them. Parker, Woods, and Tubbs (1977), for example, have shown that the figure may move independently of the ground when a bright trace moves across a less luminous oscilloscope screen. The separation of the figure (the bright sweep) from the ground (the dimmer screen) occurs when either the observer stamps his foot or the oscilloscope itself is oscillated. The separation in this case may also be due to luminance-determined latency differences producing apparent simultaneity of responses from retinal loci that do not correspond to the times of occurrence of the actual physical stimuli. The physical motion simply acts to translate both parts of the image across the retina.

In sum, it appears that a number of pieces of evidence support the idea that there are direct perceptual consequences of the latent period of the peripheral neural responses. Both direct and indirect behavioral measures reflect the impact of stimulus dimensions that are known to affect neural latencies. There seems to be little reason to deny the traditional suggestion that the perceptual phenomena discussed here are the direct outcome of retinal processes. Unfortunately, it is not

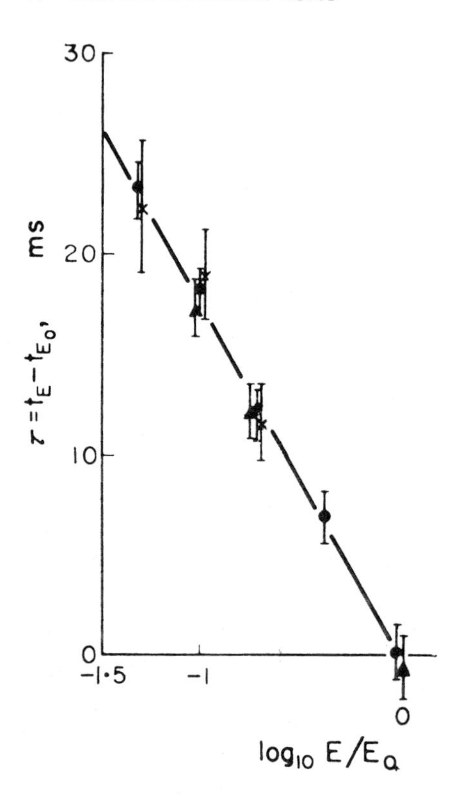

FIG. 7.10. Latency demonstrated in a two pulse experiment in which the two sequential stimuli are not of the same luminance. The criterion in this experiment is the absence of apparent motion. On this graph, t_{E0} and t_E are the latencies of the two stimuli respectively and t is the difference between the two. In this case the relationship appears to be exactly linear. (From Roufs, © 1963, with the permission of Pergamon Press.)

possible to discriminate definitively between the Level 1 and Level 2 contributions to the putative latency effect; but, as I noted, this is a quandary almost universal to the temporal phenomena that are discussed in this chapter.

One of the few bright lights in this otherwise murky picture is to be found in a recent article by Mansfield and Daugman (1978). On the basis of their studies of the electroretinogram of a toad (*Bufo marinus*), they concluded that most of the measured latency *of the retinal response* was attributable to the photoreceptor rather than more central neural interaction effects. Whereas this finding does not mean that other conduction times and central processing delays may not influence the psychophysical latency, it does suggest that Level 1 processes may be more important than Level 2 in determining the latency of the neural response at least in the periphery.

D. ARE THERE ANY PERCEPTUAL EFFECTS OF ON AND OFF TRANSIENTS?

If the reader refers back to Fig. 7-1, he will note that after the latent period has passed, there are usually some further transient fluctuations in the neural response before a stable state is achieved. The response does not typically simply rise to some asymptotic value; rather, many kinds of electrophysiological recording (e.g., from the individual receptor or the whole retina) reveal that the neural response may overshoot or even oscillate once or twice before stabilizing. A number of neurons, particularly the ganglion cells in the optic nerve, display such strong transient effects that they must be considered to produce only "on" responses, "off" responses, or some combination of the two, as shown in Fig. 7-11.

This particular sensitivity to the stimulus onset and offset in the nervous system is a highly adaptive evolutionary development. The information in the stimulus is concentrated in the regions at which the signal changes. The information in unchanging regions is intrinsically redundant, and little advantage is gained by tuning up the system to communicate this noninformation continuously during the stable periods of any stimulus. (In Chapter 8 a comparable encoding economy is observed as a result of spatial interactions in the nervous system.)

This much is neurophysiological fact and quantifiable information theory. Whether or not there are any perceptual implications of these transient responses is not quite so straightforward. The question that remains in this context of transient responses and efficient codes is whether or not there is any measurable perceptual correlate of the on and off transients that have been measured in the nervous system. In other words, do we respond perceptually to the neural tran-

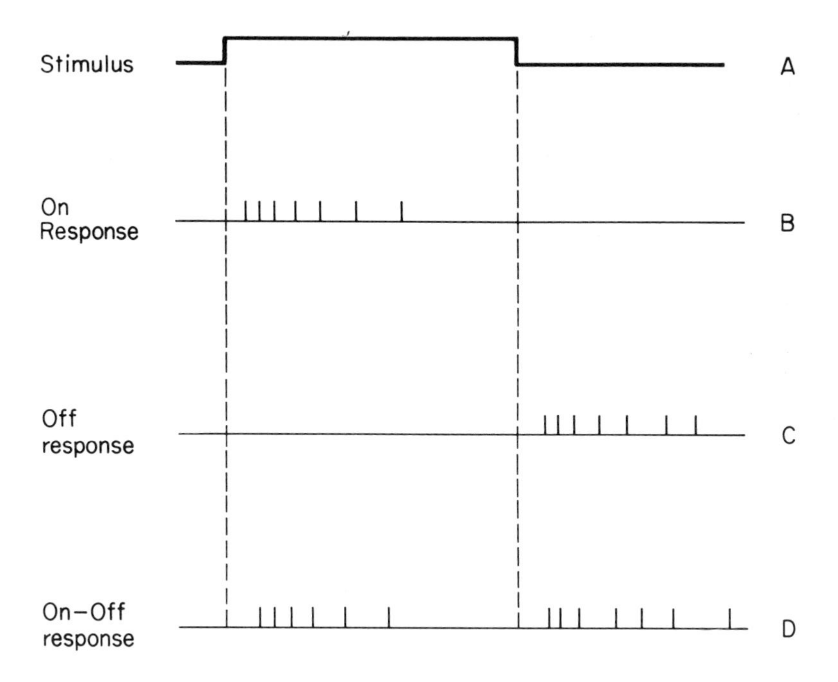

FIG. 7.11. A schematic drawing defining "on," "off," and "on-off" responses to a stimulus A respectively in B, C, and D.

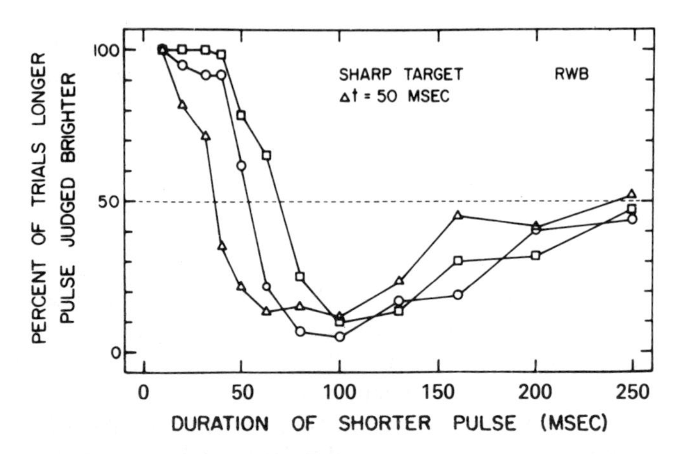

FIG. 7.12. The magnitude of the Broca-Sulzer effect as a function of stimulus duration. (From Bowen and Pokorny, © 1978, with the permission of Pergamon Press.)

sients? Are they, in other words, signs or codes?[5] Although traditional theory has long suggested such an association, it turns out that in empirical fact, as we shall see, it is only in the rarest instances that corresponding perceptual effects of these on and off transients can be observed.

One perceptual phenomenon that has often been attributed to on and off transients is the Broca–Sulzer effect (Broca & Sulzer, 1902; McDougall, 1904), an illusion in which shorter stimuli often appear to be brighter than those that are equally intense but of longer duration.[6] A typical result exhibiting this phenomenon is shown in Fig. 7-12. The classic explanation of this effect (Ebbecke, 1920; Rabelo & Grüsser, 1961) correlated this perceptual phenomenon with the initial transient responses in the neural mechanism of the kind just mentioned. Some researchers (e.g., Alpern & Barr, 1962) have even suggested a more particular hypothesis; namely, that it is the transient neural response in the receptor itself that is responsible for the Broca–Sulzer Effect.

The usual explanation of this Broca–Sulzer phenomena goes something like this: The shorter stimuli appear to be brighter than longer ones because they are *on the average* brighter. The response to a short stimulus terminates before the transients have settled down and before the lower level stable phase of the response is established. Thus the neural events produced by the short-duration

---

[5]The concept of signs and codes has been dealt with in detail in my earlier works (Uttal, 1973, 1978) and will not be exercised again at this point. The interested reader may refer there for a fuller explanation.

[6]A negative Broca–Sulzer effect in which a brief transient diminishment in luminance produces a darker experience than a longer lasting diminishment has also been reported by Björklund and Magnussen (1979). And, as we soon see, intermediate duration stimuli are actually brighter than either very long or very short stimuli.

stimulus consist only of the relatively high-level transients, whereas the longer-duration stimulus produces a neural response that consists of both a high-level transient phase and a more subdued stable phase. The average response level of both phases is less than that of the transient phase alone, and ipso facto the perceptual responses defined by the average response level are as described by Broca and Sulzer. This illusion may occur even in those conditions in which the integral of the energy absorbed during the long stimulus is substantially greater than the integral of the energy absorbed during the short stimulus.

There are two ways to explain the heightened transient phase. The first is that same retinal mechanism acts as a ''high-pass filter,'' allowing relatively more neural energy to pass when the stimulus is changing than when it is constant. The other, enunciated by Baumgardt and Segal (1947) is that there are two neural processes—one inhibitory and one excitatory—that add together in a way that produces a temporal contour intensification. In fact, both of these explanations may be considered to be identical; the former is descriptive of the process, and the latter is analytic and reductionistic. In either case there is a strong isomorphic relationship assumed between the perceptual experience and the peripheral neural response.

It is now clear (Arend, 1973; Bowen & Pokorny, 1978) that it is not the shortest flashes that are necessarily the brightest, but rather, under certain conditions a stimulus with an intermediate duration (approximately 60 to 150 msec, depending on conditions) usually has the greatest subjective magnitude as shown in Fig. 7-12. Stimuli that are either shorter or longer than this intermediate duration appear to be somewhat dimmer even when the physical luminance remains constant over all durations. There is some controversy over the putative influence of the spatial shape of the stimulus on the Broca–Sulzer phenomenon. Arend believes that the shape is important. If the stimulus fields in his experiments were blurred at the edges, for example, the brightness enhancement of the intermediate durations stimuli did not occur. He speculates, therefore, that the response is not likely to be a receptor phenomenon but should be attributed to properties of the retinal neural network. In other words, Arend feels that the Broca–Sulzer effect is the result of a Level 2 rather than a Level 1 transformation.

Further support for the idea that the Broca–Sulzer phenomenon is dependent upon the spatial configuration of the stimulus and is thus mediated by higher-level processes than those occurring in the receptor is forthcoming from the work of Kitterle and Corwin (1979). These workers showed that the magnitude of a related phenomenon—the perceived contrast of grating—was dependent upon the spatial frequency of a stimulus of this type. High spatial frequency stimuli (5.6 and 10 cycles/deg.) did not lead to the expected brightness enhancement at intermediate durations (80–100 msec) in situations in which low spatial frequency (.45 and .95 cycles/deg.) stimulus did.

On the other hand, Corwin and Green (1978) have reported that the Broca–Sulzer phemonenon can be observed when the observer views a Ganzfeld (see

Chapter 10 for a discussion of this viewing situation). Therefore edge and form effects are not necessary and, if anything, may be secondary. Indeed, Bowen and Pokorny's form effects are exactly opposite to those reported by Arend.

A severe challenge to the classic explanation of the Broca–Sulzer phenomenon is a conceptual issue raised by Wasserman and Kong (1974). These workers have called attention to the fact that the phenomenon and the process—the Broca–Sulzer effect and the transient neural response—are not comparable analogs as they had initially seemed to be. The Broca–Sulzer effect is a function of the *duration* of the stimulus but the neural transients so often associated with them are in fact functions of the *time* following the onset of the stimulus. According to Wasserman and Kong's analysis these two independent variables are not identical, and their misidentification has led to a persistent error in the level of explanation.

Figure 7-13 suggests the superficial similarity in time course between the responses to the two different independent variables, but a more careful examination also points up the mismatch between the two. Wasserman and Kong went on to show that if different durations were used to elicit the neural responses (making the experiment more comparable to the usual psychophysical paradigm), the corresponding nonmonotonicity in the relationship between stimulus duration and response magnitude did not, in fact, appear! These data are shown in Fig. 7-14. The Broca–Sulzer effect may not, therefore, be explicable in terms of the transient component of the neural response after all.

For these and other reasons many other explanations of the Broca–Sulzer phenomenon have been hypothesized. It has been associated with backward masking exerted by the later parts of the stimulus on the earlier parts (Raab, 1963), as an epiphenomenon of adaptation (LeGrand, 1957), or as a result of asynchronous activity in parallel channels (Bartley, 1969). In fact, we must admit that, like so many other "simple" perceptual phenomenon, the Broca–Sulzer illusion remains remarkably recalcitrant to theoretical analysis.

One other possible candidate phenomenon that has often been explained as a correlate of the transient characteristics of the neural response is brightness enhancement—the increased brightness of a flickering light compared to the response to a continuous light of equivalent average intensity. However, the same criticism raised by Wasserman and Kong in the case of a single flash (the Broca–Sulzer effect) may also hold in the case of multiple flashes. Indeed, it seems as if the nervous system may indeed have learned to encode (or better, ignore) the transients that occur during regions of changing stimulus intensity, just as it is so often unresponsive to the accommodation[7] of the neural response. It would, in other words, be perfectly plausible and possible for the visual system to take full advantage of an efficiently coded representation of the time course of

[7]Neural (as opposed to ocular) accommodation is the progressive reduction in a continuing neural response to a persistent stimulus of constant amplitude.

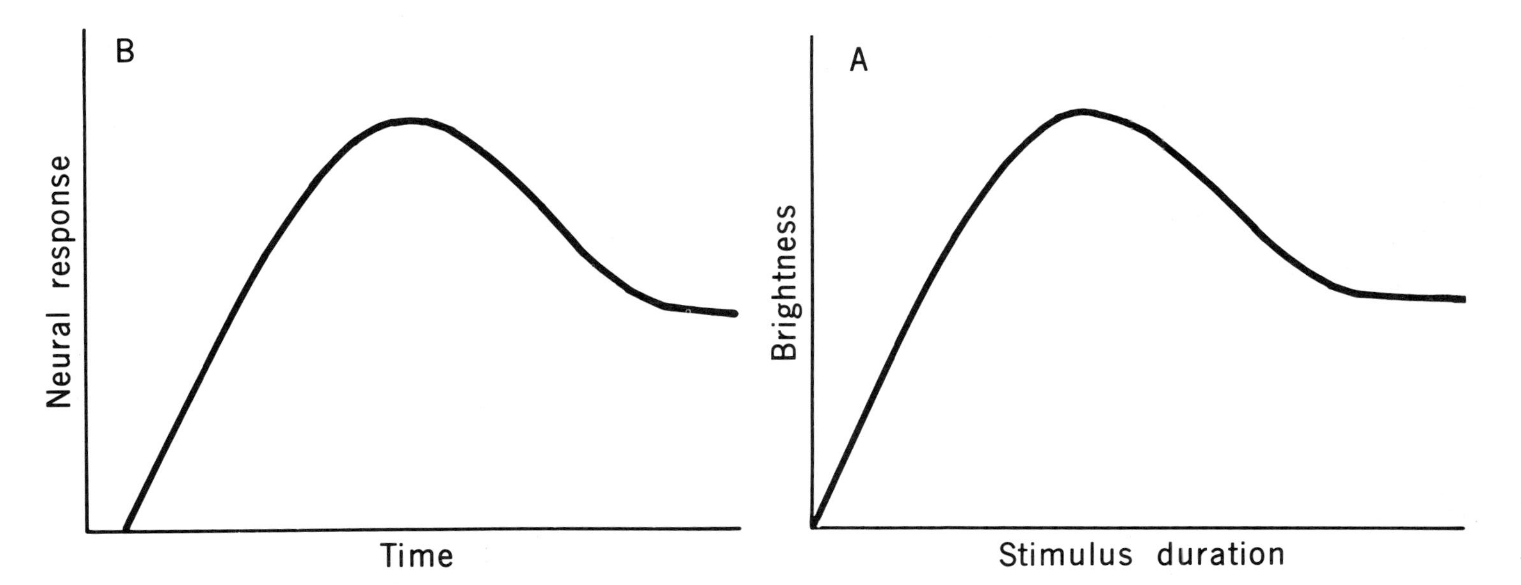

FIG. 7.13. Two curves showing an obvious analogy of response form but resulting from totally different stimulus dimensions. If stimulus duration is used to evoke the neural response, the analogy is no longer apparent. See text for complete discussion. This suggests that a superficial similarity between response forms has been overextended to generate a spurious theory of this aspect of visual perception. (From Wasserman & Kong, © 1974, with the permission of The American Association for the Advancement of Science.)

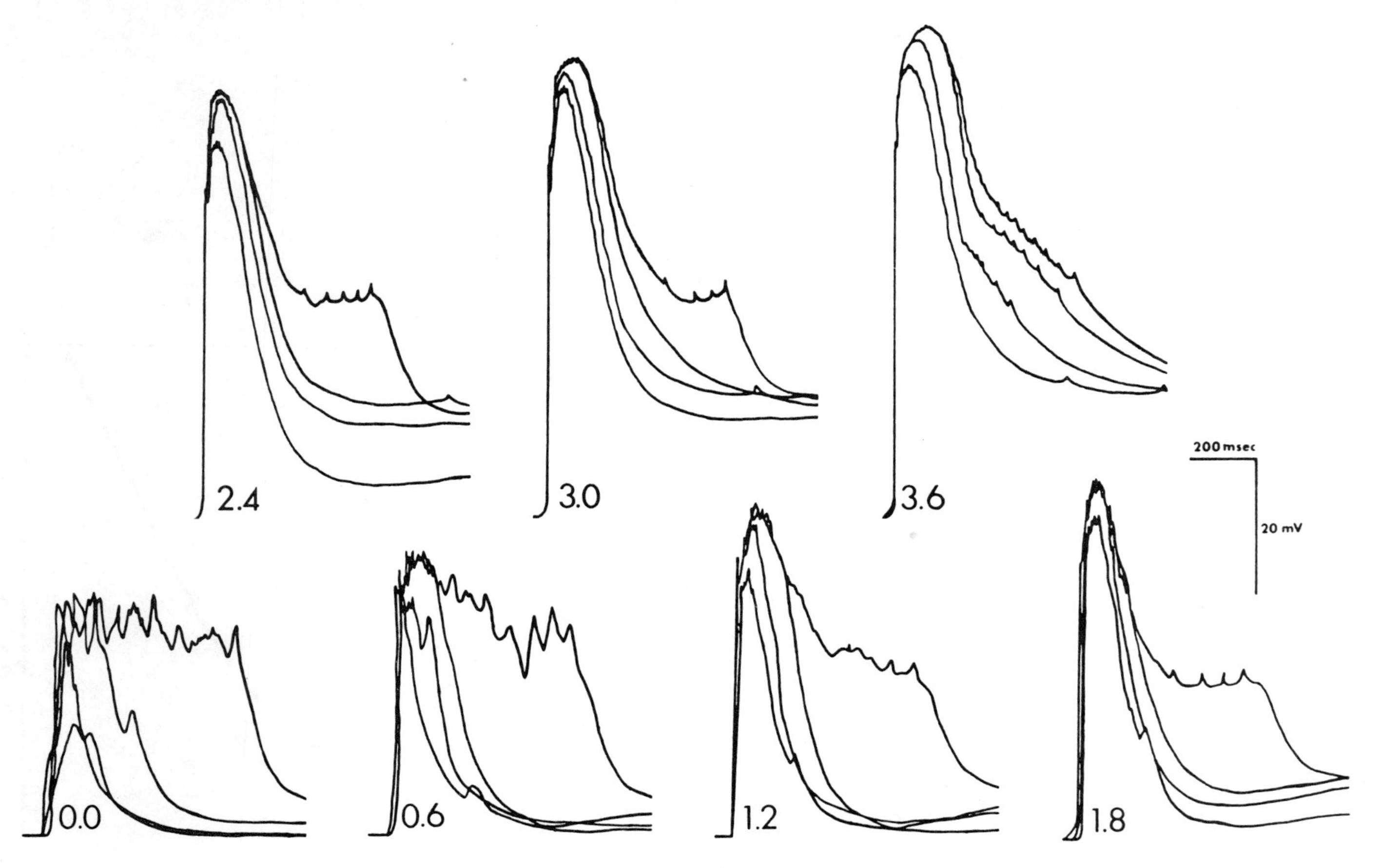

FIG. 7.14. Data obtained in a neurophysiological experiment in which duration (rather than time after stimulus onset) was measured. These data do not display any effect comparable to the Broca-Sulzer phenomenon. Numbers indicate light intensity in relative log units. (From Wasserman &

the stimulus without the perceptual experience slavishly responding to every aspect of that code. In other words, efficient coding mechanisms need not be isomorphic determinants of the peripheral response. On the contrary, if the rules of the transformation are known, coding mechanisms might be able to provide the basis for full reconstruction of the original time course of the stimulus from afferent sensory signals that only symbolically represent that original time course. For example, if a neural mechanism were tuned to filter out the low temporal frequencies—corresponding to periods in which there was little stimulus change—the fact that there was a stable level of activity at that time could be reconstructed by another level of neural processing. Thus, the original time course of the stimulus could be reconstructed from the partial information contained in the afferent message by means of compensatory neural algorithms just as deformations of the spatial stimulus pattern by optical distortions can eventually be compensated for by higher levels of perceptual processing.

True, the nervous system would not be operating as a totally passive and linear tranducer in this case, but as I have noted, demanding such isomorphic linearity may be one of the most serious conceptual errors in perceptual theorizing in recent years. The emerging realization that such a radical isomorphism is neither desirable nor necessary to explain the relationships between neural and perceptual functions is one of the most important conclusions emerging from the many experiments supporting sensory coding theory. In short, the key premise is that *any code can represent any perceptual or logical construct* (although with varying degrees of efficiency). Relentlessly searching for isomorphic relationships may blind the researcher's eye to less obvious but equally valid nonisomorphic representations and codes, particularly in a brain in which economy in the utilization of logical units is not a primary concern. The key premise also implies that the nervous system is perfectly capable of constructing a perceptual response pattern from a neural response pattern displaying a time course with which it may differ. In the case of perceptual transients, this may be exactly what is happening.

In sum, in spite of the fact that traditional perceptual theorizing has repeatedly suggested that phenomena such as the Broca–Sulzer phenomenon and the brightness enhancement of flickering stimuli may be due to the a heightened neural sensitivity to stimulus transients, abundant reasons to question this association have been forthcoming in recent years.[8]

There are other phenomena, however, that do suggest that there may be other instances in which the neural transients may exert some influence on perception.

---

[8]It is also interesting to note that brightness enhancement also seems to occur in the spatial domain (Helson, 1963; Walker, 1978); that is, when spatial frequency patterns in the range of one to eight spatial cycles per degree of visual angles are presented to an observer, the perceived brightness of the light bands between the dark bands is higher than the brightness of a uniform field with the same physical luminance. Discontinuous spatial patterns can produce illusory brightening, therefore, just as temporally discontinuous stimuli can.

Perhaps the strongest evidence in favor of the perceptual efficacy of the on and off transients is a 30-year-old study reported by Crawford (1947). Crawford tested the detectability of a small and dim test spot centered in a large and more intense conditioning field. The two stimuli were concentric and thus the smaller one appeared in a region of the retina in which the more intense stimulus was activating the same receptors. The more intense larger stimulus lasted for about .5 sec and established the time base of the experiment. The dimmer test stimulus was then presented at various times preceding, during, and after the longer flash, and the just-detectable luminance was measured as a function of that time of presentation.

The results of Crawford's experiment, shown in Fig. 7-15, indicate an obvious increase in the intensity required for detectability of the test flash at the beginning and at the end of the longer flash. This suggests that the effective background brightness produced by the longer flash was greater at these times of stimulus change than at its middle. This type of experiment is perhaps the most compelling example of a perceptual correlate of the on and off transients that are observed neurologically. It seems likely that the criticism that Wasserman and Kong have raised for the conceptually closely related Broca–Sulzer phenomenon may not be applicable here. Because the effect is maximal only when the test and masking flash are presented to the same eye, these findings do also support a peripheral explanation of this phenomenon.

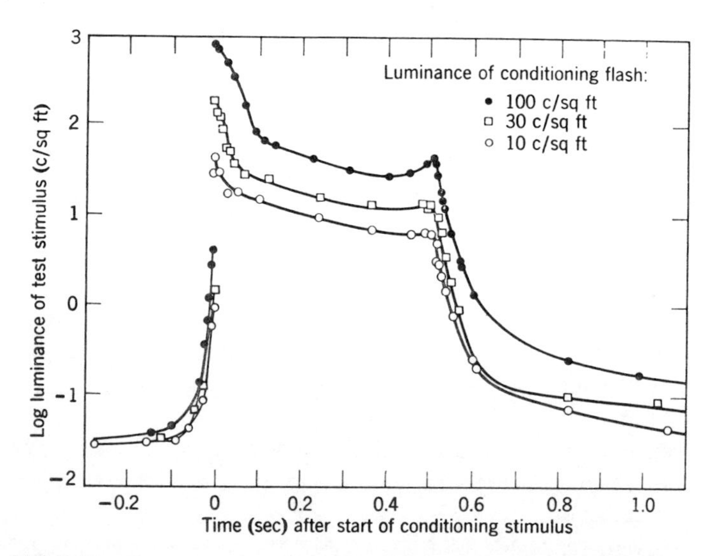

FIG. 7.15. The change in the absolute threshold as a function of the position of a test spot on a longer lasting and larger conditioning spot. (From Brown and Mueller, © 1965, after Crawford, 1947, with the permission of John Wiley & Sons, Inc.)

Some neurophysiological data also support this peripheral explanation of this bright flash masking. Fehmi, Adkins, and Lindsley (1969), Schiller (1968, 1969), Coenen and Eijkman (1972), and Felsten and Wasserman (1978, 1979) have all shown that the correlated diminution in neural response magnitude in this experimental design is very peripheral and most likely is a receptor process.

E. THE DURATION OF THE VISUAL EXPERIENCE

Once the latent period has passed and the effects of the initial transients have settled down, another characteristic of the neural response depicted in Fig. 7-1 is apparent. That characteristic is that the duration of the neural response, in almost all cases, exceeds the duration of the stimulus. This fact suggests that the perceptual response should also be prolonged; it, too, should last longer than a very brief stimulus. In fact we can go even further and assert that, for very brief stimuli, the duration of the percept should be a function of some minimum duration of the neural mechanism and be virtually independent of the duration of the stimulus.

When a brief, or impulsive, stimulus produces a response that is characteristic of the responding tissue, the shape and duration of the response can be thought of as a temporal analog of the spatial point spread function discussed in Chapter 5. This "impulse function" can be quite complex as well as variable for the different neural levels, and for the perceptual one as well. Therefore, no simple formula analogous to those shown on p. 338 has yet been proposed to describe it in general. It is worthwhile, however, to note that such a formula can exist for particular cases and that the conceptual similarity of the minimum perceived duration in psychophysics and impulse testing in the engineering sciences.

The shape of the perceptual impulse function has been measured by Sperling (1965). He presented a stimulus that could have any one of three luminances superimposed on a 9.3 deg wide background adapting field. This stimulus lasted for about 40 msec and was 1.8 deg in spatial extent. A second, smaller (in spatial extent) test stimulus about .24 deg wide also lasting 40 msec (this being the minimum duration possible with the experimental apparatus available to Sperling at that time) was presented at various times in relation to the larger and brighter flash. Figure 7-16B indicates the spatial and temporal relation of the background and the two flashes. The magnitude of the just-detectable test flash required at each delay was measured to produce an estimate of the duration and amplitude of the perceptual response at any instant. Sperling's technique suggested that the impulse response of the entire perceptual system was such that the experience of the brief 40 msec flashes was extended to as long as 250 msec as also shown in Fig. 7-16A. As we later see, other techniques suggest somewhat different durations but clearly there is a substantial elongation of the duration of the perceptual

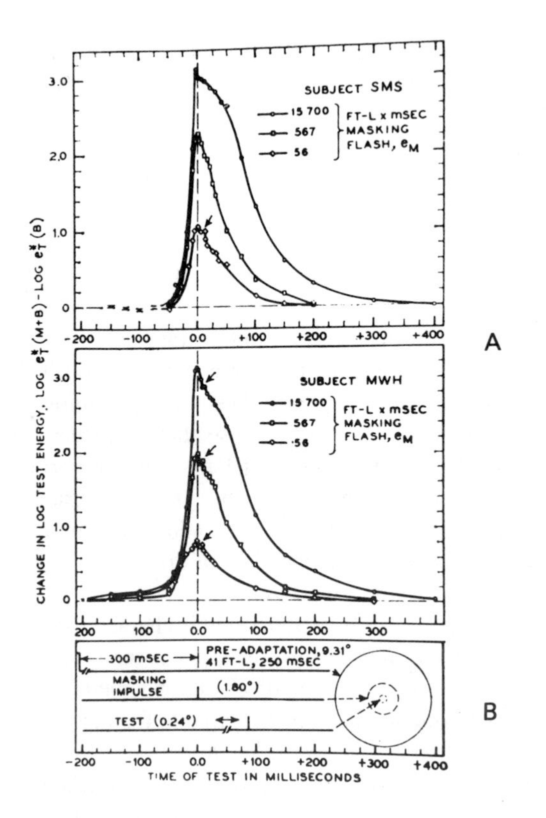

FIG. 7.16. Tracking out the course of the visual impulse function. A small test probe is used to plot the threshold relative to the time of occurrence of a larger, but also brief, flash. The function reflects the impulse response of the visual system to the larger flash. (From Sperling, © 1965, with the permission of the American Institute of Physics.)

response beyond the duration of the physical stimulus, probably as a result of the prolongation of the neural response in the visual system.

A major portion of the persistence of the perceptual experience beyond the duration of the physical stimulus is, as I have noted, attributed by most researchers to peripheral processes. However, the simple attribution of perceptual duration to critical processes occurring in the periphery is at best an incomplete explanation of the phenomena of visual persistence that make up this section. The reader should be forewarned that there are at least two premises that must be assumed to bridge the logical gaps in this conceptually difficult problem area. First, we must not forget that whatever the measured duration of a percept, it is a phenomenological event that must ultimately be defined in terms of central mechanisms. The neural event that is the equivalent of this aspect of experience, like any other, probably occurs centrally, not in the retina or optic nerve. Subjective time, no matter how elastic to the introspective observer, must thus be linked to some central neural process that displays some equivalent temporal course. In other words, there can be no persistence of perception without an equivalent persistence of some central neural response.

The second premise is that these central neural equivalents of the perceptual experience must themselves be affected by the temporal properties of the more peripheral mechanisms. Thus, if the effects of the impulse function of the peripheral mechanisms are to be exerted on the duration of the perceived event, the peripheral prolongation must be transmitted to and converted into a central prolongation.

Now that I have expressed these esoteric principles and assumptions, it is necessary to express the empirical facts of the matter. That principal fact is that we still have no idea what the central neural processes are that are associated with the perception of time. Therefore, for the best of all practical reasons, it is currently impossible to use any known neural process as a surrogate for psychophysical measurement of the phenomenological time course of a percept. Furthermore, because physical stimulus time is not directly linked to psychological time, this lack of a neural or stimulus anchor leads to a great deal of uncertainty when one asks specific empirical questions concerning perceived duration. Indirect cross-modal comparisons are often invoked in many of the studies I describe in the following sections. But these indirect comparisons themselves involve untested premises of corresponding temporal topology. All too often, the results of such comparisons are qualitatively, as well as quantitatively, inconsistent from one experiment to the next.

The point of this discourse is to forewarn the reader concerning this uncertainty. Though the psychology of time has been a topic of great interest to psychologists for many years (e.g., Paul Fraisse's, 1963, outstanding book, *The Psychology of Time* is an excellent summary), many questions concerning perceptual duration that seem at first glance to be very simple and direct remain unanswered. Thus forewarned, we can proceed by noting that there are two fundamental questions concerning the duration of the visual experience that must be considered separately:

1. What is the minimum duration of a visual experience?
2. How long does a given visual experience last?

In the following pages I look at each of these questions in turn.

1. What is the Minimum Duration of a Visual Experience?

The fact that the shortest possible visual experience outlasts by far the shortest possible photic stimulus leads directly to the idea that there should be a minimum duration of visual experience, within which all stimulus events should appear to be simultaneous and which the visual system should encode as a psychological instant or indivisible temporal quantum. The minimum apparent duration, however, is not actually instantaneous but has a palpable nonzero duration. This line of logic further implies that there should be a range of brief stimulus durations starting at the shortest possible physical flash and ranging up to the minimum perceived duration that appear to be of equal length. In this section, I review the literature that suggests that, to a first approximation, this is exactly what happens.

Although the minimum duration of a visual experience has been a classic perceptual problem (e.g., Piéron, 1923b; Richet 1898), it has recently received renewed attention by a number of investigators. Lichtenstein (1961), for example, sought an estimate of the minimum duration of an experience by asking subjects at what interval a set of four lights (arranged to form a diamond-shaped array) appeared to be simultaneous. His subjects reported simultaneity when the total interval was 125 msec, a value that Lichtenstein said corresponded to the minimum visual duration.

Some important modern work on this problem, however, has been done by Robert Efron (1970a, 1970b, 1970c). Efron attempted to measure the minimum duration of the experience produced by brief flashes of light as a function of the stimulus duration. He called the minimum perceptual response to such a stimulus the "duration of the present (Efron, 1967)." In one of his research reports Efron (1970c) studied the effect of the duration of the stimulus on perceived duration by using a cross-modality matching task in which two auditory stimulus clicks were used to demarcate the perceived onset and offset of the experience.

The observer's task in Efron's experiment was to adjust two auditory clicks so that the first appeared to be simultaneous with the onset of the stimulus and the second appeared to be simultaneous with its offset. The time between the two acoustic clicks was considered to be equal to the "duration" of the visual response. Although this process involves certain assumptions that may not be justified, for the moment let us accept this procedure as a valid one and consider only the empirical results of the experiment.

Efron found that all stimulus flashes lasting for less than 130 msec seemed to the observer to be equally long as measured by the interval between the auditory clicks. The most immediate implication of this result is that even the briefest stimulus produces a phenomenal response that lasts for approximately this magnitude of time. Efron and Lee (1971) have also used a stroboscopic type of experiment comparable to one used earlier by D. Allport (1968) to measure the duration of a percept. The results in this case, although utilizing a totally different procedure, were close to the values obtained with the two-acoustic-click method—about 140 msec.

Other investigators (Servière, Miceli, & Galifret, 1977), using other psychophysical methods, have shown that the duration of the minimum perceptual response varies, not unexpectedly, with the degree of training of the subject and such other stimulus factors as its luminance. Using very well-trained subjects and two alternative psychophysical procedures—one in which the subjects made category judgments of durations and one in which subjects were required by a forced-choice psychophysical procedure to choose the longest flash duration from among three brief flashes—Servière and his colleagues found that their trained subjects were able to discriminate 60 msec stimulus durations from even shorter ones. While Servière's estimate was only about half of Efron's, the order of magnitude of these independent estimates of a minimum duration are actually not that different; both bracket a tenth of a second—a magic number that recurs frequently in the duration literature.

The idea of a psychological "instant" with a minimum and nonnegligible duration has been proposed repeatedly in a number of different guises. One idea, known as the "Perceptual Moment Hypothesis," sought to explain why several closely spaced stimuli may appear to be simultaneous even though they may be spread over many milliseconds. According to this hypothesis, originally formalized by Stroud (1949, 1955) and later championed by White (1963) and Kristofferson (1967), there was a discrete chunking of psychological time by some central clocking mechanism such that indivisible units of perceptual simultaneity were strung together like boxcars in a train. All events occurring within the confines of one of these temporal boxcars appeared to be simultaneous, regardless of any actual time intervals between them, whereas events occurring in separate boxcars would appear to be separate regardless of how close they might actually be in time. The apparent simultaneity of two events, therefore, did not depend directly on the interval between the events, but on the statistical accident of their occurrence within the same perceptual moment. Closely spaced stimuli would be statistically more likely to fall within the limits of a single moment and more widely spaced stimuli would be less likely to do so. Because almost all experiments use multiple trials (with one notable example as we see shortly), the statistical central tendencies are measured in any experiment and the details of each trial are lost. Stroud's idea of discrete time units is illustrated in Fig. 7-17A. His estimate of the physical duration of a perceptual moment was one tenth of a second.

Stroud's ideas had a substantial influence on thinking in the psychology of time during the 1950s. But when others attempted to confirm Stroud's hypothesis (for example, Shallice, 1964), they discovered that they had to appeal to such very poorly defined criteria as "the least computation load on the brain (Shallice, 1964, p. 113)" when comparing it with the major alternative hypothesis describing simultaneity. This alternative hypothesis, often attributed to William James, asserted that time was not organized into discrete "boxcars" but rather was arranged as a continuously sliding moment or temporal window in which apparent simultaneity depended exclusively upon the interval between the stimuli as shown in Fig. 7-17B. According to this hypothesis, which has received support from D. Allport (1968), Efron and Lee (1971), and Uttal (1973), perceptual time is composed of an instant or moment that continuously changes its temporal contents. In fact, according to the sliding-window hypothesis, this one moment,

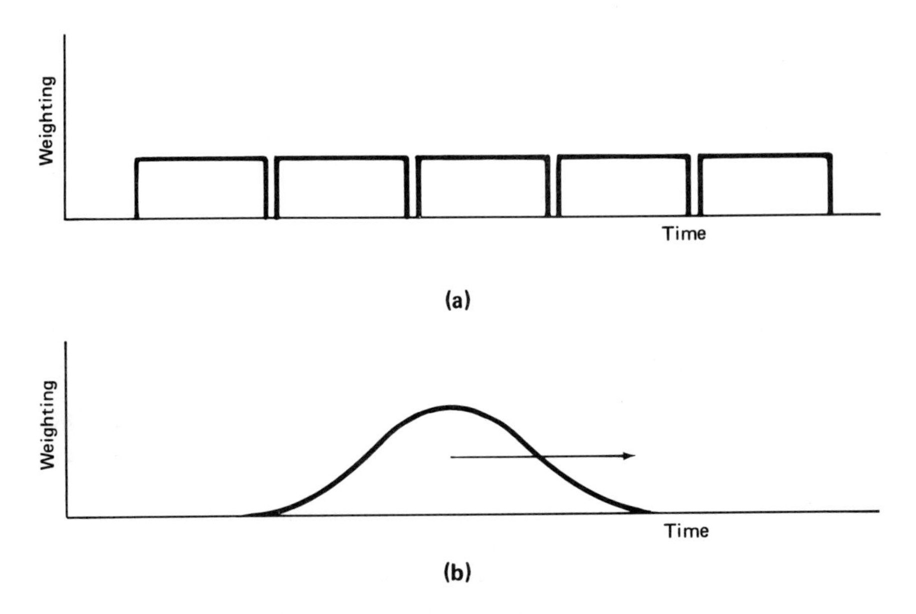

FIG. 7.17. Two drawings suggestive of the alternative models of the psychological moment. (A) The discrete, nonoverlapping, rectangular nonstimulus related moment. (B) The sliding and weighted moving window closely linked to stimulus events. (From Uttal, 1973.)

which appears in experiments as a period of interaction between sequential stimuli, drops off old information and adds new information as it progresses along the time axis. Quite unlike the Stroudian discrete perceptual moment, the main implication of the sliding-moment hypothesis is that stimuli interact as a direct function of their propinquity rather than as a result of a statistical accident that fortuitously determines the moment into which they fall. Each event, in other words, is surrounded by an area of potential interaction consisting of its own trace and the trace of the events that preceded it.

I shall not pursue the topic of perceptual moments any more deeply here. The main point to be made is that the shortest measurable perceptual moments may be much longer in duration than the stimuli that generate them when the stimuli are very brief. This perceptual moment, whatever its nature, exhibits properties that suggest that it has a persistence of something like a tenth of a second and thus defines a psychological instant for which terms like *simultaneity* and *instantaneity* are proper descriptors. The essential point is that the concepts of the moment and of the interactions of sequential stimuli may be just other ways of expressing the basic fact that a visual response outlasts a brief stimulus.

This does not mean, of course, that the human observer cannot discriminate very fine times visually if other response modes are involved. I have shown (Uttal & Hieronymus, 1970) that gaps as small as 10 msec can be detected in a stream of flashes, probably on the basis of a brightness discrimination. But this is not a pure temporal discrimination of the kind just discussed. In other instances fine temporal discrimination can be obtained if the response is analyzed in terms of stereoscopic depth (Burr & Ross, 1979). In both of these cases, the fine sensitivity is not in the time dimension but exists only to the extent that time is recoded into perceived space or brightness.

2. How Long Does A Percept Last?

Beyond the question of the minimum amount of time that a percept may last, we must also inquire into the related issue—how long a nonminimum percept lasts. Although easily stated, this question has been one of the most refractory problems in the psychology of time. The empirical and logical difficulties that arise when one attempts to measure the duration of a percept or of a thought are enormous. As I have already noted, it is not at all certain that there is an isomorphism between the perceived duration of an event and the actual physical clock time that must be used to measure some correlate of its duration. The indicators that are used to measure mental time are not rigorously linked to those mental processes. It is entirely possible, in fact very likely, that there may be a substantial delay between the psychological experience and the reported behavior. It is, in addition, not unlikely that there may even be nonlinear relationships that grossly distort the temporal topology of the external report of the internal process—the order of two events may not even be maintained within the mental domain.

Beyond these difficulties, it is obvious that mental time is enormously elastic. It is a truism that pleasant and busy periods are subjectively perceived as passing more quickly than unpleasant or boring periods of the same physical duration. This raises at least the possibility that at a more microscopic level, the duration as well as the order, of psychological events may not be congruent with the physical time.

Fraisse (1963) discusses the more macroscopic aspects of time perception in his thoughtful book. For the most part, however, these topics are not germane to the discussion of either Level 1 or Level 2. The matters that concern us now include only those more microscopic phenomena associated with very brief stimuli that clearly are influenced by the temporal, spatial, and intensive dimensions of the stimulus that would be expected to exert their influence at the most peripheral levels of processing.

As noted, the measurement of the duration of a brief perceptual experience is a difficult and perplexing problem. Because we have no direct meter for measuring mental time, attacks on the problem, like those searching for the minimum duration, can be made only by indirect procedures which themselves depend upon untested and unproved assumptions of putative associations between different modalities in different domains of discourse.

Cross-modality matching technique similar to those used by Efron (1970a, 1970b, 1970c) to measure the shortest perceived duration has also been used by Haber and Standing (1970) to determine the apparent duration of a longer-than-minimal percept. Like Efron, Haber and Standing attempted to delimit the duration of a percept by perceptually bracketing it between two clicks—one that was adjusted to occur at the "beginning" of the visual experience, and one that was placed at its apparent "termination." As I have noted, such a procedure is fraught with conceptual difficulties. We know that in some auditory situations (e.g. Warren, R. M., 1970) sounds can actually be transposed from one part of a sentence to another and that context can have a strong influence on the perception of sounds that are not even physically present. This suggests that the use of acoustic reference clicks to demarcate particular instants in visual time may be far less rigorous and precise a measurement procedure than it was previously believed to be.

Haber and Standing's results, nevertheless, were quite startling and deserve special attention. They found that the shorter the flash of light, the longer was the persistence of the experience following the cessation of the stimulus. The perceptual duration of their briefest flash (10 msec) outlasted the stimulus by as much as 175 msec whereas the response to intermediate length flashes (200 msec) persisted for only 60 msec after the termination of the stimulus. Furthermore, when the stimuli were very long (over 0.5 seconds), they found that the persistence was negligible, and in fact, the percept did not seem to outlast the stimulus to any measurable degree. Figure 7-18 plots the functional relationship between the additional persistence and the stimulus duration as well as demonstrating their experimental paradigm. This decrease in visual persistence following the cessation of the stimulus flash with increased stimulus duration has also been confirmed by Bowen, Pola, and Matin (1974).

Other techniques, however, give different answers to the same questions, sometimes even to the same investigators. In another study Haber and Standing (1969) themselves, using a procedure in which a subject was asked if a stimulus was continuous or intermittent, determined that the persistence following the offset of a stimulus was constant up to a stimulus duration of about 200 msec. Clearly, measures of persistence are highly task-dependent and thus extremely equivocal.

In this second visual persistence experiment Haber and Standing also noted another paradoxical result—the measured persistence was longer for dimmer stimuli or for stimuli on perfectly dark backgrounds than for brighter stimuli or stimuli on luminous backgrounds. However the answer to the questions of the impact of the luminance of a brief stimulus on the persistence of the visual response remains equivocal. Bowen, Polen, and Matin also found that the visual persistence decreased with increases in luminance. However, Sakitt (1976) observed that for low stimulus intensities there was little persistence. However, after a stimulus level 5 log units above threshold was reached, she discovered

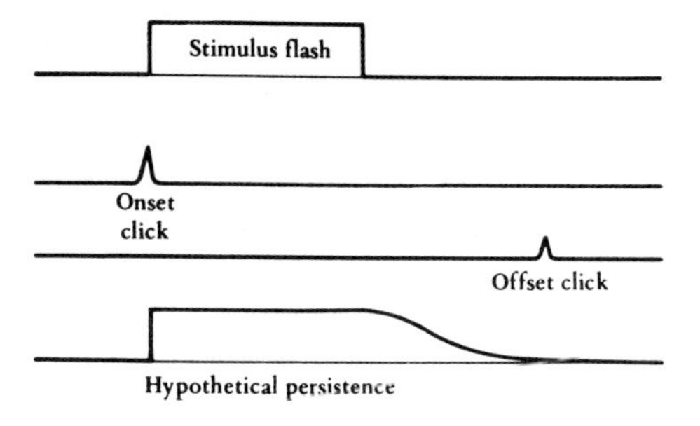

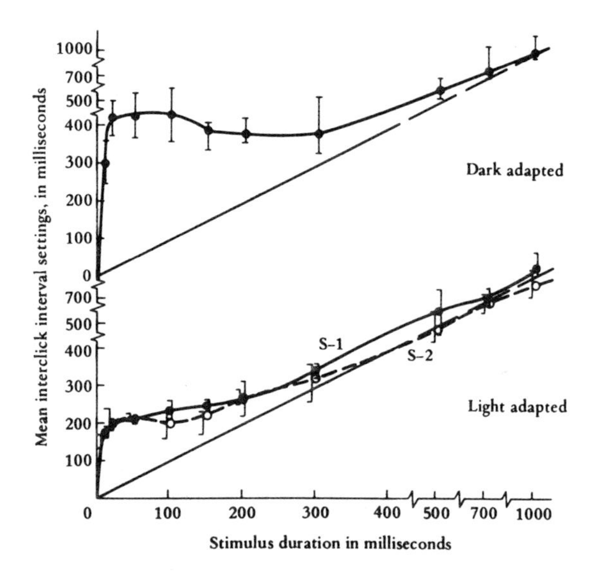

FIG. 7.18. Graph showing the decline in visual persistence as the stimulus duration increases. (From Haber and Standing, © 1970, with the permission of Holt, Rinehart and Winston.)

that a monotonic increase in persistence resulted from further increases in stimulus luminance. This finding is shown in Fig. 7-19. To further complicate the matter, it is now well known that visual persistence is also a function of the spatial properties of the stimulus. Meyer and Maguire (1977) have shown that the short-term storage of a grating depends on its spatial frequency.

Inconsistent and paradoxical results like these obviously indicate that the idea of persistent or reverberatory neural aftereffects is much too simple a concept to explain totally the outcome of these perceptual duration experiments. It is a truism to note that a phenomenal persistence varying as a function of stimulus duration requires some sort of mechanism able to regulate persistence, and a simple impulse response mechanism does not fulfill that need. It is possible,

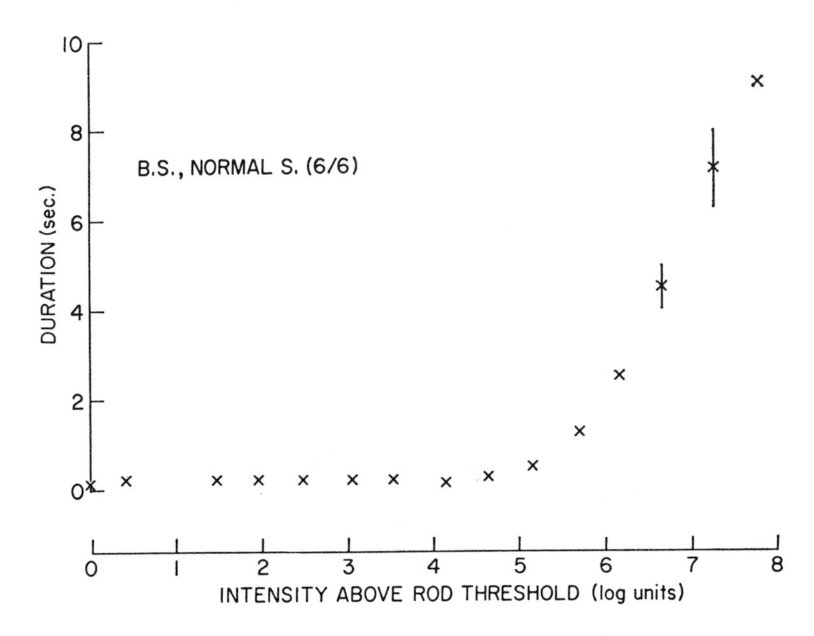

FIG. 7.19. Estimates of stimulus duration plotted as a function of the stimulus intensity. (From Sakitt, © 1976, with the permission of the American Psychological Association.)

however, to speculate that some sort of feedback process might achieve such a regulatory process. The increased duration of a stimulus could lead directly to the increased duration of the peripheral response. This "nonpersistent" or direct portion of the response could also lead to the accumulation of some state or product that inhibited the mechanism accounting for the persistent portion of the response. However, at this stage in our knowledge of the physiological mechanisms that might be involved, such speculation concerning underlying mechanism is merely clutching at straws in the wind.

What is important to note is that any such process (as opposed to the mechanism) capable of regulating the duration of persistence as a function of the duration of the direct response is a highly useful and adaptive evolutionary development that can provide persistence where needed (for short stimuli) and turn it off where it would be a handicap (for long stimuli). We should also not overlook the fact that variable persistence may be closely related to the equally paradoxical Broca–Sulzer effect in which brief stimuli (which display longer persistence) appear brighter than longer stimuli. Variable persistence may be related as well as temporal summation where two or more sequential dim stimuli can unite to produce a more powerful response than either alone would evoke.

In the light of such uncertain findings and nebulous explanations, the simple question—how long does a percept last?—remains both conceptually refractory and empirically unresolved. Although it is clear that, in general, the visual system in many situations is capable of elongating the duration of both the neural and perceptual responses far beyond that of the physical stimulus, we still do not have a satisfactory means of providing a complete answer to the question of how long any particular percept lasts. Indirect methods of measuring this intrapersonal perceptual response, the difficulty of generating a precise operational definition of perceptual time, and the variation of experimental results as a function of many task and stimulus factors makes a definitive answer to this question highly elusive.

F. AFTERIMAGES

Afterimages, the lasting responses to very bright lights, represent some of the earliest observations of persistent visual experience. In the simplest case, a burning ember, when spun around on the end of a rope or stick, produced the illusion of an arc or, if the ember were spinning rapidly enough, a circle of fire. Such observations have probably entertained people around campfires since time immemorial and continue to do so today. Later in human history there was a much more formal interest in the problem of afterimages among many different kinds of scientists. Sir Isaac Newton (1829), Robert Darwin (1786), Gustav Fechner (1838b), Herman von Helmholtz (1856), and Ernst Wilhelm von Brücke (1851) all studied the phenomenon and helped to at least specify it, if not to provide a universally adequate explanation.

In recent years there has been a relatively modest amount of research activity concerning the persistent visual images that are called afterimages. Nowadays, most research interest in this area has dealt with other classes of persistent effects, such as the visual icon produced by much dimmer stimuli, contingent aftereffects, or the problem of the duration of the percept that I have just discussed. Whether or not the icon and afterimage represent the activity of a single mechanism or process is still not definitely known although a consensus seems to be emerging that they do not. The classic studies of afterimages are, however, still interesting and instructive, and brief mention of this older work is not inappropriate in the present context.

The classic afterimages, produced by intense visual stimulation, go through a regular series of stages following the termination of the stimulus. Today these phases can be most clearly demonstrated as they were originally—by means of back illuminated rotating radial lines, which translate the temporal series of sequential stages into spatial patterns, as shown in Fig. 7-20. A representation of the same sequence of afterimage stages is shown in Fig. 7-21 as a function of time rather than of space. In both figures, it can be seen that immediately following the initiation of the stimulus some transient fluctuations in the intensity of the response are usually reported. These initial perceptual experi-

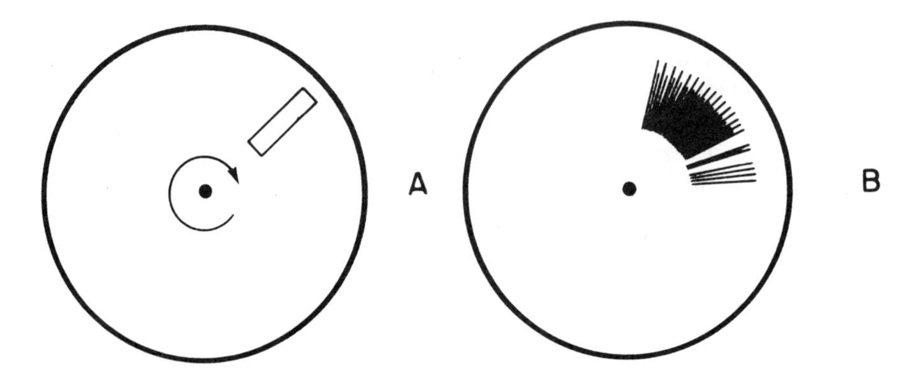

FIG. 7.20. Artist's impression of a classic after-image. (A) The actual physical stimulus a rotating radial illuminated rod. (B) The subjective impression produced by a stimulus of this sort. (Redrawn after Brown, © 1965, from McDougall, 1904.)

ences, perhaps related to those other transient fluctuations in brightness often reported at the onset of a stimulus, appear as bands on the spatial display of Fig. 7-20. After these initial perceptual oscillations have stabilized, the response is usually fairly stable in subjective magnitude until the stimulus is terminated. But following a further delay of about 200 msec, a strong violet afterimage is often reported. This violet afterimage has been referred to as ''Bidwell's Ghost'' (Bidwell, 1899) or the ''Purkinje image.'' If the stimulus is very intense, for example, as a photographic flash bulb may be, the visual afterimage may persist for several minutes.

Other colored afterimages following stimulation with strong white lights can also occur. Positive afterimages with the same luminous and chromatic properties are seen in some conditions, and negative afterimages with reversed properties are reported in other cases. Brücke has also described a ''flight of color''—a late afterimage—in which a sequence of variously colored afterimages occurs.

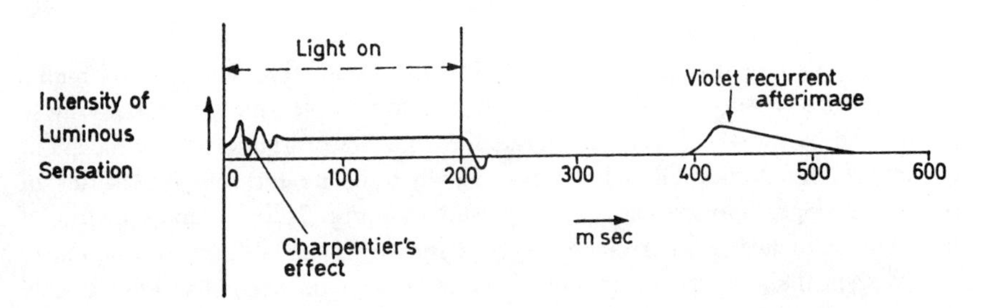

FIG. 7.21. The time course of the sequence of after-images. (From Robinson, © 1972, after Bidwell, 1899, with the permission of Hutchinson University Library.)

Negative and positive afterimages, the flight of colors, and Bidwell's ghost all entertained parlor scientists for decades in the nineteenth and early twentieth centuries. Unfortunately, this was also the period in which research activity concerning this family of persistent afterimages was most extensive, and little has been added in recent years to our understanding of them. J. Brown's (1965) comprehensive review is still sufficiently up-to-date that I do not attempt to replicate the full story of the classic work on afterimages here.

However, a body of recent data with which most Western perceptual psychologists are unfamiliar has accumulated in the Japanese literature. A discussion of some of this work can be found in Obanai (1977). Among the most interesting findings is the observation by Obanai and Kawashima (1961) that the size of the afterimage also oscillates in the period following the stimulus in a way that is associated with the chromatic and brightness oscillation.

Afterimages to high-intensity stimuli have traditionally been attributed to the photochemical bleaching processes (Alpern & Barr, 1962; Craik, 1940b). However a considerable amount of controversy concerning this attribution has recently surfaced. This controversy has mainly been the result of the increased interest in the visual icon—a shorter term visual persistence produced by lower-luminance stimuli. Virsu and Laurinen (1977) distinguish between "bleaching" afterimages (which includes the classic afterimages) and a "sensitivity" image that they attribute to neural, as opposed to photochemical, processes. Similarly, Wade (1978) and Forde and Mackinnon (1975) attribute the oscillating and fading of patterned afterimages to interaction between cortical columns and cortical neurons, respectively.

Furthermore, recent work on afterimages has dealt with the ways the spatial geometry of the stimulus affects the fading of the afterimages. Much of this work is reviewed by Wade (1978). In brief, like stabilized retinal images, afterimages tend to fade in "meaningful units" (Atkinson, 1972a, 1972b; Mackinnon, 1971). That is, lines and corners fade as units rather than in a blotchy, random fashion. Such a datum also suggests that there may be some higher-level processes influencing persistent afterimages beyond the peripheral ones traditionally emphasized.

And then there are the persistent reports of afterimages in the unstimulated eye. Obanai (1977) mentions the long, but nearly forgotten, history of the Bocci afterimage which appears in the contralateral eye after exposure to a bright light in the other eye. Such a phenomenon represents a strongly nonparadigmatic piece of evidence and is thus usually overlooked by contemporary theorists. However, there have been sufficient replications (ranging from Titchener, 1893, to Ohwaki & Kihara, 1953) of the experiment to confirm that it is fundamentally a valid observation. Unless its properties can be shown to be substantially different from those of the monocular afterimages, the Bocci afterimages represents a severe challenge to the peripheral model that has such wide currency today. In sum, there are still too many uncertainties concerning the origins of the sequence of afterimages to attribute them unequivocally to a peripheral mechanism. If there is a consensus, it is that they are more likely to be the result of Level 1 processes; but this is far from certain.

In the next section I consider in detail the persistent *iconic* response to weaker stimuli and discuss the significant differences in approach that have characterized this more recent research.

G. VISUAL PERSISTENCE AND SHORT-TERM MEMORY—ICONIC STORAGE

1. Iconic Storage—The Process

If a neural response and the associated visual experience last considerably longer than a brief stimulus, then the possibility arises that the persistent processes can act as a short-term sensory store or memory. Such a mechanism exists and is called *iconic storage*. Therein lies a considerable difference in conceptualization of the otherwise closely (phenomenologically) related problems of afterimages and iconic storage. Heretofore the study of afterimages has always progressed from the point of view of sensory scientists, who used the rest of the visual system merely as a means of evaluating these peripheral mechanisms and processes. More recent research into the nature of the icon has concentrated on the role of this kind of visual persistence as a short-term storage medium for the cognitive system. Thus the connotation of the phrase "short-term visual memory" is different from that of the phrase "visual persistence" even though both phrases may denote exactly the same thing. The latter suggests that the persistent image may be used to store temporarily information that can be selectively accessed at a later time and used in subsequent cognitive processing whereas the former emphasizes the sensory storage media itself.

Much of this change from a sensory to a cognitive emphasis and the very high level of research activity that has resulted from this reconceptualization of the problem of visual persistence was stimulated by what was clearly one of the most influential experiments of recent times—the doctoral dissertation of George Sperling. This seminal work, made generally available in a later publication (Sperling, 1960), was remarkable for the number of important methodological and conceptual contributions it made. First, it played an unusually significant role in linking together two previously conceptually well-separated topics—memory (a subfield of cognitive psychology) and visual afterimages (a subfield of sensory psychology). Prior to Sperling's sterling paper most researchers did not appreciate the close linkage between the two topics. Second, Sperling made an important methodological contribution by inventing (and demonstrating the power of) the "partial report" technique. Third, and perhaps most important, his work revolutionized the conceptual status of the problem of visual persistence by highlighting the essential fact that "we can see more than we can remember."

The novel concept implicit in the statement that we can see more than we can remember was especially fruitful. It turned out to be one of those innovative yet simple ideas that all agreed, after the fact, was self-evident. Nevertheless, once explicitly stated, it was powerful enough to lead to a complete restructuring of an entire intellectual movement. To Sperling this idea meant that the visual system is able to receive and store, for a brief period of time, a very substantial amount of information from the image projected on the retina. In fact there is a compelling argument that, for a brief time, as much information is stored as can be transduced by the photoreceptor mosaic. Quite out of balance with the ability to load this enormous, but transient, storage capacity (i.e., to see) is the very limited ability of the observer to read information out of this memory (i.e., to remember) in the brief period during which the signal persists. The bottleneck in the process is therefore a central one rather than any limit on the information capacity of the peripheral storage mechanism.

Sperling's ingenious use of the partial report method allowed him to disentangle the properties of the peripheral sensory store from those of the more central cognitive processing mechanisms. He accomplished this important analytical feat by not requiring the observer to process all of the information presented in a complex, yet brief, visual display in order to access only a small portion of it. It had long been known that if observers were briefly presented with a string of letters, such as the display shown in Fig. 7-22A, they would be unable to report all of the letters following the termination of the display. The observer's usual performance in such an experiment was to report the first few stimuli correctly and then to trail off to virtually chance behavior for the later items in the string. Sperling suggested that the problem was not one of a "span of apprehension"—a concept that implied that subjects literally could not "see" the stimuli—but rather, that the inability to report all of the characters was due to the fact that the stored information, which had in fact been successfully entered (i.e., seen) in a short-term storage medium of some sort, faded before it could be read out. He suggested further that, following the offset of the stimulus, observers literally read the letters in serial order from this short-term visual store by means of a limited capacity accessing mechanism. Thus, to recapitulate his major conclusion, we can *see everything,* but it is available only for a brief period of time beyond which *we cannot remember* what we saw.

To distinguish between the sensory and memorial components in this task, Sperling suggested that the traditional experiment should be restructured so that a rectangular stimulus array of letters, rather than a line, was briefly presented. This new stimulus design is shown in Fig. 7-22B. Now, instead of asking his observers to read out the letters from the beginning to the end of the array (which would inevitably lead to very poor reporting of the lower portion of the array if

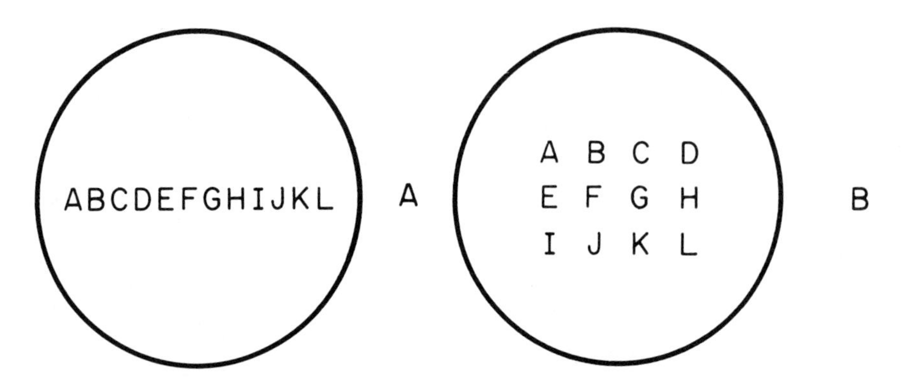

FIG. 7.22. Two displays of alphabetic characters used in short term memory experiments. (A) The traditional display. (B) The partial report display.

read in the usual order), Sperling asked his observers to read out only one of the three lines of three letters. Which particular line was to be read was signaled by a high-, medium-, or low-pitched cuing tone presented after the stimulus was terminated.

The results obtained using this partial report method were astounding. Sperling's observers could read any one of the three lines perfectly *if* they started reading at the beginning of that particular line. Obviously all of the information contained in the array was "seen" (or acquired); it required only a switching of attention from one line or another (which apparently could be done very quickly) to produce perfect reproduction of that particular line before it faded from this short-term store. In other words, the failure of his observers to report the content of large arrays accurately had nothing to do with their ability to *see* those arrays, or even to *store* them briefly. Instead, the difficulty lay in the time it took to *read* the letters from that short-term storage before it decayed. Operationally, this is another way of expressing what Sperling meant when he said that the visual system "could see more than it could remember." This reconceptualization represented a fundamental change in viewpoint with regard to the problem of processing brief visual displays.

In this type of research, the practical tasks become those of determining the duration of the short-term visual storage and the rate at which characters could be read out of it. Though a simple and universal answer cannot be given to the question of duration—it is, as we soon see, dependent upon a number of stimulus and task variables—a general picture of the persistence of the short-term store under Sperling's experimental condition is shown in Fig. 7-23. In this figure, Sperling has plotted the number of characters that are "available" in the short-term visual store as a function of the number of characters in the display. The family of curves varies parametrically with the delay between the termination of the stimulus presentation and the beginning of the cuing signal, which denoted

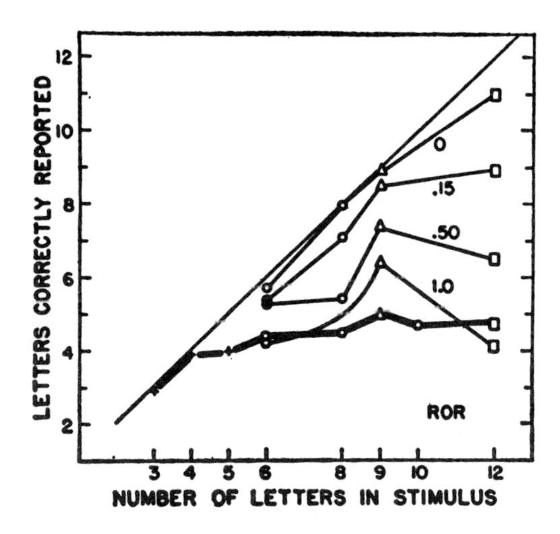

FIG. 7.23. Letters correctly reported as a function of the number of letters in the display plotted parametrically for several different delays of the partial report cue. (From Sperling, © 1960, with the permission of the American Psychological Association.)

the line to be partially reported.[9] The diagonal straight line in this figure represents perfect performance, assuming an ideal observer correctly reporting everything. The other curves indicate the progressive decline in performance with increased delay of the signal tone. After a one-second delay there is literally no difference between the score obtained by tbe partial report method and the subject's performance when asked to report the whole display.

Goryo and Kawai (1972) have reported the results of a very similar experiment and have plotted their data in a way that provides a better picture of the time course of the decay of the short-term visual store. The relative values they obtained, which are shown in Fig. 7-24, are about one half (500 msec) of Sperling's original measurements (1 sec). Thus we can assert that short-term storage lasts at most for about 1 sec under the conditions used in the Sperling experiment and one half sec in the Goryo and Kawai experiments. As we shall see, other investigators have obtained different estimates varying from a tenth of a second to several seconds with other methods. The range of these durations can be considered to be a fair estimate of what the adjective *short-term* means in the phrase "short-term sensory storage."

Several years later, Sperling (1963) followed up his 1960 study with one that answered another very important pair of questions—how long does it take to read

[9]Note in this figure that "letters correctly reported" actually means the number that can be correctly reported with the partial report procedure and not the score that could be obtained in a whole report.

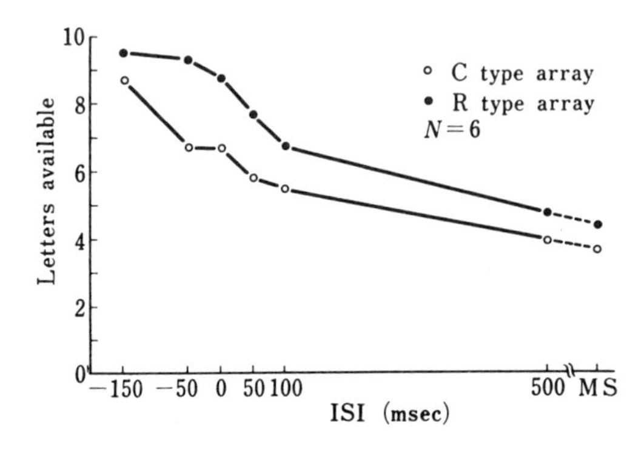

FIG. 7.24. An estimate of the duration of iconic storage for two different kinds of display. C indicates a circular array of letters and R indicates an array similar to that shown in 7.22B. (From Goryo and Kawai, © 1972, with the permission of the Japanese Psychological Association.)

a single character of the short-term store, and is the process one that can go on simultaneously for several characters? Sperling's technique, in this case, was similar to the earlier one except that he used a masking technique (a burst of random visual "noise" followed the stimulus material after a variable delay) to limit the time the subject had to read characters from the short-term visual store.

Figure 7-25 displays the very regular results of this experiment. The number of characters correctly reported was a linear function of the interval between the offset of the stimulus and the onset of the mask. Each 10 msec added to the interval on the average allowed an additional character to be reported. It is clear, therefore, that the process is not a parallel one, but that in the context of this experiment each character is read out in serial order from the short-term store. On the basis of this experiment, Sperling suggested then, that the fundamental reason that we "remember" less than we "see" is the finite amount of time required by the serial read-out process that actually retrieves information from the short-term store. If the number of characters to be read multiplied by 10 msec defines a duration that extends beyond the persistence of the short-term store, then all information requiring access times beyond the period of persistence will be lost; the short-term store simply fades before it can be read out by more central mechanisms. The only way that larger amounts of information can be absorbed is to use chunking or encoding[10] procedures that represent the message contained in the stimulus in some symbolic or semantic manner.

---

[10]By an "encoding process" in this context I am not referring to the problems of afferent neural codes but to a symbolic representation in which a large number of bits can be chunked or represented by a small number of symbols. The word *chair,* for example, is a symbol for a detailed kind of retinal map. The suggestion is that we think by such symbolic information-reducing concepts rather than in terms of isomorphic pictures or echoes. In fact there is a vigorous debate among cognitive theorists concerning the nature of the internal representation. Some (Anderson & Bower, 1973; Pylyshyn, 1976) have supported the idea that percepts and images are represented by propositional systems comparable to verbal strings that need bear no spatial relation to the percept. Others (Kosslyn & Pomerantz, 1977) have suggested that the internal representation is made up of spatially isomorphic reconstructions comparable to pictures. Sensory coding theory tells us, however, that propositional or symbolic representation is at least possible, and likely to be prevalent. I will deal with the problem of internal representation of percepts in greater detail in the next volume in this series.

This experiment, perhaps better than any other, reflects the very low information capacity of that part of the visual communication system modeled by the metaphorical plumb line in Fig. 1-1. It is only by processes that condense and symbolically represent information that we can function at all in the environment in which we are embedded; we simply cannot depend on any ability to communicate totally the large amount of information transduced by the receptor array.

The concept of a peripheral short-term storage process of the kind proposed by Sperling has become an important component of modern psychological theory. It has, as I have already noted, served the particularly important role of linking the sensory and cognitive psychological sciences. Since Sperling's original papers the process has come to be called *iconic storage* by most psychologists (following a suggestion by Ulrich Neisser, 1967, in his influential book *Cognitive Psychology*) to emphasize that this short-term sensory storage mechanism is a truly pictographic kind of storage. Iconic storage may be assayed by a number of different tasks, but the important general point to which all such studies speak is that there exists an entirely uncoded and isomorphic persistent representation of the stimulus falling on the retina. Thus it does seem to differ in fundamental

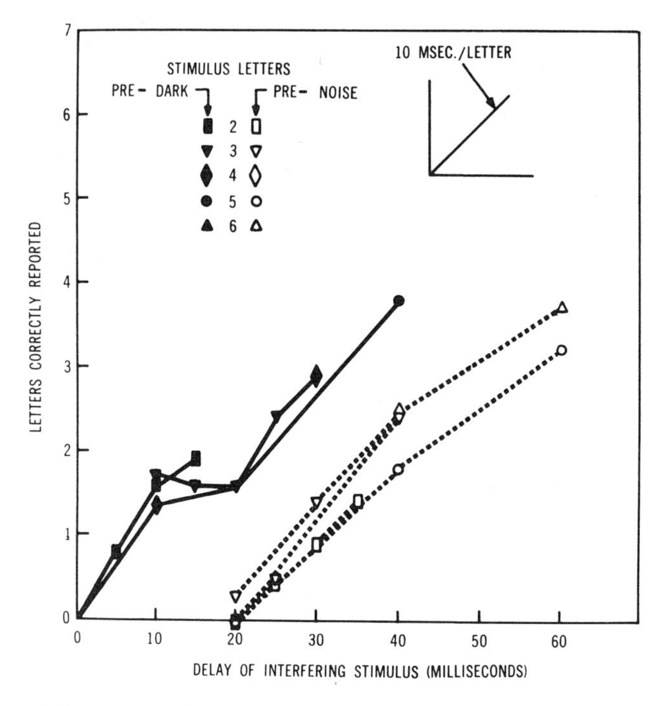

FIG. 7.25. A plot of the number of letters correctly reported as a function of the interval between the offset of the stimulus array and the onset of a masking flash. This data suggests that it takes 10 msec to organize each character and that each character is processed serially. (From Neisser, © 1967, after Sperling, 1963, with the permission of Appleton-Century-Crofts, Inc.)

principle from the higher-level, but often equally brief, cognitive stores in which such highly symbolic properties as name identity (e.g., the same name serves to denote both an uppercase and a lowercase version of the same alphabetic character) or semantic similarity (e.g., different words may have the same meaning) may be involved. The icon, to put it in a nutshell, is very much like a quickly fading photograph.

In recent years much research attention has been directed at the stimulus dimensions that can and cannot influence the duration of iconic storage. In general, the most effective factors have included luminance of the stimulus (Keele & Chase, 1967) and background and exposure duration (Bowen, Pola, & Matin, 1974). However, such factors as the familiarity of the material, its spatial arrangement (Garner, 1972), or the statistical fluctuations in letter sequence (Mewhort, 1967) fail to affect the duration of the icon or the subject's performance in partial report experiments. Furthermore, the icon also appears to move with eye movements (Hochberg, 1968).

In addition, there is only a small effect of the position of the stimulus characters, in a circular array, on the duration of the icon (Goryo & Kawai, 1972). The magnitude of the position effect is so modest that this finding predicts that there shall be little sensitivity to the usual reading order or any other similar quasi-linguistic factor. Furthermore, Wickelgren and Whitman (1970) have shown this brief visual memory is nonassociative; that is, there is little advantage gained by cuing the recall of a particular character with the same or a similar character.

Thus, in general, iconic storage is unaffected by the cognitive factors that we usually attribute to central integrative mechanisms, but the process is very dependent upon the physical properties of the stimulus thought to affect the peripheral mechanisms most directly. Each point in the iconic image space is dealt with much like any other, and the information is not compressed by any coding or chunking. Each point in the image space is also more or less independent of any other. Dick (1974) provides a good review of the independent variables that have been used to study iconic storage, adding further support for the peripheral basis of the process.

Short-term iconic storage, however, should not be misconstrued as the only form of pictographic visual memory. A much less well-understood process referred to as eidetic memory or eidetic imagery has many of the same properties. Eidetic imagery, however, differs in one extraordinary way from the icon—the persistence of the image, may last for many hours or even longer. Eidetic imagery is manifested by the ability to maintain over a long time a mental image of a briefly seen stimulus, which may be as complex as a page of print or a natural scene. A relatively small number of observers exhibit this ability, but those who do seem to be able to use the image as if it were an actual photographic record of the original stimulus scene. Pages from books can be read and even details of the typography reported from the eidetic image in a way that supports the idea that this process depends on an isomorphic representation of the original stimulus.

There are many uncertainties concerning eidetic imagery; and because the relative rarity and complexity of the phenomenon has always made it difficult to study, the process has remained a little suspect and more often subject to anecdote than experiment. Contrary to popular notion, there appears to be little change over the life cycle in those few individuals who seem to possess this kind of long-term pictographic memory. Leask, R. N. Haber, and R. Haber (1969) have demonstrated a high degree of stability in the eidetic imagery ability of children as they mature.

The rare subjects who do have good eidetic imagery are sometimes capable of extraordinary feats. Stromeyer and Psotka (1970) report the case of a unique observer who was able to maintain an eidetic image so well that she could reconstruct a random dot stereogram by combining a stimulus currently presented to one eye with one presented to the other eye more than 24 hours earlier! The fact that these stereograms were made up of random dot patterns makes it extremely implausible that the observer had been able to recode the day-old stimulus symbolically and rehearse it for later recall and use. Unless this observer used some undetected trickery, it does seem from this demonstration that some individuals can maintain an isomorphic eidetic image of a stimulus scene for incredibly long periods of time.

2. The Locus of Iconic Storage

Although the eidetic imagery process remains a mysterious and unexplained phenomenon, some progress has been made in understanding the nature of the processes underlying the shorter-term visual icon. After the general properties of short-term iconic storage were described during the late 1960s, most research attention in the field was reoriented towards the explanation and localization of the critical processes to which the transient icon should be attributed. As already indicated, there is considerable agreement[11] that the relevant processes underlying the phenomenon of iconic storage are to be found at either Level 1 or Level 2 of the taxonomy used in this book; that is, it is agreed by most workers that iconic storage is a retinal process. The phenomenology of this short-term storage process seems to argue compellingly that there is little likelihood that the icon is mediated by any more central mechanism. Thus there are three main plausible answers to the question of its localization; the icon may result from either persistent rod or cone activity or from neural reverberations in the retinal network.

The most vigorous champion of a rod explanation of iconic storage has been Barbara Sakitt (1975, 1976). In a series of ingenious experiments and abetted by some good luck in her sample of observers, Sakitt was able to demonstrate the presence of a normal iconic storage process in an individual with rod-

[11]Although as we later see, it is not a universal consensus.

monochromatism. Her experiments show that the rods are at least sufficient, if not necessary, to maintain a normal short-term visual storage.

Sakitt's fortuitously found rod-monochromat also exhibited another extraordinary phenomena that further supported the idea that rods themselves were especially important in maintaining the icon. With both a bright prestimulus and poststimulus field, this observer could see none of the letters presented in the stimulus. The bright backgrounds preceding and following the stimulus essentially saturated the retinal response so that any further brightness increase (white letters on a black background were used as stimuli in this part of Sakitt's experiment) produced no visual effect. However, when this rod-monochromatic observer closed her eyes after the stimulus, thus effectively turning off the poststimulus field, an iconic image of the stimulus could be perceived. The subject's impressions have been portrayed by an artist in Fig. 7-26 for both the eyes-open and the eyes-closed conditions. Sakitt interpreted this result to mean that the iconic image must be stored in the photoreceptors themselves prior to the point at which the saturation of the response occurred. Because saturation is known to occur in the photoreceptor (from physiological studies cited by Sakitt), she then concluded that the rod itself must be the locus of the persistent iconic process.

Further support for her contention that the rods were predominant and that the cones play only a minor role in establishing the icon, was provided when Sakitt measured the stimulus intensity necessary to produce an icon that lasted for a criterion duration (either 500 or 1000 msec) as a function of the wavelength. Sakitt measured the duration of the icon in a way with which we are already familiar—an acoustic comparison probe was set by the subject to be perceptually

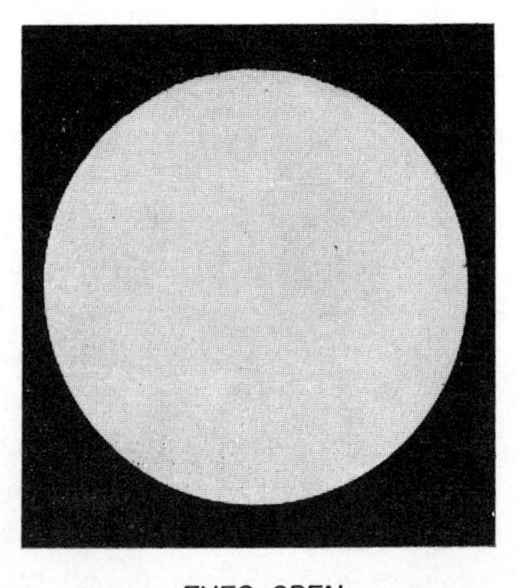

FIG. 7.26. Artist's impression of a rod monochromat's subjective experience in a study of iconic storage in which the stimuli have been superimposed on a bright stimulus that saturated the rods. The left panel depicts the experience with the eyes open and the right panel depicts the experience with the eyes closed. (From Sakitt, © 1976, with the permission of the American Psychological Association.)

coincident with the final fadeout of the icon. The results of this experiment for two normal trichromatic observers, as well as for the rod-monochromatic one, are shown in Fig. 7-27A and B, superimposed on typical photopic and scotopic curves. The spectral sensitivity of the processes underlying the visual icon is obviously fit far better by the scotopic than by the photopic curve. This result fortified Sakitt's argument that the icon measured in this case is, in fact, almost entirely dependent on the properties of rods rather than cones.

This attribution of the icon to the rod mechanism in particular, nevertheless has not been accepted by all investigators working in the field. For example, studies by Jacewitz and Lehmann (1972) showed a substantial reduction in a Sperling-type partial report of a matrix of letters presented to one eye when a masking stimulus (either a repetitive train of stimuli or a grid) was presented to the other eye. These experimenters believe this result suggests a more central explanation for the icon. However, the results of such a dichoptic experiment, in which fusion of the two monocular images occurs, are not sufficient to reject the hypothesis of the possible peripheral locus of the icon; it simply shows that dichoptic masking of the icon is possible, presumably in the same way that sequential images presented to a single eye could also result in visual masking.

A much stronger criticism of Sakitt's conclusion that the rods are the main locus of the icon comes from a pair of experiments that used gratings rather than alphabetic characters as stimulus materials. Meyer and Maguire (1977) have shown that the duration of the icon is dependent upon the spatial frequency of a grating stimulus, and Virsu and Laurinen (1977) have indicated that an alternating presentation of two gratings that are 180 deg out of phase produces an icon whose spatial frequency is twice that of the stimulus gratings. Both studies indicate that the spatial pattern of the icon is an essential factor in the mediation of the storage process in a way that is not explicable in terms of the simple photoreceptor persistence model. To the contrary, Meyer and Maguire's results suggest that persistence is defined by the spatial pattern of the stimulus and thus that at least the retinal, and possibly higher-level neural interactions must be involved. Virsu and Laurinen's results suggest that the spatial stimulus pattern may not even be the necessary and sufficient antecedent of the icon but that the incoming spatial pattern encoded by the receptor mosaic must be processed by transformations that also could only be mediated by neural interactions at a higher level than the photoreceptor. Both of these findings place the icon in the neural plexus of the retina, rather than in the photoreceptors.

McCloskey and Watkins (1978) also argue against a peripheral receptor locus for the phenomenon. They base their argument on the fact that we are able to see complete objects moved past a slit in a way that precludes presentation of the entire object at any one time. McCloskey and Watkins argue that a receptor process would require that the receptor both store old information and acquire new information simultaneously, a capability that seems unlikely to them. They, therefore, champion a more central locus for iconic persistence.

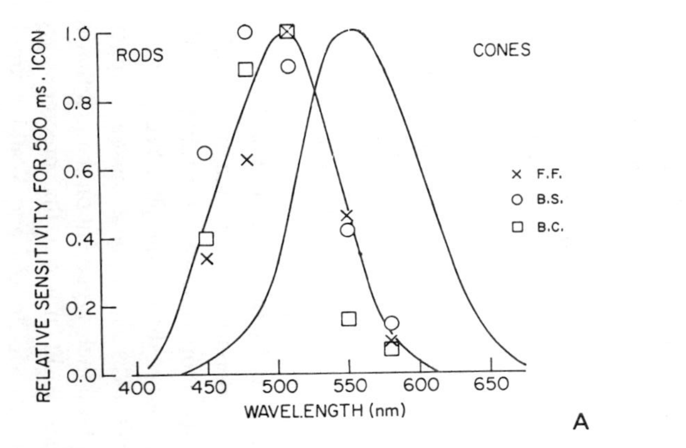

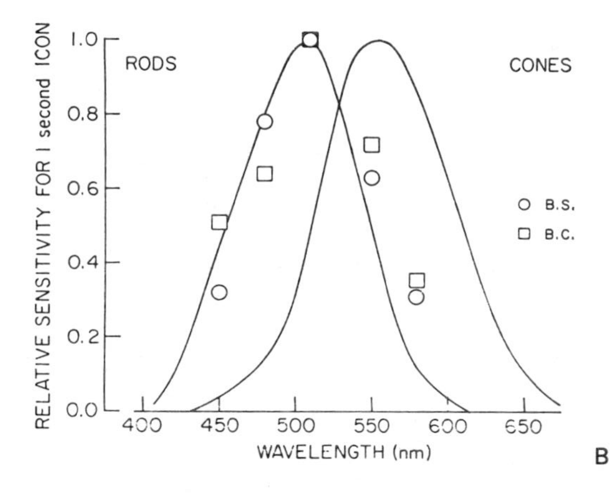

FIG. 7.27. These two graphs, each of which has a photic and scotopic curve superimposed upon it, reflect the spectral sensitivity of the mechanisms producing a criterion 500 msec (A) and a criterion 1 sec (B) visual icon. The spectral sensitivity of the iconic mechanism seems identical to that of the rods. (From Sakitt, © 1976, with the permission of the American Psychological Association.)

Furthermore, Banks and Barber (1977) have shown that the color of the stimulus affects the persistence of the icon in a way that cannot be accounted for solely by a model invoking rod sensitivity alone. They show that the Stroop effect (in which the color of stimulus words may differ from the words that are names of colors) can affect the persistence of the icon as measured with the partial report method. This latter result is particularly startling because its direct implication is that the icon may actually be affected by cognitive factors in a way that is highly incongruent with the thinking so far discussed.

A further argument against a icon specifically mediated by rods has been proposed by Adelson (1978). He used a partial report technique similar to Sperling's original procedure and showed that the partial report advantage continued to be observed even in conditions in which the rods were not operative. Rather than attributing the process to cones, Adelson remains open-minded and accepts the possibility that the critical level of processing may be somewhat more central.

At present, even Barbara Sakitt (Sakitt & Long, 1978) seems to have accepted the fact that there may be a cone icon as well as the rod icon she studied earlier. In this paper, as well as in an even more recent one (Sakitt and Long, 1979) Sakitt and Long argue that a longer-lasting rod icon could obscure a shorter cone icon since the ultimate persistence of perception would be determined by the longer lasting process. However, by means of ingenious procedures involving the use of a forced-choice psychophysical design and white and colored stimuli, they were able to separate the rod and cone contributions to the icons. Under the circumstances their results indicated that the cones may actually dominate in maintaining the icon for periods up to 100 msec. However, for longer durations, they confirmed that the rods, as suggested earlier by Sakitt, seemed to play the dominant role in determining the duration of the short-term storage of the stimulus information. Finally, an explicitly Level 2 neural network theory of the icon has been proposed by Bridgeman (1978). He expands upon a lateral interaction model of metacontrast (see Chapter 9) and my own autocorrelation model (Uttal, 1975a) to postulate a system that could also maintain a signal by means of circulating neural activity.

Obviously the problem of the locus of the icon is in a great state of flux, and this flux is one of the reasons that I have chosen not to attempt to preempt the empirical and theoretical status of the problem by assigning this process exclusively to either Level 1 or Level 2 at the present time. Although there seems to be a majority view that at least some of this short-term storage is mediated by retinal processes be they rod, cone, or network, the suggestions of such workers as Banks and Barber that there may be a more central component cannot be completely disregarded at this point.

The problem may be ultimately resolved as such controversies so often are by demonstrations that there are several different contributions to iconic storage and perhaps, as suggested by Adelson, several different kinds of iconic storage. We may eventually arrive at an explanation of the icon that, like dark adaptation, will invoke both receptor and neural process in the retina and some even more central mechanisms, in order to explain fully the many phenomena of visual short-term storage of stimulus information.

H. SEQUENTIAL INTERACTIONS OF VISUAL STIMULI

In the previous three sections of this chapter I considered the various perceptual phenomena associated with critical processes that affected the persistence of the neural response to a brief stimulus. I discussed a number of experimental paradigms that have been used to examine the subjective duration of a response and, in general, observed that perception may last far beyond the objective duration of the stimulus. I argued that the consensus in this particular area of perceptual research was that a major portion of the phenomenological prolongation was due to events occurring in the retina if not indeed in the photoreceptors themselves.

In this section I turn to another closely related set of phenomena—those involved in the interaction between sequential stimuli. In light of the prolonged duration of both the neural and the psychophysical responses, it is not surprising that the responses to two closely spaced (in time) stimuli should overlap and interact even when the physical stimuli do not. Many years of research using a large number of different experimental procedures have clearly demonstrated the nature of this interaction. We now know, for example, that the perceptual responses to sequential stimuli may either be enhanced or inhibited depending upon the task, the stimulus parameters, and the measurement procedure.

In this section I review some of what is known of interactions between sequential stimuli. It is important to note that, although in the subsections that follow I have separated these experiments and findings into separate categories for organizational reasons, from one perspective this is probably conceptually incorrect. It is essential for the reader to appreciate that, regardless of the experimental paradigm, it appears that all of the phenomena I incorporate within the rubric of temporal interaction probably reflect the action of only a single process. That critical process, which unites all of the material in this section, is the interactive addition of multiple sequential stimuli that occurs directly as a result of the prolongation of the response to single stimuli. In other words, this section concerns itself in general with the degree to which integration occurs when stimuli occur close together in time.

All of the phenomena that I shall discuss in the following sections reflect the process of interaction between prolonged responses. Whether I am considering the phenomena of intermittency detection or temporal summation, an analysis of the actual processes that underlie either phenomenon indicates that all such processes share a common origin. Even when it cannot be said with certainty exactly where the relevant processes occur, it does seem certain that most of these processes discussed in this section are very much like those others described in the previous section in terms of their peripheral origins. The point I am making is that the difference between measures of duration and measures of sequential interaction is an operational one, defined by the particular methods used by the investigator, and not a psychobiological one reflecting different underlying mechanisms and processes. With that caveat in mind, I can now turn to the topics discussed in this section on interactions between sequential stimuli. These topics include: (1) the critical duration; (2) temporal summation; and (3) intermittency detection.

1. The Critical Duration

A prototype of all of the other interactions between sequential stimuli can be discerned in the phenomenon known as the critical duration. The critical duration is defined as the integrating period within which the temporal distribution of the energy of a stimulus is purported to have little or no effect. Within the critical duration, to a first approximation, only the integral of the stimulus energy influences the visual response. The energy may be uniformly distributed or may be presented as a series of discrete events of any temporal pattern without perceptual effect; the mind, it has traditionally been asserted, cannot tell the difference.

This, at least, is the classic view. As we consider this problem in more detail, we see that some information concerning the temporal microstructure of the stimulus is retained as evidenced in some discriminative tasks. However, in every such case, the residual discriminability reflects the recoding of the temporal stimulus information into some other dimension of perceptual experience. Thus it is not time per se to which the observer is responding, but some effect of the temporal properties of the stimulus on, for example, the brightness or spatial location of the stimulus. The generality that the human observer has very poor temporal acuity in the visual system therefore is robust. Indeed, when one considers the conversions that occur in the auditory system between stimulus frequency and spatial localization on the cochlea, it is also apparent that in that case also the observer is not directly discriminating time but a recoded response to it.

That an integrating period of some kind existed in visual perception was first suggested by Bloch (1885). His formulation of the concept for vision was a modification and extension of an analogous photochemical law suggested by Bunsen and Roscoe, which stated that, up to a certain critical interval, the effect of light on a chemical reaction was independent of the temporal pattern in which the light was delivered, depending instead on the total energy absorbed by the constituent molecule. In other words, both the Bunsen–Roscoe law and Bloch's psychological analog of it assert that

$$I \times T = K \qquad \text{for all } T \text{ less than } T_c \tag{7-1}$$

where I is the intensity of the stimulus, T is its duration, K indicates a constant optical, chemical, or visual effect, and T_c is a maximum duration of time–pattern-independent integration (i.e., the critical duration). Because this equation indicates an exact reciprocal relationship between *I* and *T*, Bloch's law has often been referred to as the reciprocity law.

Although Bloch originally formulated the visual reciprocity law in terms of the absolute threshold, and much of the classic research (e.g., Baumgardt & Hillman, 1961; Blondel & Rey, 1911; Brindley, 1952; Herrick, 1956) was framed in this context, it is now clear that Bloch's law is a far more general one that probably holds for many other kinds of visual effects and types of responses other than simple absolute detection.[12] For example, Ueno (1977) has also shown that Bloch's law holds for measurements of reaction times to suprathreshold stimuli, and Kahneman, Norman and Kubovy (1967) have shown that it applies as well to tasks involving visual acuity. Ueno's result is presumably due to the tight relationship that exists between luminance and reaction time and the fact that suprathreshold luminances also obey a reciprocal type of relationship in accord with Bloch's law. Thus, given a particular luminance, up to a certain maximum time the product of stimulus intensity and duration should be a constant; and because luminance and reaction time are also tightly related, Bloch's law also holds for reaction times as well as for absolute thresholds.

Such a relationship, however, does not mean that the critical duration itself is constant for all apparent brightnesses. In fact, Ueno demonstrated that there is a monotonic decrease in the critical duration as the stimulus intensity increases above threshold. This finding confirms earlier work by Keller (1941), Herrick (1956) and Krauskopf and Mollon (1971). For the suprathreshold values Ueno used, the critical durations were very short, ranging downwards from 30 msec at the lowest to virtually zero integration time at the highest stimulus intensities used (about 2 cd/m^2). This decline in the critical duration with increased stimulus luminosity is reminiscent of the decline in visual persistence for longer stimulus durations and may reflect the same kind of compensatory feedback controls that probably underlay that finding. Such a relationship further helps to link the empirical topics of persistence and critical duration to a common underlying mechanism.

An appreciation of the levels of critical processing underlying the critical duration can be obtained by briefly considering the types of stimulus parameter that affect its duration. Kahneman, Norman, and Kubovy (1967) and Ueno (1977) have all shown that the binocular critical duration is longer than the monocular one. Furthermore, the critical duration appears to be slightly longer in the fovea than in the peripheral retina. (See also the discussion by Bartlett, 1965, of data from studies by Karn, 1936, and Blondel & Rey, 1911). The size of the stimulus, another dimension that might initially be thought to be influential in

[12]Keep in mind, however, the fact that still other tasks may show a persistence of discriminability that violates this generality. In all cases such discriminability represents a recoding of stimulus information into some other perceptual dimension and does not actually reflect a temporal discriminability on the part of the observer.

determining the critical duration, seems not to have a significant effect until the stimulus becomes very large. Kahneman (1967) also reports that contrast has little effect on the critical duration. This lack of contrast effect extends even to the complete reversal situation in which white figures are presented on a black background. Accordingly, whether the flash is a decrement or an increment in luminance also seems to have little effect on the critical duration as reported by Roufs (1974).

An effect of contrast on the critical duration however (or, as he called it—sensing time) has been demonstrated by Ko (1938). The slope of the line representing the time required to see a stimulus at various stimulus intensities varies substantially, depending upon whether he used black figures on a white background or vice versa, as shown in Fig. 7-28. The relationship between the critical duration and contrast is, therefore, complex.

The nature of the task itself can also affect the measured critical duration. Kahneman and Norman (1964), have shown that the critical duration can differ by as much as 100 msec depending on whether a brightness-matching or an identification task was used. The results of their experiment are shown in Fig. 7-29.

The effect of the wavelength of the stimulus on the critical duration has also been extensively studied by a number of investigators. One of the earliest studies of this genre, carried out by Rouse (1952), indicated that the stimulus wavelength had little effect on the critical duration as was also shown in later studies by Sperling and Joliffee (1965), and Regan and Tyler (1971). However, when

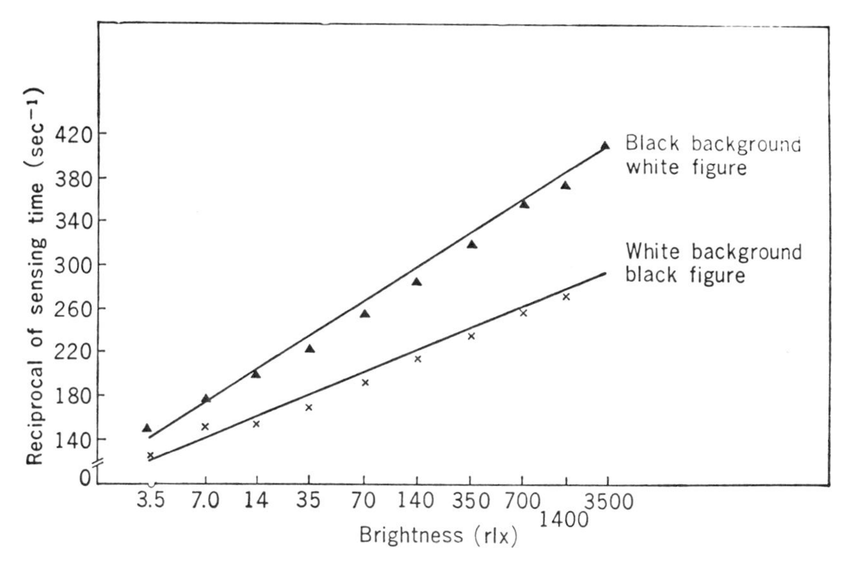

FIG. 7.28. The effect of contrast on the critical duration. (From Obonai, 1977, after Ko, 1938, with the permission of the Hokuseido Press.)

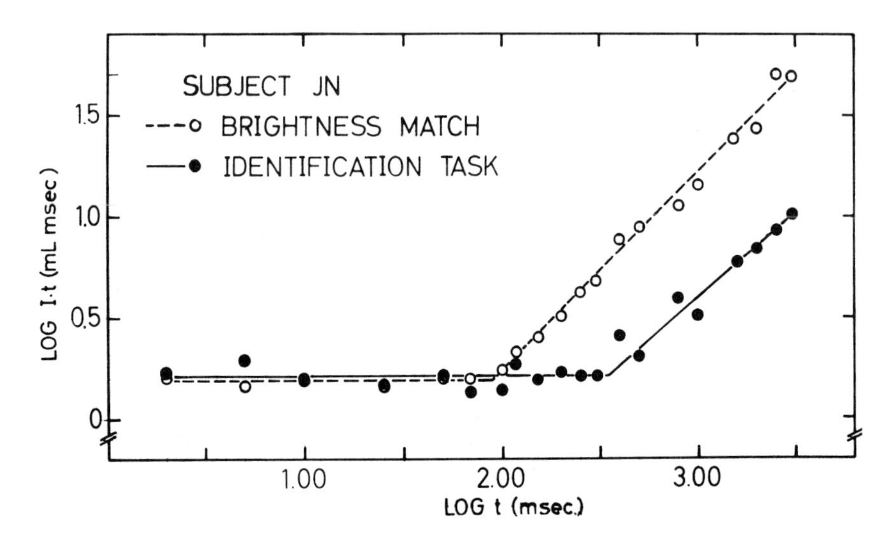

FIG. 7.29. The effect of the task on the critical duration. (From Kahneman and Norman, © 1964, with the permission of the American Psychological Association.)

Krauskopf and Mollon (1971) used the Stiles' two-color adaptation technique (described on p. 412), they observed that the different π mechanisms isolated by selective preadaptation did exhibit somewhat different critical durations. In general, the π_1 short-wavelength-sensitive system exhibited longer critical durations than the π_4 and π_5 mechanisms that have been associated with longer-wavelength-receptive functions. An important corollary of their findings is that critical duration for any one of the mechanisms depended only on its own state of adaptation, and therefore the various chromatic receptor mechanisms seemed to be functionally independent of each other in their respective temporal properties.[13] Regan and Tyler have carried this idea of independent "channels" even further by assuming that the effects on the critical duration of both luminance and wavelengths were independent of each other.

The change in the critical duration as a function of the state of dark adaptation has been studied by Stewart (1972). She observed that the critical duration was longer for eyes that were more thoroughly dark-adapted and that the critical duration progressively increased in a monotonic fashion as a function of time in the dark as shown in Fig. 7-30. Stewart also observed that the way in which the functions changed from the region in which reciprocity occurred to the region in which it did not hold, also changed as a function of time; the longer the observer was in the dark, the less abrupt was the transition.

[13]Although we see in Chapter 8 that there is ample evidence of other forms of interreceptor interactions.

In recent years, two of the most fundamental attributes of the concept of the critical duration have been called into question. First, some recent work has questioned whether the basic idea that all temporal information, other than the integral of the energy presented to the eye is lost within the critical duration, is valid. It has now been suggested that the kind of task traditionally used to measure the critical duration ignores some vestigial information that actually could be tapped to indicate a residue of psychologically usable information concerning the temporal pattern of a stimulus. Such a challenge has come from James Zacks and Joseph Lappin. Zacks (1970) and Lappin and Harm (1973) have shown that even if temporal stimulus patterns exhibit identical absolute thresholds in terms of their energy, they might well be discriminable from each other on the basis of some other criterion. Thus, for example, Zacks showed that even though two light stimulus pulses (with I_1, T_1 and I_2, T_2 such that $I_1 \times T_1 = I_2 \times T_2 = K$, and with equal detection probabilities) might be "identical" as measured with an absolute-threshold criterion, they can still be distinguished on the basis of other criteria such as apparent duration. If others can replicate this finding and substantiate the psychophysical discriminability of flashes that are equal in their reciprocal intensity–duration relationships, then reformulation of the basic idea of the critical duration would certainly be in order.

The second question raised by some of the data already described (particularly the task-dependency of the critical duration reported by Kahnemann & Norman and the difference between binocular and monocular critical durations reported

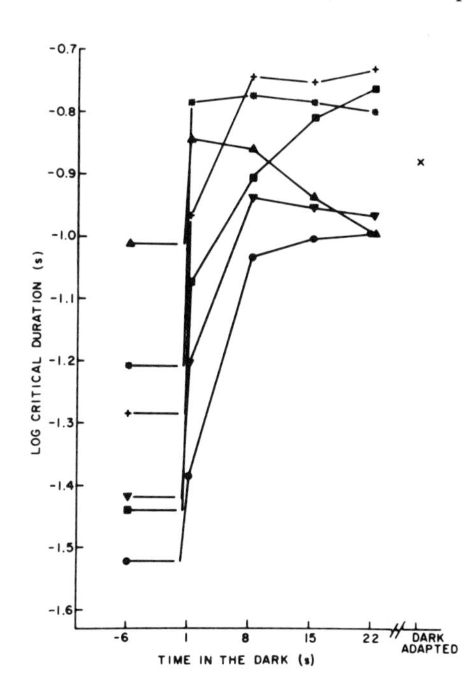

FIG. 7.30. The effect of dark adaptation on the critical duration. Light adaptation increases from bottom to top. (From Stewart, © 1972, with the permission of the American Institute of Physics.)

by Ueno, 1977) concerns the general adequacy of the very peripheral explanation of the critical duration that is usually accepted today. Perhaps other levels of processing higher than those I have invoked here may contribute further to the determination of the critical duration. Obviously there is much yet to be learned about even this simple phenomenon.

In spite of these nagging doubts, the consensus is that the phenomenon of the critical duration is primarily the result of peripheral processes. Indeed there is even some physiological evidence that adds fairly direct support to this hypothesis. Hood and Grover (1974), for example, have recorded a compound electrical potential from the retina, which they believe is entirely made up of receptor potentials from the class of cones that absorb with a peak at about 580 nm. All other retinal neural responses were blocked by perfusing the retina with aspartate, a substance that inhibits the transmitter action at the synapse but does not interfere with receptor activity. Figure 7-31 shows the results of Hood and Grover's experiments for two levels of stimulus intensity and two levels of light adaptation. In general, the reciprocity relation ($I \times T = C$) holds for all four conditions although the light-adapted preparations displayed shorter critical durations than the dark-adapted ones and the stronger responses (evoked by the stronger stimuli) produced shorter critical durations than the less intense ones. These data support the contention that a peripheral explanation of the critical duration is essentially sound by showing that the phenomenon does have a neural correlate in the receptors.

2. Temporal Summation

The critical duration can be seen in the context of the preceding discussion as one of the many ways in which the sequential portions of an extended stimulus can interact with each other. The major message of the findings I have discussed so far is that the visual response is determined by the absolute amount of energy presented to the retina within the critical duration rather than by the temporal pattern in which the stimuli are presented. These results, therefore, are essentially congruent with the idea of the perceptual moment; both assert that there is a loss of the temporal microstructure contained in a brief stimulus, at least as measured with some perceptual tasks.

But it must not be forgotten that Bloch's law and the concept of the critical duration are conceptualized in terms of a continuous stimulus, and that this is only one means of attacking the problem of temporal interactions. There is another means of looking at the same processes and mechanisms that does not demand that the stimulus be continuous as is necessitated by the formulation of Bloch's law and the paradigm of those experiments that test it. Instead, this alternative approach concentrates on those instances of summation in which sequential, but temporally discrete, stimuli become fused or integrated into a single visual experience. A wide variety of perceptual experiments falls within

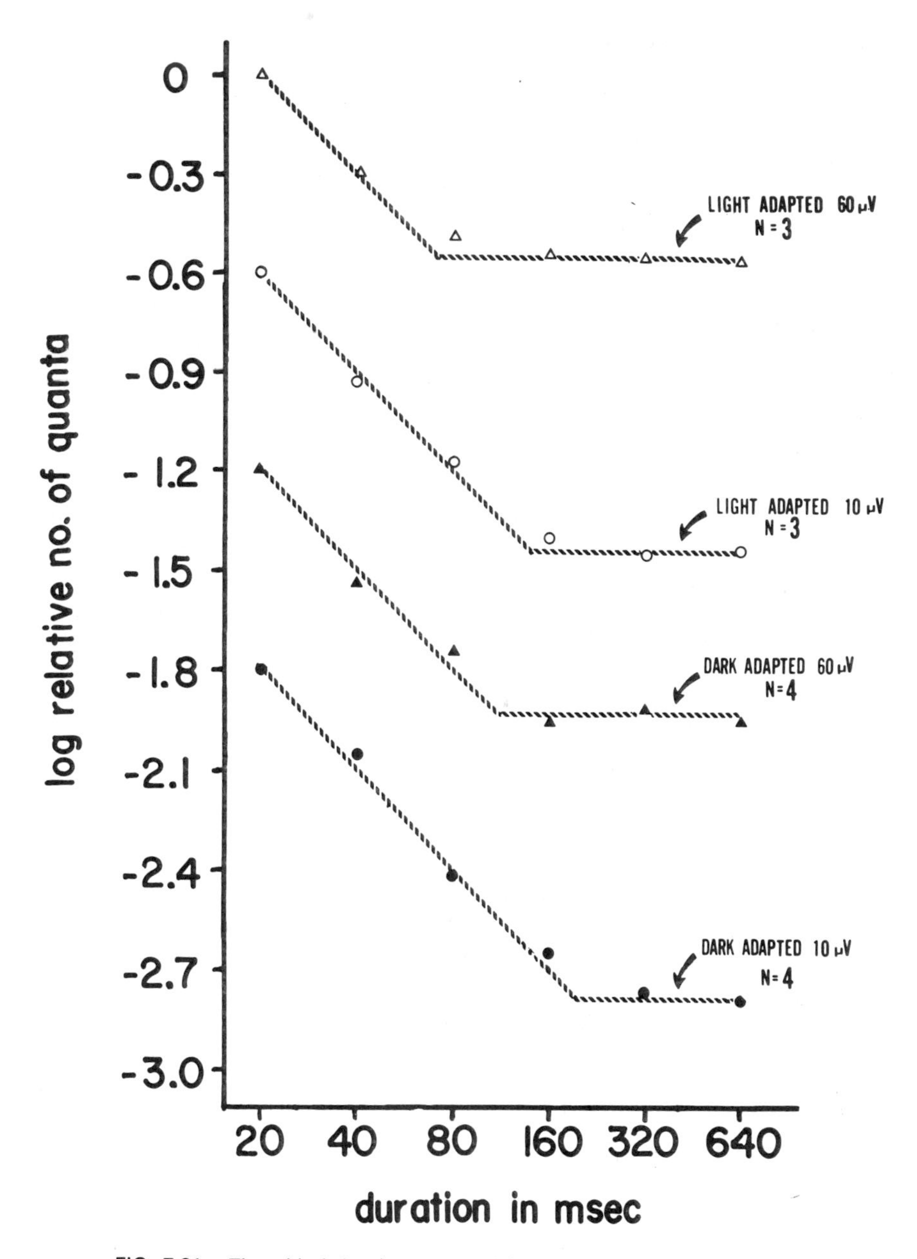

FIG. 7.31. The critical duration expressed in an electrophysiological experiment. The relative response magnitude is plotted as a function of stimulus duration. Triangles indicate a 60 microvolt response criterion, and circles indicate a 10 microvolt response criterion. Filled symbols are from a dark adapted preparation, while open symbols are from a light adapted preparation. N = the number of cells studied. (From Hood and Grover, © 1974, with the permission of the American Association for the Advancement of Science.)

this category. Two sequential stimuli may be constructively combined to produce a more detectable stimulus than either one alone, or conversely, they may combine to produce a stimulus that is less recognizable because of inhibitory camouflage or masking effects. Collectively, the class of phenomena I discuss in this section reflect the persistence or integration period of the visual system by demonstrating the perceptual results of experimental paradigms in which two or more stimuli become fused into a single perceptual experience. Although the experiment paradigms and results may differ, I find it impossible to distinguish between the mechanisms that must account for these fusion phenomena and those that must be invoked to explain the critical duration in terms of these underlying explanations and processes. As preview, it appears probable that exactly the same peripheral mechanisms must also be invoked to explain the intermittency phenomena discussed in the next section. The point is that whatever the methodology, task, or resulting phenomena, all of these topics are joined togehter in terms of a common underlying process: the persistence of the peripheral neural response beyond the duration of the stimulus.

Nevertheless, and in spite of this common origin, the topics that I deal with in this section are phenomenologically and methodologically different from those of the previous section, and for this reason (as well as to avoid conceptual confusion among them) I have separated them into separate categories.

a. Two-Pulse Interaction: Masking of the First Kind. An alternative means of measuring the temporal integration period of the visual system is to introduce two flashes of equal intensity and duration but with a variable interval between the two. The luminance that evokes a threshold sensation is then used as an index of the integration. The logic behind this approach is that when the interval between the two is great enough to preclude any temporal interaction, the threshold energy of the pair of pulses should be the same as that of either pulse presented alone. On the other hand, when the two are temporally interacting, the threshold level of the pair should differ from that of a single pulse. It should be noted that exactly this same experimental design may be used to measure the ability of the eye to resolve perceptually two suprathreshold flashes. In one case, the experimenter is interested in the additivity of two presumably subthreshold individual flashes to produce a detectable but unified response. In the other, the criterion is an intermittency detection, but the procedures and probably the mechanisms involved are identical.

The general finding of a large number of studies of the sequential interaction of two pulses has been that there is also a maximum duration beyond which summation does not occur. Estimates of the actual size of this interval have varied from 100 msec in some older studies (Davy, 1952) down to 10 msec in some more recent studies (Grossberg, 1970). However, there are exceptions to the generality that two flashes will temporarily summate to produce a better response than a single flash. Some researchers have reported that there are interflash intervals at which the interactions may actually be inhibitory, so that in order to be detected when both are presented the stimulus luminance of each pulse has to be increased rather than decreased. The literature on the two-flash experiments has been extensively discussed by Boynton (1972) in a review that covers much of the work up until about 1970; his review is summarized in Table 7-1.

An important recent study of the two-pulse interaction problem has been subsequently published by Herrick (1972a, 1972b). Herrick used an increment threshold technique (the observer was required to detect a flash of light on an illuminated background) to determine the effect of the interval between two stimuli on that detection. In the first of his experiments (Herrick, 1972a), the two light stimuli had identical durations (5 msec). The threshold luminance for the detection of the two stimuli, which appeared as a single flash, was measured as a function of the interval between them. Figure 7-32 displays the typical results of this experiment for three different background luminances. Obviously the two stimuli are summating perfectly on the left side of all three of these curves. The flat region there indicates that the total amount of energy required for detection remains constant. However, above some value, which we may consider to be the integration period in this type of experiment, perfect energy summation no longer holds and the luminance of the two stimuli must progressively increase to produce a suprathreshold response. This function, however, holds only up to a certain limit after which the threshold luminance actually declines as the interval between the two stimuli further increases. Finally, the two light pulses were so far apart that the threshold was essentially determined by the energy level of the single pulse, a value that was approximately twice that required when two stimuli were presented close together. Herrick summarized this outcome in Fig. 7-33, which is an idealization of the data he obtained. The function of interflash interval from his point of view can be represented by four straight lines, representing four different interactive processes. Table 7-2 summarizes the characteristics of the four different processes.

In more recent work, Ueno (1977), using a reaction time technique, has shown that the summation or inhibition between two flashes is dependent not only on the interval between the two flashes but also upon their respective amplitudes, a finding that was supported by Herrick's (1972b) second experiment. Ueno's index of summation, or inhibition, a change in reaction time to the first of two stimuli, although indirect, is valid because the relationship between reaction time and luminance is so tight. He defines his summation index $\Psi(\tau)$ as:

$$\Psi(\tau) = \frac{T(s) - T(\tau)}{T(s) - T(2s)} \tag{7-2}$$

where "$T(s)$ and $T(2s)$ are the reaction times to a 2 and 4 msec single pulse respectively and $T(\tau)$ represents the reaction time to a double pulse stimulus with a stimulus onset asynchrony of τ msec" (Ueno, 1977, p. 592). Figure 7-34 plots

TABLE 7.1
Summary of Two Pulse Threshold Experiments

Author	*Pulse Duration (msec)*	*Pulse Geometry*	*Pulse* λ	*Background*	*Finding* (τ = *critical duration*)
Davy (1952)	10	2′ at 15°	white	dark	$\tau = 100$ msec
van den Brink and Bouman (1954)	1	1′ at 0°, 2°, 4°, 7° and 10°	red and green	widely variable	τ decreases as adaptation level increases $\tau = 80$ msec
Blackwell (1963)	2.5	1° at 0°	white	10 ftL	inhibition at 50 msec $\tau = 20$ msec
Ikeda (1965)	12.5	30′ at 0°	red	328 td 61.2 td	inhibition at 50–70 msec (excitation for ± pulses) $\tau = 10$ to 20 msec
Battersby and Defabaugh (1968)	5	30′ at 6.5°	white	1 ml	$\tau = 10$ msec at most
Grossberg (1970)	2.5	0.5° at 0°	white	dark	$\tau = 10$ msec
Rashbass (1970)	2	17° at 0°	green	700 td	like Ikeda

From Boynton, 1972.

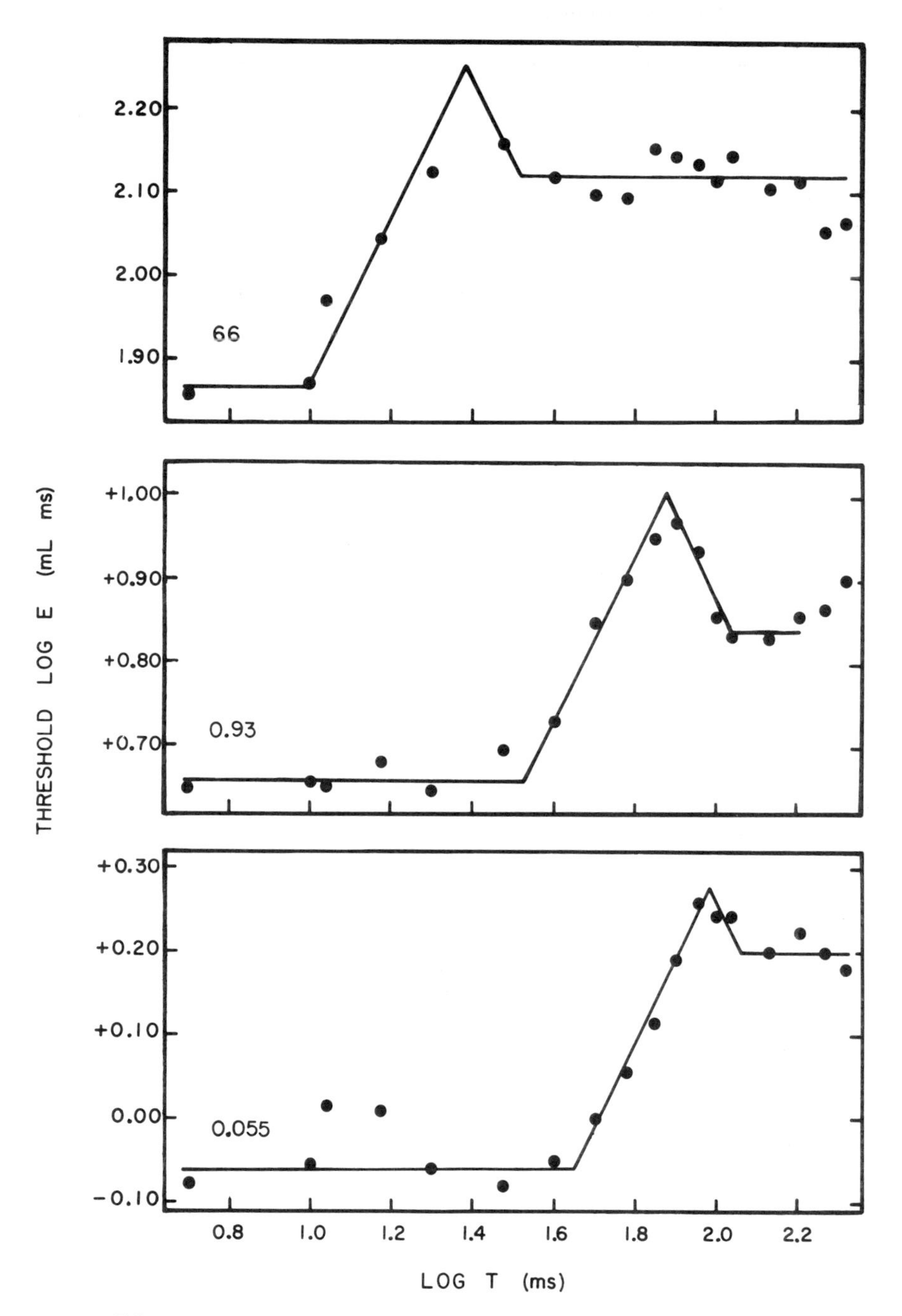

FIG. 7.32. The threshold luminance in a two pulse experiment as a function of the total display time for three different levels of adaptation (in millilamberts). (From Herrick, © 1972a, with the permission of the American Institute of Physics.)

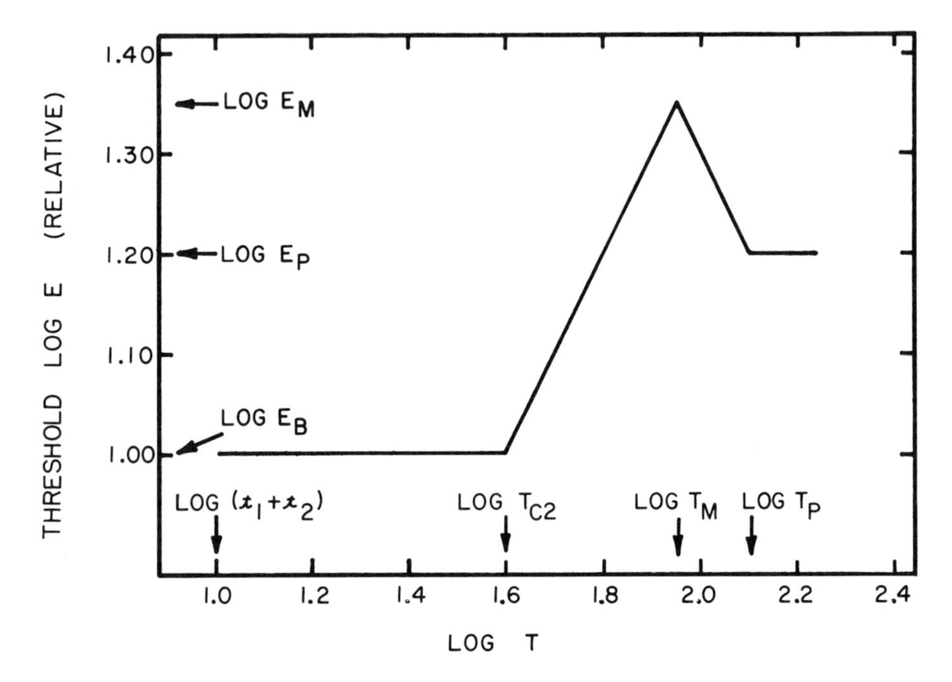

FIG. 7.33. Herrick's theoretical model of the relationship between threshold and display duration in a two pulse experiment (each of which is 5 msec in duration). (From Herrick © 1972a, with the permission of the American Institute of Physics.)

the results of Ueno's reaction time version of the two-pulse experiment. Both inhibition (values falling below the horizontal line) and summation (values falling above the line) are observed at different intervals. A further complication is implicit in the fact that the shape of the function relating interpulse interval and reaction time varies with stimulus intensity.

Ueno's demonstration of secondary effects of the amplitude of the individual pulses together with Zacks' (1970) studies of residual discriminability below the critical duration make it clear that the idea of total energy integration below some minimum duration as measured by psychophysical tests (i.e., Bloch's law) can, at best, be only a rough approximation.

I noted earlier that there are several different kinds of sequential masking experiments. They are all collectively characterized by an experimental situation in which two sequential stimuli interact in an inhibitory fashion to reduce the psychophysical detectability or recognizability of one or the other. However the various masking phenomena produced by this common experimental design may in fact be attributable to quite different processes. One of the forms of masking seems likely to be a close relative of the two-pulse interaction process I have been considering in this section. If two stimuli are presented to the same eye in rapid succession and the second is both more intense and larger in extent than the first, then the first stimulus may be obscured or masked to a degree that is a function of the interval between the two.

The classic observation of this "bright flash" type of masking was made by B. H. Crawford (1947) in the same experiment I discussed earlier as an example of transient effects. As I noted, Crawford used a long-duration (0.5 sec) masking flash and a brief, dimmer test flash, both of which were circular and concentric. In the context of our present discussion, the most interesting result of his experiment was that the bright flash could suppress detection of the dimmer flash even when it did not begin until 50 msec after the test flash was presented. In this case the differential latencies of the two different amplitude signals probably artifactually altered the period of interaction. Even if the two had had equal latencies the persistence of the response to the first stimulus would have allowed the two to interact and thus set up a situation in which the more intense flash could inhibit the less intense one by simply reducing the contrast between the target and the background. Masking of this sort is now appreciated to be effective when the two stimuli are presented to the same eye but not when the stimuli are presented dichoptically. Thus this kind of masking is most likely peripherally mediated and quite distinct from several other kinds of masking with which it shares many operational similarities. I refer here to bright flash masking as *masking of the first kind.*

The antithesis of masking—the summation of two stimuli to produce a threshold response—is, of course, a special case of the interaction of n pulses. All who have studied multipulse summation agree that, as expected, increasing the number of flashes leads to a monotonic decrease in the luminosity that is required for threshold. This experiment is usually confounded by mixing the

TABLE 7.2
Empirical Laws for Brightness Discrimination in Two Pulse Experiments at Varying Display Times

Limits of Total Display Time, T	*Empirical Law*	*Verbal Description*
From $(t_1 + t_2)$ to T_{C2}	E = constant $= E_B$	Threshold energy is constant
T_{C2} to T_M	E/T = constant $= E_B/T_{C2}$ $= E_M/T_m$	Threshold energy divided by total display time is constant
T_M to T_p	ET = constant $= E_M T_M$ $= E_p T_p$	Product of threshold energy and total display time is constant
T_p to ?	E = constant $= E_p$	Threshold energy is constant

After Herrick, 1972a.

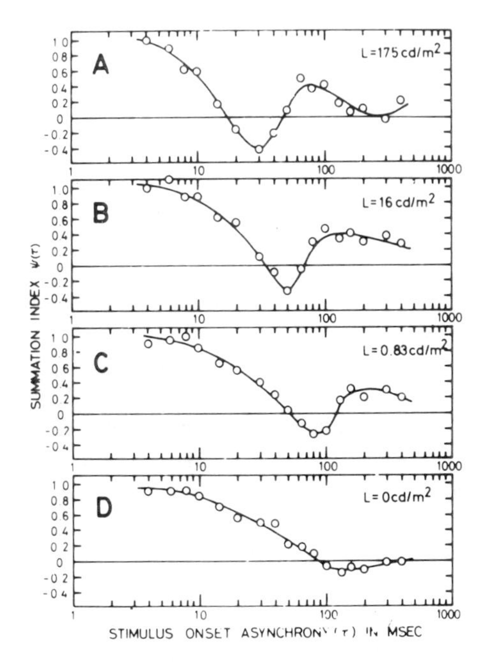

FIG. 7.34. Summation index (see text) in a two pulse experiment as a function of the stimulus onset asynchronicity for four different adaptation levels. (From Ueno, © 1977, with the permission of Pergamon Press.)

independent variable of interval between the flashes with that of a number of flashes. However, this confounding has been unravelled by Herrick in a pair of carefully executed studies of the effect of flash numerosity on the absolute threshold in the fovea (Herrick, 1973a) and in the periphery (Herrick, 1973b). In one experiment in this series he kept the flash duration equal to the interval between the flashes and simply varied the number of flashes. The results of this experiment on the threshold luminance are shown in Fig. 7-35. The function smoothly declines with the addition of each stimulus, each step producing a progressively lower threshold luminance. The curve, however, approaches an asymptotic value of less than 10% of the threshold to a single flash when all of the stimuli occur within an interval that is approximately the same as the critical duration. Other intervals and other retinal loci produced curves that were analogous though with somewhat different rates of decline.

All of these data support the outcome of a relatively straightforward summation in this type of experiment. This increase in performance with increased "sample size" is reminiscent of the higher flicker-fusion rates obtained as one increases the number of flashes in a train (Nelson, Bartley & Harper, 1964; Anderson D., Huntington, & Simonson, 1966).

b. Figural Summation: Masking of the Second Kind. The critical duration and two-pulse interaction studies are procedures for measuring temporal integration that depend mainly upon relatively simple discriminability measurements.

However, sequential visual stimuli also interact in ways that may lead to either a diminishment or enhancement in performance on certain more complex tasks. Although the basic process underlying both the simple and complex tasks may be exactly the same, the nature of the more complex task has sometimes obscured the essential identity of the responsible processes.

In this section I consider examples of more complex responses that may also arise from the integration and fusion of separate stimulus figures when they are presented in close sequential order. The most familiar example of such processes, of course, is the motion picture of the cinema or television screens in which an illusion of a continuously flowing movement is produced by presenting a series of temporal snapshots. Through a combination of apparent motion, suppression of blurred images, and temporal summation the sequence of discrete images projected on a screen can result in a perception that is as smoothly flowing as a real four-dimensional visual scene.

In the laboratory the several different perceptual processes that contribute to the illusion of moving pictures have been analyzed separately. Some of them,

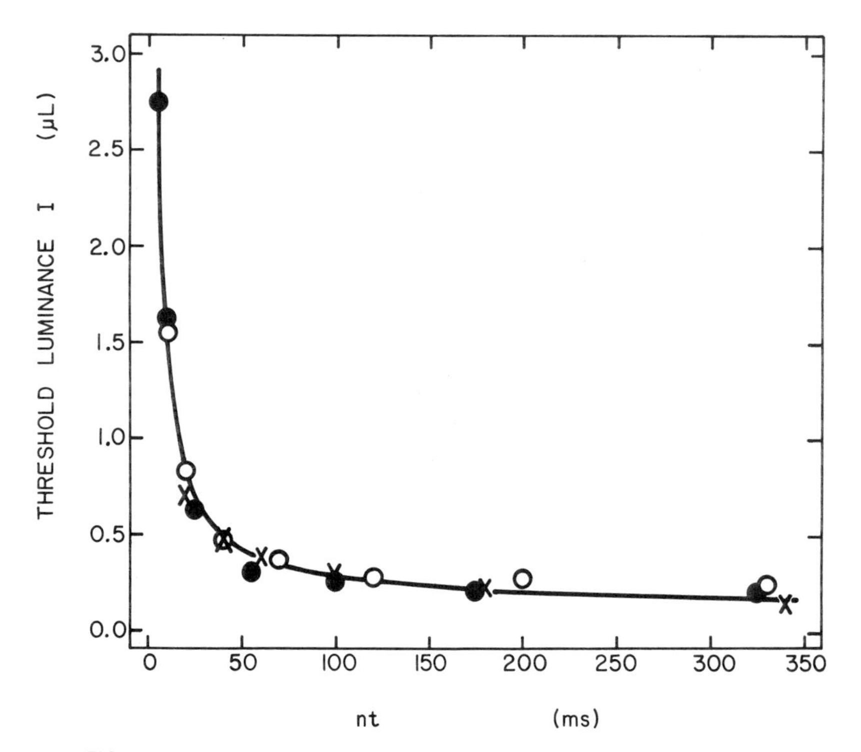

FIG. 7.35. The threshold luminance as a function of the number of flashes in a train of visual stimuli showing sequential summation. The horizontal coordinate represents the number of flashes times the flash duration. (From Herrick, © 1973a, with the permission of the American Institute of Physics.)

such as apparent motion, are high-level processes that are not discussed until later in this book. But there is also one component process that is germane to the present discussion. The persistence of the visual response to each frame in a sequence of images leads to the perceptual superimposition, or fusion, of successive images in a way that is not only subjectively comparable to the critical duration or two-flash integration but also is probably explicable in identical peripheral terms.

The essential point in this discussion, as it has been throughout this chapter, is that because the temporal acuity of the visual system is relatively poor, two stimuli that are not physically simultaneous may produce phenomenal responses that appear perceptually simultaneous. Thus as a result of this apparent simultaneity, figures that may be incomplete in two or more partial presentations may appear to be complete if the parts are presented in rapid enough succession. Furthermore, figures that were individually recognizable may be masked[14] or hidden by the camouflage that results from the mixture of a "target" and a "mask." Whether the interaction is summative and enhances perception, as it is in the former case, or inhibitory and degrades perception, as it is in the latter case, is not so much a matter of the underlying process as it is one of the nature of the stimuli and the task that the subject is required to perform.

To make this concept more concrete, let's consider two experiments that are very similar, but one illustrates temporal integration that leads to an increase in performance whereas the other results in a decrement in performance. One well-known study in which temporal summation leads to an increase in performance has been reported by Eriksen and Collins (1967). Fig. 7-36A and 7-36B show two stimuli that individually appear to be two unrecognizable random arrays of dots. However when the two stimuli are drawn on cards and presented in quick succession in a tachistoscope, the temporal integration or summation properties of the visual system combine these two incomplete stimuli into the single complete, and easily interpretable, nonsense syllable shown in the artist's rendition in Fig. 7-36C. The more rapid the succession of the two separate parts of the stimulus, the more complete the fusion and the more recognizable will be the nonsense syllables that they form. Figure 7-37, for example, shows the results of one of Eriksen and Collins' experiments determining the relationship between the percentage of correct detections and the interval between the two parts of the dotted stimulus. This graph reveals a gradual decrement in performance with an asymptotic value of about 100 msec. This curve, therefore, represents an estimate of the integration period within which the subject can use the combined information to improve his performance above the level that would be allowed by

[14]This is a new kind of masking quite distinct from the bright-flash masking discussed earlier that was probably attributable to simple contrast reduction. In this case, which we may call figural pattern masking or masking of the second kind, the contrast of the target and the mask may be identical. However, both types of masking are due to peripheral interactions between successive stimuli.

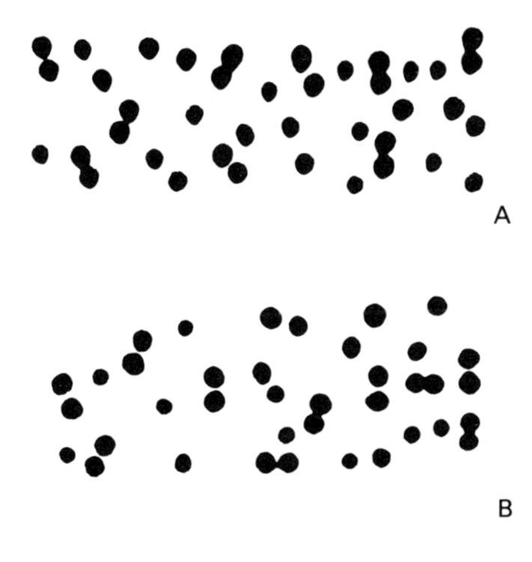

FIG. 7.36. Two "random" dot patterns (A and B) which, when superimposed, produce a complete and legible (C) nonsense syllable. (From Eriksen and Collins, © 1967, with the permission of the American Psychological Association.)

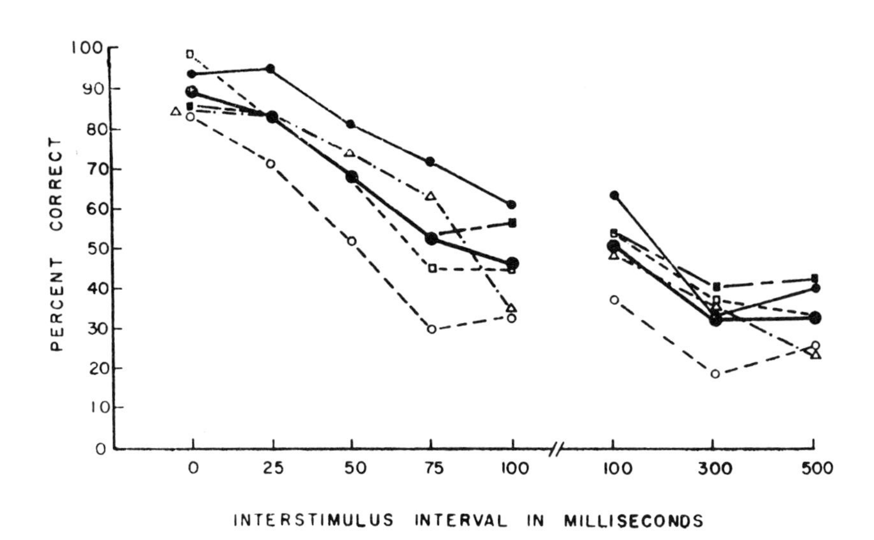

FIG. 7.37. The percentage of nonsense syllables (of the kind shown in Figure 7.36) recognized as a function of the interval between the presentations of the two parts. (From Eriksen and Collins, © 1967, with the permission of the American Psychological Association.)

the independent presentation of either of the two partial stimuli. Not too surprisingly, this estimate of the integrating period closely approximates those obtained with the critical duration or two pulse methods that I have already described.

A caveat: This estimate of the integration period seems to vary enormously with the nature of the stimulus material. For example, Ikeda and Uchikawa (1978), using cartoon-type figures, found that the average period of integration within which a fully coordinated figure was perceived was about 500 msec. Clearly at some upper limit of figural complexity and redundancy, signal persistence becomes confounded with contextual and cognitive cues.

In the case of the Eriksen and Collins experiment, the effect of temporal summation was to enhance the recognizability of the stimulus. I have published a series of experiments (Uttal, 1969a, 1969b, 1970a, 1970c, 1971a, 1975a; Uttal & Hieronymus, 1970) that demonstrate that the same kind of figural interaction can degrade rather than improve the detection of a stimulus. The stimulus materials used in my experiments were also dotted patterns but were plotted on the face of a cathode-ray tube oscilloscope rather than drawn on cards and flashed in a tachistoscope. A typical experimental stimulus is shown in Fig. 7-38A, along with some representations of how it would appear when mixed with a subsequently presented mask composed of an increasingly numerous array of randomly positioned visual noise dots.

The stimuli used in my experiments are presented in a way that produces exactly the same sort of sequential interaction exemplified in the Eriksen and Collins study. Phenomenally, however, the results are just the opposite; because of the nature of the stimuli and the task, the perceptual intermingling of the two stimuli—the target square and the random dot mask—leads to a dimunition in the ability of the subject to recognize the form rather than an increase in performance.

Figure 7-38B, C, and D show how the target form is progressively degraded in recognizability or detectability as the number of noise dots with which it is mixed[15] is increased. It really makes no difference how the visual noise dots are added to the regular pattern. They can be added simultaneously all at once in a burst, as is done in presenting Fig. 7-38 here (Uttal, 1971a), by taking advantage of the integration period of the eye so that serial sequences of dots appear as a dancing background field of apparently simultaneous dots (Uttal, 1969a), or even by presenting all of the masking dots simultaneously at some variable interval following the target. Regardless of the means of presenting these multiple stimuli, the results of many experiments all converge on one powerful conclusion—the more visual noise dots are superimposed on the target form in time and space, the more difficult it is to recognize that target form.

[15]In the example I describe here, the mask follows the target; this is an example of backward masking. In other experimental situations I have also studied the forward-masking situation in which the mask precedes the target. With the exception of the anomaly of weak dichoptic forward masking, everything I say holds equally true for both forward and backward masking.

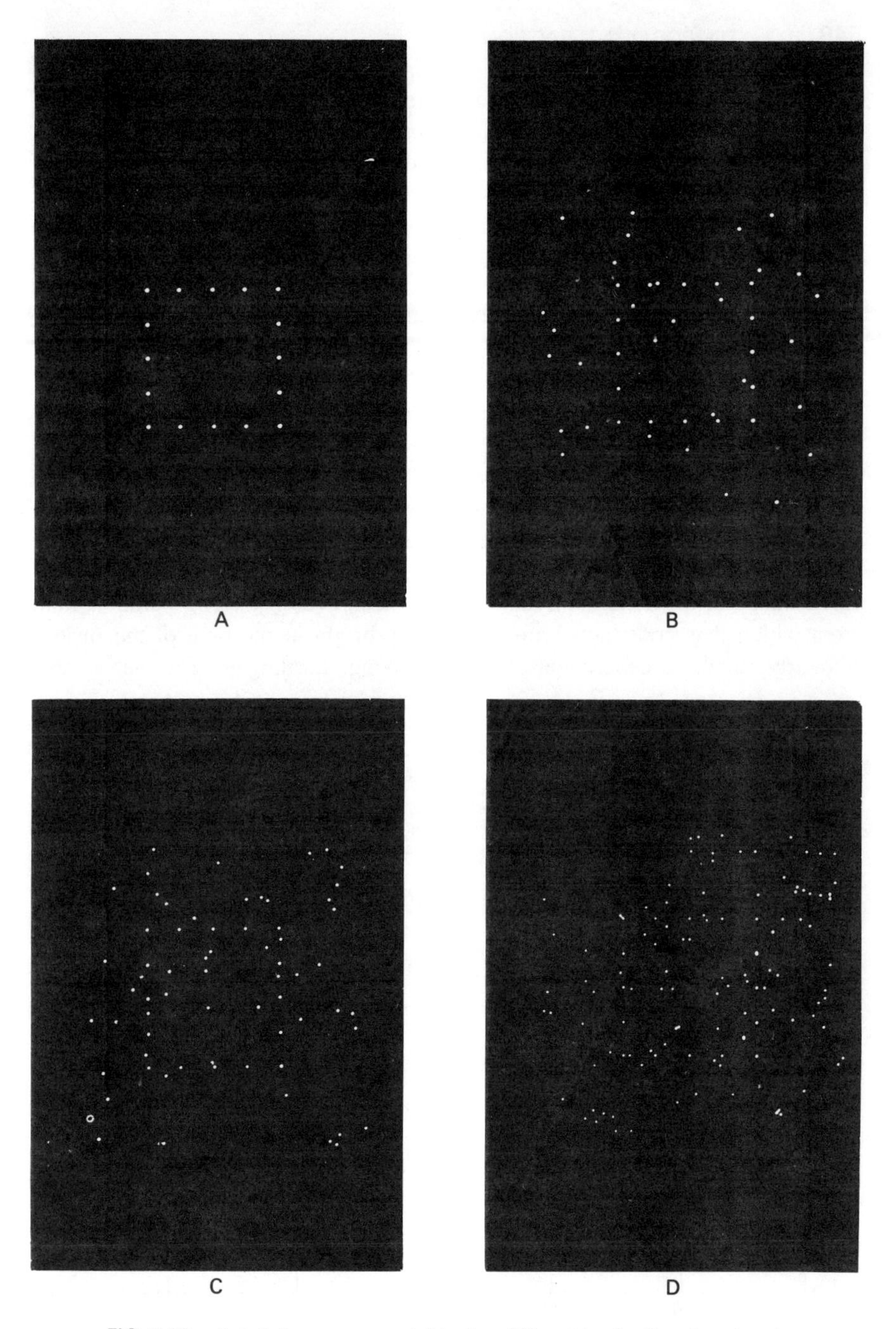

FIG. 7.38. A dotted square presented in four different levels of random dotted noise. Stimulus displays have the appearance of one of these to the subject in the experiments reported in this study: (A) no masking dots, (B) 30 masking dots, (C) 50 masking dots, and (D) 100 masking dots. Note the progressive decline in the detectability of the target square as the number of masking dots increases. (From Uttal, © 1975a.)

If the stimulus and the masking dots are both presented in the form of brief bursts, then a functional graph relating interval and detectability can be plotted. This new graph, shown in Fig. 7-39, indicates that the effect of a burst of masking dots on the detectability of the target is a function of the interval between the two. The degree to which the performance is degraded as a function of the interval between the target and the mask is also an estimate of the integration period of the visual system. Though the methods are different, if biologically valid this approach should produce results comparable to those obtained with summation procedure, a two-pulse interaction procedure, or a critical duration paradigm.

However, Fig. 7-39 indicates that the effect of the masking dots is negligible after 40 msec, a period that is considerably briefer than that usually indicated by other procedures. The differences between the estimates of the duration of the integrating period obtained in either the Eriksen and Collins or the Uttal paradigm and those other paradigms, of course, are totally explicable if one considers the nature of the two tasks. In the Erickson and Collins-type task the fused image of the nonsense syllable can be seen even if the two partial stimuli from which it is constructed are not equally bright at the time of the fusion. Similarly, in these experiments on dot masking, the target form can be read

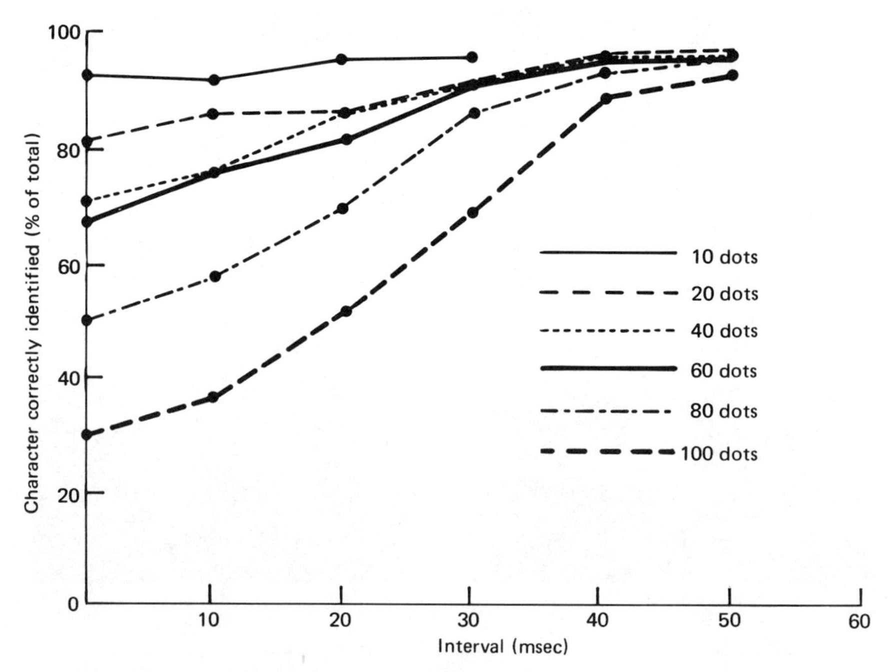

FIG. 7.39. Character recognition plotted as a function of the interval between the presentation of the character and the single noise burst. The curves are parametric in the number of dots contained in the noise burst. (From Uttal, © 1971a.)

through a substantial level of noise whenever there is any noticeable brightness difference between the two parts of the stimuli. Thus in one case, even though differential fading may have occurred, the effect (summation) is still present and the task can be accomplished, but in the other case, the effect (masking) is partially mitigated even when there may be some residual effect of both parts of the stimuli. Clearly the estimates of persistence are not contradictory in principle from those using other paradigms even though they do differ somewhat in quantitative value.

The literature on the kind of figural masking described here is too vast to attempt to review it all here. Suffice it to say that substantial interference with form recognition arises when physically sequential stimuli are perceptually superimposed. The dot-masking technique I have described here is but one example of masking due to stimulus summation as a result of response persistence. Kinsbourne and Warrington's (1962a) work with checkerboard masks, or Sperling's (1963) and Schiller and Smith's (1966) work with random fragments are also of this same genre. Whether the mask and the target are presented in the same eye or in different eyes, the phenomena are comparable (with the possible exception of forward dichoptic masking, as I have already mentioned); the target is hidden in the confusion of the superimposed binocular-fused image. The critical factor in producing the superimposition, it seems, is the prolongation of the psychoneural response long past the duration of the stimulus.[16]

It must be remembered that the kinds of masking that require spatial overlap of the stimulus and the mask should not be attributed to the same processes that must be invoked to explain those that do not. For example, metacontrast (see Chapter 11) is a form of sequential interaction and masking that does not require any spatial overlap between the stimulus and the mask. However, if the dot-masking experiment is done with random noise masks that do not overlap the target, as shown in Fig. 7-40, then there is virtually no masking (see Fig. 7-41) even though a similar nonoverlapping spatial arrangement of continuous target and mask stimuli may lead to a strong metacontrast type of suppression. The phenomenal differences exhibited here strongly suggest that these operationally similar phenomena must be mediated by different levels of processing.

---

[16]I return to reconsider the phenomena of dot masking in several contexts in this book. At first, the fact that these experiments could not be easily classified at one level or another caused me some considerable concern. However, after a little thought I was able to convince myself that this multilevel involvement is not totally inappropriate. The phenomenal superimposition of the target and the mask certainly results from the temporal persistence of the neural responses at Levels 1 and 2, as described in this chapter. The extraction of the pattern, however, represents a separate phenomenon that has been modeled by the neural net Level 2 autocorrelation theory I describe in Chapter 9. On the other hand, the neural net theory is not the only way in which it may be considered. Dot signal extraction can also be considered simply to be a Level 3 phenomenon akin to the other statistical computational abilities exhibited by the human nervous system. Level 5 processes also may be involved in the process in some way.

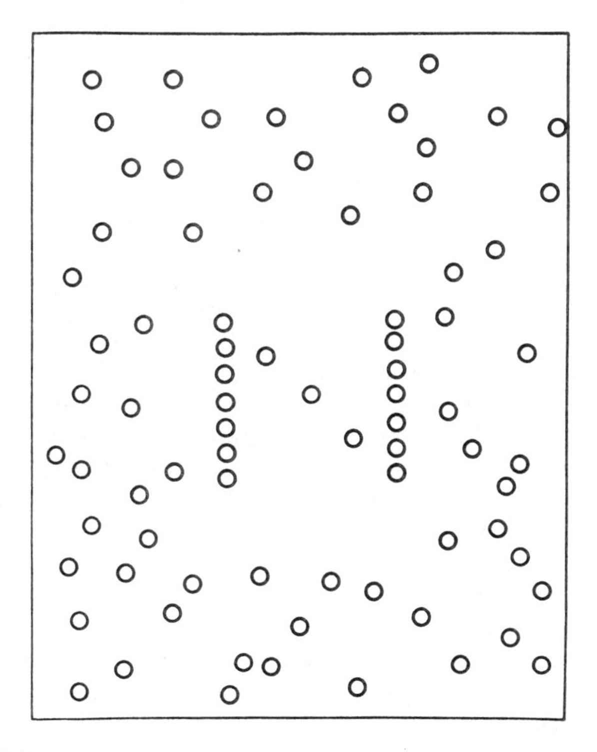

FIG. 7.40. A character formed from dots placed within a "masking" stimulus region composed of similar dots. Masking dots are excluded from the central region in which the character appears. (From Uttal, © 1970c.)

An excellent review of the very extensive pattern-masking literature up to 1968 can be found in Kahnemann (1968). However the most significant paper of this decade in the field of masking has clearly been Turvey's (1973) experimental and theoretical analysis of pattern masking. Turvey carried out a series of 19 experiments that led him to conclude that there were two levels of processing involved, even when identical stimuli and tasks were used. His experimental design was a simple one. He used either random noise or a field of letter fragments as a mask, alphabetic characters as targets, and determined both the forward or backward masking effects. Samples of Turvey's stimulus materials are shown in Fig. 7-42.

Turvey concluded from this extensive study that both peripheral and central phenomena were involved in the masking paradigm, but that these processes were not sequential in time; that is, he suggested that they were essentially simultaneous and operated in parallel, although the central process depended, of course, on whatever transformations had been made by the peripheral one. To Turvey, the word *peripheral* has meaning similar to my Levels 1 and 2, and he

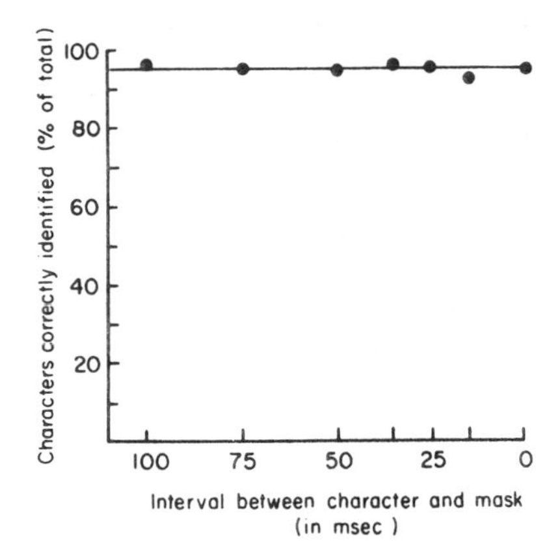

FIG. 7.41. Over a 100-msec range, there is little evidence of any masking effect by the nonoverlapping noise pattern. (From Uttal, © 1970c.)

included the visual cortex in his peripheral mechanisms in much the same way as I have in my taxonomy.

For the moment, let us consider only Turvey's conclusions about the peripheral masking processes. Peripheral masking, according to Turvey, is very similar to what I have called "masking of the second kind" in this chapter. According to Turvey, peripheral masking is characterized by a multiplicative law; that is, the energy of the target, multiplied by the minimum interstimulus interval between the target and the mask that allowed the masking effects to be completely overcome is a constant for peripheral masking. Central masking, according to Turvey's model, is better described by an additive law in which the target duration *plus* the minimum interstimulus interval equals a constant.

More specifically, Turvey's (1973, p. 48) conclusions for the central and peripheral masking processes were (in excerpt) as follows:

1. Although energy variables significantly affected the degree and direction of peripheral masking, they were relatively immaterial to masking arising centrally.

2. Forward masking of peripheral origin was more pronounced than backward masking of peripheral origin; moreover, the severity of peripheral forward

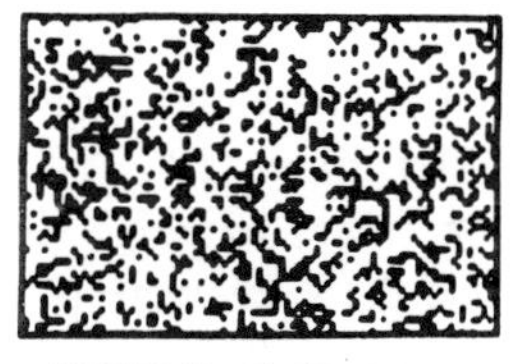

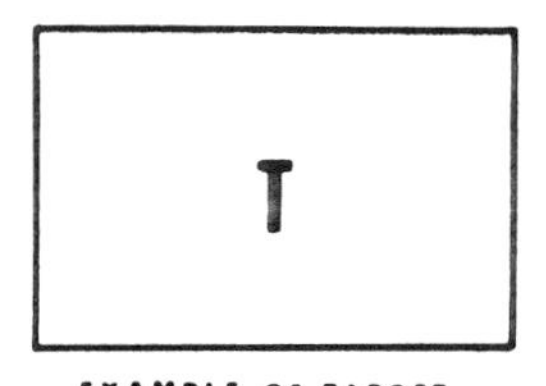

FIG. 7.42. Examples of the target stimuli and the two kinds of mask used in Turvey's experiment. (From Turvey, © 1973, with the permission of the American Psychological Association.)

masking increased with increases in mask intensity, whereas the severity of peripheral backward masking did not.[17]

3. When two stimuli, target and mask, were presented monoptically in a backward masking arrangement, the upper limit on masking was set by either peripheral or central processes depending on the energy of the target and the relation between the target and mask patterns.

4. A nonmonotonic U-shaped function was obtained monoptically with overlapping target and mask when the target energy was greater than mask energy. It was hypothesized that this function reflected the transition from peripheral to central masking with increasing delay between the two stimuli.

5. Individual differences were more obvious in central than in peripheral masking.

There are, of course, experimental paradigms other than masking that also reflect the same mechanisms of visual persistence and summation underlying these visual noise-masking results. John Hogben's (1972) dissertation utilizes an ingenious task in which missing dots must be detected in a rectangular dot matrix that is presented distributed over time. The temporal distribution is achieved by interjecting a constant interval between the sequential plotting of the dots of the matrix. The general result in Hogben's studies was that the longer the interval between the dots, the less likely the subject was to detect a missing dot. The implication of this finding is exactly the same as the others I have just described—if the temporally distributed presentation of the stimulus dots takes place quickly enough, the entire matrix is simultaneously visible because of the persistence of the visual response. The subject is thus able to use global organization cues to locate the missing dot in a way that is not available to him when the stimulus dots are spread over so great a time that the pattern cannot be seen as a whole. Figure 7-43 shows the deterioration in performance in Hogben's study as a function of the length of the period over which 25 dots were presented.

In sum, there is a broad class of different experiments that seem to be well explained by simple superimposition or fusion of two stimuli presented in quick succession occurring as a result of response persistence. Depending upon the nature of the stimulus material and the task, there may either be an inhibition (masking) or an increase in the detectability or recognizability of the form resulting from this fusion. It should be noted, however, that there is some limited evidence that contradicts the simple temporal persistence and summation explanation of the phenomena that I have emphasized here. McFarland (1965), for example, designed an experiment in which he asked observers to judge the apparent simultaneity of triangles in which the corners and the sides were presented in sequential order rather than physically simultaneously. He found that there was a difference in the judgments of simultaneity when the corners, as

[17] I do not necessarily agree with this conclusion. See Uttal 1969b.

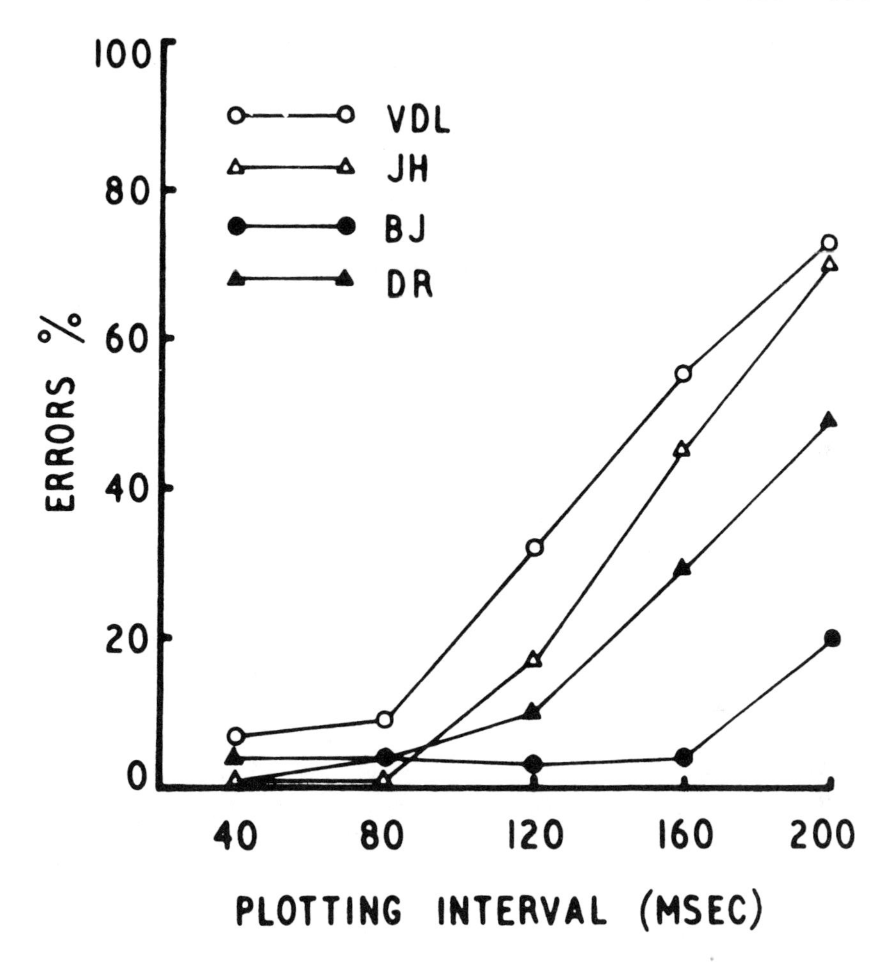

FIG. 7.43. The results of Hogben's experiment for four different subjects. (Courtesy of Dr. John Hogben of the University of Western Australia.)

opposed to the sides, were presented. Similarity, in another study using the sides of squares rather than triangles, McFarland and Prete (1969) went on to show that the presence of other lines in the field surrounding the square could alter the judgment of simultaneity when the sides of the square were presented in sequential order. The fact that the simultaneity judgments were affected by both the form and the nature of the surround supports Turvey's suggestion that some components of the masking processes may be due to a level of processing higher than Level 1 or 2.

Another aberrant result further mitigates the simple peripheral integration period explanation of these summative phenomena. For some unexplained reason, dichoptic forward masking situations (target to one eye and noise mask to the other eye) do not produce a substantial masking effect comparable to either a dichoptic backward mask or a forward or backward monocular mask. This result has been replicated too many times for there to be any doubt of its validity. The absence of forward dichoptic masking has been shown by Smith and Schiller (1966), Greenspoon and Eriksen (1968), Turvey (1973), and Uttal (1975a).

Thus the theoretical situation is still somewhat equivocal and the explanation of what leads to these effects of fusion somewhat uncertain. In general, however, there does seem to be a consensus in the theoretical literature suggesting that they are mainly due to persistent responses in peripheral portions of the visual system.

3. Intermittency Detection

In the previous section I discuss several empirical approaches to the problem of visual persistence and integration in which the goal of the experimenter was to demonstrate some perceptual effect of the neural fusion of sequential stimuli. Another traditional way of attacking the problem has been to determine the threshold stimulus conditions under which stimuli just fuse. To say the same thing from the opposite point of view—under what conditions is the stimulus just intermittent? Clearly both of these approaches are equivalent inquiries into the fundamental nature of the same biological process—the integration period. Whereas one uses just-detectable intermittency as a criterion, the other uses the first appearance of fusion. Obviously these data are the outcome of approaching a single region of demarcation between fused and unfused stimuli from opposite directions. Thus the detection of intermittency between a pair of flashes, or within a longer train, should be conceptually indistinguishable from the measurement of the critical flicker-fusion rate (CFF) or of the critical interval at which fusion occurs. Both, in fact, use the same independent variable; only the criteria differ. Indeed I propose here that they are not only conceptually identical but also attributable to the same underlying mechanism—response persistence.

A major portion of the research on the temporal properties of vision, therefore, has concerned itself with a problem that can be stated in the following way: Under what conditions and at what frequency does a flashing light appear to be continuously illuminated? The classic parameters of the answer to this question are well established. The main points of a very large amount of data concerning the critical flicker-fusion frequency (CFF) or the two-pulse fusion interval can be briefly summarized as follows:

1. The larger the number of flashes in a train, the shorter the CFF. (See Boynton, 1972, p. 205, for a list of the experiments that speak to this conclusion.) But this effect seems to asymptote at about 20 flashes (Nelson & Bartley, 1964).
2. The higher the luminance, the higher the CFF. In general, in a middle range of stimulus luminance, CFF increases with increased luminance in accord

with the Ferry–Porter law (Ferry, 1892; Porter, 1898), which can be expressed in the following simple form:

$$\mathrm{CFF} = K \times \log (I_s) \qquad (7\text{-}3)$$

where K is a constant and I_s is the luminance of the stimulus.

3. The larger the spatial extent of the stimulus, the higher the CFF (Hecht & Smith, 1936).
4. At low luminances, the peripheral retina has a higher CFF than does the fovea, but at high luminances the fovea has a higher CFF than does the periphery (Hecht & Verrijp, 1933).
5. The wavelength of the stimulus has little effect on the CFF at high luminances, but a substantial effect (shorter wavelengths fuse at higher frequencies) for low luminances (Hecht & Shlaer, 1936).
6. In the fovea, dark adaptation leads to a progressive decline in the CFF as a function of the state of dark adaptation. However, in the far periphery, the function is reversed and dark adaptation leads to an increase in the CFF when measured there. In middle portions of the retina the effect of dark adaptation may be nonmonotonic (Lythgoe & Tansley, 1929).
7. Above fusion it seems generally true that the brightness of a physically intermittent stimulus is equal to the average luminosity of that stimulus. This is known as the Talbot–Plateau law (Talbot, 1834), but this law does not generally hold for short bursts of fewer than 20 flashes (Nelson & Bartley, 1964).
8. If the surround of a flickering test light is itself flickering, the CFF for the test light is altered. If the background is flickering at a rate above the CFF, it elevates the CFF for the test spot. If the background is flickering at a rate below the CFF, the CFF for the test spot is lowered (Alpern & Sugiyama, 1961).
9. The shape of the flickering light is important. An annulus displays a lowered CFF compared to a disk with the same area and luminosity in a way that seems not to be associated with the retinal locus (Robinson, 1970).

Many of these empirical relationships are discussed in great detail in reviews by Landis (1954), Brown (1965), and Kelly (1972), and it is not necessary to recapitulate the entire story of flicker fusion at this point. It is sufficient to note that the various theories of CFF are, in general, mathematical descriptions involving hypothetical systems composed on the one hand of analogs of cascaded resistance-capacitance (RC) units of varying time constants (Ives, 1922; Kelly, 1961; Levinson, 1968; Sperling & Sondhi, 1968), or on the other hand, involving temporal Fourier analysis procedures (Brown & Forsyth, 1959; Forsythe, 1960). It must not be forgotten, in the primarily stimulus–response context in which the problem is usually posed, that the Fourier and RC models are not in fact neuroreductionistic theories; they simply describe the mathematical functions that seem to fit the empirical data best.

One important conclusion to be drawn from these data is that the interaction between the spatial properties of the stimulus and its temporal parameters, as measured by the CFF procedure, strongly suggests there is a very strong Level 2 component to this type of phenomenon. This further suggests that the receptor itself is not likely to be the sole site of the critical process underlying flicker fusion. Quite the contrary, neural interactions between different regions must affect the temporal processes measured by the flicker-fusion procedures.

Flicker-fusionlike processes have been observed in certain electrophysiological preparations. Kelly (1972) reviews most of the salient studies up to 1970 and Van de Grind, Grüsser, and Lunkenheimer (1973) also review this field in a comprehensive fashion. The most significant work up to that time, in my opinion, was done by such workers as Devoe (1962, 1964), who studied the eye of the wolf spider, and Hughes and Maffei (1966), who examined ganglion cell responses in the cat. All of these neurophysiologists reported that the spike action potential firing rate was maximum at some intermediate frequency rather than at a very low or high frequency. Figure 7-44, for example, shows a sample result from Hughes and Maffei (1966) showing what happens to both the phase relationship between the stimulus and the response and the firing rate of spike action potential as one varies the stimulus frequency. The higher the stimulus frequency, the greater the phase lag between stimulus and response. The most interesting aspect of this response, however, is the fact that the ganglion cell fired at a maximum rate of a stimulus frequency of about 50 Hz—a value quite close to the prototypical human CFF.

More recently, Baron and Boynton (1975) have reported new data that support the contention that the receptor is not the locus of fusion but that at least some component of the fusion occurs somewhere more centrally. These neural findings have been directly compared with the temporal properties of the visual system as

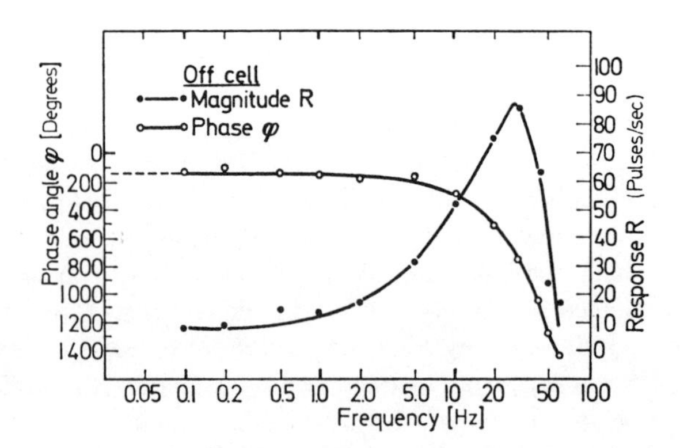

FIG. 7.44. The phase angle and spike rate of a cat retinal ganglion cell plotted as a function of stimulus frequency. (From Kelly, © 1972, after Hughes and Maffei, 1966, with the permission of Springer-Verlag, Inc.)

reported psychophysically (Kelly, Boynton, & Baron, 1976). These authors conclude that the neurophysiological data from monkey cones and the psychophysical data from human subjects agree only when the eye is strongly light-adapted. In dark-adapted conditions, there is a substantial discrepancy between the psychophysical and neurophysiological findings—a result they also interpret to mean that the locus of the fusion process must be at least partially more central than the receptor.

In most recent paper in this series (Kelly & Wilson, 1978) it is proposed that the flicker phenomenon is in fact mediated by a two-stage process and that the two stages are the receptor and bipolar neurons, respectively. Under this assumption, discrepancies between the long psychophysical time constant and that of the receptor and the differences in flicker function at high and low adaptation levels, respectively, could easily be accounted for.

A few electrophysiological studies have also been carried out on more central regions of the nervous system but, not too surprisingly, it turns out (Schneider, 1968b) that the compound cortical responses evoked by flashing lights do not in general agree with corresponding psychophysical tests (Schneider, 1968a). Psychophysically, rabbits appear to be unable to distinguish between a continuous light of about 25–30 Hz and a flickering light having Talbot–Plateau-equated luminances. The electrophysiological responses collected at those flicker rates indicated, however, that there was still a substantial (10–20%) ripple amplitude detectable in the evoked brain potentials at these flicker frequencies. Thus these compound potentials appear to maintain some information about the temporal characteristics of the stimulus even though psychophysical tests indicate that the experimental animal cannot use that information.

This vestige of coded information concerning the flicker frequency of the stimulus in the electrophysiological response is congruent with other (i.e., other than the CFF) measures of our ability to process temporal information. Accordingly, the fact that a train of stimulus flashes is fused according to one criterion and yet is reported as a continuous sensation should not be misinterpreted to mean that all of the information contained in the temporal intermittency of the stimulus is lost. It is possible under some conditions to measure an effect of flickering lights even when the intervals between sequential flashes are as brief as 1 msec. In 1970, working with Ramelle Hieronymous (Uttal & Hieronymous, 1970) I was able to show that the detectability of a gap in a train of flashes depended on the number and interval of the flashes before and after the gap. Figure 7-45A shows the design of this stimulus train. The duration of the just-detectable gap varied from 10 msec for 1 msec intervals between flashes up to about 30 msec for 20 msec intervals. The results of this experiment are shown in Fig. 7-45B. The larger the interval between the flashes in the trains on either side of the gap, the larger the gap had to be in order to be detected. The function relating flash interval and just-detectable gap size was virtually linear and did not asymptote even at very brief (1–5 msec) intervals.

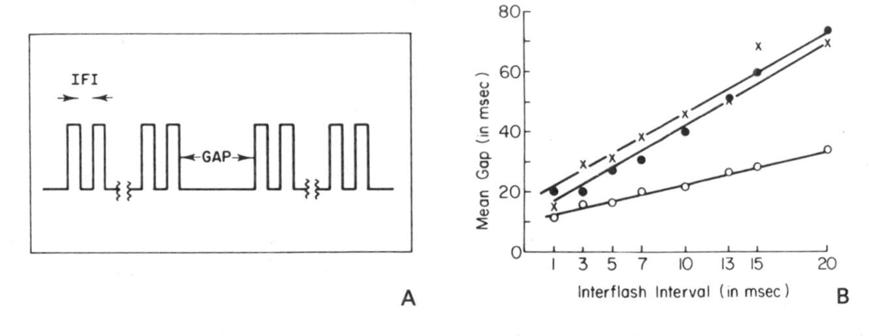

FIG. 7.45. (A) The stimulus pattern used in the Uttal and Hieronymus experiment. (B) The results of three experimental conditions in the Uttal and Hieronymus experiment. The filled circles depict the results of an experiment in which the S was required to detect a gap in dispersed random visual noise. The empty circles represent the results of an experiment in which all the dots in the pulse train were plotted on top of each other in a central location. The x's plot the results of an experiment in which an ultrashort-persistence (P-15) CRT was replaced with a medium-short-persistence one (P-31), and the first paradigm repeated. (From Uttal and Hieronymus, © 1970.)

The absolute size of the just-detectable gap in this experiment is not its most important parameter in the current context. What is important is that the intervals between the stimulus flashes, either prior to or succeeding the gap, could differentially affect the size of the discriminable gap even though intervals as small as 1 msec (1000 Hz) were being used and this is well above the CFF. I do not believe, however, that this discrimination was performed on the basis of a judgment of some temporal criterion but rather that the temporal information had actually been transformed or recoded in a way that turned this task into a brightness discrimination in much the same way that some residual discrimination persists below the critical duration. The key cue to detection of the gap, according to this hypothesis, is the contrast between the dark gap and the apparent brightness produced by the flickering lights before and after the gap rather than the dynamic temporal sequence itself. Because a more rapidly flashing light produces a brighter perceptual experience, in accord with the Talbot–Plateau law, the gap is easier to see (i.e., can be seen at a shorter duration) when the pulses are crowded together. Thus a temporal independent variable, the flash rate, has been converted to one of magnitude—apparent brightness—in a way that can affect a temporal dependent variable, the duration of the just-detectable gap. Although one criterion task (the CFF) would clearly indicate essentially perfect fusion and temporal summation at relatively low frequencies, another (gap detection) would suggest that there may be some residual coded information concerning the temporal pattern of the stimulus maintained beyond fusion. That this occurs through an intermediary (brightness) does not minimize the fact that there is a highly imperfect sensitivity to sequential temporal information.

I should also note that there is another way of representing the flicker-fusion data that has a number of advantages in the interpretation of these phenomena. This alternative method makes use of what are known as de Lange plots (de Lange, 1958a, 1958b), or in the language with which we are already familiar, the Temporal Modulation Transfer Function (TMTF). In the discussion of flicker so far, the reader will note that most of the reported results were displayed using fusion frequency as a dependent variable to determine the effect of some independent variable such as retinal locus or state of dark adaptation. Suppose, however, that instead of using fusion frequency as the dependent variable, we use frequency of a sinusoidally fluctuating (in amplitude) stimulus as the independent variable and that we then use as the dependent variable the depth of temporal modulation or contrast (where contrast is defined as it was on p. 340) at which that particular stimulus frequency appears to fuse. The diagram so formed, like the spatial modulation transfer function described in Chapter 5, represents a comprehensive statement of the sensitivity of the eye but in this case to a temporally fluctuating pattern rather than to a spatial frequency pattern. As we later see, simply altering the graphic means of plotting the data obtained in flicker experiments in this way led de Lange and a number of other workers to reconceptualize the problem in a highly fruitful way.

A sample TMTF is shown in Fig. 7-46A. One interesting general result obtained from this type of display in both de Lange's original work (1958a, 1958b) and in the subsequent work of Kelly (1969) and others is that the psychophysically measured TMTF appears to have a resonant peak; that is an intermediate flicker frequency at which the visual system is more sensitive than it is at either end of the frequency range, just as did the SMTF shown in Fig. 5-37. This psychophysical resonant or peak frequency varies from subject to subject and from condition to condition, but it appears that in humans the most sensitive part on the TMTF is generally to be found between 10 and 20 Hz. The position of this peak changes substantially as a function of the luminance of the flickering stimulus or its background (Kelly, 1961; Van Nes, 1968). The shape of the TMTF also depends very much on which of the three color systems is responding. This can be shown by individually enhancing the response of the three systems using Stiles' adaptation technique (Green, D., 1969). Figures 7-46A, 7-46B, and 7-46C show the respective curves for the three different systems at two different levels of luminances. Two of these curves—those for the red and green systems—although different in shape, do exhibit roughly the same sensitivity (a modulation threshold of about 2%) at their peaks or most sensitive point. The blue system is substantially less sensitive to temporal fluctuation than the other two—at peak its modulation threshold is almost 30%. In spite of some disagreement with the conclusion that the peak sensitivities of the red and green mechanisms are identical (e.g., Kelly, 1974, proposes that the green system is more than five times as sensitive as the red system), Cicerone and Green (1978) have provided compelling evidence to support D. Green's (1969) original contention concerning their essential similarity.

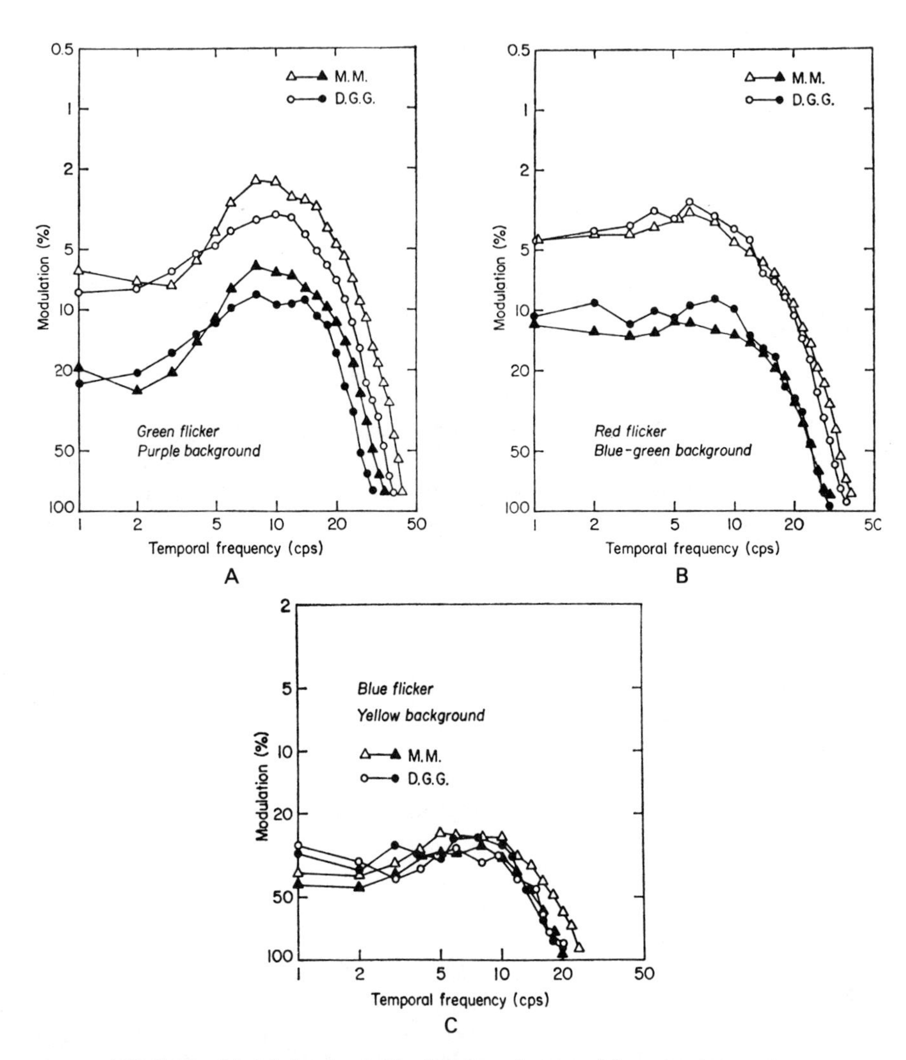

FIG. 7.46. Modulation thresholds plotted as a function of the spectral properties of the stimulating light and the background for two subjects. Open symbols represent high stimulus intensity while closed symbols represent low stimulus intensity. (A) Green flicker on purple background; (B) red flicker on blue green background; (C) Blue flicker on yellow background. (From Green, © 1969, with the permission of the Pergamon Press.)

The new perspective suggested by de Lange when he proposed the use of the TMTF has led to a conceptual revolution in flicker research. The procedure clarifies and emphasizes a number of temporal properties of the visual system that are not made explicit in conventional flicker-fusion curves. As we can see in Fig. 7-46A, B, and C, the sensitivities to flicker are not all equal below the CFF. Rather there are substantial differences in the modulation required for temporal flicker discrimination over the full range of the TMTF. A great deal of additional information is, therefore, present in the TMTF that is not available in the single value of the CFF.

Furthermore, the application of the TMTF concept allows one to explore the dynamic linearity of the visual system. Linearity is defined in terms of the relationship between the amplitude of the response and the summed amplitude or modulation level of a compound stimulus formed of two or more temporal frequencies. If the response to the compound stimulus is the sum of the responses to the individual stimuli, the visual system would be considered to be dynamically linear. However the visual system does not appear to be linear according to such an analysis at low frequencies. This is but another way of making the point that for longer durations the reciprocity law does not hold. Furthermore, as exemplified by the cutoff region at the right-hand side of all of the three curves in Fig. 7-46, for example, where no degree of modulation can be found that will allow the observer to detect flicker, we are reminded that at higher frequencies the visual system is not able to pass any temporal information. This is a close corollary of the reciprocal relationship between stimulus intensity and duration. In other words, any transient stimulus whose duration is less than the critical duration will essentially produce the impulse response of the visual system.

The de Lange TMTF technique uses the frequency of oscillation of stimulus intensities as the independent variable. However, intensive modulation is not the only way in which the temporal dynamics of the visual system can be measured. Regan and Tyler (1971) have pursued a different approach, which has some interesting implications for the temporal dynamics of color vision. These researchers modulated the *wavelength* of an alternating pair of stimuli at the same time that they kept the respective luminances equal and constant. To do so, Regan and Tyler developed a special device capable of producing sinusoidally modulated stimulus wavelengths while at the same time continuously compensating the photopic luminances of the stimuli to maintain constant brightness irrespective of stimulus wavelength. The results of one of Regan and Tyler's experiments, in which a subject was asked to detect when the colors were just chromatically (as opposed to intensively) flickering, are shown in Fig. 7-47. Clearly the depth of modulation (the degree to which the wavelength of the incident stimuli had to vary to be detected as a chromatic change) was highly dependent on the rate at which the wavelength varied. Though no resonant peak of sensitivity is indicated in this figure, as there was in the amplitude-modulated case (see Fig. 7-46), there is a progressive decrease in the observer's sensitivity to wavelength changes as the frequency of alteration increases. Where 1 or 2 nm of wavelength difference are sufficient to allow a color discrimination at low flicker frequencies, the observer requires differences as great as 10 (and in some observers, 20) nm to discriminate at chromatic flicker frequencies of 10 Hz.

The important point made by this experiment is that the ability to make color discriminations depends at least in part on the temporal properties of the stimulus. In the next section of this chapter, we also see that the perceived color

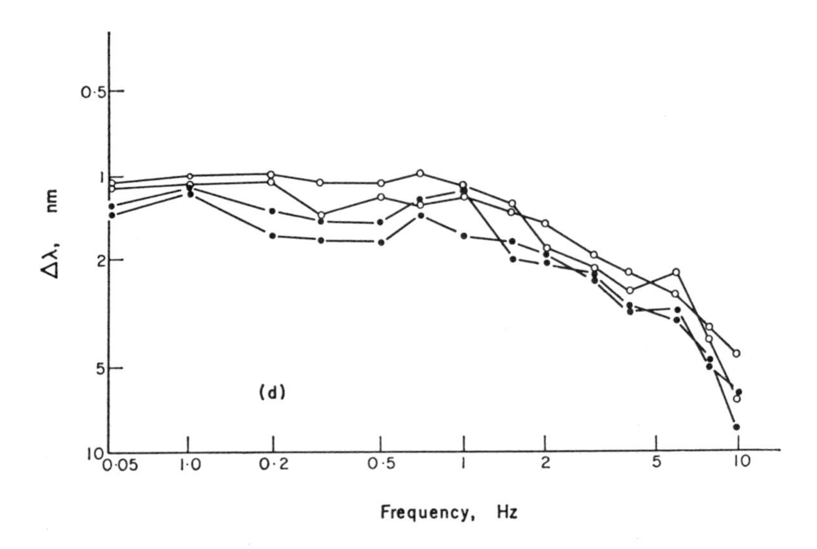

FIG. 7.47. Color discrimination thresholds as a function of very low frequency alternation between a reference color and a slightly different color for several different conditions. (From Regan and Tyler, © 1971, with the permission of Pergamon Press.)

of the stimulus, as well as the ability to discriminate wavelength, may also vary as a function of the temporal properties of the stimulus.

In the late 1970s for more or less inexplicable reasons, interest in the study of temporal intermittencies has flagged. There has been considerably less interest in flicker fusion and the two-flash intermittency discrimination problem than in previous decades. As we see in the next chapter, there has been, however, a corresponding explosion of interest in the spatial characteristics of the visual system. Because of this slowdown in new information, Kelly's (1972) review of the problem is still more or less up-to-date and can be referenced for a more complete discussion of the problem of flicker fusion and intermittency detection. Brown's (1965) review, though considerably out-of-date now, is still an excellent survey of the classic data concerning flicker.

I. SUBJECTIVE COLORS

Many other perceptual phenomena are also powerfully influenced by the temporal pattern of the stimulus, and for these other time-sensitive processes as well it is not always clear exactly at which levels of processes the critical transformations are occurring. For example, if the image of a stimulus scene is projected on the retina in such a way that the image always remains exactly fixed with respect to the retinal coordinate system, there is a gradual fading of the percept after a few minutes. It is possible to conceive of this fading as resulting from the fatigue of some peripheral neural network that is especially sensitive to the temporal gradient (in much the same way as lateral inhibitory interactions have been shown to be sensitive to spatial gradients), but there is considerable evidence that such fading cannot be solely the result of a Level 1 or Level 2 transformation. Among the most compelling arguments against a peripheral explanation is the fact that figures appear, according to most students of this phenomenon, to fade out in meaningful sub units. (The reader is referred to Fig. 10-19 for a more graphic depiction of this point.) For this reason alone—the influence of cognitive factors—it appears that the fading of stabilized retinal images is probably not mediated by peripheral mechanisms but should be classified as a Level 3 process. I therefore defer further discussion of this topic until Chapter 10.

Another inadequately explained phenomena known as subjective color, in which the temporal properties of the stimulus play a critical role, is of considerable interest in this context. Subjective colors can be seen in many different stimulus situations, but in general it occurs when luminous achromatic stimuli flicker in various temporal patterns. In such a situation, colorless stimuli take on chromatic qualities that are dependent on the temporal and spatial properties of the stimulus. The phenomenon was first observed early in the nineteenth century by a number of scientists including Prevost (1823–1826), Fechner (1838b), and Brewster (1834). Wade (1977a) briefly reviews the history of their separate discoveries of the phenomenon and notes that slightly different versions of the subjective colors phenomenon appeared in the reports of several of the early researchers, all of whom failed to realize that they were all actually studying what was essentially the same illusion. The most comprehensive review of knowledge concerning subjective color up until the middle of the twentieth century is J. Cohen and Gordon's (1949) thoughtful and still useful consideration of the subject. Another more recent review of the problem has been written by Sheppard (1968). Somewhat surprisingly, there has been a relatively rich resurgence of interest in the problem of subjective colors in recent years, most vigorously stimulated by Campenhausen's (1968a, 1968b, 1968c) work and then by Festinger, Allyn, and White's (1971) elegant study.

The classic technique used to produce these relatively strong visual impressions of pastel colors is to rotate a patterned stimulus such as one of those shown in Fig. 7-48. If the reader places any one of these patterns on the spindle of a variable speed electric drill, he can easily demonstrate the compelling chromatic illusion of subjective colors. For almost a century such a device has been called Benham's top (Benham, 1894). Some of the earlier investigators had used moving cards (Prevost, 1823–1826) or even printed material (Wheatstone, 1831) to elicit the effect, but there is some question whether or not they may have confused this illusion with the flight of colors occurring in afterimages—probably a completely distinct phenomenon.

FIG. 7.48. A variety of Fechner-Benham-Prevost "tops" used to produce subjective colors. (From Robinson, © 1972, with the permission of Hutchinson and Co., Ltd.)

Festinger, Allyn, and White made a particularly important contribution when they showed that the actual physical rotation of the stimulus pattern on one of Benham's tops was not critical to the perception of subjective colors. A stationary but flickering light source of appropriate form could produce the same phenomenal illusion if its time course were properly controlled. Obviously, as their experiment demonstrates, the rotary motion had simply been a means of temporally modulating the stimulus. Figure 7-49 shows the temporal patterns of the flickering lights that seemed to produce the strongest illusion of particular subjective pastel colors in Festinger, Allyn, and White's experiment.

The spatial configuration of the stimulus was critical in this experiment. A simple round spot did not display any appreciable subjective colors effect, but if a spatial pattern such as that shown in Fig. 7-50 was used, the illusion was very compelling. Even more dramatic was Festinger, Allyn, and White's discovery that it was not necessary for the color-specific temporal patterns shown in Fig. 7-49 to be repetitive. A single exposure of any of these temporal patterns was capable of producing the associated subjective color.

Another subjective color phenomenon has recently been reported by Mayzner (1975), who discovered that if a substantial number of alphabetic characters was plotted on a cathode-ray tube arranged in a hollow square, triangle, or circle, and the characters were sequentially presented so that there was a strong impression of apparent movement of about four characters moving around the figure, after about 30 seconds, the *interior* of the figure appeared to become colored. In this case, according to Mayzner, the subjective colors passed through a progression that included green, blue, and orange in succession. The subjective colors could be enhanced if a series of two or more concentric figures was used in which the apparent movement was in the opposite direction. The salient point of Mayzner's demonstration is that the colors appeared in the dark region inside the square rather than along the perimeter where the moving stimulus characters were plotted; in this regard, this finding is quite unlike the effect produced by the Benham top. If authenticated, this result suggests that the subjective colors need not appear to be in the same retinal locus that receives the temporally fluctuating inducing stimuli and, therefore, that subjective colors should not be attributed to receptor processes.

A number of parametric studies of the subjective color phenomenon has led to a fairly complete understanding of the stimulus factors upon which it is dependent. Young (1977), for example, has shown that reversing the rotation of a Benham top can dramatically change the color of certain sectors from blue to red. This finding means that it is not just the mixture of a set of Fourier equivalent

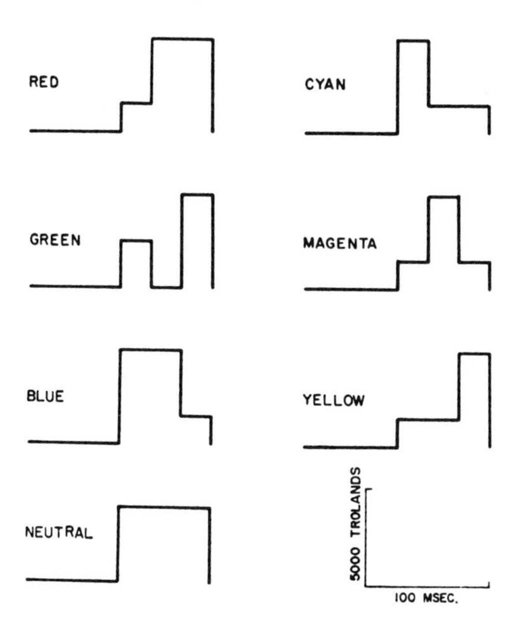

FIG. 7.49. The time course of the physical signals used by Festinger, Allyn, and White to produce subjective colors. (From Festinger, Allyn, and White, © 1971, with the permission of Pergamon Press.)

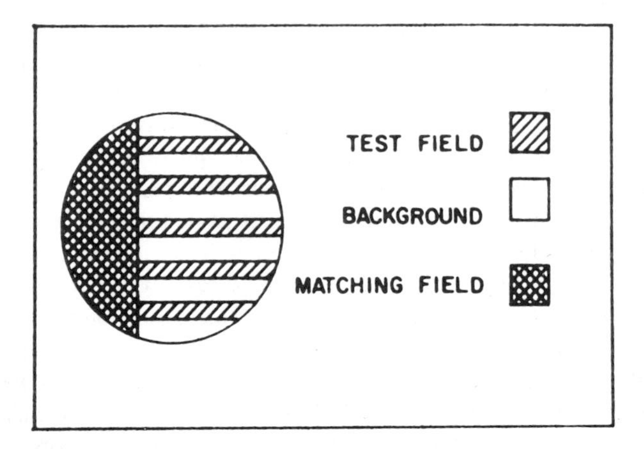

FIG. 7.50. The spatial stimulus pattern used by Festinger, Allyn, and White to produce subjective colors. (From Festinger, Allyn, and White, © 1971, with the permission of Pergamon Press.)

frequencies that determines the perceived color but that the relative order or phase of the various temporal components is necessarily influential in the specification of the perceived colors. Another important factor in eliciting the colors has been highlighted by Jarvis (1977), who showed that the spatial pattern used as a stimulus by Festinger and his colleagues could be even further reduced to two simple bars, or even to an annulus. Jarvis determined that as long as the stimulus spatial pattern was composed of at least two spatial elements, the Festinger, Allyn, and White temporal patterns (see Fig. 7-49) were capable of inducing different subjective colors. However, if the pattern is reduced to a single figural element or if its extent is constrained by a reduction screen (Hasegawa, 1972), the subjective color effect is minimal. This dependency on spatial extent suggests that the phenomenon is influenced by interactions between relatively distant retinal loci. This spatial-temporal interaction may also explain why only certain of the segmented patterns used in the original Benham top demonstration were effective in producing subjective colors, and the necessity for multiple objects in the modern experiments.

Jarvis further suggests that the spatial variable critical to the evocation of subjective colors may be the relationship between the form and the surround in which it is embedded. The extent of the surround (as shown in Fig. 7-51) was highly influential in determining the saturation of each perceived color as was the size of the stimulus object. Hasegawa, on the other hand, has suggested that the subjective colors are mainly edge effects. In his experiments a 4 mm wide segment was uniformly colored with a highly saturated color; but if the segment were broadened, the saturation decreased and a dark central region without color appeared between the colored edges. However, one should not overlook the

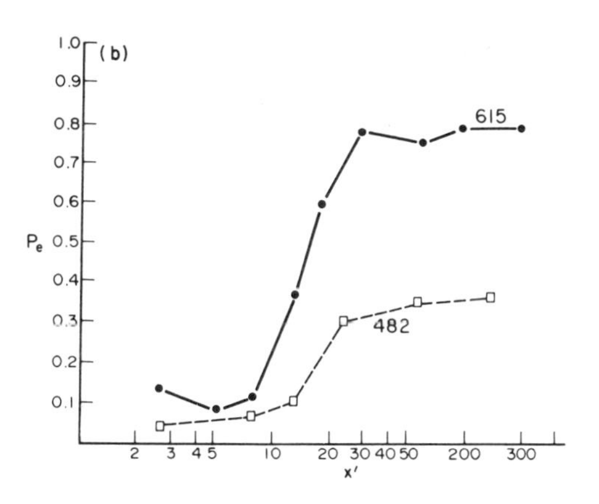

FIG. 7.51. The purity of subjective colors plotted as a function of the size of the surround (x′ = minutes of visual angle). Two stimulus patterns have been used to produce the two color experiences by the approximate dominant wavelengths indicated on the graph. (From Jarvis, © 1977, with the permission of Pergamon Press.)

inconsistency of this result with Mayzner's finding that subjective colors need not be coextensive with the stimulus.

Although the subjective colors occur only below the flicker threshold and above 2 Hz (they are optimum between 3 and 30 Hz, according to Hasegawa), their use in a subjectively colored television system has not only been suggested but even implemented. Butterfield (1968) has described the design of such a device. Because the saturation of these subjective colors was not as good as conventional color TV and the subfusion frequencies required to produce the illusions led to a distracting amount of picture flicker, there is apparently little future for this system. Nevertheless, it was an interesting demonstration of the stability and ubiquitousness of the phenomenon of subjective colors and deserves a place in their history. Not unexpectedly, even ordinary monochromatic television pictures can produce subjective colors (Gerjouy & Clarke, 1953), and this phenomenon can be a disturbing artifact in viewing this medium.

In terms of an explanatory model of subjective colors, the phenomenon's dependence on both the spatial and temporal aspects of the stimulus suggests that it is highly unlikely to be the result of Level 1 processes. It seems far more likely that these illusory colors are the result of modulations of the output of the three chromatic mechanisms somewhere deeper within the retina.[18] Other than Mayzner's unreplicated finding that response and stimulus can occur in different loci, there seems to be little evidence of any higher-level factors influencing their evocation. No reports have come to my attention that suggest that subjective colors are influenced by any cognitive components of the stimulus scene. However there is equally little direct evidence to support any particular neural model

[18]Subjective colors produced by stationary patterns usually only occur when the stimulus has a finely detailed spatial structure. In that case, (Stanley & Hoffman, 1976; Wade & Day, 1978) small eye movements may provide the necessary temporal modulation. However, Wade and Day suggest that there may also be a role for astigmatism and thus static blur, in any complete explanation of these interesting phenomena.

or level attribution. In spite of this, it is remarkable to note that over the years almost everyone has been willing to say something very specific about the level of the processes that may underlie the phenomenon.

Almost from the very beginning (e.g., Fechner, 1838a), the suggestion was made that subjective colors are due to different temporal properties or time constants[19] of the receptors themselves. Such a theory reached its epitome in Piéron's (1923a) model. Modern time–pattern theories that depend on the effect of the flickering patterns on the retinal network have been invoked by such a distinguished visual scientist as the late Glenn Fry (1945).

With the development of knowledge concerning the specific nature of neural interactions and the emerging awareness of the importance of the spatial components of the stimuli that are effective in producing subjective colors, lateral interaction theories have come to the fore. Among the leading lateral interaction theorists have been Campenhausen (1968a, 1968b, 1968c) and Festinger, Allyn, and White (1971) themselves. Finally, Jarvis (1974) has proposed a theoretical explanation of subjective colors that depends upon the center-surround organization of the receptive fields of the ganglion cells.

All of these theories have two features in common. The first is that they are all essentially peripheral in their critical locus, and thus they collectively represent a consensus that the subjective color phenomena are retinal effects. The other is that they are all highly speculative theories; there seems to be little if any electrophysiological evidence that speaks directly to the problems of the critical locus of subjective colors. Thus, I include them here with some trepidation and must, at least, leave open the possibility that they may have more in common with simultaneous contrast or the Land phenomena (see Chapter 11) than presently seems to be the case. All of these phenomena are similar in some regard and may indeed be influenced by some higher-level process that is ignored in all of the existing theories of subjective color. Clearly the problem is not yet resolved, and a considerable amount of further analysis must be carried out in order to rigorously identify the critical locus of the processes underlying apparent colors evoked by temporally varying stimulus patterns.

J. AN INTERIM SUMMARY

This chapter provides a review of an area of perceptual research into a family phenomena, mainly associated with temporal processes, for which there is not yet sufficient evidence to permit a definite determination of the critical level to which they may best be attributed. It is entirely possible that there will be no

[19]In electrical engineering circles, the time constant is the measure of the length of time it takes a system to arrive at 63.2% of the final response level following the introduction of a step input stimulus. In the looser sense, long time constants simply describe slowly responding systems whereas short time constants are associated with rapidly responding ones.

exclusive answer to the question of level for many of these temporal phenomena. Rather, there may be enormous redundancy built into the system, and such phenomena as visual persistence may result from equivalent processes occurring at several different levels. The ultimate origins of many of the phenomena I have discussed in this chapter, therefore, may eventually be discovered to be multiple. In general, however, it appears that most of the temporal processes described here exhibit few properties that are inconsistent with a peripheral (Level 1 or 2) explanation, and most of the neurophysiological data are not in disagreement with this conclusion. Considered as a group, these phenomena are highly dependent on the physical properties of the stimulus, and only a few, usually idiosyncratic, studies suggest any effectiveness of symbolic or semantic variables. But those that do are nagging reminders of how little progress neuroreductionism has made in this domain and how little we really know of the specific origins of these time-based phenomena.

It would, of course, be most satisfying if a coherent pattern of answers to the questions of critical processing levels emerged from the widely divergent methodologies used in these studies of temporal interactions. Unfortunately, it appears that this will not be the case even for some of the most basic questions concerning the temporal properties of the visual system. For example, even though it seems straightforward enough to ask if there are any temporal differences between the channels encoding stimuli of different wavelengths, the answer is frustratingly elusive. D. Green's (1969) study certainly suggests that the temporal modulation transfer function does differ from one color system to another. However when one looks at a very wide range of studies all of which can be thought of as contributing to the answer to this question, there is utter chaos.

To further illustrate this difficulty, consider the following specific formulation of the general questions I have just posed: Does the time constant of the visual system vary for different wavelength stimuli? A large number of studies that have, in one way or another, attacked this form of the question, are all in substantial disagreement with regard to an answer to this question. This makes it clear that there is no consensus concerning the question of the dependence of visual time constants on stimulus wavelength in human vision.

Other equally simple-sounding questions concerning the psychology of time remain even more refractory and lack even a contradictory and inconsistent data base from which to make a stab at an answer. Wassermann and Kong (1979) for example have inquired into the the absolute timing of mental events. Their answer to the question of when a mental event occurs is, at best, a preliminary one. They compare the critical duration in a *Limulus* with the period of interaction in human psychophysical experiments. But wisely and cautiously, they note that this association is highly tentative and fragile, depending on a chain of assumptions that cannot be rigorously proven. These assumptions (abstracted from Wassermann & Kong, 1979) include:

1. The relevant processes in man and *Limulus* are the same.
2. The relevant processes in the peripheral nervous system are the same as those in the central nervous system.
3. An isomorphism exists between neural and psychological processes.

Clearly this is a long and indirect logical pathway, but these authors appreciate this fact. Their explicit statement of the difficulties involved in such an analysis is a refreshing change from many other psychobiologists' simplistic theorizing that each and every phenomenon is the result of some special sensitivity on the part of a "feature detector." Wasserman and Kong remind us once again of the very great difficulty in measuring the temporal properties of the mind.

The problem of temporal influences on perception, therefore, remains one of the most difficult areas of modern psychological research. I have not touched on the more complex problems of temporal perception that obviously are not peripheral but are ultimately much more likely to be explained in terms of higher levels of processing. That is a topic for chapters yet to come. A number of reviews exist for the reader who would like to delve more deeply into the literature on the range of topics that I have considered here. Among the most useful are J. Brown (1965), Boynton (1972), Kelly (1972), and Ganz (1975).

8 Level 2: Neural Interaction Processes Affecting Perception

A. INTRODUCTION

So far in my discussion of the proposed multilevel taxonomy of visual perception, I have considered the physical processes that modulate the proximal stimulus (Level 0) and the receptor processes that initially transform the afferent information flow (Level 1). In Chapter 7 I digressed to consider a number of topics related to the temporal properties of the stimulus that cannot be exclusively analyzed into either receptor or neural network processes. The situation, however, is far clearer when we consider the set of phenomena that are best encompassed within the Level 2 rubric.

Level 2 processes are implemented by neural interactions occurring within the three-dimensional space of the visual nervous system. These interactions impose certain relatively well-known transformations on the communicated information patterns. We now know, for example, from the enormous data base provided by modern neurophysiology, that the afferent visual pathways (including the primary projection regions of the cerebral cortex) do not produce a pattern of neural activity that perfectly reproduces the proximal stimulus pattern falling on the retinal receptor mosaic. The various neurons lying between the retina and the brain are not independent of each other; rather, they interact heavily at many levels of synaptic interconnection to alter the communicated information. The result of this interaction is that the retinal signal is encoded in what may often be a highly distorted form at higher levels of the pathway. Some of this distortion is highly adaptive. For example, the set of spatial contour intensification processes that emphasizes the rich informational content of a gradient or contour while de-emphasizing the redundant regions of constant stimulus intensity between contours is a highly useful and biologically "economical" neural distortion. Correlates of the contour enhancement observed in the neural response with electrophysiological recording techniques can also be detected psychophysically; that is, the distortion in the neural response produces an associated perceptual nonveridicality or illusion. Although the nonveridical perceptual response may serve no useful function or may be innocuous, it is an unavoidable concomitant of a neural coding mechanism that may otherwise be highly useful to the organism. Other neural distortions, however, are the direct antecedents of nonveridical perceptions that can, in some cases, reduce the value of the perceptual experience to the organism and seriously interrupt selection of an appropriate response. An example of such a disadvantageous perceptual outcome of a neural interaction is the loss of acuity in the periphery of the normal human retina.

The thesis of this chapter is that certain of these Level 2 critical processes, occurring as a direct result of the interactions between the component neural elements, are the direct, necessary, sufficient, and essential causes of a particular group of perceptual phenomena. It must be remembered, however, that this thesis is being asserted only for certain specific phenomena. There is a considerable amount of confusion in the quasi-theoretical literature of perceptual psychobiology concerning which phenomena should in fact be associated with these Level 2 processes. It is my feeling that many more phenomena have been attributed to this relatively peripheral level of neural interactions than properly should be. More complex neural interactions, more plausibly described in terms of the interpretive and symbolic processes to be invoked in Levels 3, 4, and 5, may be more appropriate models than Level 2 network processes in many cases. I expand upon this problem as I distinguish between the two classes of response in the next chapter. For the moment, the reader is forewarned that this chapter excludes many of the phenomena previously attributed to Level 2 type interactions by other perceptual theorists. Some are omitted because no known neural correlate at this level of analysis could plausibly accommodate the theoretical needs of the particular phenomenon in my opinion. Others are omitted because the relevant stimuli that are effective in modulating the percept appear, to me at least, to be more complicated than those driving the relatively simple spatial interactions typical of the Level 2 rubric.

In sum, the following criterion statement can be asserted for phenomena putatively associated with Level 2 processes. If it can be shown that a particular perceptual phenomena can be modulated by some semantic or cognitive aspect of the stimulus, we should not assign that phenomenon to Level 2. If these cognitive influences are relatively large and prominent and the effects of variations of the more physical, as opposed to symbolic, aspects of the stimulus (e.g., size, luminance, duration) are relatively small, then the phenomena is probably better attributed to a higher level of processing. On the other hand, the possibility of Level 1 influences should also not be overlooked. Here too the physical aspects of the stimulus can be important. Neurophysiological data are usually adequate to make the distinction between Level 1 and Level 2 attributions.

And finally, I should also note that whereas Level 2 processes are explicitly network interactions, all higher levels are implicitly so: Psychoneural monism and modern science point to the neural network as the mechanism of all mental processes. As we see in subsequent chapters, these higher-level networks are so complex as to be beyond neuroreductionistic analysis. This is, however, a practical and quantitative matter and not one of principle.

1. The Nature of Neural Interaction

A major lexigraphic issue that must be considered at the beginning of this chapter concerns the meaning of the term *neural interaction*. The term has been used so often without clear definition that it has become an ambiguous shorthand for any integrative activity of the nervous system. A satisfactory definition of neural interaction must necessarily specify the exact nature of the processes that allow one neuron to affect another. Another important aspect of such a definition should be its ability to distinguish between relevant and psychoneurally effective interactions and irrelevant interactions having no perceptual impact. Thus a better answer to the question of what constitutes a neural interaction involves the concept of a collaborative action of more than one neuron such that the significance of the conveyed message is modified. Although the information passing through a single neuron may be represented by a slow graded potential, a rapidly propagating spike action potential, or even by the amount of some chemical transmitter substance that is released from its terminal arborizations, the biochemical details of the function of an individual neuron are simply not germane to the present discussion of neural informational interaction. Such matters concern the biochemical "technology" of which neurons are constructed, not the logical processes they execute. Nor, for that matter, are the internal codes used by each neuron to represent momentarily the information passing through it particularly germane to the present discussion. The essential idea at Level 2 is that no neuron exists in isolation. In the peripheral nervous system, as well as in the central nervous system, the significant process is determined by the way that the network acts to pass information back and forth between neurons. The critical fact is that, in general, stimulus-borne information does not leave any neural plexus in the same form in which it entered. Neurons are not connected in a direct serial sequence comparable to a telephone line which conveys information with high fidelity. Not only are the codes representing information different at each stage of the afferent pathway, but there are also powerful transformations occurring in the "meaning" of the message as it passes up the parallel-organized afferent pathway. These transformations are the ultimate contribution of neural networks and the basis of all adaptive mental activity.

The effective points of interconnection between neurons, of course, are the synaptic junctions. These electrically or chemically mediated interfaces between the membranes of two cytoplasmically discontinuous cells are, for all practical purposes, the only points through which neurons can interact. Though there have from time to time been suggestions of *en passant* "ephaptic" interactions,[1] clearly most of the normal information processing done by the nervous system occurs at the synapse. The types and locations of the synaptic connections and the spatial and temporal pattern through which information impinges upon them must be thought of as the ultimate mediator of virtually all neural interactions. Synapses, therefore, regulate the state of the neural network, and thus it is not too farfetched to attribute to the synapse, rather than to the rest of the neuron, the essential control functions of the nervous system. Indeed, if one concentrates on the neuron's information-processing role rather than on its own internal physiology, the neuron might be considered properly as a *logically inactive* element. Within the neuron, little happens to alter the information content of the message. The signal usually has the same meaning and represents the same information pattern when it enters the cell at some postsynaptic region as when it exits from some presynaptic region. Only when the signals from several neurons converge is the information flow modified, integrated, or critically processed in the manner

---

[1]Later in this chapter, I discuss the blue arcs of the retina. Although the origins of this phenomenon are not completely understood, at least some investigators believe that the arcs are due to ephaptic interactions between a particular bundle of ganglion cell fibers and other neurons in the retina. Not only is this possibly the only known visual example, but in fact it may be the only example of an ephaptic interaction that leads to a detectable biological response in vivo.

that significantly transforms the meaning of the signal. Although some self-inhibition, amplification, or accommodation may occur within the confines of a single neuron, the assertion that what goes into the neural net is not likely to be what comes out does not hold for the individual neuron. Informationally what comes out of the individual neuron is, by and large, pretty much what went into it even if recoded into a new neural language. For all practical purposes, if treated as a part of an information-processing network, the neuron can be considered to be a point or a node, perhaps inserting some transmission delay but still repeating at the output what essentially was asserted at the input.

The essential mechanism of neural interaction, therefore, is the pattern of synaptic interconnections between and among the various neurons in the network. The afferent visual system does not function, as is commonly implied, as a linear transmission line conveying information from the periphery to the central portions of the nervous system but, quite to the contrary, must itself be considered to be a highly active three-dimensional array powerfully transforming the signal passing through it. One has only to look at Fig. 3-24 and 3-25 depicting the complexity of the synaptic interconnections at the foot of even a single photoreceptor to appreciate the enormous information-processing possibilities inherent in such a heavily intertwined network. Nevertheless, these pictures are just as misleading in one way as are the hypersimplistic diagrams of the prototypical retina shown in Fig. 8-1. The retina is neither as incredibly complicated as suggested by the former picture nor as trivially simple as suggested by the latter. The retina and, for that matter, all of the higher levels of neural processing are in principle quite orderly.

The possible interactions in the prototypical neural network can be relatively completely characterized by the three-dimensional array shown in Fig. 8-2. This figure emphasizes that any neural network exhibits forward, backward, and sideways interactions among the various neurons. Collectively, these interactions specify that the output of the matrix will differ from the pattern of stimulus information that falls on the receptor array that constitutes its input but in a lawful way.

2. Processing Elements Versus Network Functions

Two seemingly contradictory statements must be made about the prototypical interaction matrix shown in Fig. 8-2. One is that the matrix is constituted from logical and organizational elements that are not themselves very complicated and whose nature can be relatively easily understood and appreciated. The other is that such a three-dimensional neural network is capable of interactions and computations that are usually very difficult and often impossible to analyze. These two aspects of the network can be characterized by emphasizing the simple logical elements of the matrix, on the one hand, and the overall functions of which the network is capable, on the other.

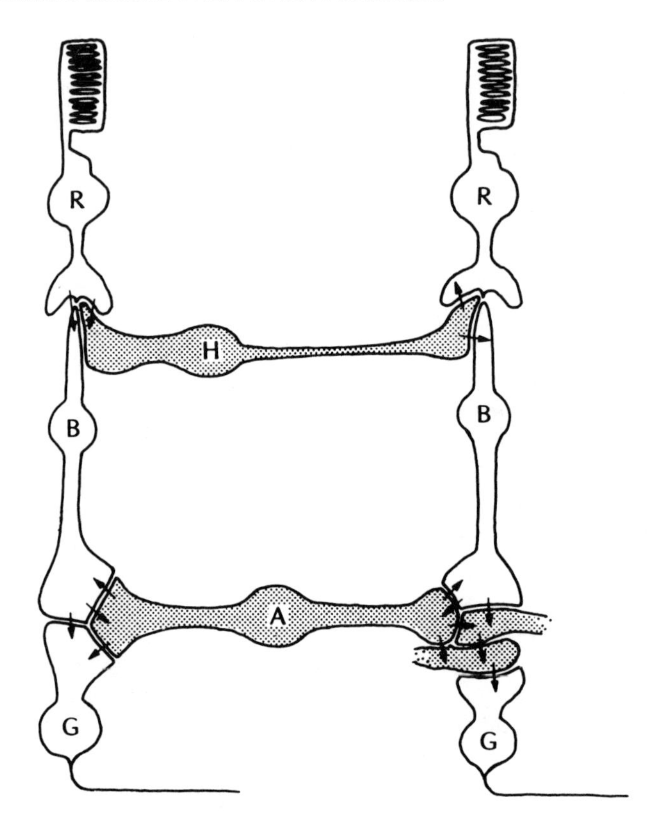

FIG. 8.1. A prototypical circuit of the basic organization of the vertebrate retina. (From Dowling, © 1968, with the permission of The Royal Society of London.)

a. Processing Elements

Consider the implication of the first statement. I have asserted that the basic logical elements of neural interaction are relatively orderly and simple. To expand upon this point, it is necessary to specify those basic interactive processes that characterize any neural network, whether it be the retinal plexus or any other higher level of the central nervous system.

One of the most important general characteristics of the model neural network shown in Fig. 8-2 is that it is a parallel-processing computational device. However regularly the neurons may be arranged and however specifically predetermined are the logical rules that the network obeys, it is unlikely that any single part of the network is critical or essential. All parts of the network simultaneously carry out a portion of the computational and integrative functions in a distributed fashion. There are many indications in the neurophysiological literature that there is such a widespread interaction between the elements at each level that the processing at any point in the network is affected by activity at many other points. This distributed processing is a highly useful mechanism. It represents an intrinsic redundancy that minimizes the importance of any single neuron and in many cases allows a satisfactory level of functioning to be maintained even where there may be some localized damage.

The important point is that for any given level of visual processing, in general, and for the retinal plexus, in particular, it is clear that the neural activity that goes on at each point within the network is a function of many points on the receptor mosaic. A corollary of this functional axiom is that likewise there is no point within the network that does not affect many points on the output mosaic. Indeed, each output point of this matrix is likely to be, within broad limits, influenced by many points on the input pattern.

Another general characteristic of this prototypical three-dimensional neural network array is that the units at the various horizontal levels are usually inter-

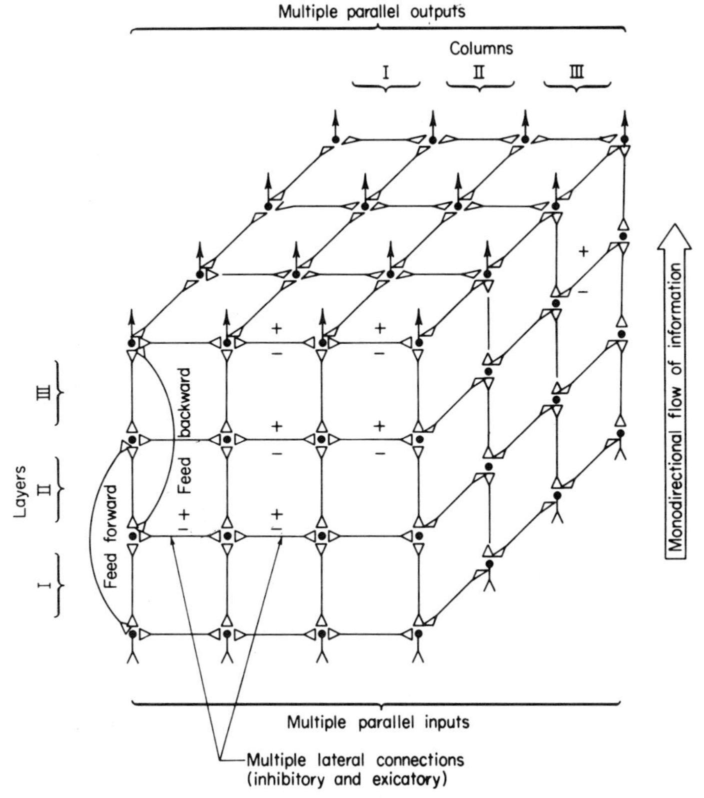

FIG. 8.2. A conceptual model of the arrangement of neurons in the nervous system. Although the nervous system never looks as neat and orderly as shown, there is a great deal of intrinsic order. (From Uttal, 1978.)

connected by strong lateral interactive mechanisms. Some of these interconnections may be excitatory (thus allowing the spread of information from one vertical column to another), and others may be inhibitory and actually act to reduce the magnitude of the activity that is conveyed in a parallel vertical column. Another important function of inhibition is to stabilize the entire system so that the neural network does not suffer from a persistent epileptiform neural explosion every time a single punctate stimulus is presented to it.

Although for conceptual simplification the lateral connectives in this diagram are drawn as if regularly spaced and of a constant length, such lateral connectives are not all of uniform length. Even in primitive organisms such as the horseshoe crab, lateral connectives vary in the distance they traverse and the extent of their influence. In the avian retina, some workers (e.g., Holden, 1977) have shown that the receptive field of an as-yet-unidentified neuron in the inner plexiform layer can apparently exert a direct effect over very great retinal distances. Holden demonstrated inhibitory interactions in his study between stimuli placed as far apart as 20 deg of visual angle.

On the other hand, local or microcircuits may involve lateral reciprocally interactive connections that may be responsive only over regions a few micra in diameter. Though exciting in its own right, the topic of neural network microcircuits is not relevant to the present discussion except as another specific example of the general concept of neural network interaction. The reader who wishes to learn more about these newly discovered logical elements in the retina should look at Rakic (1975) or, for a more popular view, Shepherd (1978).

Another major feature of this cubical array network model is that, in principle, signals can skip ahead from one horizontal level to another by processes of feedforward. Information can also be passed backward by feedback processes.[2] The mathematics of control engineering has shown how much more adaptive is a system embodying some form of feedforward or feedback (such that the output can be modified as a function of the input) compared to an open loop system with its fixed output.

Finally, there is an intrinsic directionality in this system that can only be suggested by the arrows in the diagram but that depends mainly on the refractory periods of the individual neurons and the rectification action of the synapses. This intrinsic directionality means that any neural network will, on the average, convey signals only from a well-defined input level to an equally well-defined output level, even though individual neuronal exceptions (e.g., horizontal cells) may exist.

There is an elegantly simple and even quasi-crystalline structure apparent in neural networks if they are analyzed at a relatively global level rather than at high

---

[2]Within the retina itself, however, there is no known means by which feedforward can occur. The bipolar cells, conveying information from the outer to the inner plexiform layers, constitute the only signal pathway. Feedback in the retina, on the other hand, may be accounted for by the newly discovered interplexiform cells.

magnification and in microscopic detail. Various models of the organization of nervous tissue have also been considered by such neuroscientists as Shepherd (1974) and Szentágothai (see Chapter 3 in Uttal, 1978, for a comprehensive review of his work; Chapter 3 in the present work; as well as three very recent papers, Szentágothai 1978a, 1978b, 1978c). Although there may be some differences with regard to particulars, neuroscientists have made it clear that certain fundamental and simple computational and interactive mechanisms make up the superficially chaotic nervous system that appears under the microscope. These are some of the fundamental logical processing elements of the neural network.

b. Network Functions

Now let us consider the other side of this issue. In spite of the fact that neural networks and their elements are, in principle, regular and simple, it is not necessarily an equally simple matter to describe the dynamic function of realistically complex networks. Very small concatenations of the logical elements described in the previous section can quickly lead to such intricate and complex interactions (and interactions of interactions) as to preclude neurophysiological or conventional mathematical analysis. Our technology and mathematics, therefore, fails us rather badly at this point, and we must turn to a simulation model to deepen our understanding of even the simplest neural interactions that can occur within prototypical networks of this type. Figure 8-3, for example, shows the progressive stages in the spread of activity through a simulated neural network in which a single stimulus input is initially inserted at the lower-left front corner of a cubical matrix. (The two pictures shown in each frame are the left and right eye views, respectively. If viewed in an appropriate stereoscope, the three-dimensional space defined by the matrix becomes evident.) This particular network has been designed so that backward firing of the simulated neurons is not possible, but the model does allow lateral interactions, thus permitting divergence and convergence of the signal flow. Although the spread of activity in this simulated network is not characteristic of any particular neural structure, this simulation helps to provide at least the glimmering of an intuitive appreciation of what the information flow in such a matrix might be like. Clearly at each point in the temporal sequence more than one neuron is responding, and there is a substantial spatial spread of information beyond the point of initial stimulation.

This display does not, of course, embody all of the properties usually considered to be typical of even the simplest real neural network. Inhibitory interactions, refractory periods, and feedback, for example, have not been programmed into this conceptual neural structure. However, the idea of a spreading wave of neural activity, the specific characteristics of which will depend on the particular logic of the simulated "synaptic" interconnections, is made much more explicit using this kind of model than it would otherwise be. Simulations of this sort can be used to display the result of interactions between simultaneous or sequential inputs and, if the missing properties are added, can thus become useful models of neural interactions at least in restricted regions of the nervous system. On a more

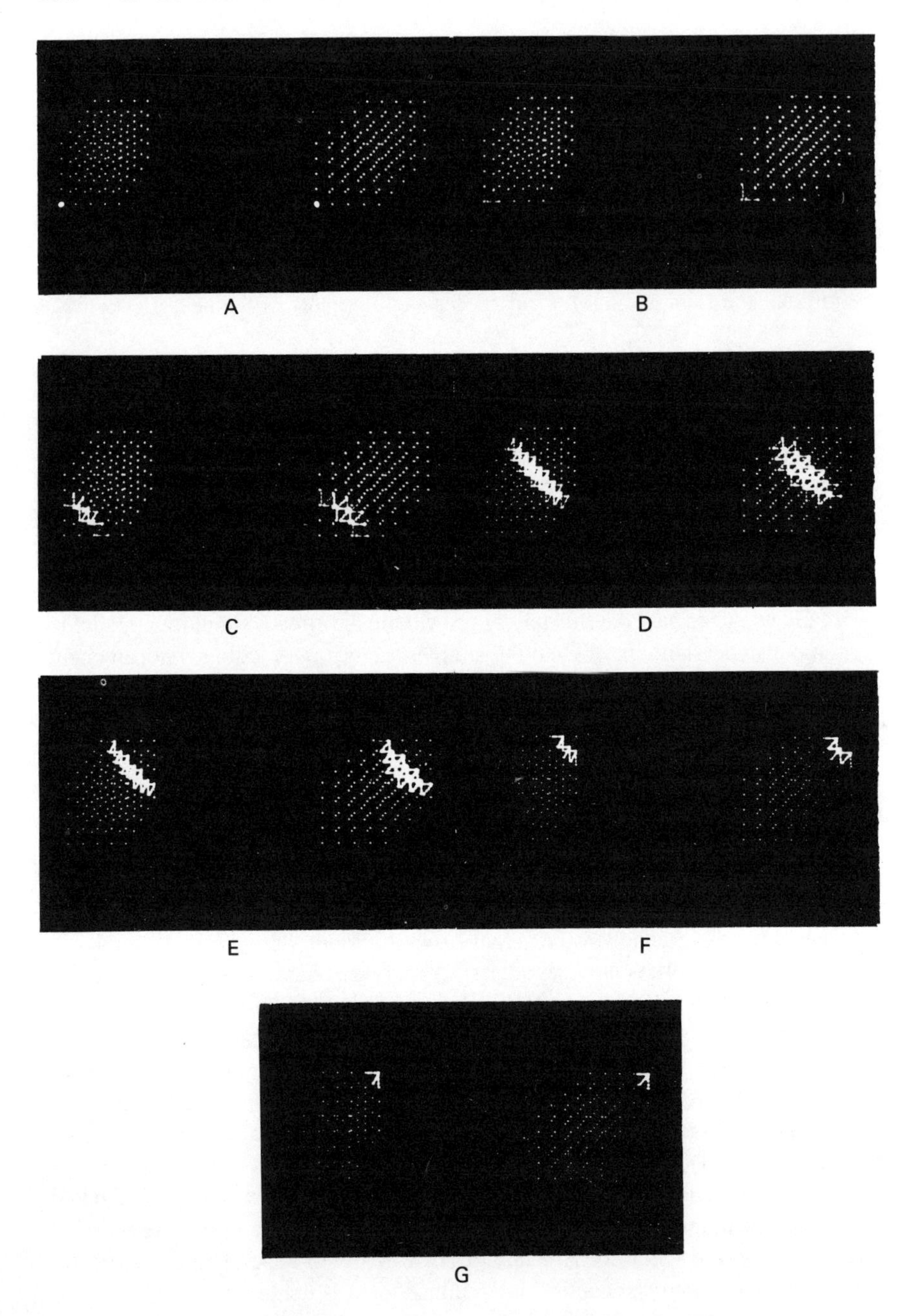

FIG. 8.3. A series of stereoscopic pictures that can be used to demonstrate the computed spread of activity through a stimulated neural network with refractory periods but no lateral inhibition.

realistic level of complexity even this artifact fails, and we simply have no insight into the nature of the network interactions that represent most psychological processes. It is only in the rare instances described in this chapter that the interactions are simple enough to link directly with the perceptual outcome.

3. Other Issues of Interaction

In the preceding paragraphs I have concentrated on the nature of the spatial interactions that are likely to occur in a neural network. There are other dimensions of the neural response, however, that may also be modified by these spatial interactions in ways that are not at all a priori obvious. The spatial interactions in the neural network can affect many other dimensions of the perceptual experience other than its subjective spatial properties. For example, because of the feedforward and feedback processes that I have described, it is possible that the temporal properties of the neural and perceptual response can be altered. I have already alluded to many of these temporal transformations in Chapter 7. Another class of spatial interactive processes—the neural re-encoding of the messages due to the specific structural interactions between the receptors and subsequent neural layers—can also have surprising effects on data obtained in studies of color vision; thus neural interactions can have qualitative as well as temporal and spatial effects.

The important point I am making here is that the neural interaction effects of the kind that I have classified as Level 2 processes, though basically interactions occurring in a three-dimensional neural *space,* are not necessarily also reflected in the *spatial* dimensions of the perceptual phenomena. Temporal, intensive, and qualitative phenomena can also be critically influenced by the nature of the neural interactions in the spatial network, as we see repeatedly in the later sections of this chapter.

There are, as I mentioned, several other phenomena that, although often attributed to Level 2 processes, are not in fact really very well linked to this level of neural processing. For example, many of the so-called chromatic, spatial, or contingent adaptation effects, however well documented as perceptual phenomena, are not likely to be Level 2 processes, in my opinion, even though some theorists would make strong claims for their inclusions in this category. A raft of contraindications, many of which I discuss in Chapter 9, suggests that any overly simplistic Level 2 explanation of such a striking phenomena as the McCulloch effect (a color and spatial-frequency-contingent aftereffect) or the waterfall illusion in terms of ''fatigued'' neural mechanisms does not seem plausible.

Similarly, there is a traditional body of evidence and theory that concerns certain spatial interactions between stimuli (the so called induction phenomena) that has long been assumed to be the result of lateral interactions (see, for example, the summary in Obanai, 1977). I believe that these phenomena are not properly categorized within Level 2 either. It seems more likely that they are actually reflections of very much more complicated interpretive mechanisms occurring at much higher levels of neural processing.

The general point is that a subjective spatial interaction in the perceptual world does not necessarily imply the existence of an isomorphic spatial interaction between cells in the nervous system. The sort of reasoning that suggests that such an isomorphism is so implied is a modern version of the overemphasis on psychoneural isomorphism that led to the demise of the Gestalt influence on perceptual theory. A similar overemphasis could prove equally lethal to modern neural interaction theories of spatial perception. I also expand upon this point in the next chapter. For the moment, I only warn the reader not to be disconcerted by the absence of some phenomena that conventional wisdom would place within the context of this chapter.

4. Plan Of This Chapter

In each of the subsequent sections of this chapter I consider as a group those phenomena that I believe are due to a common aspect of neural interaction. The first subsection includes those phenomena for which there is plausible argument that they result from the convergence or lateral excitation of one neuron by another. The excitatory mechanisms involved are those that allow one point of a stimulus array to enhance the perception of some other point by means of spatial summation or convergence.

The next subsection deals with those perceptual phenomena that can plausibly be considered to be the result of inhibitory neural interactions between adjacent neural regions. This type of process is responsible for a large number of perceptual phenomena, including those in which edge or contour enhancement occurs.

The third subsection is concerned with interactive situations which are more complex and may simultaneously involve divergent, convergent, excitatory, and inhibitory mechanisms in processing neural information. In this section I discuss the phenomenal effects of the neural recoding of color information, among other topics. The chapter concludes with a discussion of these interactions that influence such diverse phenomena as dark adaptation and visual phosphenes.

Once again I must emphasize an important organizational principle guiding the flow of this book. My taxonomy, both in terms of the six levels and in terms of their respective subdivisions, as exemplified by the sections of this chapter, is based upon common explanations, rather than common dimensions, of the perceptual experience. The main criterion for collecting together several phenomena into a single section is my judgment that each exemplar reflects the operation of a shared underlying mechanism or process. It is for this reason that discussions of some aspects of visual masking or color vision, for example, are found here as well as in several earlier and later chapters. Though the phenomenal dimensions of these effects are quite similar, the explanatory critical processes are scattered through many levels of the taxonomy that organizes this book.

B. THE PERCEPTUAL IMPACT OF NEURAL CONVERGENCE

1. The Mechanisms

The various phenomena discussed in this section are joined together by the hypothesis that they share a common underlying mechanism—convergent pooling. This idea asserts that there is a focusing of the neural signals from many units at any anatomic level onto a single unit at some subsequent anatomic level. Although I have already considered the neuroanatomy and physiology of convergence briefly in Chapter 3 and in the introduction to this chapter, a few comments must be made before considering the details of the perceptual phenomena that seem most likely to be attributable to this kind of neuronal processing.

The first point to be made is that Fig. 8-4 can be used to demonstrate neural convergence equally as well as it can be used to denote the receptive field of any neuron. The concept of the receptive field, I remind the reader, is, therefore, functionally and denotatively synonymous with the concept of convergence. Receptive fields, which are properties of individual neurons, exist because the signals elicited by stimuli in any large part of a stimulus field all feed into (i.e., converge on) neural units at higher levels of processing. This convergence can either be mediated by diagonal connectives as indicated in Fig. 8-4 or by lateral and ascending connectives as indicated in Fig. 8-5. In either case, the effect is to broaden the region in the external environment that is capable of producing activity in any particular neuron of the network. Of course, more complex receptive field structure can exist in which the interaction is not only summative but also inhibitory. These complex receptive fields themselves are undoubtedly due to a combination of convergent excitatory and inhibitory connections.

The second point I emphasize here is that the degree of convergence is not constant across the retina. In general there is considerably more convergent interaction as one passes from the fovea to the periphery of the retina, and receptive field size increases correspondingly. Specifically, Fisher (1973) has shown that there is actually a near-linear increase in ganglion cell receptive field size as a function of the distance from the fovea at which the center of the field occurs.

A related generality is that receptive field size and thus information convergence usually increase as the point of inspection moves to higher levels of the nervous system. Although this is not entirely true, any lack of field size increase at higher levels may not be due so much to an absence of convergence as to a subsequent reduction in field size by local inhibition. Thus, for example, Guillery (1966) does report ample convergence from ganglion cells onto the neurons of the lateral geniculate nucleus of the thalamus even though there is little increase in receptive field size between these two levels. Nevertheless, higher

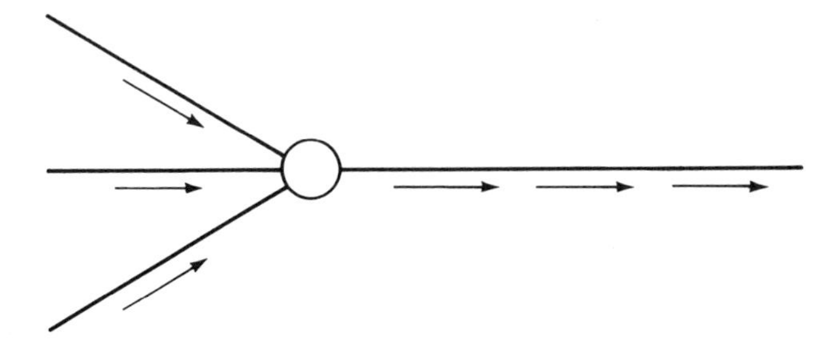

FIG. 8.4. Convergent neural interaction in a simple planar network.

levels of the visual pathway do generally contain neurons that exhibit larger receptive fields than do lower levels. McIlwain (1976) has reviewed the many studies that support this general conclusion, and the interested reader is directed there for a more detailed consideration of the problem of receptive field size.

There is another reason that this progressive increase in receptive field size, as one ascends the visual pathway, is interesting: There is no corresponding perceptual evidence of an associated loss of acuity. The most molar psychophysical evidence suggests that overall visual acuity in the fovea, at least, is even better than the theoretical limit defined by the size of the retinal elements. Thus, in spite of the general sequential summation of convergent processes, we are still able to see with a spatial sensitivity that indicates that there has not been the expected loss of information due to the increased convergent interactions. This preliminary finding also suggests that it is probably something of a logical error to associate facilely the perceptual phenomena described in this section solely with convergent processes or with the size or shape of the receptive fields of individual central neurons. Obviously there must be statistical considerations involved that go far beyond the role played by single cells.

The discussion that I present here, phrased as it is in terms of convergent mechanisms onto individual neurons and receptive field size must, therefore, be interpreted in a somewhat qualified sense. We must not overlook the fact that there is always the possibility of the intervention of interactive (i.e., multicellular) mechanisms that may act to compensate collectively for the information degradation occurring in individual neurons. Even if one were confronted with an array of neurons with large receptive fields and thus intrinsically poor acuity, the array of units might perform better than the individual cells as a result of averaging or some other statistical process.

The next preliminary point concerns neural divergence rather than convergence. As noted in the introduction to this chapter, there are also divergent excitatory processes present in addition to the convergent excitatory interactions among the neurons of the visual system. However, the most likely effect of an unmitigated divergent excitation—the dramatic spread of response ultimately resulting in a widespread activation of all of the neurons in a network as soon as any one of them is stimulated—is not observed in the normal organism; we are not all in a constant state of stimulus-triggered epilepsy. The reason that this disastrous situation does not occur is because of the inhibitory nature of other lateral interactions that compensate and regulate these divergent excitatory effects. The main effect of excitatory neural divergence, then, is a recruitment or amplification of the number of neurons that are involved in any response. However, this recruitment is moderated by inhibitory divergent mechanisms to occur in an orderly way as signals ascend the afferent pathway. Thus even though there is a progressive spread of the response—the excitation of one rod may lead to the activation of literally billions of central nervous system neurons—there is no explosive, uncoordinated response (*status epilepticus*) of all of the neurons that are divergently interconnected. Instead there is a massive, yet controlled, and highly coordinated central response from which perceptual order can be extracted.

With the divergent processes so well controlled by inhibitory mechanisms, there are few perceptual effects that seem to be exclusively due to a simple excitatory divergent spread of response. I appreciate that this statement flies in the face of the thinking of a number of classical theories and concepts such as the "spread of effect" and "retinal induction" that have been recalled to current attention by the recent publication of the book by Torao Obanai (1977), the distinguished late Japanese perceptual psychologist. However, such field interactions, which were the mainstay of the theories of the Gestalt tradition, no longer seem to have any empirical basis. Most of the instances in which spatial percepts appear to be distorted because of the presence of other objects in the scene (including many of the geometrical illusions) are better classified as the result of

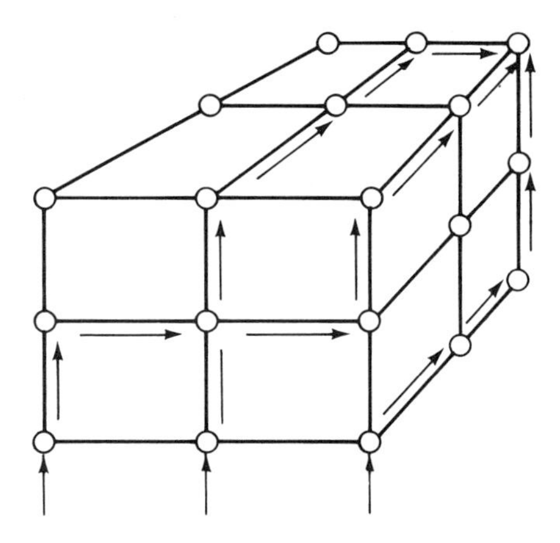

FIG. 8.5. Convergent neural interaction in a three-dimensional network.

interpretive processes at Level 4 of my taxonomy rather than as the result of any ''attractive neural forces'' operating at the level of the retina or the occipital cortex. There simply is no physiological evidence of such ''inductive processes'' in the periphery, and there are many signs (see Chapter 9) that the phenomenology does not agree, even to a first approximation, with such a simplistic neural interaction hypothesis.

On the other hand, there are well-established phenomena that do seem to be heavily influenced by critical processes mediated by convergent mechanisms in the visual system. Spatial summation, visual acuity, and peripheral color blindness are three of the most likely candidates for this kind of explanation. The remaining parts of this section deals in turn with each of these phenomena.

2. Spatial Summation

The phenomenon of spatial summation is, in many ways, analogous to the temporal summation or integration processes discussed in Chapter 7. The basic idea of spatial summation is that the energy of a stimulus can be spatially distributed within a given area (rather than within a given unit of time) without any effect on such a criterion as the amount of energy required to produce a threshold sensation. The relationship between threshold and stimulus area has traditionally been described by a system of three laws.

The first, Ricco's law (Ricco, 1877), was asserted to hold for all stimuli that subtended less than about 40 min of visual angle. Within this small area the relationship between stimulus luminance (I) and the area of the test spot (A) followed a reciprocal relation, much like Bloch's law for time and intensity, of the form

$$A \times I = C \tag{8-1}$$

In this equation, C is a constant. Such workers as Hallet, Marriott, and Rodger (1962) and Weale (1958) have carried out modern studies that have confirmed Ricco's law as a good first approximation when the stimulus is a simple, small, circular field of varying diameter and intensity.

The simplest implications of Ricco's law of spatial summation are similar to those of Bloch's temporal law. If the stimulus is small enough, there is a perfect spatial summation for all portions of the area upon which it impinges just as there is a perfect summation over short periods of time. Photic stimuli that lead to the elicitation of the threshold experience (it should not be forgotten that Ricco's law is based upon a threshold criterion) could be placed anywhere in the area of summation without differential effect. However, as we soon see, significant exceptions analogous to those mitigating the meaning of Bloch's law, have also been discovered to Ricco's law.

Spatial summation of this kind is traditionally assumed to be due to the pooling of the responses of the individual receptors onto a higher-level neuron as a result of simple convergence. Ricco's law is usually interpreted, therefore, in anatomical terms. One early inference drawn from the fact that there was an upper limit of approximately 40 min on spatial summation was that the region of spatial pooling or convergence of the corresponding neural elements was of about this magnitude. The extent of the area at which Ricco's law fails is known as the "Ricco size" for any particular set of experimental conditions.

For larger stimuli, therefore, the simple reciprocal relationship embodied in Ricco's law does not hold. To the contrary, for stimuli that vary from about 40 min of visual angle up to about 15 deg, no single descriptive law rigorously holds although most spatial summation functions in this region (Bartlett, 1965) are fit to a first approximation by a general power function of the form

$$A^n \times I = C \tag{8-2}$$

where n is the exponent of which the area is raised, and the other terms are as defined for Ricco's law. Within this broad region there is a range of stimuli of intermediate sizes (from about 2 deg up to about 10 deg in diameter) for which a square root (i.e., $n = \frac{1}{2}$) relationship, known as Piper's law (Piper, 1903), holds. Between 40 min of visual angle and 2 deg there is a gradual diminution in the exponent from $n = 1$ (Ricco's law) to $n = \frac{1}{2}$ (Piper's law) as the size of the summation area increases. When even larger stimuli are used (i.e., those that subtended 15 deg or more of visual angle), there is no summative effect of stimulus size, and a third law, characterized by $n = 0$ (i.e., $A^0 = 1$), holds, as follows:

$$I = C \tag{8-3}$$

Although it has not been specifically measured to my knowledge, the transition from Piper's law ($A^{1/2} \times I = C$) to this third law ($I = C$) for increasingly large stimuli is also probably characterized by a further progressive reduction in exponent magnitude. The transition in the descriptive law of spatial summation from very small stimuli to very large ones may therefore be better conceptualized as a single general law of the form $A^n \times I = C$, where n is a function of spot size. The value of n can be seen to vary something like the function shown in Fig. 8-6. The smooth curve drawn through the three well-established points (i.e., $n = 1$, $\frac{1}{2}$, 0) is not intended to be prescriptive; I know of no research that has empirically tracked out the full range of this function, but it does suggest a likely course.

So far I have only considered the summative effects involved in areal interactions. Some new evidence (Martinez, Sturr, and Schmalbach, 1977) suggests, however, that there may also be an inhibitory interaction. If stimuli whose onset and offset are not abrupt, but rather gradual as shown in Figure 8-7, are used, then data are obtained that can only be explained in terms of some inhibitory interaction among the neural units within the area subtended by the stimulus.

A somewhat surprising and yet very exciting finding that gives a deeper insight into the nature of the spatial summative process has been reported by Barbara Sakitt (1971). The classic notion of spatial summation, as I have noted, is analogous to the classic, but now disputed, idea of temporal summation; namely, that it did not matter how the physical energy was distributed in the spatial area in which summation was occurring. One could pile up all of the incident quanta at any one point or distribute them equally over Ricco's area, according to the prediction of Ricco's law, without differential effect. The spatial pooling produced by the neural convergence processes was assumed to be such that the absolute threshold would be determined strictly by the integral of the energy falling within the critical area. All microstructural information concerning the spatial distributions of the energy would, therefore, be lost according to this point of view. However, in another thoughtful experiment, Sakitt has shown that the spatial configuration of the stimuli within Ricco's area does, in fact, matter. She reports that there is some information retained concerning the spatial arrangement of the stimuli within Ricco's area, just as there was some information retained about the temporal pattern within the critical duration if one probed deeply enough with the appropriate tasks.

Sakitt placed her stimuli within a 20 min (of visual angle) square region about 7 deg from the fovea. She was, therefore, operating within a retinal region and with a stimulus size for which spatial summation should be well represented by the simplest version of the spatial summation rule—Ricco's law. However, following up on some earlier suggestions (Bouman & Van den Brink, 1952; Oliva & Aquilar, 1956), Sakitt did not use a circular spot of homogenous illumination to test for spatial summation but used instead a pair of small discrete spots

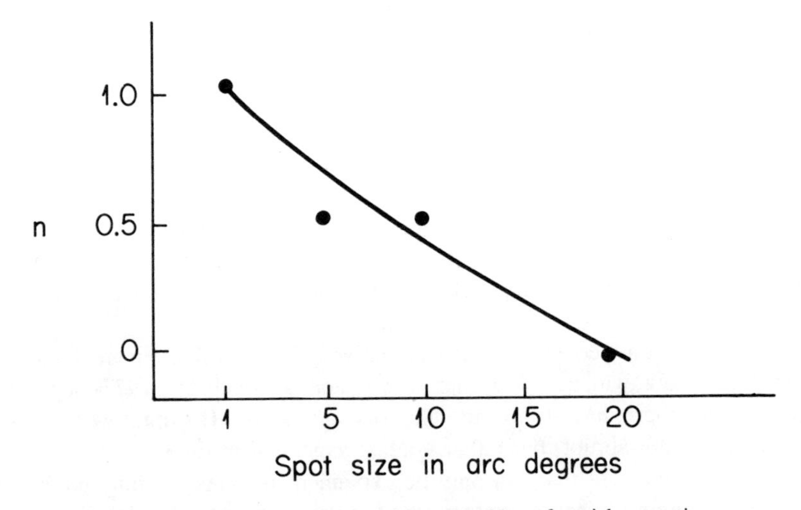

FIG. 8.6. The size of the exponent of the general law of spatial summation as a function of the size of the stimulus.

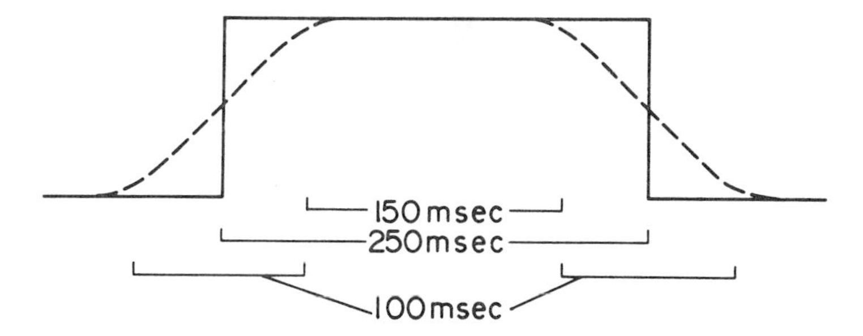

FIG. 8.7. The temporal shape of the stimuli used by Martinez and his colleagues to demonstrate inhibitory spatial interaction in vision. (From Martinez, Sturr, and Schmalbach, © 1977, with the permission of Pergamon Press.)

that were placed at several different loci within the Ricco area for that region of the retina. Figure 8-8, for example, shows the shape of several stimuli and the threshold luminances that were measured for each of these spatial configurations. Quite contrary to the classical idea of a strict spatial summation, actual physical contiguity of the separate small squares (each of which was only 3.4 min of visual angle on a side) was required for the subject to display the straightforward kind of spatial summation implied by the classic version of Ricco's law. When two spots were not touching, then the threshold was considerably elevated even though the total amount of energy was the same and the two separate spots were well within Ricco's area. This finding means that the stimulus energy was not being simply summated in the way that seemed to occur when the stimulus was a continuous oval or circular spot.

Sakitt extended her experimental design from one that utilized a pair of stimulus squares to one that involved many (up to 25) small squares. She then compared the absolute threshold of this multiple array with that of a single stimulus in which an equivalent amount of photic energy was concentrated into a contiguous area. Once again, the thresholds for the array were higher than for the single spot, indicating something less than perfect spatial summation when the array was used as the stimulus.

The implications of these experiments to any neural theory of spatial summation based on simple convergence are profound. Sakitt argues that her findings indicate that spatial summation cannot simply be the reflection of a convergent interaction in which the collective response of some hypothetical cell to all stimuli falling in its receptive field signal the total number of absorbed quanta. These data say, at the very least, that the configuration of the stimulus is important and this fact definitely means that there is information preserved about the spatial pattern of the stimulus in a way that is contrary to the most simple interpretation of Ricco's law. Ricco's law, therefore, must be considered only as a first approximation, subject to further secondary pertubations by other, more subtle forms of retinal or higher interaction.

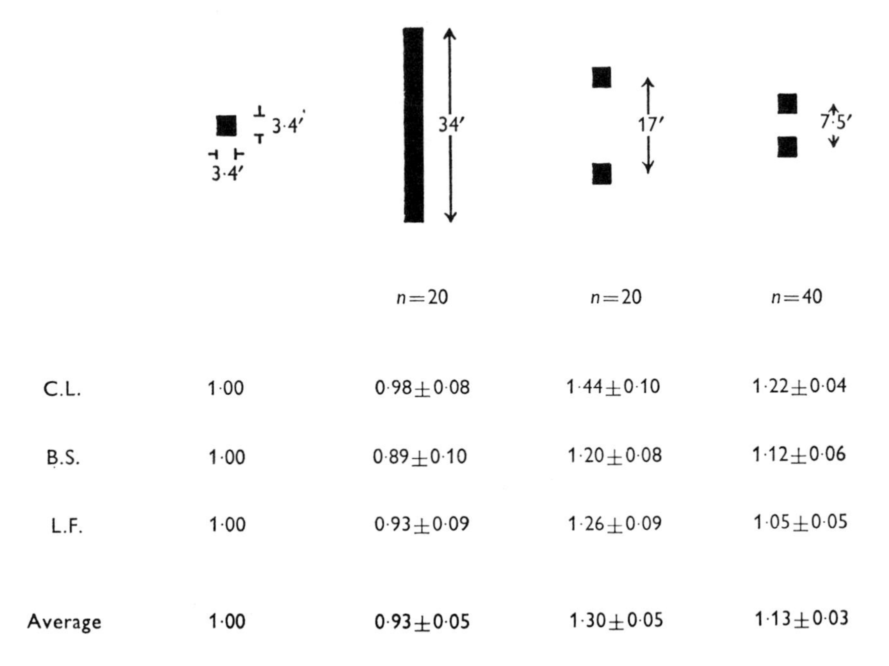

		$n=20$	$n=20$	$n=40$
C.L.	1·00	0·98±0·08	1·44±0·10	1·22±0·04
B.S.	1·00	0·89±0·10	1·20±0·08	1·12±0·06
L.F.	1·00	0·93±0·09	1·26±0·09	1·05±0·05
Average	1·00	0·93±0·05	1·30±0·05	1·13±0·03

FIG. 8.8. The stimuli used in Sakitt's experiment and the resulting absolute thresholds for three observers. (From Sakitt, © 1971, with the permission of the *Journal of Physiology*.)

It would neatly tie up this discussion if we could turn to some analogous physiological experiments and show that the response to two small spots was less than the response to a single spot of equal overall luminance. Unfortunately the physiological data are in total disagreement with the psychological findings. Easter (1968) has shown in the goldfish and Grüsser (1971) has shown in the cat that the neural response to two spots is actually greater than the response to a single spot of equal total energy. This is another one of those distressing and disappointing findings for perceptual psychobiology. Nevertheless, both sets of data—the physiological as well as the psychophysical—speak to the fact that spatial summation is a far more complicated process than is embodied in the simple expression of a pattern-independent spatial summation. Obviously, there are nonlinear interactions in the neural network that complicate any such pure energy-integration model. This is not to say, however, that the existing spatial summation is not mainly the result of convergent mechanisms. The psychophysical literature contains ample evidence of some degree of summation, and it seems closely linked to degree of neural convergence. The conclusion to which we must come, however, is that such spatial summations can be incomplete and heavily modulated by other processes that are sensitive to the geometry of the stimulus.

3. Visual Acuity

I have already introduced and discussed several of the pertinent processes that regulate visual acuity—the ability to resolve closely spaced stimuli—in Chapter 6. I noted that there are several levels of critical processes that obviously must interact to determine the thresholds of spatial resolvability that are measured with psychophysical methods. Acuity probably is influenced by Level 0 processes, including the optical aberrations of the eye; Level 1 processes, including the size and spacing of the receptors; Level 2 processes, including the pooling and convergence of stimulus signals; and probably even very central Level 5 effects that control the criterion level involved in decision making. All of these processes must contribute to the collective resolvability measured under various experimental conditions. In this section I concentrate on those aspects of the acuity problem that seem to be due to Level 2 spatial interaction processes. These are the processes that typically involve the neural interaction of different portions of the retinal projection of the stimulus pattern.

One does not have to look deeply into the literature to appreciate that spatial interactions in the visual pathways are an absolutely obligatory part of any theory of acuity. The typical cross-sectional diameter of a human rod or cone is about 12 sec of visual angle. The sampling theorem tells us that such a retina should therefore be able to resolve about a 24 sec gap between adjacent stimuli if all of the other optical properties of the eyes are perfect and if the observer is very close to ideal in all other regards. In fact, however, it is now well appreciated that the acuity of the human eye can be as good as 2 or 3 sec of visual angle under optimum conditions.[3]

Acuity that is finer than the calculated capability of the photoreceptor mosaic has been termed *hyperacuity* by Gerald Westheimer of the University of California at Berkeley. Hyperacuity is a category that includes as a subset, the classic observations that were carried out on a two-bar stimulus such as that shown in Fig. 8-9A. The minimum misalignment that can be detected in the pair of such stimuli is referred to as the vernier acuity threshold of the subject. Even the earliest measurements of the phenomenon by Wulfing (1892) indicated that vernier acuity was surprisingly good. Subsequently Baker and Bryan (1912) reported acuity thresholds for this type of stimulus as small as 4 sec of visual angle, and acuity thresholds as low as 2 sec have more recently been reported (Berry 1948). Clearly this is at least 12 times as small as would be allowed by a simple retinal mosaic calculation.

---

[3]In fact, as we later see, the nature of these interactions may not only be more complex than those heretofore considered but may also be processed at such a high level that it may be necessary to classify this exceptionally precise acuity as a result of even higher-level processes than the ones described in this chapter. I include the following material on hyperacuity at this point, therefore, with some uncertainty.

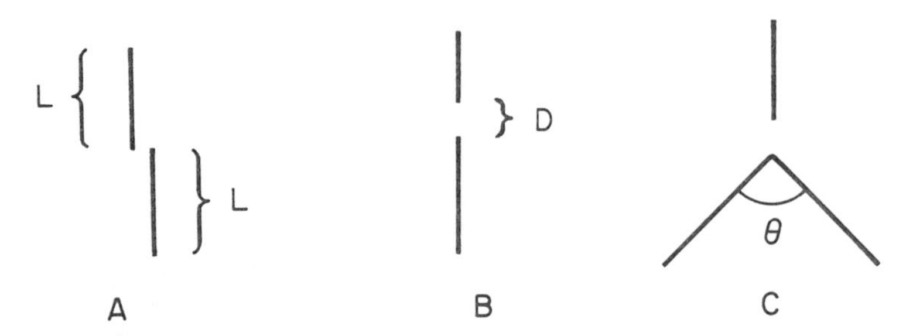

FIG. 8.9. The stimulus configurations used in the Westheimer and McKee (1977b) experiment. These figures define the length (L), and distance (D), and the angle (θ) used in these experiments.

The traditional explanation of this hyperacuity is attributed to Hering (1899). He formulated a theory that asserted that vernier hyperacuity was due to a retinal "averaging process." This hypothetical averaging process, of course, is just another way of saying that the various neurons of the retina must be interacting to produce a response sensitivity that exceeds the capacity of the individual elements. Another traditional explanation has been that the shape of the test object was also very important in determining visual acuity. This assertion is supported by the differences in the observed values of acuity measured with the Landolt C and a grating respectively by S. Shlaer (1937) and by Wilcox's (1932) comparison of acuity measured with white-on-black, and black-on-white, bars, respectively. The conclusion towards which we are impelled by these data is that there must be some kind of neural interactive effect like those now known to mediate spatial summation that is also sensitive to the organization or geometry of the stimulus.

In recent years, however, Hering's theory has been strongly challenged by some new findings. For example, Ludvigh (1953) showed that the same degree of precision observed in the vernier test shown in Fig. 8-9A could be achieved if the subject was asked simply to detect a misaligned center dot in a row of three dots, rather than a pair of continuous lines. Such a configuration of dots should not allow any averaging of the kind proposed by Hering. More recently, Westheimer and McKee (1977b) repeated and extended this paradigm for several different spatial configurations and found that:

1. For stimuli longer than about 5 min of visual angle, there was in fact very little advantage gained simply as a function of line length (L) in a vernier acuity task (Fig. 8-9A).

2. The distance (D) between the ends of the two lines in a vernier task did not monotonically affect the acuity threshold. The threshold lateral separation first decreased and then increased with increasing vertical separation. (Fig. 8-9B).

3. The angle (ϕ) of a chevron-shaped stimulus did not affect the vernier alignment of a vertical line with the apex of the chevron (Fig. 8-9C).

4. And finally, there was virtually no effect on acuity measures when the light–dark pattern configuration varied as greatly as shown in Fig. 8-10.

The implications of all of these studies is that the configuration of the stimulus actually plays only a minor and local role in the vernier acuity task. Thus, extended spatial averaging is an unlikely hypothesis to explain this form of hyperacuity.

However the facts that the simple line length is not a significant factor in determining vernier acuity and, therefore, that Hering's original hypothesis about

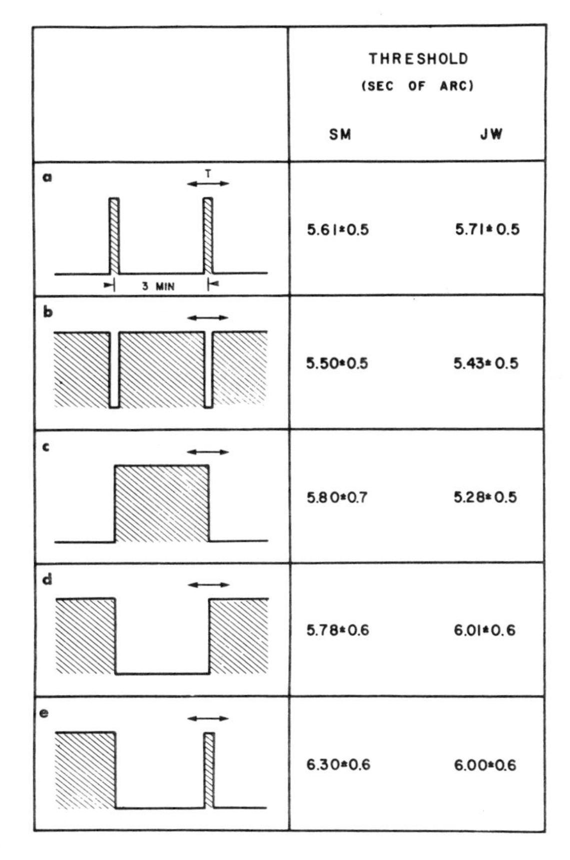

FIG. 8.10. The stimulus configurations used in the other portions of the Westheimer and McKee (1977b) experiment. The threshold spacing for various conditions of contrast and contour type are also presented. (From Westheimer and McKee, © 1977b, with the permission of Pergamon Press.)

spatial averaging leaves much unexplained should not be misinterpreted to mean that there is no interactive processing of any kind going on in this visual process. Clearly, for closely spaced retinal images (less than 5 min of visual angle), the Hering type averaging is working—but, equally clearly, it is a very short-range process. Furthermore, in another paper, Westheimer and McKee (1977a) showed that although there was not any substantial averaging along the length of the venier lines, there did appear to be a comparable statistical interaction of a system of parallel lines across the *width* of the pattern as shown in Fig. 8-11. Such an interaction indicates some form of neural integration even though it may not be conceptually identical to the kind of linear statistical averaging proposed so many years ago by Hering.

Westheimer has recently begun to interpret these findings and comparable dichoptic studies to mean that this averaging is actually carried out in the neural network of the central rather than the peripheral nervous system. Westheimer and McKee (1975) have also shown the phenomena of both vernier and stereoscopic hyperacuity to be remarkably insensitive to the degree of movement-induced blur of the retinal image. A recent paper from their laboratory (McKee and Westheimer, 1978) has also reported that the precision of hyperacuity improves with practice. It is interesting to speculate that the hyperacuity findings may, therefore, not actually reflect Level 2 processes, but rather may be more comparable to the quasi-statistical judgments observed at Level 3 where texture appears to be analyzed (see p. 761).

Westheimer and McKee's acuity measurements were almost exclusively carried out at the foveal fixation point. However, ordinary acuity, as opposed to hyperacuity, is known to vary as a function of the retinal location on which the image falls. Psychophysical data describing the relationship between acuity and retinal locus are shown in Fig. 8-12 for the whole retina and in Fig. 8-13 for the circumfoveal region.

A graphic picture of the decline in visual acuity as one projects a stimulus farther and farther onto the periphery has been presented by Anstis (1974). He has developed an acuity chart (see Fig. 8-14) composed of alphabetic characters that exhibit a constant level of identifiability even though they fall on retinal regions of varying acuity. The variation in size necessary for equal identification of the characters is a good measure of the varying acuity of the visual system at different loci.

The decline in acuity with increasingly peripheral localization, however, could result from the interaction of a number of different processes at several different levels of perceptual processing. Without doubt, acuity does partially depend (Green D., 1970) upon aberrations produced by the optics of the eye. But D. Green has also shown that such optical aberrations limit visual resolution only out to about 5° of visual angle from the fovea, as shown in Fig. 8-15. Beyond that limit the image quality determined by the optics of the eye has little effect—the

FIG. 8.11. Diagram of the stimulus configuration used in the Westheimer and McKee experiment. (From Westheimer and McKee, © 1977a, with the permission of Pergamon Press.)

image quality is better than the other receptor and neural network factors that degrade acuity. Thus it seems most likely that the phenomena of the decline in acuity with increasing eccentricity is closely related to the degree of convergence (or receptive field size) at the various retinal loci in much the same way as is spatial summation.

Some of the major processes that contribute to the determination of visual acuity have already been considered. Level 0 optical mechanisms were discussed in Chapter 5; Level 1 receptor mechanisms were discussed in Chapter 6; and interactive processes related to Level 2, and possibly Level 3 processes, have been considered here. It would be useful to summarize now what is currently known about the stimulus factors that influence acuity. These psychophysically measured relationships between the dimensions of the stimulus and visual acuity represent the collective result of critical processes that occur at all relevant levels of processing. Because there is an enormous body of older information concerning the various phenomena of visual acuity, I have used a number of secondary sources (including Graham, 1965a; Jameson & Hurvich, 1972; Stevens, 1951a) in compiling the list that is presented here as well as some newer literature that

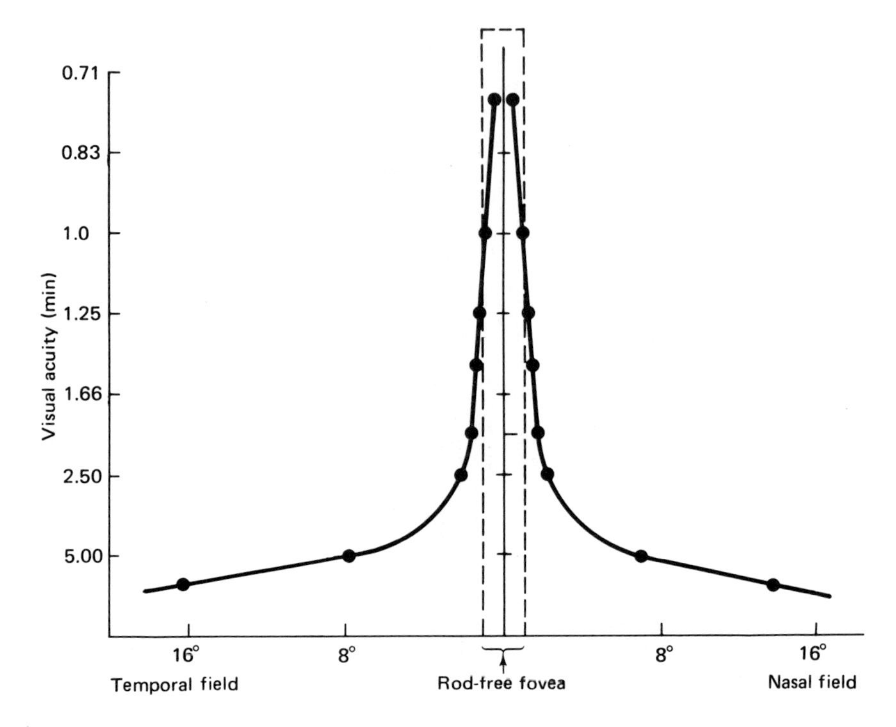

FIG. 8.12. Visual acuity plotted as a function of visual angle. Note that away from the central 4-deg region, there is little further decline in acuity out to 16 deg of visual angle. (From Uttal, 1973, redrawn from Alpern, 1969.)

was not available to these earlier reviewers. This brief summary attempts to bring all of this important perceptual material together without swamping the reader with more detail than is needed in the present context. In this listing I have also indicated, where appropriate, the processing level to which I feel each of these phenomena most plausibly should be attributed:

1. In general the more luminous the stimulus the better the acuity. This is probably associated with the signal to noise considerations discussed in Chapter 6 (Hecht, 1934; Hecht, Hendley, Frank, & Haig, 1946; Hecht & Mintz, 1939). (Level 1)

2. Although many early workers thought that the shape of the acuity target was a strong determinant of acuity (e.g., Shlaer, S., 1937; Wilcox, 1932), more recent work (e.g., Westheimer & McKee, 1977a) has clearly demonstrated that shape matters in an acuity task only over a very small region of interaction. (Levels 2 and 3)

3. The longer the exposure duration, the better the acuity (Niven & Brown, 1944). (Level 1)

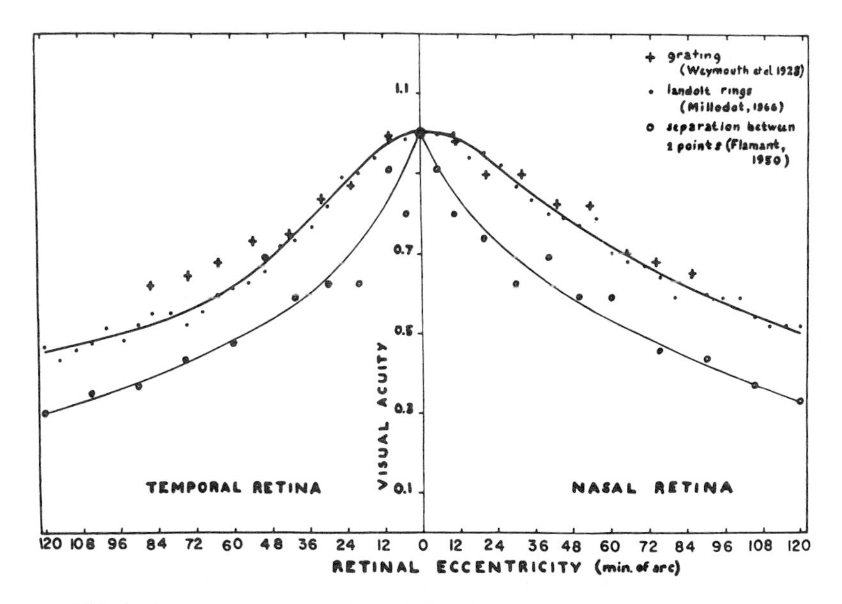

FIG. 8.13. A more microscopic (than Fig. 8.12) look at visual acuity in the region of the fovea. (From Millodot, © 1972, with the permission of the British Optical Association.)

FIG. 8.14. A novel way to demonstrate the varying acuity of the retina. Each letter is printed at the relative threshold size for the region of the retina upon which it is projected given that the observer is fixating the center of this chart. (From Anstis, © 1974, with the permission of Pergamon Press.)

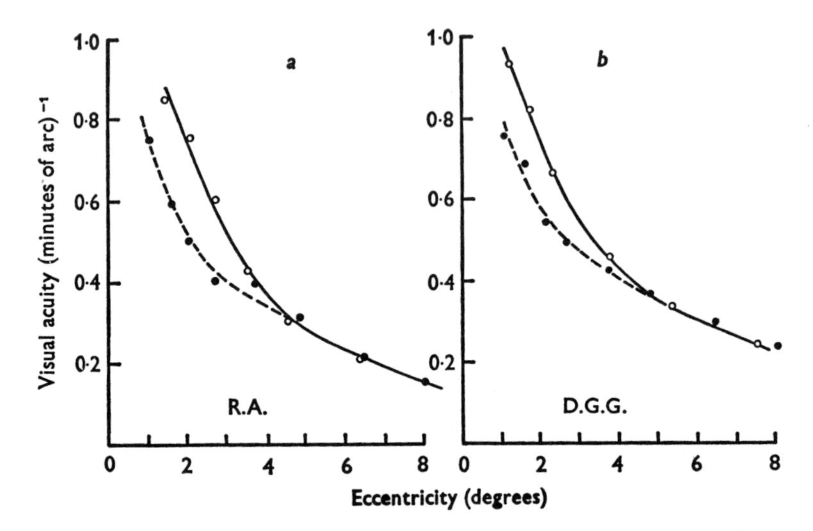

FIG. 8.15. In this experiment Green demonstrates for two observers that the optical properties of the visual system limit acuity only out to about 5 deg retinal eccentricity. Beyond that eccentricity neural convergence is a more influential factor on the threshold of acuity. Open circles are for interference fringes projected with a laser device directly on the retina. Filled circles are for an image projected through the optics of the eye. (From Green, © 1970, with the permission of the *Journal of Physiology*.)

4. Acuity declines monotonically the farther the stimulus is from the fovea (Jones & Higgins, 1947; Kitterle, Kaye, & Samuels, in press; Mandlebaum & Sloan, 1947; Sloan, 1968). (Level 2) (See Figs. 8-12 and 8-13 also.)

5. The orientation of the lines used to test acuity can strongly affect the acuity measure. In general it has been observed that horizontal and vertical orientations of the vernier test lines, for example, produce better acuity than when the lines are oblique (Campbell, Kulikowski, & Levinson, 1966; French, 1920; Leibowitz, 1953; & Millodot, 1972; Nachmias, 1960; Ogilvie & Taylor, 1958; Taylor, M., 1963). However it has recently been shown that this decline in acuity with oblique orientation only occurs within about 12° of the fovea and can be simulated by blurring the image of the stimulus (Berkley, Kitterle, & Watkins, 1975). I suspect that this ''oblique effect'' is actually the result of a very high level process, perhaps even at Level 5. It has been conclusively shown with a laser light source that produces a retinal image that is completely insensitive to optical aberrations that the dependence on orientation is not a Level 0 process (Mitchell, Freeman, & Westheimer, 1967).

6. The wavelength of the stimulating light has also been shown to have a substantial effect on acuity thresholds. Brindley (1954), using Stiles' selective adaptation techniques to isolate the long-, medium-, and short-wavelength-sensitive mechanisms, respectively, found that acuity was substantially worse

when the eye was selectively adapted to be more sensitive to the short than to the medium or long wavelengths. This was so in spite of the fact that a priori optical considerations suggest that shorter wavelengths should be expected to allow better resolution than longer ones. Obviously, the analogy to optical and microscopic resolution fails here because the wavelength of the light is not the critical factor; it is less important than the spacing and convergent interactions among the receptors. Indeed, Brindley suggests that this chromatic effect could be accounted for by the fact that the short-wavelength-sensitive mechanisms are more highly convergent than are the other two. (Level 2)

7. Kitterle, Kaye, and Samuels (in press) have shown that the superior retina has slightly better acuity than the inferior retina when stimuli are placed at the same eccentricity from the fovea. (Level unknown but possibly Level 5.)

8. Visual acuity is independent of the dynamic movement of the stimulus within broad limits (Westheimer & McKee, 1975). Those workers report that the acuity threshold is not affected by velocities up to 4 deg per sec. (Level uncertain)

9. At high spatial frequencies there obviously must be a limit on acuity defined by the diffraction effects and refractive properties of the eye to the extent that they are influenced by such factors as the pupil size and the accommodative status of the eye. The pupil size, in particular, is well known to be inversely correlated with visual acuity. The larger the pupil, the lower the spatial acuity down to about 2.4 mm, a fact known for 60 years (Cobb, 1915) and repeatedly replicated. The effect, of course, is mediated by the degradation in the quality of the retina image because of the increase in the blur circle with increasing pupil size. The reversal of the relationship between blur and pupil size below 2.4 mm is due to diffraction-induced blur (see Chapter 5). (Level 0)

10. Finally, I should also note the very large number of studies in which threshold modulation contrast is used as a dependent variable for acuity-type tests involving the detection of gratings. Obviously, with all other factors held equal, acuity would also vary with contrast. Many studies of this kind are considered in subsequent chapters.

This tenth point also reminds us that the Spatial Modulation Transfer Function (*SMTF*), discussed earlier in Chapter 5, is as equally satisfactory a means of measuring the acuity of the visual system as the Landolt C. Contrast thresholds of various spatial frequencies must be informationally equivalent to the resolvability threshold. Thus the *SMTF*, like the simpler acuity measures that I have concentrated on in this section, is affected by many levels of processing and would be sensitive in a comparable way to each of these same stimulus dimensions.

The "resonant" peak in the *SMTF* (shown in Fig. 5-37) represents, therefore, a serious challenge to theoreticians of acuity. Why should the eye be more sensitive to the middle range of spatial frequencies than to the long or short spatial wavelengths? The answer to this important question may lie in the limits of the spread of the inhibitory interactions tending to sharpen contours. Higher spatial frequencies would, of course, require proportionately greater contrast to produce a threshold discrimination because of the many factors which tend to disperse the image and to blur the neural representation of signals that are too closely spaced. Lower spatial frequencies may require greater contrast because of the lack of contrast intensification over long distances. Thus, at some intermediate value the visual system would be optimally sensitive.

4. Color Blindness in the Normal Eye

In discussing the contribution of the three photochemicals in the cones to the initial analysis underlying normal trichromatic perception in Chapter 6, I concentrated on the effects as they were measured near the fovea. Extrafoveal color vision, because of the differing distributions and interconnections of the four types of photoreceptors, might be expected to be considerably different. And in fact there is a substantial change in the psychophysics of trichromatic color addition as one moves the test region across the retina. For example, it has been known for almost a century (König & Köttgen, 1894) that the central fovea appears to be tritanopic. The rest of the fovea (and regions out to about 25 deg away from the fovea) are normally trichromatic. Moreland and Cruz (1959), however, found that in a region beyond 25 deg from the fovea chromatic stimulus matching data appeared to behave very much as if color vision were once again being mediated by a dichromatic system. At even greater visual angles, these investigators found such abnormal color-addition data that at those most eccentric positions on the retina color vision appeared to be best described as being functionally monochromatic.

The dichromacy, or more specifically, tritanopia of the central fovea is, in general, explained by the distribution of the receptors. Marc and Sperling's (1977) data shown in Fig. 3-15 indicates that there is a downturn in the number of short-wavelength-sensitive cones as one approaches the central fovea of the primate eye. Thus, central foveal tritanopia seems likely to be the phenomenal result of a Level 1 process—the simple absence of the third kind of cone.

However it also seems clear that the distribution of the cones is insufficient to account for the variation from trichromaticity at more peripheral retinal loci. The most important contribution of Marc and Sperling's study is to show that the differences in the *proportions* of the three cone types at peripheral loci are relatively small even though the overall cone density progressively declines up to about 40 deg of visual angle away from the fovea. There is, therefore, obviously a substantial discrepancy between these anatomical data of photoreceptor distribution and the psychophysically measured dichromacy and monochromacy of the more peripheral portions of the retina.

There is, of course, another possible theoretical explanation of the anomalous color vision of the peripheral retina based on Level 2 processes rather than on a malproportioned receptor distribution—a Level 1 process. The reader may recall that earlier in Chapter 6 I indicated that the effects of a missing class of photoreceptor could be mimicked perfectly if the neural network underneath the receptors was arranged such that the outputs of two or more of the receptor types were pooled by spatial convergence into a single neural communication channel. Thus, for example, if both the long- and medium-wavelength sensitive receptors of the peripheral retina fed their output signals into the same bipolar cells, the differentially encoded neural code produced as a result of the specific spectral absorption sensitivities of these two receptors would be lost. In other words, the bipolar neurons in this hypothetical network would encode the information representing long-wavelength and short-wavelength lights indiscriminately, and the neural codes for their discrimination—the *relative* amounts of activity in each channel that had been available at the receptor level—would be totally lost. Functionally this convergent situation would result in exactly the same outcome that the absence of one or the other of the two receptors would produce.

In addition to the neuroanatomic experiments of Marc and Sperling, which indicated the presence of all three types of photoreceptors everywhere in the retina, a relevant psychophysical experiment that speaks to this problem has been carried out by Wooten and Wald (1973). These workers, using the Stiles' two-color incremental threshold procedure to measure the spectral sensitivities in the various regions of the retina, made measurements of the threshold energy as a function of stimlus wavelength following adaptation with various colored lights. Following Stiles, they assumed that adaptation with middle-wavelength light selectively bleached the receptors that are particularly sensitive to middle and long wavelengths, and thus the resulting short-wavelength end of the luminosity curve should reflect more of the properties of the short-wavelength-sensitive photoreceptor wherever they were present. Combined long- and short-wavelength (''purple'') adaptation, on the other hand, should result in the medium-wavelength-sensitive receptor being more influential in determining the response, and short wavelength adaptation should emphasize the contribution of the long-wavelength-sensitive receptor.

Figure 8-16 displays Wooten and Wald's results for the three different adaptation conditions as a function of retinal location. The findings are clear; the spectral sensitivity curves for all three types of cone mechanisms are virtually unchanged in shape across the entire retina even though they vary somewhat in their respective individual magnitudes. The implication of this study is the same as that of Marc and Sperling's experiment; though reduced in number, all three types of cone are probably present across the entire retina. The loss of color discriminability (varying from a trichromatic fovea to a dichromatic response pattern at the middle visual angles to a monochromatic pattern in the far periphery) must therefore be due to a progressive pooling (i.e., convergence) of the outputs of the three photoreceptors rather than to their absence.

Such a neural pooling (which is clearly a Level 2 process in terms of the taxonomy I have proposed in this book) is not at all surprising in the peripheral retina if one considers the logic of the anatomy. Although there are probably as

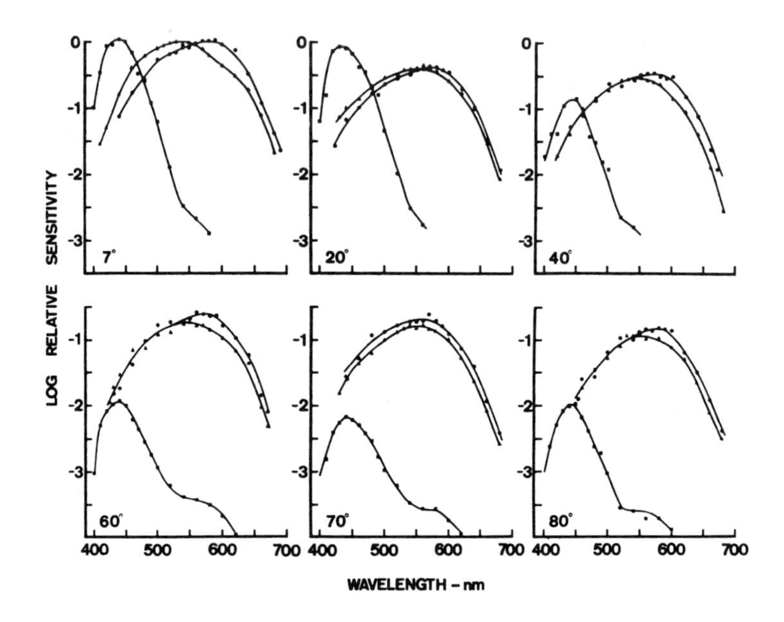

FIG. 8.16. Spectral sensitivities of the three classes of photoreceptors at various locations on the retina. Little difference can be observed in the shape of the curves across the entire retina, even though there is some difference in absolute values. (From Wooten and Wald, © 1973, with the permission of Rockefeller University Press.)

many ganglion cells as there are photoreceptors in the fovea, the ratio becomes progressively disproportionate as one moves to the periphery where there may be as many as 50 receptors for every ganglion cell (Van Buren, 1963). Obviously both the possibility and the reality of convergent information pooling in the peripheral retinal regions are very much higher than in the fovea, and most current theorists believe this convergence, rather than the presence or absence of the photochemicals themselves, largely accounts for dichromatism and monochromatism in the peripheral retinal.

C. THE PERCEPTUAL IMPACT OF LATERAL INHIBITORY INTERACTION: MASKING OF THE THIRD KIND

1. A Comment

In the previous section I considered some of the perceptual phenomena that seem to be best understood in terms of convergent excitatory summation of the receptor level signals elicited by the pattern of input stimuli onto higher-order neurons.

In this section I am considering some perceptual phenomena that appear to be based upon inhibitory rather than excitatory interactions. These theories of inhibitory interaction represent some of the best-grounded neuroreductionistic models in perceptual psychobiology. Among the phenomena covered in this section are the contour intensification phenomena known as Mach bands and some close homologs involving inhibitory interactions between and within stimulus spots of various sizes. Even though these phenomena are observed in human perception, the explanations invoked to explain them are, in large part, based upon work done on invertebrates, particularly the horseshoe crab—*Limulus polyphemus*—by H. Keefer Hartline, Floyd Ratliff, and their colleagues (Hartline & Ratliff, 1957, 1958; Hartline, Wagner, & Ratliff, 1956; Ratliff & Hartline, 1959. See Ratliff, 1965, for a summary review).

The widely accepted current model asserts that simple lateral inhibitory interactions exist in the vertebrate nervous system that are comparable to those found in the compound eye of this arachnid. Although the initial neurophysiological data confirming this model came mainly from invertebrates, in fact, most of the basic concepts had been suggested many years earlier by Ernst Mach (Mach, 1865, 1866a and 1866b) on the basis of human psychophysical findings. At present there is some neurophysiological evidence that inhibitory neural mechanisms capable of mediating contour enhancement exist in the vertebrate retina. Enroth-Cugel and Robson (1966), for example, have demonstrated a peaking of response rate in a ganglion cell of the cat retina when a step illumination was moved across it, comparable to an effect observed in the invertebrate compound eye by Ratliff and Hartline (1959). The whole problem has become exceedingly interwoven with the problem of receptive field structure, however, and much of the evidence for inhibitory interaction in the retina is couched in those terms. For our present purposes, it is sufficient to note only that there is virtually universal acceptance of the idea that such inhibitory interactions exist in the most peripheral portions of the vertebrate visual system as well as the invertebrate.

There is also considerable psychophysical evidence that the processes that lead to the Mach bands and related phenomena, in fact, are quite peripheral (see my discussion in Chapter 9). This evidence is usually obtained by comparing the results of dichoptic and monocular stimulus presentations. The repeatedly demonstrated absence of this kind of interaction between dichoptically presented stimuli is one of the most compelling arguments that the peripheral interactive processes are, at least, sufficient, if not necessary, to account for many of the phenomena I shall consider in this section.

However these findings should not be interpreted to mean that inhibitory interactions are exclusively peripheral and occur only in the inner and outer plexiform layers. Some evidence also exists indicating that central lateral inhibitory mechanisms are operative in some instances. One study seeking inhibitory neural interactions that might be associated with certain comparable psychophysical phenomena (Gardner & Spencer's, 1972a and 1972b studies of "funneling") actually found those neural interactions to be present only in the central nervous system and not in the peripheral nervous system. Although the analogy between this study and the visual system is somewhat farfetched (their study was done on the somatosensory system in which there are no synaptic interconnections that would allow lateral interactions to occur in the periphery), Gardner and Spencer's work does serve as an existence proof that lateral inhibitory interactions can occur centrally as well as peripherally.

Thus I must remind the reader that it is not my intention to assert that all Level 2 inhibitorily interactive processes are to be found only in the peripheral nervous system. Interactions with the same functional effect can, and probably do, occur in the central nervous system. Level 2 processes, therefore, must be conceived of as incorporating interactions among neurons at several anatomic levels. What this level of critical processing does emphasize is one kind of isomorphic neural interaction that may, in fact, be going on redundantly at many anatomic levels of the nervous system.

2. The Mechanisms

I have already briefly introduced the neurophysiological details of inhibitory interaction in Chapter 3 of this book and in the introduction to this chapter. I have even more extensively reviewed the development of this idea from Mach to Hartline in my earlier work (Uttal, 1973, pp. 369–400), and it is not necessary to recapitulate all of that story here. To understand the following material one should be aware of Mach's conceptualization of the problem and the history of Hartline and his collaborator's discovery of the reciprocal lateral inhibitory process in the horseshoe crab eye. One should also be aware of the fact that functionally identical lateral interactions can exist between the mutually antagonistic portions of the center-surround receptive fields of neurons in the vertebrate retina as between ommatidia in the horseshoe crab eye and should also appreciate some of the early mathematical theories that described the virtually linear interactions that occurred within the invertebrate preparation. The reader is specifically directed to Ratliff's (1965) elegant study of inhibitory neural interactions, and to von Békésy's (1967) highly integrative cross-modality analysis of the problem of sensory inhibition for further details.

The basic idea of reciprocal lateral inhibitory interaction and a discussion of the contemporary mathematical models of this process are exceedingly well presented in Graham and Ratliff (1974). To summarize the current state of theory in this well-modeled field of neurophysiology, I now briefly review the current formal models of the process as they have been presented by them. Graham and Ratliff note that the original model (Hartline & Ratliff, 1957) of the stable mutual inhibitory interaction occurring between two neurons (see Fig. 8-17) after all of the initial transients have died down can be expressed by the following pair of simultaneous equations:

$$R_1 = E_1 - K_{1,2}(R_2 - R^0_{1,2}) \tag{8-4}$$

and

$$R_2 = E_2 - K_{2,1}(R_1 - R^0_{2,1}) \tag{8-5}$$

where R_1 and R_2 are the responses of neurons 1 and 2, respectively; E_1 and E_2 are the magnitudes of the excitatory stimuli falling on these receptors; $R^0_{1,2}$ and $R^0_{2,1}$ are the thresholds of the inhibitory interaction of neuron 1 on neuron 2 and vice versa; and $K_{1,2}$ and $K_{2,1}$ are indices of interaction between the two cells. It is also most important to keep in mind that these two indices of interaction are themselves highly dependent on the distance between the two interacting cells.

The fact that these coefficients are distance-dependent and that the interactions are all negative in this case describes a particular form of lateral inhibitory interaction—the kind that is observed in the *Limulus* eye and that has become a convenient, though probably too simple, model of contour enhancement in human psychophysics. It is, however, not the only possible pattern of reciprocal lateral interaction that can approximate the data. Ratliff (1965) has tabulated

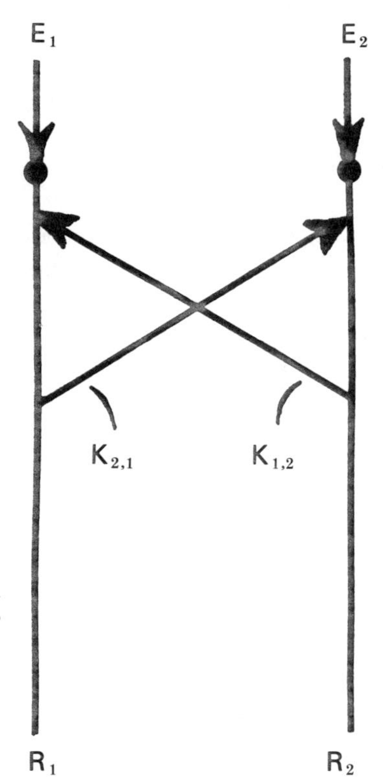

FIG. 8.17. A schematic of lateral inhibitory interactions between two neurons showing their respective excitation strengths (E), their respective response strengths (R), and the coefficient of interaction (K) between the two cells. (Redrawn from Graham and Ratliff, 1974.)

most of the published theories of such interactions proposed up to that time. Figure 8-18 is his summary of the various patterns of lateral interaction and the mathematical formula describing each of them.

For the *Limulus*, and to a first approximation, for the human, much of the data on lateral interaction has been summarized by Ratliff in the following equation. This equation describes the combined effect of all effectively inhibitory neurons on a single "pth" one.

$$R_p = E_p - \sum_{j=1}^{N} K_{p,j}(R_j - R^0_{p,j}) \qquad (8\text{-}6)$$

This equation defines the response of the pth neuron (R_p) in exactly the same way as do Eq. 8-4 and 8-5 for a pair of neurons, and the various terms have essentially the same meaning.

However this expression of the response of the pth neuron in Eq. 8-6 is, quite incomplete, as are Eq. 8-4 and 8-5. They are valid only for the steady-state condition that obtains after all of the initial transients have settled down. Further progress has been made in describing the more complicated situation occurring during the initial transient period. Those transient responses result from the dynamic properties of the system of interacting neurons when it is perturbed by a sudden illumination. Ratliff, Hartline, and Lange (1966), for example, have proposed that the following expression be used to describe the full course of the response in the horseshoe crab eye, including both the transient and stable states.

$$R_p(t) = E_p(t) - \sum_{j=1}^{N} K_{p,j}[R_j(t - T_{p,j}) - R^0_{p,j}] \qquad (8\text{-}7)$$

where $R_p(t)$ is the response of the pth neuron at time t, $T_{p,j}$ is the time lag of the action of any neuron j on neuron p, and the other terms are as previously indicated.

Graham and Ratliff (1974) have extended this analysis even further to one that models both the spatial and temporal aspects of a response to a sinusoidally modulated light stimulus as follows[4]:

$$R_p(f) = g(f) \cdot I(f) - T_1(f) \sum_{p \neq j} K_{p,j} R_j(f) \qquad (8\text{-}8)$$

where, in their words, "$R_p(f)$ or $R_j(f)$ is the peak-to-trough amplitude of the firing rate of the pth (or the jth) neuron in response to a sinusoidal light stimulus of frequency $f, I(f)$ is the peak-to-trough amplitude of the light stimulating $p, g(f)$ is the transfer function of the excitatory process, $T_1(f)$ is the transfer function of

[4]I have deleted a portion of Graham and Ratliff's formulation that deals with the self-inhibition of the receptor cell. That self-inhibition is not germane to the present discussion. It is more properly considered to be a Level 1 process.

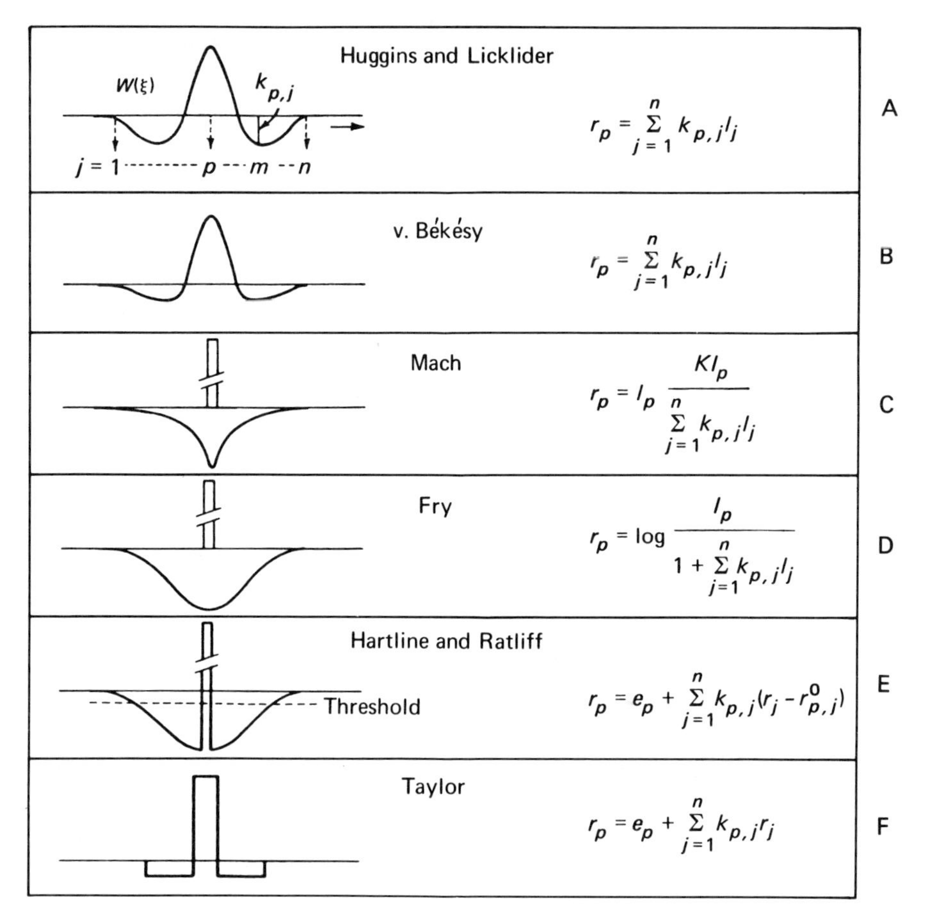

FIG. 8.18. Six alternative models of lateral inhibitory interaction. (From Ratliff, © 1965, with the permission of Holden-Day, Inc.)

the lateral inhibitory process.'' This last equation describes the dynamic response of a receptor of the type found in the *Limulus* eye to a temporally sinusoidal stimulus. If this function were evaluated for a family of sinusoids of varying temporal frequency, then a Temporal Modulation Transfer Function (TMTF) of this system would be produced. Just how extraordinarily well Graham's model works is illustrated in Fig. 8-19. This graph shows both the phase and amplitude of the response of a single *Limulus* receptor as measured in the neurophysiological labratory and predicted by Eq. 8-8.

In the vertebrate eye, of course, the neural interactions are far more complicated and are far less well understood than in *Limulus polyphemus*. However, if one utilizes the concept of the center-surround antagonistic arrangement and assumes certain excitatory and inhibitory functions such as those shown previously in Fig. 8-18A, a mathematical model of even this complex version of a lateral inhibitory visual mechanism can be formulated that is analogous to the simpler one described for the purely inhibitory interaction of the *Limulus* eye. Graham and Ratliff have summarized and reviewed a substantial body of data on the vertebrate retina and postulate the following equation as an approximation to the interactions that can occur between families of on-center, off-surround neurons.

$$R(t, x) = \int\int I(y, \tau)k_c(x - y)l_c(t - \tau)d\tau\, dy + \int\int I(y, \tau)k_s(x - y)l_s(t - \tau)d\tau\, dy \qquad (8\text{-}9)$$

In this equation, Graham and Ratliff tell us that $R(t, x)$ is the dynamic response pattern of the typical neuron at point $x, I(y, \tau)$ is the intensity of the stimulating light at the particular point y and time τ, $k_c(x - y)$ and $k_s(x - y)$ are the spatial weighting functions of the center and surround mechanisms, respectively (as indicated in Fig. 8-18a), and $l_c(t - \tau)$ and $l_s(t - \tau)$ indicate the temporal impulse functions of the response of the center and surround mechanisms to an instantaneous pulse of light, respectively. Although this equation describing the vertebrate visual system is not nearly as well substantiated by neurophysiological findings as is Eq. 8-8 for the invertebrate eye, it does provide at least a preliminary quantitative reference against which to anchor future empirical studies and with which to make at least preliminary computations.

The mathematical model so briefly paraphrased in this section is largely the work of Hartline and Ratliff and their early collaborators, along with extensions proposed by Lange, Ratliff, and Graham in recent years. It not only describes the details of a particular neural information-processing network, but also explicitly assumes that the simple computational processes carried out by that network have direct phenomenal implications. This level of analysis is now generally accepted as the most appropriate one to explain the particular set of perceptual phenomena I consider in this section. Though the mathematics may seem somewhat complicated, in fact it mainly involves only simple arithmetic and the most elementary integral calculus. Indeed, the most important part of these equations, once one has understood the nomenclature, is the minus sign indicating which terms detract from, rather than enhance, the response. A little effort in reading these equations will be amply rapid in terms of a good intuitive appreciation of the nature of these lateral interactions. A much richer discussion and a more detailed view of the relevant neurophysiological data can be found in Ratliff (1965), Jung (1973), or better still, in the source I have depended on here, Graham and Ratliff (1974).

In the following section I consider those phenomena that seem to be best explained by the invocation of neural inhibitory interaction processes such as those modeled here. An important general point to keep in mind throughout this discussion is that, for all theoretical purposes, both the excitatory center and inhibitory surround organization of receptive fields in the vertebrate visual sys-

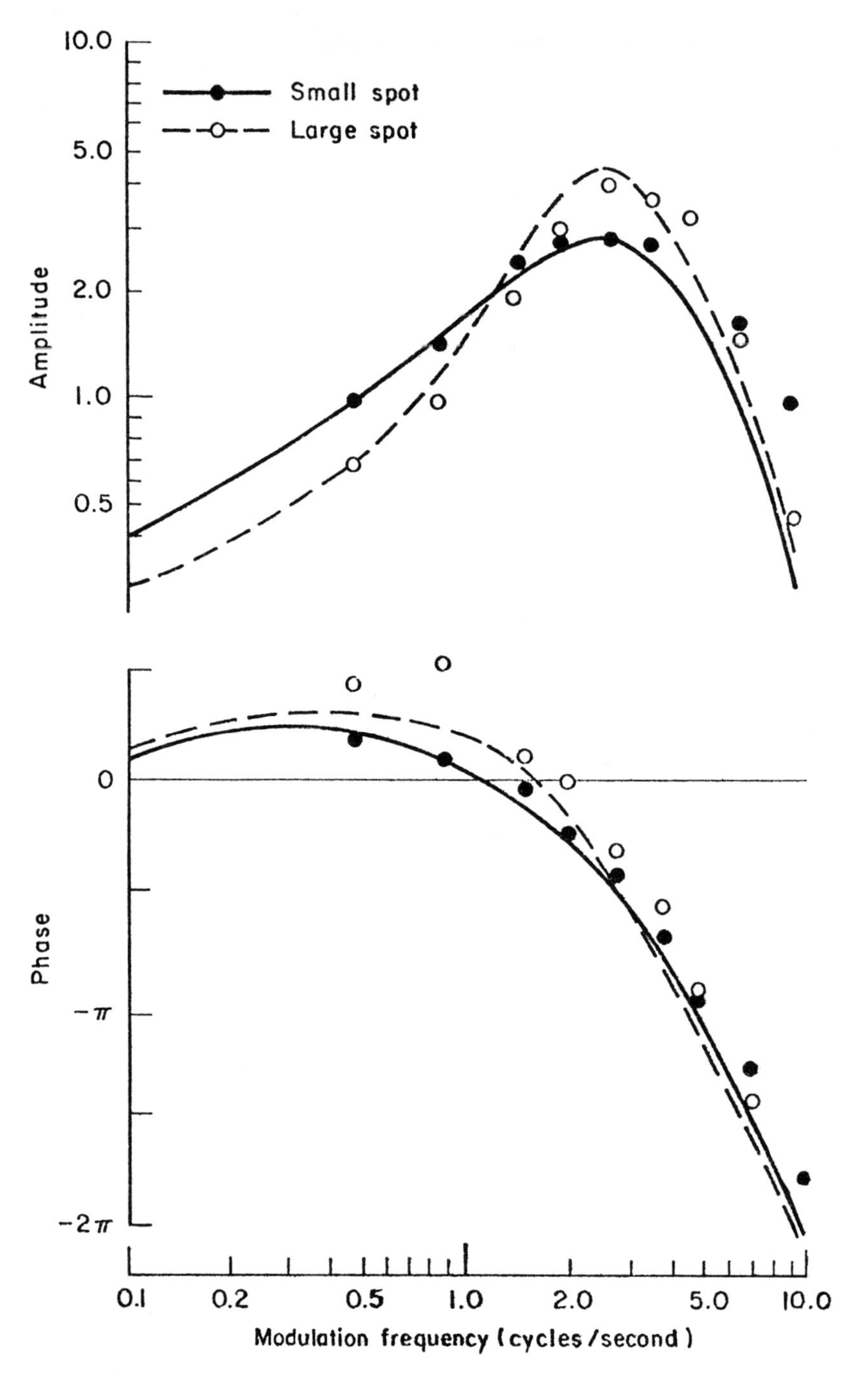

FIG. 8.19. A comparison of phase and amplitude properties as a function of the modulation frequency of two size spots. Data points are empirical; curves are theoretical predictions. (From Graham and Ratliff, © 1974, with the permission of W. H. Freeman & Co.)

tem and the purely inhibitory lateral inhibition model that describes the invertebrate compound eye are functionally equivalent. This equivalence is demonstrated by comparing Hartline and Ratliff's model shown in Fig. 8-18E with the equivalent map of an excitatory-center–inhibitory-surround receptive field shown in Fig. 8-18A. The major difference between these two fields is that the vertebrate summatory center is comparatively wider than the width of the individual ommatidium of the invertebrate eye. Summation in the former case results from excitatory interactions between a number of small photoreceptors rather than within one large one, as in the latter case. Though the dimensions are different, the principle is the same in both the invertebrate and the vertebrate visual systems. Either mechanism could be used to model any of the phenomena that will now be discussed.

3. The Phenomena

A wide variety of perceptual phenomena, with considerable justification, have been attributed to reciprocal lateral inhibitory interactions in the peripheral portions of the human visual system. Unfortunately, so have a number of other phenomena that seem to bear some superficial similarities to those appropriately classified ones but do not actually seem to possess the properties that would make them reasonable Level 2 candidates. One particularly confusing analogy concerns the misidentification of global spatial contrast effects with local contour interactions. This is due, I believe, to the fact that the word *contrast* has been used ambiguously in visual perception. One way in which this word has traditionally been used is in the context of "simultaneous contrast," the global phenomenon illustrated in Fig. 11-2A. On the other hand, some authors, for example Alpern (1963), have also used the term to denote the much more localized interaction that occurs between two or three small lines that are separated by only a fraction of a degree of visual angle as shown in Fig. 8-20. I believe this to be an incorrect analogy and that global simultaneous contrast is not mediated by the same processes to which the local interaction between the small bars should be attributed. The two phenomena have significantly different properties (described more fully in Chapter 9).

The fact that there may be more than one type of inhibitory interaction—one highly localized and one more broadly diffuse—was also alluded to by one of the arch proponents of lateral inhibition theory, the late Nobel laureate George von Békésy. von Békésy (1968) distinguished between two kinds of inhibition—the Mach and Hering types. He believed that these two types differed mainly in terms of the spatial extent over which they exerted their influence. He also (p. 1497) refers obliquely to "central" inhibition, thus at least acknowledging the possibility of several different kinds of inhibitory interaction, not all of which need necessarily follow the mathematical models introduced at the beginning of this section.

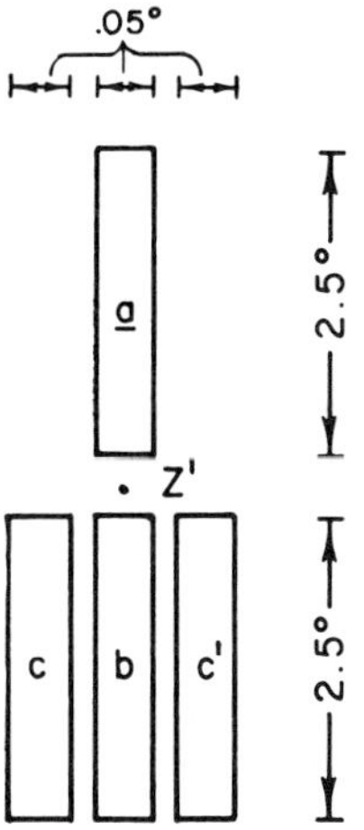

FIG. 8.20. The stimulus pattern used in Alpern's pioneering study of simultaneous brightness contrast. As noted, it is not clear that this stimulus assays the same mechanisms as those measured when the stimulus used in Fig. 11.2 is used. (From Alpern, © 1963, with the permission of the Association for Research in Opthalmology.)

The problem has also been recognized by others. R. DeValois and K. De Valois (1975), put it this way:

> An important characteristic of contrast effects—and one which presents an intriguing puzzle to understand physiologically—is that objects of virtually any size have their lightness and color determined by their relation to the surround. Thus, when we look at a nearby white wall, it may subtend 20 [deg] or more visual angle. Yet our percept of it as being white (rather than gray or even black) depends completely on the amount of light from it with respect to other surrounding objects, that is, on the contrast relationships. Furthermore, our immediate percept of the wall is of its being uniformly white. This may seem like a nonproblem until we consider, as we discuss further later, that all the likely retinal processes for explaining contrast effects only operate over much smaller distances—a degree or less of visual angle. So the white appearance of the center of the wall is determined by the contrast situation 10 [deg] or more in the periphery, whereas neurons signaling information about the center of the visual field are quite uninfluenced by stimuli even 1 [deg] away. [p. 157)

Similarly such perceptual phenomena as "irradiation," "induction," and "spatial contraction or expansion,"[5] although often attributed to distorting interactions in the retina, do not seem actually to be Level 2 processes but, from my point of view, are more likely examples of more central interactions (Level 4 or 5). In this section I deal only with the phenomena for which there is substantial supporting evidence that localized lateral inhibitory interactions, constrained to

[5]All of these phenomena are characterized by widespread spatial interactions between different parts of the visual field. These topics, although of less than central interest in visual psychology these days, were among the core topics discussed in the heyday of Gestalt psychology.

relatively local regions of the peripheral nervous system, are involved.

To provide some order in the following discussion, I have divided the various phenomena into three classes on the basis of the stimuli that are used to trigger the percept. The first class consists of those phenomena resulting from interactions between small, spotlike stimuli. The second class includes those that provide evidence of inhibitory interaction within somewhat larger, but still singular, spots and disks. The third class includes those phenomena that have substantial spatial extent, particularly involving edges and contours. This trichotomy is an arbitrary one, to be sure, and clearly the classes are not mutually exclusive. It is based on the stimulus and task aspects of the experimental paradigm and not on the underlying neural interaction processes. Thus while it may be somewhat useful as a heuristic taxonomy, such a classification schema should not be allowed to obscure the fact that all of these phenomena are probably the results of exactly the same process—lateral inhibitory interaction.

a. Inhibitory Interactions Between Discrete Small Spots

The prototypical experiment of this first class involves the presentation of two small, discrete test stimuli in close proximity to each other. One stimulus is typically defined as the inducer or masker, and the other is usually called the test or target stimulus. The general object of this prototypical experiment is to determine the effect of the inducer on the test stimulus. Typically the experiment is carried out using some sort of an absolute threshold measure to determine the magnitude and polarity of the effect. In some instances, however, evaluations of the apparent brightness of suprathreshold stimuli may be made.

If the two stimuli are very small, there is usually very little interaction observed between the two. At least one of the two stimuli must have some appreciable spatial extent for lateral interactions to become effective. This point was made most eloquently by von Békésy (1968), when he said:

> As an example, it can be demonstrated that stimuli with a small lateral spread do not produce large changes in the local sensation as a consequence of inhibition. If the stimuli consisted of two very sharp and narrow sections, even when the distance between the two point stimuli is inside the width of the Mach band type of inhibition, the reduction in sensation magnitude is quite small.

The fact that small stimuli do not appreciably interact represents one of the first deviations from the simple linear mathematical model of the lateral inhibitory interaction effects described in the introduction to this section. The central excitatory region, represented either by the width of an invertebrate ommatidium or by the central excitatory portion of a vertebrate neuronal receptive field, is not a perfect integrator; the visual information apparently must be sufficiently distributed so that it exceeds some spatial threshold of extent for the inhibitory mechanism to be energized.

Let us assume that either one or both of the two spots is large enough to produce some inhibitory effect in the other. The next question to which our attention should be directed concerns the spatial extent of the inhibitory effect itself. In other words, what is its distance function? This function has been measured in a number of different ways. For example, Beyerstein and Freeman (1977) have recently reported a study in which the inhibitory effects of a 3.5-min (of visual angle) inducing spot on the increment threshold of a 1.5-min test spot were determined. They found that the larger spot elevated the threshold of detection of the smaller one only when the separation between the two spots was less than 6 or 9 min, respectively, for two observers. The results of their experiment are shown in Fig. 8-21. Thus these relatively small spots do interact but in a

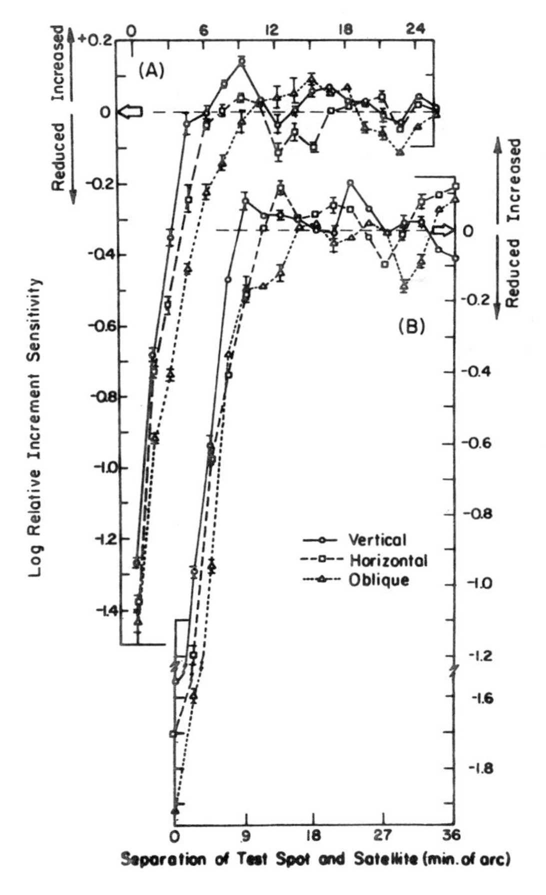

FIG. 8.21. Increment threshold sensitivity as a function of the separation of the test spot and another "satellite spot." (From Beyerstein and Freeman, © 1977, with the permission of Pergamon Press.)

way that is so narrow in its extent that any theorist would be hard pressed to suggest how this process could account for the broad global brightness alteration observed in the simultaneous contrast paradigm.

However, as the masking and test spots increase in size, as predicted by von Békésy, the distance over which the inhibitory interaction may occur also increases. A now near-classic study by Leibowitz, Mote, and Thurlow (1953) shows that the interactive effect of an inducing field that is 30 min in extent on a similar sized test field can still be measured as far apart as 10 deg. However, the distance function (the progressive decrease in the inhibitory effect as measured in terms of the luminance of a matching light) seems to asymptote at about 1 deg of angular separation as shown in Fig. 8-22. Because there is still some effect of luminance at separations greater than 1 deg, even though the distance effect seems to have become asymptotic, it is possible that this experiment is also actually sampling two different kinds of inhibition—one comparable to the geometry sensitive process I am considering here, which may extend out to 1 deg for large stimuli, and one more comparable to simultaneous contrast that may have a much broader extent. Figure 8-22 also illustrates another important fact about this kind of inhibition. The higher the inducing luminance, the greater the inhibitory effect, but only above a threshold of about 1 mL of luminous intensity.

Processes comparable to disinhibition (the reduction in effective inhibition produced by an inhibitor when it is itself inhibited by a third stimulus) has also been psychophysically demonstrated for stimuli of this class. Mackavey,

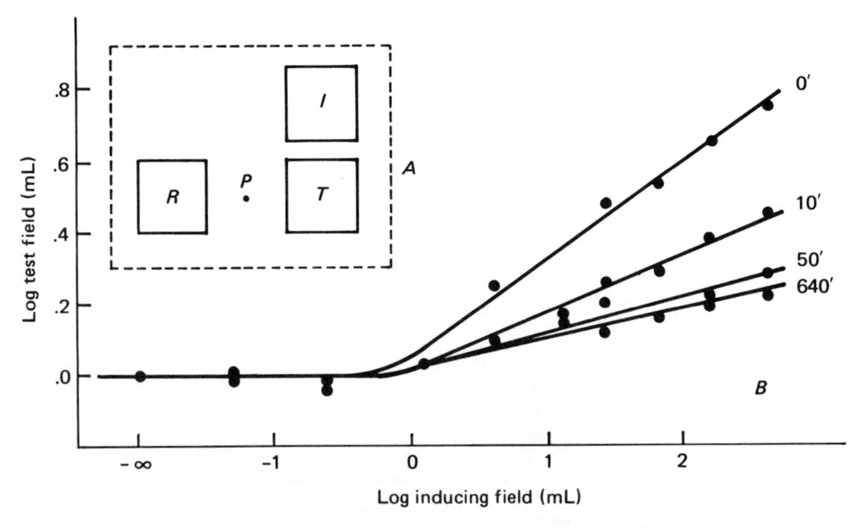

FIG. 8.22. A graph (B) showing the lateral inhibitory interaction that can be observed in a human visual psychophysical experiment using a stimulus as shown in (A) as a function of the spatial separation between the test (T) and "inducing stimuli" (I). (Redrawn from Leibowitz, Mote, and Thurlow, 1953.)

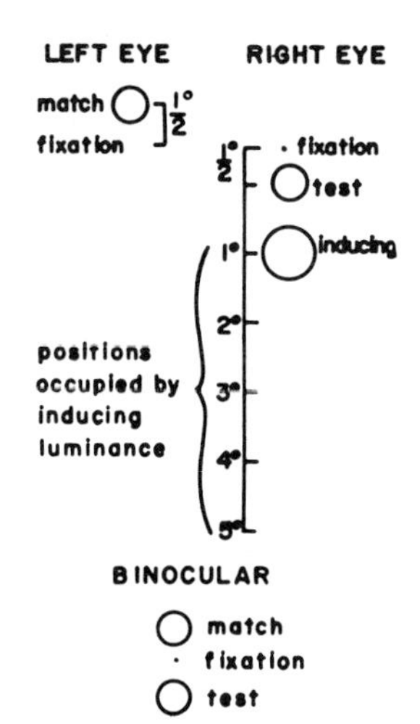

FIG. 8.23. The stimulus used by Mackavey and his colleagues. (From Mackavey, Bartley, and Casella, © 1962, with the permission of the American Institute of Physics.)

Bartley, and Casella (1962) have shown that if two or more stimulus spots (each .75 deg in diameter) are used as inducers (as shown in Fig. 8-23), the general effect is to reduce the subjective brightness of a nearby, but smaller, (0.5 deg) test spot to a greater extent than when only one inducing spot is used. These data are displayed in Fig. 8-24. Though this experiment was carried out using a suprathreshold brightness criterion, the implication is exactly the same as in most of the other studies cited in this section; spatial inhibitory mechanisms exist in the human visual system that mimic those observed in the *Limulus* eye; and their effects summate in some relatively simple manner.

When the test stimulus is small enough to fit within the expanse of the inducing stimuli, as shown in Fig. 8-25, the observed spatial interaction effects may be quite different from the phenomenon occurring as a result of interactions between two similarly sized and spatially separated stimuli. The general result of this alternative paradigm is that there is an optimum middle size of the larger background-inducing field for the detection of the smaller enclosed test spot. This result is now known as the Westheimer function, and it is quite unlike the monotonic decline in inhibitory interaction between two small spots typically observed as they are moved further apart in the human visual field.

Crawford (1940) and Westheimer (1965, 1967) have both shown that the threshold for the smaller spot when it is inhibited by a surrounding large spot is a nonmonotonic function of the size of the surrounding spot. Westheimer's results, for example, indicated that the optimum threshold was achieved for an inducer that extended about 5 min of visual angle and that the test spot was less detectable for both larger and smaller spots. The general form of the Westheimer function and the general design of the experiment is shown in Fig. 8-26. The dependent variable is the background illuminance just strong enough to hide the small inner test light when it is flashing. The major inference drawn by Westheimer from his

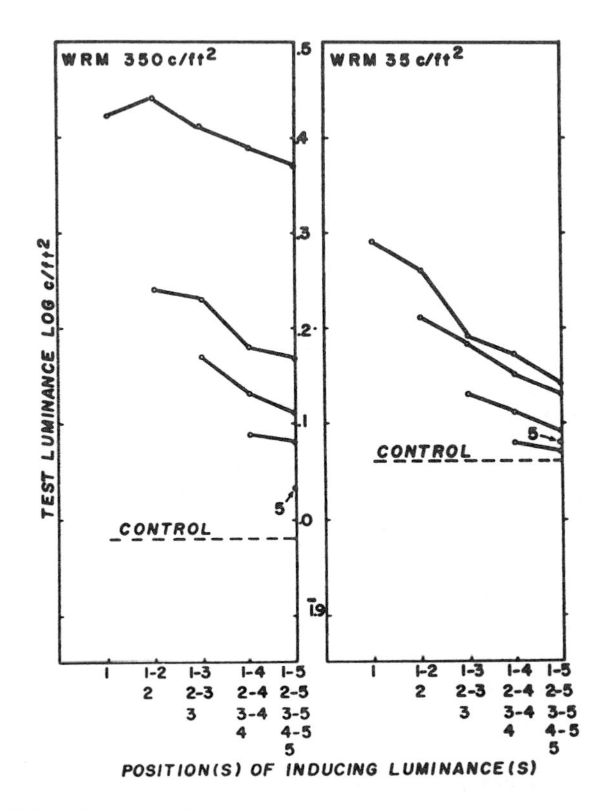

FIG. 8.24. The results of Mackavey, Bartley, and Casella experiment carried out on two observers at two different luminance levels. (From Mackavey, Bartley, and Casella, © 1962, with the permission of the American Institute of Physics.)

studies of spatial interaction in the scotopic system (Westheimer, 1965) and in the photopic system (Westheimer, 1967) is that his results directly reflect the receptive field organization of neurons in the retina. The implication is that the optimum size of the inducer spot should be roughly the same as the summatory center of the center-surround receptive field of the neurons in the retinal locus that the inducer stimulates. For an inducer that is larger than this, there should be some involvement of the inhibitory surround in a way that would reduce the detectability of the test spot. Of course, this must be at best a rough approximation because there are other processes, such as edge effects, that could perturb this effect.

The general concept that psychophysical data of this kind directly reflect the properties of individual retinal neurons has been pursued in an elegant series of studies emanating from the laboratory of Jay Enoch. He has attempted to more precisely localize the neurophysiological site of the Westheimer function shown in Fig. 8-26. Enoch (Enoch, Berger, & Birns, 1970a, 1970b; Enoch & Johnson, 1976; Enoch, Sunga, & Bachmann, 1970a, 1970b; Johnson & Enoch, 1976a,

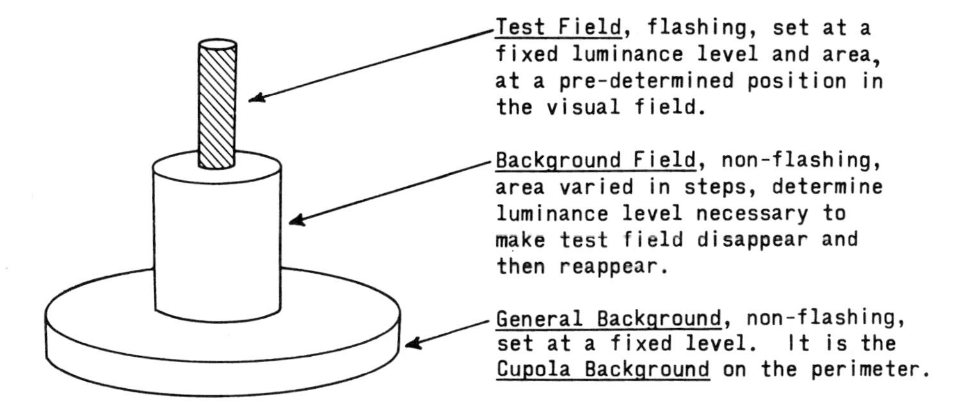

FIG. 8.25. A schematic drawing of the stimulus arrangement used in the Westheimer type of experiment. (From Enoch and Sunga, © 1969, with the permission of Dr. W. Junk N. V. Publishers.)

1976b, 1976c, 1977; Sunga & Enoch, 1970), after many psychophysical experiments and comparisons with known pathological conditions, is now convinced (see his summary paper, Enoch, 1978) that the Westheimer function can be localized exactly to the outer plexiform layer of the retina. He believes that it is here that, in our terms, the critical processes occur that lead to this important

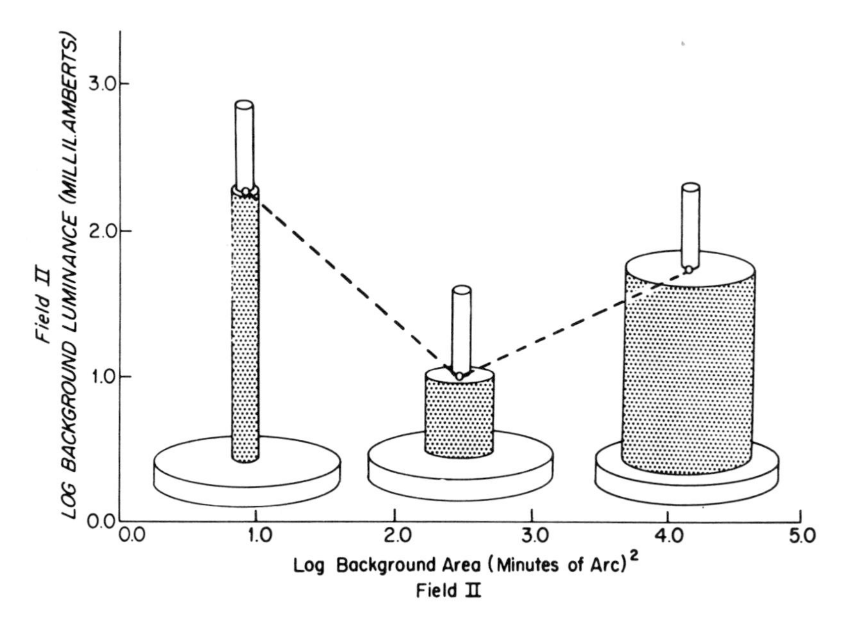

FIG. 8.26. Data from a Westheimer type experiment plotted using the schematic stimuli to provide both an insight into the outcome and the experimental design. (From Enoch and Sunga, © 1969, with the permission of Dr. W. Junk N. V. Publishers.)

phenomenon. According to Enoch and his co-workers, the Westheimer function is also related to the portion of the retino-geniculate pathway that contains sustained (X-unit) types of neuron.

It seems likely that the sustained-transient dichotomy may not result from the internal characteristics of individual neurons, as is often suggested, but from the way generalized neurons are interconnected at the outer plexiform layer. In other words, the properties of sustained and transient neurons themselves may be a reflection of the interactions in this retinal layer rather than any property of the isolated cell. In this they share a common origin with the psychophysically measured phenomena I have just described.

If the response of a sustained neurophysiological channel leads to a psychophysical correlate in the Westheimer function, is it also possible the transient channels might be associated with some equally specific perceptual response? Enoch has also pursued this question and indeed has identified a phenomenon that he believes does display some similarities to the transient channel function. To do so he adapted the stimulus paradigm used by F. S. Werblin in a series of neurophysiological studies on the mudpuppy retina (Werblin, 1972a, 1972b, 1974; Werblin & Copenhagen, 1974; Werblin & Dowling, 1969). Werblin substituted a dynamic inducing pattern consisting of a tiny windmill-shaped pattern for the static, circular, inducing disk of the Westheimer paradigm, as shown in Fig. 8-27. The basic idea is that, when rotated, the windmill would activate neurons that were selectively sensitive to transient stimuli.

Enoch pursued this hypothesis in another series of papers using both visually normal and abnormal observers (Enoch, Johnson, & Fitzgerald, 1976a, 1976b; Enoch, Lazarus, & Johnson, 1976; Johnson & Enoch, 1976a). The results of these experiments indicated that the detectability of the smaller inner light was in fact a function of the diameter and velocity of the windmill and (in later experiments) also of the proportion of light and dark areas of the windmill (Johnson & Enoch, 1977). The prototypical response curve in this case is known in Fig. 8-28. In these papers Enoch used the difference between the responses to the stationary and the moving windmill as the particular measure of the contribution of the transient channels. This difference was mediated, he suggested, by Y-type

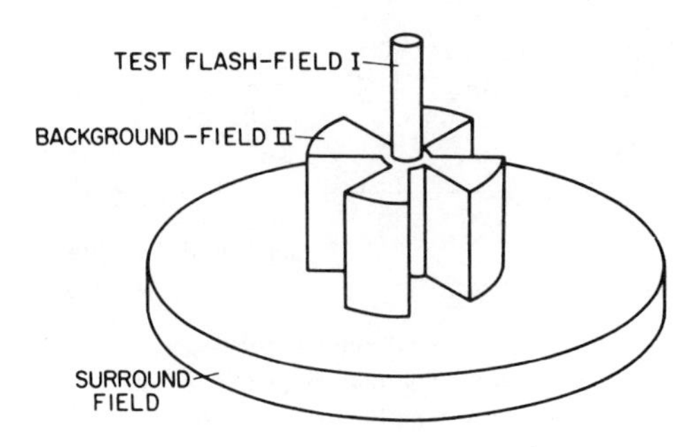

FIG. 8.27. Schematic diagram of the stimulus arrangement used in the Werblin type of experiment. (From Johnson and Enoch, © 1976b, with the permission of Pergamon Press.)

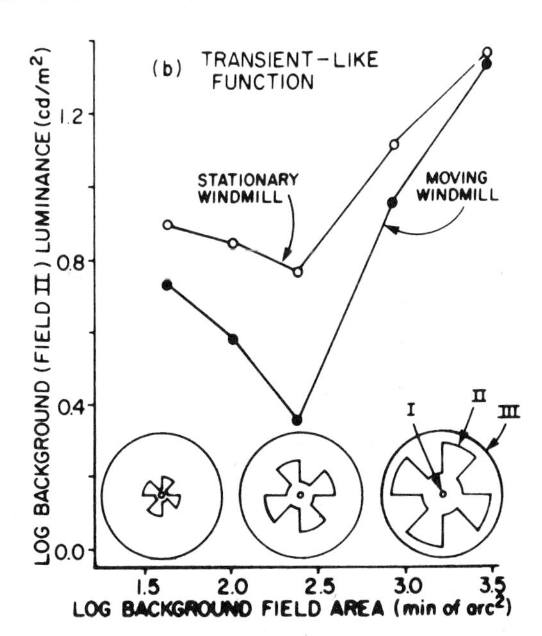

FIG. 8.28. Results of a Werblin type experiment. I = test field; II = inducing field; III = large surround. (From Johnson and Enoch, © 1977, with the permission of Dr. W. Junk N. V. Publishers.)

units. Enoch and his colleagues have adopted Werblin's attribution of their psychophysical data to neural processes occurring in the inner plexiform layer.

An important point about these putative associations between specific neural levels and particular psychophysical phenomena is that they provide a means of isolating processes not only to Level 2 but also possibly to particular sublevels within that rather large and ill-defined taxonomic level. Some might question my willingness to accept Enoch's highly specific attribution of these psychophysical phenomena to Level 2 at the same time that I assign phenomena such as simultaneous contrast to Level 4. The major difference that allows me to separate them in my own thinking is that Enoch's data describe a highly localized phenomenon; but simultaneous contrast is a broad global effect. A visit to Enoch's laboratory emphasized this point: I was able to observe firsthand just how small the windmill-type stimuli are compared to the typical simultaneous contrast display.

b. Inhibitory Interactions Within Single Large Spots

The spatial interactions of which I have just spoken occur between relatively small, discrete spots of light. Although the individual spots may overlap (or one may be enclosed by the other), in each case a separate test stimulus was used as a probe of the inhibitory interactive forces exerted by an inducing stimulus. It is not a long logical leap to the idea that some very similar spatial interactions may also be occurring between the different portions of a single larger spot of light. The theoretical contention I express here is that such intraspot inhibitory processes, which have indeed been demonstrated, are mediated by neural inhibitory processes that are homologous, if not identical, to those underlying the findings for multiple small spots. Clearly such processes are closely related to the summatory interactions occurring between different regions of a single visual stimulus leading to Ricco's and Piper's laws.

One example of such an intraspot, rather than interspot, interaction is a phenomenon that has been called the "spatial Broca–Sulzer effect" by Kent Higgins (Higgins & Knoblauch, 1977; Higgins & Rinalducci, 1975a, 1975b). Higgins and his co-workers have shown that at both long and short durations the apparent brightness of a spot of light is strongly determined by its size. However the obtained data are quite contrary to the predictions of the spatial summation. Specifically they demonstrated that, even though of equal luminance, a smaller spot (about 5 min of visual angle) appears brighter than a larger one presented for an equal duration. The optimum size at which this paradoxical effect varied, not too surprisingly, was a function of retinal location. The more peripheral the stimulus, the larger the size producing the optimum brightness. The effect, however, extended over a very broad range of stimulus durations. Stimuli as brief as 10 msec exhibited the effect as did those that lasted a second or longer.

The most plausible explanation of this spatial Broca–Sulzer phenomenon is the same as the one invoked for all of the rest of the topics discussed in this section. Higgins attributes this phenomenon to inhibitory interactions occurring within and among the several internal regions of the single stimulus spot. The larger the stimulus, the greater the likelihood of intraregional inhibitory interactions. Thus the same amount of photic energy distributed over a wide area would produce a lower average neural, and thus psychophysical response.

c. *Inhibitory Interactions at Edges, Gradients, and Contours*

Mach Bands. Perhaps no phenomenon putatively based on Level 2 neural interactions has been as frequently and persistently researched as have been the Mach bands—the contour enhancements that occur at spatial regions in which the slope of the luminance gradient changes. The Mach bands were originally observed in the scientific laboratory by Ernst Mach (1838–1916) over a century ago (Mach, 1865, 1866a, 1866b), but the impact of contours and edges on visual perception had been known for many centuries prior to their formal description. Artists of almost all eras have consciously or unconsciously altered their paintings in ways that indicate either an implicit or explicit appreciation of the contour effects.

On the basis of his psychophysical observations, however, Mach suggested that these illusory bands were probably the result of lateral inhibitory interactions most likely occurring in the retina itself. There is, perhaps, no more consistently agreed upon neuroreductionistic theoretical explanation of any perceptual phenomena than this one originally proposed by Mach for the intensified bands.

In preview, he asserted that the immediate antecedents (the critical processes) of the Mach bands are the lateral inhibitory interactions occurring between neighboring elements in the retina.

The story of the history of Mach band research has been well told by Floyd Ratliff in his elegant and scholarly work (Ratliff, 1965) and need not be recapitulated here. However, a brief description of the prototypical phenomenon and the factors that influence it will serve to make the foregoing comments and subsequent discussion more concrete. In general, Mach bands are most noticeable when a stimulus containing a gradient of spatial luminance, such as that shown in Fig. 8-29A, is presented to the observer. The prototypical stimulus consists of a region of gradually increasing luminance separating two regions of constant luminance, one of which is quite bright and the other of which is quite dim. At the intersection between the dim constant region and the lower portion of the gradient, a darker-than-expected band is observed. At the intersection between the brightest portion of the gradient and the constant bright region, a darker than expected band is also seen. Figure 8-29B plots the cross section of the corresponding spatial brightness distribution that is perceived by the observer. Ratliff discusses (Ratliff, 1965, p. 46) many different optical methods of producing the spatial luminance patterns required to produce the illusion.

The generally accepted explanation of the origin of the Mach band is depicted in Fig. 8-29C. In this figure I assume, for simplicity, that each of 10 neural units is excited only by the light falling on it and is inhibited only by its immediate neighbors. The response of the nth neuron (R_n), therefore, will be defined by the following simplification of Eq. 8-6:

$$R_n = S_n - (I_{n-1} + I_{n+1}) \qquad (8\text{-}10)$$

where S_n is the stimulus intensity falling on that unit, and I_{n-1} and I_{n+1} are the inhibitory forces exerted on it by its two immediate neighbors. To avoid negative numbers in the outcome of the demonstration calculation I am about to present, let us also assume (quite arbitrarily) that:

$$I_n = 0.25\, S_n \qquad (8\text{-}11)$$

In other words, the inhibitory force exerted by any neuron on its immediate neighbor is equal to one-fourth of the excitation falling on that unit.

If one evaluates these simple equations for each unit of a line of simulated neural units, as shown in Fig. 8-29C, it quickly becomes clear that not all units that receive the same amount of excitatory stimulation will respond at the same level. The difference can only be attributed to the differences in inhibitory interaction with their neighbors. For example, consider unit 3, which is placed at the intersection of the constant dim region and the bottom of the gradient of increasing luminance. It will be receiving disproportionately large amounts of inhibition compared to units 2 and 1. This results from the fact that it not only receives a "standard" amount of inhibition from unit 2, but also a larger-than-standard amount of inhibition from unit 4, which itself is being stimulated more

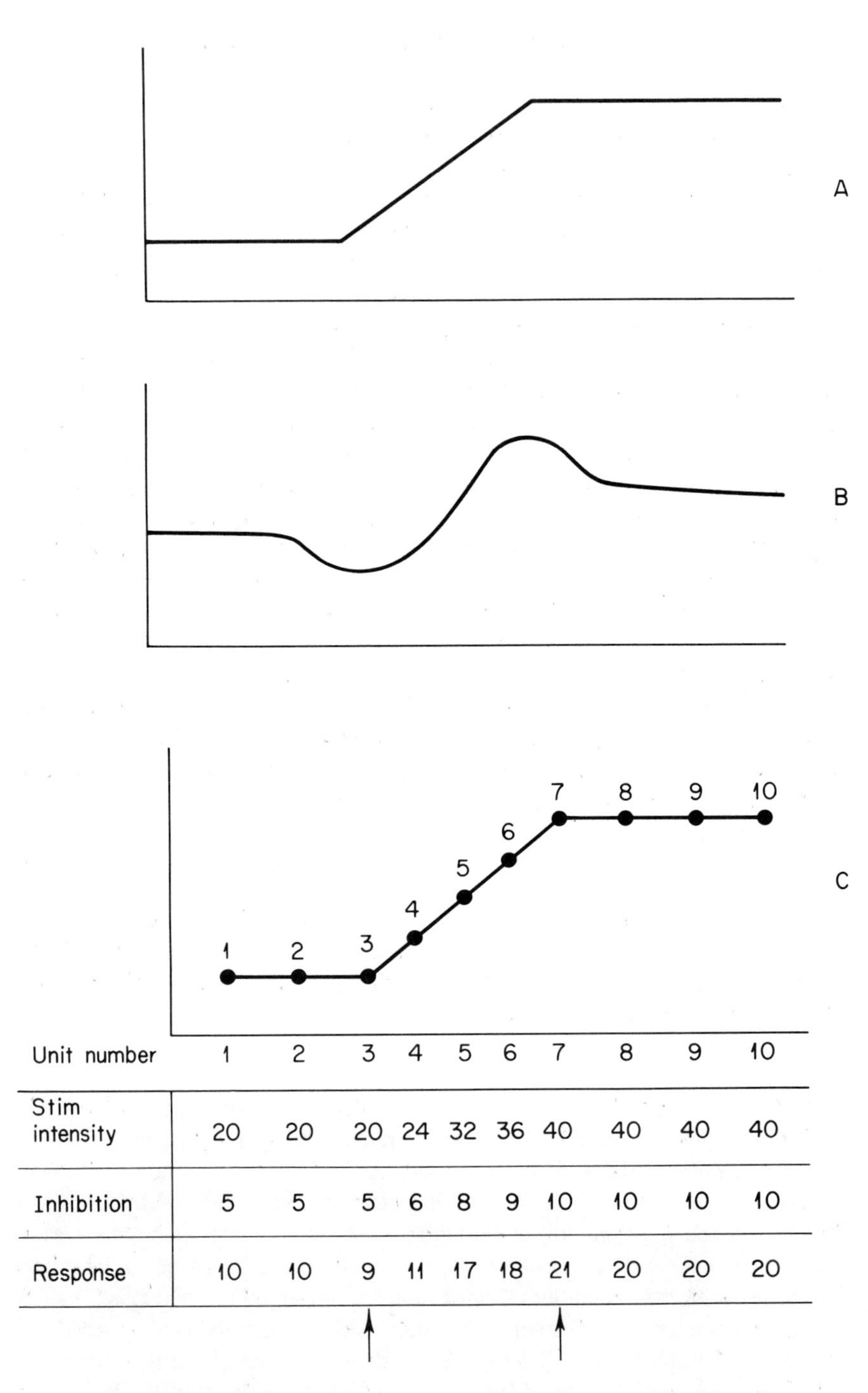

Unit number	1	2	3	4	5	6	7	8	9	10
Stim intensity	20	20	20	24	32	36	40	40	40	40
Inhibition	5	5	5	6	8	9	10	10	10	10
Response	10	10	9	11	17	18	21	20	20	20

FIG. 8.29. A graphical explanation of the Mach Band effect. (A) The physical stimulus; (B) the perceived brightness pattern; (C) the computations (described in text) converting (A) to (B).

heavily than units 1 or 2. Therefore, at the point of inflection of the spatial stimulus distribution function, there will be a decrease in the response of any unit (or units if the grain of the neural network is dense enough and the inhibitory interaction extends beyond immediate neighbors). The diminution of the neural response at this site is, according to contemporary theory, the direct antecedent of a perceived dark band.

A similar calculation can be carried out at the other point of inflection—where the gradient of increasing illumination meets the region of constant high illuminance. At this point on the stimulus luminance distribution, the inhibition exerted on unit 7 by unit 6 is less than the inhibition exerted by 8 on 7 (or by any unit in the constant bright region on its neighbors). Thus, unit 7 will respond more strongly than any unit to its right. Therefore there is an abnormal enhancement of neural activity at this point. This hyperactivity is directly transformed, according to conventional theory, into the perceived bright band.

There is little current argument (though there is some, as noted further on in this discussion) against the hypothesis that these illusory Mach bands are created by lateral inhibitory interactions occurring among neurons in the neural network of the retina. The reader who is interested in a more detailed analysis of the origins of these Mach bands is referred to Jung (1973), Fiorentini (1972), or, probably best of all, Ratliff's (1965) delightful and still up-to-date book with its many references to the early work of Mach and Hartline, as well as to the latter's co-workers.

It must not be forgotten that essentially the same argument for the genesis of these bands can be made with an excitatory-center–inhibitory-surround receptive field hypothesis (which is probably more characteristic of the vertebrate retina) as has been made with the strictly inhibitory interaction characteristic of the invertebrate eye. The issues and concepts involved are exactly the same. Glezer, Bertulis, Ivanov, Kostelyanets, and Podvigin (1971) carried out such an analysis using a center-surround receptive field arrangement and arrive at exactly the same satisfactory conclusion concerning the origin of the Mach bands.

I alluded above to the fact that there was some modest disagreement with the general idea of lateral inhibitory interaction as the explanation of the Mach bands. Although Ratliff never explicitly disagrees, he does (in Chapter 4) discuss the possible contribution of the optical properties of the eye to the elicitation of contour enhancement. The idea that what I call Level 0 processes are involved in the Mach band phenomenon has been made totally explicit in a recent letter to the *Journal of Theoretical Biology* (Ciures, 1977). Ciures noted that enhancement of contours would also occur if the optics of the eye were acting as a low-pass optical filter selectively attenuating the high spatial frequencies associated with a contour. He pointed out that if the high spatial frequency components of the signal were not being passed by the optical elements of the eye, then the pattern of information transmitted centrally would correspond to a highly distorted rendition of contours in particular. Figure 8-30 displays what the distorting effect of not passing the high frequency components would be. Such a low-pass filter property would lead directly to a bright-band enhancement and a dark-band diminishment that would be indistinguishable from those that would be produced by a neural lateral inhibitory interaction process. Indeed, the low-pass optical filtering process is a direct analog of lateral inhibitory interaction. Although each is implemented by a totally different mechanism, both are represented by the same mathematical function.

There is an important general point that should be made once again in this context. It is actually not very likely that the Mach bands are produced by the limited optical band-pass characteristic of the kind suggested by Ciures. The neurophysiological evidence is too compelling to support such an alternative hypothesis. However, once again we see an example of how *analogous* processes at a different level *could* have led to the same phenomenal outcome. Thus it is not completely absurd to accept the fact that the optical properties of the eye may in some minor way contribute to the formation of Mach bands, and we see in the following summary that in fact they do.

Finally, in this highly abbreviated discussion of the Mach band phenomenon, let us summarize the stimulus factors that affect the magnitude and breadth of the bands. In no particular order of importance, the known psychophysical facts concerning the Mach bands are:

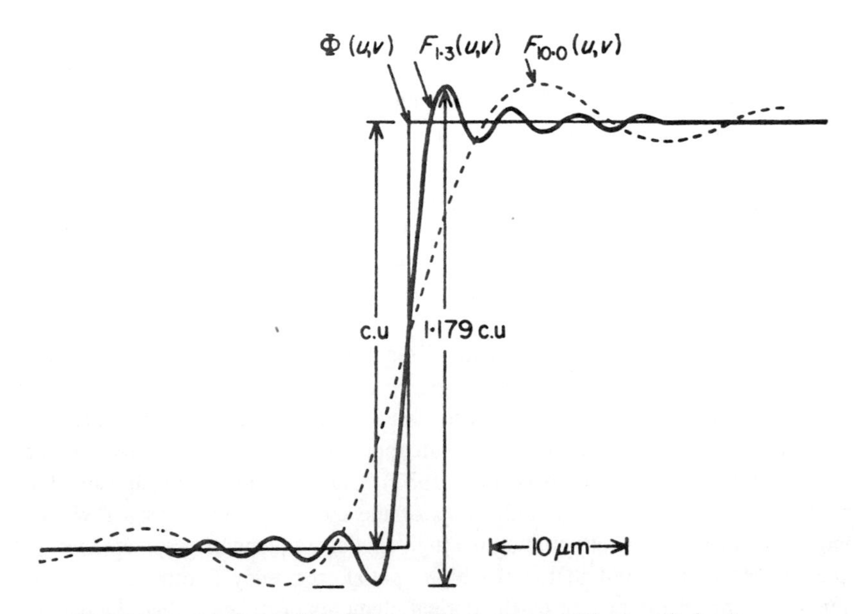

FIG. 8.30. Calculated values of the spatial pattern produced by an optical system not passing the highest spatial frequencies in the Mach band stimulus situation. (From Ciures, © 1977, with the permission of Academic Press.)

1. The luminance of the pattern plays an important role in determining the characteristics of the band but in complicated ways. The widths of both the dark and the light Mach bands are differentially dependent upon the overall illumination level of the stimulus as shown in Fig. 8-31. The dark bands increase dramatically in width as the luminance decreases, but the bright band is much less affected by such a change (Shipley & Wier, 1972). This increase in width eventually results in a corresponding decrease in the magnitude of the band. The ultimate outcome is the disappearance of the bands in very bright light. Similarly, at very low luminances, the Mach bands do not appear. Within an intermediate range of luminances, the higher the luminance, the steeper the slope of the gradient between the dim and bright regions must be to produce a just-detectable band (Ercoles & Fiorentini, 1959).

2. Another stimulus factor powerfully affecting the width and magnitude of the Mach band is the slope of the gradient between the constant dim and constant intense regions. In general, the steeper the gradient, the brighter are both the dark and bright bands (Fiorentini, Jeanne, & di Francia, 1955; Thomas, J. P., 1966). At the same time that the bands are becoming brighter with increased slope, however, they are also narrowing (Shipley & Wier, 1972).

3. Shipley and Wier have shown, furthermore, that the retinal position upon which the stimuli are projected is an effective factor in determining the width of the Mach band. The bands are narrower at the fovea and wider at any eccentricity greater than 30 min of visual angle.

4. Shipley and Wier also note that the optical properties of the eye affect the width of the bands. Adding two diopters of refractive error in either direction (i.e., making the eye more myopic or hypertropic) leads to a doubling of the width of bands. Doubling the size of the pupils also roughly doubles the width of the bands. All of these factors may either be involved in determining the width of the area in which lateral inhibitory interactions occur or, as I noted earlier, may have a more direct impact on optical processes redundant with the neural ones. Either receptive field size or optical blur are capable of recruiting more and more retinal loci into the interactive process. The general point made by this finding is that the broader the field of interaction, the broader the Mach bands are likely to be.

5. There is general agreement that luminance differences are the critical stimulus factor in producing the Mach band phenomenon and that if luminance is held constant, there can be wide variation in such qualitative stimulus factors as the wavelength spectrum without producing any comparable contour enhancement effects. Pease (1978) carefully reviewed the literature on colored Mach bands and has concluded that there is very little justification for assuming they exist. Only one of many studies even suggested the presence of bands in the absence of luminosity gradients. Considering the now well-established interactions between the chromatic receptors, why they do not occur remains something of a mystery.

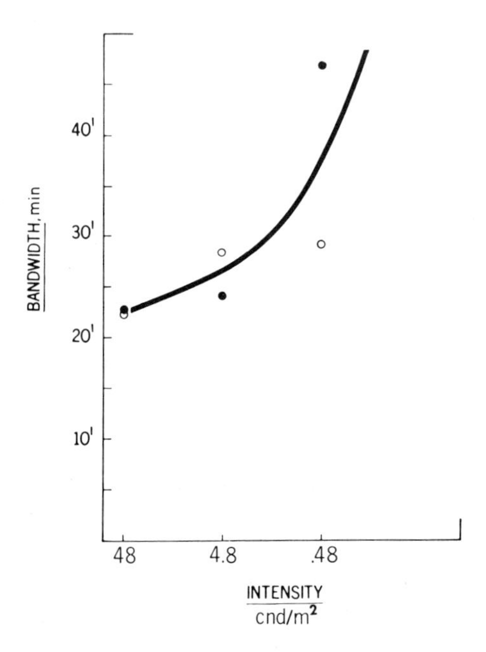

FIG. 8.31. The width of the Mach band as a function of the stimulus intensity. (From Shipley and Wier, © 1972, with the permission of Springer-Verlag.)

6. Mach bands are almost certainly a monocular and therefore peripheral, retinal effect. Koppitz (1957) has definitively shown that the bands cannot be produced by simulating the standard stimulus with dichoptically presented stimuli that when fused, produce the typical gradient pattern. His experimental design is shown in Fig. 8-32.

7. The size of the Mach band stimulus seems to be an important determinant of the shape of the bands. When the stimulus is very small, the dark band may appear to have multiple peaks (Watrasiewicz, 1963). Based on a computer simulation experiment that I carried out many years ago, I believe that this "spatial oscillation" is specifically due to the fact that the interactions are limited in their spatial extent. If the computer model allowed inhibitory interaction only between adjacent units, then multiple peaks similar to those observed in the psychophysical experiment occurred in the computer-simulated output. If the modeled inhibitory interactions were allowed to extend between simulated neurons many units apart, then the response more clearly approximated the single band of the classical psychophysical response. For very small stimuli, the neural inhibitory interactions may, in fact, be severely limited in extent, thus approximating the former condition of my simulation and leading to multiple (though progressively dimmer) bands. It is only when the lateral inhibitory interactions are spread over many units at progressively greater distance by a larger stimulus that the classic smooth single band observed is obtained.

8. In general, the dark and light bands are not symmetrical (Shipley & Wier, 1972) even though the simplest mathematical model represented by Eq. 8-6

suggests that they should be. This may partially be due to a nonlinearity in the amplitude of the response to the different levels of luminances but may also reflect some more complex aspect of the interaction.

9. The point in time at which the evaluation is made is also important in determining the characteristics of the Mach bands. Hasegawa (1972) has shown that the bands seem to be brightest (and darkest) when an evaluation of their magnitude is made about 100 msec following the time at which a stimulus of 1 sec duration is first presented. For shorter intervals between the stimulus, the stimulus onset, and the brightness test, there is a progressive reduction in the strength of the Mach bands just as there is for those very long duration stimuli in which the pattern is left on continuously.

10. The duration of the stimulus can also be an important factor in determining the strength of the Mach bands. To make the brightness of the fairly weak bands seen at an exposure duration of a few milliseconds equal to the fairly strong bands observed with durations greater than 50 msec, the gradient must be made substantially steeper (J. P. Thomas, 1965).

More complete discussions of the phenomenal effects of these stimulus factors can be found in Ratliff (1965), Fiorentini (1972), and, of course, Shipley and

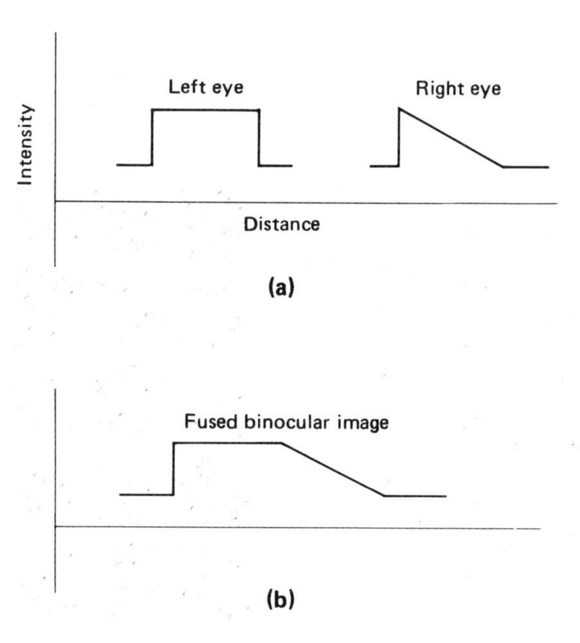

FIG. 8.32. The design of an experiment to determine if Mach bands could be produced binocularly. When the two monocular stimuli are combined in binocular fusion to produce the usual gradient, there is no observable enhancement. This indicates that the Mach band effect is mediated by neuronal interactions in the peripheral retina. (Courtesy of Dr. Werner Koppitz, Mt. Kisco, New York.)

Wier (1972) who have contributed so much to our knowledge of these parametric influences.

Finally, to reiterate a word of caution. As one reads through the literature of Mach bands, one finds a recurrent theme that these contour-enhancement effects are identical with the more expansive simultaneous contrast effects. I believe this is not the case and warn the reader again against such misidentification of the two phenomena. The arguments behind my belief are developed in the next chapter.

The Hermann Grid. Closely related to the Mach band phenomenon, and explicable in exactly the same terms, is the Hermann grid, another classic illusion, discovered over one hundred years ago by Hermann (1870). Two versions of this illusion drawn by Jung (1973) are shown in Fig. 8-33. The phenomenon, though with reversed contrast in each of these two figures, is conceptually the same and has been analyzed in identical, though opposite valence, terms. First, consider Fig. 8-33A. In this plate, which has black lines forming a grid on a white background, the illusory experience is of a system of gray (lighter than black) regions at the intersection of each of the black lines. In Fig. 8-33B, on the other hand, the illusion is a system of gray (darker than white) regions at the intersections of the white lines on the black background.

Jung has analyzed these two types of Hermann grid phenomena in terms of interactions among many of the "Mexican hat" type of receptive fields shown in Figure 8-18A. The conceptual development of Jung's analysis using receptive

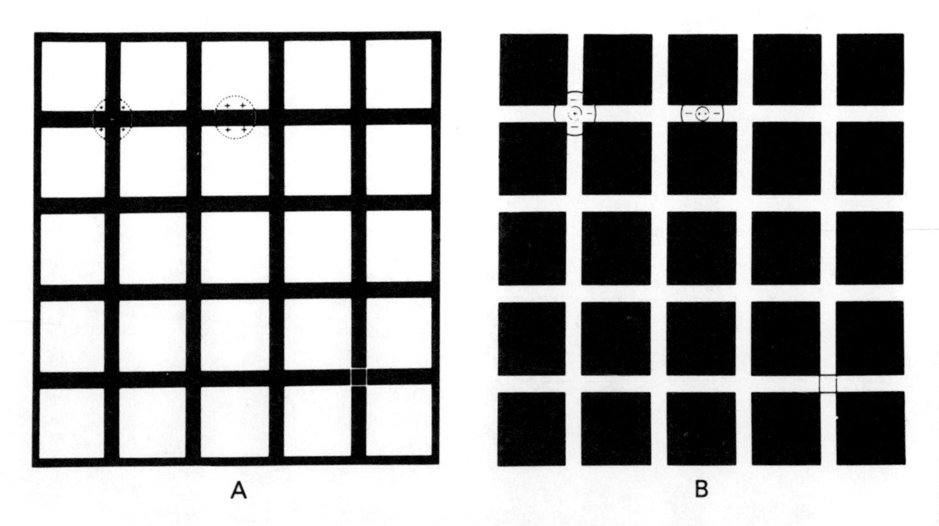

FIG. 8.33. Hermann grids presented in negative and positive contrast. The small circles and the indicated inhibitory forces can be used (as described in the text) to explain this phenomenon. (From Jung, © 1973, with the permission of Springer-Verlag.)

fields is exactly the same as either the use of lateral inhibitory interactions or receptive fields was for the Mach band. The prototypical receptive field pattern inset in these two figures is the essential aspect of his analysis. If one adds up the inhibitory and excitatory influences on two regions—at the intersections of two white (or two black) lines—and compares it with the excitation or inhibition at a point on one of the lines that is not at an intersection, it turns out that the response magnitude at the intersection will be less than (due to greater cumulative inhibition) or more than (due to less cumulative inhibition) other portions of the white or black lines (respectively) that are not at an intersection. The net result of this differential inhibition is to produce the phenomenal gray regions at the intersections of the grid lines. Thus, though the stimulus and the resultant phenomenon are different in this case from the Mach band demonstration, the nature of the underlying interaction process is exactly the same.

Relatively little formal experimentation has been done on the Hermann grid phenomenon. For a number of reasons, it has not attracted the same degree of attention as the Mach band and is usually simply presented as a demonstration. However there are a number of obvious experiments that should be done on it. A study of the effects of the size of the black or white squares, the width of the white on black lines, and the respective contrast of the lines and squares might help us to gain a clearer insight into the mechanisms and processes that underly these interesting illusions.

In conclusion, it seems certain that the Hermann grid, like the Mach band, is the result of a peripherally mediated Level 2 process. One strong argument to support this contention is that the grey spots do not occur (Uttal, 1973, p. 453) when alternate lines of black squares are presented to the subject in a dichoptic presentation, as shown in Fig. 8-34.[6] This means that, like the Mach bands, the Hermann grid cannot be produced in a centrally fused image, and therefore, ipso facto, it must be the result of a peripheral interaction.

The discussion so far presented would be particularly complete and would permit us to assert unequivocally that the Mach bands and the Hermann grid phenomena were but two aspects of one and the same process except for one major difficulty. That difficulty is that the Hermann grid spots, as can be seen when one inspects Fig. 8-33, do not appear near the region of foveal fixation; the phenomenon, unlike the Mach band, is present only in peripheral vision. Jung (1973) believes that this absence of the Hermann grid gray spots at the point of fixation is explained by the difference in size of the receptive fields in the fovea and in the periphery. The width of the lines of the grid, according to his point of

---

[6]Although the consensus still seems to be that the Hermann grid is a peripheral effect, a recent research note (Lavin & Costall, 1978) suggests that if the pattern shown in Fig. 8-35 is enlarged beyond the size that I used, the dichoptic Hermann grid stimulus will, in fact, produce the gray spots. "This report awaits further verification," as we say when confronted with a challenge to our own pet theories.

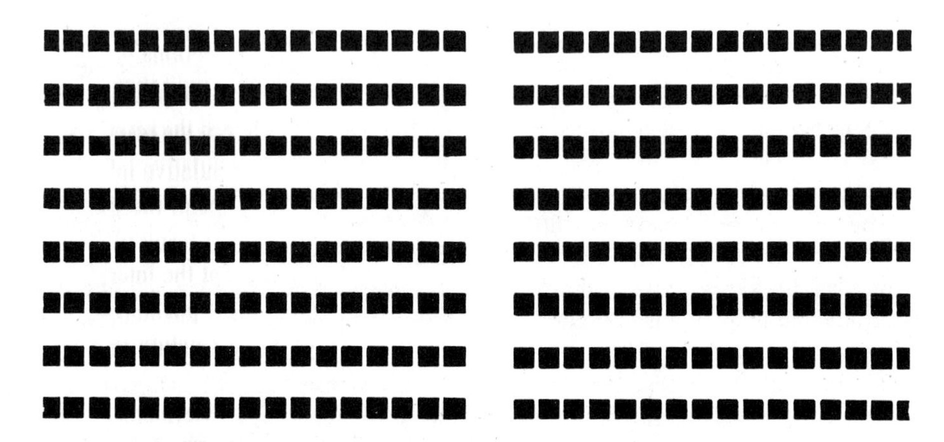

FIG. 8.34. A stereoscopic slide prepared to determine if the Hermann grid effect can be produced dichoptically. Although this slide is difficult to fuse because of a strong retinal rivalry effect, during the stable periods there is no evidence of the grey spots. The suggestion, therefore, is that the Hermann grid, like the Mach band, is mediated by neuronal interactions in the periphery. (From Uttal, 1973.)

view, are simply too wide for the interactive effects to be effective at the fovea—the effects of small inhibitory regions are simply swamped out by the relatively broad expanse of the lines here. In spite of the appeal of this suggestion, it is not completely satisfactory, and this discrepancy has not, in my opinion, been satisfactorily explained. Further empirical research and thoughtful theory is required to explain this very important difference between the two phenomena.

Edge Effects. Another paradigm that has been used to study the effect of edges on the perception of extended areas requires that the experimenter probe the region near the edges of a large field with a very small stimulus to determine local variations in such parameters as the detection threshold. Figure 8-35, in which the several small dots represent various placements of the test stimulus, depicts the typical stimulus configuration used in this experimental design. The incremental luminance (above that of the portion of the field on which it is presented) required for this test spot to be just detected is measured as a function of the distance to the edge. In general, for relatively large stimuli, the threshold luminance of a small test probe is highest when it is placed near the edge and declines when it is farther away, either in the surround or within the large field. This result, like so many of the others I have already discussed, suggests that the reduced inhibitory influence exerted by the dimmer region outside the large luminous field elevates the effective brightness of the region around the edge (an analog of a bright Mach band). Because of the well-established fact that an increment must be greater to be detected when the background is brighter, the threshold of the test spot is correspondingly elevated.

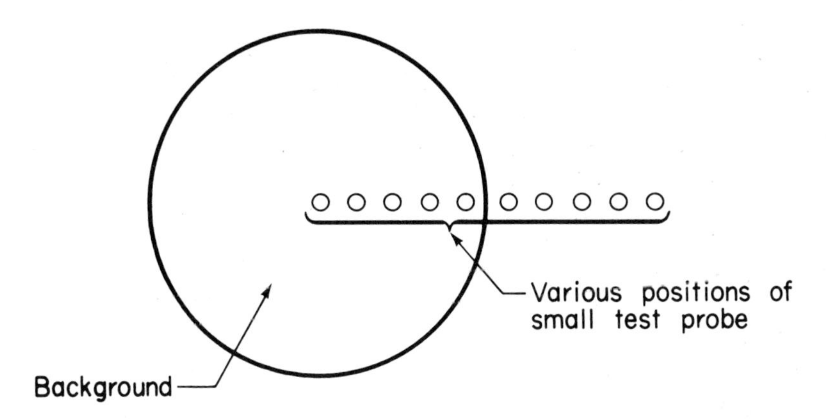

FIG. 8.35. The stimulus situation used to measure spatial interaction effects at the edge or large spot. The small test spot may be positioned at any of the indicated points.

Figure 8-36 shows a typical result, as obtained in one of the many studies of the effect of edges on the increment threshold (Fiorentini & Zoli, 1966, 1967). At low contrast (i.e., when the bright interior of the large field is not too dissimilar in luminance from the darker exterior) the edge effect looks very similar to the Mach bands; there is both a region of enhanced threshold luminances outside the edge and a region of lowered thresholds inside on the luminous spot. This bimodal response function occurs in spite of the fact that the slope of the gradient across the edge is virtually infinite (a step discontinuity). On the

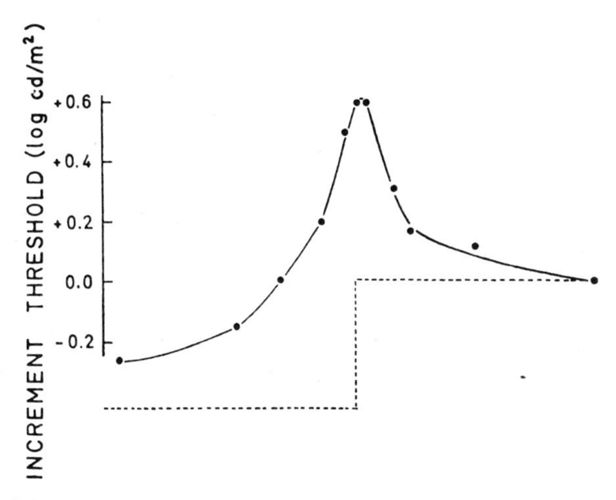

FIG. 8.36. The increment threshold as a function of the spatial relationship between the test spot and an extended edge. (From Fiorentini and Zoli, © 1966, with the permission of Springer-Verlag.)

other hand, when the luminance difference between the large field and its surrounding is very great, a somewhat different functional relationship between the increment threshold and the placement of the test spot is obtained: in this case, a single peak indicating a uniformly elevated threshold on both sides of the edge.

When the background field is small, however, a surprisingly different result is obtained. Matin and Kornheiser (1977) have demonstrated that for a background field that subtends only 25 min of visual angle, the peak threshold elevation (i.e., the lowest sensitivity) does not occur near the edge, but rather at the center of the field. To produce this displacement of the region of lowest sensitivity, Matin and Kornheiser had to use a small 2.5-min-wide test spot. Their plot of the relation of the test spot location and threshold energy is shown in Fig. 8-37. It does not take an elaborate mathematical model to suggest that such a shift of the elevated threshold from the edge to the center of the field is easily explained by assuming that the inhibitory processes from the opposite edges of a 25-min-wide spot themselves interact.

Once again, the important point is that even though this experimental paradigm is slightly different from that producing the spatial Broca–Sulzer effect, the Mach band, or the Hermann grid, it is cut from the same cloth as those other phenomena. All of these perceptual phenomena are believed by most contemporary perceptual theorists to be the direct results of inhibitory interactions that probably occur within the retina itself. There is an abundance of neurophysiological data that supports the hypothesis that either simple inhibitory interaction or its receptive field equivalents exist that are fully capable of producing these phenomena.

Because the inhibitory processes underlying these phenomena are generally agreed to be well localized in the retina, the presence or absence of such a sensitivity to lateral interaction can also be a compelling clue to where the critical processes underlying other phenomena may occur. For example, L. Marks (1972) has shown that the size of a stimulus spot exerts only a small effect on the function relating stimulus luminance and brightness. This finding suggests that there is a relatively small contribution to the suprathreshold function from the lateral inhibitory interaction processes of Level 2. Coupled with what we know about the dynamics of the receptor (Level 1 process), it seems fairly safe to conclude that the suprathreshold dynamic is primarily influenced by receptor properties.

On the other hand, Ratliff, Knight, Toyoda, and Hartline (1967) have shown that the flicker-fusion properties of the neurons of the horseshoe crab eye are substantially changed by the size of a test spot that is oscillating sinusoidally (in time). The response to a low-frequency (less than 2 Hz) stimulus was attenuated and the response to intermediate (between 2 and 7 Hz) frequencies were enhanced in their experiments as the spot size was increased from .25 mm to 1.5 mm. Because the *Limulus* eyes have no interactive mechanism other than an inhibitory one, this result directly implies the existence of a lateral inhibitory effect on this temporal response and suggests that the flicker phenomenon is, at least in this case, influenced by Level 2 processes. Similarly, in man the critical flicker-fusion frequency has been demonstrated to be dependent on the area of the test stimulus by Hecht and Smith (1936) and, more recently, by Kelly (1959). Figure 8-38 compares the results of the Ratliff et al. (1967) neurophysiological study and the psychophysical study of Kelly. The implication of this close correspondence, although not conclusive, is that the flicker-fusion phenomenon is also closely related to the lateral inhibitory interactions among the retinal elements and is, therefore, the result of a Level 2 process.

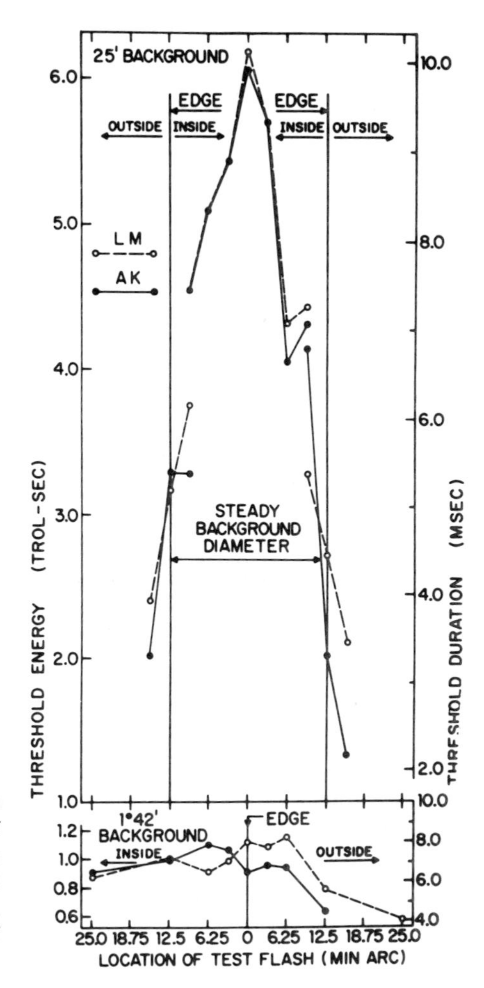

FIG. 8.37. The results of an experiment in which the threshold of a test spot was determined on an intermediately sized background spot. (From Matin and Kornheiser, © 1977, with the permission of Pergamon Press.)

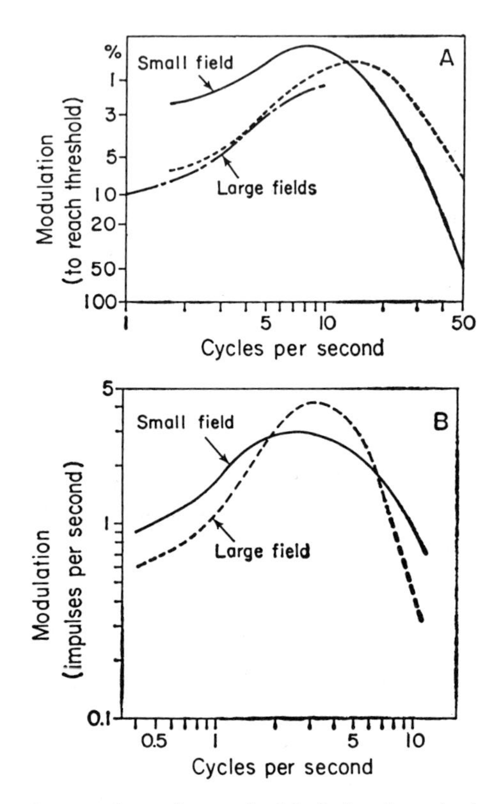

FIG. 8.38. A comparison of neurophysiological and psychophysical spatial modulation transfer functions for different size fields. (From Ratliff, Knight, Toyoda, and Hartline, © 1967, with the permission of the American Association for the Advancement of Science.)

D. THE PERCEPTUAL IMPACT OF MORE COMPLEX NETWORK INTERACTIONS

1. A Comment

Although there are clearly phenomenal traces of the peripheral inhibitory and convergent processes in the perceptual responses of man, it is obvious that these phenomena represent only a partial picture of the rich variety of neural interactions possible in the afferent nervous system. The variety of man's thoughts does not result only from such simple processes, but more likely, from a hierarchy of many levels of concatenated interactions—some inhibitory, some excitatory, and certainly some that perform such complex forms of neurophysiological logic that they will forever be beyond the limits of human analysis. It is not too surprising, therefore, to realize that even in the peripheral nervous systems there exist complex network interactions that are not simply summatory or inhibitory but constitute higher-level combinations of these primitive logical elements into more elaborate information-processing mechanisms. In this section I consider some phenomena that probably result from these more complex peripheral neural interactions. These kinds of neural processing, though somewhat more intricate and involved than those I have already discussed, are still well within the Level 2 rubric.

There is, however, a difficulty concerning these more complex interactions that should be explicitly reiterated at this point. Though we have a substantial amount of information about the neurophysiology of inhibition and convergence, there is a paucity of direct neurophysiological data concerning the concatenated interactions in vertebrates that constitute the topic of this section. Because of the difficulties of studying such interactions in vertebrates, and the limitations of the available analytic technology, neurophysiological evidence for the complex interactions I am about to discuss is for the most part indirect or, even worse, nonexistent. Thus there is a considerable amount of controversy concerning what must, at best, be considered to be the speculative theory that is invoked to explain the phenomena I consider here. In Chapter 9 I deal more specifically with the problems involved in such conceptual constructs as "channels" and "detectors" and the role they play in current theory. For the moment the reader is forewarned not to expect too much precision in the way these words are used in this section.

2. Interactions Between Receptor Systems

A long-standing debate in visual science concerns the possibility of reciprocal interactions among the signals generated by the four types of receptors of the retina. In previous sections of this chapter, I emphasized those aspects of the problem of lateral inhibition and summation that arise as a function of the spatial distribution of the stimuli on a relatively macroscopic scale; two spots of light either interacted or did not as a function of the distance between them. However, neither the spectra of the light used in those experiments (which was, in almost all instances, white) nor the specific receptors upon which that light acted was treated as a significant variable in the experiments I have considered so far.

However, this problem must also be studied at another, more microscopic level at which stimulus spectra and receptor type becomes salient. The retina is not, as we have repeatedly seen, composed of a homogenous distribution of identical receptors. It is, rather, composed of four different kinds of receptors filled with four different kinds of photochemical and exhibiting four different absorption spectra.

Most germane to the present discussion, given the existence of the four interdigitated systems, is the question of whether the elements of these four systems spatially interact in a way that is comparable to the spatial interactions of different retinal regions. In other words, this question concerns the nature of interactions between the rods and cones as well as between the different types of cones. At least two answer to this question might seem equally plausible a priori. One could imagine a system in which only like receptors interacted, as well as one in which any receptor type could interact with any other. It is the purpose of this section to consider the empirical evidence related to this question.

The visual system provides ample anatomical opportunities for interactions between any of the four receptor types. There seem to be synaptic connections between the rods and all three kinds of cones (Sjöstrand, 1974), furthermore, electrophysiological recordings from many types of ganglion cells indicate that they are often activated by signals that come from both rods and cones. A very complete review of the manifold variety of retinal neural interconnections has also been presented by Stell (1972). One cannot read his remarkable essay without coming to the conclusion that the machinery is certainly present for the interaction of just about any retinal neuron with any other. A fine, though brief, review of anatomical and physiological data supporting interreceptor interactions has also been presented by Makous and Boothe (1974).

However, the reader must appreciate by now that the mechanical possibility is not tantamount to the operational fact. And indeed, until recently, the psychophysical side of the question of receptor interaction has been quite equivocal. There are well-thought-out and executed experiments that demonstrate interaction and equally well-designed studies that demonstrate a lack of interaction between the various receptor types; some investigators are convinced that interaction occurs and others that it does not. In preview, it is probably fairest to say only that there are conditions in which interaction can be unequivocally demonstrated and others in which it is unequivocally absent. Perhaps the unusually rancorous tone of this controversy in the visual literature can be alleviated in part by reminding all concerned that there really is no intrinsic inconsistency of results but rather an emerging diversity of opinion as different experimenters use different conditions. If one assumes that all are correct at least within their own sets of conditions, one quickly arrives at a reasonable consensus and begins to appreciate the richness of the processes probed by the question—do receptors interact?

The major technical problem in such an experiment, of course, is to actually isolate the rods and different kinds of cones from each other so that any measured effects can be definitively attributed to neural interactions rather than to the overlapping spectral sensitivities of the four receptors. A number of different approaches have been used to isolate receptors. One simple method is to present a stimulus (to a dark-adapted eye) whose luminance is below the cone's absolute threshold but above that of the rods. Such a stimulus has been referred to as a "pure scotopic stimulus." If such a scotopic stimulus is used as the "inducer" to test for an effect on cone vision, then any alteration on the response produced by a photopic stimulus must be attributable to an interaction between rods and cones.

To study interactions between the three different kinds of cones is more difficult. The usual way this problem has been attacked is to use Stiles' preadaptation–increment threshold technique to emphasize the response of one or another of the triad of receptor types. The reader should keep in mind, however, the many conceptual and empirical difficulties involved in interpreting the results of this type of experiment discussed in Chapter 6. Conversely, it should not be overlooked at this point that the meaning of the results obtained with Stiles' technique is itself very much dependent upon the assumed independence of the three systems! If, as seems to be the case, there is a great deal of interaction between the three cone systems, then much of the traditional theory underlying those results becomes equivocal. As I noted earlier, the π mechanisms were originally considered to reflect the properties of single cone systems. Now most workers in this field appreciate that many of the π mechanisms represent more complex composites of the properties of all three receptor types. Nevertheless, this procedure is still the most effective method that can be applied to the solution of the problem of photopic receptor interactions.

The basic issues of the controversy surrounding the possibility of interactions between rods and the three types of cones can be illustrated by considering some of the major early studies of the problem. Two studies, the results of which were interpreted to mean that there was no interaction between the various receptors, were reported by Alpern (1965) and Alpern and Rushton (1965). Another, which did report complex interactions between the four types of retinal receptors, was published by Boynton, Ikeda, and Stiles (1964). The totally opposite conclusions to which the respective authors came, although later rationalized, represent an interesting example of the flow of ideas in science.

Alpern (1965) attacked the problem by using an experimental paradigm in which a later, larger, surrounding stimulus was used to mask the effects of an earlier and smaller one. A constantly illuminated background stimulus of 625 nm (a light which appeared reddish-orange) was presented continuously to the observer. The test stimulus was a small (2.5 deg by 2.5 deg) square placed approximately 2 deg eccentric to the fovea. It had a dominant wavelength of about 527 nm and appeared to be green. The inhibiting, or masking, afterflash was a large circular spot, identical in shape to the contrast background except that it was blacked out in the region in which the test stimulus occurred. It occurred, and this is most important, 50 msec after the test flash. The wavelength spectrum and luminance of the afterflash were the major independent variables in the experiment. Figure 8-39 shows the various components of the stimulus used in Alpern's experiment.

Selecting the wavelength and luminance of the afterflash so that it was a pure scotopic stimulus, Alpern reported that the incremental energy required for the subject to detect the green-appearing (photopic) test stimulus on the reddish-orange background did not change as a function of the presence or absence of the afterflash. However, when a photopic afterflash, which was effective in activat-

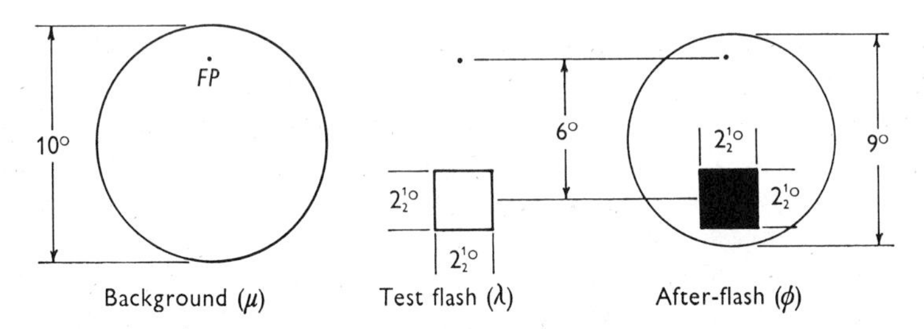

FIG. 8.39. The stimulus patterns used in Alpern's study of rod-cone interaction. (From Alpern, © 1965, with the permission of the *Journal of Physiology*.)

ing the cone systems, was used, there was a measurable additional effect on the threshold beyond the normal increase in the increment threshold produced by the background luminance per se. Similarly, if the experiment was carried out on an appropriately light-adapted observer who was responding mainly to cone signals, an inhibitory interaction of cones on cones was reported. Alpern's conclusion was that "There was no interaction between rods and cones," but he did feel that at least some kind of intercone or intracone interaction existed.

In a follow-up study, Alpern and Rushton (1965), using essentially the same test flash–afterflash experimental design (with the exception that a somewhat smaller test flash placed within the fovea was used), studied the interaction of the three "isolated" cone systems. Once again, they used the Stiles preadaptation procedure to enhance at least partially the activity of the three cone systems relative to the normal balance. The results of this study led Alpern and Rushton to reverse Alpern's original conclusion on intercone interaction and to assert that not only were the rods independent of the cones, but that the three cone systems were independent of each other as well! The interactions between cones observed in the earlier study (Alpern, 1965) were attributable, they speculated, only to interactions between the same kind of cones. That is, they asserted that the elevation in the incremental threshold for any of the π_1 π_4, or π_5 mechanisms depended only on the degree to which that system was activated and was independent of the degree to which the other two systems were activated.

Diametrically opposed results, however, had been obtained by Boynton, Ikeda, and Stiles (1964) only a year previously. Their experiments, which also used a Stiles preadaptation procedure, led to the conclusion that there were, in fact, very complicated patterns of interaction between the three cone mechanisms and that they were not, as Alpern and Rushton were subsequently to suggest, by any means independent.

It is important to note that in spite of the similarity of the general approach of Alpern and Rushton on the one hand, and of Boynton and his colleagues on the other, there were still some fundamental differences in procedure that suggest that the two studies were not directly comparable. The major difference was that the Boynton, Ikeda, and Stiles study did not use an afterflash or masking paradigm. They used an experimental design in which the stimuli for each of the three cone systems were presented at the same time and the same place—within a small spot of 10 min of visual angle in the middle of a 10 deg adapting field. The critical factor was the degree to which two simultaneous stimuli added together or inhibited each other as measured in terms of the respective independent and combined increment thresholds.

As a result of the outcomes of a comprehensive series of experiments that tested many conditions, Boynton, Ikeda, and Stiles concluded, unlike Alpern and Rushton, that a wide variety of different interactions existed among the three different cone systems. The types of interactions they observed were varied and included both inhibitory and summatory interactions reflected by respective elevations or depressions of thresholds. Although some evidence for probability summation was obtained, they also found psychophysical evidence of what they believed were genuine interreceptor interactions as well as other interneural interactions within the retina.

In recent years the controversy has continued without complete resolution, although a consensus does seem to be forming for the position that all types of receptors can interact with all others. A few investigators such as Westheimer (1970) have continued to report independence of rod and cone responses under some conditions. However, the preponderance of new data suggests that, in general, Boynton, and his colleagues were correct and that there are many conditions in which interreceptor interactions can be demonstrated. Indeed, it is the unusual and offbeat situation in which they are not so demonstrable. The afterflash or masking paradigm, which is one of them, seems to have an unfortunate choice with which to seek an answer to the question of receptor interaction.

The preponderance of recent research, as I noted, supports the idea that there are many conditions in which the four receptor systems interact with each other. For example, Makous and Boothe (1974), once again using the Stiles preadaptation technique, have shown that even when the scotopic luminance of different wavelength backgrounds are made equal, there is still a detectable difference in the incremental threshold of a superimposed test spot as the spectral properties of the background are varied. When coupled with other data showing that, in general, Boynton and his colleagues were correct and that there are many produce different rod thresholds, this evidence makes a compelling case for the presence of cone effects on rod responses. Ingling, Lewis, Loose, and Myers (1977) have also shown strong effects of cones on the rod threshold, as have Frumkes and Temme (1977), Barris and Frumkes (1978), and Blick and MacLeod (1978). Finally, Sternheim, Gorinson, and Markovits (1977) have also provided additional evidence that there is an effect of the various cones on each other.

Thus it seems certain now that there is a high degree of psychophysically observable interaction that corresponds to the well-established anatomical and neurophysiological opportunities for interactions between the four kinds of receptors. Why, then, in the light of the substantial mass of data that is now available demonstrating the presence of such interaction, was it missed in some of the earlier studies? The answer to this question is also now becoming clear. The newer studies make it clear that the interaction between the different kinds of receptors is strongly dependent upon two stimulus parameters—time and space—that were not adequately sampled in Alpern's (1965) and Alpern and Rushton's (1965) studies. Frumkes and Temme, for example, have shown that the interaction effect is substantially affected by the size of the stimuli. Any interreceptor effects, these investigators report, are washed out when the adapting field subtends an area greater than 6 or 8 deg of visual angle. It is only for smaller stimuli that any dependence on wavelength, and thus of cones on each other or on rods, can be measured. Similarly, Ingling, Lewis, Loose, and Myers (1977) have shown that the interaction effect is severely limited in time. These workers replicated Alpern's experiments, but instead of using a constant interval of 50 msec between the target and the afterflash, they varied the interval within a range of 0 to 60 msec. The results of this experiment showed that there was very little interaction between the receptors when the interval was equal to or greater than 50 msec, the very interval that Alpern had unfortunately chosen for his study, but that interaction did appear at shorter intervals.

In a similar way Makous and Peeples (1979) have resolved another discrepancy between two earlier studies that used virtually the same experimental paradigm but found opposite results. Makous and Boothe (1974) had found rod–cone interaction wherever Flamant and Stiles (1948) had not. Makous and Peeples have now shown that Flamant and Stiles had unfortunately chosen to work within a range of luminances and wavelengths in which the interaction was minimal. However, when the range was expanded (in the Makous and Peeples study), the interaction appeared.

Though these studies of the receptor interactions may seem like a relatively esoteric exercise, it turns out that the results of these studies have some very profound implications for many other areas of perceptual research. First, these findings speak directly to the problem of the nature of the four receptor systems. Because, as now seems clear, the degree of interaction between the various receptor systems is high, further support is provided for reconsidering the rationale behind Stiles' concept of the so-called π mechanisms themselves. Stiles' initial idea of selective adaptation, as I noted previously, depended upon the assumption of a relatively independent set of receptor channels. If they are not independent, exactly what the relationship is between the π mechanisms and the receptor absorption spectra becomes more and more uncertain and equivocal. Perhaps the π mechanisms are not neural mechanisms after all but interactive processes.

Another important implication of this now well-demonstrated interaction between the four receptor systems lies in the fact that the interreceptor interactions are lost at great distances and at substantial time differences. Yet these are exactly the conditions in which metacontrast and simultaneous brightness and color contrast, so often attributed to these mechanisms, are most powerfully seen. These data provide another compelling argument for the suggestion that these global phenomena are not, in fact, well explained by the type of peripheral network interaction I have been discussing here.

3. Chromatic Recoding[7]

a. The Mechanism

Another form of complex neural interaction that is now appreciated to exert a considerable impact on visual perception is the recoding of the afferent neural message that occurs as a result of interneuronal interactions in the retina. By *recoding,* I am referring to the translation that occurs in the neural signals and codes that represent such stimulus parameters as wavelength or intensity. In this section, I am concerned exclusively with the recoding of wavelength information and the psychophysics of the color-vision phenomena that seem to result from this recoding.

It is now well established (Baylor & Hodgkin, 1974; Marks, W., 1965; Tomita, Kaneko, Murakami, & Pautler, 1967) that the response of the vertebrate photoreceptor is a transient monophasic increase in the polarization of the plasma membrane. It is an equally secure conclusion that the responses of many, if not most higher-order neurons—including the second-order bipolars (Tomita, 1965), the ganglion cells (Wagner, MacNichol, & Wolbarscht, 1960), the neurons of the lateral geniculate body (DeValois, R., Abramov, & Jacobs, 1966; DeValois, R., and DeValois, K., 1975), and at least some cortical neurons—are opponent type cells that respond with either an increase or a decrease (in frequency or amplitude) in whatever electrophysiological response they are generating, depending upon the stimulus conditions. Because the coding ''language'' used at the receptor level differs from that at subsequent levels, there must be a transformation of codes inherent in the way in which the receptor feeds signals into the bipolar layer. It is the thesis of this section that these neural interactions also affect the molar properties of color perception and, thus, leave traces that can be detected in appropriately designed psychophysical experiments.

It has been hypothesized by Hurvich and Jameson (1957)[8] that the recoding of chromatic information as it passes from the receptors to the bipolar layer occurs as a result of interactions between the signals generated by the receptors. According to this model, there is a selective convergence of the signals from more than

---

[7]Some of the material discussed in this section has been adapted and updated from Uttal (1973).

[8]The classic zone or stage theories of color vision also implied such a recoding. However, Hurvich and Jameson's (1957) paper can be considered to be the first modern and specific model of this kind. Most recent interpretations take this paper as the jumping-off point into the modern era of opponent-color theory.

one kind of receptor onto a set of several opponent mechanisms. The basic idea is that although the receptors represent color by the relative amount of activity in three monophasic chromatic mechanisms, the opponent system represents chromatic information by means of the relative amount of activity in two chromatic and one luminance multiphasic mechanisms.

It is appropriate that I digress here for a moment to consider some important nomenclature. The word *trichromatic* is used in the present context to refer to a coding language in which three neural systems selectively and differentially sensitive to wavelength represent chromatic stimulus information. The ensemble of the activity in all three systems represents luminance, and all three of the systems respond monophonically. In other words the amount of induced neural activity is directly proportioned to the stimulus intensity.

The word *opponent,* on the other hand, refers to a neural coding language in which the activity in each of two systems may increase or decrease depending upon the wavelength of the light; in other words, the response is biphasic or even triphasic. In such a system a separate third black–white luminance system must be invoked.

The word trichromatic can also be used to describe the psychophysical fact that three degrees of freedom are necessary to match any color. In this sense, both the trichromatic and the opponent neural systems are trichromatic. This is not the way I use the term here.

These two encoding schemata—the opponent and the trichromatic systems—and the transformation logic that converts one code to the other are diagramed in Fig. 8-40. The details of this figure should not be taken too literally. There are many different variations on the same theme that would produce informationally identical mechanisms. The particular version that I present here differs from the one originally proposed by Hurvich and Jameson (1957) as well as from some newer models of these chromatic recoding circuits proposed by Guth and Lodge (1973), Massof (1977), and Ingling (1977). Figure 8-41, for example, presents two other alternative, but equally plausible, models that also explain how a trichromatic receptor layer could feed into an opponent-color secondary layer.

Another even more comprehensive and detailed model has been proposed by Ratliff (1976). This model (depicted in Fig. 8-42) suggests six levels of processing from the receptors to the opponent cells, some of which involve such neurally complex processes as differentiation and compression. Clearly, we are not simply talking about simple lateral inhibition and convergent summation, but neural interaction of a much more complicated kind, when we consider the translation from a trichromatic receptor to an opponent bipolar code.

However, other models involving more than three types of opponent mechanism at other levels of the visual pathway have also been suggested. A good summary of the current status of the problem is presented by DeValois and DeValois (1975). They assume six different kinds of opponent cells in the fourth layer (the lateral geniculate body) on the basis of Russel DeValois' classic studies

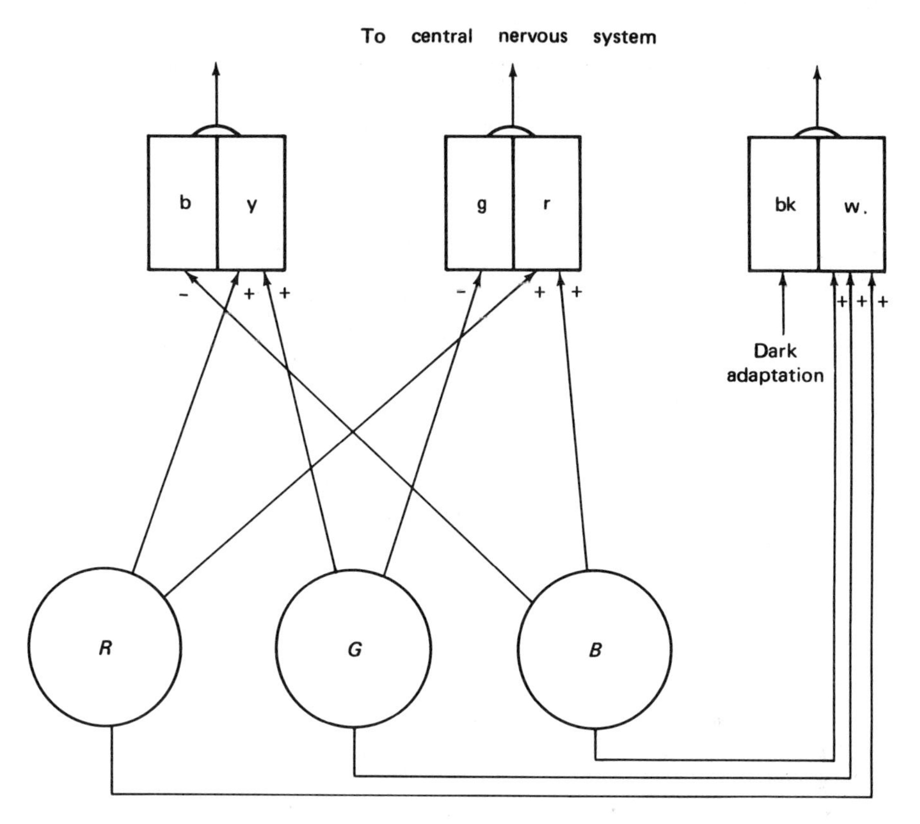

FIG. 8.40. A schematic sketch of a plausible neural mechanism, which could convert a trichromatic (R, G, and B) photoreceptor coding scheme to a more central opponent mechanism (b-y, g-r, and bk-w). (From Uttal, 1973, as adapted and modified from Hurvich and Jameson, 1957.)

(DeValois, Abramov, & Jacobs, 1966) of the responsivity of neurons at that level. Of course the existence of six different kinds of opponent cells does not mean that more than three degrees of freedom are required for a psychophysical color match, only that some combinations of these neural mechanisms are redundant with other combinations.

To add to the elegance of the system, it has even been suggested that the recoding accomplished within such a system is not stable but can vary as determined by the momentary state of dark adaptation (Ingling 1977). Such a finding also raises the possibility that this recoding process involves interactive inputs, not only from the three cones but perhaps also from the rods.

It should not be overlooked, however, that the various boxes in Figs. 8-41 and 8-42 need not necessarily indicate individual neurons. The flow of information in this case may be between larger units of organization; each block in these hypothetical diagrams may represent a functional *system* of neurons rather than a

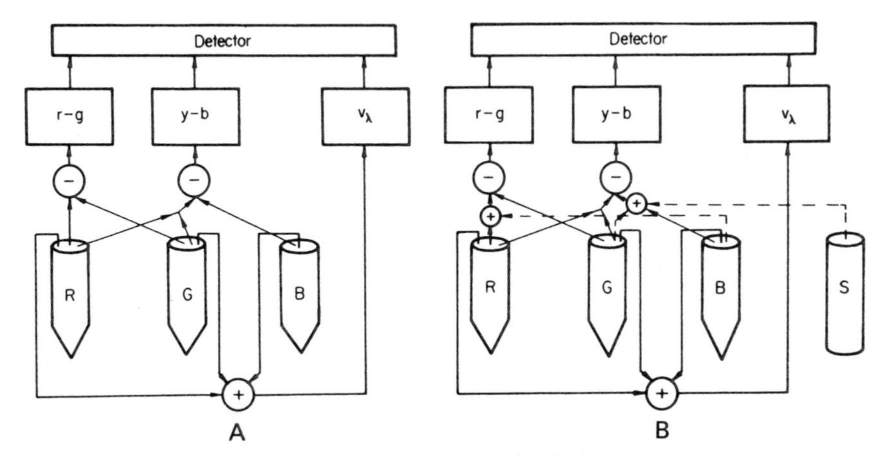

FIG. 8.41. Two alternative models of the neural network converting trichromatic to opponent codes in the retina. (From Ingling, © 1977, with the permission of Pergamon Press.)

single cell. Nevertheless there is strong evidence, as I have noted, that the recoding is carried out at least once between the receptors and the bipolars even though further transformations, it seems likely, must occur at higher anatomic levels.

In spite of the transformation from a trichromatic *code* to an opponent one at the receptor–bipolar interface, a trichromatic representation can be regenerated at higher levels of the nervous system by appropriate inverse transformations. It is possible, for example, to identify some trichromatically encoded neurons in the visual cortex (Anderson, Buchmann, & Lennox-Buchthal, 1962; Lennox-Buchthal, 1962; Motokawa, Taira, & Okuda, 1962), even though most cortical neurons appear to be opponent types if they are differentially sensitive to color at all.

It is, therefore, important to appreciate that the trichromatic information initially introduced as a result of the characteristic absorption spectra of the receptors is not lost when this information is recoded into an opponent set of symbols by the kind of neural network interactions exemplified by Figs. 8-41 or 8-42. The existence of the psychophysical "trichromatic fact" (any color experience can be matched by a mixture of any other three fundamentals) clearly shows that some properties of the *message* created by the receptors is maintained at the highest neural levels even if the neural language in which it is encoded is no longer trichromatic in the other sence of this word. Thus, despite the recodings, the trichromatic receptors have left this trace in the visual message in a way that has subsequent psychophysical implications.

In exactly the same sense, it is not unreasonable to assume whenever the neural signals are recoded from one neural coding language (e.g., trichromatic) to another (e.g., opponent) that the new coding schema will also insert some new properties into the message that can also have an observable psychophysical result. Indeed, present theory and empirical fact imply that this is exactly what happens. One has only to look back over the history of research in color vision to appreciate that the controversies that existed between the two major theoretical positions—the Young–Helmholtz trichromatic theory and the Hering opponent-color theory—could have been maintained only because both were at least partially valid. There are some psychophysical experiments that reflect the impact of the trichromatic receptors as I have previously noted; there are, in addition, some psychophysical experiments that reflect neural interactions and recoding of the signals from trichromatic to opponent-color mechanisms. There was, in fact, no fundamental inconsistency between the two theories (other than their detailed hypotheses concerning the nature of the receptors) but, quite to the contrary, a substantial complementarity. The key idea behind the contemporary rationalization of the two theories is that each describes a different level of coding and analysis. There were real differences between the two theories, of course, but only in terms of the physiological implementation that each assumed. Hering was

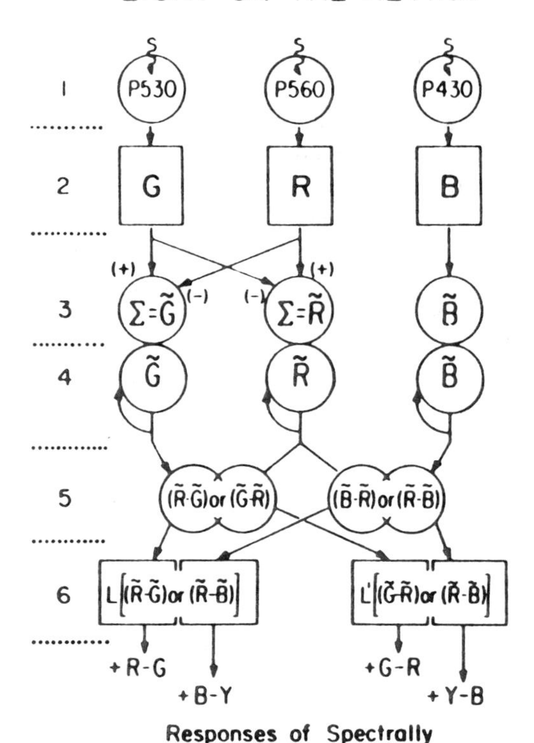

FIG. 8.42. An even more complicated neural model explaining the conversion of trichromatic to opponent codes in the retina. This model consists of six stages: 1. photoreception; 2. transduction; 3. lateral summation; 4. adaptation; 5. differentiation; and finally, 6. compression. (From Ratliff, © 1976, with the permission of MIT Press.)

wrong—we now know that there are no opponent receptors—but this was an anatomical detail that could not be ascertained until the advent of microelectrophysiology in the 1960s. He was entirely correct in assuming however, that *at some level* in the nervous system opponent mechanisms existed. But so were the proponents of the Young–Helmholtz theory correct in assuming that *at some level* trichromatic mechanisms also exist. The levels and sites at which the various mechanisms were actually operating were anatomical and electrophysiological details to be worked out later.

Our concern here, though, is with the perceptual phenomena that arise from the neural interactions underlying this recoding. In this category I would place all of the substantial body of data that pertains to opponent-color psychophysics as well as those anecdotal reports that suggest that there may be a fourth "primary" color, yellow, beyond the usual triad suggested by trichromatic theory. In the remainder of this section I consider the phenomenal traces of the opponent mechanism that occur as a result of this Level 2 recoding process.

b. The Phenomena

As one scans the historic literature of color vision, the idea constantly recurs that there is something special about yellow, so that it is not "perceived" in psychological experiments as a mixture of other colors as are such colors as greenish-blue or yellowish-red (orange). Rather, some visual scientists in the field have traditionally considered yellow to be "psychologically" just as primary as red, green, and blue. This statement is difficult to interpret, for at first glance it is not exactly clear why other color-naming situations might not lead to a wide variety of other so-called fundamental colors.

In spite of the vagueness and confusion regarding the definition and existence of a "fundamental yellow," there is a substantial amount of hard psychophysical data that supports the idea that there are links between certain color pairs that either operate together or in opposition. These kinds of data have been far more compelling than the possible existence of a vaguely defined "fundamental yellow." One of the most important of these pieces of evidence, the existence of complementary colors, is represented on the chromaticity diagrams shown in Fig. 6-8 and 6-9. Complementary colors are defined as those pairs of colors which, when mixed in appropriate amounts, produce a completely colorless or unsaturated white light. Complementary colors are represented on the diagram as the colors at the ends of any straight line whose colorimetric center of gravity lies in the central white region. Thus there are many colors that tend to cancel out the chromaticity of a complementary partner and that, therefore, presumably may be linked at some physiological or anatomical level.

A number of other ways in which pairs of colors seemed to behave in opposition have been summarized by Hurvich and Jameson (1957) as they argue for an opponent-color theory:

> how can a system of three independent processes be made to account, for example, for the apparent linkages that seem to occur between specific pairs of colors as either the stimulus conditions or the conditions of the human observer are varied? Why should the red and green hues in the spectrum predominate at low stimulus levels, and the yellow and blue hue components increase concomitantly as the spectrum is increased in luminance (von Bezold, 1873)? Why, as a stimulus size is greatly decreased, should discrimination between yellow and blue hues become progressively worse than that between red and green (Farnsworth, 1955; Hartridge, 1949)? Why should the hues drop out in pairs in instances of congenital color defect or when the visual system is impaired by disease (Judd, 1949; Köllner, 1912)? [pp. 384–385]

It has also been noted (Hurvich & Jameson, 1957; Linksz, 1964), that it is impossible to conceive of or to find words to describe a reddish-green hue or a yellowish-blue hue. The difficulty in finding a color for which we would use such color names, they believe, reflects the biological fact that the relationship between the percepts of blue and yellow, on the one hand, is different from that between yellow and red, on the other. But such data also suffer from the same difficulties as does the distinction of yellow as a primary color—color names are based on word usage and subjective judgments that are peculiarly elusive when one attempts to precisely define the operations involved in their elicitation. All we can say with some assurance now is that all of these questions and difficulties that I have just mentioned are probably explained in terms of opponent-type mechanisms.

A more compelling and quantitative body of supporting data has been developed by Jameson and Hurvich (1955) in their attempt to develop a quantitative opponent-color theory. Noting that a relatively wide range of spectral hues produces a partial experience of yellowishness, blueness, greenness, and redness, they attempted to determine the relative strength of each of these qualities by mixing varying amounts of a postulated opponent color with each hue-inducing wavelength until all traces of the original color disappeared. Thus, for example, a band of stimulus wavelengths varying from about 500–700 nm would produce color responses that were reported by the subject to have at least some yellowish tone. Various amounts of blue light would then be mixed with each of a series of wavelengths within this band, and the amount of blue required to cancel completely any "yellowishness" was measured as an indicator of the strength or chromatic valance of the yellow response at each wavelength.

Figure 8-43 shows a sample set of cancellation data for the visible spectrum. These data are plotted in terms of the amount of the opponent color that had to be added at each wavelength to eliminate any residual "redness, yellowness, greenness, or blueness." On this graph, it can be seen that the maximum amount of blue required to cancel yellowishness from one band (varying from 490–650 nm)

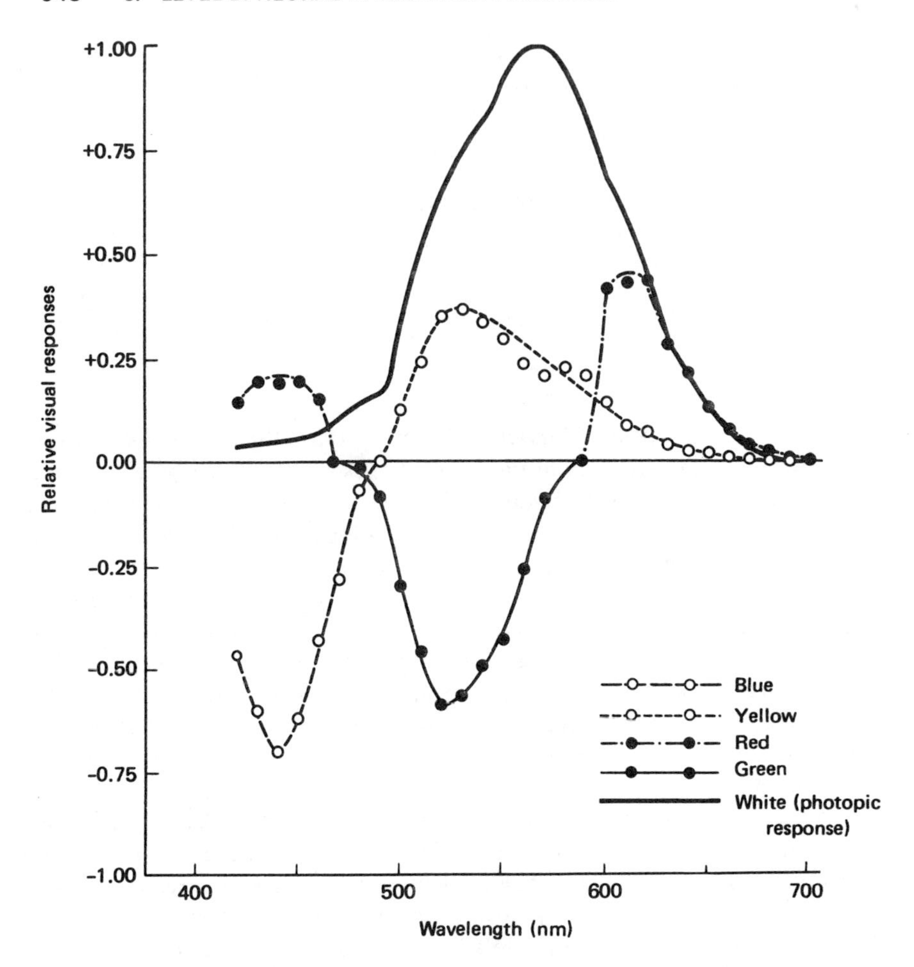

FIG. 8.43. Chromatic response functions for a single subject, indicating how much opponent color must be added to eliminate the residual chromatic effect of the colors indicated. The photopic luminosity curve is also shown for this subject. (From Jameson and Hurvich, 1955.)

was required at about 530 nm and that the function dropped off on both sides of this wavelength.

A wavelength band varying from 480–580 nm, on the other hand, elicited some green experience, which had to be neutralized with a red, the largest amount of which was required at about 520 nm. The fact that a single wavelength should produce some green and some yellow should not be too surprising. There is a range of wavelengths whose color names include greenish-yellow and yellowish-green, for example. When adequate amounts of red had been introduced to completely neutralize the green, the residual color would be a yellow.

When adequate amounts of blue had been introduced to completely neutralize the yellow, the residual color would be a green.

The curve also shows that the band of wavelengths that induces blue color experiences runs from 430–480 nm. These colors had to be neutralized with yellows, and maximal amounts of yellow were required at about 450 nm. The red curve, on the other hand, is somewhat peculiar because reddishness is an experience that is introduced by both long and short wavelengths. At the shorter wavelengths, the experience of violet includes chromatic experiences that most people describe as including some reddishness. At the longer wavelengths, the sensations are color-named as red or orange. To remove all of the reddishness from a short wavelength of about 400–470 nm, green light had to be added, peaking in the amount required for neutralization at about 440 nm. At the longer wavelengths, the range of red-inducing stimuli was about 580–700 nm, and the peak amount of green required for neutralization occurred at about 620 nm.

It should be noted that there are a number of difficulties with the Jameson and Hurvich neutralization procedure that preclude a very simple explanation of these data. First, it was both necessary and practically difficult to define, for each of these basic colors, exactly what the bandwidth of spectral wavelengths is that evokes the particular sensation. How can you be sure there is no yellowishness at a particular wavelength? Second, it is difficult to determine exactly when all of that yellowishness might be gone. The neutralized color often became an unsaturated rather than a saturated version of one of the other opponent pair. Thus, blue and a yellowish tone could be mixed together, and the observer might be faced with deciding whether there was any yellow in a resulting green or red field. Third, a more direct problem is that the data obtained with Jameson and Hurvich's hue cancellation do not agree with the data obtained in direct matching techniques (Ingling, Russell, Rea, & Tsou, 1978). Short-wavelength sensitivity is drastically overestimated by the former technique. It is possible, therefore, that the basic empirical facts as well as their interpretation may be open to question. Nevertheless, these experimental results are considered to be classic demonstrations of phenomena in color vision that are more likely to be attributable to the opponent coding mechanisms that exist at higher levels of the visual pathways than to the receptors.

It is important to note, furthermore, that there are really two quite distinct ways in which the idea of opponent mechanisms plays an important role in color vision research. First, there are the well-documented electrophysiological observations that indicate the existence of neurons whose wavelength codes are clearly opponent in nature. Second, there are the opponent-color models that are used to explain and describe a wide variety of different data ranging from the Bezold–Brucke effect through color blindness to adaptation to color cancellation. The richness of the controversy in color theory these days is at least partially due to the fact that both a trichromatic and an opponent model can do a fairly good job of representing much of the data that has been obtained. In this section I have concentrated on the phenomena that seem to reflect most directly opponent mechanisms and thus neural interactions in the visual pathway. It is likely, however, depending upon their personal orientations, that many of my colleagues would not necessarily agree with the attributions that I have made here. For reasons that are more or less convincing to each individual theoretician, these phenomena may be classified differently by others. The existence of theoretical explanations based on opponent mechanisms (which are contrary to the receptor level hypothesis I have championed) of such phenomena as the threshold for color (Massof, 1977) or of the Bezold–Brucke phenomenon (Krantz, 1975b) are two examples of the kind of difference in attribution to which I allude.

In any discussion of opponent theory, the special role of Dorothea Jameson and Leo Hurvich in promoting opponent-type theories should not be overlooked. Their leadership as latter-day proponents of opponent models of many visual phenomena is surely evidenced by their fine analyses in Volume VII/4 of the monumental *Handbook of Sensory Physiology* (1972; Chapter 14 by Jameson; Chapter 22 by Jameson and Hurvich; Chapter 23 by Hurvich).

Others have also helped to extend the opponent hypothesis far beyond Hering's original intent. In an exciting series of articles, Carl Ingling and his colleagues have expanded upon the Hurvich and Jameson (1957) transformation model to show how the recoding of the information from the three chromatic receptor channels combined with the center-surround properties of higher-order neurons lead to opponent mechanisms that seem to explain such diverse phenomena as the specific spectral sensitivities of the opponent mechanisms, Stiles' π mechanisms (processes?), color saturation, and hue discrimination (e.g., Ingling and Tsou, 1977). Figure 8-44, for example, shows the theoretically predicted spectral sensitivities of the two opponent mechanisms and the luminance mechanism based upon one model of recoding for both light and dark adapted states. This figure should be compared to the psychophysical data previously obtained by Jameson and Hurvich (1955, Fig. 8-43) to show the power of Ingling's model. Note also the great difference in spectral sensitivity between the light- and dark-adapted states in Fig. 8-44, another finding suggestive of a rod input to the opponent mechanism. The specific details of Ingling's theory of the convergent interaction leading to these phenomena are spelled out in a companion article (Ingling, 1977).

Another important theoretical development is the work of David Krantz of the University of Michigan. In two very important papers (Krantz, 1975a, 1975b), he proposed a formal mathematical model of opponent-color processes. Krantz' model represents every color experience as a multidimensional vector. These vectors represent the degree of correlation occurring between the different opponent processes (red-green, blue-yellow) as described in Jameson and Hurvich's classic study. Although Krantz' model is not phrased in anatomical or neurophysiological terms, it is explicit in its assertion that color experiences arise as a result of opponent mechanisms somewhere in the nervous system.

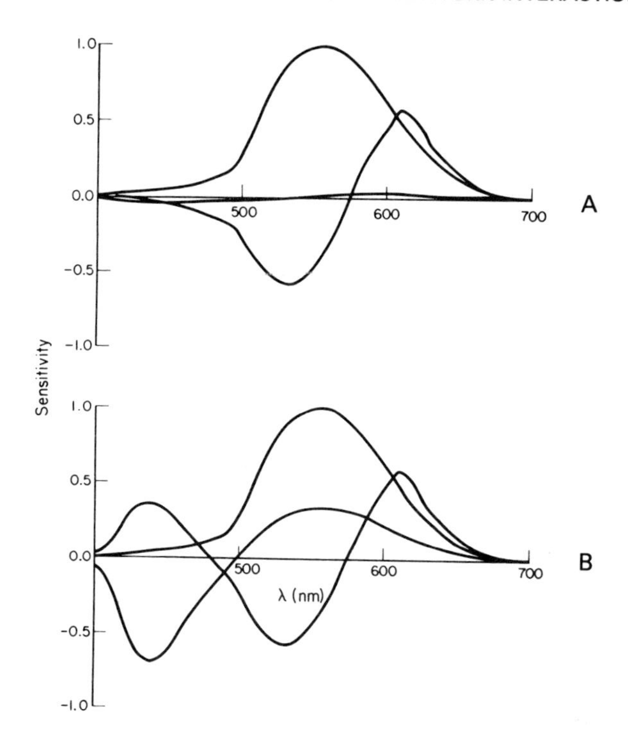

FIG. 8.44. Changes in the opponent color mechanisms as a function of stimulus intensity. (A) indicates the curves obtained using a dark adapted threshold measure. (B) indicates the curves obtained using a light adapted suprathreshold measure. (From Ingling and Tsou, © 1977, with the permission of Pergamon Press.)

In recent years there has been a high degree of activity in both opponent theory and in the empirical observation of opponent mechanisms and phenomena. These two approaches have complemented each other and, coupled with the striking breakthroughs that have been made in determining the properties of the receptors, have led to a much more mature and consensual idea of the nature of coding in the peripheral visual pathways than had been present prior to the last few decades of the 1960s and 1970s. The microspectrodensitometry measurements (see p. 403), which have definitively established the trichromatic properties of the receptor, and the electrophysiological data, which have unequivocally shown the existence of opponent mechanisms as early as the bipolar as well as at higher levels, have now led to an eclectic appreciation of the multiple codes used at the various stages of the afferent pathway. We are all both trichromatic and opponent theorists these days; we are all adherents of what have traditionally been called *zone* or *stage* theories.

In the final analysis, however, it should not be forgotten that we are emphasizing the neural communication codes of the afferent pathways when we discuss either trichromatic or opponent neural *mechanisms* and that we are not considering the central psychoneural equivalents of color perception. The important point, in spite of that limitation, is that the peripheral neural interactions described in this section do leave some traces in the perceptual response; and although the perceptual response cannot definitively specify the structure of the underlying mechanisms (for the logical reasons I have mentioned earlier), they do give behavioral clues to the nature of the constraints imposed by the various levels of recoding as the signal passes up the afferent pathway.

E. MISCELLANEOUS EFFECTS OF NEURAL INTERACTIONS

1. Dark Adaptation

In several earlier sections of this book, I discuss the impact of lower levels of processing on dark adaptation and indicated that the progressive increase in an observer's ability to detect low-level visual stimuli as a function of the time spent in the dark seemed to have multiple origins. I describe research demonstrating, somewhat surprisingly, how the amount of photochemical that is available can affect the threshold only when the level of light adaptation is very high. Research in the last decade has clearly shown that at lower luminances photochemical availability is not a significant determinant of the threshold. Thus some neural (as opposed to photochemical) processes must also be involved in determining the level of the minimum detectable stimulus. Some of the neural processes are, like the availability of the photochemical, Level 1 receptor effects; they reflect the internal properties of the receptor neuron itself rather than its role as a repository of the photochemical. Such mechanisms as self-inhibition of a receptor response due to the electrochemical effects of that response itself, perhaps mediated by some kind of a gain-controlling feedback mechanism, exemplify the type of intrareceptor neural mechanisms to which I alluded.

Now, however, I consider some Level 2, interneural interaction influences on the dark-adaptation process. From as far back as the early 1950s, there has been abundant psychophysical evidence available to support the idea that the spatial extent of the test spot or background field substantially effects the shape of the dark-adaptation function. Ratoosh and Graham (1951), for example, showed that the threshold for the detection of an incremental flash was lowered as the size of the adapting field was increased (up to about 1.34 deg), even when the adapting field's luminance remained constant. This impact of adapting-field size on the threshold of a test stimulus is clear evidence that interneural interaction in the retina is a significant contributor to the dark-adaptation process.

Westheimer (1965) has suggested that the functional relationship between the size of the adapting field and the threshold is much more complex and that it is only at low and high luminances that the process behaves in the way described by Ratoosh and Graham. At intermediate luminances he reports that the curve is nonmonotonic. From the smallest field size used (approximately 0.2 deg) up to an extent of about 1 deg, the size of the intensity increment required to achieve threshold grew as described by Ratoosh and Graham. However, for larger-sized adapting fields Westheimer found that the effect actually reversed and further increases in adapting-field diameter led first to a decline in the threshold and then to a region of no effect. Obviously, if Ratoosh and Graham had used larger adapting fields, they too probably would have observed a U-shaped function.

Other more recent experiments have supported the contention that there are substantial effects of the spatial pattern of the stimulus on the dark-adaptation process. Kitterle, Leguire, and Riley (1975) have demonstrated a modest effect of the orientation of a target on dark adaptation, and I have already mentioned Kitterle and Leguire's (1975) demonstration of the effect on dark adaptation of what were presumed to be lateral interactions between different portions of a stimulus. Other studies showing that the size of the region of spatial summation varies with the state of dark adaptation (e.g., Hallett, 1971) also support the idea that dark adaptation must be at least partially attributable to a Level 2 spatial interaction process.

Another way to support this same contention would be to demonstrate the spread of adapting effects from a relatively localized stimulus to other portions of the retina. Such an experiment was first carried out by Pirenne (1958), who used an annular adapting ring and a central test spot smaller than the blacked-out central region of the annulus. The adapting effect of the annulus was clearly evident in threshold measurements of the test spot even though the adapting field had not directly stimulated the test region itself. Ipso facto, there must have been some spread of effect, and Level 2 neural interaction effects on the state of dark adaptation seem certainly to be involved.

Rushton (1965), who also studied the problem of the spatial spread of adaptation, has shown that the integrated activity of the many receptors in a field of very dim light must be considered to account for the measured effects of background luminance and not just local adaptation effects alone. Such a result led him to suggest the existence of an adapting pool of neurons (such as that shown in Fig. 8-45) that is analogous to the excitatory pool observed in spatial summation experiments.

Ample neurophysiological evidence exists to back up Rushton's idea of an adaptation pool and the hypothesis that Level 2 interactive processes must also be responsible for some of the attributes of the dark-adaptation phenomenon. Many of these neurophysiological findings are reviewed by Green, Tong, and Cicerone (1977) in the introduction to their study of the lateral spread of light adaptation in

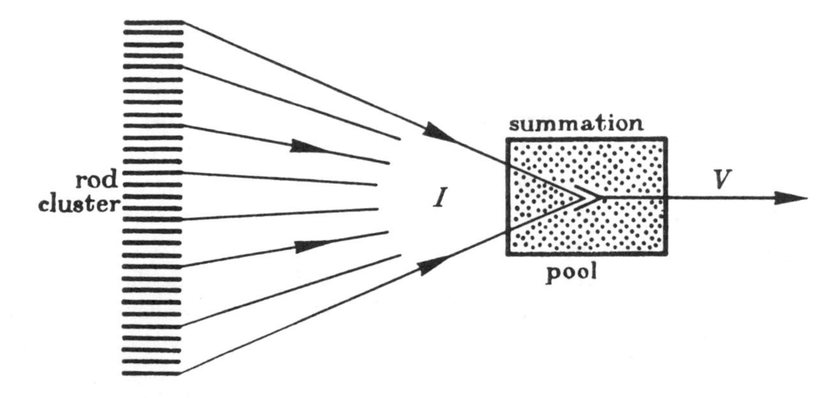

FIG. 8.45. A diagrammatic representation of dark adaptation consisting of many rods converging on a "summation pool." (From Rushton, © 1965, with the permission of The Royal Society of London.)

the rat's retina. An important outcome of their experiment was that the adaptation pool operating on any neuron in the rat's retina is not identical to the receptive field or summation pool. Thus, somewhat different interactive linkages between the various retinal neurons probably underlie the Level 2 dark-adaptation effects than underlie the receptive field properties of any ganglion cell.

Green, Tong, and Cicerone also determined that the pooling was not constant; that is, they showed that different experimental conditions could actually lead to a situation in which a more distant spot produced a larger effect than a closer one, or vice versa, on the same neuron. The specific nature of the effect could also change from one lighting condition to the next. Obviously this introduces a further complication into the dark-adaptation process. The idea of establishing an exact and fixed wiring diagram of the retinal plexus becomes even more elusive in the light of this plasticity. Furthermore, other workers have demonstrated that the difference between receptive fields and adaptation pools may be species-specific. Enroth-Cugell and Shapley (1973) have shown that in cats the adaptation and receptive fields are roughly the same size, and Burkhardt and Bernston (1972) have demonstrated that the adaptation pools are significantly smaller than the receptive fields in frogs.

Regardless of these species and situational differences, it is clear that lateral interaction processes among the neurons of the retina also contribute to the dark-adaptation process. These network interactive mechanisms are, along with the neural (but not the biochemical) processes within the receptors, likely explanations for some of the more rapid adaptive changes that occur in the early part of the dark- and light-adaptation cycles.

2. Blue Arcs and Phosphenes—Effects of Neural Geometry

Virtually all of the interactive processes discussed so far in this chapter are presumably mediated by synaptic interconnections within the latticelike neural network. However, in this section I describe two instances in which the structural organization of the visual system may itself be the proximal cause of certain visual phenomena in a way that does not involve synapses; that is, in this section I note that it is also possible to attribute certain visual phenomena to the static anatomical arrangement of the various neural units in the retina even when no synaptically mediated network functions occur. The emphasis in this section, therefore, is on the otherwise informationally passive nodes (i.e., neurons) of the neural network, rather than on the points of synaptic interconnection upon which the discussion has previously concentrated.

Consider first the phenomenon known as the Purkinje or blue arc of the retina. The blue arc is produced when a small and dim (preferably red) light is presented to an eye that has been previously adapted to a medium level of illumination. Flashing the dim red light seems to help produce the maximum brightness of a pattern of relatively dim gray or blue arcs (Ingling & Drum, 1977). Figure 8-46 shows the characteristic shape and location of the blue arcs and one way in which they can be produced by a moderately strong stimulus. The important fact in the present context, according to Alpern and Dudley (1966) and all other contemporary workers, is that the blue–gray arcs appear to be coextensive with the course of the arcuate bundle of ganglion cell fibers that pass between the fovea and the optic disk. This fact has been interpreted to mean that the perceived shape of the arcs is a direct outcome of the shape of this bundle of axons. Somehow, it is

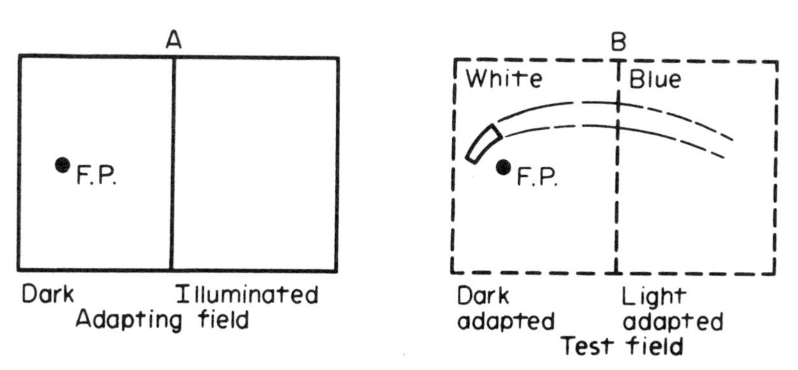

FIG. 8.46. (A) The stimulus used to elicit the blue arcs of the retina, and (B) an artist's impression of the subjective impression of the phenomenon. (From Ingling and Drum, © 1977, with the permission of Pergamon Press.)

proposed, neural activity in the arcuate bundle is communicated to the underlying neurons. How activity in this bundle is so communicated, however, remains a matter of some mystery.

The beginnings of a general explanation of this blue arc phenomenon have, nevertheless, begun to emerge. The basis of the explanatory hypothesis is that the dim red light, which is presented near but not on the fovea, produces neural activity in the arcuate bundle. This neural activity somehow stimulates other nearby receptors or second-order neurons as the spike action potentials pass through this fiber bundle. Since these ganglion cell axons are not endowed with any synaptic connections over the course of this passage, the interaction must be in the form of a direct axon-to-cell body or axon-to-axon ephaptic (i.e., nonsynaptic) communication of neural signals.

Alpern and Dudley (1966) consider several possible explanations for the transfer of information from the arcuate fiber bundle to the underlying neurons. These include secondary photoradiations by the arcuate fibers, electrotonic coupling, and local ionic depletion. However, they agree that there still is no truly compelling explanation of the blue arcs. If they are truly the result of an ephaptic interaction, the process is probably unique in being associated with a measurable perceptual phenomenon. Although such workers as Alpern and Dudley have suggested that cones must be the key receptors in the process, and Ingling and Drum (1977) have suggested that the bluish color of the arcs can be explained best in terms of an opponent-color type system, no one has yet successfully explained how the arcuate fibers activate the other involved retinal neurons. What is central to the present discussion, however, is that whatever the means of intercommunication between the arcuate fibers and other neurons, the shape of the phenomenon is directly determined by the shape of the arcuate bundle. Thus this rare phenomenon is a characteristic signature of the anatomy of the retina.

Another phenomenon that may also be a direct reflection of the anatomy of the retina is the visual phosphene. Phosphenes are the visual experiences that are produced by inadequate (i.e., nonphotic) stimuli. Electrical currents passed directly through the retina (Motokawa, 1950; Motokawa, & Akita, 1957) or through the cortex (Brindley & Lewin, 1968; Dobelle, Mladejovsky, & Girvin, 1974) can produce visual phosphenes. These often colorful geometric phenomena, however, can also be produced by applying mechanical pressure to the eyeball (Tyler, 1978b). Sometimes what seem to be irrelevant visual stimuli such as flickering homogeneous (Young, Cole, Gamble, & Rayner, 1975) or checkerboard light patterns (Welpe, 1975) can also produce similar patterns. However it is the mechanically induced phosphenes that are particularly interesting because they seem often to occur as highly regular, geometrical patterns that some students of the topic (e.g., Oster, 1970) believe may also reflect the orderly arrangement of the neurons of the retina. If Oster's speculation is correct, then these regular patterns reflect a much more regular neural pattern than is obvious in the microanatomy of the retina I discussed in Chapter 3. It may be, therefore,

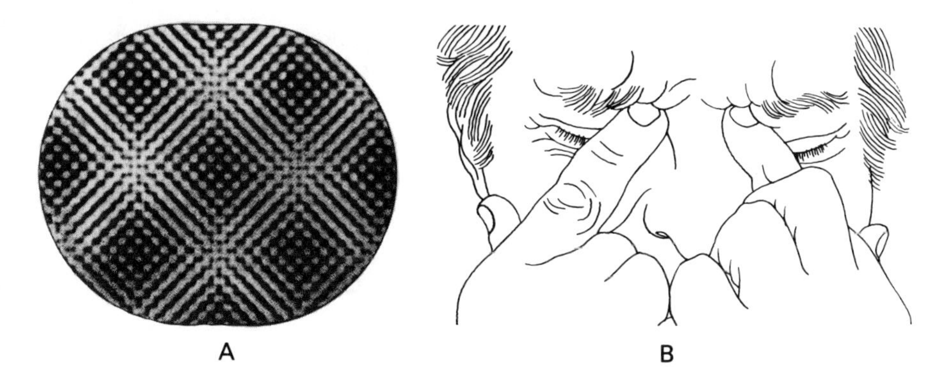

FIG. 8.47. (A) An artist's impression of the visual phosphenes produced by applying mechanical pressure as shown in (B). (From Oster, © 1970, with the permission of *Scientific American*.)

that these patterns do not reflect regularity at the individual cellular level but at some higher level of retinal organization. In other words, one might better attribute the phenomenon to the geometrical regularity of groups of neurons rather than of individual cells. Oster believes that these phenomena are strictly retinal, and thus functionally anatomical in origin, and that they may provide the basis for the design similarities observed in ancient specimens of pottery from different cultures, as well as in the regular patterns so commonly observed in children's art, so often seemingly independent of cultural origins.

Tyler, on the other hand, believes that the binocular properties of the mechanical pressure phosphene relegates it to a geniculate, or possibly even a cortical, level. He suggests that the phosphene is "a kind of a functional Golgi stain by which certain neural activities are elevated into consciousness while the majority of possible discharges remain ignored." Both Oster and Tyler agree, however, that the basis of the phosphene is the well-organized structure of the visual nervous system.

3. Others

There are a large number of other examples of interactive effects whose origins are not yet well understood. But clearly many dimensions of the stimulus may interact with each other either intracellularly or intercellularly to produce sometimes surprising cross-dimensional effects. For example, it has been shown that both the spectral properties (Sharpe, 1974) and the duration of a stimulus (Kitterle & Rysberg, 1976) can affect the contrast threshold of a grating. Similarly the spatial frequency of a grating can affect judgments of its brightness (Walker, 1978). We have already discussed the general interplay between dominant wavelength, purity, and luminance on hue, saturation, and brightness and new data continue to support that concept (Bauer & Rohler, 1977). The effects of contours on thresholds have long been known and repeatedly confirmed (Fry & Bartley, 1935; Kitterle & Leguire, 1975; Markoff & Sturr, 1971). Many of these effects seem to be Level 2 processes, but as we see in Chapter 11, there are many analogous Level 4 processes.

F. AN INTERIM SUMMARY

In this chapter, I have continued my analysis and classification of the processes that underlie perceptual phenomena. I hope by now it is absolutely clear to the reader that the taxonomy that I am developing here is based upon the underlying processes and the most plausible explanatory models rather than upon the phenomena themselves. In this chapter I have mainly dealt with those aspects of psychoneural processing that can be understood best in terms of the interactions carried out within the network of neurons that constitute the afferent visual pathway. As I argue in the next chapter, not all phenomena that are conventionally attributed to this second level of psychoneural processing are properly classified within this rubric, from my point of view. The reasons for excluding particular processes are explained in the next chapter, but for the moment, the reader is urged to suspend judgment about what may appear to be inadvertent omissions from this chapter.

I have tried to define exactly and explicitly what I mean by a network interaction process in this chapter and have spelled out the various kinds of interactions that seem to be plausible candidates to explain certain relevant and appropriate phenomena. Perhaps the key idea implicit in all discussions of these Level 2 processes is that they are intrinsically isomorphic; i.e., in most cases, spatial interactions led to corresponding alterations in the spatial nature of the perceived phenomena. In general, the network is behaving in a dimensionally straightforward or veridical way for most of the processes considered here. The processing discussed is direct, spatiotemporally compatible, and not symbolic or interpretive in any sense. This is the last level of processing at which this kind of isomorphism is observed.

As I conclude this discussion of the lower three levels (0, 1, and 2) of visual processes, it is important for the reader to appreciate that these singular, deterministic, and isomorphic relationships between such stimulus factors as wavelength, luminance, or contour, on the one hand, and the dimensions of the perceptual experience, such as color, brightness, and edges, on the other, hold only in the most highly abstract and unrealistic laboratory conditions. As we see in subsequent chapters, the actual perceptual experience is not, in general, so uniquely defined by the physical properties of each region of the stimulus scene. Rather, contextual and experiential factors can and do override or modulate the perceptual dimensions in ways so profound that at times there may appear to be no actual relationship at all between the transformations that occur at these lower levels and the final nature of the percept.

Another important general principle that emerged from the evidence reviewed in this chapter is the extreme experimental importance of adequately scanning the full range of each independent variable. I noted a number of false controversies that arose because of an inappropriate choice of the range over which some independent variable was manipulated. In some cases the discrepancy was not simply quantitative, an underestimation or overestimation of the magnitude of the response, but qualitative, a completely incorrect expression of the nature of the interaction (or noninteraction) between the dependent and independent variables.

Having discussed the possible types of neural interactions, I considered a number of phenomena that are attributable to one of the simplest kinds of neural interaction—spatial convergence. Spatial summation, color perception, and acuity were all found to be at least partially influenced by the convergence of signals from different portions of the ascending visual pathway even though they differ substantially in their subjective characteristics. Thus, in terms of the best current explanatory model, these phenomena share a common origin and represent a single class of perceptual response.

Next I considered a number of perceptual topics, all seeming to arise from the ubiquitous inhibitory interactions of the neural network. These phenomena are all more obviously related to each other than were those elicited by convergent mechanisms. Such phenomena as the Mach band, the Hermann grid, and certain other edge and contour effects fall easily within this category of processes. One important general point made here, which is expanded upon in Chapter 9, is that such short-distance-limited spatial interactions as those that underlie the Mach band, for example, are not good models for more global phenomena, such as simultaneous contrast, with which they may share a modicum of superficial similarity.

However the eye does not see by convergence or inhibition alone, and more complex forms of interactions involving combinations of several different logical processes were also discussed and categorized. The problem of receptor interaction was considered as was the phenomenal impact of neural recoding and certain other interdimensional interactions.

In conclusion, I must observe that this chapter is briefer than I would have predicted. A major portion of the experimental and theoretical literature in vision today is based upon spatial interactive models of the kind I have emphasized here. It is my conclusion, however, after reviewing this literature, that many of the associations that have been drawn between phenomena and peripheral network processes are spurious and that far fewer phenomena are appropriately classified here than is generally appreciated. As we see later, nonisomorphic neural interactions of much more complex kinds may better explain such phenomena as pattern recognition or simultaneous contrast–phenomena that are frequently misclassified as the result of Level 2 processes.

This, then, concludes the neuroreductionistic phase of my analysis. In the next chapter, I deal with the logic of the transition between those levels that are patently neural, and those which I believe are complex beyond the most radical limits of this kind of psychobiological reductionism. When I return, in Chapter 10, to further the development of the taxonomy that is the central theme of this book, the discussion will be predominantly descriptive and phenomenological.

9 Mezzolog: On The Limits of Neuroreductionism—A Heretical View

A. INTRODUCTION

1. An Orientation

This chapter is intended to be a transistional mezzolog. It is an explicit effort to establish a line of demarcation between the two major kinds of theoretical explanation in perceptual psychology—neoempiricistic neuroreductionism and neorationalistic constructionism. In this chapter I lay aside the neurophysiological theories that were the modal form of explanation in Chapters 5 through 8 and turn to more descriptive and molar models for consideration of the remaining levels of perceptual processing. As I do so, however, it is necessary to spell out the reasons for this transition and, perhaps even more important, to justify with data and logic why I do not find some of the popular neuroreductionistic theories to be compelling explanations of Level 3 and Level 4 phenomena.

The transition to nonreductive models that I hope to accomplish in this chapter is virtually total, and I hope to maintain it consistently throughout the rest of this book. Nevertheless, this does not mean that I have also abandoned my emphasis on process as opposed to phenomena. It remains my intent to concentrate on the common explanatory processes underlying the plethora of phenomena that have been observed by perceptual scientists. The explanatory processes used to explain perceptual phenomena associated with Levels 3 and 4, however, are not couched in the logic or language of neurons, synapses, and networks. Rather, the vocabulary to which I now turn denotes functions that, in general, have no specific neurological constructs associated with them. The main rationale behind this transition from neural to molar process is the very practical one to which I have alluded several times in previous chapters—the conceptual, instrumentational, and mathematical tools necessary to model the extremely complex neural networks that must underlie these higher-level perceptual processes are not yet, and may not ever be, developed to a level sufficient to accomplish the task we ask of them. Hopefully, at this point, it is redundant for me to reassert that this failure of analysis in a practical sense is in no way a renunciation of the principle implicit in the primary monistic premise of psychobiology. No matter how refractory the practical aspects of the problem, the implicit commitment of modern perceptual science to psychobiological monism remains intact; most of us in the field act as if we still believe that all mental processes are, in the final analysis, nothing more or less than another set of functions of the neural substrate. That we cannot yet understand the nature of the links between the neural and the mental should in no way subvert the principle of psychoneural monism that is the central metaphysical premise of this science.

Because I am going to be especially critical of a pervasive and popular, but I believe false, kind of neuroreductionism, I have a special responsibility to explain the reasons behind the antireductionistic bias that permeates the remainder of this book. In this mezzolog, therefore, I intend to pinpoint the conceptual basis and implicit or explicit premises and implications of the various neuroreductionistic theories. This is done in order to define their respective terminology more completely and to consider why I believe some of these neural models are inadequate "explanations" of many of the phenomena to which they have been applied. I also try to indicate why I believe contemporary perceptual psychology has so often been susceptible to this form of pseudoexplanation. After having considered these issues and pointing out some counterindications to the most popular of the neuroreductionistic dogma, I continue with the development of the multilevel taxonomy that I commenced in Chapter 4 but in terms of neorationalistic rather than neoempiricistic explanations.

2. Some Basic Concepts

To appreciate fully the inadequacy of perceptual neuroreductionism in so many areas of perception requires that we reconsider some of the basic concepts underlying reductive theory in science generally and in perception particularly. Let us start by considering the fundamental difficulty of applying reductive explanation to any system that is not amenable to dissection and analysis in their most literal sense.

The brain of all vertebrates, and of man in particular, is immensely complicated. Some estimates place the number of neurons as high as 10^{13}. (This number is three orders of magnitude higher than that usually given because of the emerging appreciation of the enormous numbers of small cells in the cerebellum.) Yet each of these 10 trillion neurons may itself have many thousands of synaptic connections with other neurons. The totality of this maze of interactions defines a system intrinsically so complex that it may not be computable or analyzable in any practical sense. Thus even though microelectrodes may be inserted into single cells, the recorded responses can only poorly reflect the activity of the very complex network of other neurons of which that neuron is an interacting part. The responses recorded from the individual neurons can at best provide only the most incomplete indication of the true functional complexity of the neural net. In vertebrates, in particular, neurons are small and idiosyncratic, and recordings of their responses are ephemeral at best. Even if there were some specific functional role played by each neuron in vertebrate preparations, it is virtually impossible to recover a particular cell after the tip of recording microelectrode has moved on, and thus improbable within one preparation to replicate any observation. How much less likely it would be to replicate the recordings obtained from any particular neuron as one moves from one preparation to another!

The problem of repeated probing of even well-identified units may be even further complicated by the fact that an individual neuron may not, in fact, play the same role from one moment to the next. Many modern theorists, notably E. Roy John (1972), have suggested that the statistics of the ensemble are more important than the responses of the individual neurons. Thus even if it were possible to record repeatedly from a particular neuron, experimenters cannot be certain that a given neuron will be doing the same thing each time they record from it. This is so even in those cases in which the relevant molar behavior or mental process is extremely stable.

It is, therefore, not simply the "black box"[1] arrangement of most psychological experiments that makes the unique specification of internal function so difficult. It is also possible that even when one "opens" a black box, the complexity of the internal structure may be so enormous that the box may remain functionally "closed." A black box, therefore, may be functionally defined not only as one whose cover cannot be violated but also as one whose internal structure is too complex to be interpretable.

---

[1]The term *black box* has been borrowed from engineers by psychologists. A black box, to the engineer, denotes any mechanical system that cannot be opened up to allow direct examination of its internal structure. Therefore, in both engineering and psychological experiments, the only avenue to understanding a black box is to compare its input and its output. The present discussion asserts that profound constraints on analysis and understanding emerge directly from that limitation.

Given the enormous number of neurons and synapses in any brain and the limits of electrophysiological technique at its best, the conceptual question can responsibly be asked whether or not a neuroeductionistic approach is likely to be fruitful in the study of those great neural networks that must be the equivalents of most interesting perceptual processes. This question is, of course, probably unanswerable in general; no science should be limited in terms of its ultimate destiny a priori. Nevertheless, in terms of its current practical limits, it is quite clear that the neuroreductionistic approach is patently incapable of explaining most phenomena of visual perception. No matter how strong the desire or how suggestive the neural analogy, this is an undeniable fact.

Another conceptual issue, closely related to this problem of the limits of neuroreductionism, concerns the equally limited capacity of mathematics to analyze the internal mechanisms of complex systems. A profound misunderstanding is rampant among psychologists concerning the role of mathematics in modeling perceptual phenomena. Mathematics is essentially a descriptive tool when used in the context of psychological theory. Mathematical models describe processes and functional interrelationships between stimulus and response variables. They do not, however, uniquely specify particular internal structure no matter how precise their descriptions of the molar phenomena. One has only to work with analog computers in order to appreciate that many different mechanisms and physical implementations are capable of producing identical patterns of functional response. The equation $y = \sin x$, for example, is a mathematical model that can describe the behavior of a swinging pendulum, a vibrating spring, an oscillating electronic circuit, a digital calculation, or a perceptual phenomenon like the Pulfrich effect. In all of these cases there is a close *functional analogy* between the similar response patterns, but a totally different *physical mechanism* underlies the sinusoidal function in each. The key implications of this state of affairs is the one to which I have alluded earlier in this book—there is in principle no way to go from a specific external stimulus—response function to a unique statement of specific internal mechanism or even to a limited class of plausible alternatives. Mathematical models always allow virtually infinite numbers of alternative possible internal structures. Other criteria must be applied to ascertain first, which of the possible mechanisms are plausible, and then, which actually exist.

It is further true that many different mathematical models that seem at first glance to be distinct turn out to be identical to each other when appropriately transformed. For example, the autocorrelation representation of a signal is identical to the Fourier transform of the power spectrum, and vice versa. Thus, autocorrelation domain and frequency domain models of perceptual phenomena are, for all purposes, informationally identical. The information contained in each domain *must* be the same as the information contained in the other even though the expressions used by each model may look quite different. This is so in spite of the fact that the mechanisms capable of performing an autocorrelation or a Fourier analysis are not identical.

The point is that one cannot tell from the output of the system anything about the actual internal mechanism; either an autocorrelator or a Fourier analyzer could produce the same "behavioral" outcome. Indeed, it is not even possible in a strict sense to tell what mechanical implementation may be responsible for a process as simple as addition. Addition may be carried out within a system in any one of a number of internal arithmetic languages and yet still be converted to exactly the same final sum by some terminal translator. Binary, octal, decimal, or hexidecimal machine languages can all be used to calculate the sum of any pair of numbers with equal accuracy.

A nonnegligible amount of effort has been directed in recent years to showing the equivalences among such neural models as the receptive field, Fourier channel, and lateral interaction theories of perception. It is entirely possible that, within the limits of explanation reasonably attributable to such neuroreductionistic models, they too are all equally correct or incorrect in exactly the same sense. Each may be transformable into any of the others by the appropriate logical and mathematical manipulations. To the extent that these different neural models can be represented by the same mathematical expressions, this intertransformability would be but another example of the intrinsic equivalence that is built into such quantitative or quasiquantitative models even when the physiological and anatomic axioms of each theory are quite distinct.[2]

Another equally disconcerting limitation of any mathematical analysis is that it may sometimes carry surplus meaning. Many years ago, when I was first introduced to quantum mechanics, I was told by my instructor that even though the solutions to certain equations had both negative and positive roots, some of these roots must be physically meaningless. Barring any new developments in matter and antimatter theory of which I am not aware, it is probably still the case that the negative roots of mathematical representations of certain physical systems are simply thrown out as being more characteristic of the modeling mathematics than of the system under investigation.

In exactly the same way, one of the most popular contemporary theories of perception—the Fourier spatial frequency channel theory—is considered by some to possess invalid anatomical implications that are manifestations of the surplus meaning of the analytical mathematics rather than of the true biology of the visual system. It must be kept in mind that the basic Fourier theorem says only that *any* function (as long as it meets the conditions of linear superimposition and the Drichelet criteria of continuity) can be represented by the sum of a series of orthogonal functions. The fact that *any* function can be so analyzed

[2]We see later how the anatomical and mathematical propositions of any theory are usually independent and can be treated separately.

mathematically has led a number of investigators to infer (erroneously, I believe) that there must also exist a family of "frequency-filtering channels" within the afferent nervous system. Whether or not this biological hypothesis is acceptable is a matter that I discuss a few pages later, but for the moment I call attention only to the fact that the existence of the specific spatial frequency filter *mechanisms* is not a necessary derivative of the existence of an analytical mathematical method that allows the representation of complex *functions* as sums of simple sinusoids, square waves, or even pulse trains. As with the negative roots in quantum mechanics, the inferred anatomical implementation may be an example of surplus meaning erroneously inferred by the mathematical modeler. The point is that there is an enormous difference between the use of the Fourier mathematics, or any other mathematical system, as a means of generating or describing well-defined stimuli, or as a means of analyzing response data, and the logically unrelated hypothesis of a specific neuroanatomic implementation.

Linguistic issues also intrude into any discussion of the plausibility of any neuroreductive analysis of perceptual processes. As I mentioned in Chapter 4, it is not well appreciated how often the links between a neural and a mental construct are based only on some very weak pun—a play on words that sound alike, but that may have quite different meanings. The classic pun in psychobiology, of course, is on the word *conditioning*. The term originally arose in early Pavlovian learning theory and denoted a change in behavior due to a pairing of a naturally effective stimulus with a naturally ineffective stimulus. This use of the word is a linguistic construct at a molar psychological level representative of a very complex network of millions, if not billions, of neurons. However, with the advent of microelectrophysiology, the same word has come to be applied to describe somewhat similar processes within simple neurophysiological preparations involving only a few cells. Nothing is inherently wrong with this dual denotation, but a serious problem occurred when psychobiologists assumed, partly on the basis of the common vocabulary, that the neural conditioning process *is* the basis of the psychological conditioning process.

The contemporary analog of the conditioning pun is embodied in the term "feature detection." Selective responding to particular geometric properties by an individual neuron (feature detection in the first sense) *does not necessarily* correspond to pattern recognition as a discriminative molar response by an entire organism (feature detection in a second sense). Indeed, there is still poor support for the idea that exhaustive listing of the properties of a stimulus form is the best or only method by means of which an organism could recognize patterns. There is ample evidence in the psychological literature, as well as in common knowledge, that man sees not by features but rather by global forms, no matter what the neurons of his retina, lateral geniculate body, or even striate cortex are individually doing. Figure 1-2 makes this point very clearly by demonstrating a collection of figures that are classified under a common rubric yet have virtually no local features in common.

Linguistic pitfalls of this sort have been brought into sharp relief by the noted neurophysiologist Eric Kandel. His words were paraphrased as follows by the organizers of a meeting at which he spoke about this same problem of the psychoneural pun (Teyler, Baum, & Patterson, 1975, p. 67):

> The vocabulary used to describe the alterations seen at a cellular level should be distinguished from the vocabulary used to describe alterations in the behavior of an intact organism. Even if a cellular response showed all the features associated with behavioral habituation, Kandel argued the cellular alteration is not habituation and should not be called that. Rather the cellular change should be referred to by its mechanisms or its properties: excitatory synaptic decrement, inhibitory recruitment, etc. This would avoid the difficulties inherent in (incorrectly) applying behavioral terms to physiological processes. Habituation is an animal process much like walking and talking. One would certainly not say that a cellular change is walking. Why then should it be habituating? The fact that we sometimes speak colloquially about the ''behavior'' of cells should not mislead us into thinking that this is logically equivalent to the ''behavior'' of an organism. Unless the definition of behavior is to become meaningless, it should be restricted to the movement of muscles, secretion of glands, etc.
>
> The tendency to apply behavioral terms to cellular processes is unfortunate even when the behavioral function of the cell is known. It is worse, as is usually the case, when there is no demonstrable relationship between overt behavior and cellular processes being examined. Here one could be in the position of calling a synaptic change ''habituation at the cellular level'' without knowing what the cell actually contributes (if anything) to the behavior or its habituation. Thus, it is possible that a change called habituation at the cellular level might ultimately be shown to be directly involved in producing reflex sensitization! It was Kandel's contention that the rational development of behavioral psychology and neurobiology and their merger requires that critical distinctions at different levels of discourse be maintained.

The lack of a clear conceptual and empirical distinction between the communicative and integrative roles of the various parts of the nervous system represents another source of conceptual confusion that is of considerable consequence in any attempt to define the limits of neurophysiological reductionism. The basic problem, in this case, is the nature and location of the essential psychoneural equivalence between the neural state and the perceptual process. There is, of course, no detailed answer to this rephrasing of the fundamental mind–body problem but it can be said with some assurance that the neural states that are the essential and equivalent correlates of our mental states (as opposed to afferent communication codes) occur only within the brain itself. It is only there, as Warren McCulloch (1951) pointed out, that the synaptic connections are rich enough to account plausibly for the great variability, adaptability, and diversity of human thought. The more peripheral portions of the nervous system, on the other hand, are more or less specialized for the communication of information into and out of this central structure.

There is, furthermore, a residual uncertainty concerning where the line of demarcation should be drawn between the peripheral and central nervous systems. In fact, if we apply functional, as opposed to the most obvious anatomical criteria, it is not unreasonable to assume that the primary sensory projection regions of the cerebral cortex, such as visual area 17, are in fact a part of the peripheral communication system. If this is an acceptable assumption, then we can draw the further general conclusion that the great preponderance of neurophysiological data has been obtained from the peripheral communication system and that in fact we know very little about the operation of the central integrative system where the true psychoneural equivalents reside. If we also accept the possibility that the peripheral and central nervous systems may not even operate on the same organizational basis, then a further source of conceptual confusion can be identified. We have been, perhaps erroneously, assuming that the properties of the communication system are identical to those of the integrative system. Have we been erroneously assuming that the functional properties of the isomorphically encoded sensory (including the primary projection regions of the cortex) and motor (including the motor areas of the cortex) communication pathways are the same as the symbolically encoded central integrating systems?

If we have, such a source of conceptual confusion has two implications for current theory. First, as I have indicated, it may be that contemporary psychobiology is misinterpreting the organization and nature of the coding processes that occur in the central nervous system by incorrectly extrapolating what we know about the peripheral nervous system to central processes. Isomorphic coding, feature selectivity, and receptive field organization, all well-established properties of the peripheral nervous system, may play far less important roles in the central nervous system where symbolically encoded (i.e, nonisomorphic), inferential, and global mechanisms may predominate.

Second, and what may be a much more fundamental aspect of the misidentification of communication with integration processes, is that we may be misattributing the psychoneural equivalent of a percept to the peripheral nervous system when in fact our attribution should be much more deeply central. Thus even though a specific pattern of neural response in the retina, the lateral geniculate body, or the striate visual cortex, may correlate with some stimulus pattern, we need not necessarily assume that peripheral activity to be the neural state equivalent of a psychological process—pattern recognition—also correlating with the stimulus. Even though few would argue that the feature-selective mechanisms that have been indisputably observed in the retinae of some animals are the equivalents of form perception, many perceptual theorists implicitly suggest that the activation of similar feature-selective neurons in the striate cortex is the necessary and sufficient equivalent of that psychological process. The point I make here is that the striate cortex may be no more the location of the psychoneurally equivalent state than the retina; it may be no more than another portion of the peripheral communication system.

Support for the point of view that denies perceptual psychoneural equivalence to the primary projection visual regions comes from a somewhat unexpected source. Speaking of some of the interpretations made by psychobiologists of the neurophysiological data from his (and Torsten Wiesel's) pioneering studies, David Hubel (1978) writes with extraordinary good sense and clarity: "Of course, this information (Hubel and Wiesel's findings) by no means tells us how we recognize a hat, or a boat, or a face. The information from cells at this stage is fed onto subsequent stages, and at some point sense must be made of it. *We have no idea how this is done* [p. 25]." (Ital. added).

A further conceptual difficulty that permeates any discussion of neural models of perception concerns the relative credence that should be given to serial and parallel models, respectively. Conventional digital computers serve as proofs that serial logical machines exist that can accomplish many of the information-processing feats of which man is capable. Alternatively, modern array processors (computers specifically designed to manipulate arrays of information by parallel calculations) as well as the rapidly increasing body of knowledge of network interactions in neural structures are equally convincing proof that parallel processes exist that can also perform essentially the same functions. Because both modes of processing are not only plausible, but also extant, the theoretician is faced with another question—is there any way to determine which is the most likely type of processing mechanism to underlie any given perceptual phenomenon? Because there must always be a serial system that can execute any logical process that a parallel system can manipulate (and vice versa), a formal and rigorous answer to this question is elusive! I must, however, express a prejudice that is based upon my subjective evaluation of the psychophysical and neurological literature.[3] It seems to me that parallel processing, and its associated network modes of operation, have been underemphasized when psychobiologists have considered possible explanations of perceptual phenomena. There are many reasons for this, but the most influential may simply be our inability to conceptualize parallel-processing mechanisms.

The general history of the search for mechanisms of mind should alert us to another potential conceptual problem in the reductive analysis of perceptual phenomena. Throughout the scientific past, man's search for explanations of mental phenomena has been based on the available concepts that have emerged

---

[3]Actually there is no empirical or theoretical proof of the following statement, and there may never be. However, as all except the most naive appreciate, science does not operate on the basis of rigorous proofs alone.

from whatever technology is momentarily dominant. At the present, having passed through hydraulic, electric, telephonic, and computer interpretations of mind, the dominant and most relevant technology for modern perceptual theory has come to be neurophysiology. There are an enormous number and variety of exciting observations reported each year in the literature that appear to have perceptual implications. Because of this diversity of data, it is possible to find in the neurophysiological literature almost any kind of neural response to support almost any neuroreductionistic model of any perceptual phenomena. Perceptual theoreticians are free to select from a bag of neural tricks that contains virtually every conceivable class of cellular response. In short, there is a very large number of candidate codes that have been observed in the laboratory.

Furthermore, it is often possible to take the same piece of data and to interpret it in a way that supports two superficially antagonistic points of view. How difficult it is in this context, for one so inclined, not to find neurons that seem to be sensitive to different spatial frequencies when there are neurons present that are obviously sensitive to different receptive-field sizes. The problem is that few sensory neurons exhibit only one dimension of sensitivity. Rather there are usually multiple dimensions of the stimulus pattern that can selectively activate a neuron. In any case, the definition of the *critical* stimulus dimension, therefore, is often very much a function of the theoretical proclivities of the experimenter and the emphasis of a particular experimental design.

Thus, in the absence of a good taxonomy of neural responses and a sharply defined set of criteria for the stimuli capable of eliciting a response from a neuron, the reductionistically predisposed theoretician can read almost anything into a particular neurophysiological finding. Furthermore, the definitive establishment of necessary and sufficient causal relationships between specific neural and perceptual data is not the same as simply plotting a correlation. It takes much more elaborate tests of causation that are almost never carried out by researchers in this complex field of psychobiological analysis. As a result many psychoneural theories are, at best, only suggestive metaphors and, at worst, totally misleading and spurious.

In summary, I think that the conceptual issues involved in neuroreductionism are far more complex than is ordinarily appreciated and that the limits of this approach are more constrained than usually acknowledged. The hierarchy of levels that I have invoked in the taxonomic level theory presented in this book is intended to help clarify and concretize many of these otherwise fuzzy issues.

The purpose of the introduction to this chapter has been to sound a note of caution concerning careless neuroreductionism. I believe that we have been carried along by the dramatic and exciting results emanating from neurophysiological laboratories to make erroneous attributions of psychoneural equivalence to the more peripheral Levels 1 and 2 rather than to Levels 3 and 4 where the weight of psychophysical evidence suggests that many perceptual phenomena should properly be classified. I hope I am able to provide a sufficiently compelling argument to support this point of view in the remainder of this chapter. First, however, I would like to consider in detail the meaning of some of the terms used so frequently (and so glibly) in contemporary perceptual theory.

B. SOME BASIC VOCABULARY

In subsequent sections of this chapter I am critical of some of the premises and points of view of several currently popular neuroreductionistic theories of visual perception. As preparation for that critique, it is important to be as specific as possible concerning the use of certain terms central to this discussion. Whereas the use of some of these words has become commonplace if not ubiquitous, their use is often unclear or ambiguous. The major problem that prompts this lexographic excursion is that the mechanisms that are invoked are often highly speculative and have not, in all cases, been empirically substantiated. The kind of neural interactions I am discussing lie at the outer limits of our technological capability, and there is often a tendency to invent pseudoanatomical entities that, although plausible and reasonable, are based on only the flimsiest empirical foundation. New conceptual mechanisms, partially anatomical and partially operational, are sometimes introduced into theoretical discussion on the basis of analogies that have little direct support from the laboratory. This section is designed to distinguish between process and structure on the one hand, and the well established and the speculative on the other.

1. Features and Feature Detectors

Central to most neuroreductionistic theories of perception stressing the role of individual neurons is the idea that certain neurons of the visual system respond selectively to certain features of the stimulus. And indeed a substantial body of empirical knowledge compellingly demonstrates that many neurons of the visual pathway do, in general, respond most vigorously to stimuli possessing certain spatial temporal properties rather than simply to the flux of light falling upon them. The pioneering work of Lettvin, Maturana, McCulloch, and Pitts (1959) and the continuing series of experimental reports from the laboratory of Hubel and Wiesel (e.g., 1962, 1968, 1970, 1972) leave no doubt about this physiological fact. The impact of these discoveries on speculative theory as well as on empirical laboratory research has been immense. A host of microtheoretical statements attributing one or another perceptual phenomenon to such feature-detecting neurons has been forthcoming in recent years.

For the moment, before turning to the details of these theories, let us consider only the vocabulary of this relatively new theoretical paradigm. What are the denotations and connotations of the words *feature detector,* and what does a deeper inquiry into the meaning of the word *feature* reveal?

It turns out that the word *feature* has a number of different meanings dependent upon one's theoretical persuasion. In some more extreme points of view, a feature is considered to be a specific localized geometrical component of a pattern. A triangle is made up of features called sides and corners. A radical feature theory (such as Donald Hebb originally proposed in his milestone book *The Organization of Behavior,* Hebb, 1949) attributes the perception of a whole form to a simple compilation or concatenation by the nervous system of the component parts or features of a stimulus into a wholistic percept. "Cell assemblies" responding to local features (corners) were aggregated into "phase sequences" in a hierarchial manner, but the critical stimulus elements in Hebb's theory were the local features. Kenneth Laughery's (1969) theory of letter recognition, also based on the component parts of alphabetic characters such as angles and vertical lines, is another example of this approach. The word *feature,* in these cases, does not imply any wholistic organizational attribute of the stimulus pattern but rather a localized geometrical component.

A somewhat more eclectic view has recently emerged suggesting that we include as "features" more than only the local component parts of a form. These theories propose that there can be wholistic features such as pattern, triangularity, or melody. In this case, the term *features* has been expanded to include the organization of the component parts of the stimulus as well as the component parts themselves.

James Howard, Jr. and James Ballas (Howard & Ballas, 1978) have made a very important point concerning these two alternative interpretations of the word *feature.* They distinguish between the property-list approach emphasizing local component parts on the one hand, and on the other, the process-oriented approach, emphasizing the broader meaning of the word I described in the preceding paragraph. The important fact, Howard and Ballas assert, is that, depending only on the meaning of *feature,* each approach can logically lead to a very different theoretical orientation.

Specifically, Howard and Ballas note that the property-list approach, based on an elementalistic philosophy and the results of single-neuron feature selectivity, leads compellingly to an associationistic type of theory in which tuned "feature detectors" play the central role. They note that the twin concepts of stimulus features or properties and of feature-detecting neurons are complementary to each other and are in positive feedback. Thus these two ideas act synergistically to support a theoretical orientation emphasizing elements, features, and an algorithmic kind of neoempiricism. Although it is usually acknowledged by theorists of this persuasion that the particular feature sensitivity of any individual neuron may depend upon its interactions with its neighbors (a network concept), interaction is de-emphasized in this theoretical approach and the component parts of the stimulus are considered to exert their influence independently of each other. A feature is extracted from the environment by virtue of its own properties, and is only secondarily influenced by those of its neighbors. Finally

Howard and Ballas point out that the property-list approach leads to the anatomic idea of quasi-independent single-cell feature filters for even the most complex ideas as expressed in that most radical version of single-cell neuron reductionism—Konorski's (1967) theory of a hierarchy of gnostic neurons.

The alternative process approach finds its roots in psychophysical data (as especially exemplified by the Gestalt tradition). Howard and Ballas distinguish it from the property-list orientation in two ways. First, they note that proponents of this view attribute a very different meaning to *feature*. A feature, to the process theorist, includes the arrangement of the parts and other aspects of the pattern as well as the local geometrical elements. Second, the processing is done not by feature filters, according to this viewpoint, but rather by general-purpose algorithmic mechanisms that can act on any input pattern. Such a process approach, Howard and Ballas assert, leads logically to different predictions concerning the most appropriate mode of neuroreductionistic explanation. No longer are the individual neuronal sensitivities important. Instead the hypothesis that there must be a broad interactive network of neurons to implement the processing algorithms gains contextual support. The network is more likely to be composed of individual neurons that differ little in their respective sensitivity, one from the other, rather than specialized neurons responding selectively to the component local features of a stimulus. The unspecialized neurons of the network respond collectively, though differentially, to transform the signals passing through them rather than simply acting as a selective filter. It is only in the ensemble that they collectively implement a specific algorithmic processor that can analyze, encode, extract, or even recognize a form. Such network theories as my own autocorrelation theory of form detection (Uttal, 1975a, also see pp. 711) are of this latter category and do not require the postulation of any special sensitivity on the part of individual neurons to any particular aspect of the geometry of the stimulus.

Beyond any argument over the relative validity of each theory, the important point made by Howard and Ballas is that depending only on one's initial premise (e.g., "local features are most important," versus "global pattern is most important"), there is a compelling logical sequence that leads to distinctly different theoretical outcomes. Careful specification of the premises is, therefore, particularly important in perceptual theory.

Further difficulties intrinsic to the attributed meaning of feature have also been noted by J. Anderson, Silverstein, Ritz, and Jones (1977) in a slightly different context. Anderson et al. (1977) consider the differences in the word as used by perceptual theorists and by neurophysiologists as follows:

> *A Regrettable Misapprehension*
>
> It is apparent from reading the literature in this area that the word "feature" as used by psychologists and by neuroscientists has come to mean different things. When a psychologist discusses features, what seems to be meant is a complex kind of perceptual atom which is independent of other atoms and constitutes an elemen-

> tary unit out of which perception is built. The feature lists that have been proposed for both letter perception and speech perception involve many different aspects of the input stimulus. Their simplicity is deceiving when considered in light of the properties of the single cells of the nervous system.
>
> It is also apparent, regrettably, that when a neurobiologist refers to a "feature detector," he is typically referring to a single neuron which displays a certain amount of selectivity in its discharge, often for the biologically important and relevant aspects of the stimulus. This does not mean that this cell has the specificity of response to be a detector of the psychological feature. Something more is involved [p. 442].

For the purposes of the following discussion, I would like to identify my use of the word: I join the camp of the property listers with regard to the meaning of feature. I define a feature as a component part of the stimulus pattern. It is something like a corner of a triangle (or its side) or a specific phoneme in an oral utterance. A feature, in the sense I use here, is not something that pertains to the organization of a figure such as its triangularity or its melody, that is, its global pattern, the overall organization of the features of the stimulus. Organizational pattern, for the purposes of my discussion, is not a feature. To call such global properties features is to confuse the issue by making the class of features all-inclusive for geometry and thus nondiscriminative of the several layers of attributes that define a stimulus form. A feature theory including such attributes would by definition include all other theories of form and thus would be not only indiscriminable from any of the others but meaningless by virtue of its inclusiveness.

A feature detector, on the other hand, is a mechanism for processing features and not the process or the feature itself. Thus merely to hypothesize the existence of a feature detector inside the human perceptual system begs the question of how we perceive patterns. It would always be possible to construct an analog of a pattern-perceiving system out of a family of feature detectors (for the same reason the Fourier analysis works in general) even if there were no such mechanisms actually present. The feature detector can play the same analytical role played by any member of the orthogonal family of functions in Fourier analysis. A system of specific feature detectors is only one of many possible internal mechanisms that might be present that are equally capable of processing the stimulus information for a satisfactory perceptual outcome.

In sum, there is probably no logically compelling way to validate (or invalidate) a hypothetical model that invokes feature mechanisms or postulates feature-detection processes with psychophysical methods alone just as there is no definitive way to establish the internal structure of any other black box. Similarly, the abundant evidence that feature-sensitive neurons exist in the nervous system is not definitive evidence that they are the psychoneural equivalents of pattern perception. It is even moot whether or not they are critical processors; these neural elements may simply generate transmission codes!

2. Channels

Another word that has become very important in our neuroreductionistic vocabulary is *channel.* This word has already crept into several of the previous discussions in this chapter. I have previously used the term as a short hand for those anatomically distinguishable portions—the families of long-, medium-, and short-wavelength-sensitive receptors, respectively—of the afferent visual system that initially encode the chromatic aspects of visual stimulus information. A bit of reflection, however, suggests the important idea that the information from the three kinds of color receptors need not necessarily be traveling along independent structural ''channels,'' but rather may be represented by three modes of activity in a single channel—a structurally indistinguishable visual pathway that responds differently to various stimulus properties.

In other words, there are two ways to define a channel. One is specifically an anatomical concept. A channel, in this case, is a spatially isolable communication link that conveys information from one place to another in the nervous system. It is literally a different spatial entity or a separate piece of tissue. Such a definition would include Norma Graham's (1980) definitions of a channel as a ''two-dimensional array, or in terms of its physiological analog, a collection of receptive fields that are identical except in position.'' Though there might be great difficulty in disentangling any one of this type of channel from the others, it is still anatomically distinct.

The other way to look upon a channel is in a more functional sense. In this case the channel has no independent structural existence. It may be simply a different mode of communication, pattern of activity, or encoding within the confines of otherwise anatomically unitary structures. In other words, a channel from this point of view is a process, not an anatomical structure. Interestingly, if the number of channels becomes very large, then there is no way to distinguish a unitary channel of this class from a very large array of parallel channels of the preceding class. I deal with this issue later when I discuss some of the details of channel models and here in the following paragraphs.

It appears to me that the former (anatomical) definition is the way the word is implicitly used by many channel theorists in spite of the fact that the empirical evidence is largely limited to the latter (process) sense. It is my conviction that the attribution of anatomical significance to mechanisms that are actually defined on the basis of process criteria also leads to a number of logical and semantic difficulties. The surplus meaning of the word *channel* has become a part of the channel theorists' thinking even when they may have originally set out to use it strictly in its normative, descriptive, or functional sense. The end product of absorbing the surplus connotation of this word into one's conceptual structure is that a number of perceptual psychobiologists spend an inordinate amount of time looking for ''channels'' at the tip of their microelectrodes when, in fact, they may not exist except in a functional sense.

In some of its roles in theory, the hypothetical channel has little theoretical uniqueness; it is not possible to distinguish between such a quasi-anatomical "channel" and an algorithmic network process, given the limits of current physiological methodology. Arnold Towe has made this same point abundantly clear in his brilliant article (Towe, 1975) discussing the meaning of a related hypothetical concept—the cortical column of neurons with common function. He noted that only randomly arranged columns would be distinguishable from a perfectly homogenous organization. In other words, fields of cortical columns containing neurons with continuously varying orientation sensitivities (from one column to the next) would not be distinguishable from a system devoid of columnar organization on the basis of any criterion, given the discreteness and finite size of individual neurons.

The same important point holds specifically for the spatial frequency channel model; given the generality of the Fourier theorem, there is no way to distinguish between actual channels and mathematical channels unless certain highly specific criteria of narrowness of tuning and independence analogous to the criterion of randomness hold. Channels, in the absence of satisfaction of these criteria, are nothing more than fancy puns! In other words, whatever phenomena could be explained in terms of frequency-sensitive channels could equally well be explained by means of a more general algorithmic processing of the global attributes of a stimulus pattern as mediated by one great channel—the visual system.

In a more positive vein it must also be appreciated that, whatever their limitations, the ideas of neural organization implicit in the concept of channels or feature detectors have been powerful heuristics for thinking in contemporary neuroreductionistic perceptual theory. However slight the evidence for the anatomical existence of this or that kind of channel, the idea, cum idea, of channels, has been one of the truly seminal ideas of modern perceptual theory. One cannot escape that fact; to pick up a journal like *Vision Research*—the major outlet for articles dealing with Level 1 and Level 2 visual processes—is to be confronted directly with the massive amount of current effort that is directly derived from the ideas of chromatic and spatial frequency "channels." To what extent this impact is conceptually misdirected is yet to be determined.

3. Receptive Fields

Another term that has become deeply enmeshed in perceptual theory is *receptive field*. The original use of the phrase was in a strictly neurophysiological context; the receptive field was originally defined (as far as I can tell by Kuffler, 1952) for a given neuron as the area of the external scene in which a stimulus may occur and effectively activate that neuron. The receptive field exists, as I noted in Chapter 8, as a result of neural convergence and lateral interactions, but the important point is that it was originally defined in terms of the responsiveness of a single neuron—not as a point on the retina and certainly not as a psychophysical construct.

However the term has crept into psychophysical thinking in two ways. First, it has provided the conceptual basis for a particular type of psychophysical experiment. In the prototypical "receptive field" experiment in psychophysics a small test stimulus is presented to a particular locus of the retina. The experimenter then determines the effect of other punctate stimuli in the surrounding area on the perceptual response to this small stimulus. To the extent that the stimuli in the immediate surround affect the perception of the central spot, they are said to fall within its receptive field.

Note, however, that the criterion in this psychophysical experiment for defining the receptive field is based on the molar response of the observer and not upon the responsivity of a single neuron. There remains, therefore, a major question concerning the parallelism of the neurophysiological and psychophysical uses of the term. It is not at all an a priori certainty that the perceptual field of interaction about a stimulated point defined in the psychophysical experiment is of the same genre as that defined in the unicellular electrophysiological study. In none of the psychophysical experiments is the central stimulus spot so small that it activates only a single receptor. Even if it did, we must not forget that the effect of the surround on the psychophysical responses arising from stimulation of the central region is not localizable to the same neural level to which the neural interaction is usually attributed. Rather the psychophysical criterion involves the entire perceptual nervous system and, therefore, is replete with the multitude of other transformations and interactions that are possible at other levels of perceptual processing.

Thus the psychophysical experiment does not define the receptive field of a single neuron, as does the neurophysiological experiment but, at best, the field of interaction surrounding a localized functional region of the entire afferent visual system. Because there is so much interaction, divergence, and convergence within and between all levels, it is not at all certain that the psychophysically defined receptive field means the same thing as the neurophysiologically defined one. Nor, for that matter, would the confirmed existence of both directly imply the identity of each with the other. The psychophysical interaction may well be the result of interaction processes that are much more complex than those simple inhibitory interactions mediated by the shape of a neural receptive field. The issue here is, does the term receptive field link two vastly different kinds of experiment in any more profound way than as a distant metaphor?

In sum, it is not at all obvious that the two types of experiment are actually probing the same mechanism in spite of analogous experimental designs. Obviously the difficult problem of the possible identification of neural and psychophysical receptive fields cannot be completely resolved at present. I raise the semantic and conceptual issue now merely as another example of the way in which terms in one domain of discourse may be inadvertently and inappropriately transferred to another domain without sufficient thought being given to their surplus denotive baggage—baggage that may not, in fact, be applicable to the new domain.

4. Lateral Interactions

Now let's consider another vocabulary item that has great currency in modern neurophysiological theory—*lateral inhibitory interaction*. This phrase also has been applied as a model in many different psychophysical situations. Because the evidence for lateral inhibitory interactions between neurons is so strong and because inhibitory interactions of one kind or another certainly occur in perceptual processing, the concept has proven to be a powerful heuristic for the psychophysical study of spatially interactive visual processes. However, once again, I must raise the caveat about surplus meaning whenever the neural concept is extended to the perceptual domain without adequate, empirically based, coordinating linkages. It is all too often forgotten that interactions can also occur between stimuli because of similarity in symbolic meaning or significance (as a result of complex neural logic that is totally beyond our understanding) as well as between spatially interconnected neurons. The issue here is the same as in the previous sections—how to justify the transition from neural concept to psychophysical theory on a firmer basis than simple process analogy.

The meaning of the term *lateral interaction* in the neural context, on the other hand, is quite clear. Lateral inhibitory interaction refers to the reduction of activity in one neuron as a result of an increase in activity in another, most often at the same level in the afferent chain. Excitatory interaction between neurons has also been observed, of course; in that case, an increase in a neighboring neuron increases the activity in the neuron under observation. It is, however, far more likely to observe mutual inhibition than mutual excitation. One should also appreciate in this context that lateral interaction is a purely spatial process occurring in the same geometrical space as the stimulus.

The analogous perceptual interactions are not so clearly defined. As I mentioned, interactions can occur between ideas, concepts, and forms in a way that is not "spatial," but deals with much more symbolic aspects of the stimulus pattern. The meaning of one word can lead to the inhibition of the perception of other words (e.g., the phenomena of perceptual defense), and geometrical forms can interact in manners that are not directly consistent with the spatial geometry per se (e.g., metacontrast). In short, as we later see, interactions between spatial patterns need not be mediated by the same spatial interactions observed in neural nets; it is entirely possible that the inhibition be due to a conflict in meaning instead. The problem faced in this area of research is to discriminate between those that are isomorphically and those that are symbolically mediated.

5. Miscellaneous

In previous portions of this book, I have several times alluded to some of the other terms that have also come to be used as puns or loosely linked metaphors in different areas of analysis—some of which are appropriately considered to be neural, and others of which exceed any presently conceivable neurophysiological reductive model. The words *conditioning, threshold, masking, acuity,* and *adaptation* are but a few examples of an ill-defined multilevel vocabulary that must be very critically analyzed to avoid the kind of semantic error I have been considering here.

I shall not reiterate the argument I have made for these terms. I hope the general nature of the possible conceptual errors I have mentioned—argument by analogy, surplus meaning, erroneous identification, incomparable levels, etc.—is now apparent and that the reader will be cautious in the use of this transitional vocabulary.

With this general introduction to a few of the concepts and vocabulary items of perceptual neuroreductionism, let us briefly review the neuroreductionistic approach to determine just how broadly it is accepted in contemporary perceptual theory.

C. SOME CURRENT NEUROREDUCTIONISTIC THEORIES OF PERCEPTUAL PHENOMENA[4]

Two fair questions are: (1) In raising the specter of rampant and unreasonable neurophysiologizing in perceptual theory, am I building a straw man? and (2) Have channels, feature detectors, and lateral inhibitory interactions actually become as deeply embedded in perceptual theory as I have suggested? Fortunately, these are among the few questions in this book that are as easy to answer as to

---

[4]In this section I am citing and, by implication, if not directly, criticizing the work of a number of my professional colleagues. In preparing this chapter I have intentionally aimed my criticism at those studies that I believe extend the idea of neuroreductionism in perceptual phenomenon to an extent not justified by the data. This is part and parcel of the scientific method—generation of hypotheses followed by a free and open dialogue concerning the ideas. Each side marshals its own supporting data and logic to the greatest extent possible. Nevertheless, each study or theory that I cite is regarded with respect. Some of the workers I criticize most strongly are my personal friends, and some have even subsequently indicated their agreement with the general approach that I champion here. There are, nevertheless, often substantial theoretical disagreements that I could no more ignore because of personal relationships than I would allow any *ad hominem* aspersion to enter into this discussion. It would be naive for me to expect that everyone who is criticized here will accept this criticism with equanimity (people are as deeply committed to their ideas in science as in any other aspects of their lives), but I hope I have never violated the limits of professional courtesy that I would expect from someone who disagrees with me on some controversial theoretical point.

ask. The prevalence of the neuroanatomic terms and concepts I discussed in the previous section in contemporary perceptual theory is easily documented. To do so does not resolve the question of the validity of these ideas but does establish the need for discussing them and specifically sets the stage for the empirical counterindications of perceptual neuroreductionism that I cite later in this chapter.

In order to provide a fair sampling of the extent of the application of such neuroreductionistic thinking in perceptual theory, I surveyed the 1977 volume (Vol. 6) of *Perception,* a major journal of research covering those phenomena that I feel are best allocated to Levels 3, 4, and 5. A survey of this type can give a valid indication of the current prevalence of this type of thinking.

Of the approximately 77 articles in Volume 6, 16 explicitly invoked some kind of neuroreductionistic theory and several others made reference to it as a plausible alternative to explain phenomena interpreted in other ways. Of the 16 papers, 2 were reports of cellular electrophysiological experiments that were considered sufficiently relevant to the problems of perception to be included in this predominantly psychophysical journal. Furthermore, both of the two controversies that erupted in the form of challenge and rebuttal articles in this volume of *Perception* were deeply concerned with just this use of neuroreductionistic models in perceptual theory. In sum, 21% of the articles in this single volume of one leading perceptual science journal invoked neuroreductionistic explanatory models for a wide variety of phenomena. A brief survey of these reports reveals the types of theory that have currency in today's perceptual research.

The major theme in this volume was the explanation of perceptual phenomena on the basis of the behavior of single neurons as revealed in microelectrode experiments. This single-cell approach was the theoretical theme of Bacon and King-Smith's (1977) study of the detection of line segments. They note that the probability of detecting a line segment in a masking task increases with line length up to a length of about 30 min of visual angle. They attribute this increase specifically to probability summation of the responses of a family of Hubel and Wiesel-type neurons that display a common orientation sensitivity. Bacon and King-Smith also allude to the influences on their work of earlier studies by Andrews (1967a, 1967b), Blakemore and Nachmias (1971), and Campbell and Kulikowski (1966), all of whom also invoke single-cell feature sensitivity to explain simple visual detection tasks.

Single-cell sensitivities are also used to explain a demonstrated perceptual tilt of stereoscopically perceived space by Breitmeyer, Battaglia, and Bridge (1977). These researchers go even further than did Bacon and King-Smith, however, when they speculate that the neuronal properties, which they believe underlie this tilt, are acquired during the early days of life when the infant is more or less continuously supine. The resulting geometrical perspective, according to their hypothesis, selectively sensitizes neurons in a way that leads to the perceptually tilted stereoscopic space in the adult.

Other articles in this 1977 volume of *Perception* also link the properties of neurons that are known to be specifically sensitive to binocular input to the properties of visual space perception. Influenced by the pioneering studies of the neural representations of binocular input (which is discussed in Chapter 11), Ninio (1977) derives a neuromathematical model of the perceptual geometry of the stereoscopic space constructed from the two monocular image projections on the retina.

The two purely neurophysiological studies in this volume of *Perception* link the properties of specific neurons that are sensitive to moving stimuli to the molar perceptual phenomena of motion detection (Flandrin & Jeannerod, 1977, Orban, 1977). One other more theoretically oriented paper (Bonnet, 1977) argues that the feature-filtering single neuron and the frequency-filtering channel are both equivalent explanatory models of visual motion detection. In this same volume, Tadasu Oyama (1977) attributes illusions of size to the activity of size-sensitive single neurons in the visual cortex. Then two studies (Denton, 1977; Keck & Pentz, 1977) invoke selective adaptation and fatigue of cortical neurons that have been shown elsewhere to be selectively sensitive to movement to explain psychophysically demonstrated motion aftereffects, a suggestion that they note was made very early after the original discoveries of feature-sensitive neurons by such notables as Barlow and Hill (1963) and Sutherland (1961).

If the single-neuron model is the dominant theme in this symphony of neuroreductionism, then a rapidly accentuating secondary theme can be discerned in the increasingly popular invocation of the idea of spatial frequency analysis. Anatomical equivalents of Fourier transformations and filters, as originally proposed by Blakemore and Campbell (1969), are often cited as an explanatory model in this volume of *Perception*. For example, one repeated implicit or even explicit hypothesis in this sample of studies is that visual aftereffects (defined as a perceptual experience resulting from preconditioning with some related stimulus) are a result of the induced fatigue of these neural frequency filters. Although this idea of neural fatigue is not necessarily restricted to the concept of frequency-sensitive channels (many other reports in recent years have attributed aftereffects to the comparable fatigue of individual neurons), the idea, in this sample at least, was most often applied to the Fourier filter theory. Indeed, Smith (1977) distinguishes between non-Fourier types of aftereffects and the selective fatigue of frequency-specific Fourier channels as two separate mechanisms. He concludes that his experiments support the Fourier hypothesis in particular and not a mechanism involving exhausted single cells. Others, although not interested in exploring aftereffects, also invoke the Fourier hypothesis to explain other phenomena. For example, Frisby and Mayhew (1977), following up on a suggestion made a couple of years earlier by Julesz and Miller (1975), attribute the organization of stereoscopic space to a similar pattern of organization of spatial frequency-sensitive channels.

Beyond single cells and Fourier filters, a tertiary neuroreductionistic theme, lateral interaction, is evident in this brief sample of perceptual studies. Lateral interaction differs somewhat from the single-cell and frequency-sensitive channel ideas in that models of this genre concentrate on the interaction processes between the quasi-anatomical units rather than the neural units or structures themselves. Nevertheless, the theoretical philosophy is that similar well-substantiated neurophysiological processes—in this case, lateral interactions—are utilized to explain psychological phenomena with which they may share some analogous behavior.

An example of the lateral interaction approach is found in Coren and Theodor's (1977) report which seeks an explanation of the brightness differences between different regions of "subjective patterns" such as illustrated by the Kaniza illusion (see Fig. 10-34). Coren and Theodor, following a suggestion by Brigner and Gallagher (1974), propose that there are inhibitory interactions between different parts of the retinal image. Because this brightness difference is further confounded by an apparent difference in depth and the perception involves contours that are not physically present,[5] this is phenomenologically a somewhat more complex situation than that involved in a phenomenon like the Mach bands. Commendably, although somewhat unusual for papers of this sort, Coren and Theodor express an all-too-often overlooked caveat in their discussion. They note that the fit between their psychophysical data and their lateral interaction model "does not rule out other explanations necessarily." This is an important acknowledgment from these perceptual scientists, and another expression of the main point I seek to make in this chapter.

In this same issue of *Perception,* lateral interactions are also invoked to explain the misperception of geometrical angles, as occurs in the Zollner and the Hering illusions, by Oyama (1977). Another paper seeks to explain the colored halo that can be seen under certain viewing conditions around the Fechner–Benham top (used to produce subjective colors) in terms of this same neural mechanism. Then, Wenderoth and Beh (1977) invoke lateral inhibitory interactions to explain the rod and frame illusion and some related spatial interactions between pairs of parallel lines and among the lines of the crisscrossing grid. They, however, do suggest an interesting twist to this point of view. Even though the fundamental process involved in these illusions are lateral interactions according to them, they assert that these lateral interactions may provide the underlying processes from which Fourier-type spatial frequency channels are generated. They thus have incorporated both of these neuroreductionistic themes within a single theory.

Another theme regularly played out in these psychobiological models of perception is that of the channel. What a channel is, however, as I noted in the previous section, is often poorly defined. Some authors refer to it rather loosely in quasi-anatomical terms: They seem to imply that a channel is a structural

---

[5]A more detailed discussion of subjective contours and surfaces is presented in Chapter 10.

entity. Others use the term in an even less precise way, implying that it is only distinguishable in terms of its function. Gregory (1977), for example, suggests that the signals from the three color "channels" are brought into registration under the influence of a "master" luminance channel. However registration itself may be a false issue. It seems likely that the *problem* of registration of three channels of information arises as a manifestation of the hypothesising of channels themselves, rather than as a real biological problem. The technical analogy from which the idea of registration is drawn, of course, is the usual color television receiver with its three sets of colored dots. There the problems of alignment and registration are severe. However the analogy of registration may not be a valid one for the human chromatic perceptual system with its finely interleaved and naturally registered receptor mosaic. "Registration," in the latter case, is directly and simply accomplished by the design of a system that does not have these three anatomically distinct channels. On the other hand, the whole issue of registration may be a false one in a system like the brain in which spatial locus may not have the same meaning as in a television set.

Perhaps a harbinger of what is yet to come in perceptual neuroreductionism is Camisa, Blake, and Lema's (1977) attribution of the oblique effect (the diminished visual capacity for stimuli not aligned vertically or horizontally) to the action of sustained channels of information communication in the sensory pathways. New knowledge about different classes of afferent neurons (i.e., sustained and transient channels) in the geniculo-striate pathway has obviously been very quickly put to use in psychobiological theory.

In the previous few paragraphs I have taken, as a single sample, one recent volume of an important perceptual science journal and analyzed it to determine if, in fact, neurobiological theorizing is prevalent. It was possible, of course, that the problem that I have called attention to here—excessive and uncritical neuroreduction—might have been just a phantom and not a serious problem. However, in light of the theoretical approach characteristic of at least a fifth of the articles in this journal, it is clear that the neuroreductionistic approach is very commonplace and that the problem posed is not a red, green, or even blue herring or a straw man of any other color.

It is clear that neuroreductionistic theory has been, and remains, a widely accepted mode of explanation of perceptual data in exactly the same way that models of mind have traditionally followed whatever else was the contemporary technology throughout the course of history. Although valid in some instances, this approach is often utilized even when the phenomena are so complex and high level that the analogy to neuronal function is very farfetched. One is reminded of the comment by Thomas Brown quoted on p. 27. It seems to be still the case that theorists are all too likely to seize upon "... traces in the sensorium, vibrations, vibratiuncles, animal spirits, electricity and galvanism" as explanatory models of perception. Although what I am about to say may provoke considerable contentious reaction, I believe that much of this theorizing is carried out without careful consideration of the presence or absence of plausible logical or empirical links between the neurophysiological and perceptual domains of discourse. Channels, lateral inhibitory interactions, and feature detectors have become the new "vibratiuncles."

The point made by the overall organization of this book and by my eclectic taxonomy is the same as the one made here: Although there are many phenomena that are satisfactorily reduced to the terms of neuroreductionistic concepts (I have already alluded to many of them in the previous chapters in which I discussed Levels 1 and 2), it is my opinion that many higher-level processes are just too complex or too susceptible to symbolic, cognitive, or semantic influences to be plausibily incorporated within the radical neuroreductionistic approach so prevalent in the literature.

I am not sure if the kind of neuroreductionistic thinking I considered in this section can be eliminated, and it is possible that new empirical and conceptual breakthroughs will establish the logical bridges that seem to be missing now. Nevertheless, the state of neuroreductionistic theorizing reflected in the 1977 volume of *Perception* leaves much to be desired in terms of its logical completeness.

In the following sections of this chapter I detail my criticisms of the neuroreductionistic approach that has been exemplified in the preceding paragraphs. To do so effectively, however, requires a more precise statement than has been available of exactly what is being criticized. The next section, therefore, is specifically intended to clarify what I believe are the origins and the fundamental premises of each of the currently popular neuroreductionistic theories. As I begin this critique I want once again to remind the reader that my criticism of neuroreductionistic modeling is not intended to deny the general metaphysical monism that asserts that, in principle, all mental phenomena are the outcome of neural processes. The point I now make is that most perceptual processes (those best classified in Levels 3, 4, and 5) are so complex as to make any application of neuroreductionism impossible in practice even if it is correct in principle.

D. A CRITIQUE OF NEUROREDUCTIONISTIC THEORIES OF PERCEPTUAL PHENOMENA[6]

In this section I trace the historical roots and isolate the essential premises of the various neuroreductionistic theories that emerged as contenders during the minireview conducted in the previous section and describe some of the most

[6]Once again, I am in the position of introducing certain concepts and phenomena that are not fully described until later in the book. I hope the reader will bear with me and, if necessary, consult the index for a guide to a more complete discussion of whatever terms seem cryptic.

significant applications of each in explaining particular perceptual phenomena. Discussion of these theories is ordered in a rough chronology, beginning with a brief discussion of the lateral inhibitory interaction model, the eldest of the neuroreductionisms (discussed more fully in Chapter 8), and followed by a more detailed discussion of the other more recent ,theoretical approaches.

1. The Lateral Inhibitory Interaction Model

The history of the lateral inhibitory interaction approach is reviewed in detail in Chapter 8 where, I believe, it provides a valid and appropriate model for many Level 2 processes. There is, perhaps, no more fully substantiated neuroreductionistic model of any perceptual phenomena than the lateral inhibitory interaction theory of the Mach band and the Herman grid even though the foveal absence of the grids gray spots and some other discrepancies remain unsolved. I would now like to extract what appears to me to be the key and essential premises of this model. Whether implicitly or explicitly, any lateral interaction theory seems to imply the following dogma:

1. There exist horizontal connections between neural units at the same anatomical level. This is the essence of what is meant by the term *lateral.*
2. These interconnections are primarily inhibitory. However, over short distances most current expressions of the theory allow that the interactions may be excitatory.
3. The degree of interaction is dependent upon the distance between the mutually inhibiting units.
4. The lateral inhibitory interactions in the neural space are the direct and immediate precursors (the critical processes) of similarly organized phenomena in the subjective space.
5. All lateral interaction theories assume that the subjective magnitude of the percept is monotonically related (i.e., is topologically isomorphic) with the amplitude of the neural response, and that reduction in the magnitude of the neural response is a necessary correlate of the reduction in perceived amplitude. According to these theories some afferent information is irretrievably lost as a result of the lateral inhibitory interactions.

These premises collectively describe a theoretical system that, as I have noted, seems to justify their application to a number of Level 2 phenomena. However I do not believe that their application to higher-level phenomena such as simultaneous contrast or metacontrast is equally well justified.

Nevertheless, lateral interaction has been applied as a model of metacontrast in recent years by a group of perceptual psychobiologists including Naomi Weisstein, Bruce Bridgeman, Bruno Breitmeyer, and Leo Ganz. Because of the importance and influence of this work, let us now consider their approach in

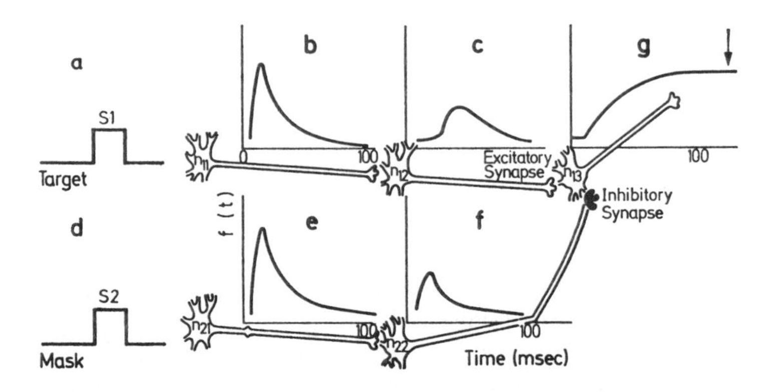

FIG. 9.1. Weisstein's model of metacontrast. This model involves several hypothetical "neurons" or "functions," some purported to be peripheral (n_{11} and n_{21}), and some to be central (n_{12}, n_{22}, and n_{13}). The small curves labelled b, c, g, e, and f represent the time course of the spike firing rate of each neuron. The difference in the time course of the various neurons is used to provide the necessary degrees of freedom to simulate the psychophysical function. (From Weisstein, © 1972, with the permission of Springer-Verlag.)

detail. Weisstein's model (Weisstein, 1968, 1972), the outstanding exemplar, hypothesizes that the interaction of five prototypical neurons produce the metacontrast output function. A critical factor in the most current version of her metacontrast theory[7] (Weisstein, 1972) is that at least one of the neurons of the five-neuron system must exhibit a time constant with respect to its excitatory and inhibitory influences that is different from the other four. Specifically, Weisstein has hypothesized a network with a fast inhibitory neuronal factor and a slow excitatory neuronal factor to produce the proper output response characteristic. (See Fig. 9-1.) One advantage of a model in which the terms have been quantitatively specified is that it can be simulated on a computer to test its plausibility. By varying the parameters of the equations that represent the neural interactions, it is possible for Weisstein to produce either the classic U-shaped psychophysical function or a monotonic response form. (I describe the various conditions that lead to these alternative response forms in greater detail on p. 902.)

Another lateral inhibitory interaction theory of metacontrast that is also directly derived from the classic Hartline findings in *Limulus* has been proposed by

[7]Although the Weisstein model still has wide currency, Naomi Weisstein herself has recently revaluated many of the aspects of her early neural model in personal conversations and public talks. Her recent papers (e.g., Weisstein and Harris, 1974) stress a more configurational and cognitive approach than is evident in the original neural interaction model. It should not be forgotten that the Weisstein neural postulates and the Weisstein mathematics are separable, and one can reject the former while retaining the latter. A good discussion of the conceptual changes and data that have led to this new point of view on her part can be found in Weisstein and Maguire (1978).

Bruce Bridgeman. Bridgeman's (1971, 1977) model used a graphical construction to demonstrate the interaction between a central target disk and a metacontrasting annulus as shown in Fig. 9-2. The amplitude of each of the curves shown in this figure represent the firing rate of the simulated neurons. Bridgeman assumes the neural amplitude directly determines the perceptual amplitude. This latter isomorphic assumption, of course, is common to all theories of this class. In particular, Bridgeman asserts that because the response patterns in the situation with both stimuli (the masked disk and the masking annulus) are more like the response of annulus alone than of the disk alone, this model is a valid analog of the metacontrast phenomena in which the disk would be perceptually masked.

Another twist to the lateral inhibition explanation of metacontrast has been proposed by Breitmeyer and Ganz (1976). Their theory merges the lateral interaction idea with recent observations of the nature of the sustained and transient channels within the afferent visual pathways. Conceptually, this approach is very similar to the Weisstein model in that it invokes neural components with differing time constants. However, Breitmeyer and Ganz proceed further than did Weisstein by suggesting much more specific neural mechanisms to account for the variation in time constants. Breitmeyer and Ganz also distinguish (as was originally done by Kolers, 1962) between the neural origins of type A (monotonic) and type B (nonmonotonic) forward and backward masking.

Metacontrast, with which we are specifically concerned here, is an example of the type B backward-masking phenomenon (i.e., the nonmonotonic response form characterized by a U-shaped perceptual suppression exerted by the second of two stimuli on the first). A sample of such a response function is shown in Fig. 11-28. Breitmeyer and Ganz propose that metacontrast is mediated by a lateral inhibition of the response of transient neurons in one geniculo-striate "channel"

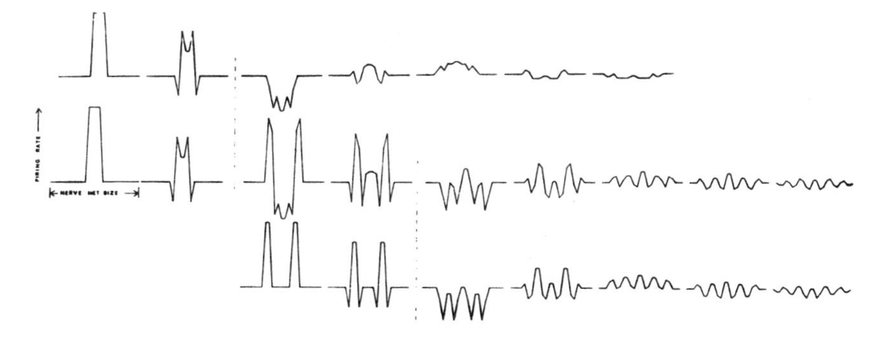

FIG. 9.2. Bridgeman's model of metacontrast. The top curves represent the response produced by the target at different times. The bottom curves represent the response produced by the mask. The middle curves are purported to be the metacontrasted response at various times, computed as an algebraic sum of the responses to the target and of the mask. (From Bridgeman, © 1971, with the permission of the American Psychological Association.)

by sustained cells in another. Breitmeyer and Ganz, like Bridgeman, use a graphical procedure for simulating the interaction between a ''mask'' and a ''target'' rather than the analog computer procedure used by Weisstein, but this is a trivial technical detail; the key issue is that the three models are conceptually very similar indeed.

The Bridgeman model has been criticized by Weisstein, Ozog, and Szoc (1975) on relatively minor technical grounds, and Bridgeman's (1977) rebuttal is in kind—it deals only with experimental details. A more serious general criticism of this kind of modeling lies in the nature of the mathematics utilized in this kind of model. Just as the perceptual response function simulated by the respective computational procedures of Weisstein, Breitmeyer and Ganz, or Bridgeman, can be implemented by several different neural mechanisms, all that is required to reproduce any U-shaped function is any one of the many mathematical formulations that possess two degrees of freedom or, equivalently, is at least a second order polynomial. Further mitigating the uniqueness of any such model is the fact that any neurophysiological process that incorporates two time constants essentially provides the necessary two degrees of freedom. The mathematical functions that are used are merely descriptions of the form of such processes and, by themselves, say nothing about the underlying neural mechanisms.

It is essential for the reader to appreciate that the mathematical and the neural assumptions of all of these models are not linked in any concrete way! All of these theories depend upon neurophysiological data that are only weakly related to the metacontrast phenomena in order to generate the particular neural background required by their individual models. Obviously the neural data are, at best, acting as heuristics, suggesting analogous computational mechanisms; conversely, these theories do not constitute a tightly linked ''proof'' of any of the neural hypotheses. The important point, therefore, is whether or not the mathematical descriptions used in this kind of model building are adequate to distinguish between the various alternatives on the basis of goodness of fit. In my opinion the models of metacontrast considered here are all so flexible, and thus equivalent, that they cannot be discriminated from each other in terms of their respective assumptions.

Lateral inhibitory interaction has also been invoked as an explanatory model of a wide variety of perceptual phenomena other than metacontrast and those described in Chapter 6. For example, von Békésy (1967) suggested that the perceived distortions of physical stimuli that occur in the classic geometrical illusions result from lateral interactions among the peripheral neural representations of the various portions of the stimulus objects. Ganz (1966a, 1966b) has suggested that they are also the basis of figural aftereffects by invoking lateral interactions between current and delayed responses. (But see J. Robinson's, 1972, devastating critique of this idea.) Schoenberg, Katz, and Mayzner (1970) have applied a lateral inhibitory interaction model to explain the psychophysical field of interaction that they believe reflects the shape of the inhibitory field surrounding a point on the retina. Wade (1978), although at the same time expressing deep reservations about any neuroreductionistic models in the context of our present knowledge, also suggests that lateral interactions between cortical columns may be the origin of afterimages.

Attempts have also been made to explain binocular rivalry, the alternation of perception in the presence of competing dichoptic inputs, with lateral inhibitory interaction models by a number of neurophysiologists and psychologists (Abadi, 1976; Thomas 1977, 1978; Wade, 1975b). None of these, as we see in subsequent chapters, seems to satisfactorily account for the behavioral data.

2. The Single-Cell Feature-Detector Model

If any two groups of neurophysiologists can honestly have been said to have revolutionized modern psychobiology, it is without doubt D. H. Hubel and T. N. Wiesel, on the one hand, and J. Y. Lettvin, H. R. Maturana, W. S. McCulloch, and W. H. Pitts on the other. These outstanding scientists revolutionized perceptual theory by discovering neurons[8] in the visual system that responded more vigorously to specific spatiotemporal patterns (trigger features) of the stimulus than to the simple luminous flux. In my previous two books in this series (Uttal, 1973, 1978) I have discussed their pioneering work and the continuing development of these ideas by Hubel and Wiesel in great detail and will not repeat that discussion here. To summarize their accomplishment briefly, however, the major concept emphasized in their seminal studies was that the afferent nervous system has evolved in such a way that its constituent neurons are selectively responsive to the ecologically significant aspects of the stimulus rather than simply to luminosity per se. Ecologically significant stimuli are spatial or temporal transients, in general, and thus it is not too surprising that patterns of changing illumination in space (e.g., contours and corners), time (brightening and dimming), or combinations of spatial and temporal transients are the most effective stimuli in evoking nervous activity in the visual system. This is an easily accepted concept in the physiological domain. but when applied uncritically to the findings of molar psychophysics, serious conceptual difficulties emerge that make the perceptual significance of these neurophysiological data quite equivocal.

[8]It should not go unremarked that these spatiotemporal sensitivities on the part of individual neurons are indubitably the result of the way in which they are hooked together and thus interact with each other. Therefore in the final analysis the feature sensitivity of single cells is very much a function of exactly the same kind of interaction mechanisms that I described in the previous section and consider when I discuss the neural net hypothesis. The critical aspect distinguishing between these single-cell models of perception and the others is none other than the emphasis of the modeler. In the former case the emphasis is on the neuron cum neuron; in the latter it is on the interconnection and the interactive processes between neurons.

To understand the nature of the arising conceptual difficulties it would be useful to know exactly what are the essential propositions and premises of the single-neuron, trigger-feature version of perceptual neuroreductionism. In this particular case, a remarkable thing has occurred: One of the archproponents of a radical single cell neuroreductionism, Horace Barlow, an eminent perceptual psychobiologist fully aware of the conceptual difficulties involved in any ill-formed neuroreductionism, has set down what he believes to be the principle axioms of the single-cell approach. Barlow's (1972) "Neuron Doctrine for Perceptual Psychology" is an important milestone in any discussion of the deep meaning of this theoretical approach, whether or not one agrees with the specific content of each axiom of his stated dogma. One of the most prolific and influential single-neuron perceptual theorists currently active, Barlow's ideas deserve careful attention. Specifically, Barlow (1972) states:

1. To understand nervous function one needs to look at interactions at a cellular level, rather than either a more macroscopic or microscopic level, because behavior depends upon the organized pattern of these intercellular interactions.
2. The sensory system is organized to achieve as complete a representation of the sensory stimulus as possible with the minimum number of active neurons.
3. Trigger features of sensory neurons are matched to redundant patterns of stimulation by experience as well as by developmental processes.
4. Perception corresponds to the activity of a small selection from the very numerous high-level neurons, each of which corresponds to a pattern of external events of the order of complexity of the events symbolized by a word.
5. High impulse frequency in such neurons corresponds to high certainty that the trigger feature is present [p. 371].

It is the fourth of Barlow's dogmas, of course, that most explicitly concretizes the thinking found in single–cell-oriented neuroreductionism. One must admire Barlow's intellectual sally into the conceptual tangle of neuroreductionism, for in this single sentence he explicitly states a guiding premise that is usually only implicit in the theoretical speculations of many less thoughtful psychobiologists. The identification of the perceptual experience with the feature-triggered response of a single neuron is, for once, made overt. Nevertheless, to some of us this is exactly the point at which the serious conceptual error that has misdirected so much thinking in modern perceptual theory has occurred.

Indeed, stated as explicitly as it is, it is here that the internal inconsistency between the first and the fourth of Barlow's dogmas becomes most evident. The network vocabulary that is used in the first (e.g., "interactions," and "organized pattern") are all, from my point of view, much more compatible with the neural network brand of sensory neuroeductionism (described shortly) than with the single-cell hypothesis expressed in Barlow's fourth dogma. Clearly, however, Barlow is asserting a neurophysiological philosophy emphasizing information convergence (on single neurons). Equally clearly, however, the explosive magnification of the number of cortical neurons activated by a miniscule peripheral stimulus is a strong argument that this approach must be fundamentally in error.

Because the purpose of this section is to introduce the essential premises of each theoretical approach I defer responding to these tenets individually until later in this chapter. For the moment let me only reiterate that this dogma is the core of a very widespread neuroreductionistic point of view in perceptual theory. The ramifications of this point of view are manifold, and these ideas have been applied in efforts to explain a wide variety of perceptual phenomena.

Perhaps the most extreme development of these ideas is to be found in the hierarchical neuronal theory of mind proposed by Konorski (1967). He proposed that all levels of cognitive activity, *no matter how complex,* were encoded by the activity of *individual* neurons. Feature-sensitive neurons of increasing complexity fed successive levels of increasing specificity, each successive level of cellular response representing a more complex concept, until one arrived at an individual cell whose activity encoded any concept even the most complex idea.

Though Konorski's is the most extreme version of a theory based upon the concept of single-cell representation, many others have proposed equally drastic, although less well defined, versions of the same approach. After all there is very little difference in principle between Konorski's ideas and any other hypothesis that identifies single-neuron activity with any percept, no matter how simple the percept may seem to be. Other theories invoking single-cell explanation of perceptual phenomena have evolved from the work of Celeste McCollough (1965). Her discovery of the orientation-specific color aftereffect now bearing her name was another of the exceedingly fruitful developments in the 1960s. The McCollough effect, as it is now appropriately known, (see p. 895 for a more detailed discussion) was originally attributed by her to the fatigue of edge-detecting neurons of the types described by Hubel and Wiesel. The Harris and Gibson (1968) model of the McCollough phenomena, although hypothesizing a special type of neural unit they referred to as a "dipole," is also of this same genre. Fidell (1970), Lovegrove and Over (1972), and Murch (1972) have all also proposed single-cell theories of the McCollough effect that are also similar in principle to these earlier ones.

Campbell and Kulikowski's (1966) well-known paper on the psychophysics of orientation sensitivity also suggested, although more cautiously than was typical at the time, that the Hubel and Wiesel observations described cellular behavior that was the probable cause for the diminished detectability of lines following presentation of a conditioning field of similarly oriented lines. Gilinsky and Doherty (1969) believed that the interocular transfer of masking effects was also accounted for by the action of individual, though binocularly sensitive, neurons in the human brain. Sutherland's (1968) theory of pattern recognition also depended, in large part, on the concept of feature-detecting single neurons.

Since the observation of binocular sensitivity on the part of neurons in the cortex of both cats and monkeys by Hubel and Wiesel (1962, 1968, 1970), and by Barlow, Blakemore, and Pettigrew (1969), a number of perceptual scientists have invoked this type of single-cell sensitivity as the mechanism underlying stereopsis. Such papers as those by Blakemore and Hague (1972); and Blake, Camisa and Antoinetti (1976) explicitly make the association between stereoscopic perception and binocularly sensitive single neurons in the primary cortical receiving areas. Lema and Blake (1977), furthermore, extend the concepts to other binocular summation effects as measured with contrast thresholds. In fact, because they showed that binocular summation and stereopsis were linked (stereoblind subjects showed no contrast summation) they concluded that the same neuronal mechanism was involved in both cases.

Barlow and Hill (1963), furthermore, invoked single-cell sensitivity in seeking an explanation of the waterfall illusion, and Blakemore and Campbell (1969) formulated their paper on orientation and size sensitivity in the same theoretical context. Even as complex a process as sensitivity to changes in the size of visual illusions has bcen attributed to the selective sensitivity of single neurons by Regan and Beverly (1978).

Another such single-cell neuroreductionistic explanation of perceptual constancies has been proposed by Richards (1977). In this rather extreme application of the cellular neurophysiological model, Richards attributes such phenomena as brightness, color, motion, and size constancy all to the action of single neurons in the visual cortex. His approach is to identify analogies in the perceptual constancies and in the single-cell data and to suggest that the latter might encode the former. Though there is no question that such logical units could, in principle, represent the constancies, the impact of symbolic and semantic variables on these phenomena suggests that Richards is operating at far too low a level of neural complexity to make his model plausible.

Finally, Estes (1972, 1974) has also proposed a theory of form detection in which feature-sensitive receptive fields are the major processing mechanisms. His theory was designed to explain the detection of single-target characters in a field of nonoverlapping dissimilar, "noise" characters. For example, the subject may be asked to locate a *T* in a field of *F*s. Bjork and Murray (1977) have elaborated on this general idea in research exploiting a paradigm of sequential visual masking rather than parallel search.

It would, of course, be possible to continue listing studies in which some allusion to a single-cell explanation of some relatively complex perceptual phenomena is made. There are, however, several reasons why this is not necessary. First, I hope I have presented enough examples to make it clear that this approach had wide currency in the 1960s and early 1970s and that I have thus made my point.

Second, in spite of all this activity, there has been no real progressive development of theory in this movement. Rather, single-cell neuroreductionism started out and has continued to be more of a metaphor than a formal theory. It has become, in fact, a convenient vocabulary rather than an analytic tool in our search for understanding of the nature of perceptual processes. The single-cell concept shares with information theory both the high level of promise and the low level of fulfillment.

Third and finally, I believe that the radical single-cell approach has diminished somewhat in popularity in recent years among many thoughtful perceptual theorists. Unfortunately, a part of this abatement in interest is a result of the very great increase in the popularity of Fourier analysis, the spatial-frequency filter model, an approach that suffers from similar conceptual difficulties. The purpose of the next section, therefore, is to continue this review of the history and current state of neuroreductionistic models by identifying the main premises of the Fourier model.

3. The Spatial-Frequency Filtering Model

In several earlier parts of this book I discussed the Spatial Modulation Transfer Function (*SMTF*). The *SMTF* can be measured by determining the contrast of a sinusoidal stimulus required to exceed the detection threshold as function of the spatial frequency of a stimulus grating. The *SMTF* obtained in this type of experiment could have been considered merely as a convenient means of characterizing the discriminative responses of the visual system. However, data that are formulated in this way also raise the possibility of another type of neuroreductionistic theory. Because the perceptual experience can be investigated with spatial frequency patterns so easily, why, some could not resist asking, is the internal anatomic mechanism not also organized in the same way? The logic behind an affirmative answer to this question is relatively simple, terribly seductive, and probably totally incorrect.

The basic neuroreductionistic premise of this spatial-frequency filter approach is derived from the Fourier theory of mathematical analysis. Fourier, in postulating his enormously useful and influential theorem, asserted that any linear and continuous function or system could be *mathematically represented* by the sum of a family of orthogonal functions. The associated but clearly distinguishable neuroreductionistic hypothesis is that the visual system is made up of a system of more or less functionally or even structurally independent anatomic channels. The distinguishing characteristic of channels according to this hypothesis, is that each is selectively sensitive to only a narrow band of spatial frequencies; this is the analog of each orthogonal function in the mathematical model. The main idea, therefore, is that a family of anatomically isolable channels, acting as spatial-frequency filters, performs the equivalent of two-dimensional Fourier analysis on the stimulus pattern. In this manner, according to this theory, they convert the retinal image from the two-dimensional space in which it was originally represented to a multidimensional vector consisting of components encoding the relative responses of a family of spatial-frequency filters.

It must be remembered that there are vast differences among the various ways in which this complex of ideas revolving around spatial-frequency analysis can be used in visual analysis. To use spatial frequency as a medium of quantifying what are otherwise quite complex stimuli is incontestably valid. It is, furthermore, not unreasonable to assume that the very general Fourier mathematics is a valid means of analyzing the behavior of a complex optical system. However, in this section I am not dealing with these uses of Fourier analysis but rather with the more specific neuroreductionistic concepts that are implicit in the anatomical hypothesis that *structurally* isolated spatial-frequency filtering channels actually exist in the visual nervous system. That is a quite distinct and separate idea. The point to be made here is that the successful use of Fourier analysis as a research tool does not necessarily imply that anatomically distinct spatial-frequency channels exist in the visual system.

The initial expression of the anatomical postulate that separable frequency-selective channels capable of analyzing input stimulus forms actually exist in the visual nervous system, has usually been attributed to Campbell and Robson (1968). Campbell and Robson carried out psychophysical experiments in which they measured the *SMTF* of several different kinds of spatial-frequency patterns presented on the face of oscilloscopes. The main finding of their study was that the contrast thresholds obtained in their study were all predictable on the basis of the equivalent sinusoidal components obtained by a Fourier analysis. This outcome was obtained regardless of whether the original stimulus was a sinusoidal, rectangular, or even a sawtooth waveform. On the basis of these psychophysical data, Campbell and Robson hypothesized that anatomically distinct Fourier channels actually existed in the nervous system.[9]

Campbell and Robson's suggestion of the existence of multiple spatial-frequency-sensitive channels was, of course, stimulated by earlier work in which the *SMTF* idea had been developed and subsequently applied to the visual system. Schade (1956) had apparently been the first to measure the *SMTF* in nonbiological optical systems, but Arnulf and Dupuy (1960) and Westheimer (1960) had been the first to apply the idea to the ocular optics. These perceptual scientists, however, apparently conceptualized the *SMTF* (see Fig. 5-37) as the

---

[9]I must admit to a certain uncertainty concerning Campbell and Robson's personal attitude towards the practical, as opposed to the theoretical, isolability of these channels. Nevertheless, the subsequent search for channels in the neurophysiological laboratory, though still unsuccessful, suggests that many visual scientists believe they can be dissected out in one way or another.

overall response of a single-channel system that simply displayed different sensitivities at different frequencies. That single-channel model was more analogous to the response of the optical system with which Schade had worked—optical pathways having no microstructure comparable to channels even though they can be easily modeled by Fourier theory. Campbell and Robson's multichannel model thus was a major conceptual leap. It embodied the truly novel suggestion that the *SMTF* was in fact the aggregated effect, not of a single channel, but of a family of virtually independent subchannels.

There now exists a wealth of psychophysical data that purports to support Campbell and Robson's Fourier-channel hypothesis, and some that is said to deny it. Irrespective of its validity, this conceptual paradigm has certainly become one of the most influential theoretical approaches in visual perception since the publication of their exceedingly important and seminal paper. To a considerable extent, as I have noted, the Fourier model has supplanted the single-cell approach invoking Hubel and Wiesel-type receptive fields that dominated the field in the 1960s.

Because of the generality of the Fourier mathematics and the ease with which mathematical and anatomical concepts can be confused, it is especially important to be precise about the premises of such a multiple-channel model. Without a clear specification of the specific premises of the model, this idea too could fade into one of those gray metaphors that is indistinguishable from any other mathematically equivalent but anatomically irrelevant, theory. No one, to my knowledge, has ever explicitly spelled out the tenets of the specific Fourier *neuroanatomic* model proposed by Campbell and Robson, but it seems that the following must be included among its major premises if one is to distinguish it from other theoretical constructions:

1. There exist anatomically discrete channels in the nervous system that selectively respond to the two-dimensional component spatial frequencies of the stimulus. The whole visual stimulus is thus analyzed by a Fourier-type process implemented by these channels acting as spatial frequency filters.
2. The channels are relatively narrowly tuned. They respond only to a narrow bandwidth of spatial frequencies.
3. These channels are relatively independent of each other.
4. Perceptual information is represented by the relative amount of activity (a multidimensional vector) in the channels.
5. Different stimulus patterns produce different vectors, and different vectors are equivalent to different perceptual experiences.
6. The channels are each individually sensitive to spatial frequencies across broad areas of the visual field.

It is very important to appreciate that without the premises of narrow tuning and independence of channels, Campbell and Robson's neuroanatomical channel hypothesis would be virtually untestable and merely an abstraction. In the absence of such criteria the theory would blend into all other analogous ones and simply reflect the great generality of the Fourier mathematics.[10] Unfortunately, as we shall see, tests of the independence and narrowness of the tuning of the channels have been less than fully supportive of these two premises of Campbell and Robson's theory. Notwithstanding the existence of data that may be interpreted as rejecting the neuroanatomical idea, remember that the Fourier mathematics is so general that we should be able to find considerable support from a spatial-frequency model almost anywhere in psychophysical data if approached solely from a molar point of view. To do so, however, is not supportive of the quite separate hypothesis of underlying neuroanatomical channels. The acid test of the structural hypothesis can only come from neuroanatomical studies themselves. As we later see, however, such proof has also been very elusive.

Another important limitation of the Campbell and Robson-type model (and all other feature analytic theories) is that the analysis that is performed at this level of abstraction (i.e.. transforming the stimulus pattern into a vector representing the respective responses of system of parallel "channels") does not, in fact, solve the greater problem of pattern recognition. Instead a complicated pattern in one space has merely been transformed into a corresponding pattern in another space, but the challenge posed by the recognition or classification problem remains unsolved. Although it has been suggested (e.g., Ginsburg, 1975) that some transformational artifacts may be introduced into the neural message by such a Fourier transformation that may ultimately lead to illusions of one kind or another, the fact that a spatial transformation has occurred is hardly a complete solution to the very refractory and separate problem of pattern recognition. The theoretician must invoke other mechanisms such as template matching, cross correlation, autocorrelation, or much more complex ideas of statistical network theory to explain how the final categorizations and recognitions are, in fact, made. A Fourier model, therefore, even if it is correct in general principle, leaves much to be explained and is no more a full theory of spatial perception than is any other microtheory. It is a highly limited idea that at best is concerned with the coding and representation of stimulus patterns in the afferent pathways.

Given the neuroanatomic nature of the Fourier theory posed by Campbell and Robson, a major question one must also ask concerns the physiological and

[10]It is possible, however, to conceive of a "softer" version of the theory in which broad-band and interacting channels might be present. Here space might be encoded in a manner comparable to that used by the triad of cone receptors to encode chromatic information. Such a system is certainly possible, and much of the psychophysical data that I discuss later in this chapter supports the possibility of broadly tuned and interactive channels, but their neuroanatomical demonstration remains elusive. Furthermore, at best the observed neural correlates of "channels" seem to have a breadth of field that is no better than the receptive fields measured for individual cells and not the required broad spatial extent. Thus even this softer version of the channel theory is yet to be placed on a firm empirical foundation.

anatomic identifiability of the hypothetical channels. Unfortunately for supporters of this structural premise of the spatial-frequency hypothesis, direct neurophysiological searches for the discrete frequency-filtering channels have generally not been successful. Some investigators have, nevertheless, proposed that their findings are suggestive of (or "not inconsistent with") the presence of the anatomical equivalents of channels. For example, Campbell, Cooper, and Enroth-Cugell (1969); Campbell and Maffei (1970); Maffei and Fiorentini (1973); Pollen and Ronner (1975); Glezer, Ivanov, and Tscherbach (1973); Glezer, Cooperman, Ivanov, and Tscherbach (1976); R. DeValois, K. DeValois, Ready, and von Blanckensee, (1975); and Pollen, Andrews, and Feldon (1978) have all reported neurophysiological data that they believe indirectly support the frequency filter idea. However almost all of these data have been framed in terms of neuronal receptive fields that are comparable to "frequency-filtering" channels rather than to the channels themselves. No channels cum channels have yet been identified that are globally sensitive to broad expanses of total stimulus field and independent of stimulus position within it to the best of my knowledge. Even the best work in this field—specifically, the recent studies by Russell DeValois (in press)—indicates that the demonstrated spatial-frequency sensitivity is limited to relatively narrowly localized regions of the visual field. The "broad field channel," so often postulated, is nowhere in evidence in this distinguished work.

It should be noted that with the exception of the DeValois work, data collection in this field is usually based on a very small number of cells. For example, Campbell, Cooper, Enroth-Cugell (1969); Glezer, Cooperman, Ivanov, and Tscherbach (1976); and Glezer, Ivanov, and Tscherback (1973) do not discuss the large population of other neurons they must have observed in their experiments that do not behave in the way their putative "frequency channel" neurons seem to behave. Furthermore, even if a large porportion of the cells could, in fact, be shown to be selectively sensitive to the dimension of spatial frequency, this would not necessarily imply a Fourier-type transformation of the type proposed by Campbell and Robson. As Kripke (1972) points out, an infinity of other neural transforms would display this characteristic sensitivity to spatial frequencies equally as well as a Fourier system. The neurophysiological data, therefore, remains equivocal and inconclusive with regard to the actual existence of spatial-frequency-sensitive channels.

Perhaps the best organized criticism of the putative neurophysiological evidence for Fourier channels has come from C. W. Tyler. He notes (Tyler, 1975, 1978a), in a compelling critique of the work of Glezer and his colleagues, that the tests to distinguish adequately between a true spatial-frequency-sensitive system and a more conventional system of feature-detecting neurons responsive to nonrepetitive aspects of the stimulus are severe. The concept of distinguishability raised by Tyler is very similar in principle to Towe's (1975) critique of cortical columns as a putative model of brain organization. Specifically, Tyler (1978a) suggests that the following (paraphrased, in part) three criteria must be met before one can accept a neuron as being selectively sensitive to various spatial frequencies rather than as merely exhibiting a general sensitivity to linear patterns:

1. The neuron must exhibit "a preferential response to a grating in comparison with a bar."

2. "The spatial frequency tuning of neurons should be narrower or at least different from the type of center-surround receptive field" described in the classic studies of Kuffler (1952) or Hubel and Wiesel (eq. 1968).

3. There must be "an adequate number of cells with peak responses over a range of spatial frequencies in each retinal area." [p. 121]

Even in the more recent of the electrophysiological studies that I have studied (Pollen, et al. 1978), the authors find that the Campbell and Robson version of the neuroreductionistic Fourier model does not do very well according to these criteria. In general, Tyler's criteria are not well met by the population of neurons sampled in visual area 17 by Pollen and his co-workers. Furthermore, a continuation of their search for neurophysiological indications of spatial-frequency-sensitive neurons to other areas (area 19) of the cortex led this same group (Feldon, Andrews, and Pollen, 1978) only to more frustration and, ultimately, to the acceptance of the fact that there was still little electrophysiological evidence for such neural "channels." Feldon and his colleagues (1978) say, for example, in concluding their report:

> However, because the response density at the narrow-band frequency is so very low, we do not know whether the selective responsiveness at this frequency is of special significance for information processing as required for the hypothesis proposed by Pollen, Lee and Taylor (1971). It is disappointing that this question could not be settled in these studies [p. 350].[11]

Clearly the electrophysiological and/or anatomical status of the hypothetical spatial frequency-tuned neurons in the visual nervous system remains equivocal. It is further possible that the electrophysiologists who have set themselves the task of identifying neural correlates of Fourier channels have chosen the wrong tools. The word *channel* is not necessarily identical with the word *neuron* and it may be that, if they exist, the channels are of a level of network complexity that would preclude their being discerned in the responses of an individual cell with the microelectrode technology. Be this as it may, there seems to be little direct support in the current literature for the very popular hypothesis that a Fourier spatial frequency analysis is carried out within the perceptual system in the specific way proposed by Campbell and Robson.

---

[11] I return in a few paragraphs to give the background of Pollen, Lee and Taylor's original work.

In spite of this low level of neurophysiological and anatomical support, the simplistic idea that any of the psychophysical experiments using gratings (or other stimuli in which the spatial frequency characteristics have been specified) are directly supportive of the Fourier channel theory continues to have wide currency. Only recently has the relevant scientific literature evidenced some emerging appreciation of the logical difficulties in using such psychophysical data to support specific neuroanatomical models. Regan and Beverly (1978), for example, begin an interesting paper with a long footnote describing the role of psychophysical data in supporting models of this sort. In this footnote they assert that such findings can only be "consistent with," but never "definitive of" internal structure. Though this is a step in the right direction I do not believe that they have gone far enough. In fact, although psychophysical evidence may be sufficient to reject some implausible model, it can never provide any more support for any one of the many plausible models that are functionally analogous to each other than for any other. In spite of this caveat, the literature abounds with psychophysical papers asserting that their findings are consistent with one or another particular form of the spatial-feature filtering neuron or channel theory. It is only in a few cases that one of the necessary criterion premises of the Fourier channel theory is specifically tested. An increasing body of evidence (see p. 724) suggests that the radical form of the hypothesis, in which narrowly tuned anatomically distinct channels are proposed, cannot be valid.

The history of this explosive current enthusiasm for the hypothesis of multiple Fourier channels as an explanatory model of visual psychophysical findings is clear. It can be specifically dated from Campbell and Robson's (1968) very influential paper. Since then the Cambridge school, revolving around Fergus Campbell, has continued to be the most vigorous champion of this approach. The Blakemore and Campbell (1969) and Blakemore and Nachmias (1971) studies of grating adaptation (and, by implication, the selective fatigue of Fourier-like channels) set the stage for a number of experiments that use this paradigm. Kerr and Thomas (1972), Jones and Tulunay-Keesey (1975), and Burton and Ruddock (1978) are among the many others who have argued for the existence of independent channels by using the well-documented fact that psychophysical sensitivity to a test grating is reduced more for a test grating that is similar in spatial frequency to an inspection grating than for a test grating that is different.

Another psychophysical approach purported to be supportive of Fourier channel theory has been the use of the spatial sine wave summation technique. In such studies the threshold sensitivity to the sum of several different spatial frequencies is measured. If the threshold to the sum of the spatial frequencies can be predictable on the basis of the sensitivities to the individual spatial frequency components, then, according to the logic behind the experiments, this is a compelling argument in favor of independent channels. The work of Graham and Nachmias (1971), and of Graham, Robson and Nachmias (1978) is illustrative of this approach. Other psychophysical paradigms have also been used. The application of Schade's original invention of the Spatial Modulation Transfer Function to vision, of which I have already spoken, is an important case in point. Such studies show that the depth of modulation required for a stimulus to be perceived as a grating (rather than as a continuously illuminated region) varies as a function of the spatial frequency of the stimulus.

Many other perceptual phenomena measured in psychophysical experiments have also been attributed to Fourier filters in the nervous system. Mansfield (1974) sees such channels as the basis of orientation perception. The masking of gratings by gratings has also been linked to neural Fourier channels by Stromeyer and Julesz (1972). Complex interactions between spatial frequencies and color aftereffects have been attributed to spatial-frequency filters in the nervous system by a number of workers. Obviously this latter attribution is another spin-off of the very influential discovery of the orientation-specific color afteraffects by Celeste McCollough (1965). Among those who see evidence for the Fourier model in such spatial frequency-color contingent aftereffects data are Stromeyer, (1972) and May, Matteson, Agamy, and Castellanos (1978).

A most interesting application of the Fourier idea to the problem of stimulus equivalence has been proposed both by Pollen, Lee, and Taylor (1971) and by Cavanaugh (1978). These workers have noted that because the Fourier transform is insensitive to some of the translation and magnification transformations in exactly the same way as is the human, the former may be an explanation of human visual phenomenon. Although neither of these papers presents any specific psychophysical evidence to support this hypothesis, these workers do believe that the nervous system is organized to produce such a Fourier transform and that the logic of the process justifies the linkage between psychophysically demonstrated stimulus equivalence and the Fourier model.

An important paper by Weisstein, Harris, Berbaum, Tangney, and Williams (1977) raises another interesting issue. These workers showed that patterns that did not look very much like other patterns (e.g., a bull's-eye and a grating) could mask each other if the Fourier components of the two patterns were alike. Although these authors were very careful to avoid any unique linkage between the idea of the Fourier channels and their psychophysical findings, they did note that the idea of a sensitivity to nonlocalized and distributed aspects of the stimulus is a property that the Fourier model does possess—even though it does share this property with some other mechanisms. It does not, however, share this property with the model of a retinotopic system of receptive fields responsive only to local regions of retinal imagery.

Another approach to the problem of visual spatial frequency channels has ignored both psychophysical and neurophysiological data. In their stead some theoreticians of a more mathematical persuasion have tried to show that the Fourier transformations produced by optical or electronic systems introduce new properties into the signal that are analogous to visual phenomena. A persistent problem with this approach is establishing that the new properties, indisputably produced by such transformations, are actually phenomenologically significant. It is, therefore, a matter of considerable debate whether the diagonal "lines" introduced into a Fourier processed pattern are perceptually present or not. The reader is referred to an illuminating confrontation between Rudee (1977), Boulter (1977), and Ginsburg and Campbell (1977) on the one side and Schachar, Black, Hartfield, and Goldberg (1977) on the other. As the authors on the latter side properly assert (after taking their lumps for an oversight in an original article), "the presence of diagonal Fourier Components in the pincushion grid does not necessarily account for the presence of the illusory diagonal lines nor prove that the visual system performs a two-dimensional Fourier transform. [Schachar et al. 1977, p. 962]."

It is interesting to note how often supporters of Fourier models, when pressed on this matter, revert to a somewhat more conservative point of view and acknowledge that their psychophysical data or computer or optical analogs are, at best, plausibility tests and not necessary and sufficient proofs of the truth or falsity of the Fourier hypothesis. The same, somewhat forced, conservative tone is taken in another debate over the origins of checkerboards and color aftereffects by M. Green, Corwin, and Zemon (1977) and May and Matteson (1977), following a devastating critique of their work by F. Smith (1977) and Tyler (1977a). For example, Green et al. (1977) state:

> Our goal was to compare the explanatory value of two alternative ways of specifying a visual stimulus, rather than to establish the details of possible neural coding mechanisms. As we stated, "The purpose of our experiment is to demonstrate that Fourier analysis can better account for the processing of patterns than an analysis which treats spatial stimuli as collections of visual features. [p. 209]"[12]

May and Matteson (1977) add:

> We did not feel that our results constituted direct support for such a notion and consequently were quite tentative in our statements about whether patterned information is processed by Fourier analysis as opposed to feature detection mechanisms. We felt that it would be just as premature to attribute perceptual responses to single cortical units as it would be to state that the brain performs Fourier analysis. Our experiments examined perceptual responses as they relate to one of many heuristic methods of describing visual inputs [p. 209].

---

[12]I do not agree with these authors that their quoted earlier sentence is quite as clear in limiting their contribution to "alternative ways of specifying a visual stimulus" as they suggest. The stress on visual process in their original statement suggests that they believed, at least at that time, that this was the way the visual system actually encoded the stimulus, not just how the experimenter found it convenient to represent it.

Unfortunately, it is only when pressed that this highly laudable conservatism becomes overt. The amount of controversy itself is indicative of both the impact this approach has had and the fragility of the model. (See also p. 698 for my discussion of the critique of Pollen, Lee, & Taylor's 1971 hypothesis).

To sum up this minireview, there is an enormous enthusiasm at the present time for this kind of spatial-frequency-filter model. Even though many of the papers I have cited simply invoke the Fourier idea as a way of conceptualizing the data that are obtained in each of the respective experiments, obviously the extreme neuroreductionistic version of the model is taken literally, and not just as a metaphor, by many at the present time.

Now I would like to turn to some more specific theoretical models that push the idea of frequency-filtering channels further than do most of these earlier papers. One of these, to which I briefly alluded a few pages earlier, has been proposed by a group of highly regarded neurophysiologists—Pollen, Lee, and Taylor (1971). In this paper, they attempt to make the neurophysiological details implied by the Fourier hypothesis much more specific. The other, presented by an outstanding mathematical psychologist, Norma Graham, pursues the formal implications of the psychophysical data far more deeply than any of the other supporters of the Fourier model.

Pollen, Lee, and Taylor (1971) have proposed what is still, to my knowledge, the most specific Fourier-analysis-based neurophysiological theory of visual function. They proposed in this early study (in which, incidentally, they also reported neurons that they believed displayed the properties required of the hypothetical filter elements) that the information in the retinal image was conveyed in a retinotopic[13] fashion to the lateral geniculate body of the thalamus. However, according to their hypothesis, when signals are sent from the thalamus to the visual cortex the information contained in the pattern is transformed by simple cells (of the type identified by Hubel and Wiesel) into a series of "strip integrals", each of which represents the stimulus energy in a linearly shaped field. The transformed "value" of these strip integrals is thus reflected in the activity of neurons whose primary axes of sensitivity are oriented along that field. Figure 9-3 represents the alignment of three (of many possible) of these fields. Of course, all orientations would have to be represented in a complete system. The pattern of the output of all of the simple neurons would correspond

---

[13]In the present context I use the word *retinotopic* to refer to a subsequent representation that is at least topologically, if not geometrically, isomorphic to the retinal image. In other words a retinotopic representation can still be plotted in the same x, y space as the original stimulus image, even though highly distorted. Each point of a retinotopic representation corresponds to a point on the retinal stimulus map. To the contrary, the Fourier transformation, like others of its genre, converts the stimulus representation to one in another space with which it is no longer isomorphic. In the specific case of a Fourier transform, the transformation is to a two-dimensional space in which the proportion of the stimulus energy distributed at different spatial frequencies is plotted rather than the energy at each of the x, y coordinates of the original stimulus space.

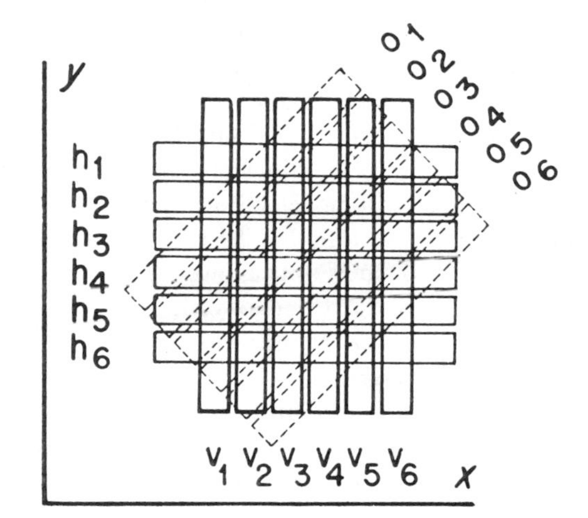

FIG. 9.3. A representation of the strip integrals, purported to be computed by simple cells in the more peripheral portions of the visual cortex. (From Pollen, Lee, and Taylor, © 1971, with the permission of the American Association for the Advancement of Science.)

to the distribution of neural activity in the entire retinotopic *x, y* space and the activity of each would represent the distribution of energy in a single strip.

The next step in the process, as proposed by Pollen, Lee, and Taylor, is the integration of the outputs of families of parallel strip integrators (i.e., as reflected in the accumulated response patterns of many simple cells) by complex cells presumed to be at a higher level of the visual cortex. This is, of course, the necessary stage at which a field of broad extent would become available to the "Fourier channels." They propose that the complex cells are performing a spatial Fourier transform of the information contained in the parallel strip integrals. The information that had been represented in the thalamus in the *x, y* domain is now represented by a transformed pattern in the spatial frequency domain.

To sum up Pollen, Lee, and Taylor's model, the stimulus pattern has been transformed from one domain (*x, y*) to another (spatial frequency) by a two-stage process; the first stage—the construction of the strip integrals—is carried out by simple cells of the visual cortex, and the second—the Fourier transformation of the strip integrals—by the complex cells.

Unfortunately, from our previous observations of Pollen's more recent work, it seems that the neurophysiological details of the model are difficult to substantiate. Pollen, Lee, and Taylor's model has also been criticized not only by Mittenthal, Kristan, and Tatton (1972), and Kripke (1972), but also, as I have noted, by Feldon, Andrews, and Pollen himself (1978). Pollen's group, much to their credit, has expressed disappointment that even 7 years after proposing the model they had not been able to establish more rigorously an empirical basis for the neural mechanisms that might underlie the necessary global aspects of their hypothetical transformational mechanism.

In retrospect, it is not too surprising that this should be the state of their detailed neural hypotheses at the present time. Pollen, Lee, and Taylor's model was almost too detailed for the neurophysiological data that had been accumulated at the time it was enunciated. No matter how consistent the psychophysical data may be with the Fourier transform hypothesis, there is no way to go from these behavioral data to the detailed internal structure of the visual portions of the brain. Because the neural data remain inconclusive, their most explicitly stated neurophysiological model still lacks a concrete foundation. The recent collapse of support for the idea that the responsivity of complex cells is defined by the convergence of inputs from a lower echelon of simple cells in a hierarchy of cells of increasing complexity (Kelly, J., & Van Essen, 1974) has also resulted in a lessened confidence that these workers were on the right track with their hierarchial neural hypothesis.

This, however, is a difficulty that the mainly descriptive Fourier theories do not share. In theories that are not so specifically neurophysiological, the emphasis is on the processes. The mathematical apparatus, in that case, need not be encumbered by any specific hypothesis of neural implementation. Among those who have chosen to use the Fourier model as a descriptive rather than as a neuroreductive model, perhaps the most eloquent has been Norma Graham (1980). Regardless of whether or not one agrees with her analysis (and any evaluation of it depends upon criteria of elegance and goodness of fit more than any neurophysiological validation per se) one cannot help but be impressed by the clarity with which Graham has identified and expressed the major issues.

Graham set out to establish that a Campbell and Robson-type of Fourier theory (multiple and independent narrow-band channels selectively sensitive to spatial frequencies) fits the data of a number of experiments better than any single-channel theory involving a broad distribution of receptive field sizes associated with Hubel and Wiesel-type feature-detecting neurons. The single-channel[14] theory, against which Graham tests her Fourier model is made up of a uniform field of neurons whose receptive fields individually display either an inhibitory or summatory "Mexican Hat" sensitivity characteristic like that shown in Fig. 8-18A but over a continuous range of field sizes. The major argument against such a single-channel theory, according to Graham. is that though the single-channel theory predicts otherwise, the contrast threshold has been shown psychophysically to be actually defined by the individual component to which the visual system is most sensitive. In other words, the threshold does not change as much as it should with the addition of a second component. This partial insensitivity to the properties of the sum of the two waves exists in spite of the fact that the summation of the peaks and troughs of the two sine waves may result in a peak-to-trough contrast that is much higher than that of an individual

[14]It should not go unmentioned that the "single-channel" model can actually be better conceptualized as an "infinite-channel" model involving a continuous distribution of receptive field sizes or channels. Clearly the Fourier multiple channel model must coverge upon this theory at its limit as the number of channels increases.

wave. Again according to Graham. such a summative contrast would be expected to activate selectively at least some of the feature detectors implied by the single-channel model.[15] That model is, therefore, less likely to be correct in Graham's view.

Graham's particular version of the Fourier theory invokes narrow-band, independent, spatial-frequency-sensitive channels of the classic kind originally proposed by Campbell and Robson (1968). To this basic foundation she adds a new concept: probability summation among the several channels. This is an idea that was originally proposed by Sachs, Nachmias, and Robson (1971) but is fundamental in Graham's thinking. Probabilistic summation seemed to be a likely candidate to be incorporated into the model because of the high degree of variability of a positive response when the stimuli contrasts are close to the threshold. Thus, as Graham explains the process, if a compound stimulus made up of two spatial sinusoids has a probability a of evoking a response in one channel, and a probability b of evoking a response in another channel that has some other center frequency, then the probability c of a response for the entire two-channel system would be somewhat greater than for either individual channel (but not for the sum of the two). For example, the probability c would be expressed as

$$c = a + b - ab \qquad (9\text{-}1)$$

Such an expression suggests some lowering of the threshold when two independent spatial-frequency channels interact but not as much as that predicted by a great single channel made up of a wide distribution of sizes of Hubel and Wiesel-type feature detectors. As noted, the latter theory would predict that the increase in detectability would be more closely related to the new peak-to-trough height of the summated stimulus pattern that is generally observed in the appropriate psychophysical experiments.

It is at this point that the theoretical and empirical difficulties in modeling complex perceptual processes of this kind begin to mount. First, the probability

---

[15]In presenting this material here I am not going to try to spell out the counterarguments against each of Graham's propositions. In fact, she explicitly acknowledged in this paper, in an eminently reasonable way, the limitations of each of the steps in her logic and that alternative, if not equally parsimonious, explanations were possible. The important point here is not that each point of logic is correct or incorrect per se but that the reader remember that the reason that so many of these arguments end up as discussions of parsimony or aesthetic pleasingness is that there is a fundamental equivalence of many of the models. Either a single-channel theory based on feature detectors or a theory implying a parallel system of independent spatial frequency detectors is, in principle, capable of explaining any and all of the data if a sufficient number of degrees of freedom are allowed in the formulation. At the very least, there could be a feature detector for every stimulus and a Fourier analysis of anything is possible in any system that is continuous and linearly supremative. The mathematical equivalences of the formal models, however, should not be allowed to divert the reader's attention from the possibility that alternative "neural implementations," which are not equivalent, may also be a part of each theory's premises.

model does not precisely predict the data in summation experiments either. Graham notes that observers do increase their sensitivity to a greater degree with summating stimuli than they should according to this simple probability summation model. It is little solace that the single-channel, feature-detecting model fails to a greater degree in its even greater overprediction of the extent of expected improvement in compound grating detection. Another difficulty quickly became evident, as Graham so fairly makes clear. Different experimental procedures give different estimates of the bandwidth of the channels. It is always a disappointing result when the most fundamental parameters of a model turn out to depend on the method used to measure them. Such a result leaves much to be desired in any search for biological reality.

Graham goes on, nevertheless, to propose and test a more elaborate mathematical formulation of the multiple spatial frequency-sensitive channel probability summation model she champions. Her model is based upon two assumptions. First, for the summation type experiment, in which one is interested in the effect of additional spatial sinusoids on the contrast threshold, she proposes that the added effectiveness is porportional to the fraction of the total response that is added by the newly activated channel. Second, Graham assumes that the response of any channel is proportional to the contrast sensitivity of that channel multiplied by the proportion of the stimulus energy that is distributed at the center frequency of that channel.

The first of these two assumptions has been expressed[16] by Graham in the following equation:

$$\frac{\Psi\ (w_0)}{S\ (w_0)} = K_1 \frac{R\ (w_0)}{\Sigma\ R_n} \tag{9-2}$$

where $\Psi\ (w_0)$ is the perceptual effectiveness of an additional spatial sine wave of frequency w_0 in reducing the threshold contrast of a complex test stimulus; $S(w_0)$ is the sensitivity of a channel centered at w_0; $R(w_0)$ is the response of a channel centered at w_0; and $\Sigma\ R_n$ is the response of all of the channels in the system. K_1 is a constant. Assumption 2 was expressed in the following form:

$$R(w_n) = K_2 f(w_n) \times S(w_n) \tag{9-3}$$

where $R(w_n)$ is the response of a channel centered at frequency w_n; $f(w_n)$ is the amount of frequency w_n present in the stimulus; $S(w_n)$ is the sensitivity of the channel to frequency W_n; and K_2 is another constant.

Using these two equations Graham was able to derive the following expression for the perceptual effectiveness $\Psi\ (w_0)$ of adding an additional sine wave stimulus, $f(w_0)$, to an existing compound stimulus on the modulation threshold

[16] I have changed the symbols in these equations to make the presentation somewhat clearer than in the original.

of a system composed solely of such probability-summating Fourier channels when the sensitivity of the channel for w_0 is $S(w_0)$.

$$\Psi\,(w_0) = \frac{K_1 K_2}{\Sigma\, R_n} \times f(w_0)[S(w_0)]^2 \tag{9-4}$$

And indeed the expression in Eq. 9-4 did predict the data obtained in experiments on sine-wave summation by Kulikowski and King-Smith (1973) fairly well. It is interesting to note that those perceptual scientists, however, had originally proposed a neuroreductionistic model that not only included spatial frequency-sensitive channels, but edge and line detectors of the more conventional kind as well, to explain their data when it was originally obtained.

Graham, continuing her open-minded discourse, acknowledges that there are many other models of various forms that also might predict the data she has considered perhaps equally as well. It is possible, for example, to invoke broadband channels, as opposed to her narrow-band channels, that are sensitive to wide ranges of frequencies if one also incorporates geometrical feature sensitivity to such properties as edges and slits in their repertoire of trigger features. It is her judgment, however, that the model she proposes is able to fit the data better than any of the other approaches and with the fewest assumptions.

To sum up this discussion, Graham's particular model is one of several nearly equivalent ones that invoke narrow-bandwidth, spatial-frequency-tuned channels to perform a Fourier analysis on the stimulus pattern. The novel contribution that she makes is to consider the role that probability summation might play in the process. Whether or not Graham's model is entirely correct in detail is almost incidental. The clarity and evenhandedness of her discussion is a model of this kind of scientific discourse. Many of the key issues were highlighted and at least preliminary steps taken towards quantitative evaluation of alternative approaches.

However, as we see elsewhere in this chapter, despite its apparent parsimony there is a substantial body of data suggesting that the Fourier model is not likely to be correct in its basic neuroanatomical axioms, no matter how good the fit of the mathematical model. Dominating any such discussion of the plausibility of such a Fourier model, however, is the essential limitation on the analysis of internal structure by input–output methods of the kind exemplified by visual psychophysics.

4. The Neuronal Network Model

The final theoretical approach to perceptual neuroreductionism that I shall discuss is the neuronal network model. This approach represents another attempt to explain and conceptualize the neural substrate of perceptual function. However, rather than concentrating on lateral interactions, on the selective responsiveness of individual neurons, or on the filtering action of hypothetical Fourier channels, the neuronal network approach emphasizes the general ability of a network consisting of an ensemble of more or less unspecialized neurons to carry out logical operations that critically process incoming information. The roots of this relatively recent approach toward neuroreductionistic theory can be found in the pioneering work of a group of scientists at the Research Laboratory of Electronics at MIT in the years following World War II. Men such as Warren McCulloch and Walter Pitts were enormously influenced by the wartime work on computer logical circuits and the emerging analogies with brain function that seemed, at the time, to be all too evident. The McCulloch and Pitts (1943) and Pitts and McCulloch (1947) papers were among the first attempts to represent psychophysical phenomena as the output of a network of nearly homogenous neurons. Hebb's (1949) model, incorporating the concepts of cell assemblies and phase sequences also included some ideas of this genre. Farley and Clark's (Clark & Farley, 1955; Farley & Clark, 1954) simulation of a self-organizing pattern recognizer set the stage for a large amount of subsequent work, much of which was also influenced by contemporary work that stressed the adaptive learning of pattern recognition skills as simulated on a digital computer by such pioneers as Selfridge (1955) and Dinneen (1955). The work of the grand old man of mathematical biophysics, Nicholas Rashevsky was also important in the development of the network tradition.[17] (See the relevant chapters in Rashevsky's heroic book on mathematical biophysics, Rashevsky, 1948.)

In the recent past, studies of specific networks have proliferated using several different approaches. Some workers (Harmon, 1959; Harmon & Lewis, 1966) have tried to simulate network functions with electronic devices while others (note especially the work of Pellionisz, Llinás, & Perkel, 1977; Pellionisz, 1970; Pellionisz & Szentágothai, 1973) have simulated the action of neural nets with general purpose digital computers. Still others have gone about the task analytically using noncomputerized mathematical models. This latter group includes some exceedingly interesting work by Teuvo Kohonen and his colleagues (Kohonen, Lehtiö, & Rovamo, 1974; Kohonen, Lehtiö, Rovamo, Hyvärinen, Bry, & Vainio, 1976) at the University of Helsinki in Finland.

There is, of course, an enormous overlap between the neuonal net approach and all of the other neuroreductionistic models that I have already discussed in this chapter. Lateral interaction processes must necessarily be a part of any neuronal net model and, conversely, some would also say that interactions in the

---

[17]I am grateful to Frederick A. Webster of South Pomfret, Vermont, who, in a lengthy personal communication, helped me to understand the complex history of the neural net simulation approach during the decade after the second World War. Of particular interest to me in the present context was his recollection that Walter Pitts, one of the leaders of the MIT group, had also spoken vigorously against psychoneural isomorphism at a meeting at the National Institute of Cardiology in Mexico in 1947.

net are the underlying causes of the specific feature sensitivity of any single-cell or Fourier channel. Furthermore, many of the Fourier ideas I have described were derived from postulates based upon the well-established and validated neurophysiological observations of feature-sensitive neurons or the known properties of their characteristic receptive fields. So there is a fundamental conceptual link between all these schools of thought. Because of this conceptual link, it is possible for others (e.g., Bonnet, 1977) to see feature, network interaction, and spatial frequency explanations of perceptual processes as being "consistent" if not identical, and certainly not antagonistic, with each other. Other theoretical psychobiologists (e.g., Anderson, Silverstein, Ritz, & Jones, 1977) seek neuronal net explanations of how a brain could extract features rather than depending on the vaguely described discriminative properties of selectively sensitive cells. Obviously only a matter of emphasis separates each model from its neighbors, and no categorization of the type I present here can ever consist of mutually exclusive classes.

The invocation of a neuronal network, however, does imply that neurons interact to process stimuli by algorithmic and general-purpose means that are less dependent on the particular nature of the local features of the input stimulus than are some of the other models. Both the single-cell and the Fourier approaches imply the opposite hypothesis—namely, that the neurons (or channels) have adapted (presumably on the basis of ecological and adaptive utility) in particular ways to respond to selected local aspects or features of the stimulus. This different emphasis is not a trivial consideration! It was, as I noted earlier, appreciated by Howard and Ballas (1978), that one's initial emphasis can be the basis of a fundamental divergence in subsequent steps of theoretical development, one path leading to theories stressing local analysis and the other to theories stressing global synthesis.

What then are the fundamental premises that distinguish the neural network approach from the others? To my knowledge there has been no explicit statement of the foundation premises of network theory comparable to Barlow's important contribution to single-cell theory. However, I propose that an analogous set of dogmas, characterizing the prototypical network approach, can be summarized as follows:

1. Perceptual information is represented by patterns of activity in distributed networks of neurons.
2. The state of the system at any moment represents the current state of the perceptual process.
3. The state of the system is determined by statistical considerations. No particular neuron or set of neurons is critical; what matters is the central tendency of all of them. Any neuron can be replaced by many others in any given process.
4. Even the simplest perceptual process involves many millions of neurons.

5. Most neurons are innately unspecialized in logical function and depend upon the nature of their interconnections as to what their role will be in the network.

6. Any individual neuron may participate in several different network functions, perhaps even simultaneously.

The major difficulty with the neuronal network approach is that it is essentially untestable neurophysiologically for practical reasons.[18] The reasons for this have already been discussed. We simply do not have the technical equipment, the descriptive mathematics, or the conceptual superstructure to handle the unspeakable complexity of even the simplest mammalian neuronal network. Although some progress has been made in analyzing the action of simple nerve nets in invertebrates (e.g., the fine work of Kandel, 1977, 1979, on aplysia) there has not been a single study reported that deals with vertebrate neurophysiology at a level of detail comparable to the one implied by the premises of the neuronal network hypothesis.

It is indeed also possible that there is an even more fundamental barrier to progress in this field than the practical one to which I alluded in the previous paragraph. We probably have yet to fully appreciate the full implications for neuroreductionism of Gödel's (1930) famous theorem that the internal consistency of any mathematical system cannot be proven using the axioms of the system itself. One possible implication of Gödel's theorem was suggested by John von Neumann (1966). He interpreted (p. 54) Gödel's theorem to require that after a system had reached a certain level of complexity, any model of it would have to be *more* complex than the system itself. In other words, von Neumann asserted that any system could be best modeled by itself and that any further interpretation or explanation would require more than itself. He also suggested that any verbal or "literary" description of a complex system must necessarily be less than adequate.

A further implication of this very important theorem is, therefore, that the human mind cannot in principle understand its own internal structure, but philosophers and logicians still argue this point. As J. R. Lucas (1961) points out, this theorem may mean that we should not "ask, and cannot obtain, complete formalization" of a system like the human brain when we have only the system itself to do the analysis. This is a theoretical subtlety, however, that may not be presently germane simply because of the fact that the lower level practical barriers have themselves not yet been overcome. For example, some relatively easily stated and finite problems generate computational requirements that are beyond practical obtainability. Stockmeyer and Chandra (1979) say with regard to this point, that problems such as checkers, chess, certain topological prob-

---

[18]This is a judgment with which all of my colleagues will not agree, of course, but I am convinced that current facts support this contention for the moment as well as in the foreseeable future.

lems, and those of number theory in particular would require "a computer as large as the universe running for at least as long as the age of the universe" for their complete solution.[19] Many of the problems that perceptual theoreticians ask seem also to be of this class; even though finite, such a computer is, of course, practically impossible.

The current status of the problem is that however plausible the neural network model seems, it is especially beset by substantial practical and conceptual limitations that prevent it from being either totally refuted or accepted at the present time. Thus though the neural network theory is, in principle, sufficiently complex to provide a mechanism for the representation of the full majesty of human perception and cognition in situations where the other theories are not, it remains an expression of hope and belief rather than of well-established fact. The other theoretical approaches, of course, are so limited in the maximum extent of their potential application that they do not, even in principle, provide the same opportunity for generalization to other than the highly specialized microsystems for which they were specifically invented.

In spite of these serious concerns with the limits of neuroreductionism, there has been a considerable amount of activity in recent years and attempts have been made to explain perceptual processes in terms of models that involve distributed processing by networks of unspecialized simulated neurons. The emphasis in this approach has been on the overall configuration of the interconnections between the elements of the neural net or, in the absence of details of that configurational information, on the statistical properties of a quasi-random network. If there is any single property that is most characteristic of the neuronal network model it is the fact that all such models incorporate some kind of parallel processing; that is, processing of incoming information from different parts of the visual field is assumed to be going on simultaneously in many different parts of the neural network. It is even possible to conceive of the processing of all parts of the visual field going on in *all* parts of the network simultaneously. It is this concept that is connoted by the word *distributed,* another defining characteristic of network theory.

Such a distributed, parallel-processing network approach is, I believe, exemplified in the proposed neuronal implementation of my own autocorrelational theory of form detection (Uttal, 1975a). Figure 9-4 is a diagram of a possible, and not too implausible, neuronal network that could extract regular patterns from irregular background noise on the basis of a two-dimensional autocorrelation transformation carried by the ensemble of unspecialized neurons depicted there. The main premise of this neural network hypothesis is that un-

---

[19]The fact that humans can play chess does not negate this conclusion. We do not produce complete (exhaustive) solutions, only partial solutions to particular situations. Nor does the existence of chess playing microcomputers: Their approximations cannot be considered to be complete solutions either.

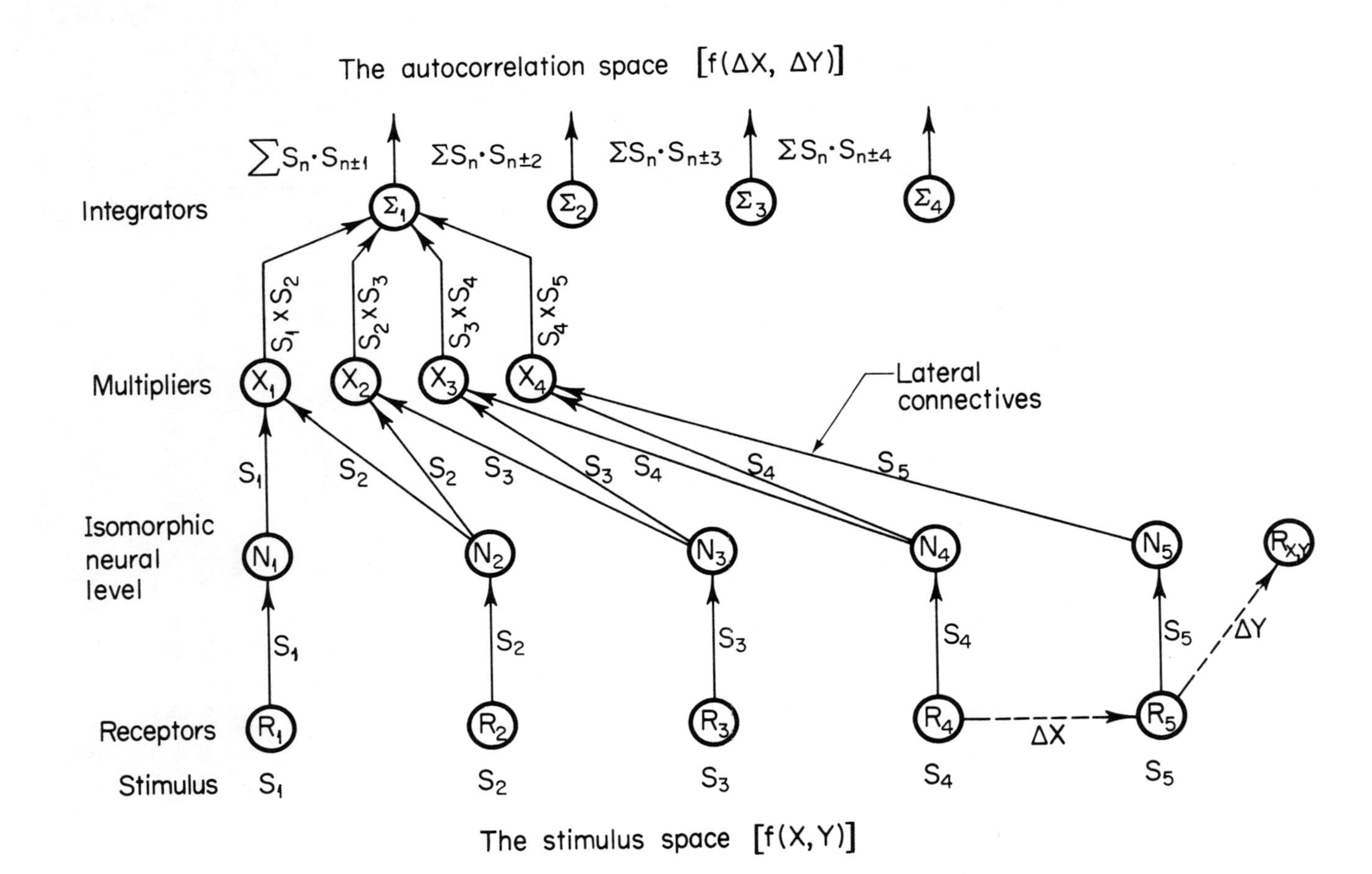

FIG. 9.4. A plausible neural network that could accomplish an autocorrelation transform. (From Uttal, 1975a.)

specialized neurons can be interconnected such that they process the incoming stimulus information in a way that is comparable to the mathematical transform carried out during a two-dimensional autocorrelation. The major corollary is that this is the way that the perceptual system actually processes incoming visual information.

As I noted earlier, there is nothing mathematically unique about the autocorrelation process in spite of the fact that I found it to be especially useful in modeling the detection data. It is well established that if the autocorrelation function works, then the Fourier transform must also succeed in accomplishing the same task. However, the autocorrelation theory is associated with a particular neural implementation that is distinct from the Fourier models described in the previous section. The network proposed in Fig. 9-4 is specific to an autocorrelational transform. It implies that the neurons are interconnected into a parallel-processing and distributed lattice without any intrinsic specialized sensitivity to particular geometrical features in the x, y domain (as would be implied by the single-cell theory), and without any channels sensitive to spatial frequencies (as would be implied by the Fourier theory). The neuronal mechanism suggested by the autocorrelation model would, to the contrary, operate on the global properties of the incoming information in a way that is particularly sensitive to periodicities. In this manner certain regular and repetitive geometric features of the target stimulus can be enhanced or extracted while random noise is ignored. The autocorrelation model can be formalized by the following equation:

$$A(\Delta x, \Delta y) = \int\int f(x, y) \times f(x + \Delta x, y + \Delta y)\, \mathrm{dy}\, \mathrm{dx} \tag{9-5}$$

where Δx and Δy are shifts in the positions of the stimulus pattern $f(x, y)$ and $f(x, y)$ is the original stimulus pattern. A family of $A(\Delta x, \Delta y)$ values is then computed to fill out the various points in the autocorrelation space. An example of a set of simulated stimuli and computer plots of their autocorrelations are shown in Fig. 9-5.

The autocorrelational transformed stimulus is seen in this figure to be made up of a number of peaks distributed in the Δx, Δy space. By applying the following expression:

$$F_m = \frac{\sum_{i=1}^{I} \cdot \sum_{n=1}^{N} \frac{A_i \cdot A_n}{D_{i,n}}}{N} \tag{9-6}$$

a single numerical "figure of merit" (F_m) representing the relative psychophysical detectability of patterns can be generated for each autocorrelation. In this expression, A_i and A_n are the amplitudes of peaks in the autocorrelation space, D is the pythagorean distance in that space between the two peaks, and N is the number of peaks. In Fig. 9-5, the four-digit numerals represent the figure of merit for the four autocorrelations. As described earlier (Uttal, 1975a), the model

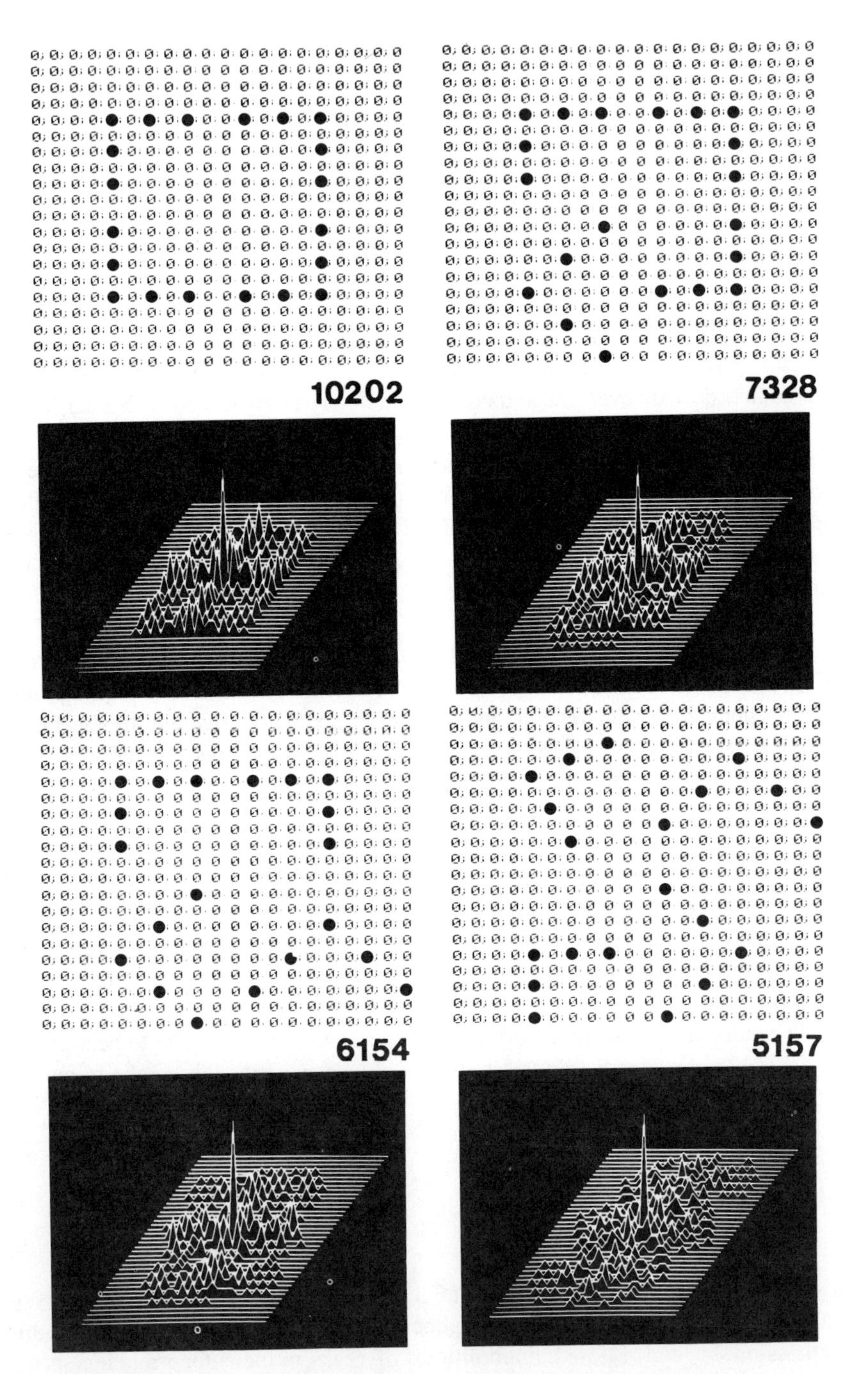

FIG. 9.5. Four autocorrelations showing the effect of disorganizing the corners of triangles on the figure of merit. The greater the disorganization, the lower is the figure of merit. (From Uttal, 1975a.)

was highly successful in predicting the rank order of detectibility within a large number of stimulus sets.

A very general mathematical statement of the limits and capabilities of neuronal-network-like devices called *perceptrons* (the use of the term perceptron was first proposed by Rosenblatt, 1962) has been presented by Minsky and Papert (1969). Their work generalizes the concept of a randomly (randomness being the sine qua non of the original Rosenblatt perceptron) interconnected network consisting of receptors, reinforcers, and responders (or categorizers) operating on the basis of selective reinforcement to a more general theory of threshold logic and decision processors of geometrical patterns. In Minsky and Papert's view, Rosenblatt's idea of simply building such a gadget to test the properties of such a mechanism was a highly limited approach. By providing a more highly formal theoretical basis for the generalized perceptron, they have greatly enhanced our understanding of the fundamental capabilities and limitations of such networks.

Minsky and Papert showed, for example, that there were many other kinds of perceptrons with properties quite different from the randomly interconnected type originally proposed by Rosenblatt. They went on to show under which specific conditions each type of perceptron could accomplish a particular task (e.g., a "diameter limited perceptron" cannot, in principle, tell if all of the parts of a pattern are connected to each other). Other perceptrons were shown by Minsky and Papert's derivations not to be able, in basic principle, to "recognize" certain types of patterns, a conclusion expanded upon by Abelson (1976) for a class of perceptron-like devices he calls "linear threshold machines." All in all, these computer scientists have made an important contribution to understanding the limits of these types of networks. Clearly, however, the human mind itself stands as an existence proof of the ability of some types of networks to accomplish an enormous range of similar tasks.

Another formal approach to a neural-network model like Minsky and Papert's has been formulated by Sejnowski (1976). His analysis also deals primarily with the mathematical properties of the network rather than the perceptual applications. This work, however, is especially interesting because it concentrates on the processing of the global properties of stimuli by such nets.

More recently other investigators have used neural-network ideas in less formal ways as heuristic metaphors that suggest how the storage of information in the nervous system might be carried out. A thoughtful, but neither mathematically nor even simulation-orientated approach, stressing the statistical properties of the network, has been presented by E. Roy John (1967, 1972). John's own words are the best brief summary of his network approach. Although in this excerpt his emphasis is on the temporal aspects (the common mode of activity) of the network state, the general concept of a statistical network state is eloquently presented by John (1972):

> These considerations and related data led me to propose (John, 1967) an alternative to switchboard theories: the statistical configuration theory. The critical event in learning is envisaged as the establishment of representational systems of large numbers of neurons in different parts of the brain, whose activity has been affected in a coordinated way by the spatiotemporal characteristics of the stimuli present during a learning experience. The coherent pattern of discharge of neurons in these regions spreads to numerous other regions of the brain. Sustained transactions of activity between participating cells permit rapid interaction among all regions affected by the incoming sequence of stimuli as well as the subsequent spread. This initiates the development of a common mode of activity, a temporal pattern which is coherent across those various regions and specific for that stimulus complex. As this common mode of activity is sustained, certain changes are presumed to take place in the participating neuronal populations, which are thereby established as a representational system. Whether such changes are alterations of "synaptic efficiency" or not, it is assumed that the critical feature of these changes is to increase the probability of recurrence of that coherent pattern in the network. Certain types of preexisting neuronal transactions become more probable, but no new connections are assumed to be formed.
>
> This tyeory is statistical, in that the informational significance of an event is represented by the average behavior of a responsive neural ensemble rather than by the exclusive behavior of any specifiable neuron in the ensemble. The same ensemble can represent many different items, each with a different coherent pattern of deviation from randomness or from its baseline pattern. The theory is configurational in that new responses are based upon the establishment of new temporal patterns of ensemble activity rather than upon the elaboration of new pathways or connections. Learning increases the probability that particular temporal patterns of orderly activity will occur in coupled ensembles of neurons. By this process, the representational system acquires the capability of releasing the specified common mode of activity as a whole if some significant portion of the system enters the appropriate mode.
>
> It should be emphasized that this is not a "field" theory, nor does it deny the highly organized structure of the brain. The firing pattern of neural ensembles undoubtedly depends upon connections between neurons. Configurations of activity in representational systems are presumed to become established by modification of interneuronal relationships, perhaps by changes located at the synapse although other alternatives are conceivable. However, in this laboratory we doubt that memory is based upon the establishment of new connections rather than upon the modification of existing relationships. We consider representation of information by statistical features of temporal patterns of ensemble behavior more likely than by the localized activity of specific cells [pp. 853–854].

Although many contemporary psychobiologists would disagree with John's presentation with regard to a number of particular details concerning the mechanisms by which the network state is achieved, this lucid statement effectively expresses one view of the statistical nature of neuronal network function; it is a contribution that seems to adequately describe what is probably the most plausible basis for all mental activity.

However, when a more detailed examination of the principles of neural interaction in a highly interconnected network is made, then the difficulties of concretizing some of the verbal assumptions that John has proposed become evident. One example of a more specific attempt to spell out the details of such a neural net model has been presented by J. Anderson, Silverstein, Ritz and Jones (1977). In developing their model, Anderson and his colleagues make two assumptions that were among the most important of the premises that I presented on p. 709. First, they propose that the processes they are modeling occur as a result of simultaneous activity in a large number of neurons; and second, they assume that any one neuron may be a part of several different processes.

Anderson and his colleagues proceed from these assumptions through the use of simple linear algebraic equations to describe the action of neural networks of the sort shown in Fig. 9-6. In this model network, an especially important role is played by feedback signals from neurons later in the chain onto neurons situated

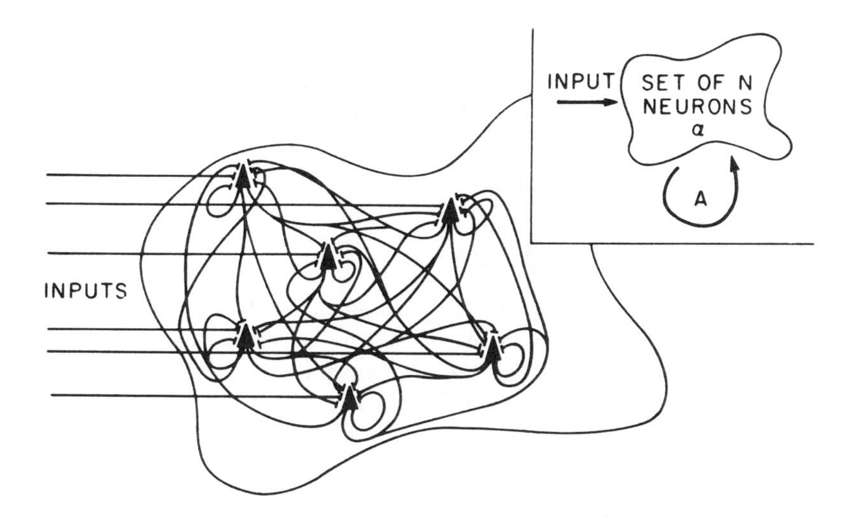

FIG. 9.6. A "simple" neural network consisting of only six neurons. Each cell feeds back on itself as well as on its neighbors, producing a very complex pattern of responses. (From Anderson, Silverstein, Ritz, and Jones, © 1977, with the permission of the American Psychological Association.)

closer to the input. Anderson and his colleagues assume that as a result of this feedback and other interactions, the network can operate as a feature analyzer. This hypothetical system responds most strongly to features of the stimulus for which it is tuned as a result of the pattern of "neural" interconnection. This network thus emphasizes features in the same way as the autocorrelational model responds to the periodic aspects of the stimulus, not because of any property of individual neurons but rather as a result of the general organization of the network.

Anderson, Silverstein, Ritz, and Jones go on to discuss how such hypothetical networks could account for several other kinds of psychological processes that are not particularly germane to our present discussion of theories of visual perception. But the important point is the basic conceptual nature of their model. They do not attempt to simulate the full neural network in all its richness. Rather, they have worked out the mathematics of interaction among a very small number of neurons (only a half dozen in the case of Fig. 9-6). Even so, the computational requirements for their simulation are very high. Matrix manipulations requiring elaborate and extensive computational power were needed to carry out even this simulation of a trivial neuronal network. Their results show that such operations as might be carried out by a more realistically numerous network system can, at best, only be remotely approximated in this simple microcosm. Nevertheless, this model is one of the most specific of the genre I am considering here, and a careful reading of their paper leads to an appreciation of both the strength and limitations of the network approach.

5. The Continuous Field Model

Field theories are essentially dead, representing a theoretical approach that has a very modest, if any, following these days. Even the holographic theory proposed by Pribram, Nuwer and Baron (1974), which uses the field terminology of the interference hologram as a metaphor for brain activity, is actually based upon a set of assumptions that are very difficult to distinguish from the other neuronal network theories I have already described. The essential point is that the neuron theory predominates in perceptual neuroreductionistic theory as thoroughly as it does in the electrophysiology laboratory. That theory is that the nervous system is composed of independent functional units (neurons) that are cytoplasmically discontinuous. Neurons are also functionally independent except through the highly specialized points of conjunction we know as synapses. Any theory of brain function that is based upon either local ephaptic or broad electrotonic interaction as a major means of communication between different regions is inconsistent with this most basic premise of modern neurobiology—the neuron theory. All electrotonic field theories involving electrotonic spread (as opposed to those reducible to neuronal network concepts) were effectively laid to rest by the definitive studies of Sperry, Miner, and Myers (1955) and Lashley, Chow, and Semmes (1951) that showed that the insertion of short-circuiting metallic foils, pins, and wires into the cortex did not disrupt visual discriminations to any significant degree.

Fields, therefore, are descriptions that are at best wholistic metaphors of, or molar approximations to, what is actually going on in the nervous system, in much the same way as is the mentalistic vocabulary of psychology. In spite of this analogy between molar fields and molar minds, there is little interest in this approach these days. I exclude the work on evoked brain potentials and electroencephalographs from this statement—they constitute a somewhat different conceptualization of the problem. Nevertheless, they are also best understood as cumulative, quasi-statistical processes reflecting the overall behavior of networks consisting of millions and millions of discrete neurons. Be that as it may, the notion of the electrotonic field as a means of processing sensory information and representing perceptual processes has few adherents in the late 1970s. All of us have been irretrievably influenced by the microelectrode and the electron micrograph in spite of the lack of correspondence in scale and time between the mechanisms these devices probe and molar psychological processes.

E. COUNTERINDICATIONS TO CONTEMPORARY DOGMA IN PERCEPTUAL NEUROREDUCTIONISM

In the several preceding sections of this book I have sought to present a relatively straightforward discussion of the various neuroreductionistic theories that have some currency among perceptual scientists these days. Although I could not fully restrain my doubts—in a number of places I have indicated my skepticism with the logic or empirical status of elements of the various theories—my critical comments were not expanded upon and any criticisms certainly not documented. In this section, however, I intend to fill this gap and present a more detailed consideration of the empirical data base that I believe specifically counterindicates some of the premises of contemporary neuroreductionistic theory and the dogmas that have followed from them.

It is sometimes startling to realize how speculations initially proposed as very tentative hypotheses can, in some inexplicable way, be transformed into rigidly held dogmas. The problem is especially severe in this field of perception because there is still a totally inadequate logical and empirical bridging of the psychological and neurophysiological domains. Indeed, one of the major criticisms of this entire endeavor is that, in fact, many of the popular neuroreductionistic theories are beyond logical or empirical establishment or refutation. This dismal possibility becomes evident in a number of different situations: (1) The enormous generality of the Fourier mathematics makes it highly unlikely that we would not be able to find some such representation in any nervous system even if that nervous system does not contain anything structurally like a spatial frequency-sensitive channel; and (2) the single-cell feature detector hypothesis is probably unrejectable in a neural universe of such an enormous variety of neural sensitivities that anything, including a "monkey's hand" or a "yellow Volkswagen" can be found to elicit activity selectively in at least some neurons. In each case, the problem remains that of identifying the *critical* set of properties to which a certain single neuron or channel will respond rather than of finding *any* of the many stimulus properties that may activate it. Logically, the rigorous establishment of what are the *essential* trigger features of a neuron or a channel and the establishment of any candidate neural response as a true code (See Uttal, 1973) are much harder goals to achieve than seems to be generally appreciated by many perceptual theoreticians. Only a few psychobiologists, such as John and Schwartz (1978), explicitly discuss this fundamental difficulty with the neuroreductionistic approach.

This section of the present Chapter is going to attack the problems of neuroreductionism using a somewhat unusual tactic. I first identify some of the dogmas that have wide currency in our thinking concerning perceptual neuroreductionism but which I believe are open to question. I then present brief discussions of some data that seem to me to counterindicate those dogma. In so doing I am admittedly taking a dogmatic and one-sided position and largely ignoring the data that speak for the other side. This is at least partly justified by the fact that much of that supportive data and logic have already been presented in the preceding sections or exists in the literature that I have already cited or will cite in subsequent chapters. Furthermore, supportive discussions have often been equally unbalanced in the other direction. My presentation in this section is not, therefore, intended to be evenhanded but rather to emphasize a point of view that is all too often ignored in the research literature.

One of the main motivations for this critical discussion is to lay a solid foundation for the major principle that guides the remainder of this book. That principle, of course, is that, in spite of the existence of some more or less plausible speculation, there are few satisfyingly solid neuroreductionistic explanations of the Level 3 and 4 processes to be discussed in subsequent pages. Quite the contrary, it seems to me that many of the popular neuroreductionistic metaphors may actually mislead and divert attention from the true complexity of perceptual processes. For one example, many of these models of higher-level processes involve totally inadequate isomorphic concepts that grossly misjudge the nature of the symbolic representation that probably occurs. In some cases, errors as gross as attributing a given perceptual phenomenon to a peripheral rather than a central process may be committed. As another example, the metaphors drawn from the neurophysiological laboratory lead to an erroneous stress on elementalistic feature detection (in the property-list sense) and divert attention from the abundance of empirical facts that point to a more wholistic processing by the human perceptual system.

In this section, therefore, I identify the specific dogmas of contemporary perceptual neuroreductionism and indicate those counterindications that *suggest* that these dogmas may not be totally valid. It is necessary, however, once again to reiterate the major premise of perceptual psychobiology in order to guarantee that there be no misunderstanding about my goals. However critical I may be of the individual neuroreductionistic theories and dogma that abound today, I am in no way denying the essential physicalistic, monistic identity of mental functions, on the one hand, and the processes and states of central neural tissue, on the other. Now Let's consider the dogmas themselves and the counterindications that should insert a cautionary note into our acceptance of them.

Questionable Dogma Number 1

The actions of single cells encode or represent complex perceptual behavior.

As I noted earlier, this very general dogma, most explicitly expressed by Barlow (1972), is the keystone of a substantial portion of contemporary neuroreductionistic theory. In spite of the fact that neurons responding to specific trigger features of the stimulus are ubiquitous in the nervous system, many logical and empirical counterarguments argue against the validity of such a dogma. It is clear that in many cases we have confused the role of the peripheral nervous system as communicator with the role of the central nervous system as interpreter and psychoneural equivalent. In accepting this questionable dogma, many perceptual scientists have thus violated in a particularly extreme manner the sign-code caveat I have previously highlighted (Uttal, 1975a). Furthermore, the identification of individual neuronal feature sensitivity with perceptual experience is simply not justified on logical grounds. As John and Schwartz (1978) point out, the logical difficulty involved in the invention of a ''pontifical'' neuron was appreciated by Sherrington (1906) over seventy years ago. His caveat apparently fell on deaf ears.

There is, without doubt, an abundance of neurophysiological data that demonstrate feature sensitivity in a wide variety of sensory neurons. The argument against this dogma, therefore, has to be mainly couched in logical terms; there is no empirical procedure by means of which this hypothesis could be totally rejected any more than there is a methodology with which it could be rigorously established.

The main logical argument involves discrepancies between the time constants of the responses of individual neurons and the psychological phenomena they purport to model. Similarly, the principle of stimulus equivalence (many versions of the same stimulus can elicit the same response) suggests a flexibility and computational power that does not seem to be within the capabilities of single neurons. One could, of course, simply increase single neuron ''concept detectors'' to a number equal to all possible versions of a stimulus, but frankly, this seems an inelegant solution to the problem. Logically, it also seems unlikely that the kind of cellular functions that are to be found in the primary projection regions, where most of our data on single-cell sensitivity have been obtained, are the psychoneural equivalents of perceptual processes. The impact of statistical ideas concerning brain organization is another reason for doubting the role of the individual neuron as a mediator of perceptual experience. And finally, only rarely have psychobiological experiments been carried out in which a direct association has been demonstrated between any single neuronal response and any perceptual experience.

Though many of these arguments are patently "logical," there also are some empirical findings that can be interpreted as strong arguments against the single-cell hypothesis. Even the archproponent of single cell theory, Horace Barlow, sees some experimental counterindications to this approach. For example, Barlow (1978) reports his inability to find any differential sensitivity to form in a texture-discrimination task and notes the inconsistency of such a finding with a single-cell theory of form perception.

Similarly, Timney and MacDonald (1978) raised an important question concerning feature detectors in the visual nervous system. They sought to determine whether curvature detectors per se, as opposed to multiple line detectors sensitive to the tangents of curves, were responsible for the adaptive desensitization to curved gratings as a result of prolonged exposure to other curved gratings. They concluded that their experiments did not distinguish between the two hypotheses and also alluded to the fact that the overall structure of the pattern—and thus, "higher" levels of processing—must be involved. Pomerantz, (1978) also raises another difficulty for a simplistic single-cell feature detection theory in his experimental findings showing that stimuli varying in slope alone are difficult to discriminate. Although Pomerantz' main goal was to show that more complex elements than lines (such as angles) are more likely to be the basis of form perception, his results do dissociate the cellular neurophysiological data from the psychophysical in a way that challenges the tenets of the most simplistic of the pontifical cell theories.

The most complete body of empirical evidence counterindicating this dogma, however, is the large amount of data I present in Chapters 10 and 11 of this book. In general, these data deal with the effect of the configuration, meaning, or global pattern of a stimulus on many different phenomena. Features, unless redefined to a point of generality at which they are no longer local "properties," but rather become global aspects of the stimulus, are woefully inadequate in explaining most of the phenomena discussed in these two subsequent chapters.

Clearly the single-cell feature detector paradigm, if not rejectable outright, is seriously in need of some close scrutiny. Many investigators are beginning to appreciate this fact even though none of the present data are themselves compelling counterarguments against the pontifical neuron hypothesis.

Questionable Dogma Number 2

The nervous system operates by greater and greater degrees of feature extraction and abstraction, mapping concepts of ever-greater complexity onto the responses of an ever decreasing number of neurons.

This proposition is Barlow's (1972) second dogma; unlike the first, it seems clearly to be incorrect on a strictly empirical basis. The mass of neurophysiological evidence indicates that activity initially elicited in even a single peripheral receptor neuron is magnified and distributed by neural divergence in time and space in such a way that an uncountably large number of neurons are ultimately activated in the brain. Rather than an increasing specificity and convergence on a small number of neurons, just the opposite seems to be happening; responses to stimuli, mediated by both the ascending reticular formation and the classic sensory pathways, are generated in widely distributed regions of the brain. The call for some kind of "neural economy" by Barlow is a spurious one in a system that has many neurons (and, perhaps more important, synapses) to spare, and in which individual neurons can be simultaneously involved in so many different circuits. In short, economy need hardly be a driving force in a system so richly endowed with structural elements.

Questionable Dogma Number 3

High frequency in neural response rate encodes high stimulus certainty.

This proposition, Barlow's (1972) fifth dogma, stating that high-frequency nerve action potentials (or large ones, etc.) encode higher certainty of a stimulus being present, can also be criticized on empirical grounds. The weight of evidence has always suggested that strong stimuli may be encoded in several parts of the nervous system either as increases or decreases from the resting level of action potential firing rates, as differential rates of firing in adjacent loci, or by the relative magnitude of graded responses. The opponent-color mechanisms in the visual system is one obvious example of this differential encoding as is the differential responsivity of binocularly sensitive neurons in the visual cortex. Such opponent or differential mechanisms probably occur in many other portions of the nervous system. The inherent isomorphism of *positive* correlations between neural and mental responses is simply not justified by current neurophysiological knowledge. A strong negative correlation may be just as "significant" as a strong positive one, and ample evidence suggests that the nervous system is capable of encoding signals in just this way.

Questionable Dogma Number 4

The trigger features of neurons change as the result of experience.

Stryker and Sherk (1975) and Mize and Murphy (1973) have shown that in spite of the repeated "demonstration" of experiential effects on neuronal orientation selectivity, many previously reported results of early experience may have been due to poor sampling and wishful thinking on the part of the experimenters. In their important experiment, for example, Stryker and Sherk showed that if the usual experiment was done with a double-blind procedure, and if the experimenter was very careful about using a standard sampling rule with which to gather data, then the effects of early experience on cortical neuron orientation selectivity seemed to disappear.

In spite of this caveat, there is still a considerable flurry of controversy and new studies purporting to demonstrate experiential effects on neuronal orientation selectivity are continuously being published. However the data are in substantial disagreement and vary considerably with the particular methodology (see Gordon, Presson, Packwood & Scheer, 1979, for a good discussion of these discrepancies). A far more plausible idea has been proposed by Stryker, Sherk, Leventhal, and Hirsch (1978). They suggest that rather than having their orientation *modified* by experience, neurons require experience to *maintain* innate patterns of organization. The experiential modification findings, they suggest, are actually due to a variation in the sample of neurons as some are selectively deactivated by a lack of experience. Thus they argue that the preferred orientation of a neuron is not affected by experience; it can only be deactivated by a lack of experience.

Questionable Dogma Number 5

Neuroanatomically distinct channels selectively sensitive to spatial frequency exist in the visual nervous system.

This, of course, is the prototypical dogma of the Fourier analysis type of neuroreductionistic theories. As I have noted in the discussion of this theory earlier in this chapter, the Campbell and Robson model holds only if three main properties of the channels can be validated; the channels must be narrowly tuned, must have broad receptive field sensitivity, and must be independent. Without these three properties, as Towe (1975) has noted in the analogous case of cortical columns, there is no way to distinguish between this putative theoretical mechanism and a host of others that are also able to represent spatial frequencies. Almost any nervous system made up of neurons arranged in some sort of spatial array or composed of a field of various size receptive fields will exhibit some properties that are analogous to the Fourier channels. Thus the rigorous proof of the Campbell and Robson Fourier-type theory demands neurophysiological and psychophysical validation of narrow tuning, broad sensitivity, and channel independence, validations which I have already indicated are not yet available.

As I have already indicated, in my opinion there is still little neurophysiological evidence that unequivocally supports the existence of anatomically discrete spatial frequency sensitive "channels" with the proper properties. By far the best data comes from the work of R. DeValois (e.g. DeValois, Albrecht, and Thorell, 1977). But they have shown that spatial frequency-sensitive neurons are sensitive to only relatively narrow regions of the receptive field.

Psychophysical evidence that the molar behavior is "consistent" with these properties is not a proof of this, or any other model, for reasons already noted. However any psychophysical evidence showing that the molar performance is not consistent with the Campbell and Robson version of the channel hypothesis would be compelling. And, indeed, there is substantial evidence of inconsistency that argues against the prerequisite Fourier premises. For example, Stromeyer and Klein (1975)[20] have presented evidence that seems to support the idea that the channels, if they exist, must be very broadly (and not narrowly) tuned. On the other hand, Tolhurst (1972), Stetcher, Sigel, and Lange (1973), Henning, Hertz, and Broadbent (1975), Nachmias and Weber (1975), and Tolhurst and Barfield (1978) have presented equally compelling evidence that the channels, if they exist, must be interacting.

A wide variety of other inconsistent psychophysical data is also available to counterindicate the neuroanatomical-channel postulate in a way that goes far beyond the assumptions of the most radical version of Fourier channel theory. Indeed, the following data seem to argue against any version of the spatial frequency tuned channel, be they narrowly or broadly tuned. The bandwidths of any channels that might exist seem to vary quite a bit depending upon the method used to measure them (see Graham, 1980, for discussion of this point), and the theory typically fails (like most theories) to provide a good fit for the psychophysical data at the high- and low-frequency limit of the range. Furthermore, Coffin (1978) has shown that the Fourier theory fails very badly when it is confronted with a task that does not involve stimuli already represented as spatial frequency patterns. If stimuli such as block letters are used and the Fourier analysis is only done ex post facto, Coffin reports that the confusions among such letters obtained in psychophysical experiments are not well predicted by the Fourier components of the stimuli. Indeed, the predictions of a more convential feature similarity model fit the data much better. A further counterindication to this dogma can be found in the work of Growney (1978). He has shown that the Fourier model does equally poorly in explaining the metacontrast phenomenon even when the stimuli are explicitly spatial frequency patterns.

Another counterindication to the Fourier channel hypothesis has been reported by Greenwood (1973). In an interesting study he compared the contrast sensitivity of patterns that were composed either of linear or dotted grating patterns. In this experiment the dots were arranged to produce patterns with the same overall spatial frequencies as the gratings. The results of this experiment showed that the linear gratings were detected at contrasts less than 40% of that required to detect the dotted patterns even when the two were matched for brightness. Obviously the visual system does not depend on Fourier channels alone, if at all; other dimensions of the stimulus such as the local microstructure are also very impor-

---

[20]A counterargument to Stromeyer and Klein's paper has been presented by Graham and Rogowitz (1976). They criticize Stromeyer and Klein both on the basis of the supportive empirical evidence they presented and on the basis of their theoretical deductions. But Graham and Rogowitz do not reject the contention out of hand that the channels are broadly tuned; in fact, they themselves call attention to other research that supports such a viewpoint.

tant. Furthermore, in a backward-masking experiment (Zamansky & Corwin, 1976) in which scattered letter fragments were used to mask letters, fragments of the same stroke width as the letters were not the best maskers, as would be predicted by a spatial frequency-sensitive channel hypothesis. Clearly the Fourier model seems to work best in the context of gratinglike stimuli and even then not universally as proposed by its proponents.

Another phenomenon that is very difficult for the radical theory of Fourier channels to handle is Gregson's (1976) observation that the afterimages produced following persistent viewing of a grating have an apparent spatial frequency 1.5 octaves *greater* than the adapting one. Despite a somewhat tortuous bit of neural backsliding on his part, invoking hypothetical lateral inhibition between the hypothetical channels, Gregson's data remain, for some of us, another discrepancy in the conceptual structure surrounding Fourier channel theory.

An even more serious difficulty is a startling and paradoxical result reported by Levinson and Frome (1979). They showed that, in a grating adaptation experiment, the width of a single bar may appear to increase at the same time that the grating frequency appeared to increase! This physical impossibility was coupled with, what would have been from the point of view of the radical Fourier channel theorists, a perceptual impossibility—observers could, by selective attention, *"restrict their spatial frequency analysis to a limited region of the visual field"* (italics added). This attentive control over the putative "channels" raises another question about their very existence; this is a far more serious conclusion than Levinson and Frome's concluding suggestion that spatial frequency analysis and selective attention are only "linked" by this finding.

There are many other logical and mathematical arguments against the strong neuroanatomical Fourier channel idea. T. Poggio, (1979) has noted the following:

1. It is impossible to represent Fourier coefficients by means of cells with receptive fields that are spatially localized.
2. Vision is generally nonlinear and the role of Fourier analysis in nonlinear systems is equivocal.[21]
3. The number of channels (12) generally reported does not seem to be large enough to carry out the analysis.
4. No convincing demonstration has yet been made showing that phase information (a necessity for perceptual reconstruction) is encoded and yet pictures with identical power spectra may appear quite different to the human observer.

All in all the Fourier model leaves much of form perception to be explained in spite of the spirited defense of it to be found in such sources as DeValois and

[21]Bela Julesz has gone even further. At a recent meeting he noted that since linear theories do not selectively attenuate information, no linear theory can adequately model vision—a constellation of processes that is inherently nonlinear.

DeValois (1980), and the many publications of the group surrounding Fergus Campbell.

Questionable Dogma Number 6

Metacontrast results from peripheral lateral inhibitory interactions that diminish the strength of the conducted neural signals.

This dogma is perhaps one of the most pervasive in modern perceptual psychobiology. Surprisingly it is also the one for which the most abundant body of counterindications exist. A 15-year accumulation of solid findings argues against all of the lateral interaction theories of metacontrast that I previously described. Unfortunately these data are largely ignored in the enthusiastic debates concerning which version of the lateral interaction model best represents the psychophysical data. Yet, over a decade and a half ago, Fehrer and Raab (1962) raised a very important caveat when they noted that the reaction time to a metacontrasted stimulus (which is presumably perceptually less intense) did not differ from those measured to the same, but uncontrasted, stimulus. Because the link between brightness and reaction time is so tight, this should have been a prominent warning that the diminution in the metacontrasted percept should not be equated with a diminution in the afferent signal strength. The phenomenon is obviously much more complex than the simple lateral inhibition model suggests if its impact on reaction time can remain constant even though the "brightness" varies downward to virtually zero.

Several more recent studies have also shown that the process is dramatically dependent upon higher levels of cognitive processing than are dealt with by the simple lateral interaction model. Mayzner and Tresselt (1970a), for example, in studying the powerful form of metacontrast they called sequential blanking, should have had their suspicions raised about the lateral interaction model when they discovered that a sequential series of letters blanked each other only when the letter sequence did not form a word. My own study of metacontrast (Uttal, 1970c) was prima facie evidence that lateral inhibition was an inadequate explanation. In that case the contrast effect seemed to depend on the contrasted and the contrasting parts of the stimuli sharing a common overall form and not simply on common features or contours that would have been expected to interact laterally in the traditional sense of the word. Because the contrast effects require that a priori form recognition and comparison be made, it is hard to appreciate how the metacontrast suppression could be as peripheral and passive as suggested by the lateral interaction model. Thus, unless one is willing to put such complex cognitive functions as form recognition in the retina, the model fails rather badly.

Additional evidence arguing against that version of the lateral interaction theory that asserts specifically that contours are the components that interact and are suppressed is reported by Stoper and Mansfield (1978). They showed that metacontrast-type masking occurs over broad areas entirely free of contours.

Over a decade ago it was known that the suppressed response to a metacontrasted stimulus could be recovered by subsequently suppressing the metacontrasting pattern. This was originally shown by D. Robinson (1966) and then further supported by Dember and Purcell (1967). This temporal "disinhibition," as they called it, is not, however, directly analogous to the spatial disinhibition observed in the *Limulus* eye by Hartline and his collaborators (see p. 603). In the metacontrast paradigm the time difference between the original stimulus and the disinhibitor is so great that a lateral interaction theory would have to involve some kind of storage mechanism that is not a part of that simple spatial model. Such a storage mechanism immeasurably complicates the lateral interaction explanation to the point, I believe, of converting it into a more constructionistic type explanation.

Furthermore, the suppression of the contrasting stimulus by a disinhibitor is not a requirement to restore the original stimulus to visibility. Such a trick can be performed simply by changing one's research methodology! Schiller and Smith (1966) and Pollack (1972), using forced-choice experimental designs, have both shown that the metacontrasted information, even though suppressed to invisibility, could be recovered simply by manipulating the observer's criterion level. This is also strong evidence that the neural signal information is not passively inhibited but is actively suppressed in some way that it loses perceptual significance without a physicalistic kind of signal degradation.

Hernandez and Lefton (1977) have further shown that there is a profound shift in the criterion used by the subject at exactly the place where the slope reverses in the typical U-shaped metacontrast curve. This result also suggests that there is a strong cognitive or interpretive component to the nonmonotonic metacontrast function that is totally ignored by the lateral interaction hypothesis.

Additional counterindications to this dogma are available. Hogben and Di-Lollo (1978) have found substantial practice effects in the metacontrast paradigm as well as an absence of any effect of the number of contours that are interacting. The net impact of their results is to reinforce the view that the metacontrast function is not the result of simple spatial interactions. The geometrical factor (number of inhibitors) that should be effective is not, and the experiential factor (practice) that should not be effective actually is.

A further substantial counterindication to the peripheral lateral interactions hypothesis of metacontrast can be found in experiments that have varied the apparent depth between the inducing field and the target. It is now well established (Fox & Lehmkuhle, 1978) that the metacontrast effect diminishes as the difference in depth between the two increases. Because the effect diminishes despite the fact that monocular retinal images still maintain the same spatial adjacency (and thus the potential for peripheral lateral interaction), once again it seems unlikely that the simplistic lateral interaction hypothesis is valid.

The general conclusion to be drawn from all of these data is that there are sufficient cognitive, symbolic, and relational factors involved to raise a serious question about the isomorphic, passive, lateral interaction explanation of the metacontrast phenomenon. To this counterindicative psychophysical data we can couple the fact that there are virtually no well-substantiated physiological findings that unequivocally show metacontrast-like effects in peripheral nervous tissue. Even Bruce Bridgeman, a strongly committed neural interaction theorist, was unable to find (Bridgeman, 1975) any backward masking in the cat's optic tract or lateral geniculate nucleus that corresponded to metacontrast, though he did find some attenuation of a delayed burst of activity in the cortex that he felt might be comparable in some ways to this psychological experience.

Finally, recall that the mathematical assumptions of the various lateral interaction theories are separable from the physiological ones, and even the fact that it is possible to fit the psychophysical data relatively well with such equations does not necessarily support the neurophysiological postulates of the model.

Questionable Dogma Number 7

Simultaneous contrast is a result of the same kind of lateral inhibitory interaction mechanisms that seem to adequately explain the Mach band and the Hermann grid.

It has been virtually axiomatic among visual scientists that the Mach band and simultaneous contrast are expressions of one and the same process—reciprocal lateral inhibitory interactions. As distinguished a visual scientist as Floyd Ratliff (1965) has suggested that Mach bands and simultaneous contrast "share some underlying physiological mechanisms in common." However, a closer examination of the similarities and differences between these two sets of phenomena suggests that they are actually very different. Simultaneous contrast of the kind shown in Fig. 11-2 is a global effect that occurs over the entire enclosed region regardless of distance from the edge, but the Mach bands are highly localized effects, very sensitive to the distances between the interacting regions, and occurring only at contours. Indeed, our very successful theoretical understanding of the Mach band effect depends entirely upon this strong relationship between the strength of the interaction and the distance between the interacting objects.

Another discrepancy concerns the location of the processes underlying the two effects. I have previously presented a demonstration (Uttal, 1973 therein see Fig. 8-17 on page 451) that suggests that the simultaneous contrast effect is quite central and can be produced by a dichoptic display in which neither eye alone receives the information necessary to give rise to the effect. Julesz (1971) makes this same point with a random dot stereogram on p. 323 of his delightful book on the cyclopean eye. On the other hand, Werner Koppitz (1957) has shown that the Mach band does not appear when the parts of the stimulus are shown separately to each eye. Koppitz' conclusion was reinforced by another stereoscopic demonstration of my own (see Fig. 8-34 herein) in which it was shown that the Hermann grid illusion could not be produced by dichoptic fusion. These latter two phenomena, therefore, must be the result of quite peripheral processes. A very interesting paper by Kanizsa (1975) provides further support for the idea that simplistic lateral inhibitory interactions do not adequately explain that brightness contrast. Kanizsa presents a wide variety of brightness contrast displays in which the form or configuration of the stimulus plays a critical role in defining the effect above and beyond considerations of local luminance and geometry.

Furthermore, Geisler (1978) has suggested that the amount of simultaneous contrast that occurs at high luminances is so great that it could not be accounted for by lateral inhibition alone. Although he attributes the effect to photopigment depletion due to eye movements and I, to a higher level "computational" factor, both of us agree that lateral inhibition is an inadequate model for this phenomenon.

Additional counterindications are available. Gogel and Mershon (1969), Mershon and Gogel (1970), Mershon, (1972), and Gilchrist (1977) have all shown that the simultaneous contrast effect, as well as the metacontrast phenomenon, depends on apparent adjacency in depth, and that if the induced and inducing fields are separated (in depth), the effect is substantially reduced. The argument here is the same as for metacontrast—because monocular retinal adjacency is maintained in a dichoptic stimulus situation and yet no contrast occurs, no peripheral mechanism could account for this phenomenon. Other studies have shown strong cognitive components in the simultaneous contrast paradigm that are not consistent with the lateral interaction model. Festinger, Coren, and Rivers (1970) demonstrated that the degree of effort with which the subject attended to a stimulus could result in a modulation of the magnitude of the simultaneous contrast phenomenon. The entire literature on lightness contrast, if considered to be parallel to the kind of brightness contrast effect I have been discussing, constitutes another major counterindication to the most fundamental premises of the passive lateral inhibitory model by involving active relational processes. It has been known for over a hundred years that the lightness of an object depends on our knowledge of what it is or on our knowledge that it is a continuation of an object that may exhibit a widely different luminance in some other region. Recent research has supported this classic observation by manipulating the apparent spatial position (Beck, 1965) or the figure–ground relations (Coren, 1969a).

Finally, specific searches (e.g., DeValois, R., & Pease, 1971) for a neural correlate of simultaneous contrast have also been unsuccessful in the peripheral nervous system of mammals, even though the localized neural interactions corresponding to the Mach band have regularly been observed.

Questionable Dogma Number 8

Prolonged viewing leads to figural aftereffects that are the direct result of fatigued neural components.

There is perhaps no more generally accepted dogma in psychology than that which proposes that figural aftereffects such as the waterfall illusion or the McCollough effect[22] are the result of some kind of neuronal fatigue. In particular, a differential adaptation in an otherwise balanced bivalent or opponent system has often been proposed as the locus of such aftereffects. In recent years, however, some extraordinarily powerful counterindications have been forthcoming that also challenge this dogma. These counterindications typically involve thc extraordinary persistence of the effect of adaptation or fatigue. Specifically, we have known (and apparently have overlooked the knowledge) for nearly a decade, since the work of Stromeyer and Mansfield (1970), that aftereffects produced by prolonged viewing of spirals or stripes can last for over 6 weeks! More recently, this extreme persistence of aftereffects has been shown to last even longer. Jones and Holding (1975) demonstrated that the McCollough effect could last for up to 6 months, as long as the subject was not exposed to the specific stimuli used to test for the persistence of the effect during that time. Once tested, however, the effect rapidly diminished following the same time course that would have been followed if the test had commenced at the end of the adaptation period. Others who have provided evidence supporting this extraordinarily long persistence of the McCollough effect include Riggs, White, and Eimas (1974), Skowbo, Gentry, Timney, and Morant (1974), MacKay and MacKay (1975), Heggelund and Hohmann (1976), Thompson and Movshon (1978), and K. White (1978). The prolonged durations of these aftereffects are hardly consistent either with what is known electrophysiologically about the recovery of function of individual neurons or what might be plausibly inferred about the recovery of complex networks from fatigue alone.

Further support that these perceptual adaptation or conditioning effects are underlain by processes much more complicated than simple neural fatigue has been presented by Sharpe and Teas (1978). They have demonstrated a remarkable lack of influence on the figural aftereffects when stimuli are blurred or interrupted in time! Additionally they were unable to demonstrate any difference between early and later conditioning trials—a difference that would have been predicted by a simple fatigue model.

The fatigue explanation of contingent aftereffects is also challenged by the demonstration that the McCollough effect can be induced by simply imagining the bars of a conditioning pattern (Finke & Schmidt, 1977). Though the effect is weaker than the standard phenomenon produced by a real conditioning stimulus, it is clear that any model invoking relatively peripheral single-cell processes would be hard pressed to account for this influence of mental imagery. Murch's (1979) demonstration that the color of the background of the test stimulus does not affect the McCollough effect is also interpreted by him as an argument against an explanation of this phenomenon based on the fatigue of a color-

[22]The reader will find a complete description of these phenomena in Chapter 11.

sensitive receptor or other neuron. He too turned to the vocabulary of a central nervous system "conditioning" model to account for this lack of impact of the background color.

Another counterindication suggesting that the McCollough effect is not mediated by tired neurons is Jenkins and Ross's (1977) demonstration that the effect switches in and out as a function of the subjective state when the figure is a reversible one as shown in Fig. 9-7. This reversible figure can be seen either as a set of triangles or a set of squares. If the McCollough effect was induced by inspection of a green vertical and a red horizontal grating, the phenomenon occurs when the figure is organized into triangles. However when the stimulus is perceived as a set of concentric squares, the effect disappears. Because the subjective organization and interpretation of the inspection figure plays such an important role, it is unclear how any simple theory of neural fatigue could account for this finding. (But see note added at the end of this chapter.)

And, finally, White, Petry, Riggs, and Miller (1978) have shown that the McCollough effect is binocularly transferable under some conditions. If the effect is due to neural fatigue, it clearly is a very peculiar kind of high-level central "fatigue" of which we know very little, occurring above the point of binocular fusion.

Obviously, simple fatigue models do not perform well in explaining aftereffects of the kind considered here. One has to look elsewhere, most probably at higher-order cognitive effects in which inferences about or interpretations of the stimulus become salient, for a more appropriate answer to the difficult problem raised by the phenomena of figural aftereffects.

FIG. 9.7. A stimulus pattern that can be used to demonstrate that the subjective organization of an ambiguous pattern can affect the McCollough phenomenon. (From Jenkins and Ross, © 1977, with the permission of Pion, Ltd.)

Questionable Dogma Number 9

Stabilized retinal images lead to percept fading due to fatigued retinal components.

A perceptual dogma closely related to the one just described, also probably false, concerns the oft-reported fading of retinal images that are stabilized by contact lens–mirror arrangements. The explanatory hypothesis most often invoked also involves the decreased responsiveness of neurons that are exposed to a constant contourless illumination. However, a considerable amount of data counterindicates this dogma, too. One body of knowledge indicates that the perceived pattern in such a stabilized viewing situation fades in meaningful subunits (such as corners or sides) rather than in random blotches (Evans, 1965; Davies, 1973; Pritchard, Heron & Hebb, 1960). Such a context-dependent fading could hardly be mediated entirely by a simple peripheral mechanism. This finding, quite to the contrary, also suggests the involvement of higher-level processes. The point is, fading seems not to be due to a loss of the peripheral signal, but rather to a "designification" of a continuing signal by a more complex central mechanism.

Questionable Dogma Number 10

Evoked brain potentials are direct reflections of perceptual states.

Few, if any, students of the compound evoked brain potentials have specifically spelled out the nature of the relationship they perceive to exist between these signals and perceptual responses. Nevertheless, there is implicit in this entire research program the unspoken premise that the electrical brain response directly reflects something about the psychological state that a similar electrical response from the liver, for example, would not. In other words, the prevailing dogma with regard to these evoked potentials is that they are actually psychoneural equivalents, or codes, and not simply systemic signs of a generalized brain activity or arousal.

This dogma is especially frail and would fall victim to any findings that show disassociation of the perceptual response and the evoked potential. And indeed several such disassociation studies have now appeared. One extraordinary case of psychoneural dissociation involving visual perception and evoked brain potentials has been reported by Bodis-Wollner, Atkin, Raab, and Wolkstein (1977). They carried out a more or less conventional evoked potential study on a very unconventional subject. The subject was a six-year-old boy who had massive destruction of the occipital lobe of his brain. The damage, however, was restricted in a way that spared the primary visual projection regions of Area 17. In spite of this damage, a normal evoked potential to a checkerboard stimulus pattern could be obtained. Their data were especially remarkable in that the evoked potential was normal in *all* regards. Not only were the initial transients (generally associated with activity in the primary projection regions) present, but the later potentials (200 msec following the stimulus) that have been associated with cognitive manipulation of the afferent information were also normal. Psychophysically, however, the child was totally blind in terms of the results of a battery of behavioral tests. Thus, even though these evoked signals did indicate the presence of neural activity in the afferent pathway and the primary projection regions of the cortex, the recorded microvoltages seem to be totally unrelated to any perceptual experience. This is strong evidence that the evoked potential is not a direct equivalent of the percept but probably only reflects the activity of the afferent communication system. Though this distinction may seem trivial, the dogma that the evoked potential is a psychoneural equivalent of perception has already been developed into the practice of clinical testing of vision or audition. Results such as that of Bodis-Wollner and his colleagues make this a highly doubtful procedure in doing anything other than testing the integrity of the afferent pathways.

Questionable Dogma Number 11

Many geometric illusions and other related perceptual phenomena are due to peripheral distortions of the neural representation of the stimulus.

Among the most mysterious, and yet most familiar, phenomena of visual perception are the geometric illusions. Although theories of visual illusions are ubiquitous, we have but the vaguest idea of the mechanisms that underlie these intriguing and fascinating perceptual distortions. A masterful compilation of the various kinds of illusions and review of the state of theories purporting to explain them has been presented by J. O. Robinson (1972). Robinson describes a number of neuroreductionistic theories of geometric illusions, most notably those of Eriksson (1970), Motokawa (1950), Motokawa and Akita (1957), Chiang (1968), W. Köhler and Wallach (1944), and Ganz (1966a, 1966b). All these theories share a common feature—they all invoke a spatial interaction somewhere in the (presumably) more peripheral portions of the nervous system among the encoded representations of parts of the stimulus pattern as the necessary and sufficient cause of this class of illusions. The theories invoke isomorphic distortions, rather than interpretive ones, and see the peripheral distortion remaining a constant influence as the coded signals ascend to the central nervous system where they are transformed into the perceptual experience itself.

It is difficult to designate generalized experimental evidence that attacks all of these theories collectively. There are general logical or conceptual arguments that can be marshaled against them as a group, however. First, the implicit and radical isomorphism that is a part of all of these theories ignores the abundant evidence that suggests that isomorphism is a treacherous foundation upon which to build any perceptual theory. Second, there is a total absence of first-class physiological evidence to support the idea that the perceived spatial distortions are present in the peripheral neural interactions. In spite of the many traditional models and theories of these neural "induction" effects (e.g., Obanai, 1977), no trace of anything remotely comparable to this type of spatial interaction process has yet been found in the electrophysiological laboratory.

There is, to the contrary, some specific evidence that each of the neuroreductionistic theories of geometrical illusions individually fails in one way or another. Robinson adequately describes the weakness of the experimental methods utilized and their failure to predict properly outside of a very narrow range of phenomena. He notes, for example, that Ganz' lateral interaction theory comes to grief in incorrectly predicting the relations between simultaneous and successive effects as well as in underpredicting the spatial extent of the illusions, that Chiang's diffraction theory clashes with the true nature of phenomena other than the ones with which he specifically dealt, and that Motokawa's electric–photic interaction experiments have proven difficult to replicate. Others, like Eriksson's field theory, seem to be no more than the invocation of a physical analogy as a metaphorical description rather than as a true reductionistic explanation.

Other studies that show that the "inducing" effects of one stimulus on another are reduced if the two are at different stereoscopic depths also present difficulties to lateral interaction theories of illusions. The argument is the same as that for lateral interaction theories of simultaneous contrast and of metacontrast. For example, Gogel and Newton (1975) have shown a marked diminishment in the rod and frame illusion when the rod and frame are presented at different depths.

Another general difficulty for any theory of geometrical illusions invoking local spatial interactions between parts of the stimulus is that the stimulus components that must supposedly interact need not be physically present in order to effectively "distort" some other feature of the stimulus scene—they need only be suggested. Coren (1970), for example, has shown that the Müller–Lyer illusion occurs even though the stimulus lines are reduced to dot patterns, as shown in Fig. 11-14K. In other experiments (e.g., those of Goldstein & Weintraub, 1972; Kanizsa, 1976; Weisstein, Matthews, & Berbaum, 1974) illusory contours have been shown to possess the same perceptual effectiveness as real contours even though they are present, so to speak, only "in the eye of the beholder." Similarly, the tilt illusion can be produced by subjective contours (Smith & Over, 1977). Spatial interaction between the electrotonic fields produced by nonexistent stimulus parts becomes a nonsensical concept, and if suggestion and symbolic construction play such a great role in this case, why not also in the case in which the contour happens to be physically present?

A similar counterindication to a peripheral explanation of movement illusion can be found in the work of G. Robinson and Moulton (1978). They showed that the induced apparent movement exerted by a moving dot on a stable one occurred after a lag of 0.33 sec! They too concluded that no simple peripheral isomorphic explanation would account for such a phenomenon. In sum, geometrical illusions, although clearly responsive to the spatial properties of the stimulus, do not so clearly involve any kind of spatial interactions between isomorphic neural representations of those spatial properties.

Questionable Dogma Number 12

Humans see by analyzing stimulus pattern into features.

The entire single-cell neuroreductionistic approach feeds back and forth onto the idea that features (to which neurons are supposed to be selectively sensitive) are more important in human perception than the global organization of the stimulus. The great historical debate between elementalism and wholism might never have occurred, so great is the commitment to feature detection in current perceptual theory; perceptual theorists seem to have taken up, more or less uncritically, the concepts of local feature detection, feature recognition, and feature analysis. This enthusiasm is obviously stimulated by exciting progress in the neurophysiology laboratory as well as in computer science; the microelectrode technology and the logic implicit in present-day programming arts both emphasize such an elementalistic approach.

In spite of this wholesale commitment to a feature-oriented elementalism in current theory, it seems clear that there has been ample evidence for many years in the visual literature that humans perceive not by features, but mainly by the global configuration of the stimulus. However disappointing the theoretical contributions of Gestalt psychology were, they nevertheless called attention to the many instances that argued strongly for a wholistic, as opposed to a featuristic, processing of visual stimuli by the human perceiver.

The classic fractured figures of Leeper (1935), and Kolers' (1970) famous chairs (see Fig. 9-8 and 1-12) also clearly indicate that the particular angles, curves, and lines from which a pattern may be constructed are less important than the overall configuration into which the "features" are arranged. Unless one wishes to play a word game and call global organization just another feature, these demonstrations obviously are strong counterindications to the idea that man sees by processing features. My own work on an autocorrelational analysis of form detection (described on p. 711) also makes this same argument for a wholistic approach as does the work on the superiority of line detection that occurs when the line is part of a configuration as demonstrated by Weisstein and Harris (1974). Other workers have also shown strong spatial context effects in perception (e.g., Pomerantz, Sager, & Stoever, 1977; and Prinzmetal & Banks, 1977). All such experiments speak against the basic premises of the radical feature analytical model of perception.

Questionable Dogma Number 13

It is possible to tell from behavioral studies whether any particular coding scheme is used to represent stimulus quantity and, for that matter, what code is used in the nervous system to encode any perceptual dimension.

FIG. 9.8. A sample of a fractured figure emphasizing the importance of the overall configuration rather than local features in the determination of the perceived form. (From Leeper, 1935, after Street's Gestalt Completion Test.)

Many perceptual theorists (e.g., Luce & Green, 1972) seem to have overlooked the fact that internal structural analysis on the basis of external behavior is simply not possible for the purest mathematical and logical reasons. Plausible mechanisms may be suggested, implausible ones rejected, and demonstrations made of the processes that must be executed within some device, but in the final analysis, no behavioral test can say anything definitive about internal neural codes, many different versions of which can equally effectively represent any concept or idea. The many behavioral studies that purport to demonstrate neuronal receptive fields, channels, feature sensitivity, orientation detectors, or counting or timing internal codes in the human nervous system are all logically inadequate in the light of this fundamental constraint.

Questionable Dogma Number 14

Apparent motion produces an internal neural response that is identical to real motion.

Kolers (1964) has shown that an apparently moving object is not able to inhibit the detection of a small probe stimulus in the same way that a real moving object does. Thus, apparent motion, like geometric illusions, must involve higher-level interpretive processes than the isomorphic ones invoked by a simplistic neuroreductionism. An important general implication of this specific result is, therefore, that no isomorphic neural signal need be associated with a perceptual response; symbolic interpretations of suggestive stimuli can suffice to produce a compelling perceptual experience. This is a strong argument for a constructionalistic, and inferential if not rationalistic, model of human perception. In short, identical perceptual experiences can be produced by both isomorphic and nonisomorphic stimuli.

Questionable Dogma Number 15

Binocular rivalry is the result of reciprocal lateral inhibition between the afferent signals from the two eyes.

In a comprehensive review of the problem of binocular rivalry, Walker (1978) masses a substantial amount of evidence that argues against a lateral inhibition explanation of the binocular rivalry phenomenon. I review many of his arguments in Chapter 10. For the moment, I simply challenge the dogma and refer the impatient reader to p. 828.

Questionable Dogma Number 16

Stereopsis is the result of either suppression or fusion of the two monocular images.

It seems to me that both psychophysical and neurophysiological data counterindicate both sides of the false debate between suppression and fusion theories of stereopsis. There are compelling phenomenological reasons to assume that stereopsis is not a result of either the suppression of one or the other monocular image or the fusion of the two because the stereoscopic percept is neither the sum of nor the difference between the two dichoptic images. Nor is it the manifestation of one "unsuppressed" image alone. Rather, the three-dimensional experience is a *totally new* psychological construct that *takes the place* of the two monocular impressions. There is no way that the two-dimensional *images* impinging on the two retinae can themselves be added or subtracted from each other to produce a three-dimensional *image*. Instead the transformation has to be one in which the two stimuli provide informational cues (concerning the invariances common to both) to some interpretive or quasi-computational mechanism to be recoded into a new three-dimensional percept. The search for a residual two-dimensional percept that no longer exists (and may never have existed) in the stereoscopic image is a search for a chimera. The three-dimensional image is but another reasonable perceptual construction of the available two-dimensional cues from both of the eyes. However, when sufficient information is available to construct the third dimension, the stereo percept is the one constructed and the two two-dimensional percepts simply do not exist.[23]

A specific empirical counterindication to the suppression hypothesis can be found in the work of Blake and Camisa (1978). These workers showed that there was no reduction in visual sensitivity to either eye during stable stereoscopic (cyclopean) vision comparable to the reduction in sensitivity found during retinal rivalry. Thus, the vision from each eye is not suppressed during binocular vision, and a suppression hypothesis of stereopsis is patently untenable.

Questionable Dogma Number 17

The perceived color of a stimulus is solely defined by the relative amount of activity in three-cone receptor systems or by the stimulus spectrum.

Although there is considerable evidence that the wavelength spectrum emitted by or reflected from an isolated object in space is mainly encoded by the relative degrees of activity induced in the three-cone systems, as extensively discussed in Chapter 6, it is clear that the spectral properties of the stimulus are not, in a more

---

[23]I am aware as I write these words of the extraordinary work that has been done on the encoding of binocular information by early stages in the peripheral nervous system (see p. 951). These data do not, I believe, contradict my argument but rather suggest one way in which the transformation from two-dimensional to three-dimensional information may be achieved. These data do not speak to the nature of the mental responses—only to one means of transforming the information from the two-dimensional retinal images into a three-dimensional code, i.e., one means of extracting the invariances. It is interesting to note, even in these neurophysiological data, that the monocular neural signals themselves are neither "fused" nor "suppressed" during this transformation. Rather, it is a combination of information from both eyes that leads to a coded representation of a totally different nature than that to be found in the responses of each optic nerve.

general sense, the only determinants of perceived color. Color-contrast effects, the influences of the surrounding environment, are supplementary influences. Color constancy, in which the color of an object may depend in complex ways upon the ability of the human to compute the chromatic reflectivity or lightness of the object, represents another counterindication to the simple idea of a direct determination of the color of a percept by the physical spectrum.

Perhaps the most compelling counterargument to this particular dogma comes from the work of Edwin Land (see particularly, Land, 1977) in which he showed that red, green, or blue experiences can all be produced by exactly the same flux of spectral energies. The chromatic experience in this case depends heavily upon the reflectance relationships among the various objects in the stimulus. These effects, though not yet completely understood, seem to be directly ''computed'' from the respective reflectances of the objects and do not depend, as often as suggested, on any knowledge of what the color ''should'' be. However, the known color of an object (e.g., an egg or a piece of coal) also can affect perceived color or lightness in other situations and, therefore, represents an additional counterindication to the dogma asserting that the spectral properties of the stimulus as the sole determinants of perceived chromaticity.

The point is that the detailed knowledge that we have of trichromatic color addition and receptor function should not be overgeneralized as the sole determinant of all aspects of color perception. The evidence is overwhelming that those trichromatic addition data only represent the outcome of a highly specific and abstract experimental situation.

Questionable Dogma Number 18

There is an isomorphic relation between certain dimensions of the stimulus and certain dimensions of the perceptual response.

Dogma 17 can in fact be generalized to most other perceptual dimensions. A major conclusion from much of the perceptual research that has been done on illusions, contrast, and constancy (summarized in Chapter 11) is that there is no direct deterministic link between any particular aspect of a stimulus and the associated percept even though they may be closely correlated in tightly constrained experimental situations. Whether it be in the domain of space, time, quality, or quantity, we see innumerable examples of stimulus–percept nonveridicality. In some cases the correlation between the stimulus properties and the perceptual experience may be exactly zero; a single stimulus property may be interpreted in many different ways, depending on the context and significance of other parts of the stimulus scene. We apparently have been devastatingly misled by the design of the typical unidimensional laboratory experiment to assume that the neat relationship observed between a single aspect of the stimulus and a single aspect of the percept holds in general. Systematic relationships between stimuli and percepts do exist, but they usually occur in contexts in which all other factors have been held constant or removed from the stimulus scene. In situations that are more ecologically valid, the one-for-one relationship between stimulus and phenomenal dimensions almost always breaks down. As a result we see such discrepancies as size, lightness, or color constancy in which the percept deviates substantially from the physically defined stimulus pattern. In short, no stimulus dimension uniquely defines a perceptual dimension. Each stimulus dimension or aspect contributes to the aggregate of cues from which the perceptual experience is constructed as the "best solution" to the problem posed by those cues.

In this section I have challenged some of the deeply held and popular dogma of current perceptual theory. Although many other widely accepted microtheories or dogma of the kind I have described here might also justifiably be classified as questionable, it is not necessary to push this discussion further. I hope by now that I have made the general point that many beliefs in contemporary perceptual neuroreductionism are highly suspect. Although each of the arguments I have presented here could be countered by an abundance of what many believe are supportive data, the simple fact is that a substantial body of empirical counterindications and logical counterarguments does exist that strongly suggests that we may have prematurely adopted a more accepting point of view about neuroreductionism than is currently justified. I propose that the complexity of the neural mechanisms underlying most perceptual processes has been grossly underestimated in current thought. Unsupported but widely accepted metaphors and analogies have seduced us to profoundly overestimate both the level of understanding of perceptual phenomena we have achieved and what it will be possible to achieve within the limits of the neuroreductionistic approach.

Now that this point has (hopefully) been made, it would be well to look at an important general problem raised by this criticism. If I am correct so far, how does one account for the propensity on the part of so many very bright people to accept so uncritically these unsubstantiated dogma? The answer to this question is psychological in another sense of that word.

The factors contributing to the contemporary overcommitment to empiricistic neuroreductionism can be briefly tabulated. Although I have spoken of some of these factors in general in Chapter 4, it would be useful to reconsider them in this specific context:

1. First and foremost, of course, is that the problem of how internal mechanisms represent perceptual phenomena is both important and unsolved. Because of its importance, people want answers to this great epistemological issue. It is the essence of the human spirit to search out answers and sometimes to invent them when they are not yet actually available. Thus we tend to deal with whatever answers have been proposed as a "final solution" rather than a tentative hypothesis.

2. Throughout history the response to the great psychobiological perplexity—the mind-brain problem—has been to invoke whatever is the con-

temporary technology as the model of mind in general or perception in particular. Today's most powerful and relevant technology for perceptual theory—a particularly well-structured subquestion of the more general problem of the relationship between mind and brain—appears to be single-cell neurophysiology. Because neurons do encode mental processes in some way, our knowledge of individual cells in the afferent and efferent communication system has become a model of central processes in exactly the same way that hydraulic systems, vapors, telephones, and computers did earlier.

3. We tend to confuse superficial process analogies with true structural homologies. Lateral interactions between contours and simultaneous contrast are not homologs, only partial analogs of each other.

4. We tend to misunderstand the intended range of application of an idea. There is considerable confusion in the literature concerning the Fourier channel theory. Is it only an abstract mathematical description of the stimulus or its internal representation, or does it assert the actual existence of anatomically distinct spatial frequency channels in the brain?

5. There are, in fact, few direct neurophysiological and psychophysical comparisons of truly comparable experimental situations. The linkage being so poor, we have a tendency to accept isomorphic similarity and analogs for solid relationships. We lack appreciation of the fundamental message of coding theory, namely, that any code can represent any message, and its implicit rejection of the need for isomorphic representation.

6. At the same time, we also tend to underappreciate the possible role of symbolic representation in perception—a symbolic representation that is not mediated by individual neurons, but rather by myriads of neurons interconnected in a network of such complexity that we may never be able to link the neural logic with the mental processes for reasons of simple practical computability.

7. We have a tendency to accept overly simplistic peripheral explanations of what are, in fact, central mechanisms of a degree of complexity that makes them qualitatively different from the peripheral mechanisms.

8. There is a semantic confusion in the use of key words (e.g., thresholds, learning, masking). Neural and psychological processes are sometimes described with the same vocabulary in a way that can only be described as punning.

9. The perceptual constructs that people are trying to model are poorly defined. Only recently, for example, has signal detection theory made clear that both discriminative and criterion factors contribute to thresholds, masking, etc.

10. We overlook the great differences in time constants between proposed neural explanations and the supposedly similar psychological processes.

11. We misidentify stimulus dimensions in what are actually noncomparable situations.

12. We ignore basic perceptual data.

13. Neuroreductionistic theories in perception are usually not presented as well-defined propositions that can be tested for logical clarity or consistency; the verbal analogies and models are often very loosely formulated.

14. There is a serious lack of a good classification system of perceptual processes.

As negative as this tabulation is, there is another side to it. Even though the errors of logic and concept that I have alluded to here may all have been committed, it may have been a necessary stage through which any science must pass. However sincerely we may disagree as to the range of application of the neuroreductionistic philosophy, we all learned a great deal, even from its frailest version. As I noted in Chapter 1, many other perceptual scientists are now becoming aware of the limits of neuroreductionism, and an increasingly critical (in the good sense) body of thoughtful literature is appearing concerning this problem. In particular, the reader is referred to the stimulating discussion of a target paper by Wasserman and Kong (1979) by a large number of commentators in the remarkable journal, *The Behavioral and Brain Sciences*. To have been brought to the point of retrospective criticism the way we have may have been far more useful than never having passed through this stage. Furthermore there may have been no alternative. We must acknowledge the incredible complexity of the perceptual nervous system and the frailty of our intellectual and instrumental armamentarium. However the important fact is that we have to move on, and one of the most important tasks ahead is to define the point beyond which we must admit that neuroreductionism fails us. All are in agreement with this statement. The major problem in this area is to identify that point of demarcation between the plausibly reductionistic and the practically irreducible. This chapter and the general organization of this book is an attempt to do just that.

F. AN INTERIM SUMMARY—A CONTEMPORARY VIEWPOINT

In this chapter I have mounted a critical attack, not on the basic postulate of psychoneural monism, but rather on the unsatisfactory state of contemporary neuroreductionistic theory in perception. I have pointed out some of the conceptual problems and some of the empirical counterindications to dogma of wide popular currency. I have sought to highlight the ill-defined nature of some of the language used by neuroreductive theorists in explaining perceptual phenomena. I have also tried both to sharpen that vocabulary and to clarify the essential aspects of the theories by redefining some of the words and extracting what I believe are the essential premises that are implied, if not made explicit, in the enunciation of each of the theories. Finally, I have struck out at what I perceive to be a set of dogma that are particularly frail, yet virtually ubiquitous in contemporary thought. In all of this, I have intentionally presented a very one-sided "devil's advocate" argument against these dogma, leaving for others the task of marshaling the data supporting the other side of the argument. Hopefully, this is equally as forgivable as are those lapses in the arguments for the other viewpoint.

Another goal of this chapter was somewhat more ambitious but also more directly relevant to the remainder of this book. I strongly believe that many perceptual phenomena that have been subject to neuroreductionistic modeling are, in fact, the manifestation of neural systems so complex that the language of single-cell feature selectivity, lateral interactions, and spatial frequency filters is entirely inappropriate. Instead these perceptual processes are, in my opinion, better expressed in the vocabulary of molar phenomenology and psychological processes. Words like inference, construction, interpretation, and cognition are part of this more appropriate vocabulary for most interesting perceptual phenomena, not because these processes and phenomena are nonneural but because the complexity of the mechanisms underlying these processes is so great as to preclude any reasonable hope for a microscopic and neuroreductionistic analysis in the foreseeable future.

I would like to conclude this chapter by drawing the reader's attention to the general properties of the four main neuroreductionistic theories that I have presented here and compare these properties with the comparable attributes of perception. Table 9-1 will help us to guide this concluding discussion. In this table, I have indicated the main premise of the theory, the locus of the unit of representation, the fundamental processing element, the mode of operation, and the way in which each theory deals with form recognition—one sample perceptual process.

Upon examination of this table, it quickly becomes clear that neither the single-cell nor the channel theories compare well with the psychological experience. Both of these theories are inherently elementalistic with regard to the analysis of a stimulus pattern. Both implicitly (and sometimes explicitly) assume that the elements of the stimulus, regardless of how they may be organized, are the essential stimulus aspects. Yet, to the contrary, most visual psychophysical data, as we see more forcibly in the next two chapters, seem to argue for the wholistic or Gestalt nature of the processes carried out by the human visual system. The field theory, though it is known to be inadequate because of physical considerations (the hypothetical fields cannot be short-circuited nor distorted by imposed electrical currents), does share this wholistic orientation with the neural network theory and the perceptual experience.

The single-cell and the feature-filtering theories also implicitly place the critical processing mechanism in highly localized places in the nervous system. In this regard they are also discrepant with the massive body of data showing that the neural responses to visual stimuli are widely distributed in the brain and that substantial chunks of the brain have to be damaged before any perceptual experience is disrupted.[24] In other words, a considerable amount of psychobiological

---

[24]Although the reader may want to dispute this comment by pointing out the damage that can be done by a small lesion in the optic nerve, tract, or even in the occipital cortex, I believe all of these effects arise from interference with the communication of information to the locus of psychoneural equivalence rather than disruptions of the mechanisms of equivalence themselves.

TABLE 9.1
A Summary of the Characteristics of the Various Neuroreductionistic Theories of Perception

Main Premise of Theory	*Locus of Representational Unit*	*Fundamental Processing Element*	*Mode of Operation*	*Deals with Forms by*
1. Single Cell Feature Selectivity	Local	Discrete Neuron	Elementalistic (Feature)	Feature Analysis
2. Fourier Channel Spatial Frequency Analysis	Local	Discrete Channel	Elementalistic (Feature)	Feature Analysis
3. Neuronal Network State	Distributed	Discrete Neuron	Wholistic (Gestalt)	Algorithmic Global Synthesis
4. Neuroelectric Field	Distributed	Homogeneous Block of Tissue	Wholistic (Gestalt)	Global Inhomogenities
5. Cognitive-Constructionistic-Symbolic-Molar-Behavioral	Not Specified	Not Specified	Wholistic (Gestalt)	Global Relations

data indicates that central perceptual processes are not well localized in the brain either in the form of single pontifical cells or in the form of channels that can be characterized by discrete anatomical localization. Thus these two theories also fail to conform with the known first principles of neuroanatomic organization in this regard.

In conclusion, if we exclude the physically unlikely field theory, the neural network approach seems best to fit the general principles of organization of the perceptual system. Neural networks are, in principle, distributed mechanisms, sensitive to the global organization of the stimuli and operate on the basis of general purpose algorithmic mechanisms. These properties seem to be more in line with what is known of such phenomena as stimulus equivalence, and with the abundance of psychophysical data suggesting that specific features of a stimulus are not as important in modulating our perceptual experiences as is its global organization.

I can now sum up this discussion by expressing a new set of premises (or dogma, if you wish) comparable to those proposed by Barlow (1972) concerning the neuroreductionistic foundations of perception. This set of new tenets represents what I believe is a more acceptable view of how the perceptual system works in the context of modern neurophysiological and psychophysical research. This dogma consists of the following generalizations of the premises of the neural network approach discussed earlier:

1. Transformational processes affecting perceptual phenomena may occur at any level of the nervous system.

2. Most perceptual phenomena are the result of processes occurring at several levels but may directly result from an isolated transformation at a single level.

3. Most processes (with the exception of those of preneural Level 0 and receptor Level 1) result from the interaction of very large numbers of neurons in a probabilistic manner in what may best be characterized as a statistical network.

4. The nervous system is abundantly supplied with neurons and neurons can be used for several different functions. Therefore the nervous system can be and is extravagant and wasteful in their use. Rather than minimizing the number of neurons for any process, neural nets tend to be highly redundant as a result of widespread divergence.

5. The psychoneural equivalent of any perceptual phenomenon is the dynamic state of some network. Even the simplest phenomenon is represented by an innumerable number of neurons.

6. No individual neuron is critical. The statistical nature of the process is such that no neuron is uniquely involved in a single percept, nor is any percept uniquely dependent on any small number of neurons.

7. No neural code is intrinsically optimal nor is it necessarily isomorphic. Any neural dimension can change in any direction to represent any dimension of the message.

8. Though neural nets may simulate continuous field processes because of their small size and great number, the fundamental logical processes are discrete and only locally interactive.

9. The perceptual nervous system does not work by analyzing stimulus scenes into parts or features but rather by an algorithmic sensitivity to its global aspects.

10. In the main, a description of the function of the neural network involved in most perceptual processes is still beyond the power of contemporary neurosciences. Therefore the global, wholistic, molar, synthetic approach of the psychologist must still remain preeminent for understanding all but the most simple phenomena. Though we remain *metaphysical* reductionists, practicality dictates that we assert a new *epistemological* antireductionism. An eclectic and mixed approach to perception, involving both neural and psychological concepts, is, therefore, still required. We should not be seduced by the superficial similarities of some single-neuron observations and some much more complicated perceptual processes into oversimplifying the enormity of the problem faced by those interested in discovering neural explanations of perceptual phenomena.

In summary, the goal of this chapter has been to consider the limits of the neuroreductionistic approach in perceptual theory. It now seems certain that, regardless of technical sophistication in the neurophysiological laboratory or analogical similarity between mental process and proposed neural mechanism, neuroreductionism is, in practical fact, currently incapable of providing biologically valid explanations of most interesting perceptual phenomena. The essential limitation involves our ability to deal with networks of great complexity. This practical fact in no way mitigates my conviction that all psychological processes are, in principle, the result of neural mechanisms; it simply expresses the results of the limited computational, technical, and conceptual power we can bring to bear on the problem.

What then are the alternatives to an overly ambitious neuroreductionism? Certainly we do not want to throw up our hands and abandon our search for understanding of this complexity. Such a response would be neither intellectually satisfying nor necessary. Physics has dealt with similar problems and has developed a rich body of theory based on the more molar aspects of ensembles too large to be studied at an elemental level. We must not forget that the classic traditions of psychology developed in just such a molar manner; phenomenological description guided the thoughts of researchers for centuries. In recent years we have also developed a rich mathematical psychology, which is also nonreductive, to model and describe the molar behavior of the organism. Few mathematical models are explicitly related to any neurophysiological presumptions, and none need necessarily be so linked. Descriptive mathematics can stand on its own feet as a powerful means of interpreting perceptual phenomena.

We see in the following chapters that description and phenomenology can be satisfying means of analysis. The search for the rules that govern, the factors that influence, and the functions that fit various perceptual phenomena have led to the development of a high level of understanding in many of the research areas that we study next. The point is that neural explanations, although desirable wherever possible, are not entirely necessary to the fulfillment of the epistemological quest. An understanding of the processing of information, independent of the underlying neural codes, is a both satisfying and acceptable solution to the problem posed at the outset of this book.

As I turn now to the higher, but no less immediate, levels of perceptual processing that are less susceptible to neuroreductionism, the need for an explicit classification system becomes even more critical. In the next two chapters in particular, I present two further stages in this taxonomy of visual processes. This discussion presents a taxonomy that is based upon criteria that are much more difficult to make intuitively satisfying than were the classification criteria of the previous three levels. The problem is that many of these higher-level processes are redundant and overlap with each other to affect the phenomena that I shall be describing. Nevertheless, it is essential for the reader to keep in mind that the classification system that I propose is still based upon processes not phenomena. This is still the only way, in my opinion, it is possible to construct a plausible classification system for perception. This emphasis on process allows us to proceed with the task before us even in the absence of the physical, physiological, or anatomical anchors that graced Levels 0, 1, and 2.

Level 3 mainly encompasses those processes that lead to the organization of visual fields on the basis of a single dimension of the system. It is in this category that I place all of those processes that are largely determined by a single aspect of the stimulus scene even when the aspect may be very complicated. In general, the percepts resulting from Level 3 processes are not quantitative—a scene may be appreciated as involving subregions, but the properties are not metricized in any way at this level of processing. Level 4, on the other hand, is characterized by an interaction among multiple aspects of the stimulus scene and the development of quantified values of size, distance, color, brightness, and so on. It is at these higher levels of processing that the lack of veridicality between the stimulus and the percept will be most clearly evident and in which the neorationalistic, inferential, and constructionistic aspects of perception will be seen to be most evident.

Note added in proof: The validity of the conclusion drawn in Jenkins and Ross's (1977) report discussed on page 732 has been challenged by Milewski, A. E., Iaccino, J., and Smith, D. Perception and Psychophysics, 1980, *28*, 329–336.

10 Level 3: Unidimensional Processes Affecting Prequantitative Spatial and Figural Organization

A. INTRODUCTION

This chapter is concerned with what I have designated Level 3 processes. In general, Level 3 processes are categorized in terms of the effects they exert on the organization of visual space and form. I expand shortly upon this very general criterion to define more specifically the nature of the processes to be included within this chapter's rubric. However, before I proceed, it is important to emphasize that the material of this chapter differs from the discussions in the previous chapters in several important ways. Chapter 9 alerted the reader to one important distinction—most of the phenomena to be considered here are beyond neuroreductionistic explanation.

There is, however, another difference that must also be highlighted; the discussion that follows is presented in a language and from the point of view of a foundation philosophy very different from those characterizing my discussions of the earlier levels of processing. When Levels 1 and 2 were discussed, the sample interactions between the stimulus and the organism were typically both isomorphic and deterministic. That is, the transformations that occurred were exerted on some spatial representation of the message that maintained the dimensional structure of the physical stimulus. For example, a complex chromatic signal might have been analyzed by the differential wavelength sensitivities of the cones, or a contour might have been enhanced by lateral interactions in the neural net. However, in both cases it was possible to consider these processes in terms of strictly deterministic spatial relationships in which the stimulus and the properties of the nervous system passively interacted in a more or less direct way to produce the critical transformations. The discussion, in the terms used earlier in this book, was essentially neoempiricistic and mechanistic. The symbolic value or meaning of the stimulus played little or no role in the experiments discussed; only the naked geometry of the stimulus and its subsequent neural representations and the algorithms inherent in simple neural networks affected the outcome. This sort of processing defined a particular point of view or philosophy concerning the nature of the visual system.

As we turn to the higher levels ofperceptual processing, however, the foundation philosophy changes in a profound way. There is an increasing emphasis on the inferences, interpretations, and constructions that are carried out by an active nervous system. No longer is there a direct, passive, algorithmic processing of the spatial attributes of the stimulus; at Levels 3 and 4, stimulus geometry seems to act much more like a vehicle to convey significance than as an essential stimulus dimension in its own right. Thus, for example, the characters used in the many written languages of the modern world can all convey exactly the same meaning or significance in spite of a bewildering diversity of alphabetic type fonts or pictographic styles and systems of grammar. It is the meaning associated with the symbol rather than the symbol itself that now becomes the focus of our attention. In this chapter I assert, therefore, that Level 3 (and higher) critical processes mediate transformations of such complexity that the classical empiricistic philosophical approach fails us completely; of necessity, rationalism (or better, some appropriate neorationalism) becomes the point of view of all future analysis. Terms like "inferential," "ambiguous," "interpretive," and "subjective," which had little utility in the discussions of the previous chapters, must now be introduced to maintain any coherence in the analysis of perceptual topics to follow.

Such a neorationalistic approach is hardly my own innovation, of course. Many perceptual scientists have continued to stress the interpretive, inferential, and cognitive aspects of many phenomena in spite of the monumentally influential developments in modern neurophysiology and information science. Many contemporary perceptual psychologists, including Irvin Rock, Paul Kolers, Richard Gregory, Daniel Weintraub, and Ulric Neisser among others, will find much of what I have to say in the next few chapters consistent with their own perspectives.

Weintraub (1971, pp. 1–2) in particular sums up this idea in one context with the following words:

> Percepts are in no sense copies of real-world objects or events. Percepts must be reconstructions. The perceiver may profitably be considered as a decision making

system in which the incoming array of stimulation is compared with stored information in order to reach a decision about what is ''out there.'' For those who boggle at the decision making conception of perception, the approach can be considered as an analogy or model of process rather than in any more literal sense.

This trend towards a rationalistic language is, of course, a pragmatic response to the limits of scientific knowledge and of its technology. There is no intended implication of a dualistic metaphysics in this transition from a neuroreductionistic empiricism to a nonneuroreductionistic neorationalism. It is merely a practical response to a difficult methodological problem. Simply put, the history of research on perceptual problems of the types that I consider in this chapter has shown them to be intractable to other than descriptive and neorationalistic forms of analysis. The words *interpretive* and *constructive* are used, not as a cryptic means of introducing some intellectual demon or homunculus who carries out these complex information-processing tasks but rather as a means of describing the awesome and so far impenetrable complexity of the information-processing capacity of the human brain.

As we make this transition from a neoempiricistic to a neorationalistic model, there will be costs that have to be paid. The rationalistic vocabulary is by no means as precise as the empiricistic, and its referents are often much more obscure. It is sometimes difficult to adhere to process as the basis of the taxonomy as opposed to phenomena, as readers of this chapter will almost certainly become aware. It is particularly important, therefore, as we move away from the physical and anatomical anchors that characterized Levels 0, 1, and 2 that the criteria for a process being attributed to any particular level, rather than to any particular level, rather than to any lower or higher level, be as explicitly spelled out as possible. The distinguishing criteria for the higher levels discussed in Chapters 10 and 11 are by no means as intuitive as they were at the lower levels. For Level 0, the preneural and pretransductive criteria were straightforward and the line of demarcation between Levels 0 and 1—the primary sensory action—was very explicit. For Level 1, the anatomical criterion implicit in the boundaries of the receptor cell was also close to self-evident and certainly intuitively obvious. Even Level 2 networks had a substantive concreteness about them that led to a relatively direct and easy appreciation of how these processes could be distinguished from the previous two stages.

For higher levels of processing, however, such neat physical and anatomical conceptual anchors are not available, and the taxonomic scheme from this point on involves a considerably higher degree of arbitrariness. Not the least source of this arbitrariness is that *all* subsequent levels of processing, if one adheres to a strictly monistic solution to the mind–brain problem, could actually be considered to be subclasses of Level 2. Clearly, all of those molar processes that are incorporated within Levels 3, 4, and 5 of my taxonomy also have a neural basis and that neural basis however complicated can be conceptualized in terms of logical and computational interactions going on within the great networks of the brain.

The main criterion, therefore, distinguishing Levels 3, 4, and 5 from 0, 1, and 2 is the practical one of complexity—complexity of the neural mechanisms and complexity of the stimulus factors that determine the response but, most important of all, complexity of the relationship between the stimulus and the response. As a result of all three kinds of complexity, Level 3 processes are characterized, as are all subsequent levels, by an even further reduction in the apparent deterministic relationship between the stimulus and the perceptual experience. Stimuli involved in these higher-level processes are more frequently described as being ambiguous; that is, the information that they present to the observer is capable of eliciting different perceptual experiences depending on that observer's state. Observers use the physical aspects of the stimulus only as general guides, cues, or hints to the nature of the experience. The construction of the percept is, in the terms of this new vocabulary, mediated by processes that are not amenable to the deterministic stimulus–response language that characterized all three of the earlier levels.

There is, therefore, a considerably greater opportunity for the perceptual response to be nonveridical with the stimulus, as well (presumably) as with the pattern of information that is conveyed along the peripheral sensory pathways. This lack of veridicality, however, is not necessarily a negative feature of perception in the same way that low fidelity might be in a music system; it is the positive basis for constructing responses that may in some cases actually exceed the absolute information content conveyed by the afferent stimulus. For example, the ability to construct three-dimensional depth from monocular cues adds considerable ecological utility, as well as richness, to the two-dimensional array imaged on one retina.

Given these criteria for distinguishing between Levels 0, 1, and 2 on the one hand and 3, 4, and 5 on the other, what then are the features that distinguish among Levels 3, 4, and 5, and which ones do they share in common? Like Level 3, Level 4 processes are relatively insensitive to attention and effort. Though it is often possible, as we see later in this chapter, to modulate the experience produced by a Level 3 or 4 process, in the main the respective transformations are automatic and immediate in much the same sense as were those of the prior levels of perceptual processing. It is usually impossible for an observer to suppress completely the illusions attributable to these levels of processing, no matter how great his knowledge of physical stimulus reality; it is only in the rarest incidents that verbal instructions or previous experience can reduce the power of an illusion produced by a Level 3 or 4 process.

Level 5, on the other hand, includes a class of processes that involve active, manipulative, cognitive transformations by an attentive mind. I mention only briefly this level of perceptual processes in this book because I believe that the analytic approach changes so substantially when one crosses the boundary between Levels 4 and 5 that Level 5 processes are not within the rubric of automatic percepts that I have chosen to consider here.[1] An example of the distinction I make here is that existing between a Level 3 figure–ground separation and the search for a word with a particular meaning in a list of similar words, the latter being presumably mediated by a Level 5 process.

This distinction between the perceptual or preattentive levels of processing and the cognitive or attentive level has also been noted by others. For example, Bela Julesz (1975, p. 34) has stated: ''Any visual task that cannot be performed spontaneously, without effort or deliberation, can be regarded as a cognitive task rather than a perceptual one.''

A. J. Marshall made the same distinction in his presidential address to the Australian Psychological Association in 1969, when he distinguished between ''sensory and attentional devices in perception'' (Marshall, 1969), as did Jacob Beck (1972b) and Ulric Neisser (1967), among many others. The same meaning can also be imputed to the distinction made between ''perceptual'' and ''decision'' levels of processing by Bjork and Murray (1977) and G. Gardner (1973). Clearly the line that I have drawn here is in agreement with the thinking of many contemporary psychologists.

Now that the difference between the lower levels and Level 5 is somewhat clearer, it is important to consider further how Levels 3 and 4 differ from each other. Specifying the criteria of distinquishability between these two levels was among the most difficult tasks I faced in developing the taxonomy that organizes this book, and I am not yet entirely satisfied with the outcome. I must acknowledge that there are many other alternative classification schemata that could have been constructed to organize ''Level 3'' and ''Level 4'' processes. This is so for the simple reason that there is no single simple distinguishing criterion upon which to make this classification—there is no concrete anatomical concept that distinguishes Levels 3 and 4 and probably no natural chronological order in which the respective processes take place to use as a basis for classification.

Therefore, the criteria that must be used to distinguish between Levels 3 and 4 are, of necessity, quite arbitrary and unanchored to any natural anatomic, physiological, or temporal reference. The two major distinguishing criteria I have chosen are framed in terms of the number of dimensions or aspects of the stimulus that are involved in each of the processes at each level, and the degree of perceptual ''quantification'' obtainable in the resulting experience. In general (but as the reader subsequently sees, not exclusively) Level 3 processes act upon a single aspect of the stimulus. This aspect need not be exclusively unidimensional in spatial or temporal sense. For example, the texture or extent of a stimulus may be characterized as extending in both the x and y dimensions, and, perhaps, even in the z dimension as well. However texture itself is a unitary

---

[1]To which I must also add, of course, the observation that the immense magnitude of the literature concerning Level 5 exceeds the practical limits of size for this book.

property or aspect of the visual stimulus in the sense I use the word here. So also are spectrum, size, duration, monocular view, arrangement, shape, contour, spatiotemporal dynamic, and luminosity. One discriminating property of a Level 3 process is that the perceptual response that is produced is dependent not on any interaction between several of these factors or aspects but on only one such property of the stimulus.

On the other hand, the main distinguishing property of Level 4 processes in this taxonomy is that they are dependent on interactions between several of these unitary aspects of the stimulus. Stereopsis arises from the interaction of the signals from each eye; apparent size is defined by the interaction between the retinal image size and the cues suggesting the distance to an object. In each of these cases and in other Level–4-based phenomena as well, the result of such interactions may be a substantial disagreement between the most salient image dimension or aspect and the percept. In the case of Level 3 processes, however, the most salient aspect of the stimulus is more often found to be the main determinant of the perceptual experience, and stimulus–percept veridicality is the far more usual outcome.

Thus in this taxonomy, the major distinguishing criterion between Level 3 and Level 4 is the degree to which multidimensional interaction occurs. Obviously this is not, and cannot be, a totally exclusive means of characterizing the broad range of processes included within these two levels. To a certain extent these dimensions or aspects must be arbitrary and defined in terms of the specific conditions of the viewing situation. Nevertheless, in my opinion, this criterion better than any other, does help to connote the difference in meaning between these two classes of perceptual processing.

The other major discriminating property of Level 3 processes is that they result in *nonquantitative* percepts. Virtually none of the phenomena attributable to this level of processing are concerned with such factors as perceived size, distance, color, or lightness in any kind of a metrical sense. Instead the perceptual experiences that characterize this level of processing mainly involve the qualitative establishment of a percept of the objects in the scene as an organized pattern or form, that is, with the establishment of stimuli as discrete things rather than as things of a certain size or color. On the other hand, as we later see, Level 4 processes, resulting from multidimensional relationships, seem to underlie the perceptual computations that go into the perceptual experience of such quantitative factors of the stimulus as size and lightness. They are highly dependent on comparisons and thus suggest that a kind of perceptual "relativity" is operating. An important general point is that these relational processes occur within the nervous system of the observer, not in the external stimulus world or in the theorists' description of phenomena. They are just as real in a neurophysiological sense as lateral inhibitory interactions.

There are other phenomenological criteria that help to characterize Level 3 processes. In the main, this level of processing is associated with the organization of the spatial aspects of the visual experience. This chapter emphasizes those processes that lead to the awareness and appreciation of the arrangement of space and the objects it contains and will be concerned with those aspects of visual perception that allow us to distinguish between different objects in complex scenes or between foreground objects of great salience and background objects that are not relevant at the moment. It deals with the organization of the parts of the stimulus into a coherent and organized percept.

In sum, Level 3 processes, although sharing many features with Level 4 (automaticity, immediacy, complexity, interpretive constructionism, and reversals of alternative responses to ambiguous stimuli) can be distinguished from Level 4 processes mainly on the basis of the following two criteria:

1. Level 3 processes are more sensitive to single aspects or dimension of the stimulus than are Level 4 processes.
2. Level 3 processes are mainly concerned with the organization of prequantitative aspects of the visual scene.

The implicit nature of these criteria for distinguishing between Levels 3 and 4 has led many perceptual theoreticians to ask whether what I call Level 3 processes are necessary and more primitive perceptual precursors that must be executed before what I call Level 4 processes can function. My personal answer is that they are, and that Level 3 processes represent a necessary qualitative preprocessing of the stimulus environment before that environment can be evaluated in more quantitative terms by Level 4 processes.

This predilection, however, I must admit, is not buttressed by any solid arguments. Despite strong feelings, the plain facts of the matter are that this is an immensely complicated issue that has not yet been resolved empirically. Experiments that purport to detect a sequence in the order of the two levels of processing are never completely convincing. In my opinion, any glib answer to the question of the temporal sequence of levels of processing at the present time is unsupportable at the present state of our knowledge mainly because we do not know enough about the inner neural workings of these processes. It is, therefore, only on "logical" grounds that arguments for "sequence" or "primitiveness" can be made with regard to Level 3 and Level 4 processes. One may argue that before one could quantify the dimensions of an object one would have to appreciate the existence of the object and to segregate it from its background. Any conceivable computer simulation of such processes would certainly have to be designed to operate in this way. However, computer programs operate by means of logical and computational mechanisms that are far different from those apparently working within the confines of the very complex neural networks of the brain. With such weak insights into the logical mechanisms underlying Level 3 and 4 processes we cannot be certain that such an argument for sequentiality is actually a valid one. It is entirely possible that both processes may be going on simultaneously or even that Level 4 processes precede Level 3 processes in some instances.

Nevertheless, even within the acknowledged limits of this unresolved argument, and in the absence of any other more compelling alternative, it seems that sequence is a good heuristic for organizing the various levels and sublevels discussed in this chapter. The sequential assumption, which asserts that in some way Level 3 processes precede Level 4 processes, also implies the possibility that there may be a similar sub-sequence existing within Level 3 itself. The sequence that seems most evident would be a two-stage one, including: (1) Processes involved in the initial segregation of objects and other subdivisions of complex scenes (i.e., scenes including more than a single field or object); (2) Processes involved in the organization of the shape and extent of these specific objects and subdivisions.

Once again, it should be noted that the dichotomy of substages that I have just proposed is hardly novel. For many years perceptual psychologists have raised the possibility that the establishment of visual perception proceeds through a series of successive stages in just this manner. Obanai (1977, p. 64) calls to our attention the summation enunciated by M. D. Vernon (1952) of what he perceived to be a consensus at that time:

> there seems to be a fair amount of agreement as to the fundamental stages which may be observed in the development of full apprehension and knowledge of the nature of the objects exposed. The first of these stages seems to consist of a vague awareness or knowledge that there is something in the visual field . . . (the next stage) has been called by Dickinson and Freeman the stage of the generic object—the awareness that the visual stimulation is connected with some kind of object with an existence in the visual field. . . . As this organization becomes more and more detailed and complete, the relevant and important parts rise out of the field, the rest of which fades into the background (Freeman). These parts . . . are recognized as appertaining to some particular and specific object; and this stage is called the stage of the specific object. . . . The last essential stage of the perceptual process then is that of the identification and understanding of meaning. . . . The essential nature of this stage is clearly shown in the introspection of the observers in Bartlett's experiments on perception; they experienced an ''effort after meaning,'' a conative drive towards the completion of the perceptual process by the attribution of meaning.

More modern information-processing theories with their ''flow charts'', one of which is illustrated in fig. 10-1, also implicitly adhere to the same idea of a sequence of processes that must be executed in a certain order for full-blown perception to occur. In both these cases many more stages are proposed than have been considered here. It may be that they exist in some way; however sufficient evidence to justify such a detailed analysis is not yet available in my judgment.

In the next section of this chapter I consider the first category of Level 3 processes—the processes that are concerned with the initial segregation of the

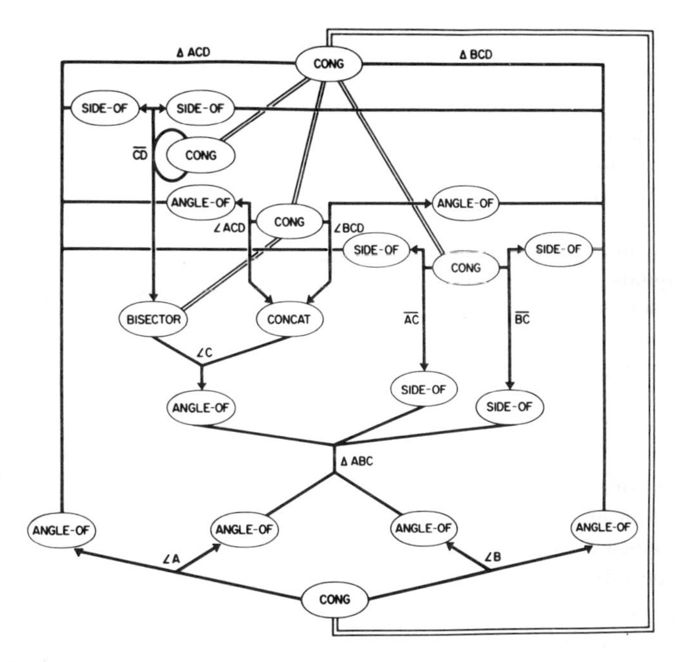

FIG. 10.1. A ''cognitive map'' of the thought processes involved in proving that the base angles of an isosceles triangle are equal. (From Greeno, © 1977, with the permission of Lawrence Erlbaum Associates, Inc.)

subregions of a complex stimulus scene on the basis of their texture and the boundaries between them. An important topic in this section, one that gives many clues to the processes that are involved in the segregation of portions of a scene into individual objects, concerns those conditions in which this perceived organization can disintegrate and in which what had been a clearly perceived image can fade. I am referring here to the image-fading that occurs with stablized retinal images and the perceptual disorganization that occurs in the classic ganzfeld experiments.

I then turn to the other major subdivision of Level 3 processes, those topics dealing with the perceived arrangement and organization of visual scenes. In this section I am concerned with the ability of the observer to perceive individual objects or organized clusters of objects in complex scenes or interfering backgrounds as well as one's ability to establish figure–ground relationships. Another kind of masking is introduced at this point that is essentially equivalent to the communication engineer's problem of extracting a signal from noise. The problem of camouflage and the awareness of hidden figures in scenes in which the background may break up the texture, boundaries, or other clues to the specification of the individual object is also considered here.

Another major section of this chapter deals with stimuli that can be appropriately organized in more than a single way by the perceiver. The responses to such ambiguous objects as the Necker cube represent not only interesting and amusing illusions, but these phenomena also speak directly to the point that active perceptual construction is a major characteristic of visual processing at these levels. Binocular rivalry in this context is also considered, somewhat unconventionally, in a discussion that emphasizes its dependence on central integrative interpretations rather than on the suppression of afferently flowing neural signals.

The phenomena of subjective contours is also discussed within this second subdivision of Level 3 processes. These phenomena—additional exemplars of the powerful ability of the perceptual system to extrapolate and interpolate over stimulus discontinuities—are particularly instructive because they show how the segregation of an individual object can occur even when all of the stimulus conditions necessary to define that object are not physically present. The indirect clues and hints that are provided by the stimulus scene can lead to a compelling awareness of an object that may have subjective lightness, contour, and depth characteristics that are distinguishable from adjacent regions of the surround even though the physical properties of the two regions are indistinguishable on an objective basis. The classic Gestalt laws, long-standing enigmas of perceptual research, are also discussed in this section along with the relatively new field of perceptual research concerning stimulus figures that are physically "impossible."

B. PROCESSES AFFECTING THE INITIAL SEGREGATION OF OBJECTS AND FIELDS

It takes no extreme stretch of logic to support the idea that any segregation of a complex scene into its constituent subregions must be based on discriminable differences between those subregions and that all subsequent acts of form processing must be based upon the ability of the observer to discriminate those differences. It is not yet fully established what all of the contributing stimulus characteristics of a visual scene are that lead to such a segregation; however two general classes are clearly important. The first, the properties of the surface, consists of overall differences between subregions. Whole areas of a stimulus scene may differ in their chromatic, luminous, or textural nature, and these surface differences are obviously strong cues on which the observer bases the organization of the parts of a complex field. The second class is based on the fact that even areas of identical chromatic, luminous, and textural characteristics may be demarcated from each other by contours or boundaries, and these contours may have profound effects on the perception of the entire region. Of course, these two properties are not entirely separable from each other; clearly any two areas that differ in some surface property will also be separated by some kind of implied, if not actual, boundary. As we later see, this region of discontinuity may exert the same effect as an actual physical outline.

1. Surface Cues: Masking of the Fourth Kind

The physical properties of an extended stimulus are, of course, limited to the same set of dimensions that must characterize any other physical stimulus. The stimulus characteristics of a surface are limited by the wavelength spectrum, luminosity, spatial extent, and the patterned variations of these properties within the region being examined. The phenomenal response to a surface, however, may have many more degrees of freedom. *Surface color* is the term that has been traditionally used to describe the wide variety of experiences attributable to an extended region. Jacob Beck, in a virtually unique, analysis of surface colors (Beck, 1972b), has listed a very large number of dimensions along which surface appearances may vary. The range of dimensions of surface-color appearance can be best appreciated by listing some of the attributes Beck mentions:

1. Gloss.
2. Chromaticity.
3. Fluorescence.
4. Brightness.
5. Lightness.
6. Expressiveness.
7. Impressiveness.
8. Insistence.
9. Pronouncedness.
10. Transparency.
11. Fluctuation in time.

Beck also extends this list by citing Katz (1935), who suggested that our perception of surface color could be characterized by the following ''modes of experience'':

1. Film colors.
2. Volume colors.
3. Mirror colors.
4. Luminous colors.
5. Space illumination.
6. Object illumination.

These lists contain some terms familiar to most of us, but also some (e.g., Impressiveness) that are both difficult to define and no longer of serious interest to many perceptual psychologists.

The vagueness of some of these terms is clearly evidenced in the paucity of relevant empirical research. Whatever the complex of factors that lead to each of them, it is clear that only with regard to such stimulus variables as wavelength, purity, and luminance have we begun to achieve an empirical basis for understanding the limits of discriminability, and thus of the limits to segregation of subregions of a visual field on the basis of their surface properties. In the following paragraphs I consider the three major areas in which our knowledge is relatively complete—wavelength, luminance, and texture discrimination.

The classic wavelength discrimination function is shown in Fig. 6-16. This curve depicts the ability of an observer to distinguish between two closely spaced wavelengths. The experimental paradigm traditionally used to generate this type of data in both chromatic and luminance discrimination tests utilizes a stimulus consisting of a reference monochromatic wavelength projected on one side of a bipartite field and a sequence of other similar monochromatic stimuli that vary in wavelength projected on the other side. By means of some appropriate same–different psychophysical test, the just-discriminable difference is established at which the two halves of the field appear to the observer to be different. This just-noticeable–different type of experiment establishes the differential threshold curve for wavelength (as shown in Fig. 6-16) to be a nonmonotonic function of stimulus wavelength and thus not to be directly related to the energy or frequency of a quantum of the stimulating light. The saturation (purity) discrimination curve shown in Fig. 6-20 exhibits a similar kind of nonmonotonicity.

The luminance discrimination function is also equally well known. The prototypical question in that case is how small a change in the luminance of a stimulus can be detected as a function of the absolute level of the luminance. I have already discussed this problem in Chapter 6, where I showed that there is a substantial compression of neural signals representing the stimulus intensity even at the level of receptor processes and that the differential threshold for brightness varies in a way that is only a rough approximation to Weber's ratio.

The form of the luminance discrimination function is strongly affected by the level of light adaptation to which the eye has been exposed. Figure 10-2 displays the generally accepted function relating the differential threshold for luminance to the state of dark adaptation as obtained by Hecht, Peskin, and Patt (1938). This curve plots the logarithm of the ratio of the increment to the background luminance that is necessary for discrimination as a function of the background illumination level to which the eye has been adapted. Clearly, luminance discrimination improves substantially[2] as the eye is adapted to more and more intense background levels. Nevertheless this is but the most general statement about luminance discrimination studies; the ability of the eye to discriminate between different levels of luminance is strongly affected by many other conditions of the viewing situation. Brown and Mueller (1965) have fully reviewed the conditions that affect brightness discrimination, and it is not necessary to recapitulate their entire story here. It is sufficient to note only that such additional factors as stimulus size, duration, and even the design of the psychophysical

[2]Of course, in an absolute sense the increment of light that has to be added becomes larger with higher background illuminances and, from this perspective, discriminability becomes poorer.

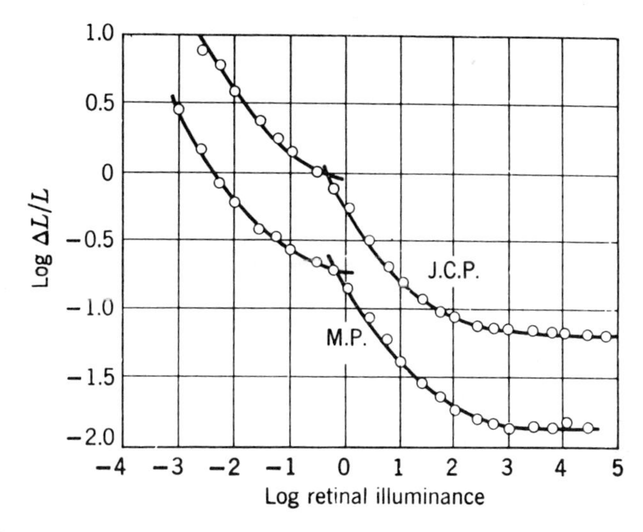

FIG. 10.2. Brightness discrimination for two obsevers plotted as the Weber fraction as a function of retinal illuminance. (From Graham, © 1965a, after Hecht, Peskin, and Patt, 1938, with the permission of John Wiley & Sons, Inc.)

procedure can affect the just-detectable magnitude of the difference between two stimuli in an experiment of this type.

The ability of the eye to discriminate different wavelengths, purities, and luminances constitutes a well-known and generally accepted body of scientific knowledge and requires only brief mention here. The basis of these discriminations is probably a Level 1 process, but clearly these three dimensions of the stimulus are important cues for the visual observer's segregation of the subregions within a visual scene. However, as I have noted, they constitute only some of the possible surface clues to regional segregation. In recent years, primarily as a result of the availability of digital computers capable of displaying the output of extensive computations in the form of graphic displays, a renewed interest has been kindled in other properties of extended stimuli. The main interest and the topic to which I devote most of my attention in this section concerns those statistical properties of the regions that can be summed up by the term *texture*.

Texture denotes the systematic arrangement of the elements of a spatial pattern. Texture may vary absolutely—two patterns may differ totally from each other in the density or size of the elements—or relatively, there may be a gradient of change in the density or size of the pattern elements within a single scene. Gradients of texture have been extensively discussed by J. J. Gibson (1950) among others as a cue to depth. However this is not the context in which I am interested at this point. For the moment, let us consider the ability of an observer to segregate subregions of a field from each other on the basis of discriminable differences in the texture of the field, in much the same way he made a distinction on the basis of wavelength or luminance.

A major breakthrough in the experimental study of texture as a cue for regional segregation has occurred in recent years. The study of texture had been complicated by the fact that however intuitively clear the meaning of the word may have been there were no simple ways to vary the "texture" of a pattern in a controllable and quantitative fashion. Without such control of the independent variables, as workers in the field of form perception have realized for a long time, it is very difficult to do systematic psychophysical experiments on this or any other stimulus dimension. It is now, however, becoming appreciated that the statistical description of the local properties of a surface can be used as a quantitative independent variable in this type of research. A key step in the study of texture occurred, therefore, when Bela Julesz (Julesz, 1962; Julesz, 1975; Julesz, 1978b; Julesz, Gilbert, Shepp, & Frisch, 1973) introduced the idea of *orders* of statistical complexity into the texture problem. The orders of statistical complexity that he and his colleagues proposed are comparable to the moments (mean and variance, etc.) of descriptive statistics, but, as we soon see, these two kinds of statistics are not identical.

The significance of each of the orders can best be understood if described in terms of dot patterns. The first order of complexity defined by Julesz (1975) is closely associated with the mean number of dots in the stimulus, i.e., the mean density. Because dot densities are related to the energy being emitted by a surface, whether there are black dots on a white background or vice versa, first-order texture is also linearly related to the luminance of a dotted stimulus pattern. This is a straightforward extrapolation of a simple statistical idea, and it is intuitively obvious just what this first order signifies. Two samples with different first-order statistics are shown in Fig. 10-5.

Julesz' second statistical order is not quite so obvious, but it is still possible to achieve a relatively direct appreciation of what it means. The second-order statistics describes an aspect of a dot pattern that is most closely related to the average spacing between dots—a textural property perceived as the "clumpiness" or "laciness" of the dots. It is analogous to the variance in ordinary descriptive statistics. Thus two textures might have identical first-order statistics (equal numbers of dots in equal areas) but may differ in their second-order statistics (as reflected in the degree to which the dots are bunched and separated) in a way that makes them appear very different, as shown in Fig. 10-3. It is also important to appreciate that the second-order statistics describe much the same information that is described by the autocorrelation function or the spatial frequency spectrum. The vast literature that relates those kinds of mathematical processes to vision must also necessarily relate the second-order statistics of texture.

Third-order textural statistics are much less easily described in a simple, intuitive say. Julesz described a statistical test in which a sample triangle is "thrown" onto a number of places on two dot patterns. If, on the average, the

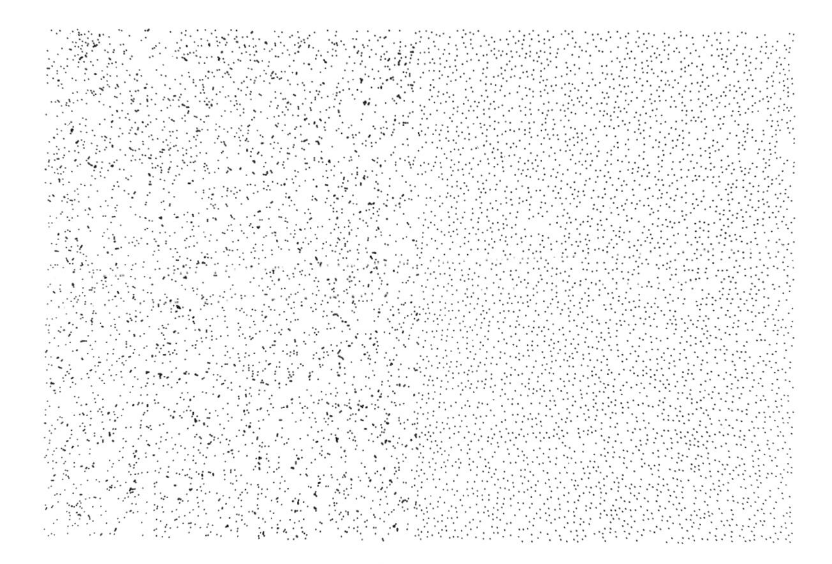

FIG. 10.3. Two textured regions having the same first order statistics (average density), but different second order statistics (regularity of spacing). Discrimination is easy in this case. (From Julesz, Gilbert, Shepp, and Frisch, © 1973, with the permission of Pion, Ltd.)

triangle's corners fall on three dots the same number of times in the two patterns, then the patterns are said to possess the same third-order statistics.

Another way to conceptualize the idea of the third-order statistics of a pattern more intuitively is to consider it as a common property of the local geometry of the elements that make up the pattern as opposed to the global measures—density and clustering—described by the first two orders. For example, Julesz has shown that if a texture is made up of U-shaped objects, a third-order statistical difference can be produced between two subregions even if the objects are rotated in a way that maintains the same lengths of horizontal and vertical line components in the two parts of the scene. Textures varying in the third-order statistics, but with equal first- and second-order statistics, are shown in Fig. 10-4 A and B. Appropriate selection of the elements of the pattern can thus produce patterns with equal first- and second-order but quite different third-order statistics.

Julesz notes another important general property of these patterns with regard to their statistical rather than their perceptual role. First, if two patterns have identical statistics at one order, then all lower orders must also be identical. However, as we have seen, the opposite is not true—higher-order statistics are independent of those of lower order. One can straightforwardly produce patterns that are identical in their first order yet differ in their second- and third-order statistics as easily as patterns that are identical in their second-order statistics

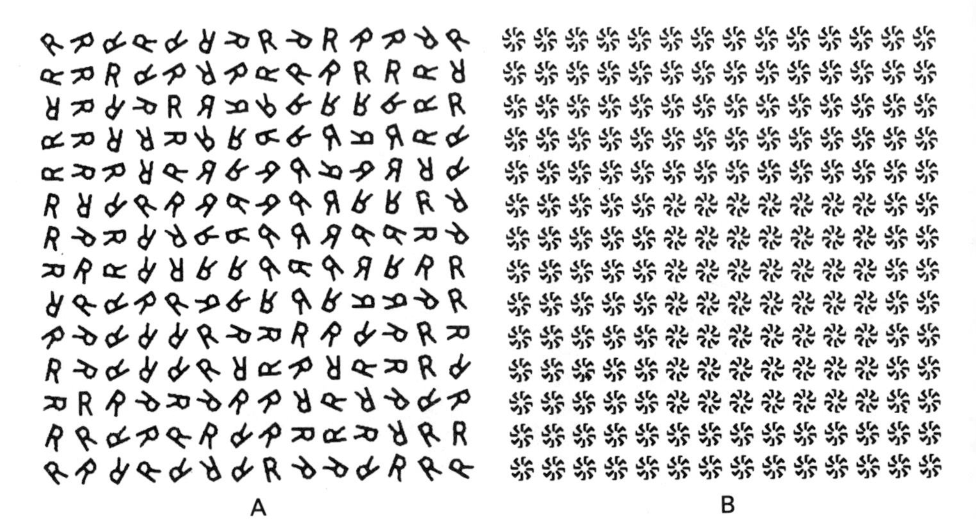

FIG. 10.4. Mirror transformations produce differences in third order, but not second order statistics. In patterns (A) and (B) a subset of the elements are mirror images of the surrounding elements, yet no discrimination is possible. (From Julesz, Gilbert, Shepp, and Frisch, © 1973, with the permission of Pion, Ltd.)

(and thus necessarily in their first-order statistics), yet differ in their third-order statistics.

So far, I have only described the statistical properties of these quasi-random patterns. More germane to the present discussion is their impact on human perception—in particular on the ability of an observer to discriminate between different regions that vary in one or another order of statistical regularity. A major study of the discriminability of dotted patterns that differ in their first-order statistics (i.e., in dot density) has recently been reported by Barlow (1978). Barlow was concerned with the ability of observers to detect shaped regions of dots within and beside other dotted patterns that differed only in dot density. Barlow proposed a measure (F) of the statistical efficiency of the human observer based on the ratio of the sample size (i.e., the number of dots) required by an ideal observer and the sample size required by the typical human observer to determine that two patterns were different purely on the basis of the respective dot densities. This ratio is equal to the square of the ratio of d' (discriminability in a signal detection theoretical sense) that would be exhibited by an ideal observer (d'_{ideal}) and the d' that is exhibited by real observers in his experiments (d'_{exp}). Formally, according to Barlow, the efficiency of discriminability is therefore represented by the following expression:

$$F = \left(\frac{d'_{ideal}}{d'_{exp}}\right)^2 \tag{10-1}$$

A sample of the stimuli used in Barlow's experiments is shown in Fig. 10-5. In this sample, the reference and the test patterns are placed side by side. In other experiments, however, the test might be a square or rectangular area embedded in the middle of the reference pattern. The reference pattern always consisted (in each experiment) of a standard number (N) of dots although this constant number of dots was randomly distributed across the stimulus field in a different fashion in each trial. The adjacent test pattern, to which the observer had to respond "same" or "different," contained the same number of dots (N) plus a constant number of additional dots δN. A variable number of other dots σ_n was either added to or subtracted from the test pattern to introduce variability so that the signal detection measure d' could be computed. Thus each test pattern had a number of dots equal to $N + \delta N = \sigma_n$. Figure 10-6 shows the visual effect of the variation in the number of dots and the associated changes in the d'_{exp} that occured as δN varied as well as the changes in d'_{ideal} (defined as $\delta N/N$) that should have occured.

The results of Barlow's psychophysical experiment indicated that observers were not, however, ideal; they rarely performed better than a 50% efficiency. The only condition in which his observers approached ideal discrimination of these first-order statistics occurred in those limiting conditions in which the dot densities were so low and exposures so long that they could actually count the individual dots. At higher dot densities, or shorter durations, their efficiency fell off substantially from the ideal. This result indicated an inability on the part of the observer to carry out this kind of statistical processing at high dot densities at anywhere near ideal levels. Specifically, the relationship between dot density and efficiency is shown in Fig. 10-7. Thus, whereas observers can process first-order statistics under some conditions, there is a progressive deterioration in their

100 ± 10

20

2

FIG. 10.5. Two random dot patterns that differ in their first order statistics. The left half of this figure may have 100, plus or minus 10, plus a variable number of dots (in this case 20), while the right side always has 100 dots. Discrimination on the basis of density, the first order statistic, is excellent. (From Barlow, © 1978, with the permission of Pergamon Press.)

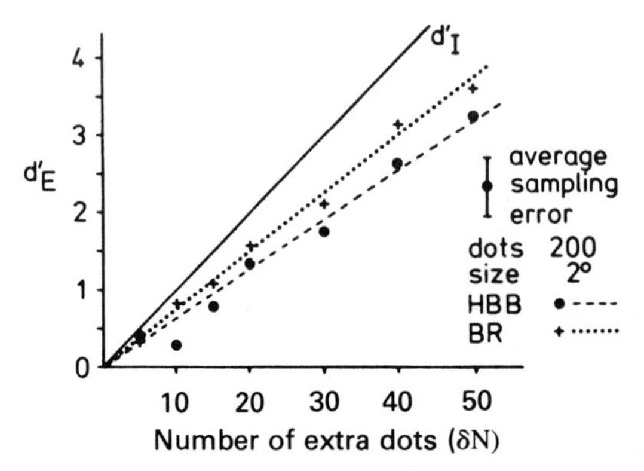

FIG. 10.6. Barlow measured the discrminability of dot density in terms of d′(d′$_E$ being the experimentally determined index). This graph relates d′$_E$ to the different number of dots, as shown in Fig. 10.5. At greater dot densities, the curve deviates from d′$_I$ (the ideal observer's index of discriminability as shown). (From Barlow, © 1978, with the permission of Pergamon Press.)

ability to discriminate between different dot densities when the mean number of dots is high. This is not just a matter of a constant Weber ratio but a more profound decline in efficiency (as defined by Eq. 10-1) with increases in dot density.

Another important outcome of Barlow's experiment was the lack of any effect of the shape of the stimulus (when it was embedded within the reference region) on d'_{exp}. This is an important result because it dissociates this kind of overall pattern information processing from the kind of simplistic feature detection theory that is all too often misapplied to this kind of finding.

Barlow's data are probably definitive in describing the processing of first-order statistics, but I must now turn to other experimental reports to consider the ability of observers to process the higher-order statistical properties of those quasi-random dot patterns. However an important technical difficulty with the higher-order statistical properties, highlighted by Julesz and his co-workers, must be mentioned at this point. Even though it is relatively easy to generate, in a

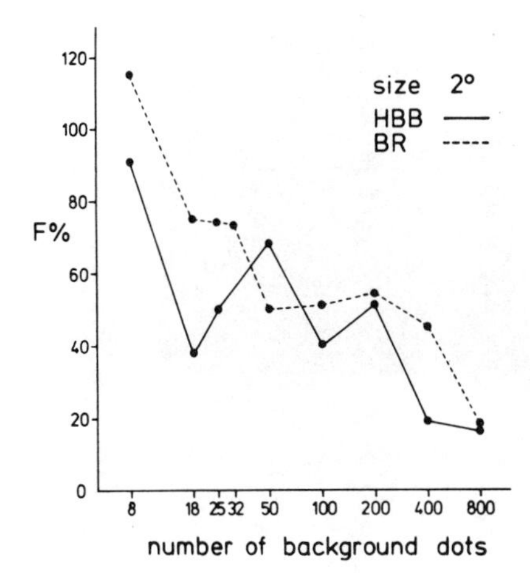

FIG. 10.7. F defines the square of the ratio of d′$_I$ and d′$_E$. The index is plotted here to show the decline in efficiency of discrimination as the number of dots increases. (From Barlow, © 1978, with the permission of Pergamon Press.)

precisely controlled way, patterns that differ in their first-order statistics (one needs only a two-dimensional random number generator to calculate the x and y coordinates and an appropriate display, because the location of each dot is independent of all others), it requires somewhat more elaborate computer processing power to develop stimuli that differ in their second- and higher-order statistics. This escalation of difficulty is fundamentally due to the fact that control of the higher-order statistics of a quasi-random pattern involves the computation of local interactions between the individual components of the display. In other words, where a dot is plotted on such a display depends on the location of at least some of the other nearby dots in the display. Unlike Barlow's (1978) experiments using easily generated stimuli, studies of the effects of differences in the second-order statistics on the discriminability of various regions of the stimulus require stimuli for which the total number of dots in the pattern is held constant, in order to avoid discrimination based on a first-order difference; then the spacing among this constant number of dots must be manipulated to vary the second-order statistics. It has now also been shown that it is possible for the observer to discriminate between patterns if the second-order statistical difference is large enough. The question is, what are the limits of the human observer in processing such second-order statistical differences?

One good quantitative study of the ability of observers to process the second-order statistical properties of a stimulus pattern (as opposed to a qualitative demonstration that is possible) has been reported by Pollack (1971). Although he did not use dot patterns in his experiments, but a matrix of printed letters instead, Pollack's work serves as an excellent complement to the present discussion. Pollack overcame the previously mentioned difficulty of generating a two-dimensional field with known second-order statistical (Markov) properties by using a computer-executed probabilistic rule that determined the presence or absence of a typewritten X in the lower right corner of a series of sliding local 2×2 arrays embedded within a larger matrix of letters. A sample stimulus is shown in Fig. 10-8. The determination of whether or not an X would be printed in any position was based on a rule that evaluated the presence or absence of Xs in the other three corners of the 2×2 grid and the number of characters to be presented in each stimulus. Because the two-dimensional pattern was initiated by generating a random series of Xs across the top row and down the left-hand column of the large matrix, it was only necessary to apply this generation rule sequentially starting at the upper left corner and to slide the 2×2 matrix along to fill up the entire area to generate an appropriate sample. With proper constraints on the number of Xs that appeared in the larger matrix, a pattern that had a constant first-order statistic but a variable second-order statistic could be automatically generated using this simple algorithm.

Pollack asked his observers to rank order a set of these patterns in terms of their "lumpiness" or "laciness." Because observers could do so in a lawful way, these studies showed that they were able to discriminate between patterns of

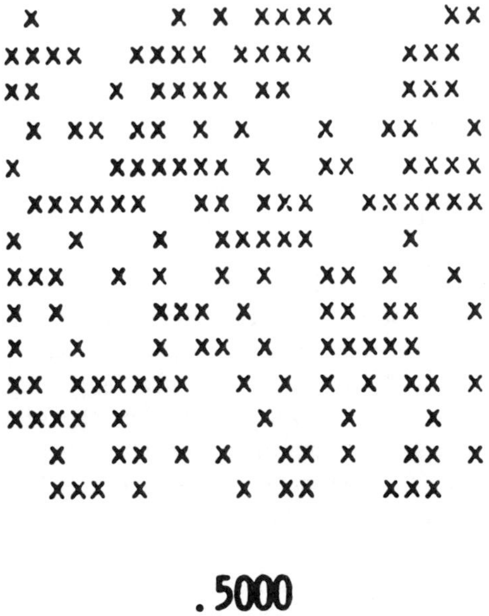

```
X        X X XXXX      XX
XXXX   XXXX XXXX     XXX
XX     X XXXX XX     XXX
 X XX XX X X    X   XX   X
X      XXXXXX X   XX   XXXX
 XXXXXX   XX XXX   XXXXXX
X  X    X  XXXXX     X
XXX   X X   X X   XX X   X
X X     XXX X    XX XX   X
X  X    X XX X   XXXXX
XX XXXXXX  X X X X XX X
XXXX X       X    X    X
  X  XX X X  XX X   XX X
  XXX X      X XX   XXX
```

.5000

FIG. 10.8. A sample stimulus with a two-dimensional Markov spatial constraint. (From Pollack, © 1971, with the permission of The Psychonomics Journals, Inc.)

this kind that varied only in their second-order statistics. As in Barlow's (1978) experiment, Pollack found that his observers did not perform at the level of a theoretically ideal observer. According to Pollack's estimates, his observers could only discriminate among eight different levels of variation in the second-order statistics. His data also indicated that there is an apparent saturation of second-order discriminability that occurs when high dot density levels are used.

Pollack's method of generating the Markov constrained patterns differs considerably from that used by Julesz to produce the patterns shown in, for example, Fig. 10-3, which also vary only in their second-order statistics. Julesz used a decision rule to control second-order statistics that said that no dot could appear within 10 dot diameters of a previously plotted dot. Nevertheless the effect is the same, and both Julesz' demonstrations and Pollack's more formal experiment make it clear that observers are to a certain, though certainly not to an ideal, degree capable of processing second-order statistical information. The internal mechanisms used to compute these perceptual statistical estimates, of course, remain obscure.

Now let's turn to the problem of stimulus patterns that have identical first-and second-order properties but different third-order statistics. Julesz presents a compelling argument supporting the "conjecture" that, in most instances, human beings are not capable of evaluating third-order statistical computations. Thus, in a number of ingenious demonstrations (Julesz, 1975; Julesz, 1978b; Julesz,

Gilbert, Shepp and Frisch, 1973) he has shown that, in general, observers are not able to discriminate between textures that differ only in third-order statistical properties. The pattern shown in Fig. 10-9, for example, consisting of *U*-shaped elements, is particularly interesting since the textures are not discriminable when the *U*-shaped elements are simply inverted (thus keeping the second-order statistics of horizontal and vertical line lengths identical) even though such an inversion produces a change in the third-order statistics. However when some of the *U*s are laid on their sides, the second-order statistics of the local elements (the proportion of horizontal and vertical lines, respectively) change and the differing local regions (horizontal *U*s versus vertical *U*s) are immediately apparent. This demonstrates that it is only when second-order differences exist that the regions become discriminable; we simply do not seem to be able to see the third-order difference in this and most other cases.

As noted, the third-order statistics of a pattern are mainly defined by the properties of the local elements rather than by their distribution over the whole scene. However the properties of local elements do not only contribute to the third-order but can also influence the lower-order statistics. This problem has been specifically studied by Julesz, Gilbert, Shepp, and Frisch (1973), and by Fox (in press). Fox, for example, has shown that easily distinguishable textures, such as the *V*-shaped patterns shown in Fig. 10-10A, can become indistinguishable simply by adding a circle around each *V* as shown in Fig. 10-10B. Clearly the distinctive second-order differences in the former case are degraded by these additional microstructural features—the circles.

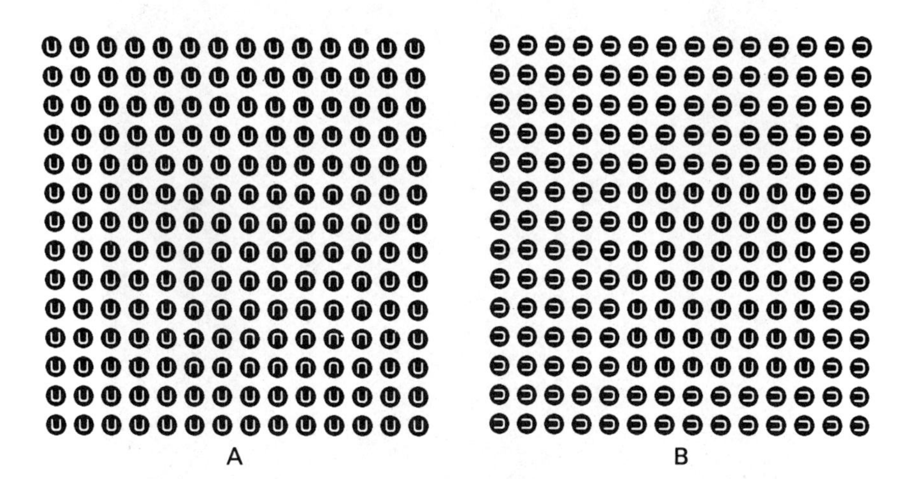

FIG. 10.9. Two patterns made up of identical elements. However, in (A) some of the U's have been rotated 180°, while (B) some have been rotated 90°. Rotation of 90° changes the second order statistics of the patterns, making the subarea discriminable, while rotation of 180° does not. (From Julesz, Gilbert, Shepp, and Frisch, © 1973, with the permission of Pion, Ltd.)

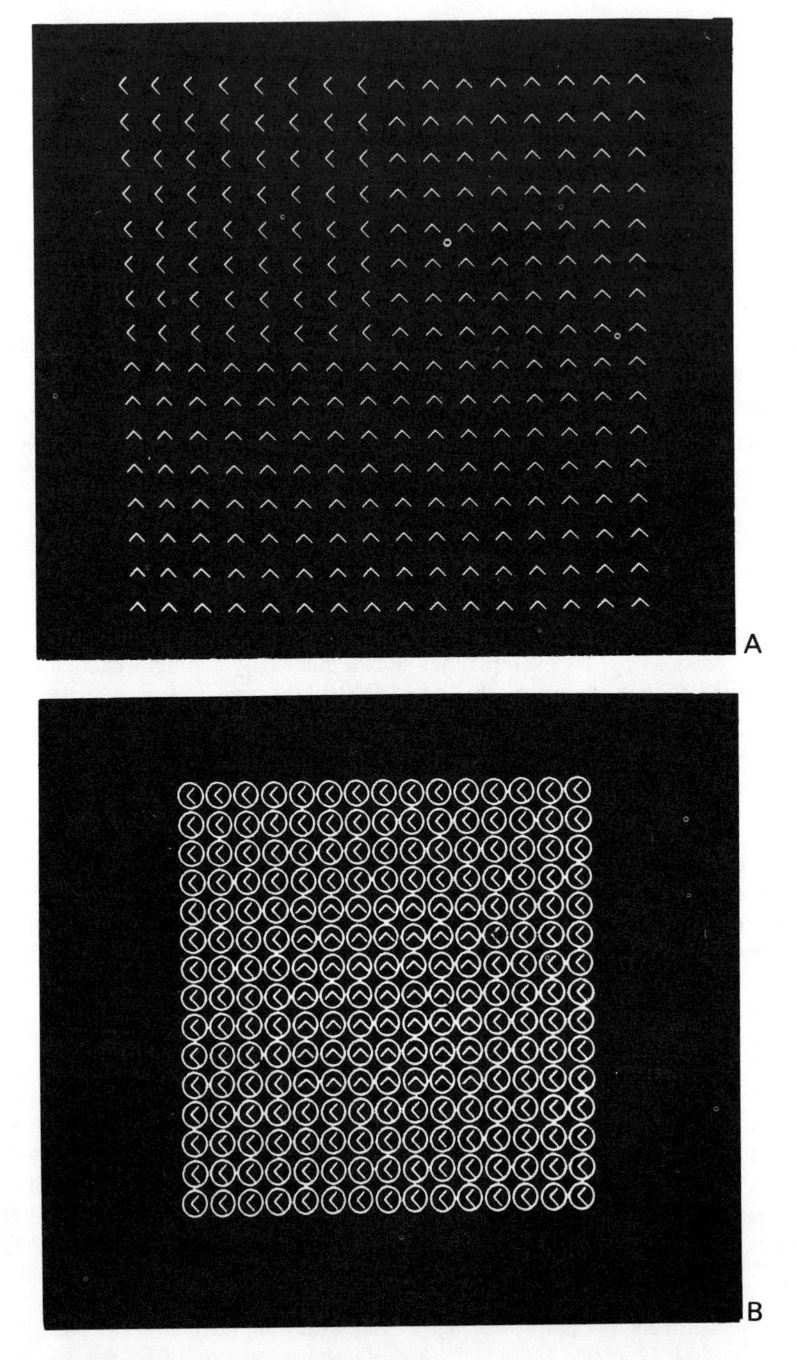

FIG. 10.10. Adding circles to a textured pattern in which discrimination was originally possible (A) destroys that ability on the part of the observer (as shown in (B). (From Fox, in press.)

The most extensive studies of the third-order statistical properties of dot patterns, however, have been carried out by Caelli and Julesz (1978), and Caelli, Julesz, and Gilbert (1978) who have specifically manipulated the microstructure of the elements of the textured pattern. Fig. 10-11A, for example, indicates two microelements (among many other possible examples of these two classes) that can be grouped to produce textured regions with identical first- and second-order but different third-order statistics. A very few patterns of this type have been shown by Caelli, Julesz, and Gilbert (1978) to violate Julesz' conjecture of the indiscriminability of third-order patterns. For example, when many of the two kinds of microelements shown in Fig. 10-11A are used to form a textured stimulus, then two regions, differing only in their third-order statistics, do become immediately segregated as effectively as if they had differed in their first- or second-order statistics, as shown in Fig. 10-11B.

Caelli, Julesz, and Gilbert (1978) have examined a wide variety of such dotted patterns but have found only a few types of stimuli that have identical first- and second-order (but different third-order) statistics that are so discriminable. They discuss four properties that seem to violate the general conjecture that third-order differences are not discriminable. These types include those exhibiting the following properties: (1) variations in iso-dipole statistics; (2) quasi-colinearity; (3) corners; and (4) closure.

The last three items on this list are reminiscent of the classic Gestalt properties discussed later in this chapter), and are exemplified by the drawings in Fig. 10-11 C, D, and E respectively. The first—iso-dipole statistics—is more subtle and has to do with the statistics of the arrangements of pairs of the constitutent dots of the micropattern. These are among the very few exceptions to Julesz' conjecture that have been discovered so far, and each seems to work because it simulates some "good figure" (in the Gestalt sense) in a way that transcends the statistical aspects of stimuli emphasized so far. Caelli, Julesz, and Gilbert (1978 pp. 208, 210) suggest two ways in which the original conjecture should be modified to take these exceptions into account: (1) ". . . If a texture has identical dipole statistics and if quasi-collinearity, corner, and closure properties are excluded, no discrimination is possible"; and (2) given that the exceptions are so rare, ". . . texure pairs that were randomly selected from a pool of textures with identical dipole statistics have a very large probability of not being discrimnable."

Another related finding concerning the human observer's ability to process statistical properties of a visual stimulus has been reported by Pollack (1973). He also showed that certain patterns consisting of a 32 × 32 dot matrix generated on the basis of differing third-order statistical constraints could be reliably discriminated from each other if the difference were great enough. Pollack defined the texture of the two dimensional dot array in terms of the probability of repetition—$P(\Sigma_e/\Sigma_e)$—of a 2 × 2 subarray with an even parity sum (i.e., 0, 2, or 4 dots present out of a possible 4) or with an odd parity sum (1 or 3 dots present

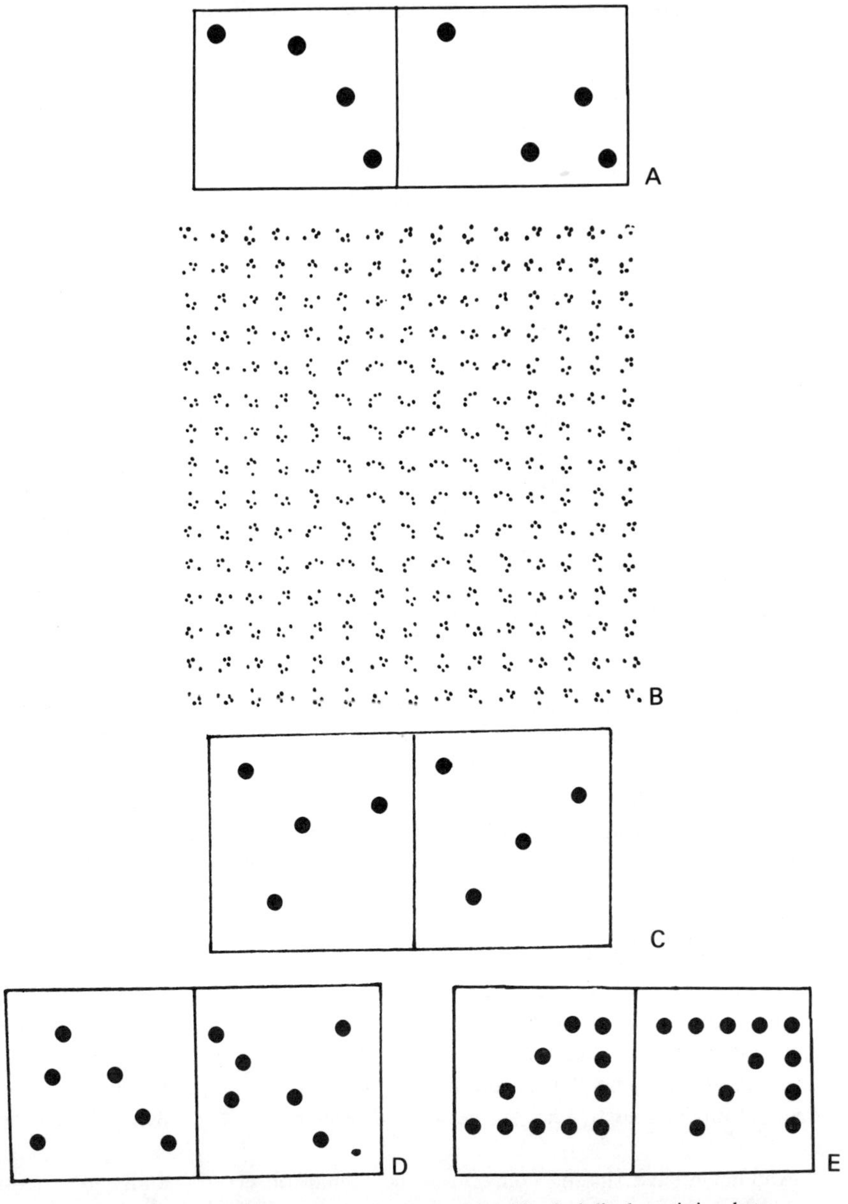

FIG. 10.11. (A) Two texture elements that have identical dipole statistics, but one of which is quasi-colinear. (B) Textures made up of these two patterns are discriminable. (C) Another example of a pattern of micro elements, one of which displays a quasi-colinear pattern, and thus would allow discrimination. (D) Two texture elements whose dipole statistics are equal, but one of which forms a "corner." Regions made up of the corner would be discriminable from regions made up from the other texture element. (E) Two texture elements whose dipole statistics are alike, but differ in that one forms a closed figure. Textures made up of these two elements can also be discriminated. (From Caelli, Julesz, and Gilbert, © 1978, with the permission of Springer-Verlag, Inc.)

out of a possible 4). This probabalistic regulation of the texture of the reference pattern was the independent variable in his experiment. The dependent variable was the equivalent probabalistic rule describing the variable comparison matrics (there were three of them—the observer's task was to find the odd one).

Figure 10-12 shows the results of Pollack's experiment. Clearly the higher the probability of the repetition of odd or even parity, the higher the probability of repetition of the comparison figure had to be to be discriminated. Like Caelli and his colleagues, Pollack also asserts that these results may be based on the observer's use of local anomalies rather than statistical processing of the overall pattern.

The main question arising at this point concerns why the human observer is not in general able to make use of the third-order statistical properties of a textured pattern when he so easly handles the statistical puzzle posed by patterns varying in the lower two orders.[3] Julesz postulates what is probably the most plausible and straightforward answer. He notes that the calculations required to process statistical information increase exponentially as the order increases. That means that evaluations of third-order statistics require roughly 1000 times more neural information processing power than first-order computations. It is not at all certain that such an investment in neural circuitry could have evolved without degrading other, even more necessary, aspects of human perception. So the answer is simply a practical one: Our brains are probably just not powerful enough. We have already encountered corroborative support for this overload hypothesis. Recall the practical problem of generating stimuli of increasingly higher order. It is only when there are some exceptional figural properties such as corners, quasi-linearity, or closure, or vast differences in the iso-dipole statistics, factors which actually "preprocess" some of the statistical aspects of the stimulus, that the computational requirements are sufficiently modest to allow immediate segregation by the observer.

Can our failure to process third-order statistics be interpreted more microscopically? Caelli, Julesz, and Barlow all relate their findings to the action of single-cell feature detectors in the visual system. From my point of view, however, this is certainly an inappropriate attribution. To the contrary, it seems that any plausible neural model of second- and third-order processing must necessarily involve a very elaborate neural network and not feature detectors in the sense the word is

[3]Needless to say, in the vigorously bubbling turmoil of perceptual theory, even Julesz' refined and beautiful approach to the processing of statistical orders has not gone unchallenged. Martin and Pomerantz (1978) suggest that Julesz' conjecture (that people can process first- and second-order statistics but cannot handle the computational requirements of third-order statistics) does not hold. They present some data that counterindicate the idea of statistical processing per se and allude to the importance of such factors as spatial overlap, border differences, and even that old favorite—figural goodness. Martin and Pomerantz assert that although there may be some superprinciple that incorporates all of these factors, including the statistical discriminations, it is yet to be found. In fact, this is not too different an idea from the concept behind the exceptions described in Caelli, Julesz, and Gilbert's (1978) paper.

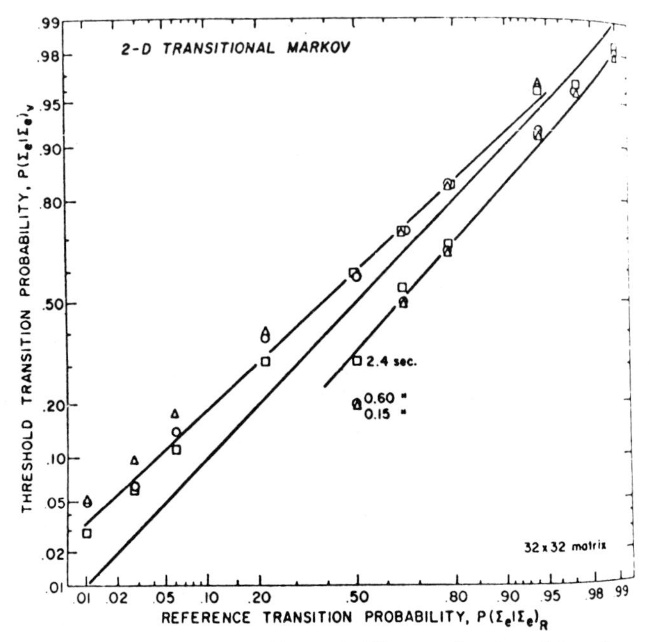

FIG. 10.12. The threshold transition probability as a function of the reference transition probability resulting from Pollack's study of two-dimensional Markov constraints. The shape of the points encodes different display durations. (From Pollack, © 1973, with the permission of The Psychonomics Journals, Inc.)

usually used. Caelli and Julesz, in particular, specifically invoke a hierarchical model of Hubel and Wiesel-type feature-detecting neurons that, I believe, can no longer be considered to be a serious contender to explain these phenomena.

Barlow also invokes the concept of single "dot number estimating" neurons that have specific spatial and temporal sensitivity to the first-order statistics of a displayed pattern. However this minitheory is so qualitative that his metaphor could equally as well describe any analyzing system at any level of complexity, from the single-cell level to a level that, in principle, is not distinguishable from the entire visual system. As I indicated in the previous chapter, I find these pseudoneurophysiological explanations to be singularly uncompelling, and prefer a more phenomenological description, even though the latter are not reductive in a satisfying manner at the present time.

Barlow (1978, p. 649) does, at least in part, qualify his position among the most radical of single-cell neuroreductionists when he says:

> The failure to find any improved efficiency for elongated test objects can be explained in a number of ways, one of which is to suppose that we are on the wrong track in thinking of the cortical neurons as responding in proportion to the linear sum of weighted contributions from the parts of their respective fields. Sooner or

later the nervous system must perform more interesting logical operations, and these cannot be modeled by simple linear summation.

Another way, independent of texture, in which the ''statistical'' processing capacity of the visual system has been studied is exemplified by the model proposed to explain the results of one of my own studies (Uttal, 1975a). Although the confusions introduced into the dot-masking experiments that I described in Chapter 9 (see pp. 711–715) are clearly due to the temporal superimposition of the dots of the mask and the dots of the target, extracting the target from the visual noise involves an autocorrelation type of processing that is closely related to the statistical capabilities I have just discussed. The observer is able to extract a target on the basis of regularities in the target dots that the noise dots do not possess. Thus even though overall dot density may be the same in target trials and pure noise trials; and thus the same first-order statistics obtained, there are residual differences in the second-order statistics, such as spacing and regularity, that allow the signal to be extracted from the noise. I refer to this type of signal-in-noise masking in particular, and to camouflage in general, as masking of the fourth kind. I believe this kind of experiment assays the ability of an observer to process second-order visual pattern statistics.

The autocorrelation model applied to this type of dotted target detection task, although presented in the form of a neural network implementation in Chapter 9, need not necessarily be considered in those neuroreductionistic terms. It is also possible to consider it independently simply in terms of the necessary mathematical operations and transformations. Indeed, the operators depicted in the network model shown in Fig. 9-4 are not likely to be individual neurons but large functional units, possibly involving very large numbers of neurons. The point in the present context is that whatever the particular neural implementation the autocorrelation model invokes a set of mathematical processes that operate on the second-order statistics of dot patterns to simulate how an observer might discriminate target from noise, and therefore, by analogy, how the human observer may also be acting as a global statistical processor. It is a specific alternative to the single-cell feature detector hypothesis and one particular embodiment of the concept of a statistical processor.

The autocorrelation model has been successful in predicting the detectability of target patterns that varied in ways that are directly comparable to the various order statistics I described in the preceding section. Specifically, the effect of each of the following dimensions of the dotted targets were considered with the results indicated:

1. Dot numerosity—more dots, more detectable.
2. Line orientation—no effect.
3. Deformation of straight lines into curves and angles—more deformation, less detectable.

4. Colinear dot-spacing irregularity—more irregular, less detectable.
5. Traverse dot-spacing irregularity—more irregular, less detectable.
6. Missing parts in triangles—sides more important than corners.
7. Polygonal orientation—no effect.
8. Distortions of squares into parallelograms—more distortion, less detectability.
9. Organized straight-line patterns versus ''pick up stix'' patterns composed of the same lines—more organized, more detectable.
10. Distortions of squares and triangles by misplacing one or more corners—more distortion, less detectable.
11. Figural goodness—no effect.

This psychophysical data base was then compared to the results of a computer simulation model based upon an autocorrelation transformation that operated on simulated samples of the stimuli, as shown in Fig. 9-5. In all the cases listed here the data were in substantial agreement with the prediction of the model.

Unfortunately, substantial discrepancies from the predictions of the model (but in a way that actually helped to suggest the specific weakness of it) have begun to appear in more recent reports (e.g., Uttal & Tucker, 1977). In that report we discovered that the complexity of the pattern varied in a way that was not predicted satisfactorily by the autocorrelation theory.

Other researchers have used this same paradigm and have studied the extraction of target signals from noisy backgrounds. Although I did not know of their work until 1976, J. Simon and Camillerapp (1968) had also been pursuing a similar line of research utilizing quasi-random dot patterns and stressing a correlational type approach. Two other studies that antedated my own but were of very much the same spirit (and conclusions) were those of Van de Geer and Levelt (1963) and French (1954).

More recently, Bell and Handel (1976) have also studied the effects of pattern goodness in a related paradigm, using reconstruction rather than detection as the task, and have discovered that a substantial effect of pattern goodness appears to be exerted on the rate of encoding a stimulus pattern rather than on one's memory of that pattern. The difference between Bell and Handel's positive finding regarding goodness and my own negative one can be attributed to the different tasks required of the observers in each case. In my experiment, observers were merely required to detect the target patterns; they did not even have to say which one of the several possible alternatives they saw. In Bell and Handel's study, the observer had to reproduce the target pattern, a response requiring a higher degree of perceptual awareness of the detailed characteristics of the target form and this is presumably aided by figural goodness.

These studies, in common, explore the ability of the observer to act as an implicit statistician and his power to analyze the statistics of quasi-random dot patterns. All attest to the fact that the human visual system is capable of carrying out such computations. As another example of this power, consider the remarkable ability of the human, originally described by Richard Kirkham of the University of Western Australia, to detect a single discrepant element in Fig. 10-13. When the pattern is held at a distance, or degraded by squinting, the ''localized error'' becomes immediately evident.

In sum, as a result of mechanisms that are still obscure, the human visual system has been shown to be able to perform some complex and wonderful evaluations of the statistical properties of quasi-random stimuli. The suggestion is that the psychophysical findings reflect the action of a parallel-processing system of considerable power. Though there are definite limits to these statistical processing mechanisms (they do not seem to be capable of supplying the enormous computational power required to process third-order statistical differences), they do exhibit remarkable capabilities in a wide variety of other quasi-statistical tasks.

2. Contour Cues

The importance of the texture, color, and brightness surface properties of visual scenes in the present context is that they all provide cues to the segregation of different regions of complex visual scenes as a precursor to the establishment of figure–ground relations. All of the processes I have discussed so far depend upon properties that extend over the entire surface or subregion. It is obvious, however, that surface properties are not the only cues to spatial segregation; simple line drawings or even suggestions of lines that do not exist physically can also lead to the awareness of distinct regions of the visual scene.

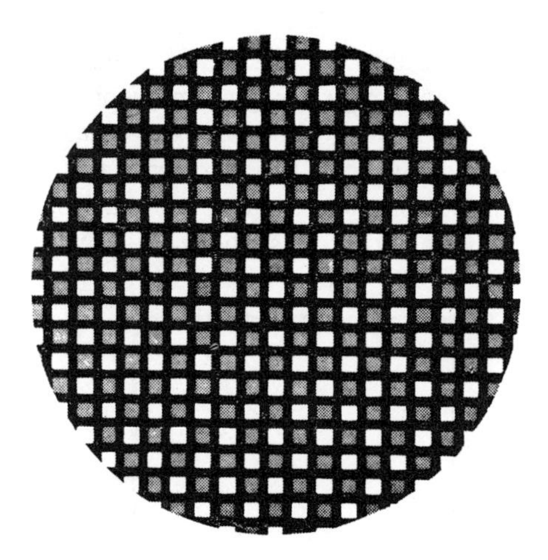

FIG. 10.13. In this textured pattern only one square is the wrong shade, yet it is quickly and easily detected. (From Marshall, © 1969, with the permission of the Australian Psychological Association.)

In this section I consider the little that is known of such cues to regional segregation and their contribution to the organization of visual scenes. Unfortunately, almost nothing in a formal experimental sense has been done with line drawings per se. Rather they have merely been the object of a number of those innumerable demonstrations that grace the history of perceptual science; demonstrations that intrigue and excite but do woefully little to explicate the nature of the underlying mechanisms and processes. What we do know can be summed up in a few words.

First, regions of identical surface properties can be demarcated from each other by means of outline contours. Figure 10-14, for example, shows an outline drawing of a square. Not only are two regions of the field (the inside and the outside of the square) segregated from each other, but very often this stimulus scene leads to subjective impressions of differences in lightness, brightness, and spatial position between the square and its surround.

It is not even necessary that a contour be physically present to produce the same segregation effects. If two areas of identical texture are conjoined in such a way that the components of the texture in the two regions are not in alignment, then a strong ''subjective'' contour will be produced that is equally effective in demarcating the two regions. Such a stimulus pattern is presented in Fig. 10-36C. Outline caricatures (silhouettes) as exemplified in Fig. 10-15 are other examples, of the powerful influence of simple linear contours to define not only different regions of a stimulus but also to convey enormous amounts of information with the simplest and most stylized features. Another class of contour effects is typified by Fig. 10-16. Here the presence or absence of a trivial thread can have a profound effect on the way in which the constant luminance of the two halves of the ring are interpreted.

Contours and outlines are thus ubiquitous and influential in structuring our visual world. However, even though they play an important role in a considerable portion of contemporary theoretical thinking (because of the implications of many neurophysiological studies of ''line detectors'' that have dominated the literature in that domain for so many years), it is amazing how little specific perceptual research has been carried out studying their impact on regional segre-

FIG. 10.14.

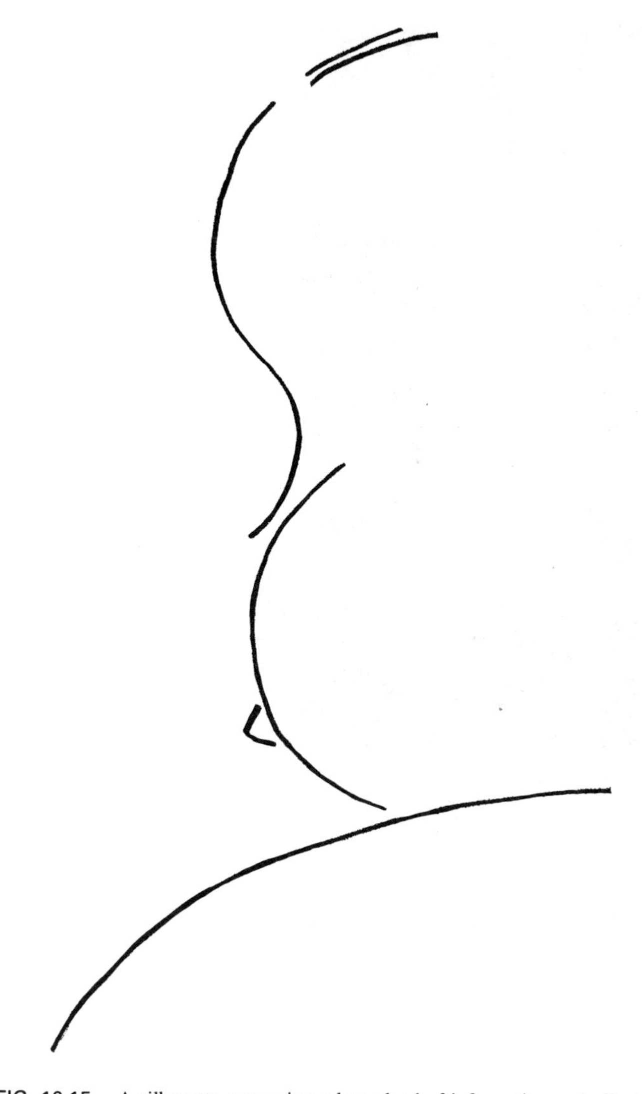

FIG. 10.15. A silhouette conveying a large load of information and affect.

gation. Perhaps calling attention to these examples in this context, even as briefly as I have here, will help someday to remedy this deficiency.

3. On the Fading of Segregated Areas

In the previous section, my discussion concentrated on those cues that help us to perform the initial segregation of different regions of the stimulus scene. It is also true, however, that there are certain conditions in which areas that have been so segregated can lose that figural organization, and a breakdown in regional per-

FIG. 10.16. If a fine line is drawn (or a thread placed) along the vertical intersection of the black and white regions, there is a striking change in the lightness of the two halves of the ring. (From Gregory, © 1966, with the permission of the McGraw-Hill Company.)

ceptual differentiation occurs. An examination of such figural breakdown phenomena may also help us to understand the normal processes that lead to the segregation of objects and regions in the visual field in the first place. Four such phenomena fall within this particular subcategory of Level 3 processes:

1. The fading of the ganzfeld.
2. The Shurcliff blotch.
3. The fading of stabilized retinal images.
4. Alterations of nonstabilized periodic patterns.

A ganzfeld, as classically defined by Koffka (1935), is a totally homogenous visual stimulus. Whereas it may have some measurable overall luminance and spectral characteristics, it has no *stimulus-defined* subregions. A close approximation to a ganzfeld can be achieved by attaching one half of a plastic table tennis ball to each eye to form a pair of opaque goggles (a technique probably first utilized by Hochberg, Triebel, & Seaman, 1951); or by seating an observer a meter or so from a uniformly illuminated wall and dimming the right until the surface appeared homogenous (a technique probably originally utilized by Metzger, 1930). Natural stimuli approximating ganzfelds can also occur in the form of snow fields or cloud banks in which the glare produced by moderately high illumination and a uniformly white environment produces a nearly featureless visual environment.

The perceptual response to a ganzfeld can be quite dramatic. After viewing such a stimulus for a period as short as 2 or 3 minutes, even those limited luminance and spectral properties of the visual stimulus field that had been present lose their ability to produce the corresponding brightness and color experiences evoked under more ordinary conditions. What had been an evenly illuminated surface with specific chromatic values fades to what has been described as "a featureless volume filled with a gray fog." This fog is not a *surface* nor does it possess any brightness, lightness, or color characteristics. What may have originally appeared as a uniformly colored surface becomes, after a few minutes, an achromatic *space*.

It is difficult to find either dimensions or a vocabulary describing a "featureless gray fog" that could be used as independent variables in a formal experiment; therefore, formal studies of the ganzfeld are few and far between and demonstrations still reign supreme. To my knowledge, the most recent experimental studies are those reported by Hochberg et al. (1951), W. Cohen (1957, 1958), and Weintraub (1964). The work of Hochberg and his colleagues, using the Ping-Pong ball goggles, led to several specific conclusions about the perceptual response to the ganzfeld stimulus conditions that still seem to have validity:

1. They confirmed that chromatic stimuli did fade to achromatic gray.
2. They showed that the aftereffects of viewing a ganzfeld did not transfer from one eye to the other.
3. They showed that the fading of lightness and color was not due to a interruption of the neural communication process. The introduction of shadow objects into the ganzfeld led to their immediate perception; therefore the afferent pathway was still working.
4. They showed that eye movements were not capable of restoring the faded chromatic experience.
5. They showed that interruption of a colored ganzfeld (i.e., a darkening of the field) led to the strong experience of the complementary color even though the ganzfeld had faded to a featureless gray.

The most interesting aspect of Cohen's work, on the other hand, was his introduction of a small test spot varying in wavelength, luminance, or both into the stimulus. Surprisingly, the introduction of a small spot of a different spectral composition (than the ganzfeld) into the ganzfeld seemed to affect only minimally the already faded field. The only effect was a highly localized increase in saturation in a region of the ganzfeld immediately surrounding the test spot. This often led to the formation of a chromatic halo of a different color around the smaller colored spot.

Weintraub's (1964) study of the ganzfeld demonstrated just how powerful the fading effect could be. The color and then the brightness faded so quickly (in some cases as quickly as 2 sec) and so completely that observers often asked, "Why has the light been turned off?" Curiously, the greater the purity of the light, the quicker and more completely the ganzfeld faded.

The general impression given by these sets of data is that the ganzfeld fading is not mediated by relatively peripheral processes, although this conclusion is still moot. No one has yet provided a comprehensive explanation of the localized impact of the off-colored spot observed in Cohen's study, nor the failure of the ganzfeld-induced fading to transfer from one eye to the other in the study reported by Hochberg and his colleagues. On the other hand, the immediacy of the recovery upon introduction of shadows rules out Level-2-type network processes as a complete explanation of these phenomena. Clearly, we do not yet have a full and satisfactory appreciation of the origins of ganzfeld fading.

One other important fact about the ganzfeld-type experiment is that it illustrates the tight relationship that exists between different dimensions of the visual experience. It is, it seems, necessary for the observer to have some spatially segregated regions in the visual field for brightness and color to be appreciated. This is so in spite of the fact that these latter dimensions of visual experience are usually thought to be independent of the spatial attributes of the stimulus and to depend mainly on the luminance and wavelength, respectively.

Prolonged gazing at a uniform surface, however, does not always lead to the fading of that field and the appearance of a formless gray space. Shurcliff (1959) reported a little-known phenomenon that suggests that there are some conditions in which a uniform field may, quite to the contrary, take on the appearance of two quite differently colored areas. Although "Shurcliff blotches" exhibit many similarities to receptor-mediated afterimages, they also share some common features with the responses to the ganzfeld I have just described. The blotches can be generated by looking through a reddish filter at a diffuse light source. After about 5 sec of viewing, a purplish, amorphous shape suddenly emerges in the middle of the image where nothing initially had been perceived. According to Shurcliff, the shape fades to invisibility after about 20 sec. The Shurcliff blotch response to a uniformly illuminated field is of interest mainly because it is the complete antithesis of the ganzfeld phenomenon. Unfortunately, it too remains an obscure and mysterious phenomenon; no one, including Shurcliff in his original report, to my knowledge, has even speculated about the underlying mechanisms that may account for this illusion.

A phenomenon closely related to these just discussed is the fading of the experience of form that occurs when complex images are stabilized in position on the retina. Images of objects in the stimulus scene can be held rigidly positioned on a fixed retinal locus by means of an optical system such as that shown in Fig. 10-17. The stabilization results from the compensation of the optical pathways by the double reflection along the indicated optical pathway. Barring slippage of the contact lens, the image may be held virtually constant in its position on the retina by this apparatus. An alternate means of stabilizing the retinal image is to mount a tiny slide projector onto a contact lens as shown in Fig. 10-18, but this is cumbersome and does not allow as rapid interchange of stimulus materials as does the mirror arrangement.

Any stimulus scene, no matter how rich, viewed through an image-stablizing optical system quickly begins to induce perceptual anomalies similar to those produced in the ganzfeld viewing situation. Considerable portions of the visual experience simply fade away until nothing is seen and the percept finally approximates the featureless response to the ganzfeld. This phenomenon was originally described by Ratliff and Riggs (1950), and then further studies by Riggs, Ratliff, Cornsweet, and Cornsweet (1953), Pritchard, Heron, and Hebb (1960), and Evans (1965). However, by far the most comprehensive discussion of the many effects produced during stabilized image-viewing can be found in R. W. Ditch-

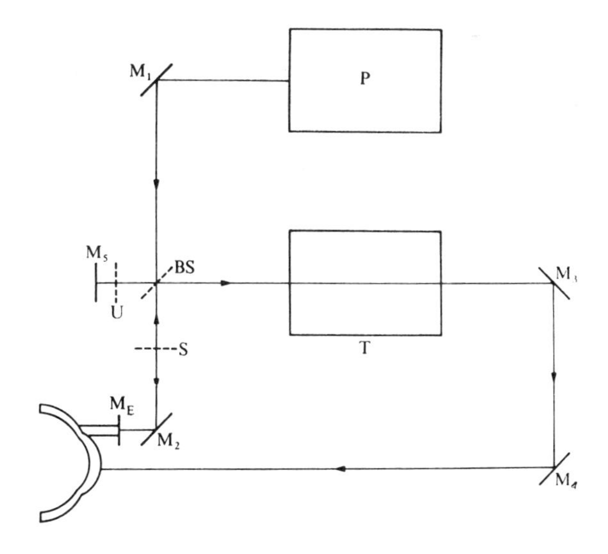

FIG. 10.17. A mirror system for stabilizing the retinal image. BS is a beam splitter. Source and target are in the unit P. Shutter S is opened to view the unstabilized image. (Figure and caption abbreviations from Ditchburn, © 1973, with the permission of the Oxford University Press.)

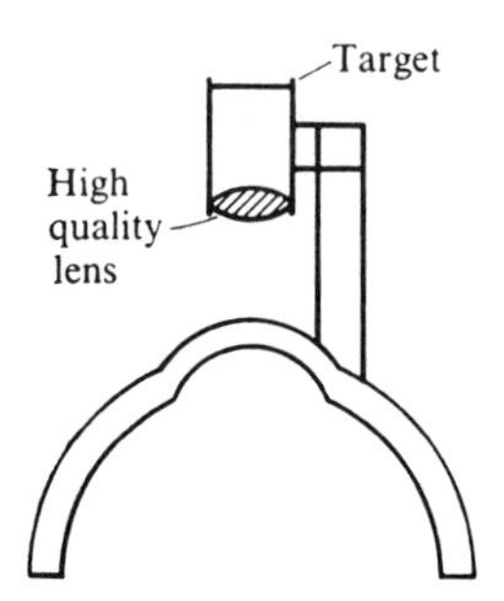

FIG. 10.18. A contact lens mounted miniature projector system for stabilizing the retinal image. (From Ditchburn, © 1973, with the permission of the Oxford University Press.)

burn's magnum opus, *Eye Movements and Visual Perception* (Ditchburn, 1973). Ditchburn (1973, pp. 132–135) lists four different types of vision that can occur under stabilized viewing conditions, which (paraphrased) are:

Type I - If exposures are short, clear and virtually normal vision occurs, even though the image is perfectly stabilized.

Type II - Under conditions of moderately good stabilization and prolonged exposure duration, a hazy, featureless gray or slightly colored field is usually perceived.

Type III - Under conditions of excellent stabilization and relatively large stimuli with low constrast and blurred contours, a total blackout of visual experience occurs in *both eyes* simultaneously.

Type IV - Under conditions of moderate stabilization, alternation of Type II gray out and Type I normal vision often occur for various parts of the visual scene.

Although Ditchburn cites many instances of experimental results that suggest a central locus for the phenomenal fading of the percepts generated by stabilized retinal images, he too is unable to propose a full answer to the question of the origin of this phenomenon. In a few places in his book he attributes these processes to ''pattern perception units (p. 309).'' In other places, he alludes to what must be interpreted as a more peripheral explanation attributing the Type II process to the failure of transmission of ''on-off'' signals that should have been sent from the retina (p. 194). Elsewhere (p. 196) the Type IV blackout is attributed to the development of a positive feedback loop in which weakened afferent signals attenuate something closer to visual ''attention.''

Although Ditchburn has amassed an abundance of data and seems committed to a single-cell-type theory to explain the fading of stabilized retinal images, in my opinion no neuroreductionistic theory of any compelling force yet exists to account for this impressive phenomenon any better than for the Ganzfeld or the Shurcliff blotch. It seems probably, however, that the fading of the stabilized retinal image is beyond the scope of any simple retinal neural fatique explanation. The main argument for this rather poorly supported presumption is that the fading does not occur in a random fashion but rather that specific meaningful subportions of the scene fade away as organized units. (Davies, 1973; Pritchard, Heron, and Hebb, 1960). For example, Fig. 10-19 shows an artist's impression of the way in which a number of different kinds of stimuli typically fade away. Admittedly, however, there is a widespread feeling of uncertainty concerning the robustness of these findings among many perceptual scientists.

In conclusion, it seems likely that the fading and instability of stabilized retinal images reflect the action of far more complex and central interpretative mechanisms than can be encompassed within any plausible single-cell or retinal-fatique model. The important phenomenological implication of the stabilized retinal image phenomenon is that movement of the stimulus image on the retina seems to be absolutely necessary to maintain the integrity of the visual experience. Without such movement there is a profound collapse of pattern and form perception.

The perceptual literature reports many other instances in which substantial changes can occur in the perceptual organization of a stimulus merely as a result of prolonged viewing. Wade (1977) lists over 30 different phenomena (see Table 10-1) in which the characteristics of some patterned stimulus have been reported to change after a relatively short period of viewing. These changes include

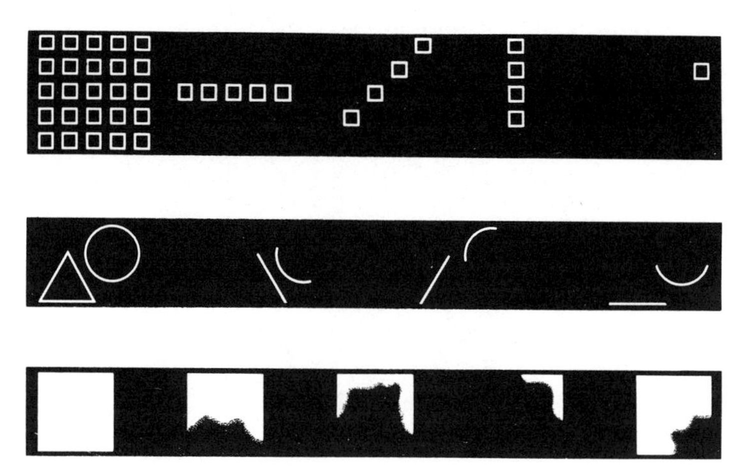

FIG. 10.19. Various ways in which stabilized retinal images can dissolve. (From Pritchard, © 1961, with the permission of Scientific American.)

TABLE 10.1
A Summary of Aftereffects Produced by Prolonged Observation of Constant Stimuli

Reference	*Pattern*	*Viewing Conditions*[a]	*Effects Reported*	*Interpretation*
Distortions				
Purkinje (1823)	grating	? binocular	lines appear wavy	overlap of image and afterimage
Brewster (1825)	grating	monocular	lines appear broken and serpentine	interference fringes on retina
Helmholtz (1860)	grating	? monocular	lines appear wavy	lines finer than retinal mosaic
Hensen (1867)	grating	? monocular	lines appear wavy and varicose	retinal irradiation
Fleischl (1883)	grating	? binocular	lines appear wavy and oscillating	eye movements
Schilder (1912)	lines, gratings, afterimages	monocular and binocular	waviness and movement	retinal irradiation
Purkinje (1825)	concentric circles	? monocular	cloudy bands radiating from centre	variations in accommodation
Helmholtz (1856)	concentric circles	? monocular	radiating and rotating spokes	asymmetry of eye (astigmatism)
Disappearances				
Troxler (1804)	peripheral shapes	monocular	shapes disappear and reappear	none
Brewster (1818)	peripheral shapes	monocular and binocular	partial and complete disappearances	none

Purkinje (1823)	peripheral shapes	monocular	shapes disappear and are replaced by moving cloudy streaks	cloudy streaks in dark field mask peripheral shapes
McDougall (1901)	centrally fixated lines	monocular	partial and complete disappearances and reappearances	binocular rivalry
Monocular rivalry				
Breese (1899)	orthogonal gratings	monocular	gratings fluctuate in clarity	none
McDougall (1901)	orthogonal lines	monocular	lines fragment or alternate in visibility	cortical inhibition
Tscherning (1904)	grid	? monocular	disappearances of parts of vertical or horizontal lines	none
Gellhorn (1928)	orthogonal line afterimages	monocular or binocular	lines tended to alternate in visibility	intracortical rivalry
Campbell and Howell (1972)	orthogonal gratings	monocular or binocular	gratings alternate in clarity	interaction between cortical channels for spatial frequency and orientation
Streaming over, and scintillation of, pattern				
Purkinje (1823)	grating	monocular	indefinite scintillation of pattern	variations in accommodation
Brewster (1825)	grating	monocular	moving, broken lines	interference fringes on retina

(continued)

TABLE 10.1 (*Continued*)

Reference	*Pattern*	*Viewing Conditions*[a]	*Effects Reported*	*Interpretation*
Hensen (1865)	grating	? monocular	lines appear beady and checkered	none
Zehfuss (1880)	sectored disc	? monocular	moving, weak light sparks	circulation of blood in retina
Pierce (1901)	grating	monocular	streaming across lines, cobwebby lattice	impuses to movement aroused by lines
Rollett (1910)	grating	monocular	black and white points moving perpendicularly to lines	electrical currents in retina
Erb and Dallenbach (1939)	grating	? binocular	streaming, random movement, zigzag bands, wavy lines, circular movement, shimmer	none
Streaming over, and scintillation of, pattern (continued)				
MacKay (1957a)	ray figure, concentric circles	monocular	moving wavy lines perpendicular to pattern (complementary image)	directional satiation and rivalry

Howard (1959)	grating	monocular	lattice obliterating pattern, foveal line afterimage	interaction between afterimage and random activity from closed eye
Welpe (1975)	grating	binocular	lattice or rhombic patterns, mostly coloured	interactions between channels for orientation, spatial frequency and colour
Aftereffect				
Purkinje (1823)	grating	monocular, then eyes closed or white field	shadowy zigzag forms moving perpendicular to lines	alternating light and shade of afterimage
Pierce (1901)	grating	binocular then black card	dust drift perpendicular to lines	impulses to movement aroused by lines
MacKay (1957a)	ray figure, concentric circles	binocular then blank field	wavy streams moving perpendicularly to lines	directional satiation
Georgeson (1976)	sine wave grating	binocular then white screen	streaming perpendicular to lines, diagonal lattice, broader and finer bands in same orientation	cortical inhibition between pattern and movement channels

From Wade, 1977a.

distortions of geometry, streaming of gratings, and brightness scintillations, but Wade also describes the phenomenon of peripheral image disappearance that was reported (Troxler, 1804) 150 years prior to the first reports of fading due to retinal stabilization. All of the phenomena discussed in Wade's review occur in the absence of any explicit attempt to stabilize, desaturate, or lower the contrast of the stimuli.

Although all of the perceptual experiences described in this section are enjoyable demonstrations in their own right, the major issue is to what may the ganzfeld phenomenon, the stabilized retinal image, and these other less well-known fading and disorganizing experiences be attributed? And as a corollary, is there a common explanation for all of them? Unfortunately, there is little possibility of a neat answer to these questions emerging in the near future. Like other Level 3 phenomena, it is my judgment, based on what is admittedly a paucity of solid data, that the central nervous system simply turns off the significantion of the stimulus in some way when highly redundant stimuli are presented to the eyes. In some respects, this ''turnoff'' seems to be independent of peripheral communication processes, and like binocular rivalry (discussed later in this chapter) and stereoscopic fusion (discussed in Chapter 11) it is a function of central, interpretive, and constructive mechanisms that are beyond our ken at the present time.

Apparently the most important thing we can learn from these phenomena is that, whatever the underlying mechanism, it is necessary for the nervous system to be stimulated with both time- and space-varying stimulus patterns to maintain normal function; constant simuli quickly become ineffective and lose their perceptual significance. One adaptive function of the statistical variability inherent in textured patterns may be to provide a modicum of stimulus variability in the spatial domain. Miniature eye movements (microsaccades), on the other hand, may be a corresponding means of providing stimulus variability in the temporal domain. That the two domains are closely related is self-evident. Spatial variability (textured grain) can be converted to temporal variability as a result of the microsaccades. Some perceptual scientists have raised the possibility that the constant small eye movements (microsaccades) may play an important role in maintaining vision in exactly this manner when low contrast and poorly detailed stimuli are presented.

In sum, we are at the very beginning of the path towards achieving any understanding of the processes that underlie regional segregation as well as the subsequent failure of segregation exhibited in the various fading phenomena. The strong dependence on the molar or statistical properties of the entire pattern make it clear, however, that whatever processing is done is the result of the action of many neurons, probably interconnected into a complex net—a net of such complexity that any reductionistic analysis is beyond reasonable expectations at the present time.

C. FIGURAL ORGANIZATION

In the previous section I considered those processes that seemed to be involved in the initial segregation of the subregions of the visual scene into separate fields and areas. Once these primitive operations have been performed the organization of the visual scene can develop further. The ecologically or symbolically significant portions of the scene can be identified and emphasized in the visual experience while background and environmentally irrelevant aspects can, at the same time, be de-emphasized. The mechanisms that account for the discrimination of a figure from a ground, though more complex than anything we have spoken of so far, still seem to depend on processes that are as automatic and immediate as any of the others previosuly discussed; it takes no greater attentional effort to achieve these perceptual organizations than it did to discriminate between two regions of a stimulus field. Nevertheless, the phenomena to which I now turn are not totally passive network responses to the stimulus configuration. In almost all of the instances that I discuss in this section various aspects of the stimuli are organized by processes that require some kind of preattentive, constructionistic, or rationalistic *interpretation* of the meaning of the parts of the stimulus in a way that transcends the information provided by its physical dimensions. What is to be perceived as the salient foreground, or figure, and what is to be perceived as the irrelevant background, or ground, is not totally explicable in terms of the properties of the stimulus. As we shall see, figure–ground relationships are highly susceptible to reversal in situations in which the relevant cues may be ambiguous.

The central point to be made in introducing this section, therefore, is that the processes that I describe here are the result not only of the stimulus information but also of the central state of the organism. We organize stimuli into figures and grounds not only because of any cues for organization that are implicit in the stimulus or in the peripheral mechanisms but also as a result of central processes of great complexity. Figure and ground are not solely characteristics of stimuli but of the observer's mind. In general, therefore, we shall see that the relationships between stimuli and perceptual responses become continuously less veridical as we proceed through the discussion. In this section I am considering the relatively well-known phenomena involved in the establishment of figure–ground relations, extrapolation and interpolation of incomplete figures, and the interpretation of those currently popular curiosities called "impossible figures."

1. Figure–Ground Organization

Following the segregation of subregions that occurs when any complex scene is presented to an observer, there is a more or less immediate separation of the salient and perceptually significant parts of the stimulus from the irrelevant or insignificant parts. The amount of time required to achieve this functional separation depends on such a wide variety of stimulus and observer factors that it is not possible to give a more precise estimate of exactly what "more or less immediate" means. Clearly, however, in optimal situations figure–ground organization can occur in as little as a 10th of a second. Sperling's (1963) study, extensively discussed on p. 520, makes it clear that the organization of alphabetic characters can occur in at least this brief an interval.

The salient part of a stimulus—the figure—is perceptually distinguished from the insignificant part—the ground—in several ways. Most noticeable is that the figure is more clearly organized in terms of outlines and detail than is the ground in all but the most ambiguous cases. The internal microstructure of the figure is also clearer than that of the ground. In fact, the ground may appear as a more or less blurred and featureless region in a way that cannot be accounted for in terms of the physics of the retinal projection. Though figures are usually smaller and more central than grounds, this is not an absolute criterion; ambiguous figures, such as the famous Rubin vases shown in Fig. 10-20, may induce reversals of the figure–ground organization in such a way that the "figure" may very often be the more peripheral and larger of the two regions. This demonstration also makes it clear that there is no absolute relationship between foveal locus and the resulting figure–ground organization even though we do tend to fixate and attend to the figure more than to the ground.

Another major attribute of the figure is that it usually appears to be closer to the observer than does the ground. This apparent depth difference is often also associated with a marked brightness difference (the figure appears brighter than

FIG. 10.20. The rubin vase/face stimulus.

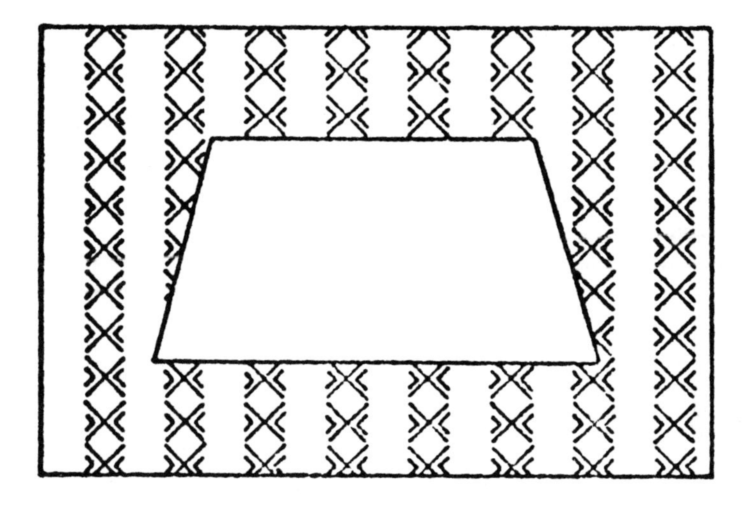

FIG. 10.21. A stimulus producing moving phantom motion through the central rectangle when the vertical columns of x's move horizontally. (Courtesy of Dr. Naomi Weisstein of the State University of New York at Buffalo.)

the ground) in much the same way that a subjective surface (see Fig. 10-34) appears to be both brighter and closer than its surround.

A major perceptual feature of the ground is that it possesses the appearance of being continuous (i.e., it appears to extend "in back of" the figure and over the edges of the scene). The figure, on the other hand, usually is perceived to have a limited spatial extent. I have elsewhere noted how powerful this perceived continuity of the background can be when I described Naomi Weisstein's (1970) experiment in which she showed that an implied "background" grating could actually inhibit the detection of test gratings in much the same way, if not to the same extent, that a real grating could. (See Uttal, 1973, p. 455.)

In a similar vein, Weisstein, Maguire, and Berbaum (1977), among others, have shown that there may be a continuity of the apparent motion of objects passing through a region that is obstructed by some intervening object as shown in Fig. 10-21. There may also be an aftereffect corresponding to the nonexistent moving phantoms in this stimulus situation. Weisstein and her collaborators have shown that if a small stationary grating of black and white stripes is presented in the obstructed region after viewing the illusory motion, the lines of this grating will appear to move in a direction opposite to that of the phantom. Clearly the perceptually implied "in back of" status of the ground can have powerful perceptual effects of its own, even in the absence of the associated real physical stimulus itself.

A modest amount of experimental effort has gone into identifying the factors that determine which part of a stimulus scene will appear as figure and which will appear as ground. The following list summarizes some of this research and identifies a few of the influential factors. However, it is important for the reader to remember that these "rules" only reflect tendencies and proclivities. It is entirely possible for an observer to reconfigure a visual scene by an attentive effort, or for one factor to be overridden by another. In general, no single stimulus factor totally determines or even dominates figure-ground organization. However, in the absence of specific instructions and when all other factors are held constant, most observers report that their figure–ground segregation occurs in accord with the following general rules:

1. If two portions of the scene are of different sizes, the smaller one tends to be seen as the figure.

2. If the two regions are of different degrees of figural goodness (see the definition of goodness presented later in this chapter), the better figure tends to be seen as figure. Symmetry, one example of figural goodness, leads to the selection of a symmetrical, in preference to an unsymmetrical, region as the figure in an unambiguous situation, as shown in Fig. 10-22.

3. If one portion of a scene encloses or surrounds another portion, the enclosed region tends to be perceived as the figure.

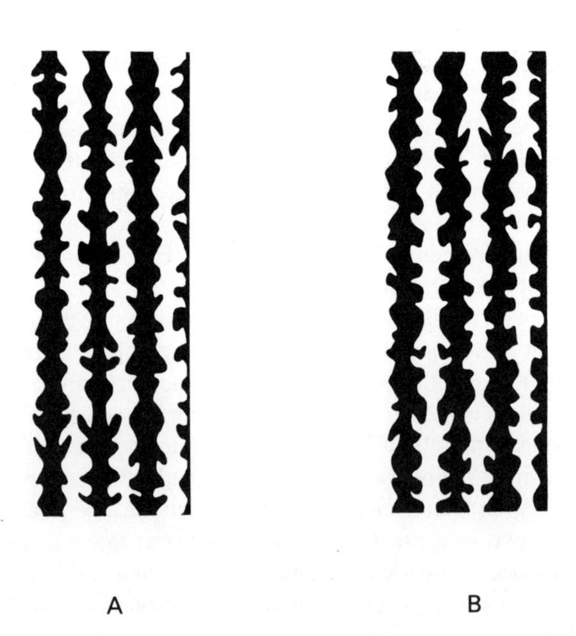

FIG. 10.22. Symmetrical (A) and nonsymmetrical (B) Rubin type figures displaying the tendency for symmetrical patterns to be seen as figure in preference to nonsymmetrical figures. (From Rock, © 1975, with the permission of the Macmillan Publishing Company.)

4. Portions of a stimulus that are aligned along the horizontal or vertical axis tend to be seen as figure more often than parts aligned obliquely.

5. If two regions of a scene differ in their texture or degree of blur, then the one that is sharper or more regular tends to be seen as the figure.

6. If two otherwise equal regions of a scene intersect in such a way that one region is concave and the other convex, the convex region is more often seen as the figure.

These rules for figure-ground segregation have been accepted by most perceptual scientists in recent years. However, there is actually little direct experimental evidence to support these more or less anecdotal principles. These rules, which were originally formulated in the pioneering work of Rubin (1921), have nevertheless become widely accepted perceptual folklore. I must reiterate that these principles are only tendencies and the observer's set and expectations (traditionally referred to as his ''einstellung'') may play an even more important role in determining figure–ground organization. Such observer factors as individual differences, sex, motivation, previous experience, as well as expectation have all also been shown to contribute to figure–ground organization. Such observer factors as individual differences, sex, motivation, previous experience, as well as expectation have all also been shown to contribute to figure–ground organization. A good review of the contribution of such observer variables to the figure–ground organizational process is given by Zusne (1970) in his monumental review of form perception. So little research on figure–ground organization has been done since that date that his review is reasonably current.

Given that the tendency to form figure–ground organizational relationships is governed by rules that are only approximately valid and that the process is affected by so many factors internal to the observer, it is obvious that there will be many instances in which the figure–ground relations are susceptible to reversal. Reversal will be especially evident in those situations in which the individual cues are ambiguous or are in conflict with other cues in other parts of the visual scene. At the most primitive level, a scene such as that shown in Fig. 10-23 is totally ambiguous; either side of this ''ying–yang'' could be perceived as the figure. More complicated stimuli can also be equally ambiguous with regard to figure-ground relations, as shown in Fig. 10-24—another of the masterpiece etchings of the maestro of visual illusions, Maurits C. Escher (1898–1971).

In spite of the great interest in, and the many demonstrations of, figure–ground organization, one searches the visual literature in vain for a satisfying theoretical explanation of this basic perceptual process. Virtually all research is, at best, barely descriptive; researchers are prone to assert only that their findings ''may help to understand the factors involved'' when pressed for theoretical details. Nor is there any relief from this difficulty to be found in the classic Gestalt approach to the figure–ground problem, as exemplified in the writing of Kohler (1929/1947) or Rubin (1921). Though replete with laws, rules, and

FIG. 10.23. The ying-yang reversible figure.

demonstrations, neither of these giants of Gestalt psychology had much to say about underlying mechanisms. More modern invocations of such mechanisms as ocular convergence and accommodation by such workers as Hochberg (1971) are hardly satisfying when one considers that the figure and ground, even though they may appear to be in different depths, are actually at the same depth in the stimulus plane.

FIG. 10.24. A reversible figure from the pen of the extraordinary graphic artist, Maurits Escher.

Thus, though profoundly interesting, studies of the principles of figure-ground organization, like those of so many other high-level perceptual processes, have not fulfilled their promise as a guide to understanding the underlying *mechanisms* of visual perception. Studies of these phenomena are virtually non-reductionistic. Nevertheless it is clear that, prior to the perceptual organization of the details of individual forms, segregation of subregions is an essential process for the specification of what the forms are. These processes must be appreciated and described, if not analyzed in reductionistic terms, for progress to be made in this field.

2. The Gestalt Rules of Grouping: Masking of the *Fifth* Kind

Once the subregions of a stimulus figure have been segregated and the figure-ground relationships established, it seems likely that the next step in the organization of the scene should be the organization of the various components of the figure into pattern-significant groupings. By grouping I am referring to the functional clustering by the observer of a subset of figural components so that they are perceived as "belonging" together. The belongingness may be expressed either in terms of the static or dynamic aspects of the perceptual response. It is in this regard that, once again, we are confronted with a further reminder of the fact that the organization of the stimulus is an active mental process of the observer and not a property of the stimulus. Though various stimulus factors, as we soon see, may suggest an order and thus may influence the observer's response to a multicomponent pattern, the grouping of components like those shown in Fig. 10-25 into a meaningful perceptual structure is purely a psychological action.

In emphasizing the observer's role in grouping, I am deviating considerably from the emphasis made by Gestalt psychologists. Their codification of the rules, laws, or principles of grouping mainly emphasized stimulus properties. Never-

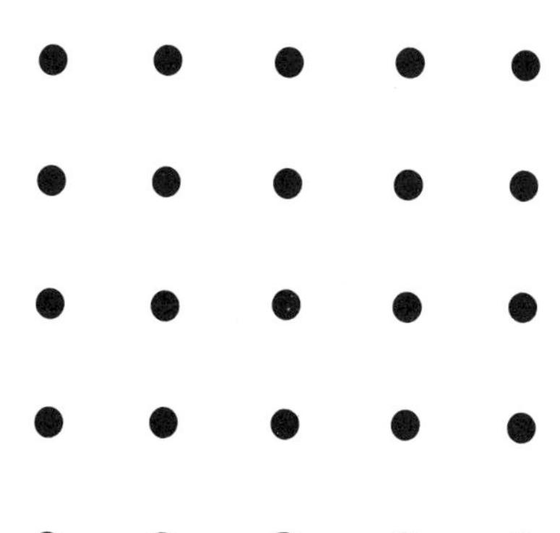

FIG. 10.25. A sample of an ambiguously grouped figure that may be grouped in many different ways.

theless, this difference in emphasis I believe is a valid one. The difference is subtle, but it is important. The global attributes of a stimulus assume perceptual and functional reality only in terms of the processes carried out in the observer.

The rules of grouping the figural components of a complex scene have been a matter of concern to the Gestalt psychologists since the inception of their school of psychological theory. Study of the Gestalt "rules of grouping" was the keystone around which most of the rest of their wholistic theory was itself organized. The word *Gestalt* itself is virtually synonymous with the terms *pattern, form,* or *group*. An explicit search for the rules of grouping was, therefore, an important part of Gestalt psychology's research program and has been one of its most lasting contributions. Eleven main rules, first explicitly enunciated by Max Werthheimer (1923), governing the perceptual grouping of the elements of a multielement display, are usually tabulated. Of these, ten refer to influential properties of the stimulus pattern, and the eleventh to an internal state of the observer: The first ten are:

1. The rule of spatial proximity: All other things being equal, elements of a pattern that are close together in space tend to be grouped together.
2. The rule of temporal proximity: All other things being equal, elements of a pattern that occur close together in time tend to be grouped together.
3. The rule of similarity: All other things being equal, elements of a pattern that are geometrically similar tend to be grouped together.
4. The rule of continuity: All other things being equal, elements of a pattern that represent a continuation of a pattern defined by the organization of other elements of the pattern tend to be grouped with those other elements.
5. The rule of closure: All other things being equal, elements that form a closed pattern (i.e., a pattern without discontinuous boundaries) tend to be grouped together.
6. The rule of uniform density: All other things being equal, elements of a pattern that are distributed with equal spacing tend to be grouped together better than irregularly spaced elements.[4]
7. The rule of common fate: All other things being equal, elements of a dynamic pattern that are moving in the same direction and at the same velocity tend to be grouped together.
8. The rule of symmetry: All other things being equal, the elements of a pattern that form a symmertrical form will be grouped together.
9. The rule of common orientation: All other things being equal, elements sharing a common orientation (i.e., vertical, horizontal, oblique) tend to be grouped together.

---

[4]The relationship between this rule of uniform density and my own work on an autocorrelational analysis (Uttal, 1975a, and see pp. 711 and 775 of this book) should not be overlooked. The uniform density rule implies a special sensitivity to periodically spaced elements in exactly the same way as does the autocorrelation theory.

10. The rule of pragnanz: All other things being equal, the elements of a pattern that produce the "best" figure (the figure with the highest degree of "goodness" or minimum amount of "structural stress") tend to be grouped together.

Pragnanz is, as so many others have noted, a terribly difficult term to translate from the language (German) and, perhaps more important, from the linguistic philosophy in which it was originally formulated by Koffka (1935). In an attempt to catch the flavor of this word, we can only say that the Gestalt psychologists believed that each stimulus figure has inherent in it one best form that was the easiest for the observer to organize. Thus, an equilateral arrangement of three dots displays the highest degree of "pragnanz" for a triangle, even though it could be forced or perceptually stressed to represent three points on a circle or other curve. Pragnanz has also been defined as the minimally complex figure into which a pattern can be organized. In that context, it has close denotative relations with such terms as entropy and information. However, to this date, no one has yet been able to propose a quantitative metric for pragnanz; the use of this word is still highly qualitative and somewhat arbitrary. The important thing about this concept is that the Gestalists assumed that it was a property of the stimulus whereas modern though is more likely to attribute it either to the properties and characteristics of the observer or to an "interaction" between the stimulus and the observer.[5]

All of the ten laws, principles, or rules of grouping and figural organization that I have mentioned so far are characteristics of the stimulus scene or, more properly, of the observer's response to those characteristics. Each can be illustrated by a drawing (with the exception of rules 2 and 7, which would require a motion picture, and 10, which is a little too subtle a concept to be depicted in a single picture). On the other hand, the eleventh rule of grouping is a general property of the observer and cannot be depicted in any kind of a pictorial representation:

11. The rule of einstellung: All other things being equal, elements of a pattern will be grouped in accord with the "objective" set (einstellung) of the observer. If the observer has been preconditioned to expect a triangle, when three dots are presented, he is indeed more likely to see a triangle; and if he has been preconditioned to see a bear in an astral constellation, the bear is more likely to be apparent than any other form. (This, of course, was the Gestaltists only bow to

[5]The idea of interaction between stimulus and observer is an intrinsic part of J. J. Gibson's ecological optics and transactional functionalism. It is also a part of the perceptual philosophies of such current notables as Joseph Lappin, Michael Turvey, and Robert Shaw. Interaction implies (to me) a two-way flow of information between the observer and the observed. However I am unable to discern any effect in the macroscopic world of the observation on the observed distal stimulus object. My personal judgment, therefore, is that the putative interaction is but another metaphor and that the "action" is mainly on the monodirectionally flowing afferent information.

the experiential and attentional factors that now dominate thinking about perceptual grouping.)

All of these rules of grouping interact strongly with each other, and it is by no means certain at this point which would dominate in any particular stimulus scene in which conflicting rules were brought into play. Traditional Gestalt psychology never embarked on a programmatic attack on the myriad problems posed by conflict or ambiguity with respect to the different rules. What they did provide, instead, was an extensive listing of what they observed to be the principles of perceptual organization among which are included the grouping laws I have mentioned. In what is now considered to be a classic paper, Harry Helson (1933) listed over 100 of these Gestalt principles—an encyclopedia of discriptive wisdom that has yet to be associated with any integrative theoretical metastructure or synthesized into a more concentrated set of of more general principles.

In recent years a few investigators have, however, begun to follow up the important line of research that concerns the relative dominance of the grouping rules. The most energetic effort to study the interactions of the different factors that contribute to grouping has come from the laboratory of Julian Hochberg. In a pair of studies (Hochberg & Hardy, 1960; Hochberg & Silverstein, 1956) he and his co-workers found that there was a compensatory interaction between the luminance of the individual elements of a rectangular array of small squares (similarity) and the distance between the rows and columns (proximity). As the brightness of a single row of squares increased with respect to their neighbors, the spacing between the columns had to decrease to maintain a column, as opposed to a row, pattern of perceived organization. Conversely, if the spacing increased between the rows, the squares in the columns had to be brightened to maintain perceived columnar organization. Figure 10-26 shows some of the results of this interesting experiment.

Jacob Beck (1966), on the other hand, has compared the effects on grouping patterned textures of element orientation and element similarity. His results present clear evidence for the dominance of orientation over similarity in determining the perceptual organization of the pattern he used.

One of the few other modern examples of a study of the interactions of the grouping rules is Yamada and Oyama's (1972) report of the relative effectiveness of spatial and temporal proximity. They studied the grouping of an array of 16 dots arranged with a constant horizontal spacing but with a vertical spacing that varied from trial to trial. The dots were presented in two sequential tachistoscopic exposures—the first and third columns in the first exposure, and the second and fourth columns in the second exposure. Yamada and Oyama thus set up a situation in which spatial proximity (vertical spacing) competed with temporal asynchrony in the definition of either row or column organization. They found that the spatial cue dominated up to a 40 msec interval between the two exposures, but there was a progressive reduction in the proportion of the trials that were

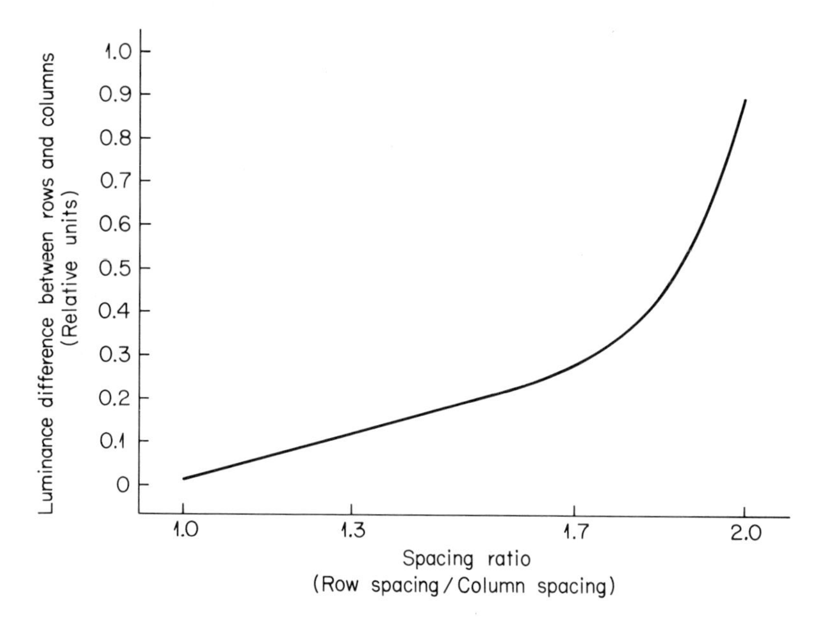

FIG. 10.26. The effect of row and column spacing on the grouping of stimulus elements. (Plotted from data collected by Hochberg and Hardy, 1960.)

reported to be horizontally grouped as the interval increased. The function relating the interval between the two exposures and the proportion of horizontal row groupings reported was, however, very much dependent upon the nature of the dots. If the "dots" were unfilled circles, then the distance between them did not matter, but if they were luminous spots on a black background, then spacing effects were considerable. Yamada and Oyama's experiment thus both demonstrates an interaction between spatial and temporal propinquity and shows that the crossover from dominance by spatial factors to dominance by temporal factors is dependent on such other factors as the type of pattern element (similarity). This type of research, though rare, is highly useful in establishing the nature of the interaction between the various influences on perceptual grouping and the relative power of each influence.

Oyama (1961) has also provided important data in an earlier study of the effect of dot spacing per se on perceptual grouping. This study is particularly significant because it is one of the few actually to quantify the impact of any individual factor on the grouping process as opposed to a qualitative demonstration. In Oyama's experiment, observers were asked to report the occurrence of grouping dots into perceived horizontal rows or vertical columns for two series of stimuli. In the first series, the horizontal spacing between columns of dots was kept constant and the vertical spacing varied; in the second, the situation was reversed—the vertical spacing was kept constant and the horizontal varied. The independent variable in this experiment—distance—was plotted as the logarithm of the ratios of the variable horizontal or vertical distance and the constant distance along the orthogonal axis. The dependent variable was the ratio of the observation time during which the perceived organization was in the direction of the variable dimension and the time during which they were perceived in the orthogonal direction in which spacing was held constant.

Figure 10-27 shows the results of this experiment. The major finding is the highly linear (on a log–log scale) relationship between the direction of perceived organization and the interstimulus spacing. Indeed, Oyama suggested that these data were well fit by a power function with a very steep negative slope (−2.88). The major implication of this unusually quantitative result is the suggestion that grouping is not just generally, but in fact exquisitely sensitive to spacing. The overall magnitude of the effect was also quite large—only a relatively small change in the ratio of the variable and constant dot separations was required to produce a thousandfold change in the proportion of observation time committed to one or the other mode of perceptual grouping.

Oyama's quantitative results have considerably more significance than the usual qualitative demonstration of the effect of spacing on grouping. These findings show that the Gestalt psychologists (and modern workers of the same

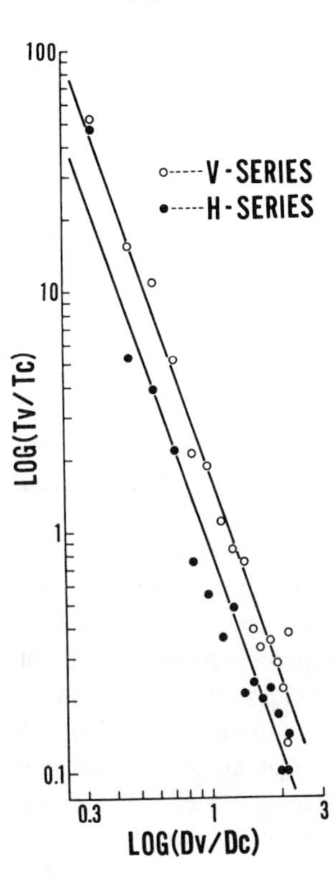

FIG. 10.27. The ratio of the time that a figure was grouped in the variable direction (T_v) compared to the time it was grouped in the constant spacing direction. (Reprinted with permission of Author and Publisher from: Oyama, T. Perceptual grouping as a function of proximity. *Perceptual and Motor Skills*, 1961, *13*, 305–306, Figure 1.)

persuasion) were dealing with phenomena that were as inherently regular and quantifiable as any other in the repertoire of perceptual science. It is especially disappointing from this point of view that there should have been no continuing systematic effort to establish programmatically either the magnitude or the priority of the relationships between the other stimulus factors in this important subarea of perceptual research.

In recent years, the emphasis in the study of these rules of perceptual organization has changed dramatically. The current stress is on how to use them as independent variables rather than to measure them as dependent variables. The goal in the most modern research is usually to determine the effect of grouping on a task such as target detection or memory rather than to study the factors that influence grouping. A general outcome of this emphasis has been to highlight further the fact that simple feature-detection models are not, in general, adequate as models of target-detection behavior and to show that the influence of configurational or organizational factors on memory and detection is even more powerful than the influence of local features.

The theory tested in many such studies has been the specific feature-detection model proposed by such workers as Estes (1972, 1974) and Bjork and Murray (1977). The general philosophy expressed by these psychologists is that there are independent channels (conveying feature-specific information) that interact to account for the masking effects of letterlike stimuli[6] on each other. Samples of the type of stimuli typically used are shown in Fig. 10-28. I refer to this type of masking paradigm as masking of the fifth kind—that is, a reduction in visibility produced by the entanglement of an element of a target pattern in a Gestalt or grouped pattern in a way that reduces the probability of its being detected or recognized as an independent element.

The major counterargument to the Estes, Bjork, and Murray feature-sensitive channel theory, which clearly is of a genre similar to those that I criticized in the previous chapter, has been the demonstration that the Gestalt configurational effects, which are not well accounted for in such theories, are in fact dominant in modulating the detection of letters in this kind of experiment. Such an argument has been presented by Banks, Bodinger, and Illige (1974); Banks and Prinzmetal (1976); and Prinzmetal and Banks (1977). In the first of these papers, Banks and his colleagues (1974) reported that increasing the separation between a target *T* letter and a set of masking *F* letters increased the detectability of the target by perceptually extracting it from a group in which it had been embedded. This

[6]There is good evidence to support the idea that letter masking of this type and dot masking are not due to the same underlying processes. I (Uttal, 1975a) have shown minimal effect of figural goodness on random dot pattern masking and Banks and Prinzmetal (1976) and Prinzmetal and Banks (1977) have shown strong effects of goodness on letter-masking situations of the type referred to here. On this basis I consider these two phenomena to be masking of different kinds and to represent an even further subdivision of the masking taxonomy.

FIRST DISPLAY
(PREMASK)

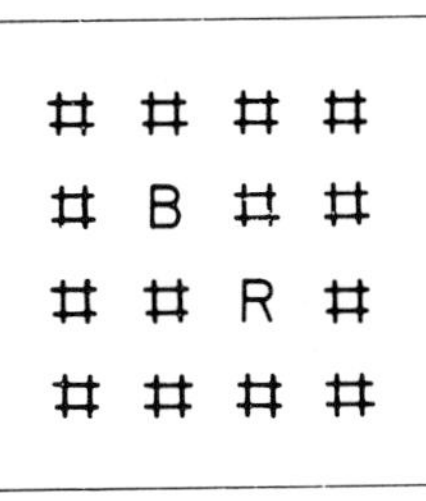

SECOND DISPLAY
(STIMULUS)

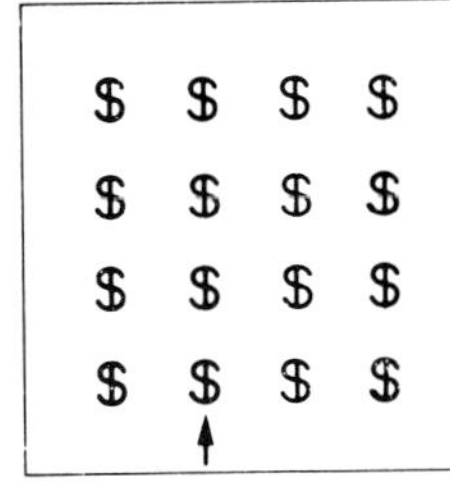

THIRD DISPLAY
(POSTMASK and CUE)

FIG. 10.28. The sequence of stimuli presented in a single trial in Bjork and Murray's experiment. (From Bjork and Murray, © 1977, with the permission of the American Psychological Association.)

experiment was well controlled for lateral interaction effects; the authors thus felt confident in attributing the release-from-masking effect purely to the reduction of a Gestaltlike proximity factor rather than to a reduced spatial interaction between any putative feature sensitive channels.

In the second of these studies, Banks and Prinzmetal showed that the grouping of the elements in the target and the mask strongly affect both the speed and accuracy with which a target letter could be detected and recognized. If the stimulus pattern was organized so that the target letter was a part of a Gestalt or perceived grouping that included the noise characters, then the target letter was detected less well than when it was separated from the group. This reduction in visibility of the target occurred even when the number of masking letters was larger in the well-grouped stimulus than in the poorly grouped condition, as shown in Fig. 10-29A and B, respectively.

In the third study, Prinzmetal and Banks (1977) discovered that a target character could be hidden by being made a perceptual part of a pattern that exhibited good continuity, as shown in Fig. 10-30A. The target letter *F* in this case is far less easily detected when it is at the end of a line of characters (of which it becomes a perceptual part) than when it is placed alongside the line of

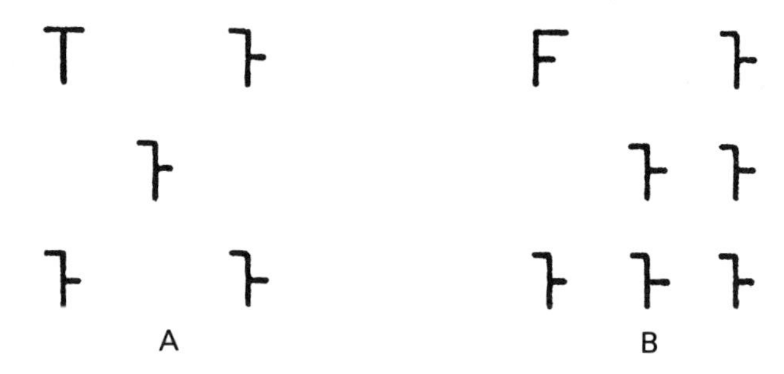

FIG. 10.29. (A) An example of a stimulus in a "gestalt" masking trial. (B) An example of a stimulus with a larger number of masking characters. (From Banks and Prinzmetal, © 1976, with permission of The Psychonomics Journals, Inc.)

masking characters. This result is so robust that it holds even when the latter discontinuous positioning would bring the target into closer proximity to a larger number of masking characters (as shown in Fig. 10-30B) than when it was at the end of the line.

The important point made by three of these experiments is that the global configuration of the stimulus exerts a powerful, if not dominating, effect even on such processes as target detection, which are often considered only in terms of the details of their local geometry. From my perspective, there is no way that such phenomena can be satisfactorily attributed to the function of hypothetical "channels" or "feature detectors" in the way that the Estes, Bjork, and Murray theories attempt.

The masking of characters by characters, as described in the experiments I have just discussed, is not the only way in which powerful configurational effects, akin to the Gestalt factors, on target detection can be demonstrated. In another kind of experiment, Weisstein and Harris (1974), Williams and Weiss-

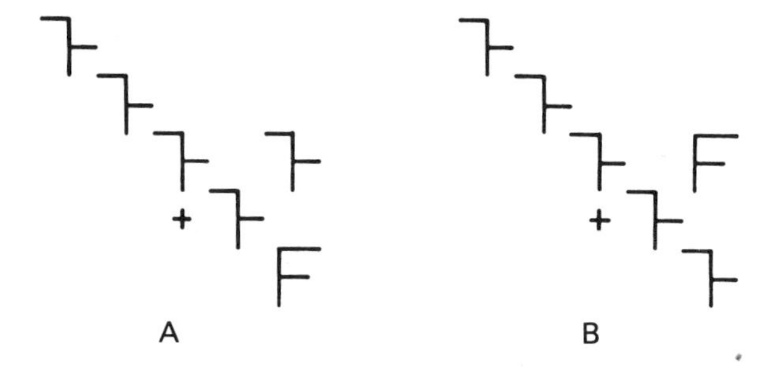

FIG. 10.30. An example of a situation in which a target letter might become less detectable if it is part of a "group" (A) than when it is isolated (B), even though the spatial relations of the latter case bring the target into greater proximity with the elements of the mask. (From Prinzmetal and Banks, © 1977, with the permission of The Psychonomics Journals, Inc.)

tein (1978), McClelland and Miller (1979) have all demonstrated a similar configurational impact on the detection and recognition of straight-line segments. The observer's task in Weisstein and Harris' study, for example, was to report which one of four straight-line segments (as shown in Fig. 10-31A) had been tachistoscopically presented. The lines could be flashed separately or as parts of patterns that had "good" organizational properties (as shown in Fig. 10-31B). Control stimuli, made up of the same number of adjacent straight-line segments but in less well-ordered patterns, made it clear that this was not just an effect of the additional lines, but truly one of "object" (or Gestalt) superiority of the organized pattern over the disorganized ones.

As powerful and well substantiated as are the organizational influences on perception, it is disappointing to note that, beyond the Gestaltist's "rules," there are few modern metatheories of perceptual grouping. Perhaps the most interesting approach to what is actually such a theory of grouping is presented, incorrectly I believe, in an entirely different context. I am referring here to the work on the "interpolation" of dotted contours reported by T. M. Caelli and his colleagues at the University of Melbourne. This work (Caelli, Preston, & Howell, 1978; Caelli & Umansky, 1976) also provides an interesting set of psychophysical data concerning completion and closure processes.

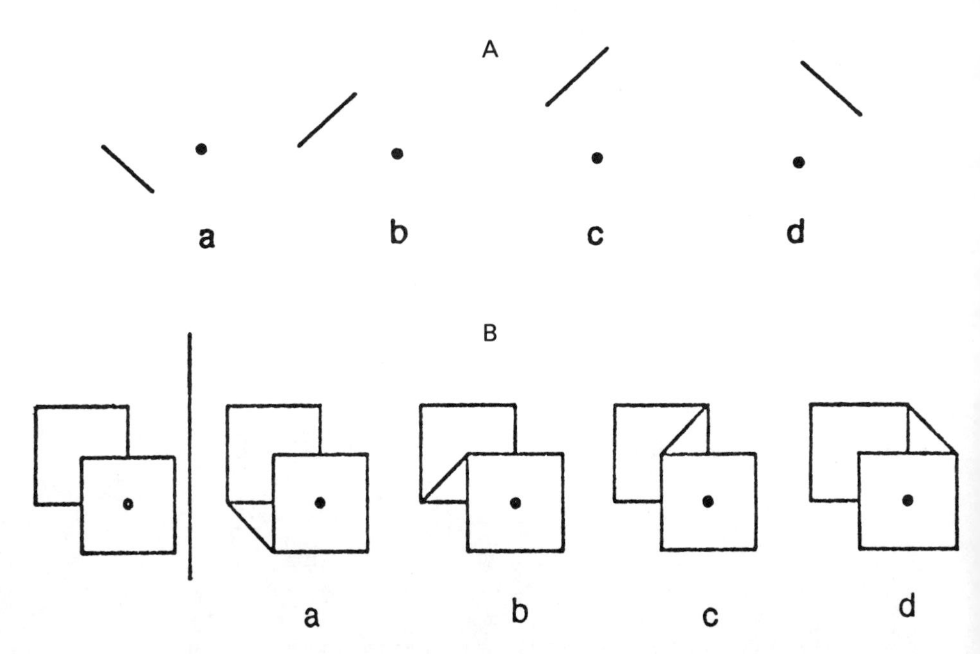

FIG. 10.31. (A) Sample of the line segments used as targets in the Weisstein and Harris experiment. (B) The same line embedded in a spatial context. (From Weisstein and Harris, © 1974, with the permission of the American Association for the Advancement of Science.)

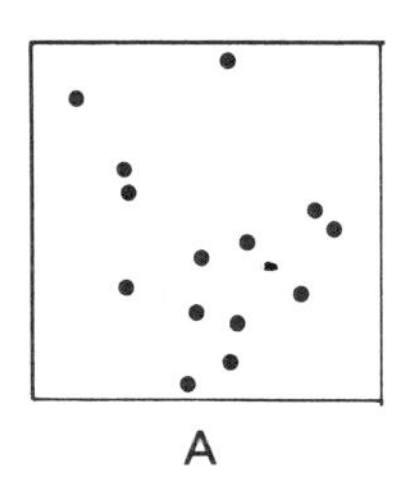

FIG. 10.32. (A) A sample of the stimuli used in the Caelli, Preston, and Howell experiment. (B) The tangent vectors purported to be computed by the visual system. (From Caelli, Preston, and Howell © 1978, with the permission of Pergamon Press.)

Before I begin this discussion, I should note that Caelli may well feel that I am misplacing his experiments and theory in my taxonomy. As I understand his work, he suggests that his data describe the emergence of percepts of continuous contours from discontinuous stimuli as a result of interpolative processes. However I maintain that the work of Caelli and his colleagues does not, in fact, involve the perception of *continuous contours* but rather the *perceptual grouping* of discrete points better described as a constellation of those points. To make this criticism clearer, consider the experimental design. In Caelli, Preston, and Howell's experiments (1978, p. 728), the observer is typically asked to: "Join up the dots (with a pencil on a paper test sheet) which correspond to the contours or shapes which spontaneously appeared when looking at each display." One of their typical displays is shown in Fig. 10-32A.

The point of my criticism is that both the response and the instructions in this experiment are actually ambiguous. The observer probably does not actually *see* continuous contours, nor does any part of the task or the response delve into the issue of continuity or discontinuity. Rather, the observer is more likely to be seeing groupings of dots akin to a stellar constellation without the awareness of continuous contours suggested in Caelli's interpretation of the findings. In other words, the observer is *not* interpolating between the dots. Instead, he is organizing and grouping them in much the same way as in any of the other Gestalt-type phenomena I have just described. The perceived patterns are still discontinuous, however, and not completed in the same way as in the closure phenomena discussed later in this section.

Caelli's mathematical theory, on the other hand, which is based upon the development of tangent vector fields determined by the spatial positions of the dots, does provide one of the few good descriptions of how dots might interact in visual (as opposed to physical or neural) space to produce organized patterns. The tangent vector in Caelli's theory is a mathematical construct that describes possible perceptual interactions among the components of a dotted stimulus. Figure 10-32B, for example, shows the tangent vector field associated with the stimulus that I previously presented in Fig. 10-32A. These vectors are formed, according to Caelli's theory, primarily as a result of a summation of the interdot interactions that are most heavily, but not exclusively, influenced by the distances between pairs of the dots. Thus the vectors associated with widely separated dots will be very small, whereas those associated with closely spaced dots will tend to be both longer and, most important, aligned along the major organizational axis defined by the stimulus. Caelli thus is asserting that these vectors are not solely depedent on the local distance between pairs of dots but, because the distance between many pairs of dots is taken into account in defining the vector, also on the global organization of the pattern.

Caelli's "vectors" effectively describe "figural forces" directly comparable to Pragnanz or proximity that are known to affect grouping, but there is little basis for his assertion that these vectors themselves come into awareness in the form of continuous contours. What he has done is to sharpen our language and to provide a more formal description of the Gestalt ideas. We also must not forget, however, that Caelli's vectors in no sense should be considered to be actual properties of the stimulus. Instead they describe the outcome of interactive processes in the brain. Whether these processes reflect the function of local neural interactions in the visual cortex or more subtle symbolic interactions of higher perceptual levels is moot at the present time. But my intuition tells me that the latter language is probably more appropriate.

3. Interpretive Processes

In the preceding sections I have dealt with the various ways by which the perceptual system responds to stimuli that are relatively well defined and unambiguous. The perceptual responses to these stimuli are analogous to those that could be generated by some ideal automaton. In that discussion it was often implicit that it was against such an automaton that a human observer was compared and evaluated. There are, however, many other situations in visual perception in which the stimuli are incomplete or ambiguous rather than definitive of a unique perceptual response. In those cases the percept depends to a much more substantial degree on the interpretations that the observer, as an active, inferential agent, may place on the incomplete or ambiguous stimuli. In some cases, the perceptual process may actually fill in lacunae and gaps in an incomplete stimulus so that the observer perceives a physically incomplete stimulus to be complete. In some cases, the resulting interpretation may not be stable but may periodically alternate between equally plausible perceptual constructions.

Demonstrations of such figural reversals and completions have been a popular part of any discussion of visual perception for many years. These demonstrations, however, play a much more important role in the theory of perceptual science than simply as parlor games or examples of the virtuosity of the human mind in elementary textbooks. The major theoretical impact of these illusions of completion, reversibility, extrapolation, or alternative perceptual constructs is that they collectively reflect the ubiquity of the constructionistic role played by the higher levels of the visual nervous system on what may seem to be relatively primitive and automatic phenomena. These interpretive illusions, perhaps better than any other artifact of perceptual science, illustrate the need for the neorationalistic or constructionistic component in any metatheory of perception. In the most graphic and direct way, illusions of the class I consider here indicate that many perceptual responses are actively constructed from the symbolic cues and clues provided by the stimulus rather than passively determined by any aspect of the geometry of the stimulus acting strictly deterministically on the nervous system. The fact that there can be alternative and reversible perceptual constructions while the stimulus and, presumably, the state of the afferently transmitted neural signal remain nearly constant, is another strong argument for considering the nervous system as an active participant in the perceptual process rather than some kind of automaton that is merely passively responsive to the stimulus-borne information.

The phenomena to be considered in this section are well known to anyone who has had an introductory course in psychology, but in spite of that familiarity there has been little effort to organize them in a way that highlights the similarities and differences of the processes that acount for them. In order to provide some order to the discussion, I propose the following microtaxonomy of what I call here interpretive processes. Two main subclasses of these phenomena are identified. The first consists of processes that lead to the phenomena of closure, extrapolation, and completion. In other words, these are the processes that lead to percepts that are more complete than the stimuli that elicited them. The second has to do with processing of stimulus conditions that are intrinsically ambiguous and that, therefore, are often interpreted as alternative perceptual experiences. This second subclass therefore includes the wide variety of processes leading to what have come to be called reversal phenomena.

a. Closure and Completion. One of the most impressive perceptual processes displayed by the human observer is the ability to transform an incomplete stimulus into a full and complete experience. This completion, closure, or filling in (any of these words will do), can be amazingly thorough; great gaps in the physical stimulus are perceptually closed up by mechanisms of which we have very little knowledge. A universally observed instance of such a completion process is evidenced by the absence of any awareness of the substantial blind spot (approximately 3 deg of visual angle) on the retina. This large lacuna results from the absence of receptors in the retinal region where the retinal blood vessels and the optic nerve enter and leave the eye. Under most normal conditions of viewing, however, we are oblivious to this broad hiatus in the temporal portion of the external visual field (corresponding to the nasal location of the blind spot) in each eye. Even structured fields, such as checkerboards, appear to be complete when viewed under other than the most abnormal conditions. Retinal lesions can also produce pathological lacunae that have functional properties very similar to the normal blind spot. Both normal and pathological ''blind spots'' have been well known and the object of psychological research for over a century. Hermann von Helmholtz had written about it in his magnum opus on physiological optics

(Helmholtz, 1867) and Poppelreuter (1917) had studied completion in patients with visual field defects due to neurological damage.

One explanation that has often been proposed to explain the continuity of vision across the blind spot is characterized by a radical isomorphic premise. This hypothesis assumes that because there are no brain regions corresponding to the blind spot, the regions geometrically adjacent to where it would have been are actually in anatomical contact with each other—the brain space and the perceptual space are congruent. In other words, because there is no missing cortical tissue, there is no discontinuity of neural representation to be perceived. This hypothesis, however, is counterindicated by the strong completion process that can occur equally as well elsewhere in the visual scene. Completion is not restricted to the blind spot; there are many other examples of closure that occur even when the retinal ''blind spot'' is not involved. For example, we tend to ''see'' grounds continue behind figures and figures continue behind interpositioned objects. In those cases there is no ''missing'' neural tissue to be used as a conceptual crutch to explain this phenomenon. Completion, therefore, is not just an aberration of one localized region on the cerebral cortex but rather is a general property of visual processing throughout the entire visual field.

The remaining questions are: How are the missing components, without regard to retinal locus, completed and filled in; and how can we be so insensitive to missing parts of the visual scene? Once again, it must be acknowledged that thc underlying mechanisms of these powerful perceptual processes elude us. There is certainly no network hypothesis sufficiently complex to handle these phenomena and thus they can only be discussed phenomenologically. Even the best available analyses often turn out to be little more than recitation of the many instances in which the phenomena occur.

Thus what we can best do is simply to tabulate the wide variety of exemplars of completion and the conditions under which they occur. Indeed, there are many instances in both art and the technical literature to reinforce our appreciation of the ubiquity of the processes underlying perceptual completion whatever they may be. As one example, the fractured figure shown in Fig. 9-11, though initially difficult to perceive as a complete and unitary form, becomes whole once the perceptual problem it represents is solved. The Belgian artist Rene Magritte (1898–1967) has also used the powerful perceptual tendency to fill in figures as the basis for his curiously disturbing paintings. One of these, shown in Fig. 10-33, is at first glance totally reasonable, yet the reasons for our discomfort with this picture become evident when it is examined in detail. The reader interested in more of these elegant examples of the completion process should refer to the work of Gombrich (1960); Carraher and Thurston (1969); and Parola (1969).

Another striking illusion of completion—the subjective contour—has been brought to current attention by the work of Kanizsa (1955, 1974), although the original description of this phenomenon can be dated back to Schumann (1904)

FIG. 10.33. A painting by Réné Magritte showing the extraordinary amount of perceptual filling and closure that can occur in a very incomplete stimulus display.

and Rubin (1915). Figure 10-34 illustrates one example of this intriguing phenomenon. It should be noted that the phrase "subjective contour" is something of a misnomer. In fact, the illusion is often not just of contours but, as is clearly evident in this figure, of extended surfaces. The central rectangle in each of the drawings shown in Fig. 10-34 is not simply outlined by apparent edges; rather, each rectangular surface possesses illusory properties that are clearly different from their surrounds in spite of the fact that the physical properties of the two regions are identical. In particular:

1. There is a marked brightness difference between the illusory area and the surrounding area. The subjective rectangle in Figure 10-34A, for example, is brighter than the background. This brightness difference occurs even though both regions are of exactly the same luminance.
2. The depth of the illusory areas appear to be different from that of the backgrounds.[7] This difference in apparent depth occurs even though all of the usual monocular and stereoscopic cues are identical in the two regions.
3. The illusory surface appears to be opaque and visually to obstruct the background. The background appears to continue behind the subjective surface.
4. Two or more subjective contours may exist simultaneously in the same region of space, as shown in Fig. 10-35.
5. The illusory surface tends to be the figure in the figure–ground relationship established for the scene and like the figure in an ordinary scene to be sharper in contour, more dense in texture, and more saturated in color than the ground that surrounds it.

Because subjective contours are not an essential part of our existence, what rationale is there for the development of such a mechanism? Kanizsa (1974) notes that the only feature that is common to all of the many subjective contour demonstrations is that there must be an incomplete figure in the original stimulus. It seems possible, therefore, that the most logical way for the observer to construct a rational model of an incomplete object is to infer the existence of another intervening object. Thus, while the current enthusiastic interest in subjective

[7]This difference in apparent depth between the illusory foreground and the background has led some perceptual psychologists (e.g., Coren, 1972) to link the mechanisms underlying subjective contours with those of stereoscopic vision. There seems little justification for this association, however, because the illusory or subjective contours are, if anything, enhanced in monocular viewing while stereoscopic perception is abolished. Spatial disparities play no role in the depth differential observed in the Kaniza "subjective" triangle. The depth differences observed in the illusory contour seems to be more closely associated with some of the monocular cues to depth that I consider in Chapter 11. It seems likely that all of these mechanisms simply represent alternative means of providing information to the interpretive mechanisms constructing the depth experience. The error here, once again, appears to be the fallacy of arguing from analogy of phenomena rather than homology of process.

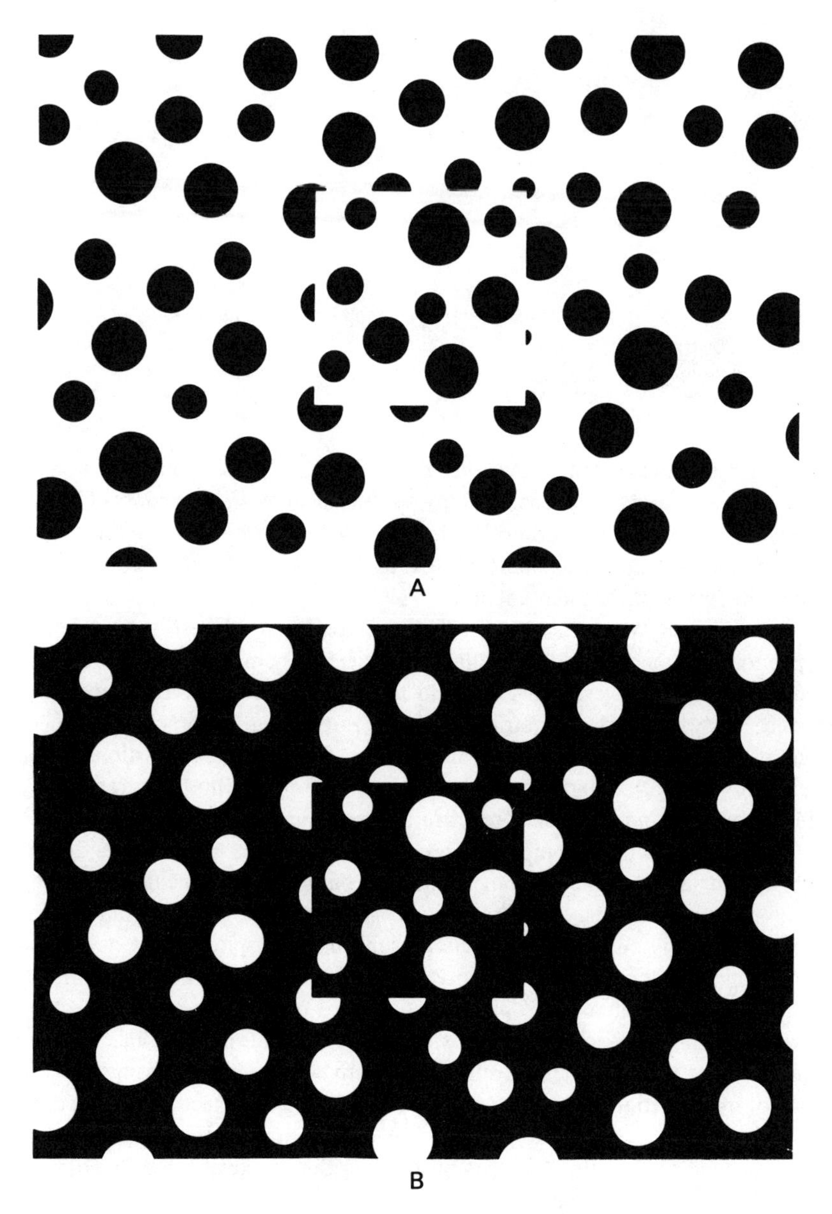

FIG. 10.34. Two subjective surfaces generated by patterns of opposite contrast. (Courtesy of Dr. Gaefano Kanizsa of the University of Trieste.)

FIG. 10.35. Stimultaneous generation of two subjective surfaces in an overlapping manner. (From Kennedy and Lee, © 1976, with the permission of Pion, Ltd.)

contours may be directed at the illusory surface, the perception of this surface may actually be epiphenomenal—a curious, but secondary, byproduct of the very strong tendency to fill in incomplete, but real, stimulus objects. It is this completion process that may be the adaptive and useful basis of the otherwise insignificant subjective surface phenomenon.

Regardless of what the primary focus of research interest should be, and epiphenomenal or not, it is clear that the subjective contours and surface generated by this process are powerful and compelling percepts. It is possible to produce such standard geometrical illusions as the Poggendorf and Ponzo illusions with illusory contours (see Fig. 10-36A & B), and I have already noted Weisstein's (1970) demonstration of the ability of an illusory grating in an inferred background to mask a real grating in a subsequent test.

Clearly the powerful completion processes giving rise to the subjective contours and surfaces are the outcome of neural computational mechanisms that are so complex that there is yet no satisfactory neuroreductionistic explanation nor, in my opinion, is one possible at the present time. In spite of this neuroreductionistic models abound. Some theoreticians have suggested that these illusions may arise as a result of the "partial activation" of "line segment detectors." However, Kaniza has convincingly shown this hypothesis to be inadequate by demonstrating the existence of curved subjective contours occurring in the absence of even partial activation of any putative contour detectors. Furthermore, even dot patterns, presumably incapable of stimulating line-sensitive detectors, can lead to the illusion. Demonstrations that make these two points are shown in Figs. 10-36C and D.

Further evidence that narrowly defined line detectors are not involved in the elicitation of subjective contours is to be found in an illusory surface that does not produce a contour but a diffusely terminating surface that approximates a glowing object. This illusion, invented by Kennedy (1976), is shown in Fig. 10-37.

Another important aspect of this demonstration is the additional support it provides for Kanizsa's conjecture that textured dot patterns, as well as lines, are capable of producing illusory surfaces. Kennedy and Ware (1978) have developed a wide variety of other illusory contours that can also be produced with dot patterns. The ability of observers to construct such elaborate subjective experiences from dot patterns argues strongly against a simplistic extrapolation

FIG. 10.36. (A and B) Demonstrations that geometric illusions can be produced by subjective surfaces. (C) Demonstrations that subjective contours can be evoked without ''partial activation'' of ''line detectors.'' (D) Demonstrations that even as incomplete a stimulus as three dots can produce complex subjective surfaces. (Courtesy of Dr. Gaetano Kanizsa of the University of Trieste.)

FIG. 10.37. A stimulus pattern producing a subjective surface in the absence of sharp contours. (From Kennedy, © 1976, with the permission of Pion, Ltd.)

from Hubel and Wiesel's data on single-cell feature sensitivity to "line detector" explanations of subjective contours.

Coren and Theodor (1977), another pair of proponents of neuroreductionistic theory for this aspect of perception, have suggested that lateral interactive processes may play a role in the brightness difference between the brighter illusory surface and the background, but they carefully qualify this hypothesis by asserting only that the current state of empirical knowledge "does not rule out this type of explanation." Another example of a different kind of neuroreductionism is Ratliff's (1965) and Ginsburg's (1975) proposal that the illusory figures in the Kaniza patterns are a natural byproduct of a Fourier transform carried out by the visual nervous system as a result of its limited band-pass characteristics. Ginsburg, in particular, argues that the "subjective figure" is actually present in the physical stimulus and is extracted by the Fourier transformation. This hypothesis has been severely criticized on the following basis by Tyler (1977b), and also strongly cautioned against by Becker and Knopp (1978). Tyler's arguments, in abstract, are:

1. The Fourier processed simulation of the Kanizsa triangle produces a roughly textural surface not the homogeneous surface reported by observers.

Why should we disregard this aspect of the transformation while at the same time accepting some others?

2. Ginsburg asks us to compare the filtered image visually with our perceptual response to the original image. This is, in fact, a double filtering that represents a "serious philosophical error."

3. Contours appearing in the Fourier-filtered image appear to be an artifact of Ginsburg's process, apparently involving a filter with an abrupt cutoff. Such a filter produces lines but is physiologically implausible.

4. Most of Ginsburg's simulations seem to be due to high-frequency cutoff, but when this is simulated by viewing a stimulus at a distance, the illusion does not occur.

5. Finally, even if it is true that the illusion is mainly associated with a particular band of frequencies, this does not mean that the illusory figure is "physically present in the stimulus."

I believe that Tyler's criticism is correct. It seems to me that what Ginsburg has done is to *simulate* an illusion, not to *explain* it. Indeed, Becker and Knopp (1978) demonstrate another similar model based on a convolution process that simulates the illusion equally well. What Ginsburg, Tyler, and Becker and Knopp all agree upon is that the high-frequency characteristics of the stimulus are necessary for seeing the edges and the low-frequency characteristics are necessary for its uniform surface brightness.

In general, however, other more molar theories invoked to explain the properties of subjective contours are equally unsatisfying. A good summary review of theories of subjective contours is provided by Bachmann (1978). He lists the following molar approaches:

1. Gregory's (1975) and/or Kennedy and Lee's (1976) cognitive theories.
2. Kanizsa's (1974) and/or Pastore's (1971) Gestalt theories.
3. Coren's (1972) and/or Kaufman's (1974) depth-perception theories.
4. Frisby and Clatworthy's (1975) contrast theory.
5. Bachmann's (1978) own proposed resonance-by-feedback theory.

None of these, from my point of view, really help very much in understanding the mechanisms underlying this compelling phenomenon. For example, there is considerable experimental evidence that the Gestalt model fails to provide a satisfactory explanation for subjective contours or surfaces. In particular, Elizabeth Warrington (1965) has studied the completion of figures across defective regions of the visual fields in patients with some sort of retinal or cerebral damage. The independent variable in Warrington's experiments was the type of stimulus that had to be completed across the field defect. The major finding of her study was that completion of figures that were not good (in the Gestalt sense) and that contained no internal cues to what the absent portion of the figure might be occurred almost as well as figural completion processes in which the cues to completion were more obvious. Examples of these two kinds of stimuli are shown in Fig. 10-38. Nonsymmetrical figures were completed at a rate very close to that observed for the simple geometrical objects used as controls. The major factor determining the completion of any figure was the degree of the observer's previous experience with it. In other words, the Gestalt hypothesis proposed by Kanizsa was not substantiated. Warrington's results are important because they help to shift the locus of the completion phenomenon, of which subjective contours are only one important component, from the geometry of the stimulus to the interpretive and constructionistic capabilities of the observer. In this regard they argue also against both the simplistic single-cell theories invoking partial triggering as well as the Gestalt "stimulus pragnanz" explanation.

So far I have restricted this discussion to the completion of static spatial patterns. However, perceptual filling need not be considered only in a static and spatial context. It is also possible to observe perceptual filling and completion in dynamic temporal stimulus situations. Our ability to fuse the sequence of slightly differing sequential image frames in a cinema is an example of the visual system's powerful ability to interpret temporally incomplete stimulus information in a way that produces a continuous perceptual experience. When considered in this context, the phenomenon of saccadic suppression, so often alluded to in the literature as an explanation of the "cinema phenomenon," can be interpreted from a different point of view. This alternative asserts that we ignore the stops between each frame of a movie or the blur in retinal images during eye movements, not because afferently conducted signals are suppressed but, at least in part, because these irregularities are smoothed out by a perceptual filling process. (Do not forget, however, that Matin, 1974, has identified a wide variety of other influences beyond "filling in" as contributing to saccadic suppression—see Chapter 5.)

There are other more precisely measured effects involving subjective contours that reflect their temporal properties. For example, von Grünau (1979) has shown that apparent movement can exist between subjective contours, and Smith and Over (1979) have shown the existence of a motion aftereffect induced by moving subjective contours. Along with the facts that gratinglike subjective contours can mask gratings and that subjective contours can produce geometric illusions, these

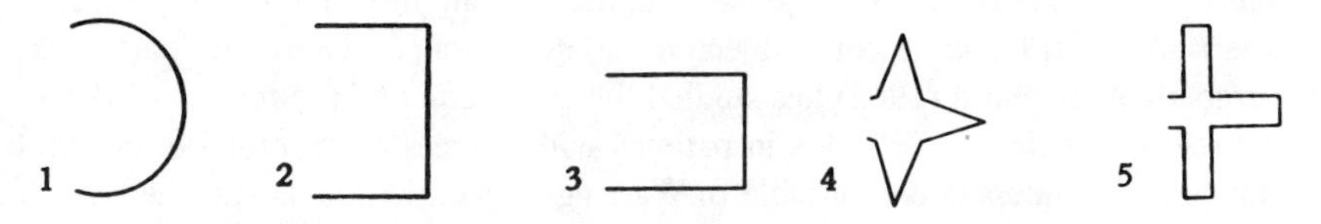

FIG. 10.38. 1, 2, and 3 are figures that are good in a Gestalt sense. 4 and 5 are not. Yet both are completed over retinal lacuna equally well. (From Warrington, © 1965, with the permission of the British Psychological Society.)

findings all attest to the fact that these perceptual filling-in processes can produce "virtual" stimuli that themselves can lead to responses comparable to those produced by real stimuli.

In conclusion, the visual system exhibits a powerful ability to complete and fill in, in both time and space, missing parts of a visual stimulus. The processes underlying these phenomena, in spite of suggestions to the contrary, clearly seem to depend on exceedingly complex neural mechanisms, probably beyond current understanding in any truly reductionistic sense. It seems that they are best considered to be the result of interpretive and symbolic processes described with a neorationalistic theoretical vocabulary.

b. Reversible Figures. In the proceding section I considered a number of visual processes in which the failure of stimulus–percept veridicality was so great that the resulting phenomena had to be considered to be the outcome of interpretive or constructive processes that transcended the informationally incomplete cues provided by the stimulus. That is, the information contained in the stimulus was so incomplete that only by invoking logical constructions based on interpretations of object continuity could we explain how we perceive. My discussion of these processes and phenomena was intended to make one major point, namely, that the properties of the stimulus and simple passive network transformations alone cannot fully explain the nature of the resulting percepts. The conclusion seems inescapable—they must also be influenced by symbolic and interpretive processes, no less neural but so complex as to embody a kind of logic of which we have virtually no understanding.

Another category of perceptual phenomena incorporated within Level 3 makes this same point but from a somewhat different perspective. This category involves those instances in which the stimulus may be complete, but in which it is so ambiguous that two or more alternative perceptual constructions are probable outcomes. Examples of reversible perceptual processes, capable of flipping back and forth between alternative interpretations, are legion in the popular literature on visual perception and ubiquitous in any introductory discussion of visual perception. Most of these intriguing demonstrations can be classified within the following five categories:

1. Reversal of figure–ground organization.
2. Reversal of depth.
3. Reversal of figural meaning.
4. Reversal of grouping.
5. Reversal resulting from binocular rivalry.

The first four types of reversible phenomena are essentially monocular; only one eye is necessary to observe the reversal of the ambiguous figure. The fifth type, however, although phenomenally quite similar, is a binocular process that occurs when two images are so disparate that no meaningful combination of them, comparable to that occurring during normal binocular fusion or stereopsis, is possible. All five categories, however, represent situations in which ambiguous or paradoxical stimuli are subsequently disambiguated by the visual system by alternation between alternative perceptual interpretations. To a greater or lesser degree, and depending on many factors including the nature of the ambiguity, the proportion of time allocated to each alternative percept may vary. Some alternative states are, therefore, said to be dominant over others. Reversal rate or the proportion of time spent perceiving each alternative state are often used as dependent variables in research on these phenomena.

The first class of reversible figure, involving alternations in figure–ground relationships, has already been discussed. For example, Fig. 10-23 and Fig. 10-24 show two examples of figures in which the information leading to the establishment of the figure–ground relations is sufficiently ambiguous to allow alternative organizations to be constructed by the observer. Figure 10-24, the etching by the extraordinary Maurits Escher, demonstrated a profound reversibility that extends over an entire scene. It is now firmly established that Escher was well acquainted with the Gestalt demonstrations and that this scientific knowledge as well as his early contact with the highly geometric Moorish art in Spain were major influences on the development of his graphic artform. Those interested in this topic should read the delightful article by Marianne Teuber (1974), "Sources of Ambiguity in the Prints of Maurits C. Escher," to learn of this extraordinary interaction between art and science.

The second type of alternation—depth reversal[8]—is illustrated by the three stimuli shown in Fig. 10-39. All three of these line drawings are strongly suggestive of, but not definitive of, depth. The first (fig. 10-39A) is the famous Necker cube, first described in 1832 as an artifact in the work of the crystallographer, Louis Necker. This object may be interpreted so that the upper right-hand corner (in the two-dimensional projection) may lie either on the front or the back plane of the perceived three-dimensional cube. The second (fig. 10-39B); the equally famous Schroder staircase, exhibits this same property of depth reversal. Figure 10-39C shows a third classic reversible figure known as the Thiery illusion. This ambiguous stimulus may be organized in either of two ways, which can best be appreciated by inspection of this figure.

A few recent empirical studies of Necker cube reversal have been published. One of special interest has been reported by Kawabata, Yamagami, and Noaki (1978). They showed that the perceived three-dimensional organization of the

[8]Although I emphasize the reversal aspects of the illusions now to be discussed, it is clear that all of these stimuli must also be influenced by the kind of Level 4 spatial and temporal interaction cues that are considered in the next chapter. In this regard, others may find the inclusion of this material at this point somewhat inconsistent with the rest of my taxonomy. However, the emphasis in this case is on a part of the perceptual processing of these figures that I believe is organizational, rather than relational, and it is for this reason that these phenomena are placed at this point in the discussion.

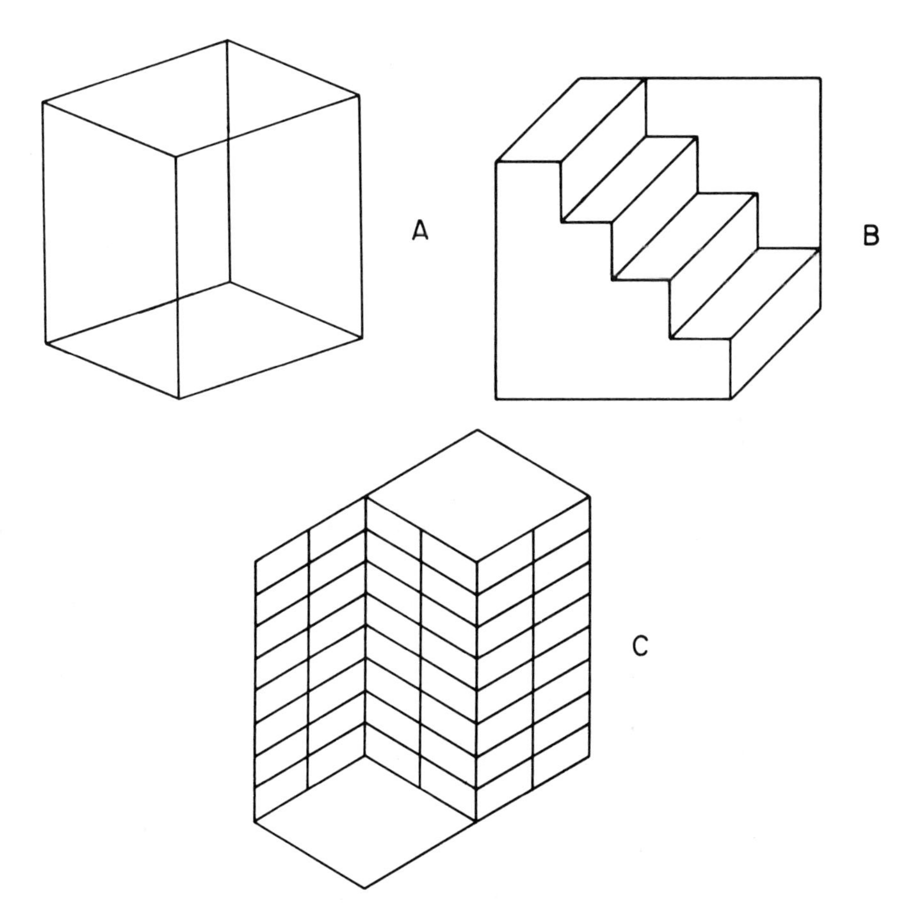

FIG. 10.39. Three reversible figures: (A) The Necker cube. (B) The Schroeder staircase. (C) The Thiéry Blocks.

Necker cube depended on the point of fixation taken by the observer. If, as shown in Fig. 10-40, the observer fixated the corner marked *A*, then virtually all of the time the surface *ABCD* appeared in front of surface *A'B'C'D'*. On the other hand, if the observer fixated the corner marked *A'*, then *ABCD* appeared to be in front of *A'B'C'D'* only a small proportion of the time. Furthermore, it is now certain (Ellis, Wong, & Stark, 1979) that accommodation plays no role at all in the Necker cube response.

Dynamic properties can also influence the interpretation of depth of objects like the Necker cube. If a rotating wireframe object is back-lighted so that a two-dimensional projection falls on a screen, the sequence of the projected images also helps to produce the perception of a solid object. In some instances, however, these dynamic two-dimensional projections can also be ambiguous,

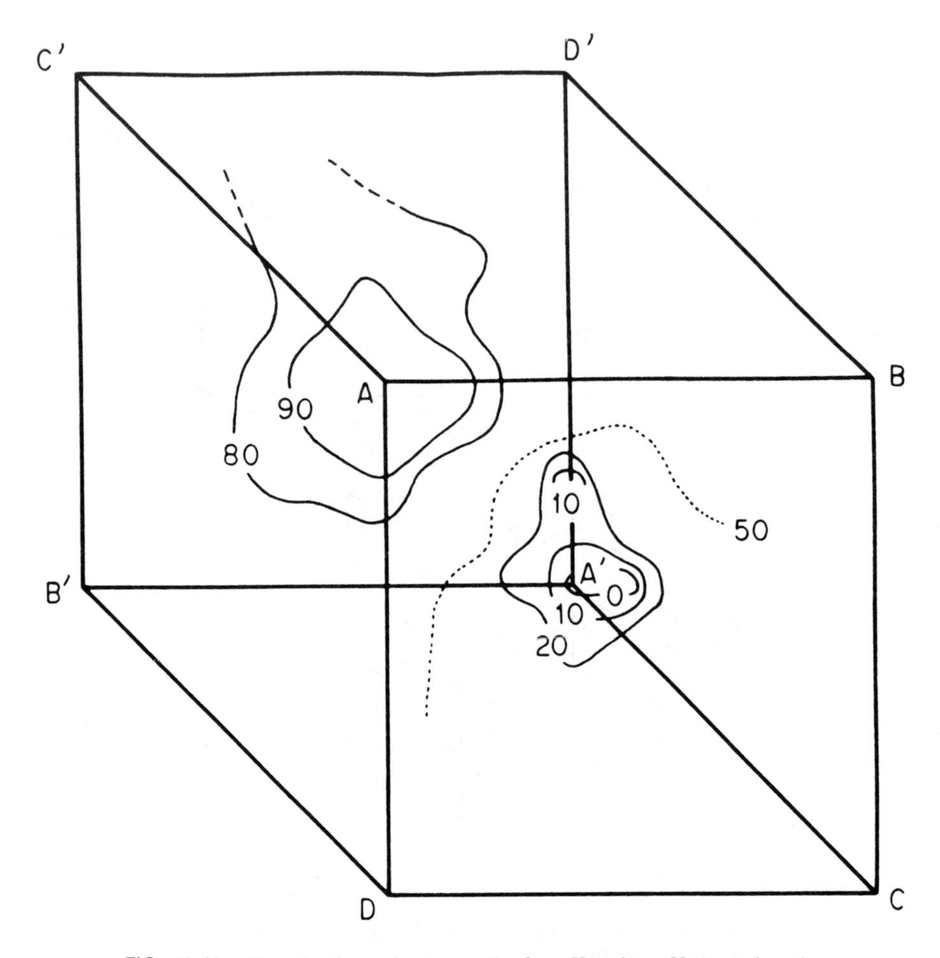

FIG. 10.40. The stimulus and some results from Kawabata, Yamagami, and Noaki's experiment. The location of the fixation point has a powerful influence on the proportion of times that the surface ABCD is seen as the front face of the cube, i.e., closer to the observer, as indicated by the "iso-reversal curves." (From Kawabata, Yamagami, and Noaki, © 1978, with the permission of Pergamon Press.)

and reversible directions of rotation can result. I have more to say about this Level 4 process in the next chapter.

The third type of reversible figure includes drawings that may be interpreted to have totally different meanings in alternate reversals. Figures 10-41, for example, show a piece of art work that exhibits this type of reversal; a woman is sitting in front of a mirror in which we see either her own reflection or, alternatively, a skull. Other familiar reversals of this class, such as the rabbit–duck reversal, the old woman–young woman reversal, and the kneeling-nude–man's-

FIG. 10.41. A reversible figure drawn by the artist C. Allan Gilbert.

face reversal need not be reproduced here, they are sufficiently well known. This category shares many features in common with simple figure–ground reversal.

Figure 10-25 exemplifies the fourth kind of reversible figure. If a regular array of small geometric components is presented to an observer, the components can be subjectively grouped in a number of different ways; columns, rows, diagonals, or sets of small subarrays are all possible alternative perceptual organizations of these stimuli. An astonishing natural reversible grouping figure of this type has been identified by Kennedy (1977). The small triangles in the electron micrograph of kidney tissue shown in Fig. 10-42 can be grouped with others into alternative "Stars of David" by the observer.

These first four types of visual alternation have been extensively discussed in an eminently readable article by Fred Attneave (1971), to which the reader is directed for a more complete description of the various kinds of monocular reversible figure. Unfortunately, neither Attneave nor any other perceptual psychologist has provided any theoretical insight into the mechanisms that may underlie these reversals of figure–ground, depth, meaning, or grouping. The responsible mechanisms are just as obscure and mysterious as those underlying the completion processes described in the previous section of this chapter. Attneave's allusion to an electronic analog that can also "flip-flop" between two quasi-stable states is not a substitute for an analytic theoretical explanation. It is but another one of those physical analogies that makes the phenomena somewhat more intuitively clear but does not illuminate the underlying mechanisms or processes. But perhaps that is about all our science can do now; describe the processes as well as possible and determine those stimulus factors that influence

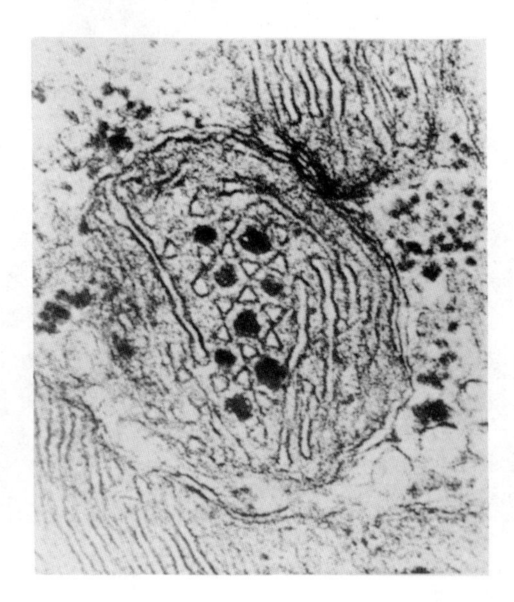

FIG. 10.42. Reversible grouping in a natural setting. The small triangles can be grouped with alternative stars of David in this micrograph of kidney tissue magnified 80,000 times. (From Kennedy, © 1977, with the permission of Pion, Ltd.)

such behavioral dimensions as the reversal rate. In light of the extremely complex central mechanisms of construction and interpretation that obviously must be involved in these processes, it is unnecessary to debate whether the processes are central or peripheral—they must be central!

One of the most exciting developments in the mathematical *description* of reversible figures has come from the application of a relatively recent development in mathematics—catastrophe theory. Catastrophe theory, originally developed by Rene Thom (1975), is a branch of mathematics that is especially suited to the analysis of systems in which there are sharp discontinuities in response. For example, catastrophe theory was applied early in its short history to the study of collapses in the stock market and stress failures in metallurgy. An analogy has been drawn between these discontinuous processes and the sudden reversals that occur when ambiguous figures of the sort I have been discussing snap back and forth between two or more alternative perceptual interpretations. Catastrophe theory thus provides a descriptive model of the process and many of the phenomenological aspects of the reversal process can be incorporated within this framework. Figure 10-43A, from Poston and Stewart (1978) shows a "cusp" model of the multistable perceptual experiences induced by various forms of the man–woman reversal stimulus shown in Fig. 10-43B. These versions of the stimulus that are reversible are enclosed within the *V*-shaped area. These correspond to the cusp in Fig. 10-43A, for which two alternative perceptual states may occur. These few words hardly do justice to the full capabilities of catastrophe theory; the reader is referred to Thom's treatise or to any of a number of newer texts for a fuller description of the ideas embodied in this model.

Though there has been some controversy over the general utility of catastrophe theory, this application of the model seems natural and in the absence of any other more detailed mathematical model, it may prove to be useful in at least providing a formal means of describing the course of the process. Any further progress in analyzing underlying mechanisms will depend in large part on the presence of some such suitable descriptive methodology.

The fifth type of reversible figure—binocular rivalry—is dissimilar from the first four in that it necessarily involves both of the eyes. If the two eyes are presented with stimuli that are so nonconjugate, or so disparate that they cannot be merged or dealt with in combination, then there tends to be a rivalry or alternation in which the visual experience alternates between the two monocular views with virtually total suppression of the unseen stimulus.

Binocular rivalry has been both an amusing parlor game and a stimulus for serious scientific research for over a century. The phenomenon was originally discovered and reported by Charles Wheatstone (1838). Helmholtz (1867) devoted a chapter of his famous and influential work on physiological optics to the topic, and the phenomenon has played an important role in the writing and thinking of such major figures in perceptual and physiological theory as William James and Charles Sherrington.

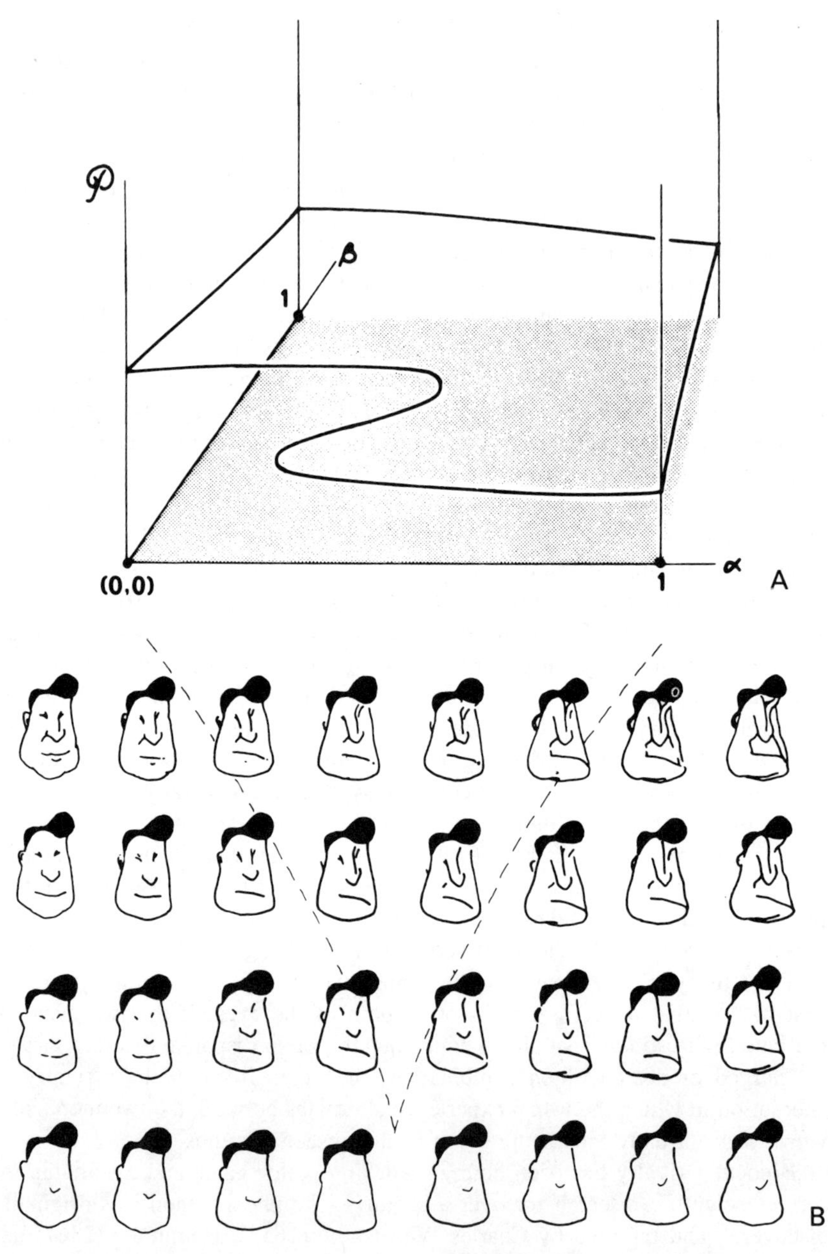

FIG. 10.43. (A) A diagram of the cusp model from catastrophe theory. Note that a particular point on the horizontal plane may be associated with two alternative values, which may catastrophically interchange. (B) A sample of a set of stimuli that exhibits properties modeled by the Cusp model. (From Poston and Stewart, © 1978, with the permission of the Society for General Systems Research.)

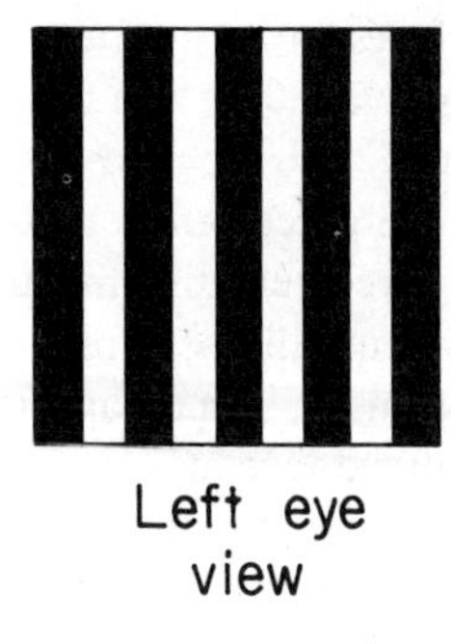

FIG. 10.44. Left and right eye stimuli that will not fuse, but that will produce strong rivalry.

It seems to me, however, that a serious miscalculation has been made by many authors when they identify the processes underlying binocular rivalry with those that must account for stereopsis. Though both processes involve inputs from both eyes, the resulting phenomena are entirely different. Rivalry results in the perception of either one or the other of the two inputs; the image conditions are so disparate that no meaningful compound or mixture can be constructed from the two inputs. In such a situation, the visual system tends to alternate back and forth between two percepts, suppressing in some way, one or the other. In the case of stereopsis, the disparities are small enough so that it is possible for the visual system to construct a meaningful percept that is not the direct reflection of either one of the individual monocular inputs but rather is a combination of the two. Stereopsis, therefore, does not involve the suppression of information[9] from either eye, but binocular rivalry does. This profound difference demands that we distinguish between these two phenomena and the processes that underlie them. For me, binocular rivalry is best classified within the Level 3 rubric, whereas stereopsis belongs in Level 4.

With this brief introductory comment concluded, let's consider binocular rivalry in more detail. Figure 10-44 shows two monocular stimuli that are strongly rivalrous. The resulting percept may be of one or the other of the two patterns or a mosaic-like mixture of the two. However, both are never seen wholy at the same time, and no locus in the mosaic may incorporate parts of both simultaneously. In those cases in which it is possible to combine parts of the two monocular images into a collage-type percept, the effect can sometimes be quite startling. My friends at the University of Western Australia have constructed a remarkable device that demonstrated the properties of the rivalrous mixture better than any other of which I know. This device—the ''humanscope,'' based on an idea first proposed by A. L. Austin in 1877—is a binocular viewing system that

[9]See my discussion of this issue in the next chapter.

is large enough to allow two different human faces to be inserted in two windows; mirrors are arranged in such a way that only one face can be viewed with each eye. As just noted, there is no way to "fuse" two faces to give an "average" of the two, nor can both of the faces both be perceived in their entirety at the same time. The escape from this logical and perceptual dilemma to which the human visual system retreats is that the observer usually sees one or the other face—binocular rivalry. However, in some instances, a montage made up of parts of both faces is perceived. Thus, the combined face at one moment might consist of the eyes and chin of one face, and the hair, mouth, and nose of the other. This "construction" might then reverse and another combination take its perceptual place.

The important thing about this amusing demonstration is that the parts (eyes, chin, nose, etc.) that are utilized in each construction *are always taken as meaningful wholes.* Both eyes (sometimes complete with eyeglasses), and the whole chin (sometimes complete with bread) are utilized in constructing the perceived face. However automatic the mixture might be, it is the result of a process that is sensitive to the meaning and logical wholeness of the component parts.

Unlike the first four kinds of reversible phenomena, which have not stimulated much formal experimentation, a considerable amount of research has been carried out on binocular rivalry. The major theoretical controversy concerning binocular rivalry has, of course, revolved around the problem of the locus of the phenomenon. As with so many other perceptual topics, the wave of enthusiasm for neuroreductionistic explanation in the 1960s and 1970s stimulated by dramatic discoveries in the neurophysiological laboratory, led a number of contemporary perceptual theorists to suggest that, among other phenomena, binocular rivalry was the result of a relatively peripheral inhibitory interaction between the two monocular channels. This point of view was probably first proposed by Sherrington (1906), but was reintroduced in psychological thinking by Jung (1961) and has been developed further by Bishop (1973), Wade (1975b), and, most recently, by Abadi (1976). The "peripheral" mechanism these workers invoke to explain binocular rivalry was not necessarily retinal. Abadi, for example, attributes it to inhibition among cortical feature-detecting neurons.

The major alternative to such a peripheral lateral inhibition hypothesis is that interpretive (i.e., cognitive, inferential, constructionistic) processes representing the output of a much more complex level of neural processing must be invoked to explain these phenomena. A major review of the available data pertaining to this problem and these two major opposing theories has appeared recently (Walker, P., 1978). After reviewing a wide variety of literature, Walker comes to the conclusion that only a constructionistic model is capable of explaining most of the data. In his review, Walker considers the following findings (abstracted) to be most supportive of a centralist–interpretive model of the processes underlying rivalrous phenomenon and most damning to a peripheralist–inhibitory approach:

1. There can be a substantial degree of voluntary control over the reversals in binocular rivalry (Breese, 1899).

2. The periods of rivalrous suppression do not alter other retinal aftereffects (Lehmkuhle & Fox, 1975).

3. There is no statistical evidence of sequential dependency between the rivalrous images (Blake, Fox, & McIntyre, 1971; Fox & Herrmann, 1967; Walker, P., 1975).

4. Rivalry can occur between different regions of a monocular field as well as between the images from the two eyes (Walker, P., 1976). This phenomenon may link the fading of the stabilized retinal images to rivalry, according to Walker.

5. Information suppressed during a period of rivalry may still actually be used in determining stereoscopic depths (Kaufman, 1964b). Therefore it is not lost or inhibited; it is simply "designified" at the moment in forming the perceptual construct.

6. Neither the focus, nor luminance, nor any other such physical dimension of the stimulus to the unsuppressed eye determines how long the image in the other eye will be suppressed. The duration of suppression is more effectively determined by the properties of the stimulus to the suppressed eye (Levelt, 1966).

7. The reversals in a rivalry situation are dependent upon the observer's "personality, cultural background and sex" (Reitz & Jackson, 1964).

8. The reversal rate in a rivalry situation depends upon the meaning of words in the display (Rommetreit, Toch, & Svendsen, 1968).

I have abstracted this set of findings from Walker's review because it represents one of the most comprehensive arguments against any simple lateral interaction theory of binocular rivalry. He asserts, and certainly not without disagreement, that each of these studies in one way or another (see Walker's paper for a complete discussion of the implication of each) is beyond the explanatory power of any such simplistic peripheral neural model. All these findings emphasize the independence of rivalry from the physical properties of the stimulus and the possibility of a continued psychological impact of the "suppressed" information, even when the observer momentarily does not perceive it.

Other data that seem to make the same argument include:

1. Which of two binocular-presented figures is perceived depends on the observer's previous experience with both (Toch & Schulte, 1961). In other words, there is a strong effect of familiarity on dominance; the more familiar stimulus is the more dominant.

2. Stimuli containing more detail (such as lines) or of a more complex texture tend to be dominant over texturally homogeneous stimuli (Breese, 1899).

3. Moving stimuli tend to dominate stationary ones (Breese, 1899).

4. Prior inspection of one stimulus in a rivalry task can affect the duration of the period in which it is dominant (Goryo, 1969; Kakizaki, 1950a, 1950b).

5. There is considerable debate in the literature concerning the purported sensitivity of the rivalry phenomenon to such factors as grating orientation and spatial frequency. Some work (e.g., Wade, 1974; Blake & Fox, 1974b) has been reported that suggests that orientation differences between rivalrous gratings are not effective in varying the rate of alternation. On the other hand, Thomas (1977, 1978) reports such a sensitivity, as do Kitterle, Kaye and Nixon (1974). Their general result is that as the orientation difference increases the alternation rate decreases. Kitterle and his co-workers also find a strong effect of spatial frequency on alternation. Obviously this problem is far from settled.

6. Meaningful stimuli, such as words, tend to be dominant over meaningless stimuli, such as nonsense syllables (Ogle, 1950).

7. The region of suppression extends beyond the area in which the two rivalrous stimuli overlap. In other words, the inhibition of a stimulus is not dependent on the presence of an inhibitor but occurs in a way that maintains "reasonable" unity of the percept (Kaufman, 1964b).

8. Changes in the frequency or contrast of the suppressed stimulus near the beginning of the suppression period can lead to the immediate reversal of the rivalrous percept (Walker, P., & Powell, 1979).

Thus, in general, the physical characteristics of the stimulus, such as its orientation, luminosity, contrast, color, physical overlap, or spatial frequency, seem not to be influential determinants of the dominance. The factors that seem to be influential, on the other hand, involve complex pattern aspects of the stimulus or symbolic dimensions that are closely related to the observer's state. Once again, the conclusion toward which we driven is that no lateral inhibition theory can possibly explain this highly interpretive process.

Now let us consider in more detail some of the empirical data forthcoming from research on binocular rivalry. One of the most prolific contributers to research on binocular rivalry in recent years has been Randolph Blake of Northwestern University. In several experiments, Blake has also shown that the reversal or alternation process is remarkably insensitive to the physical properties of the stimulus. In one particularly interesting study Blake (1977) demonstrated that two low contrast gratings can act as effective stimuli in a binocular rivalry situation, even when the gratings are very close to their contrast threshold. In other words, even gratings that are very difficult to see can be effective in "suppressing" the image from the contralateral eye. Considering that lateral inhibition mechanisms are known to depend strongly on the amplitude of the excitatory signal, this is further damning to an argument based on such simple neural network interactions. Figure 10-45 makes this point more concretely, showing the virtually complete absence of any effect of contrast of a grating

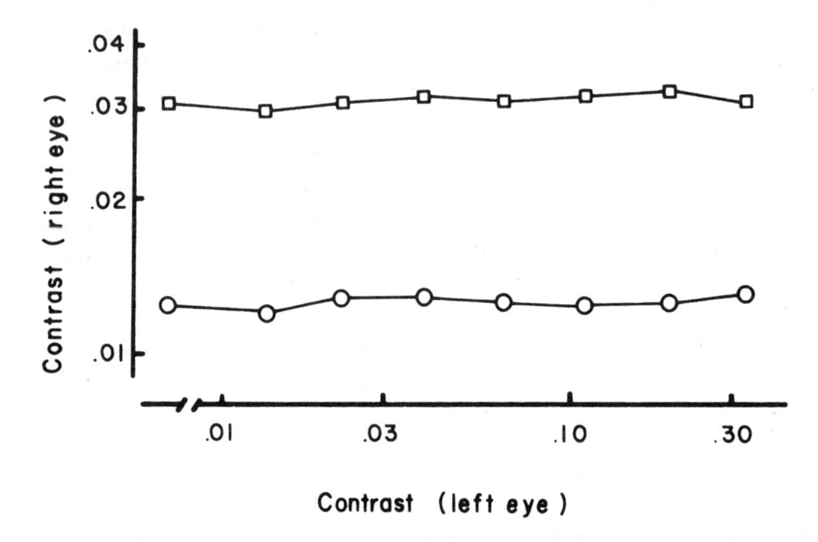

FIG. 10.45. Threshold contrast to the right eye as a function of contrast to the left eye in a rivalry situation. Obviously the contrast to the left eye exerts no influence on the threshold of reversal. (From Blake, © 1977, with the permission of The American Psychological Association.)

presented to the right eye on the threshold of response to a much higher contrast grating presented to the left eye.

This lack of increased influence with increased stimulus contrast is another case of what I have referred to previously as an information-saturation effect. Once the detection threshold of the grating has been exceeded, the grating has exerted its maximum ability to influence the threshold of the rivalry response. The reason for this outcome is that the increases in contrast do not affect this high-level process, the essential information having been conveyed even at low contrast levels.

Blake went on to show that although under some conditions the contrast of grating could be effective in altering the *duration* of the suppression, one had to raise the stimulus contrast to over four times the threshold value before it would become effective in altering this aspect of the response. This insensitivity to such an important physical characteristic—contrast—of the stimulus, which should affect neural interactions so strongly, is another datum strongly supporting the argument against any simple inhibition theory of binocular rivalry.

Using two gratings with variable orientation as the rivalrous stimuli, Blake and Lema (1978) have also shown that the detection of a brief and dim test stimulus, presented to one eye during the period of suppression of the image from that eye, was inhibited to a degree but that the magnitude of this inhibition was independent of the orientation of the suppressed grating. Such a result is also contrary to the implications of any inhibitory interaction theory that invokes reciprocal spatial interaction among orientation-sensitive neural units (e.g., Abadi, 1976) as an explanation of binocular rivalry. This finding indicates, to the contrary, that putative interactions among hypothetical orientation detectors actually play, at best, a minimal role in determining the magnitude of the suppression. Blake and Lema note that the reduction they observed in detection sensitivity in the suppressed eye, which amounted to only about 20%, is a common feature of the binocular rivalry situation. Other perceptual researchers, had previously shown this also to be the case (e.g., Wales & Fox, 1970) in other contexts.

Blake and Lema, therefore, came to the eminently reasonable conclusion that the measured insensitivity to orientation exhibited in this experiment must be a characteristic of a system that operates at a very high level of perceptual processing. Though the word *inhibition* may be used in this context, it is almost a pun; it does not have the same meaning as it does when used in the network context. In that latter context, Abadi (1976), for one, uses the word to refer to a highly specific neurophysiological interaction in which the neural representation of the stimulus is inhibited and the afferent signal actually diminished. In the former case, "inhibition" refers to a much more generalized interpretive suppression of the perceptual significance of the response, probably without a physical suppression of the neural signal. The inhibition in this case is between conflicting constructs and percepts, or between alternative possible meanings of the stimulus; such processes are represented by neural networks of such complexity that they mock comparison with the simple peripheral neural networks invoked in the lateral inhibition theory.

In sum, the various kinds of reversible figures provide powerful and compelling evidence that the visual system acts to construct a plausible and reasonable mental model of the visual environment on the basis of stimuli that convey only partial information. This kind of interpretation stresses the indeterminacy of stimuli and the inferential and constructionistic nature of perception. All these reversible phenomena arise because the stimuli are impoverished, contradictory, or ambiguous in a way that allows the construction of plausible alternative percepts to solve the problem posed by the environment. Despite the prevalence of simplistic neuroreductionistic theories invoking low-level neural networks as explanatory mechanisms, it is my judgment that these phenomena reflect the operation of far more complex neuronal nets than our available neuroreductionistic theory and technology can possibly handle. The organization of figures, forms, and scenes, though characteristically preattentive and automatic, involve high-level factors (e.g., the semantic and symbolic content of the stimulus) in a way that reflects the action of computational mechanisms of enormous complexity for which we have little knowledge or insight.

At present, although some efforts have been made to develop a hierarchy or sequence of visual processing mechanisms (e.g., Blake & Fox, 1974a, and

Blake, Fox, & Westendorf, 1974, suggest that afterimages, rivalry, and size constancy represent serial steps in visual processing), we still have only fragmentary evidence that would justify such a view. All Level 3 and 4 processes could be operating in a parallel mode equally well. Our theory and technology simply do not yet provide a means to discriminate between serial and parallel alternative modes of operation.

c. Impossible Figures (Paradoxical Stimuli). Closely related to the illusions of reversal are the so-called "impossible figures" most recently brought to modern attention by Penrose and Penrose (1958). The typical impossible figure is a drawing of some object in which there are internally inconsistent or paradoxical cues regarding its figural organization. The most familiar of these paradoxical stimuli—a better descriptor than the term "impossible figures"—are the Devil's tuning fork (first published in the psychological literature by Schuster, 1964) and the Penrose figures (Penrose & Penrose, 1958). Examples of these stimuli are depicted in Fig. 10-46A and B, respectively. The perceptual organization of the entire object in each case is difficult; of this there is no question. But there is no illusion involved in the conventional sense of the word (our response to the ambiquous cues is verdical.) Nor are the objects physically impossible in at least of sense—the Devil's tuning fork, for example, has actually been built by Masterson and Kennedy (1975), as shown in Fig. 10-47. Rather, there is a perceptual reversal from one form of organization to another as fixation (attention?) is moved from one part of the paradoxical stimulus defining one figural organization to a region of contrary cues defining the alternative organization. Indeed, there is a great deal of verdicality in the perceptual response between either of the two alternative constructions and their respective stimuli. The "impossibility" resides in the perceptual inability of the observer to maintain both contradictory organizations simulataneously.

Surprisingly, for such complex perceptual phenomena, a relatively deep understanding of the nature of paradoxical stimuli themselves has accumulated. This wisdom has mainly come from the mathematical analyses of paradoxical figures carried out by Thaddeus Cowan. In a pair of exceedingly interesting papers (Cowan, 1974, 1977), he develops a classification system of paradoxical figures that not only allows him to classify a particular set of known versions of these stimuli, but also to predict others that had not yet been discovered or invented by less formal approaches.

Cowan works mainly with a particular kind of paradoxical object—a four-cornered torus—made up of the four possible kinds of corner shown in Fig. 10-48A. Depending on how the four corners are put together, however, either a paradoxical (impossible) or nonparadoxical (possible) figure may result. In fact, of the 27 objects that can be formed from these corners 23 are paradoxical in the sense used here. The 27 figures are shown in Fig. 10-48B, along with several standard transformations of each. Those standard transformations are indicated

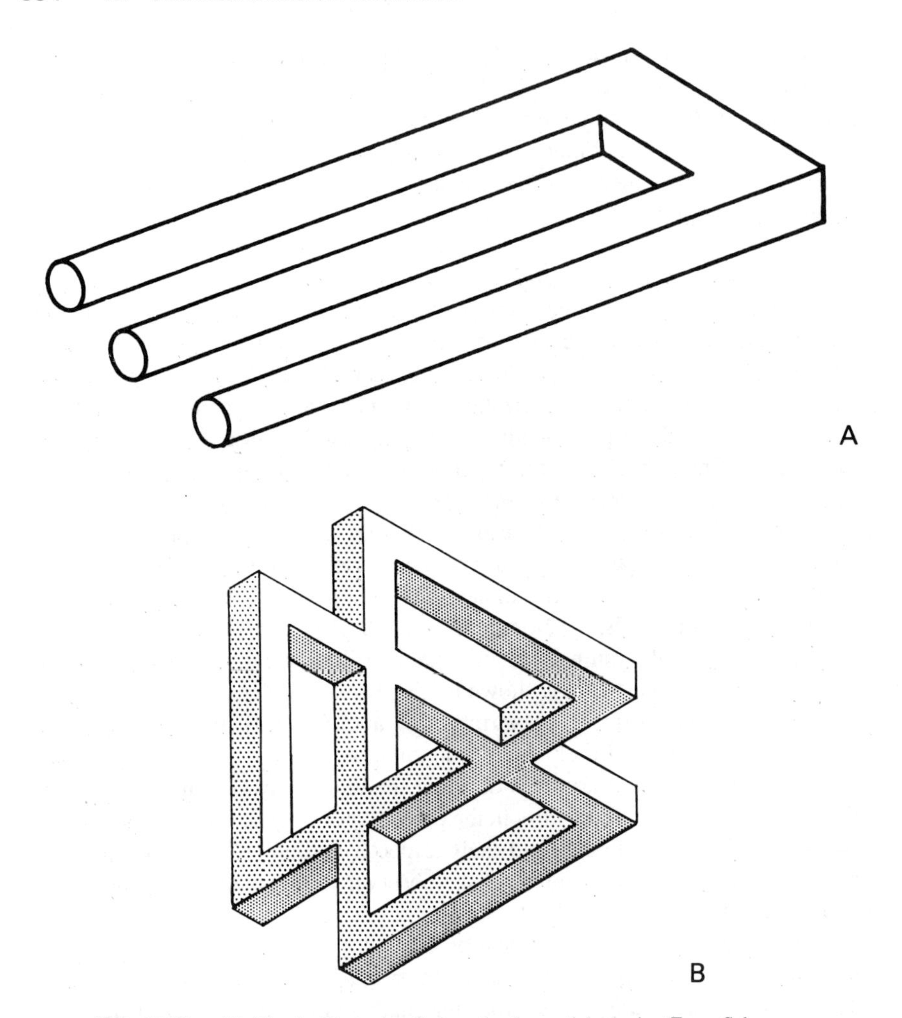

FIG. 10.46. (A) The devil's tuning fork or the three-stick clevis. (From Schuster, © 1964, with the permission of the University of Illinois Press.) (B) A multiple "impossible" triangle. (From Penrose and Penrose, © 1958, with the permission of the British Psychological Society.)

by the terms *inverse, everse, observe,* and *unit* forms in this figure. Unit forms are identical to the standard, but the other transformations are the result of specific manipulations. For example, the inverse of one figure is produced by replacing each corner with its own inverse. The transforms of each type of corner are also indicated in Fig. 10-48B. For example, in that figure we see that the corners z and z^{-1} are each other's inverse and M and N are their own inverses.

Cowan proposes, as a general rule, that a paradoxical figure will be produced whenever a transition is made on a torus from one corner to another against the direction of the arrows shown in Fig. 10-48A. This rule makes the paradoxical nature of a stimulus figure, so vaguely alluded to in the psychological literature, concrete.

It must be remembered, however, that this system is a quantitative means of representing stimuli, but it is not an explanatory or reductionistic model of the underlying perceptual processes. What Cowan has done is to provide a system for representing and classifying paradoxical stimuli; he has not proposed a model of how we perceive or process them. A discussion of how these figures generate the peculiar perceptual reversals, on the other hand, has been presented by Draper (1978). After a comprehensive review of the class of paradoxical figures, of which the examples that I have given so far are only representative, he proposed that the "impossibility" of perceiving the figures arises from the limits of the perceiver's ability to process the geometry of the figure. This limited ability is due to the conflict in the direction and destination of each of the component parts. The mental calculations involved in organizing these forms are anchored to a coordinate system that, according to Draper, is defined by the stimulus scene itself. When a portion of the figure terminates in two different ways, depending on the direction in which the mental calculation is proceeding along the object, then the paradoxical impossibility of the figure obtains, and the observer is forced to alternate, for perfectly reasonable grounds, between two alternative constructions. Like all other theories of such complex perceptual phenomena, this is not so much an explanatory theory as it is a description of a plausible logic that must necessarily underlie all such perceptual processes.

Paradoxical cues arising from a conflict in the linear geometry of a stimulus

FIG. 10.47. The "impossible" devil's tuning fork physically constructed. (From Masterson and Kennedy, © 1975, with the permission of Pion, Ltd.)

scene are not the only source of "impossible" figures. Figure 10-49 reproduces a famous painting by William Hogarth, dated 1754, that is also paradoxical. The paradox in this case, however, arises from the many conflicts among interposition cues. Objects are seen simultaneously both *in front of* and *in back of* other objects in the scene in a way that defies three-dimensional reality. The paradox in this painting is not so much a matter of "false perspective," as is usually asserted but, rather, a result of inconsistent interposition cues.

D. AN INTERIM SUMMARY

In this chapter I have sought to bring together a number of perceptual processes and phenomena involved in the early stages of the organization of visual forms. All of the Level 3 processes I have described underlie the initial prequantitative organization of the visual response that probably must occur prior to the perceptual quantification mediated by Level 4 processes. Unlike Level 4 processes, which seem, in general, to depend on comparisons or relations among the various aspects, attributes, or dimensions of the stimulus, Level 3 processes seem to act upon single dimensions or aspects of the stimulus. Here, only the texture, color, simple geometry, or some other single aspect of the stimulus is significant in determining the response. The salient Level 3 dimensions may be global, as we have seen, representing the entire area of the stimulus or the statistics of major subregions of it, but there is no explicit interdimensional comparison involved in any of these processes.

Level 3 processes, unlike lower levels, however, share with higher levels a high degree of "constructive interpretation" in the production of the percept.

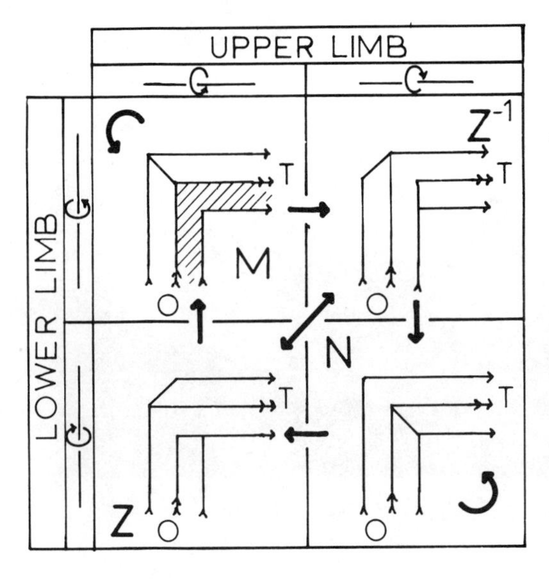

FIG. 10.48. (A) The four basic corners that can be used to construct four-sided toruses. (B) The twenty-seven four-sided toruses that can be constructed from the four basic corners and their possible transformations; i = inverse; e = everse, o = obverse, and u = unit forms. (From Cowan, © 1977, with the permission of Pion, Ltd.)

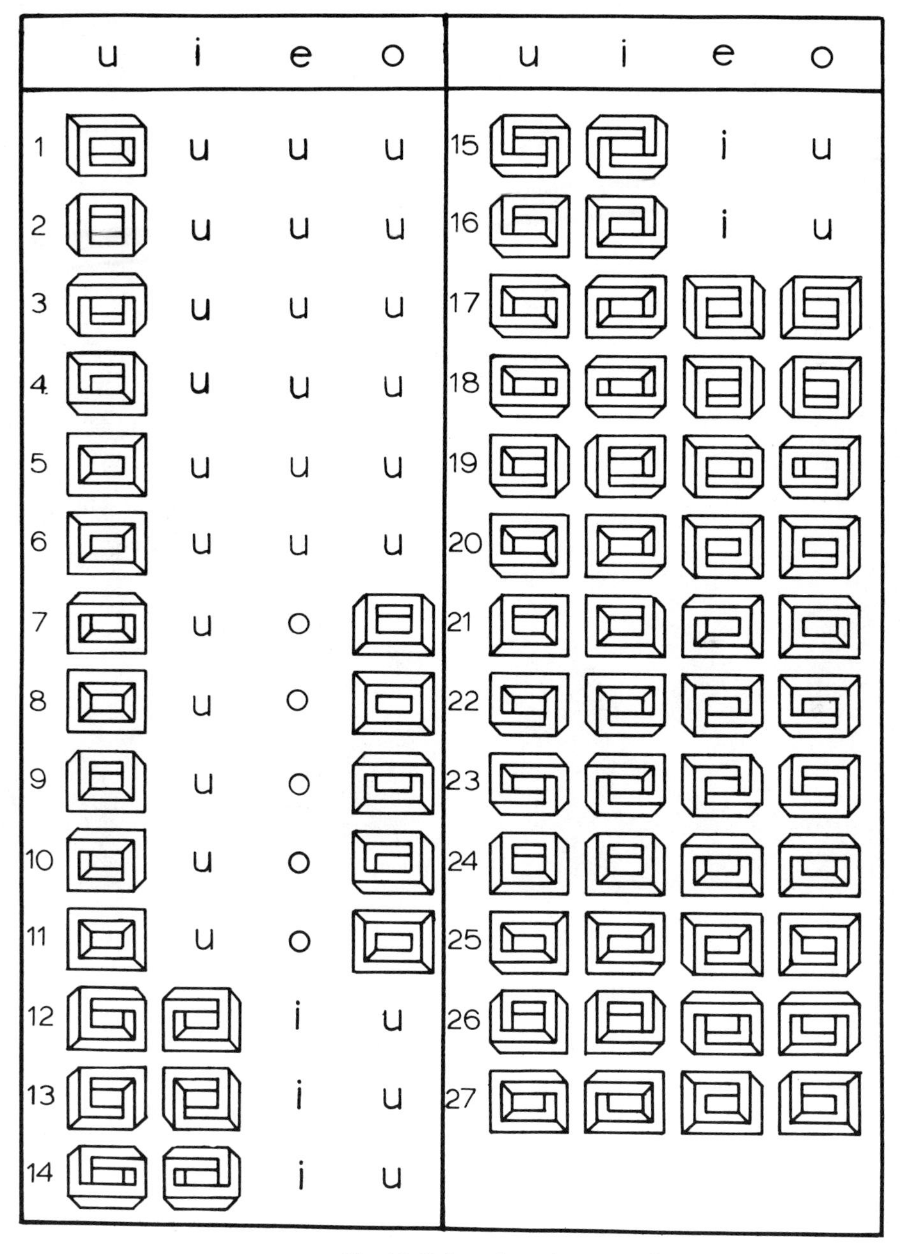

Fig. 10.48 (*continued*) B

FIG. 10.49. A figure that is impossible in a physical sense because of false interposition, not, as usually suggested, because of false perspective. (This is a painting by William Hogarth, 1754.)

Stimuli often only suggest the perceptual experience, rather than definitively determine it, and the processes of this level may best be thought of as solutions to a complex problem rather than as automatic responses to the stimulus.

As a result of this constructionistic overtone, and despite some presisting theoretical expressions to the contrary, all of the processes and phenomena described in this chapter seem to be beyond neurophysiological explanation. It is important to reiterate that this is not because they are in any sense fundamentally nonneural but because the complexity of neural computations that must underlie this kind of "mental" processing is so great as to preclude any attempts at neuroreductionistic explanation.

Admittedly, the words *interpretation* and *construction,* are part of a neorationalistic vocabulary that is not as easily specifically defined and made intuitively clear as was the more concrete, physicalistic, and neuoanatomic vocabulary that characterized the lower levels of the taxonomy proposed in this book. No longer do we have the anchors to the external world or references to the neural and anatomic substrate with which to conceptualize these terms. The vocabulary of neorationalism is only able to describe processes, and it fails to delineate mechanisms. As we saw in most of the instances in this chapter, the opaqueness of meaning was further complicated by the absence of good operational constructs and/or metrics for many of the phenomena when subjected to experimental scrutiny. Interpretative and constructionistic processes, whatever they are, disassociate the stimulus world from the mental world in a profound way; the vocabulary itself precludes deterministic links between the external physical and the internal mental worlds. This disassociation makes any attempt to define specifically the relevant processes much more difficult than when one is dealing with the concepts involved in the lower levels of processing. With regard to the outcome of Level 3 processes, the phenomenon is always "more" than the stimulus or any straightforward transformation of it. Information from previous experience or from the current state of the organism has been added or subtracted by censors and filters of one kind or another; the transformations between the stimulus and the percept, therefore, are neither linear nor nonlinear, nor, for that matter, even algebraic in any sense that would allow us to apply any of the much simpler stimulus–response philosophy that permeated early chapters of this book.

What we see emerging at Level 3 is phenomenal evidence of very powerful computational processes. Some of these processes are describable in the language of stochastic processes or differential discriminations, but others involve the elaboration of the *meaning* or symbolic significance of the stimulus in a way that probably will forever exceed the techniques and theories of deterministic empiricism. We may never be able to unravel the neural logic underlying the establishment of say, figure–ground relationships, nor understand how a "computational engine" like the brain could possibly accomplish the magnificent feats of perceptual computation and construction I have described here.

The initial process in visual form perception at Level 3 appears to be the segregation of the various subregions of a visual field on the basis of whatever discriminable differences exist. Once these discriminations are made and the primitive subregional partitions thus established, the perceptual field is "organized" into salient and nonsalient components. Like the words *interpretation* and *construction,* the word *organize* also eludes explicit definition. What is meant by "organize" is probably best appreciated by the many fascinating phenomena described rather than by any tortured effort to make the definition any more precise. The difficulty in conceptualizing these processes is reflected in the disappointing paucity of a good base of solid experimental findings concerning figure–ground construction, the priority of the various factors in grouping, or any satisfying estimates of the magnitude of most of the effects. Descriptive statements, like the classic Gestalt rules of grouping, and parlor-pleasant demonstrations, tend to substitute for quantitative or comparative studies when one searches for understanding in the field of figural organization.

It is also the reason that this chapter is necessarily weaker in adhering to the criterion of a process-oriented taxonomy than any other in this book. All too often in this discussion I have had to fall back on phenomenological discussions, rather than strictly process-oriented explanations. To put it simply, this is, unfortunately, the state of the art, and it represents an acknowledged weakness in the taxonomy I present here.

However difficult to explain, Level 3 phenomena cannot be ignored in any comprehensive description of perceptual processes. Their existence and nature are important parts of the best evidence of the limits of the empiricistic approach to perception. We have seen how the visual system is able to create the perception of depth where there was only a monocularly viewed, incomplete, two-dimensional stimulus, carry out complex statistical processing, and respond to stimuli that are so ambiguous that they do not uniquely define a specific perceptual outcome. All these high-level processes transcend isomorphism and determinism, and despite some farfetched and wildly speculative theories, the resulting phenomena make implausible any simple "neural-network-logic"-type explanations of the associated phenomenon. The major implication of all of the data described in this chapter, therefore, is that the visual nervous system involves logical processes about which we now know, and perhaps can only know, very little. These data, perhaps better than any other level of processing, reflect the great gulf between our current ideas of neural mechanism and perceptual process and demand a neorationalistic approach for this realm of perceptual science.

11 Level 4: Interdimensional Interactions Leading to Quantitative Perceptual Experiences—Perceptual Relativism

A. INTRODUCTION

The processes discussed in the previous chapter can all be characterized by the fact that, in general, they led to unmetricized and qualitative phenomena of figural segregation and organization. In this chapter, I consider a family of perceptual processes that, though similar in many ways to those encompassed within the Level 3 rubric, differ substantially in their outcomes. Level 4 processes typically induce quantified experiences (i.e., they lead to perceptual experiences that allow us to make judgments of the value of magnitude, quality, space, and time) rather than only qualitative differences in figural organization or regional discriminations. In other words, all Level 4 phenomena are capable of being scaled along perceptual dimensions in a way that was not, in general, possible with the outcomes of Level 3 processes.

There is, however, another very important criterion that distinguishes Level 4 from Level 3 processes in this taxonomy. In every case to which I allude in this chapter, the phenomenal outcome of a Level 4 process is the result of an interaction between two or more aspects or dimensions of the total stimulus scene. This intrinsic multidimensionality is an essential criterion for identifying a Level 4 process. Interdimensional interactions and quantitative percepts are, therefore, the joint characteristics of this level of perceptual processing. Indeed, as I surveyed the perceptual literature, it became clear that it may be impossible for an observer to develop any quantified estimate of any dimension of perceptual experience without some means of relating and comparing multiple aspects of the stimulus.

To further clarify this key point, let's consider some familiar analogous systems. Optical range finders used in the days prior to the development of electronic ranging devices (e.g., RADAR) required that two points of view be compared to determine the range to a target. These two points of view were obtained in this particular instrument by aligning the lines of sight of two lens systems on a target in such a way that a single fused image could be formed by an observer as shown in Fig. 11-1. This criterion of fusion determined the point at which measures should be made of the orientation angles, ϕ and θ, of the two lens systems. Simple trigonometry then could be applied to determine the exact range of the target.

The point is that a single-lens system is intrinsically incapable of producing this quantified range information.[1] In spite of a perfectly good optical image, the determination of range (or for that matter size) is not, in principle, possible without some intradimensional or intra-aspect comparison in this optical system.

When optical range finders were supplanted by electronic ranging systems that depended on the reflection of a transmitted radio wave from a target, the requirement for a relational process was not mitigated; it was still necessary to make a comparison to allow accurate ranging. In the case of the RADAR system, however, the comparison was made between the time it took for a transmitted signal to return from a target and the passage of time itself as a surrogate for

[1] In some instances it might have been possible to use a single lens and to obtain quantified range information by comparing the visual angle subtended by a known target with a set of standard size targets, but this is merely another means of implementing a comparison process.

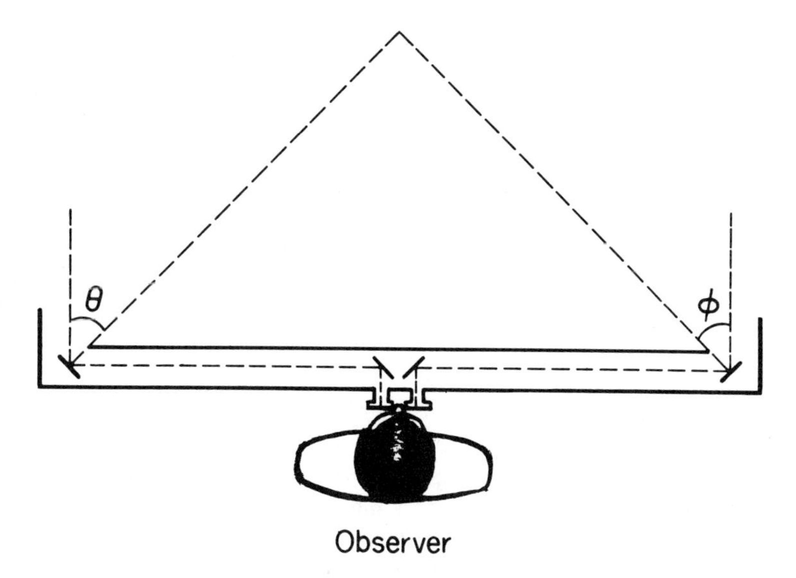

FIG. 11.1. An old fashioned optical range finder whose principle of operation is the comparison of the angles (θ and ϕ) of the two lines of sight.

distance. No matter how perfect the reception of a return signal, without the use of the time base as a reference standard no range data could be calculated.

In both of these two examples—the optical and the electronic systems—either a simulataneous spatial (relative angular positions) or a sequential temporal (relative delay) comparison had to be made between two information-bearing signals to determine range. In neither case could the absolute value of one singal provide sufficient information about the distance to the target.

I propose that this property of target-ranging equipment is illustrative of a much more general law of perception. The force of the argument in this chapter is that whereas we are able to organize stimuli into qualitative patterns on the basis of a single dimension of the stimulus, quantitative estimates of the value of any perceptual dimension depend entirely on comparisons made between two or more aspects or dimensions of the relevant stimulus. Each of the phenomena that I have collected within the Level 4 rubric in this chapter, whether it involves motion, color, lightness, or any dimension in any other experiential domain, depends on some kind of an underlying multidimensional comparison process.

The premise that perceptual quantification must depend on relational or comparative processes is hardly novel; many other psychologists, as early as Wundt (1894/1907) and as recently as Weintraub (1971), have suggested some variation of this idea. There seems to be substantial agreement that the concept of perceptual relativism is fundamental and that comparison processes are ubiquitous, if not always obvious, in all of the phenomena I discuss in this chapter. It is, in short, the essential idea around which this chapter is built.

This general principle of perceptual relativity, which suggests that we can only construct quantified dimensions of experience when multiple dimensions or aspects of a stimulus allow relational comparisons, is entirely consistent with what we have seen at other levels of neurophysiological encoding and perceptual processing. The experience of trichromatic color is but one example of a relational representation of information by signals (from three kinds of photosensitive photoreceptors) at a lower level. I have already shown on p. 401 how the nearly universally accepted trichromatic receptor theory suggests that activity in any one of the three wavelength-sensitive systems is indeterminate with regard to the resulting color experience. It is only when the three chromatic receptor outputs are compared and contrasted against each other that color code becomes unique.[2]

I cited another relevant example in Chapter 10. Without some sort of gradient or differential texture in a stimulus scene, there is a virtually immediate and progressive breakdown in the perceptual experience. Without multiple stimulus dimensions (as exemplified by a single luminous disk placed against an extensive dark background), only vague and ambiguous percepts can be generated, and these often do not persist—they rapidly fade away. What I am suggesting here, in sum, is that relational comparisons are the sine qua non of any quantified experience.

However, an extremely important caveat must be explicitly expressed at this point. Unfortunately, we know very little about the nature of these comparative and relational mechanisms, and I am no more qualified than any other student of perception to define specifically what is meant by a Level 4 "interactive process." We do not yet comprehend the internal neural logic and computational processes that actually integrate the various dimensions of stimulus information. The problem is that any current analysis of these processes is not only neurophysiologically nonreductive but possibly nonreductive in a logical sense as well. We are left only with approaches such as verbal and mathematical description to analyze Level 4 processes and phenomena. For example, we may measure the impact of the various stimulus factors that go into the determination of any perceptual experience. This is the traditional psychophysical approach well exemplified by the recent work of Naomi Weisstein and William Maguire (1978) in which ingenious new experimental paradigms were developed to study the impact of various aspects of stimulus organization on perceptual tasks.

Alternatively, we may fall back on formal mathematical description, using algorithms often originally developed to describe other physical mechanisms to represent more complicated psychological processes. Such an approach is well exemplified by Foster's (1978) application of the calculus of variations to the problem of apparent motion. However, applications of various systems of math-

---

[2]Although, as we see when we discuss color and lightness constancy, color is still not totally defined even in the case of this unique peripheral trichromatic representation. It is the code that is unique not the final perceptual interpretation of the information represented by that code.

ematics as descriptive tools involve process premises that are totally independent of any neurophysiological assumptions. Furthermore, the mathematical model may be based on farfetched, if not absurd, analogies to physical mechanisms to which they are equally poorly linked in terms of underlying mechanisms. Nevertheless, mathematical description plays an especially important role when the microelectrode is no longer effective in studying the higher levels of perceptual processing. The recent publication of Leeuwenberg and Buffart's (1978) compendium of models of visual perception is an excellent guide to the current status of this theoretical approach. I return to several of the formal theories described there in the more detailed discussions of later parts of this chapter.

No matter how badly reductive analysis fails us, it is only by continuing to concentrate on the nature of the processes, as opposed to the phenomena and as embodied in the nature of the relevant interactions, that order can be brought to the jumble of phenomena that are collected within the Level 4 rubric. This chapter, therefore, is organized around the theme of interactions as processes. I propose the following subclassification scheme for the processes specific to Level 4.

1. Static interactions between different objects located in different portions of space—Spatial Context.
2. Dynamic interactions between sequential representations of the same objects at different points in time—Temporal Context.
3. Interactions between disparate binocular representations of the same stimulus object—Binocular Disparities.
4. Compound interactions between different dimensions or aspects of the same stimulus.

The remainder of this chapter presents detailed discussions of the processes and phenomena I have allocated to each of these four major subclassifications. The significance of each category becomes clearer as we proceed. However, I also have a more general goal in mind. By juxtaposing phenomena I can show that in many cases they represent unappreciated, but equivalent, manifestations of virtually identical processes.

This chapter is an especially long one. Simply enumerating the awesome body of empirical facts demands a substantial number of pages. Unfortunately, there is only a modest amount of wisdom available with regard to underlying processes. This necessarily means that this chapter is going to be more encyclopedic than analytic. It is my hope that the proposed taxonomy will alleviate some of the discomfort associated with such a plethora of facts and that the reader will not find the conclusions and generalizations too distant as he proceeds through the empirical material.

Partially to ameliorate the difficulty to distant generalizations, I now briefly state one major conclusion toward which the substance of this chapter progressively leads. That yet-to-be-drawn conclusion is that Level 4 perceptual processes seem characteristically to involve the extraction of invariant information from the multiple stimuli or dimensions. This invariance extraction is based on logical computations that, although not particularly mysterious, are more or less invisible to the researcher as well as to the observer. Nor is the idea of invariance mysterious. The invariant information contained in the various stimulus configurations with which I deal can be precisely specified in almost all cases. Indeed, mathematicians frequently deal with patterns in which the critical information can be extracted only on the basis of comparisons among objects transformed in either space or time. Information of this sort, covert in the individual image, is often referred to as being invariant under transformation. The mathematician's task is to develop computational procedures that will extract that invariant information as various transformations of the object are compared with each other.

An analogous concept—the comparison of transformed objects by the perceptual system to extract invariances—is another way to make more concrete the perceptually relativistic and interactionistic processes referred to earlier in this chapter. It gives more specific substance to the idea that quantitative perceptual estimates can only be generated by relational, comparative, or, in this new terminology, invariance-sensitive procedures; it also provides some insight into these ideas that is not forthcoming from the simple assertion of the existence of a "perceptual relativity."

Of course this does not mean that we are, therefore, going to be handed the golden key to understanding the deep structure of perceptual processes. The task of understanding the intrinsic nature of the precognitive computational processes that mediate our ability to extract invariances is gargantuan. Nevertheless, they are understandable in principle, and we actually have fairly good ideas nowadays of the nature of some of the computations that must be carried out if not the exact details of how our brains actually do it. Progress has been substantial in this regard, as we shall see, particularly concerning the problem of constructing three-dimensional percepts from two-dimensional projections. In other instances, comparisons may be made between symbolic aspects of multiple stimuli and the invariance extraction is based on symbolic rather than mathematical comparisons.

The magic of the perceptual system is that it is able to carry out logical and quasi-mathematical calculations of great complexity to extract a wide variety of invariances. Clearly, the full explanation of how we do so is one of the great goals of perceptual psychology. There are, no doubt, many obstacles to achieving this goal, not the least of which is the fact that the computational processes are themselves entirely invisible, even to the perceiver, and must be inferred on the basis of indirect evidence. We do not personally have any introspective insight into the nature of the invariant extracting computations that underlie our experiences. I have mentioned several times in the preceding pages of this book that we perceive only the outcome of perceptual processing not the processes themselves.

In spite of these difficulties, the concepts of invariance and of the extraction of invariances under temporal and spatial transformations (by processes aptly described as computational comparisons or interactions) are central to this chapter. In those instances in which formal models are available, I acknowledge their existence. However, the caveat against confusing analogies with homologies is especially pertinent in this chapter and success in simulation must not be confused with success in explanation. Even though formal mathematical or nonnumerical computer algorithms capable of extracting the invariances can be identified, such mathematical solutions to the problem posed by perception are not unique—they provide no unequivocal information about the nature of the mechanisms actually executing the same tasks in the brain.

B. SPATIAL CONTEXT

In this section I consider a number of Level 4 interactions that occur among spatially separated objects or regions simultaneously present in a stimulus scene. It is important for the reader to appreciate that these Level 4 spatial interactions are vastly different from those only distantly analogous Level 2 processes discussed earlier. It is essential to remember that the perceptual interaction of objects in space can be of several different kinds. The first kind involves interactions within the space of relatively simple neural networks and includes the reciprocal lateral inhibitions discussed in Chapter 8. The kind of spatial interactions discussed in this section, however, consist of a substantially different class of processes. These processes may be better denoted by the use of the term *spatial context* than by *spatial interaction*. The interpretive and inferential processes that occur are much more complex; they take into account the nature of the meaningful or contextual relationships between objects in the same stimulus space, not on a strictly spatially isomorphic or geometrical basis as in the simple neural net but rather in a manner that involves nonisomorphic spatial relationships of a less topographic and more symbolic nature. All contrast and assimilation demonstrations, regardless of the specific dimension involved—spatial or otherwise—seem to reflect the activity of interactions in which the significance or value of a given dimension is more important than its physical geometry. In spite of this difference, the result of such interpretive interactions may be equally profound. Distortions of the shape of an object can be induced by another object, or an alteration in the perceived brightness or lightness of an object can result from its interaction with its spatial context. Spatial interactions at this level may also result in the attribution of a property that was not inherent in the original stimulus (such as depth, to an otherwise two-dimensional stimulus), or the emergence in the percept of features not physically present in the stimulus. The point is that such interactions can occur as a result of what a stimulus means, in addition to such parameters as its shape or its distance from its neighbors, yet still result in modifications of the perceptual experience compared to what would have been perceived if the object were isolated.

It is my belief that few of the spatial-context effects considered in this section could be adequately explained in either simplistic arithmetic or neuroreductionistic terms. The processes that underlie these phenomena transcend any simple additive or multiplicative interactions, of which lateral interaction is an example. Quite the contrary, most involve a kind of nonnumeric interaction more akin to the mental processing of the meaning of language. The great variety of dimensions (e.g., numerosity and shape as well as brightness and size) that are subject to the influence of spatial context is another strong argument against attributing any particular one of them (i.e., brightness) to local spatial interactions. As I have indicated in Chapter 9, not all of my colleagues would agree with this belief, and many have proposed Level 2 explanations of some of the phenomena described here. The analogies that exist between Level 2 and Level 4 processes are terribly seductive—both involve spatial dimensions, and both reflect a common geometry. However, for reasons briefly discussed in the previous chapter, the argument against such simplistic Level 2 neural network or field explanations of most of these phenomena seems to me to be compelling. I add additional counterarguments against Level-2-typc explanations of various phenomena as we proceed.

I now propose three major subclasses of Level 4 spatial-context processes. The first subclass includes the mechanisms that give rise to contrast or assimilation phenomena in which the color, brightness, size, lightness, or even the numerosity of a stimulus varies as a result of the spatial context in which it is embedded. Briefly, spatial-contrast effects are those in which one object or region in a stimulus scene is perceived less like its surround than would have been predicted had it been presented in isolation. Assimilation effects are those in which the spatial context exerts an influence in the opposite direction: The object is perceived as more like its surround than would have been predicted had it been presented in isolation. The prototype of this first subclass is, of course, that familiar phenomenon known as simultaneous contrast.

The second subclass of Level 4 spatial interactions includes those processes that lead to what have been termed the classic geometrical illusions. Although there are many kinds of illusiions (if the reader has bought my argument so far, he will agree that all perception is illusory), I am concerned here with only a specific subset of illusory phenomena. To circumscribe more precisely the class to which I refer, I limit the relevant geometrical illusions of this subclass to those spatial distortions of length, direction, or shape that are induced by their respective static spatial context. The famous Müller–Lyer and Poggendorff illusions are examples of this second subclass. Temporal, or dynamic, illusions are dealt with in a later section.

The third subclass of Level 4 spatial interactions includes processes that elicit the experience of depth from monocular cues. These must be distinguished from the processing of stereoscopic and dynamic cues to depth that are dealt with elsewhere in this chapter. The processing of static, monocular cues to depth is also a spatial interaction even though the final phenomenal outcome is quite different from the results of contrast processes. In this second subclass we see instances in which spatial interactions lead to the generation or construction of three-dimensional percepts from two-dimensional stimuli. Differences in image clarity, perspective, and interposition, among other factors, are all powerful cues to the elicitation of an experience of depth in such instances.

Obviously, in some cases a particular illusion may fall into two of the subclasses I have defined, depending on the point of view from which they are analyzed. For example, size contrast, itself an illusory phenomenon, has often been incorporated into explanations of certain geometric illusions of length or size. I try, however, to discriminate between different processes and phenomena in a way that minimizes these overlaps. In almost all cases, such redundant classifications result from a confusion of process with phenomenon. Let's now consider these three subclasses in greater detail to make clear the processes that are included within each one.

1. Spatial Contrast

If two or more objects or regions are present in a visual stimulus scene the response tends to be determined by the relationship that exists between the objects or regions as well as by their individual properties. One way in which this relational interaction can be mediated is through a process that has been generically referred to as *contrast*. Although the most familiar contrast illusion is the well-known simultaneous brightness-contrast demonstration shown in Fig. 11-2, almost any dimension of the perceptual response is susceptible to a similar kind of interaction. Contrast can affect the perceived size, shape, numerosity, or color, and probably any other dimension of perception that would ever be tested. In the following pages I consider various contrast effects according to a subclassification scheme based on the subjective dimension being influenced.

a. Brightness Contrast. The prototypical question asked in the simultaneous brightness-contrast experiment is what is the effect of the luminance of the surround on the perceived brightness of a stimulus object? In this context, the brightness-contrast paradigm can be seen to highlight a fundamental perceptual principle; that is, *the experience does not depend entirely on the local properties of the stimulus object itself but on the object's relationship with its perceptual environment as well.* Whatever other role contrast plays, this profoundly important concept must never be overlooked in discussions of perceptual processes. The impact of this principle is to dissociate experience from the local physical

FIG. 11.2. The prototypical simultaneous contrast stimulus.

attributes of the stimulus and to place it in the higher-level context alluded to when one invokes such an idea as perceptual relativity.

The classic brightness-contrast experiment was reported 90 years ago by Hess and Pretori (1894). In their pioneering study, they established the most general principle of simultaneous brightness contrast; namely, that the brighter the surround, the dimmer an enclosed test stimulus appeared. More modern research on the problem has been carried out by Heinemann (1955), Horeman (1963), and Jameson and Hurvich (1961), among many others to whom I shortly refer. The general stimulus arrangement that Heinemann and subsequent experimenters all used is virtually the same. A constrasting stimulus surround and an enclosed

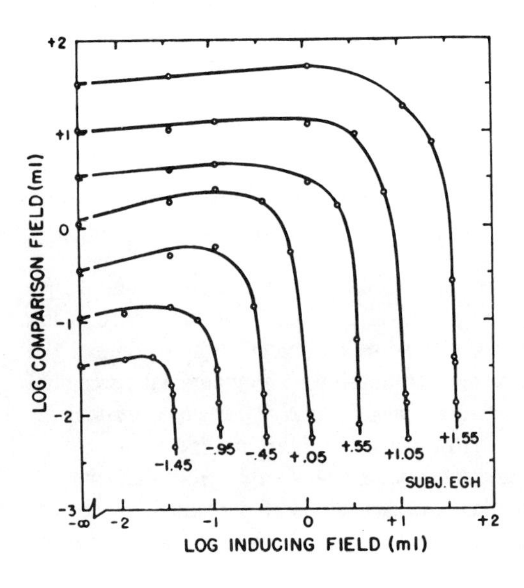

FIG. 11.3. Typical results from a simultaneous contrast experiment. The observer's admustment of the luminance of a comparison field is plotted as a function of the luminance of the inducing field. The parameter is the luminance of the test field. (From Heinemann, © 1955, with the permission of the American Psychological Association.)

contrasted stimulus (usually a concentric annulus and a disc-shaped spot respectively) are placed at some distance from a matching stimulus. To measure the subjective magnitude of a contrasted test stimulus, the observer adjusts the intensity of a matching stimulus so that the matching brightness appears equal to that of the enclosed test stimulus. Thus, a key premise in this and related experiments is that although the effect of the contrasting stimulus on the brightness of the contrasted stimulus is substantial, its influence on the brightness of the matching stimulus is minimal. The change in the setting of the matching stimulus produced by the surround is used as a measure of the surround's contrast effect.

The general results of the Heinemann-type experiment are shown in Fig. 11-3 for various levels of the test spot's luminance. In general, we see from this figure that the luminance of the surrounding annulus does not appreciably affect the brightness of the test spot until the luminance of the annulus is roughly half that of the test spot.[3] However, after that threshold has been exceeded, there is a remarkable reduction in the brightness of the test spot for increasing annulus luminance. The slope of this decline is quite steep; it is possible to reduce the apparent brightness of the test spot by contrast until the luminance of the matching light has to be less than one-thousandth of that of the test light to achieve a good match.

An even more useful representation of the effect of contrasting luminance in simultaneous contrast paradigms has been suggested by Horeman (1965). As shown in Fig. 11-4, he constructed a three-dimensional graph showing the measured apparent brightness that resulted when various values of both test luminance and contrasting luminance were used. The resulting surface depicts, better than any single two-dimensional curve, the interaction effects of varying both contrasting and contrasted luminance. Furthermore, Oyama (1967) has noted that this is only one of a class of surfaces that can be constructed using such other dependent variables as the luminance of a matching stimulus or any single multiplicative transform of subjective brightness. He says that although the choice of dependent variable will affect the shape of the surface, all such surfaces will be linear transforms of each other.

Despite the fact that workers such as Fry (1948), Diamond (1960), Ratliff (1965) and Cornsweet (1970) have associated this kind of simultaneous brightness-contrast with lateral inhibitory interactions, the neural inhibition model is woefully inadequate to handle this contrast phenomenon, as I argued in Chapter 9. Another dramatic example counterindicating such a simplistic Level 2

[3]Although I concentrate here on the diminishing effects of a brighter contrasting stimulus on a dimmer test one. it should at least be noted in passing that it is also possible to produce a reverse effect. If the contrasting stimulus is much dimmer than the test stimulus, the latter may appear brighter than it would in isolation. This reversed contrast, enhancement, or assimilation phenomenon has been known for many years (von Bezold, 1874) and has been discussed in detail by J. O. Robinson (1972) and by R. DeValois (1973). Reversed contrast can also result when the size of the contrasting stimulus is reduced (Helson, 1943).

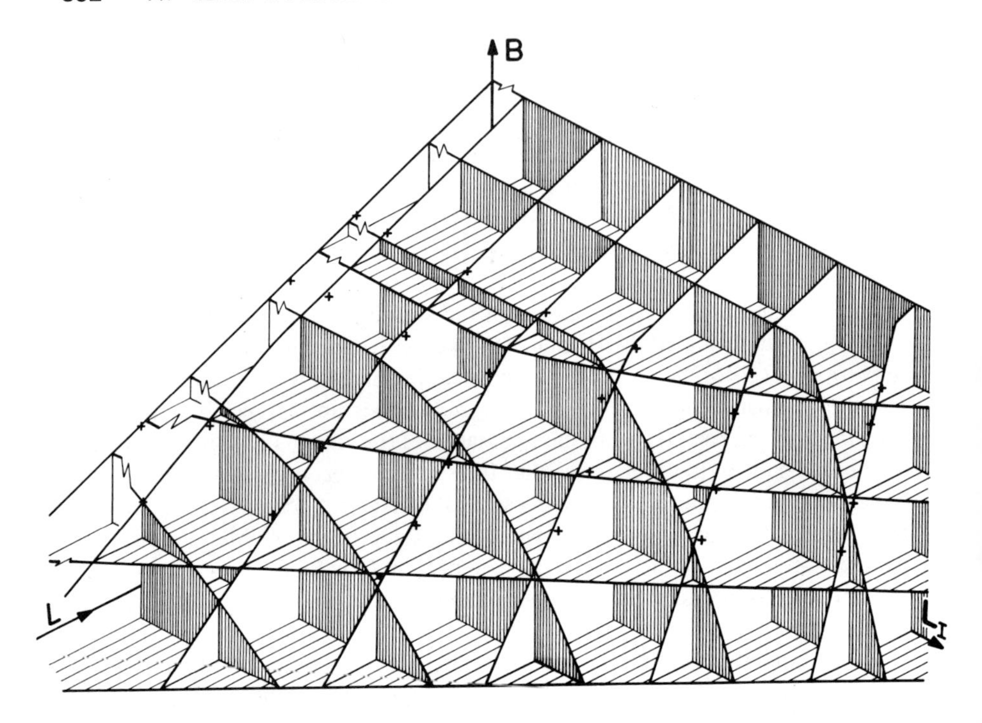

FIG. 11.4. A three-dimensional plot of the relationship between perceived brightness (B), the luminance of the inducing field (L_I) and the luminance of the test field (L). (From Horeman, © 1965, with the permission of Pergamon Press.)

theory of contrast was shown in Fig. 10-16. If this unusual contrast display is shown to an observer, despite the difference in the bipartite surround, the central spot will appear to be of constant brightness across its entire extent. However if even the slenderest vertical thread is placed to divide the test spot into equal halves, then the two sides change their apparent brightness substantially. It would be hard to develop a spatial "inhibitory" interaction model to explain this startling over all change. Obviously, in this case, the thread plays a role quite different from that of a modifier of "lateral inhibitory interactions." To the contrary, it has acted to alter substantially the "contexts" and perhaps even more importantly, the "meaning" of that context. Much higher-level processes must thus be invoked to explain the nature of this kind of perceptual experience.

A closely related phenomenon is the so-called Craik–O'Brien–Cornsweet illusion. Here too, the nature of the discontinuity between two regions can produce different perceived brightness even when the luminance of the two regions is identical. If a stimulus characterized by the cross-sectional luminance distribution shown in Fig. 11-5A is presented to an observer, the stimulus is transformed in such a way that it is perceived as being made up of two areas of different, though uniform, brightness, as shown in Fig. 11-5B. The entire area to the left of the region of discontinuity appears dimmer than the entire area on the right.

This illusion was first reported by Craik (1940a) and then by O'Brien (1958). It has subsequently been developed in several other forms by Cornsweet (1970) among others. Although repeated allusions to a lateral interaction explanation of this phenomenon have been made by many perceptual psychobiologists, the important thing to note about this illusion is that the global change in brightness over such broad areas is not well predicted by any plausible lateral inhibitory interaction theory. The extreme breadth of the regions over which the phenomenon occurs seems to place it in another domain, one in which the overall "context" is responsible for the phenomenon rather than any local spatial interactions.

Further evidence against considering this illusion as the outcome of a simple lateral spatial interaction is the fact that this same illusion can be produced along many other stimulus dimensions that do not involve brightness. MacKay (1973), for example, has shown that an analog of the Craik–O'Brien–Cornsweet illusion exists for line spacings (in which case the perceived distortion is on apparent line spacing rather than on brightness). Furthermore, Crovitz (1976) has shown that such an interaction exists for line lengths, and Anstis, Howard, and Rogers (1978) have even shown that an analog of the illusion exists in stereoscopic space in spite of the fact that the depth dimension does not even exist in the two-dimensional retinooptic representation space in which the inhibitory interactions are conventionally supposed to be located. An analogous phenomenon can also

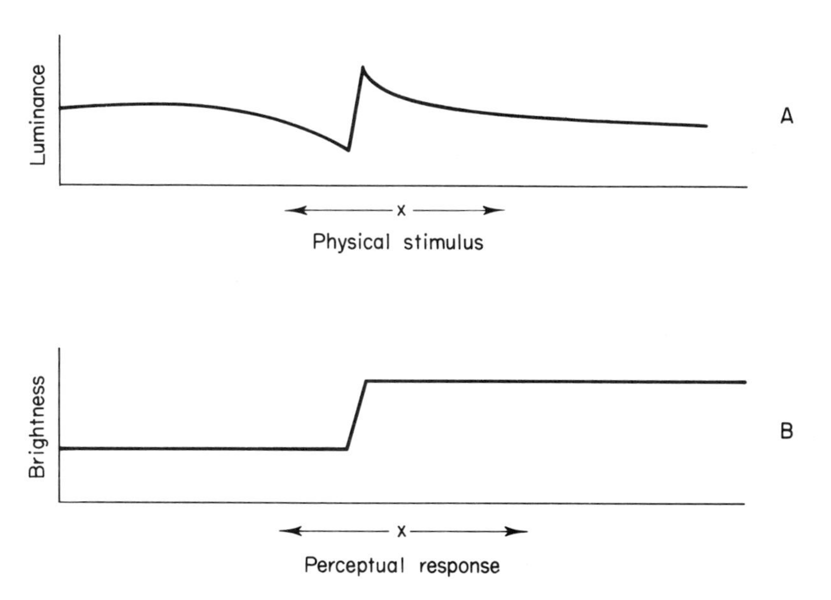

FIG. 11.5. The Craik-O'Brien-Cornsweet illusion. (A) A plot of the luminance of the physical stimulus. (B) A plot of the perceived brightness.

be produced in an auditory loudness context (Jesteadt, Green, & Wier, 1978; Rawdon-Smith & Grindley, 1935).

The point of all of these examples is to stress that contrast effects are neither simple nor local. They are produced by relational factors that extend over very broad regions, and they are compelling in situations in which simple concepts of lateral inhibitory interaction cannot possibly apply. These illusions, quite to the contrary, must be the outcome of very broad global processes that depend on spatial "symbols" and "interpretations" of the global organization of stimuli more than on local inhibitory interactions.

The fact that higher-order (i.e., Level 4) processes are seemingly better explanations of the simultaneous contrast phenomenon that Level 2 processes does not mean, of course, that analogous systematic laws of spatial interaction do not hold for these higher-level processes as well as for the lower-level ones. Indeed, it has been repeatedly shown that the distance between the test stimulus and a simultaneously contrasting stimulus is also a critical factor in determining the magnitude of the contrast effect. For example, in experiments similar in design to that of Heinemann's classic experiment, but with the added independent variable of distance between a circular test target and a circular (i.e., nonannular) contrasting target, Leibowitz, Mote, and Thurlow (1953), as well as Mackavey, Bartley, and Casella (1961), have shown that the farther the two stimuli are separated from each other the greater thc decrease in the contrast effect.

A fascinating and thoroughly illuminating corollary of this phenomenon, to which I alluded in Chapter 9, is that the decline in the brightness-contrast effect with spatial separation also occurs when the test and contrasting stimuli are increasingly separated in stereoscopic depth (Gilchrist, 1977; Gogel & Mershon, 1969; among others). Because depth is itself a constructed perceptual experience and because the two-dimensional projections on the retina are actually physically adjacent, this important finding also argues strongly against any kind of a peripheral neural interaction explanation of contrast.

This finding—reduction in contrast efficacy with increase in depth separation—is also closely related to the continuing controversy concerning the possible binocularity of the simultaneous contrast phenomena. As noted in Chapter 9, there is some evidence (Uttal, 1973, p. 454) that brightness contrast occurs even when the test and contrasting portions of the stimulus are presented dichoptically. However, I must also acknowledge that this is not universally accepted. Many experimenters have interpreted their experimental results to indicate that dichoptic brightness contrast does not in fact exist. This point, of course, is critical, for it would require a severe stretch of a peripheral lateral inhibition model to explain any simultaneous contrast effects if the phenomena were definitively shown in this manner to be present with dichoptic stimuli. However, as we see later in this chapter, there are many other instances of binocular interactions that do support a centralist explanation for this general class of phenomenon.

Geometrical factors other than spatial separation also play an influential role in defining the magnitude of the simultaneous contrast phenomenon. Increases in either the number or size of the contrasting stimuli increase the brightness-contrast effect in the same way as does an increase in luminance (Torii & Uemura, 1965). The reader is also directed to Kitterle (1972) for both new data and a good minireview of the effects of size and number of the contrasting stimuli on the simultaneous contrast phenomenon.

Thus both spatial and areal factors play an important role in defining the extent of the brightness-contrast effect. However they too are not totally definitive of the resulting percept. Organizational and configurational properties of the stimulus also influence simultaneous contrast effects even when luminance, distance, and area are kept constant. It is, for example, even possible to reverse contrast to assimilation while holding the luminance and areal relations constant simply by altering the spatial configuration.

An example of the influence of configuration on simultaneous contrast can be found in the Benary cross illusion shown in Fig. 11-6. In this figure, it can be seen that the triangular area external to the body of the cross is apparently brighter than the one lying within the perimeter of the cross. However, both are surrounded by exactly the same amount of black and white and have exactly the same black–white contour length. Kanizsa (1975) explains this paradoxical illusion by noting that the triangle inside the cross appears to "belong" to the cross and the one outside the perimeter is not a "part" of the figure. Thus, according to Kanizsa, the difference in the degree of "belongingness" (a symbolic and certainly not a geometric concept) is the immediate precursor of the difference in contrast effects.

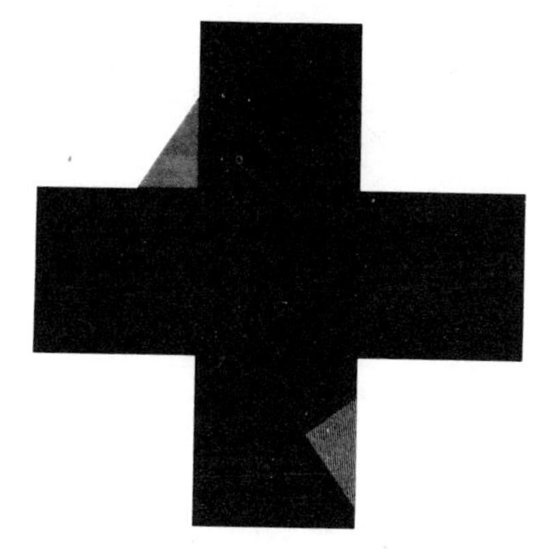

FIG. 11.6. The Benary cross illusion showing paradoxical contrast. Though both gray triangles should have the same inhibitory forces operating on them, they tend to be seen with different brightness because of their configurational relationship (inside versus outside) to the large cross. (Courtesy of Dr. Gaetano Kanizsa of the University of Trieste.)

Just how complex the contrast interactions can be is perhaps best illustrated by an important study reported by Jameson and Hurvich (1961). In their experiment the stimulus used was a complex pattern involving five different square regions arranged as indicated in Fig. 11-7. The reflectance of each of the five regions was kept constant; therefore, the *relative* luminance of all of the areas remained constant, however much the overall illumination varied. The pattern was presented at three different levels of illumination, and observers were asked to make brightness judgments (as measured by the setting of a matching light) about each region at each of these three levels of illumination.

Jameson and Hurvich obtained a rather startling result in this experiment. As would have been expected from what we already know about contrast, there was no simple relationship between the luminance of each region and its respective apparent brightness. For example, no power law was able to define the relationship between the luminance of each area and the perceived brightness of that area. The brightness function of each area depended on its relations with its neighbors, much more than on the absolute level of illumination and its reflectance. Contrast affects were, therefore, complex among the different areas and no single function could account for the brightness changes of all five regions at the three levels of illumination. Indeed, the perceptual responses to the various stimulus regions were not even all qualitatively alike; i.e., they were not in the same direction. The stimulus square with the lowest reflectance descreased in brightness as the overall illumination of this complex scene increased. On the other hand, the three highest reflectance squares substantially increased in preceived brightness as the overall illumination increased. Not surprisingly in such a

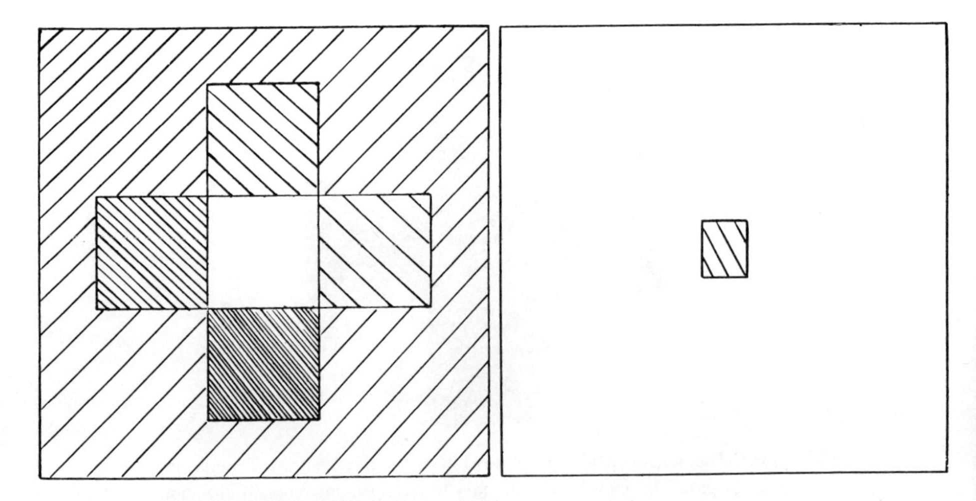

FIG. 11.7. The stimulus pattern used in the Jameson and Hurvich experiment. (From Jameson and Hurvich, © 1961, with the permission of the American Association for the Advancement of Science.)

situation, with some increases and some decreases there must be a neutral point and, indeed, the remaining stimulus, the second least reflective, remained relatively constant in brightness over wide ranges of illumination. All of these results are shown graphically in Figs. 11-8A–E. Such diverse results led Jameson and Hurvich to reject both a "ratio" and "adaptation level" explanation of contrast. Although seeing some promise for neural interaction models, they too concluded that "interpretive" processes must be invoked to explain contrast.

Simultaneous brightness contrast, therefore, seems to be a highly complex, and probably a very high-level, central effect in which the dominant processes are best incorporated within the Level 4 rubric. There certainly are significant perturbations inserted into the spatial interaction process by lower-level processes (Mach type lateral neural interactions may modify the effect near contours, and blur may affect the brightness-contrast phenomenon to some degree—Coren and Girgus, 1978). Nevertheless, there is little doubt that by far the major portion of the phenomena I have discussed here must be attributable to perceptual computations that work according to the rules of a logic of which we know very little. Given the contextual and paradoxical properties of wide area contrast, one can only conclude that the substantial confusion found in the literature of these Level 2 and Level 4 processes is based on little more than a superficial analogy. Walter Gogel (1978) has put it much better. Recalling and generalizing Kirschmann's (1891) and Titchener's (1915) earlier laws of proximity, he notes that many perceptual phenomena display a sensitivity to variations in the spatial separation between the interacting objects; Gogel refers to this very general sensitivity as the "adjacency principle." The important point about the adjacency principle is that Gogel has conceptualized it as a very general concept denoting a wide variety of perceptual processes that, although are all dependent on distance, are not necessarily identical in terms of underlying mechanisms. Some of these processes certainly are mediated by peripheral and local neural interactions; others, however, are mediated by perceptual processes of a much greater level of complexity. Some are relatively automatic in the sense that Helmholtz referred to as "unconscious inference" (and I believe that simultaneous contrast falls well within the limits of such a subtle and invisible computational process); others may indeed involve attentive cognitive processing of an even more complicated nature.

b. Color Contrast. A generalization of the concept of simultaneous spatial contrast beyond the dimension of brightness is illustrated by the effects on perceived color that occur when a colored object is surrounded by objects or surrounds of other colors. The realization that, like brightness, the chromatic response to a stimulus is not determined solely by the wavelengths of light emitted or reflected from it, but also by its context, was appreciated very early in the history of experimental psychology. Meyer (1855), Helmholtz (1866), and Hering (1887) are among the great names of 19th century visual science that

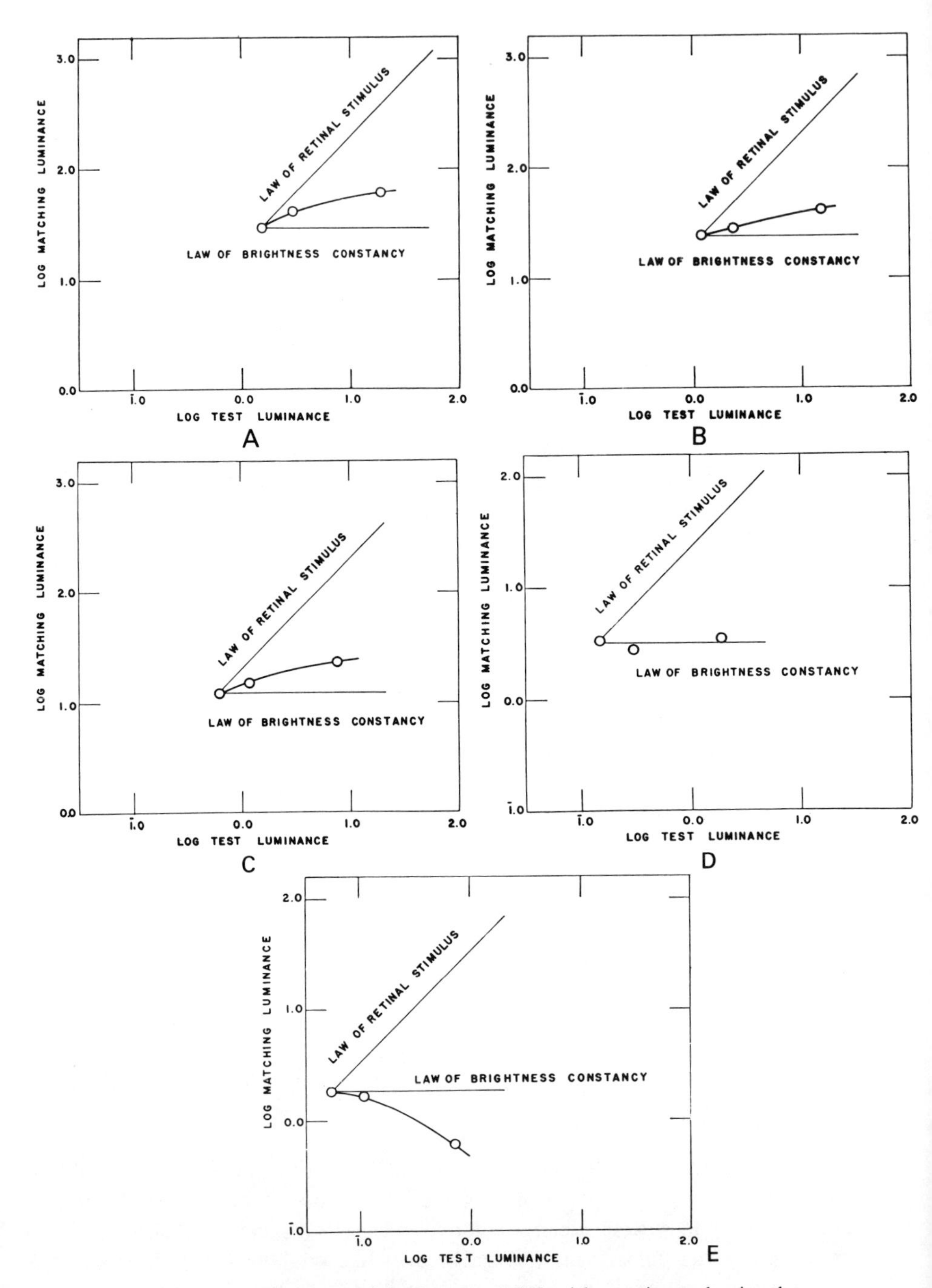

FIG. 11.8. The results of the Jameson and Hurvich experiment showing the luminance to which the matching stimulus had to be set as a function of the overall luminance for (A) the center square in Fig. 11.7; (B) the right square; (C) the upper square; (D) the left square; and finally, (E) the lower square. (From Jameson and Hurvich, © 1961, with the permission of the American Association for the Advancement of Science.)

considered the problem of color contrast to be of substantial import. Subsequently, Pretori and Sachs (1895) showed that color assimilation—i.e., situations in which the test stimulus acquires the color of the contrasting stimulus—could also be obtained even if the test area were black. The spatial interactions that mediate color contrast, therefore, share one of the main characteristics of brightness contrast—when the test stimulus is dim or dark, it tends to adopt the color of the inducing surround rather than to contrast with it.

As early as 1891 Kirschmann felt that knowledge of color contrast was sufficiently complete to formulate five general rules governing the phenomenon. They have been summarized by Graham and Brown (1965 p. 460, abstracted) as follows:

1. Color contrast increases when the area of the contrasting region increases.
2. Color contrast increases when the area of the contrasted region decreases.
3. Color contrast declines when the contrasting regions are increasingly separated.
4. Color contrast is at a maximum when brightness contrast is minimal.
5. Color contrast increases with increasing saturation of the contrasting region.

These general rules not only describe the dynamics of the spatial interactions involved in color contrast but also represent a fairly complete expression of the factors (distance, purity, area, luminance difference) that are effective in defining the magnitude of these particular contrast phenomena. Most recent research has been an attempt to determine the quantitative details of each of Kirschmann's rules. For example, Helson and Rohles (1959) have made detailed measurements of the effect of the size of the contrasting region and have generally confirmed Kirschmann's first law. As another example, Oyama and Hsia (1966) specifically attacked the problem of the effect on color contrast of the distance separating the contrasted and the contrasting stimulus. Using a procedure in which the observer had to adjust the color of a stimulus to the best perceived blue, green, yellor, or red appearance, they measured the changing magnitude of the contrast effect when a contrasting annulus was separated by various spacings from a concentric disk. The results of this experiment are shown in Fig. 11-9. Depending on the spectral properties of the contrasting stimulus and the separation, the adjustment of the test stimulus to produce the best color varied considerably. Oyama and Hsia found that the color-contrast effect, as suggested by Kirschmann, decreased with greater separation according to the functions shown in this figure.

Kirschmann's law dealing with the impact of the spectral purity of the contrasting stimulus was studied quantitatively by Schjelderup-Ebbe (1926) in a study that remains definitive. He reported a strong positive and linear relationship between the magnitude of the contrast effect and the purity of the contrasting light. Another major finding of Schjelderup-Ebbe's experiment was that the

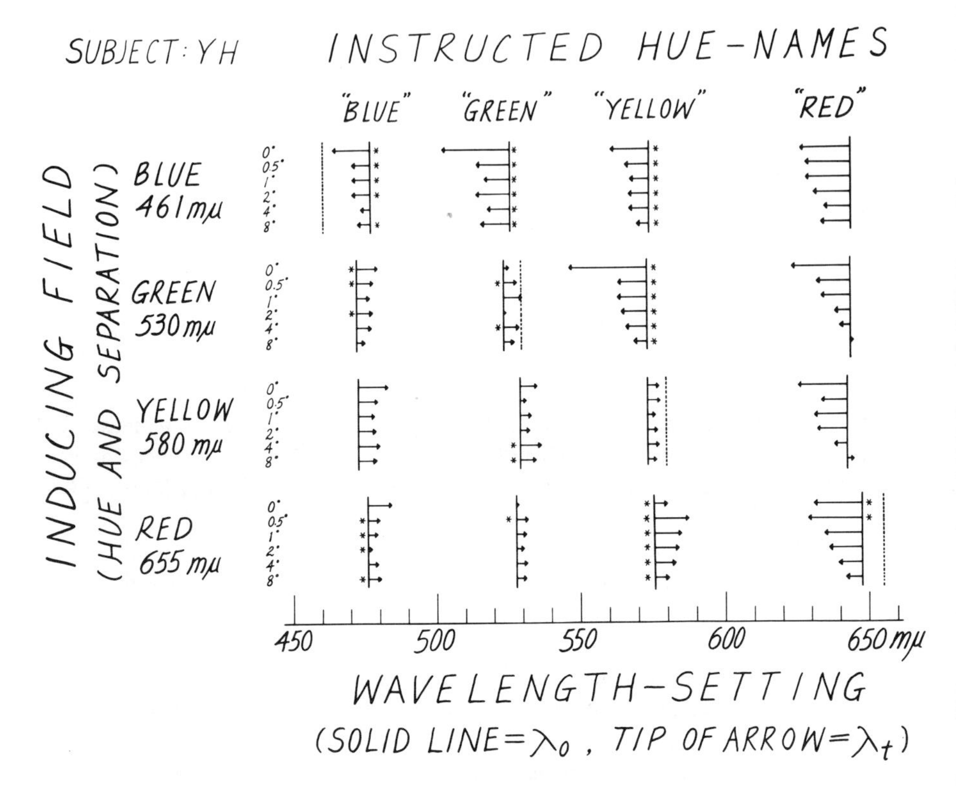

FIG. 11.9. The shift in hue produced by color contrast as a function of wavelength for various separations of the inducing and induced stimuli. The vertical lines indicate the wavelength settings for the test stimuli without the contrasting stimuli to match a particular reference color name. The small horizontal lines indicate the amount the wavelength of the test stimulus had to be shifted to maintain the reference color in the presence of the inducer. (From Oyama and Hsia, © 1966, with the permission of the American Psychological Association.)

contrast effect was very much a function of the dominant wavelength of the contrasting stimulus. Long-wavelength stimuli produced much less dramatic contrast effects than did shorter-wavelength ones.

These more recent quantitative empirical elaborations of Kirschmann's rules have generally supported the empirical findings that came from the early research on color contrast. However, there has been a paucity of good theory to explain the phenomena of color assimilation or contrast. Such Gestalt field-type theories as Obonai's (1977) "psychophysical induction model" have not stood up well to the test of modern neurophysiological research. Nor, for that matter, do the lateral interaction theories (which are usually based upon experiments in which very small and closely spaced stimuli are used as an approximation to the larger regions of the classic stimulus) do well when it is appreciated that they are probably not assaying the same mechanisms and processes. However some progress has been made in developing formal descriptive theories of color contrast. Unfortunately, complex mathematico-descriptive theories of contrast (e.g., Buffart, 1978), do not entirely satisfy our need for a neurophysiological explanation either, because they often involve so many degrees of freedom and so few essential neurophysiological assumptions that they would allow a host of possible mechanisms to embody the processes described in that type of model. However, such mathematical descriptions may be highly realistic from one point of view in their expression of the enormous computational complexity of the visual nervous system.

c. Other Spatial-Contrast Processes. Brightness and color do not exhaust the family of perceptual dimensions that exhibit the common property of being affected by their spatial surrounds. Indeed, the fact that so many other nonspatial dimensions are so affected by spatial context is itself strongly supportive of the hypothesis that no simplistic spatial interaction model could account for the manifold effects of spatial context on perception. For example, many of the classic geometric illusions can be most coherently classified as contextual alterations of size, length, or shape due to contrast interactions with their surrounds. In a quick scan through J. O. Robinson's (1972) excellent compilation of visual illusions, one easily identifies some that are clearly of this genre. A particularly clear example is shown in Fig. 11-10A. This is an example of a spatial-contrast illusion in which the perceived length of a line segment varies substantially as a function of the length of adjacent segments. Figure 11-10B shows, furthermore, the effect on the perceived curvature of one line that results from differences in curvature of other lines in the stimulus scene (Oyama, 1960b). The classic Titchener circles (as described by Wundt, 1898) are clearly of this same category: Circles of physically identical size can be substantially altered in their perceived size, depending on the size of other circles by which they are surrounded. This striking illusion is shown in Fig. 11-11A. Many other familiar

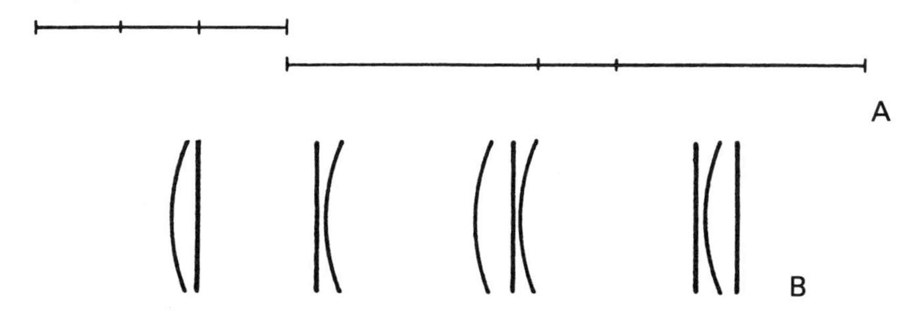

FIG. 11.10. Some geometrical illusions of spatial contrast. (A) An illusion of length; (B) an illusion of curvature. (From Robinson, © 1972, with the permission of Hutchinson University Library.)

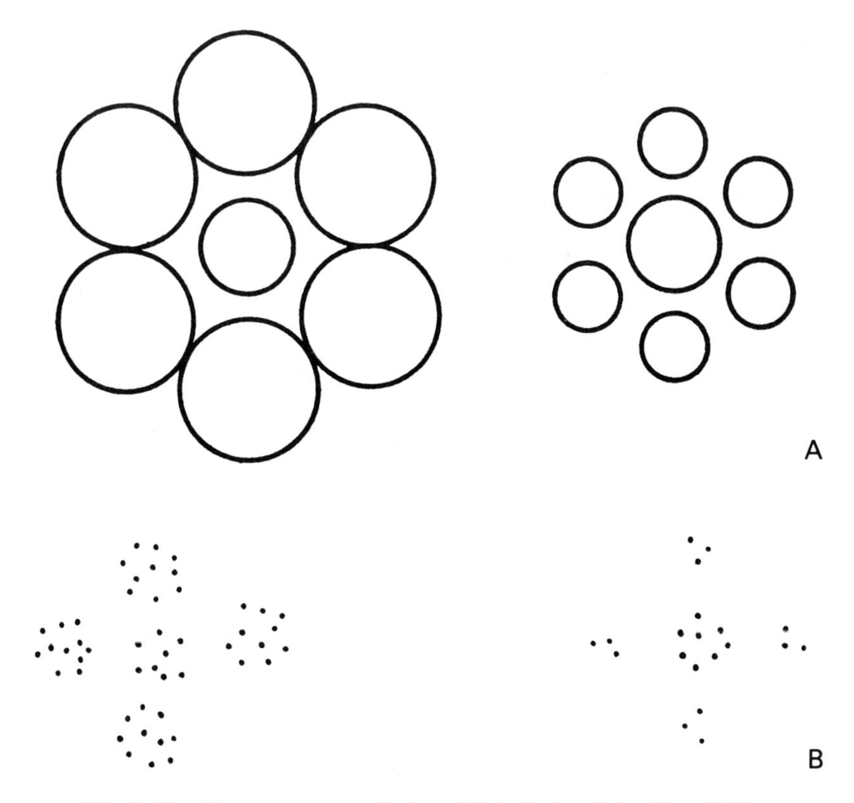

FIG. 11.11. Some more contrast illusions. (A) An illusion of size. (From Robinson, © 1972, with the permission of Hutchinson University Library.) (B) An illusion of numerosity. (Courtesy of Professor Tadasu Oyama of the University of Tokyo.)

illusions in which the geometrical properties of the perceptual response are altered from those of the stimulus, though not traditionally attributed to the same processes that underlie spatial-contrast effects, can be considered to be examples of this same kind of interaction.

Then there are other illusions, not so well known, that also fit in the spatial contrast rubric. Tadasu Oyama (1979) reports a contrast effect in which the apparent numerosity of a cluster of dots depends strongly on the numerosity of other clusters of dots in the surround. This phenomenon is shown in Fig. 11-11B. Clearly, numerosity is a nonspatial dimension that makes any spatial interaction theory of lateral inhibition extremely implausible.

This brings us to the major conclusion of this section on spatial-contrast interactions. My thesis here has been that it is essential to appreciate that even though adjacent objects in a stimulus scene may interact, it is not necessary to attribute that interaction to isomorphic interactions in some hypothetical neural net. Rather, the diversity of the dimensions that are subject to contrast effects, as well as the properties of those that have been quantitatively measured, make it clear that interactions along nonspatial dimensions (e.g., redder than or more numerous than) may be more important in determining the magnitude of some of these spatial interaction effects than the physical attributes of distance or spectral components. The impact of this line of logic is to shift putative explanations from concentrating excessively on isomorphic, passive, neural interactions toward considering processes so complex that they can only be characterized by neorationalistic terms and concepts.

But it must also be admitted that, in general, contemporary rationalistic theories of contrast are also not convincing. Theories such as Helson's (1948) adaptation level approach or the even older "ratio" models are but descriptions that do not attempt to analyze mechanisms and processes deeply. The substitution of a constructionistic–neorationalistic theory for those primitive lateral interaction ideas is also not completely satisfactory, but at least it places the discussion in what I believe is the proper context.

2. Static Geometrical Illusions

Perhaps no area of perceptual research has achieved such enormous popularity (it also epitomizes the subject for the lay public) as has the study of the "classic" geometrical illusions. Although I have already indicated that some of those illusions seem to fit in well with the concept of spatial contrast, there are many others that do not conveniently do so. Nevertheless, contrast or not, many of the illusions to which I now refer represent the results of other spatial interactions between different parts of the scene. A major point I wish to make here is that contrast phenomena alone do not exhaust the possible variations contained within the term *spatial interaction*.

Because of the popularity of visual illusions, there has always been an abundant supply of good review books on the topic, and I shall not attempt to summarize the many fine discussions of geometrical illusions that are more competently and fully presented elsewhere. Among the books dealing specifically with geometrical illusions are works by Luckiesh (1922), Tolansky (1964), J. O. Robinson (1972), and more recently, Coren and Girgus (1978). Other books also deal—to a lesser degree of completeness—with the problem posed by visual illusions (e.g., Gregory & Gombrich, 1973), but not in such detail as the first four mentioned with regard to the data or theory of the particular kind of spatial-interaction illusion that I will emphasize in this section.

I have previously asserted that all perception is more or less illusory, and therefore that the term "geometrical illusion" must be further delimited in its denotation for the purposes of the following discussion. Perhaps the best way to do this is through Fig. 11-12. This figure presents the prototypes of many of the classic geometrical illusions that have attracted so much lay and professional

Name	Illusory stimulus	Effect
Vertical—horizontal	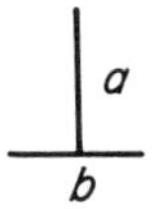 a b	*a* appears longer than *b*
Müller—Lyer	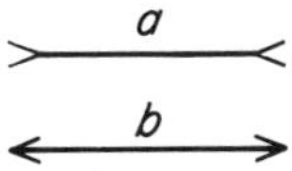 a b	*a* appears longer than *b*
Fat lady	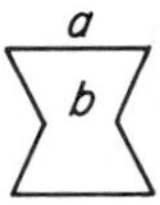 a b	*b* appears greater than ½ of *a*
Convergence—divergence	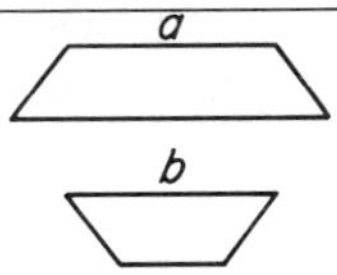 a b	*a* looks longer than *b*
Wundt's area	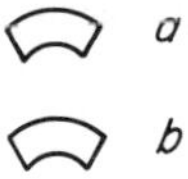 a b	*b* looks larger than *a*
Filled—empty space a	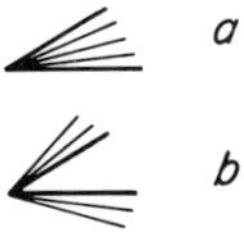 a b	*b* looks larger than *a*
b	 a b	*b* looks longer than *a*
Curvature	 a b c	Even though all arcs have same curvature, shorter appears less curved
Poggendorff	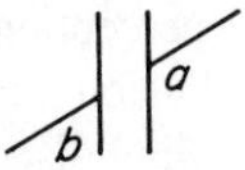 a b	*a* nd *b* do not appear to be colinear

FIG. 11.12. A sampler of spatial geometric illusions.

Name	Illusory stimulus	Effect
Zöllner	 a b	Lines *a* and *b* appear nonparallel
Ebbinghaus (size contrast)*	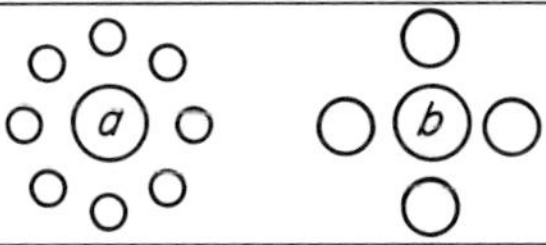 a b	*a* looks larger than *b*
Angle contrast	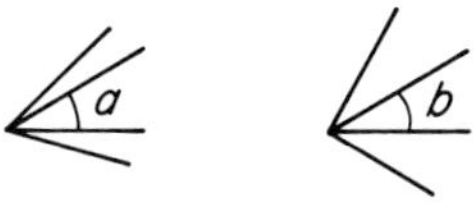 a b	∠*a* looks larger than ∠*b*
Perspective	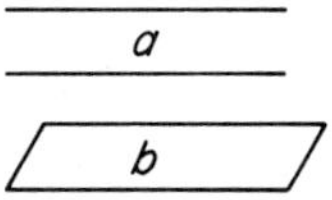 a b	Lines in *a* look further apart than lines in *b*
Wundt's lines‡	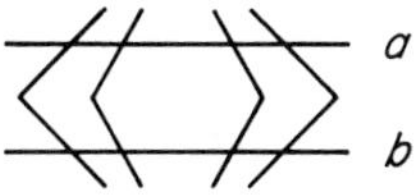 a b	*a* and *b* look curved
Wundt's curves		Line *a* looks curved
Winged lines	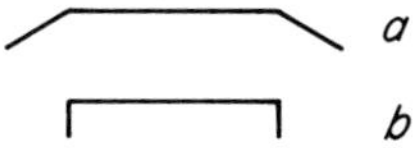 a b	*a* looks longer than *b*
Ponzo	 a b	*a* looks longer than *b*
Divided line	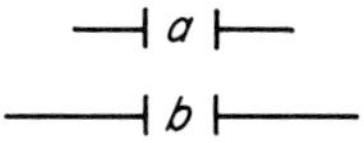 a b	Gap *a* looks larger than gap *b*
Baldwin	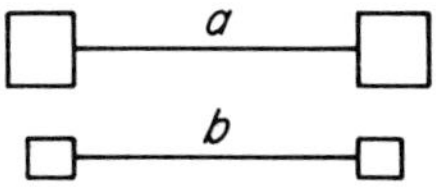 a b	*b* looks longer than *a*

* Related to Delboeuf illusion

‡ Simple case of twisted chord illusion

Fig. 11.12 (*continued*)

Name	Illusory stimulus	Effect
Rod and frame	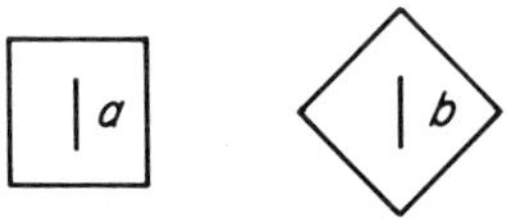 a b	b looks nonvertical
Schumann square	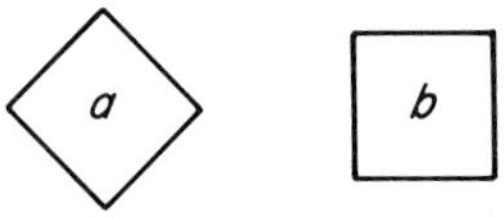 a b	a looks larger than b
Shepard	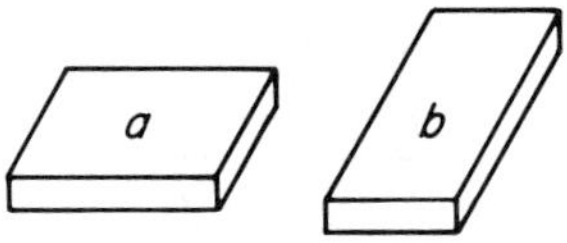 a b	b looks larger than a
Jastrow–Lipps	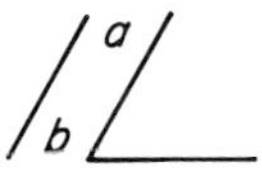 a b	Lines appear closer at b than at a
Sander parallelogram	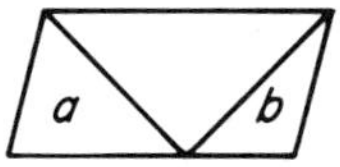 a b	a looks longer than b
Orbison	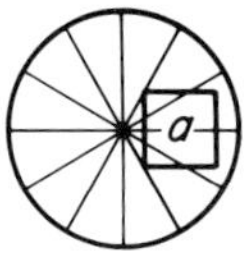 a	Square a distorted in parallelogram

Fig. 11.12 (*continued*)

attention and stimulated so much research activity for so many years. This tabulation is presented without any attempt at categorization.[4] It is obvious that there is great diversity in this collection of illusions, even when those attributable to spatial contrast are removed. Nevertheless, all of those presented in Fig. 11-12 share one common feature—they all represent the perceptual responses resulting from processes that compellingly distort the shape (defined by objective evaluations) of an isolated stimulus.

[4]The reader should also remember that some peculiar visual experiences are quite veridical with the proximal stimulus and can be better attributed to processes other than those of Level 4. Most notable among such ''nonillusions'' are the perceptual responses to moiré patterns and ''impossible'' figures. These are not illusions of the class I consider here.

Beyond the stark facts of this compendium of illusions, there are two important conceptual questions to be considered in this section. The first question concerns the plausibility of the development of a taxonomy of the visual illusions. For reasons that should be obvious in the context of this book, it would be highly desirable to classify these interesting phenomena so that their perceived differences do not distract our attention from what may be their close similarities in underlying processes.

The second question concerns a more fundamental matter—the nature of explanation in visual illusion theory. A wide variety of theoretical explanations has been offered—some neuroreductive and some only descriptive. I would like to consider these theories as a class, as another way of developing some insight into the limits imposed on our understanding of Level 4 processes.

Consider the first of these issues. Taxonomic classification of the visual illusions, in spite of their great diversity, has in fact been attempted for many years. Since the time of the great 19th century perceptual scientists, it has been appreciated that some of these phenomena may be closely related to others. One consistent error made in the development of these taxonomies of illusions, however, has been to base that classification on the nature of the stimuli or on phenomenological criteria—i.e., in terms of the nature of the stimulus or of the response rather than in terms of the intervening processes that may plausibly be considered to account for them. Thus, for example, Tolansky (1964) groups his discussion of the geometrical illusions in chapters with such titles as "The Effect of Weak Wings," "Crossed-Bar Illusions," and "Illusions Produced by Hatched Lines." This is obviously an attempt at systemization based on the characteristics of the illusion-generating stimuli, rather than on the phenomena themselves. Luckiesh's (1922) older book is somewhat more analytic—he concentrates on the impact of various organizational factors in his classification scheme. For example, we see chapters entitled "The Influence of Angles," and "Irradiation and Brightness Contrast." Nevertheless, both volumes are singularly devoid of attempts at process-oriented classification. Perhaps Luckiesh's engineering background and his specific effort to make this volume practically useful (as spelled out in his introduction) diverted him from such esoteric pursuits. As psychologists seeking explanation and understanding, however, we are left with a feeling of incompleteness when reading either of these books.

The problem of classifying illusions is more explicitly faced by Robinson. In his comprehensive and well-organized work (J. O. Robinson, 1972, pp. 20–24), he discusses the shortcomings of many of the taxonomies that had been previously proposed. Yet in spite of, or perhaps because of, this concern with classification, his exhaustive compilation of the geometrical illusions seems also to avoid any explicit attempt to organize or categorize. Indeed, Robinson goes so far as to apologize for his own lack of conviction about the suitability of the few categorizations he does infrequently propose. Most other perceptual taxonomists (e.g., Oyama, 1960b; Boring, 1942) are purely stimulus-bound in their modest efforts to categorize, and allude to illusions of angle, extent, size, direction, or length in a way that does not delve deeply into the manifold processes that must underlie and account for the distortions encompassed within the rubric defined as "geometrical illusions."

A major exception to this dearth of taxonomic effort in illusion research, however, can be found in the recent work of Coren, Girgus, Erlichman, and Hakstian (1976), a system that is also described in Coren and Girgus (1978). These psychologists factor-analyzed the results of a very extensive experiment involving many different geometric illusions as well as a family of different versions of the Müller–Lyer illusion. Their stimuli are shown in Fig. 11-13 and 11-14, respectively. In general, Coren and his collaborators discovered that two major factors discriminated among the illusory stimuli in their sample. The two factors identified a family of illusions of linear extent on the one hand and a family of illusions of area, shape, and direction on the other. However, a deeper level of factor analysis indicated that five distinguishable groups of illusions can be identified. Coren and his colleagues believe that these five factors are much more useful in suggesting the underlying causes of clusters of different illusions than is the crude dichotomy. Table 11-1 shows their correlation matrix for the various illusions used in their experiments. Very few negative correlations were found, and all were insignificant. Thus no inverse relation seemed to be present between any of the illusions and any of the five factors. On the other hand, the high positive correlations suggested the existence of five major illusion clusters, thus implying five separable causal influences on these geometric illusions.

Coren, Girgus, Erlichman, and Hakstian interpreted these five factors in the following ways. The first factor, which characterized such illusions as the Poggendorff phenomenon, seemed to cluster together a number of illusions that were experienced as deviations in the direction of lines or distortions in the shapes of objects. They interpreted the underlying causes for this group of illusions to be lateral interactions among contours in a way that is close to the concept I have denoted as Level 2 interactions.[5]

The second factor, which characterized a cluster of such size-contrast illusions as the Ebbinghaus illusion (otherwise known as the Titchener circles), seemed to them to reflect the results of a process in which relational judgments were dominant. (This is the group I have already classified in the previous sections as a separate class of contrast-type illusions.) The third and fourth factors were very closely correlated with each other and, therefore, difficult to disentangle. Coren's group separated them by noting that the third cluster primarily involved

[5]As I have indicated, I do not agree with this interpretation; interaction, I believe, can occur between the meanings of stimuli (e.g., linearity as a concept) equally well as between isomorphic neural representations (e.g., the geometrical linearity of a line). However, this difference in interpretation does not mitigate the power of this factor analysis. The clusters, obtained from an analysis of the empirical data, would exist regardless of their theoretical interpretation.

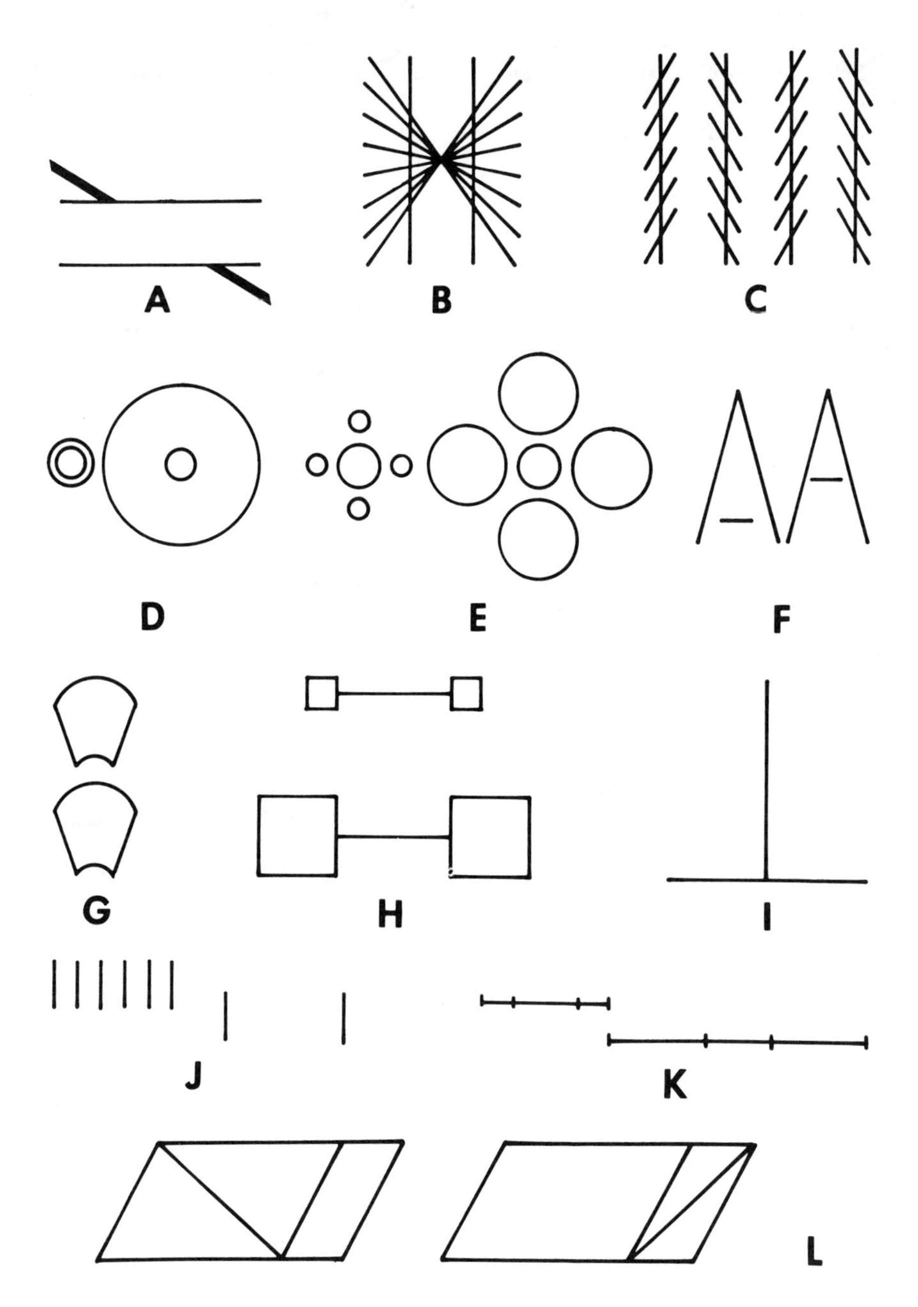

FIG. 11.13. The stimulus patterns used in the experiment of Coren and his colleagues. Poggendorff (A); Wundt (B); Zoellner (C); Delboeuf (D); Ebbinghaus (E); Ponzo (F); Jastrow (G); Baldwin (H); horizontal-vertical (I); Oppel-Kundt (J); divided line (K); and Sander parallelogram (L). (Figure and caption code from Coren, Girgus, Erlichman, and Hakstian, © 1976, with the permission of the Psychonomics Journals, Inc.)

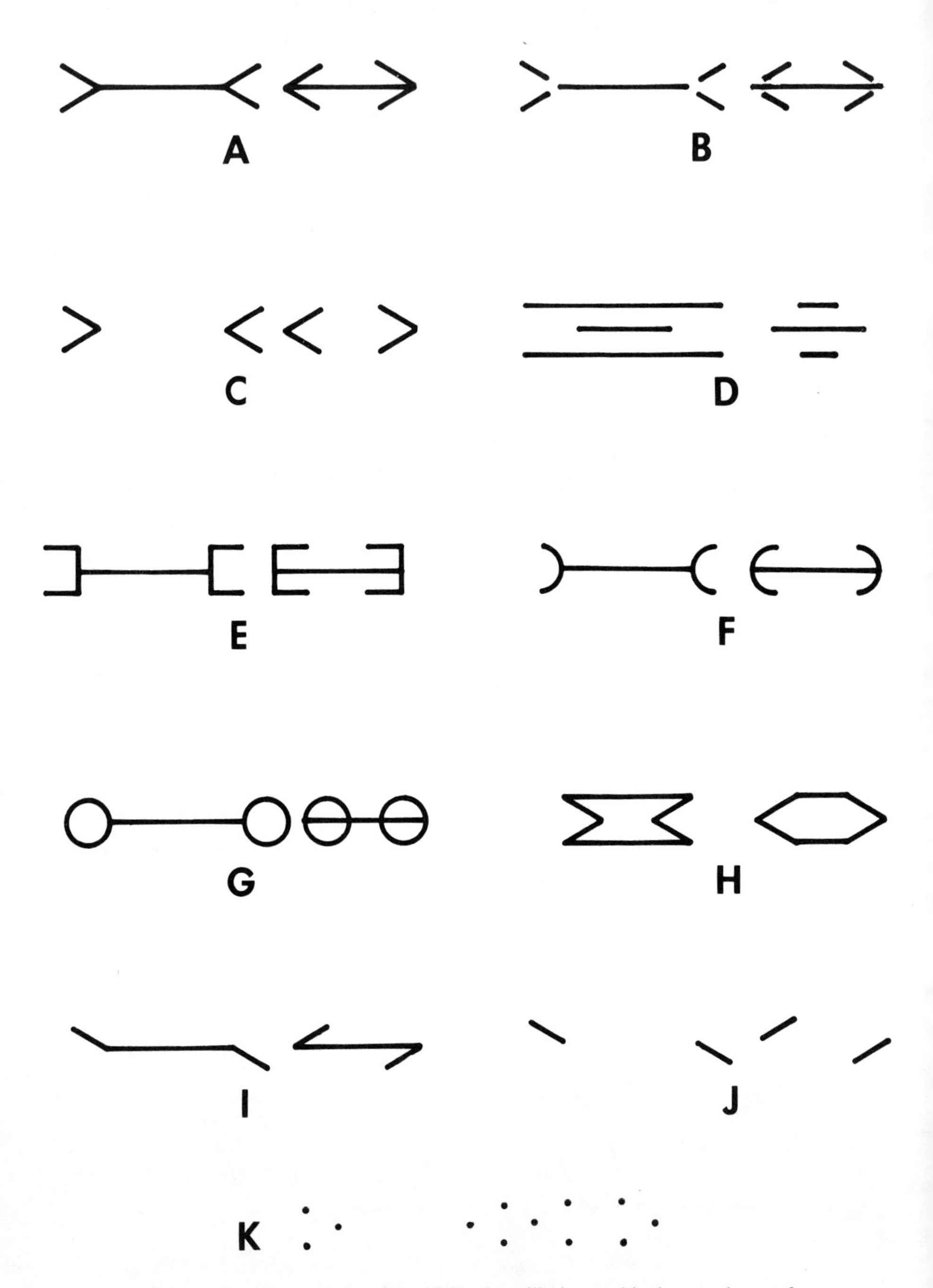

FIG. 11.14. The varieties of the Müller-Lyer illusion used in the experiment of Coren and his colleagues. Standard form (A); exploded (B); Piaget form (D); curved (E); box (F); lozenge (H); Sanford form (I); minimal (J); Coren form (K). (Figure and code caption from Coren, Girgus, Erlichman, and Hakstian, © 1976, with the permission of the Psychonomics Journals, Inc.)

TABLE 11.1
Correlations and Factors for 45 Illusion Measures

	I	*II*	*III*	*IV*	*V*	h^2
Pogaendorff	*.42*	.07	.01	.03	.05	.65
Wandt +	*.76*	.13	−.05	.03	.09	.50
Wandt −	*.51*	.39	.05	−.20	−.05	.55
Zoellner +	*.84*	.02	−.28	.16	−.04	.59
Zoellner −	*.74*	.11	.01	−.04	.00	.63
Delboeuf −	−.08	*.81*	.16	−.19	.13	.59
Delboeuf +	−.10	*.62*	−.04	.29	−.10	.23
Ebbinghaus −	.23	*.57*	.01	.01	.07	.64
Ebbinghaus +	.15	*.69*	−.25	.07	.04	.51
Ponzo +	.07	*.62*	.09	.08	.04	.77
Ponzo −	.05	.20	.13	−.03	*.66*	.61
Jastrow +	.08	*.49*	.15	.27	.08	.48
Jastrow −	.01	.38	.07	.29	.15	.54
Baldwin +	.02	−.22	*.58*	.30	.13	.27
Baldwin −	.02	.21	*.64*	.04	−.02	.68
Horiz-Vert +	.24	−.06	*.67*	.00	−.10	.55
Horiz-Vert −	.05	.12	.36	.38	−.08	.64
Oppel-Kundt +	.07	.07	*.46*	.15	.12	.58
Oppel-Kundt −	.04	−.05	.21	*.68*	−.05	.06
Standard ML +	.04	−.03	*.69*	.18	−.16	.52
Standard ML −	−.12	.16	.23	*.49*	.00	.68
Exploded ML +	−.05	−.12	*.51*	.36	.15	.64
Exploded ML −	.12	.13	.15	*.62*	.07	.55
No Shaft ML +	−.07	−.07	*.74*	.14	.00	.65
No Shaft ML −	.02	.17	.14	*.50*	.06	.67
Piaget ML +	.24	−.03	*.70*	.06	.05	.67
Piaget ML −	.05	−.10	.11	*.68*	.20	.54
Curved ML +	−.11	.04	*.62*	.24	.19	.66
Curved ML −	−.12	.03	.11	*.59*	.30	.66
Box ML +	−.10	.11	*.59*	.17	−.02	.65
Box ML −	−.19	.19	.34	.39	−.04	.66
Circle ML +	−.08	−.07	*.64*	.16	.19	.57
Circle ML −	−.33	.06	.49	.31	−.01	.54
Lozenge ML +	−.15	−.07	*.70*	−.04	.12	.62
Lozenge ML −	.02	.00	−.23	*.96*	.01	.59
Sanford ML +	.07	.13	*.81*	−.03	−.02	.52
Sanford ML −	.05	.02	.05	.62	.27	.66
Minimal ML +	.03	.12	*.49*	.28	.25	.72
Minimal ML −	−.07	.22	.01	*.63*	.21	.66
Coren ML +	−.03	.02	*.85*	.20	.04	.56
Coren ML −	.22	.00	.19	*.56*	−.03	.50
Divided Line +	*.45*	.09	.13	.05	.30	.52
Divided Line −	.02	.16	−.06	.15	*.69*	.61
Sander Parallelogram +	*.56*	−.09	.28	.27	−.10	.59
Sander Parallelogram −	.18	−.06	.00	−.08	.16	48
Factor Variance	3.57	3.99	9.04	7.43	1.84	

From Coren, Girgus, Erlichman, and Hakstian, 1976.

illusions of overestimation, whereas the fourth cluster incorporated illusions of underestimation of size or length. Finally, they attribute the fifth cluster, represented only by the perceived distortion of the shorter lines of the Ponzo and divided-line illusions, to a "frame of reference" misinterpretation.

It is important to reiterate, as Coren, Girgus, Erlichman, and Hakstian themselves carefully noted, that even though the mathematics of the factor-analytical procedure does segregate clusters, such a clustering does not in itself say anything about the underlying causes of the illusions. However, the nature of the clusters suggests explanations and directs our attention to groups of illusions arising from what may be a common origin. The attribution of particular processes to each of these clusters represents another layer of analytic interpretation by the investigators.

This then brings us to the crux of the second question to which I alluded—is any satisfactory "explanation" of an illusion possible? The answer to this question can be approached by considering the various theories of illusion that have been proposed. Not too surprisingly, in light of their great popular interest, theories of illusion are abundant. Indeed, theories of the classic geometrical illusions have abounded since the phenomena were first brought to the attention of perceptual researchers by Oppel in 1855. Once again, we are fortunate that discussions of the classical theories of geometrical illusions are abundant (see Over, 1968; J. O. Robinson, 1972, Ch. 6; Coren & Girgus, 1978, Ch. 11; Gillam, 1980) and, therefore, it is necessary only to mention briefly a few of the most important or recent, to identify the main themes of thought.

A number of contemporary workers have proposed specific explanations for various individual phenomena. For example, Zanuttini (1976) has discussed the possiblity that a shrinkage of the perceptual space due to the perceptual completion of a physically discontinuous stimulus might explain the Poggendorff illusion, and Oyama (1977) has attributed the Zöllner and Hering illusions to lateral interactions among Hubel and Weisel-type orientation-detecting neural subsystems. Specific microtheories of this kind do not, however, really fill the need for a general statement concerning the origins of this major class of geometrical illusions. In my opinion, most of these theories are a patchwork of narrowly useful physical or neural analogies or mathematical descriptions mistakenly interpreted as reductionistic explanations. Nor do the many neuroreductive approaches that I mentioned in previous sections and chapters fill the need that now exists for a comprehensive metatheory of illusions.

A few contemporary psychologists have attempted to fill this metatheoretical gap and propose broad global theories of the geometric illusions. For example, Day (1972) has suggested that a wide variety of spatial geometric illusions are due to a constancy transformation that itself is a reflection of the apparent distance to the perceived object. This metaprinciple is expressed by Day (1972, p. 1340) in the following terms: "I conclude that any stimulus which serves to maintain perceptual constancy of a property of an object as the visual representation of that property varies will, when independently manipulated with the retinal image not varied, produce an illusion.''

The attribution of geometric illusions as a class to a sometimes inappropriate constancy has had wide currency ever since it was originally proposed by Helmholtz (1867). For example, the Müller–Lyer illusion has often been attributed to the subjective interpretation of these lines as either interior or exterior corners. In this case, the ''more distant'' corner is misconstrued to appear smaller than the ''closer'' corner. Psychologists who have taken this approach include Gregory (1966; 1968) and Gillam (1971). It takes no great insight, however, to appreciate that this ''general'' constancy principle cannot possible explain all of the geometric illusions incorporated within this category. Nevertheless, this approach exemplifies a kind of thinking in which the theoretician eschews peripheral neural interactions and attributes the illusion to a high-level central act of interpretive construction.

Others who argue for a spatial contour interaction theory of illusions (e.g., G. H. Fisher, 1973) often express this belief in terms of symbolic spatial interactions that are not necessarily the same kind of neural network interactions as are those invoked by Blakemore, Carpenter, and Georgeson (1970), J. O. Robinson (1968), or by E. Walker's (1973) formal mathematical model. It is often said that the spatial interaction models, in general, are antithetical to the distance–size constancy models proposed by Helmholtz, Day, Gregory, and others. It is probably the case, however, that this is but another example of a false controversy. In each case, the essential causal factor is neither constancy (which, in fact, is merely another phenomenological response and thus hardly a satisfactory explanation for an illusion) nor some isomorphic spatial interaction between nearby contours. In fact, the key causal factor underlying geometrical illusions, I believe, is that some misinterpretation is made on the basis of spatial context. A corollary of this assertion is that the information describing that context may be provided to the observer in many different ways.

A highly eclectic theoretical approach of particular interest to the explanation of visual illusions has been taken by Coren and Girgus (1978) in developing the theme of their book on visual illusions. Unlike many of the restricted and specialized theories in this field, their approach has been to emphasize the fact that many different levels of processing can and do contribute to the evocation of geometrical illusions. They believe that it is even possible to demonstrate that a Level 0 process—the degree of blur of the retinal image (Ward and Coren, 1976)—can affect such phenomena as the Müller–Lyer illusion.[6] Coren and

[6]A bizarre corollary of this observation is that there may be a difference in the magnitude of this illusion as a function of the pigmentation of the iris of the eye. Coren and Porac (1978) report that the Müller–Lyer illusion is significantly greater in people with blue eyes than in people with dark eyes. According to them, this is due to the greater light scattering (and thus greater blur) in light-eyed individuals.

Girgus also accept the principle that lateral interactions among mutually inhibitory neurons (Level 2 processes) also contribute to some illusions and that major influences are exerted as well by cognitive, judgmental, or "adaptation level" processes in the form most recently proposed by Restle and Merryman (1968), and Restle (1971).

I am not sure, however, if this multilevel argument is entirely compelling for all levels and for all illusions. For example, consider the claim that optical blur partially explains the Müller-Lyer illusion. I believe this is a misleading concept. In its stead I would like to propose that what Coren, Ward, and Porac have done when they blurred the stimulus and observed an elongation was to "simulate" the perceptual illusion. The blurred images that they present in drawings such as the ones shown in Fig. 11-15 show an actual physical elongation in the photographic images of the subjectively longer of the Müller-Lyer lines as the blur increases. But this is not because the illusion is enhanced—it is because the stimulus is actually elongated—the phenomenal result is veridical, not illusory! Therefore, to assert that the peripheral process contributes to the nonveridical illusion seems fallacious.

The point is that whereas the Müller-Lyer illusion may be approximated or simulated by the actual physical elongation of the lines in a badly blurred image, this is not the same process as the subjective distortions reported for well-focused images. This seems to be another example of the danger of identifying analogous phenomena with each other. Although both processes result in what are superficially the same perceptual outcomes, the underlying mechanisms are, in fact, quite different. The Level 0 blur processes underlying the "simulation" of the illusion are not involved, in most practical situations, in the subjective distortion of the more interesting Level 4 transformation. A separate argument can be made that lateral inhibitory interactions are also not a significant part of the causal influences involved in the classic Müller-Lyer illusion, in spite of the fact that such interactions could, in principle, contribute in some small measure to an analogous phenomenon under abnormal conditions.

The few examples of geometrical illusion theory I have presented document the contention that there has been a rich tradition of theory concerning the origins and causes of geometric illusions. However, it is also clear that in spite of this activity few important theoretical breakthroughs have occurred. Most psychologists, even as they propose their own pet hypothesis about this or that illusion, usually retreat at some point in their writing to acknowledge that the fundamental mechanisms of most illusions remain highly mysterious. Without denying the ultimate neural origins of geometrical illusions, it seems to me that the weight of the experimental evidence argues compellingly for a neorationalistic or constructionistic (in the sense implied by the Level 4 concept) approach to the problem of illusions. Alternative approaches stressing peripheral neural network factors seem to be totally incapable of handling such phenomena as the persistence of illusions in the face of transformations of the Müller-Lyer prototype as profound as those shown in Fig. 11-14, or the lack of robustness of an illusion to such an apparently trivial transformation is a 45 deg rotation. The studies reported by Krantz and Weintraub (1973), Oyama (1975), and Avery and Day (1969), in which the effect of the orientation of the Poggendorff, Zöllner, and horizontal-vertical illusions, respectively, was shown to be extensive, are damning to any simplistic neural interaction model. For example, Krantz and Weintraub's results, shown in Fig. 11-16, indicate that the effect is so great (the magnitude of the displacement error in the Poggendorff illusion can vary eightfold as a result of a 45 deg rotation of the whole pattern) as to preclude a simple single-cell or network explanation.

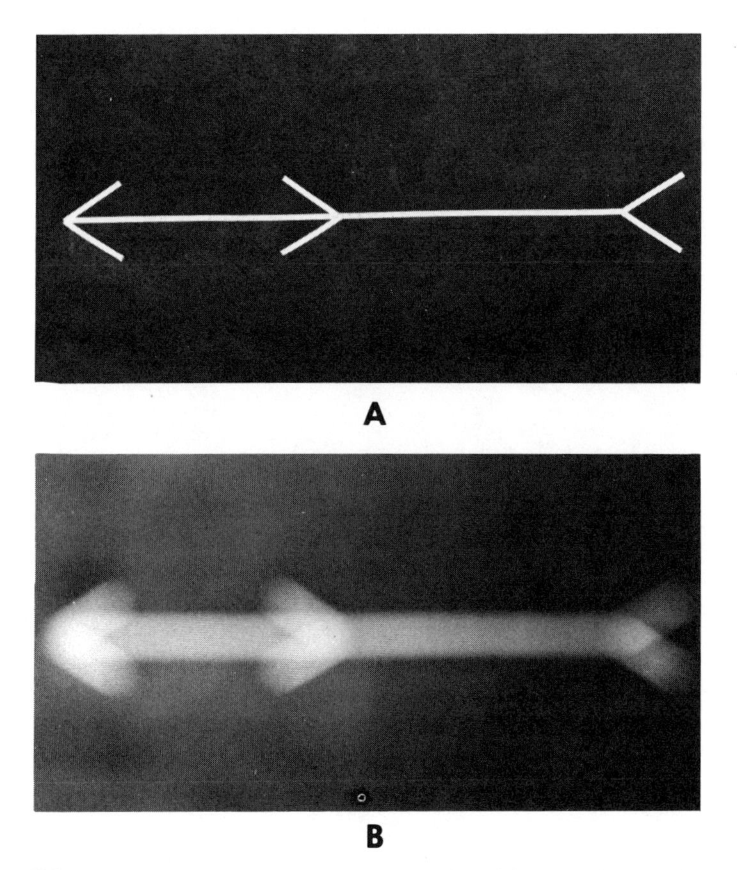

FIG. 11.15. Standard (A) and a blurred (B) version of the Müller-Lyer illusion. (From Ward and Coren, © 1976, with the permission of the Psychonomics Journals, Inc.)

We must, therefore, turn to an entirely different theoretical domain to achieve understanding. It must be that the general context plays the most significant role in defining the magnitude of this illusion and not some local interaction as proposed by theorists such as E. Walker (1973) in his technically elegant but, from my point of view, conceptually flawed neuromathematical model. Simi-

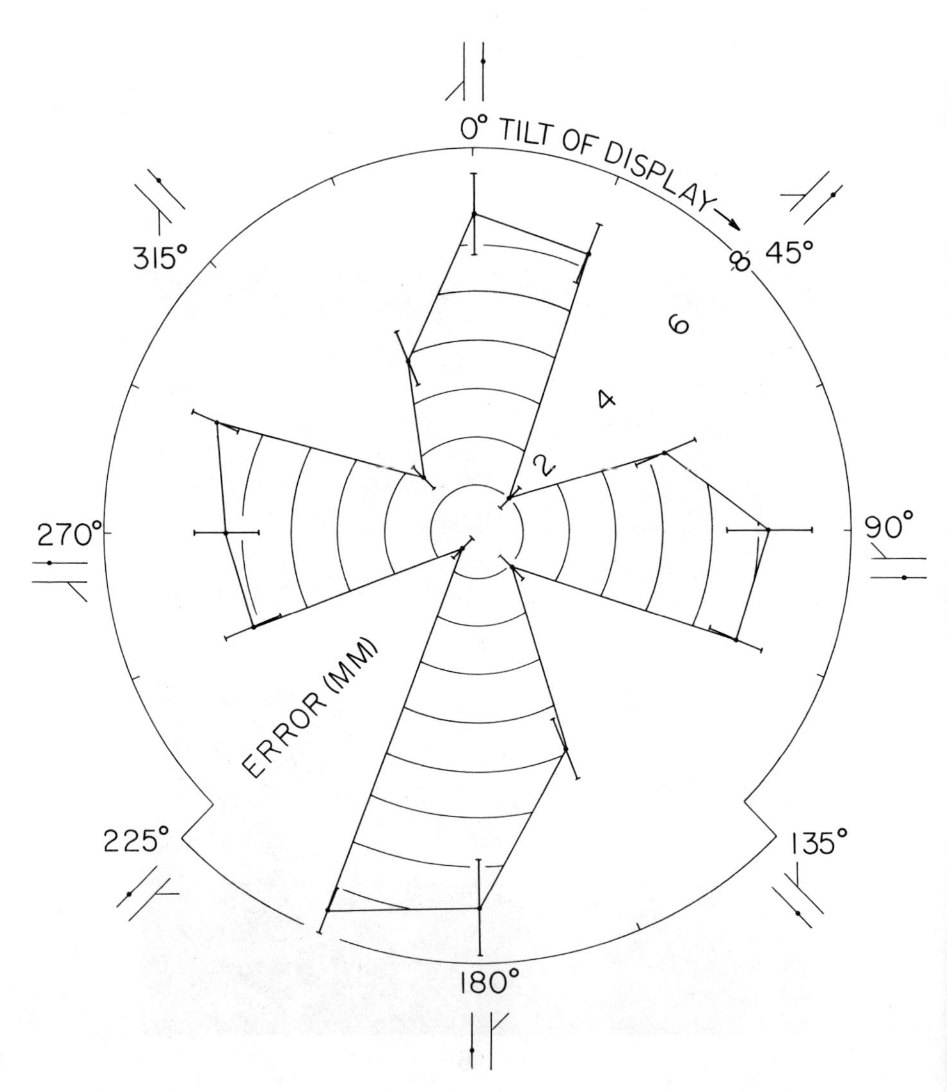

FIG. 11.16. The effect on the Poggendorff illusion of the angle at which the stimulus is presented. (From Weintraub and Krantz, © 1971, with the permission of the Psychonomics Journals, Inc.)

larly, the modern field theories, which evolved out of the classic Gestalt idea of "inductive" interactions, find little support in the empirical literature. The absence of any physiological correlates of such fields and the efficacy of even subjective contours to distort perceived objects is lethal to any such ideal. Models invoking such fields are reduced to the status of rather loose metaphors or physical analogies that have little to offer in the way of explaining the fundamental origins of these interesting phenomena.

The experimental literature on geometric illusions is so immense and generally disorganized that no useful purpose would be served by reviewing such a clutter of data in detail here. For readers interested in these studies, J. O. Robinson (1972) and Coren and Girgus (1978) do an especially good job of considering the effects of the various stimulus parameters on many of the classic illusions. For the moment, I not only that there are many studies showing that various dimensions of the stimulus can affect geometric illusions and that, equally as well, many observer variables (e.g., adaptive state, experience, set, age, and ethnic background) also are known to influence illusions of this class. In many cases the magnitude of some such effect is often so large and discontinuous that the respective illusions become meaningful only in terms of interpretations of a shift from one perceptual "interpretation" to another.

One excellent example of a sophisticated experimental approach to the problem posed by geometrical illusions deserving a mention, however, is the program of research carried out by my colleague, Daniel Weintraub, at the University of Michigan. In an extensive series of papers he shows, for example, that the efficacy of the Poggendorff illusion depends on an actual intersection of the transverse and parallel lines (Weintraub & Krantz, 1971), that subjective contours can also produce the Poggendorff illusion (Goldstein & Weintraub, 1972), that at least four stimulus factors contribute to misperception of the apparent point of convergence of nonparallel lines (Weintraub & Virsu, 1972), and that the Ebbinghaus illusion involves both contour "attraction" and context effects (Weintraub, 1979). In general, Weintraub agrees, it is the cognitive and interpretive factors that dominate in illusions. Weintraub's empirical data, in aggregate, argue against all of the neural net theories that have recently been proposed.

In sum, spatial context-dependent geometrical illusions, like many other kinds of nonveridical percepts, still pose highly refractory theoretical problems to perceptual psychologists. Many attempts to identify the underlying causes of illusions that may at first glance have appeared useful often turn out to be worthless. For example, the old standby—dichoptic presentation of the different parts of the stimulus—typically results in a reduced or negated illusory effect (Coren & Girgus, 1977; Day, 1961; Ohwaki, 1960; Schiller and Weiner, 1962; Springbett, 1961). Such a well-substantiated empirical result would, under ordinary circumstances, be considered to be strong evidence for a peripheral basis of the relevant illusions. Most investigators, however, now follow Day's lead in considering these experiments to be heavily confounded by binocular rivalry and apparent depth differences, themselves indisputably central processes that are well known to reduce the magnitude of such other perceptual phenomena as contrast. Thus, even the standard localization test—dichoptic versus monocular viewing—fails to provide unequivocal clues to the unraveling of the theoretical knot presented by illusions.

Another suggestion made about geometric illusions is that they work only within a relatively narrow size range. John Ross of the University of Western Australia recently supported this hypothesis by demonstrating the following phenomenon: Visual phenomena, such as the Poggendorff illusion, cease producing the expected effect when retinal image size becomes very small. Size constancy, a compelling response when relatively large stimuli are used, also fails, he suggested, when the stimuli subtend small retinal angles. Interestingly, according to Ross, the stimuli producing the moon illusion seem to be just about at the threshold of this transition between the size at which the constancy effect holds and the size at which it is not effective. The main implications of Ross's demonstrations are that illusions are representative of a kind of processing that acts only at relatively large sizes and over long retinal distances. On the other hand, the Ross hypothesis (later published as Ross, J., Jenkins, B., and Johnstone, J. R. Size constancy fails below half a degree. *Nature,* 1980, 283, 473–474) has been severely criticized by Day, R. H., Stuart, G. W., and Dickinson, R. G. (Size constancy does *not* fail below half a degree. *Perception and Psychophysics,* 1980, 28, 263–265). Day and his colleagues find no empirical support for the Ross hypothesis.

My opinion is that, unfortunately, the study of these visual illusions has not, in general, fulfilled the promise repeatedly made by those who have pursued this research topic over the years—namely, to provide more profound insights into other mechanisms of perception. Illusions are fun and intrinsically interesting but the mystery surrounding their origins remains for the most part intractable. It seems unlikely, in light of the type of research now being done, that further exploration of these phenomena will tell us very much more of a fundamental nature about the underlying mechanisms of visual perception than they have already provided.

The one exception of this gloomy evaluation of the science of geometrical illusions is that it has provided some insights into the nature of the metrics of visual space and the relation between that subjective space and external physical space. The phenomenology of illusions does reflect the way in which transformations occur between what is an essentially euclidean stimulus space and a perceived world of which non-euclidean geometries seem to be the best descriptive models. In this context, theories such as W. Hoffman's (1966) or A. Watson's (1978) mathematical formulations are of particular interest. They describe the form of the spatial transformations that lead to the classic static visual illusions with only a minimum of unlikely, implausible, or farfetched neuroreductionistic speculation. These mathematical psychologists have provided formal systems that describe the nature of the transformations occurring between the external stimulus space and the internally perceived visual space without attemption to detail the nature of the mechanisms that might account for them. This is an emphasis on process and transformation with which I am particularly comfortable.

An excellent way to conclude this discussion of geometrical illusions is to simply list the formal assumptions of Watson's theory to delineate one view of the nature of the spatial transformations that occur during illusions. Watson's (1978) main assumptions concerning geometric illusions can be paraphrased as follows:

1. The intended realm of application of Watson's model is constrained to static phenomena occurring on two-dimensional surfaces on which lines and curves have been drawn.
2. Visual space (i.e., the apparent phenomenological space that is perceived) in the absence of any lines or curves is euclidean.
3. Visual space in the presence of lines and curves is best described by a Riemannian (non-euclidean) geometry.
4. Objects spatially interact over distance to distort visual space from euclidean to Riemannian.
5. The distance across visual space remains constant, so if there is a contraction at one place (due to the presence of objects) there must be an expansion elsewhere.
6. The units of length in the vertical and the horizontal directions are the same.

Each of these verbal statements was formalized by Watson into a mathematical expression. When these mathematical expressions were applied to the interactions of stimuli in this field, close approximations to a number of the classic geometric visual illusions were simulated, including the Poggendorff, Müller-Lyer, and Ponzo phenomena.

Thus in a manner very similar in principle to the general theory of relativity proposed by Einstein (space, physical or visual, is distorted by the presence of objects contained within it), Watson has provided a model that predicts a wide variety of visual illusions. The model finesses the physiological nature of the interactions in exactly the same way that Einstein's general theory of relativity finesses the underlying mechanism by providing a geometric interpretation of physical space. In the physical world the geometry is distorted by some force, which need not necessarily be specifically described, but which is probably gravity. Likewise the perceptual "interactions" presumably reflect the action of some unknown "force", which is far more likely to be of a nonisomorphic nature than not and which tends to distort our subjective space away from the geometry defined by the euclidean space of the external physical world within which we are embedded. The beauty of this model is that it does not rely upon specific neurophysiological mechanisms, and yet it does bring many of the static geometric illusions within the framework of a single descriptive model.

Watson's model is certainly not complete—his first assumption limits its application to a small sample of the full range of visual illusions. Nevertheless, it is a stunning success as an example of a much more general and explicit theoretical approach to illusions than is usually available. Watson's theory is a rare example of coherence in a discipline in which verbal speculation and disorganized concatenation, rather than crisp analysis and general principle, are the rule.

3. Static Monocular Cues to Depth

Depth—another major dimension of visual experience—is also strongly influenced by spatial interactions among the components of the stimulus. It has long been appreciated that the experience of depth is not solely dependent on dichoptic (stereoscopic) viewing but that strong impressions of depth can also be generated by a number of cues that are essentially monocular. Each of these cues, nevertheless, is spatially relativistic in exactly the same sense I have invoked in the previous sections of this chapter; the impact of the cue is dependent upon a comparison of different aspects, dimensions, or parts of the stimulus.

There is perhaps no better single illustration of the variety of monocular cues to depth than Fig. 11-17, another of Maurits Escher's extraordinary etchings. In this exquisite drawing, a powerful and compelling illusion of depth is produced by a two-dimensional drawing as a result of a number of monocular cues. Three classes of this kind of cue to depth can be designated: (1) cues due to the relative geometry of visual angles;[7] (2) cues doe to relative blur; and (3) cues due to pictorial relations. All three of these classes of cues occur in still pictures and do not depend on motion in any way. I have, therefore, further characterized them as being static, as well as monocular, cues to depth. (I deal with dynamic cues to

---

[7]It is necessary for the reader to appreciate the distinction made here between Level 0 physical processes, which lead to apparent perspective, on the one hand, and Level 4 interpretations of that apparent perspective in generating depth, on the other. Geometrical perspective is the direct phenomenological outcome of the nature of physical space as described in Chapter 5. The reduced visual angle subtended by distant stimuli, for example, clearly leads to a reduction in the retinal image size and thus to a reduction in the apparent size of the stimulus (all other factors being equal or controlled). However, the construction of depth from differences in retinal size, or from the visual angles subtended by objects at various distances, represents a subsequent and deeper level of processing.

It is also important to remember that because the distance between the lens of the eye and retina is constant, visual angle and retinal size are related by multiplicative constant (see Eq. 3-20). Use of the term *visual angle* is, therefore, equivalent to a statement of retinal size. The fact that visual angle is directly specifiable in terms of externally measured size and distance makes its use preferable.

FIG. 11.17. Another example of Maurits Escher's work in which many monocular cues have been incorporated to produce a strong impression of depth.

depth later in this chapter as examples of temporal or sequential interactions.) Now let's consider these three classes of static spatial monocular cues to depth in greater detail.

a. Cues Associated with Visual Angles. Because of the spatial relations defining the visual angle (see Eq. 3-19) an object located farther away will project a smaller image on the retina than will the same object located closer to the observer. There exists a cluster of monocular cues to depth that derive directly from this simple fact, including: (1) relative retinal size; (2) linear perspective; (3) texture gradients; and (4) relative elevation.

There is a substantial similarity between the first three of these cues. Indeed, when considered in the context of this class of cues, they can all be thought of as manifestations of a single process. However, because they have traditionally been considered separately and because there is a slight difference in the connotation of each term, I consider each in turn.

Consider relative retinal size first. In general, when objects apparently of the same physical size are presented in a way such that they subtend different retinal angles, our visual system tends to interpret differences in retinal image size as differences in depth or distance from the objects to the eye. On the other hand, objects that provide no clues to their actual size tend to be located at either an indeterminate depth or at some "default" depth, usually about one meter. Both of these empirical facts reinforce the conjecture that the perception of depth depends upon a relational, differential, or comparative interaction, and that without such a relative evaluation specific quantitative judgments of depth are not well perceived. To the contrary, however, if a relational comparison is possible, depth is easily achieved even if we do not have any way to estimate the absolute size of each element in the pattern. To exemplify this latter point, consider that in Escher's drawing (Fig. 11-17), the relative size of the fish is a usable cue to depth even though their physical size is indeterminate, there being so many different-sized fishes of this same general shape in the world's waters.

Exactly the same dimension, relative size (though in a continuous rather than a discrete version), is referred to as linear perspective. Here the convergence of lines (see Fig. 11-17) provides exactly the same basis for a relational comparison and the awareness of depth as is illustrated in the Escher drawing with discrete objects. Texture gradients act according to this same principle to provide cues to depth (see Fig. 5-5).

The nature of external space and the nature of the visual angle lead directly to another monocular cue to depth—relative height. As noted in Chapter 5, in general, objects that are farther away are seen placed higher in the two-dimensional projected plane. Conversely, the inference usually made by an observer is that objects that are higher in the visual field are farther away. How wonderfully easily we override this interpretation when we are in a situation in which a series of objects extending away from us are on the ceiling (see Fig. 5-6).

The important unifying principle about all of the static monocular cues to depth that I have just mentioned is that they are all (a) relational, and (b) atributable to the simple geometry of visual angles. All are manifestations of the natural geometry of the scene and demonstrate not only how perspective geometry can provide depth cues to the observer but also that the observer can process those cues.

b. Cues Associated with Relative Blur. Just as many of the traditional static monocular cues to depth that I have just considered may be attributed to a single visual angle factor, it is also possible to cluster a number of other depth cues within the single category of blur effects. In this instance, we also see the phenomenological uselessness of absolute blur levels. Rather, the same generalization that characterizes this whole chapter also operates here—only relative values obtained from comparisons of different absolute degrees of blur can provide depth information.

In spite of the conceptual identity of the blur cues, blur is produced by a number of distinguishable mechanisms, and this has led to separate discussions of the various "kinds" of blur. For example, the air, even on the best of days, is not entirely clear—it is filled with light-absorbing and light-scattering molecules and particles of one kind or another. Two kinds of scattering are known to exist. The first is produced by relatively large particles and is simply produced by a series of reflections and the attendant edge diffraction effects. This kind of scattering simply distributes light uniformly and blurs images. A second kind of scattering occurs when the particles are small (down to individual molecules) relative to the wavelength of light. In this kind of scattering (Rayleigh scattering) the degree to which light is scattered depends upon its wavelength. Specifically, the intensity of scattered light is proportional to $1/\lambda^4$. Therefore short wavelengths of light will be scattered more than will long wavelengths. The net effect is to make the atmosphere and large bodies of water look blue because the molecules making up liquids and gases meet the size requirement for Rayleigh scattering.

The results of physical scattering by atmosphere or underwater effects are increasingly desaturated colors as well as blurred retinal images, the greater the distance to the stimulus object. The differing levels of desaturation and blur at various distances—aerial perspective—is the basis of another powerful static monocular cue to depth. Aerial perspective is also an artistic device often used to imply depth in two-dimensional graphics: a particularly striking example is illustrated in Escher's drawing shown in Fig. 11-17.

Similarly, the image differences introduced by interposing transparent foreground objects in front of background objects can also be thought of as a relative blur cue. This diffusive difference can also lead to successfully discriminating surfaces that are in front of others in much the same way as does aerial perspective. Here too, as shown in Fig. 11-18, there is a softening of the clarity of the background image's color, texture, and contours in a way that is interpreted as a depth difference by the observer. The best discussion of the use of the transparency cue to create the experience of depth is to be found in an article by Metelli (1974).

Incidentally, a similar explanation, the absorption of light by the atmosphere, is the only explanation of the diminution in brightness of a luminous surface with increased distance. Only a few perceptual psychologists (including Kaufman, 1974, p. 36) seem to appreciate that the luminance of a lighted surface does *not* decrease with distance. Rather, the reduction in surface area in accord with the inverse square law as distance increases is exactly compensated by an increase in the luminous area contained within each degree of visual angle. Thus, in a perfectly clear environment, the luminance of a surface would remain constant. It

FIG. 11.18. A demonstration of the transparency effect on perceived depth. (From Metelli, © 1974, with the permission of Scientific American.)

is only the increased absorption of light by the atmosphere that diminishes light intensity with distance. Brightness-difference cues to depth, therefore, must be considered to be actually special cases of aerial perspective.

Relative blur is also involved in what are often considered to be more ''physiological'' cues to depth. Blur is a powerful and compelling cue to the visual system to stimulate the ciliary muscles of the lens to vary the accommodative focusing power of the eye. The relative degree of ciliary muscle tension is also believed to act as a cue for the construction of a depth experience although a direct experimental report of this conjecture is elusive.

Blur also interacts with astigmatism to provide a depth cue. The major impact of astigmatism on image focus is that objects aligned along different meridians are brought to focus at different focal distances (see Fig. 5-28). Somehow, by means of mechanisms about which we are not yet very knowledgeable, these meridian differences in blur and focal length are transformed into apparent depth. It seems that the relative degree of defocusing along the different axes can be evaluated either during sequential accommodative steps or all at once.

In spite of the variety of mechanisms involved in producing and processing blur information, the critical clue in all of these cases is the relative degree of retinal image clarity. This differential blur may be processed simultaneously at different points in space (as occurs in the processing of aerial perspective) or during sequential sampling of the image (as probably occurs in the processing of astigmatic blur), but in principle, all of the examples I have mentioned are based on a common sensitivity to differences in image clarity.

c. Cues Associated with General Pictorial Relations. Finally, there are a number of static monocular cues to depth that also depend upon the spatial relationships of the stimulus pattern but are not easily categorized as either blur or visual angle effects. Escher's drawing (Fig. 11-17) can also be used to illustrate the effect of some of these ''pictorial'' cues to depth. For example, stimulus components that obscure or intersect other components are perceived as lying in front of the object. This spatial relationship cue is referred to as *interposition*. How then, in an otherwise ambiguous figure such as that shown in Fig. 11-19, is the observer able to determine which are the obscuring and which are the obscured portions of the pattern? Although not a complete answer, Ratoosh (1949) has proposed a quantification of the Gestalt notion of good continuation that helps us to understand this process. He suggests that the interruption of contour determines that an object will be seen in the background. Specifically, Ratoosh says that if the contours of two objects intersect, the object having a contour with a continuous first derivative will appear to be in front of an object having a contour with a discontinuous first derivative.

The nature of shadowing in a complex scene can also be a strong cue to depth. Figure 11-20, for example, depicts an instance in which a dislocation line may appear to be either a depression or a protrusion on the surface of a crystal depending only on the shadowing. For reasons that are long lost in our combined cultural and genetic heritage, light is generally assumed by our perceptual computer to come from above. Thus a stimulus like the one shown in this figure appears as a convex protrusion when the shadows are located on what is interpreted to be its lower side. If the picture is turned over, however, the shadow relations are reversed and the dislocation line in this crystal reverses to appear as a segmented series of concave depressions.

To summarize the general conclusion to which we are led by these static monocular cues to depth: No absolute value of a single dimension of a stimulus is sufficient to produce depth experiences. Like the geometrical illusions or the contrast phenomena, the experiences resulting from the cues I have described in

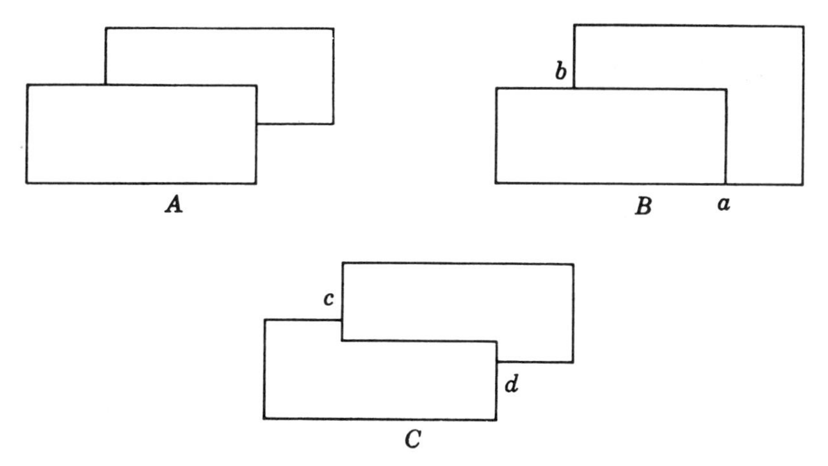

FIG. 11.19. Interposition as a cue for depth. (A) and (B) are unambiguous, but (C) creates a conflict. (From Ratoosh, © 1949, with the permission of the National Academy of Sciences.)

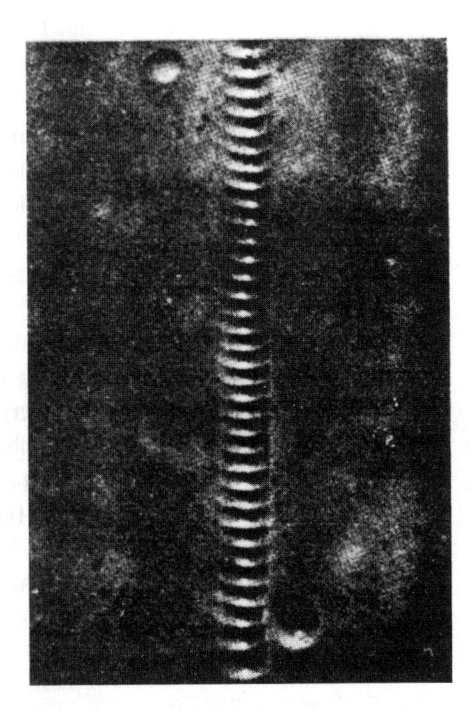

FIG. 11.20. A physical system (a crystal dislocation line, greatly magnified) which, when photographed, produces a figure that may reverse from a convex to a concave shape depending upon the lighting. If the picture is turned upside down, it will reverse its depth relations. (From Hull, © 1965, with the permission of Pergamon Press.)

this section reflect processes that must involve computations of differences, invariances, and relationships among multiple dimensions or aspects of the stimulus. That such spatial computations are made in some way by the nervous system does not necessarily mean, of course, that any simple isomorphic spatial interactions are being executed. Rather, the very diversity of these relation-computing processes suggests that the significance, meaning, or implication of the relationships are more important than the topological properties of the stimulus itself. It is almost as if the comparison processes that are ubiquitous at Level 4 produce dimensionless values comparable to mathematical ratios. These perceptual ratios do not directly quantify representations of size, blur, or position in a spatially isomorphic domain but rather define values in a nonspatial domain. It is these dimensionless values that provide the cues for the appreciation of depth in the situations that I have described in this section.

C. TEMPORAL CONTEXT

We have just seen how various objects simultaneously present in the stimulus scene can interact to distort or modify the dimensions of visual experience away from the values that would have been predicted a priori on the basis of the physical properties of the relevant stimulus objects. Such distortions or non-veridicalities between the properties of the stimulus and the properties of the experience are ubiquitous in visual perception. Spatial interactions were identified capable of producing distortions of brightness, color, and shape or providing cues sufficient to allow the interpretive construction of depth in situations in which only two-dimensional information was actually present. This section is dedicated to the principle that we do not live only in a spatial world; there are also temporal contexts and interactions to be considered when we attempt to understand perception. It takes no great effort to demonstrate convincingly that the interactions between sequentially presented stimuli can be equally as powerful as those between simultaneously presented ones.

The purpose of this section, therefore, is to discuss the many Level 4 processes and phenomena that are illustrative of perceptually influential temporal interactions. These temporal interactions may compellingly lead to spatial, chromatic, and intensive distortions and, like spatial contrast and assimilation, the sequential effects may be in either direction. In some instances, the aftereffects of viewing one stimulus may lead to attributing properties to a subsequently viewed stimulus that are exactly the reverse of the initial experience. In other words, strong temporal "contrast" effects are also possible. In other equally dramatic and compelling illusions, the perception of a stimulus object may be totally suppressed or masked just as other kinds of temporal interactions seem to provide the information necessary for the psychoneural mechanism to construct experiences corresponding to physical objects or events that did not actually exist.

The four major classes of processes that I believe encompass the wide variety of temporal interactions are those underlying the following phenomena: (1) aftereffects; (2) metacontrast—masking of the sixth kind; (3) apparent movement; and (4) monocular motion-induced depth. In the following sections, I consider each of these in detail.

1. Aftereffects

Many experiments and demonstrations over the years have repeatedly illustrated an important perceptual generality: Our visual experiences are not determined solely by the immediate stimulus but also by stimuli that have been previously presented. Obviously our recollections and logically generated knowledge (based on previous experience) about what currently presented stimuli should be also have a direct effect on what we perceive. However, in this section, I am concerned with the more transient effect of the prior inspection of figures that are similar in form to the current stimulus on perception. The upshot of the discussion to follow is that local temporal context effects can drastically distort apparent shape, color, and size just as well as can the spatial contexts discussed in the previous section.

Unfortunately the word "aftereffect" has already been usurped to describe a very narrow class of phenomena in perceptual research (the so-called figural aftereffects), so it must be made clear that I am using the term with a much broader meaning in the present context. Four major categories of aftereffects are included within the limits of this broader definition of aftereffects: (1) the classic figural aftereffects; (2) effects of long-term adaptation; (3) contingent aftereffects; and (4) aftereffects of illusions.

a. Figural Aftereffects. I would like to commence this section by recalling the effects of prolonged viewing of a single stimulus. An excellent review of the effects of prolonged viewing of a single stimulus has been provided by Wade (1977a) and discussed in Chapter 10. If the stimulus pattern is a regular, finely drawn grating (i.e., with relatively high spatial frequency), a number of distortions and disappearances regularly occur after prolonged viewing even in the absence of any change in the stimulus (see Table 10-2). This family of perceptual aftereffects of a stimulus on itself was characterized by Wade as including fading, shimmering, scintillating, and spatial distortions. Such self-aftereffects are not well understood even though Table 10-2 indicates they are widespread, if not ubiquitous, in sustained viewing of stimuli with substantial fine detail.

On the other hand, a variety of aftereffects with which we are more familiar appears to be somewhat different in origin from those produced by sustained viewing of a single stimulus. These aftereffects occur when an observer examines a test stimulus following a moderately long (1–10 min) period of inspection of a related, but nonidentical, stimulus pattern. Such aftereffects have traditionally been collected together under the generic rubric of *figural aftereffects*. In general, although there are some exceptions, most figural aftereffects are negative, that is, the distortion of the percept is in the direction opposite to the significant dimension of the inspection or conditioning stimulus. Thus, if the inspection pattern was a set of convex lines, the figural aftereffect produced by prolonged examination would be to make a set of straight lines subjectively curve in a concave direction. If, on the other hand, if the direction of motion of a moving inspection figure were downward, then the usual aftereffect makes a stationary object appear to move upwards. Reddishness in a colored inspection stimulus, as another example, would tend to make a subsequently observed achromatic stimulus appear to be greenish.

Because of this general negative influence of such aftereffects, a wide variety of theories invoking fatigue or satiation has been suggested to explain those temporal interactions. Many of the theories propose multiple systems of balanced neural mechanisms in the nervous system comparable to the opponent-color mechanism that has been so compellingly demonstrated in the color system. As we later see, however, such satiation and component models suffer from a number of difficulties, suggesting that the applicability of this idea to the spatial domain may not be as convincing as the opponent-color model is in its domain.

To begin this discussion, let us consider the main empirical facts; Figure 11-21 presents a sampling of known figural aftereffect prototypes. An important first conclusion from this tabulation is that almost any dimension of that stimulus or, for that matter, of the perceptual experience can act to produce a measurable aftereffect.

A considerable amount of research has been carried out on aftereffects in the past century, and the phenomenology of this particular category of interactions is well established. An idea of the nature of the influential dimensions and the parameters involved in figural aftereffects can be appreciated from a sampling of some of the most significant studies of those phenomena. First we consider aftereffects involving gratings (a particularly popular class of stimuli nowadays) and then some of the other classic aftereffects:

1. An excellent recent summary (Braddick, Campbell, & Atkinson, 1978) asserts that, when gratings with regular spatial frequencies are used as both inspection and test stimuli, the following aftereffects are obtained:

a. The decline in visibility of a test grating following adaptation to an inspection grating is inversely related to the similarity in spatial frequency of the two gratings (Blakemore & Campbell, 1968).

b. The decline in grating visibility is insensitive to the light–dark phase relations (Jones & Tulunay-Keesey, 1975).

c. The inhibited system, whatever it is, does not change its band-pass properties only its sensitivity (Graham, 1972).

d. Many more spatial frequencies are able to adapt the frequency-tuned mechanism than can optimally be detected by that mechanism (Dealy & Tolhurst, 1974).

e. The grating adaptation effects occur even when the inspection figure is presented to one eye and the test figure to the other, and, furthermore, even when the adapted eye is pressure-blinded following the adaptation period (Blake & Fox, 1972).

2. Other recent studies that help to characterize the grating adaptation experiments as members of the class of figural aftereffects include:

a. When the spatial frequencies of the adapting the test gratings are very different (of the order of one or two octaves) these appears to be a paradoxical enhancement of sensitivity resulting in a lowered detection threshold for the test grating (Tolhurst & Barfield, 1978).

b. If the observer adapts to two side-by-side gratings simultaneously, the presence of one grating seems to reduce the aftereffect that would have been produced by the other (Tolhurst, 1972), suggesting that some process analogous to mutual inhibition may occur.

c. The degree of grating adaptation depends on the similarity in length of the grating lines as well as on the spatial frequency (Burton & Ruddock, 1978) when the length of the line is less than three times the width of the bar.

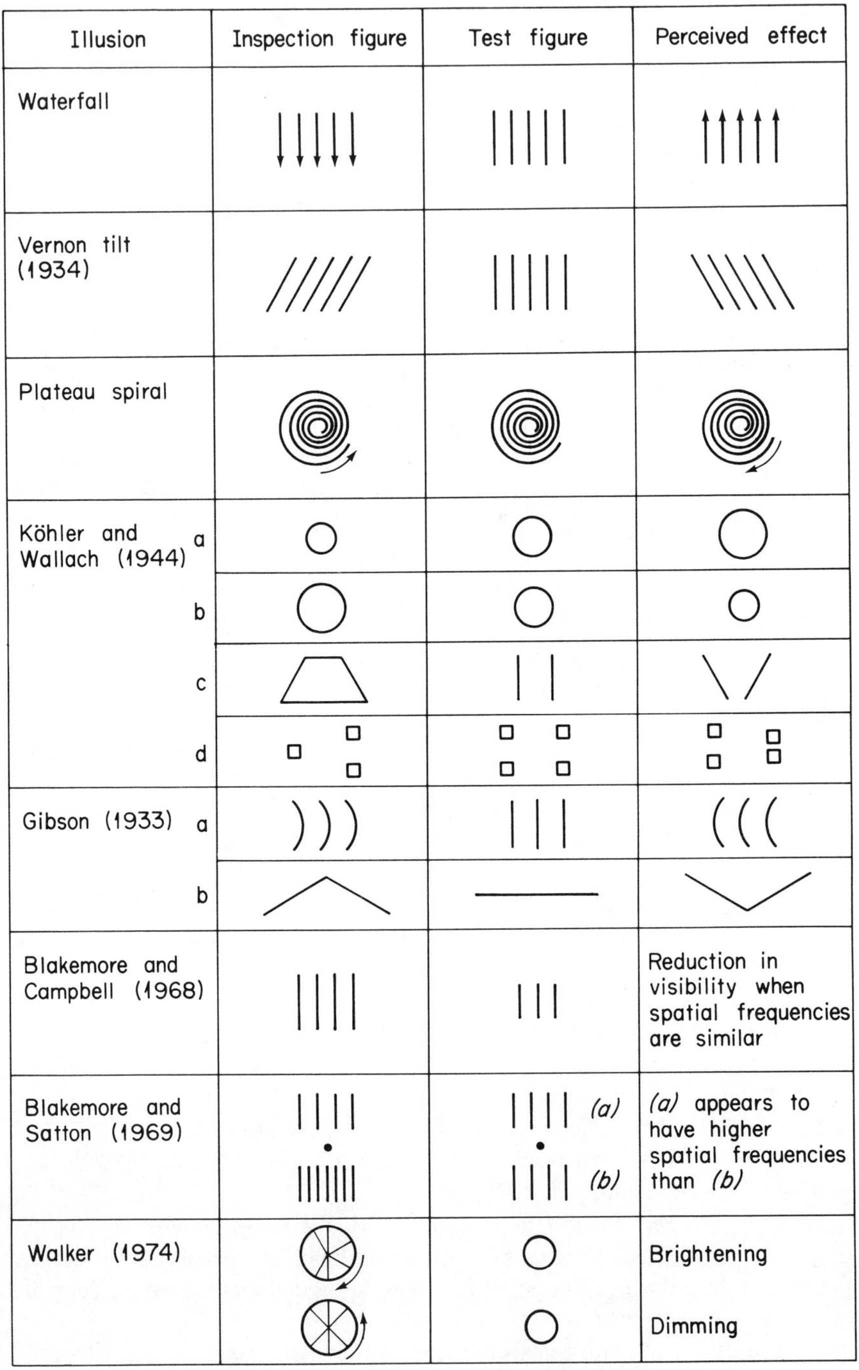

Illusion		Inspection figure	Test figure	Perceived effect
Waterfall				
Vernon tilt (1934)				
Plateau spiral				
Köhler and Wallach (1944)	a			
	b			
	c			
	d			
Gibson (1933)	a			
	b			
Blakemore and Campbell (1968)				Reduction in visibility when spatial frequencies are similar
Blakemore and Satton (1969)			*(a)* *(b)*	*(a)* appears to have higher spatial frequencies than *(b)*
Walker (1974)				Brightening Dimming

FIG. 11.21. A sampler of temporal aftereffects.

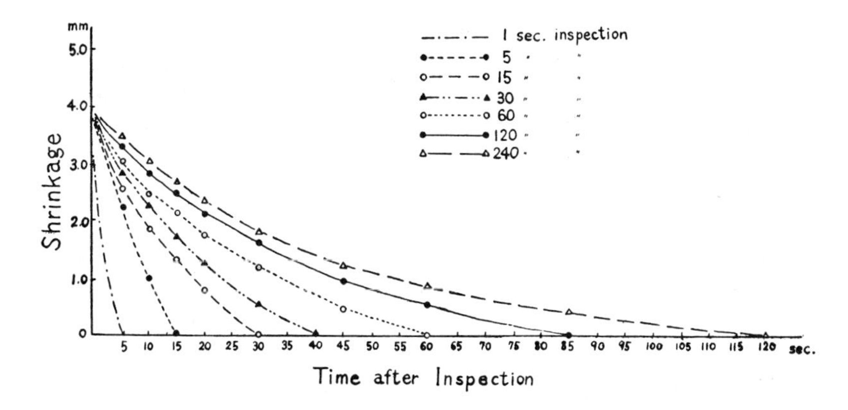

FIG. 11.22. The strength of an aftereffect as a function of the time following inspection for various durations. (From Ikeda and Obanai, © 1953, with the permission of the Japanese Psychological Association.)

These are but a few of the many experimental findings on grating adaptation that have been obtained in research stimuluated by Blakemore and Campbell's (1968) pioneering study. It would be impossible to cite them all here. One has only to look at any recent volume of *Vision Research* or the *Journal of Physiology* (London) to appreciate quickly the impact of this approach in the past decade.

3. Research on other kinds of figural aftereffects is also plentiful. A brief sample of other recent findings includes the following additional facts about aftereffects:

a. In general, the degree of similarity or dissimilarity between the inspection and test figures in terms of hue, brightness, stroke width, and contrast has little effect on the strength of a figural aftereffect (Graham, 1961; Oyama, 1960a).

b. The strength of an aftereffect declines exponentially in time—the longer the inspection period, the slower the decline, as shown in Fig. 11-22 (Ikeda & Obanai, 1953; Parducci & Brookshire, 1956).[8]

c. Figural aftereffects can occur when the inspection figure is a subjective contour or even just imagined (Kolehmainen & Crouhjort, 1970; Stadler, 1972; Weisstein, Matthews, & Berbaum, 1974).

d. The effect of the interval between the inspection period and the test period is complex; it depends on the nature of the figure and the duration of the exposure for the inspection figure as well as many other factors (Fehrer & Ganchrow, 1963).

---

[8]As we see when we discuss the McCollough effect, even this statement may reflect a gross underestimate of the persistence of aftereffects. If the test stimulus is not presented for a prolonged period of time, there may be little decline in the magnitude of the aftereffect for periods of months!

e. The effect of the duration of the inspection period on the initial magnitude of a figural aftereffect is a matter of some dispute. Some researchers (Hammer, 1949; Parducci & Brookshire, 1956) report that the longer the inspection period, the greater the initial aftereffect. But Ikeda and Obonai's (1953) data (shown in Fig. 11-22) do not indicate such a result.

f. Considerable controversy has also arisen concerning whether apparent size (suggesting a central process), or retinal size (suggesting peripheral process) is responsible for some kinds of figural aftereffects. Sutherland (1961) links phenomena of this class at least partially to the apparent size of the stimulus, although he also acknowledges the possible role of retinal size to the illusion. However, Oyama and Ichihara (1973) declare that the phenomena are solely associated with retinal size. The respective peripheral or central explanation of figural aftereffects in each of these papers is, not unexpectedly, consistent with their experimental findings, however inconsistent they are with each other. The answer to this question, therefore, also remains moot.

g. The spatial distance between the test and inspection figures also seems to affect figural aftereffects but in what are often highly complex ways. The curve relating the magnitude of the effect and spatial separation between inspection and test figures is often a nonmonotonic function with maxima occurring at intermediate distances; the effect then declines for both closer and more distant spatial separations (Köhler & Wallach, 1944).

h. Aftereffects can occur in stereoscopic depth as well as in two dimensions (Blakemore & Julesz, 1971; Köhler & Emery, 1947).

The many demonstrations and formal experiments carried out on figural aftereffects have thus led to a substantial empirical literature concerning these interesting phenomena. However little agreement yet exists with regard to a satisfactory general theory of their origins. The theories that have been proposed to explain figural aftereffects can be divided into two groups—those championing the "peripheral," isomorphic, neuroreductionistic models, and those supporting functional or symbolic models that attribute this class of temporal interactions to central processes of too great a neural complexity to be so modeled. The former class, emphasizing the isomorphic neural interactions, includes among others the lateral inhibitory interaction theories of Ganz (1966b) and R. Howard (1971), and the receptive field model of E. Walker (1973). All three of these theories invoke delayed neural interactions in relatively peripheral portions of the visual nervous system to explain the aftereffects. However, the general concept—simple neural interactions—as exemplified by Ganz' theory, has been criticized by both J. O. Robinson (1972) and Stadler (1972). Stadler specifically challenges Ganz' postulate that the aftereffects are, in fact, simultaneous contrast illusions resulting from the inhibitory interaction between the test figure and some kind of persevering afterimage of the inspection figure. Stadler specifically notes that the spatial extent of the lateral inhibitory effects proposed by Ganz as the mechanism for that interaction were greater than the limits of known neural processes. Robinson's criticism of Granz' theory is directed at another aspect of the latter's work. Robinson notes a number of instances in which the theory simply does not fit the findings of what should certainly be considered to be closely related experiments.

Other theories that can be placed in the isomorphic and peripheralist half of the theoretical dichotomy include those that involve response persistence, fatigue, or satiation of one neural component of an opponent or balanced system for the representation of spatial percepts. Köhler and Wallach's (1944) classic model, for example, involved the interaction of balanced electronic fields in the cerebral cortex. The field produced by an inspection figure persisted and distorted the spatially adjacent response to the test figure as a result of electrical forces. Osgood and Heyer's (1952) "statistical theory" used a different nomenclature but incorporated a similar concept. Instead of fields, they emphasized a somewhat more elementalistic approach in which the brain's response to a stimulus was encoded by a near-normal distribution of neuronal activity. According to Osgood and Heyer, the apparent position of the percept was associated with the neural locus at which the signal was the strongest—at the neural "mode" of the distribution. The position of the percept shifted to the degree that this neuronal response distribution could be shifted or warped by the residual response to other previously presented stimuli. Conceptually, of course, this model is virtually indistinguishable from the isomorphic field theory of Köhler and Wallach; it invokes distributions of activity and fatigue or satiation effects among neurons in exactly the same way as the earlier workers had invoked fields and field effects and is subject to the same criticisms.

The alternative class of theories, those invoking interpretive central processes, is only sparsely represented in the literature. The general approach taken by followers of this symbolic and nonneuroreductive approach is to emphasize the phenomenal rather than neurophysiological interactions. Typically this means an extreme concentration on perceptual learning and experience with regard to their role in determining the percept. According to this point of view, we learn to associate particular retinal stimuli with straightness no matter how distorted these stimuli may be. Thus, prolonged viewing of inspection figures of the type we have been considering can establish a new set, standard, or norm against which straightness is to be compared. However from this point of view it is the "meaning" and not the geometry of the stimulus that is critical in determining the perceptual outcome. Such an approach is profoundly nonisomorphic. Unlike all of the peripheral theories that I have just mentioned, it does not assume any necessary linear or even topological relationship between the brain response and the perceptual experience. In this regard, such a theoretical perspective also eschews the emphasis on spatial analogies that epitomizes much current theory.

Perhaps the best example of such a nonisomorphic, centralist approach to the problem of figural aftereffects in which learning is emphasized is still the early theory expressed by the distinguished perceptual psychologist J. J. Gibson (1933, 1937), in which he assumed that a continuous learning about or adaptation to the stimulus environment was constantly taking place. Gibson suggested that, as a result of this adaptation, ''norms that recalibrate which stimuli will be associated with which percepts are established.'' He thus asserts that there is no fixed link between retinal image maps and percepts but rather that those relationships are in a constant state of flux. Such a dissociation of stimulus and response is a premise of a theory that is fundamentally at odds with any isomorphically oriented neuroreductionistic model, of course, and is also curiously inconsistent with Gibson's ecological optical theory.

In spite of the popularity of both peripheral and central theories of figural aftereffects, my review of such theories suggests that, in fact, the origins of these phenomena, as for many of the other classic visual illusions, still remain obscure and that no satisfactory theory of these intriguing phenomena yet exists. General statements attributing figural aftereffects to the ''fatigue or conditioned fatigue'' of individual neurons at various levels of the nervous systems (e.g., the point of view expressed by Favreau & Corballis, 1976) are, at best, heuristic metaphors insufficiently supported by specific empirical evidence to justify taking them very seriously at the present time.

b. Effect of Long-Term Adaptation. Closely related to the figural aftereffects, but possibly representing an extreme case are the classic studies on the effects of profound long-term distortions of the visual scene by inverting or distorting prisms. Experiments of this sort were originally reported by Stratton (1896, 1897) and later replicated by Köhler (1951) and Snyder and Pronko (1952) among many others. Though these experiments and their interpretations have always been highly equivocal, they have played a major role in the mythology of recent and contemporary psychology. Indeed, the level of misunderstanding and confusion surrounding the long-term prism-wearing experiments is enormous. The key difficulty lies in the nature of the perceptual response following the adaptation period: Does the world actually correct itself perceptually by inverting (or ''undistorting'') after a long period of adaptation, or do we simply learn to respond appropriately to a world that is, in fact, still perceptually anomalous? Unfortunately, Stratton and the others are woefully ambiguous with regard to this matter.

The general procedure in these long-term adaptation experiments was to place inverting prisms in front of an observer's eyes and to have them worn for days and weeks at a time. The question that motivated Stratton's experiments seemed to revolve more around the necessity of an inverted retinal image rather than the problem of perceptual plasticity. Nevertheless, their major impact has proven to be more in terms of the latter than the former problem. Stratton apparently did report that the environment actually inverted perceptually after several days of vision solely through prisms, but his words are neither simple nor clear and leave us in a state of uncertainty concerning what actually happened. Did Stratton mean to imply that the observer was simply able to perform well in the new inverted environment, or was he asserting a much stronger outcome—that the observer actually saw the world rightside up after the period of adaptation? Because the upsidedownness–rightsideupness dichotomy is actually a discontinuous dimension (no one seems ever to have reported a gradual rotation in the percept), why did the performance flip-flop not occur suddenly instead of rather gradually as implied in the writing of all involved researchers? Whatever the answers to questions of this sort, it is astonishing to discover how much controversy still exists over the meaning of those experiments so many years after they were first reported. My conclusion, as with figural aftereffects, is that these long-term adaptation phenomena also remain unsolved problems of perceptual psychology. Although I do not deal further with these curious problems here, the interested reader may want to refer to an excellent discussion of them in Forgus and Melamed's (1976) fine textbook on perception.

c. Contingent Aftereffects. The aftereffects that I have just discussed represent changes in the perceptual effect of one stimulus dimension as a result of adaptation to an inspection stimulus varying in some way along the same dimension. The aftereffect appears to be present whenever the proper stimuli are presented in the appropriate order under the proper conditions. Recently, however, perceptual psychologists have come to appreciate that other aftereffects exist which may not be absolute, but rather may depend or be contingent on multidimensional interactions. The best-known contingent aftereffect is the McCollough effect, named after its discoverer, Celeste McCollough. In her exceedingly influential paper, McCollough (1965) described an orientation-contingent aftereffect in which the perceived *color* of a test grating depended on the respective orientations of that test grating when it was presented following two sequentially alternating conditioning gratings—one horizontal and one vertical.

To make this phenomenon more concrete, consider the inspection stimuli used by McCollough, which were presented in sequential alternation. One conditioning stimulus was a vertical grid with black lines and orange interstices. The other was a horizontal grid with black lines and blue interstices. For approximately 10 minutes, these two inspection figures (shown in Fig. 11-23) alternated with each other; each being presented for 10 seconds before the other was substituted. At the end of this inspection or conditioning period one of two test stimuli was presented. The first test stimulus was a horizontal grid with black lines and white interstices while the second, although also black and white, was oriented vertically. The novel aspect of McCollough's discovery was the finding that if the horizontal test grid was presented, there was a pronounced colored aftereffect in which the white interstices appeared to be a desaturated orange—a color that is, of course, close to the complement of the blue of the horizontal inspection

FIG. 11.23. The inspection stimuli pattern used in the original McCollough experiment. The interstices between the vertical lines were orange, while those between the horizontal lines were blue. (From McCollough, © 1965, with the permission of the American Association for the Advancement of Science.)

figure. So far this is hardly startling. The phenomenon I have described hardly differs from the negative chromatic afterimage described in Chapter 7. However, if the vertical black and white test grating was presented, then, most astonishingly, observers reported that the white interstices of the grating no longer appeared orangish, but rather took on a lightly colored bluish-green color. The chromatic response to the vertical grating is close to the complementary color of the grid interstices of the vertical inspection grating. The very important fact about the McCollough effect, therefore, is that the color of the afterimage is not determined solely by the color of the inspection figure but is dependent or contingent on the relative orientation of the lines in the test and inspection figures. This is an extraordinary finding, for it is obvious that a peripheral receptor or photochemical explanation, however satisfactory it may be in explaining the classic noncontingent afterimages, can only weakly explain the orientation-contingent McCollough effect. To do so would require the assumption that peripheral mechanisms were able to recognize form, a notion that most perceptual theorists, whatever their inclination, would find hard to accept. As we see shortly, peripheral neural net models also do poorly.

Furthermore, evidence (Hansel & Mahmud, 1978; Harris & Gibson, 1968) is becoming available that clearly distinguishes the McCollough effect from the classic negative afterimage even when the experimental conditions are such that their respective time courses are the same. For example, to establish this point, Hansel and Mahmud showed that the McCollough and traditional afterimage effects are independent even when elicited by stimuli presented to the same retinal locus.

Research on the McCollough effect has been extensive since her original report. Much of it has already been reviewed and summarized by Skowbo, Timney, Gentry, and Morant (1975), and by White (1978), and it is unnecessary to recapitulate that review here. The reader is referred to those sources for thoughtful and critical statements of the abundant data available concerning this interesting finding. The main point in the present context is that the phenomenon has been repeatedly validated and is now solidly accepted as a robust visual phenomenon.

McCullough's discovery has had an enormous impact on perceptual research. Not only was a substantial body of experimentation stimulated by her description of this novel aftereffect, but there was also quite a strong influence on subsequent theoretical developments. Her work suggested that our ideas about afterimages, as well as aftereffects, may be in need of thoughtful reconsideration.

Despite the attempts of some perceptual theorists to patch up the fatigue or satiation models of spatial aftereffects by invoking new knowledge about individual neurons that are sensitive to both spatial and chromatic dimensions, single-neuron fatigue models of this genre very quickly fail. The subsequent discovery of the extraordinarily long persistence of the McCullough effect by such workers as Jones and Holding (1975), as well as the sensitivity of the effect to subjective organization reported by Jenkins and Ross (1977), both previously discussed in Chapter 9, are difficult for any such simplistic neuoreductionistic interpretation to handle.

Such findings make it clear that the McCollough effect probably represents another example of a central symbolic and adaptive response to the prolonged viewing of an inspection figure rather than a phenomenal reflection of the properties of single neurons or simple neural networks in the periphery. This message now seems to be reaching contemporary theoretical consciousness. The emphasis in theoretical accounts of this phenomenon is shifting from the single-cell fatigue or satiation model to models in which the vocabulary of molar learning and conditioning is more often used. To illustrate this change, one only has to compare the differences between the early neuroreductionistic models postulating that McCollough contingent aftereffects were ''explained'' by the action of Hubel and Wiesel-type orientation detectors (e.g., Fidell, 1970; Weisstein, 1969; White & Riggs, 1974) or by network interaction processes (e.g., MacKay, D., & MacKay, V., 1975; Montalvo, 1976) on the one hand, and the school of thought emphasizing molar learning and conditioning exemplified in the work of

Mayhew and Anstis (1972) and Skowbo, Timney, Gentry, and Morant (1975) on the other. The final words of this latter group (Skowbo et al., 1975, p. 508) at the conclusion of their extensive review deserve attention:

> It would seem most reasonable, for the present, for researchers to avoid complex neurophysiological model building and to concentrate instead on using quantifiable dependent variables to examine the effects themselves more closely. Perhaps a thorough description of their characteristics will permit McCollough effects to be regarded as "missing links" between perception and learning.

Of course, there are many who would still attribute the McCollough phenomenon to peripheral neural properties. The most recent of which I am aware is Krüger's (1979) lateral geniculate network model, but this approach comes nowhere near handling the reported 6-month duration of the effect nor the effects of perceptual organization or imagery that have now been suggested.

Although the McCollough effect was the first, is the best known, and is the most thoroughly researched of the contingent phenomena, a number of others have already been identified. For example, Favreau, Emerson, and Corballis (1972) have demonstrated a color-contingent motion aftereffect that is based on the classic Plateau spiral. To observe this compelling illusion, the observer must alternate between inspection of a contracting red spiral and an expanding green spiral. When the observer is subsequently presented with a stationary green or a stationary red spiral, the former appears to be contracting and the latter to be expanding. The motion aftereffect, in this case, is, therefore, contingent upon the color of the spiral. Mayhew and Antis (1972), have also reported the existence of a motion-contingent effect that depends upon the Plateau spirals. Furthermore, Lovegrove and Over (1972) have demonstrated that the spatially contingent aftereffects are also frequency-contingent. Rather than using horizontal and vertical gratings to define two spatially distinct stimuli, as McCollough did, these psychologists chose to use two vertical inspection gratings that differed in spatial frequency as well as being, respectively, red and black, and green and black. Black and white test gratings corresponding to the spatial frequencies of the two respective inspection patterns were then presented. The phenomenal outcome depended upon the relation of the involved spatial frequencies. If the frequency of the test grating matched that of the red inspection grating, then a poorly saturated green aftereffect was reported. If, on the other hand, the spatial frequency of the test grating matched the green inspection figure, then a weak red aftereffect was reported. The contingency of color spatial frequency has been further documented by May, Agamy, and Matteson (1978) using checkerboard-type patterns. They found that spatial frequencies varying from 2–7 cycles/deg elicit this analog of McCollough's original effect.

In sum, the contingent effects and the prolonged persistence of these phenomena present a serious problem for any explanatory theory of aftereffects based on neural fatigue or satiation. First, no plausible neural "fatigue" effect could last as long as these aftereffects have been reported to persist. Second, the fatigue in this case seems to be specific to a particular stimulus; the effect may or may not occur depending on the other contingent factors. This is a substantial difficulty for any strictly deterministic theory of the kind typified by the fatigue model. Based on these and other new findings in recent years, the trend in explanatory theorizing concerning this problem has shifted away from peripheral neuroreductionistic models toward more complex central learning and/or cognitive approaches, for which there is little hope of a neural model. The "conditioning" approach to long-term contingent aftereffects championed by some psychologists is nothing other than a Level 4 model clothed in Pavlovian language.

d. Aftereffects of Illusions. Finally, in this discussion of aftereffects produced by the inspection of geometrical figures, I come to an exceedingly mysterious class of phenomena in which the aftereffects are generated by aspects of the stimulus that themselves are illusory and have no physical energy or energy discontinuities associated with them. Figural aftereffects of the type I have been discussing in this section can be produced by inspection of stimuli that produce illusory or subjective phenomena! I have already noted that it is possible to produce spatial interactions of this kind as exemplified by the sensitivity of geometrical illusions to subjective contours; the brief comment in this section extends this same concept to temporal interactions.

One of the first reports of an aftereffect to an aspect of a response that was not actually present in the two-dimensional retinal mapping was made by Blakemore and Julesz (1971). They demonstrated that a stereoscopic percept subjectively produced from two monocularly presented random dot patterns[9] could produce a substantial aftereffect following prolonged inspection. Specifically they showed that inspection of two planes at different apparent depths could alter the apparent depth of other subsequently presented stereoscopically produced planes. Because *no monocular cues* are present in such a stimulus (see Fig. 11-24A), the aftereffect can be attributed only to the processes that led to the "constructed" three-dimensional phenomenon. Blakemore and Julesz went on to vary the time that the inspection figure was presented to the observer and found that the strength of the aftereffect increased almost linearly with inspection times extending up to about 5 minures as shown in fig. 11-24B. An extension of this same kind of experiment has been carried out by Walker and Krüger (1972).

Another example of an aftereffect to an illusory stimulus can be seen in the work of Weisstein, Matthews, and Berbaum (1974)—work that I have already discussed in another context. If a stimulus like that of Fig. 11-25 is inspected by

---

[9] I detail the specifics of the stereoscopic process shortly, but for the moment the reader should simply consider disparity-cued depth only as another example of an illusory experience.

an observer for a prolonged period of time, a selective diminishment in the contrast and detectability of a test grating of similar spatial frequency occurs in much the same way that it would have if a real grating stimulus had been used as the inspection figure. Any such outcome is also a serious obstacle to any fatigue theory of visual aftereffects, of course, because the energy of the stimulus and thus the activation of the putative neural apparatus is nil.

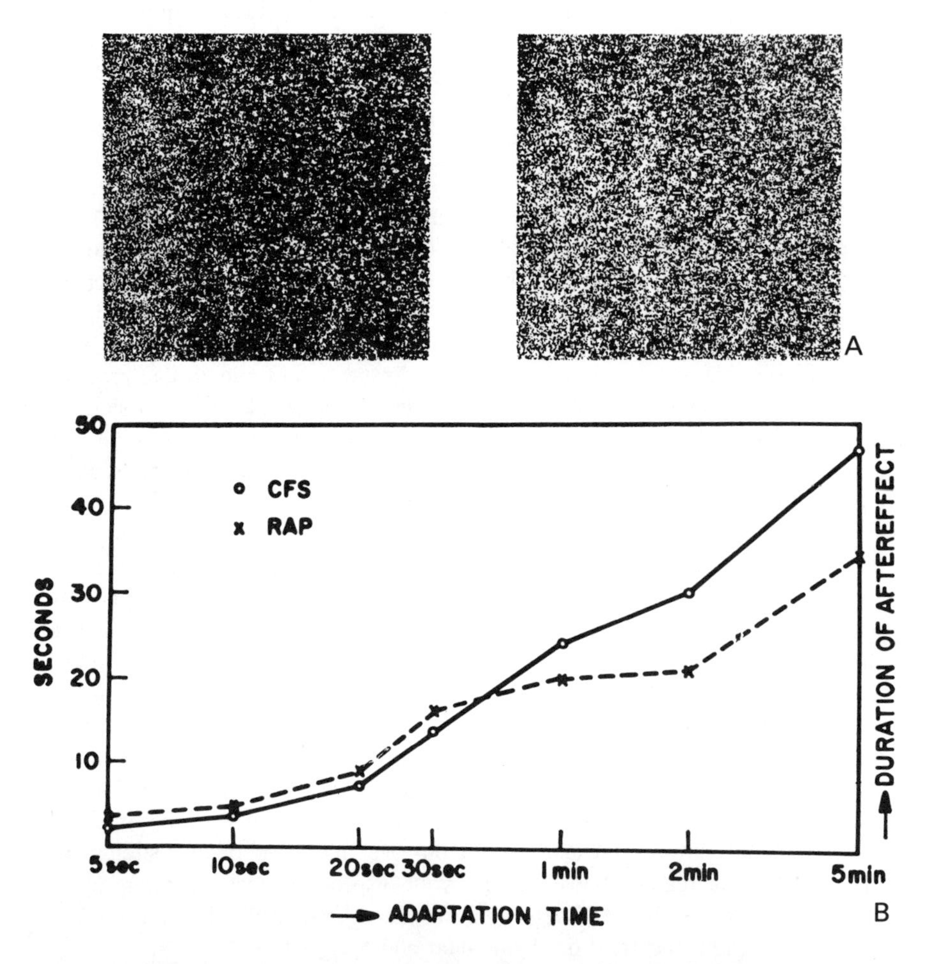

FIG. 11.24. A random dot stereogram demonstrating a dichoptic aftereffect. (A) displays the stimulus pattern (which, when viewed steroscopically, produces a pattern of two planes at different depths than the surround). Following inspection of this figure, a similar stereoscopic pattern with two planes presented at the same disparity appear to be at different depths. (B) shows the duration of the aftereffect as a function of the inspection (adaptation) time. (From Blakemore and Julesz, © 1971, with the permission of the American Association for the Advancement of Science.)

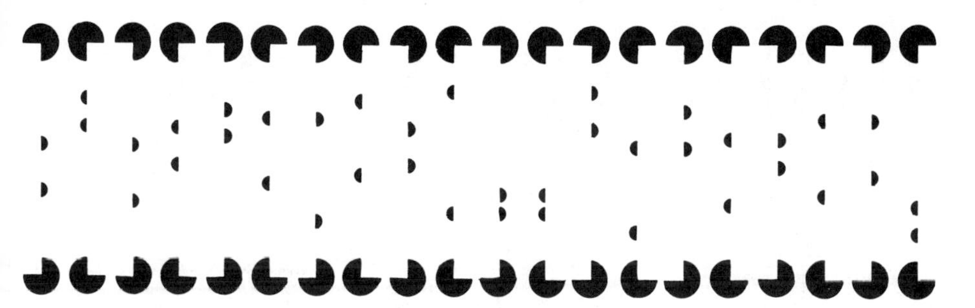

FIG. 11.25. An illusory grating. (Courtesy of Dr. Naomi Weisstein of the State University of New York at Buffalo.)

There has been considerable uncertainty concerning the efficacy of apparent motion, a related subjective phenomenon, in producing aftereffects. Some work aimed at resolving this uncertainty has been carried out by Stuart Anstis. In his earliest work on this topic (Anstis & Gregory, 1965), he concluded that the stimulus conditions underlying apparent movement were insufficient to produce an aftereffect. His data suggested that an actual transition of a physical stimulus across the retina was required to produce an aftereffect. However, in two more recent studies (Anstis & Moulden, 1970; Anstis & Reinhardt-Rutland, 1976), it did prove possible to produce movement aftereffects with a binocularly produced apparent motion (each eye saw a different random twinkle of lights) and with a very large induced movement stimulator (the observer was actually enclosed in a vertical cylinder), respectively.

In this same vein, Weisstein, Maguire, and Berbaum (1977) have reported an aftereffect of an illusory phenomenon now generally known as phantom motion. Phantom motion is perceived motion that occurs within an empty, but surrounded, region of a stimulus when the surrounding bars or lines physically move. The inspection patterns that Weisstein and her collaborators used in this experiment are shown in Fig. 11-26. The experimental conditions used are presented in this figure. Figures 11-26A and B represent control stimuli; Fig. 11-26C and D represent stimuli with horizontal interruptions; and Figs. 11-26E and F represent stimuli with vertical interruptions. The vertical lines in the test stimulus shown in Fig. 11-G were stationary. During the presentation of the test stimulus, however, most observers reported that it appeared to be moving if the inspection figure had been those shown in Figs. 11-26C and D. This subjective movement did not occur, however, when the inspection pattern was that shown in Fig. 11-26E and F, or if the moving pattern of lines was only above or only below the stimuli.

The significant outcome of Weisstein, Maguire, and Berbaum' experiment for our present discussion is that if a stationary test pattern, such as that shown in Fig. 11-26G, was presented to the observer following a period of inspection in which the phantom motion had been perceived, the test pattern appeared to move

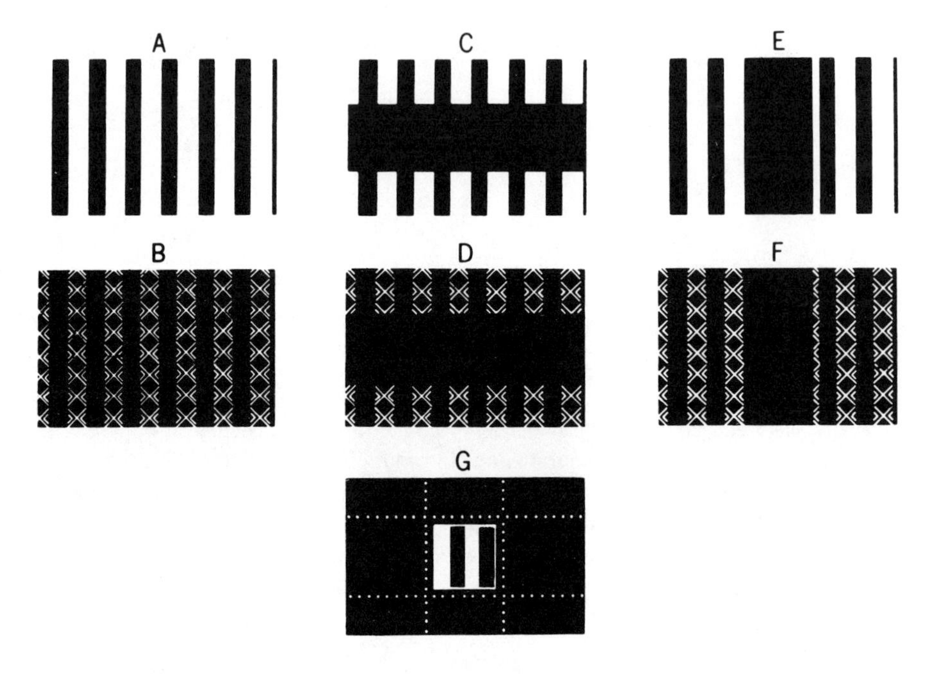

FIG. 11.26. The stimuli used in the demonstration of the phantom motion aftereffect by Weisstein and her colleagues. (Note: The frequency of the bars shown here is twice that actually used in the experiment.) A through F represent the different types of adaptation stimuli, and G is the stationary test grating. (From Weisstein, Maguire, and Berbaum, © 1977, with the permission of the American Association for the Advancement of Science.)

in the direction opposite to that of the moving phantom. The striking result here is that this aftereffect occurred in spite of the fact that the inspection or conditioning stimulus itself was a subjective phenomenon and did not actually exist in the stimulus space. Such a result is also a serious challenge to a fatigue model, to any other theory that proposes that aftereffects are the direct result of neural satiation, or for that matter, to any theory that invokes simple neural network interactions, either current or delayed, to explain aftereffects.

2. Metacontrast-Masking of the Sixth Kind

Another form of temporal interaction that has attracted considerable attention in recent years is known as metacontrast. Metacontrast is a backward-masking phenomenon in which the first of two nonoverlapping stimuli is reduced in subjective brightness (often to the point of nondetectability) as a result of its interaction with the later-coming second stimulus. The two standard stimuli used in most metacontrast experiments are shown in Fig. 11-27. Either of the two stimulus patterns shown in this figure have proven to be effective in eliciting the

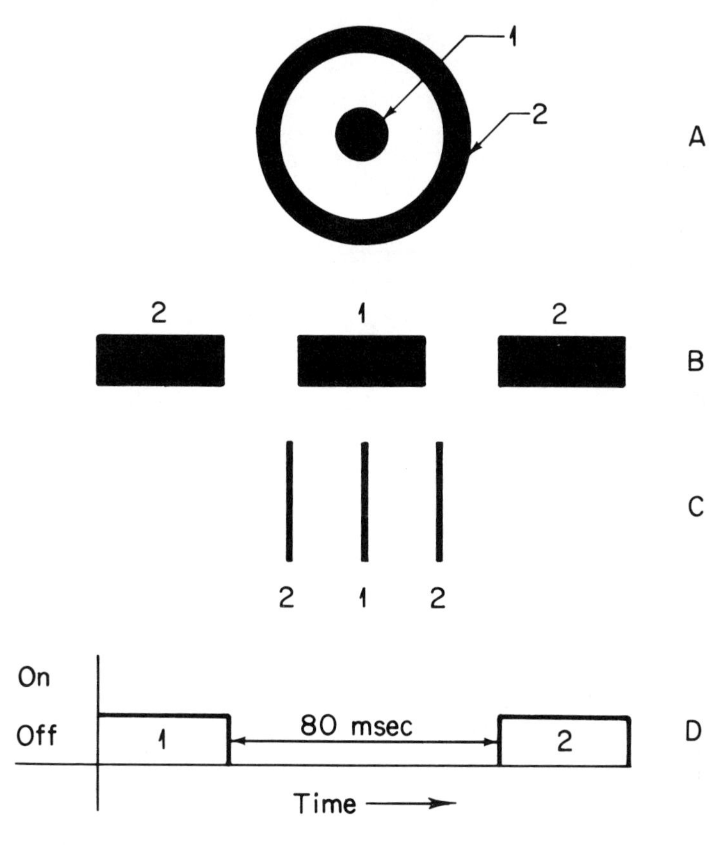

FIG. 11.27. Three (A, B, and C) different kinds of stimuli used in metacontrast type experiments and (D) the time relations of the two stimuli in each case.

phenomenon. A ''target'' or ''contrasted'' stimulus is presented *prior* to presenting a ''masking'' or ''contrasting'' stimulus. The effect usually occurs best within some specific range of intervals between the contrasted and contrasting stimulus.[10] Because this is a backward-masking effect in which a retroactive effect of a subsequent stimulus on an earlier stimulus is measured, this phenomenon has been of especially great interest to perceptual scientists; it is not intuitively obvious how one stimulus that has occurred as long as 100 msec after the presentation of another could affect that earlier stimulus. No other explanation being available, metacontrast would have had to have been considered as an example of backward causation—a process disdained by thermodynamicists, philosophers, and psychologists alike.

[10]Backward enhancement, rather than inhibition, can also be obtained in some situations (Dember and Stefl, 1972).

As we soon see, however, other explanations are available. As we saw in Chapter 9, models involving transient and sustained channels or neurons of differing conduction velocities have been invoked to reduce the need for invoking as unpalatable a concept as backward causation. Constructionistic processes in which percepts are assembled *after* all stimuli have occurred also provide another alternative solution to this dilemma. Interest in a closely related phenomenon, paracontrast, in which the contrasting stimulus occurs prior to the contrasted one, has been considerably less, simply because of its lesser challenge to our notion of the unidirectionality of time and our knowledge of the persistence of visual responses. In general, the contrasting stimuli are set at the same color and luminance and, therefore, no model invoking variable latent periods in the receptor (with the resultant possibility of one signal catching up with another) is as plausible as it was with the kind of bright-flash masking that I discussed on p. 536.

Metacontrast is a very distinct kind of masking, even though it is often confused with some of the other kinds I have already mentioned. The characteristics that distinguish this particular kind of masking effect from others are:

1. The contrasting and contrasted stimuli are similar in shape.
2. The contrasting and contrasted stimulus patterns do not spatially overlap.
3. The measured effect is exerted on the apparent brightness or detectability of the preceding stimulus; it is a backward effect.
4. The stimuli are relatively large and widely separated and the effect is global over the entire area of the masked stimulus.

It is important to reiterate that metacontrast is only one kind of backward masking and that several other backward paradigms exist (see p. 536, 542, and 603) that are similar in experimental design but do not meet all four of these criteria.

Metacontrast illusions were first reported and named as such by Stigler (1910), and were subsequently brought to modern attention in the publications of Werner (1935), Piéron (1935), Cheatham (1952), and Alpern (1953). A number of excellent reviews of this active research topic have been published in recent years, attesting to the widespread interest in this temporal interaction illusion. Among the most highly recommended ones are those by Raab (1963), Kahneman (1968), Weisstein (1972), Lefton (1973), and Scheerer (1973).

A wide variety of different psychophysical procedures have been used to assess the magnitude of the inhibition exerted on the contrasted stimulus by the contrasting stimuli. These methods have ranged from brightness-matching procedures to rank-ordering the apparent brightness using absolute judgments. The result of many of these experiments is typified by the data shown in Fig. 11-28. The maximum suppression of the contrasted stimulus occurs at an interval of about 80–100 msec between the two stimuli. In general, the metacontrast sup-

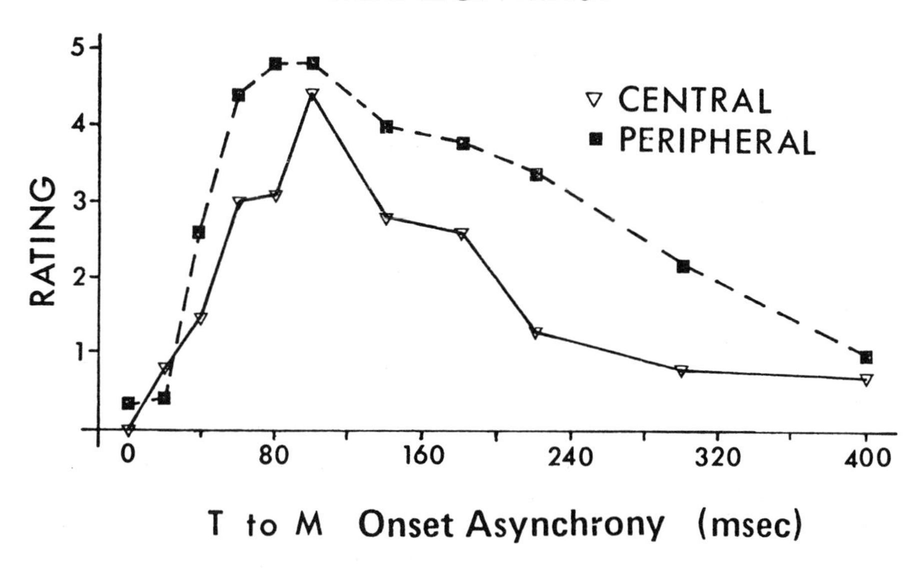

FIG. 11.28. A rating scale estimate of brightness of a metacontrasted stimulus as a function of the interval between the contrasted and contrasting stimuli. Note the inverted U-shape curve with peak contrast occurring at about 80 msec. The two curves represent the results for a central fixation of the stimulus and for a 4° eccentric viewing condition. (From Stoper and Banffy, © 1977, with the permission of the American Psychological Association.)

pression is reduced at both shorter and longer intervals, and the phenomenon has therefore been described as exhibiting a U-shaped function.

However, a considerable amount of controversy has revolved around the actual shape of the metacontrast function and its origins. This controversy takes the form of a disagreement between those who feel that the metacontrast phenomenon (and its U-shape in particular) results from high-level judgmental, or "subjective" factors on the one hand, and those who feel it is mediated by a more peripheral process, on the other. The issue has been most explicitly raised by Eriksen and Marshall (1969) and Eriksen, Becker, and Hoffman (1970), who have suggested that the U-shaped curve so often reported was an artifact of the response required of the observer. In other words, they suggest that the observer actually changed his criterion during the course of the experiment as the experimental conditions varied. This subjective explanation of the U-shaped function, which incidentally has been supported by the work of Hernandez and Lefton (1977), was supposed to occur in those experiments in which observers ranked or rated the apparent brightness of the masked stimulus using magnitude-estimation procedures. Forced-choice procedures were at first proposed to negate the U-shape outcome and produce a monotonic curve.

It must also be acknowledged, nevertheless, that there is a substantial body of information evidencing the robustness of the U-shaped function in a wide variety of experimental paradigms and with a variety of different stimuli. Weisstein, Jurkens, and Ondersin (1970) were the first to challenge Eriksen and Marshall's suggestion in experiments in which magnitude-estimation and forced-choice procedures were directly compared. And others (e.g., Andreassi, Mayzner, Beyda, & Waxman, 1970; Bachmann & Allik, 1976; Bernstein, Proctor, Proctor, & Schurman, 1973; Cox & Dember, 1972) have all subsequently found the U-shaped function appearing in a wide variety of experimental designs, including those using forced-choice methods.

Our understanding of the issue has been considerably deepened by Weisstein (1972) and Weisstein and Growney (1969), who have shown that either U-shaped or monotonic functions can be obtained with either forced-choice or magnitude-estimation procedures depending on the luminance relations of the stimulus. When the mask is very much brighter than the target, there is a tendency for monotonic functions to occur. On the other hand, if the target stimulus is adjusted to maintain a constant brightness for all values of interstimulus intervals, the function is always U-shaped. Clearly the point is that the metacontrast function, like the results of so many other Level 4 processes, is not solely determined by either interval, luminance, or any other aspect of the stimulus or response alone but is influenced rather by multiple aspects of the stimulus and experimental design. It is my judgment, after considering the data, that the central "subjective" explanation of metacontrast comes closer to a true explanation than do any of the more peripheral neural net models

The major empirical facts concerning metacontrast can be summarized as follows:

1. Metacontrast occurs dichoptically, that is, when the contrasted stimulus is presented to one eye and the contrasting stimulus is presented to the other (Kolers & Rosner, 1960).

2. Reaction times to the contrasted stimulus do not diminish under metacontrast conditions (Fehrer & Raab, 1962; Schiller & Smith, 1966).

3. Though metacontrast has often been associated with and even attributed to split apparent motion, it is possible to dissociate one phenomenon from the other in such a way that one cannot be considered to be the "cause" of the other (Stoper & Banffy, 1977).

4. The magnitude of the metacontrast suppression effect varies with retinal locus, but in a way that interacts strongly with stimulus size. The interaction has been represented in the three-dimensional space by Bridgeman and Leff (1977) shown in Fig. 11-29.

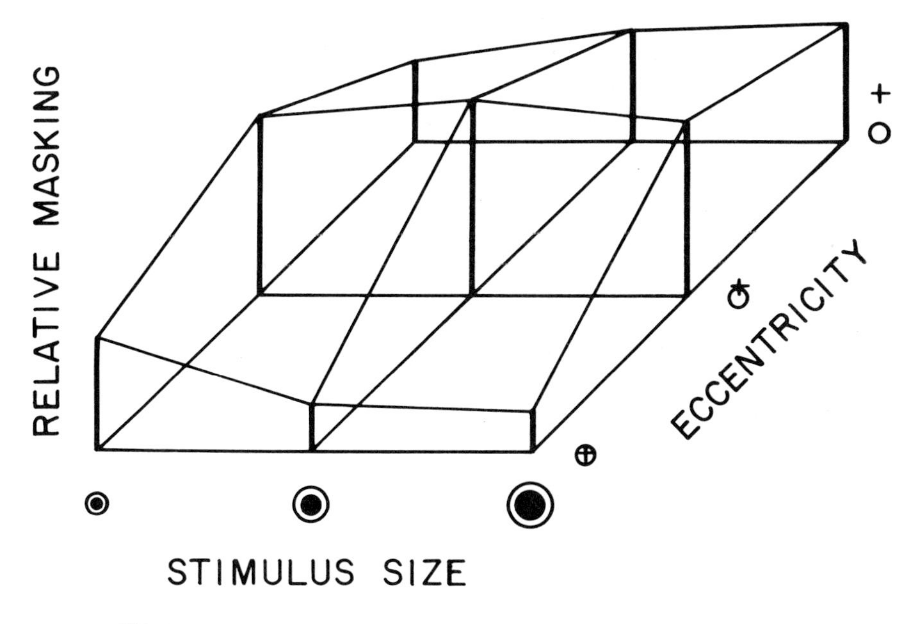

FIG. 11.29. A three-dimensional plot showing the degree of metacontrast masking as a function of stimulus size and retinal location. (Courtesy of Bruce Bridgeman of the University of California at Santa Cruz.)

5. The metacontrast effect is not localized to a small portion of the test stimulus near contours, but the entire stimulus appears to be globally and equally diminished in amplitude.

6. Identify of form and color plays an important role in metacontrast suppression in a way that also suggests that simple contour interactions are not satisfactory explanations of the phenomenon. Bevan, Jonides, and Collyer (1970) have shown that metacontrast is maximum when identical colors are used, greatly reduced when complementary colors for the contrasting and contrasted stimuli, respectively, are used, and intermediate when differing colors other than complements are used. More importantly, a considerable body of research indicates that form similarity plays a significant role in determining the magnitude of the effect. As simple a dimension as line length can be critical. Parlee (1969) and Buchsbaum and Mayzner (1969), for example, have shown that altering the linc length only a slight amount in a metacontrast experiment with two and five lines respectively can substantially mitigate the supression effect. Similarly, I showed in an earlier work (Uttal, 1970b) that identical shapes are required to produce good masking and that different froms did not mask each other well even when they shared common adjacent contours. The stimuli used in that experiment are shown in Fig. 11-30.

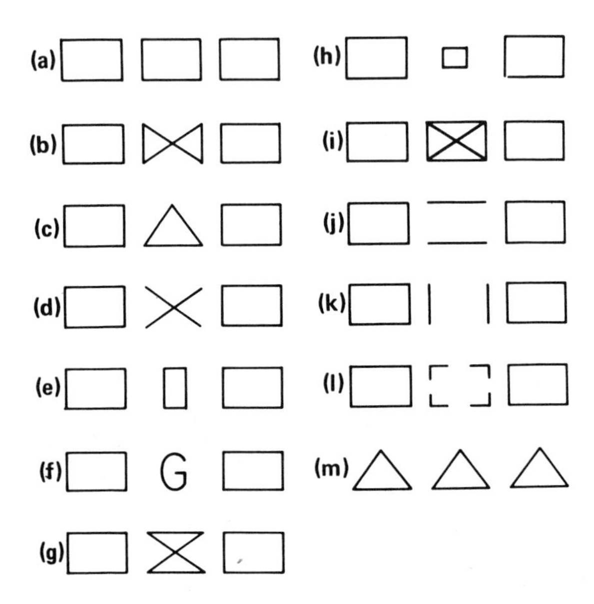

FIG. 11.30. A group of stimuli used to test whether similarity is necessary for the metacontrast effect. Only (a) and (m) produce a strong effect suggesting that the phenomenon is dependent upon prior form identification and not so much upon the geometry or the propinquity of lines. (From Uttal, 1970c.)

William Dember and his colleagues at the University of Cincinnati have shown that the spatial configuration of an annular contrasting stimulus was very important in determining the magnitude of the metacontrast effect on a central stimulus even when controlled for area. As Fig. 11-31 shows, annuli made up of small segments and small gaps regularly produced a greater masking effect on a surrounded solid disk target than when the annulus was composed of large segments and small gaps (Arand & Dember, 1974; Sherrick & Dember, 1968). Sherrick and Dember attribute this effect to the fact that the smaller-segmented, smaller-gapped ring is "a closer approximation, phenomenally, to a complete ring." Although I do not agree that it is the phenomenal difference that matters but rather that it is the stimulus difference, I do believe their argument is correct in principle. Further support for the impact of configuration on metacontrast comes from other studies reported from this same laboratory. Cox and Dember (1970), Dember and Stefl (1972), and Dember, Mathews, and Stefl (1973) have shown that the more finely a contrasted target is broken up into pie-shaped segments, the more difficult it is to mask the target with a solid annulus. However, in a more recent paper, this same group (Arand & Dember, 1976) showed that segmentation per se was not as critical in determining these results. Shape similarity between the contrasting and controlled stimuli turned out to be the essential element thus further supporting the general conjecture that form similarity is critical in metacontrast masking.

FIG. 11.31. A series of incomplete metacontrasting masks. The degree of masking is indicated in terms of the percentage of detections of an enclosed spot. (From Sherrick and Dember, © 1968, with the permission of the American Psychological Association.)

7. In general, as the distance between the contrasting and contrasted stimuli increases, there is a reduction in the magnitude of the metacontrast effect. This inverse effect of distance has been repeatedly demonstrated by a number of researchers who have worked with stimuli large enough clearly to be included within the metacontrast rubric (Cox, Dember, & Sherrick, 1969; Weisstein & Growney, 1969).

8. When the contrasting and concentrated stimuli are separated in apparent depth, there is a substantial reduction in the strength of metacontrast effect. This has been shown to be the case in a study by Lehmkuhle and Fox (In Press). They used a Julesz-type random dot stereogram to present an annular ring as a contrasting stimulus and, a Landolt C, rather than a disk, as the metacontrasted stimulus. The task of the observer was to detect the position of the break in the Landolt C under conditions of metacontrast suppression by the annular disk. The main independent variable in their study of interest in the present context was the apparent difference in depth introduced by disparity differences between the binocular images of the annulus and Landolt C, respectively. The general effect on the main dependent variable—the magnitude of metacontrast suppression—from several of their experiments is shown in Fig. 11-32. The greater the difference in depth (as determined by the controlled difference in disparity for the annulus and Landolt C, respectively), the better the observer's performance in detecting the gap in the C. This outcome implied a reduced metacontrast effect. This experiment compellingly illustrates the fact that any model of metacontrast suppression based upon lateral interaction in the periphery must be incomplete because the lateral separations between the projections of the annulus and the C in the retinal plane remain nearly constant.

9. Metacontrast may be disinhibited by a second annulus outside of, but concentric with, the first contrasting annulus. D. Robinson (1966) was probably the first to demonstrate such an effect. His paradigm was based on the suggestion emanating from the neurophysiological studies of Hartline and Ratliff (1957). Disinhibition—the perceptual phenomenon—was subsequently confirmed by Dember and Purcell (1967) and Dember, Schwartz, and Kocak (1978). Additional studies by D. Robinson (1968) demonstrated that the disinhibition effect did not, unlike the metacontrast effect itself, occur if the second ''disin-

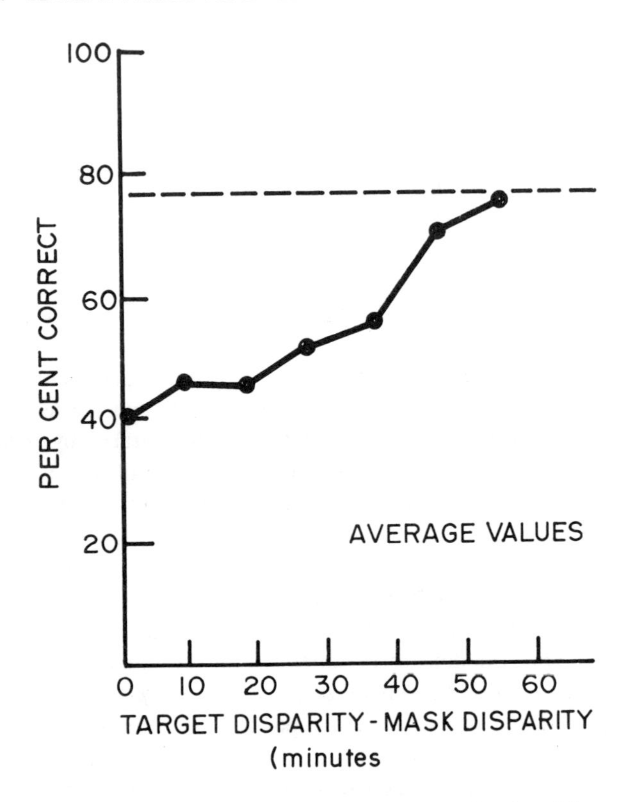

FIG. 11.32. Detectability of a metacontrasted target as a function of the stereoscopic separation in depth. (From Lehmkuhle and Fox, in press, with the permission of the American Psychological Association.)

hibiting'' annulus was presented to the eye opposite that receiving the first contrasting annulus and the contrasted disk.

10. Although metacontrast of the kind I have been describing in this section typically involves suppression by geometrically congruent stimuli of the kind shown in Fig. 11-27, other stimuli have been used in what may be very similar backward-masking experiments with comparable results. Mark Mayzner and his colleagues (e.g., Mayzner, 1972; Mayzner, 1975; Mayzner & Tresselt, 1970b; Newmark & Mayzner, 1973) and Merikle (1977) have all worked with alphabetic character strings in which sequentially presented letters appear to suppress each other in a way that seems closely related to the classic metacontrast phenomenon. The important contribution of the experiments, which use alphabetic characters rather than the geometrical patterns shown in Fig. 11-27, is their emphasis on the impact of semantic content on what had been hitherto considered to be a purely form-dependent process. It must therefore be acknowledged that a major dilemma remains after one has compared these studies with those that suggest that

metacontrast is dependent on spatial contours and form identity. Escape from the horns of this dilemma is possible if one accepts the fact that actually more than a single kind of masking is present in this letter-interaction paradigm and that two processes are being uncritically mixed in analysis of this type of experiment. Merikle (1977, p. 618) supports this speculation when he notes:

> The present results also suggest that metacontrast[11] is not a unitary phenomenon. Different aspects of the metacontrast phenomenon appear to require considerably different explanations. In particular, it appears that the nonmonotonic functions, the effects of semantic similarity, and the effects of mask complexity all reflect different underlying processes.

Intermediate experimental designs that have been included within the metacontrast paradigm, in which geometrical forms such as circles mask single alphabetic characters (e.g., Eriksen & Collins, 1964a, 1964b), introduce further levels of both stimulus and conceptual complexity that actually may define another entry into the increasingly cluttered list of backward-masking phenomena.

These, then, are some of the empirical facts concerning metacontrast. It would be a pleasure to be able to say that these findings are universally accepted, and/or that they lead irrevocably to a widely accepted theoretical explanation. However there is also a remarkable degree of controversy present in this field. Part of this controversy may be due to the fact that we are still uncritically mixing together processes that are not exactly equivalent. The masking of geometric forms by other similar geometric forms may involve processes that are different from, or only a part of, those involved in letter masking, for example. The commonality of the experimental design may have blinded us to what are actually fundamentally different underlying processes.

Many other persistent and fundamental controversies concerning metacontrast continue to occupy the attention of researchers in this field. One continuing perplexity revolves around the problem of whether or not information that has been metacontrasted is physically suppressed (as would be predicted by those championing neural net reductionistic type theories). An alternative view is that physical information is not suppressed, but rather only loses its perceptual significance as a result of interpretative processes that have nothing to do with, say, isomorphic lateral inhibitory interactions operating on the neural representation. The recurrent suggestion that information that has been metacontrasted can actually be recovered and the repeated demonstrations showing that which information is lost depends on some aspect of its meaning are, however, compelling

[11]Merikle uses the word *metacontrast* here to refer to the kind of backward masking he used in his study. According to the criteria defining metacontrast presented earlier, he may be using the word in a broader sense more akin to the implications of the term *backward masking*.

counterarguments that the metacontrast is not an act of neural signal suppression alone.

This, then, brings us to the crux of the metacontrast problem. The value and attention that have been attributed to this peculiar little phenomenon arises mainly out of the fact that it is a useful medium with which to study some of the complex problems of perceptual processing. Metacontrast is, therefore, of interest to the degree that it tells us something about the function and structure of the visual process, that is, to the degree that it becomes a vehicle for theoretical development. In this regard, metacontrast has been extremely frutiful and has stimulated the development of a rich variety of theoretical models. I have already considered in detail (on p. 685) the neuroreductionistic models, but many other models have also been proposed. Briefly, some of the more interesting theoretical explanations of metacontrast so far proposed have been Kahneman's (1968) attribution of it to the perceptual disallowance of the impossible apparent motion that must occur in several directions simultaneously when the disk and annulus (or three rectangular stimuli) are sequentially flashed; Eriksen and Hoffman's (1963) and Eriksen and Lappin's (1964) suggestion that metacontrast was an artifact of delayed simultaneous contrast between an image and an afterimage (this is generally known as the integration hypothesis); and Kolers' (1968) and Haber's (1969) proposal of an ''information overload'' hypothesis. This last hypothesis asserts that the first stimulus in a metacontrast paradigm was not allowed sufficient time to be fully processed before the contrasting stimulus ''caught up with it'' and that the latter thus interfered with the recognition of the former (this is usually referred to as the interruption hypothesis).[12]

In conclusion, metacontrast represents a prototypical form of temporal interaction characterized by a backward suppression of detectability or luminance that, despite a substantial empirical and theoretical effort, remains largely enigmatic in terms of its origins. In particular, it appears that the several currently popular neuroreductionistic models (discussed in Chapter 9) are inadequate. Their popularity persists mainly because of an absence of alternatives that incorporate knowledge of the effects of higher-level influences (e.g., the ''judged'' impossibility of split apparent motion). The metacontrast effect seems clearly not to be a peripheral one, but, rather, to be strongly dependent on central information-processing mechanisms that are considerably more complex than the simple networks proposed by the lateral inhibition theorists. It is also possible that several different processes are uncritically intermingled in the metacontrast rubric. This phenomenon is only one of at least six distinguishable kinds of

[12]Michael Turvey's very influential paper (Turvey, 1973) deals with a kind of masking that, in my opinion, is also not identifiable with metacontrast. He superimposed visual noise (both random visual noise and letter fragments) on top of alphabetic characters. Though many of his comments may be generally relevant to the problem of metacontrast, I believe that they are more appropriate to considerations of the kind of masking I have discussed on p. 551 and his work, therefore, is considered there rather than here.

masking and the significance of a given experiment is often clouded by the variety of experimental paradigms; the many different stimulus configurations that are used, many of them purporting to produce "classic" metacontrast, do not all satisfy the four criteria defining metacontrast that was enumerated at the outset of this discussion. Clearly, any current taxonomy of masking processes, in general, and understanding of metacontrast, in particular, is, at best, tentative and incomplete.

3. Apparent Movement

So far in this section, I have discussed temporal interactions either between repeated occurrences of similar geometric forms or between sequential presentations of different forms. In these cases the phenomenal response was either an aftereffect or a suppression of detectability or brightness of one or the other stimuli. Turning from these phenomenal outcomes to another quite different perceptual result of a sequential interaction, I now consider a temporal interaction whose outcome is the construction of an entirely new phenomenal dimension that was not actually encoded in the original physical stimulus. The phenomenon to which I refer is the subjective construction of a continuously moving percept as the result of the sequential presentation of two or more discrete stationary stimuli.

As noted in Chapter 1, Lloyd Kaufman has pointed out that apparent movement phenomena represent some of the most paradoxical of the visual illusions. This type of illusion requires the experimenter to explain how the direction of apparent movement can be determined *before* the stimulus that defines that direction is perceived. In other words, the dynamics of the apparent motion phenomenon suggest that we acquire information about the location of the second stimulus ("see" it in terms of one meaning of the word) before we actually become aware of the arrival of the moving object at that location ("see" it in terms of another meaning of the word). To understand the difficulties raised by this paradox, we need a deeper appreciation of the problem created by the empirical facts surrounding the perception of motion in the absence of moving visual stimuli. The term—apparent motion—as should be evident by now, incorporates a fairly broad class of phenomena. I have already spoken about the apparent motion that occurs as an aftereffect of the inspection of real motion or phantom motion. However, the apparent motion of the kind to be considered now is not dependent on the prior inspection of a moving figure; it is a perceptual construct that occurs simply as a result of the sequential presentations of stationary stimuli located in different spatial locations.

The prototypical apparent motion illusion occurs when two lighted objects are briefly presented in succession, as shown in Fig. 11-33. The perceptual impression produced by this stimulus (when the interval is correct) is of a single object moving continuously and smoothly from the position of the first stimulus to the

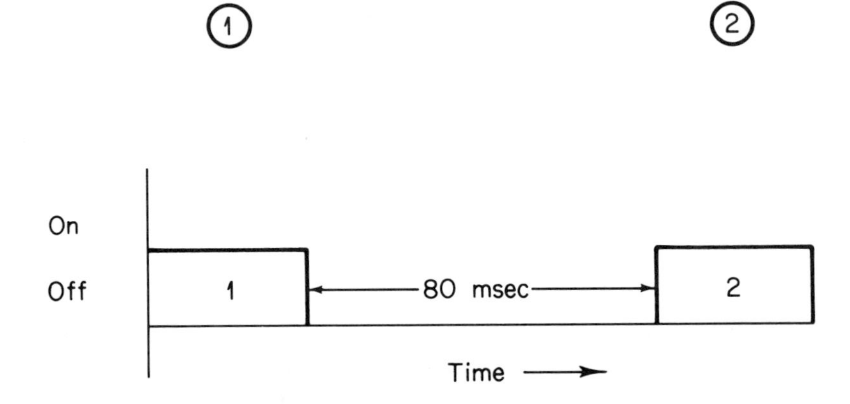

FIG. 11.33. The stimuli and timing relations in the prototypical apparent movement display.

position of the second one. Successful use has been made of disks, spots, and even random dot matrices in elicting the apparent movement phenomenon. Although the effect is enhanced by having the two luminous objects identical in geometry, it also occurs when they are of different shapes—sometimes, however, with surprising concomitant perceived shape distortions. Thus, apparent motion is not the only possible outcome when two spatially spearated stimuli are presented—perceptual distortions and deformations can often occur in addition to the induced movement.

Apparent motion and these related phenomenal outcomes have a long and distinguished history as targets of perceptual research. Graham (1965a), J. O. Robinson (1972), and Kolers (1972) review this history thoroughly enough that it need not be repeated here. In particular, the interested reader is directed to Paul Kolers' exceptional book on apparent motion. Kilers' scholarly and constructively critical analysis of the problem is by far the best of any that I have encountered in my studies.

The seminal research paper (Wertheimer 1912) on apparent motion in modern times should also be explicitly noted. This report not only stimulated a new surge in apparent motion research but also was instrumental in initiating the Gestalt school of psychological theory itself. The Gestalt psychologists were particularly influenced by the apparent motion phenomenon, and it was to play a central and continuing role in their theoretical development. Though the explanatory models they proposed to explain phenomena of this kind no longer are considered acceptable, the classic Gestalt taxonomy of the several different kinds of apparent motion phenomena is still useful in organizing modern perceptual research and theory regarding this topic. The Gestalt psychologists distinguished among the following kinds of apparent motion:

1. Alpha Motion—An apparent continuous expansion or contraction of an object when it was successively presented in two different-sized versions.

2. Beta Motion—The apparent movement of an object between two positions in which it is successively presented.

3. Gamma Movement—The apparent continuous expansion or contraction of an object when its luminance is changed.

4. Delta Movement—Apparent movement in the direction from the second to the first position in which it is successively presented. Delta movement occurs only when the second stimulus is much more luminous than the first.[13]

Another term—phi motion or the phi phenomenon—is often used to describe the best possible apparent movement. The original use of this term by Wertheimer (1912) denoted an optimum kind of apparent motion that did not involve any "awareness of the object." Rather, Wertheimer believed that a pure sense of motion (phi motion) existed that was fundamental in its own right. The idea of a pure, object-free phi motion has persisted; it can be discerned in more recent attempts to distinguish between object perception and motion perception—a distinction that many of us now feel less comfortable with than did some of our predecessors.

The empirical facts concerning apparent motion at one time were thought to be relatively straightforward. Indeed, Korte (1915), over a half century ago, had formulated a set of principles (now known as Korte's laws) that were thought to summarize the general characteristics of these phenomena. Although still frequently cited, Korte's laws are now thought to be, at best, gross approximations (e.g., Kolers' discussion). I think, therefore, that it would be better to simply list the major empirical findings of apparent motion without recapitulating the error of reciting these outmoded and inaccurate generalizations.

One of the most intricate and often ignored problems in any area of perceptual research concerns the relations between the different dimensions of the stimulus. In apparent motion research, perhaps more than in any other area, the nature of the interactions between the duration of the stimuli, their respective luminances, their physical position, and the interval between them has been central. Korte's (1915) studies, and the laws that he proposed, reflected a sensitivity to the importance of multidimensional influences that set the stage for the continuing modern interest in interactions. This was so in spite of the fact that his general "laws" now seem to be such inadequate descriptions of the actual interactions. We have learned much since Korte's time, from the work of such scholars as Neuhaus (1930) and especially Paul Kolers (as summarized in the latter's 1972

---

[13]I have already indicated on p. 488 how Delta motion may be attributable to the luminance–latency relationship. However a recent demonstration of a similar reversed apparent movement effect by Anstis and Rogers (1975) seems not to be attributable to latency differences.

book. Mainly on the basis of Kolers' discussion, much of this new knowledge can be summarized as follows:

1. In general, as Korte suggested, the longer the duration of each stimulus, the shorter the interval between the two at which the best apparent (phi) motion occurs, all other parameters held constant. However, Kahneman and Wolman (1970) have suggested that the situation is actually far more complex. They note that the visual response is always longer than the stimulus and has been considered to be constant for any stimulus duration up to about 100 msec (see Chapter 7). Therefore, they suggest that apparent motion should be considered to be a function of neural inter*response* intervals rather than physical inter*stimulus* intervals, the latter always being greater than the former due to response persistence.

2. The velocity of apparent motion, contrary to the implications of one of Korte's laws, is not constant. Kolers replots Neuhaus' data to show that the apparent velocity in the paradigm the latter used increases with the spatial separation of the two stimuli and with their durations.

3. In general, as the separation between the two stimuli increases, the interstimulus-interval at which the optimum beta motion occurs also increases. However this is bounded by the fact that after some maximum interval the two stimuli are seen as successive. This threshold interval for succession, contrary to that for apparent movement, decreases as the spatial separation between the two stimuli increases. The result is that the two curves cross over and no apparent motion can be obtained for stimuli separated by greater than 6 or 7° according to Caelli, Hoffman, & Lindman, (1978), or 3 or 4° according to Neuhaus (1930) and Kolers (1972). The enclosed area in which the best apparent motion occurs between the apparent motion threshold curve and the succession threshold curve in this separation–interval space is thus elipsoidal, as shown in Fig. 11-34.

4. Another argument that the apparent properties of the visual response may be more important than those of the physical stimulus in determining the nature of the induced apparent motion is based upon the work of Rock and Ebenholtz (1962). They showed that apparent motion would result even if the two sequential stimuli fell on the same retinal locus if that locus was associated with different apparent positions. This sensitivity to apparent position, rather than to actual retinal locus, has been confirmed for three-dimensional movements by Attneave and Block (1973) by judicious adjustment of the actual retinal disparities associated with the three-dimensional loci of a point. Such a shift in apparent position for the same retinal locus also occurs when the eye is moved between two sequential stimulus presentations to the same retinal locus. This result further supports the hypothesis that the apparent motion phenomenon is not a function of any simple neural processing in the periphery but is a construction developed from the cues provided by the stimuli that determine the apparent properties of the stimulus. Furthermore, apparent *separation* of the initial and end points is not always required to produce good *apparent motion*.

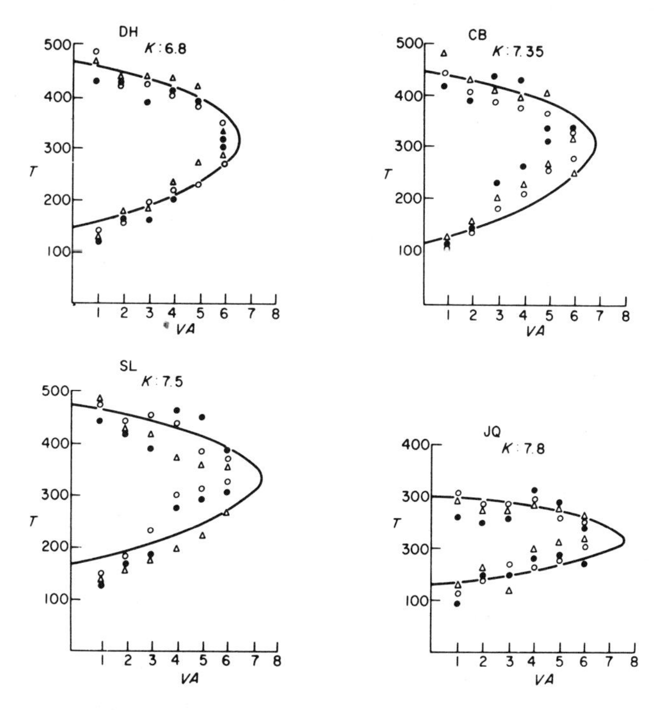

FIG. 11.34. Data (from 4 observers) depicting the narrow range of apparent motion (τ = onset time of the second stimulus minus the onset time of the first stimulus) as a function of the visual angle between the two stimuli. The three symbols represent different exposure times of each of the stimulus lights (open triangles = 10, open circles = 45, filled circles = 90 msec). (From Caelli, Hoffman, and Lindman, © 1978, with the permission of John Wiley & Sons, Inc.)

Biederman-Thorson, Thorson, and Lange (1971) have shown that an impression of motion and accurate directional judgments can occur when two dots are so close together that they cannot be resolved when they are stationary.

5. In general, similarity in shape of the first and second stimulus tends to enhance any induced apparent motion (Orlansky, 1940). However identify of form is by no means an absolute necessity. Kolers and Pomerantz (1971) have shown that only a slightly attenuated apparent motion occurs when one uses, for example, a square and an arrow as opposed to two squares. Nevertheless, at longer interstimulus intervals there is a tendency for apparent deformations (from one shape to the other), orientation changes, or even changes in apparent depth to occur instead of, or in addition to, motion. Finally, it is not necessary for any discriminable forms to be present to produce good apparent motion. Bell and Lappin (1973) have shown that good apparent motion can be produced from very small displacements of monocularly presented quasi-random patterns.

6. More complex stimulus displays can produce complex spatiotemporal responses that appear to have much in common with apparent motion. For example, Mayzner and Tresselt (1970b) showed that a series of letters, separated in space but presented serially in time, could produce both apparent displacement and movement. Geldard's (1976) saltatory (i.e., ''hopping'') visual effects in which similar sequential patterns of dots are presented in the retinal periphery may also involve the same mechanisms that underlie the more familiar forms of continuous apparent motion.

7. In his book Kolers also reports the results of a series of experiments in which stimuli with two alternative second targets produce perfectly good split or duplicate apparent motion. Similarly, he discusses other experiments that show little evidence of any ''vector addition'' in which the apparent motion appears to take an intermediate pathway between two subsequent second targets. Kolers (1972) concludes that the perceptual system does not operate on the basis of any psuedophysical forces, attractions, or fields but acts to ''resolve or rationalize the disparity between two properly timed flashes [p. 194].''

8. Apparent motion does not seem to involve the same physiological mechanisms that are activated by real stimulus motion. Kolers (1964), in what many now consider to be a classic experiment, has also shown that whereas there is a substantial masking effect on the detection of a small spot of light presented in the close proximity to the path of a real moving object, no such masking or reduction in detectability occurs when the small spot of light is presented at a point close to the path of an apparent motion.

Observations like this have led to a vigorous controversy over whether real and apparent motion should be considered to be the same or different processes. This controversy has been fully discussed and carefully analyzed by Anstis (1978), who contrasts single-component theories (which assert that real and apparent movement are attributable to the same mechanism) with dual-component theories (which assert that real and apparent movement are attributable to entirely different mechanisms). Anstis also considers the possibility that some kind of a compromise resolution of this controversy is possible, and alludes to mixed theories, proposing that (a) both real and apparent movement may be mediated by the same mechanisms over very short differences, but (b) at larger distances they have to be explained in separate terms.

An important conceptual point implicit in this controversy is germane to the argument I made in Chapter 9. If one accepts Kolers' argument that real and apparent motion, phenomenally do similar, do not in fact both involve the same neural mechanisms, then one may validly ask another obvious question: If a dissociation can be demonstrated between the neural and perceptual responses associated with apparent motion, why do we need to postulate that a dimensionally isomorphic neural response pattern is a necessary concomitant of real motion? In other words, these findings raise the possibility that the geometrically isomorphic neural signals, seemingly so closely correlated with the perceptual experience of real motion, may in fact be irrelevant to the representation of the percept. In other words, such neural signals may be signs of that activity, but not true codes in the sense I expressed on earlier (Uttal, 1973).

9. Apparent motion may occur between stimuli that are widely separated in the visual field. In general the effect occurs over far greater distances than even the widest neural interaction processes so far measured. Successful long-range apparent motion depends on very long stimulus durations but has been reported by some observers to occur when the two stimuli are separated by retinal distances as great as 150 or 160 deg in extreme cases.

10. Apparent motion, like many of the other phenomena I have discussed in this chapter, seems to depend on many subjective factors. These findings also place it outside the limits of any plausible neural interaction model. Sigman and Rock (1974) have shown, for example, that expectations, set, and "intelligence" all influence apparent motion and that such configurational factors as the observer's subjective organization of reversible objects can affect the constructed apparent motion.

11. Apparent movement also seems to depend very much on the ways in which the stimuli are grouped, in accord with the classic Gestalt laws. Braddick and Adlard (1978) have reviewed the parameters that affect group movement, as opposed to the movement of individual elements, in a stimulus display in which several alternative patterns of apparent motions are possible. They suggest, as did Braddick (1974) earlier, a two-component theory of apparent motion consisting of a short-range mechanism that operates only for interstimulus intervals less than 100 msec (attributable, according to them, to the activation of neuronal motion detectors) and a long-range process sensitive to long interstimulus intervals. Braddick and Adlard's conclusion is that the more persistent, longer-range process is so dependent on the perceptual organization of the visual scene that it can only be attributable to a "high-level interpretive process."

12. Apparent motion can occur between subjective contours. Von Grünau (1979) has demonstrated that the apparent disks occurring in two Ehrenstein figures (see Fig. 11-35) can evoke an illusion of motion when they are successively flashed that is distinguishable from the apparent motion effect induced by the lines producing the illusory contours.

13. Gamma movement, the symmetrical expansion of a light as it is being illuminated (or its inverse—the contraction of a light being dimmed), is strongly affected by the presence of other luminous objects in the visual field. Generally, according to Kanizsa (1978), the direction of apparent growth is away from a nearby object that is permanently illuminated, and this polarization is inversely proportional to the distance to that permanent object.

These are some of the empirical facts concerning apparent motion. They have been interpreted in diverse ways by theoreticians interested in explaining this compelling illusion. Because Kolers (1972) has competently reviewed and

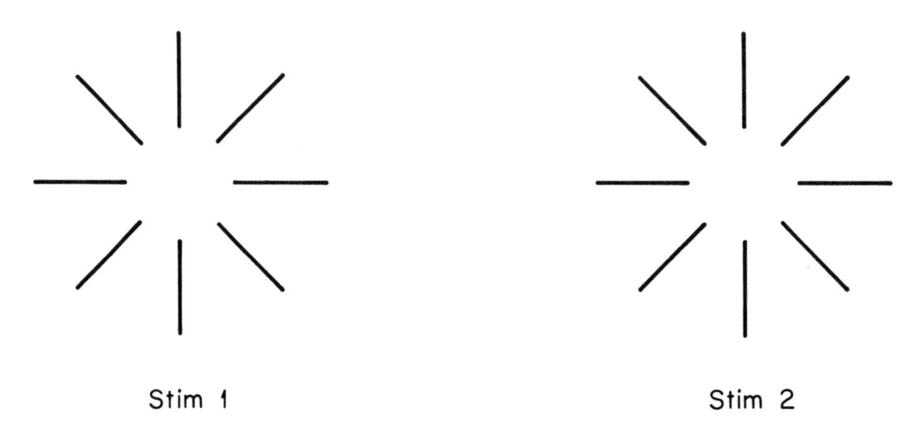

FIG. 11.35. Experimental stimulus demonstrating that apparent motion can be obtained from subjective surfaces. (Redrawn from von Grünau, 1979.)

critiqued the classic theories of apparent motion, I only briefly abstract his taxonomy of theories here. Kolers notes that there are only three truly different general types of apparent motion theory. The first type he classifies as epiphenomenal. This type, Kolers suggests, includes those putative models that adhere to a single major influence as the sole cause of the apparent movement phenomenon; from this point of view apparent movement is an "epiphenomenon" of that other process. To exemplify this first type of theory, Kolers cites Higginson's (1926) early theory invoking eye movements as the sole determinant of apparent motion. Kolers (1972) notes that theories of this class "do not fully distinguish between an influence and a mechanism [p. 172]."

Kolers' second type of apparent motion theory is denoted as "figural." This type includes those theories suggesting that apparent motion is a cognitive, although highly atuomatic, rational solution to the perceptual paradox created by what appears to be the same object appearing in subsequent instances in two different positions without a spatial translation. Apparent motion, according to this class of theories, represents a constructive solution to the physical implausibility defined by the temporally and spatially disparate stimuli.

Finally, Kolers' third type of apparent motion model is denoted by the term "excitation theories." This category includes those theories proposing that some sort of a neural process is elicited that is in isomorphic conformity with the spatial pattern of the stimulus. Köhler's (1947) electrotonic field interaction, for example, in which the neural responses to each of the stimuli were literally thought to short circuit each other, is the prototype of this theoretical approach. The many theories of spatiotemporal induction (those invoking attractive or repulsive forces among the isomorphic neural representations of sequential stimuli) would also fall within the scope of Kolers' third class of apparent motion theories.

Although Kolers (1972) does not refer to them specifically in his discussion and classification of apparent motion theories, he does allude later to a new group of theories that has become increasingly popular in recent years. This new group is also neuroreductionistic but in a single-cell sense (rather than mass action or electrical field) and is, of course, the same one we have already confronted many times in our discussion. Once again, the analogy is made between the functions of neurons that are particularly sensitive to moving stimuli and the phenomenon of apparent motion. In general, these theories assert that there is a partial activation, in some way, of these movement-detecting single cells. Such models are versions of a strong place theory that postulates that this spurious activation is tantamount to the experience of movement itself. Clearly, these single-cell models are only the most modern entries into Kolers' excitation class of apparent motion theory.

In general, however, all of these speculative, phenomenological, or physiological models of apparent motion are incomplete. There are many reasons for this pessimistic conclusion. The reader interested in a more complete critique is directed to Kolers' 11th and 12th chapters. His summary statement that "no theory of visual perception gives an answer to more than a small number of the many aspects of the apparent motion phenomena" provides a good concluding summary of this brief discussion of classic apparent motion theories.

In spite of, or perhaps because of, the absence of satisfying reductive models of apparent motion, increasing attention has been given to more sophisticated descriptive analysis than is typical in other fields of perceptual research. Of particular interest are two very elegant mathematical models of this phenomenon that have recently appeared. The first (Foster, 1978) deals both with the problem of apparent motion and the problem of the plastic deformations that occur when the two sequentially presented stimuli are not spatially congruent. Foster's main point is that the perceptual transformations that occur when an object is either apparently translated from one point to another or when it is apparently plastically deformed are in accord with a mental "calculus of variations" comparable to the classic mathematical technique. The calculus of variations in mathematics is a means of predicting the transformations that an object will undergo when subjected to a system of forces. The technique was stimulated by such problems as the determination of the minimum time of flight for a gravity-driven object proposed by Jacob Bernoulli in the 17th century. The main criterion in the physical situation is that the process progresses along a path that minimizes some dimension such as time or stress, that is, the internal reaction forces to the externally applied strain, and thus the energy expended on or within the object.

Foster applied these classic mathematical procedures to the problem of apparent motion by invoking an analogous criterion of "minimum perceptual energy" as the determining factor in shaping the perceived deformation of an object. Minimum perceptual energy, from one point of view can be considered to be nothing more than another way of expressing the concept of a symbolic constructionism. Minimum perceptual energy specifies a particular criterion that might be used by the constructionistic logic to determine what experience can be evoked that will best solve the problem posed by the stimulus. On this basis Foster is able to show that many phenomena of the kind we have been considering here can be both described and predicted. His model also deals well with more complex transformations occurring, for example, when a circle perceptually turns into a circumscribed square, or when a straight line is perceived to be deformed into a curved line as a result of sequential presentation of the two lines. Another important aspect of Foster's model is that it successfully predicts the psychophysical fact that some figures that are not topologically transformable into each other (e.g., a checkerboard and a set of concentric circles) will not exhibit apparent motion no matter how optimum the timing and separation. Thus, prior form recognition and some kind of an awareness of "physical plausibility" are important preliminary factors in specifying apparent motion and distortion, as well as in metacontrast.

The other important new development in the descriptive mathematical theory of apparent motion is Caelli, Hoffman, and Lindman's (1978) discussion (in the same volume as Foster's model) placing this phenomenon in a context of relativistic dynamics. Their work was stimulated by the fact that the perceived and physical velocities in *real* movement situations do not always correspond. They note that, instead, there is a frequent perceptual distortion of both the spatial and temporal properties of moving real stimuli just as there is in apparent movement. These empirical facts suggested to Caelli and his colleagues that the relativistic mathematics that has served physicists so well might usefully be applied to the perceptual problem. In particular, they applied the Lorentz transformation, used by Albert Einstein to describe physical contractions and expansions as a function of velocity, to the problem of how perceptual lengths contract and times dilate when objects are moving rapidly. Of course, the abstruse mathematics does not explain the functions of the neural mechanisms that account for these phenomena (the model is essentially descriptive and not reductive); and what constitute high velocities in the physical and the perceptual domains are vastly different; but it does provide an alternative descriptive framework upon which to base further analysis and research.

4. Dynamic Monocular Cues to Depth

So far in this discussion of temporal interactions, we have seen how sequential interactions between stimuli can lead to distortions, suppressions, and movement. Throughout these sections I have contended that each of these phenomenal outcomes of such interactions is best understood as a construction or interpretation of the significance of the stimuli rather than as the outcome of a strict stimulus-response or a rigid neural network process. These constructions lead to plausible mental models of the meaning of incomplete, complex, or paradoxical

FIG. 11.36. Two drawings demonstrating the dependence of the apparent velocity vector of a visual field on the point of fixation. (From Rock, © 1975, with the permission of Macmillan Publishing Co.)

stimuli. Temporal interactions, however, can also lead to other constructions that are neither distortions, suppressions, nor movement. In this section I would like to consider one of the most dramatic of these alternative constructions—the experience of depth that arises from the dynamics of interactions between sequential monocular cues.[14]

Let us consider only those monocular cues to depth that become available when moving stimuli are presented to an observer who is viewing a stimulus either monocularly or binocularly, but not dichoptically. Two major classes of such dynamic monocular cues to depth have been identified. The first is motion parallax and the second is generically referred to as either the kinetic depth effect or stereokinesis. Both of these processes become available, like many of the static monocular cues to depth previously discussed, as an outcome of the natural geometry of visual space and the restrictions and invariances that are imposed by the nature of the visual angle on the two-dimensional projection of three-dimensional objects.

For example, examine Fig. 11-36. As this diagram shows, both the magnitude and apparent direction of the velocity vector of a moving object (or an object one is moving past—the analysis is identical) is determined by the distance at which that object is located from the eye. If one fixates the most distant portion of the environment from a moving train or automobile, as illustrated in Fig. 11-36A, then the geometry of the situation determines that nearby objects will have a high velocity of translation across the retina (i.e., the visual angle traversed per second is large) and distant objects will have a low velocity of translation; however, all objects will move in the same direction. If, on the other hand, the fixation is midway in the field, then objects in the near field and the far field will

[14]I am specifically not referring to binocular stereopsis in this discussion. That important depth cue results from comparisons of inputs from the two eyes and is discussed in detail in the next section.

actually appear to move in different directions. This second viewing situation is shown in Fig. 11-36B.[15]

Differences in direction and magnitude of apparent velocity are, therefore, indicative of the distance at which an object is located and the fixation conditions. This information—monocular parallax—thus represents a potential cue to depth that could be used by any ideal mechanical computing mechanism capable of decoding the spatial significance of the velocity differences. Along with such mechanical devices, the human observer is also capable of making this calculation and transforming these velocity cues into depth experiences. Evaluations of velocity differences, representing another kind of a spatiotemporal comparison, can be and regularly are decoded in such a way that apparent depth can also be reconstructed from this information. Once again, we see an instance in which dynamic (e.g., temporal) comparison cues lead to the construction of a perceptual dimension (depth) that is not inherent in the original two-dimensional retinal mapping just as spatial comparisons accomplish the same task in binocular stereopsis. Other monocular cues, of course, contribute to experienced depth, but monocular motion parallax is among the most compelling.

Monocular motion parallax, as just described, probably also plays a particularly important role in explaining why solid objects are so much more easily interpreted as three-dimensional objects when they are moving than when they are stationary. Several mechanisms are probably involved in the increased awareness of depth in addition to including motion parallax. Among the most likely contributors are sequential interposition relations and relative size changes produced by the rotational and translational transformations occurring when an object moves in three-dimensional space.

A reduced version of motion parallax in which all three-dimensional cues have been removed is referred to as stereokinesis. If an object is placed between a projection screen and a point source of light, as shown in Fig. 11-37, the dynamics of the shadow present a constrained and limited set of cues leading to the orgainzation of the object in a perceptual three-dimensional space. When still, the two-dimensional projection appears to be just that—a projection on a flat surface. However, the sequence of different two-dimensional shadow images produced by a moving object allows some mental computational mechanism, of which we admittedly know very little, to construct a powerful illusion of depth in the absence of other object cues.

We now possess a fairly substantial foundation of psychophysical data concerning a large variety of such projected stereokinetic illusions. For example, Braunstein (1962) has shown that the impression of depth increases with the number of elements in a shadowgram-type display, and Wallach and O'Connell (1953) have shown that these shadowgrams must change in both extent and

[15]This is of course a simplified situation. The geometric relations are also dependent on the angle between the direction of locomotion and the line of sight.

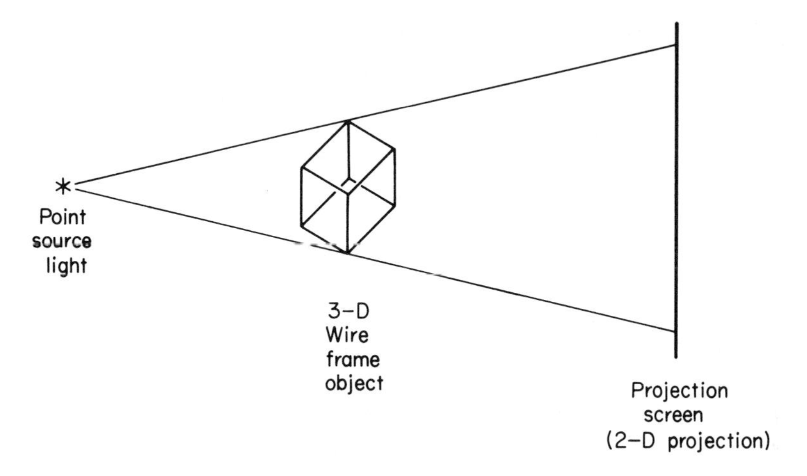

FIG. 11.37. A means of producing a two-dimensional stereokinetic display from a three-dimensional object, a point source of light, and a shadow box. Note: This can also be done mathematically by a computer without the involvement of a real solid object.

direction to be effectively transformed into percepts of solid objects. An important generalization of much of the research on the stereokinetic effect is that rotational direction judgments based on this cue are enhanced by, if not dependent on, the shadowed image being a polar (as opposed to Cartesian rectangular) projection of the original three-dimensional object (Braunstein, 1966). Physically this means the light source throwing the shadowgram must be a nearby point and not a plane or a distant point.

Experiments exploring the nature of the parallax–depth relationship have been carried out for many years by such researchers as Miles (1931) and Metzger (1934). B. Green (1959) produced simulated shadowgrams by digital computer transformation of the mathematical representation of nonexistent wire-frame-type objects. Stimulus objects capable of producing the kinetic depth effect need not, however, possess identifiable contours. Lappin, Doner, and Kottas (1980) has shown that even a quasi-random dot pattern presented on a cathode-ray tube representing the two-dimensional projection of a sphere will lead to the strong impression of the three-dimensional sphere when the dots are rapidly presented as a pair of sequential projections equivalent to two rotational positions only 5.6 deg apart. Some process, globally sensitive to the sequential positions of the quasi-random points on the surface of the only mathematically defined sphere, evokes a strong impression of a three-dimensional object.

A substantial body of evidence concerning the psychophysics of this kind of stereokinetic process has also been published in a long series of papers by R. B. Mefferd in the late 1960s. The reader is referred to the last of these papers (Mefferd, 1968) for citations to the earlier ones. Perhaps the most important aspect of Mefferd's work was his analysis of the existence of reversible percepts in this type of display. In other words, these stereokinetic cues do not necessarily define a unique spatial object; rather, the resulting percepts can be ambiguous, allowing alternative interpretations of the number of objects, axes of rotation, or perspective. Hershberger and his group (e.g., Hershberger & Carpenter, 1972; Hershberger, Carpenter, Starzel, & Laughlin, 1974) have also published extensively in the late 1960s and early 1970s on the factors affecting direction of rotation in this illusion quantifying the classic demonstration of the apparently reversing Ames (1951) trapezoidal window. In the Ames illusion the perceived direction of rotation (about a vertical axis) reverses even though the shadowed physical object continues to be rotated consistently in one direction.

The most comprehensive and up-to-date review and analysis of the stereokinetic process is to be found in a thoughtful and clearly illustrated book by Myron Braunstein (1976). Braunstein deals with the historical precedents as well as modern research on the problem of how we use motion-dependent cues to generate an appreciation of the three-dimensionality of the stimuli. He lists many types and examples of stereokinetic phenomena, discusses his own extensive research on the topic, and contributes a particularly lucid discussion of the geometry of projections of objects in rigid rotation.

In conclusion, the compelling perceptual force of a two-dimensional quasi-random dot display in evoking the experience of a three-dimensional object provides strong support for the idea that stereokinesis is mainly mediated by temporal comparisons of the sequential perspective relationships and that this process depends mainly on the cues generated by the dynamic projective geometry of the situation. It is possible to appreciate the general nature of the mathematics that must underlie this process of extracting invariant spatial information from a series of two-dimensional projections even though we do not know the nature of the actual algorithmic mechanisms carried out by the brain.

Gunnar Johansson (e.g., 1978), among the most productive and thoughtful theoreticians of stereokinesis, has noted that even though we do not yet understand the brain's algorithms, the relevant mathematical background for the study of stereokinesis is well developed. He notes that traditional projective geometry is the study of transformations in which certain spatial properties remain invariant. Johansson (1978) postulates that one function of the visual system may be to function as a "projective geometer to compute or decode the stimulus geometry so that we can extract the information characteristic of its invariant spatial structure." In other words, Johansson is asserting that the information necessary to reconstruct the solid object that gave rise to any shadowgram is inherent in the two-dimensional image but in a cryptic form that must be processed to be extracted. The major problem remaining is to determine how the invariances are actually extracted by the visual system. Though we have by no means even begun to approach that goal, it is clear that there is nothing intrinsically mysterious about the process. It is only another example of the powerful quasi-statistical and quasi-mathematical computational powers of which the brain is capable.

In a number of his important papers, Johansson (e.g., 1958, 1964, 1973, 1976) has attacked the important problem of the nature and limits of that computational power. In some of his research he has used the usual laboratory abstractions (spots of light moving in simplified trajectories on a projection screen), but in other studies he has ingeniously used an exceedingly novel display to demonstrate the extreme versatility of this internal geometer. Johansson attached small point lights to the joints, extremities, and torso of a person clad in a dark outfit walking across a darkened stage. When photographed, this scene appeared as a pattern of dots moving in accord with the idiosyncracies of the person's gait. In spite of these highly impoverished stimulus conditions, the spatiotemporal relationships among the moving dots give rise to a powerful impression of an organized constellation of dots moving in a coordinated fashion. Not only is the unity of this constellation of moving dots evident, but it is also possible to determine such other factors as the age or sex of the person who originally served as the source of the dynamic pattern of stimulus dots. Of course, such extrapolations must be extrageometric and not directly a part of the invariant information extracted by the mental geometer; rather, we have learned to attribute certain gaits to certain classes of people. In the present context, however, the important point is that an enormous amount of information remains in the two-dimensional kinetic pattern of a few rigidly interconnected dots and this information can be extracted to provide the cues to these higher-order associations.

The theoretical implications of Johansson's work are impressive. Johansson himself has noted that this work emphasizes the *relational* invariance (that which remains constant during various transformations of the stimulus pattern) rather than its momentary state. This is conceptually quite different from the classic approach to motion that more typically asked what are the *absolute* properties of the stimulus that define or determine the perceptual response? The spatiotemporal relationships that allow observers to make such exquisite judgments in Johannson's or Lappin's elegant experiments must be operated upon by perceptual processing mechanisms that extract the properties of the stimulus that remain invariant even when it is transformed rather than its absolute properties. The concept of invariance extraction is a more formal way of expressing the idea of interpretation or construction (of the form implied by the invariances), but it does not differ in principle from these near-synonyms.

Specifically, Johansson's theory asserts that in experiments of the class he has carried out, the major invariance extracted is the common vector of motion. That is, the information that is critical to organizing these motion phenomena is not what each point is doing, but rather what the aggregate is doing in common. Once again, the concept of a relational comparison rises to the surface as the basis for the extraction of the universal property or invariant.

It should not be overlooked that Johansson's point of view is not without its critics. A somewhat different orientation has been expressed by Wallach (1965). He suggests, rather than the common or invariant vector of motion being extracted, that the motion of the dots are seen *a priori* in terms of their relation to each other. Again the relational aspect is emphasized, but in this case it is the displacement between the dots that is computed rather than the "common vector fate" of the aggregate. Additional support for Wallach's point of view has been reported by Proffitt, Cutting, and Stier (1979) using the apparent motion of lights mounted on rotating (and translating) wheels. These psychologists conclude, along with Wallach, that the displacement of the lights related to each other takes procedence over the group or aggregate movement, and argue that the common vector attributes emphasized by Johansson are subsequently perceptually organized. According to Cutting, Proffitt, and Kozlowski (1978) subsequently perceived aggregate movement is dependent, they believe, on ". . . a true abstract entity, the center of movement for the system of lights," an entity they believe also accounts for Johansson's findings on gait perception.

The controversy here is over priority. Which occurs first—object relative displacement or the invariant common-motion vector? Experimental tests to discriminate such a priority are fraught with conceptual as well as perceptual difficulties. But all concerned seem to be well aware of the problems involved, and all seem to appreciate the enormous complexity of the problem of analyzing such processes.

Another, somewhat more conventional, interpretation of the stereokinetic process has been proposed by Braunstein (1972). He believes that the critical cue in the stereokinetic phenomenon in particular is the angle that exists between the projected contours of, for example, the shadowgram of a rotating stick object. In other words, Braunstein has identified a particular geometrical property that he believes in and of itself signifies the invariant attribute of the figure. That property becomes evident as the projection of the object is transformed by rotations and/or translations.

There is another critical difference between Braunstein's approach and that of either Proffitt and his colleagues or Johannson. Instead of attributing stereokinesis to the geometrical invariances of the stimulus and extraction by an unknown continuous computational process, Braunstein specifically proposes a logic diagram, much like a computer flow chart, that he believes describes the kind of discrete decision making being executed during the construction of the three-dimensional percept from the dynamic two-dimensional projection of a revolving solid object. Figure 11-38 is a sample of one of the "subroutines" carried out by the observer in determining which way one of the edges of an object is rotating.

It must be appreciated that Braunstein's logical flowchart is not necessarily antithetical to Johannson's projective geometry; it may be merely an analog of it. It is one way of modeling some of the processes that may be involved in process-

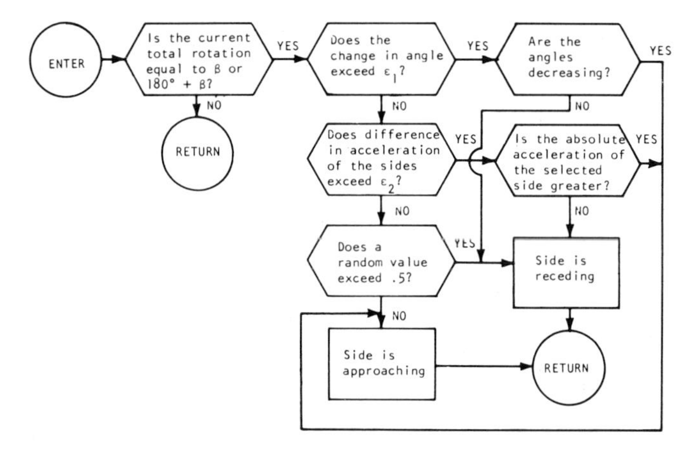

FIG. 11.38. Braunstein's model of some of the logical steps that must be executed to answer the question—is the selected side approaching? (From Braunstein, © 1972, with the permission of the American Psychological Association.)

ing stereokinetic information. It is highly unlikely, however, that the computational steps proposed in Braunstein's flowchart model are executed in the serial order he proposes. Rather, it is more likely that there exist nonverbal and parallel mechanisms that this model only vaguely analogizes. However it must be understood that Johansson's projective geometry is also a descriptive model in exactly the same way—no better, no worse, and certainly no more or less meaningful than Braunstein's discrete model. Both describe processes without reductionistic language and eschew underlying mechanisms.

In sum, both dynamic stimulus contributions to perceived depth—motion parallax and stereokinesis—contribute to a variety of compelling and powerful illusions of three-dimensional objects; both reflect our ability to reconstruct a dimension of experience that is not explicitly present in the proximal physical stimulus (the retinal image) on the basis of a computational logic that still remains largely mysterious. In the next section I deal with another powerful means of constructing three-dimensional percepts in a visual system that, in fact, has only two-dimensional information available to it—the binocular comparisons that arise because of the fact that we view the world through two eyes.

D. BINOCULAR INTERACTIONS

The fact that we have a bilaterally symmetrical visual system consisting of two eyes positioned at different points along a horizontal axis obviously has a profound effect on visual perception. One has only to close one eye to appreciate this point. The main reason for this effect is also obvious. Because each eye has a slightly different point of view, the images of a single solid object that fall on the eyes are not exactly the same. This slight difference is the basis of a number of other cues to depth. One, the binocular parallax cue, takes advantage of the same kind of natural spatial geometry as does the monocular parallax cue discussed in the previous section. Binocular parallax, however, is based upon differences in the point of view of the two eyes as either the eyes or the object move, rather than differential velocity cues that are produced by one eye alone. However, by far the most impressive binocular interaction effect, and the main topic of this section, is stereopsis—the perception of depth that emerges out of the exceedingly small spatial differences (disparities) in retinal images as a result of those differences in point of view of the two eyes. In addition, I also consider a number of other binocular interactions later in this chapter.

There is, however, one taxonomic caveat that I must make at the outset of this discussion on stereopsis. In the last few years there has been a substantial amount of neurophysiological data that suggest how the representation of space may be converted from a dual two-dimensional to a single three-dimensional code as a result of particular neural mechanisms. If this neural transformation is the critical process in the sense defined on p. 274, then the attribution of stereopsis to Level 4 may be incorrect. It may be more appropriate to consider it as a rather complex Level 2 process. However the role of these relatively peripheral neural transformations in the stereoscopic process is still moot, and for this reason I have chosen to leave this material in Level 4.

1. Stereopsis

In the previous substantive sections, I discussed a number of processes that led to the experience of quantifiable dimensions of visual experience. Each of these processes was the result of comparing two or more spatially or temporarlly disparate stimuli. If one considers the observer, in the abstract, as a single point in space, as I have implicitly been doing in the proceeding sections, then either temporal or spatial disparity of the stimulus is needed to provide the necessary information for a relational comparison. However the observer need not be considered only as a cyclopean abstraction in light of the practical fact that we are binocular. That we have two eyes is another means of comparing stimuli that require multiple stimuli neither in space or time. Two points of view provide relational information to the observer equally as well as time or space differences. The outcome is that binocularly disparate information can also be analyzed in a way that allows similar kinds of quantitative spatial percepts to be constructed.

Dichoptic vision (as opposed to binocular vision, in which the two eyes see the same thing and which for informational purposes may, therefore, be considered to be monocular) can lead to a number of perceptual experiences that cannot be predicted from some simple algebraic summation of the properties of the monocular stimuli. This is an important point that has been frequently overlooked in the past in the development of theories of stereoscopic perception. The classic theories sought to explain stereopsis by showing how the two retinal images were either summed (fused) or subtracted (suppressed). However, it is now becoming clear that the stereoscopic experience is not the result of either simple suppression or fusion but of a much more involved kind of process involving the extraction of spatial invariances implicit in the disparities between the two images. This is not to imply that there is anything nonmathematical or nonneural about the process but only that it is a considerably more complicated process than can be modeled by simple arithmetic. Here, too, invariance extraction processes more akin to projective geometry than to addition or subtraction must be involved. In some way the nervous system is able to convert two-dimensional disparity information from the two eyes into a representation that effectively symbolizes a unified three-dimensional percept. How this must be done, in principle, is clear: Computer programs are frequently used that can extract the invariances from disparity information in order to generate three-dimensional representations.

Another false concept that has often arisen is the mistaken supposition that there need be some kind of a three-dimensional neural representation someplace in the brain in order for the three-dimensional percept to exist. The idea that "there must be a toy in the head for there to be an image in the mind" is implicit in many stereoscopic theories that seek to find some way to construct a three-dimensional map in the brain to account for spatial vision. I believe that this reflects a serious misunderstanding of the nature of coding and representational processes in the brain and that no such spatially isomorphic representation is necessary. The search for isomorphic neural "toys", therefore, can be both misleading and absurd. Totally nonisomorphic (i.e., dimensionally nonveridical codes) are possible in depth perception just as they more obviously must exist in color perception.

Now that I have dealt with a few of the general conceptual issues, it is necessary to look at some of the more concrete aspects of stereoscopic vision. To help in this discussion, consider Fig. 11-39. This drawing represents the basic geometry of the stereoscopic viewing situation. Any solid object placed at a point in space will be seen from a different perspective by each of the eyes, even when the eyes are converged to fixate on the object. The pictorial differences between the two retinal images themselves may serve as an effective cue for depth as can the angle of convergence of the lines of sight itself. However most research attention has been directed at the effects of retinal disparity—slight differences in the two retinal images.

Two kinds of disparity are defined in this viewing situation. As shown in Fig. 11-40A, absolute disparity is defined by the trigonometry of the relation of the

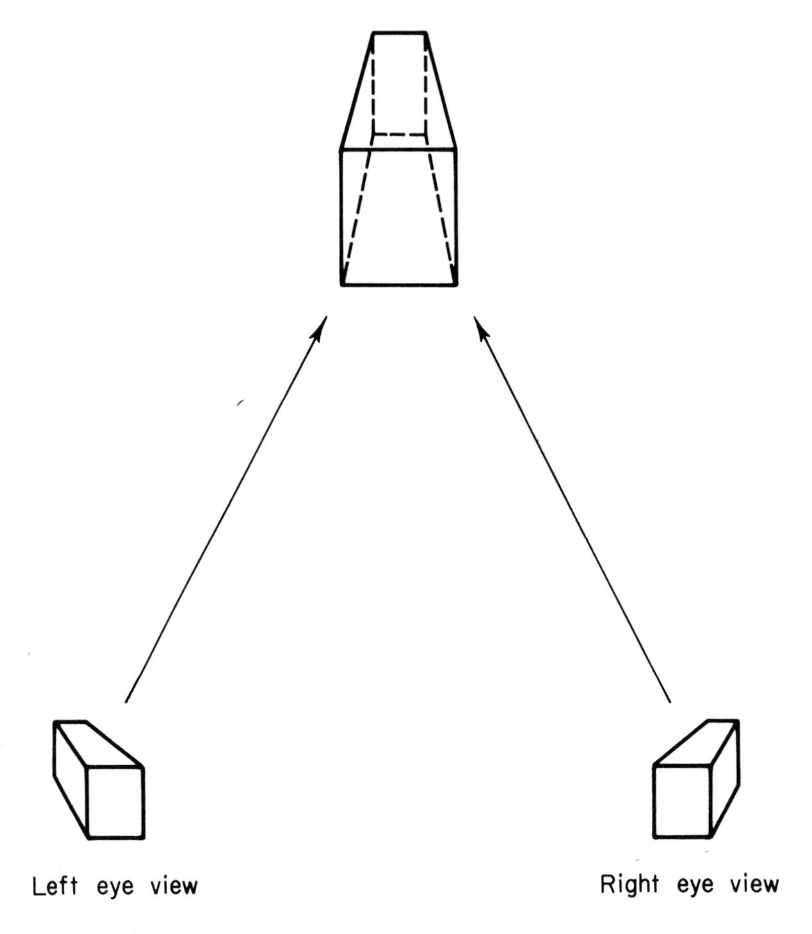

FIG. 11.39. The disparate viewpoints of the two eyes leads to different projected images of an object on the two retinae as shown.

external object to the eyes, irrespective of the convergence of the eyes and their lines of sight. The absolute disparity is conventionally defined by the symbol α and expressed by the following equation:

$$\tan \frac{\alpha}{2} = \frac{B}{2} \div D \tag{11-1}$$

or

$$\alpha = 2 \arctan \frac{B}{2D} \tag{11-2}$$

where D is the distance from the eyes to the object and B is the distance between the centers of the pupils.

Absolute binocular disparities, or parallaxes of this kind, are totally without value, however, as cues to distance. Like all the other cues to various perceptual experiences that have been discussed in this chapter, they become meaningful only when they are compared or related to other absolute disparities. This is clearly evidenced by the fact that a solitary object, from which all monocular reference cues have been removed, appears to be located at a very poorly defined distance from the observer compared to the extreme precision of stereoscopic vision. Interestingly, the apparent distance of an object that has such greatly reduced depth cues has actually been measured (Gogel, 1972). Gogel finds that observers tend to perceive such an object at an apparent depth of about a meter although there are enormous variations from one observer and one lighting condition to another. This natural apparent depth of a cue-impoverished object may be

A

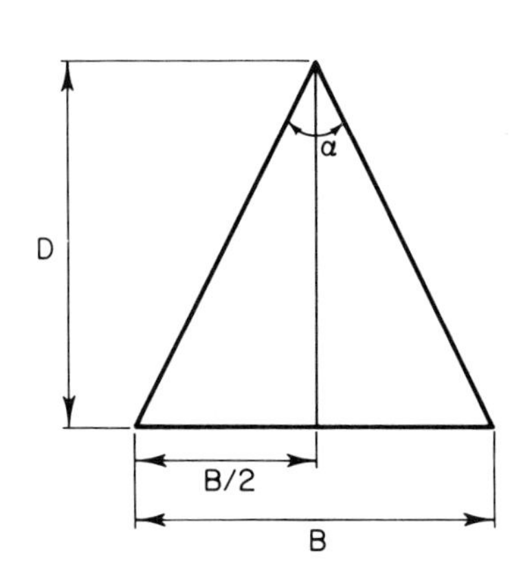

Absolute disparity $= \alpha$

$$\mathrm{Tan}\frac{\alpha}{2} = \frac{B}{2} \div D$$

$$\frac{\alpha}{2} = \arctan\frac{B}{2D}$$

$$\alpha = 2 \arctan\frac{B}{2D}$$

B

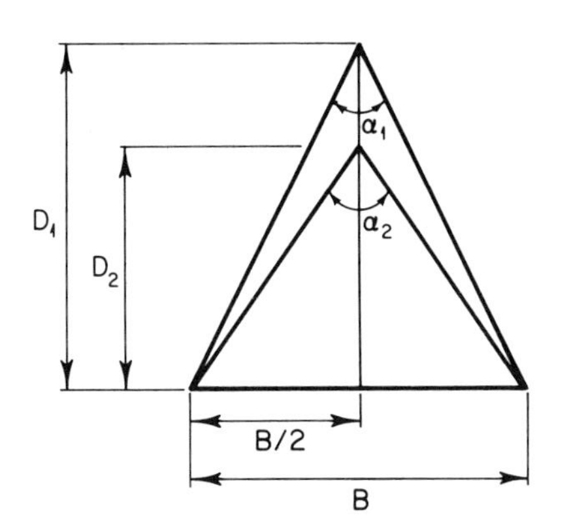

Relative disparity $= \Delta\alpha$

$$\Delta\alpha = \alpha_2 - \alpha_1$$

$$= 2 \arctan\frac{B}{2D_2} - \arctan\frac{B}{2D}$$

$$= 2 \arctan\frac{B(D_2 - D_1)}{D_1 \times D_2}$$

FIG. 11.40. Definitions of absolute and relative disparity.

considered to be the default condition—the apparent depth assumed when no reliable relative depth information is available.

The relative disparity (denoted $\Delta\ \alpha$), which is effective in establishing stereoscopic depth, is defined as the difference between two or more absolute disparities. $\Delta\ \alpha$ is straightforwardly expressed by the following equation for the geometry depicted in Fig. 11-40B:

$$\Delta\ \alpha = \text{relative disparity} = \alpha_2 - \alpha_1 \tag{11-3}$$

$$\Delta\ \alpha = 2\ \arctan \frac{B}{2D_2} - \arctan \frac{B}{2D_1} \tag{11-4}$$

$$\Delta\ \alpha = 2\ \arctan \frac{B\ (D_2 - D_1)}{D_1 \times D_2} \tag{11-5}$$

When the visual angles are relatively small (i.e., when objects are relatively far from the eyes) then the arctan and the ratio $B\ (D_2 - D_1)/(D_1 \times D_2)$ both converge to the same number, of course, and the perceived difference in the depth of the two objects is directly proportional to their relative disparity. Relative disparity, not absolute disparity, is the basis of the fundamental cue that leads to stereoscopic vision.

A complete mathematical description of depth perception could be developed based upon nothing more than the geometry that I have described so far. However, the analysis of such a system is greatly simplified if it is assumed that the eyes are, in fact, converging upon one or the other of the two objects shown in Fig. 11-41. A very important additional aspect of adopting such a convention is that it allows us to move on to the next level of analysis of the stereoscopic process and simply and elegantly to consider some other important functional properties of the organization of the retina—the properties of correspondence, fusional areas, and the threshold of diplopia.

When the eyes are converged on a point in space, the two images of that point fall on one pair of systems of what have been designated corresponding retinal points. Corresponding points can either be geometrically or functionally defined loci but they do not seem to have any special physiological or anatomical identity in the retina. The axons projecting from pairs of points, as well as from many pairs of noncorresponding points, do, however, converge on individual neurons in the brain that are exquisitely sensitive either to simultaneous activation of corresponding points or to the degree of disparity between noncorresponding points.

Retinal disparity can, in this context, also be defined as the degree of discrepancy in the projection of images onto corresponding points of the retina. This spatial misregistration on functionally designated corresponding points is the primary cue for stereoscopic depth. There is little disagreement on this point in modern theory nor has there been any since the identification of retinal disparity as a major variable in depth perception by Wheatstone (1838) almost 150 years

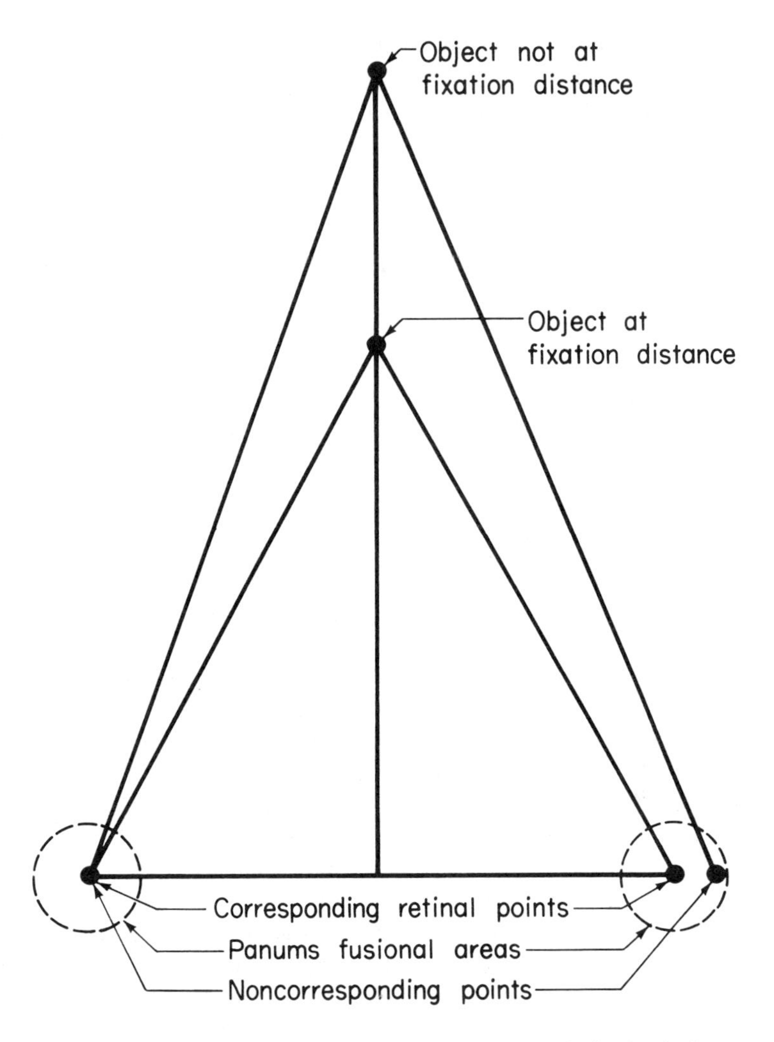

FIG. 11.41. The relationship of the convergence angle, actual stimulus depth, and coressponding points.

ago. And it must not be forgotten in the context of this chapter that disparity is very much a relational cue and that stereopsis is very much the outcome of a relational comparison. Stimuli are appreciated as falling on noncorresponding points only to the degree that some corresponding points have been defined by a reference anchored by the convergence of the lines of fixated sight. Objects, therefore, appear to be in front of or in back of other objects rather than to have any absolute depth associated with them unless cues other than pure disparity are present.

It is also important to remember that far more than a single pair of corresponding points are defined by the convergence angle. Not only is a central corresponding pair defined at the fixation point by the projection of the main lines of sight but there is also a family of other pairs of points defined on the horizontal and vertical axes. As described in Chapter 3, this is what is meant by the horopter. Traditionally, however, the horizontal line of corresponding points in visual space has been considered to be closely approximated by a circle (the Vieth–Müller or Graham horopter) whose dimensions and curvature change as a function of fixation distance.

I do not delve further at this point into the complexities of the varied definitions of the horopter. I have considered some of the issues in Chapter 5 in the context of the perceptual impact of the natural geometry of space, and other books, such as Gulick and Lawson (1976) and Ogle's (1950) still-impressive monograph, have detailed the nature of the problems involved to a much greater depth than is possible here.

An intuitive appreciation of the concept of corresponding points, however, can be approached from another point of view. An important criterion is that singleness of vision occurs when a limited region around corresponding points is stimulated. However, at some depth differences the relative disparity can become so great that single vision can no longer be maintained, and diplopia or double vision may occur. Corresponding points thus can also be defined behaviorally as the points on the retina at the center of the region in which single vision occurs. But this implies that there is also a region of some nonnegligible extent around the corresponding points within which single vision also occurs. Such perceptually defined regions have traditionally been referred to as Panum's fusional areas (honoring one of the early masters of stereoscopic research, P. L. Panum 1858). Under various experimental conditions, Panum's areas may be as large as two or more degrees of visual angle in extent.

An exceedingly important fact about stereoscopic vision is that Panum's fusional areas, defined as the region in which single vision occurs, are not constant in size. This means that they probably do not represent a built-in neural field of interaction any more than corresponding points are anatomically defined but are functionally determined regions. Indeed, the size of the area of single vision may vary greatly, depending on whether the disparity is increasing or decreasing. Fender and Julesz (1967) have referred to this phenomenon as stereoscopic hysteresis. Figure 11-42, for example, shows the results of one of their experimental runs in which stereoscopic hysteresis was demonstrated. A random dot stereogram (a class of stimuli discussed shortly) was presented to an observer with a minimum disparity. Good fusion of the two monocular images into a single visual experience was easily achieved. However the relative disparity of a subregion of this dot pattern was then gradually increased. Eventually, when the disparity was greater than 2 degrees of visual angle, the percept suddenly became diplopic, the image doubled at a disparity Fender and Julesz called the breakaway

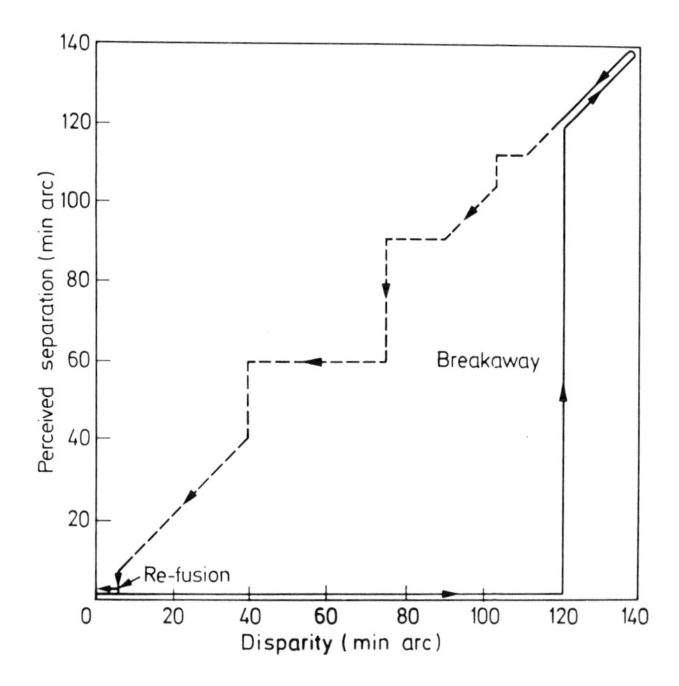

FIG. 11.42. A demonstration of hysteresis in the viewing of a random dot stereogram. (From Fender and Julesz, © 1967, with the permission of Springer-Verlag.)

threshold. Subsequent reduction of the disparity, however, did not immediately reestablish single vision at the breakaway threshold: the disparity had to be reduced to only a few minutes of arc before fusion reoccurred and single vision was reestablished. In other words, the ascending breakaway threshold was far greater than the descending refusion threshold. The results of Fender and Julesz' hysteresis experiment support the contention that no rigid, deterministic, hard-wired organizational model of the fusional areas could be valid. In short, it would be a hopeless task to search for any putative anatomical equivalents of Panum's areas.[16]

Another important outcome of Fender and Julesz' experiment was that some degree of depth discrimination was possible even when single vision did not occur. Despite some earlier speculation that "true" stereoscopic depth discrimination could occur only with single fused perceptual images, it now appears

[16]Incidentally, my colleague Daniel Weintraub reports (in a personal communication) that the hysteresis phenomenon is also exhibited in simultaneous color contrast. If a red area and a gray area are placed side by side, the gray area will appear greenish. If the two are moved apart, the gray area will maintain that illusory greenness for rather substantial separations. However, if the red and gray areas are initially widely separated, the greenness does not appear until they are almost adjacent.

certain that depth can be inferred by the observer from diplopic images. In other words, relative disparity remains a cue for depth even when fusion is not possible. A good review of modern research on large-disparity depth discrimination can be found in Foley, Applebaum, and Richards (1975). They note that absolute judgments of the magnitude of the depth encoded by relatively large disparities (i.e., greater than 2 deg) and the ability to discriminate relative depth with large disparities are two separate phenomena that must be distinguished from each other. Yet with either relative or absolute measures, depth judgments were still significantly different from zero for disparities as great as 8 deg. This sensitivity to disparity existed in spite of the diplopia that must have been present for all disparities greater than 2 deg. There was, of course, also a decline in the ability to discriminate depth for all disparities greater than 2 deg (monocular cues do help), but this does not negate the important point that stereoscopic depth perception does not depend on single fused vision and that this ability does not completely disappear even with such large disparities.

Without question, the most significant modern step forward in the study of stereopsis was the development of the random dot stereogram as a perceptual research tool by Bela Julesz (1960). Like so many other perceptual problems, the study of stereopsis has always been confounded and complicated by the simultaneous presence of cues other than the pure retinal disparity one wished to isolate and study. Even when as simple a device as the Howard–Dohlman apparatus (in which the observer must align a pair of vertical sticks) was used, there was always the possibility that information about depth that did not depend on retinal disparities could be extracted from the stimulus by the observer. The size of the stick, subtle parallax cues, or even their respective shadowing or apparent brightness, could provide clues utilizable by our remarkably effective visual systems to confound experiments aimed at determining our disparity-discrimination skills.

The considerable contribution that Julesz made was to remind us of a stimulus in which there were no extraneous cues to pollute estimates of stereoscopic sensitivity beyond pure disparity. His exploitation of this type of display to analyze stereoscopic perception is considered by all to be a modern classic. Though primitive random dot stereograms had been used earlier by Aschenbrenner (1954) as a means of interpreting air reconnaissance photographs, Julesz can quite rightly claim to be the first to use them in psychological research.

Figure 11-24A shows one of Julesz' modern computer-generated random dot stereograms. The stimuli presented to each eye appear as a featureless and random pattern of dots. However, when the two retinal images are fused (many people can accomplish this by simply crossing their eyes and paying attention to the third fused image formed between the two monocular images) after a few seconds, a very nonrandom object of startling depth and apparent solidarity can be perceptually organized by all except the most deficient stereoblind observers. The object is an illusion, as are all other such objects of course; it is totally nonveridical with the two-dimensional stimuli that induce it. Nevertheless, this percept possesses a reality that leads even the most sophisticated observer to reach out and try to touch this totally impalpable object. The perception of this solid object is elicited by what are in fact a large number of regularities in the relative retinal disparities of the individual dots that make up the monocular random dot pattern—disparities that are anchored to a reference depth defined by the fixation distance from the eyes to the page on which the stimulus patterns are printed. Random dot stereopsis is an especially interesting example of invariance extraction because of the point-by-point analysis that must be carried out to correlate the many pairs of dots.

Random dot stereograms are usually constructed by computer procedures that calculate the respective disparities for an object that may be only mathematically defined to possess a particular three-dimensional geometry. It is not at all surprising to learn that Julesz has been on the staff of the Bell Telephone Laboratories with its extensive computer facilities since the time that he began to develop his extraordinary displays. The trick is to establish, for each dot and its paired correspondent, the appropriate disparity associated with a desired depth. Systematic changes in disparity can thus produce stereoscopic percepts that appear to be varying continuously in depth—in other words, apparently solid objects of arbitrary shape. Percepts of these objects can be generated even in the absence of any other monocular or pictorial cue to their spatial nature.

A major issue that has repeatedly arisen concerning this kind of pure disparity—driven depth perception—is whether or not the process is local or global, that is, whether the processes and mechanisms are restricted in their range of operation or are the resulting phenomena of the cumulative results of spatial interactions occurring across wide ranges of the visual scene. Julesz (1978a) has argued that stereopsis actually displays both local and global properties. If isolated dots are presented sufficiently far apart, he agrees that the limits of globality must be exceeded and that they must act independently. And, indeed, there is evidence that adding dots to a sparsely populated array does not greatly increase the thresholds or precision with which depth can be judged (Uttal, Fitzgerald, & Eskin, 1975a). On the other hand, Julesz feels that some form of global stereopsis must be invoked to account for the observer's ability to resolve ambiguous complex stereograms so that only a single unified surface is seen in situations that would otherwise allow a chaotic percept. In other words, the overall rationalization of ambiguous cues is attributed by Julesz to a neural system that has wide-ranging interactive properties. In such a system many different regions of the stimulus scene collectively define the depth experience at each and every point.

One of the best pieces of experimental evidence to support the contention that this global interactive process actually exists is Julesz and Chang's (1976) demonstration of the "pulling effect" in an experiment in which ambiguous stereograms were presented. In such an ambiguous display there are often several alternative ways in which dots can be paired to produce an organized three-dimensional form. One system of pairing would result in a plane of dots that might appear to be closer to the observer than the fixation plane, whereas another might result in a plane that appears to be at a greater depth than the fixation plane. In display situations in which the disparity is ambiguous the observer tends to exhibit some bias and to resolve the ambiguity by "organizing the field" into a single plane either in front or in back of the fixation plane. He typically does not perceive the ambiguous display in another way that would be perfectly plausible for a system without global interaction—that is, as a patchwork or lacy set of partial planes or independent points at both possible depths.

In their study, Julesz and Chang found that a few unambiguous dots placed in the figure could strongly influence the direction of the bias and determine which of the two possible alternative planes would be perceived and interpreted this to mean that global interaction was occurring. Although Julesz' conceptual model of stereopsis (I discuss it in detail later) is based upon such a system of hypothetical interacting disparity detectors, the question can be raised whether such global interactions between local disparity-sensitive units would necessarily be a desirable evolutionary outcome. Stereopsis did not evolve in a context of ambiguous random dot stereograms of fronto-parallel planes but rather in a world of continuous surfaces oriented at all angles. The perception of a plane slanting away from the observer involves continuously changing disparity and one could argue that its perception would be optimal in this case at least if each depth were independently determined—i.e., if the adjacent regions did not inhibit or enhance the respective responses of their neighbors.

One thus wonders what would have happened in the Julesz and Chang experiment if the observers had been given verbal instructions that the plane was in front of or in back of the fixation instead of the cues provided by the few unambiguous dots. Would the "pulling effect" have been equally great or would it have been nonexistent? In other words, is the "pulling effect" but another example of an extremely complicated symbolic evaluation supplementing the specific local cues provided by the individual dots, or is it the reflection of a quasi-physical force operating between the neural representations of the individual dots of the stimulus stereogram? Data relevant to this question are rare indeed. However, Staller, Lappin, and Fox (in press) suggest that in stereoscopic situations with differing amounts of uncertainty about the shape of the target, stereoscopic resolution time is independent of the shape uncertainty. They thus support the quasi-physical (i.e., neural interaction) alternative answer to this question.

Shipley and Hyson's (1972) and Shipley's (1973) allusion to the problem of "global stereopsis" as a three-dimensional analog of two-dimensional Gestalt properties is also relevant to this controversy. Many of the stimuli presented in the latter of these two papers suggest an independence of the stereo responses to individual pairs of dichoptic dots even though global organization may be formed by what are presumably higher-order processes.

Obviously, like so many other perceptual questions, the problem of whether stereopsis is local or global is not yet completely resolved. "Global" stereopsis may only be another term for the so far poorly understood statistical computation properties of the visual system and only poorly modeled by the concept of interacting disparity detectors proposed as its physical analog by Julesz and Chang.

Another important phenomenon that stresses the nonisomorphic nature of the stereoscopic process has been stressed by Kaufman (1974) in his insightful discussion of stereopsis. He reminds us of the phenomenon of displacement or "alletropia"—the shift in perceived position of the fused dichoptic image away from those perceived positions that would have been associated with the individual unfused monocular retinal images. When a stereoscopic display such as that shown in Fig. 11-43 is presented, for example, the apparent position in the $x-y$ plane of the middle numeral in the lower row shifts so that it is centered immediately beneath the middle numeral in the upper row. This shift in apparent position as one changes from a monocular (or binocular) viewing condition to a dichoptic one is strong evidence against a strong "local sign" hypothesis. In other words, particular points on the retina are not associated with particular points in perceived space.

One of the few systematic studies of alletropia has been reported by Sheedy and Fry (1979). In addition to the strong individual differences, which they refer to as a psychophysical ocular dominance, the placement of the combined image is affected by the vertical position of the two monocular targets, the disparity, the duration of the exposure, and the color of the target lines. Obviously, the apparent position of the binocular image is the outcome of a complex process involving many dimensions of the stimulus scene and not just the retinal location of the image.

It is obvious in the few pages that I can devote to stereopsis in this book that I cannot fully review either the experimental or theoretical literature in the complex field or even identify all of the perplexities this phenomenon raises. However, to give at least the flavor of the state of research in the field, I list briefly some of the major empirical developments concerning stereopsis:

1. The absolute threshold of stereopsis (i.e., how small a disparity can be detected using a depth discrimination test) is incredibly small. Graham (1965c)

234 **234**

567 **567**

FIG. 11.43. A demonstration of alletropia. (From Kaufman, © 1974, with the permission of Oxford University Press.)

has reviewed the older literature and cites the work of H. Howard (1919) who, using the conventional Howard–Dohlman depth discrimination device, determined that the absolute threshold (75% criterion) was of the order of 2 sec of arc. This minute value was confirmed in a replication by Woodburne (1934). Astonishingly, this value is smaller by nearly an order of magnitude than the typical cross-sectional diameter (1.5 micra = 15 sec of arc) of a single photoreceptor outer segment. This finding definitely implies that some kind of a statistical (multicellular) process must be active in sterescopic vision.

The absolute stereoscopic threshold, furthermore, is highly dependent on the duration of the stimulus. Graham notes that when "brief (sparkflash) exposures were used by Langlands (1926), the measured thresholds varied up to 20 or 40 sec of disparity." I have confirmed this lessened sensitivity to brief stimuli in my own work (Uttal, Fitzgerald, and Eskin, 1975a), in which it was determined that measurable discriminations existed for submillisecond-long exposures of stereograms consisting of only two dots with a disparity of about 30 sec of arc.

2. The stereoscopic threshold is also a function of the luminance of the stimulus. However, the relationship is not robust. Mueller and Lloyd (1948) showed that thresholds varied only from 8–25 sec of disparity when the stimulus luminance was varied over many orders of magnitude.

3. A measurable amount of time is required for stereopsis to develop. Julesz (1964) and Uttal, Fitzgerald, and Eskin (1975a) have shown that it takes appreciably longer for the stereoscopic process to develop fully (50 msec) than it does to recognize a single two-dimensional pattern (10 msec). A sharp discontinuity in performance can be observed at an interval of about 50 msec when the test stereogram is followed by a masking burst consisting of randomly placed dots in a volume surrounding the test stimulus. Even without that subsequent stereoscopic masking stimulus, it is possible to demonstrate the need for the 50 msec period for the stereoscopic percept to fully develop. Beverly and Regan (1974b) have studied an observer's ability to detect a brief transient shift in stereoscopic depth as a function of the duration of an equivalently brief and temporary shift in disparity. Their data also show a progressive increase in sensitivity for increasing transient durations, until an asymptote was approached at a duration of about 50 msec. An interesting sidelight of Beverly and Regan's study was that the observers were also increasingly able to specify the direction of the shift as the duration of the transient increased. At very short durations, even though they were capable of detecting a depth shift, they could not tell in which direction it took place.

4. A closely related observation is that simultaneity of the two monocular images is not required for satisfactory stereopsis. Ross and Hogben (1974), and Ross (1976) have shown that the interval between the presentation of the two monocular images can be as long as 100 msec without attenuating a strong experience of stereoscopic depth. Surprisingly, adequate depth perception can also occur even when the spatial disparity between the two images is negligible if

a temporal disparity is present. This result thus represents a situation in which temporal disparities can be substituted for spatial disparities. Ross (1976) and Burr and Ross (1979) believe that this temporal disparity may be effective for intervals between left and right eye presentations as great as 2 sec. The uniqueness of the spatial disparity cue to stereopsis, therefore, is opened to question by this exceptional finding. Time differences can, in some way, substitute for space differences.

In a similar but conceptually different experiment, Beverly and Regan (1974a) have shown that sensitivity to stereoscopic depth declines for a stimulus oscillating in apparent depth but only after the period of that oscillation exceeds 500 or 600 msec. They interpret this result to mean that the stereoscopic mechanisms can integrate depth information (comparable to the integrative mechanisms that lead to the concept of the critical duration—see p. 529) over a half-second period or longer. In other words, stereoscopic integration performance declines only when the frequency of oscillation falls below 2 Hz. Thus, in general, stereopsis seems to exhibit longer time constants than two-dimensional visual processes.

5. Breitmeyer, Julesz, and Kropfl (1975) have shown that there is no difference in the threshold for stereoscopic detection of a small spot located on either side of the vertical midline. This not-too-surprising finding is made startling in light of their coincident discovery that there is a substantial difference in duration threshold between the upper and lower hemiretinae on either side of the horizontal midline. In their study they determined that the upper hemiretinae were considerably more sensitive than the lower hemiretinae when the disparity was uncrossed, but the lower were more sensitive when the disparity was crossed.

6. If a planar stereotarget consisting of a collection of dots organized in a vertical plane (as shown in Fig. 11-44A) is presented in a tachistoscopic exposure to an observer whose task it is to detect the plane in a space otherwise filled with randomly placed dots, Uttal, Fitzgerald, and Eskin (1975b) have shown that performance is equally good at all angles of rotation (other than when the target plane is virtually on edge to the observer). The stimuli and the results of this experiment are shown in Fig. 11-44B. This finding implies that the three dimensions of stereoscopic space are being processed with equal precision and in an equivalent manner; that is, dot density in the z-axis (depth) is being dealt with in exactly the same way as in the fronto-parallel (x–y) plane. This, too, is an unexpected result, since the x- and y-dimensional projections are actually explicit in the individual retinal images, whereas the perceived z dimension must be a construction based upon the interpretation and extraction of the invariant depth information from the two retinal projections. I believe that this result means that the x and y dimensions are also constructions (as opposed to deterministic responses) in the same way as is the z dimension.

7. On the other hand, in an absolute sense, if the two monocular stimuli are stabilized such that any stereoscopic image movement is seen to move only in

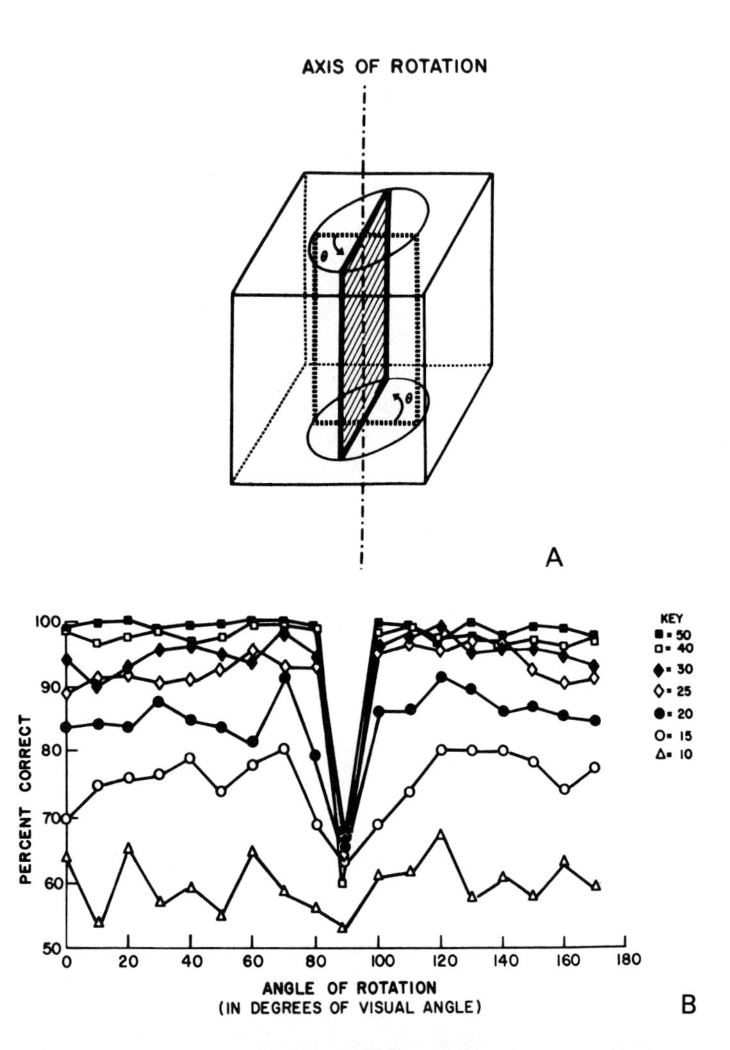

FIG. 11.44. (A) Diagram of the stimulus used to determine the effect of the angle of a plane of random dots on its detectability in stereomasking experiments. The plane could be rotated to any one of 18 positions in any triad. The outline cube defines the extent of the randomly distributed masking dots. (B) The results of the experiment showing the minimal effect of rotation of an angle on the detectability of the plane of random dots. Except for the 89° orientation there is no effect of orientation of the plane at any masking dot density, but there is a strong effect of target plane dot density. The family of curves is parametric with the number of dots in the target planes. Masking dot density is held constant at 100. (From Uttal, Fitzgerald, and Eskin, © 1975b.)

depth and not in the fronto-parallel plane, then movement is less likely to be detected, according to Tyler (1971); that is, equivalent movement is less likely to be detected in the *z* axis than in the *x* or *y* axis. It should be noted that this experiment is not designed to measure the threshold for depth but the threshold of change in depth. In this case, as Tyler whimsically titles his paper "Two Eyes (Are) Less Sensitive Than One." Obviously, there are some residual differences between the construction of depth along the *z*-axis and the construction of experiences along *x*- and *y*-axes.

8. When a stereo target plane formed from an array of dots varies in position from the front to the back of a perceptual space filled with masking dots, as shown in Fig. 11-45A, the observer's ability to detect the plane is maximum near the center of the space (the point of fixation), as shown in Fig. 11-45B. This finding is counterintuitive in view of the signal-to-noise situation because the maximum spatial density of the masking dots around the plane occurs near this central point; planes located near the edges of the volume of masking dots are less obstructed. This result (Uttal, Fitzgerald, and Eskin, 1975b) shows that the optimum ability to discriminate absolute depth occurs with small disparities, even though companion studies (Uttal, Fitzgerald, and Eskin, 1975a) have shown that the ability to discriminate relative depths increases with increasing disparity difference between two planes.

9. It does not seem necessary that the two disparate images in a stereoscopic display be of the same form. Lloyd Kaufman, in a series of papers (e.g., Kaufman, 1964b, 1965; Kaufman & Pitblado, 1965) has shown that even different alphabetic characters could be stereoscopically combined to produce a robust experience of depth. The critical cue for stereopsis, Kaufman concluded, was the disparity of the stimulus *luminance* on corresponding points rather than identical forms. Specific contours, he feels, play a small role in the process. This is of course also the main message that is telegraphed to us by the fact that we can accurately localize a single dot in space—local disparity, not global configuration, is the initial trigger to stereoscopic perception. Kaufman and Pitblado (1969) have gone on to show that, despite previous controversy, the effects of monocular image contour are so small that it is even possible to fuse opposite-contrast stereograms to produce discriminable depth experiences.

10. In situations in which binocular stimuli are very disparate in contrast, there is often a race between rivalry and depth. Levy and Lawson (1978) have shown that opposite-contrast stimuli fuse to produce an experience of depth only when the contrast difference is moderate. Great differences in contrast result in binocular vivalry. Excluded from this generalization are opposite-contrast outline figures, which have been known since Helmholtz' time to give depth perception.

11. Stereopsis seems to be remarkably insensitve to many other kinds of geometrical factors as well. Westheimer and McKee (1978) have shown that stereoscopic acuity remains unimpaired even though both monouclar targets were moving on the retina with velocities as great as 2 deg per sec. Considering the

extreme sensitivity of the stereoscopic process to disparity (as small as a few seconds of visual angle), this is an astonishing result—it suggests an extraordinary ability to keep spatiotemporal relations properly registered. However, as one reflects on this result, it seems like a highly adaptive evolutionary development. The eyes are in constant motion, and these natural motions must certainly be nonconjugate to a degree that is much greater than the precision of stereoscopic depth. Insensitivity to such ocular (or for that matter stimulus) motion is, therefore, highly useful in maintaining stereoscopic precision under many natural

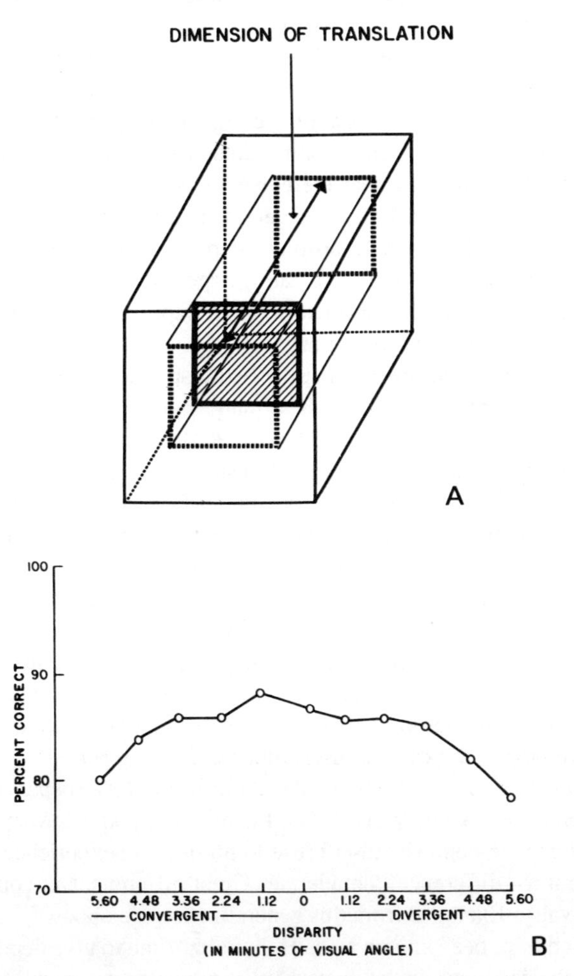

FIG. 11.45. (A) Diagram of the stimulus used to determine the effect of the translation of a plane of dots on its detectability in a random dot stereomasking experiment. (B) The results of the experiment showing detectability as a function of the stereoscopically generated disparity. (From Uttal, 1975b.)

circumstances. Of course, this kind of finding complicates the simplistic description of the function of corresponding points and Panum's areas enormously by further removing them from any anatomical anchor, for these data also stress that these terms describe functional rather than structural entities.

12. Stereoscopic acuity (measured in seconds of disparity) is relatively unaffected by the observation distance per se (Lit & Finn, 1976). These psychologists have shown virtually flat functions relating stereoscopic thresholds and distance over a range of 2–200 cm, even though there is some deterioration in performance for depths less than 20 cm.

On the other hand, there is a maximum distance at which stereopsis fails. This upper limit is determined by the trigonometry of the situation and the minimum threshold disparity. Most estimates place this maximum distance for effective stereopsis at greater than 100 meters although a rough calculation by Graham (1965c, p. 525) suggests that the maximum theroretical depth, assuming a disparity threshold as large as 30 sec of arc, should be of the order of 500 meters.

This then, is just a brief sampling of some of the more fundamental or recent experimental findings concerning stereopsis. The reader interested in more complete discussions of the stereoscopic process, or of depth vision in general, has many sources available. Among the most important books are Ogle (1950), Julesz (1971), and Gulick and Lawson (1976). Sections of other books also often present excellent discussions of the available data base. Most notably, this includes Kaufman's (1974) exceptionally lucid discussion. Several handbooks present important reviews, including Graham's (1965c) article on stereopsis in the now classic *Vision and Visual Perception,* and Foley's (1978) and Julesz' (1978a) articles in the newly published volume on perception in the monumental *Handbook of Sensory Physiology*.

There are many theoretical developments in the field of stereopsis, but even the best available today are distressingly incomplete and controversial. Explanatory models of this form of depth perception have, over the years, varied from vague statements about fusion or suppression (see Kaufman, 1974, for a good review of these classic theories) to physical analogies that do not delve into possible neural mechanisms. Unfortunately, the recent outstanding and important neurophysiological findings concerning disparity-tuned, binocularly sensitive neurons in the visual system do not yet satisfactorily explain some of the more complex psychophysical findings. To review the major theories of stereopsis fully would make demands beyond the space limits of this chapter, but it may be useful to give a capsule summary of the emphases of at least several of the more important models at this point.

a. The Classic Isomorphic Fusion Theories. For many years, indeed centuries, perceptual scientists have been aware of the discrepancy between the dimensions of perception of three-dimensional depth and the two-dimensional information that is manifest in the retinal image. Because that experience of depth was clearly attenuated when one eye was covered, obviously some combination of the information from the two eyes was required to construct the most compelling depth experience. The classic version of fusion theory has always been formulated in algebraic terms that implicitly assumed that the two images were in some way ''added'' together to produce the three-dimensional experience. The traditional isomorphic fusion theory, for example, was a typical ''toy in the head'' theory. In one form or another (Kaufman, 1974, eloquently recounts the many equivalent versions of this approach that have appeared in the past) it involves the reconstruction of a three-dimensional field of activity within the brain that is spatially similar to both the stimulus and the percept. This kind of isomorphism, as I hope I have convinced the reader by now, is not necessary in neural explanations of perception. Nevertheless, it was an integral part of all of the classic fusion theories.

Classic fusion theories, however, had multiple deficiencies as explanatory models of stereopsis. Alletropia, which I have already discussed, is one such difficulty. No simple isomorphic, deterministic, or algebraic model can account for this phenomenon; it must be attributed to some kind of a resignification process of a much higher level of complexity than simple fusion. Furthermore, the visual cortex, in which the reconstruction is usually assumed to take place, is actually more of a two-dimensional surface than a three-dimensional solid. (The columnar organization makes all cortical representation redundant along an axis normal to the surface, and thus functionally two-dimensional.) Furthermore, all fusion theories are inherently uncertain with regard to the problem posed by the successful processing of ambiguous stereoscopic images. In many viewing situations fusion theory allows disparities to be interpreted as either crossed or uncrossed (or both), and thus raises the possibility of ghost images. In spite of this theoretical possibility ghost images are never seen, and their very absence has become a major challenge for any form of a pure fusion theory. The paradox of stereoscopic ghost images is a perfect example of a pseudoproblem arising out of the surplus meaning of a theoretical model. One may put the string of words ''why do we not see the ghost images?'' together, but this syntactical construction does not guarantee an equally meaningful semantic content. ''Ghost images'' may simple be figments of the fusion model.

Lloyd Kaufman (1974, p. 292) sums up the difficulty faced by the classic isomorphic fusion theories with the following words:

> It can be seen that existing fusional theories have difficulty with several facts. First, complete sensory or perceived fusion is not necessary to the occurrence of stereopsis. Second, partial displacement is not an unequivocal sign of sensory fusion, since there is no proof that displacement may not be caused by fixation disparity. Third, perceived displacement is not correlated with perceived depth. Fourth, fusion theories are haunted by predicted ghost images that are simply not perceptible.

b. The Classic Suppression Theories. Because only one image is seen when two eyes view a scene, might it not be possible that one of the images is suppressing or inhibiting the other? This question was answered in the affirmative by those who have proposed versions of the classic suppression theory of stereopsis. However, suppression theory must be, a priori, incorrect for the most basic of reasons—the final stereoscopic percept is not the same as either one of the two monocularly driven percepts. Thus, stereopsis in some ways depends on maintaining and using information from both monocular signals and not on diminishing one or the other. More specific experimental evidence that some form of suppression is not a plausible part of stereopsis comes from an interesting experiment carried out by Blake and Camisa (1978). They showed that there was no evidence that the detection threshold for a stimulus presented to either eye was elevated during stereoscopic fusion. In other instances (e.g., binocular rivalry) in which one of two nonfusible images was suppressed to produce a single visual response, such a decrement in the detection threshold was observed.

c. Physical Analogies. Some theoretical models of stereopsis make no attempt to analyze the system down to underlying mechanisms but resort instead to descriptive physical analogies to help us to establish intuitive appreciations of the nature of the interaction processes that give rise to the depth experience. Julesz (1971) and Julesz and Chang (1976), for example, have modeled stereopsis by invoking a frame of magnetic dipoles as a physical analogy for the stereoscopic process as shown in Fig. 11-46. In their model the magnetic dipoles are analogous to the disparity-sensitive neurons (or neural complexes) in the visual cortex. The "dipoles" from each eye interact locally by virtue of the short-range fields of interaction that are modeled by the "magnetic forces" of these hypothetical elements. The resulting "alignment" of dipoles from the left and right eye respectively correspond to the activation of binocular disparity-sensitive cells. This process describes local stereopsis, but does not explain the neural mechanisms.

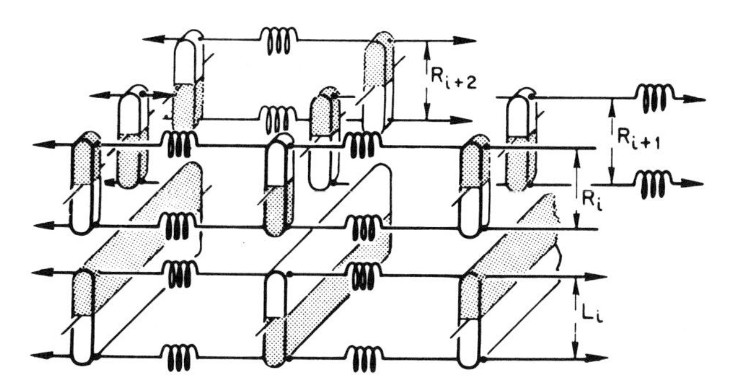

FIG. 11.46. The parallel spring model of stereoscopic vision. (From Julesz and Chang, © 1976, with the permission of Springer-Verlag.)

On the other hand, global stereopsis occurs, according to Julesz and Chang, because the dipoles are tied together by a system of "soft springs." The springs represent forces of neural interaction between widely separated regions of the field. Thus, if a dipole in one position is rotated by the visual stimulus, it not only interacts with the opposite eye's corresponding dipole via its magnetic influence but also with other dipoles associated with more distant regions of the same eye via the influence of the metaphorical springs. These interaction effects summate to develop an overall pattern of behavior in the framework of magnets that is analogous to the perceptual responses that presumably occur in the visual system. It thus provides a heuristic for understanding the nature of some of the interactions in stereoscopic processing if not the neurophysiological details of the involved mechanisms.

Julesz and Chang's model, of course, is a particularly fine example of a physical analogy. Nowhere in their articles do they suggest that there are actually magnetic dipoles and springs in the eye, but rather, that the eye is made up of units that operate according to similar functional rules. They propose that there are both intraeye and intereye interactions modeled by the springs and magnetic fields, respectively, but in fact they explicitly acknowledge that these interactions are implemented in the eye by lateral neural connectives that have not yet been identified or fully studied in the neurophysiological laboratory. This is a fair approach, quite useful, but not a reductive model in the ideal sense.

Sperling (1970), from another theoretical perspective, utilizes the mathematical apparatus of quantum mechanics to model stereopsis. He invokes concepts such as "potential wells" corresponding to stable visual states. His mathematical model and physical analogy are based on the idea of small dense spheres moving on a nonuniform surface. The model not only attempts to describe stereopsis but also accommodation and vergence responses. It deals with forces and interactions in a purely mathematical manner rather than in the more intuitively direct mechanical manner of the Julesz and Chang model.

Sperling (1970) goes on, however, to propose a neural model that parallels, but is independent of, his mathematical potential-well analogy but wisely notes that "it is not unique [p. 525]." In fact he too disassociates his model from neuroanatomy and states that it is "an hypothesis only about topology (i.e., connectivity)."

d. Neurophysiological Theories. Speculative, as well as laboratory-based, theories of stereopsis based on known properties of neurons have also been proposed. One of the most complete of the speculative models is Nelson's (1975) proposal invoking the neural processes of mutual inhibition and facilitation; he asserts four specific postulates (pp. 76–77) which can be paraphrased as follows:

Postulate 1. Disparity detectors of identical disparity interact in a facilitatory manner, but the facilitation declines with distance (i.e., likes facilitate).

Postulate 2. Dissimilar disparity detectors are mutually inhibitory. The greater the dissimilarity, the greater the inhibition, but that inhibition also declines with distance (i.e., unlikes inhibit).

Postulate 3. The visual system cannot distinguish between distributed low levels of activity and localized high levels of activity. It essentially responds only to the mean level of activity in an aggregate of neurons (i.e., globality).

Postulate 4. The mutual inhibition described in Postulate 2 is recurrent. That is, the inhibition is a function of both the activity in a neuron and the inhibition from its neighbors (i.e., reciprocal inhibition).

These four postulates are summarized in the drawing shown in Fig. 11-47.

Obviously, Nelson's model represents a concept of the nervous system that stretches the limits of knowledge available from experimental neurophysiology. However it does construct a speculative organization of a plausible stereoscopic nervous system that he feels might account for some of the phenomenology of depth perception. For example, he suggests that his first postulate explains why we see surfaces when confronted by a pattern of random dots in a Julesz type stereogram. According to this postulate the spatial facilitation that exists between the dots serves to unite the depth percepts of all of the individual dots into a continuous experience. On the other hand he feels that the second postulate explains why we do not see a surface when there is wide variation of disparities. The inhibition between the dissimilar depths overcomes whatever tendency may have existed to aggregate the dots as an irregular surface. Though framed in neurophysiological terms, Nelson's theory is, in truth, very much of the same rubric as was Sperling, Julesz, and Chang's models. It, too, is a physical analogy although the physical universe from which its central concepts are taken in this case is that of the body of neurophysiological knowledge.

There are, however, neurophysiological theories of stereopsis that are more specifically related to available laboratory findings. Nevertheless, it must be remembered that the two theories I now discuss are also extrapolations from one domain (neurophysiology) to another (psychophysics) and thus susceptible to the same kind of criticism made for any of the other types of models.

By far the most detailed neurophysiological theories of stereopsis are to be found in the interpretations made of the highly influential laboratory discoveries of such workers as Hubel and Wiesel (1962, 1970); Barlow, Blakemore, and Pettigrew (1967); Pettigrew, Nikara, and Bishop (1968); Blakemore and Pettigrew (1970); Pettigrew and Konishi (1976); and Poggio and Fischer (1977). All these experimenters have discovered and observed particular neurons in the visual areas of the brains of one species or another that are selectively sensitive, not to particular shapes or orientations but rather to highly specific spatial disparity differences (as defined on p. 933) between corresponding points on the two retina. These neurons require simultaneous inputs from the two eyes with particular disparities before they will respond. Many such neurons have been observed and a wide variety of trigger disparities noted. Thus, the system seems to encode disparity by transforming that dimension to spatial location—neurons in particular places fire when particular disparities are present. Neurons of this kind appear to be ubiquitous in the visual cortices of animals, such as primates and owls, that also show strong behavioral signs of good stereopsis. All of these data indicate

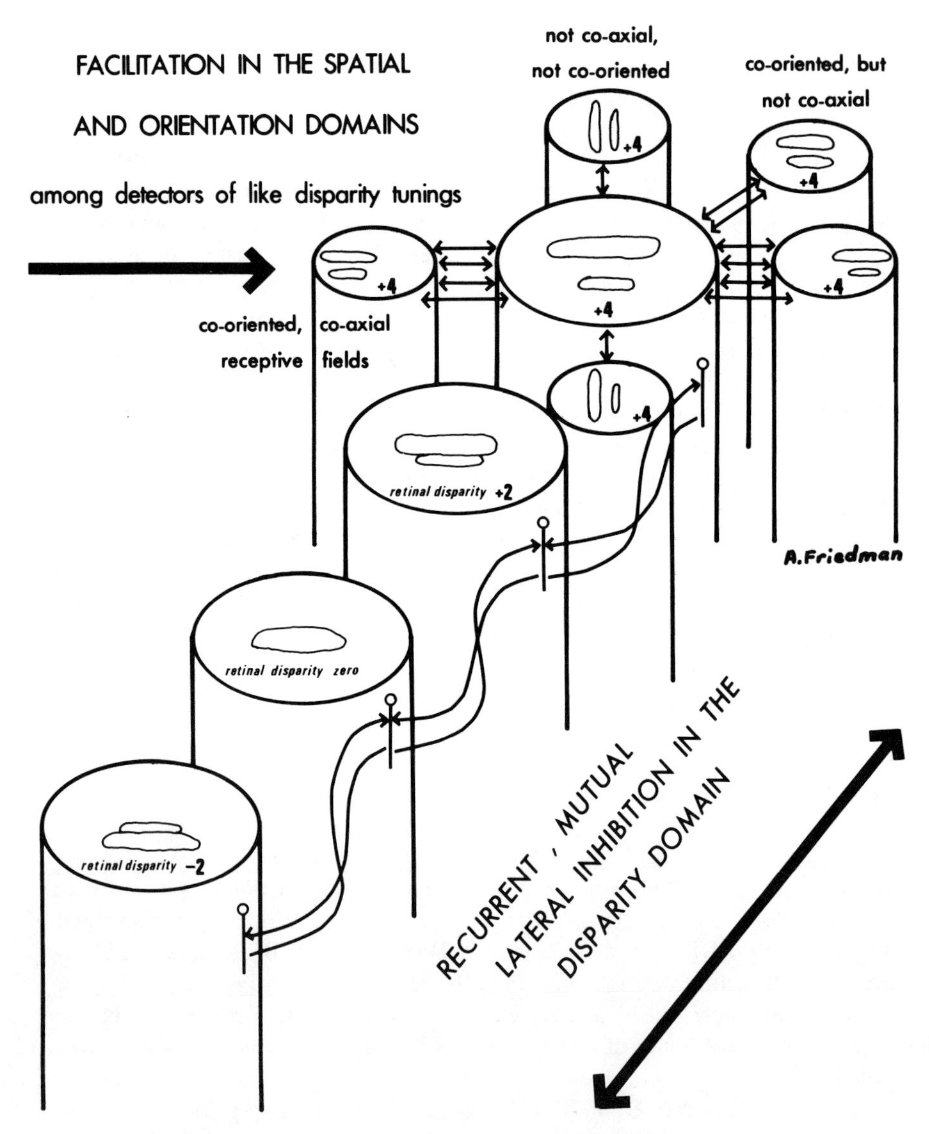

FIG. 11.47. A lateral inhibitory interaction model of stereoscopic vision. (From Nelson, © 1975, with the permission of Academic Press.)

that the transformation from the two-dimensional retinal image space to a coded representation of a three-dimensional space occurs relatively early in the visual cortex.

These neurophysiological data also support the argument that monocular images are neither suppressed nor fused to produce stereoscopic depth experiences, but that the information content from each eye is maintained in a combined form to produce a new representation that is implicit, but not explicit, in the pair of two-dimensional retinal images. In short, a modern view of stereopsis is that an invariance sensitive computational mechanism of some kind extracts information from the two monocular images and constructs a new neural model of external reality.

However some data are becoming available that argue even against this modern neural theory of fusion. For example, it has been shown by Harris and Gregory (1973) that good stereoscopic depth can be achieved by fusion of two disparate *subjective contours!* That this is possible raises doubts about the role of the physical stimulus and its direct neural representation in the stereoscopic process, and leaves us with the same kind of paradox that we had prior to the neurophysiological discoveries. It is another example of a dissociation among stimulus, neural representation, and percept that is terribly difficult for any radical neuroreductionistic theory to handle.

e. Computational Models. Some contemporary workers in the field of stereopsis assert both that the process is not susceptible to neural modeling and that it is unlikely that anything positive will come from continuing the qualitative descriptions that characterize both the classic and modern theories. They propose, instead, that computer models be developed to simulate the processes that *must* necessarily be carried out to extract invariant depth information from the two retinal image spaces. Although the work carried out by computer modelers is always intended to be within the constraints set by neurophysiological data, they often eschew any specific physiological or anatomical implications for their work other than a pro forma tip of the hat to Hubel and Wiesel. Rather, theoreticians of this persuasion seek to define the logical nature of the tasks that must be performed by the nervous system in order to generate stereoscopic vision and then propose mathematically efficient algorithms that can carry out the task. These algorithms are then implemented in the form of a computer program, and to the degree that they do finally mimic human depth perception they become more or less acceptable models of the perceptual process if not of the underlying mechanism. The more enlightened of these AI (Artificial Intelligence) scientists do not assert that their particular algorithms are the only possible solutions to the perceptual problem but rather that they represent plausible statements of the way in which the essential information processing steps may be executed. Thus the computational theories are more closely anchored to the psychophysical data than to any putative neurophysiological mechanism. In this sense, they are "informational analogs'' in which the logic of a computer program becomes the model for the perceptual process. There is, of course, no means of guaranteeing that this kind of logic is the only acceptable logic. In fact, it seems quite likely that neither the computational models embodied in the computer programs nor the computer itself are executing the same kind of logic as is utilized in the brain.

Among the most important of recent simulation models of stereopsis is that part of the more general theory of visual information processing proposed by a group of computer scientists led by David Marr of MIT (Marr & Nishihara, 1978; Marr & Poggio, 1976, 1979). The algorithm proposed in Marr and Poggio's (1979) paper involves both spatial-frequency-sensitive channels and the degree of convergence of the eyes. According to the authors, their model fits a wide variety of psychophysical data.

The essence of Marr and Poggio's theory is that contour-enhanced (by some kind of an edge detecting preprocessor) representations of the two retinal images are matched by some more central portion of the visual system according to two rules. The first rule is that each point on one eye's representation is to be matched with only a single point on the opposite eye's representation. The second rule is that visual space is continuous; that is, there is a smooth variation of disparity from one point to an adjacent one. Using these two criteria, Marr and Poggio (1976).showed how a simple algorithm could compute local disparities and how these local disparities could be translated into a single three-dimensional representation of the stimulus from the two-dimensional retinal projections.

Marr and Poggio make no claim that this algorithm represents the only way that the disparity information may be processed in the human visual system. Instead they have provided one plausible algorithm for invariance extraction that can do some of what is done by the human system in a manner that does not violate the limits of psychophysical plausibility. In that regard their computer program represents one of the most specific and detailed theories of stereopsis. Perhaps its most important contribution is that this analysis makes very clear what it is that has to be explained when one puts together a theory of stereoscopic vision.

The theories of stereopsis that I have discussed here are not presented in sufficient detail to allow the reader to understand all of their subtle implications. But my purpose is only to indicate the types of theories that are presently available to model the stereoscopic process and some of the advantages and disadvantages of each. It is clear that many aspects of stereopsis are not well accounted for by any of these theories.

Three major issues are now generally appreciated to represent the heart of the challenge faced in any further theoretical efforts. The first of these great issues has been referred to as the problem of correspondence. This problem is most directly encountered in the random dot stereogram stimuli used in the work of Bela Julesz (e.g., Julesz, 1971). Given the nature of these stereograms, one must ask—how it is possible for an observer to align or register the two different images so that disparity differences between proper pairs of points can be correctly interpreted? How, in other words, do we find the pairs of dots in the random dot stereogram that correspond to each other without an exhaustive comparison on a dot-by-dot basis—a process that seems highly implausible given the number of possible pairs that could exist in a pattern with even a modest number of dots?

Solving the problem of correspondence is central to achieving understanding of the stereoscopic process and is beginning to receive a great deal of research attention. But there are many aspects to this problem that have not yet been explored. For example, one can ask whether the edges of the random dotted areas contribute to the observer's ability to register corresponding stimulus dots.[17] A perfectly plausible experiment, and yet one that has not been carried out to my knowledge, would involve eliminating these contours by making each of the two monocular stimuli as large as the entire visual field. Then there would be no contours (other than those of the perimeter on the eye itself) to act as secondary cues to registration. So, the experimenter might ask, what would happen to the latent period for the establishment of the stereoscopic view? Is the latent period elongated by the absence of contour cues to registration thus indicating a difficulty in registration of corresponding dots where contours are absent, or is it hardly affected? It seems to me that this would be a highly useful experiment to help to resolve many of the controversies that now inhibit progress on this key issue of correspondence. Marr and Poggio's model depends in large part on the availability of such contours to achieve the registration necessary for stereoscopic depth. Do human beings also depend on the availability of contours in the same way in order to produce perceived depth? The rapidly accumulating body of data based on research utilizing random dot stereograms suggests that they do not, but the question is yet unanswered.

The human ability to register corresponding points in the presence of what would be expected to produce serious difficulty, on the other hand, comes close to being incredible. Bela Julesz presents some extraordinary demonstrations of the power of the visual system to determine stereoscopic correspondence (Julesz, 1971). On page 325 of this very special book he shows an anaglyph in which the two figures 15% different in size can be combined to give perfectly good stereopsis. On page 331 he shows a fusible anaglyph in which one of the two stimuli is badly blurred and yet, in this case too, stereopsis can be achieved relatively easily. I have already mentioned Kaufman's work with reversed contrast stereog-

[17]In any random sterogram it is physically possible to define fortuitously a large number of lacy, irregularly dotted surfaces consisting of those pairs of points across the entire plane that spuriously possess a common disparity due to an accidental misregistration of noncorresponding, but physically identical, stimulus elements in the dichoptic images.

rams on p. 945. These are only a few of the examples of the extraordinary power of the visual system to achieve correspondence—a power that still exceeds the ability of even the most sophisticated computer model.

The second important and persistent issue in stereoscopic theory involves the displacement effect alluded to earlier. The displacement effect (alletropia) is especially significant because it, in particular, also disassociates retinal location from perceived location. As noted earlier. this phenomenon suggests not only that the third dimension (depth) is the result of an act of construction or interpretation, but also that the two fronto-parrallel (x and y) dimensions are also constructions only implied, but not determined, by the nature of the proximal stimulus projected on the retinae. Again there is a paucity of relevant research beyond the simple demonstrations that have graced the classical literature on this topic and much remains to be done to understand the full implication of this important phenomenon—alletropia.

The third major issue in stereoscopic theory concerns the extent of the interactions that may or may not occur among stereoscopic elements. Is stereopsis essentially a local process or is it, to the contrary, dependent on global interactions such that active interaction occurs even among the most distant regions of the visual field? Despite many years of active research on the problem of the globality of the stereoscopic process, there is still a considerable amount of disagreement concerning this question. Some work (e.g., Uttal, Fitzgerald, and Eskin, 1975a) suggests that there is relatively little interaction; as one adds to the number of stimulus points in a random-dot stereogram, only a modest increase in the precision or reduction in latency of depth discrimination occurs. Neurophysiological evidence also generally suggests relatively localized stereoscopic processing; binocular neurons seem to interact most strongly with their immediate neighbors. However, as we have seen, others have obtained data that they interpret to mean that there is a considerable global effect across the stereoscopic space. The problem of globality, therefore, also remains a central one in future theoretical and empirical development. But solutions to all three of these perplexities—correspondence, alletropia, and globality—must be incorporated within any future theory if it is to have wide acceptance and utility.

This, then, is the story of one very important kind of binocular interaction, a binouclar process in which a comparative computation or interpretation of the inputs from two different points of view leads to a highly quantitative awareness of the depth dimension that is only implicit in the two retinal images. Relative disparity, however, is not the only way in which the two eyes can interact to alter the experience of depth. In addition a powerful binocular cue to depth is also generated by the angle of vergence of the two eyes. Fixation on nearby objects, of course, results in a highly degree of convergence, whereas fixation on objects at greater depths produces a greater and greater divergence until the lines of sight of the two eyes are virtually parallel. The proprioceptive signals from the ocular muscles are probably also converted in some way into a depth experience even in the absence of any other monocular or binocular cues. Little is known of how this proprioceptive response actually influences vision, but it is clear that this vergence angle can in no way be considered to be isomorphic to visual space percepts. The angular measurements made by the somatosensory nerves that underlie this experience are but symbols of visual depth and must be treated in the same way that the indicator values on the optical rangefinder are used. Unfortunately, contemporary visual science has not yet located the corresponding trigonometric calculator in the human brain.

2. Other Dichoptic Interactions

Disparity and vergence cues to depth, of course, do not exhaust the possible ways in which the two eyes may interact. A wide variety of other dichoptic interaction processes have been of concern to psychologists for over a century. Blake and Fox (1973) have reviewed a number of these binocular interactions and have distinguished between two major classes—threshold phenomena and suprathreshold phenomena. I only briefly summarize their findings here. The reader is directed to their comprehensive and lucid paper for a thorough discussion.

Blake and Fox note that several familiar experimental paradigms in which thresholds and suprathreshold magnitudes are measured can be studied as special cases of a generalized interocular interaction. Among the threshold processes that they have included within this rubric are dichoptic increment detection, form recognition, acuity, and flicker fusion. After comparing a wide variety of such studies in which *thresholds* were measured under dichoptic and monocular conditions, respectively, they conclude that there is little doubt that there must be some kind of facilitatory interaction between the signals from the two eyes. The main argument they propose is that the improvement (i.e., lowering) in thresholds seen in all of the dichoptic experiments is greater than would be expected on the basis of simple probability summation of the responses generated by each eye independently.

However, when Blake and Fox go on to consider the*suprathreshold* processes typified by brightness and reaction time measures, they conclude that the case for dichoptic interaction is not so clear. Since the earliest studies of dichoptic brightness interaction, for example, there has been considerable controversy concerning the very existence of the phenomenon. Some of the earlier workers—for example, Sherrington (1906) and Fechner (1860)—had denied the existence of any kind of brightness summation. Later studies by workers such as DeSilva and Bartley (1930) and Fry and Bartley (1933) seemed to support the existence of some kind of interocular interaction on the other hand. Compounding the confusion was a classic illusion known as Fechner's paradox. Early in the history of experimental psychology, Fechner discovered that if two lights of greatly dissimilar luminance were presented to the two eyes, the observer reported a fused cyclopean brightness that was intermediate between the two. If the dimmer of the two lights was then removed, a paradoxical brightening of the experience generated by the remaining light occurred, even though the total amount of luminous flux to both eyes had been lowered.

This paradoxical brightening suggested the existence of an inhibitory rather than summatory interaction between the two eyes. Clearly, suprathreshold brightness interaction is not, therefore, simply a case of summatory interaction; additive and subtractive interactions have both been reported, and in such a situation no simple rules determine the outcome of all viewing situations. And indeed, Blake and Fox conclude that the data are so equivocal for dichoptic and brightness and reaction time effects in general that no single solution to the problem of the nature of suprathreshold dichoptic interactions yet exists.

Some further insight into this problem is achieved by considering the following question: In those situations in which dichoptic brightness summation occurs, at what level is it processed? This question has been asked by Lema and Blake (1977), who concluded that such summations, when they exist, are probably mediated at the same level, if not by the same mechanism, that accounts for stereopsis. To arrive at this conclusion, they showed that stereoblind observers displayed virtually no interocular interaction in a contrast-detection task—both monocular and dichoptic thresholds were the same. Observers with normal stereopsis, on the other hand, typically showed a 30% improvement in those thresholds for the dichoptic viewing condition. The implication of this result is that binocular interactions, when they occur, are not simple algebraic peripheral processes. Like stereopsis, they may be the result of fairly high-level computations, comparable to invariance extraction, that are complex enough to alleviate at least part of the perplexity introduced by theories purporting to explain such phenomena as Fechner's paradox with simple, algebraic interactions.

Another dichoptic phenomenon, interest in which has not persisted well in the decades of microelectrodes and computers, is a putative chromatic interaction occurring when lights of different spectra are presented to each eye. In this case the effect is not necessarily slight. Reports exist of dichoptic color mixing in which the observer perceives a color intermediate between the two monocular ones (e.g., Fry, 1936). This change in dichoptic quality, as opposed to brightness or threshold, represents a problem toward which little experimental effort has recently been directed, but its existence is clear evidence that dichoptic interactions are far more complex than generally appreciated.

Thus though the problem of dichoptic interactions (in which the two eyes observe different stimuli, but the mind sees only one) has been with us for many years, there is still a considerable amount of debate over the basic empirical facts of the matter. Paradoxes, color mixing, and ambiguous suprathreshold effects make theoretical attacks on the problem difficult, and explanations that are more than simple handwaving are hard to come by. Perhaps this explains why the best theoretical models of these processes (e.g., Engel, 1969; Levelt, 1965) are still beset by uncertainty and dispute.

E. MULTIDIMENSIONAL INTERACTIONS

Finally, in this discussion of comparative and interactive Level 4 processes, we come to a set of interactions that occur between different dimensional domains rather than between attributes of the stimulus that are dimensionally homogeneous. In previous sections, I discussed interactions between properties of the stimulus that allowed the theoretician, at least, to conceive of some kind of an isomorphic model. However, I now consider interactions between attributes of the stimulus or of previous experience that are so dimensionally different as to preclude even this simplistic kind of isomorphic analogizing.

An important general point must preface this discussion of multi-dimensional interactions. The sine qua non—the critical defining criterion—of all of the multidimensional interactive processes to be considered here is the recurrent demonstration that what most psychologists would consider to be the first-order stimulus–response association does not hold; that is, although there may be an identifiable stimulus dimension (e.g., retinal size) that should be most closely related to a corresponding perceptual dimension (e.g., apparent size), we see repeated evidence that the latter can be virtually independent of the former over a wide range of stimulus variation. Multidimensional interactions, better than any other area of perceptual research, point up the fact that peripheral stimulus representations and subjective experiences can often be highly nonveridical and that any putative stimulus–response isomorphism is likely to be highly misleading criterion for evaluating theories of visual performance. These discrepancies are strong evidence for the existence of central processing mechanisms having symbolic and interpretive functions more in accord with the concept of rationalistic interpretations of partial cues and clues than with the idea of deterministic response specification by an empiricistic automation.

Thus, whether one is considering the subjective size, shape, color, direction, velocity, or lightness of the response to some stimulus, a common characteristic uniting all of the topics is nonveridicality. Some of the nonveridical phenomena I consider are referred to as constancies (i.e., objects tend to preserve their normative properties in spite of wide deviations in the properties of the stimulus). Modern television provides one familiar example of size constancy—even though the size of picture tubes, and thus of the retinal images, vary over wide ranges, there is a surprisingly modest alteration in the apparent size of objects and people. It is startling to measure objectively the visual angle of a television screen by holding a ruler at arm's length. The visual angle subtended by even a small television screen across the room is totally discrepant with the apparent size of the people cavorting on the screen.

Similarly, the color of an object remains within normative limits (a "red" apple) even though the spectrum of the light being reflected from it may contain no wavelengths comparable to the subjective colors. Distortions of the actual shape or the real distance to a physical stimulus may also be enormous without producing comparable perceptual distortions.

All of the sample nonveridicalities or discrepancies between stimulus and percept that I have just mentioned result from the operation of processes in which multiple stimulus dimensions are interacting. Distance and size, reflectance and lightness, chromatic quality and previous knowledge, and visual and gravitational stimuli all interact in situations that are comparable to those I have already discussed in previous sections of this chapter. These interactions, and the topic of this section, are distinguished by the fact that the interacting stimuli, in these cases, are heterogeneous (multidimensional) rather than homogeneous (unidimensional).

Before turning to a more detailed discussion of such heterogeneous interactions, I must first consider an exceedingly important conceptual issue. Multidimensional interactions, perhaps more than any other class of perceptual processes, remind us that we are dealing with a black box—the brain mechanisms embodying the processes that are equivalent to the human mind. Given the fundamental limitation that we can only measure external behaviors, how do we wend our way through the tangle of causal relations between stimulus, various internal representations, and interpersonally observable behavioral responses? No matter how high, it must be remembered that correlations between two or more aspects of the response do not help us out of this difficulty or provide insights into the knot of internal representations and processes. At best, such correlative associations show concommitance, but not causality.

Perhaps this point can be made a little more specific by briefly considering some of the size-distance explanations of perceptual size constancy. As I indicated above, it has been demonstrated in many different contexts that the perceived size of an object is often drastically dissociated from the projected retinal size. Retinal size, indeed, is not even a very good predictor of apparent size; perceived size can vary enormously even though retinal image size remains totally constant. This extreme dissociation has been classically demonstrated by projecting onto the retina a patterned light of sufficient intensity to produce a strong afterimage. We can assume that this retinal representation is more or less constant in extent. The afterimage can then be viewed by looking at a featureless screen placed at various real distances. Given other cues that suggest the distance between the observer and the screen, the afterimage can thus be made to appear to be "projected" at various distances from the observer. The astonishing result of this relatively simple demonstration is that the apparent size of the afterimage is more *dependent* on the stimuli that determine the distance at which it appears to be projected than on the retinal image size (which is constant). Indeed, the relationship between the factors determining apparent distance and those determining apparent size of an afterimage is highly linear and has been formulated in the perceptual rule known as *Emmert's law*. The problem, and here is the heart of the conceptual issue, is that the dependent and independent variables are often confused. Apparent size and apparent distance are all too often invoked as the causes of Emmert's law rather than the stimulus factors that jointly determine these perceptual responses.

Obviously, this allusion to perceptual response rather than to stimulus factors represents an entirely unappealing logic. What we really should be emphasizing in expressing either Emmert's or some inverse Emmert's law (which would relate apparent distance to apparent size) is that size and distance responses are joint functions of certain stimulus factors. In its usual formulation, Emmert's law misleads us concerning the involved causal relations and asserts a relationship that is contradictory to the tenets of a radical monism. In short, perceptual responses do not determine perceptual responses; stimulus and organism variables determine responses.

Is there any way around this difficulty? Although it is not yet certain that this question can yet be positively answered in the affirmative, one step towards a solution has been suggested by Simon (1954) and Blalock (1962) and applied to perceptual problems of this sort by Oyama (1974a; 1974b) and Oyama, Yoshioka, Ebihara, and Katahira (1976a, 1976b). The causal analysis system suggested by Simon (for three variable interactions) and by Blalock (for four variable interactions) depends on carefully designed experiments in which certain of the independent variables are held constant while others are allowed to vary. Subsequent computation of both cross and partial correlations allows the investigator to discriminate among various models describing the possible ways in which the stimulus and response variables may interact. For example, Blalock has suggested 43 different "models" of causation and interaction that could possible represent the interactions between a four-variable system consisting of two stimulus (independent) variables and two response (dependent) variables. Figure 11-48 shows some of these 43 models. In this figure, arrows indicate a causal relationship between variables, and the partial- and full-correlation coefficients indicate the values that would be expected to occur in a well-designed experiment should each particular model hold. The absence of an arrow (and/or a full-correlation coefficient of zero) indicates that the two variables are totally unrelated. A partial-correlation coefficient of zero indicates that the two variables are unrelated in those situations in which a third stimulus variable is held constant. Computation of the various full and partial correlation coefficients, therefore, can produce a pattern of interrelationships that can suggest which of the models *cannot* hold. However, as Oyama, Yoshika, Ebihara, and Katahira (1976b) note, it cannot definitively establish that one and only one of them *must* hold.

Oyama (1974a,) and Oyama, Yoshioka, Ebihara, and Katahira (1976b) have applied the Simon–Blalock method to the study of several versions of the size–

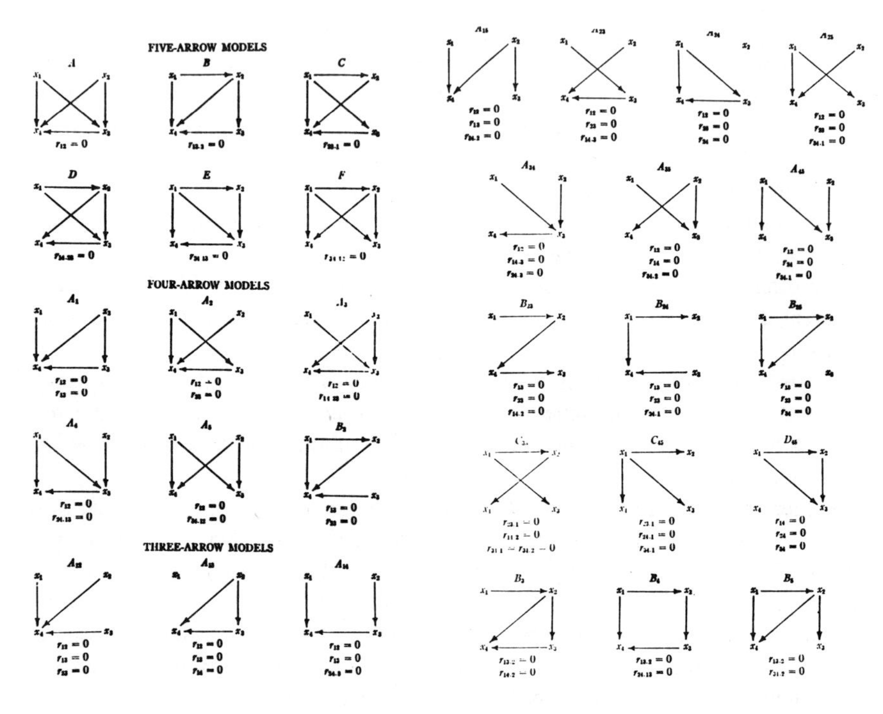

FIG. 11.48. 31 models of the possible interactions between four variables. (From Blalock, © 1962, with the permission of the University of Chicago Press.)

distance relationship in which the four involved variables are, respectively, the retinal size in degrees of visual angle (a cue to the size of the object), the angle of convergence of the two eyes (a cue to the distance to the object), the apparent distance, and the apparent size. Upon carrying out the appropriate set of control experiments and computing the required correlation coefficients, these psychologists came to some important conclusions concerning the causal interactions of these four variables.

First, they noted that there were substantial individual differences and that no single model adequately represented all observers. However, if all of the data were pooled, a specific pattern did emerge. The one model that could not be rejected and that seemed to best represent what was going on is shown in Fig. 11-49. This model tells us that both apparent size and apparent distance are jointly determined by the angle of convergence and the retinal image size, but that neither the apparent size nor the apparent distance directly influenced each other. This is an important conceptual step forward because this interpretation is quite different in meaning from the traditional expression of, say, Emmert's law, asserting a causal relationship between the apparent size and apparent distance responses. The logical, philosophical, and aesthetic difficulties inherent in Emmert's formulation—that some perceptual responses could influence other perceptual responses—is alleviated by Oyama and his colleagues' much more precise reformulation of the nature of the relationship among the four interacting variables.

The same sort of clarification is inherent in Restle's (1970) reconceptualization of the generally accepted theory of the moon illusion. The moon illusion is a natural example of the multi-dimensional, size–distance relationship that I have just been describing. When close to the horizon, the moon appears considerably larger than when it is at its apex in the sky. The illusions can also be seen in other contexts. Galanter (1972) has shown exactly the same process at work in judgments of flight path lenths of aircraft flying at various altitudes.

Although there had been some suggestions that this type of illusion might be due to the difference in proprioceptive feedbeack from neck muscles when one looked at the horizon compared to the situation in which the neck is bent to look directly up, that "motor" theory of the illusion had been totally repudiated by Kaufman and Rock (1962). Instead, they support the other classic alternative and assert that the course of the moon illusion was the same as that underlying Emmert's law, i.e., the moon appeared larger at the horizon because the horizon appeared further away than the apex. This explanation of the moon illusion, however, exhibits exactly the difficulties that bedeviled other theories of constancy: The putative causal relationships occur between two response variables rather than between two stimulus variables.

Restle (1970), however, has reanalyzed this classic problem and defined the relations among the important variables in a way that obviates this difficulty. He suggests, as did Oyama, that apparent distance and apparent size are both the result of all the involved stimulus variables. Restle clarifies the logic by asserting that the causal interactions go from the objective stimulus properties to the subjective states but not between subjective states. However, because the sky is at optical infinty over its entire extent, Restle was faced with the problem of defining the germane stimulus variable that determined different apparent distances in a situation in which convergence angle differences did not exist. His

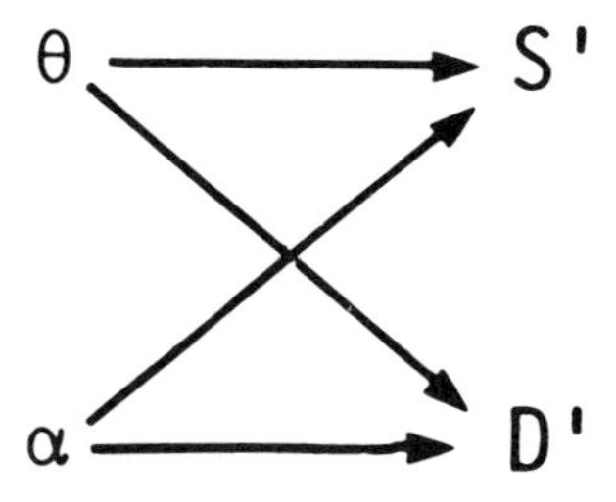

FIG. 11.49. The only plausible causal model of the interaction of visual angle (α), convergence angle (θ), apparent size (S′), and apparent distance (O′) that could not be rejected in Oyama's experiment. (From Oyama, © 1974a, with the permission of the Psychologia Society.)

eminently acceptable solution to this problem was to propose that the critical supplementary variable (in addition to retinal image size) was the local spatial contrast that existed between the moon and other objects in its immediate surround. The moon appears small (and nonverdicial with its retinal image size) not because it appears distant, says Restle. Rather, it appears both distant and small when it is at the apex because it is compared with the large empty environment that surrounds it. When the moon is near the horizon, or for that matter, at any other point in which there are objects with which to compare it, it enlarges in both perceived extent and perceived distance as a function of its multidimensional interaction with its surround.

Thus, Restle has proposed a neat and aesthetically pleasing theory in which the causal "arrows" run entirely from aspects of the objective stimulis to aspects of the perceptual responses and not between the perceptual responses. Many other examples of multidimensional interactions have also at one time or another run into the same intellectual difficulty, but Oyama's application of the Simon–Blalock procedures and Restle's analysis are milestones in clarifying the a posteriori absurd idea that the responses—perceived size and perceived distance—themselves causally interact.

Now that I have considered some general matters, let's look more closely at the details of the perceptual experiences that result from some specific multidimensional interactions.

1. Constancies in the Magnitude and Qualitative Domains—Lightness, Brightness, Hue, and Saturation

In this section I deal with a group of phenomenal dimensions that, year by year, are being appreciated as being increasingly closely related. We have already encountered the terms lightness, brightness, and color in several previous sections in which it was shown that one or another lower level of processing contributed to the determination of these perceptual properties. In this section, I consider the multidimensional Level 4 interactive processes that also contribute to the specification of these subjective dimensions.

Briefly, the reader should recall that lightness refers to the degree of grayness or blackness of an object, and brightness refers to the apparent magnitude of the chromatic (which also varies in hue and saturation) experience. The important thing in the present context with regard to all of these dimensions of experience is that they are *not* uniquely defined by any single level of processing. Neither the intensity or spectrum of the photic energy impinging upon the visual system nor the relational processes that I consider here can totally explain any of these subjective dimensions. There is a series of experiments, however, usually collected together under the rubric of constancy phenomena, that are particularly effective in demonstrating that several different levels of processing and aspects of the stimulus and/or previous experience most certainly are involved in determining what the respective lightness, brightness, hue, or saturation response to any particular physical stimulus will be.

The classic demonstration of lightness constancy was reported by Gelb (1929). In this prototypical experiment, a disk of black paper was suspended in the doorway to a darkened room. A beam of light was shone on it in such a way that the disk was fully illuminated. In spite of the fact that the disk was actually black (i.e., had a very low reflectance), it appeared to be a fairly luminous object that observers reported to be quite light in appearance, that is, it appeared to be perceptually more "whitish" than "blackish."

The dark chamber served two functions in this experiment. First, it acted very much like the physicist's "black body," absorbing practically all of the incident light not intercepted by the disk. Second, it provided a surround for the disk that was free of most relational cues. The blackness of the chamber was thus virtually constant, regardless of the intensity of the light illuminating the disk and escaping past it into the chamber. In other words, this situation provided minimal cues that could help the observer to determine the actual lightness of the object. Since the light shown on the disk was very intense, even though the reflectance of the black disk was relatively modest, a substantial amount of white light was actually reflected from it. The amount of light being reflected from the object, however, was both perceptually and physically indeterminate; that is, it could have been produced by a very intense light and a poorly reflecting disk, or by a weak light and a disk that reflected well. However, in this isolated case without some kind of a reference standard, this ambiguous reflectance was usually interpreted as a high degree of lightness by the human visual system.

In the next step of his experiment, Gelb inserted a small, highly reflecting (white) object in the same illuminating beam beside the disk. In this case, a standard was present (the white disk provided a reference), and the black disk immediately took on a much darker appearance. When the small white object was removed, the appearance of the black disk reverted to its spurious whiteness.

The import of this classic experiment is exactly the general one with which this chapter is concerned. The essential message is that any quantitative estimate of any perceptual dimension requires some kind of a comparative evaluation of the relations between different stimuli (or stimulus aspects) to specify properly the nature of the resulting percept. Situations that do not allow such comparisons are intrinsically ambiguous. Ambiguity has a very specific meaning in the case of Gelb's experiment. The amount of reflected light is clearly a joint function of the stimulating light intensity and the reflectance of interposed objects. If only a single object is present (or if all objects in the scene have the same reflectance), the situation is indeterminate. It is as if the mental computer was being asked to evaluate a situation with two unknowns but with only one equation or measurement available for that evaluation. There is, in principle, no way to do this. A mathematician can solve such a problem only by setting up a system of simultaneous equations equal in number to the number of unknowns. The mental computer, equally well, requires a second stimulus (in the Gelb experiment this is the small white object) in order to provide the basis for evaluating both the illumination and reflectance and thus for extracting the basic invariance—in this case, the lightness of the disk. Only in this manner can the veridical percept—a dark though brightly illuminated disk—be constructed.

We do not have a very good idea about how these relative reflectance computations are made by the brain, but it seems certain that such processes are fundamental to all lightness-constancy phenomena. What we do now know is something about the chain of causality, if not the details of the relationship. The essential message telegraphed by study of this causal chain is that there is no simple, isomorphic, one-to-one relationship between stimulus luminance and perceived lightness. Only in situations in which the relational factors are held constant, and in which there is little or no ambiguity does a simple algebraic relationship between luminance and lightness—or for that matter, brightness—hold. Well-controlled experiments in which only a single stimulus dimension is varied were the prototypical paradigms of research for Levels 1 and 2, but they are not, in general, appropriate to the study of Level 4 processes.

Reflectance computations, as mysterious as their underlying mechanism may be, represent the outcome of a perceptual process that influences not only the lightness or as it is sometimes called, the neutral color of an object, but also the hue and saturation of the chromatic response to a stimulus. Perhaps the importance of these reflectance computations as a cue to color has been most sharply brought to recent attention by Edwin Land. His development of the retinex theory of color vision (Land, 1959a, 1959b, 1959c, 1964, 1977) was an important development in demonstrating the role of relational cues in color vision. Land showed originally (Land, 1959a, 1959b, 1959c) that a nearly full color display could be obtained with what otherwise would have been considered a very incomplete kind of lighting arrangement.

Land's procedure involved the preparation of two black and white projection slides of a complex stimulus scene. One slide was photographed through a filter that only passed long-wavelength light; the other was photographed through a filter that passed only middle wavelengths. If the two slides were projected superimposed upon each other, illuminating the "long-wavelength" projected image with a narrow-bandwidth reddish light, and the "middle-wavelength" projected image with a a broad-band white light, a striking, color-filled scene was perceived. This is a direct contradiction of classic theory which attributes color experiences to the spectral properties of the stimulus alone.

A similar separation of perceived color and spectrum can be obtained by simply looking through a densely colored filter. As long as all of the scene is modulated by the filter, there still remains a relatively good color rendition of the original scene; that is, it is nearly veridical with both the unfiltered stimulus and color experience. Thus good color experience occurs in the case of both the filter and the Land demonstration, in which the actual physical energy characteristics of the stimulus do not present the full spectrum and, therefore, in which wide ranges of perceived color would not have been predicted by classic trichromatic theory.

Obviously some factors other than the wavelength spectrum of the stimulus must be influencing the resulting color experiences. That this is so should not have been too surprising in view of the lightness constancy phenomena that I just discussed. The Land and colored filter phenomena make exactly the same point—the absolute properties of the physical stimulus are not the complete determinants of the percept. Many other contextual cues, comparisons, and relations contribute to the percept—particularly our ability to determine the actual lightness of an object in spite of wide deviations in the amount of reflected light.

Although Land's early work was interpreted by some visual scientists as suggesting the existence of a two-component visual system capable of producing full color vision, the present version of his color vision theory, as embodied in his retinex model (Land, 1964, 1977; Land & McCann, 1971), does not stress this point. Instead the retinex model now stresses the central role of lightness computations, very similar to those illustrated by the Gelb experiment, and their impact on color perception. Indeed, Land's retinex is currently very much a trichromatic, Young–Helmholtz-type model in terms of its proposed receptor mechanisms. Land accepts the idea that three cone systems operate to produce slightly different representations of the stimulus scene by means of long-, middle-, and short-wavelength photoabsorption action, respectively. Land suggests, however, that something additional to the trichromatically coded information contributes to the determination of the respective lightnesses, and he further asserts that it is the relative lightness of adjacent areas that is the mystery factor contributing to perceived color in the impoverished spectral conditions of his classic demonstrations.

In his most recent paper, Land (1977) places considerable emphasis on the fact that the perceived color of an object can be totally independent of the physical energetics of the light reaching the eye. Using an elegant experimental stimulus reminiscent of a Mondrian painting, he demonstrates that under some circumstances, perception of red, blue, and green hues can be produced by exactly the same spectral information. He rejects contrast, in the classical sense, as well as knowledge of what the colors "should be," as explanations of this variation in perceived hues even with constant spectral output. The critical cue to color, he says, is relative reflectance.

In suggesting that it is, in fact, the reflectance of the stimulus object that is a major contributing cue for color perception, Land (1977) poses the perplexing problem of how the respective lightnesses of a complex scene, such as his Mondrian-like stimulus, are calculated. Although he proposes computer-like logical programs that can carry out such calculations, there is little evidence that the serial queries employed in this model are actually homologous to those used in the human visual system any more than were Braunstein's (1972) for stereokinetic processing. It is also possible that some kind of a global, more parallel kind of processing of incoming relative spectral information occurs comparable to the spatial statistical computations that were discussed in the previous chapter.

In all fairness, however, we simply do not know anything about the underlying mechanisms of these perceptual computations. The main contribution of Land's studies and of his retinex theory is the fact that they have decoupled color experience from rigid determination by the wavelength spectrum of the stimulus. Simplistic psychophysical laws relating color and wavelength are once again shown to be woefully inadequate as descriptions and explanations of the full-fledged complexity of even what may have seemed to have been the most automatic aspects of our perceptual system. Unfortunately, as the complexity of the stimulus response increases, we are forced to fall back on allusions to ill-defined computational mechanisms of unknown characteristics[18] or to statements about the interpretation and construction of responses to complex stimuli. Obviously, there is an enormous gaps in our understanding of these multidimensional perceptual processes.

It is also necessary to appreciate that many other factors other than the reflectance computations of which I have spoken so far contribute to the quantitative perception of lightness or color. The spatial arrangement of the object is also critical to the perception of lightness and color, just as it is to the perception of depth. For example, Gilchrist (1977, 1979) has shown that the perceived lightness of two parts of the stimulus scene depends on whether or not they are organized as parts of the same object. If, for example, a surface appears to be partially obscured by a shadow, he notes that the shadowed and the unshadowed portions of the surface are perceived as exhibiting the same lightness. On the other hand, he reports that if two objects or surfaces are presented to the observer in such a way that they appear to lie at different depths, their lightnesses are independent of each other, in much the same way that the simultaneous contrast mechanism fails when the contrasted and contrasting fields are separated in depth (see p. 730).

Collectively, these multiple and multidimensional influences on surface lightness, brightness, and color tell us that there is no simple one-to-one relationship between stimulus and response. Isomorphism along these quantitative and qualitative dimensions seems no more necessary here than in the spatial domain. Most important, in light of these data it is obvious that any simple deterministic neuroreductionistic model must fail to fit the true range of constancy data beyond the grossest first approximation.

---

[18]There is no question, of course, that these computational mechanisms exist; the fact that we can perceive information that exists only in the form of invariances in alternative, adjacent, or subsequent presentations of transformed versions of a stimulus is an existence proof in itself.

2. Constancies in the Spatial Domain—Size and Shape

In the previous section I discussed how color, lightness, and brightness are affected by stimulus dimensions other than the one to which they might a priori seem most closely related, and the need for multidimensional comparisons to resolve many perceptual ambiguities. In this section, I will consider how the geometrics of size and shape are similarly affected by multidimensional influences. Once again, there is ample evidence that the geometry of the perceptual response can be drastically dissociated from the geometry of the retinal projection. For example, I have already briefly considered the implications of the moon illusion in the introduction to this part of this chapter. The moon illusion is a natural demonstration of the power of multidimensional interactions in the spatial domain. There is, furthermore, a long list of somewhat better-controlled laboratory experiments that more compellingly demonstrate the same point than do demonstrations in open fields. The classic laboratory study of the ''size–distance'' interrelationship was reported by Holway and Boring (1941). Briefly, these two psychologists set up a viewing situation composed of two corridors at right angles to code other. One corridor contained a comparison stimulus situated at a fixed distance (approximately 3 m) from the observer. This comparison stimulus could be varied in size by the observer to match a test stimulus that was positioned at various distances, ranging from approximately 3–40 m down a second corridor perpendicular to the first. The test stimulus was arranged so that by varying its size as a function of its distance from the observer it always subtended a visual angle of one deg. The observer's task was to set the size of the comparison stimulus so that it appeared to be the same size as the test stimulus. In this way the apparent size of the test stimulus could be evaluated as the distance along the corridor varied.

The results of the Holway and Boring experiment are shown in Fig. 11-50. One can assume that if the retinal size of the test stimulus was the sole predictor of its apparent size, then the setting of the comparison disk should remain constant, because the visual angle of the test stimulus was always constant. Such a result would be represented by the horizontal line on the figure. On the other hand, if the observer compensated his perception in some way to take into account the actual or perceived distance to the object, then he would exhibit size constancy to a greater or lesser extent. The further the constant one-deg-wide object was from the observation point, the larger it would appear to be. Perfect constancy in such a case would be represented by the diagonal line in this figure. The observer, in other words, would be setting the comparison stimulus to a larger and larger size relative to the unchanging visual angle; this performance would reflect some sort of a computation of what the actual object size must be to produce a one-deg retinal image size at the various distances.

Figure 11-50 shows the actual results of the Holway and Boring experiments as a function of the distance to the test stimulus. The set of curves is parametric for several conditions in which there was a progressive reduction in the

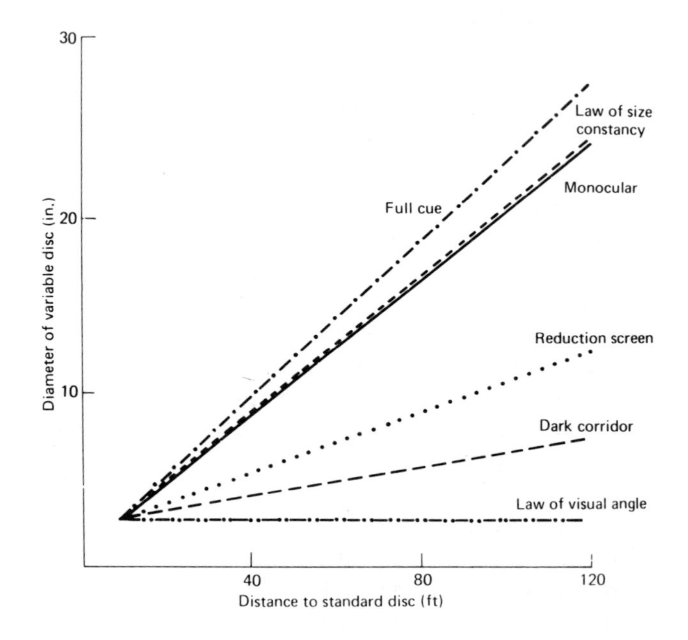

FIG. 11.50. The results of the Holway and Boring experiment. (From Kaufman, © 1974, with the permission of the Oxford University Press.)

availability of distance cues. Clearly, with both of the two utilized distance cues present (binocular viewing cues and monocular depth cues), the observer not only exhibited constancy but actually exhibited a kind of "superconstancy," setting the comparison stimulus to a value that was larger than the object size would have to be at that distance to produce the one-deg visual angle spot size. As available binocular cues were removed and a reduction screen (a viewing tunnel that obstructed monocular adjacency cues) was introduced, there was a progressive reduction in the degree of constancy exhibited. At the limit at which neither of those cues to distance was present, the resulting curve converged on the horizontal line that reflected size judgments depending on retinal image size alone.

Again I must remind the reader that the perceived distance is not the direct causal modifier of apparent size; rather, what this experiment is saying in this regard is that the stimulus cues that contribute to distance perception *also* contribute to size perception. The most important aspect of this classic experiment, however, is that the retinal image size, which to a first approximation would be thought to be the determining factor in apparent size, can actually be totally dissociated from that perceptual experience. In fact, we see in this exceptionally well-remembered experiment wide variations in apparent size with literally no variation in actual retinal image size.

It should not be misunderstood, however, that the observed relationship between size- and distance-determining cues is itself rigid and invariant. A large number of further experiments have shown that the procedures and the conditions under which the experiments are carried out can produce functions vastly different from those obtained in the Holway and Boring (1941) experiments. Some subsequent experimenters have discovered, for example, that it is possible for observers to separate apparent and retinal image estimates and to give perfectly good, though independent, judgments of each when properly queried (e.g., Gilinsky, 1955).

The situation described so far still only partially suggests the full complexity of the size-constancy phenomenon and the wide variety of available knowledge. The cues that contribute to distance are not the only cues that contribute to apparent size. The following list summarizes a number of major discoveries of other multidimensional stimulus effects on apparent size:

1. Tadasu Oyama and his colleagues at Chiba University in Japan have been among the most diligent students of the various factors that influence apparent size. In an extensive series of studies, they have shown that:

a. In a size-illusion experiment in which the size of an inner circle was measured as a function of the properties of a concentric annulus, no effect of any color difference was found between the disk and the annulus (Oyama, 1962). Similarly, the apparent size of circular colored figures on rectangular backgrounds of other colors did not seem to be influenced by color variables (Oyama & Nanri, 1960).

b. However, when isolated (i.e., presented on black backgrounds), substantial differences were observed in apparent size as a function of the color of those fields. Red and yellow fields appeared to be larger than equivalently luminous greys, and blues tended to be smaller than comparison grays. (Oyama & Anzai, 1973).

c. Oyama and Iwawaki (1972) and Oyama (1974b)[19] have also shown that apparent size varies with the degree of convergence of the two eyes but is independent of binocular disparity per se. This is a modern confirmation of the classic work of Helmholtz (1860) who first described this result.

2. As would be expected, a strong aftereffect follows examination of stimuli of other sizes prior to the presentation of the test stimulus. Kitterle (1975) has shown that adaptation with small stimuli leads to an overestimation of the size of a subsequent stimulus object and vice versa.

3. Common knowledge asserts that familiar objects are perceived closer to their objective size than are unfamiliar objects. The classic case is the "over-

---

[19]Other modern workers who have made this same association include McCready (1967) and Richards (1969a).

size'' playing card that is perceived normal size, but relegated to a distant locus to compensate for its hypertrophy.

4. Size is strongly affected by context and the self-context provided by simple figures. Size differences are less effective than shape differences in discrimination tasks (Weintraub, 1971).

A similar analysis can be made for the multidimensional influences on perceived shape. Shape, in short, is not determined solely by the shape of the projected retinal image any more than is the size of an object. Demonstration of shape constancy (in which an object appears as it should rather than in accord with the shape of the projected image) are also ubiquitous. Clearly the problem of stimulus equivalence, stated in Chapter 1, is but another way of highlighting the fact that the perceived shape of an object is far more stable than it should be on the basis of the retinal mapping.

Perceived shape is also driven by multidimensional interactions. Knowledge of what the object should look like is a powerful determinant of the shape of an object. That television set, of which I spoke a few pages earlier, cannot only be moved to a distant locus and still maintain apparent size stability but can also be rotated in a way that introduces a substantial degree of distorting perspective into the two-dimensional retinal image without a comparable distortion in the shape of the percept.

In more formal experiments, Leibowitz and Bourne (1956), for example, have shown that shape constancy is intimately tied to the duration of exposure and the luminance of the object. The shorter the duration of exposure, the more likely an observer was to follow the dictates of the shape of the retinal image; as the exposure duration increased, the constancy effect became more pronounced. The same relationship also occurred between luminance and constancy. Dim stimuli produced percepts that followed the retinal image dimensions much more closely than did brighter ones.

Eye movement can also produce a substantial discrepancy between the perceived shape of an object and its objective characteristics. For example, Festinger and Easton (1974), following up a discovery that had been reported several decades earlier by Fujii (1943), showed that the shape of a pathway traced out by a point moving along a square or triangular path was greatly distorted by the motor act (eye movements) of following that pathway. Sample distortions are shown in Fig. 11-51. When Festinger and Easton correlated eye position and motion information with the perceived distortions, they were able to show that the perceptual construct was highly sensitive to the direction of the eye movement but relatively insensitive to its speed.

Lappin and Preble (1975) have shown that the perception of shape depends on the observer's ''conception'' of the organization of the three-dimensional space in which it was embedded more than upon the properties of the projected retinal

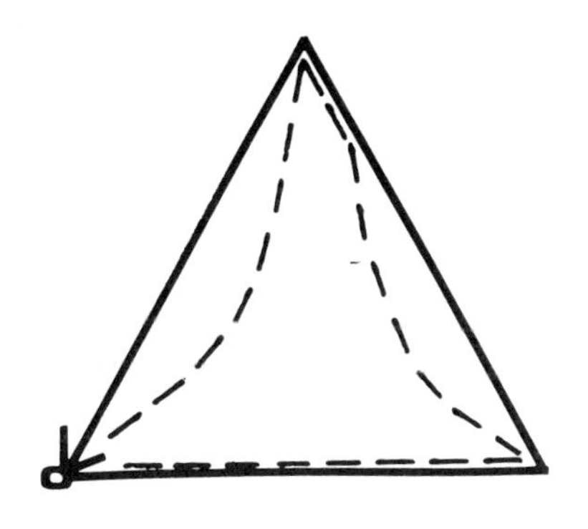

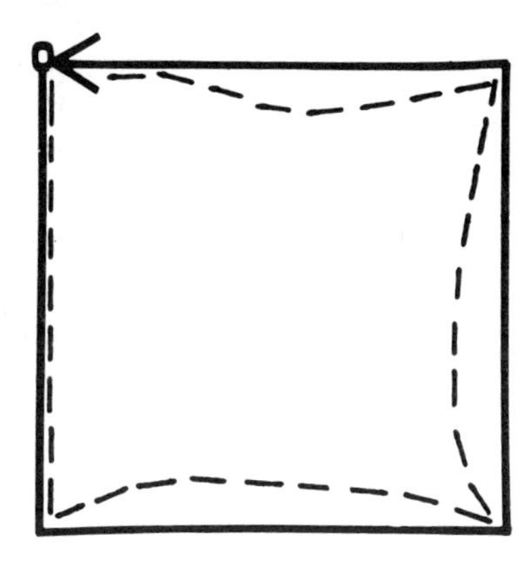

FIG. 11.51. Distortions in the apparent path of a moving luminous point stimulus. The solid line is the physical path and the dotted line denotes the perceived path. (From Festinger and Easton, © 1974, with the permission of the American Psychological Association.)

image. In their ingenious experiment, the constituent angles of polygons had to be judged in a naturalistic environment consisting of many different real objects that provided several monocular cues to the spatial organization of the scene. An example of one of their stimuli is shown in Fig. 11-52. They repeatedly observed the primacy of spatial organization over retinal projection in determining the perceived size of those angles.

FIG. 11.52. One of Lappin and Preble's stimulus displays. (From Lappin and Preble, © 1975, with the permission of The Psychonomics Journals, Inc.)

As Lappin and Preble also note, there is a paucity of formal experimental studies of shape constancy, but the few studies and demonstrations that I have cited make it clear that, in this domain too, there is no more intrinsic need for an isomorphic relationship between the stimulus shape and the perceived shape than among any of the other aspects discussed earlier. The experiments referred to repeatedly demonstrate the same sort of disassociation between the external stimulus and the perceived response that was observed in studies of lightness, color, or size. In conclusion, it appears that a lack of veridicality is the *rule,* rather than the *exception,* in all these perceptual domains if veridicality is defined in terms of correspondences between the physical stimulus and the perceptual response.

F. AN INTERIM SUMMARY

And thus, with broad stroke and an acknowledged incompleteness, a review and critique of Level 4 processes has been presented. There is a large body of additional research literature that does not need to be reviewed in detail here to make the same point that all of the discussions I have presented so far were intended to emphasize—perceptual responses, in most natural situations, eliciting quantitative percepts are usually the result of the compound interaction of several dimensions or aspects of the stimulus scene. In other words, I am asserting that the relative value of some dimension with regard to other dimensions is more important than its absolute value in cuing the perceptual experience throughout all of the Level 4 processes I have discussed in this chapter. A corollary of this conclusion is that the essential information in a stimulus pattern may exist only in the form of invariances between the alternative dimensions or representations and may require some kind of logical or quasi-numeric "computation" in order to be made explicit. Evidence for these assertions can also be found in the abundant literature on visual direction, on the oculogravic and tilt illusions, and in studies of the perception of movement and velocity that I have not considered in detail here. An exceedingly good summary of the current status of research in some of these areas of multidimensional interaction can be found in Epstein (1977) as well as in Dichgans and Brandt's (1978) and Lackner's (1978) reviews in the eighth volume of the *Handbook of Sensory Physiology* (Held, Leibowitz, & Teuber, 1978).

Another collective implication of all these findings is their repeated demonstration of the dissociation between the single stimulus dimension that may seem, at first glance, to be most closely associated with a given perceptual dimension and the dimensions of the perceptual response. The dissociation is so great in so many cases that it challenges the very conceptual foundations of the stimulus-determined perception that has dominated modern psychophysical theory. Instead of an empiricistic perceptual system, in which the stimulus determines the response, we must now begin to think about situations in which the stimulus merely implies or provides cues to some kind of a highly complex, problem-solving mechanism capable of generating solutions to the puzzle posed by a complex visual scene. This dissociation of stimulus and response in realistic natural scenes particularly reminds us of the profound separation between the external physical and the internal mental worlds. Not only are we isolated by the transductive and subsequent neural coding processes that only partially maintain information (certainly not energy) isomorphism, but more profoundly, we are isolated by the fact that information does not, as we have seen here, directly trigger or elicit mental states. Rather, stimuli lead to percepts through processes that are analogous to what electrical engineers would call isolation transformers. These perceptual isolation transformers do not convert voltages from one level to another but rather convert external information patterns encoded in physical energy into nonisomorphic representations encoded not only in different energies but also different patterns. The brain, in all its complexity, is a ''transformer'' of meaning, symbolisms, and constructed interpretations of what are at best only hints and cues provided to it about what is going on in the outside world.

In this chapter I have completed the case, I trust, against any kind of absolute stimulus determination of perceptual responses. We have seen how the effects of almost any single stimulus dimension could be overridden by interdimensional relations. It was repeatedly demonstrated that there was no link between any single response dimension and any single perceptual dimension that was not subject to alteration when other stimulus aspects became involved in the process. Those experiments that had traditionally demonstrated tight, absolute, unidimensional relationships between stimuli and responses can now be viewed as merely highly constrained abstractions in which most independent variables had been held constant but not as realistic expressions of the actual relationship between perceptual experience and all contributing stimuli in the natural world. Recall the many instances in which retinal image size or spectral content, as examples of many other ''primary'' stimulus dimensions, remained constant while substantial changes occurred in the respective perceptual experience following the influence of ''secondary'' independent variables. The point is the one that I raised at the outset of this book—no matter how many unidimensional graphs may exist in the perceptual literature, there is, in fact, no such thing as a unidimensional relationship between stimulus and response. Any psychophysical law of the form, *Response* = *f*(*Stimulus*), is apt to be highly misleading. A corollary of this conclusion also asserts that isomorphism is not an acceptable criterion for perceptual analysis. If all responses are determined by multiple stimulus dimensions, then no stimulus dimension is critical, and a one-for-one dimensional isomorphism is thus patently impossible.

Another general conclusion that emerges from the material surveyed in this chapter is the need to make comparative judgments in order to specify quantitative perceptual experiences. I presented a large body of evidence implying that it was unlikely that a quantitative estimate of any subjective dimension could be achieved unless it was possible to relate and compare alternative dimensions or aspects of the stimulus. In the absence of such relational judgments, there was a strong tendency for the response to be ambiguous, ill-defined, or illusory. Judgments of color, brightness, and shape all seemed to demand that some sort of relational comparison be made before a perceptual magnitude could be established.

Perhaps the key word in this whole chapter is *nonveridicality*. This entire discussion was, in fact, a presentation of a wide variety of nonveridical illusions—of percepts that deviated from what some kind of a machine incapable of interdimensional interactions would have measured on the basis of the given stimulus information. We have seen many instances in which the effects of lower levels of processing were mitigated, attenuated, or altered as a result of Level 4 processes. We have also seen how these Level 4 processes, though complex, still appear to be relatively automatic and preattentive. In concluding this discussion of Level 4 processes, however, we come to the boundary of such passive perceptual processing. The practical size limit of a book like this and the magnitude of the task of analyzing visual attentive and cognitive processes require that a discussion of Level 5 be postponed until the next volume in this series.

12 Epilog: Emerging Principles of Visual Processing

A. INTRODUCTION

This book opened with the fundamental epistemological question: How do humans acquire information about the external world? This all-too-general query was quickly particularlized to the more limited topic of visual perception and to a series of questions of somewhat greater specificity. It would be most satisfying if I were able to close this book with a summary chapter that answered the questions that I posed in Chapter 1. Unfortunately, this is not to be, as I am sure any reader of this book must have been aware from the very beginning. Those questions constitute the skeleton of a program of inquiry that has hardly begun. In concluding this book I acknowledge that there is as yet no grand metatheory of the more automatic, preattentive aspects of visual perception, any more than there is of its active and attentive components; this book fills the great need for a global ''explanation'' of perception no better than any of its predecessors.

What this book offers instead is an organizing taxonomy of visual processes and a set of general conclusions about where we are today in our attack on the many problems of visual perception. A satisfactory, process-oriented taxonomy,

I am convinced, is a necessary antecedent to any comprehensive metatheory. Nevertheless, over the past few decades the perceptual-research community has not shown sufficient interest in the development of such a classification system. Yet it is becoming increasingly clear to some of us that without such a system the continued chaotic accumulation of empirical data threatens to collapse the entire scholarly scientific enterprise under the weight of its own information overload. Regardless of what may or may not have been accomplished in this book, it is clear that systematization and generalization are the only plausible solutions to this problem. It is equally obvious that no information retrieval system could solve the problem created by the glut of disorganized research reports in this active field of research. Even a modestly effective information retrieval system would simply exacerbate the problem rather than alleviate it. Imagine what would happen if each of us arrived at our desks or laboratories each day to find all of the documents that we ''should'' be reading. The only solution to the information overload in modern scientific psychology is the construction of a conceptual superstructure—in other words, first a taxonomy and then a metatheory—that orders and systematizes the material so that the intrinsic patterns of organization are made apparent. After all, individual experiments are inconsequential; the general principles, of which they are but exemplars, are what really matter in the historical course of science.

The proposed taxonomy has already been presented in several ways in this book; it is presented in brief outline form in Chapter 4 and in an even more abstract and diagramatic form in Table 4-1. However, by far the most complete outline of the proposed taxomony is the entire contents of this book. The table of contents and the discussions presented in Chapters 5, 6, 7, 10, and 11 represent a detailed statement of one possible taxonomy of the first five levels (0, 1, 2, 3, 4) of perceptual processing. Chapter 8, of course, is an important adjunct; it acknowledges that certain temporal processes cannot yet be isolated in any way that would allow them to be classified within the context of the taxonomy.

At the outset of this epilog, I should also acknowledge that I do not believe this particular taxonomy will either be fully accepted initially or preserved intact very long by my perceptual science colleagues. Some will find certain arbitrary criteria applied in developing this classification system to be less than fully satisfactory. Some levels of analysis are probably more robust than others. For example, I do not believe that anyone could dispute the fact that there are external, preneural, Level 0 processes that influence visual perception. On the other hand, as I progressed deeper into the more central levels of perceptual processing, I became increasingly aware that the particular criteria I had chosen to discriminate between levels were not the only ones possible. It would not require much effort for someone to convince me that Levels 3 and 4 should have been organized on some other basis than the unidimensional, qualitative, figural organization, and multidimensional, relational, quantification criteria that I chose to use. I think the main reason for this uncertainty is that these more central processes are, in fact, not yet well understood and no natural criteria comparable to the neuroanatomical and physical ones of the lower levels have yet appeared. On the other hand, I am equally convinced that I have used acceptable, if not unique, criteria and that any other selection would have been either equivalent or subject to the same uncertainties.

There is one general criterion, however, to which I am still deeply committed; that criterion is that the main basis of any satisfactory perceptual taxonomy must be *underlying process* rather than *experienced phenomenon*. To classify on the basis of phenomena, as have most texts and other analyses of the field of visual perception in the past, is tantamount to confusion from the outset. In other words, whenever possible, I have tried to organize the material in this book in accord with the best available explanations of what causes the percept rather than the nature of the percept itself. Thus a phenomenon such as the experience of color appears in several chapters in this book as befits an experience depending on several levels of processing. Although the higher levels (3 and 4) presented some difficulties because they are not subject to neuroreductionistic analysis, discussion of the organizational and interactive processes still predominated. I hope that this book has successfully established that a hierarchy of processing levels is the most orderly dimension along which a taxonomy of visual perception can be construction. From my perspective this single fact—the inappropriate choice of the criterion of phenomenon rather than the appropriate choice of process—may alone be responsible for much of the chaos that typifies so much of the literature on visual perception. Using process rather than phenomena was the key that helped me personally to disentangle the empirical literature, and I feel I can now see some pattern within the chaos and can much more easily understand where a newly encountered experiment fits into the grand scheme of this science. It is my hope that this taxonomy will also serve a similar function for my readers; indeed, that is the major contribution I hope this book will make.

The main purpose of this epilog, therefore, is to survey broadly what has been discussed in detail in previous chapters. The goal is to extract a list of generalizations that represent the collective implications of this topic as an integrated science rather than the specific details of individual experiments. To do so justifies the empirical research. We seem often to forget that we do not carry out well-controlled univariate experiments solely for their own sake. The reason we perform these sometimes silly experiments (which exist in a microcosm that is so terribly isolated from complex reality) is a practical one: Multidimensional reality makes it difficult for our limited conceptual and research tools to describe what is happening when several variables are simultaneously varying. The impact of each study, no matter how abstract the experimental situation, has to be measured in terms of what it contributes to the overall perspective not what it says in isolation. If one accepts this argument, it is obligatory that some conscious effort be made to extract those broader implications.

In this epilog, I list, without further argument or citation, the major emerging principles of perceptual research as I see them at the conclusion of my studies. This approach, which I have used in the two preceding books in this series (Uttal,

1973, 1978), of course represents a highly personal evaluation, but I do not believe that it is aberrantly idiosyncratic. In my opinion, and in that of many of the perceptual psychologists who have influenced me, the present state of perceptual science is fairly represented by the list of principles presented here. There may be disagreement concerning specific issues or conclusions, but I believe the resulting overall metatheory is one most of my colleagues can accept without great difficulty.

In this epilog, I distinguish between two levels of emerging principle—the metaprinciple and the general principle. The metaprinciple makes a statement that extends across many issues and describes a global aspect of perceptual processing. As its name suggests, a metaprinciple is a major organizing conclusion that encompasses many of the less "general" principles themselves. Metaprinciples are the universals that emerge when one studies visual perception; they reflect the tenets of a global epistemology of visual knowledge acquisition. On the other hand, the less comprehensive "general" principle transcends the conclusions of an individual experiment but is not intended to be quite so universal; it speaks more to the process level than to the level of global doctrine. I do not try to summarize detailed conclusions concerning the effect of particular independent variables on specific dependent variables; that task, I hope, was accomplished in the text of the preceding chapters, in the many detailed discussions of individual experiments, and in the lists of findings that I presented earlier.

B. METAPRINCIPLES OF VISUAL PERCEPTION

The following metaprinciples represent the doctrines and canons of a modern perceptual metatheory. Implicit or explicit, I believe they can be identified in the thinking of most contemporary perceptual scientists. What follows in this section is, in fact, a perceptual credo.

1. Materialistic Realism

Perceptual psychologists consider the external world to be real in the sense that it does not need to be perceived to exist.[1] Pragmatic concerns dictate that the internal perceptual state must be referenced or anchored to the external physical state simply because the latter is measured in less ambiguous and more consistent terms than other perceived stimuli.

---

[1]Much to my surprise, and assuredly to that of many of my colleagues, an argument has now been presented against the kind of radical realism that has heretofore been axiomatic for materialists. d'Espagnat (1979) asserts that modern quantum theory and some of its derivative experiments actually suggest that realism of this genre is not correct!!

2. Psychobiological Monism

Percepts and other mental responses are also real in that, in principle, some neural state must be identifiable with every mental response. No matter how inadequate contemporary neuroreductionistic models may be (the reader should be well aware of my biases in this regard at this point), this should not detract from the fundamental metaphysical premise that mind is based upon the brain—solely, uniquely, and irrefutably. The only foundation for mental process yet known is the neural substrate, and without the brain (or some equally complex logical engine), mental process could not exist. Mind is but one property of the neural functioning of the brain; the two are inseparable. I restate this metaphysical metaprinciple at this point to make absolutely certain that there be no suggestion that my rejection of neurophysiological models of some perceptual processes is also a rejection of the materialistic, physicalistic, and realistic monism implicit in the psychobiological approach to the study of mental processes.

A somewhat subtle corollary of this metaprinciple is that all of the psychoneural processes (i.e., those of Levels 1 through 5) produce perceptual transformations purely as a function of the action of the nervous system. I reject the concept of a transaction or interaction between the stimulus and the brain proposed by some perceptual theorists today. The stimulus is not modified by the brain state—the brain state is modified by the stimulus. Physics makes this unidirectional influence imperative; to assume otherwise is to virtually imply that certain supraphysical principles operate in vision.

3. Methodological Dualism

In spite of my conviction that a radical metaphysical monism is basic to any modern perceptual metatheory, the survey of data and theory presented in this volume has also made it clear that neuroreductionism cannot be applied in most practical situations. The links between neurophysiology and perception are, for the most part, unknown, and the complexity of the neural networks that must be involved in even the simplest percepts is often so great as to preclude any reductionistic analysis. Intrapersonal mind is not directly examinable; only interpersonally communicated behavior can be examined. Thus a modern perceptual metatheory or taxonomy must be methodologically dualistic; that is, it must invoke concepts, methods, and elements from both the neural domain and from a molar domain that is patently nonreductionistic. It must, in other words, be dualistic in its methodology. It must be emphasized again that this is a practical epistemological consideration, and it does not extenuate the psychobiological monism that takes precedence in the metaphysics of modern psychobiology. There is no inconsistency in being a metaphysical monist (in answer to the question of the ultimate nature of reality) and being an epistemological dualist (in answer to the question of the ways in which we can learn about that reality). One result of this epistemological or methodological dualism is that any comprehensive taxonomy or theory of perception must be an eclectic one. Physical, neural, and rational transformations must all be invoked to explain the full range of perceptual phenomena; the perceiving mind must be dealt with as if it were an active, inferential, constructionistic engine in at least part of any metatheory.

Accumulating empirical evidence is beginning to show that both low level deterministic neural and high-level inferential processes can exert similar effects. von Békésy's (1968) invocation of Mach and Hering types of lateral interaction, Turvey's (1973) allusion to peripheral and central masking, and Braddick's (1974) concept of a dual mode of apparent motion detection are contemporary indications of the increasing tendency to invoke what may considered to be both neural and constructionistic processes in perceptual theory.[2] Once again, however, I must warn that the fact that we must treat mind, in at least some cases, as an inferring, constructing, symbolizing, interpreting *process,* does not mean that mind is in any way assignable to some different metaphysical reality than the brain.[3] It only means that the mechanisms underlying those particular high-level processes are beyond our means of analysis, currently and possibly in the future. Rationalism, like statistical mechanics, is a molar expedient that is used when one is faced with enormous complexity or numerosity. Though complex, a rationalistic process is no less a function of the brain, in principle, than one describable in deterministic or empiricistic terms.

4. Multilevel Processing

The next important emerging metaprinciple asserts that perception is the result of transformations that occur at many different levels of processing. I have identified six levels, and it seems evident that each is capable of influencing some aspect of quality, quantity, extent, or duration of the mental responses to external stimulus patterns we call percepts. The implications of this multilevel metaprinciple go far beyond the mere organization of this book. This metaprinciple imples further that there are opportunities at several levels for any aspect of the afferent stimulus information to be transformed. The phenomena of color, for example, cannot be solely attributed to transformations at any single level even though the critical processes that occur at each level can be localized. This means that explanations and theories of perception cannot be limited to either peripheral or central factors alone. Eclectic theory thus reflects the intrinsic biological nature of the process and is not just a taxonomic convenience.

A corollary of this metaprinciple is that because all percepts are multidimensionally caused (i.e., all percepts result from the impact of many dimensions of past and present stimulus scenes), no unidimensional psychophysical law is valid

[2]This is true even though none of these authors expressed the dichotomy in these terms.

[3]An expanded statement of two contradictory points of view concerning the solution to the classic mind–body problem can be found in Popper and Eccles' (1977) and Eccles' (1979) books on the one hand, and in my earlier work (Uttal, 1978) on the other.

except as the roughest of approximations in a ridigly controlled experimental situation. At the very least, and even this may be a poor solution to the problem, expressions describing the relationships between stimuli and perceptual responses must be multidimensional. Other forms of laws that are, for example, statements of the statistical and physical properties of the stimulus alone ignore the basic fact that *perceptual transformations* are the results of the functions of the nervous system and not of the organization of the stimulus. The best "laws" of psychophysics are the theoretical explanations describing the processes that most likely mediate the transformations.

5. Invisible Invariance Computations

Many of the processes described in this book involve the extraction of information or invariances that exist only in terms of the differences between two or more dimensions, presentations, or transformations of the stimulus. The mental computations that must be carried out (in order to construct percepts from stimuli in which the information is not explicit) are themselves extremely elusive objects of scientific inquiry for two reasons. First, they are invisible to the perceiver, who is aware only of the outcome of the process and not the process itself. Second, the process is never directly open to interpersonal examination, and the nature of the process must, in general, be inferred from its outcome. The latter reason imposes a severe restriction under which to search for the characteristics of a putative internal mechanism; many (in fact, an infinite number) analogous mechanisms can produce the same outcome. It is also for this latter reason that the application of mathematics to perceptual analysis is inherently indeterminate. Mathematical theory, in much the same way as behavior, is intrinsically incapable of uniquely specifying the internal structure of a "black box." I cannot stress too strongly, however, that this restriction is not special to psychology. The invisibility of the objects of inquiry is just as common in many other sciences, including the most macroscopic (astronomy) and the most microscopic (basic particle physics). These sciences also must make inferences about the nature of their own invisible realities on the basis of indirect evidence. Their theories can also only be tested for plausibility and consistency; the mathematical models of physics are no more susceptible to tests of exclusive validity than are those of psychology. On the other hand, psychology is no less susceptible to scientific analysis than are any of the simpler sciences.

6. No Need for Isomorphic Representation

Throughout this book, as well as in the literature of sensory coding mechanisms in the peripheral nervous system, there is ample evidence that any dimension of the stimulus or percept may be represented by any dimension of the neural response. The efficacy of symbolic and quasi-cognitive factors in altering the percept is also well demonstrated at the higher levels of perceptual processing.

The impact of all these data is to stress that there need not be a dimensionally isomorphic ''toy in the head'' for there to be a ''picture in the mind''; dimensional isomorphism between the stimulus, the neural response, and the perceptual response is not necessary for the representation of mental experience. Nor, for that matter, neither is isomorphism in a more mathematical sense (i.e., one-for-one mapping from dimension to dimension) necessary. We have seen many instances in which one stimulus may be perceived in a number of ways (e.g., contrast) or, conversely, situations in which a wide variety of stimuli may evoke a single experience (e.g., constancy). Even spatial concepts can be suggested by stimuli in a way that is so compelling that it is often hard to distinghish between the inferred subjective surface or contour and the response to a stimulus that is actually physically present. Stereoscopic space need not be represented by a three-dimensional array of neural circuts in the brain—it is equally well represented, according to this metaprinciple, by a sequence of printed symbols such as c-u-b-e or by an equivalent set of highly transformed neural symbols. Lord Adrian's advice to psychobiologists—''seek isomorphisms''—was simply wrong.

7. The Perceptual Indeterminacy of Stimuli

The multidimensional and inferential nature of perception makes it clear that traditional stimulus–response psychology, although a convenient expedient, also drastically misled psychological theorists in their search for the relationship between the external physical and the internal mental worlds. Percepts are not determined by stimuli but instead are cued by what are, at best, partial and incomplete hints and clues provided by the stream of afferent information in the peripheral communication pathways. Perception is, for the most part, an act of inferential construction—a mental model-making of the external world on the basis of limited, but multidimensional, information. For the most part, true veridicality does not really exist. The degree of veridicality that does exist is, to a large extent, fortuitous and stimulus–response determination is more apparent than real.

A corollary of this metaprinciple is that the visual system does not have a means of adequately dealing with lacunae cum lacunae. Ignorance (missing information) can be as invisible to the perceiver as are the processes that underlie perception. As philosophers have told us for millenia, we cannot appreciate what it means to ''not know''; we usually fill in any missing parts of a stimulus configuration.

C. SOME DISAPPOINTMENTS

These, then, are the major metaprinciples that have emerged during the writing of this book. All of these doctrines are essentially positive and reflect some kind of a conclusion to which I was directed by the press of the data. It would be incomplete, however, if I did not acknowledge that there were some disappointments in carrying out this research—some questions that I posed for which neither I nor anyone else seems to have found satisfactory closure. Even worse, some of these disappointments reflect fundamental uncertainties concerning the possibilities of progress in the immediate future. The following list tabulates some of these disappointments.

1. The Failure of Neuroreductionism

Despite my own theroretical predilections, one cannot escape the fact that neurophysiology does not provide an adequate model for most aspects of perception, nor can one ignore the argument inherent in the data summarized in Chapters 9, 10, and 11. In general, current neural models are less robust than their originators have usually supposed. Many neural models are so remotely linked to the perceptual phenomena they purport to explain that they must be considered to be no more than remote metaphors or distant physical analogies based on neurophysiological, as opposed to hydraulic, concepts. The proportion of the neurophysiologically explicable phenomena versus those that were inexplicable moved ever lower as I proceeded through the task of developing the taxonomy. I have placed many more processes at Level 3 or 4 than I thought I would have at the outset of this project, and like most other perceptual scientists, I have been forced to shift to a nonreductionistic and neorationalistic vocabulary using words like *symbolic, inferential, constructionstic,* and *interpretive* ever more frequently in the discussion of these higher levels of perceptual processing.

It is worthwhile to consider in retrospect what is meant by these terms. All more or less synonymously denote molar mental processes. Their use is required, not because the underlying neural mechanisms are not real and do not exist but because of the complexity of those mechanisms. These terms may be considered to be the names of "programs" implemented by the logic implicit in the unimaginably complex neural networks of the brain. They are the action algorithms of those mechanisms, in other words. These programs or action algorithms do not exist separately from that neural substrate but as a fully determined result of it. Nevertheless, the complexities are beyond us and, despite the metaphysical identity of these molar processes and states of neural networks someplace in the brain, we may be limited for the practical and foreseeable future to this type of descriptive molar analysis.

2. The Failure of Any Theory at the Higher Levels

I must also admit to a profound disappointment with regard to the explanations that were advanced for the more central processes of visual perception surveyed in Chapters 10 and 11. What had been a vague feeling, prior to beginning my studies, became a conviction by the time that research was complete: Solid explanatory theories at these levels of processing are few and far between. We know shockingly little about the mechanisms underlying the powerful ability of the nervous system to integrate various aspects of a stimulus scene, to extract invariances, and to construct or infer what might be a plausible solution to the problem so posed. We saw in Chapters 10 and 11 that the internal logic remained invisible not only to the observer but also to the perceptual psychologist. Instead, heuristic physical analogies and descriptive models, not too far removed in concept or meaning from the data themselves, dominated the "theoretical" scene. We can assume that nonisomorphic computational processes must extract invariances (the fact that we can perceive certain phenomena is a proof of the existence of some such process) but the nature of these processes remains obscure. Few successful efforts have been made to attack directly the great mystery that these intrapersonal processes represent. Although descriptive microtheories abound, no general model yet exists, and although a number of highly complex mathematical descriptions have now begun to appear, their ability to describe the outcome of a process greatly exceeds their ability to give deep insight into its underlying mechanisms. Often, when an analogous mathematical procedure is able to extract the same invariances the perceptual system does, it is mistaken for an explanation of the brain's methods regardless of obvious differences in the strategy used. The pseudoidentification of two equally successful and analogous procedures—one computational and descriptive, one psychological—is without merit as a logical argument for the uniqueness of the descriptive model as an explanation of the psychological processes.

Although the perceptual literature is replete with the statement—"investigation of this particular phenomenon may tell us something in general about visual perception"—very little of general interest has been learned from even the most extensive description of many phenomena. For example, however fascinating the study of geometric illusions may be, it actually tells us little more than the nature of the illusions. This is perhaps the greatest disappointment in the study of visual perception; the manifest failure of generalization from the huge amount of data now available. It is also a major motivation behind the development of a taxonomy of perceptions.

3. The Vast Areas of Ignorance in Perceptual Science.

Despite the enormous amount of empirical research on perceptual topics, the extent of our ignorance in certain areas of this important scientific area is surprising once one delves below the surface of glib superficialities. There are five major distinguishable areas of ignorance. First, as was pointed out in Chapter 9, we know very little about the links between the neurophysiological mechanisms and perceptual processes. How the action of a neuronal net, however complex, can be transformed into a conscious experience is still as much a mystery as it was before the development of today's ultrasophisticated electrophysiological research technology.

Second, we still know very little about the nature of the suppression of the meaning of a stimulus or about its antithesis, the attribution of perceptual reality and significance to a stimulus that is only suggested but not physically present. How can we utilize the information signified by a stimulus without "seeing it," as we seem to do in the construction of apparent motion? How do we see "subjective" contours?

Third, we do not yet understand the nature of the attentive, conscious, and willful manipulations that occur in what I have designated as Level 5 processes but have not discussed in this book. We are not only ignorant, in general, about the processes themselves but also about why these Level 5 manipulations have such a minimal effect on the more automatic processes of the Levels 0 through 4.

Fourth, though perceptual science is well aware of the many interactions that occur between various aspects of the stimulus scene, there have been relatively few systematic programs in which multidimensional interactions were the main object of study. The major empirical effort has been characterized by a paradigm in which all variables except one are held constant, and the effect of that one is then determined. We still know very little about the mechanisms and processes through which multiple dimensions are integrated to influence collectively the perceptual outcome.

Fifth and finally, we know very little about the nature of the internal mental algorithms that actually extract invariances from temporal or spatial arrays of stimuli. Although we can simulate these mechanisms with analogous processes, we have no means yet of determining what is actually going on when these elaborate mental computations are carried out.

In sum, it should be clear from these comments and from the many instances in the text of this book that identified broad disagreements among theorists concerning the origins of various phenomena that there is still an enormous amount of controversy, uncertainty, and ignorance about the processes underlying perceptual mechanisms. There is perhaps no single phenomenon on which there is a universal consensus, even with regard to as fundamental an issue as whether a particular percept is mediated by a central or a peripheral mechanism. Clearly, perceptual science is beset with problems of enormous difficulty, and an appreciation of the legitimacy of alternative and contradictory points of view is mandatory among practitioners in this field. Arrogant dogmatism is especially inappropriate in perceptual science.

4. The Indeterminacy of Mathematical and Behavioral Models with Regard to Internal Structure and Representation

I have alluded several times to the inability of either mathematical models or behavioral data to define uniquely internal structures and mechanisms. This too is a major disappointment, even more so in light of the general analysis of cognitive processes sought by so many of my colleagues today. J. R. Anderson (1978) and Palmer (1978) have both made the same point in a slightly different context. They are concerned with the problem of the nature of the representation of memory-stored information. In recent years considerable controversy has evolved among congitively oriented psychologists concerning the way information is stored in memory. One side suggests a pictorial (imaginal) mode while the other champions a symbolically encoded mode. Arguments for and against isomorphism notwithstanding, Anderson has suggested that it is intrinsically impossible to resolve this issue, a position with which I concur. Despite disagreement with this position (Hayes-Roth, 1979; Pylyshyn, 1979), it seems to me that Anderson's thesis that the issue is unresolvable is impeccable on the most fundamental logical grounds and that none of the tools that psychologists can bring to bear on this problem can possible resolve this particular issue.

5. The Irresolvability of the Issue of the Feasibility of Perceptual Theory

One of the major disappointments as I complete this work is that I have not been able to provide even a preliminary estimate of the likelihood of ever developing a plausible theory of visual perception, i.e., one that is satisfactorily explanatory, reductionistic (in the sense that terms at one level are defined in terms of a lower level, neurophysiological or otherwise), and comprehensive. The dreary outlook for ultimate success of a research effort in this direction may be nothing more than a pessimistic and discouraged response to the state of the science at present rather than a valid epistemological inquiry. Just asking the question raises doubts about the future, but the negative tone can always be countered with a naive and optimistic hope—an attitude that I, like most people, would prefer to embody in my own philosophy. Nevertheless, the issue of the logical and practical limits of our scientific knowledge is a valid one, and it must be dealt with. After all, the Heisenberg uncertainty principle and the speed of light represent real physical limits; a unified perceptual theory may be equally impossible because of similar limits on practical computability or because of the logical difficulties expressed by such rich concepts as Gödel's theorem (see p. 24). We do not know whether perceptual theory is ultimately possible, and the failure to ascertain at least the beginning of a satisfactory answer to the question of plausibility itself is deeply disappointing.

D. GENERAL PRINCIPLES

So far I have tabulated the broad positive metaprinciples of perceptual theory and some of the major negative disappointments that have emerged during the course of this project. There is also a set of somewhat more specific conclusions or percepts that represent a much more detailed view of the meaning of the vast body of perceptual data now available. In the following list, these ''general'' principles are stated as specific examples of the progress perceptual science has made and as an expression of my own personal estimate of the contemporary status of the field. Justification for each of these dogmas (or in some cases heresies) will have to be found in the preceding chapters; their presentation here is without further support. I hope these principles will help readers to establish their own viewpoints whether in agreement or rejection, about each of the individual principles.[4]

1. Perception is defined as the relatively immediate, intrapersonal, mental response evoked as a partial, but not exclusive, result of impinging multidimensional stimuli and modulated by the transforms imposed by the afferent communication system, previous experience, and contextual reasonableness. Each percept is the conscious end product of both simple passive transformations and more complex constructionistic ''interpretations.'' However the underlying neural and symbolic processes are not part of the observer's awareness. Although this definition is not an operational one (I have defined perception as an intrapersonally private event), this is, in fact, the appropriate approach to the problem. This mental process is private and only indirectly observed through the medium of behavior.

2. Visual perception, in large part, is an active process dependent on global properties, multiple dimensions, and the state of the perceiver. Percepts are solutions to the complex problems posed by the stimulus environment and involve processes that give rise to reasonable and plausible models of the external world. They are not passively determined responses to prepotent single stimulus dimensions.

3. Relationships are exceedingly important, not only in terms of the interactions between different parts of the stimulus but also in terms of the relative amount of activity in coded neurons. Percepts in space and time are all ''relativistic'' in this sense. When only a single dimension or code is available and no relational comparisons are possible the result is usually a nonquantitative and ambiguous experience.

4. For millenia philosophers, scientists, and laymen alike have felt a deep-seated urge to explain the phenomena of perception. Such explanations take the

[4]This list of general principles, though probably more extensive than most other previous attempts to tabulate perceptual wisdom, is not unique. Readers who would like to consider other points of view will find briefer examples of similar summaries in Gregory's (1974) chapter in Volume I of Carterette and Friedman's (1974) *Handbook of Perception* and in Rock's (1975) text.

form of theories, a word that does not connote unwarranted speculation or extrapolation but, rather, an integrative extension from the bare facts of individual observations to a comprehensive explanation. Theoretical integration, not the unadorned collection of facts, is the *raison d'être* of science in general and of perceptual science in particular. No perceptual theory, however, has ever withstood the test of time. Theories come and go along with the prevailing technology and scientific Zeitgeist.

5. Historically, theories of perception may be divided into two major classes: The first includes those theories that are empiricistic, passive, and deterministic; the second includes those that are rationalistic, constructionistic, interpretive, inferential, and active. Both classes of theory are presently required in order to give a comprehensive explanation of visual perception. The ebb and flow of both over the years is ample evidence of their respective contributions.

6. Perceptual theories typically deal with a restricted universe of experimental data. As such they often do not intercommunicate with each other and are, for the most part, highly restrictive in their coverage. Macrotheories of perception are therefore not in general antagonistic to each other; rather, in most instances, they are complementary and/or supplementary.

7. The major characteristics of any macrotheory of perception can be characterized by its position in a three-dimensional query space that depicts the stance of each theory's response to three great questions: (a) Is perception mainly innate or mainly learned? (b) Is perception mainly empiricistic or mainly rationalistic? and (c) Is perception mainly holistic or mainly elementalistic?

8. There is a wide variety of empirical, logical, and conceptual obstacles to theory development in perceptual psychology. An appreciation of the nature of these obstacles leads us to understand why the search for satisfactory explanation has been so difficult. The only practical response to these difficulties at present is a multilevel, eclectic, taxonomic theory of the kind presented in this book. In fact, this is the consensus; no alternatives exist, and all perceptual metatheoreticians are implicitly or explicitly multilevel and eclectic, if not taxonomic, in their approach.

9. The key to a satisfactory taxonomic theory is the concept of the critical process—a transformation that alters the information content of an afferent signal, not in terms of the neural language in which it is encoded but in terms of its meaning or significance. Many processes and transformations within the nervous system are not critical in this sense but may simply be changes in code without changes in meaning. The definition of a critical process also implies the existence

of an isolable critical level at which that process occurs. The particular criteria for each level of processing are:

Level 0: The critical process transforming the distal stimulus to the proximal stimulus occurs in the physical environment prior to sensory transduction.

Level 1: The critical process occurs in the receptor cells.

Level 2: The critical process occurs as a result of interneural interactions in simple neuronal nets.

Level 3: The critical process is essentially dependent on a single dimension or aspect of the stimulus and results in a nonquantitative experience. (The complexity of the process exceeds neuroreductionistic plausibility from Level 3 onwards.)

Level 4: The critical process is essentially dependent on multiple dimensions or aspects of the stimulus and results in a quantitative experience.

Level 5: The critical process, unlike the preceding levels, requires an attentive effort.

10. The concept of processing levels may say something about the constraints and transformations that the nervous system imposes on the flow of coded information, but it does not say anything about the level at which psychoneural identity occurs, i.e., where the neural equivalent of a perceptual experience is actually located. Many studies of the nervous system show a correlation, transformation, or analysis of an afferent signal at one or another level, but this does not mean that such a locus is the site of the psychoneural equivalent of the resulting percept. The fact that information is encoded at all levels does not mean that psychoneural identity between perceptions and neural states exists at all levels.

11. The anatomy of the retina shows that elaborate information processing occurs within the eye, but it is unlikely that an isolated eye would be able to perceive anything. It simply modulates the incoming signal, sharpens contours, and removes redundant information among other transformations. Similar neural net processes occur at other levels of the visual pathway.

12. The initial photochemical reaction in vision is well understood as the isomerization of rhodopsin from the stable 11-*cis* form to the unstable all-*trans* form. All subsequent photochemical processes are thermally-driven dark reactions following their course without further photic stimulation. This isomerization is the "primary sensory action" in vision.

13. There appear to be multiple pathways from the eye to the brain. The retinallateral geniculate-cortical pathway seems to be concerned mostly with

fine-form perception, and the retinal-collicular-cortical pathway seems to be associated with eye movements (foveation), alerting, and general orientation. As many as a dozen visual pathways are to be found in some vertebrates, and in mammalian brains many cortical areas are devoted to vision. The functions of all of the various areas are not definitively known.

14. Many perceptual phenomena are wrongly attributed to processes within this multilevel processing system when, in fact, they are the result of highly veridical responses of the perceptual system to transformations that occur prior to the initial sensory transduction. These preneural transformations, referred to as Level 0 processes, may have colossal perceptual impact, but they do not say anything about the properties of the perceptual system. Level 0 processes have been generically referred to as *mirages* in this book to contrast them with the *illusions* produced by nonveridical transformations within the nervous system.

15. The first level of truly perceptual processing occurs in the receptors, where physical energy from the external world is transduced and encoded into the electrochemical energies of the nervous system. Both the photochemical and neural properties of the receptor can affect perceptual experience.

16. Rushton's law of univariance, a corollary of Müller's law of specific energies, is fundamental to understanding photoreceptor action. This law states that once transduced the neural signal carries no trace of the wavelength or intensity of the stimulating photic energy.

17. The absolute energy threshold of a single receptor appears to approximate closely that of a single quantum of light; and in some cases the whole observer appears to be also sensitive to even this low level of energy. Therefore, the human visual system is very close to being as sensitive as it possible can be in the context of modern quantum theory.

18. Temporal summation may sometimes mimic spatial summation in the retina. Both occur within limits, however, leading to the postulation of such hypothetical entities as the "area of spatial summation" and the "critical duration." In fact, however, both of these entities may represent regions of interaction probability rather than sharply demarcated spatial or temporal regions.

19. The absorption spectra of the receptor photochemicals, the state of adaptation, and the availability of receptors account for a wide variety of perceptual phenomena, including the luminosity curves, trichromatic color addition, increment thresholds, and abnormal color vision. However none of these responses is totally determined by the stimulus or the momentary state of the peripheral portions of the perceptual system, both of which can be overridden by higher levels of processing.

20. The three dimensions of the chromatic stimulus (dominant wavelength, spectral purity, and luminosity) all jointly affect the three dimensions of the perceptual response (hue, saturation, and brightness). Thus there is no strict association between any single attribute of the stimulus and any single attribute of the chromatic response.

21. Though a fundamental limit on visual acuity is set by the size and density of the receptor mosaic, other factors, such as neural convergence, contribute to visual acuity. On the other hand, hyperacuity as exemplified by vernier acuity, and which seems at first glance to exceed the limits set by the properties of the retinal mosaic, may result from quasi-statistical processing at a considerably higher level of the perceptual system.

22. Extreme depletion of the photochemical must occur before the threshold is affected. The fact that measurable effects of adaptation can be obtained at relatively low light levels (at which photochemical depletion is modest) is a compelling indication that there must be both photochemical and neural components to light and dark adaptation and that the neural processes dominate at low to moderate luminance levels.

23. The suprathreshold dynamics of the function relating perceptual magnitudes and stimulus intensity appears also to result at least in part from receptor-level processes. In this case, however, the function is a result of the dynamic compression occurring in the neural mechanisms subsequent to the receptor's photoabsorption process rather than of photoreception itself. Higher levels of processing, without doubt, also contribute to the suprathreshold function.

24. Whereas information conducted along the sensory communication pathways does not entirely define the percept any more than do the properties of the receptors, the characteristics of the pathways also constrain and modulate what is seen and can leave their own traces in the perceptual response.

25. Afferent neural codes and representations need not be dimensionally isomorphic to the percept. This is sometimes forgotten when dealing with spatial forms for which there is a natural isomorphism in the peripheral portions of the system. However colors are certainly not coded by isomorphic representations (perceived colors are not dimensionally the same as photon wavelength); this disassociation raises doubts about the necessity of isomorphism where it does fortuitously occur, for example, in the spatial domain. The ubiquitous disassociations of perceptual and neural dimensions found elsewhere strongly suggest that all experiences can be represented by nonisomorphically encoded stimuli.

26. Current neuroreductionistic theories of "perception" are more applicable as descriptions of the properties and capabilities of the peripheral communication

network than of the more central aspects ofintegration and psychoneural equivalence.

27. All psychophysical tests are influenced by two kinds of processes: (a) the sensory or discriminatory processes; and (b) the criterion-selection processes. Superimposed on the determinations of sensory limits are the criteria applied by the observer to determine what will be accepted as a valid stimulus. Analyses using signal detection theory are unique in that they tease these two processes apart in a way that allows them to be measured independently. Forced-choice experimental design minimizes the criteria effects.

28. Perceptual time displays some peculiar qualities. It apparently is not always processed in the same way as external clock time. Phenomena can occur in reverse order to stimuli. For example, apparent motion occurs in a direction that is defined by the ''awareness'' of where a second stimulus is but well before that stimulus is ''perceived'' as being there. We clearly do not yet understand the relation between psychological and physical time.

29. It is extremely difficult to attribute temporal processes to a particular level of processing because of a fundamental difficulty, namely that receptor (Level 1) and neural network (Level 2) processes may either be redundant or, though produced at the receptor level, indistinguishably exhibited at both neural levels.

30. In general, the neural and perceptual responses to even the briefest stimulus are substantially prolonged. The prolongation is progressive as the signal ascends the afferent pathways and more and more neurons become involved. Many perceptual effects can be directly attributed to this prolongation of the neural response. Most obvious examples include a decline in temporal resolvability, an increase in apparent duration, afterimages, iconic storage, and temporal summation.

31. Other perceptual phenomena, such as the elongation of reaction times with decreased stimulus intensities and the Pulfrich effect, seem to be in part attributable to variations in the latency of the peripheral neural response.

32. Several distinguishable classes of visual masking exist. Though examined in the context of a single experimental paradigm—sequential presentation—the various kinds of masking arise from vastly different underlying processes scattered through all levels of the perceptual system. The main classes of masking are:

a. Bright flash masking.
b. Camouflage as a result of figural summation.

c. Signal diminution as a result of lateral inhibitory interaction.
d. Textural masking.
e. Masking as a result of Gestalt grouping.
f. Metacontrast.

A considerable amount of confusion exists in the perceptual literature because these phenomena are not usually distinguished as the respective outcomes of different processes but are uncritically identified with each other on the basis of the common experimental design. This is another example of the logical disorder that can result if one bases one's classification of perception on phenomena or on experimental design rather than on the best possible judgment of underlying processes.

33. Simple neural interactive mechanisms such as convergence, divergence, and reciprocal summatory and inhibitory interactions represent the logical elements in the brain's computational system. It is clear that all other mental processes are generated from these simple logical elements by myraid concatenation. From one point of view, all higher-level perceptual and other mental processes are, therefore, Level 2 neural network interactions. Higher levels of processing, framed in the vocabulary of psychological, rationalistic, and molar terms, do not deny this fundamental neuroreductionistic reality only the practical difficulty of attacking the problem at this level.

34. Lateral inhibitory interactions play an important role in reducing the redundancy of the transmitted neural signal by emphasizing contours. This contour intensification modifies the signal in a way that is perceptually significant. Among other phenomena, simple neural network interactions result in such illusions as the Mach bands and the Hermann grid.

35. Neural convergence (lateral excitatory interaction) is the proximal cause of a number of perceptual phenomena. These include spatial summation, limited spatial acuity, and color blindness in the periphery of the normal retina. Lateral inhibitory interactions appear to be the proximal causes of several kinds of spatial inhibitions, including those occurring between small spots and within larger spots and at edges, contours, and gradients.

36. Although there was some initial suggestion that each of the four kinds of retinal photoreceptors interacted only with their own kind, it now seems certain that interactions occur among the four types as well as within types. Such interactive processes are necessarily implicated in the recoding that occurs as information passes from the trichromatic receptors to the opponent bipolar cells.

37. Neural interaction mechanisms in the retinal plexus must also be invoked to explain fully dark adaptation and phosphenes.

38. Neural interactions leave traces in the afferent signal that affect subsequent perceptual constructions. These traces are mediated by actual denotative alterations of the afferent sensory signal; i.e., the significance of the communicated information is changed, it is not just recoded by these transformations. These neural interaction processes are the prototypes of the deterministic, passive, empiricistic processes that occur throughout the perceptual system.

39. Though a wide variety of neuroreductionistic explanations of other perceptual phenomena have been based on the same neural interaction concepts to which I have just alluded, there is in fact an abundance of evidence that many of these models exhibit only the loosest kind of physical analogy with perceptual processes. These analogies are based only upon similarities of form; they are often devoid of the solid empirical and conceptual links required for a definitive explanation of perceptual performance. Many phenomena, often attributed to simple neural interactions, exhibit properties totally inconsistent with such an approach. A wide variety of empirical counterindications denude many such neuroreductionistic "dogma" of any validity. This has led to some counter-dogma (or heresies) that are becoming increasingly palatable to an ever larger number of perceptual scientists.

40. A modern metaphysical monism must accept the facts that the proximal cause of most perceptual phenomena is the state of activity in a very large number of neurons and that the statistics of these networks is so complex as to require a molar and rationalistic approach to most of the problems of perceptual science. In perceptually significant neural networks, no neuron is uniquely necessary, and most neurons probably are involved simultaneously in many processes. For these reasons, and because of simple numerosity, real neural networks probably must be classified as representing intrinsically noncomputable problems even though they are formally finite.

41. Though neural nets may simulate continuous field processes and action at a distance because of their small size and great numerosity, the fundamental logical manipulation in such nets is discrete and only locally interactive.

42. The higher levels of perceptual processing are characterized by a lack of linear veridicality; that is, perceptual responses tend not to replicate independently obtained estimates of the dimensions of the stimulus array. For example, the perceptual dimension may be profoundly dissociated from the stimulus dimension with which a priori it would have been expected to have been most closely related; the percept may not vary with wide variations in the stimulus, or conversely it may vary even though the stimulus remains constant.

43. Level 3 processes seem to represent a qualitative stage of processing that must occur prior to Level 4 processes. However the idea of a sequence of

perceptual processing from Level 3 to Level 4 is not clear cut; both levels may occur simultaneously or in a way in which order does not matter. Nevertheless, the key phenomenal outcome of a Level 3 process is the qualitative segregation of the component parts of a complex scene and the organization of those parts into, among other formats, figure and ground.

44. Both surface cues (textural and chromatic properties) and contours can help to segregate areas of a visual scene.

45. The human observer seems capable of perceptually processing the statistical properties of a texture only up to the second order. Although differences in density (first-order statistics) and distribution eveness (second-order statistics) seem to be quite discriminable, in only a few exceptional cases can differences in third-order statistics be discriminated. The fact that our language has no simple words comparable to *density* and *evenness* with which to describe third-order statistics is another indication that we cannot directly (i.e., immediately) process variations in this statistical order.

46. Both textural gradients and stimulus motion (across the retina) seem to be necessary for continued operation of the visual system. For reasons that probably span several levels of processing, retinal images that are stabilized in either time or in texture quickly (in a few seconds) fade away.

47. Regularities and periodicities of organization seem to be powerful cues for extracting patterns from irregular backgrounds even when the patterns and the background are composed of identical elements.

48. Monocular stimuli that are ambiguous or dichoptic stimuli which are different tend to be alternatively perceived. The rate of reversal depends on many different factors that clearly have nothing to do with any simple neural network type of inhibitory interaction or with the physical properties of the stimulus.

49. Elements of a figure tend to be organized as described by the classic Gestalt laws of grouping. We have no idea what processes and mechanisms mediate these organizational actions. In general, however, the "better" the figure the easier it is perceived or remembered. There is a gradual tendency for figures to improve in "goodness" the longer they reside in memory.

50. Many compelling percepts can be generated from very incomplete stimuli as a result of constructionistic processes sensitive to "suggestions" made by other portions of the stimulus. Perceptual filling, closure, and subjective contours and surfaces all represent percepts that go beyond the information explicitly carried by the stimulus. The extraordinary fact is that the processes underlying these constructs can themselves exert powerful influence on other perceptual

processes. For example, a subjectively generated contour can often mask or inhibit a real contour just as well as a real contour can.

51. Many figural organization processes demonstrate a remarkable insensitivity to the physical properties of the stimulus. Familiarity with the stimuli may be a stronger cue than stimulus luminance in some cases. The physical attributes of the stimuli seem to have become informationally saturated long before Levels 3 and 4, and other organizational, meaningful, and cognitive factors dominate at these higher levels.

52. Impossible figures are not impossible to perceive. Rather, these are examples of figures in which there is a clash of cues producing specific and well-defined reversals as the observer selectively attends to the respective inconsistent parts. In general, the perception is quite veridical to whatever part of the paradoxical figure attention is directed.

53. All Level 3 and Level 4 processes reflect the ability of the perceptual system to perform complex analysis and to extract invariances by carrying out extensive computations. However the nature of the logical steps by which these computations are carried out remains obscure. By no stretch of the imagination does a stimulation of such processes (e.g., in an artificial intelligence experiment) provide a definitive description of the algorithm actually used by the brain. In fact, an infinite number of possible algorithms may underlie any perceptual phenomenon, all of which can effectively extract the same invariances with greater or lesser efficiency. Such simulations only test the plausibility of one of that infinite number of possibilities. However, careful simulations can highlight the general nature of the task and specifically identify the kind of processing steps that must be achieved to extract the invariances.

54. Quantitative experience of any perceptual dimension seems to depend on relative comparisons of two or more dimensions or aspects of the stimulus scene. A stimulus in which all but a single dimension have been removed (by minimizing contextual cues) is essentially ambiguous and leads to percepts that are highly uncertain and ill defined.

55. An inhibitory interaction can take place between the meanings or significances of two stimuli equally as well as between two spatial patterns. Such a conclusion further implies that symbolic rather than isomorphic encoding is probably ubiquitous in the perceptual system.

56. In general, Level 4 spatial interactions seem to be broadly global and not to be functions of distance as are analogous Level 2 spatial interactions. A very minor modification of the physical stimulus, such as the introduction of a thread-like contour, can often alter a percept mediated by a Level 4 process in astonish-

ing ways. Such a result clearly argues against simple, spatial, Level 2 models of such processes as simultaneous contrast.

57. In general. simplistic unidimensional arithmetic laws of the form $\psi = f(S)$ are misleading and hold only in highly impoverished experimental situations.

58. Geometric visual illusions appear to be remarkably insensitive to cognitive or experiential interference yet still exhibit many properties of interpretive construction. Many illusions of this type are intimately related to perceptual constancy and may be abortive attempts to maintain some perceptual dimension at its normative value. Illusions may, therefore, be examples of erroneous, maladaptive, and extraneous responses that arise under certain conditions for which the perceptual system has evolved useful mechanisms to handle other, more ecologically significant tasks.

59. The magnitude of many illusions depends on the orientation of the pattern. Variations in magnitude may be enormous, perhaps magnifying the effect eightfold when the figure is horizontally or vertically rather than obliquely oriented. Such a variation is totally inconsistent with any neuroanatomically identified anisotropy of the retinal plexus or any other known neural net.

60. Perceived space is best described as non-euclidean, even though the external stimulus environment (at the level of common experience) is euclidean. The transformation from a physical euclidean space to a perceived Riemannian space is itself a visual "illusion." As in the macroscopic space–time described by Einsteinian general relativity, perceptual distortion is closely related to the presence of objects in the stimulus space.

61. Many cues to depth exist. Some are monocular and some are binocular. The most compelling cue is the spatial disparity that exists between the projections of images on the two retinae. All depth cues seem to involve some kind of a relative comparison.

62. Disparity-driven stereopsis is explicable neither in terms of suppression nor fusion. A theory incorporating highly nonlinear constructions based on the extraction of disparity-borne invariances comes closer to modeling validly the stereoscopic process. Unlike most other Level 4 processes, this informational (as opposed to image) fusion process now appears to have a relatively well-understood neural basis in terms of binocularly responsive neurons directly sensitive to disparities.

63. Panum's fusional areas and corresponding points, concepts used to explain dichoptic stereopsis, appear to be functional rather than true anatomic

entities. Further evidence that this is so lies in the fact that there is no fixed threshold for stereoscopic fusion. Instead, the disparity at which dichoptic stimuli will "break away" or fuse seems to depend on the conditions of the viewing situation.

64. The search for possible ghost images in the coded representation of stereoscopic perception is a search for a chimera, stimulated by the mistaken idea that spatial perception must be modeled by spatially isomorphic neural models in the brain. In fact, ambiguous stimuli of this sort are resolved (as are all other ambiguous stimuli) by interpretive mechanisms that construct a single stable or quasi-stable perceptual state from among the plausible alternatives. Ghost images do not exist except in the mind of the hyperisomorphic theorist.

65. Many kinds of temporal interactions exist that seem to transcend simple temporal recovery from satiation. The course of recovery of an aftereffect is often coningent on the presentation of the test stimulus; the aftereffect may persist for extraordinarily long periods of time in the absence of a test. This outcome, among others, argues against any simple fatigue or satiation explanation of aftereffects.

66. Apparent motion is not the only perceptual response possible when two stimuli are presented in quick succession. In addition to apparent motion, a plastic deformation of the first into the second stimulus may occur when the two are not identical in shape. In this case, all intermediate shapes are perceived as the first is transformed into the latter even though there is no physical correlate of any of these intermediate shapes. In general, many other Level 3 and Level 4 processes result in percepts that have no physical correlates and thus must reflect the outcome of some constructionistic or inferential processes in which the stimulus does not determine but, rather, only cues the construction of a "plausible" perceptual experience.

67. Many perceptual phenomena are affected by multiple dimensions of the *stimulus*. In many previous theories it has been fashionable to attribute such phenomena to the interaction between different dimensions of the perceptual *response*. This has been shown to be incorrect in principle. For example, even though apparent size may seem to be affected by apparent distance, the logic is in fact compelling that it is actually affected by a single stimulus dimension that simultaneously influences both apparent distance and apparent size. In other words, there are multiple stimulus influences on a percept not interactions between percepts. Such interresponse interaction would imply a dualism that is not palatable to modern psychobiological monisms.

These, then, are the general principles that have emerged during my research for this book. Many other more specific facts or relationships have been detailed in the various lists, tables, and discussions in this book, and still others can be found in the much larger body of knowledge that exists in the experimental literature that I was not able to review. It would be ostentatious for me to claim that either the enormous literature in this field or the taxonomy and summary that I have presented here have really brought us much closer to solving the great epistemological question of how we gain information about the external world. What we do know now is that perceptual science, particularly at the higher levels, is primarily a descriptive rather than a reductive or analytic science. In the main, the nature of the processes that underlie the graphs and equations describing the phenomena that fill the literature remains obscure. This is especially sad because neither descriptions of the phenomena nor measurement of the functional relations between stimuli and phenomena are the essential answers to the great epistemological perplexity. Ultimately, the solution to this great problem must be framed in terms of the processes that account for those relations—an understanding of why and how we see, rather than what we see.

I sincerely believe that the development of a satisfactory taxonomy will play an important antecedent role in developing such an understanding about perceptual processes. But it must not be forgotten that a taxonomy is not an explanatory theory in the truest sense of the word. It is, at best, a prototheory that may provide some of the organization that is necessary before a truly analytic and reductionistic explanation can be constructed. If this book no more than raises our awareness of the need for an acceptable taxonomy and thus begins to set the stage for that next step in the development of perceptual science, it will have achieved the primary goals I had set for it at the outset.

REFERENCES

Abadi, R. V. Induction masking—a study of some inhibitory interactions during dichoptic viewing. *Vision Research,* 1976, *16* 269–275.

Abelson, H. *Computational geometry of linear threshold functions.* (Artificial Intelligence Memo No. 76) Cambridge, Mass.: MIT Press, 1976.

Abelson, R. P. The structure of belief systems. In R. C. Schank and K. M. Colby (Eds.), *Computer models of thought and language.* San Francisco: Freeman, 1973.

Abney, W. *Researchers in colour vision and the trichromatic theory.* London: Longmans, Green, 1913.

Aborn, M., & Rubenstein, H. Information theory and immediate recall. *Journal of Experimental Psychology,* 1952, *44,* 260–266.

Adelson, E. H. Iconic storage: The role of the rods. *Science,* 1978, *201,* 544–546.

Adolph, A. R. Spontaneous slow potential fluctuations in the *Limulus* photoreceptor. *Journal of General Physiology,* 1964, *48,* 297–322.

Ahern, S., & Beatty, J. Pupillary responses during information processes vary with scholastic aptitude scores. *Science,* 1979, *205,* 1289–1292.

Allman, J. M., & Kaas, J. H. The organization of the second visual area (VII) in the owl monkey: A second order transformation of the visual hemifield. *Brain Research,* 1974, *76,* 247–265. (a)

Allman, J. M., & Kaas, J. H. A visual area adjoining the second visual area (VII) on the medial wall of the parieto-occipital cortex of the owl monkey (Aotus trivirgatus). *Anatomical Record,* 1974, *178,* 297–298. (b)

Allman, J. M., & Kaas, J. H. Representation of the visual field on the medial wall of occipital–parietal cortex in the owl monkey. *Science,* 1976, *191,* 572–575.

Allport, D. A. Phenomenal simultaneity and the perceptual moment hypothesis. *British Journal of Psychology,* 1968, *59,* 395–406.

Allport, F. H. *Theories of perception and the concept of structure.* New York: Wiley, 1955.

Alpern, M. Metacontrast. *Journal of the Optical Society of America,* 1953, *43,* 648–657.

Alpern, M. Relation of visual latency to intensity. *Archives of Ophthalmology,* 1954, *51,* 369–374.

Alpern, M. Simultaneous brightness contrast for flashes of light of different durations. *Investigative Ophthalmology,* 1963, *2,* 47–54.

Alpern, M. Rod–cone independence in the after-flash effect. *Journal of Physiology,* 1965, *176,* 462–472.

Alpern, M. Movements of the eyes. In H. Davson (ed.), *The eye.* 2nd ed. Vol 3. *Muscular mechanisms.* New York: Academic Press, 1969.

Alpern, M. What is that confines in a world without color? *Investigative Ophthalmology,* 1974, *13,* 648–674.

Alpern, M., & Barr, L. Durations of the after-images of brief light flashes and the theory of the Broca and Sulzer phenomenon. *Journal of the Optical Society of America,* 1962, *52,* 219–221.

Alpern, M., & Campbell, F. W. The spectral sensitivity of the consensual light reflex. *Journal of Physiology,* 1962, *164,* 478–507.

Alpern, M., & Dudley, D. The blue arcs of the retina. *Journal of General Physiology,* 1966, *49,* 405–421.

Alpern, M., & Rushton, W. A. H. The specificity of the cone interaction in the after-flash effect. *Journal of Physilogy,* 1965, *176,* 473–482.

Alpern, M., & Sugiyama, S. Photic driving of the critical flicker frequency. *Journal of the Optical Society of America,* 1961, *51,* 1379–1385.

Ames, A. Visual perception and the rotating trapezoidal window. *Psychological Monographs,* 1951, *65*(Whole No. 324).

Anderson, D. A., Huntington, J., & Simonson, E. Critical flicker frequency as a function of exposure time. *Journal of the Optical Society of America,* 1966, *56,* 1607–1611.

Anderson, D. H., & Fisher. S. K. Disc shedding in rodlike and conelike photoreceptors of tree squirrels. *Science,* 1975, *187,* 953–954.

Anderson, D. H., & Fisher, S. K. The photoreceptors of diurnal squirrels: Outer segment structure, disc shedding, and protein renewal. *Journal of Ultrastructure Research,* 1976, *55,* 119–141.

Anderson, J. A., Silverstein, J. W., Ritz, S. A., & Jones, R. S. Distinctive features, categorical perception, and probability learning: Some applications of a neural model. *Psychological Review,* 1977, *84.* 413–451.

Anderson, J. R. Arguments concerning representation for mental imagery. *Psychological Review,* 1978, *85,* 249–277.

Anderson, J. R., & Bower, G. H. *Human associative memory.* Washington, D.C.: Hemisphere Press, 1973.

Anderson, V. O., Buchmann, B., & Lennox-Buchthal, M. A. Single cortical units with narrow spectral sensitivity in monkey (*Cercocebus Torquatus Atys*). *Vision Research,* 1962, *2,* 295–307.

Andreassi, J. L., Mayzner, M. S., Beyda, D., & Waxman, J. Sequential blanking: A U-shaped function. *Psychonomic Science,* 1970, *18,* 319–321.

Andrews, D. P. Perception of contours in the central fovea, Part I: Short lines. *Vision Research,* 1967, *7,* 975–997. (a)

Andrews, D. P. Perception of contours in the central fovea, Part II: Spatial integration. *Vision Research,* 1967, *7,* 999–1013. (b)

Andrews, H. C. *Computer techniques in image processing*. New York: Academic Press, 1970.

Anstis, S. M. A chart demonstrating variations in acuity with retinal position. *Vision Research,* 1974, *14,* 589-592.

Anstis, S. M. Apparent movement. In R. Held, H. W. Leibowitz, & H. L. Teuber, (Eds.) *Handbook of sensory physiology: Perception (Vol. 8),* Berlin: Springer-Verlag, 1978.

Anstis, S. M., & Gregory, R. L. The aftereffect of seen motion: The role of retinal stimulation and of eye movements. *Quarterly Journal of Experimental Psychology,* 1965, *17,* 173-174.

Anstis, S. M., Howard, I. P., & Rogers, B. A Craik-O'Brien-Cornsweet illusion for visual depth. *Vision Research,* 1978, *18,* 213-217.

Anstis, S. M., & Moulden, B. P. Aftereffect of seen movement: Evidence for peripheral and central components. *Quarterly Journal of Experimental Psychology,* 1970, *22,* 222-229.

Anstis, S. M., & Reinhardt-Rutland, A. H. Interactions between motion aftereffects and induced movement. *Vision Research,* 1976, *16,* 1391-1394.

Anstis, S. M., & Rogers, B. J. Illusory reversal of visual depths and movement during changes of contrast. *Vision Research,* 1975, *15,* 957-961.

Arand, D., & Dember, W. N. Masking effectiveness and number of segments in the masking ring. *Bulletin of the Psychonomic Society,* 1974, *3,* 127-128.

Arand, D., & Dember, W. N. Metacontrast with internal contours in target and mask. *Bulletin of the Psychonomic Society,* 1976, *7,* 370-372.

Arbib, M. A. Parallelism, slides, schemas and frames. In M. A. Arbib, *Two papers on schema and frames* (COINS Technical Report 75C-9). Department of Computer and Information Sciences, Amherst: University of Massachusetts, 1975.

Arbib, M. A., & Riseman, E. M. *Computational techniques in visual systems, Part I: The overall design* (COINS Technical Report 76-10). Department of Computer and Information Sciences, Amherst: University of Massachusetts, 1976.

Arden, G. B., & Weale, R. A. Variations of the latent period of vision. *Proceedings of the Royal Society of London, Series B,* 1954, *142,* 258-267.

Arend, W. E. Spatial factors in the Broca-Sulzer phenomenon. *Journal of the Optical Society of America,* 1973, *63*(7), 879-883.

Armstrong, D. M. *Berkeley's theory of vision*. Melbourne: Melbourne University Press, 1960.

Armstrong, D. M. *Perception and the physical world.* Atlantic Highlands, N.J.: Humanities Press, 1970.

Arnheim, R. *Art and visual perception*. Berkeley, Los Angeles: University of California Press, 1971.

Arnulf, A., & Dupuy, O. La transmission des contrastes par le systeme optique de l'oeil les seuils de contrastes retiniens. *Academie Des Sciences, Paris, Comptes Rendus,* 1960, *250,* 2757-2759.

Aschenbrenner, C. M. Problems in getting information into and out of air photographs. *Photogrammetric Engineering,* 1954, *20,* 398-401.

Atkinson, J. The effect of size, retinal locus, and orientation on the visubility of a single afterimage. *Perception & Psychophysics,* 1972, *12,* 213-217. (a)

Atkinson, J. Visibility of an afterimage in the presence of a second afterimage. *Perception & Psychophysics,* 1972, *12,* 257-262. (b)

Atkinson, R. C., & Shiffrin, R. M. Human memory: A proposed system and its control process. In K. W. Spence & J. T. Spence (Eds.), *The psychology of learning and motivation.* New York: Academic Press, 1968.

Attneave, F. Some informational aspects of visual perception. *Psychological Review,* 1954, 61, 183-193.

Attenave, F. *Applications of information theory to psychology*. New York: Holt, Rinehart, & Winston, 1959.

Attneave, F. Perception and related areas. In S. Koch (Ed.), *Psychology: A study of a science* (Vol. 4). New York: McGraw-Hill, 1962.

Attneave, F. Multistability in Perception. *Scientific American,* 1971, *225*(6), 62–71.

Attneave, F., & Arnoult, M. D. The quantitative study of shape and pattern perception. *Psychological Bulletin,* 1956, *53,* 452–471.

Attneave, F., & Block, G. Apparent movement in tridimensional space. *Perception & Psychophysics,* 1973, *13,* 301–307.

Aulhorn, E., & Harms, H. Visual perimetry. In D. Jameson & L. M. Hurvich (Eds.), *Handbook of sensory physiology: Visual psychophysics* (Vol. VII/4). New York: Springer-Verlag, 1972.

Auslander, L., & Mackenzie, R. E. *Introduction to differentiable manifolds.* New York: McGraw-Hill, 1963.

Avant, L. L., & Helson, H. Theories of perception. In B. B. Wolman (Ed.), *Handbook of General Psychology.* Englewood Cliffs, N.J.: Prentice-Hall, 1973.

Avery, G. C., & Day, R. H. Basis of the horizontal–vertical illusion. *Journal of Experimental Psychology,* 1969, *81,* 376–380.

Bachmann, T. Cognitive contours: Overview and a preliminary theory. In J. Allik, M. Kotik, A. Lunge, & K. Toim (Eds.), *Problems of communication and perception 474.* Tartu, Estonia, U. S. S. R.: Tartu State University, 1978.

Bachmann, T., & Allik, J. Integration and interruption in the masking of form by form. *Perception,* 1976, *5,* 79–97.

Bacon, J., & King-Smith, P. E. The detection of line segments. *Perception,* 1977, *6,* 125–131.

Baker, H. D. Initial stages of dark and light adaptation. *Journal of the Optical Society of America,* 1963, *53,* 98–103.

Baker, T. Y., & Bryan, G. B. Errors of observation. *Proceedings of the Optical Convention 2.* London: Hodder & Stoughton, 1912.

Banks, W. P., & Barber, G. Color information in iconic memory. *Psychological Review,* 1977, *84,* 536–546.

Banks, W. P., Bodinger, D., & Illige, M. Visual detection accuracy and target noise proximity. *Bulletin of the Psychonomic Society,* 1974, *2,* 411–414.

Banks, W. P., & Prinzmetal, W. Configurational effects in visual information processing. *Perception & Psychophysics,* 1976, *19,* 361–367.

Barlow, H. B. Retinal noise and absolute threshold. *Journal of the Optical Society of America,* 1956, *46,* 634–639.

Barlow, H. B. Increment thresholds at low intensities considered as signal/noise discriminations. *Journal of Physiology,* 1957, *136,* 469–488.

Barlow, H. B. Temporal and spatial summation in human vision at different background intensities. *Journal of Physiology,* 1958, *141,* 337–350.

Barlow, H. B. The physical limits of visual discrimination. In A. C. Geise (Ed.), *Photophysiology* (Vol. 2). New York: Academic Press, 1964.

Barlow, H. B. Single units and sensation: A neuron doctrine for perceptual psychology *Perception,* 1972, *1,* 371–394.

Barlow, H. B. The efficiency of detecting ranges of density in random dot patterns. *Vision Research,* 1978, *18,* 637–650.

Barlow, H. B., Blakemore, C., & Pettigrew, J. D. The neural mechanism of binocular depth discrimination. *Journal of Physiology,* 1967, *193,* 327–342.

Barlow, H. B., & Hill, R. M. Evidence for a physiological explanation of the waterfall illusion and figural aftereffects. *Nature,* 1963, *200,* 1434–1435.

Barlow, H. B., & Levick, W. R. The mechanism of directionality selective units in the rabbit's retina. *Journal of Physiology,* 1965, *178,* 477–504.

Barlow, H. B., & Levick, W. R. Three factors limiting the reliable detection of light by retinal ganglion cells of the cat. *Journal of Physiology,* 1969, *200,* 1–24.

Barlow, H. B., Levick, W. R., & Yoon, M. Response to single quanta of light in retinal ganglion cells of the cat. *Vision Research,* 1971, *11* (Suppl. 3), 87–101.

Baron, W. S., & Boynton, R. M. Response of primate cones to sinusoidally flickering homochromatic stimuli. *Journal of Physiology,* 1975, *246,* 311–331.

Barris, M. C., & Frumkes, T. E. Rod-cone interaction in human scotopic vision-IV cones stimulated by contrast flashes influence rod threshold. *Vision Research,* 1978, *18,* 801–808.

Bartlett. F. C. *Remembering.* London: Cambridge University Press, 1932.

Bartlett, F. C. *Thinking.* New York: Basic Books, 1958.

Bartlett, N. R. Thresholds as dependent on some energy relations and characteristics of the subject. In C. H. Graham (Ed.), *Vision and visual perception.* New York: Wiley, 1965.

Bartley, S. H. *Principles of perception* (2nd ed.). New York: Harper & Row, 1969.

Bass, L., & Moore, W. J. An electrochemical model for depolarization of a retinula cell of *Limulus* by a single photon. *Biophysical Journal,* 1970, *10,* 1–19.

Battro, A. M., Netto, S. di P., & Rozestraten, R. J. A. Riemannian geometries of variable curvature in visual space: Visual alleys, horopters, and triangles in big open fields. *Perception,* 1976, *5,* 9–23.

Bauer, H. D., & Rohler, R. Brightness generation in the human visual system. Colour brightness: A contribution of cortical colour channels to brightness sensation. *Visual Research,* 1977, *17,* 1211–1216.

Baumgardt, E. Threshold quantal problems. In D. Jameson & L. M. Hurvich (Eds.), *Handbook of sensory physiology: Visual psychophysics* (Vol. VII/4). New York: Springer-Verlag, 1972.

Baumgardt, E., & Hillman, B. Duration and size as determinants of peripheral retinal response. *Journal of the Optical Society of America,* 1961, *51,* 340–344.

Baumgardt, E., & Segal, J. Facilitation et inhibition, paramètres de la fonction visuelle. *Anneé Psychologique,* 1947, *43,* 54–102.

Baumgardt, E., & Smith, S. W. Facilitation effect of background light on target detection: A test of theories of absolute threshold. *Vision Research,* 1965, *5,* 299–312.

Baumgardt, E., & Smith, S. W. Comparaison de la sensibilité des cônes et des bâtonnets de l'oeil humain. *Academie Des Sciences, Paris. Comptes Rendus,* 1967, *264,* 3041–3044.

Baylor, D. A., & Fuortes, M. G. F. Electrical responses of single cones in the retina of the turtle. *Journal of Physiology,* 1970, *207,* 77–92.

Baylor, D. A., & Hodgkin, A. L. Changes in time scale and sensitivity in turtle photoreceptors. *Journal of Physiology,* 1974, *242,* 729–758.

Baylor, D. A., Hodgkin, A. L., and Lamb, T. D. The electrical response of turtle cones to flashes and steps of light. *Journal of Physiology,* 1974, *242,* 685–727.

Beck, J. Apparent spatial position and the perception of lightness. *Journal of Experimental Psychology,* 1965, *69,* 170–179.

Beck, J. Perceptual grouping produced by change in orientation and shape. *Science,* 1966, *154,* 538–540.

Beck, J. Similarity grouping and peripheral discriminability under uncertainty. *American Journal of Psychology,* 1972, *85,* 1–19. (a)

Beck, J. *Surface color perception.* Ithaca, N.Y.: Cornell University Press, 1972. (b)

Becker, M. F., & Knopp, J. Processing of visual illusions in the frequency and spatial domains. *Perception & Psychophysics,* 1978, *23,* 521–526.

Bedford, R. E., & Wyszecki, G. Axial chromatic aberration of the eye. *Journal of the Optical Society of America,* 1957, *47,* 564–565.

Békésy, G. von. Sensations on the skin similar to directional hearing, beats, and harmonics of the ear. *Journal of the Acoustical Society of America,* 1957, *29,* 489–501.

Békésy, G. von. Interaction of paired sensory stimuli and conduction in peripheral nerves. *Journal of Applied Physiology,* 1963, *18,* 1276–1284.

Békésy, G. von. *Sensory inhibition.* Princeton, N.J.: Princeton University Press, 1967.

Békésy, G. von. Mach- and Hering-type lateral inhibition in vision. *Vision Research,* 1968, *8,* 1483–1499.

Bell, H. H., & Handel, S. The role of pattern goodness in the reproduction of backward masked patterns. *Journal of Experimental Psychology: Human Perception and Performance,* 1976, *2,* 139–150.

Bell, H. H., & Lappin, J. S. Sufficient conditions for the discrimination of motion. *Perception & Psychology,* 1973, *14,* 45–50.

Bender, W. R. G. The effect of pain and motional stimuli and alcohol upon pupillary reflex activity. *Psychological Monographs,* 1933, *44,* 1–32.

Benham, C. E. The artifical spectrum top. *Nature,* 1894, *51,* 200.

Bennett, A. G., & Francis, J. L. The eye as an optical system. In H. Davson, (ed.), *The eye.* Vol. 4. *Visual optics and the optical space sense.* New York: Academic Press, 1962.

Bergson, H. [*Matter and memory*] (N. M. Paul, & W. S. Palmer, trans.). New York: Macmillan, 1911.

Berkeley, G. *An essay towards a new theory of vision and other writings.* New York: Dutton, 1954. (Originally published as *An essay towards a new theory of vision,* 1709.)

Berkley, M. A., Kitterle, F., & Watkins, D. W. Grating visibility as a function of orientation and retinal eccentricity. *Vision Research,* 1975, *15,* 239–244.

Bernstein, I. H., Proctor, J. D., Proctor, R. W., & Schurman, D. L. Metacontrast and brightness discrimination. *Perception & Psychophysics,* 1973, *14,* 293–297.

Berry, R. N. Quantitative relations among vernier, real depth, and stereoscopic depth acuities. *Journal of Experimental Psychology,* 1948, *38,* 708–721.

Besharse, J. C., Hollyfield, J. G., & Rayborn, M. E. Photoreceptor outer segments: Accelerated membrane renewal in rods after exposure to light. *Science,* 1977, *196,* 536–537.

Bevan, W., Jonides, J., & Collyer, S. C. Chromatic relationships in metacontrast suppression. *Psychonomic Science,* 1970. *19,* 367–368.

Beverly, K. I., & Regan, D. Temporal integration of disparity information in stereoscopic display. *Experimental Brain Research,* 1974a, *19,* 228–232.

Beverly, K. I., & Regan, D. Visual sensitivity to disparity pulses: Evidence for directional sensitivity. *Vision Research,* 1974b, *14,* 357–361.

Beyerstein, B. L., & Freeman, R. D. Lateral spatial interaction in humans with abnormal visual experience. *Vision Research,* 1977, *17,* 1029–1036.

Bezold, W. von. Ueber das Gesetz der Farbenmischung und die physiologischen Grundfarben. *Annalen der Physik and Chemie,* 1873, *150,* 221–247.

Bezold, W. von. *Die farbenlehrer im Hinblick auf Kunst und Kuntsgewerbe.* Brunswick: Westermann, 1874.

Bidwell, S. Curiosities of light and sight. London: Sonnenschein, 1899.

Biederman-Thorson, M., Thorson, J., & Lange, G. D. Apparent movement due to closely spaced sequentially flashed dots in the human peripheral field of vision. *Vision Research,* 1971, *11,* 889–903.

Bindra, D. *A theory of intelligent behavior.* New York: Wiley, 1976.

Bishop, P. O. Neurophysiology of binocular single vision and stereopsis. In R. Jung (Ed.) *Handbook of sensory physiology: Central Processing of Visual Information, A Integrative Function 5 and Comporative Data.* (Vol. VII/3). New York: Springer-Verlag, 1973.

Bjork, E. L., & Murray, J. T. On the nature of input channels in visual processing. *Psychological Review,* 1977, *84,* 472–484.

Björklund, R. A., & Magnussen, S. Decrement versions of the Broca–Sulzer effect and its spatial analogue. *Vision Research,* 1979, *19,* 155–157.

Blackwell, H. R. Neural theories of simple visual discrimination. *Journal of the Optical Society of America,* 1963, *53,* 129–160.

Blake, R. Threshold conditions for binocular rivalry. *Journal of Experimental Psychology: Human Perception and Performance,* 1977, *3,* 251–257.

Blake, R., & Camisa, J. M. Is binocular vision always monocular? *Science,* 1978, *200,* 1497–1499.

Blake, R., Camisa, J. M., & Antoinetti, D. N. Binocular depth discrimination depends on orientation. *Perception & Psychophysics,* 1976, *20,* 113–118.

Blake, R., & Fox, R. Interocular transfer of adaptation to spatial frequency during retinal ischaemia. *Nature. New Biology,* 1972, *240,* 76–77.

Blake, R., & Fox, R. The psychophysical inquiry into binocular summation. *Perception & Psychophysics,* 1973, *14,* 161–185.

Blake, R., & Fox, R. Adaptation to invisible gratings and the site of binocular rivalry suppression. *Nature,* 1974, *249,* 488–490. (a)

Blake, R., & Fox, R. Binocular rivalry suppression. *Vision Research,* 1974, *14,* 1–5. (b)

Blake, R., Fox, R., & McIntyre, C. Stochastic properties of stabilized-image binocular rivalry alternation. *Journal of Experimental Psychology,* 1971, *88,* 327–332.

Blake, R., Fox, R., & Westendorf, D. Visual size constancy occurs after binocular rivalry. *Vision Research,* 1974, *14,* 585–586.

Blake, R., & Lema, S. A. Inhibitory effect of binocular rivalry suppression is independent of orientation. *Vision Research,* 1978, *18,* 541–544.

Blakemore, C., & Campbell, F. W. Adaptation to spatial stimuli. *Proceedings of the Physiological Society,* 20–21 September, 1968, 11P–13P.

Blakemore, C., & Campbell, F. W. On the existence of neurons in the human visual system selectively sensitive to the orientation and size of retinal images. *Journal of Physiology,* 1969, *203,* 237–260.

Blakemore, C., Carpenter, R. H. S., & Georgeson, M. A. Lateral inhibition between orientation detectors in the human visual system. *Nature,* 1970, *228,* 37–39.

Blakemore, C., & Cooper, G. F. Development of the brain depends on the visual environment. *Nature,* 1970, *228,* 477–478.

Blakemore, C., & Cooper, G. F. Modification of the visual cortex by experience. *Brain Research,* 1971, *31,* 366.

Blakemore, C., & Hague, B. Evidence for disparity detecting neurons in the human visual system. *Journal of Physiology,* 1972, *255,* 437–455.

Blakemore, C., & Julesz, B. Stereoscopic depth aftereffect produced without monocular cues. *Science,* 1971, *171,* 286–288.

Blakemore, C., & Nachmias, J. The orientation specificity of two visual aftereffects. *Journal of Physiology,* 1971, *213,* 157–174.

Blakemore, C., Nachmias, J., & Sutton, P. The perceived spatial frequency shift: Evidence for frequency sensitive neurons in the human brain. *Journal of Physiology,* 1970, *210,* 727–750.

Blakemore, C., & Pettigrew, J. D. Eye dominance in the visual cortex. *Nature,* 1970, *225,* 426–429.

Blalock, H. M. Four variable causal models and partial correlations. *American Journal of Sociology,* 1962, *68,* 182–194.

Blank, A. A. Axiomatics of binocular vision. *Journal of the Optical Society of America,* 1958, *48,* 328–334.

Blank, A. A. The Luneberg theory of binocular space perception. In S. Koch (Ed.), *Psychology: A study of a science* (Vol. 1). New York: McGraw-Hill, 1959.

Blank, A. A. Metric geometry in human binocular perception: Theory and fact. In E. L. J. Leeuwenberg & H. F. J. M. Buffart (Eds.), *Formal theories of visual perception.* Chichester, England: Wiley, 1978.

Blank, K., & Enoch, J. M. Monouclar spatial distortions induced by marked accommodation. *Science,* 1973, *182,* 393–395.

Blank, K., Provine, R. R., & Enoch, J. M. Shift in the peak of the photopic Stiles–Crawford function with marked accommodation. *Vision Research,* 1975, *15,* 499–507.

Blick, D. W., & MacLeod, D. I. A. Rod threshold: Influence of neighboring cones. *Vision Research,* 1978, *18,* 1611–1616.

Bloch, A. M. Expériences sur la vision. *Societe de biologie, Paris, Comptes rendus hebdomadaires des seances et memoires,* 1885, *37,* 493–495.

Blondel, A., & Rey, J. Sur la perception dus lumières brèves à la limite de leur portée. *Journal de Physique* (Series 5), 1911, *1,* 530–550.

Bobier, C. W., & Sivak, J. G. Chromoretinoscopy. *Vision Research,* 1978, *18,* 247–250.

Bodis-Wollner, I., Atkin, A., Raab, E., & Wolkstein, M. Visual association cortex and vision in man: Pattern-evoked occipital potentials in a blind boy. *Science,* 1977, *198,* 629–631.

Boehm, G. Über maculare (Haidinger'seche) polarisationsbüschel and über einen polarisatinoptischen fehler des auges. *Acta Ophthalmologica,* 1940, *18,* 109–142.

Bonds, A. B. Optical quality of the living cat eye. *Journal of Physiology,* 1974, *243,* 777–795.

Bonds, A. B., Enroth-Cugell, C., & Pinto, L. H. Image quality of the cat eye measured during retinal ganglion cell experiments. *Journal of Physiology,* 1972, *220,* 383–401.

Bonnet, C. Visual motion detection models: Features and frequency filters. *Perception,* 1977, *6,* 491–500.

Bonting, S. L., & Bangham, A. D. On the biochemical mechanism of the visual process. *Experimental Eye Research,* 1967, *6,* 400–413.

Boring, E. G. *Sensation and perception in the history of experimental psychology.* New York: Appleton-Century-Crofts, 1942.

Boring, E. G. *A history of experimental psychology* (2nd ed.). New York: Appleton-Century-Crofts, 1950.

Boulter, J. F. Optical transforms and the "pincushion grid" illusion. *Science,* 1977, *198,* 960–961.

Bouman, M. A., & Van den Brink, G. On the integrate capacity in time and space of the human peripheral retina. *Journal of the Optical Society of America,* 1952, *42,* 617–620.

Bowen, R. W., Pola, J., & Matin, L. Visual persistence: Effects of flash luminance, duration, and energy. *Vision Research,* 1974, *14*(4), 295–303.

Bowen, R. W., & Pokorny, J. Target edge sharpness and temporal brightness enhancement. *Vision Research,* 1978, *18,* 1691–1696.

Bower, G. H. Cognitive psychology: An introduction. In W. K. Estes (Ed.), *Handbook of learning and cognitive processes.* Hillsdale, N.J.: Lawrence Erlbaum Associates, 1975.

Boycott, B. B., Dowling, J. E., Fisher, S. K., Kolb, H., & Laties, A. M. Interplexiform cells of the mammalian retina and their comparison with catecholamine-containing cells. *Proceedings of the Royal Society of London* (Biology Series), 1975, *191,* 353–368.

Boycott, B. B., & Wässle, H. The morphological types of ganglion cells of the domestic cat's retina. *Journal of Physiology,* 1974, *240,* 397–419.

Boyer, C. B. *The rainbow: From myth to mathematics.* New York: Thomas Yoseloff, 1959.

Boynton, R. M. Color vision. In J. W. Kling & L. A. Riggs (Eds.), *Woodworth and Schlosberg's experimental psychology.* New York: Holt, Rinehart, & Winston, 1971.

Boynton, R. M. Discrimination of homogeneous double pulses of light. In D. Jameson & L. M. Hurvich (Eds.), *Handbook of sensory Physiology: Visual psychophysics* (Vol. VII/4). New York: Springer-Verlag, 1972.

Boynton, R. M., & Clarke, F. J. J. Sources of entoptic scatter in the human eye. *Journal of the Optical Society of America,* 1964, *54,* 110–119.

Boynton, R. M., Ikeda, M., and Stiles, W. S. Interactions among chromatic mechanisms as inferred from positive and negative increment thresholds. *Vision Research,* 1964, *4,* 87–117.

Boynton, R. M., & Whitten, D. M. Visual adaptation in monkey cones: Recordings of late receptor potentials. *Science,* 1970, *170,* 1423–1426.

Braddick, O. A short-range process in apparent motion. *Vision Research,* 1974, *14,* 519–528.

Braddick, O., & Adlard, A. Apparent motion and the motion detector. In J. C. Armington, J. Krauskopf, & B. R. Wooten (Eds.), *Visual Psychophysics and Physiology.* New York: Academic Press, 1978.

Braddick, O., Campbell, F. W., & Atkinson, J. Channels in vision: Basic aspects. In R. Held. W.

Leibowitz, & H-L. Teuber (Eds.), *Handbook of sensory physiology: Perception* (Vol. 8). Berlin: Springer-Verlag, 1978.

Brain, W. R. *The nature of experience*. London: Oxford University Press, 1959.

Brauner, J. D., & Lit, A. The Pulfrich effect, simple reaction time, and intensity discrimination. *American Journal of Psychology,* 1976, *89,* 105–114.

Braunstein, M. L. Depth perception in rotating dot patterns: Effects of numerosity and perspective. *Journal of Experimental Psychology,* 1962, *64,* 415–420.

Braunstein, M. L. Sensitivity of the observer to transformations of the visual field. *Journal of Experimental Psychology,* 1966, *72,* 683–689.

Braunstein, M. L. Perception of rotation in depth: A process model. *Psychological Review,* 1972, *79,* 510–524.

Braunstein, M. L. *Depth perception through motion.* New York: Academic Press, 1976.

Breese, B. B. On Inhibition. *Psychological Review Monographs,* 1899, *3,*(Whole No. 2).

Breitmeyer, B. G., Battaglia, F., & Bridge, J. Existence and implication of a tilted binocular disparity space. *Perception,* 1977, *6,* 161–164.

Breitmeyer, B. G., & Ganz, L. Implication of sustained and transient channels for theories of visual pattern masking, saccadic suppression, and information processing. *Psychological Reveiw,* 1976, *83,* 1–36.

Breitmeyer, B. G., Julesz, B., & Kropfl, W. Dynamic random-dot stereograms reveal up-down anisotrophy between cortical hemifields. *Science,* 1975, *187,* 269–270.

Brentano, F. [*Psychology from an empirical standpoint*] (O. Kraus & L. L. McAlister, Eds.; A. C. Rancurello et al., trans.). Atlantic Highlands, N.J.: Humanities Press, 1973. (Originally published, 1874.)

Brewster, D. Account of an affection of the eye. *Thomson's Annals of Philosophy* (Proceedings at the Royal Society of Edinburgh), 1818, *11,* 151.

Brewster, D. On some remarkable affections of the retina, as exhibited in its insensibility to indirect impressions, and to the impressions of attenuated light. *Edinburgh Journal of Science,* 1825, *3,* 288–293.

Brewster, D. On the influence of successive impulses of light upon the retina. *London, Edinburg, and Dublin Philosophical Magazine and Journal of Science,* 1834, *4,* 241–245.

Bridgeman, B. Metacontrast and lateral inhibition. *Psychological Reveiw,* 1971, *78,* 528–539.

Bridgeman, B. Correlates of metacontrast in single cells of the cat visual system. *Vision Research,* 1975, *15,* 91–99.

Bridgeman, B. A correlational model applied to metacontrast: Reply to Weisstein, Ozog, and Szoc, *Bulletin of the Psychonomic Society,* 1977, *10,* 85–88.

Bridgeman, B. Distributed sensory coding applied to simulation of iconic storage and metacontrast. *Bulletin of Mathematical Biology,* 1978, *40,* 605–623.

Bridgeman, B., Hendry, D., & Stark, L. Failure to detect displacement of the visual world during saccadic eye movements. *Vision Research,* 1975, *15,* 719–722.

Bridgeman, B., & Leff, S. Interaction of stimulus size and retinal eccentricity in metacontrast masking. Paper presented at the meeting of the Psychonomics Society, November, 1977.

Brigner, W. L., & Gallagher, M. B. Subjective contour: Apparent depth on simultaneous contrast. *Perceptual and Motor Skills,* 1974, *38,* 1047–1053.

Brindley, G. S. The Bunsen–Roscoe law for the human eye at very short durations. *Journal of Physiology,* 1952, *118,* 135–139.

Brindley, G. S. The summation areas of human colour-receptive mechanisms at increment threshold. *Journal of Physiology,* 1954, *124,* 400–408.

Brindley, G. S. *Physiology of the retina and the visual pathway.* London: Edward Arnold, 1960.

Brindley, G. S., & Lewin, W. S. The sensations produced by electrical stimulation of the visual cortex. *Journal of Physiology,* 1968, *196,* 479–493.

Broadbent, D. E. *Perception and communication.* Oxford: Pergamon Press, 1958.

Broadbent, D. E. The hidden preattentive processes. *American Psychologist,* 1977, *32,* 109–118.

Broca, A., & Sulzer, D. La sensation lumineuse fonction du temps. *Journal de Physiologie et de Pathologie Generale,* 1902, *4,* 632–640.

Brown, C. R., & Forsythe, D. M. Use of a Fourier model in describing the fusion of complex visual stimuli. *Journal of the Optical Society of America,* 1959, *49,* 760–763.

Brown, D. R., & Owen, D. H. The metrics of visual form: Methodological dyspepsia. *Psychological Bulletin,* 1967, *68,* 243–259.

Brown, J. L. Flicker and intermittent stimulation. In C. H. Graham (Ed.), *Vision and visual perception.* New York: Wiley, 1965.

Brown, J. L., LaMotte, R. H., Shively, F. D., & Sechzer, J. A. Color discrimination in the cat. *Journal of Comparative and Physiological Psychology,* 1973, *84,* 534–544.

Brown, J. L., & Mueller, C. G. Brightness discrimination and brightness contrast. In C. H. Graham (Ed.), *Vision and visual perception.* New York: Wiley, 1965.

Brown, K. T., & Murakami, M. A new receptor potential of the monkey retina with no detectable latency. *Nature,* 1964, *201,* 626–628.

Brown, P. K., & Wald, G. Visual pigments in single rods and cones of the human retina. *Science,* 1964, *144,* 42–52.

Brücke, E. W. von Untersuchungen über subjective Farben. *Poggendorff's Annalen der Physik und Chemie,* 1851, *84,* 418–452.

Bruner, J. S. Personality dynamics and the process of perceiving. In R. R. Blake & G. V. Ramsey (Eds.), *Perception: An approach to personality.* New York: Ronald Press, 1951.

Bruner, J. S., & Postman, L. Emotional selectivity in perception and reaction. *Journal of Personality,* 1947, *16,* 69–77.

Bruner, J. S., & Postman, L. An approach to social perception. In W. Dennis (Ed.), *Current trends in social psychology.* Pittsburgh, Pa.: University of Pittsburgh Press, 1948.

Bruner, J. S., & Postman, L. Perception, cognition, and behavior. *Journal of Personality,* 1949, *18,* 14–31.

Brunswik, E. Representative design and probabilistic theory in a functional psychology. *Psychological Review,* 1955, *62,* 193–217.

Buchsbaum, W. H., & Mayzner, M. S. The effects of line length on sequential blanking. *Psychonomic Science,* 1969, *15.* 111–112.

Buffart, H. F. J. M. *A coding language for patterns.* Nijmegan, The Netherlands: University of Nijmegen Press, 1974.

Buffart, H. F. J. M. Brightness and contrast. In E. L. J., Leeuwenberg & H. F. J. M. Buffart (Eds.) *Formal theories of visual perception.* Chichester, England: Wiley, 1978.

Burg, A. Visual acuity as measured by dynamic and static tests: A comparative evaluation. *Journal of Applied Psychology*, 1966, 50, 460–466.

Burkhardt, D. A. Cone action spectra: Evidence from the goldfish electroretinogram. *Vision Research*, 1968, *8*, 839–853.

Burkhardt, D. A., & Bernston, G. G. Light adaptation and excitation: Lateral spread of signals within the frog's retina. *Vision Research,* 1972, *12,* 1095–1111.

Burr, D. C., & Ross, J. How does binocular delay give information about depth? *Vision Research,* 1979, *19,* 523–532.

Burton, G. J., & Ruddock, K. H. Visual adaptation to patterns containing two-dimensional spatial structure. *Visual Research,* 1978, *18,* 93–99.

Butterfield, J. F. Subjective (induced) color television. *Journal of the Society of Motion Picture and Television Engineers,* 1968, *77,* 1025–1028.

Caelli, T., Hoffman, W., & Lindman, H. Apparent motion: Self-excited oscillation induced by retarded neuronal flows. In E. L. J. Leeuwenberg & H. F. J. M. Buffart (Eds.), *Formal theories of visual perception.* New York: Wiley, 1978.

Caelli, T., & Julesz, B. On perceptual analyzers underlying visual texture discrimination: Part I. *Biological Cybernetics,* 1978, *28,* 167–175.

Caelli, T., Julesz, B., & Gilbert, E. On perceptual analyzers underlying visual texture discrimination: Part II. *Biological Cybernetics,* 1978, *29,* 201-214.

Caelli, T. M., Preston, G. A. N., & Howell, E. R. Implications of spatial summation models for processes of contour perception: A geometric perspective. *Vision Research,* 1978, *18,* 723-734.

Caelli, T. M., & Umansky, J. Interpolation in the visual system. *Vision Research,* 1976, *16,* 1055-1060.

Camisa, J. M., Blake, R., & Lema, S. The effects of temporal modulation on the oblique effect in humans. *Perception,* 1977, *6,* 165-171.

Campbell, F. W., Cooper, G. F., & Enroth-Cugell, C. The spatial selectivity of the visual cells of the cat. *Journal of Physiology,* 1969, *203,* 223-235.

Campbell, F. W., & Green, D. G. Monocular versus binocular visual acuity. *Nature,* 1965, *208,* 191-192. (a)

Campbell, F. W., & Green, D. G. Optical and retinal factors affecting visual resolution. *Journal of Physiology,* 1965, *181,* 576-593. (b)

Campbell, F. W., & Gubisch, R. W. Optical quality of the human eye. *Journal of Physiology,* 1966, *186,* 558-578.

Campbell, F. W., & Howell, E. R. Monocular alternation: A method for the investigation of pattern vision. *Journal of Physiology,* 1972, *225,* 19P-21P.

Campbell, F. W., & Kulikowski, J. J. Orientation selectivity of the human visual system. *Journal of Physiology,* 1966, *187,* 437-445.

Campbell, F. W., Kulikowski, J. J., & Levinson, J. The effect of orientation on the visual resolution of gratings. *Journal of Physiology,* 1966, *187,* 427-436.

Campbell, F. W., & Maffei, L. Electrophysiological evidence for the existence of orientation and size detectors in the human visual system. *Journal of Physiology,* 1970, *207,* 635-652.

Campbell, F. W., & Robson, J. G. An application of Fourier analysis to the visibility of gratings. *Journal of Physiology,* 1968, *197,* 551-566.

Campenhausen, C. Über die Farben der Benhamschen Scheibe. *Zeitschrift fuer vergleichende Physiologie,* 1968, *60,* 351-374. (a)

Campenhausen, C. Über den Ursprungsort von musterinduzierten Flickerfarben im visuallen System des Menschen. *Zeitschrift fuer vergleichende Physiologie,* 1968, *61,* 355-360. (b)

Campenhausen, C. Untersuchung des Fechner-Benhamschen Farbphänomens. *Pfüger's Archiv fuer die Gesamte Physiologie des Menschen und der Tiere*, 1968, *300*, R98-R99. (c)

Capra, F. Quark theory without quarks: A review of recent developments in S- matrix theory. *American Journal of Physics*, 1979, *47*, 11-23.

Carpenter, M. B. *Human neuroanatomy* (7th ed.). Baltimore: Williams & Wilkins, 1976.

Carraher, R. G., & Thurston, J. B. *Optical illusions and the visual arts.* New York: Van Nostrand Reinhold, 1969.

Carterette, E. C., & Friedman, M. P. (Eds.). *Handbook of perception: Historical and philosophical roots of perception* (Vol 1). New York: Academic Press, 1974.

Carterette, E. C., & Friedman, M. P. (Eds.). *Handbook of perception, Vol. 5: Seeing.* New York: Academic Press, 1975.

Cavanagh, P. Size and position invariance in the visual system. *Perception,* 1978, 7, 167-177.

Charman, M. N., & Jennings, J. A. M. Objective measurements of the longitudinal chromatic aberration of the eye. *Vision Research,* 1976, *16,* 999-1005.

Charpentier, A. Différence de temps perdu suivant les couleurs. *Archive de Physiologique* (Series 5), 1893, *5,* 568-570.

Cheatham, P. G. Visual perceptual latency as a function of stimulus brightness and contour shape. *Journal of Experimental Psychology,* 1952, *43,* 369-380.

Chew, G. F., & Rosenzweig, C. Dual topological unitarization: An ordered approach to hadron theory. *Physics Reports,* 1978. *41,* 263-327.

Chiang, C. A new theory to explain geometrical illusions produced by crossing lines. *Perception & Psychophysics,* 1968, *3,* 174-176.

Cicerone, C. M., & Green, D. G. Relative modulation sensitivities of the red and green color mechanisms. *Vision Research,* 1978, *18,* 1593–1598.

Cicerone, C. M., Krantz. D. H., & Larimer, J. Opponent-process additivity—III. Effect of moderate chromatic adaptation. *Vision Research,* 1975, *15,* 1125–1136.

Ciures, A. The Mach bands: The visualization of Gibbs phenomenon in the space domain. *Journal of Theoretical Biology,* 1977, *66,* 195–197.

Clark, W. A., & Farley, B. G. Generalization of pattern recognition in a self-organizing system. *Proceedings of the Western Joint Computer Conference, I.R.E.,* 1955, 86–91.

Clark-Jones, R. Quantum efficiency of human vision. *Journal of the Optical Society of America,* 1959, *49,* 645–653.

Cleland, B. G., Dubin, M. W., & Levick, W. R. Sustained and transient cells in the cat's retina and lateral geniculate nucleus. *Journal of Physiology,* 1971, *217,* 473–496.

Cleland, B. G., & Levick, W. R. Physiology of cat retinal ganglion cells. *Investigative Ophthalmology,* 1972, *11,* 285–290.

Cleland, B. G., & Levick, W. R. Brisk and sluggish concentrically organized ganglion cells in the cat's retina. *Journal of Physiology,* 1974, *240,* 421–456.

Cleland, B. G., Levick, W. R., & Sanderson, K. J. Properties of sustained and transient cells in the cat retina. *Journal of Physiology*, 1973, *228*, 649–680.

Cline, D. B., Mann, A. K., & Rubbua, C. The search for new families of elementary particles. *Scientific American*, January 1976, *234* (1) 44–54.

Cobb, P. W. The influence of pupillary diameter on visual acuity. *American Journal of Physiology*, 1915, *36,* 335–346.

Coenen, A. M. L., & Eijkman, E. G. J. Cat optic tract and geniculate unit response corresponding to human visual masking effects. *Experimental Brain Research,* 1972, *15,* 441–451.

Coffin, S. Spatial frequency analysis of block letters does not predict experimental confusions. *Perception & Psychophysics,* 1978, *23,* 69–74.

Cogan, D. G. Some ocular phenomena produced with polarized light. *Archives of Ophthalmology,* 1941, *25,* 391–400.

Cohen, J., & Gordon, D. A. The Prevost–Fechner–Benham subjective colors. *Psychological Bulletin,* 1949, *46,* 97–136.

Cohen, W. Spatial and textural characteristics of the ganzfeld. *American Journal of Psychology,* 1957, *70,* 403–410.

Cohen, W. Color perception in the chromatic ganzfeld. *American Journal of Psychology,* 1958, *71,* 390–394.

Cohn, P. M. *Lie groups*. London: Cambridge University Press, 1957.

Cone, R. A. Early receptor potential: Photoreversible charge displacement in rhodopsin. *Science,* 1967, *155,* 1128–1131.

Cone, R. A., & Brown, P. K. Dependence of the early receptor potential on the orientation of rhodopsin. *Science,* 1967, *156,* 536.

Cone, R. A., & Cobbs, W. H., III. Rhodopsin cycle in the living eye of the rat. *Nature,* 1969, *221,* 820–822.

Coren, S. Brightness contrast as a function of figure–ground relations. *Journal of Experimental Psychology,* 1969, *80,* 517–524. (a)

Coren, S. The influence of optical aberrations on the magnitude of the Poggendorf illusion. *Perception & Psychophysics,* 1969, *6,* 185–186. (b)

Coren, S. Lateral inhibition and geometric illusions. *Quarterly Journal of Experimental Psychology,* 1970, *22,* 274–278.

Coren, S. Subjective contours and apparent depth. *Psychological Review,* 1972, *79,* 359–367.

Coren, S., & Girgus, J. S. Density of human lens pigmentation *in vivo* measures over an extended age range. *Vision Research,* 1972, *12,* 343–346.

Coren, S., & Girgus, J. S. Illusions and constancies. In W. Epstein (Ed.), *Stability and constancy in visual perception: Mechanisms and processes*. New York: Wiley, 1977.

Coren, S., & Girgus, J. S. *Seeing is deceiving: The psychology of visual illusions*. Hillsdale, N.J.: Lawrence Erlbaum Associates, 1978.

Coren, S., Girgus, J. S., Erlichman, H., & Hatstian, A. R. An empirical taxonomy of visual illusion. *Perception & Psychophysics*, 1976, *20*, 129–137.

Coren, S., & Porac, C. Iris pigmentation and visual-geometric illusions. *Perception*, 1978, *7*, 473–477.

Coren, S., & Theodor, L. H. Neural interaction and subjective contours. *Perception*, 1977, *6*, 107–111.

Cornsweet, T. N. *Visual perception*. New York: Academic Press, 1970.

Corwin, T. R., & Green, M. A. The Broca–Sulzer effect in a ganzfeld. *Vision Research*, 1978, *18*, 1675–1678.

Cowan, T. M. The theory of braids and the analysis of impossible figures. *Journal of Mathematical Psychology*, 1974, *11*, 190–212.

Cowan, T. M. Organizing the properties of impossible figures. *Perception*, 1977, *6*, 41–56.

Cox, S. I., & Dember, W. N. Backward masking of visual targets with internal contours. *Psychonomic Science*, 1970, *19*, 255–256.

Cox, S. I., & Dember, W. N. U-shaped metacontrast functions with a detection task. *Journal of Experimental Psychology*, 1972, *95*, 327–333.

Cox, S. I., Dember, W. N., & Sherrick, M. F. Effect on backward masking of spatial separation between target and mask contours and of target size. *Psychonomic Science*, 1969, *17*, 205–206.

Craik, F. I. M., & Lockhart, R. S. Levels of Processing: A Framework for memory research. Journal of Verbal Learning and Verbal Behavior, 1972, *11*, 671–684.

Craik, K. J. W. The effect of adaptation on subjective brightness. *Proceedings of the Royal Society of London* (Series B), 1940, *128*, 232–247. (a)

Craik, K. J. W. Origin of visual afterimages. *Nature*, 1940, *145*, 512. (b)

Craik, K. J. W. *Visual adaptation*. Unpublished doctoral dissertation, Cambridge University, 1940. (c)

Craik, K. J. W. *The nature of explanation*. Cambridge, England: Cambridge University Press, 1967.

Crawford, B. H. The effect of field size and pattern on the of visual sensitivity with time. *Proceedings of the Royal Society of London* (Series B), 1940, *129*, 94–106.

Crawford, B. H. Visual adaptation in relation to brief conditioning stimuli. *Proceedings of the Royal Society of London*, 1947, *134*, 283–302.

Crawford, B. H. The Stiles–Crawford effects and their significance in vision. In D. Jameson & L. M. Hurvich (Eds.), *Handbook of sensory physiology* (Vol. VII/4). Berlin: Springer-Verlag, 1972.

Crovitz, H. F. Perceived length and the Craik–O'Brien illusion. *Vision Research*, 1976, *16*, 435.

Cutting, J. E., Proffitt, D. R., & Kozlowski, L. T. A biomechanical invariant for gait perception. *Journal of Experimental Psychology: Human Perception and Performance*, 1978, *4*, 357–372.

Dartnall, H. J. A. The interpretation of spectral sensitivity curves. *British Medical Bulletin*, 1953, *9*, 24–30.

Darwin, C. *Origin of species* (A facsimile of the 1st ed.). Cambridge, Mass.: Harvard University Press, 1975. (Originally published, 1859.)

Darwin, R. W. New experiments on the ocular spectra of lights and colours. *Philosophical Transactions of the Royal Society of London*, 1786, *76*, 313–348.

Davies, P. The role of central processes in the perception of visual afterimage fragmentation. *British Journal of Psychology*, 1973, *64*, 325–338.

Davy, E. The intensity–time relation for multiple flashes of light in the peripheral retina. *Journal of the Optical Society of America*, 1952, *42*, 937–941.

Daw, N. W., & Enoch, J. M. Contrast sensitivity, Westheimer function, and Stiles–Crawford effect in a blue cone monochromat. *Vision Research*, 1973, *13*, 1669–1680.

Day, R. H. On the stereoscopic observation of gemoetrical illusions. *Perceptual and Motor Skills*, 1961, *13*, 247–258.

Day, R. H. Visual spatial illusions: A general explanation. *Science*, 1972, *175*, 1335–1340.

Dealy, R. S. & Tolhurst, D. J. Is spatial adaptation an aftereffect of prolonged inhibition? *Journal of Psychology* (London) 1974, *241*, 26–270.

deGroot, S. G., Dodge, J. M., & Smith, J. A. *Factors in night vision sensitivity: The effect of brightness*. Medical Research Laboratory Report No. 194, 1952, *11*, 1–17.

de Lange, H. Research into the dynamic nature of the human fovea–cortex systems with intermittent and modulated light. I. Attenuation characteristics with white and colored light. *Journal of the Optical Society of America*, 1958, *48*, 777–784. (a)

de Lange, H. Research into the dynamic nature of the human fovea–cortex systems with intermittent and modulated light. II. Phase shift in brightness and delay in color perception. *Journal of the Optical Society of America*, 1958, *48*, 784–789. (b)

Dember, W. N., Mathews, W. D., & Stefl, M. Backward masking and enhancement of multisegmented visual targets. *Bulletin of the Psychonomic Society*, 1973, *1*, 45–47.

Dember, W. N., & Purcell, D. G. Recovery of masked visual targets by inhibition of the masking stimulus. *Science*, 1967, *157*, 1335–1336.

Dember, W. N., Schwartz, M., & Kocak, M. Substantial recovery of a masked visual target and its theoretical interpretation. *Bulletin of the Psychonomic Society*, 1978, *11*, 285–287.

Dember, W. N., & Stefl. M. Backward enhancement? *Science*, 1972, *175*, 93–95.

Dember, W. N., & Warm, J. S. *Psychology of perception*. New York: Holt, Rinehart and Winston, 1979.

deMonasterio, F. M. Macular pigmentation and the spectral sensitivity of retinal ganglion cells of macaques. *Vision Research*, 1978, *18*, 1273–1277.

DeMott, D. Direct measures of the retinal image. *Journal of the Optical Society of America*, 1959, *49*, 571–579.

Denton, G. G. Visual motion aftereffect induced by simulated rectilinear motion. *Perception*, 1977, *6*, 711–718.

de Robertis, E. Electron microscope observations on the submicroscopic organization of the retinal rods. *Journal of Biophysics, Biochemistry, and Cytology*, 1956, *2*, 319–330.

Descartes, R. [Discourse on the method, Part II.] In E. S. Haldane & G. T. R. Ross (Eds. & trans.), *The philosophical works of Descartes*. Cambridge, England: Cambridge University Press, 1967. (Originally published, 1637.)

DeSilva, H. R., & Bartley, S. H. Summation and subtraction of brightness in binocular perception. *British Journal of Psychology*, 1930, *20*, 241–252.

DeValois, R. L. Central mechanisms of color vision. In R. Jung (Ed.), *Handbook of sensory physiology* (VII/3A). New York: Springer-Verlag, 1973.

DeValois, R. Paper presented at University of Texas symposium on pattern perception. March, 1979, (In press).

DeValois, R. L., Abramov, I., & Jacobs, G. H. Analysis of response patterns of LGN cells. *Journal of the Optical Society of America*, 1966, *56*, 966–977.

DeValois, R. L., Albrecht, D. G., & Thorell, L. G. Spatial tuning of LGN and cortical cells in monkey visual system. In H. Spekreijse & L. H. Van der Tweel (Eds.), *Spatial contrast*. Amsterdam: North Holland, 1977.

DeValois, R. L., & DeValois, K. K. Neural coding of color. In E. C. Carterette & M. P. Friedman (Eds.), *Handbook of perception Seeing* (Vol. 5). New York: Academic Press, 1975.

DeValois, R. L., & DeValois, K. K. Spatial vision. *Annual Review of Psychology*, 1980, *31*, 309–341.

DeValois, R., DeValois, K., Ready, J., & Blanckensee, H. von. Spatial frequency tuning of macaque straite cortex cells. *Proceedings of the Association for Research in Vision and Ophthalmology*, Spring, 1975.

DeValois, R. L., & Pease, P. L. Contorus and contrast: Response of monkey lateral geniculate nuclear cells to luminance and color figures. *Science*, 1971, *171*, 694–696.

Devoe, R. D. Linear superposition of retinal action potentials to predict electrical flicker responses from the eye of the wolf spider, *Lycosa Baltimoriana* (Keyserling). *Journal of General Physiology,* 1962, *46,* 75–96.

Devoe, R. D. Linear electrical flicker responses from the eye of the wolf spider. *Documental Ophthalmologica,* 1964, *18,* 128–136.

Dewey, J., & Bentley, A. F. *Knowing and the known.* Boston: Beacon Press, 1949.

Diamond, A. L. A theory of depression and enhancement in the brightness response. *Psychological Review,* 1960, *67,* 168–199.

Dichgans, J., & Brandt, T. Visual-vestibular interaction: Effects on self-motion perception and postural control. In R. Held, H. W. Leibowitz, & H-L. Teuber (Eds.), *Handbook of sensory physiology: Perception* (Vol. 8). Berlin: Springer-Verlag, 1978.

Dick, A. O. Iconic memory and its relation to perceptual processing and other memory mechanisms. *Perception & Psychophysics,* 1974, *16,* 575–596.

Diener, H. C., Wist, E. R., Dichgans, J., & Brandt, T. The spatial frequency effect on perceived velocity. *Vision Research,* 1976, 169–176.

Dinneen, G. P. Programming pattern recognition. *Proceedings of the 1955 Western Joint Computer Conference,* Institute of Radio Engineers, New York, 1955, 94–100.

Ditchburn, R. W. Eye movements in relation to retinal action. *Acta Ophthalmologica,* 1955, *1*(4), 171–176.

Ditchburn, R. W. *Eye movements and visual perception.* Oxford: Clarendon, 1973.

Dobelle, W. H., Mladejovsky, M. G., & Girvin, J. P. Artificial vision for the blind: Electrical stimulation of visual cortex offers hope for a functional prosthesis. *Science,* 1974, *183,* 440–443.

Dodge, R. Visual perception during eye movement. *Psychological Review,* 1900, *1,* 454–465.

Dodge, R. The illusion of clear vision during eye movement. *Psychological Bulletin,* 1905, *2,* 193–199.

Dodwell, P. C. Contemporary theoretical problems in seeing. In E. C. Carterette & M. P. Friedman (Eds.), *Handbook of perception Seeing* (Vol. V). New York: Academic Press, 1975.

Dowling, J. E. Chemistry of visual adaptation in the rat. *Nature,* 1960, *188,* 114–118.

Dowling, J. E. The site of visual adaptation. *Science,* 1967, *155,* 273–279.

Dowling, J. E. Synaptic organization of the frog retina: An electron microscopic analysis comparing the retinas of frogs and primates. *Proceedings of the Royal Society, Series B,* 1968, *170,* 205–228.

Dowling, J. E. Organization of vertebrate retinas. *Investigative Ophthalmology,* 1970, *9,* 655–680.

Dowling, J. E., Ehinger, B., & Hedden, W. L. The interplexiform cell: A new type of retinal neuron. *Investigative Ophthalmology,* 1976, *15,* 916–926.

Draper, S. W. The Penrose triangle and a family of related figures. *Perception,* 1978, *7,* 283–296.

Drell, S. D. Electron-positron annihilation and the new particles. *Scientific American,* 1975, *232*(6), 50–62.

Dubin, M. W. The inner plexiform layer of the vertebrate retina: A quantitative and comparative electron microscopic analysis. *Journal of Comparative Neurology,* 1970, *140,* 479–506.

Easter, S. S. Excitation in the goldfish retina: Evidence for a nonlinear intensity code. *Journal of Physiology,* 1968, *195,* 253–271.

Ebbecke, U. Über das Sehen im Flimmerlicht. *Pflügers Archiv fuer die Gesumte Physiologie des Menschen und der Tiere,* 1920, *185,* 196–223.

Ebrey, T. G., & Honig, B. New wavelength dependent visual pigment nomograms. *Vision Research,* 1977, *17,* 147–151.

Eccles, J. C. *The human mystery.* Berlin: Springer-Verlag, 1979.

Efron, R. An extension of the Pulfrich stereoscopic effect. *Brain,* 1963, *86,* 295–300.

Efron, R. The duration of the present. *Annals of the New York Academy of Sciences,* 1967, *138,* 713–729.

Efron, R. Effect of stimulus duration on perceptual onset and offset latencies. *Perception & Psychophysics,* 1970, *8,* 251–254. (a)

Efron, R. The minimum duration of a perception. *Neuropsychologia,* 1970, *8,* 57–63. (b)

Efron, R. The relationship between the duration of a stimulus and the duration of a perception. *Neuropsychologia,* 1970, *8,* 37–55. (c)

Efron, R., & Lee, D. N. The visual persistence of a moving stroboscopically illuminated object. *American Journal of Psychology,* 1971, *84,* 365–375.

Einstein, A. On the generalized theory of gravitation. *Scientific American,* 1950, *182*(4), 13–17.

Ekman, G., Eisler, H., & Kunnapas, T. Brightness scales of monochromatic light. *Scandinavian Journal of Psychology,* 1960, *1,* 41–48.

Ellis, S. R., Wong, J. H., & Stark, L. Absence of accommodation during perceptual reversal of Necker cubes. *Vision Research,* 1979, *19,* 953–955.

Encyclopedia of Philosophy, Vol. 1–8. New York & London: Macmillan & Collier, 1967.

Engel, G. R. The autocorrelation function and binocular brightness mixing. *Vision Research,* 1969, *9,* 1111–1130.

Enoch, J. M. Response of a model retinal receptor as a function of wavelength. *Journal of the Optical Society of America,* 1960, *50,* 315–320.

Enoch, J. M. Waveguide modes in retinal receptors. *Science,* 1961, *133,* 1353–1354.

Enoch, J. M. Retinal receptor orientation and the role of fiber optics in vision. *American Journal of Optometry and Archives of American Academy of Optometry,* 1972, *49,* 455–469.

Enoch, J. M. Marked accommodation, retinal stretch, monocular space perception, and retinal receptor orientation. *American Journal of Optometry and Physiological Optics,* 1975, *52,* 376–392.

Enoch, J. M. Vertebrate photoreceptor orientation. *International Journal of Quantum Chemistry,* 1976, *3,* 65–88.

Enoch, J. M. Quantitative layer-by-layer perimetry. *Investigative Ophthalmology and Visual Science,* 1978, *17,* 208–257.

Enoch, J. M., Berger, R., & Birns, R. A static perimetric technique believed to test receptive field properties: Extension and verification of the analysis. *Documenta Ophthalmologica,* 1970, *29,* 127–153. (a)

Enoch, J. M., Berger, R., & Birns, R. A static perimetric technique believed to test receptive field properties: Responses near visual field lesions with sharp borders. *Documenta Ophthalmologica,* 1970, *29,* 154–167. (b)

Enoch, J. M., & Hope, G. M. An analysis of retinal receptor orientation: IV Center of the entrance pupil and the center of convergence of orientation and directional sensitivity. *Investigative Ophthalmology,* 1972, *11,* 1017–1021. (a)

Enoch, J. M., & Hope, G. M. An analysis of retinal receptor orientation: III Results of initial psychophysical tests. *Investigative Ophthalmology,* 1972, *11,* 765–782. (b)

Enoch, J. M., & Hope, G. M. Directional sensitivity of the foveal and parafoveal retina. *Investigative Ophthalmology,* 1973, *12,* 497–503.

Enoch, J. M., & Horowitz, B. R. The vertebrate retinal receptor as a waveguide. In J. Fox (Ed.), *Symposium on optical and acoustical micro-electronics.* New York Microwave Research Institute, 1974, *23,* 133–159.

Enoch, J. M., & Johnson, C. A. Additivity of effects within sectors of the sensitization zone of the Westheimer function. *American Jounral of Optometry and Physiological Optics,* 1976, *53,* 350–358.

Enoch, J. M., Johnson, C. A., & Fitzgerald, C. R. Human psychophysical analysis of receptive fieldlike properties: V. Adaptation of stationary and moving windmill target characteristics to clinical populations. *Documenta Ophthalmologica,* 1976, *41,* 347–370. (a)

Enoch, J. M., Johnson, C. A., & Fitzgerald, C. R. Human psychophysical analysis of receptive fieldlike properties: VII. Initial clinical trials of psychophysical transient-like function. *Documenta Ophthalmologica Proceedings Series, Second International Visual Field Symposium,* Tübingen, Sept. 1976. (b)

Enoch, J. M., & Laties, A. M. An analysis of retinal receptor orientation: II Predictions for Psychophysical tests. *Investigative Ophthalmology,* 1971, *10,* 959–970.

Enoch, J. M., Lazarus, J., & Johnson, C. A. Human psychophysical analysis of receptive fieldlike properties: I. A new transient-like response using a moving windmill (Werblin-type) target. *Sensory Processes,* 1976, *1,* 14–32.

Enoch, J. M., & Sunga, R. N. Development of Quantitative perimetric tests. *Documenta Ophthalmologica,* 1969, *26,* 215–229.

Enoch, J. M., Sunga, R. N., & Bachman, E. Static perimetric technique believed to test receptive field properties: II. Adaptation of the method to the qunatitative perimeter. *American Journal of Ophthalmology,* 1970, *70,* 124–137. (a)

Enoch, J. M., Sunga, R. N., & Bachman, E. Static perimetric technique believed to test receptive field properties: I. Extension of Westheimer's experiments on spatial interaction. *American Journal of Ophthalmology,* 1970, *70,* 113–126. (b)

Enroth-Cugell, C., & Robson, J. G. The contrast sensitivity of retinal ganglion cells of the cat. *Journal of Physiology,* 1966, *187,* 517–552.

Enroth-Cugell, C., & Shapley, R. M. Flux not retinal illumination, is what cat retinal ganglion cells really care about. *Journal of Physiology,* 1973, *233,* 311–326.

Epstein, W. (Ed.). *Stability and constancy in visual perception.* New York: Wiley, 1977.

Erb, M. B., & Dallenbach, K. M. "Subjective" colors from line-patterns. *American Journal of Psychology,* 1939, *52,* 227–241.

Ercoles, A. M., & Fiorentini, A. Visibility of the Mach bands as a function of field luminance. *Fondazione "Giorgio Ronchi," Florence, Atti,* 1959, *14,* 230–235.

Eriksen, C. W., Becker, B. B., & Hoffman, J. E. Safari to masking land: A hunt for the elusive U. *Perception & Psychophysics,* 1970, *8,* 245–250.

Eriksen, C. W., & Collins, J. F. Backward masking in vision. *Psychonomic Science,* 1964, *1,* 101–102. (a)

Eriksen, C. W., & Collins, J. F. Investigation of the effect of a priming stimulus on backward masking. *Psychonomic Science,* 1964, *1,* 249–250. (b)

Eriksen, C. W., & Collins, J. F. Some temporal characteristics of visual pattern perception. *Journal of Experimental Psychology,* 1967, *74,* 476–484.

Eriksen, C. W., & Hoffman, M. Form recognition as a function of adapting field and interval between stimulation. *Journal of Experimental Psychology,* 1963, *66,* 485–499.

Eriksen, C. W., & Lappin, J. S. Luminance summation-contrast reduction as a basis for certain forward and backward masking effects. *Psychonomic Science,* 1964, *1,* 313–314.

Eriksen, C. W., & Marshall, P. H. Failure to replicate a reported U-shaped visual masking function. *Psychonomic Science,* 1969, *15,* 195–196.

Eriksson, E. S. A field theory of visual illusions. *British Journal of Psychology,* 1970, *61,* 451–466.

d'Espagnat, B. The quantum theory and reality. *Scientific American,* 1979, *241*(5), 158–181.

Estes, W. K. Interactions of signal and background variables in visual processing. *Perception & Psychophysics,* 1972, *12,* 278–286.

Estes, W. K. Redundancy of noise elements and signals in the visual detection of letters. *Perception & Psychophysics,* 1974, *16,* 53–60.

Estes, W. K. *Handbook of learning and cognitive processes, Vol. 5: Human information processing.* Hillsdale, N.J.: Lawrence Erlbaum Associates, 1978.

Estevez, O., & Cavonius, C. R. Human color perception and Stiles' π mechanisms. *Vision Research,* 1977, *17,* 417–422.

Evans, C. R. Some studies of pattern perception using a stabilized retinal image. *British Journal of Psychology,* 1965, *56,* 121–133.

Fain, G. L., & Dowling, J. E. Intracellular recordings from single rods and cones in the mudpuppy retina. *Science,* 1973, *180,* 1178–1181.

Farley, B. G., & Clark, W. A. Simulation of a self-organizing system by a digital computer. *Institute of Radio Engineers Transactions of Information Theory,* 1954, *4,* 76–84.

Farnsworth, D. Tritanomalous vision as a threshold function. *Die Farbe,* 1955, *4,* 185–196.

Favreau, O. E., & Corballis, M. C. Negative aftereffects in visual perception. *Scientific American,* 1976, *235*(6), 42–48.

Favreau, O. E., Emerson, V. F., & Corballis, M. C. Motion perception: A color contingent aftereffect. *Science,* 1972, *176,* 78–79.

Fechner, G. T. Ueber eine Scheibe zur Erzeugung subjectiver Farben. *Poggendorff's Annalen der Physik and Chemie,* 1838, *45,* 227–232. (a)

Fechner, G. T. Ueber die subjectiven complementer Farben. *Poggendorff's Annalen der Physik und Chemie,* 1838, *44,* 513–535. (b)

Fechner, G. T. *Elemente der psychophysik.* Leipzig: Breitkopf & Hartel, 1860.

Fehmi, L. G., Adkins, J. W., & Lindsley, D. B. Electrophysiological correlates of visual perceptual masking in monkeys. *Experimental Brain Research,* 1969, *7,* 299–316.

Fehrer, E., & Ganchrow, D. Effects of exposure variables on figural aftereffects under tachistoscopic exposure. *Journal of Experimental Psychology,* 1963, *66,* 506–513.

Fehrer, E., & Raab, D. Reaction time to stimuli masked by metacontrast. *Journal of Experimental Psychology,* 1962, *63,* 143–147.

Feigl, H. The mental and the physical. In H. Feigl et al. (Eds.), *The Minnesota studies in the philosophy of science, Vol. II: Concepts, theories and the mind–body problem.* Minneapolis: University of Minnesota Press, 1958.

Feldon, S. E., Andrews, B. W., & Pollen, D. A. Periodic complex cells in cortical area 19 of the cat. *Vision Research,* 1978, *18,* 347–350.

Felsten, G., & Wasserman, G. S. Masking by light in *Limulus* receptors. *Journal of Comparative and Physiological Psychology,* 1978, *92,* 778–784.

Felsten, G., & Wasserman, G. S. Masking induced sensitivity changes in *Limulus* photoreceptors. *Vision Research,* 1979, *19,* 943–945.

Fender, D. H., & Julesz, B. Extension of Panum's fusional area in binocularly stabilized vision. *Journal of the Optical Society of America,* 1967, *57,* 819–830.

Ferry, E. S. Persistence in vision. *American Journal of Science,* 1892, *44,* 192–207.

Festinger, L., Allyn, M. R., & White, C. W. The perception of color with achromatic stimulation. *Vision Research,* 1971, *11,* 591–612.

Festinger, L., Coren, S., & Rivers, G. The effect of attention on brightness control and assimilation. *American Journal of Psychology,* 1970, *83,* 189–207.

Festinger, L., & Easton, A. M. Inferences about the afferent system based on a perceptual illusion produced by eye movements. *Psychological Review,* 1974, *81,* 44–58.

Fidell, L. S. Orientation specificity in chromatic adaptation of human "edge detectors." *Perception & Psychophysics,* 1970, *8,* 235–237.

Finch, D. Hyperbolic geometry as an alternative to perspective for constructing drawings of visual space. *Perception,* 1977, *6,* 221–225.

Finke, R. A., & Schmidt, M. J. Orientation-specific color aftereffects following imagination. *Journal of Experimental Psychology: Human Perception and Performance.* 1977, *3,* 599–606.

Fiorentini, A. Mach band phenomena. In D. Jameson & L. M. Hurvich (Eds.), *Handbook of sensory physiology: Visual psychophysics* (Vol. VII/4). New York: Springer-Verlag, 1972.

Fiorentini, A., Jeanne, M., & Toraldo di Francia, G. Measurements of differential threshold in the presence of spatial illumination gradient. *Fondazione "Giorgio Ronchi," Florence, Atti,* 1955, *10,* 371–379.

Fiorentini, A., & Zoli, M. T. Detection of a target superimposed to a step pattern of illumination. *Fondazione "Giorgio Ronchi," Florence, Atti,* 1966, *21,* 338–356.

Fiorentini, A., & Zoli, M.T. Detection of a target superimposed to a step pattern of illumination. II. Effects of a just-perceptible illumination step. *Fondazione "Giorgio Ronchi," Florence, Atti,* 1967, *22,* 207–217.

Fisher, B. Overlap of receptive field centers and representation of the visual field in the cat's optic tract. *Vision Research,* 1973, *13,* 2113–2120.

Fisher, G. H. Towards a new explanation for the geometrical illusions: II. Apparent depth or contour proximity. *British Journal of Psychology,* 1973, *64,* 607–621.

Flamant, F. Etude de la réportition de lumiere dans l'image retinienne d'une fente. *Revue D'optique Theorique et Instrumentale,* 1954, *34,* 433–459.

Flamant, F., & Stiles, W. S. The direction and spectral sensitivities of the retinal rods to adapting fields of different wavelengths. *Journal of Physiology,* 1948, *107,* 187–202.

Flandrin, J-M., & Jeannerod, M. Development constraints of motion detection mechanisms in the kitten. *Perception,* 1977, *6,* 513–527.

Fleischl, E. Physiologisch-optische Notizen, 2. Mittheilung. *Sitzungsberichte der Wiener Academie der Wissenschaften,* 1883, *86,* 8–25.

Foley, J. M. Primary distance perception. In R. Held, H. W. Leibowitz, and H-L. Teuber (Eds.), *Handbook of sensory physiology, Perception* (Vol. 8): Berlin: Springer-Verlag, 1978.

Foley, J. M., Applebaum, I. & Richards. W. Stereopsis with large disparaties: Discrimination and perceived depth. *Vision Research,* 1975, *15,* 417–421.

Forde, J., & Mackinnon, G. E. Binocular stimulation and the fragmentation of afterimages. *Quarterly Journal of Experimental Psychology,* 1975, *27,* 565–577.

Forgus, R. H., & Melamed, L. E. *Perception: A cognitive-stage approach.* New York: McGraw-Hill, 1976.

Forsythe, D. M. Use of a Fourier model in describing the fusion of complex visual stimuli. *Journal of the Optical Society of America,* 1960, *50,* 337–341.

Foster, D. H. Visual apparent motion and the calculus of variations. In E. L. J. Leeuwenberg & H. F. J. M. Buffart (Eds.), *Formal theories of visual perception.* Chichester, England: Wiley, 1978.

Fowles, G. R. *Introduction to modern optics.* New York: Holt, Rinehart, and Winston, 1975.

Fox, J. Continuity, concealment, and visual attention. In G. Underwood (Ed.), *Strategies of information processing.* New York: Academic Press, in press.

Fox, R., & Check, R. Binocular fusion: A test of the suppression theory. *Perception & Psychophysics,* 1967, *1,* 331–334.

Fox, R., & Herrmann, J. Stochastic properties of binocular rivalry alternations. *Perception & Psychophysics,* 1967, *2,* 432–436.

Fox, R., Lehmkuhle, S. W., & Westendorf, D. H. Falcon visual acuity. *Science,* 1976, *192,* 263–265.

Fraisse, P. *The psychology of time.* New York: Harper & Row, 1963.

Fraser, A. B. Theological optics. *Applied Optics,* 1975, *14*(4), A92–A93.

Fraser, A. B., & Mach, W. H. Mirages. *Scientific American,* January 1976, *234*(1), 102–112.

Freedman, D. Z., & Van Nieuwenhuizen, D. Supergravity and the unification of the laws of physics. *Scientific American,* 1978, *238*(2), 126–143.

French, J. W. The unaided eye: III. *Transactions of the Optical Society, London,* 1920, *21,* 127–156.

French, R. S. Pattern recognition in the presence of noise. *Journal of Experimental Psychology,* 1954, *47,* 27–31.

Friedman, R. B., Kaye, M. G., & Richards, W. Effect of vertical disparity upon stereoscopic depth, *Vision Research,* 1978, *18,* 351–352.

Frisby, J. P., & Clatworthy, J. L. Illusory contours: Curious cases of simultaneous brightness contrast. *Perception,* 1975, *4,* 349–357.

Frisby, J. P., & Mayhew, J. E. W. Global processes in stereopsis: Some comments on Ramachandran and Nelson (1976). *Perception,* 1977, *6,* 195–206.

Frisch, K. von. *The dance language and orientation of bees.* Cambridge, Mass.: Harvard University Press, 1967.

Frumkes, T. E., & Temme, L. A. Rod-cone interaction in human scotopic vision. II: Cones influence rod increment thresholds. *Vision Research,* 1977, *17,* 673–679.

Fry, G. A. Binocular integration of hue and brilliance. *Archives of Ophthalmology,* 1936, *15,* 443–456.

Fry, G. A. A photoreceptor mechanism for the modulation theory of color vision. *Journal of the Optical Society of America,* 1945, *35,* 113-135.

Fry, G. A. Mechanisms subserving simultaneous brightness contrast. *American Journal of Optometry,* 1948, *25,* 162-178.

Fry, G. A. Blur as a factor in form discrimination. In J. Wulfeck & J. Taylor (Eds.), *Form discrimination as related to military problems.* Washington, D.C.: NAS-NRC Publication No. 561, 1957.

Fry, G. A., & Bartley, S. H. The brilliance of an object seen binocularly. *American Journal of Ophthalmology,* 1933, *16,* 687-693.

Fry, G. A., & Bartley, S. H. The effect of one border in the visual field upon the threshold of another. *American Journal of Physiology,* 1935, *112,* 414-421.

Fujii, E. Forming a figure by movement of a luminous point. *Japanese Journal of Psychology,* 1943, *18,* 196-232.

Galanter, E. *Range and time estimates of dynamic visual targets* (Tech. Rep. PLR-27). New York: Psychophysics Laboratory, Columbia University, 1972.

Ganz, L. Is the figural after aftereffect an aftereffect? A review of its intensity, onset, decay and transfer characteristics. *Psychological Bulletin,* 1966, *66,* 151-165. (a)

Ganz, L. Mechanism of the figural aftereffect. *Psychological Review,* 1966, *73,* 128-150. (b)

Ganz, L. Temporal factors in visual perception. In E. C. Carterette & M. P. Friedman (Eds.). *Handbook of perception Seeing* (Vol. 5): New York: Academic Press, 1975.

Gardner, E. P., & Spencer, W. A. Sensory funneling. I. Psychophysical observations of human subjects and responses of cutaneous mechanoreceptive afferents in the cat to patterned skin stimuli. *Journal of Neurophysiology,* 1972, 35, 925-953. (b)

Gardner, E. P., & Spencer, W. A. Sensory funneling. II. Cortical neuronal representation of patterned cutaneous stimuli. *Journal of Neurophysiology,* 1972, 35, 954-977. (a)

Gardner, G. T. Evidence for independent parallel channels in tachistoscopic perception. *Cognitive Psychology,* 1973, *4,* 130-155.

Garner, W. R. An informational analysis of absolute judgments of loudness. *Journal of Experimental Psychology,* 1953, *46,* 373-380.

Garner, W. R. *Uncertainty and structure as psychological concepts.* Huntington, N.Y.: R. E. Krieger, 1962.

Garner, W. R. Information integration and form of encoding. In A. W. Melton & E. Martin (Eds.), *Coding processes in human memory.* Washington, D.C.: Winston, 1972.

Garner, W. R. *The processing of information and structure.* Hillsdale, N.J.: Lawrence Erlbaum Associates, 1974.

Geisler, W. S. The effects of photopigment depletion on brightness and threshold. *Vision Research,* 1978, *18,* 269-278.

Gelb, A. Die Farbenkonstanz der sehfinge. *Handbuch der Normalen und Pathologischen Physiologie,* 1929, *12,* 594-678.

Geldard, F. A. *Sensory saltation.* Hillsdale, N.J.: Lawrence Erlbaum Associates, 1975.

Geldard, F. A. The saltatory effect in vision. *Sensory Processes,* 1976, *1,* 77-86.

Gellhorn, E. Über den Wettstreit im Nachbild. VI. Über Intracorticale Errengungsvorgünge in der Sehrinde des Menschen. *Pfügers Archiv fur Gesamte Physiologie des Menschen und der Tiere,* 1928, *218,* 54-82.

Gell-Mann, M. A schematic model of baryons and mesons. *Physics Letters,* 1964, *8,* 214-215.

Georgeson, M. A. Antagonism between channels for pattern and movement in human vision. *Nature (London),* 1976, *259,* 413-415.

Gerjouy, H., & Clarke, F. R. Fechner colors on television. *American Journal of Psychology,* 1953, *71,* 606-607.

Gibson, E. J. *Principles of perceptual learning and development.* New York: Appleton-Century-Crofts, 1969.

Gibson, J. J. Adaptation, aftereffect, and contrast in the perception of curved lines. *Journal of Experimental Psychology,* 1933, *16,* 1–31.

Gibson, J. J. Adaptation with negative aftereffect. *Psychological Review,* 1937, *44,* 222–244.

Gibson, J. J. *The perception of the visual world.* Boston: Houghton Mifflin, 1950.

Gibson, J. J. What is a form? *Psychological Review,* 1951, *58,* 403–412.

Gibson, J. J. Perception as a function of stimulation. In S. Koch (Ed.), *Psychology: A study of a science, Vol. I.* New York: McGraw-Hill, 1959.

Gibson, J. J. *The senses considered as perceptual systems.* Boston: Houghton Mifflin, 1966.

Gibson, J. J. The information available in pictures. *Leonardo: Art, Science, and Technology,* 1971, *4,* 27–35.

Gibson, J. J. *The ecological approach to visual perception.* Boston: Houghton Mifflin, 1979.

Gibson, J. J., & Gibson, E. J. Perceptual learning: Differentiation or enrichment? *Psychological Review,* 1955, *62,* 32–41.

Gilbert, M. Colour perception in parafoveal vision. *Proceedings of the Physical Society, London,* 1950, *63,* 83–89.

Gilchrist, A. L. Perceived lightness depends on perceived spatial arrangement. *Science,* 1977, *195,* 185–187.

Gilchrist, A. L. The perception of surface blacks and whites. *Scientific American,* 1979, *240*(3), 112–124.

Gilinsky, A. S. The effect of attitude on the perception of size. *American Journal of Psychology,* 1955, *68,* 173–192.

Gilinsky, A. S., & Doherty, R. S. Interocular transfer of orientational effects. *Science,* 1969, *164,* 454–455.

Gillam, B. A depth processing theory of the Poggendorff illusion. *Perception & Psychophysics,* 1971, *10,* 211–216.

Gillam, B. Geometrical illusions. *Scientific American,* January 1980, *242*(1), 102–111.

Ginsburg, A. P. Is the illusory triangle physical or imaginary? *Nature,* 1975, *257,* 219–220.

Ginsburg, A. P., & Campbell, F. W. Optical transforms and the ''pin-cushion'' illusion. *Science,* 1977, *198,* 961–962.

Girgus, J. S., Coren, S., & Porac, C. Independence of *in vivo* human lens pigmentation from u.v. light exposure. *Vision Research,* 1977, *17,* 749–750.

Glezer, V. D., Bertulis, A. V., Ivanov, V. A., Kostelyanets, N. B., & Podvigin, N. F. Functional organization of the receptive fields of the retina. In G. V. Gersuni (Ed.), *Sensory processes at the neuronal and behavioral levels.* New York: Academic Press, 1971.

Glezer, V. D., Cooperman, A. M., Ivanov, V. A., & Tscherbach, T. A. An investigation of spatial frequency characteristics of complex receptive fields in the visual cortex of the cat. *Vision Research,* 1976, *16,* 789–797.

Glezer, V. D., Ivanov, V. H., and Tscherbach, T. A. Investigation of complex and hypercomplex receptive fields of visual cortex of the cat as spatial frequency filters. *Vision Research,* 1973, *13,* 1875–1904.

Gödel, K. Einige metamathematische resultate über entscheidungsdefinitheit und widerspruchsfreiheit. *Anzeiger der Akademie der Wissenschaften, Vienna Mathematischnaturwissenschaftliche Klasse,* 1930, *67,* 214–215.

Gogel, W. C. Scalor perceptions with binocular cues of distance. *American Journal of Psychology,* 1972, *85,* 477–497.

Gogel, W. C. The adjacency principle in visual perception. *Scientific American,* 1978, *238*(15), 126–139.

Gogel, W. C., & Mershon, D. H. Depth adjacency in simultaneous contrast. *Perception & Psychophysics,* 1969, *5,* 13–17.

Gogel, W. C., & Newton, R. F. Depth adjacency and the rod-frame illusion. *Perception & Psychophysics,* 1975, *18,* 163–171.

Goldsmith, T. H. The effects of screening pigments on the spectral sensitivity of some crustaceans with scotopic (superposition) eyes. *Vision Research,* 1978, *18,* 475–482.

Goldstein, M. B., & Weintraub, D. J. The parallel-less Poggendorff: Virtual contours put the illusion down but not out. *Perception & Psychophysics*, 1973, *11*, 353–355.

Goldstein, M. J. A test of the response probability theory of perceptual defense. *Journal of Experimental Psychology,* 1962, *63,* 23–28.

Gombrich, E. H. *Art and illusion: A study in the psychology of pictorial representation.* London: Phaidon Press, 1960.

Gordon, B., Presson, J., Parkwood, J., & Scheer, R. Alteration of cortical orientation selectivity: Importance of asymmetric input. *Science,* 1979, *204,* 1109–1111.

Gorrand, J. M. Diffusion of the human retina and quality of the optics of the eye on the fovea and the peripheral retina. *Vision Research,* 1979, *19,* 907-912.

Goryo, K. The effect of past experience upon binocular rivalry. *Japanese Psychological Research,* 1969, *11,* 46–53.

Goryo, K., & Kawai, R. Short-term visual storage and the position effect in the stimulus display. *Japanese Psychological Research,* 1972, *14,* 209–218.

Gourlay, K., Gyr, J. W., Walters, S., & Willey, R. Instrumentation designed to simulate the effects of prisms used in studies of visual rearrangement. *Behavior Research Methods and Instumentation,* 1975, *7*(3), 294–300.

Grabowski, S. R., Pinto, L. H., & Pak, W. L. Adaptation in retinal rods of axolotl: Intracellular recordings. *Science,* 1972, *176,* 1240–1245.

Graham, C. H. Figural aftereffects as functions of contrast, area, and luminance. *Psychologia,* 1961, *4,* 201–208.

Graham, C. H. Perception of movement. In C. H. Graham (Ed.), *Vision and visual perception.* New York: Wiley, 1965. (a)

Graham, C. H. (Ed.). *Vision and visual perception.* New York: Wiley, 1965. (b)

Graham, C. H. Visual space perception. In C. H. Graham (Ed.), *Vision and visual perception.* New York: Wiley, 1965 (c)

Graham, C. H., & Brown, J. L. Color contrast and color appearances: Brightness constancy and color constancy. In C. H. Graham (Ed.), *Vision and visual perception.* New York: Wiley, 1965.

Graham, N. Spatial frequency channels in human vision: Effects of luminance and pattern drift rate. *Vision Research,* 1972, *12,* 53–68.

Graham, N. Spatial frequency channels in human vision: Detecting edges without edge detectors. In C. S. Harris (Ed.), *Visual coding and adaptability.* Hillsdale, N.J.: Lawrence Erlbaum Associates, 1980.

Graham, N., & Nachmias, J. Detection of grating patterns containing two spatial frequencies: A comparison of single channel and multiple channel model. *Vision Research,* 1971, *11,* 251–259.

Graham, N., & Ratliff, F. Quantitative theories of the integrative action of the retina. In R. E. Atkinson, D. L. Luce, & P. Suppes (Eds.), *Contemporary developments in mathematical psychology.* San Francisco: W. H. Freeman, 1974.

Graham, N., Robson, J. G., & Nachmias, J. Grating summation in fovea and periphery. *Vision Research,* 1978, *18,* 815-825.

Graham, N., & Rogowitz, B. E. Spatial pooling properties deduced from the detectability of FM and quasi-AM gratings: A reanalysis. *Vision Research,* 1976, *16,* 1021-1026.

Granit, R. The components of the retinal action potential in mammals and their relation to the discharge in the optic nerve. *Journal of Physiology,* 1933, *77,* 207–239.

Granit, R. *The purposive brain.* Cambridge, Mass.: MIT Press, 1977.

Grassman, H. On the theory of compound colours. *Philosophical Magazine,* 1854, *7,* 254–264.

Graybiel, A. M. Some ascending connections of the pulvinar and nucleus lateralis posterior of the thalamus of the cat. *Brain Research,* 1972, *44,* 99–125.

Graybiel, A. M. Studies on the anatomical organization of posterior association cortex. In F. O.

Schmitt & F. G. Worden (Eds.), *The neurosciences: Third study program*. Cambridge, Mass.: MIT Press, 1974.

Green, B. F. *Kinetic depth effect*. Massachusetts Institute of Technology, Cambridge, Mass.: Lincoln Laboratory, 1959. (Quarterly Progress Report)

Green, D. G. Sinusoidal flicker characteristics of the color-sensitive mechanisms of the eye. *Vision Research*, 1969, *9*, 591-601.

Green, D. G. Regional variations in the visual acuity for interference fringes on the retina. *Journal of Physiology*, 1970, *207*, 351-356.

Green, D. G. Light adaptation in the rat retina: Evidence for two receptor mechanisms. *Science*, 1971, *174*, 598-600.

Green, D. G., & Campbell, F. W. Effect of focus on the visual response to a sinusoidally modulated spatial stimulus. *Journal of the Optical Society of America*, 1965, *55*, 1154-1157.

Green, D. G., Tong, L., & Cicerone, C. M. Lateral spread of light adaptation in the rat retina. *Vision Research*, 1977, *17*, 479-486.

Green, M. A., Corwin, T. R., & Zemon, V. Checkerboards and color aftereffects. *Science*, 1977, *198*, 209.

Greeno, J. G. Process of understanding in problem solving. In N. J. Castellan, Jr., D. B. Pisoni, & G. R. Potts (eds.), *Cognitive theory*. Vol. 2. Hillsdale, New Jersey: Lawrence Erlbaum Associates, 1977.

Greenspon, T. S., & Eriksen, C. W. Interocular nonindependence. *Perception & Psychophysics*, 1968, *3*, 93-96.

Greenwood, R. E. Visibility of structural and unstructural images. *Journal of the Optical Society of America*, 1973, *63*, 226-231.

Gregory, R. L. Visual Illusions. In B. M. Foss (Ed.), *New horizons in psychology*. Harmondsworth, England: Penguin, 1966.

Gregory, R. L. Visual Illusions. *Scientific American*, 1968, *219*(5), 66-76.

Gregory, R. L. *The intelligent eye*. London & New York: Weidenfeld, 1970.

Gregory, R. L. Choosing a paradigm for perception. In E. C. Carterette & M. P. Friedman (Eds.), *Handbook of perception: Historical and philosophical roots of perception* (Vol. 1). New York: Academic Press, 1974.

Gregory, R. L. Do we need cognitive concepts? In M. S. Gazziniga & C. Blakemore (Eds.), *Handbook of psychobiology*. New York: Academic Press, 1975.

Gregory, R. L. Vision with isoluminant colour contrast: 1. A projection technique and observations. *Perception*, 1977, *6*, 113-119.

Gregory, R. L., & Gombrich, E. H. (Eds.). *Illusion in nature and art*. London: Duckworth, 1973.

Gregson, M. A. Psychophysical hallucinations of orientation and spatial frequency. *Perception*, 1976, *5*, 99-111.

Grice, G. R., Nullmeyer, R., & Schnizlein, J. M. Variable criterion analysis of brightness effects in simple reaction time. *Journal of Experimental Psychology: Human Perception and Performance*, 1979, *5*, 303-314.

Gross, C. G., Bender, D. B., & Rocha-Miranda, C. E. Inferotemporal cortex: A single unit analysis. In F. O. Schmitt & F. G. Worden (Eds.), *The neurosciences: Third study program*. Cambridge, Mass.: MIT Press, 1974.

Grossberg, M. Frequencies and latencies in detecting two-flash stimuli. *Perception & Psychophysics*, 1970, *7*, 377-380.

Growney, R. Metacontrast as a function of the spatial frequency composition of the target and mask. *Vision Research*, 1978, *18*, 1117-1124.

Grünau, M. W. von. The involvement of illusory contours in stroboscopic motion. *Perception & Psychophysics*, 1979, *25*, 205-208.

Grüsser, O. J. A quantitative analysis of spatial summation of excitation and inhibition within the receptive field of retinal ganglion cells of cats. *Vision Research*, 1971, *3*, 103-127.

Guillery, R. W. A study of Golgi preparations from the dorsal lateral geniculate nucleus of the adult cat. *Journal of Comparative Neurology,* 1966, *125,* 21–50.

Gulick, W. L., & Lawson, R. B. *Human stereopsis: A psychophysical analysis.* New York: Oxford University Press, 1976.

Guth, S. L. The effect of wavelength on visual perceptual latency. *Vision Research,* 1964, *4,* 567–578.

Guth, S. L. Nonadditivity and inhibition among chromatic luminances at theshold. *Vision Research,* 1967, *7,* 319–328.

Guth, S. L. Photometric and colorimetric additivity at various intensities. R. M. Musterschmidt (Ed.), *Proceedings, First A.I.C. Congress,* Stockholm, Sweden. Berlin: June 1969.

Guth, S. L., Donley, N. J., & Marrocco, R. T. On luminance additivity and related topics. *Vision Research,* 1969, *9,* 537–575.

Guth, S. L., & Lodge, H. R. Heterochromatic additivity, foveal spectral sensitivity, and a new color model. *Journal of the Optical Society of America,* 1973, *63,* 450–462.

Gyr, J. Is a theory of direct visual perception adequate? *Psychological Bulletin,* 1972, *77,* 246–261.

Haber, R. N. Repetition, visual persistence, visual noise, and information processing. In K. N. Leibovic (Ed.), *Information processing in the nervous system.* New York: Springer-Verlag, 1969.

Haber, R. N. Information processing. In E. C. Carterette & M. P. Friedman (Eds.), *Handbook of perception: Historical and philosophical roots of perception* (Vol. 1). New York: Academic Press, 1974.

Haber, R. N., & Standing, L. G. Direct measures of short-term visual storage. *Quarterly Journal of Experimental Psychology,* 1969, *21,* 43–54.

Haber, R. N., & Standing, L. G. Direct estimates of the apparent duration of a flash. *Canadian Journal of Psychology,* 1970, *24*(4), 216–229.

Hagen, M. A. Picture perception: Toward a theoretical model. *Psychological Bulletin,* 1974, *81,* 471–497.

Hagins, W. A., Penn, R. D., & Yoshikami, S. Dark current and photocurrent in retinal rods. *Biophysical Journal,* 1970, *10,* 380–412.

Haidinger, W. Über das directe Erkennen des polarisierten lichts und der lage der polarisationsebene. *Annalen der Physik,* 1844, *64,* 29–39.

Hake, H. W., Rodwan, A., & Weintraub, D. Noise reduction in perception. In K. R. Hammond (Ed.), *Psychology of Egon Brunswik.* New York: Holt, Rinehart, & Winston, 1966.

Hakerem, G., & Sutton, S. Pupillary response at visual threshold. *Nature,* 1966, *212,* 485–486.

Hallett, P. E. Rapid changes and hysteresis in spatial integration for human rod vision. *Journal of Physiology,* 1971, *215,* 433–447.

Hallett, P. E., Marriott, F. H. C., & Rodger, F. C. The relationship of visual threshold to retinal position and area. *Journal of Physiology,* 1962, *160,* 364–373.

Hamlyn, D. W. *Sensation and perception: A history of the philosophy of perception.* London: Routledge & Kegan Paul, 1961.

Hammer, E. R. Temporal factors in figural aftereffects. *American Journal of Psychology,* 1949, *62,* 337–354.

Hammond, A. L., Maugh, T. H., II. Stratospheric pollution: Multiple threats to earth's ozone. *Science,* 1974, *186,* 335–338.

Hansel, C. E. M., & Mahmud, S. H. Comparable retention times for the negative colour afterimage and the McCollough effect. *Vision Research,* 1978, *18,* 1601–1605.

Hanson, A. R., & Riseman, E. M. *A progress report on VISIONS: Representation and control in the construction of visual models* (COINS Technical Report 76-9). Amherst: University of Massachusetts, 1976.

Hardy, A. C., & Perrin, F. H. *The principles of optics.* New York: McGraw-Hill Book Company, 1932.

Harker, G. S. A saccadic suppression explanation of the Pulfrich phenomenon. *Perception & Psychophysics,* 1967, *2,* 423–426.

Harmon, L. D. Artificial neuron. *Science,* 1959, *129,* 962–963.

Harmon, L. D., & Lewis, E. R. Neural modeling. *Physiological Reviews,* 1966, *46,* 513–591.

Harris, C. S., & Gibson, A. K. Is orientation-specific color adaptation due to edge detectors, afterimages, or "dipoles"? *Science,* 1968, *162,* 1506–1507.

Harris, J. P., & Gregory, R. L. Fusion and rivalry of illusory contours. *Perception,* 1973, *2,* 235–247.

Hartline, H. K., & Ratliff, F. Inhibitory interaction of receptor units in the eye of *Limulus. Journal of General Physiology,* 1957, *40,* 357–376.

Hartline, H. K., & Ratliff, F. Spatial summation of inhibitory influences in the eye of the *Limulus,* and the mutual interaction of receptor units. *Journal of General Physiology,* 1958, *41,* 1049–1066.

Hartline, H. K., Wagner, H., & Ratliff, F. Inhibition in the eye of *Limulus. Journal of General Physiology,* 1956, *39,* 651–673.

Hartridge, H. The limit to peripheral vision. *Journal of Physiology,* 1919, *53,* xvii–xviii.

Hartridge, H. The polychromatic theory. *Documenta Ophthalmologica,* 1949, *3,* 166–193.

Hasegawa, T. Temporal transition of Mach bands. *Abstract Guide of XXth International Congress of Psychology,* 1972.

Hayes-Roth, F. Critique of Turvey's "Contrasting orientations to the theory of visual information processing." *Psychological Review,* 1977, *84,* 531–535.

Hayes-Roth, F. Distinguishing theories of a representation: A critique of Anderson's "Arguments concerning mental imagery." *Psychological Review,* 1979, *86,* 376–382.

Hebb, D. O. *The organization of behavior.* New York: Wiley, 1949.

Hecht, S. Vision II. The nature of the photoreceptor process. In C. Murchison (Ed.), *A handbook of general experimental psychology.* Worchester, Mass.: Clarke University Press, 1934.

Hecht, S. Rods, cones, and the chemical basis of vision. *Physiology Reveiw,* 1937, *17,* 239–290.

Hecht, S., Haig, C., & Wald, G. Dark adaptation of retinal fields of different size and location. *Journal of General Physiology,* 1935, *19,* 321–337.

Hecht, S., Hendley, C. D., Frank, S. R., and Haig, C. Anoxia and brightness discrimination. *Journal of General Physiology,* 1946, *29,* 335–351.

Hecht, S., & Mintz, E. U. The visibility of single lines at various illuminations and the retinal basis of visual resolution. *Journal of General Physiology,* 1939, *22,* 593–612.

Hecht, S., Peskin, J. C., & Patt, M. Intensity discrimination in the human eye, II: Relation between ΔI/I for different parts of the spectrum. *Journal of General Physiology,* 1938, *22,* 7–19.

Hecht, S., & Shlaer, S. Intermittent stimulation by light. V. The relation between intensity and critical frequency for different parts of the spectrum. *Journal of General Physiology,* 1936, *19,* 965–977.

Hecht, S., Shlaer, S., & Pirenne, M. H. Energy, quanta, and vision. *Journal of General Physiology,* 1942, *25,* 819–840.

Hecht, S., & Smith, E. L. Intermittent stimulation by light. VI. Area and the relation between critical frequency and intensity. *Journal of General Physiology,* 1936, *19,* 979–988.

Hecht, S., & Verrijp, C. D. Intermittent stimulation by light. III. The relation between intensity and critical fusion frequency for different retinal locations. *Journal of General Physiology,* 1933, *17,* 251–265.

Heggelund, P., & Hohmann, A. Long-term retention of the "Gilinsky effect." *Vision Research,* 1976, *16,* 1015–1017.

Heinemann, E. G. Simultaneous brightness induction as a function of inducing and test-field luminance. *Journal of Experimental Psychology,* 1955, *50,* 89–96.

Held, R., Leibowitz, H. W., Teuber, H.-L. *Handbook of sensory physiology, Vol. 3: Perception.* New York: Springer-Verlag, 1978.

Heller, J., Ostwald, T. J., & Bok, D. Effect of illumination on the membrane permeability of rod photoreceptor discs. *Biochemistry,* 1970, *9,* 4884–4889.

Helmholtz, H. von *Handbuch der physiologischen optik.* Zweiter Band, Leipzig: Voss, 1856/1860/1866/1867/1924/1962.

Helson, H. The fundamental propostion of Gestalt psychology. *Psychological Review,* 1933, *40,* 13–32.

Helson, H. Some factors and implications of color constancy. *Journal of the Optical Society of America,* 1943, *35,* 555–567.

Helson, H. Adaptation-level as a basis for a quantitative theory of frames of reference. *Psychological Review,* 1948, *55,* 297–313.

Helson, H. Studies of anomalous contrast and assimilation. *Journal of the Optical Society of America,* 1963, *63,* 179–184.

Helson, H. *Adaptation-level theory: An experimental and systematic approach to behavior.* New York: Harper & Row, 1964.

Helson, H. Perception. In H. Helson & W. Bevan (Eds.), *Contemporary approaches to psychology.* Princeton, N.J.: D. Van Nostrand, 1967.

Helson, H., & Rohles, F. H., Jr. A quantitative study of reversal of classical lightness contrast. *American Journal of Psychology,* 1959, *72,* 530–538.

Hennessy, R. T., & Leibowitz. Laser optometer incorporating the Badal principle. *Behavioral Research Methods and Instrumentation,* 1972, *4,* 237–239.

Henning, G. B., Hertz, B. G., & Broadbent, D. E. Some experiments bearing on the hypothesis that the visual system analyzes spatial patterns in independent bands of spatial frequency. *Vision Research,* 1975, *15,* 887–897.

Hensel, H., & Boman, K. K. Afferent impulses in cutaneous sensory nerves in human subjects. *Journal of Neurophysiology,* 1960, *23,* 564–577.

Hensen, V. Über eine Einrichtung der Fovea centralis retinea, welche bewirkt, dass feinere Distanzen als solche, die dem Durchmesser eines Zapfens entsprechen, noch unterschieden werden konnen. *Archiv für Pathologische Anatomie und Physiologie und für Klinische Medizin,* 1865, *34,* 401–411.

Hensen, V. Über das Sehen in der Fovea centralis. *Archiv für Pathologische Anatomie und Physiologie und für Klinische Medizin,* 1867, *39,* 475–492.

Hering, E. Über die theorie des simultanen contrastes von Vhelmholtz. *Pflüger's Archiv für die Gesamte Physiologie des Menschen und der Tiere,* 1887, *41,* 1–29.

Hering, E. Uber die Grenzen der Sehscharfe. *Berichte uber die Verhandlungen der Koniglich Sachsischen Gesellschaft der Wissenschaften zu Liepzig, Mathematisch-Physische Classe, Naturwissenshaft-Lichertheil,* 1899, 51, 16–24.

Hering, E. [*Outlines of a theory of the light sense.*] (L. M. Hurvich & D. Jameson, trans.). Cambridge, Mass.: Harvard University Press, 1964. (Originally published, 1905–1920.)

Hermann, L. Eine erscheinung des simultanen contrastes. *Pflüger's Archiv* für die Gesamte Physiologie des Menschen und der Tiere, 1870, 3, 13—15 .

Hernandez, L. L., & Lefton, L. A. Metacontrast as measured under a signal detection method. *Perception,* 1977, *6,* 695–702.

Herrick, R. M. Foveal luminance discrimination as a function of the duration of the decrement or increment in luminance. *Journal of Comparative and Physiological Psychology,* 1956, *49,* 437–443.

Herrick, R. M. Increment threshold for two identical flashes. *Journal of the Optical Society of America,* 1972, *62,* 104–110. (a)

Herrick, R. M. Increment thresholds for two nonidentical flashes. *Journal of the Optical Society of America,* 1972, *62,* 588–593. (b)

Herrick, R. M. Foveal increment thresholds for multiple flashes. *Journal of the Optical Society of America,* 1973, *63,* 870–878. (a)

Herrick, R. M. Increment thresholds for multiple identical flashes in the peripheral retina. *Journal of the Optical Society of America,* 1973, *63,* 1261-1265. (b)

Herrick, R. M. Psychophysical methodology: VI. Random method limits. *Perception & Psychophysics,* 1973, *13,* 548-554. (c)

Hershberger, W. A., & Carpenter, D. L. Veridical rotation in depth in unidimensional projections devoid of three motion-parallax cues. *Journal of Experimental Psychology,* 1972, *93,* 213-216.

Hershberger, W. A., Carpenter, D. L., Starzel, J., & Laughlin, N. K. Simulation of an object rotating indepth: Constant and reversal projection ratios. *Journal of Experimental Psychology,* 1974, *103,* 844-853.

Hess, C., & Pretori, H. Messende untersachungen uber die gesetzmassigkeit des simultanen Helligkeits-contrastes. *Albert von Graefe's Archiv fur Klinische und Experimentelle Ophthalmologie,* 1894, *40,* 1-24.

Hess, E. F. Attitude and pupil size. *Scientific American,* April 1965, *212,* 46-54.

Higgins, K. E., & Knoblauch. K. Spatial Broca-Sulzer effect at brief stimulus durations. *Vision Research,* 1977, *17,* 332-334.

Higgins, K. E., & Rinalducci, E. J. The spatial Broca-Sulzer and sensitization effects for foveal viewing. *Vision Research,* 1975, *15,* 423-425. (a)

Higgins, K. E., & Rinalducci, E. J. Suprathreshold intensity-area relationships: A spatial Broca-Sulzer effect. *Vision Research,* 1975, *15,* 129-143. (b)

Higginson, G. D. The place of ocular movements in stroboscopic perception. *American Journal of Psychology,* 1926, *37,* 408-413.

Hinton, H. E., & Gibbs, D. F. Diffraction gratings in phalacrid beetles. *Nature,* 1969, *221,* 953-954.

Hinton, H. E., & Gibbs, D. F. Diffraction gratings in gyrinid beetles. *Journal of Insect Physiology,* 1971, *17,* 1023-1035.

Hirsch, H. V., & Spinelli, D. N. Visual experience modifies distribution of horizontally and vertically oriented receptive fields in cats. *Science,* 1970, *168,* 869-871.

Hirsch, H. V., & Spinelli, D. N. Modification of the distribution of receptive field orientation in cats by selective visual exposure during development. *Experimental Brain Research,* 1971, *12,* 509-527.

Hirst, R. J. *The problem of perception.* London: Humanities Press, 1959.

Hirst, R. J. (Ed.). *Perception and the external world.* New York: Macmillan, 1965.

Hobbes, T. *Leviathan.* (M. Oakeshott, ed.). New York: Macmillan, 1962. (Originally published, 1651.)

Hochberg, J. In the mind's eye. In R. N. Haber (Ed.), *Contemporary theory and research in visual perception.* New York: Holt, Rinehart, & Winston, 1968.

Hochberg, J. Perception. In J. W. Kling & L. A. Riggs (Eds.), *Experimental Psychology* (3rd ed.). New York: Holt. Rinehart, & Winston, 1971.

Hochberg, J. E., & Hardy, D. Brightness and proximity factors in grouping. *Perception and Motor Skills,* 1960, *10,* 22.

Hochberg, J. E., & Silverstein, A. A. A quantitative index of stimulus similarity: Proximity vs. differences in brightness. *American Journal of Psychology,* 1956, *69,* 456-458.

Hochberg, J., Triebel, W., & Seaman, G. Color adaptation under conditions of homogeneous stimulation (ganzfeld). *Journal of Experimental Psychology,* 1951, *41,* 153-159.

Hochheimer, B. F. Polarized light retinal photography of a monkey eye. *Vision Research,* 1978, *18,* 19-23.

Hoffman, K. P., Stone, J., & Sherman, S. M. Relay of receptive-field properties in dorsal lateral geniculate nucleus of the cat. *Journal of Neurophysiology,* 1972, *35,* 518-531.

Hoffman, W. C. The Lie algebra of visual perception. *Journal of Mathematical Psychology,* 1966, *3,* 65-98.

Hoffman, W. C. Higher visual perception as prolongation of the basic Lie transformation group. *Mathematical Biosciences,* 1970, *6,* 437–471.

Hoffman, W. C. Visual illusions of angles as an application of Lie transformational groups. *Society for Industrial and Applied Mathematics,* 1971, *13,* 169–184.

Hoffman, W. C. The Lie transformation group approach to visual neurophysiology. In E. L. J. Leeuwenberg & H. Buffart (Eds.), *Formal theories of visual perception.* London: Halsted Press, 1978.

Hogben, J. H. *Perception of visual pattern with components distributed in time.* Unpublished doctoral dissertation, University of Western Australia, 1972.

Hogben, J. H., & DiLollo, V. Practice induced decrement of suppression in metacontrast and apparent motion. University of Western Australia, personal communication, 1978.

Holden, A. L. Extensive lateral transmission in the inner plexiform layer of the pigeon retina. *Vision Research,* 1977, *17,* 665–666.

Holt, E. B. Eye movement and central anaesthesia. *Harvard Psychology Studies,* 1903, *1,* 3–45.

Holway, A. H., & Boring, E. G. Determinants of apparent visual size with distance variants. *American Journal of Psychology,* 1941, *54,* 21–37.

Hood, D. C., & Grover, B. G. Temporal summation of light by a vertebrate visual receptor. *Science,* 1974, *184,* 1003-1005.

Horeman, H. W. Inductive brightness depression as influenced by configurational condition. *Vision Research,* 1963, *3,* 121–130.

Horeman, H. W. Relations between brightness and luminance under induction. *Vision Research,* 1965, *5,* 331-340.

Howard, H. J. A test for the judgment of distance. *American Journal of Optometry,* 1919, *2,* 656–675.

Howard, I. P. Some new subjective phenomena apparently due to interocular transfer. *Nature (London),* 1959, *184,* 1516–1517.

Howard, J. H., & Ballas, J. A. *Feature selection in auditory perception* (Technical Report ONR-78-5). Department of Psychology; The Catholic University of America: Human Performance Laboratory, 1978.

Howard, R. B. Neurophysiological models of figural aftereffects and visual illusions. *Psychonomic Monograph Supplements,* 1971, *4,* 57–72.

Hubel, D. Vision and the brain. *Bulletin of the American Academy of Arts and Sciences,* 1978, *XXXI,* 17–28.

Hubel, D. H., & Wiesel, T. N. Receptive fields of single neurons in the cat's striate cortex. *Journal of Physiology,* 1959, *148,* 574–591.

Hubel, D. H., & Wiesel, T. N. Receptive fields, binocular interaction, and functional architecture in the cat's visual cortex. *Journal of Physiology,* 1962, *160,* 106–154.

Hubel, D. H., & Wiesel, T. N. Shape and arrangement of columns in cat's striate cortex. *Journal of Physiology,* 1963, *165,* 559-568.

Hubel, D. H., & Wiesel, T. N. Receptive fields and functional architecture in two nonstriate visual areas (18 and 19) of the cat. *Journal of Neurophysiology,* 1965, *28,* 229–289.

Hubel, D. H., & Wiesel, T. N. Receptive fields and functional architecture of monkey striate cortex. *Journal of Physiology,* 1968, *195,* 215–243.

Hubel, D. H., & Wiesel, T. N. Stereoscopic vision in macaque monkey. *Nature,* 1970, *225,* 41–42.

Hubel, D. H., & Wiesel, T. N. Laminar and columnar distribution of geniculo-cortical fibers in the macaque monkey. *Journal of Comparative Neurology,* 1972, *146,* 421–450.

Hughes, G. W., & Maffei, L. Retinal ganglion cell response to sinusoidal light stimulation. *Journal of Neurophysiology,* 1966, *29,* 333-352.

Hull, C. L. *Principles of behavior.* New York: Appleton-Century-Crofts, 1943.

Hull, C. L. *Essentials of behavior.* New Haven, Conn.: Yale University Press, 1951.

Hull, C. L. *A behavior system*. New Haven, Conn.: Yale University Press, 1952.

Hull, D. *Introduction to dislocations*. Oxford: Pergamon Press, 1965.

Hume, D. *A treatise of human nature* (L. Selby-Bigge, Ed.). Oxford: Oxford University Press, 1941. (Originally published, 1739.)

Hume, D. *Enquiry concerning human understanding* (2nd ed.) (T. J. McCormack & M. W. Calkins, Eds.). LaSalle, Ill.: Open Court Publishing, 1966. (Originally published, 1748.)

Hurvich, L. M. Color vision deficiencies. In D. Jameson & L. M. Hurvich (Eds.), *Handbook of sensory physiology: Visual psychophysics* (Vol. VII/4). New York: Springer-Verlag, 1972.

Hurvich, L. M., & Jameson, D. Spectral sensitivity of the fovea. I. Neutral adaptation. *Journal of the Optical Society of America,* 1953, *43,* 485–494.

Hurvich, L. M., & Jameson, D. Some quantitative aspects of an opponent-color theory. II. Brightness, saturation, and hue in normal and dichromatic vision. *Journal of the Optical Society of America,* 1955, *45,* 602–616.

Hurvich, L. M., & Jameson, D. An opponent-process theory of color vision. *Psychological Review,* 1957, *64,* 384–404.

Ikeda, H., & Obonai, T. The qualitative analysis of figural aftereffects: I. The process of growth and decay of figural aftereffects. *Japanese Journal of Psychology,* 1953, *23,* 246–260.

Ikeda, H., & Wright, M. J. Receptive field organization of "sustained" and "transient" retinal ganglion cells which subserve different functional roles. *Journal of Physiology,* 1972, 227, 769–800.

Ikeda, H., & Wright, M. J. Evidence for "sustained" and "transient" neurons in the cat's visual cortex. *Vision Research,* 1974, *14,* 133–136.

Ikeda, M., & Uchikawa, K. Integrating time for visual pattern perception and a comparison with the tactile mode. *Vision Research,* 1978, *18,* 1565–1571.

Ingling, C. R., Jr. The spectral sensitivity of the opponent-color channels. *Vision Research,* 1977, *17,* 1083–1089.

Ingling, C. R., Jr., & Drum, B. A. Why the blue arcs of the retina are blue. *Vision Research,* 1977, *17,* 498–500.

Ingling, C. R., Jr., Lewis, A. L., Loose, D. R., & Myers, K. J. Cones change rod sensitivity. *Vision Research,* 1977, *17,* 555–563.

Ingling, C. R., Jr., Russell. P. W., Rea, M. S., & Tsou, B. H. P., Red-green opponent spectral sensitivity: Disparity between cancellation and direct matching methods. *Science,* 1978, *201,* 1221–1223.

Ingling, C. R., Jr., & Tsou, B. H. P. Orthogonal combination of the three visual channels. *Vision Research,* 1977, *17,* 1075–1082.

Ives, H. E. A theory of intermittent vision. *Journal of the Optical Society of America and Review of Scientific Instruments*. 1922, *6,* 343–361.

Jacewitz, M. M., & Lehmann, D. Iconic memory, dichoptic interference and short-term consolidation. *Neuropsychologia,* 1972, *10,* 193–198.

Jaeger, W. Genetics of congenital colour deficiencies. In D. Jameson & L. M. Hurvich (Eds.), *Handbook of sensory physiology, Visual psychophysics (Vol. VII/4).* New York: Springer-Verlag, 1972.

James, W. *The principles of psychology*. New York: Dover, 1890.

Jameson, D. Theoretical issues of color vision. In D. Jameson & L. M. Hurvich (Eds.), *Handbook of sensory physiology: Visual Psychophysics* (Vol. VII/4). New York: Springer-Verlag, 1972.

Jameson, D., & Hurvich, L. M. Some quantitative aspects of an opponent-colors theory. I. Chromatic responses and spectral saturation. *Journal of the Optical Society of America,* 1955, *45,* 546–552.

Jameson, D., & Hurvich, L. M. Complexities of perceived brightness. *Science*, 1960, *133*, 174–179.

Jameson, D., & Hurvich, L. M. Color adaptation: Sensitivity, contrast, afterimages. In D. Jameson & L. M. Hurvich (Eds.), *Handbook of sensory physiology: Visual psychophysics* (Vol. VII/4). New York: Springer-Verlag, 1972. (a)

Jameson, D., & Hurvich, L. M. (Eds.). *Handbook of sensory physiology: Visual psychophysics* (Vol. VII/4). Berlin: Springer-Verlag, 1972. (b)

Jarvis, J. R. *A study of temporally based subjective colour phenomena*. Unpublished doctoral dissertation, City University, London, 1974.

Jarvis, J. R. On Fechner–Benham subjective colour. *Vision Research,* 1977, *17,* 445–451.

Jenkins, B., & Ross, J. McCollough effect depends on perceptual organization. *Perception,* 1977, *6,* 399–400.

Jesteadt, W., Green, D. M., & Wier, C. C. The Rawdon–Smith illusion. *Perception & Psychophysics,* 1978, *23,* 244–250.

Johansson, G. Rigidity, stability, and motion in perceptual space. *Acta Psychologia,* 1958, *14,* 359–370.

Johansson, G. Perception of motion and changing form. *Scandinavian Journal of Psychology,* 1964, *5,* 181–208.

Johansson, G. Visual perception of biological motion and a model for its analysis, *Perception & Psychophysics,* 1973, *14,* 201–211.

Johansson, G. Spatiotemporal differentiation and integration in visual motion perception. *Psychological Research,* 1976, 38, 379–393.

Johansson, G. About the geometry underlying spontaneous visual decoding of the optical message. In E. L. J. Leeuwenberg & H. F. J. M. Buffart (Eds.), *Formal theories of visual perception.* Chichester, England: Wiley, 1978.

John, E. R. *Mechanisms of memory*. New York: Academic Press, 1967.

John, E. R. Switchboard versus statistical theories of learning and memory. *Science,* 1972, *177,* 850–864.

John, E. R., & Schwartz, E. L. The neurophysiology of information processing and cognition. *Annual Review of Psychology*, 1978, *29*, 1–29.

Johnson, C. A. & Enoch, J. M. Human psychophysical analysis of receptive field-like properties. II. Dichoptic properties of the Westheimer function. *Vision Research,* 1976, *16,* 1455–1462. (a)

Johnson, C. A., & Enoch, J. M. Human psychophysical analysis of receptive fieldlike properties. III. Dichoptic properties of a new transient-like psychophysical function. *Visual Research,* 1976, *16,* 1463–1470. (b)

Johnson, C. A., & Enoch, J. M. Human psychophysical analysis of receptive fieldlike properties. II. Dichoptic properties of the Westheimer function. *Vision Research,* 1976, *16,* 1455–1462. (c)

Johnson, C. A., & Enoch, J. M. Human psychophysical analysis of receptive fieldlike properties. IV. Further examination of the psychological transient-like function. *Documenta Ophthalmologica,* 1976, *41,* 329–345. (d)

Johnson, C. A., & Enoch, J. M. Human psychophysical analysis of receptive fieldlike properties. VI. Current summary and analysis of factors affecting the psychophysical transient-like function. *Documenta Ophthalmologica Proceedings Series,* Second International Visual Field Symposium, Tübingen, September, 1977.

Johnson, K. A. The bog model of quark confinement. *Scientific American,* 1979, *241*(1), 112–121.

Jones, D. D., & Holding, D. H. Extremely long-term persistence of the McCollough effect. *Journal of Experimental Psychology: Human Perception and Performance,* 1975, *1,* 323–327.

Jones, L. A., & Higgins, G. C. Photographic granularity and graininess. III. Some characteristics of the visual system of importance in the evaluation of graininess and granularity. *Journal of the Optical Society of America,* 1947, *37,* 217–263.

Jones, R. M., & Tulanay-Keesey, U. Local retinal adaptation and spatial frequency channels. *Vision Research,* 1975, *15,* 1239–1244.

Judd, D. B. Chromaticity sensibility to stimulus differences. *Journal of the Optical Society of America,* 1932, *22,* 72–108.

Judd, D. B. Current views on colour blindness. *Documenta Ophthalmologica,* 1949, *3,* 251-288.

Judd, D. B. Basic correlates of the visual stimulus. In S. S. Stevens (Ed.), *Handbook of experimental psychology.* New York: John Wiley & Sons, 1951.

Julesz, B. Binocular depth perception of computer generated patterns. *Bell System Technical Journal,* 1960, *39,* 1125-1162.

Julesz, B. Visual pattern discrimination. *Institute of Radio Engineers Transactions on Information Theory,* 1962, 1T-8, 84-92.

Julesz, B. Binocular depth perception without familiarity cues. *Science,* 1964, *145,* 356-362.

Julesz, B. *Foundations of cyclopean perception.* Chicago: The University of Chicago Press, 1971.

Julesz, B. Experiments in the visual perception of texture. *Scientific American,* 1975, *232*(4), 34-43.

Julesz, B. Global stereopsis: Cooperative phenomena in stereoscopic depth perception. In R. Held, H. W. Leibowitz, & H-L. Teuber (Eds.), *Handbook of sensory physiology, Vol. 8: Perception.* Berlin: Springer-Verlag, 1978. (a)

Julesz, B. Perceptual limits of texture discrimination and their implications to figure-ground separation. In E. L. J. Leeuwenberg & H. F. J. M.Buffart (Eds.), *Formal theories of visual perception.* New York: Wiley, 1978. (b)

Julesz, B., & Chang, J. J. Interaction between pools of binocular disparity detectors tuned to different disparities. *Biological Cybernetics,* 1976, *22,* 107-119.

Julesz, B., Gilbert, E. N., Shepp, L. A., & Frisch, H. L. Inability of humans to discriminate between visual textures that agree in second order statistics—revisited. *Perception,* 1973, *2,* 391-405.

Julesz, B., & Miller, J. Independent spatial frequency-tuned channels in binocular fusion and rivalry. *Perception,* 1975, *7,* 125-143.

Jung, R. Neuronal integration in the visual cortex and its significance for visual information. In W. A. Rosenblith (Ed.), *Sensory communication.* New York: Wiley, 1961.

Jung, R. Visual perception and neurophysiology. In R. J-ng (Ed.), *Handbook of sensory physiology: Central processing of visual information, A: Integrative functions and comparative data* (Vol. VII/3). New York: Springer-Verlag, 1973.

Kahneman, D. Temporal effects in the perception of light and form. In W. Wathan-Dunn (Ed.), *Models for the perception of speech—visual form.* Cambridge, Mass.: MIT Press, 1967.

Kahneman, D. Metacontrast: Method, findings, and theory in studies of visual masking. *Psychological Bulletin,* 1968, *70,* 404-425.

Kahneman, D., & Beatty, J. Pupil diameter and load on memory. *Science,* 1966, *154,* 1583-1585.

Kahneman, D., & Norman, J. The time-intensity relation in visual perception as a function of observer's task. *Journal of Experimental Psychology,* 1964, *68,* 215-220.

Kahneman, D., Norman, J., & Kubovy, M. Critical duration for the resolution of form: Centrally or peripherally determined? *Journal of Experimental Psychology,* 1967, *73,* 323-327.

Kahneman, D., & Wolman, R. E. Stroboscopic motion: Effects of duration and interval. *Perception & Psychophysics,* 1970, *8,* 161-164.

Kakizaki, S. The effects of proceding conditions upon binocular rivalry (I). *Japanese Journal of Psychology,* 1950, *20,* 11-17. (a)

Kakizaki, S. The effects of preceding conditions upon binocular rivalry (II). *Japanese Journal of Psychology,* 1950, *20,* 24-32. (b)

Kandel, E. R. *Cellular basis of behavior.* Sna Francisco: W. H. Freeman, 1976.

Kandel, E. R. Cellular basis of behavior: *An introduction to behavioral neurobiology.* San Francisco: Freeman, 1977.

Kandel, E. R. *Behavior of biology of aplysia.* San Francisco: W. H. Freeman, 1979.

Kaniza, G. Margini quasi-percettivi in campi con stimolaxione omogenea. *Rivista di Psicologia,* 1955, *49,* 7-30.

Kaniza, G. Contours without gradients or cognitive contours. *Italian Journal of Psychology,* 1974, *1,* 93-112.

Kaniza, G. Some near demonstrations of the role of structural factors in brightness contrast. In S. Ertel, L. Kemmler, & M. Stadler (Eds.), *Gestaltheorie in der moderne psychologie*. Stuttgart: Steinkopf, 1975.

Kaniza, G. Subjective contours. *Scientific American*, April 1976, *234*(4), 48–52.

Kaniza, G. The polarization of gamma movement. *The Italian Journal of Psychology*, 1978, *5*, 265–285.

Kaplan, S. The role of location processing in the perception of the environment. *Proceedings of the Annual Conference of the Environmental Design Research Association,* 1970, Pittsburgh, Pa.

Karn, H. W. Area and the intensity-time relation in the fovea. *Journal of General Psychology,* 1936, *14,* 360–369.

Katz, D. *The world of color.* London: Kegan Paul, 1935.

Kaufman, L. On the nature of binocular disparity. *American Journal of Psychology,* 1964, *77,* 393–402. (a)

Kaufman, L. Suppression and fusion in viewing complex stereograms. *American Journal of Psychology,* 1964, *77,* 193–205. (b)

Kaufman, L. Some new stereoscopic phenomena and their implications for the theory of stereopsis. *American Journal of Psychology,* 1965, *78,* 1–20.

Kaufman, L. *Sight and mind.* New York: Oxford University Press, 1974.

Kaufman, L., & Pitblado, C. Further observations on the nature of effective binocular disparities. *American Journal of Psychology,* 1965, *78,* 379–391.

Kaufman, L., & Pitblado, C. Stereopsis with opposite contrast contours. *Perception & Psychophysics,* 1969, *6,* 10–12.

Kaufman, L., & Rock, I. The moon illusion, I. *Science*, 1962, *136*, 953–961.

Kawabata, N., Yamagami, K., & Noaki, M. Visual fixation points and depth perception. *Vision Research,* 1978, *18,* 853–854.

Keck, M. J., & Pentz, B. Recovery from adaptation to moving gratings. *Perception,* 1977, *6,* 719–725.

Keele, S. W., & Chase, W. G. Short-term visual storage. *Perception & Psychophysics,* 1967, *2,* 383–386.

Keesey, U. T. Effect of involuntary eye movements on visual acuity. *Journal of the Optical Society of America,* 1960, *50,* 769–774.

Keller, M. The relation between the critical duration and intensity in brightness discrimination. *Journal of Experimental Psychology,* 1941, *28,* 407–418.

Kelly, D. H. Effects of sharp edges in a flickering field. *Journal of the Optical Society of America,* 1959, *49,* 730–732.

Kelly, D. H. Visual responses to time-dependent stimuli. II. Single-channel model of the photopic visual system. *Journal of the Optical Society of America,* 1961, *51,* 747–754.

Kelly, D. H. Flickering patterns and lateral inhibition. *Journal of the Optical Society of America,* 1969, *59,* 1361–1370.

Kelly, D. H. Flicker. In D. Jameson & L. M. Hurvich (Eds.), *Handbook of sensory physiology: Visual psychophysics* (Vol. VII/4). New York: Springer-Verlag, 1972.

Kelly, D. H. Spatiotemporal frequency characteristics of color vision mechanisms. *Journal of the Optical Society of America,* 1974, *64,* 983–990.

Kelly, D. H., Boynton, R. M., & Baron, W. S. Primate flicker sensitivity: Psychophysics and electrophysiology. *Science,* 1976, *194,* 1077–1079.

Kelly, D. H., & Wilson, H. R. Human flicker sensitivity: Two stages of retinal diffusion. *Science,* 1978, *202,* 896–899.

Kelly, J. P., & Van Essen, D. C. Cell structure and function in the visual cortex of the cat. *Journal of Physiology,* 1974, *238,* 515–547.

Kennedy, J. M. Sun figure: An illusory diffuse contour resulting from an arrangement of dots. *Perception,* 1976, *5,* 475–481.

Kennedy, J. M. Natural reversing figure: Interleaving Stars of David. *Perception*, 1977, *6*, 231-232.

Kennedy, J. M. Illusory contours not due to completion. *Perception*, 1978,*7*, 187-189.

Kennedy, J. M., & Lee, H. A figure density hypothesis and illusory contour brightness. *Perception*, 1976, *5*, 387-392.

Kennedy, J. M., & Ware, C. Illusory contours can arise in dot figures. *Perception*, 1978, *7*, 191-194.

Kerr, L. G., & Thomas, J. P. Effect of selective adaptation on detection of simple and compound parafoveal stimuli. *Vision Research*, 1972, *12*, 1367-1379.

Kidd, M. Electron microscopy of the inner plexiform layer of the retina in the cat and the pigeon. *Journal of Anatomy*, 1962, *96*, 179-187.

Kinchla, R. A., & Wolfe, J. M. The order of visual processing: "Top-down," "Bottom-up" or "middle-out." *Perception & Psychophysics*, 1979, *25*, 225-231.

Kinsbourne, M., & Warrington, E. K. The effect of an after-coming random pattern on the perception of brief visual stimuli. *The Quarterly Journal of Experimental Psychology*, 1962, *14*, 223-234. (a)

Kinsbourne, M., & Warrington, E. K. A variety of reading disability associated with right hemisphere lesions. *Journal of Neurology*, 1962, *23*, 339-344. (b)

Kirschmann, A. Ueber die quantitativen verhaltnisse des simultanen Helligkeits und farben contrastes. *Philosophische Studien*, 1891, *6*, 417-491.

Kitterle, F. L. The effects of simultaneous and successive contrast on perceived brightness. *Vision Research*, 1972, *12*, 1923-1931.

Kitterle, F. L. The effect of adapting and test field color on the perception of size. *Vision Research*, 1975, *15*, 883-885.

Kitterle, F. L., & Corwin, T. R. Enhancement of apparent contrast in flashed sinusoidal gratings. *Vision Research*, 1979, *19*, 33-39.

Kitterle, F. L., Kaye, R. S., Nixon, H. Pattern alternation: Effects of spatial frequency of orientation. *Perception & Psychophysics*, 1974, *16*, 543-547.

Kitterle, F. L., Kaye, R. S., & Samuels, J. Grating acuity along the vertical meridian as a function of grating orientation and mean luminance. In press.

Kitterle, F. L., & Leguire, L. E. The effect of borders and contours on threshold during early dark adaptation. *Vision Research*, 1975, *15*, 1217-1224.

Kitterle, F. L., Leguire, L. E., & Riley, J. A. The effects of target orientation on threshold during early dark adaptation. *Vision Research*, 1975, *15*, 1-3.

Kitterle, F. L., & Rysberg, J. A. The effect of exposure duration on the apparent contrast of sinusoidal gratings. *Perception & Psychophysics*, 1976, *19*, 335-338.

Kleinschmidt, J., & Dowling, J. E. Intracellular recordings from gecko photoreceptors during light and dark adaptation. *The Journal of General Physiology*, 1975, *66*, 617-648.

Knuth, D. E. Mathematics and computer science: Coping with finiteness. *Science*, 1976, *194*, 1235-1242.

Ko, T. Measurement of visual acuity in terms of sense time (continued). *Japanese Journal of Ophthalmology*, 1938, *42*, 705.

Koffka, K. *Principles of Gestalt psychology*. New York: Harcourt, Brace, 1935.

Köhler, I. *Über Aufbau und Wandel lungen der wahrnehmungswelt: Insbesondere über "bedingte" empfindungen*. Vienna: Rohrer, 1951.

Köhler, W. Zur Theorie der storbosk-opischen bewegung. *Psychologische Forschung*, 1923, *3*, 397-406.

Köhler, W. *Gestalt psychology: An introduction to the new concepts in modern psychology*. New York: Liveright, 1947. (Originally published, 1929.)

Köhler, W., & Emery, D. A. Figural aftereffects in the third dimension of visual space. *American Journal of Psychology*, 1947, *60*, 159-201.

Köhler, W., & Wallach, H. Figural aftereffects: An investigation of visual processes. *Proceedings of the American Philosophical Society,* 1944, *88,* 269–357.

Kohonen, T., Lehtiö, P., & Rovamo, J. Modelling of neural associative memory. *Annales Academiae Scientiarum Fennicae* (Series A), 1974, *167,* 1–18.

Kohonen, T., Lehtiö, P., Rovamo, J., Hyvärinen, J., Bry, K., & Vainio, L. *A principle of neural associative memory.* Helsinki University of Technology: Department of Technical Physics, Report No. TKK-F-A274, 1976.

Kolehmainen, K. & Crouhjort, R. Apparent properties of inspection figures as determiners of figural aftereffects. *Scandinavian Journal of Psychology,* 1970, *11,* 103–108.

Kolers, P. A. Intensity and contour effects in visual masking. *Vision Research,* 1962, *2,* 277–294.

Kolers, P. A. The illusion of movement. *Scientific American,* 1964, *211*(4), 98–106.

Kolers, P. A. Some psychological aspects of pattern recognition. In P. A. Kolers & M. Eden (Eds.), *Recognizing patterns.* Cambridge, Mass.: MIT Press, 1968.

Kolers, P. A. The role of shape and geometry in picture recognition. In B. S. Lipkin & D. Rosenfeld (Eds.), *Picture processing and psychopictorics.* New York: Academic Press, 1970.

Kolers, P. A. *Aspects of Motion Perception.* Oxford: Pergamon Press, 1972.

Kolers, P. A., & Eden, M. (Eds.). *Recognizing patterns: Studies in living and automatic systems.* Cambridge, Mass.: MIT Press, 1968.

Kolers, P. A., & Pomerantz, J. R. Figural changes in apparent motion. *Journal of Experimental Psychology,* 1971, *87,* 99–108.

Kolers, P. A., & Rosner, B. S. On visual masking (metacontrast): Dichoptic observation. *American Journal of Psychology,* 1960, *73,* 2–21.

Köllner, H. *Die storungen des farbensinnes.* Berlin: S. Karger, 1912.

Kong, K-L., Fung, Y. M., & Wasserman, G. S. Filter-mediated color vision with one visual pigment. *Science,* 1980, *207,* 783–786.

König, A., & Köttgen, E. Über den menschlichen Sehpurpur und seine Bedeutung für das Sehen. *Sitzungsberichte der Königlich Preussischen Akademie der Wissenschaften zu Berlin,* 1894, 577–598.

Konorski, J. *Integrative activity of the brain.* Chicago: University of Chicago Press, 1967.

Koppitz, W. J. *Mach bands and retinal interaction.* Unpublished doctoral dissertation, Ohio State University, 1957.

Korte, A. Kinematoskopische untersuchungen. *Zeitschrift fur Psychologie,* 1915, *72,* 193–296.

Kosslyn, S. M., & Pomerantz. J. R. Imagery, propositions, and the form of internal representations. *Cognitive Psychology,* 1977, *9,* 52–76.

Krantz, D. H. Measurement structures and psychological laws. *Science,* 1972, *175,* 1427–1435.

Krantz, D. H. Color measurement and color theory. II: Opponent-colors theory. *Journal of Mathematical Psychology,* 1975, *12,* 304–327. (a)

Krantz, D. H. Color measurement and color theory. I. Representation theorem for Grassman structures. *Journal of Mathematical Psychology,* 1975, *12,* 283–303. (b)

Krantz, D. H., & Weintraub, D. J. Factors affecting perceived orientation of the Poggendorff transversal. *Perception & Psychophysics,* 1973, *14,* 511–517.

Krauskopf, J. Light distribution in human retinal images. *Journal of the Optical Society of America,* 1962, *52*(9), 1046–1050.

Krauskopf, J., Graf, V., & Gaarder, K. Lack of inhibition during involuntary saccades. *American Journal of Psychology,* 1966, *79*(1), 73–81.

Krauskopf, J., & Mollon J. D. The independence of the temporal integration properties of individual chromatic mechanisms in the human eye. *Journal of Physiology,* 1971, *219,* 611–623.

vonKries, J., & Eyster, J. A. E. Uber die zur Erregung des Sehorgans erforderlichen Energiemengen. *Zeitschrift fur Sinnesphysiologie,* 1907, *41,* 373–394.

Kripke, B. Does the striate cortex begin reconstruction of the visual world? *Science,* 1972, *176,* 317.

Kristofferson, A. B. Attention and psychological time. *Acta Psychologica,* 1967, *27,* 93–100.

Krüger, J. McCollough effect: A theory based on the anatomy of the lateral geniculate body. *Perception & Psychophysics,* 1979, *25,* 169–179.

Kuffler, S. W. Neurons in the retina: Organization, inhibition, and excitation problems. *Cold Spring Harbor Symposium on Quantitative Biology,* 1952, *17,* 281–292.

Kuhn, T. S. *The structure of scientific revolutions.* Chicago: University of Chicago Press, 1962.

Kuhn, T. S. *The essential tension: Selected studies in scientific tradition and change.* Chicago: University of Chicago Press, 1978.

Kühne, W. Chemical processes in the retina. *Vision Research,* 1977, *17,* 1269–1316.

Kulikowski, J. S., & King-Smith, P. E. Spatial arrangement of line edge and grating detectors revealed by subthreshold summation. *Vision Research,* 1973, *13,* 1455–1478.

Kurtz, D. *Eye movements of monkeys with superior collicular lesions during visual discrimination performance.* Unpublished doctoral dissertation, University of Michigan, 1977.

Lackner, J. R. Some mechanisms underlying sensory and postural stability in man. In R. Held, H. W. Leibowitz, & H-L. Teuber (Eds.), *Handbook of sensory physiology: Perception* (Vol. 8). Berlin: Springer-Verlag, 1978.

Lana, R. E. *The foundations of psychological theory.* Hillsdale, N.J.: Lawrence Erlbaum Associates, 1976.

Lancaster, W. Aniseikonia. *Archives of Ophthalmology,* 1938, *20,* 907–912.

Land, E. H. Color vision and natural image: I. *Proceedings of the National Academy of Sciences,* 1959, *45,* 115–129. (a)

Land, E. H. Color vision and the natural image: II. *Proceedings of the National Academy of Sciences,* 1959, *45,* 636–644. (b)

Land, E. H. Experiments in color vision. *Scientific American,* 1959, *200*(5), 84–99. (c)

Land, E. H. The retinex. *American Scientist,* 1964, *52,* 247–264.

Land, E. H. The retinex theory of color vision. *Scientific American,* December 1977, *237,* 108–128.

Land, E. H., & McCann, J. J. Lightness and retinex theory. *Journal of the Optical Society of America,* 1971, *64,* 1–11.

Landis, C. Determinants of the critical flicker-fusion threshold. *Physiological Reviews,* 1954, *34,* 259–286.

Langlands, H. M. S. Experiments in binocular vision. *Transactions of the Optical Society, London,* 1926, *28,* 45–82.

Langley, S. P. Energy and vision. *The London, Edinburgh, and Dublin Philosophical Magazine and Journal of Science. Fifth Series,* 1889, *27,* series 5, 1.

Lappin, J. S. Personal communication, 1979.

Lappin, J. S. Analytic and functional paradigms in psychological research. In C. W. Deckner (Ed.), *Introduction to behavioral research: Perspectives in methodology.* Springfield, Ill.: Charles C. Thomas, in press. (a)

Lappin, J. S. Perception and choice. In C. W. Deckner (Ed.), *Introduction to behavioral research: Perspectives in methodology.* Springfield, Ill.: Charles C. Thomas, in press. (b)

Lappin, J. S., Doner, J. F., & Kottas, B. L. Minimal conditions for the visual detection of structure and motion in three dimensions. *Science,* 1980, *209,* 717–719.

Lappin, J. S., & Harm, O. J. On the rate of acquisition of visual information about space, time, and intensity. *Perception & Psychophysics,* 1973, *13,* 439–445.

Lappin, J. S., & Preble, L. D. A demonstration of shape constancy. *Perception & Psychophysics,* 1975, *17,* 439–444.

Larimer, J., Krantz, D., & Cicerone, C. M. Opponent process additivity: II. Yellow–blue equilibria and nonlinear models. *Vision Research,* 1975, *15,* 723–732.

Lashley, K. S. The problem of cerebral organization in vision. In *Biological Symposia, Vol. 7: Visual mechanisms.* Lancaster, Pa.: Jacques Cuttell Press, 1942.

Lashley, K. S., Chow, K. L., & Semmes, J. An examination of the electrical field theory of cerebral integration. *Psychological Review,* 1951, *58,* 123–136.

Laties, A. Histochemical techniques for the study of photoreceptor orientation. *Tissue and Cell,* 1969, *1,* 63–81.

Laties, A. M., & Enoch, J. M. An analysis of retinal receptor orientation: I. Angular relationship of neighboring photoreceptors. *Investigative Ophthalmology,* 1971, *10,* 69–77.

Laties, A. M. & Liebman, P. A. Cones of living amphibian eye: Selective staining. *Science,* 1970, *168,* 1475–1476.

Latour, P. L. Visual threshold during eye movements. *Vision Research,* 1962, *2,* 261–262.

Laughery, K. R. Computer simulation of short-term memory: A component decay model. In G. H. Bower & J. R. Spence (Eds.), *The psychology of learning and motivation (Vol. 3).* New York: Academic Press, 1969.

LaVail, M. M. Rod outer segment disk shedding in rat retina: Relationship to cyclic lighting. *Science,* 1976, *194,* 1071–1073.

Lavin, E., & Costall, A. Detection thresholds of the Hermann grid illusion. *Vision Research,* 1978, *18,* 1061–1062.

Leask, J., Haber, R. N., & Haber, R. Eidetic imagery in children: II. Longitudinal and experimental results. *Psychonomic Monograph Supplements,* 1969, *3,* 25–48.

Lederman, L. M. The upsilon particle. *Scientific American,* September 1978, *239,* 72–80.

Leeper, R. A study of a neglected portion of the field of learning—the development of sensory organization. *Journal of Genetic Psychology,* 1935, *46,* 41–75.

Leeuwenberg, E. L. J. Quantitative specifications of information in sequential patterns. *Psychological Review,* 1969, *76,* 216–220.

Leeuwenberg, E. L. J. A perceptual coding language for visual and auditory patterns. *American Journal of Psychology,* 1971, *84,* 307–349.

Leeuwenberg, E. L. J. Quantification of certain visual pattern properties: Salience, transparency, similarity. In E. L. J. Leeuwenberg & H. F. J. M. Buffart (Eds.), *Formal theories of visual perception.* Chichester, England: Wiley, 1978.

Leeuwenberg, E. L. J., & Buffart, H. F. J. M. *Formal theories of visual perception.* New York: Wiley, 1978.

Lefton, L. Metacontrast: A review. *Perception & Psychophysics,* 1973, *13*(1B), 161–171.

LeGrand, Y. *Light, colour, and vision.* New York: Dover, 1957.

Lehmkuhle, S. W., & Fox, R. Effect of binocular rivalry suppression on the motion aftereffect. *Vision Research,* 1975, *15,* 855–859.

Lehmkuhle, S. W., & Fox, R. Effect of depth separation on metacontrast masking. *Journal of Experimental Psychology* (in press).

Leibowitz, H. Some observations and theory on the variation of visual acuity with the orientation of the test object. *Journal of the Optical Society of America,* 1953, *43,* 902–905.

Leibowitz, H., & Bourne, L. E. Time and intensity as determiners of perceived shape. *Journal of Experimental Psychology,* 1956, *51,* 277–281.

Leibowitz, H., Mote, F. A., & Thurlow, W. R. Simultaneous contrast as a function of separation between test and inducing fields. *Journal of Experimental Psychology,* 1953, *46,* 453–456.

Lema, S. A., & Blake, R. Binocular summation in normal and stereoblind humans. *Vision Research,* 1977, *17,* 691–695.

Lennox-Buchthal, M. A. Single units in monkey, *Cercocebus Torquatus Atys,* cortex with narrow spectral responsiveness. *Vision Research,* 1962, *2,* 1–15.

Lettvin, J. Y., Maturana, H. R., McCulloch, W. S., & Pitts, W. H. What the frog's eye tells the frog's brain. *Proceedings of the Institute of Radio Engineers,* 1959, *47,* 1940–1951.

Levelt, W. J. M. *On binocular rivalry.* Unpublished doctoral dissertation, Leiden University, 1965.

Levelt, W. J. M. The alternation process in binocular rivalry. *British Journal of Psychology,* 1966, *57,* 225–238.

Levine, D. M., & Mayzner, M. S. Effects of density of noise field and delay on information processing of patterned inputs. *Perceptual and Motor Skills,* 1976, *42,* 819-824.

Levinson, J. Z. Flicker fusion phenomena. *Science,* 1968, *160,* 21-28.

Levinson, J. Z., & Frome, F. S. Perception of size of one object among many. *Science,* 1979, *206,* 1425-1426.

Levy, M. M., & Lawson, R. B. Stereopsis and binocular rivalry from dichoptic stereograms. *Vision Research,* 1978, *18,* 239-246.

Liàng, T., & Piéron, H. Recherches sur la latence de la sensation lumineuse pour la méthode de l'effet chronostétéoscopique. *Anneé Psychologigue,* 1947, *43-44,* 1-53.

Lichtenstein, M. Phenomenal simultaneity with irregular timing of components of the visual stimulus. *Perceptual and Motor Skills,* 1961, *12,* 47-60.

Lindberg, D. C. *Theories of vision from Al-Kindi to Kepler.* Chicago: University of Chicago Press, 1976.

Linksz, A. The horopter: An analysis. *Transactions of the American Ophthalmological Society,* 1954, *52,* 877-946.

Linksz, A. *Essay on color vision.* New York: Grune & Stratton, 1964.

Linnaeus, C. *Systema Naturae.* Lugduni Batavorum: Apud T. Haak, 1735.

Lipetz, L. E. The transfer functions of sensory intensity in the nervous system. *Vision Research,* 1969, *9,* 1205-1234.

Lipkin, B. S., & Rosenfeld, A. (Eds.). *Picture processing and psychopictorics.* New York: Academic Press, 1970.

Lit, A. The magnitude of the Pulfrich stereophenomenon as a function of binocular differences of intensity at various levels of illumination. *American Journal of Psychology,* 1949, *62,* 159-181.

Lit, A. Magnitude of the Pulfrich stereophenomenon as a function of target thickness. *Journal of the Optical Society of America,* 1960, *50,* 321-327. (a)

Lit, A. The magnitude of the Pulfrich stereophenomenon as a function of target velocity. *Journal of Experimental Psychology,* 1960, *59,* 165-175. (b)

Lit, A. Illumination effects on depth discrimination. *The Optometric Weekly,* 1968, *59,* 42-55.

Lit, A., & Finn, J. P. Variability of depth discrimination thresholds as a function of observation distance. *Journal of the Optical Society of America,* 1976, *66,* 740-742.

Lit, A., Finn, J. P., & Vicars, W. M. Effect of target-background luminance contrast on binocular depth discrimination at photopic levels of illumination. *Vision Research,* 1972, *12,* 1241-1251.

Lit, A., & Hamm, H. D. Depth-discrimination thresholds for stationary and oscillating targets at various levels of retinal illuminance. *Journal of the Optical Society of America,* 1966, *56,* 510-516.

Lit, A., & Hyman, A. The magnitude of the Pulfrich stereophenomenon as a function of distance of observation. *American Journal of Optometry,* 1961, *28,* 564-580.

Lit, A., Young, R. H., & Schaffer, M. Simple time reaction as a function of luminance for various wavelengths. *Perception & Psychophysics,* 1971, *10*(6), 397-399.

Locke, J. *An essay concerning human understanding.* In P. H. Nidditch (Ed.), Clarendon edition of the works of John Locke, Oxford: Oxford University Press, 1975. (Originally published, 1690.)

Loop, M. S., & Bruce, L. L. Cat color vision: The effect of stimulus size. *Science,* 1978, *199,* 1221-1222.

Loop, M. S., Bruce, L. L., & Petuchowksi, S. Cat color vision: The effect of stimulus size, shape, and viewing distance. *Vision Research,* 1979, *19,* 507-513.

Lovegrove, W. J., & Over, R. Color adaptation of spatial frequency detectors in the human visual system. *Science,* 1972, *176,* 541-543.

Lucas, J. R. Minds, machines, and Gödel. *Philosophy,* 1961, *36,* 112-127.

Luce, R. D., & Green, D. M. A neural timing theory for response times and the psychophysics of intensity. *Psychological Review,* 1972, *79,* 14-57.

Luce, R. D., & Mo, S. S. M. lMagnitude estimation of heaviness by individual subjects: A test of a probabilistic response theory. *British Journal of Mathematical and Statistical Psychology,* 1965, *18* (Part 2), 159–174.

Luckiesh, M. *Visual illusions: Their causes, characteristics, and applications.* Princeton, N.J.: D. Van Nostrand, 1922.

Ludvigh, E. Direction sense of the eye. *American Journal of Ophthalmology,* 1953, *36,* 139–142.

Luneberg, R. K. *Mathematical analysis of binocular vision.* Princeton, N.J.: Princeton University Press, 1947.

Luneberg, R. K. Metric methods in binocular visual perception. In *Studies and essays, Courant anniversary volume.* New York: Interscience, 1948.

Luneberg, R. K. The metric of binocular visual space. *Journal of the Optical Society of America,* 1950, *40,* 627–642.

Luria, S. M., & Kinney, J. A. S. Underwater vision. *Science,* 1970, *167,* 1454–1461.

Lythgoe, J. N. The adaptation of visual pigments to the photic environment. In H. J. A. Dartnall (Ed.), *Handbook of sensory physiology: Photochemistry of vision* (Vol. VII/1). Berlin: Springer-Verlag, 1972.

Lythgoe, R. J., & Tansley, K. The relation of the critical frequency of flicker to the adaptation of the eye. *Proceedings of the Royal Society* (London), 1929, *105,* 60–92.

MacAdam, D. L. Visual sensitivities to color differences in daylight. *Journal of the Optical Society of America,* 1942, *32,* 247–274.

Mach, E. Über die wirkung der räumlichen vertheilung des lichtreizes auf die Netzhaut, I. *Sitzungsberichte der Mathematisch-Naturwissenschaftlichen Classe der kaiserlichen Akademie der Wissenchaften,* 1865, *52,* 303–322.

Mach, E. Über den physiologischen Effect räumlich vertheilter Lichtreize, II. *Sitzungsberichte der Mathematisch-Naturwissenschaftlichen Classe der kaiserlichen Akademie der Wissenschaften,* 1866, *54,* 131–144. (a)

Mach, E. Über die physiologische Wirkung räumlich Vertheilter Lichtreize. *Sitzungsberichte der Kaiserlichen der Akademie der Wissenshaften. Mathematisch-Naturwissenshaftliche Classe. Wien,* 1866, *54* (Abt. 2), 393–408. (b)

Mach, E. Über die physiologische Wirkung räumlich vertheilter Lichtreize, III. *Sitzungsberichte der Mathematisch-Naturwissenschaftlichen Classe der kaiserlichen Akademie der Wissenschaften,* 1866, *57,* 393–408. (c)

Mackavey, W. R., Bartley, S. H., & Casella, C. Measurements of simultaneous brightness contrast across the retina. *The Journal of Psychology,* 1961, *52,* 241–250.

Mackavey, W. R., Bartley, S. H., & Casella, C. Disinhibition in the human visual system. *Journal of the Optical Society of America,* 1962, *52,* 85–88.

MacKay, D. M. Moving visual images produced by regular stationary patterns. *Nature,* 1957, *180,* 849–850. (a)

MacKay, D. M. Some further visual phenomena associated with regular patterned stimulation. *Nature,* 1957, *180,* 1145–1146. (b)

MacKay, D. M. Lateral interactions between neural channels sensitive to texture density. *Nature,* 1973, *245,* 159–161.

MacKay, D. M., & MacKay, V. What causes decay of pattern-contingent chromatic aftereffects. *Vision Research,* 1975, *15,* 462–464.

MacKay, D. M., & MacKay, V. Multiple orientation-contingent chromatic aftereffects. *Quarterly Journal of Experimental Psychology,* 1977, *29,* 203–218.

Mackinnon, G. E. Steadily fixated figures and prolonged afterimages: Further evidence that fragmentation occurs nonrandomly. *Canadian Journal of Psychology,* 1971, *25,* 384–393.

Maffei, L., & Fiorentini, A. The visual cortex as a spatial frequency analyzer. *Vision Research,* 1973, *13,* 1255–1267.

Makous, W., & Boothe, R. Cones block signals from rods. *Vision Research,* 1974, *14,* 285–294.

Makous, W., & Peeples, D. Rod–cone interaction: Reconciliation with Flamant and Stiles. *Vision Research,* 1979, *19,* 695–698.

Mandelbaum, J., & Sloan, L. L. Peripheral visual acuity. *American Journal of Ophthalmology,* 1947, *30,* 581–588.

Mansfield, R. J. W. Brightness function: Effect of area and duration. *Journal of the Optical Society of America,* 1973, *63,* 913–920.

Mansfield, R. J. W. Neural basis of orientation perception in primate vision. *Science,* 1974, *186,* 1133–1135.

Mansfield, R. J. W., & Daugman, J. G. Retinal mechanisms of visual latency. *Vision Research,* 1978, *18,* 1247–1260.

Marc, R. E., & Sperling, H. G. Chromatic organization of primate cones. *Science,* 1977, *196,* 454–456.

Marg, E. Recording from single cells in the human visual cortex. In R. Jung (Ed.), *Handbook of sensory physiology* (Vol. VII/3). Berlin: Springer-Verlag, 1973.

Markoff, J. I., & Sturr, J. F. Spatial and luminance determinants of the increment threshold under monoptic and dichoptic viewing. *Journal of the Optical Society of America,* 1971, *61,* 1530–1537.

Marks, L. E. Visual brightness: Some applications of a model. *Vision Research,* 1972, *12,* 1409–1421.

Marks, L. E. *Sensory processes: The new psychophysics.* New York: Academic Press, 1974.

Marks, W. B. Visual pigments of single goldfish cones. *Journal of Physiology,* 1965, *178,* 14–32.

Marks, W. B., Dobelle, W. H., & MacNichol, E. F. Visual pigments of single primate cones. *Science,* 1964, *143,* 1181–1183.

Marr, D. Early processing of visual information. *Philosophical Transactions of the Royal Society of London. Series B,* 1976, *275,* 483–519.

Marr, D., & Nishihara, H. K. Representation and recognition of the spatial organization of three-dimensional shapes. *Proceedings of the Royal Society, London, Series B,* 1978, *200,* 269–294.

Marr, D., & Poggio, T. Cooperative computation of stereo disparity. *Science,* 1976, *194,* 283–287.

Marr, D., & Poggio. T. A theory of human stereo vision. *Proceedings of the Royal Society, London,* 1979.

Marriott, F. H. C. The foveal absolute threshold for short flashes and small fields. *Journal of Physiology,* 1963, *169,* 416–423.

Marshall, A. J. Sensory and attentional devices in visual perception. *Australian Psychologist,* 1969, *3,* 124–139.

Martin, C., & Pomerantz, J. R. Visual discrimination of texture. *Perception & Psychophysics,* 1978, *24,* 420–428.

Martin, L. C., Warburton, F. L., & Morgan, W. J. The determination of the sensitiveness of the eye to differences in the saturation of colours. Great Britain Medical Research Council, *Special Report Series,* 1933, 1–42.

Martinez, J. M., Sturr, J. F., & Schmalbach, N. L. The luminance difference threshold as a contrast threshold: Evidence for inhibitory interactions in spatial summation. *Vision Research,* 1977, *17,* 687–689.

Marx, M. H., & Hillix, W. A. *Systems and theories in psychology* (2nd ed.). New York: McGraw-Hill, 1973.

Massof, R. W. A quantum fluctuation model for foveal color thresholds. *Vision Research,* 1977, *17,* 565–570.

Masterson, B., & Kennedy, J. M. Building the devil's tuning fork. *Perception,* 1975, *4,* 107–109.

Matin, E. Saccadic suppression: A review and an analysis. *Psychological Bulletin,* 1974, *81,* 899–917.

Matin, L., & Kornheiser, A. S. Reversal of the edge effect for the increment threshold with a small background. *Vision Research,* 1977, *17,* 742–747.

Maxwell, J. C. On the unequal sensibility of the Foramen Centrale to light of different colours. *Report of the British Association for the Advancement of Science,* 1856, 12.

May, J. G., Agamy, G., & Matteson, H. H. The range of spatial frequency contingent color aftereffects. *Vision Research,* 1978, *18,* 917–921.

May, J. G., & Matteson, H. H. Checkerboards and color aftereffects. *Science,* 1977, *198,* 209–210.

May, J. G., Matteson, H. H., Agamy, G., & Castellanos, P. The effect of differential adaptation on spatial frequency-contingent color aftereffects. *Perception & Psychophysics,* 1978, *23,* 409–412.

Mayhew, J. E. W., & Anstis, S. M. Movement aftereffects contingent on color, intensity, and pattern. *Perception & Psychophysics,* 1972, *12,* 77–85.

Mayzner, M. S. Visual information processing of alphabetic inputs. *Psychonomic Monograph Supplement,* 1972, *4,* 239–243.

Mayzner, M. S. Studies of visual information processing in man. In Solso, R. L. (Ed.), *Information processing and cognition: The Loyola symposium.* Hillsdale, N.J.: Lawrence Erlbaum Associates, 1975.

Mayzner, M. S., & Tresselt, M. E. Visual dynamics of a novel apparent motion effect. *Psychonomic Science,* 1970, *18,* 331–332. (a)

Mayzner, M. S., & Tresselt, M. E. Visual information processing with sequential inputs: A general model for sequential blanking, displacement, and overprinting phenomena. *Annals New York Academy of Science,* 1970, *169,* 599–618. (b)

McCann, J. J. Rod–cone interactions: Different color sensations from identical stimuli. *Science,* 1972, *176,* 1255–1257.

McCann, J. J., & Benton, J. Interaction of the long-wave cones and the rods to produce color sensations. *Journal of the Optical Society of America,* 1969, *59,* 103–107.

McClelland, J. L. Perception and masking of wholes and parts. *Journal of Experimental Psychology: Human Perception and Performance,* 1978, *4,* 210–223.

McClelland, J. L., & Miller, J. Structural factors in figure perception. *Perception & Psychophysics,* 1979, *26,* 221–229.

McCloskey, M., & Watkins, M. J. The seeing-more-than-is-there phenomenon: Implications for the locus of iconic storage. *Journal of Experimental Psychology: Human Perception and Performance,* 1978, *4,* 553–564.

McCollough, C. Color adaptation of edge-detectors in the human visual system. *Science,* 1965, *149,* 1115–1116.

McCulloch, W. S. Why the mind is in the head. In L. A. Jeffress (Ed.), *Cerebral mechanisms in behavior (The Hixon Symposium).* New York: Wiley, 1951.

McCulloch, W. S., & Pitts, W. A logical calculus of the ideas immanent in neural nets. *Bulletin of Mathematical Biophysics,* 1943, *5,* 115–137.

McCready, D. W. Size–distance perception and accommodation–convergence micropsia—A critique. *Vision Research,* 1967, *5,* 189–206.

McDougall, W. Some new observations in support of Thomas Young's theory of light- and colour-vision.I. *Mind,* 1901, *10,* 52–97.

McDougall, W. The variation of the intensity of visual sensation with the duration of the stimulus. *British Journal of Psychology,* 1904, *1,* 151–189.

McFarland, J. H. Sequential part presentation: A method of studying visual form perception. *British Journal of Psychology,* 1965, *56,* 439–446.

McFarland, J. H., & Prete, M. The effect of visual context on perception of a form's parts as successive. *Vision Research,* 1969, *9,* 923–933.

McIlwain, J. T. Large receptive fields and spatial transformations in the visual system. In R. Porter (Ed.), *International review of physiology, Neurophysiology II, Vol. 10.* Baltimore: University Park Press, 1976.

McKee, G., & Westheimer, G. Improvement in Vernier acuity with practice. *Perception & Psychophysics,* 1978, *24,* 258–262.

McKee, S. P., McCann, J. J., & Benton, J. L. Color vision from rod and long-wave cone interactions: Conditions in which rods contribute to multicolored images. *Vision Research,* 1977, *17,* 175–185.

Mefferd, R. B., Jr. Perception of depth in rotating objects. *Perception and Motor Skills,* 1968, *27,* 1179–1193.

Meisel, W. S. *Computer-oriented approaches to pattern recognition.* New York: Academic Press, 1972.

Merikle, P. M. On the nature of metacontrast with complex targets and masks. *Journal of Experimental Psychology: Human Perception and Performance,* 1977, *3,* 607–621.

Mershon, D. H. Relative contributions of depth and directional adjacency to simultaneous whiteness contrast. *Vision Research,* 1972, *12,* 969–979.

Mershon, D. H., & Gogel, W. C. The effect of stereoscopic cues on perceived whiteness. *American Journal of Psychology,* 1970, *85,* 55–67.

Metelli, F. The perception of transparency. *Scientific American,* April 1974, *230*(4), 90–98.

Metz, W. D. Elusive quarks: Hints of two from a Stanford experiment. *Science,* 1977, *196,* 746–747.

Metzger, W. Untersuchungen am Ganzfeld: II. Zur phänomenologie des homogenen Ganzfelds. *Psychol. Forsch.,* 1930, *13,* 6–29.

Metzger, W. Tiefenerscheinungen in optischen Bewegungsfeldern. *Psychologische Forschung,* 1934, *20,* 195–260.

Metzler, J. *Systems neuroscience.* New York: Academic Press, 1977.

Mewhort, D. J. K. Familairity of letter sequences, response uncertainty, and the tachistoscopic recognition experiment. *Canadian Journal of Psychology,* 1967, *21,* 309–321.

Meyer, D. R., Miles, R. C., & Ratoosh, P. Absence of color vision in cats. *Journal of Neurophysiology,* 1954, *17,* 289–294.

Meyer, G. E., & Maguire, W. M. Spatial frequency and the mediation of short-term visual storage. *Science,* 1977, *198,* 524–525.

Meyer, H. Über kontrast and komplementarfarben. *Annalen der Physik und Chemie,* 1855, *95,* 170–171.

Meyer-Rochow, V. B. Axonal wiring and polarisation sensitivity in eye of the rock lobster. *Nature,* 1975, *254,* 522–523.

Michaels, C. F., Carello, C., Shapiro, B., & Steitz, C. An onset to onset rule for binocular integration of the Mach–Dvorak illusion. *Vision Research,* 1977, *17,* 1107–1113.

Miles, W. R. Movement interpretations of the silhouette of a revolving fan. *American Journal of Psychology,* 1931, *43,* 392–405.

Mill, J. S. Essay on Bentham. In F. R. Leavin (Ed.), *Mill on Bentham and Coleridge.* London: Chatto & Windus, 1950.

Miller, G. A. *Language and communication.* New York: Appleton-Century-Crofts, 1951.

Miller, G. A., & Frick, F. C. Statistical behavioristics and sequences of responses. *Psychological Review,* 1949, *56,* 311–324.

Miller, G. A., Galanter, E., and Pribram, K. N. *Plans and the structure of behavior.* New York: Henry Holt, 1960.

Miller, G. A., & Johnson-Laird, P. N. *Language and perception.* Cambridge, Mass.: Harvard University Press, 1976.

Millodot, M. Variation of visual acuity in the central region of the retina. *British Journal of Physiological Optics,* 1972, *27,* 24–28.

Minsky, M. L. A framework for representing knowledge. In P. H. Winston (Ed.), *The psychology of computer vision.* New York: McGraw-Hill, 1975.

Minsky, M., & Papert, S. *Perceptions: An introduction to computational geometry.* Cambridge, Mass.: MIT Press, 1969.

Mitchell, D. E., Freeman, R. D., & Westheimer, G. Effect of orientation on the modulation sensitivity for interference fringes on the retina. *Journal of the Optical Society of America,* 1967, *57,* 246–249.

Mitrani, L., Mateeff, St., & Yakimoff, N. Smearing of the retinal image during voluntary saccadic eye movements. *Vision Research,* 1970, *10,* 405–409.

Mitrani, L., Mateeff, St., & Yakimoff, N. Is saccadic suppression really saccadic? *Vision Research,* 1971, *11,* 1157–1161.

Mittenthal, J. E., Kristan. W. B., Jr., & Tatton, W. G. Does the striate cortex begin reconstruction of the visual world? *Science,* 1972, *176,* 316–317.

Mize, R. R., & Murphy, E. H. Selective visual experience fails to modify receptive field properties of rabbit striate cortex neurons. *Science,* 1973, *180,* 320–323.

Mollon, J. D., & Polden, P. G. Absence of transient tritanopia after adaptation to very intense yellow light. *Nature,* 1976. *259,* 570–572.

Mollon, J. D., & Polden, P. G. An anomaly in the response of the eye to light of short wavelenths. *Philosophical Transactions of the Royal Society of London,* Series B, 1977, *278,* 207–240.

Montalvo, F. S. A neural network model of the McCollough effect. *Biological Cybernetics,* 1976, *25,* 49–56.

Moreland, J. D., & Cruz, A. Colour perception with the peripheral retina. *Optica Acta,* 1959, *6,* 117.

Mostow, G. D. The extensibility of local Lie groups of transformations and groups on surfaces. *Annals of Mathematics,* 1950, *52,* 606–636.

Motokawa, K. Field of retinal induction and optical illusion. *Journal of Neurophysiology,* 1950, *13,* 413–426.

Motokawa, K., & Akita, M. Electrophysiological studies of the field of retinal induction. *Psychologia,* 1957, *1,* 10–16.

Motokawa, K., Taira, N., & Okuda, J. Spectral responses of single units in the primate visual cortex. *Tohoku Journal of Experimental Medicine,* 1962, *78,* 320–337.

Mountcastle, V. B. Modality and topographic properties of single neurons of cat's somatic sensory cortex. *Journal of Neurophysiology,* 1957, *20,* 508–534.

Mueller, C. B., & Lloyd, V. V. Stereoscopic accuity for various levels of illuminace. *Proceedings of the National Academy of Sciences,* 1948, *34,* 223–227.

Murch, G. M. Binocular relationships in a size and color orientation specific aftereffect. *Journal of Experimental Psychology,* 1972, *93,* 30–34.

Murch, G. M. The role of test pattern background hue in the McCollough effect. *Vision Research,* 1979, *19,* 939–942.

Murphy, G., & Kovach, J. K. *Historical introduction to modern psychology* (3rd ed.). New York: Harcourt Brace Jovanovich, 1972.

Nachmias, J. Meridional variations in visual acuity and eye movements during fixation. *Journal of the Optical Society of America,* 1960, *50,* 569–571.

Nachmias, J., & Weber, A. Discrimination of simple and complex gratings. *Vision Research,* 1975, *15,* 217–222.

Naka, K. I., & Rushton, W. A. H. S-potentials from colour units in the retina of fish (Cyprinidae). *Journal of Physiology,* 1966, *185,* 536–555.

Nambu, Y. The confinement of quarks. *Scientific American,* 1976, *235*(5), 48–60.

Natsoulas, T. Consciousness. *American Psychologist,* 1978, *33,* 906–914. (a)

Natsoulas, T. Residual Subjectivity. *American Psychologist,* 1978, *33,* 269–283. (b)

Navon, D. Forest before the trees: The precedence of global features in visual perception. *Cognitive Psychology,* 1977, *9,* 353–383.

Neisser, U. *Cognitive psychology.* New York: Appleton-Century-Crofts, 1967.

Neisser, U. *Cognition and reality.* San Francisco: Freeman, 1976.

Nelson, J. I. Globality and sterescopic fusion in binocular vision. *Journal of Theoretical Biology,* 1975, *49,* 1–88.

Nelson, T. M., & Bartley, S. H. The Talbot–Plateau law and the brightness of restricted numbers of photic repetitions at CFF. *Vision Research,* 1964, *4,* 403–411.

Nelson, T. M., Bartley, S. H., & Haprer, E. S. Cff. for short trains of photic stimulation having various temporal distribution and separations. *Journal of Psychology, the General Field Psychology,* 1964, *58,* 333–341.

Neuhaus, W. Experimentelle untersuchung der scheinbewegung. *Archiv für die Gesamte Psychologie,* 1930, *75,* 315–458.

Neumann, J. von. *Theory of self-reproducing automata.* Urbana, Ill.: University of Illinois Press, 1966.

Newell, A. Artificial intelligence and the concept of mind. In R. C. Schank & K. M. Colby (Eds.), *Computer models of thought and language.* San Francisco: W. H. Freeman, 1973.

Newman, J. R. Commentary on the periodic law and Mendeleev. In J. R. Newman (Ed.), *The world of mathematics, Vol. II.* New York: Simon & Schuster, 1956.

Newmark, J., & Mayzner, M. S. Sequential blanking effects for two interleaved words. *Bulletin of the Psychonomic Society,* 1973, *2,* 74–76.

Newton, I. Letter to John Locke, 1691. In Lord King, *The life of John Locke* with extracts from his correspondence, journals, and common-place books. London: Henry Colburn, 1829.

Nihm, Sue Doe. Polynomial law of sensation. *American Psychologist,* 1976, *31,* 808–809.

Nilsson, S. E. G. Receptor cell outer segment development and ultrastructure of the disk membranes in the retina of the tadpole (*Rana pipiens*). *Journal of Ultrastructure Research,* 1964, *11,* 1–40.

Nilsson, S. E. G. The ultrastructure of the receptor outer segments in the retina of the leopard frog. *Journal of Ultrastructure Research,* 1965, *12,* 207–231.

Nilsson, S. E. G. The ultrastructure of photoreceptor cells. *Rendiconti della Scuola Internazionale di Fisica "E. Fermi,"* 1969, *XLIII,* 69–115.

Ninio, J. The geometry of the correspondence between two retinal projections. *Perception,* 1977, *6,* 627–643.

Nisbett, R. E., & Wilson, T. D. Telling more than we can know: Verbal reports on mental processes. *Psychological Review,* 1977, *84,* 231–259.

Niven, J. L., & Brown, R. H. Visual resolution as a function of intensity and exposure time in the human fovea. *Journal of the Optical Society of America,* 1944, *34,* 738–743.

Nussenzveig, H. M. The theory of the rainbow. *Scientific American,* April 1977, *236*(4), 117–128.

Obanai, T. *Perception, learning, and thinking: Psychophysiological induction theory.* Tokyo: The Hokuseido Press, 1977.

Obanai, T., & Kawashima, K. Temporal characteristics of size change of colored afterimage. *Japanese Psychological Research,* 1961, *3,* 138–145.

O'Brien, V. Contour perception, illusion, and reality. *Journal of the Optical Society of America,* 1958, *48,* 112–119.

Ogilvie, J. C., & Taylor, M. M. Effect of orientation on the visibility of fine wires. *Journal of the Optical Society of America,* 1958, *48,* 628–629.

Ogle, K. N. *Binocular vision.* Philadlephia: Saunders, 1950.

Ogle, K. N. The problem of the horopter. In H. Davson (ed.), *The eye,* Vol. 4. *Visual optics and the optical space sense.* New York: Academic Press, 1962.

Ohwaki, S. On the destruction of geometrical illusions in stereoscopic observation. *Tohoku Psychologica Folia,* 1960, *29,* 29–36.

Ohwaki, Y., & Kihara, T. A new research on the socalled "Bocci" image. *Tohoku Psychological Folia,* 1953, *13,* 157–180.

Ohzu, H., & Enoch, J. M. Optical modulation by the isolated human fovea. *Vision Research,* 1972, *12,* 245–251.

Oliva, J., & Aguilar, M. Zones de sommation partielle. *Optica Acta,* 1956, *3,* 90–93.

Oppel, J. J. Über geometrisch-optische tauschungen. *Jahresbericht der Frankfurt* (Vereins), 1855, *55,* 37–47.

Orban, G. A. Area 18 of the cat: The first step in processing visual movement information. *Perception,* 1977, *6,* 501–511.

Orlansky, J. The effect of similarity and difference in form on apparent visual movement. *Archives of Psychology,* 1940, *35*(246), 1–85.

Osgood, C. E., & Heyer, A. W. A new interpretation of figural aftereffects. *Psychological Review,* 1952, *59,* 98–118.

Oster, G. Phosphenes. *Scientific American,* February 1970, *222*(2), 82–87.

Osterberg, G. Topography of the layer of rods and cones in the human retina. *Acta Ophthalmologica* (supplement), 1935, *6,* 1–103.

Over, R. Explanations of geometrical illusions. *Psychological Bulletin,* 1968, *70,* 545–562.

Oyama, T. Figural aftereffects as a function of hue and brightness. *Japanese Psychological Research,* 1960, *2,* 74–80. (a)

Oyama, T. Japanese studies of the so-called geometrical optical illusions. *Psychologia,* 1960, *3,* 7–20. (b)

Oyama, T. Perceptual grouping as a function of proximity. *Perceptual and Motor Skills,* 1961, *3,* 305–306.

Oyama, T. The effect of hue and brightness on the size-illusion of concentric circles. *American Journal of Psychology,* 1962, *75,* 45–55.

Oyama, T. Three-dimensional representation of brightness-contrast effect and Stevens' scale of subjective brightness. *Vision Research,* 1967, *7,* 503–505.

Oyama, T. Inference of causal relations in perception of space and motion. *Psychologia,* 1974, *17,* 166–178. (a)

Oyama, T. Perceived size and perceived distance in stereoscopic vision and an analysis of their causal relations. *Perception & Psychophysics,* 1974, *16,* 175–181. (b)

Oyama, T. Determinants of the Zöllner illusion. *Psychological Research,* 1975, *37,* 261–280.

Oyama, T. Feature analyzers, optical illusions, and figural aftereffects. *Perception,* 1977, *6,* 401–406.

Oyama, T. How many objects can we see in one glance? Span of perception. *Scientific American* (Japanese Edition), September 1978, 23–33.

Oyama, T. *Personal communication,* 1979.

Oyama, T., & Anzai, C. A further study on the effects of hue and luminance on the size perception. *Acta Chromatica,* 1973, *2,* 164–169.

Oyama, T., & Hsia, Y. Compensatory hue shift in simultaneous color contrast as a function of separation between inducing and test fields. *Journal of Experimental Psychology,* 1966, *71,* 405–413.

Oyama, T., & Ichihara, S. Which determines figural aftereffect, retinal size or apparent size? *Japanese Psychological Research,* 1973, *15,* 92–98.

Oyama, T., & Iwawaki, S. Role of convergence and binocular disparity in size constancy. *Psychologische Forschung,* 1972, *35,* 117–130.

Oyama, T., & Nanri, R. The effects of hue and brightness on the size perception. *Japanese Psychological Research,* 1960, *2,* 13–20.

Oyama, T., & Yamamura, T. The effect of hue and brightness on the depth perception in normal and color-blind subjects. *Psychologia,* 1960, *3,* 191–194.

Oyama, T., Yoshioka, I., Ebihara, N., & Katahira, M. Author's reply to comments. *Hiroshima Forum for Psychology,* 1976, *3,* 43–44. (a)

Oyama, T., Yoshioka, I., Ebihara, N., & Katahira, M. Causal relations between perceived size and perceived distance in various experimental conditions. *Hiroshima Forum for Psychology,* 1976, *3,* 29–37. (b)

Pacey, A. *The maze of ingenuity.* New York: Holmes & Meier, 1975.

Palmer, S. E. Fundamental aspects of cognitive representation. In E. H. Rosch & B. B. Lloyd (Eds.), *Cognition and categorization.* Hillsdale, N.J.: Lawrence Erlbaum Associates, 1978.

Panum, P. L. *Physiological investigations concerning vision with two eyes.* Kiel, Germany: Schwering, 1858.

Parducci, A., & Brookshire, K. Figural aftereffects with tachistoscopic presentation. *American Journal of Psychology,* 1956, *69,* 635–639.

Parker, D. E., Woods, D. L., & Tubbs, R. L. Illusory displacement of a moving trace with respect to the grid during oscilloscope motion. *Perception & Psychophysics,* 1977, *21,* 439–444.

Parks, T. E. A control for ocular tracking in the demonstration of postretinal visual storage. *American Journal of Psychology,* 1970, *83,* 442–444.

Parlee, M. Visual backward masking of a single line by a single line. *Vision Research,* 1969, *9,* 199–205.

Parola, R. *Optical art: Theory and practice.* New York: Van Nostrand Reinhold, 1969.

Pastore, N. *Selective history of theories of visual perception: 1650–1950.* New York: Oxford University Press, 1971.

Pease, P. L. On color Mach bands. *Vision Research,* 1978, *18,* 751–755.

Pellionisz, T., Llinas, R., & Perkel, D. H. A computer model of the cerebella cortex of the frog. *Neuroscience,* 1977, *2,* 19–48.

Pellionisz, T. Computer simulations of the pattern transfer of large neuronal fields. *Acta Biochimica et Biophysica Academiae Scientiarum Hungaricae,* 1970, *5,* 71–79.

Pellionisz, T., & Szentágothai, J. Dynamic single unit simulation of a realistic cerebellar network model. *Brain Research,* 1973, *49,* 83–99.

Penn, R. D., & Hagins, W. A. Kinetics of the photo current of retinal rods. *Biophysics Journal,* 1972, *12,* 1073–1094.

Penrose, L. S., & Penrose, R. Impossible objects: A special type of illusion. *British Journal of Psychology,* 1958, *49,* 31–33.

Perkel, D. H., & Bullock, T. H. Neural coding. *Neurosciences Research Program Bulletin,* 1968, *6,* 221–347.

Perl, M. L., & Kirk, W. T. Heavy leptons. *Scientific American,* March 1978, *238*(3), 50–57.

Pettigrew, J. D., & Daniels, J. D. Gamma-aminobutyric acid antagonism in visual cortex: Different effects on simple, complex, and hypercomplex neurons. *Science,* 1973, *182,* 81–83.

Pettigrew, J. D., & Konishi, M. Neurons selective for orientation and binocular disparity in the visual wulst of the barn owl (Tyto Alba). *Science,* 1976, *193,* 675–678.

Pettigrew, J. D., Nikara, T., & Bishop, P. O. Binocular interaction on single units in cat striate cortex: Simultaneous stimulation by single moving slit with receptive fields in correspondence. *Experimental Brain Research,* 1968, *6,* 391–410.

Piaget, J. [*The mechanisms of perception*] (G. N. Seagrim, trans.). New York: Basic Books, 1969.

Pierce, A. H. *Studies in auditory and visual space perception.* New York: Longmans, Green, 1901.

Piéron, H. Le méchanisme d'apparition des couleurs subjectives de Fechner–Benham. *Année Psychologique,* 1923, *23,* 1–49. (a)

Piéron, H. Les problèmes psychophysiologiques de la perception du temps. *Année Psychologique,* 1923, *24,* 1–25. (b)

Piéron, H. Le processus de métacontraste. *Journal de Psychologie Normale et Pathologique,* 1935, *32,* 5–24.

Piper, H. Über die Abhängigkeit des Reizwertes leuchtender Objekte von ihrer Flächen-bezw. Winkelgrösse. *Zeitschrift für Psychologie und Physiologie der Sinnesorgane,* 1903, *32,* 98–112.

Pippenger, N. Complexity theory. *Scientific American,* June 1978, *238,* 114–124.

Pirenne, M. H. Some aspects of the sensitivity of the eye. *Annals of the New York Academy of Sciences,* 1958, *74,* 377–384.

Pirenne, M. H. Visual acuity. In H. Davson, (Ed.), *The eye, Vol. 2.* New York: Academic Press, 1962.

Pirenne, M. H. *Vision and the eye* (2nd ed.). London: Chapman & Hall Ltd. & Science Paperbacks, 1967.

Pirenne, M. H. *Optics, painting, and photography.* Cambridge, England: Cambridge University Press, 1970.

Pitts, W., & McCulloch, W. S. How we know universals: The perception of auditory and visual forms. *Bulletin of Mathematical Biophysics*, 1967, *9*, 127–147.

Plateau, J. Sur la mesure des sensations physiques, et sur la loi qui lie l'intensité de ces sensations à l'intensité de la cause excitante. *Bulletin de l'Académie Royale des Sciences, des Lettres, et des Beaux-Arts de Belgique, Series 2,* 1872, *33,* 376–388.

Platt, J. R. Strong inference. *Science,* 1964, *146,* 347–353.

Poggio, G. F., & Fischer, B. Binocular interaction and depth sensitivity of striate and prestriate cortical neurons of behaving Rhesus monkeys. *Journal of Neurophysiology,* 1977, *40,* 1392–1405.

Poggio, T. Trigger features or Fourier analysis in early vision: A new point of view. Paper presented at the University of Texas Conference on Feature Detection, Austin, Texas, March 22–24, 1979.

Pollack, I. Perception of two-dimensional Markov constraints within visual displays. *Perception & Psychophysics,* 1971, *9,* 461–464.

Pollack, I. Visual discrimination of "unseen" objects: Forced choice testing of Mayzner–Tresselt sequential blanking effects. *Perception & Psychophysics,* 1972, *11,* 121–128.

Pollack, I. Discrimination of third-order Markov constraints within visual displays. *Perception & Psychophysics,* 1973, *13,* 276–280.

Pollack, J. D. Reaction time to different wavelengths at various luminances. *Perception & Psychophysics,* 1968, *3,* 17–24.

Pollen, D. A., Andrews, B. W., & Feldon, S. E. Spatial frequency selectivity of periodic complex cells in the visual cortex of the cat. -Vision Research, 1978, *18,* 665–682.

Pollen, D. A., Lee, J. R., & Taylor, J. H. How does the striate cortex begin the reconstruction of the visual world? *Science,* 1971, *173,* 74–77.

Pollen, D. A., & Ronner, S. F. Periodic excitability changes across the RF of complex cells in the striate and parastriate cortex of the cat. *Journal of Physiology,* 1975, *245,* 667–697.

Polyak, S. L. *The retina.* Chicago: University of Chicago Press, 1941.

Polyak, S. L. *The vertebrate visual system.* Chicago: University of Chicago Press, 1957.

Pomerantz, J. R. Are complex visual features derived from simple ones? In E. L. J. Leeuwenberg & H. F. J. M. Buffart (Eds.), *Formal theories of visual perception.* New York: Wiley, 1978.

Pomerantz, J. R., Sager, L. C., & Stoever, R. J. Perception of wholes and their component parts: Some configurational superiority effects. *Journal of Experimental Psychology: Human Perception and Performance,* 1977, *3,* 422–435.

Poppelreuter, W. *Die psychischen Schadigungen durch kopfschuss im kriege (1914–1916).* Leipzig: Voss, 1917.

Popper, K. R., & Eccles, J. C. *The self and the brain.* New York: Springer-Verlag, 1977.

Porter, T. C. Contributions to the study of "flicker." *Proceedings of the Royal Society, London,* 1898, *63,* 347–356.

Posner, M. I. *Chronometric exploration of mind.* Hillsdale, N.J.: Lawrence Erlbaum Associates, 1978.

Postman, L. Toward a general theory of cognition. In J. H. Rohrer & M. Sherif (Eds.), *Social psychology at the crossroads.* Plainview, N.Y.: Books for Libraries, Inc., 1951.

Postman, L., & Tolman, E. C. Brunswik's probabilistic functionalism. In S. Koch (ed.), *Psychology: A study of a science.* Vol. 1. *Sensory, perceptual, and physiological formulations.* New York: McGraw-Hill Book Company, 1959.

Poston, T., & Stewart, I. Nonlinear models of multistable perception. *Behavioral Science,* 1978, *23,* 318–335.

Powers, W. T. *Behavior: The control of perception.* Chicago: Aldine, 1973.

Pretori, H., & Sachs, M. Messende untersuchungen des farbigen simultancontrastes. *Pflueger's Archiv fuer die Gesamte Physiologie des Menschen und der Tiere,* 1895, *60,* 71–90.

Prevost, B. Sur une apparence de décomposition de la lumière blanche par le mouvement du corps qui la réfléchit. *Mémoires de la Société de Physique et d'Histoire naturelle de Genèva,* 1823–26, *3,* 121–129.

Pribram, K. H., Nuwer, M., & Baron, R. L. The holographic hypothesis of memory structure in brain function and perception. In D. H. Krantz (Ed.), *Contemporary developments in mathematical psychology* (Vol. II). San Francisco: Freeman, 1974.

Price, H. H. *Hume's theory of the external world.* Oxford: Clarendon Press, 1940.

Priest, I. G., & Brickwedde, F. G. The minimum perceptible colorimetric purity as a function of dominant wavelength. *Journal of the Optical Society of America,* 1938, *28,* 133–139.

Prinzmetal, W., & Banks, W. P. Good continuation affects visual detection. *Perception & Psychophysics,* 1977, *21,* 389–395.

Pritchard, R. M. Stabilized images on the retina. *Scientific American,* June 1961.

Pritchard, R. M., Heron, W., & Hebb, D. O. Visual perception approached by the method of stabilized images. *Canadian Journal of Psychology,* 1960, *14,* 66–77.

Proffitt, D. R., Cutting, J. E., & Stier, D. M. Perception of wheel-generated motion. *Journal of Experimental Psychology: Human Perception and Performance,* 1979, *5,* 289–302.

Provine, R. R., & Enoch, J. M. On voluntary ocular accommodation. *Perception & Psychophysics,* 1975, *17,* 209–212.

Pugh, E. N., Jr., & Mollon, J. D. A theory of the π_1 and π_3 color mechanisms of Stiles. *Vision Research,* 1979, *19,* 293–312.

Pulfrich, C. Die stereoskopie im dienste der isochromen und heterochromen photometrie. *Naturwissenschaften,* 1922, *10,* 553–564, 569–574, 596–601, 714–722, 735–743, 751–761.

Purdy, D. M. *Chroma as a function of retinal illumination.* Unpublished doctoral dissertation, Harvard University, 1929.

Purdy, D. M. The Bezold–Brücke phenomenon and contours for constant hue. *American Journal of Psychology,* 1937, *49,* 313–315.

Purkinje, J. *Beobachtungen und versuche zur physiologie die sinne. Beiträge zur kenntniss des sehens in subjecktiver hinsicht* Erstes Bändchen. Prague: Calve'schen Buchhandlung, 1823.

Purkinje, J. *Beobachtungen und Versuche zur Physiologie der Sinne. Neue bieträge zur kenntniss des sehens in subjecktiver hinsicht* Zweites Bändchen. Berlin: Reiner, 1825.

Pylyshyn, Z. W. Imagery and artificial intelligence. In W. Savage (Ed.), *Minnesota Studies in the Philosophy of Science* (Vol. 9). Minneapolis, Minn.: University of Minnesota Press, 1976.

Pylyshyn, Z. W. Validating computational models: A critique of Anderson's indeterminacy of representation claim. *Psychological Review,* 1979, *86,* 383–394.

Raab, D. Backward masking. *Psychological Bulletin,* 1963, *60,* 118–129.

Rabelo, C., & Grüsser, O.-J. Die abhängigkeit der subjektiven Helligkeit intermittierender Lichtreize von der Flimmerfrequenz (Brücke-Effekt, "brightness enhancement"): Untersuchungen bei verschiedener Leuchtdichte und Feldgrösse. *Psychologische Forschung,* 1961, *26,* 299–312.

Rakic, P. Local circuit neurons. *Neurosciences Research Program Bulletin,* 1975, *13*(3), 291–446.

Rashevsky, N. *Mathematical biophysics.* Chicago: University of Chicago Press, 1948.

Ratliff, F. *Mach bands: Quantitative studies on neural networks in the retina.* San Francisco: Holden-Day, 1965.

Ratliff, F. On the psychophysical basis of universal color terms. *Proceedings of the American Philosophical Society,* 1976, *120,* 311–330.

Ratliff, F., & Hartline, H. K. The responses of *Limulus* optic nerve fibers to patterns of illumination on the receptor mosaic. *Journal of General Physiology,* 1959, *42,* 1241–1255.

Ratliff, F., Hartline, H. K., & Lange, D. The dynamics of lateral inhibition in the compound eye of *Limulus* I. In C. G. Bernhard (Ed.), *The functional organization of the compound eye.* Oxford: Pergamon Press, 1966.

Ratliff, F., Knight, B. W., Toyoda, J., & Hartline, H. K. Enhancement of flicker by lateral inhibition. *Science,* 1967, *158,* 392–393.

Ratliff, F., & Riggs, L. A. Involuntary motions of the eye during monocular fixation. *Journal of Experimental Psychology,* 1950, *40,* 687–701.

Ratoosh, P. On interposition as a cue for the perception of distance. *Proceedings of the National Academy of Sciences,* 1949, *35,* 257–259.

Ratoosh, P., & Graham, C. H. Areal effects in foveal brightness discrimination. *Journal of Experimental Psychology,* 1951, *42,* 367–375.

Rawdon-Smith, A. F., & Grindley, G. C. An illusion in the perception of loudness. *British Journal of Psychology,* 1935, *26,* 191–195.

Rayleigh, Lord. Experiments on colour. *Nature*, 1881, *25*, 64–66.

Reed, S. K. *Psychological Processes in Pattern Recognition*, New York: Academic Press, 1973.

Regan, D., & Beverly, K. I. Looming detectors in the human visual pathway. *Vision Research*, 1978, *18,* 415–421.

Regan, D., & Tyler, C. W. Some dynamic features of colour vision. *Vision Research,* 1971, *11,* 1307–1324.

Reichardt, W. (Ed.). *Processing of optical data by organisms and by machines.* (Proceedings of the International School of Physics "Enrico Fermi," Course XLIII, Varenna on Lake Como, Villa Monastero, July 15–27, 1968.) New York: Academic Press, 1969.

Reitz, W. E., & Jackson, D. N. Affect and stereoscopic resolution. *Journal of Abnormal and Social Psychology,* 1964, *69,* 212–215.

Restle, F. Moon illusion explained on the basis of relative size. *Science,* 1970, *167,* 1092–1096.

Restle, F. Visual illusion. In M. H. Apley (Ed.), *Adaptation level theory.* New York: Academic Press, 1971.

Restle, F., & Merryman, C. T. An adaptation level theory account of a relative size illusion. *Psychonomic Science,* 1968, *12,* 229–230.

Ricco, A. Relazione fra il minimo angolo visuale e l'intensitá luminosa. *Annali di Ottalmologia*, 1877, *6,* 373–479.

Richards, W. *The influence of oculomotor systems on visual perception.* Air Force Office of Scientific Research Tech. Rep. No. 69-1934TR, 1969. (a)

Richards, W. Saccadic suppression. *Journal of the Optical Society of America,* 1969, *59,* 617–623. (b)

Richards, W. Lessons in constancy from neurophysiology. In W. Epstein (Ed.), *Stability and constancy in visual perception.* New York: Wiley-Interscience, 1977.

Richards, W., & Luria, S. M. Color-mixture functions at low luminance levels. *Vision Research,* 1964, *4,* 281–313.

Richet, C. Forme et durée de la vibration/nerveuse/et l'unité psychologique de temps. *Revue Philosophique de la France et de l'Etranger,* 1898, *45,* 337–350.

Richter, B. From the psi to charm: The experiments of 1975 and 1976. *Science,* 1977, *196,* 1286–1297.

Riggs, L. A. Light as a stimulus for vision. In C. H. Graham (Ed.), *Vision and visual perception.* New York: Wiley, 1965.

Riggs, L., A., Merton, P., & Morton, H. Suppression of visual phosphenes during saccadic eye movements. *Vision Research,* 1974, *14,* 997–1011.

Riggs, L. A., Ratliff, F., Cornsweet, J. C., & Cornsweet, T. N. The disappearance of steadily fixated visual test objects. *Journal of the Optical Society of America,* 1953, *43,* 495–501.

Riggs, L. A., White, K. D., & Eimas, P. D. Establishment and decay of orientation-contingent aftereffects of color. *Perception & Psychophysics,* 1974, *16,* 535–542.

Ringo, J., Wolbarsht, M. L., Wagner, H. G., Crocker, R., & Amthor, F. Trichromatic vision in the cat. *Science,* 1977, *198,* 753–755.

Robinson, A. L. High energy physics: A proliferation of quarks and leptons. *Science,* 1977, *198,* 478–481.

Robinson, A. L. Particle physics: New evidence from Germany for fifth quark. *Science,* 1978, *200,* 1033–1034.

Robinson, D. N. Disinhibition of visually masked stimuli. *Science,* 1966, *154,* 157–158.

Robinson, D. N. Visual disinhibition with binocular and interocular presentation. *Journal of the Optical Society of America,* 1968, *58,* 254–257.

Robinson, D. N. Critical flicker-fusion of solid and annular stimuli. *Science,* 1970, *167,* 207–208.

Robinson, D. N. *An intellectual history of psychology.* New York: Macmillan, 1976. (a)

Robinson, D. N. Thomas Reid's Gestalt psychology. In S. F. Barker & T. L. Beauchamp (Eds.), *Thomas Reid: Critical interpretations* (Vol. 3). Philadelphia: Philosophical Monographs, 1976. (b)

Robinson, D. N. (Ed.). *Significant contributions to the history of psychology 1750–1920*. Washington, D.C.: University Publications of America, Inc., 1977.

Robinson, D. N. *Thomas Reid's Gestalt psychology*. In press.

Robinson, G. M., & Moulton, J. A delayed induced-motion illusion. *Perception,* 1978, *7,* 85–89.

Robinson, J. O. Retinal inhibition in visual distortion. *British Journal of Psychology,* 1968, *59,* 29–36.

Robinson, J. O. *The psychology of visual illusion*. London: Hutchinson & Co., Ltd., 1972.

Robson, J. G., & Enroth-Cugell, C. Light distribution in the cat's retinal image. *Vision Research,* 1978, *18,* 159–173.

Rock, I. *An introduction to perception*. New York: Macmillan, 1975.

Rock, I., & Ebenholtz, S. Stroboscopic movement based on change of phenomenal location rather than retinal location. *American Journal of Psychology,* 1962, *75,* 193–207.

Rock, I., Shallo, J., & Schwartz, F. Pictorial depth and related constancy effects as a function of recognition. *Perception,* 1978, *7,* 3–20.

Rodieck, R. W. *The vertebrate retina: Principles of structure and function*. San Francisco: W. H. Freeman, 1973.

Rollett, H. Über ein subjektives optisches Phänomen bei der Betrachtung gestreifter Flächen. *Zeitschrift für Psychologie und Physiologie der Sinnesorgane, Abteilung II. Zeitschrift für Sinnesphysiologie,* 1910, *46,* 198–224.

Rommetreit, R., Toch, H., & Svendsen, D. Semantic, syntactic, and associative context effects in a stereoscopic rivalry situation. *Scandinavian Journal of Psychology,* 1968, *9,* 145–149.

Rose, A. The sensitivity performance of the human eye on an absolute scale. *Journal of the Optical Society of America,* 1948. *38,* 196–208.

Rosenblatt, F. Two theorems of statistical separability in the perception. *Proceedings of a Symposium on the Mechanization of Thought Processes*. Her Majesty's Stationary Office, London, 1959, 421–456.

Rosenblatt, F. *The principles of neurodynamics*. Washington, D.C.: Spartan Books, 1962.

Rosenfeld, A. *Picture processing by computer*. New York: Academic Press, 1969.

Ross, J. Stereopsis by binocular delay. *Nature,* 1974, *248,* 363–364.

Ross, J. The resources of binocular perception. *Scientific American,* March 1976, *234*(3), 80–84.

Ross, J., & Hogben, J. H. Short-term memory in stereopsis. *Vision Research,* 1974, *14,* 1195–1201.

Roufs, J. A. J. Perception lag as a function of stimulus luminance. *Vision Research,* 1963, *3,* 81–91.

Roufs, J. A. Dynamic properties of vision: IV. Thresholds of decremental flashes, incremental flashes and doublets in relation to flicker fusion. *Vision Research,* 1974, *14*(9), 831–851.

Rouse, R. O. Color and the intensity-time relation. *Journal of the Optical Society of America,* 1952, *42,* 626–630.

Rowe, M. H., & Stone, J. Naming of neurons. Classification and naming of cat retinal ganglion cells. *Brain Behavior and Evolution,* 1977, *14,* 185–216.

Rubin, D. C., & Rebson, D. J. A halo visual illusion. *Perception,* 1977, *6,* 227–236.

Rubin, E. *Synsoplevede figurer*. Copenhagen: Gyldendalske, 1915.

Rubin, E. *Visuelle wahrgenommene figurer*. Copenhagen: Gyldendalske, 1921.

Ruch, T. C. Vision. In T. C. Ruch & H. D. Patton (Eds.), *Physiology and biophysics*. Philadelphia: Saunders, 1965.

Ruddock, K. H. Evidence for macular pigmentation from colour matching data. *Vision Research,* 1963, *3,* 417–429.

Rudee, M. L. Optical transforms and the "pincushion grid" illusion. *Science,* 1977, *198,* 960.

Rumelhart, D. E. A multicomponent theory of the perception of briefly exposed visual displays. *Journal of Mathematical Psychology,* 1970, *7,* 191–218.

Rushton, W. A. H. The rhodopsin density in the human rods. *Journal of Physiology,* 1956, *134,* 30–46.

Rushton, W. A. H. Kinetics of cone pigments measured objectively on the living human fovea. *Annals of the New York Academy of Science,* 1958, *74,* 291–304.

Rushton, W. A. H. Rhodopsin measurement and dark adaptation in a subject deficient in cone vision. *Journal of Physiology,* 1961, *156,* 193–205.

Rushton, W. A. H. Visual pigments in man. *Scientific American,* November 1962, *207*(5), 120–132.

Rushton, W. A. H. Flash photolysis in human cones. *Photochemistry and Photobiology,* 1964, *3,* 561–577.

Rushton, W. A. H. The Ferrier lecture, 1962: Visual adaptation. *Proceedings of the Royal Society of London, Series B,* 1965, *162,* 20–46.

Russell, B. R. *Analysis of matter.* New York: Harcourt Brace & Co., 1927.

Sachs, M. B., Nachmias, J., & Robson, J. G. Spatial frequency channels in human vision. *Journal of the Optical Society of America,* 1971, *61,* 1176–1186.

Said, F. S., & Weale, R. A. The variation with age of the spectral transmissivity of the living human cyrstalline lens. *Gerontologia,* 1959, *3,* 213–231.

Sakitt, B. Configuration dependence of scotopic spatial summation. *Journal of Physiology,* 1971, *216,* 513–529.

Sakitt, B. Counting every quantum. *Journal of Physiology,* 1972, *223,* 131–150.

Sakitt, B. Locus of short-term visual storage. *Science,* 1975, *190,* 1318–1319.

Sakitt, B. Iconic memory. *Psychological Review,* 1976, *83,* 257–276.

Sakitt, B., & Long, G. M. Relative rod and cone contributions in iconic storage. *Perception & Psychophysics,* 1978, *23,* 527–536.

Sakitt, B., & Long, G. M. Spare the rod and spoil the icon. *Journal of Experimental Psychology: Human Perception and Performance,* 1979, *5,* 19–30.

Salzmann, M. *The anatomy and physiology of the human eyeball in the normal state.* Chicago: University of Chicago Press, 1912.

Sambursky, S. (Ed.). Physical thought from the pre-Socratics to the quantum physicists. New York: Pica Press, 1975.

Schachar, R. A., Black, T. D., Hartfield, K. L., & Goldberg, I. S. Optical transforms and the "pincushion grid" illusion. *Science,* 1977, *198,* 961–962.

Schade, O. H. Optical and photoelectric analog of the eye. *Journal of the Optical Society of America,* 1956, *46,* 721–739.

Schank, R. C., & Colby, K. M. (Eds.). *Computer models of thought and language.* San Francisco: W. H. Freeman, 1973.

Scheerer, E. Integration, interruption, and processing rate in visual backward masking: 1, Review. *Psychologische Forschung,* 1973, *36,* 71–93.

Schilder, P. Über autokinetische Empfindungen. *Archiv für die Gesamte Psychologie des Menschen und der Tiere.* 1912, *25,* 36–77.

Schiller, P. H. Single unit analysis of backward visual masking and metacontrast in the cat lateral geniculate nucleus. *Vision Research,* 1968, *8,* 855–866.

Schiller, P. H. Behavioral and electrophysiological studies of visual masking. In K. N. Leibovic (Ed.), *Information processing in the nervous system.* New York: Springer-Verlag, 1969.

Schiller, P. H., & Koerner, F. Discharge characteristics of single units in superior colliculus of the alert Rhesus monkey. *Journal of Neurophysiology,* 1971, *34,* 920–936.

Schiller, P. H., & Smith, M. C. Detection in metacontrast. *Journal of Experimental Psychology,* 1966, *71,* 32–39.

Schiller, P. H., & Wiener, M. Binocular and stereoscopic viewing of geometrical illusions. *Perception and Motor Skills,* 1962, *15,* 739–747.

Schjelderup-Ebbe, T. Der kontrast auf dem gebiete des licht-und farbensenness (I). *Neue Psychologische Studien,* 1926, *2,* 61-126.

Schneider, C. W. Behavioral determinations of critical flicker frequency in the rabbit. *Vision Research,* 1968, *8,* 1227-1234. (a)

Schneider, C. W. Electrophysiological analysis of the mechanisms underlying critical flicker frequency. *Vision Research,* 1968, *8,* 1235-1244. (b)

Schneider, G. E. Two visual systems. *Science,* 1969, *163,* 895-902.

Schoenberg, K. M., Katz, M., & Mayzner, M. J. The shape of inhibitory fields in the human visual system. *Perception and Psychophysics,* 1970, *7,* 357-359.

Schultz, D. *A history of modern psychology.* New York: Academic Press, 1975.

Schumann, M. Einige Beobachtungen über die zusammenfassung von gesichtseindrücken zu einheiten. *Psychologische Studien,* 1904, *1,* 1-32.

Schuster, D. H. A new ambiguous figure: A three-stick clevis. *American Journal of Psychology,* 1964, *77,* 673.

Schuyt, M., & Elffers, J. *Anamorphoses: Games of perception and illusion in art.* New York: Harry N. Abrams, 1975.

Schwarz, J. H. Dual-resonance models of elementary particles. *Scientific American,* 1975, *232*(2), 61-67.

Schwitters, R. F. Fundamental particles with charm. *Scientific American,* 1977, *237,* 56-70.

Sejnowski, T. J. On global properties of neuronal interaction. *Biological Cybernetics,* 1976, *22,* 85-95.

Selfridge, O. G. Pattern recognition and modern computers. *Proceedings of the 1955 Western Joint Computer Conference, Institute of Radio Engineers,* New York, 1955, 82-85.

Selfridge, O. G. Pandemonium: A paradigm for learning. In *Mechanization of thought processes,* Proceedings of a symposium held at the National Physics Laboratory, November 1958, London: Her Majesty's Stationery Office, 1959.

Servière, J., Miceli, D., & Galifret, Y. A psychophysical study of the visual perception of "instantaneous" and "durable." *Vision Research,* 1977, *17,* 57-63.

Shallice, T. The detection of change and the perceptual moment hypothesis. *The British Journal of Statistical Psychology,* 1964, *17,* 113-135.

Shannon, C. E. A mathematical theory of communication. *Bell System Technical Journal,* 1948, *27,* 379-423; 623-656.

Sharpe, C. R. The colour specificity of spatial adaptation: Red-blue interactions. *Vision Research,* 1974, *14,* 41-51.

Sharpe, L. T., & Teas, R. C. Contour specificity of the McCollough effect. *Perception & Psychophysics,* 1978, *23,* 451-458.

Shaw, R., & Bransford, J. Introduction: Psychological approaches to the problem of knowledge. In R. Shaw & J. Bransford (Eds.), *Perceiving, acting, and knowing: Toward an ecological psychology.* Hillsdale, N.J.: Lawrence Erlbaum Associates, 1977.

Shaw, R., & Turvey, M. T. Coalitions as models for ecosystems: A realist perspective on perceptual organization. In M. Kubory & J. Pomerantz (Eds.), *Perceptual Organization.* Hillsdale, N.J.: Lawrence Erlbaum Associates, 1981.

Sheedy, J. E., & Fry, G. A. The perceived direction of the binocular image. *Vision Research,* 1979, *19,* 201-211.

Shepard, R. N., & Chipman, S. Second-order isomorphism of internal representations: Shapes of states. *Cognitive Psychology,* 1970, *1,* 1-17.

Shepherd, G. M. *The synaptic organization of the brain: An introduction.* New York: Oxford University Press, 1974.

Shepherd, G. M. Microcircuits in the nervous system. *Scientific American,* 1978, *238(2),* 93-103.

Sheppard, J. J. *Human color perception.* New York: Elsevier, 1968.

Sherman, S. M., Wilson, J. R., Kaas, J. H., & Webb, S. V. *X*- and *y*-cells in the dorsal lateral geniculate nucleus of the owl monkey (*Aotus trivirgatus*). *Science,* 1976, *192,* 475-476.

Sherrick, M. F., & Dember, W. N. Configurational factors in visual backward masking. *Proceedings of the 76th Annual Convention of American Psychological Association,* 1968, 111–112.

Sherrington, C. S. *The integrative action of the nervous system.* New Haven: Yale University Press, 1906.

Shipley, T. The stereoscopic pattern signal: Gestalt processes in the binocular field. *Pattern Recognition,* 1973, *5,* 109–120.

Shipley, T., & Hyson, M. The stereoscopic sense of order—a classification of stereograms. *American Journal of Optometry and Archives of the American Academy of Optometry,* 1972, *49,* 83–96.

Shipley, T., & Rawlings, S. C. The nonius horopter I. History and theory. *Vision Research,* 1970, *10,* 1225–1262.

Shipley, T., & Wier, C. Asymmetries in the Mach band phenomena. *Kybernetik,* 1972, *10,* 181–189.

Shlaer, R. An eagle's eye: Quality of the retinal image. *Science,* 1972, *176,* 920–922.

Shlaer, S. The relation between visual acuity and illumination. *Journal of General Pysiology,* 1937, *21,* 165–188.

Shurcliff, W. A. New visual phenomenon: The greenish-yellow blotch. *Journal of the Optical Society of America,* 1959, *49,* 1041–1048.

Shute, C. C. D. Haidinger's brushes and predominant orientation of collagen in corneal stroma. *Nature,* 1974, *250,* 163–164.

Shute, C. C. D. Haidinger's brushes—A letter. *Vision Research,* 1978, *18,* 1467.

Sigman, E., & Rock, I. Stroboscopic movement based on perceptual intelligence. *Perception,* 1974, *3,* 9–28.

Simon, H. A. Spurious correlations: A causal interpretation. *Journal of the American Statistical Association,* 1954, *49,* 467–479.

Simon, J. C., & Camillerapp, J. Recherche d'une «forme» dans un fond. *Comptes Rendus Academie des Sciences, Paris,* 1968, *267,* 946–949.

Simonelli, N. M. *Polarized vernier optometer* (BEL-79-4/AFOSR-79-8). New Mexico State University, Las Cruces: Behavioral Engineering Laboratory, Department of Psychology, November 1979.

Sirovich, L., & Abramov, I. Photopigments and pseudopigments. *Vision Research,* 1977, *17,* 5–16.

Sjöstrand, F. S. The outer plexiform layer and the neural organization of the retina. In. B. R. Straatsma, M. O. Hall, R. A. Allen, & F. Crescitelli (Eds.), *The retina: Morphology, function, and clinical characteristics* (UCLA Forum in the Medical Sciences No. 8). Berkeley & Los Angeles: University of California Press, 1969.

Sjöstrand, F. S. A search for the circuitry of directional selectivity and neural adaptation through three-dimensional analysis of the outer plexiform layer of the rabbit retina. *Journal of Ultrastructure Research,* 1974, *49,* 60–156.

Sjöstrand, F. S. The outer plexiform layer of the rabbit retina, an important data processing center. *Vision Research,* 1976, *16,* 1–14.

Skinner, B. F. The operational analysis of psychological terms. *Psychological Review,* 1945, *52,* 270–277.

Skowbo, D., Gentry, J., Timney, B., & Morant, R. B. The McCollugh effect: Influence of several kinds of visual stimulation on decay rate. *Preception & Psychophysics,* 1974, *16,* 47–49.

Skowbo, D., Timney, B. N., Gentry, T. A., & Morant, R. B. McCollough effects: Experimental findings and theoretical accounts. *Psychological Bulletin,* 1975, *82,* 497–510.

Sloan, L. L. The photopic acuity—luminance function with special reference to parafoveal vision. *Vision Research,* 1968, *8,* 901–911.

Smith, A. T., & Over, R. Orientation masking and the tilt illusion with subjective contours. *Perception,* 1977, *6,* 441–447.

Smith, A. T., & Over, R. Motion aftereffect with subjective contours. *Perception & Psychophysics,* 1979, *25,* 95–98.

Smith, F. D. Checkerboards and color aftereffects. *Science,* 1977, *198,* 207-208.

Smith, M. C., & Schiller, P. H. Forward and backward masking: A comparison. *Canadian Journal of Psychology,* 1966, *20,* 191-197.

Smith, R. *A compleat systems of opticks.* Cambridge, 1738.

Smith, R. A., Jr. Spatial frequency adaption and afterimages. *Perception,* 1977, *6,* 153-160.

Smythies, J. R. *Analysis of perception.* New York: Humanities Press, 1956.

Snyder, A. W., Laughlin, S. B., & Stavenga, D. G. Information capacity of eyes. *Vision Research,* 1977, *17,* 1163-1175.

Snyder, F. W., & Pronko, N. H. *Vision with spatial inversion.* Wichita, Kans.: University of Wichita Press, 1952.

Solomon, R. L., & Howes, D. H. Word frequency, personal values, and visual duration thresholds. *Psychological Review,* 1951, *58,* 256-271.

Southall, J. P. C. *Introduction to physiological optics.* New York: Oxford University Press, 1937.

Spekreijse, H., Wagner, H. J., & Wolbarsht, M. L. Spectral and spatial coding of ganglion cell responses in goldfish retina. *Journal of Neurophysiology,* 1972, *35,* 73-86.

Sperling, G. The information available in brief visual presentations. *Psychological Monographs: General and Applied,* 1960, *74,* 1-29.

Sperling, G. A model for visual memory tasks. *Human Factors,* 1963, *5,* 19-31.

Sperling, G. Temporal and spatial visual masking. I. Masking by impulse flashes. *Journal of the Optical Society of America,* 1965, *55,* 541-559.

Sperling, G. A physical and neural theory. *American Journal of Psychology,* 1970, *83,* 461-534.

Sperling, G. The description and luminous calibration of cathode ray oscilloscope visual displays. *Behavior Research Methods and Instrumentation,* 1971, *3,* 148-151. (a)

Sperling, G. Flicker in computer generated visual displays: Selecting a CRO phosphor and other problems. *Behavior Research Methods and Instrumentation,* 1971, *3,* 151-153. (b)

Sperling, G. Stereoscopic visual displays: Principles, viewing devices, alignment procedures. *Behavior Research Methods and Instrumentation,* 1971, *3,* 154-158. (c)

Sperling, G., & Sondhi, M. M. Model for visual luminance discrimination and flicker detection. *Journal of the Optical Society of America,* 1968, *58,* 1133-1145.

Sperling, H. G., & Joliffe, C. L. Intensity-time relationship at threshold for spectral stimuli in human vision. *Journal of the Optical Society of America,* 1965, *55,* 191-199.

Sperry, R. W., Miner, R., & Myers, R. E. Visual pattern perception following subpial slicing and tantalum wire implantations in the visual cortex. *Journal of Comparative and Physiological Psychology,* 1955, *48,* 50-58.

Springbett, B. M. Some stereoscopic phenomena and their implications. *British Journal of Psychology,* 1961, *52,* 105-109.

Stabell, U., & Stabell, B. Chromatic rod vision—X. A theoretical survey. *Vision Research,* 1973, *13,* 449-455.

Stadler, M. Figural aftereffects as optical illusions. *American Journal of Psychology,* 1972, *85,* 351-375.

Staller, J. D., Lappin, J. S., & Fox, R. Stimulus uncertainty does not impair stereopsis, *Perception and Psychophysics,* 1980, *27,* 361-367.

Stanley, G., & Hoffman, W. C. Orientation-specific color effects without adaptation. *Bulletin of the Psychonomic Society,* 1976, *7,* 513-514.

Stark, L. Nonlinear operator in the pupil system. *Quarterly Progress Report* 72, Research Laboratory of Electronics, Massachusetts Institute of Technology, 258-260, 1964.

Stark, L. *Neurological control systems: Studies in bioengineering.* New York: Plenum Press, 1968.

Stark, L., Campbell, F. W., & Atwood, J. Pupil unrest: An example of noise in a biological servomechanism. *Nature,* 1958, *182,* 857-858.

Steinman, R. M., Haddad, G. M., Skavenski, A. A., & Wyman, D. Miniature eye movement. *Science,* 1973, *181,* 810-819.

Stell, W. K. The morphological organization of the vertebrate retina. In M. G. F. Fuortes (Ed.),

Physiology of photoreceptor organs. New York: Springer-Verlag, 1972.

Sternheim, C. E., Gorinson, R., & Markovitz, N. Visual sensitivity during successive chromatic contrast: Evidence for interactions between photopic mechanisms. *Vision Research,* 1977, *17,* 45–49.

Stetcher, S., Sigel, C., & Lange, R. V. Composite adaptation and spatial frequency interaction. *Vision Research,* 1973, *13,* 2527–2531.

Stevens, J. K., McGuire, B. A., & Sterling, P. Toward a functional architecture of the retina: Serial reconstruction of adjacent ganglion cells. *Science,* 1980, *207,* 317–319.

Stevens, S. S. (Ed.). *Handbook of experimental psychology.* New York: Wiley, Inc., 1951. (a)

Stevens, S. S. Mathematics, measurement, and psychophysics. In S. S. Stevens (Ed.), *Handbook of experimental psychology.* New York: Wiley, 1951. (b)

Stevens, S. S. On the psychophysical law. *Psychological Review,* 1957, *64,* 153–181.

Stevens, S. S. The psychophysics of sensory function. In W. A. Rosenblith (Ed.), *Sensory communication.* Cambridge & New York: MIT Press, Wiley, 1961.

Stevens, S. S. Sensory power functions and neural events. In W. R. Loewenstein (Ed.), *Principles of receptor physiology.* New York: Springer-Verlag, 1971.

Stewart, B. R. Temporal summation during dark adaptation. *Journal of the Optical Society of America,* 1972, *62*(3), 449–457.

Stigler, R. Chronophotische studien über den umgebungs kontrast. *Pfluüger's Archiv für die Gesamte Physiologie des Menschen und der Tiere,* 1910, *134,* 365–435.

Stiles, W. S. The luminous efficiency of monochromatic rays entering the eye pupil at different points and a new colour effect. *Proceedings of the Royal Society of London, Series B,* 1937, *123,* 90–118.

Stiles, W. S. The directional sensitivity of the retina and the spectral sensitivities of the rods and cones. *Proceedings of the Royal Society of London, Series B,* 1939, *127,* 64–105.

Stiles, W. S. Increment thresholds and the mechanisms of human color vision. *Documenta Ophthalmologica,* 1949, *3,* 138–163.

Stiles, W. S. The basic data of colour matching. *Physical Society Year Book,* 1955, 44–65.

Stiles, W. S. Color vision: The approach through increment threshold sensitivity. *Proceedings of the National Academy of Sciences,* 1959, *45,* 100–114.

Stiles, W. S., & Burch, J. M. National Physical Laboratory colour matching investigation: Final report. *Optica Acta,* 1959, *6,* 1–26.

Stiles, W. S., & Crawford, B. H. The luminous efficiency of rays entering the eye pupil at different points. *Proceedings of the Royal Society of London, Series B,* 1933, *112,* 428–450.

Stockmeyer, L. J., & Chandra, A. K. Intrinsically difficult problems. *Scientific American,* May 1979, *240,* 140–159.

Stoper, A. E., & Banffy, S. Relation of split apparent motion to metacontrast. *Journal of Experimental Psychology: Human Perception and Performance,* 1977, *3,* 258–277.

Stoper, A. E., & Mansfield, J. G. Metacontrast and paracontrast suppression of a contourless area. *Vision Research,* 1978, *18,* 1669–1674.

Stratton, G. Some preliminary experiments on vision without inversion of the retinal image. *Psychological Review,* 1896, *3,* 611–617.

Stratton, G. Upright vision and the retinal image. *Psychological Review,* 1897, *4,* 182–187.

Stromeyer, C. F., III. Edge contingent color aftereffects: Spatial frequency specificity. *Vision Research,* 1972, *12,* 717–734.

Stromeyer, C. F., III, & Julesz, B. Spatial frequency masking in vision: Critical bands and the spread of masking. *Journal of the Optical Society of America,* 1972, *62,* 1221–1232.

Stromeyer, C. F., III, & Klein, S. Evidence against narrow-band spatial frequency channels in human vision: The detectability of frequency modulated gratings. *Vision Research,* 1975, *15,* 899–910.

Stromeyer, C. F., III, & Mansfield, R. J. W. Colored aftereffects produced both moving edges. *Perception & Psychophysics,* 1970, *7,* 108–114.

Stromeyer, C. F., III, & Psotka, J. The detailed texture of eidetic images. *Nature,* 1970, *225,*

346–349.

Stroud, J. M. The psychological moment in perception. In H. von Foerster (Ed.), *Transactions of the Sixth Conference on Cybernetics*. New York: Josiah Macy, Jr., 1949.

Stroud, J. M. The fine structure of psychological time. In H. Quastler (Ed.), *Information theory in psychology*. Glencoe, Ill.: Free Press, 1955.

Stryker, M. P., & Sherk, H. Modification of cortical orientation selectivity in the cat by restricted visual experience: A reexamination. *Science*, 1975, *190*, 904–906.

Stryker, M. P., Sherk, H., Leventhal, A. G., & Hirsch, H. V. B. Physiological consequences for the cat's visual cortex of effectively restricting early visual experience with oriental contours. *Journal of Neurophysiology*, 1978, *41*, 896–909.

Sunga, R. N., & Enoch, J. M. A static perimetric technique believed to test receptive field properties: III. Clinical trials. *American Journal of Ophthalmology*, 1970, *70*, 244–272.

Sutherland, N. S. Figural aftereffects and apparent size. *Quarterly Journal of Psychology*, 1961, *13*, 222–228.

Sutherland, N. S. Outlines of a theory of visual pattern recognition in animals and man. *Proceedings of the Royal Society of Londin, Series B*, 1968, *171*, 297–317.

Sutherland, N. S. Intelligent picture processing. In N. S. Sutherland (Ed.), *Tutorial essays in psychology, Vol. 1*. Hillsdale, N.J.: Lawrence Erlbaum, 1976.

Swartz, R. J. (Ed.). *Perceiving, sensing, and knowing: A book of readings from twentieth century sources in the philosophy of perception*. Berkeley: University of California Press, 1977.

Szentágothai, J. Glomerular synapses, complex synaptic arrangements, and their operational significance. In F. O. Schmitt (ed.), *The neurosciences: Second study program*. New York: Rockefeller University Press, 1970.

Szentágothai, J. Neural and synaptic architecture of the lateral geniculate nucleus. In R. Jung (ed.), *Visual centers in the brain*. Berlin: Springer-Verlag, 1973a.

Szentágothai, J. Synaptology of the visual cortex. In R. Jung (ed.), *Visual centers in the brain*. Berlin: Springer-Verlag, 1973b.

Szentágothai, J. The module concept in cerebral cortex architecture. *Brain Research*, 1975, *95*, 475–496.

Szentágothai, J. The Ferrier lecture, 1977: The neuron network of the cerebral cortex: a functional interpretation. *Proceedings of the Royal Society of London, Series B*, 1978a, *201*, 219–248. (a)

Szentágothai, J. The local neuronal apparatus of the cerebral cortex. In P. Buser & A. Rougeul-Buser, (Eds.), *Cerebral correlates of conscious experience*. Amsterdam; New York: Elsevier North Holland Biomedical Press, 1978. (b)

Szentágothai, J. Specificity versus (quasi-) randomness in cortical connectivity. In M. A. B. Brazier & H. Petsche (Eds.), *Architectronics of the cerebral cortex*. New York: Raven Press, 1978. (c)

Talbot, H. F. Experiments on light. *Proceedings of the Royal Society of London*, 1834, *3*(16), 298.

Tanner, W. P., Jr., & Swets, J. A. A decision-making theory of visual detection. *Psychological Review*, 1954, *61*, 401–409.

Tate, G. W., & Lynn, J. R. *Principles of quantitative perimetry*. New York: Grune and Stratton, 1977.

Taylor, M. M. Visual discrimination and orientation. *Journal of the Optical Society of America*, 1963, *53*, 763–765.

Taylor, M. M., & Creelman, C. D. *PEST: Efficient estimates on probability functions*. University of Toronto preprint, Canada, 1965.

Terdiman, T., Smith, J. D., & Stark, L. Pupil responses to light and electrical stimulation: Static and dynamic characteristics. *Brain Research*, 1969, *16*, 288–292.

Teuber, M. L. Sources of ambiguity in the prints of Maurits C. Escher. *Scientific American*, 1974, *231*(1), 90–104.

Teyler, T. J., Baum, W. M., & Patterson, M. M. Behavioral and biological issues in the learning paradigm. *Physiological Psychology*, 1975, *3*, 65–72.

Thom, R. *Structural stability and morphogenesis*. Reading, Mass.: W. A. Benjamin, Inc., 1975.

Thomas, J. A reciprocal inhibitory model for monocular pattern alternation. *Perception & Psychophysics,* 1977, *22,* 310-312.

Thomas, J. Binocular rivalry: The effects of orientation and pattern color arrangement. *Perception & Psychophysics,* 1978, *23,* 360-362.

Thomas, J. P. Threshold measurements of Mach bands. *Journal of the Optical Society of America,* 1965, *55,* 521-524.

Thomas, J. P. Brightness variations in stimuli with ramplike contours. *Journal of the Optical Society of America,* 1966, *56,* 238-242.

Thompson, P. G., & Movshon, J. A. Storage of spatially specific threshold elevation. *Perception,* 1978, *7,* 65-73.

Thomson, J. J. Cathode rays. *Philosophical Magazine,* 1897, *44,* 293-316.

Thorson, J., & Biederman-Thorson, M. Distributed relaxation processes in sensory adaptation: Spatial non-uniformity in receptors can explain both the curious dynamics and logarithmic statics of adaptation. *Science,* 1974, *183,* 161-172.

Timney, B. N., & MacDonald, C. Are curves detected by "curvature detectors?" *Perception,* 1978, *7,* 51-64.

Ting, S. C. C. The discovery of the J particle: A personal recollection. *Science,* 1977, *196,* 1167-1178.

Titchener, E. B. Über binoculate Wirkungen monocularer Reize. *Wundt Philosophische Studien,* 1893, *8,* 231-310.

Titchener, E. B. *An outline of psychology.* New York: Macmillan, 1896.

Titchener, E. B. *Experimental psychology, Vol. I: Qualitative experiments, Part I, Student's manual.* New York: Macmillan, 1915.

Tobey, F. L., Jr., & Enoch, J. M. Directionality and wave guide properties of optically isolated rat rods. *Investigative Ophthalmology,* 1973, *12,* 873-880.

Toch, H. H., & Schulte, R. Readiness to perceive violence as a result of police training. *British Journal of Psychology,* 1961, *52,* 389-393.

Tolhurst, D. J. Adaptation to square wave gratings: Inhibition between spatial frequency channels in human visual system. *Journal of Physiology,* 1972, *226,* 231-248.

Tolhurst, D. J., & Barfield, L. P. Interaction between spatial frequency channels. *Vision Research,* 1978, *18,* 951-958.

Tolman, E. C. *Purposive behavior in animals and man.* New York: Appleton, 1932.

Tolansky, S. *Optical illusions.* Oxford: Pergamon, 1964.

Tomita, T. Electrophysiological study of the mechanisms subserving color coding in the fish retina. *Proceedings of the Cold Spring Harbor Symposium on Quantitative Biology,* 1965, *30,* 559-566.

Tomita, T. Electrical activity of vertebrate photoreceptors. *Quarterly Review of Biophysics,* 1970, *3,* 179-222.

Tomita, T., Kaneko, A., Murakami, M., & Pautler, E. L. Spectral response curves of single cones in the carp. *Vision Research,* 1967, *7,* 519-531.

Toraldo di Francia, G. Per una teoria dell'effetto Stiles-Crawford. *Nuovo Cimento,* 1948, *5,* 589-590.

Torii, S., & Uemura, Y. Effect of inducing luminance and area upon the apparent brightness of test field. *Japanese Journal of Psychological Research,* 1965, *7,* 86-100.

Towe, A. L. Notes on the hypothesis of columnar organization in somatosensory cerebral cortex. *Brain, Behavior, and Evolution,* 1975, *11,* 16-47.

Treisman, M. Brightness contrast and the perceptual scale. *British Journal of Mathematical and Statistical Psychology,* 1970, *23,* 205-224.

Trevarthen, C. B. Two mechanisms of vision in primates. *Psychologische Forschung,* 1968, *31,* 299-337.

Trezona, P. W. Additivity in the tetrachromatic colour matching system. *Vision Research,* 1974, *14,* 1291-1303.

Tricker, R. A. R. *Introduction to meteorological optics*. New York: American Elsevier Publishing Co., 1970.

Troland, L. T. *The principles of psychophysiology: Vol. II-Sensation*. New York: Van Nostrand, 1930.

Troxler, D. Über das Verschwinden gegebener Gegenstände innerhalb unsers Gesichtskreises. *Ophtalmologisches Bibliothek,* 1804, *2,* 1-53.

Tscherning, M. *Physiologic optics*. Philadelphia: Keystone, 1904.

Tukey, J. W. *Halocarbons: Environmental effects of chlorofluoromethane release*. Washington, D.C.: National Academy of Sciences, 1976.

Turing, A. M. On computable numbers with an application to the entscheidungs problem. *Proceedings of the London Mathematical Society,* (Series 2), 1936, *42,* 230-265.

Turvey, M. T. On peripheral and central processes in vision: Inferences from an information-processing analysis of masking with patterned stimuli. *Psychological Review,* 1973, *80,* 1-52.

Turvey, M. T. Constrasting orientations to the theory of visual information processing. *Psychological Review,* 1977, *84,* 67-88.

Turvey, M. T., & Shaw, R. The primacy of perceiving: An ecological reformulation for understanding memory. In L. G. Nilsson (Ed.), *Perspectives on memory research: Essays in honor of Uppsala University's 500th anniversary*. Hillsdale, N.J.: Lawrence Erlabum Associates, 1979.

Turvey, M. T., Shaw, R., & Mace, W. Issues in the theory of action: Degrees of freedom, coordinative structures, and coalitions. In J. Requin (Ed.), *Attention and performance, VII*. Hillsdale, N.J.: Lawrence Erlbaum Associates, 1978.

Tyler, C. W. Stereoscopic depth movement: Two eyes less sensitive than one. *Science,* 1971, *174,* 958-961.

Tyler, C. W. Spatial frequency filters in cat visual cortex. *Vision Research,* 1975, *15,* 303-304.

Tyler, C. W. Checkerboards and color aftereffects. *Science,* 1977, *198,* 208-209. (a)

Tyler, C. W. Is the illusory triangle physical or imaginary? *Perception,* 1977, *6,* 603-604. (b)

Tyler, C. W. Selectivity for spatial frequency and bar width in cat visual cortex. *Vision Research,* 1978, *18,* 121-122. (a)

Tyler, C. W. Some new entopic phenomena. *Vision Research,* 1978, *18,* 1633-1639. (b)

Tyner, C. F. The naming of neurons: Applications of taxonomic theory to the study of cellular populations. *Brain, Behavior, and Evolution,* 1975, *12,* 75-96.

Ueno, T. Reaction time as a measure of temporal summation at suprathreshold levels. *Vision Research,* 1977, *17,* 227-232.

Uhr, L. (Ed.). *Pattern recognition*. New York: Wiley, 1966.

Uhr, L. *Pattern recognition, learning, and thought*. Englewood Cliffs, N.J.: Prentice-Hall, 1973.

Uhr, L. *A model of form perception and scene description*. Tech. Rep. No. 231. University of Wisconsin, Madison: November 1974.

Usui, S., & Stark, L. Sensory and motor mechanisms interact to control amplitude of pupil noise. *Vision Research,* 1978, *18,* 505-507.

Uttal, W. R. The character in the hole experiment: Interaction of forward and backward masking of alphabetic character recognition by dynamic visual noise (DVN). *Perception & Psychophysics,* 1969, *6*(3), 177-181. (a)

Uttal, W. R. Masking of alphabetic character recognition by dynamic visual noise (DVN). *Perception & Psychophysics,* 1969, *6*(2), 121-127. (b)

Uttal, W. R. Masking of alphabetic character recognition by ultrahigh-density dynamic visual noise. *Perception & Psychophysics,* 1970, *7,* 19-22. (a)

Uttal, W. R. On the physiological basis of masking with dotted visual noise. *Perception & Psychophysics,* 1970, *7,* 321-327. (b)

Uttal, W. R. Violations of visual simulataneity. *Perception & Psychophysics,* 1970, *7,* 133-136. (c)

Uttal, W. R. The effect of interval and number on masking with dot bursts. *Perception & Psychophysics,* 1971, *9*(6), 469-473. (a)

Uttal, W. R. The psychological silly season or what happens when neurophysiological data become psychological theories. *Journal of General Psychology*, 1971, *84*, 151–166.

Uttal, W. R. *The psychobiology of sensory coding*. New York: Harper & Row, 1973.

Uttal, W. R. *An autocorrelation theory of form detection*. Hillsdale, N.J.: Lawerence Erlbaum Associates, 1975. (a)

Uttal, W. R. *Cellular neurophysiology and integration: An interpretive introduction*. Hillsdale, N.J.: Lawrence Erlbaum Associates, 1975. (b)

Uttal, W. R. *The psychobiology of mind*. Hillsdale, N.J.: Lawrence Erlbaum Associates, 1978.

Uttal, W. R., & Cook, L. Systematics of the evoked somatosensory cortical potential. *Annals of the New York Academy of Science*, 1964, *112*, 60–81.

Uttal, W. R., Fitzgerald, J., & Eskin, T. E. Parameters of tachistoscopic stereopsis. *Vision Research*, 1975, *15*, 705–712. (a)

Uttal, W. R., Fitzgerald, J., & Eskin, T. E. Rotation and translation effects on stereoscopic acuity. *Vision Research*, 1975, 939–944. (b)

Uttal, W. R., & Hieronymus, R. Spatiotemporal effects in visual gap detection. *Perception & Psychophysics*, 1970, *8*, 321–325.

Uttal, W. R., & Smith, P. Recognition of alphabetic characters during voluntary eye movements. *Perception & Psychophysics*, 1968, *3*(4A), 257–264.

Uttal, W. R., & Tucker, T. E. Complexity effects in form detection. *Vision Research*, 1977, *17*, 359–365.

Valeton, J. M., & Van Norren, D. Transient tritanopia at the level of the ERG b-wave. *Vision Research*, 1979, *19*, 689–693.

Van Buren, J. M. *The retinal ganglion cell layer*. Springfield, Ill.: Thomas, 1963.

Van de Geer, J. P., & Levelt, W. J. M. *Detection of visual patterns disturbed by noise*. *Quarterly Journal of Experimental Psychology*, 1963, *15*, 192–204.

Van de Grind, W. A., Grüsser, O-J., & Lunkenheimer, H-U. Temporal transfer properties of the afferent visual system: Psychophysical, neurophysiological, and theoretical investigations. In R. Jung, R. (Ed.) *The Handbook of Sensory Physiology: Central processing of visual information. A.: Integrative functions and comparative data* (VII/3) Berlin: Springer-Verlag, 1973.

Van Loo, J. A., & Enoch, J. M. The scotopic Stiles–Crawford effect. *Vision Research*, 1975, *15*, 1005–1009.

Van Nes, F. L. *Experimental studies in spatiotemporal contrast transfer by the human eye*. Unpublished doctoral dissertation, University of Utrecht, Netherlands, 1968.

Vernon, M. D. The perception of inclined lines. *British Journal of Psychology*, 1934, *25*, 186–196.

Vernon, M. D. *A further study of visual perception*. Cambridge, England: Cambridge University Press, 1952.

Vernon, M. D. The functions of schemata in perceiving. *Psychological Review*, 1955, *62*, 180–192.

Virsu, V., & Laurinen, P. Long-lasting afterimages caused by neural adaptation. *Vision Research*, 1977, *17*, 853–860.

Volkmann, F. Vision during voluntary saccadic eye movements. *Journal of the Optical Society of America*, 1962, *52*, 571–578.

Vos, J. J. 25 years of the Stiles–Crawford effect. *Advances in Ophthalmology*, 1960, *10*, 32–48.

Wade, N. J. The effect of orientation on binocular rivalry of real images and afterimages. *Perception & Psychophysics*, 1974, *15*, 227–232.

Wade, N. J. Fragmentation of monocular afterimages in individuals with and without normal binocular vision. *Perception & Psychophysics*, 1975, *18*, 328–330. (a)

Wade, N. J. Monocular and binocular rivalry between contours. *Perception*, 1975, *4*, 85–95. (b)

Wade, N. J. Distortions and disappearances of geometrical patterns. *Perception*, 1977, *6*, 407–433. (a)

Wade, N. J. Letter to the editors: A note on the discovery of subjective colours. *Vision Research*, 1977, *17*, 671–672. (b)

Wade, N. J. Thomas S. Kuhn, revolutionary theorist of Science, 1977, 197, 143–145. (c)

Wade, N. J. Why do patterned afterimages fluctuate in visibility? *Psychological Bulletin,* 1978, *85,* 238–352.

Wade, N. J., & Day, R. H. On the colors seen in achromatic patterns. *Perception & Psychophysics,* 1978, *23,* 261–264.

Wagner, H. G., MacNichol, E. F., Jr., & Wolbarscht, M. L. The response properties of single ganglion cells in the goldfish retina. *Journal of General Physiology,* 1960, *43,* 45–62.

Wald, G. Vitamin A in the retina. *Nature,* 1933, 132, 316–317.

Wald, G. Human vision and the spectrum. *Science,* 1945, *101,* 653–658.

Wald, G. The photochemistry of vision. *Documenta Ophthalmologica,* 1949, *3,* 94–137.

Wald, G. The receptors of human color vision. *Science,* 1964, *145,* 1007–1017.

Wald, G. Reflective color vision and its inheritance. *Proceedings of the National Academy of Sciences,* 1966, *55,* 1347–1363.

Wald, G. Molecular basis of visual excitation. *Science,* 1968, *162,* 230–239.

Wales, R., & Fox, R. Increment detection thresholds during binocular rivalry suppression. *Perception & Psychophysics,* 1970, *8,* 90–94.

Walker, E. H. A mathematical theory of optical illusions and figural aftereffects. *Perception & Psychophysics,* 1973, *13,* 467–486.

Walker, J. The amateur scientist. *Scientific American,* December 1977, *237,* 172–180.

Walker, J. T. A new rotating gradient disk: Brightness, flicker, and brightness aftereffect. *Vision Research,* 1974, *14,* 223–228.

Walker, J. T. Brightness enhancement and the Talbot level in stationary gratings. *Perception & Psychophysics,* 1978, *23,* 356–359.

Walker, J. T., & Krüger, M. W. Figural aftereffects in random-dot stereograms without monocular contours. *Perception,* 1972, *1,* 187–192.

Walker, P. Stochastic properties of binocular rivalry alternations. *Perception & Psychophysics,* 1975, *18,* 467–473.

Walker, P. The perceptual fragmentation of unstabilized images. *Quarterly Journal of Experimental Psychology,* 1976, *28,* 35–45.

Walker, P. Binocular Rivalry: Central or peripheral selective processes? *Psychological Bulletin,* 1978, *85,* 376–389.

Walker, P., & Powell, D. J. The sensitivity of binocular rivalry to changes in the nondominant stimulus. *Vision Research,* 1979, *19,* 247–249.

Wallach, H. Visual perception of motion. In G. Kepes (Ed.), *The nature and art of motion.* New York: George Braziller, 1965.

Wallach, H., & O'Connell, D. N. The kinetic depth effect. *Journal of Experimental Psychology,* 1953, *45,* 205–217.

Walls, G. L. *The vertebrate eye.* Bloomfield Hills, Michigan: Cranbrook Institute of Science, 1942.

Ward, L. M., & Coren, S. The effect of optically induced blur on the magnitude of the Müller–Lyer illusion. *Bulletin of the Psychonomic Society,* 1976, *7,* 483–484.

Warnock, G. J. (Ed.). *The philosophy of perception.* Oxford, England: Oxford University Press, 1967.

Warren, R. M. Perceptual restoration of missing speech sounds. *Science,* 1970, *167,* 392–393.

Warren, R. M., & Warren, R. P. Helmholtz on perception: Its physiology and development. New York: Wiley, 1968.

Warrington, E. K. The effect of stimulus configuration on the incidence of the completion phenomenon. *British Journal of Psychology,* 1965, *56,* 447–454.

Wasserman, G. S. Invertebrate color vision and the tuned-receptor hypothesis. *Science,* 1973, *180,* 268–275.

Wasserman, G. S. *Color vision: An historical introduction.* New York: Wiley, 1978.

Wasserman, G. S., Felsten, G., & Easland, G. S. The psychophysical function: Harmonizing Fechner and Stevens. *Science,* 1979, *204,* 85–87.

Wasserman, G. S., & Kong, K. L. Illusory correlation of brightness enhancement and transients in the nervous system. *Science,* 1974, *184,* 911–913.

Wasserman, G. S., & Kong, K. L. Absolute timing of mental activities. *The Brain and Behavioral Sciences,* 1979, *2,* 243–304.

Watanabe, S. (Ed.). *Methodologies of pattern recognition.* New York: Academic Press, 1969.

Waterman, T. H. Responses to polarized light: Animals. In P. L. Altman, & D. S. Dittmer (Eds.), *Biology data book, Vol. II* (2nd ed.). Bethesda, Md.: Federation of American Societies for Experimental Biology, 1973.

Watrasiewicz, B. M. Measurements of the Mach effect in microscopy. *Optica Acta,* 1963, *10,* 209–216.

Watson, A. A Riemann geometric explanation of the visual illusions and figural aftereffects. In E. L. J. Leeuwenberg & H. F. J. M. Buffart (Eds.), *Formal theories of visual perception.* New York: Wiley, 1978.

Watson, A. B., & Nachmias, J. Patterns of temporal interaction in the detection of gratings. *Vision Research,* 1977, *17,* 893–902.

Watson, R. E., & Perlman, M. L. Seeing with a new light: Synchrotron radiation. *Science,* 1978, *199,* 1295–1302.

Weale, R. A. Retinal summation and human visual threshold. *Nature,* 1958, *181,* 154–156.

Weale, R. A. Note on the photometric significance of the human crystalline lens. *Vision Research,* 1961, *1,* 183–191.

Webb, N. G. X-ray diffraction from outer segments of visual cells in intact eyes of the frog. *Nature,* 1972, *235,* 44–46.

Webster's third new international dictionary of the English language, unabridged. Springfield, Mass.: Merriam, 1963.

Wehner, R. Polarized-light navigation by insects. *Scientific American,* 1976, *235*(1), 106–115.

Weinberg, S. Unified theories of elementary-particle interaction. *Scientific American,* July 1974, *231* (1), 50–59.

Weinberg, S. The search for unity: Notes for a history of quantum field theory. *Daedalus,* 1977, *106,* 17–35.

Weinstein, G. W., Hobson, R. R., & Baker, F. H. Extracellular recordings from human retinal ganglion cells. *Science,* 1971, *171,* 1021–1022.

Weintraub, D. J. Successive contrast involving luminance and purity alterations of the ganzfeld. *Journal of Experimental Psychology,* 1964, *68,* 555–562.

Weintraub, D. J. Rectangle discriminability: Perceptual relativity and the law of prägnanz. *Journal of Experimental Psychology,* 1971, *88,* 1–11.

Weintraub, D. J. Ebbinghaus illusion: Context, contour, and age influence the judged size of a circle amidst circles. *Journal of Experimental Psychology: Human Perception and Performance,* 1979, *5,* 353–364.

Weintraub, D. J., *Personal communication,* 1980.

Weintraub, D. J., & Krantz, D. H. The Poggendorff illusion: Amputations, rotations, and other perturbations. *Perception & Psychophysics,* 1971, *10,* 257–264.

Weintraub, D. J., & Virsu, V. Estimating the vertex of converging lines: Angle misperception? *Perception & Psychophysics,* 1972, *11,* 277–283.

Weisstein, N. A Rashevsky-Landahl neural net: Simulation of metacontrast. *Psychological Review,* 1968, *75,* 494–521.

Weisstein, N. What the frog's eye tells the frog's brain: Single-cell analyzers in the human visual system. *Psychological Bulletin,* 1969, *72,* 157–176.

Weisstein, N. Neural symbolic activity: A psychophysical measure. *Science,* 1970, *168,* 1489–1491.

Weisstein, N. Metacontrast. In D. Jameson & L. M. Hurvich (Eds.), *Handbook of sensory physiology: Visual psychophysics* (Vol. VII/4). New York: Springer-Verlag, 1972.

Weisstein, N. Tutorial: The joy of Fourier analysis. In C. S. Harris (Ed.), *Visual coding and adaptability*. Hillsdale, N.J.: Lawrence Erlbaum Associates, Inc., 1980.

Weisstein, N., & Bisaha, J. Gratings mask bars and bars mask gratings: Visual frequency response to aperiodic stimuli. *Science*, 1972, *176*, 1047–1049.

Weisstein, N., & Growney, R. L. Apparent movement and metacontrast: A note on Kahneman's formulation. *Perception & Psychophysics*, 1969, *5*, 321–328.

Weisstein, N., & Harris, C. S. Visual detection of line segments: An object superiority effect. *Science*, 1974, *186*, 752–755.

Weisstein, N., Harris, C. S., Berbaum, K., Tangney, J., & Williams. A. Contrast reduction by small localized stimuli: Extensive spread of above-threshold orientation-specific masking. *Vision Research*, 1977, *17*, 341–350.

Weisstein, N., Jurkens, T., & Ondersin, T. Effect of forced choice vs. magnitude-estimation measures on the waveform of metacontrast type functions. *Journal of the Optical Society of America*, 1970, *60*, 978–980.

Weisstein, N., & Maguire, W. Computing the next step: Psychophysical measures of representation and interpretation. In E. M. Riseman & A. R. Hanson (Eds.), *Computer vision systems*. New York: Academic Press, 1978.

Weisstein, N., Maguire, W., & Berbaum, K. A phantom motion aftereffect. *Science*, 1977, *198*, 955–958.

Weisstein, N., Matthews, M., & Berbaum, K. Illusory contours can mask real contours. *Bulletin of Psychonomics Society*, 1974, *4*, 266.

Weisstein, N., Ozog, G., & Szoc, R. A comparison and elaboration of two models of metacontrast. *Psychological Review*, 1975, *82*, 325–343.

Welpe, E. Das Schachbrettmuster: Ein nur binokular antegbares Flimmermuster. *Vision Research*, 1975, *15*, 1283–1287.

Wenderoth, P., & Beh, H. Component analysis of orientation illusions. *Perception*, 1977, *6*, 57–75.

Werblin, F. S. Functional organization of a vertebrate retina: Sharpening up in space and intensity. *Annals of the New York Academy of Sciences*, 1972, *193*, 75–85. (b)

Werblin, F. S. Lateral interactions at the inner plexiform layer of the retina: Antagonistic response to change. *Science*, 1972, *175*, 1008–1010. (a)

Werblin, F. S. Control of retinal sensitivity, II. Lateral interactions at the outer plexiform layer. *Journal of General Physiology*, 1974, *63*, 62–87.

Werblin, F. S., & Copenhagen, D. Control of retinal sensitivity, III. Lateral interactions at the inner plexiform layer. *Journal of General Physiology*, 1974, *63*, 88–110.

Werblin, F. S., & Dowling, J. E. Organization of the retina of the mudpuppy, *Necturus Maculosas*, II. Intraretinal recordings. *Journal of Neurophysiology*, 1969, *32*, 339–355.

Werner, H. Studies on contour: I. Qualitative analysis. *American Journal of Psychology*, 1935, *47*, 40–64.

Wertheimer, M. Experimentelle studien über das sehen von bewegung. *Zeitschrift ür Psychologie*, 1912, *61*, 161–265.

Wertheimer, M. Unterchungen zur Lehre von der Gestalt, II. *Psychologische Forschung*, 1923, *4*, 301–350.

West, E. R., Brandt, T., Diener, H-C., & Dichgans, J. Spatial frequency effect on the Pulfrich stereophenomenon. *Vision Research*, 1977, *17*, 391–397.

Westheimer, G. Modulation thresholds for sinusoidal light distribution on the retina. *Journal of Physiology*, 1960, *152*, 67–74.

Westheimer, G. Optical and motor factors in the formation of the retinal image. *Journal of the Optical Society of America*, 1963, *53*, 86–93.

Westheimer, G. Spatial interaction in the human retina during the scotopic vision. *Journal of Physiology,* 1965, *181,* 881–894.

Westheimer, G. Spatial interaction in human cone vision. *Journal of Physiology,* 1967, *190,* 139–154.

Westheimer, G. Rod–cone independence for sensitizing interaction in the human retina. *Journal of Physiology,* 1970, *206,* 109–116.

Westheimer, G. Visual acuity and spatial modulation thresholds. In D. Jameson & L. M. Hurvich (Eds.), *Handbook of sensory physiology: Visual psychophysics* (Vol. VII/4). Berlin: Springer-Verlag, 1972.

Westheimer, G., & Campbell, F. W. Light distribution in the image in the living human eye. *Journal of the Optical Society of America,* 1962, *52,* 1040–1044.

Westheimer, G., & McKee, S. P. Visual acuity in the presence of retinal image motion. *Journal of the Optical Society of America,* 1975, *65,* 847–850.

Westheimer, G., & McKee, S. P. Interactions regions for visual hyperacuity. *Vision Research,* 1977, *17,* 89–93. (a)

Westheimer, G., & McKee, S. P. Spatial configurations for visual hyperacuity. *Vision Research,* 1977, *17,* 941–947. (b)

Westheimer, G., & McKee, S. P. Stereoscopic acuity for moving retinal images. *Journal of the Optical Society of America,* 1978, *68,* 450–455.

Wheatstone, C. (signed C. W.) Contributions to the physiology of vision, No. II. *Journal of the Royal Institute of Great Britain,* 1831, *1,* 534–537.

Wheatstone, C. Contributions to the physiology of vision: I. On some remarkable, and hitherto unobserved, phenomena of binocular vision. *Philosophical Transactions of the Royal Society of London,* Part I, 1838, *128,* 371–394.

White, C. T. Temporal numerosity and the psychological unit of duration. *Psychological Monographs,* 1963, *77* (whole number 575), 37 pp.

White, K. D. Studies of form-contingent color aftereffects. In J. C. Armington, J. Krauskopf, & B. R. Wooten (Eds.), *Visual psychophysics and physiology.* New York: Academic Press, 1978.

White, K. D., Petry, H. M., Riggs, L. A., & Miller, J. Binocular interactions during establishment of McCollough effects. *Vision Research,* 1978, *18,* 1201–1215.

White, K. D., & Riggs, L. A. Angle-contingent color aftereffects. *Vision Research,* 1974, *14,* 1147–1154.

Wickelgren, W. A., & Whitman, P. T. Visual very short-term memory is nonassociative. *Journal of Experimental Psychology,* 1970, *84,* 277–281.

Wiener, N. *Cybernetics.* New York: Wiley, 1948.

Wilcox, W. W. The basis of the dependence of visual acuity on illumination. *Proceedings of the National Academy of Sciences,* 1932, *18,* 47–56.

Williams, A., & Weisstein, N. Line segments are perceived better in a coherent context than alone: An object-line effect. *Memory & Cognition,* 1978, *6,* 85–90.

Wilson, B. C. *An experimental examination of the spectral luminosity construct.* Unpublished doctoral dissertation, New York University, 1964.

Wilson, P. D., & Stone, J. Evidence of W-cell input to the cat's visual cortex via the claminae of the lateral geniculate nucleus. *Brain Research,* 1975, *92,* 472–478.

Wist, E. R., Brandt, T., Diener, H. C., & Dichgans, J. Spatial frequency effect on the Pulfrich stereo phenomenon. *Vision Research,* 1977, *17,* 391–398.

Witkovsky, P. The effect of chromatic adaptation in color sensitivity of the carp electroretinogram. *Vision Research,* 1968, *8,* 825–837.

Wolf, E., & Gardiner, J. S. Studies on the scatter of light in the dioptric media of the eye as a basis of visual glare. *Archives of Ophthalmology,* 1965, *74,* 338–345.

Woodburne, L. S. The effect of constant visual angle upon the binocular discrimination of depth differences. *American Journal of Psychology,* 1934, *46,* 273–286.

Wooten, B. R., & Wald, G. Color-vision mechanisms in the peripheral retinas of normal and dichromatic observers. *The Journal of General Physiology,* 1973, *61,* 125–145.
Wulfing, E. A. über den kleinsten Gesichtswinkel. *Zeitschrift für Biologie,* 1892, *29,* 199–202.
Wundt, W. *Lectures on human and animal psychology.* London: Swan Sonnenschein, 1894/1907.
Wundt, W. Die geometrisch-optischen Täuschungen. *Abhandlungen der Mathematisch-Physischen Classe der Königlich Sächsischen Gesellschaft der Wissenschaften,* 1898, *24,* 53–178.
Wundt, W. [*Lectures on human and animal psychology*] (J. E. Creighton & E. B. Titchener, trans. from 2nd German ed.). New York: Macmillan, 1907. (Originally published, 1894.)
Wundt, W. *Principles of physiological psychology.* Millwood, New York: Kraus Reprint 1874/1910.
Wyszecki, G., & Stiles, W. S. *Color science: Concepts and methods, quantitative data and formulas.* New York: Wiley, 1967.
Yamada, W., & Oyama, T. Perceptual grouping between successively presented dot figures. *Abstract Guide of XXth International Congress of Psychology,* Tokyo, Japan, 1972.
Young, R. A. Some observations on temporal coding of color vision: Psychophysical results. *Vision Research,* 1977, *17,* 957–965.
Young, R. S. L., Cole, R. E., Gamble, M., & Rayner, M. D. Subjective patterns elicited by light flicker. *Vision Research,* 1975, *15,* 1289–1290.
Zacks, J. L. Temporal summation phenomena at threshold: Their relation to visual mechanisms. *Science,* 1970, *170,* 197–199.
Zamansky, H. S., & Corwin, T. R. Word length and visual noise texture in backward masking. *Perception,* 1976, *5,* 211–215.
Zanuttini, L. A new explanation for the Poggendorff illusion. *Perception & Psychophysics,* 1976, *20,* 29–32.
Zehfuss, G. Über Bewegungsnachbilder. *Wiedermann's Annalen der Physik und Chemie,* 1880, *9,* 672–676.
Zeki, S. M. Cortical projections from two prestriate areas in the monkey. *Brain Research,* 1971, *34,* 19–35.
Zigman, S. Ultraviolet light and human lens pigmentation. *Vision Research,* 1978, *18,* 509–510.
Zuber, B. L., & Stark, L. Saccadic suppression: Elevation of visual threshold associated with saccadic eye movements. *Experimental Neurology,* 1966, *16,* 65–79.
Zuber, B. L., Stark, L., & Lorber, M. Saccadic suppression of the pupillary light reflex. *Experimental Neurology,* 1966, *14,* 351–370.
Zusne, L. *Visual perception of form.* New York, Academic Press, 1970.

Author Index

Numbers in *italics* indicate pages with complete bibliographic information.

A

B

C

H

L

N

O

S

T

Y Z

Subject Index

O

P

S

W

Y